WESTMAR COLLEGE LIBRARY

THE POPULATION OF JAPAN

UNDER THE EDITORIAL SPONSORSHIP OF

OFFICE OF POPULATION RESEARCH

PRINCETON UNIVERSITY

THE POPULATION OF JAPAN

BY IRENE B. TAEUBER

PRINCETON, NEW JERSEY, 1958
PRINCETON UNIVERSITY PRESS

HB 3651 .T3
301.32 T123

Copyright © 1958 by Princeton University Press
All Rights Reserved

L.C. Card: 58-7122

✧

Publication of this book has been aided in part by the Ford Foundation program to support publication, through university presses, of work in the humanities and social sciences.

Second Printing 1965

Printed in the United States of America

61177

To my colleagues in Japan

FOREWORD

THE previous books sponsored by the Office of Population Research that deal with Asian populations have in effect represented studies of the processes of population change in agrarian regions that are either under, or just emerging from, colonial rule. Dr. Taeuber's study of Japan stands in sharp contrast to them. Her book is, first of all, a study of an island nation in which the demographic situation has been critically important for centuries. But for the demographer, the Japanese case is peculiarly important. Virtually all of our generalizations about population and social-economic change during the transition from an agrarian to an urban-industrial society have been drawn from Western experience. Because Japan has reached an advanced state of industrial development without a colonial interlude, it affords an excellent opportunity to test the extension of these generalizations to an Oriental context. It is this situation, plus the wealth of research materials available, that have justified a study in such depth as that here presented.

Dr. Taeuber's work on Japan was initiated during the war when the Geographer of the Department of State arranged for the Office to conduct certain studies of Asian populations. With the end of the war the work was continued and has resulted in books by Davis on India and Pakistan, Barclay on Taiwan, Smith on Malaya, and now the present volume on Japan.

The study has been made possible by the generous financial assistance of the Milbank Memorial Fund and the Rockefeller Foundation, which have provided the major financial support for the Office during the years in which the work on the book has been done. Of course, neither of the foundations bears any responsibility either for the topics studied or for the resulting publications. To Dr. Taeuber goes both the credit and the responsibility, together with the congratulations of her colleagues at the Office for a work that we think will prove to be a landmark of demographic analysis.

FRANK W. NOTESTEIN, *Director*
Office of Population Research
Princeton University

PREFACE

THE legends of the ancient societies and the non-literary peoples indicate the age-old interest of man in the trends of his numbers. Counts have long been taken and records have been kept, but the field enumeration and data processing that permit analysis were products of the scientific developments of recent centuries. Demographic statistics became available primarily for the industrializing and urbanizing nations of Europe or the overseas nations settled and developed by peoples of European origin. Here also were concentrated the statisticians, the social scientists, and the demographers. It is only natural, therefore, that the early studies of social, economic, and demographic relations were culturally limited descriptions rather than generalizations covering relationships without specificity in place and time.

When statistical activities were extended into colonial areas, the analyses of the data indicated persistent increases in the numbers of many of the agrarian peoples. There seemed to be a bifurcated world. People of European origin, with industrial economies, urbanized societies, and high levels of living had already or were in process of balancing their reduced mortality with reduced fertility. Other peoples with agrarian economies, village societies, and low levels of living were characterized by high fertility and reduced mortality. One of the few historical developments that permits analysis of the cultural context of demographic change occurred in Japan. Here an industrial economy and an urban society developed in an independent Asian nation. A modern statistical system that utilized the techniques of data collection, processing, and analysis learned from European people was integrated with statistical procedures that traced back to the T'ang dynasty of China. Quantitative data and a rich literate record were available for an analysis of the demography of industrialization in a population whose indigenous culture, historic evolution, and premodern social and economic structure were related to the cultures of the South Pacific and the great Confucian traditions of the Celestial Kingdom rather than to the Graeco-Roman traditions of the Western European culture area. Thus phrased, study of the demography of Japan seems far removed from relevance to the acute population problems of the present in the densely settled areas of the Pacific region. Actually, the relationship between such study and the search for means to resolve the demographic crisis that now exists in other cultures is rather direct. If the associations between industrialization, urbanization, social change, and declining fertility in Japan are comparable to those in other nations, there is presumptive evidence that similar associations may exist in the future as other peoples undergo comprehensive economic, social, and political transformations.

There were major difficulties in the way of intensive analysis of the demography of Japan. The quantitative materials for Japan and the countries formerly subject to Japan were largely unknown in this country, and in the prewar period few even of those materials known to exist were available in libraries. General apathy concerning research on Japan was replaced by widespread interest, however, as a country and a people who had seemed remote became our enemy in the Pacific War and our responsibility in the years of occupation. In the years from 1937 to 1952, most external study of the demography of Japan was operational and purposive. This was necessarily so, for research with a locus in Japan required co-operation with the demographers of Japan in a milieu of peace rather than of war or military occupation. Hence it is that an interest which has continued whenever time permitted for almost two decades has only now resulted in comprehensive publication.

Perusal of the table of contents will indicate that this study begins with the demography of the legendary period and proceeds swiftly through the twelve centuries of recorded history from the Great Reform of 650 A.D. to the Meiji Restoration of 1868. This excursion back through the centuries will doubtless be painful to historians, but it was essential if the demography of the century of industrialization was to have comparative relevance. At the time of the commercial developments under the Tokugawa *bakufu* and the early industrial developments of the Meiji era, the birth rate of the Japanese reputedly was held to low levels by rational decisions as to which of the children born would be allowed to survive. If the demographic developments in the Tokugawa period reflected a political structure, a type of man-land relationship, and a dedication to family planning unique to Japan, the results of an analysis of the demography of the decades of industrialization in Japan would have questionable significance for an assessment of the population prospects in other Asian areas. As this question of typicality was pursued back in Japan's history, it became apparent that understanding in depth of the traditional culture was essential to the analysis of the characteristics and the interrelations of economy, society, and population in the modern period. It is quite possible, even probable, that demographic research in other ancient cultures will require study of the past before the transformations of the present can be understood or the prospects for the future evaluated.

The many deficiencies in this study are due to the widely ranging curiosity and the limitations of the knowledge of the writer. Whatever merits it may have can be attributed to the many people, Japanese and American, who have contributed their knowledge and understanding through their writings and the gifts of their time. Four have contributed personally at the same time that they have provided the essential institutional facilities: Professor Frank W. Notestein, Director of the Office of Population Research of Princeton University; Dr. Luther Evans, formerly Librarian of the Library of Congress; Dr. Ayanori Okazaki, Director of the Institute of Population Problems of the Welfare Ministry of Japan; and Dr. Yoshio Koya, formerly Director of the Institute of Public Health of the Welfare Ministry of Japan.

Mr. Minoru Tachi of the Institute of Population Problems was both sponsor and critic, contributing generously of his immense knowledge of demography and demographic research. Dr. Minoru Muramatsu of the Institute of Public Health added his extraordinary linguistic ability, his keen insights, and his professional cooperation as the writer learned to know Japan, its people, and its population problem in the great cities, the ancient villages, and the frontier regions. Dr. Haruo Mizushima of the School of Public Health of the University of Kyushu not only shared his knowledge of the population of Japan and Korea but made Kyushu an understood region in the Japanese scene. Dr. Takemune Soda, former Chief of the Division of Health and Welfare Statistics, Ministry of Welfare, added to the co-operation of his staff in the pursuit of vital statistics a long and rich knowledge of the population of Taiwan. And, finally, acknowledgment of access to the demographic statistics of Japan is not a formal gesture in a situation in which there have been several censuses from which only limited data have been published, particularly when the seeker after data from the past censuses also wished complex tabulations from the current censuses. The writer expresses her indebtedness to Dr. Yuzo Morita, formerly Director of the Bureau of Statistics of the Prime Minister's Office, but absolves Dr. Morita and the members of his staff from responsibility for errors in manipulation or interpretation of the data they so generously furnished.

Dr. Edwin G. Beal, Jr., and the staff of the Japanese Section of the Orientalia Division of the Library of Congress have been indispensable guides to the vast and only partially classified holdings of the Library of Congress. Dr. Beal co-operated in the early research on Japan and related areas, and when other responsibilities became too heavy, he continued to furnish general guidance, assistance on specific points, and encouragement.

Members of the staff of the Office of Population Research have been subjected to recurrent pressures for co-operation in Far Eastern research for many years. Special assistance was given at varying times by Dr. George Barclay, Dr. Eleanor Bernert, Dr. A. H. Hobbes, Mrs. Billie King, Mr. Robert Osborn, and Dr. George Stolnitz, former staff members. The personal research assistance which permitted this study to be made in the midst of other activities was rendered successively by Dr. Paul Mundy, Dr. Chungnim C. Han, and Dr. Y. Scott Matsumoto. Mrs. Daphne Notestein prepared the maps and figures. Miss Jean MacLachlan and Mr. Warren Robinson were responsible for the editorial and management functions that transformed a manuscript into a book. I wish it were possible to mention by name all those persons here and in Japan who copied the figures and made the computations on which the analysis rests. I must note specifically the services of Mrs. Stella Sutton and Mrs. Geraldine Hancock, for they cheerfully typed and retyped copy that had become scarcely legible to its writer.

The deepest debt is that I owe to my late colleague as co-editor of *Population Index*, Dr. Louise K. Kiser. It was Dr. Kiser's dedicated acceptance of major responsibilities that enabled me to follow my interests in research both in this country and across the Pacific.

IRENE B. TAEUBER

Office of Population Research
Princeton University, July 1, 1957

CONTENTS

Foreword vii

Preface ix

PART I. THE POPULATION IN THE PREMODERN PERIOD

I. Formation and Growth: The Beginnings to the Twelfth Century 3
The Ancient Society 3
The Taika Reform: The Plans 6
The Developments, Seventh to Twelfth Century 8
Growth and Change 11
Population: The Perennial Problem 15

II. The Changing Population: Late Twelfth to Mid-Nineteenth Century 16
Change and Stability under the *Bakufu* 16
The Trend of the Population 20
The Growth of Cities 25
The Changing Class Structure 27
Birth and Death Rates 28
Family Limitation 29
Change in the Changeless State 33

PART II. THE TRANSITION, 1852-1918

III. Increase and Redistribution 37
The Movement to Modernization 37
Population Statistics 40
Population Increase 44
Redistribution and Urbanization 45
The Balance of Births and Deaths 50
The Demographic Transition 53

PART III. THE CHANGING POPULATION, 1920-1955

IV. Population Changes: The Bases and the Patterns 59
The Increasing Population 59
The Economic Transformation 61
Mobility and Cultural Change 64
Education 66
The Demographic Transformation 67
Changes in Age Groups 73

V. The Economically Active Population 80
Participation in Gainful Employment 80
The Forces of Change 82
Industrialization and Urbanization 84
The Industrial Structure 85
The Social Structure 91
The Demographic Structure 93
Labor Force, Industrialization, and Urbanization 96
The Type of Industrialization 96

VI. The Family 100
House, Family, and Household 100
Family Relations and Household Residence 105
The Composition of Households 107
Dependency Burdens in Households 111
The Roles of Women 114

PART IV. MIGRATION

VII. Migration and Industrialization 123
Migration and Migrant Status, 1920-1950 123
The Cityward Movement of the Peasant 126
Demographic Selection and Structural Impact 127
Prefectural Redistribution, from Birth to 1930 129
The Migrants Within the Prefectures, from Birth to 1930 137
The Stable Within the Communes, from Birth to 1930 141
Net Migration, Prefectures, 1920-1940 142
The Contributions and Limitations of Migration 144
War: Reversal and Restoration 146

VIII. Cities and Metropolitan Areas 148
The Metropolitan Areas 148
Metropolis and Prefectural Hinterland 151
The Great Cities 154
Net Migration, 1925-1935 157
Tokyo: City of Migrants 160
Great Cities, 1940-1955 167
Problems of Acculturation in the Cities 167
Conclusions 168

PART V. EXPANSION

IX. Frontiers of Settlement and Utilization 173
Hokkaido 173
Karafuto 175
Okinawa 179
Nanyo-gunto 180
Taiwan 181
Korea 186
The Assessment 189

X. Imperial Expansion 191
Manchuria 191
Occupied China 197
Other Areas 198

The Dispersions of Two Decades: 1920-1940 201
The Mobility of the Industrializing Region 203

PART VI. NATURAL MOVEMENTS

XI. Marriage 207
Civil Codes and Statistics 207
The Postponement of Marriage 209
The Married 213
Unrecorded Marriages 218
Marriage Rates 223
The Stabilization of Marriage 227
Divorce 228
Conclusions 229

XII. Fertility 231
Trends in National Fertility 231
Fertility in the Prefectures 238
Industrialization and Fertility 245
Urbanization and Fertility 247
Migration, Urbanization, and Fertility 256

XIII. The Control of Fertility 258
The Factors in Decline 258
Fertility Outside Marriage 261
The Fertility of the Married 264
The Planned Limitation of Fertility 269
The Means of Limitation 272
Conclusion 283

XIV. Mortality 284
Public Health and Medical Care 284
Mortality in the Nation, 1920-1955 285
Mortality in the Prefectures 289
Industrialization, Urbanization, and Mortality 293
Death and the Production of Life 300
Some Social Aspects of the Changing Mortality 303
Conclusions 308

XV. Natural Increase 310
Increase of the National Population 310
Variations and Trends in the Prefectures 313
Industrialization, Urbanization, and Natural Increase 317
The Saving of Life and the Growth of Population 319
Internal Redistribution and Growth 320
Natural Increase and the Structure of the Population 320
Growth Potential in the 1930's 324

PART VII. DEMOGRAPHY IN PEACE AND WAR

XVI. The Demography of War 329
The Armed Forces 331
The Population Behind the Front 335
Exodus and Return 343
Restoration 347
The Balance of the Decade 350
Population Increase and War 362

XVII. Problems, Projections, and Policies 364
The Formative Decades 364
Population and Food: The Commission 366
Increase for the Co-Prosperity Sphere 366
SCAP: Policies, Actions, and Evaluations 369
Japanese Moves Toward Policy: 1946-1949 371
Research, Publications, and the Decline of Fertility 373
New Moves Toward Policy on Fertility 376
The Problems of Policy 378

XVIII. Past and Future 380
Imperial Japan: 1868-1945 380
The Years of Reconstruction: 1945-1950 382
The Situation from 1950 to 1955 383
The Dimensions of the Future: 1950-1980 384

Appendices 391
Chronology 391
Glossary 391
Agencies and Institutions 392
Periodicals 393

Bibliography 395
Preface 395
Subject guide 395
Citations 396

Index 457

TABLES

1. The population of selected local areas, by sex and age, from registration records of the eighth century A.D. ... 10
2. Population reports from the fiefs of nine *daimyo*, late seventeenth and early eighteenth centuries ... 21
3. The number of commoners, Tokugawa reports, 1726-1852 ... 22
4. The commoner population of the *do*, 1750-1852 ... 23
5. The historical development of the castle towns and their status in 1950 ... 25
6. Annual changes in population, 1875-1919 ... 41
7. Per cent deviations of population, by age, in the registration compilations from those expected on the basis of the census of 1920 ... 43
8. The population of the *shi* and the *gun* in the industrialized prefectures, by type of residence allocation, 1920 and 1918 ... 44
9. The increase of the population, 1873-1918 ... 45
10. Changes in the *honseki* population, by sex and age, 1888-1918 ... 46
11. The population of the regions, 1750-1852 and 1872-1885 ... 46
12. The changing distribution of the present-resident population, 1903-1918 ... 48
13. The present-resident population, by size of commune, 1888-1918 ... 49
14. The vital rates of the Japanese, 1875-1919 ... 50
15. Ratios of children to women, 1903-1918 and 1920 ... 54
16. The population of Japan and the former Empire, 1920-1940 ... 60
17. The numbers of the ethnic Japanese, 1920-1940 ... 61
18. School attendance among youth aged from 6 to 24, by sex, prefectures by industrial type, 1950 ... 67
19. Years of school completed by persons aged 25 and over, by sex, prefectures by industrial type, 1950 ... 68
20. The populations of the regions and the prefectures, 1920-1955 ... 70
21. Population and its increase by age groups, 1920-1955 ... 73
22. The populations of the prefectures by industrial type, by age, 1920-1955 ... 75
23. The age and sex structure of the population, 1920-1955 ... 76
24. Age structures, by size of commune, 1930 and 1950 ... 77
25. Age structures in the *shi* and the *gun*, 1920, 1930, and 1955 ... 78
26. Age structures and sex ratios, prefectures by industrial type, 1920-1955 ... 79
27. The economically active population by sex, age, and military status, 1920-1955 ... 81
28. The industrial structure of the economically active population, 1920-1955 ... 87
29. The industrial structure of the gainfully occupied population, by size of commune, 1930 ... 90
30. Employed persons, by class of worker and sex, in the *shi* and the *gun*, prefectures by industrial type, 1950 ... 92
31. The industrial structure of the age groups in the gainfully occupied population, by sex, 1940 ... 94
32. Age composition of the labor force by sex, agricultural and non-agricultural industries, prefectures by industrial type, 1950 ... 97
33. The structure of relations in multi-person households, 1920 ... 105
34. Number of generations in multi-person households, 1920 ... 106
35. Private households, by number of members, *shi* and *gun*, 1920-1950 ... 108
36. Age of heads of multi-person households, by sex, prefectures by industrial type, 1950 ... 110
37. Relation to household head of all members of multi-person households, by selected industries of heads, by sex, 1930 ... 111
38. Composition of multi-person private households, by industry of head and gainful employment of persons related to head, 1930 ... 112
39. Composition of private multi-person households, by industry of head and labor force status of persons related to head, 1950 ... 113
40. The participation of regular members of farm households in the agriculture of the family, by age, prefectures by industrial type, 1947 ... 114
41. Labor force status of related persons other than the head, by industry of the head, *shi* and *gun*, 1950 ... 114
42. The industrial structure of the gainfully occupied female population, by age and marital status, 1940 ... 118
43. The prefectural interchange, place-of-birth statistics, 1920-1950 ... 125
44. Per cent distribution of the populations of the prefectures, by place of birth, 1930 ... 128
45. Sex and age structures of the populations of the prefectures, by industrial type, 1930 ... 130
46. Exodus of the native-born, from birth to October 1, 1930, by sex and age, prefectures by industrial type ... 133
47. Influx from other prefectures, from birth to October 1, 1930, by sex and age, prefectures by industrial type ... 135
48. Present population in relation to population born in the prefectures, October 1, 1930, by sex and age, prefectures by industrial type ... 136
49. The balance of inter-prefectural migration, from birth to October 1, 1930, by sex and age, prefectures by industrial type ... 138
50. Net migration by sex, prefectures by industrial type, 1920-1940 ... 144
51. Migrant status of the population in and outside cities of 100 thousand and over, males, by selected ages, 1930 ... 150

52. Migrant status of the male population in migrant and stable cities, by selected ages, 1930 151
53. Migrant status of the male population outside cities of 100 thousand and over in prefectures including cities of 100 thousand and over, prefectures by industrial type, selected ages, 1930 152
54. Stability and mobility, male population of cities of 100 thousand and over, 1930 153
55. Migrant status of the male population in the great cities, other cities of 100 thousand and over, and remainder of prefecture, by selected ages, 1930 155
56. The prefectural interchange among the great cities and their prefectures, 1930 157
57. Net gain or loss by migration, prefectures of the great cities and the remainder of Japan, 1925-1930 and 1930-1935 158
58. Net migration of Japanese aged from 10 to 64, six cities, 1925-1930, by sex 159
59. Net migration by age, four great cities and the prefectural areas outside them, 1925-1930 161
60. In-migrants in Greater Tokyo in 1935, by present age and age at arrival, age 0 to 44 163
61. Age at last migration in relation to present age, selected ages at migration, Tokyo, 1935, by sex 164
62. Inter-prefectural migrants as of 1930, enumerated in Tokyo in 1935 165
63. Migrant status of the male population of Hokkaido, 1930 176
64. The industrial composition of the in-migrant population of Karafuto, by year of arrival, 1930 177
65. Age structure of migrant status groups in Karafuto, by place of birth, 1930 178
66. Place of *honseki* of the Japanese population of Karafuto, by place of birth, 1930 178
67. The population of Nanyo-gunto, by ethnic group, 1920-1940 182
68. The population of Taiwan, by ethnic group, 1905-1940 184
69. The industrial composition of the gainfully occupied population of Taiwan by ethnic group, *shi* and *gun*, 1930 185
70. The population of Korea, by ethnic group, *shi* and *gun*, 1925-1940 187
71. The population of the provinces of Manchoukuo, by ethnic group, 1940 193
72. Educational status of Japanese with *honseki* in Japan but resident outside Japan, the Empire, or Manchoukuo, 1940 200
73. Distribution of the Japanese in the world, by sex and age, 1940 202
74. World distribution of Japanese aged from 15 to 59, 1920-1940 203
75. The proportions of the single, by sex and age, 1920-1955 211
76. The single in the *shi* and the *gun*, by sex and age, 1920-1955 211
77. The proportions of the married, by sex and age, 1920-1955 213
78. The proportions of the widowed and separated, by sex and age, 1920-1955 213
79. Proportions married among women aged from 15 to 49, prefectures by industrial type, 1925-1950 215
80. Proportions of married Japanese whose marriages were not recorded in *koseki*, by sex and age, 1920 and 1940 219
81. The unrecorded marriages among women, by age, prefectures by industrial type, 1940 221
82. The proportion of unrecorded marriages, by sex, economic status, and major economic activity, 1940 221
83. Economic activities of the Japanese, total married, unrecorded unions, and the widowed or separated, by sex and age, 1940 222
84. Rates of marriages and divorce, Japanese in Japan, 1900-1955 223
85. First marriages of the Japanese, by sex and age, from 1919-1920 to 1934-1936 225
86. Marriages of the widowed and the separated per 100 marriages of the single, by sex, from 1919-1921 to 1934-1936 226
87. Age of wives at recording of marriage, by age of husbands, age 15 to 39, 1904-1934 228
88. Divorces in relation to total population and to marriages, by age, 1920-1940 229
89. Divorces and the disappearance of the divorced, by sex and age, from 1919-1921 and 1934-1936 230
90. Annual fertility, 1920-1955 232
91. Female births per 1,000 women, 1925-1954 234
92. Number of live births per 1,000 women, by age of women and orders of birth, 1947-1954 236
93. Birth rates in the prefectures, 1920-1955 242
94. Gross reproduction rates in the prefectures, 1920-1955 244
95. Number of children ever born per 1,000 women, by age, prefectures by industrial type, 1950 245
96. Female births per 1,000 women, by age, prefectures by industrial type, 1925, 1930, and 1947 246
97. Female children under 5 (Western) or under 6 (lunar) per 1,000 women aged from 20 to 49 (Western) or 21 to 50 (lunar), 1920-1955 247
98. Children under one year of age per 1,000 women aged from 15 to 44, by size of commune, all Japan and prefectures by industrial type, 1930 248
99. Age-specific fertility of women in *shi* of 100 thousand and over and in the remainder of the country, 1925 and 1930 251
100. Age-specific fertility of women in the *shi* of 100 thousand and over, 1925 and 1930 252
101. Fertility of women in the *ku* of the six great cities, 1930 and 1935 253
102. Per cent of Japanese women ever married, prefectures by industrial type, *shi* and *gun*, 1950 259
103. Illegitimacy status of live births, by type, large cities and remainder of the country, 1923-1938 263
104. Legitimate female births per 1,000 married women, by age, prefectures by industrial type, 1925 and 1930 265
105. Stillbirths per 1,000 live births, by legitimacy status, cities of 100 thousand and over and remainder of the country, 1923-1935 270
106. Stillbirths by legitimacy status, by age of mother, 1930 and 1939-1943 271
107. The practice of contraception, 1950, 1952, and 1955 273
108. The incidence of reported induced abortions, by age of women, 1950-1954 277

109. Reported stillbirths per 1,000 live births, by age of mother, 1947-1950 ... 278
110. Stillbirths per 1,000 total women, by age, 1947-1950 ... 279
111. Reported stillbirths per 1,000 women, by order of gestation and age of mother, 1947-1950 ... 280
112. Mortality in Japan, 1920-1955 ... 287
113. Expectation of life, by selected ages, 1920-1925 to 1954-1955 ... 288
114. The ten leading causes of death, 1920-1953 ... 290
115. Expectation of life at birth in the prefectures, 1920-1925 to 1950 ... 294
116. Death rates in *shi, machi,* and *mura,* 1925-1935 ... 298
117. Expectation of life at selected ages, by cities of 100 thousand and over and areas outside such cities, 1925-1926, 1930-1931, and 1935-1936 ... 299
118. The mortality of women aged from 10 to 34, six cities and remainder of the country, 1920-1921 to 1940-1941 ... 300
119. Infant mortality in the prefectures, 1919-1920 to 1953 ... 302
120. The mortality of men aged from 10 to 34, six cities and remainder of the country, 1920-1921 to 1940-1941 ... 304
121. Natural increase of the Japanese in Japan, 1920-1955 ... 311
122. Rates of natural increase in the prefectures, 1920-1955 ... 314
123. Net reproduction rates, intrinsic and standardized rates of natural increase, prefectures, various dates, 1925-1950 ... 316
124. The armed forces of Imperial Japan, 1935-1945 ... 333
125. The population behind the front, 1940-1945 ... 336
126. The female population of the prefectures: years of concentration ... 338
127. The female population of the prefectures: years of dispersion and early return ... 341
128. Net civilian movements to and from Japan (46 prefectures), 1920-1945 ... 344
129. Non-Japanese civilians repatriated from areas of the Co-Prosperity Sphere other than Japan ... 345
130. Repatriation, civilian and military, October 1945-September 1950 ... 346
131. Repatriated population, by military status and region, 1945-1952 ... 346
132. The population of postwar Japan, by sex and age, 1945-1950 ... 349
133. The female population of the prefectures: years of restoration ... 351
134. Changes in population in Japan, 46 prefectures, October 1, 1940-September 30, 1950 ... 352
135. The population of the six great cities, other *shi*, and *gun*, 46 prefectures, 1940-1950 ... 353
136. The numbers of the Japanese enumerated in 1940 and in 1950, and the numbers "expected" in 1950, ages 15-59, by sex ... 359
137. The war losses among Japanese aged from 15 to 59 in the Repatriation Area, 1940-1950 ... 362
138. Labor force, by sex and age, October 1950 and October 1954 ... 385
139. Estimates of the future population of Japan, 1950-2000 ... 386
140. Estimates of the future population of Japan, by broad age groups, 1950-1980 ... 387
141. The population of Japan by sex and age, actual, 1920 and 1950, estimated 1980 ... 387

FIGURES

1. Probability of death, males aged from 5 to 49, registration life tables, 1891-1898, 1899-1903, and 1908-1913 ... 51
2. Annual indices of population, industrial activity, and production, 1937-1954 ... 62
3. The gainfully occupied population, by sex and age, in the six great cities and in other cities of 100,000 and over, 1930 ... 85
4. The labor force in the *shi* and the *gun*, by sex and age, 1950 ... 86
5. Labor force participation, by age and sex, prefectures by industrial type, 1950 ... 89
6. Employed persons, by class of worker and sex, selected industry groups, prefectures by industrial type, 1950 ... 93
7. Age composition of the labor force in the *shi* and the *gun*, males in selected industries, 1950 ... 96
8. Per cent distribution of the Korean population in northeast Asia, by sex and age, October 1, 1940 ... 189
9. The proportions of the single in selected boom and stable cities, by sex and age, 1930 ... 212
10. Marital status, by sex and age, prefectures by industrial type, 1950 ... 216
11. Gross reproduction rates, by size of place, 1920-1935 ... 250
12. Birth rates in *shi, machi,* and *mura* of selected prefectures, 1925 ... 255
13. Number of children ever born to ever-married women of specified ages, prefectures by industrial type, 1950 ... 266
14. Number of children ever born to mothers of specified ages, prefectures by industrial type, 1950 ... 267
15. The probability of death, males, 1920-1925, 1935-1936, 1947, and 1953-1954 ... 289
16. Age patterns in the mortality of Japanese males, selected prefectures by industrial type, and imperial areas, 1925-1930 ... 296
17. Changes in the probability of dying, ages 10-39, by sex, selected periods, 1891-1898 to 1953-1954 ... 303
18. The declining excess in the mortality of females, 1921-1925, 1935-1936, 1947, and 1952-1953 ... 305
19. Rates of natural increase in *shi, machi,* and *mura,* selected prefectures, 1925-1935 ... 318
20. Number of women in the childbearing ages, prefectures by industrial type, 1920, 1935, and 1950 .. 320
21. Japanese population in the world in 1950, by sex and age, on various assumptions as to fertility and mortality, 1920-1950 ... 321
22. The sex and age composition of the population of Japan in 1955 and 1970, assuming growth at the rates of the stable population of 1934-1936 ... 324
23. The population of Japan, estimated actual, 1955; and projected on a European model, 1935-1955 .. 325

24a. The population of Japan by single years of age, 1920 ... 329

b. The population of Japan by single years of age, 1935 ... 330

25. Population by size of commune, 46 prefectures, 1920-1950 ... 350
26. Ratio of deaths to births by months in the war period ... 354
27. The deviations of fertility from prewar trends, 1920-1953 ... 356
28. The population of Japan, by sex and age, 1950 and 1955 ... 384
29. The population of Japan, by sex and age, 1920, 1950, actual; and 1980, projected ... 388

MAPS

1. Japan. Surface features of the land 4
2. Japan. Average annual rainfall, 1931-1940 5
3. Changes in the commoner population of the *kuni*, 1750-1804 and 1804-1852 24
4. The change in the present-resident population of the prefectures, 1903-1918 47
5. Population change in the prefectures in intercensal periods, 1920-1940 69
6. Prefectures by industrial type; and the proportion of the gainfully occupied population in agriculture, 1930 88
7. Exodus of the native-born, from birth to October 1, 1930, males in selected ages, by prefectures 131
8. Net migration, prefectures, 1920-1940 143
9. Out-migrants from each prefecture resident in Hokkaido, by place-of-birth data, census of 1930 174
10. Density of population, Manchoukuo and Kwantung, October 1, 1940 192
11. Birth rates and gross reproduction rates, by prefectures, 1920-1925 238
12. Female births per 1,000 women, selected ages, by prefectures, 1925 240
13. Gross reproduction rates in the *shi* and the *gun* of the prefectures, 1925 and 1950 249
14. Birth rates in the *gun*, 1930 254
15. Death rates and expectation of life at birth, prefectures, 1920-1925 291
16. Death rates, prefectures, 1925-1930, 1947, 1950 and 1953 292
17. Population replacement ratios in the *gun*, 1930 318
18. Differential fertility in the war years. Ratios of girls to women, 1935-1940, 1940-1945, and 1942-1947 357

[*See also next page for two general maps which are intended to apply to the entire book.*]

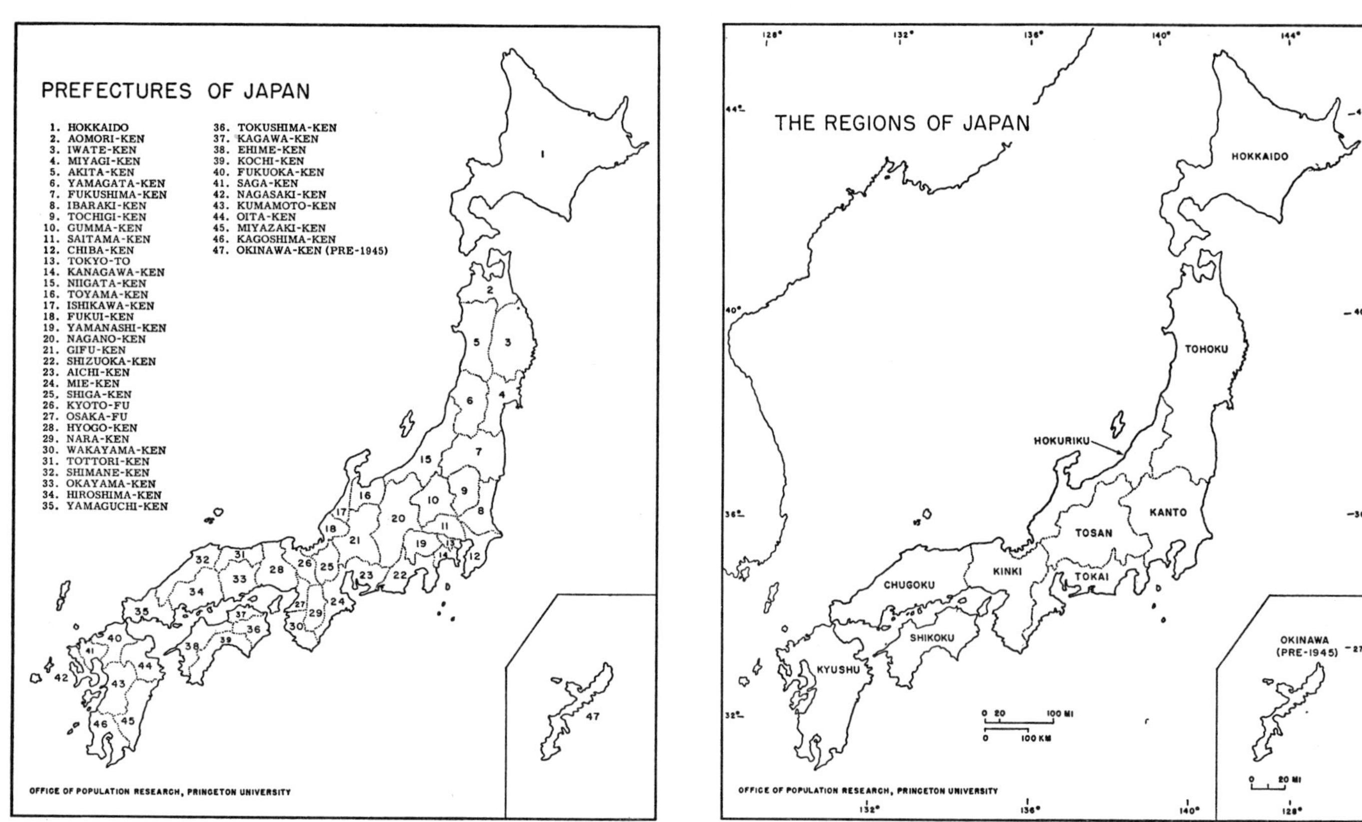

Japan: Political divisions and regional groupings

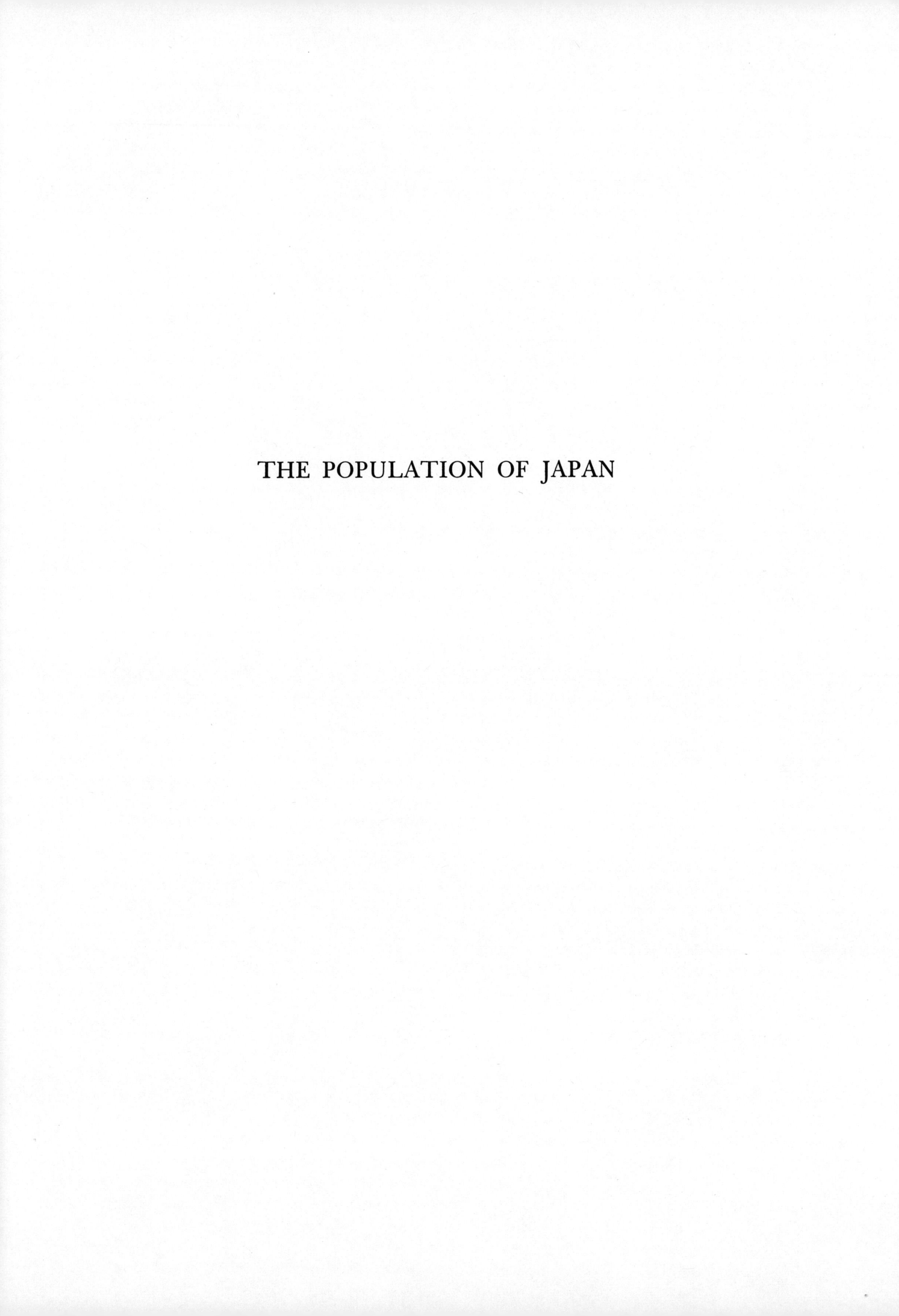

THE POPULATION OF JAPAN

CHAPTER I

Formation and Growth

The Beginnings to the Twelfth Century

THE islands of Japan are the crests of great ridges elevated from the floor of the Pacific Ocean.[1] Numerous volcanoes and frequent earthquakes reflect continuing readjustments of the rock masses. More significant perhaps than the instability of the earth itself, although related directly to it, is the mountainous terrain (Map 1). More than 65 per cent of the land area consists of hill and mountain land whose average slope exceeds fifteen degrees.[2] The largest of the lowland areas is the Kanto Plain of east-central Honshu, and it covers only 5,000 square miles. The total land area of the six other plains that are 450 square miles or more in extent is less than 4,000 square miles. The remainder of the cultivable land consists of diminutive plains created by the sediment from streams. This geographic fragmentation of agricultural land makes internal transportation and communication difficult and costly except by sea. It facilitates localism and economic self-sufficiency.

Despite the ever-present danger of catastrophe from earthquake, typhoon, or torrential rain, the climate is hospitable to man (Map 2). Warmth and rainfall are adequate for agriculture in all lowland areas except those in northern Hokkaido. Moreover, no section of Japan has either an annual or a seasonal deficiency of moisure. To the buffalo-hunting Indians of the Great Plains of the United States, or to their successors, the commercial farmers of the world's grain basket, the almost microscopic Japanese plains would pose severe if not insuperable problems of adjustment. To migrants who either had or soon acquired the agricultural techniques of mainland Asia, semitropical southwestern Japan offered almost an ideal environment.

The location of the Japanese islands was of signal importance in the evolution of the Japanese people. The islands of Kyushu, Shikoku, Honshu, and Hokkaido are separated from each other by fairly narrow straits; all are separated from mainland Asia by the Sea of Japan. In both north and south, the arc of islands curves inward toward the continent. Even for primitive boats voyages were fairly easy from Korea to Tsushima Island to Kyushu, or from Korea directly to western Kyushu or southwestern Honshu.

Japan's island position placed barriers in the paths of migrants from the mainland, but migration was possible. To the east of Japan, on the other hand, there was the Pacific Ocean. Japan, like Britain, was strategically located to receive migrants.[3] Once migrants arrived, they could either adjust to life in the new environment, return to the continent, or perish. Japan was a last frontier for the moving peoples of Asia.

[1] Trewartha, Glenn T. *Japan. A physical, cultural and regional geography*. P. 9.

[2] SCAP. GHQ. Natural Resources Section. *Japanese natural resources. A comprehensive survey*. P. 23.

[3] Sansom, George B. *Japan. A short cultural history*. P. 10.

There is little agreement concerning the origin, the physical characteristics, or the cultures of the peoples who reached Japan. The traditional interpretation involved movements of migrants with Neolithic cultures from the mainland. The modern controversy centers around the role of early migrants from the south, and it places the initial habitations in the Mesolithic or the Paleolithic period.[4] However, the migrations of the various peoples were almost completed by the beginning of the Christian era.[5] The significant factors in later periods were the interminglings of the groups already present in Japan.[6]

THE ANCIENT SOCIETY

The earliest Neolithic cultures in Japan were similar to those of the adjacent mainland areas of northeastern Asia. Neolithic sites in Korea yield stone axes, slate knives, arrowheads, swords, articles of bone and horn, and pottery similar to those found in Kyushu and western Japan.[7] A Neolithic culture persisted in southern and western Japan until the first century of the Christian era, in the central portion of Honshu until the third or fourth century A.D., and in northern Honshu until 1000 A.D. Its transformation in the south and west was associated with the diffusion of the metal culture of China by way of Korea.[8]

There are no historical writings on the initial contacts of the Japanese with the more developed culture of the Chinese. A Chinese record of the third century B.C. indicates that the Wa (Japanese) were subject to the Kingdom of Yen in North China, and coins of the Yen rulers have been found in the

[4] Groot, Gerard J. *The prehistory of Japan*. Ch. I.

[5] The problems of folk migrations and physical anthropology in Japan are a segment of the broader problems of the origins of physical types and the folk migrations within the northeast Asian region, including Korea, the Soviet Far East, Manchuria, and other areas of northern and western China. For Japan itself there is a rather large literature on skeletal anatomy, but interpretations were made difficult by the barriers implicit in the legends of origin. For instance, a great economist could write in the immediate prewar period that the Yamato race had continued ". . . to maintain its predominant place in the racial composition of our population ever since the dawn of our national history down to this very day." (Honjo, Eijiro. *The social and economic history of Japan*. P. 9.) As a Japanese student said in the anonymity of a footnote to an article published in America, ". . . in considering . . . theories of origin, it should be borne in mind that this is not a topic for free speculation in Japan." (Nishioka, Hideo, and Schenck, W. Egbert. "An outline of theories concerning the prehistoric people of Japan." *American Anthropologist*, N.S., 39: 23-31. January-March 1937.)

[6] Hulse, Frederick S. "Physical types among the Japanese." Pp. 122-133 in: Coon, Carleton S., and Andrews, James M., IV, Editors. *Studies in the anthropology of Oceania and Asia*.

[7] Sansom, George B. "An outline of recent Japanese archaeological research in Korea, in its bearings upon early Japanese history." *T.A.S.J.*, 2nd Series, 6:5-19. December 1929.

[8] Grott. *The prehistory* . . . . Ch. I. Also Sansom. *Japan* . . . . Pp. 1-13.

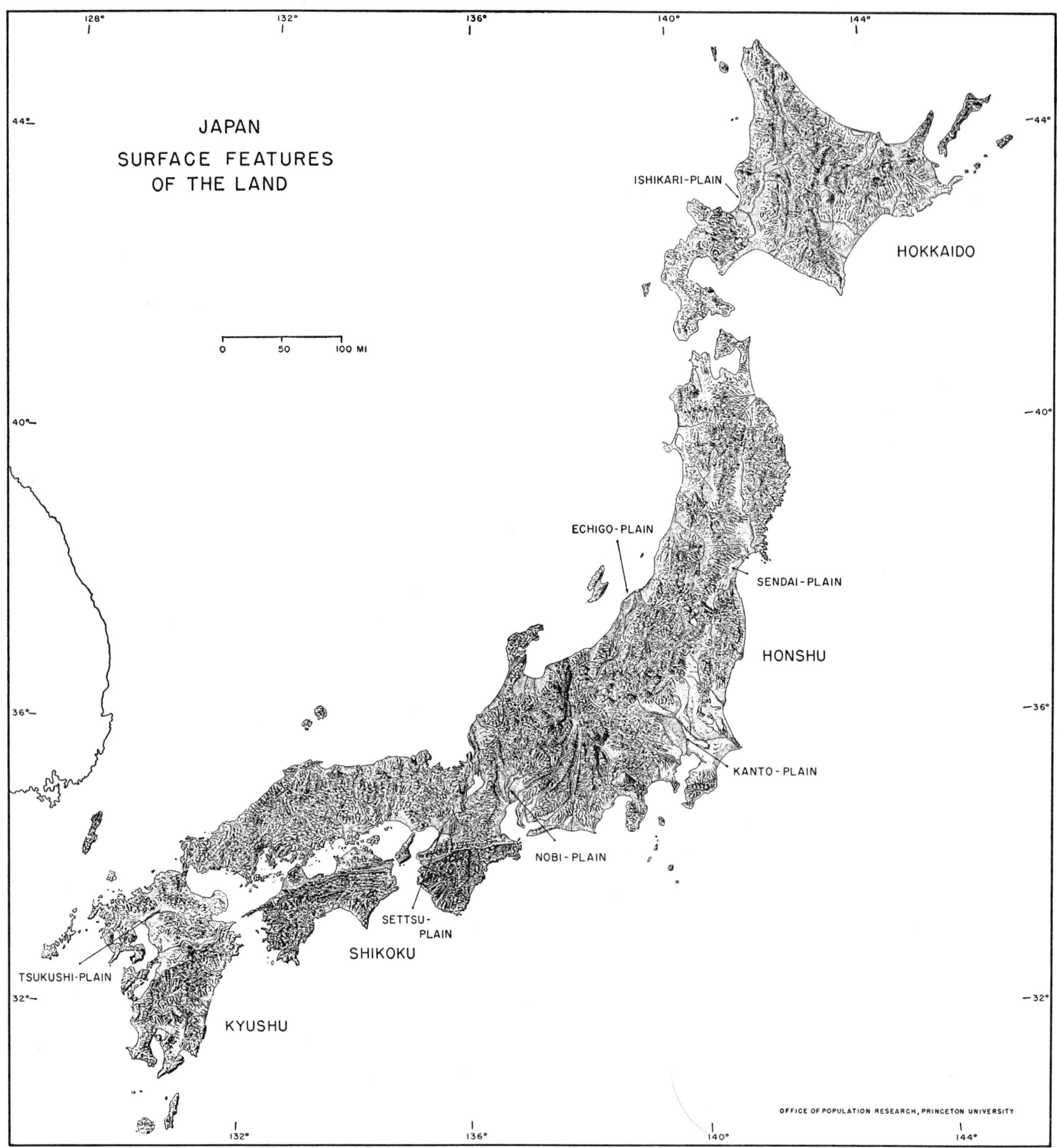

Map 1. Japan. Surface features of the land
Source: SCAP. GHQ. Natural Resources Section. *Japanese natural resources . . . . Map supplement,* Map 1.

Ryukyu Islands as well as in Korea. Direct contact between Japan and China seems to have been established by the second half of the third century B.C. However, the great expansion of Chinese culture into the northeastern region of Asia and across to Japan came with the Han dynasty.[9] The earliest direct and relatively authentic information concerning the early Japanese is contained in the Han records of 57 A.D.[10] The arrival of a Japanese mission at Loyang, the capital of

[9] The Han records, including the geographical section of *Hou han shu* (424 A.D.), the *Wei chih,* and the *Wei liao* (before 292 A.D.), were compiled from original materials now lost and contain many internal inconsistencies. Sansom observes, however, that the statements of the Wei records "are credible enough in general to furnish a fair picture of Japan as seen by Chinese observers in the first century of the Christian era." Sansom. *Japan* . . . . P. 19.

[10] In 108 B.C., northern Korea was divided into four Chinese provinces, and one of these, Lakliang, became a major center of Chinese culture. Its direct control extended to what is now middle Korea; its indirect influence reached throughout southern Korea and across to Kyushu. Archaeological research in south Korea and west Japan indicates the strong probability of fairly regular trade between Lakliang and Kyushu by the beginning of the Christian era. With the changing political situation in China, Lakliang was conquered by the Kingdom of Kokuryo, but the influence of Chinese culture persisted.

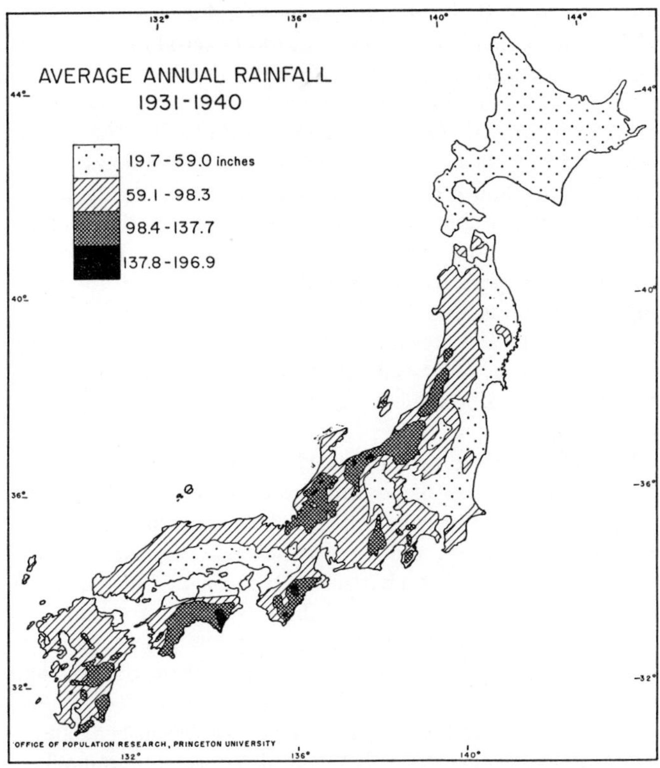

Map 2. Japan. Average annual rainfall, 1931-1940
Adapted from: SCAP. GHQ. Natural Resources Section. *Japanese natural resources* . . . . P. 22.

the Han, was noted and the following description of the country added: "The country of the Wa lies south-east of South Korea in the middle of the ocean and is formed of a number of islands. It contains more than one hundred kingdoms . . . . They understand the art of weaving . . . . Their soldiers have spears and shields, wooden bows and bamboo arrows sometimes tipped with bone. The men all tattoo their faces, and adorn their bodies with designs. Differences of rank are indicated by the position and size of the pattern . . . ."[11]

Thus the records of the literate peoples of the mainland corroborate the archaeological evidence that the peoples of southwest Japan received the metal culture of China during the early centuries of the Christian era. To the Chinese, however, the Japanese were not worthy of detailed description. An analysis of the society, economy, and demography of the preliterate era in Japan must rest primarily on deductions from the chronicles of the Japanese of later centuries.

Sometime prior to the development of written records there appeared in southwest Japan a people and a culture called the Yamato. Presumably this group possessed some of the weapons and the tools of the metal culture of the Chinese and thus had some superiority over its neighbors of Neolithic culture.[12] Both the material relics and the chronicles of later centuries indicate that the Yamato remained a minor people in a limited area of southwestern Japan for a long period of time. The development of strength for major conquest and expansion required an improved agriculture, an altered form of social organization, and centralized order. It also required an increase in population, either by natural increase of the Yamato or by the assimilation of conquered peoples.

After their long stay in southwestern Japan, the expansion of the Yamato was reasonably rapid, considering the nature of the land and the cultural levels of the period. The Yamato reached the Kinai, or Inner Provinces, of Honshu by the third century A.D. From the third to the sixth century they drove back the indigenous people called the Ezo and extended their frontiers to the Kanto Plain, the site of modern Tokyo. They had already pushed westward to the coast, defeating the people of Izumo-no-kuni, and they had driven the Kumaso of Kyushu southward. By the end of the fourth century A.D. they dominated south and central Japan and maintained some contacts with the people living in the southern part of the Korean peninsula.[13]

By the seventh century the suzerainty of the Yamato extended from Kyushu in the southwest to Sendai in the northeast. The rulers wished to consolidate the existing situation and to justify their claims to sovereignty over all the lands and peoples of Japan. Hence they ordered two official records to be compiled, the *Kojiki* (Record of ancient matters) and the *Nihon-shoki* (Chronicles of Japan).[14] These works, written in the early part of the eighth century A.D., combined myths, legends, and history in such a way as to increase the prestige of the ruling families of the Yamato and their allied clans. They were followed by massive compilations that were the official records of the Yamato rulers.

In the way of life described in the *Nihon-shoki*, the basic unit of the society and the economy was the *uji*. This was a community of families who were, or believed themselves to be, of common ancestry in direct or collateral lines.[15] Probably the people in the *uji* had once been a kin group, but by the protohistoric period the *uji* was a locality group composed of villages or a series of locality groups. The theories of consanguinity contributed to unity, but the fundamental ties that bound the people together were the organization of group living, cooperation in production, and common political allegiance.

The original *uji* was relatively self-sufficient, but the development of the larger society was achieved by the consolidation of *uji* and the formation of hierarchical relations

[11] Sansom. *Japan* . . . . P. 18.
[12] Munro, N. Gordon. *Primitive culture in Japan.*

[13] Reischauer, Robert K. *Early Japanese history, c. 40 B.C.-A.D. 1167.* Vol. I, pp. 18-19.

[14] These were compiled in the eighth century A.D. The *Kojiki* is in three volumes, the first on the era of the gods; the *Nihon-shoki* is in thirty volumes, the first two on the age of the gods. The *Kojiki* is the more specifically Japanese, for it traces back to the orally transmitted legends of the people. It seems that Temmu-tenno (672-687 A.D.) ordered a certain man of marvelous memory, Hiyeda-no-are, to learn "the genuine traditions and old languages of former ages." A quarter of a century later Gemmei-tenno ordered Yasumaro to record this history deposited in the memory of Hiyeda-no-are. The *Nihon-shoki* was compiled as an official history by imported scribes who used the Chinese style and the Chinese language. It includes an incomplete integration of various cycles of legends with elements of Japanese, Chinese, and Korean origin. Translations of the materials in each dealing with the era of the gods are available in English: Chamberlain, Basil Hall. *Translation of the Kojiki, or Record of ancient matters.* Also: Aston, W. G. *Nihongi. Chronicles of Japan from the earliest times to A.D.* 697.

The stories of the legendary period as told in the *Kojiki* and the *Nihon-shoki* were commissioned by those in political power, but they became the sources for a system of beliefs that was diffused as the underlying religion of the people and elevated at differing periods to a creed of state. Even the motives for compilation were ambivalent. Superficially, they represent a planned enhancement of the prestige of a ruling group through the identification of its members with the heroic people of the age of the gods and even with the gods themselves. It is quite possible, though, that a confused elite, conscious of its chaotic intellectual and spiritual milieu, had scholars and scribes compile and rationalize the multitudinous and conflicting legends of the past in order to make the present more rational.

[15] Honjo, Eijiro. *The social and economic history of Japan.* Ch. II, "The economic development."

between them. The Yamato became the largest and most powerful of the *uji*. As they incorporated other groups, the leaders of these groups were designated with titles and served in the Yamato court. The leader of the Yamato thus occupied a dual rule. As *uji-no-kami*, head of the Yamato, he ruled the area and the people of the imperial *uji* directly. In his role as sovereign he controlled the *uji-no-kami* of the lesser *uji*, but they retained power with reference to the members of their own *uji*. The structure was essentially one of personal relations of domination and carefully regulated submission. It was not the political structure of a national state but rather a pseudo-consanguineous relationship. It contained possibilities for friction, should any of the lesser *uji* expand in power relative to the imperial *uji*.

Economic and cultural transformations were in process as the *uji* of the Yamato approached the apex of its power. Techniques for the cultivation of the soil, the processing of commodities, manufacturing, and transportation came from China. These were economic folkways, but they were associated with a greatly increased subsistence that permitted an increase in population. Furthermore, the change from hunting and fishing to agriculture anchored people to areas and created the food surpluses that were basic to a growth of cities. As developments within Japan permitted the rise of leisure classes and urban elites, cultural currents from China reached the upper groups of the Japanese. Literature, art, and the religion of Buddhism were gifts of the Chinese to all the peoples on their frontiers, and the Japanese were receptive indeed.

The Taika Reform: The Plans

The changes that occurred in Japan in the early centuries of the Christian era were in part the by-product of fortuitous events, in part the consequence of a deliberate but limited introduction of elements of Chinese culture. Gradually the introduction of things Chinese became more conscious and more comprehensive. In the seventh century students, priests, artists, and craftsmen went to China for long periods of observation and study.[16] These cultural emissaries brought back not only new material objects and improved techniques, but reports of an empire whose frontiers extended across the fabled lands of a continent. In this empire government was centralized on a territorial basis. Officials were selected on the basis of competitive examinations rather than family position. Material splendor revealed the possibilities of a life more abundant than that in a Japan now recognized as primitive. The conclusion seemed obvious: Japan should adopt the Chinese political and economic structure and thereby secure a culture and a power equivalent to those of China.

The veneration of Chinese culture and the desire for a similar culture in Japan existed among only a small portion of the oligarchy. The intellectuals, the leaders of the imperial *uji*, and the Buddhists favored the creation of a replica of China in the Japan of the seventh century A.D. The leaders of the dissident *uji* and the Shintoists favored the maintenance of the ancient order. Civil war seemed likely under this situation, but in the seventh century, as in later periods of great crisis, reorientation proceeded by indirection and compromise. A new order was created, but the new order was in major part a rearrangement of the ancient order. Through assassination and forced abdication, it became possible to secure major reforms in the name of the head of the imperial *uji*, who thus became the emperor of a national state.

In 646 A.D. Kotoku-tenno issued the edict that has given the designation of Taika, or Great Reform, to the period 645-650 A.D.[17] Its four major articles were as follows:

I. All lands and products are the property of the state. The various granaries and hereditary corporations of the Yamato *uji* and the personal estates of imperial and local leaders are abolished. All persons of the fifth rank or above are given sustenance grants.

II. *Uji* officials are replaced by civil servants centrally appointed on a territorial basis, with communication and transportation to be established to permit movement throughout the empire.[18]

III. "Let there be now provided for the first time registers of population, books of account, and a system of the receipt and re-granting of distribution-land. Let every fifty houses be reckoned a township, and in every township let there be one alderman who shall be charged with the superintendence of the population, the direction of the sowing of crops and the cultivation of mulberry trees, and prevention and examination of offences, and the enforcement of the payment of taxes and of forced labor."[19]

IV. The old taxes and forced labor are abolished, and a system of commuted taxes introduced by which commodities produced locally are payable in lieu of labor. Contributions of post horses, weapons, and manpower are to be made in a fixed ratio to the number of houses.

Brief exploration of the significance of this edict of 645 A.D. will indicate the aptness of the designation of Taika, or Great Reform. Full implementation would have transformed the pseudo-consanguineous structure of seventh-century Japan into a national state with an all-powerful emperor who held all lands and products. The officials of the new state were to be selected on the basis of merit rather than lineage, with a consequent liquidation of the status of the *uji* leaders. Transportation and communication systems were to bring all dissident groups into a centralized political structure. These transformations in the structure of government, economy, and society would have created conditions for population growth far different from those that existed in the ancient society.

The provisions of the Great Reform most relevant to the growth of the population were those concerned with land ownership and cultivation. The third article of the Taika Reform ordered the preparation of a plan for the redistribution of land. Subsequent plans provided for a periodic redistribution in accord with the size and composition of families.[20] Hence in theory there would be equality in the relations of population and resources. Moreover, in the life cycle of the

[16] For the history of the Taika reforms, their implementation and their transformation, see: Honjo. *The social and economic history* . . . . Also: Sansom, *Japan* . . . . Reischauer, *Early Japanese history* . . . .

[17] Sansom. *Japan* . . . . Ch. IV, "The introduction of Chinese learning," and Ch. V, "Cultural relations with China and the political reform of Taika."

[18] Detailed regulations for a capital city were prescribed in this section of the code, despite the fact that the Yamato capital of the time was a rude village abandoned at the death of a sovereign.

[19] Aston. *Nihongi* . . . . Vol. II, pp. 207-208.

[20] The first recorded Japanese legislation on the Chinese model was a *ryo* in twenty-two volumes promulgated from Otsu in Omi in the year 662. Revisions were distributed in 689. The Taiho Code of 702 laid out the administrative organization. The revision of this code, issued in 718, is the first of the great codes extant. The resume given in this chapter is based on Sir George Sansom's translation and analyses of a later code, the Yoro, as published in 833. By this time there had been changes in detail, but the principles remained. Sansom, George B. "Early Japanese law and administration." *T.A.S.J.*, 2nd Series, 9:67-109, and 11:117-149. 1932 and 1934.

individual family, increases or declines in numbers would be accompanied by expansion or contraction of the land available to the family. If an agricultural society had actually developed along the lines prescribed in the Taika Reform, conditions would have been very favorable for population growth. Progress toward the goal of many sons could have proceeded without the deterrents of poverty and insecurity. Mortality might have been expected to decline as land and hence food became more plentiful for those who had lacked land or possessed it in quite inadequate amounts. Whether the planners of the Taika Reform were conscious of the demographic implications of their land reforms is doubtful. They did know, however, that land redistribution and supervision of the complex operations of a centralized state required a continuing inventory of population, land, and resources. And so the third article of the Reform of 645 A.D. also ordered the establishment of a nation-wide population register in Japan.

The effects of the Great Reform in the centuries following its pronouncement were quite different from those that would have resulted from a direct transformation of Japanese society in accord with the statement of the principles of the Reform. The principles themselves were the bases for codified regulations that specified in some detail the organization of the social structure, the economy, and the government. The great codes, like the principles of the Reform, were statements of ideal structures rather than of anything that came to exist in Japan. Actual developments in culture and hence in population were influenced by these ideals, but the developments represented adaptations and compromises that often contravened them. Thus it is essential to outline the planned new order of Japan in some detail before we consider the course of Japanese society and population during the centuries that followed the Great Reform.

The social structure prescribed in the codes was in curious contrast with the agrarian equalization implicit in the provisions for a periodic redistribution of the land. A rigid hierarchy extended from the imperial court to the slave household.[21] There were four grades of imperial princes and thirty grades of princes and subjects, the latter including both free and unfree. Free subjects were divided into those with and those without rank. The latter in turn were subdivided into *hakutei* (small cultivators) and *zoshiki* (artisans). The artisans were hereditary members of various agricultural and industrial guilds; strictly speaking, they were semi-free rather than free. The unfree people included five categories: tomb serfs, official serfs who cultivated crown land, indentured domestic workers, public slaves who worked for the government, and private slaves who worked for individuals. Members of these last two groups could be purchased or sold.

A territorial organization into *kuni* (provinces) and *gun* (districts) replaced the *uji* structure of the earlier period. The *kami* (governor) of the province was responsible for public order and public morals, military defense, economic development, labor regulation, and population registration.[22] Each *gun* had its own administrator, usually a man of influence from the local gentry. The *gun* in turn was divided into townships or villages, each of which had a headman. Households were organized in small groups, with collective responsibility for the maintenance of order and the payment of taxes.

This territorial organization with administrative lines passing from the center to the individual families was the basis for an elaborate revision of the system of land tenure and taxation. *Uji* ownership was replaced by a state tenancy that adjusted land to labor in order to produce maximum yields. Wet-rice fields were to be distributed among the cultivators on the basis of the number of members in the household, with a redistribution each sixth year.[23] Land and produce taxes were levied in relation to the normal yields of the allotted areas, but the liability of a household to personal taxes was determined by the size and composition of its membership. Exempt categories included the imperial family, persons of the eighth rank or above, males aged six or less, persons "covered" by their relationship, the aged, the deformed and the crippled, the diseased, all female members, servants, and slaves. Members of the household were further classified by age: under three, infants; 3 to 16, children; 17 to 20, youths; males 21 to 60, able-bodied; males 61 to 66, elders; males 66 and over, aged.

The small group of neighboring households was responsible for the good conduct, the economic activity, and the residential stability of its members. Members were required to notify the others in the group of their own movements and of the arrival or departure of guests. If one household moved, the remaining households in the group were responsible for the cultivation of the land and the payment of the taxes for three years, after which the allotment returned to the state. The neighborhood group as well as the members of the family concerned had to guarantee any person joining a household within the group. If a household wished to move to a less congested area, the head had to secure permission from the provincial or the national government. Vagrants whose registration in their original household had lapsed and servants or slaves who had become free were placed on the register of the place where they resided. These provisions could be used to encourage movement to the frontier provinces and to restrict reverse movements from the frontier to the inner provinces and the capital.

Periodic reallocation of land and the assessment of taxes proportionate to areas, normal yields, or number of households necessitated the maintenance of a continuing inventory of acreage and households. Likewise, the levying of individual taxes on households on the basis of the personal characteristics of their members necessitated information on such characteristics. And, finally, continuing reports on movements to and from local areas implied a registration system. Hence the third provision of the Taika code was quite appropriate: "Let there now be established for the first time registers of population, books of account, and a system of the receipt and re-granting of distribution-land."

The *koseki* (household registers) were the responsibility of the headmen of the villages. Detailed information was re-

[21] Asakawa, Kan'ichi. *The early institutional life of Japan. A study in the reform of 645 A.D.* The household laws not only specified the social classes but gave detailed instructions concerning marriage, succession, and economic status and relationships.

[22] Sansom, "Early Japanese law . . . ." Pp. 120-121. The new responsibilities of government for education and cultural advance were also allocated to the provincial governors. Each province was to have one professor of Chinese and one doctor of medicine. The students attached to each were to number perhaps fifty in a major province.

[23] Land redistribution was to be achieved through a planned redesign of rural villages patterned after the uniform land system in ancient China. Since the implementation of this redesign of the land-utilization pattern and reallocation of rural population could occur only when the power of the government was great and labor was abundant, it was limited largely to the Kinki districts. The pattern is still apparent in some agricultural villages of southwest Honshu. See Oda, Takao, and Tanioka, Takeo. "The jo-ri system . . . ." Pp. 16-17 in: Tsujimura, Taro, Compiler. *Distribution maps on the regional geographical study of Japan. Text.*

quested concerning the age and physical capacity of the members of the household; whether subject to, or exempt from, the labor tax; whether entitled to servants, etc. Tax registers were compiled annually on the basis of reports from the household heads giving the name of the household and listing its members. The household registers were compiled each sixth year. The volume or roll for each village was prepared with three copies, two sent to the national chancellor's office, one retained in the province. Registers of households of special classes, such as serfs and industrial workers, were also prepared and copies sent to the appropriate office of the central government. Household registers were kept for five periods of six years, after which they could be cancelled.[24]

To the Japanese oligarchy of the seventh and later centuries, intricate provisions for land redistribution, social organization, and human accounting were only means for the attainment of an urban culture. The city that was to be the center of this great new civilization was pictured as a replica of Ch'ang-an, the capital of the T'ang Empire. The location selected was Nara, where topography met the demands of the Chinese theory of "wind and water"; that is, there were hills for protection and rivers for transportation and contact. Nara's seven Buddhist temples, its Shinto shrines, its palaces and other public buildings were more magnificent than anything that had existed previously in Japan. Its total population reputedly reached some two hundred thousand, but dissatisfaction with its site was widespread by the middle of the eighth century. Both the sovereign and the leader of the most powerful of the great families thought that the domination of the central government by the Buddhist sects might be lessened by moving the capital. Furthermore, Nara had an inadequate physical location, potable water being insufficient and communication by river with the seaport village of Naniwa inadequate. In 793 the capital was moved to the site of the present city of Kyoto. Here it remained until the Meiji Restoration, a period of almost eleven centuries.

The new capital was named Heian-kyo, "the Capital of Peace." It was planned, as Nara had been, on the pattern of the T'ang capital of Ch'ang-an, but it was more magnificent than Nara. The chronicles describe a city that was laid out with 38,912 houses.[25] By the beginning of the ninth century the number of houses was reported as 100 thousand and the population as 500 thousand.[26] In Heian there was development of art, literature, and philosophy, even empirical study of social phenomena, but the philosophical and intellectual awakening was accompanied by prolific regulations designed to maintain an unchanging social structure. As the following sections will indicate, the creation of a great urban culture could not proceed apart from the development of the nation as a whole.

The Developments, Seventh to Twelfth Century

Legal codes promulgated by a small elite could not have created a replica of the T'ang Empire within the primitive social and economic structure of the Yamato kingdom even under ideal conditions.[27] And conditions were not ideal, for practical considerations dictated fundamental departures from the Chinese model. Since the development of a centralized government to replace the *uji* structure required the co-operation of the oligarchy, public officials were chosen from persons of rank rather than on merit as in China. An educational system was instituted as the basis for a civil service on the T'ang pattern, but the schools were few and the students were children of men of rank. Thus the implementation of the Great Reform occurred under the aegis of that small aristocracy of birth and wealth which had ruled Japan since the mythical descent of the ancestors from the Plains of High Heaven.

A similar incongruity between plans and levels of cultural development characterized activities in the political and military spheres. The planners of Taika realized that there must be a police force responsible to the central government rather than to the chiefs of the *uji*. The theoretical solution lay in universal military service, and the provisions for such service were explicit. Conscripts unable to commute their labor service by a tax in kind were to serve one year as frontier guards and three years as guards of palaces or mansions. The training of the men and the custody of military supplies were the responsibilities of district administrators. Four districts constituted a command, which was to have from 500 to 1,000 men. Thus the implementation of the Reform as originally envisioned would have yielded a disciplined army responsible to the central government. If this goal had been realized, order in the settled areas, expansion of frontiers in the north and the southwest, and the maintenance of Japanese hegemony on the Korean peninsula could have been achieved without the acquiescence of the heads of the great contending *uji*.

The actualities of the Japanese situation prohibited developments along the lines of the mainland empire. Official policy toward militarism and expansionism vacillated in the early years of the Great Reform. The leaders wished to achieve internal order and external expansion, but they suspected the people whom they trained for war and they feared that the district administrators would weld the soldiers into provincial armies. The dilemma was inescapable, for the commanders of the conscript armies were members of the *uji* whose powers the army was to check.

A plethora of regulations reveals the continuing conflict between the drive toward national power and the necessity to curb the great families.[28] By the end of the eighth century even the theory of a centrally controlled military force had lapsed. In its place were local gendarmeries, staffed primarily by younger men from the families of the district administrators. As a result, the central government could enforce its regulations only with the concurrence of the provincial officials—and these were members of the *uji* whose prerogatives the national government had intended to assume.

The deteriorating international position of Japan was a consequence of the retreat from militarism within Japan and the changing power position on the mainland. Japanese activities in

[24] The rolls of 670 A.D. were to be preserved, for they confirmed the names and titles established in an ordeal of 415 A.D.

[25] Murdoch, James. *A history of Japan*. Vol. I.

[26] Sansom. *Japan* . . . . P. 193. It is apparent that the population figures of this early period involve systematic exaggeration.

[27] This and the following sections rely for their factual content on the chronicle of events of the period as compiled by Robert K. Reischauer in his *Early Japanese history*, Part A. Pp. 123-405. Reischauer's chronicle was based on an examination of the works of eminent Japanese historians and on investigation of events noted in the source books for the period. The cultural history of the period follows Sansom, *Japan* . . . .

[28] In 675 all men from princes down to those of the lowest rank were ordered to provide themselves with weapons; in 684 all officials were ordered to store arms and practice the military arts. But in 685 it was forbidden to store great horns, drums, fifes, banners, flags, and great bows in the provinces; these were to be placed in district government storehouses and used only by the imperial armies. The chronicles of the succeeding years record the failure of centralization and unification.

Korea had served to maintain contacts with China, but the hegemony of the expanding T'ang Empire over the former Korean kingdoms of Paiksche and Kokuli gave Japan direct access to T'ang culture. The retreat from the mainland was not entirely voluntary, for a Japanese fleet was defeated by a T'ang fleet in the late seventh century. Japan withdrew her armies from the Korean peninsula and maintained guards against a possible invasion of Japan itself by the T'ang forces. Her efforts to expand on the mainland were not renewed until a thousand years later, when Hideyoshi moved an army into Korea.

Japan's need of an army for external aggression could be obviated by withdrawal to the home islands, but the problems of internal order were not so easily solved. Frontier barricades had to be maintained against the Ezo in the north and the Kumaso in the southwest. Conflicts among the great families were recurrent. Each death of an emperor brought a struggle for the succession. The suppression of vagabondage and robbery was an acute problem for a government that had neither an efficient police nor a functioning army. In fact, it was this inability to maintain order that led eventually to the replacement of the central government by strong men capable of maintaining peace, order, and security on local and regional levels.

THE POPULATION STATISTICS

If we trust the chronicles, the early rulers of the Yamato occasionally counted their subjects.[29] In 248 A.D., Sujin-tenno is reported to have issued an imperial rescript announcing a new census of the population. This census was to secure detailed information on age and occupation, and it was to be used for the establishment of population registers. The purpose was reported to be both military and economic, for Sujin-tenno levied taxes in terms of animal skins and game for men and textiles for women.

The emperors who followed Sujin-tenno are also described as engaging in statistical activities. Richu-tenno (428-432 A.D.) appointed historiographers to draw up detailed reports on each province, but there is no mention of population counts accompanying these surveys. Ingyo-tenno (438-454 A.D.) reorganized and corrected the population registers, which had been allowed to lapse after Sujin-tenno caused them to be established two centuries earlier. These and many other reports concerning statistical activities in early Japan may be inventions of Chinese sages in Japan who knew that the rulers of their own country compiled statistics and maintained registers.

It is not known when the first counts of the population of local areas or wider regions were made in Japan. The earliest surveys were probably those of the population of *miyake*, or areas where people cultivated rice for the imperial government.[30] In the year 610 A.D. Suiko-tenno ordered a census of Buddhists and a count of the general population. According to tradition, this "census" indicated a total population of 4,988,842, of whom 1,994,018 were men and 2,994,824 were women. The great surplus of women is most peculiar, especially in a society in which female infanticide was reported to exist. Later estimates of the population as of the early seventh century tend to cluster around an estimated total of five million, but all trace back to the count ordered by Suiko-tenno.

If the registration system prescribed in the codes that followed the Taika Reform had been developed, it would have provided a basis for analysis of the population of Japan from the seventh to the twelfth century. It is obvious, however, that an advanced system such as this could not be imposed on the loosely integrated structure of seventh-century Japan. It is equally obvious that no people with almost universal illiteracy could operate a detailed human inventory at the local level. Many specific factors retarded the successful operation of the *koseki* system of household registration in the Japan of the seventh to the twelfth century: the limited control exercised by the central government over many areas, difficulties in transportation and communication, the low cultural levels of the people, and various economic and political factors forcing flight from registration of people and allocation of land.

The difficulties in analysis of the population dynamics of the centuries following the Taika Reform would be immeasurably less if even the fragmentary and deficient records of the twenty-two registrations that were ordered between 645 and 790 survived, but these "censuses" were taken for administrative rather than analytical purposes. The size of the population was a state secret; records were to be preserved by the government for thirty years, then burned. The codification of Engishiki of 947 forbade the copying of the figure on the size of the reported population without the permission of the emperor.[31]

The few surviving records of the eighth century indicate systematic errors in the reporting of age and sex that reflected the compulsions to escape taxation in commodities and in labor (Table 1).[32] In most age groups females exceeded males. Moreover, while the age changes in the population of the sexes considered separately were quite irregular, the age changes in the total population were fairly regular. This would indicate a tendency to report men as women, perhaps because women received only two-thirds as large an allotment of land as men but were exempt from forced labor.

The descriptive and numerical evidence indicates that the registration system in seventh-century Japan contributed little to knowledge of the size, the structure, or the increase of the population in ancient Japan. The establishment of the system was significant, however, because the tradition of statistics became associated with others of the remote past.

LAWS AND RECORDS OF HOUSEHOLDS

In early days, as today, the attitudes and values of the Japanese people and the ways in which their lives were organized in families and communities were critical factors in the growth of the population. Analysis of attitudes and values is impossible, for illiterate people leave no written records. The law of households does survive, though, and from this expression of the ideals of the governing group it

[29] Yanagisawa, Yasutoshi. "Histoire critique des travaux statistiques au Japon depuis l'antiquite jusqu'a la restauration imperiale." *Bulletin de l'institut international de statistique*, 19(3): 249-307. 1911.

[30] A household survey of one such area of 92 sections indicated a population of 18,670 in the reign of Yuryaku-tenno (457-489 A.D.). Sixty or seventy years later, in the first year of the reign of Kimmei-tenno (539-571 A.D.), another survey indicated that this same area included 7,053 households. See Uchida. *Study of economic history of Japan.* [In Japanese.] Vol. I, p. 722. Cited in: Sugino, Wataro. "Waga kuni kodai no jinko zoka." *Keizai shi kenkyu*, No. 7, pp. 1-9. May 1930.

[31] Yokoyama, Y. "A study of Japanese population since ancient times." [In Japanese.] *Gakugei shirin*, 5:26. September 1879. Cited in: Ishii, Ryoichi. *Population pressure and economic life in Japan.* P. 2.

[32] Sekiyama, Naotaro. *Nihon jinko shi.* Pp. 20-42.

TABLE 1

The populations of selected local areas, by sex and age, from registration records of the eighth century A.D.

Age (lunar)	*Total*	*Male*	*Female*
1–5	603	309	294
6–10	431	206	225
11–15	459	226	233
16–20	458	214	244
21–25	350	182	168
26–30	292	154	138
31–35	297	116	181
36–40	230	118	112
41–45	199	84	115
46–50	152	61	91
51–55	117	45	72
56–60	93	44	49
61–65	78	23	55
66–70	62	16	46
71–75	33	10	23
76–80	15	10	5
81 and over	11	3	8
Total	3,880	1,821	2,059

Source: Sekiyama, Naotaro. *Nihon jinko shi.* Areas and dates: Mino-no-kuni, 702; Seikaido, 702; Shimobusa-no-kuni, 721; other *kuni,* 724-748.

is possible to deduce the family structure that was regarded as proper; the roles assigned to men, women, and children; the relations of the generations; and the status hierarchy based on sex, age, and relationship to the paramount ancestor. If these laws alone were available, any conclusions as to the existence or nature of a Chinese-inspired family system in the formative period of Japanese culture would be hazardous indeed. There is another source of information, however, for the relationships within the individual households were recorded in the *koseki* that were the basis for the allocation and redistribution of the cultivated land and the obligations of the household to the state. Fragments of these records survive.

The household code of Taika involved explicit acceptance of the five Confucian teachings from which the rules of pious duty were derived.[33] The duty of the father was justice, while that of the mother was affection. The duty of the elder brother was friendship, that of the younger brother respect. The duty of the child was obedience. The supreme virtue was filial piety.

The structure of the household was hierarchical. The head was responsible for the family's relations with community organizations and the government. When the head died, he was succeeded by his eldest legitimate son, even though that son was a minor. Perpetuation of the household through the eldest son was the paramount function of the family. Thus failure to produce a male child was the first of the seven grounds on which the wife could be divorced. If there was no male child, a relative in the fourth degree or closer could be adopted, provided the age difference was such that the household head could have been the "father" of the "son." Given this appropriate difference in age, the adopted son could pay proper respect to the father during his lifetime and perform the ancestral rites after his death.

In the chronicles of the legendary periods there were great empresses. The Sun Goddess herself was, of course, female. But in the period after the Great Reform, some twelve centuries ago, the proper Japanese family was patrilocal and patriarchal.[34] Description of its status structure can be derived from the laws of divorce and of grave offenses against piety. While there were no provisions for divorce of the husband, there were a variety of reasons that permitted the husband to write a notice of divorce against his wife. These included childlessness, disobeying a parent-in-law, committing adultery, stealing, or talking too much.[35] However, the wife could assure her status through appropriate filial piety. She could not be divorced if she had maintained the household during the period of mourning for her parents-in-law, if the house had risen in status since her marriage, or if there was no one to receive her.

If the wife committed a grave offense against piety, the relations between husband and wife had to be severed. The nature of the grave offenses indicates the status of the parents and more remote ancestors of the husband as contrasted with those of the wife. The first of the grave offenses against piety was striking a parent or a paternal grandparent. The husband had no alternative but to divorce his wife if she struck his mother. Divorce was also required if the wife murdered her husband's maternal grandparents, or her own uncle, aunt, brother, or sister. Similarly, it was a grave offense for a wife to strike her husband's paternal grandparents or to attempt to inflict harm on her husband.

The legal codes of the seventh and eighth centuries suggest that the subservient position of women was not as severe as in later centuries. The distribution of property at the death of the husband was as follows: wife, two shares; husband's mother, two shares; male children of the wife, two shares; male children of a concubine, one share. Daughters and concubines received half a share. The property the wife brought at her marriage was not shared.

The obligations and responsibilities of the household were carefully defined. They were inescapable, for an individual had no legal existence outside a household. The provisions for controlling mobility and preventing vagabondage were specific and rigid. Marriage and divorce were regulated by the family. Persons unable to support themselves had to be cared for by near relatives, however, and so security compensated for the lack of freedom.

The codes suggest discrepancies between behavior and propriety. Relations between male slaves or servants and kin of the owner were proscribed; children born of such relationships had no rights. However, concubinage was recognized and the concubine was protected by the family. The remarriage of widows was not approved, though a deserted wife could remarry.

The codes suggest a family structure favorable to high fertility. Marriage could occur in the early teens, but child marriage was not sanctioned. The bearing of sons was essential; failure of the woman in this function could result in divorce.

The fragments of the *koseki* records that survive cannot

[33] Sansom, George B. "Early Japanese law and administration." *T.A.S.J.*, 2nd Series, 11:117-149. Ch. VIII, "The law of households." The *Kokushi taikei* text was used first, but others were consulted.

[34] The assumption that the household was patrilocal is a deduction from the laws of *koseki,* particularly those on marriage and divorce. At marriage, the wife's name was removed from the *koseki* of her father and added to that of her husband's family. On divorce, her name was removed from the husband's register and restored to that of her father.

[35] Sansom. "Early Japanese law . . . ." Ch. VIII, Article 28.

indicate the characteristics of households in all the social-economic and status classes, but they merit careful inspection. Sir George Sansom has reproduced the following extract from a register of 702 A.D. which refers to a village in Kyushu:[36]

Relationship	*Name*	*Age*	*Category*	*Remarks*
Head of House	Urabe Nomoso	49	Able-bodied male, full age	Taxable household
Mother	Kayabe Ishi-me	74	Female, over age	
Wife	Urabe Hoshito-me	47	Female, full age	
Son	Urabe Kuromaro	19	Able-bodied male, under age	Eldest son, by wife
Son	Urabe Wakashi	6	Male child	Younger son, by wife
Daughter	Urabe Kagora-me	16	Female child	Daughter, by wife
Daughter	Urabe Kokagora-me	13	Ditto	Ditto
Brother	Urabe Katana	46	Able-bodied male, full age	
Wife	Nakatomibe Hitame-me	37	Female, full age	
Son	Urabe Kuro	17	Able-bodied male, under age	Son, by wife
Son	Urabe Akai	16	Male child	
Son	Urabe Okoji	2	Infant	
Daughter	Urabe Hisadzu-me	18	Female, under age	
Daughter	Urabe Aka-me	13	Female child	
Daughter	Urabe Hitsuji-me	9	Ditto	
Daughter	Urabe Maro-me	1	Infant	

In all 16 mouths, of which { Exempt—12; Taxable— 4 }

The head of this household was a male aged 49; his wife was 47. They had four surviving children, aged 6, 13, 16 and 19. The brother of the head lived with the household. He and his wife had a son aged 17 and six other children, whose ages were 1, 2, 9, 13, 16, and 18. The clustering of the ages here suggests concubinage. Although sons and nephews of the head aged from 16 to 19 lived in the household, they were apparently single, for no wives or concubines were recorded for them.

Professor Toda analyzed the records for two villages in the eighth century to indicate the relationship of persons living in the households to the household head.[37] There were 59 households in Oshima-mura, Chiba-ken, in the year 721 A.D. The average number of related persons per household was 8.4. The 59 heads reported 27 spouses and 10 concubines. The average number of children was almost five. The structure of relations within the households was somewhat more inclusive than that in modern Japan. High mortality had apparently reduced the number of the generations. In these 59 families there were no grandparents or great-grandparents, 13 grandchildren, and no great-grandchildren. Curiously enough, there were no spouses of children present to account for these 13 grandchildren. However, 54.5 per cent of all household members consisted of the head and lineal descendants of the head; 7.5 per cent of the members were spouses of the head or of descendants of the head. Thus, over three-fifths of all family members were in the direct patrilineal succession of the head or were spouses of persons in this line.

[36] Sansom. *Japan* . . . . P. 99.
[37] Toda, Teizo. *Kazoku kosei*. Pp. 418, 447-448.

Professor Toda presents data for another village for the year 702 A.D. The household pattern here was similar to that in Oshima-mura, but the households were more inclusive. The 109 heads had 471 children in the households, over four per man. Again there was a major deficit in the women who should have been the mothers of these sons of heads; only 31 wives and 14 concubines were reported. In this village the patrilineal line of the head and the spouses of persons in this line included only 44 per cent of all household members. Almost 43 per cent of the members were brothers, sisters, nephews and nieces, and the children of nephews and nieces of the head. The collateral relatives of spouses were again excluded. High mortality had not permitted many multi-generation families.

Growth and Change

The area effectively subject to the control of the Yamato and their allied *uji* in the middle of the seventh century is known only roughly. Outposts thrust into the territory of the Ezo had reached as far north as the present city of Sendai, but the Ezo held enclaves in the mountainous western regions of central Honshu. Their domination of northern Honshu and Hokkaido was undisputed.

Conquest of the indigenous groups was difficult. The Yamato were somewhat superior in military technology, but the Ezo fought in their own mountainous terrain, where problems of transport and supply limited the movements of the Yamato forces. Yamato expansion could occur only as a gradual process of pushing back the frontier century after century, with individual battles or even campaigns often ending in the victory of the Ezo. However, a process of accommodation and intermixture seems to have occurred over the centuries. Integration of the Ezo into Yamato communities, the assimilation of Yamato into Ezo communities, and the development of mixed settlement areas are reported again and again in the chronicles.

Expansion proceeded through the building of palisades and the stationing of frontier guards, with an outward movement from the barricades when opportunity offered, a withdrawal when the Ezo pushed downward in force. The vacillating campaigns continued throughout the seventh and eighth centuries, but there were only sporadic revolts after the early ninth century. Thus two and a half centuries after the Great Reform of 645 A.D. all the land of Japan except the Ryukyus and Hokkaido was subject to the people who believed themselves the direct and unsullied descendants of god-ancestors sent from the Plains of High Heaven to rule the sacred islands. Yamato and Japan were now synonymous.

THE ECONOMY

The artifacts indicate that agriculture was practiced in Japan by the middle Jomon period and had reached a substantial development by the late Jomon period. The pseudo-historical chronicles indicate that cultivation of the soil had replaced hunting and fishing as the major basis for the support of the Yamato people by the beginning of the Christian era.[38] In the late centuries of the *uji* society, there were increases in the acreage in lowland and in upland fields, and a development of irrigation which increased and regularized production in new areas as well as in those long utilized. The great Sujin-tenno (230-258 A.D.) and his successors struggled to advance agriculture through encouraging the digging of ponds and ditches for irrigation, the leveling of land, the creation of new rice fields, the construction of dams, and the opening of roads. Nintoku-tenno (395-427 A.D.) reportedly addressed his ministers as follows in the year 402 A.D.: "Viewing this land, the moors and marshes extend far and wide, and the cultivated fields are few and rare. Moreover, the river waters spread out to each side, so that the lower streams flow sluggishly. Should there happen to be continuous rains, the tide from the sea flows up against them so that one may ride in boats through the villages: and the highways, too, are covered with mud. Therefore do ye our ministers examine this together, and having ascertained the source of the divergence, make a channel for them to the sea, and staying the contrary flow (of the tide) preserve the fields and houses."[39] That winter the plain north of the palace was excavated and the water from the south diverted into the Western Sea. Embankments to the rivers were constructed. In 403 A.D. a great canal was built in Yamashiro to irrigate the rice fields; "by this means the peasants of that district had always years of abundance."

The extension of irrigation under the influence of the superior technology of China, often under the supervision of Korean engineers, and the use of grasses and green manures for fertilizers produced increases in the acreage and yields of the rice fields. In 292 A.D. each province was ordered to erect special granaries for the storage of grains from the imperial fields.

Developments in industry, trade, and communication paralleled those in agriculture. Roads were necessary for the expanding Yamato power. Ships moved with increasing frequency from Kyushu to Korea, and Korean migrants introduced such industrial technologies as sericulture, weaving, ceramics, carpentry, and leather manufacturing. The articles of gold and silver, the jewels, and the rich textiles that were imported from the mainland did much to make Japanese culture seem crude to its rulers.

The extent of the economic development of Japan in the early centuries of the Christian era should not be exaggerated. At the time of the Taika Reform of 645-650 A.D., the economy was largely agricultural and the techniques were crude. In succeeding centuries, central and local governments encouraged the utilization of superior agricultural implements, the diversification of crops, and the building and maintenance of irrigation facilities.[40] The chronicles indicate that the area under cultivation was increased, that more varied crops were produced, and that unit yields were increased, but measurement is difficult. The official statistics were compilations of tax records. It was natural, therefore, that as the power of the central government declined there was a decline in the amount of land reported as cultivated. Historical studies indicate that increase in cultivated acreage continued even when the records of the government indicated otherwise.

There were also developments in industry, trade, and transportation in the period after the Great Reform. The central government encouraged the weaving of damasks and brocades and the production of other luxuries. Merchants from China came to the ports of Kyushu, while a center for internal trade developed on the site of modern Osaka. There was some use of coins, but direct integration into a monetary economy was limited to small and predominantly urban groups. Developments in transportation were relatively advanced, for the surplus of the rural areas had to be transported to the cities. The Kiso-sando, a great highway through mountainous country in Mino-kuni, was opened in 703. Post stations were established in Yamashiro, Kawachi, Settsu, and Iga-kuni. A highway was built in the north country. In 754 the government in Kyushu was ordered to repair the signposts it had erected in the islands south of Kyushu and to write on each the name of the island, the places where ships could anchor, the places where drinking water could be found, the courses to be followed, and the distances. In 801 the provinces were ordered to build both ships and pontoon bridges and to make oars and rudders in order that taxes and tribute could be transported to Heian. In 835 it was ordered that the number of boats at the important ferries and harbors in Tokaido and Tosando be increased in order to improve transportation facilities.

THE EMERGENCE OF THE SHOEN

The Taika Reform was a blueprint for an ideal state in which power would be concentrated in a national government that would then regulate production and consumption. The attempt at centrally directed development continued for centuries, but the movement was toward regionalism. The land

[38] Tsuchiya, Takao. *An economic history of Japan.* Ch. I.

[39] Aston. *Nihongi* . . . . Vol. I, pp. 280-281.

[40] The following decrees indicate the type of encouragement that would have been given to agricultural development in these early centuries if the orders had been effective. In 693 the people in the provinces were commanded to plant mulberry trees, hemp, pear trees, and greens in addition to the grain crops; in 700 they were ordered to establish stock farms. And in 710 the Mountain Wardens' Hereditary Corporation was ordered to prohibit the cutting of trees. In 714 the farmers of Dewa *kuni* were ordered to promote sericulture; in 766 the farmers of the various provinces were encouraged to plant barley and wheat. In 767, and again in 840, it was ordered that agriculture be encouraged in all the provinces. In 840 also the people in the five Inner Provinces and the seven districts were ordered to plant millet, sorghum, Deccan grass, various cereals, soy beans, red beans, and sesame. In 841 the Government Headquarters in Kyushu was ordered to repair the embankments and the irrigation ponds of the provinces under its jurisdiction.

holdings of the powerful families had not been abolished even by the initial land redistributions.[41] As the power of the central government declined, there were increasing possibilities for the expansion of holdings.[42] The people found in *shoen* (manors) an escape from taxation and service that avoided the penalties of vagrancy and the difficulties of flight. The cultivator placed himself under the protection of the lord. Institutions of commendation and benefice developed. In commendation, the owner of taxable land surrendered it to the owner of the *shoen* for incorporation with tax-free land. A share of the product was given to the lord for physical protection and immunity from taxation. In benefice, the lord made grants to persons employed in the management or cultivation of land. The ownership of the land remained that of the lord of the *shoen*. Thus the cultivator became a hereditary tenant or a serf, fixed to the land and subject to taxation in kind and to compulsory labor.

The central government could not prevent the development of *shoen* and the escape of land and people from taxation, for many of the officials of the central government were also lords of *shoen*. The maintenance of national life was complicated by this duality within the central government itself. The imperial institution remained the symbol through which and for which all activities were carried on, but the emperor was not the architect of imperial policy. As the national state of Taika merged into the decentralized structure of a manorial organization, centralized power was secured by the Fujiwara family, whose founder Kamatari had fostered the Taika Reform. By the beginning of the tenth century the Fujiwara were the political dictators of Japan. The force that underlay this control was the organization of the lords of *shoen*.

The *shoen* provided enclaves of order in a period of national disorganization. However, struggles between groups were widespread by the middle of the eleventh century. Rioting spread even in the city of Kyoto. The Fujiwara could not restore order, so they appealed to powerful military families, the Minamoto and the Taira. National consolidation proceeded through the struggles of the great lords until in the twelfth century the final conflict between the Minamoto and the Taira occurred. The chronicles report that fighting spread throughout the country, that famine, pestilence, and death were widespread. After the victory of the Minamoto in the sea battle of Dannoura in 1185, the struggle of the lords was ended temporarily. There was a coalition and a consolidation of power. The manorial structure had become a feudal structure.

THE INCREASE OF THE POPULATION

The increases in acreage and the improvements of yields in the early centuries failed to solve the problems of the relation between people, food, and other products. The development of an overdense population in the settled areas and the correlated process of frontier expansion are noted again and again in the chronology of events in the legendary period. Typical of this search for additional agricultural areas is the report that Sujin-tenno (230-258 A.D.) sent an emissary to the regions of the north and east to inspect the conditions of the people and the land. The emissary returned with the news that a people called Emishi dwelt in a land that was fertile and broad—and he recommended conquering it.

While the expansion of the frontier involved frequent struggles with the Ezo, the extent of the mortality involved for either Japanese or Ezo is not ascertainable. There were continuing reports that the Ezo had been captured and settled outside the Kinai, or Inner Provinces. The following account of the "wars" of the period of expansion may not be atypical. Keiko-tenno (291-322 A.D.) ordered the Prince Mimoro-wake to ". . . 'undertake the absolute rule of the Eastern lands,' but the Yemishi [Emishi] rebelled so he raised an army and attacked them. Then the Yemishi chieftains, Ashi-furi-he, Oho-ha-furi-he, and Tohotsu-kura-ho-he bowed their heads to the ground and came; they made deep obeisance and accepted punishment, offering him all their territory without exception. Therefore he pardoned those who surrendered, and put to death those who would not submit. On this account the Eastern land was for a long time free from trouble. Therefore his descendants are to this day in the Eastern Land."[43] Whatever the direct mortality involved in the expansion, to the Yamato the net result was the virtual elimination of opposing groups, either through death or through assimilation to Yamato culture and amalgamation with its bearers.

The increase in population permitted by the development and extension of rice agriculture did not lessen the vulnerability of the Japanese to famine and epidemics. It is reported that in the reign of Sujin-tenno (230-258 A.D.) a great epidemic continued for three years, killing the majority of the people and causing farmers to desert the countryside. During a later famine Nintoku-tenno (395-427 A.D.) addressed his ministers as follows: "We ascended a lofty tower and looked far and wide, but no smoke arose in the land. From this we gather that the people are poor, and that in the houses there are none cooking their rice. We have heard that in the reigns of the wise sovereigns of antiquity, from every one was heard the songs hymning their virtue. . . . But now when we observe the people, for three years past, no voice of eulogy is heard; the smoke of cooking has become rarer and rarer. By this we know that the five grains do not come up, and that the people are in extreme want."[44]

Recognizing the suffering of his people, Nintoku-tenno freed them from forced labor and taxes in kind for three years and let his palace fall into ruins. When, years later, he saw the smoke rising again from the fires and knew that the people were prosperous, he permitted them to repair his palace. This emperor also drained the land, deepened and straightened the river, and protected his capital from floods. When he died, he was given the posthumous name of "Benevolence-Virtue-Sovereign," Nintoku-tenno. Natural disasters continued, however, for in the reign of Suiko-tenno in 627 A.D. there were heavy rains and floods, hail, and drought. The result was a great famine in which the old, the mothers, and the children died.

When Nara was established as the capital of Japan in the eighth century, the plains of southwest Honshu were already settled.[45] If the provisions of the Taika Reform for the periodic redistribution of rice fields in relation to family size had

[41] Men of rank were exempt from personal levies on production or labor. Buddhist temples and monasteries were immune from national and local levies. Allotment of land was one of the ways in which the emperor provided for his children, his friends, and the high officers of the government.

[42] In Japan, however, this did not mean the consolidation of agricultural units and a centrally directed production with greater division of labor. The unit of production remained the family enterprise.

[43] Aston. *Nihongi* . . . . Vol. I, pp. 213-214.

[44] *Ibid.* P. 278.

[45] The ancient records, particularly the *Fudoki*, preserve information on the names and products of villages, Noh, Toshio. "The development of 'Shinden' villages in Musashino upland." Pp. 23-25 in: Tsujimura, Taro, Compiler. *Distribution maps on the regional geographical study of Japan. Text.*

been widely applied, the initial effect would have been substantial growth in population, for the subsistence available to the lesser peasants would have been increased. There is some indication that such in fact was the result of land reform in the areas in which it was carried out, but the limitations to redistribution were so severe that it is doubtful whether there was any appreciable effect on the national population. The growth of manorial lands of the *shoen* was reducing the amounts of land available for redistribution at the same time that claimants were increasing in numbers. The periods of time between allotments were increased and the amounts allotted were reduced, but still there were complaints that the rice lands were inadequate. By the early years of the eighth century the government was ordering the transfer of families from the older provinces to the newer areas on the frontier. Here it was assumed that the men would extend the cultivated acreage at the same time that they served as palisade guards against the rebellious Ezo.

The *Dajokan* (Great Council of State) became concerned with the population problem. The councilors noted that princes, nobles, and Buddhist monasteries were pre-empting uncultivated lands, removing them from possible development, production, and taxation. In 722 the Council recommended that some 2.45 million acres of waste land be brought under cultivation. The project was to be under the supervision of the provincial and district governors, and the workmen were to be maintained at government expense. The execution of this plan would have meant doubling the land under cultivation, but achievements were quite limited. The Council then attempted to stimulate private enterprise in land reclamation through a decree that any person who raised at least three thousand *koku* (almost 15 thousand bushels) of rice was to be given the sixth class of merit, while anyone raising one thousand *koku* (5 thousand bushels) was to be freed from payment of personal taxes for life.

In 723, the Council decided that those who built new irrigation systems could keep the rice fields in their families for three generations. Those who developed new fields that made use of existing irrigation facilities could keep the new fields as long as they lived. In this attempt to bolster the allotment system, the Council introduced the exemptions from allotment that gradually eliminated the planned economy of Taika as a functioning economic structure.

The economic problem in Japan was not the simple one of producing a quantity of food that would maintain the people if it was evenly distributed. There was never any consideration of solving the population problem through the equalization of the distribution system. Rather, the expanding urban centers and the proliferating aristocracy generated material demands far beyond the productive capacity of the countryside at existing technical levels. The luxury of the capital city of Heian meant increasing needs for money or for wealth in the form of rice, textiles, tools, and labor. The process of social imitation complicated the problem, for the lesser peoples in the capital and the outer provinces developed standards of living modeled after those of Heian. The Buddhist priesthood and temples made heavy demands on rural production, while the campaigns against the aborigines required levies on supplies and men.

The needs of the central and local government and the Buddhist temples could be met either through an increase of the cultivated acreage and its production or through increased rates of extraction from the producers. What seems to have happened is a simultaneous decrease in the cultivated acreage subject to taxation and an increase in extraction. Tax rates were increased in quantity and in variety. By the beginning of the tenth century the tax structure was a complex system that left little alternative to the cultivator but to attempt to escape it. Agriculturalists and local officials alike could maintain themselves or achieve economic progress only to the extent that they avoided taxation by the central government.

The decrease in taxable population proceeded rapidly, especially in the ninth and later centuries.[46] An edict of 902 stated that there had been no allotments for fifty or sixty years and that the untaxable people were increasing, whereas the taxable were without land. The land reported as "not arable" was increasing year by year, while the registration reports showed disproportionate deficits of men in the taxable families. In the year 914 Miyoshi Kiyotsura reported a district in the province of Bitchu which was populous enough to have furnished 20 thousand soldiers in 660, but which in 765-767 had a taxable population of less than two thousand. In 860 its taxable population was seventy; in 893 it was nine. In 911 no taxable resident was reported. This may have been an extreme case, but reputable estimates indicate that by the ninth century not more than 100 thousand of the 300 thousand or so people who lived outside the Inner Provinces in Kyushu, Mutsu, and Dewa were taxed.[47]

Population estimates based on the number of allotted rice fields indicate that the total population of Japan declined from perhaps five million at the time of the Taika Reform of 645-650 A.D. to less than four million in 823 and only a little over a million in 923. It is obvious that this decline in the number of people registered in *koseki* reflects the collapse of the system of registration rather than the depopulation of Japan. An estimate of the actual trend of the population is difficult to make. Two Japanese students of the problem, Yokoyama Yoshikiyo and Yoshida Togo, utilized the records of the land redistributions in certain local areas to secure a multiplier to apply to the number of districts in the country. These estimates were then analyzed for consistency with the records on the size of households, the number of towns and villages, and the amounts of the rice crops. The estimates are as follows:[48]

Year	*Population*
823	3,694,331
859-922	3,762,000
990-1080	4,416,650
1185-1333	9,750,000

Although the population at any time throughout the Nara and Heian periods cannot be known with certainty, the surviving statistical and descriptive records indicate the probability of substantial increase. There can be only conjecture as to the rate of that increase, and whether it was achieved by fairly regular increments or by alternation of periods of increase and decrease. The latter is more probable, for famine, epidemic, and violence added to the hazards of natural calamities in a culture in which knowledge of medicine, sanitation, and nutrition was limited. The danger of famine was increased by Japan's continued dependence on rice. There are reported to have been national, provincial, and district storehouses where emergency rice supplies could be kept for loan to the

[46] The taxable population was that registered in the *koseki*, and hence participated in the payment of taxes and whatever redistributions of allotted land occurred.

[47] Asakawa. *The early institutional life* . . . . P. 344.

[48] Ishii. *Population pressure* . . . . P. 3.

poorer peasants, but these would have been quite inadequate if crop failures were widespread. If excessive rain, drought, or civil disorders produced poor harvests over any considerable area, there was no alternative to severe malnutrition, flight, and perhaps death.

The chronicles sometimes record famine in isolation, but reports of multiple difficulties are more common. Vagabondage, robbery, and a general disintegration of order accompanied famine conditions. With these came the great epidemics that spread among the debilitated peoples and then over wider areas as people fled the stricken area. In 764 drought and political disturbances produced an acute shortage of food. In 854 Mutsu appealed to the central government for help, for the crops had failed the previous year, the farmers were in a desperate condition, the troops were dispersed, and robbery was widespread. The government sent one thousand troops and ordered the province to distribute rice. In 877 there was famine in Kyoto and the Inner Provinces; here the government sold rice at fixed prices. Plagues, on the other hand, were often reported without famine. Neither the rich nor the powerful escaped epidemics. In 737, for instance, the heads of each of the five Fujiwara families died of smallpox.

These conditions of living and of dying were not unique to early Japan. They were the corollaries of dependence on local agriculture prior to the development of commercial and industrial economies, communication, transportation, public health measures, and sanitation. The significant factor in the early evolution of the Japanese population is not the nature of the hazards to life present in the physical and cultural environment, but the persistent upward movement of numbers to create dense settlement in the areas of occupation.

Population: The Perennial Problem

Population growth must have been quite irregular among the peoples of the early Neolithic period in Japan.[49] The first migrants found an empty country, but life did not thereby become simple. "Fertile rice lands" were of little consequence to people who either were without agriculture or had a knowledge that went little beyond the technique of the digging stick. Typhoons, floods, earthquakes, and fires were even greater hazards to ancient than to modern Japan. The possibilities for epidemics may have been limited by the barriers to mobility, but epidemics decimated the group subjected to them. There were neither doctors, knowledge of medicine, sanitation, nor folk techniques other than the magical to protect the individual against contagion or to enhance his chances for survival if stricken. There were severe economic hazards, too, for existence itself depended on current production within the local area. Drought or excessive rain might bring catastrophe, for storage facilities and transportation from other areas were undeveloped. Furthermore, the early millennia during which settlement occurred were characterized by intermittent wars between local groups, for no migrants except the first found the country empty.

Despite these continuing and major hazards to survival, the islands of Japan were hospitable to human settlement and population increase. The wide distribution of material remains indicates the increase of numbers during the Neolithic period. It would be difficult to measure the relations between population and resources in the Neolithic economy, but the answer is not too important. The introduction of elements of Chinese culture altered the balance of births and deaths and hence the rates of population growth.

The first great increase in the carrying capacity of the land occurred when agriculture replaced hunting and fishing. That change took place very gradually in Japan, spreading from the southwest northward and eastward. At first it was a process of supplementation rather than substitution, but even in this early stage the amount of food was increased. The demographic consequences involved both an increased rate of survival because of more regular and more adequate nutrition and a lessened incidence and severity of famine. Once people had increased in number, there was a strong compulsion to extend the cultivation of the soil and so secure the increased amount of subsistence essential to the survival of the greater number of people. The growing number of people whose survival was permitted by agriculture thus stimulated the further development of agriculture.

The agriculture of Japan was primarily the cultivation of rice, with an early development of irrigation and fertilization. High densities of population could be supported, provided the rural people molded their lives to the imperatives of food production. The construction of irrigation systems, the preparation of fields, the building of dykes, and the maintenance of the soil were the contributions of generations. The Japanese political and social system, with its emphasis on discipline and stability, was ideally fitted to encourage the attitudes and the behavior patterns essential to the maintenance and extension of rice agriculture—or perhaps the continuing order and the unremitting toil essential to survival in the rice areas facilitated the development of a stable social structure. Even the legends of the gods recognized the importance of rice to rulers and people, for the Sun Goddess herself cultivated her rice fields in the Plains of High Heaven.

The integrated social organization that had such high survival value in creating continuity and stability was also favorable to the creation or development of the familial values of abundant childbearing. However, even in this early period the co-existence of order, a regularized food supply, and a high birth rate made almost inevitable a rate of population increase that could not be maintained without continuing extension of the areas under cultivation. Numbers tended to increase beyond the margins of permanent subsistence at existing levels of material technologies and social-economic structure. Pressures in the settled areas forced expansion outward whenever and wherever technical and political conditions permitted.

This problem of the inadequacy of the rice lands for the maintenance of people and economy has been a recurring motif in the history of Japan. In the early centuries, as today, the difficulties were twofold: the paucity of land and the overproduction of people. Within the political and social structure of the ancient world, no culture could escape permanently from this problem of population pressure and food deficiency. Malnutrition and famine were the final results of political stability and economic advance.

Perhaps these conclusions should have been stated as hypotheses, for the chronicles of the legendary and early historical period are biased documents. However, there is a monotonous regularity in the accounts of agricultural improvements, new lands, famine, epidemic, and decline. It may be objected that many of these events occurred in China rather than in Japan. If this is so, population theory is strengthened, for China was the prototype of the relations between rice agriculture and population increase.

[49] Sugino. "Waga kuni . . . ." Pp. 1-9.

CHAPTER II

The Changing Population

Late Twelfth to Mid-nineteenth Century

IN THE late twelfth century the Japanese economy supported from six to nine million people; in the middle of the nineteenth century it supported more than thirty million. The data on the growth of the population are deficient for the early part of the period but numerous and diverse for the late part. In periods of disorder, *koseki* were maintained in some local areas, but there were no national compilations. National reporting would have been possible when the Tokugawa secured power in the early seventeenth century, but at that time there was little interest in population. Eventually there were rumors that lands lay uncultivated while people deserted the villages and roamed the countryside. The government ordered reports on the area of farm land and the number of farmers, merchants, and other commoners. This was in the year 1721. The results were alarming, for many regions seemed to have declining populations. The government then ordered a report in 1726 and each six years thereafter.

The population of Japan seems to have changed irregularly but with a general upward movement from the thirteenth through the sixteenth century. It is believed to have increased rapidly in the seventeenth and to have changed little from the early eighteenth century until 1852. In one approach common in the literature, the presumed stability of numbers in the late Tokugawa period is viewed as a classic illustration of a people who had increased to the limits of physical subsistence. In another approach, also common in the literature, the stability of numbers is ascribed to infanticide. Some interpretations combine the two approaches, infanticide being seen as the means whereby the population was kept within the subsistence limits of the economy.

If the change from population growth to stability can be demonstrated, the fact of stability in a premodern and mainly peasant population is important. Perhaps even more significant is the balance of births and deaths that prevented increase in numbers over a long period of time. It is possible that numbers had increased until there were absolute limitations to growth, any population increase being wiped out by famine and epidemic. If this situation existed, short-time fluctuations in mortality would be the means whereby a relatively unchanging population and a relatively unchanging social and economic order co-existed. If, on the other hand, fluctuations in fertility were involved in the maintenance of relatively unchanging numbers, we have at least one case of a major country in which family-planning occurred within a pre-industrial culture.

If it was the planned limitation of family size rather than fluctuating mortality that stabilized the population of Japan in the late Tokugawa period, the usual interpretations of the relations among a peasant economy, a familistic society, and human reproduction may need revision. Moreover, if the Japanese began the process of industrialization and urbanization with controlled fertility rather than the high fertility characteristic of the other cultures of Monsoon Asia, their modern demographic transition may be atypical of that to be expected in other industrializing countries.

Whether we are considering the stability of the population or the nature of the balance of births and deaths, the primary interest is not in the demographic processes as such, but in their interrelations with the changes and the stabilities in the state and the economy. Hence a résumé of the social and economic developments of the *bakufu* period must precede consideration of the more specifically demographic processes of increase, urbanization, mortality, fertility, and family limitation.

CHANGE AND STABILITY UNDER THE BAKUFU[1]

THE EVOLUTION: LATE TWELFTH TO EARLY SEVENTEENTH CENTURY

By the late twelfth century the Minamoto had secured military hegemony over Japan. Faced with the problem of consolidation of authority and the restoration of peace and stability, the new military leaders turned backward in Japanese history for their ideal. To them, urban life was dissolute and effeminate; the true virtues lay in the simple life and the virile qualities of the soldier and the peasant. The new orientation was symbolized in the establishment of a *bakufu*, an army headquarters, at Kamakura, and the imperial appointment of Minamoto Yoritomo as *seii-tai-shogun*, or barbarian-subduing-generalissimo. Representatives of the *shogun* were sent throughout the country, a constable to each *kuni* and a steward to each *shoen*. Constables and stewards were in the military service of the *bakufu*, with armed forces under their immediate control.

The *bakufu* at Kamakura lasted only a century and a half. The accumulating tensions were primarily political, but social and economic problems also arose. As the *shogun* was unable to control the military mechanism he had created, constables and stewards became lords and *shoen* became fiefs. Although the early regime had been austere, the levels of living of the eastern lords rose sufficiently to threaten the consumption-production balance of the period. The destruction of life was widespread as civil disorder spread and production declined. Earthquakes and epidemics added to the losses brought about by social disorganization and reduced food production. In

[1] The major sources are the following: Sansom. *Japan . . .*; Honjo. *The social and economic history . . .*; Tsuchiya. *An economic history . . .*; Takizawa, Matsuyo. *The penetration of money economy in Japan*; Smith, Neil Skene, Editor. *Materials on Japanese social and economic history: Tokugawa Japan.* (1), "Introduction," "Resources and population," "Communication and trade."

1259 famine and plague were so severe that the streets of Kyoto were reported to be ". . . choked with dead and dying."[2]

Internal difficulties were compounded by external events, for in the late thirteenth century the Yüan Empire demanded tribute from the Japanese. Chinese invasions of Japan in 1274 and 1281 were unsuccessful, but mobilization against the possibility of a further assault continued until the death of Khubilai Khan in the year 1300. The Mongol invasions destroyed the precarious equilibrium of the Kamakura *bakufu*. Losses of life, property, and crops were great, especially in Kyushu. The men who had participated in mobilization and war desired rewards, but, since the enemy had been external, no simple redistribution of fiefs could solve the problem. Eventually the Kyoto nobles and the discontented *daimyo* formed a coalition that led to the defeat of the Minamoto forces, the destruction of the city of Kamakura, and the transfer of the government to Kyoto. The struggles continued throughout most of the fourteenth century until a new consolidation occurred under Ashikaga *shogun*.[3] Two or three generations of relative stability preceded the intermittent civil wars that continued throughout the fifteenth and sixteenth centuries. At the end of the War of Onin, 1467-1477, the city of Kyoto was in ruins. The lords barred their domains to communications from the outside, discontinued the payment of imperial taxes, and governed as they wished. Court nobles had no revenues and government officials had no salaries. In the year 1500 the body of an emperor lay unburied for six weeks because there were no funds for the rites; his successor had to wait twenty years for his enthronement ceremony.[4] The sixteenth century was *sengoku jidai*, the age of the country at war.

The insecurities of the centuries of struggle influenced both the structure of the larger society and the cohesion of the household and the village. There was a simplification of the lines of vassalage, lords and warriors becoming vassals and rear-vassals in a hierarchical structure.[5] Local insecurities were minimized by an increase in the protective and economic functions of the family. The extended family became the basic unit in the social structure. The practices of primogeniture and the subordination of women were correlates of this integration of functions at the family level. The movements of members of the family became subject to family decisions, and social pressures to family conformity became more severe. This consolidation of family resources permitted survival in a situation in which no outside group could protect life or property.

While the consolidation of the family strengthened the forces of stability, other aspects of the changing culture furthered mobility. The landless warriors of defeated lords took service with other lords, moved into towns, or became mercenary soldiers. Peasants and serfs deserted civilian responsibilities to become foot soldiers.

Military activities and political changes disturbed the lethargy of the peasant societies. The movement of the shogunate to Kyoto showed sophisticated urban life to soldiers of peasant origin. Recruitment from all parts of Japan quickened the development of a culture that was distinctively Japanese and essentially uniform throughout the islands. There were negative aspects to the changes, however, for discontent spread among peasants and city dwellers. In times of famine or epidemic the landless *samurai* and the peasants joined in mass revolts.[6]

Eventually a reintegration of power occurred under the aegis of the Tokugawa.[7] Hierarchical feudalism was combined with a police state under a hereditary shogunate that withdrew Japan from contacts with the outside world in the early seventeenth century and governed the country until the sixth decade of the nineteenth century. Brief digressions on the development of external contacts and the withdrawal to seclusion are necessary preludes to the description of changes in Japanese society during the centuries when the Tokugawa shogunate had thought to create a society without change.

THE PERIOD OF CONTACTS

As vessels suitable for navigating the open seas replaced small junks, the merchants of Japan extended their trade to the southeast Asian region, while Japanese sailors operated ships that seized vessels on the seas and raided cities along the China coast.[8] By the first quarter of the seventeenth century there were Japanese trading settlements in Thailand, Annam, Cochin-China, Java, and the Philippines. Little is known concerning the populations of these settlements, although one near Bangkok was said to include eight thousand Japanese, while a settlement near Manila was reported to number three thousand.

Direct contact between the cultures of Europe and Japan came in 1542, when three Portuguese were driven by a typhoon to a small island off the coast of Osumi. They were received enthusiastically and the harquebus they carried was copied. Soon the Portuguese sent expeditions to sell luxurious goods to the lords of the Kyushu harbors of Kagoshima, Hirado, Omura, and Funai. Tobacco was introduced about 1590, while the English brought the potato from Java in 1615. Clocks, globes, maps, and musical instruments excited the curiosity of the Japanese, and the silk yarns, textiles, books, pictures, porcelains, drugs, spices, and perfumes of China and India had a ready market. Portuguese dress became fashionable among the women of the upper classes. Since Jesuit priests from the missions of Macao and Goa came with the traders, the secular learning and the religious faith of the West were diffused along with its material products.

When Tokugawa Ieyasu assumed control in 1598, he encouraged both foreign commerce and the growth of the merchant marine. In the first decade and a half of the seventeenth

[2] Sansom. *Japan . . . .* P. 308.

[3] The Ashikaga were former vassals of the Minamoto. They gave the name of their quarters in Kyoto, Muromachi, to the period from 1392 to 1573.

[4] Sansom. *Japan . . . .* P. 367.

[5] See especially: Asakawa, Kan'ichi. "Some aspects of Japanese feudal institutions." *T.A.S.J.*, 46(1): 76-102. 1918.

[6] The earliest of the great rice riots occurred in 1428, almost two centuries before the Tokugawa period.

[7] Three men played major roles in this new centralization: Oda Nobunaga, Toyotomi Hideyoshi, and Tokugawa Ieyasu. The struggle for control was costly, but by 1590 the conquests were relatively complete and Japan was at peace for the first time in over a century. Ancient imperial dreams revived, perhaps as a continuation of the drive that had made Hideyoshi the master of Japan, perhaps to solve the problem of armies without internal enemies to conquer. In 1592 Hideyoshi moved an army reported as numbering 200 thousand men across the Tsushima Straits to Korea. Opposition and problems of supply proved too great, so the army was evacuated in 1593. More thorough preparations were made, and another invasion was launched in 1596-1597. Hideyoshi died in 1598, and the armies were drawn home for the succession disputes that followed. Finally, in the great battle of Sekigahara in October of the year 1600, Tokugawa Ieyasu emerged victorious. He redistributed fiefs to prevent insubordination, but his position remained somewhat precarious until the siege of Osaka in 1615, when the supporters of Hideyoshi were routed. That victory insured the supremacy of the Tokugawa shogunate.

[8] Kuno, Yoshi S. *Japanese expansion on the Asiatic continent.* Vol. II, "To the end of the seclusion period."

century, Portuguese, Spaniards, English, Dutch, and Chinese traveled throughout Japan. Aliens resided in Nagasaki, Funai, Kuchinotsu, Hakata, and Kagoshima in Kyushu, and in Osaka, Sakai, Edo, Shizuoka, and Uraga in Honshu. Japanese lords and Jesuit priests might quarrel, with consequent closing of individual harbors, but on the whole Portuguese traders could go wherever they wished in Kyushu.[9] However, Tokugawa Ieyasu's contacts with the Spanish in the Philippines and the Dutch in Java and Taiwan convinced him that missionary activities would lead to conquest. Gradually, antagonism against an alien culture produced antipathy to the Jesuit priests and the Christian faith. As soon as Ieyasu had consolidated his secular power, he turned from tolerance to proscription.[10] The drive for ethnic and cultural purification began in 1615-1616. In 1624 it was decreed that all Spaniards be deported and that no Japanese travel overseas. In 1628 the Portuguese were expelled.

The decision for seclusion was not reversed until the middle of the nineteenth century. For two and a half centuries Japan lived unto herself, her people forced to find subsistence or starve within her densely settled islands. In the view of her ardent patriots, she forfeited a brilliant destiny when she turned her back on the Asian continent and severed contacts with the West. In this view, Japan was a sea-going power with a redundant population; as such, she could have seized the Pacific littoral of Asia, made the Sea of Japan a Japanese lake, and emerged as the England of the Far East.

Realistic appraisal indicates that Japan may have averted colonial status by her exclusionist policies. However, she secured the opportunity to maintain her own culture in a sovereign state only by sacrificing the technical and intellectual opportunities inherent in an identification with the onrushing tide of Western intellectual, commercial, and industrial expansion.

THE PERIOD OF SECLUSION

When Tokugawa Ieyasu became *shogun* in the early seventeenth century, his lands covered one-fourth of the area of the country. They were scattered in 47 of the 68 *kuni* into which the country was then divided.[11] He controlled all places of political or religious importance, as well as all commercial and industrial cities. Adroit policies of redistributing lands, arranging marriages among the *daimyo* families, and imposing levies on rich *daimyo* enabled the Tokugawa to extend their domains. The redistribution of land increased the power of the feudal lords in hereditary vassalage to the Tokugawa (*fudai-daimyo*) as against the lords not in such vassalage (*tozama-daimyo*) and thus guarded against hostile combinations. Perhaps the most ingenious of the provisions of the *shogun* was the system of alternate attendance (*sankin-kotai*), by which each *daimyo* had to reside in Edo during alternate years and maintain his wife and children there as hostages in his absence.

The influence of the central administration penetrated downward from the manager on the fief of the *shogun* or the *daimyo* on his own fief to the peasant on his tiny plot of land. The managers and the *daimyo* worked with the heads of the villages. The village heads in turn worked through small neighborhood groups that were responsible collectively for the enforcement of the law and the payment of taxes. The adherence of the peasant to a specific group was hereditary.

The social structure of the state was presumed to be changeless, each person being fixed in that station of life to which he was born. At the apex were the lords, the court nobility, the priests, and the students, each group minutely subclassified as to rank. At the bottom were the outcasts, the *eta* and the *hinin*. The ordinary people were divided into three major classes: the *samurai*, the farmers, and the *heimin*. The function of the *samurai* was to rule. He was to live by the military tradition, the cult of *bushido*. Subsistence and luxuries were derived from rice stipends granted to the *samurai* by the *daimyo* to whom they vowed allegiance. The peasants were the productive class. They were to maintain themselves and also to produce the rice and other crops that were collected by the agents of the *daimyo* and transported to the castles or the cities to meet the "payrolls" of rice stipends. Below the peasants were the *heimin*: traders, merchants, bankers, and early industrialists. In the views of the time, their activities were not productive.

The planners of the Tokugawa *bakufu* thought to erect an impenetrable shield around their domain and thus perpetuate a stable order. However, social mobility developed as urban residence, diffused communication, and monetary evaluations replaced the warrior virtues of the founders. The merchants increased in economic power and in social status. Some *samurai* whose rice stipends were inadequate to maintain their standard of living entered trade and industry. Others solved their personal problems by marrying the daughters or adopting the sons of merchants. Individual members of the merchant class moved upward by purchasing the status of *samurai* or acquiring fiefs as payment of debts; some merchants used surnames and carried swords. Mobility also developed in the peasant society and the sons of peasants moved to the cities.

In the oligarchic structure of Japanese society, the *samurai* were the group best equipped to lead creative change. They had traditions of leadership, and the knowledge and the administrative know-how that education and assured social position alone could give. The *tozama-daimyo*, the "outer lords," who had never submitted fully to the Tokugawa in Edo, emerged as powerful opponents to the existing structure of authority, but their interests were limited to changes in the personnel and the practices of the ruling elite.

The partial and often distorted information about the outer world that reached the Japanese was a stimulant to discontent. There was direct trade with the Netherlands and China at Nagasaki, while relations with Korea filtered through Tsushima. Chinese trade reached Satsuma through the Ryukyu Islands. Eventually the government lifted the embargo on all foreign books except those dealing with religion. Languages, chemistry, the calendar, astronomy, and military science were studied avidly, while many books describing conditions abroad were written in Japan.

The impact of the new learning was both intellectual and material. Among the upper classes there was a cultural renaissance oriented toward a return to traditional values. There was also application of the knowledge acquired from books and periodicals. Plans for establishing woolen textile factories were made in the beginning of the nineteenth century, while

[9] Reischauer, Robert K. *Alien land tenure in Japan.* Cited to p. 320 in: Takekoshi, Y. *Nihon keizai shi.* Vol. II. Tokyo, 1920.

[10] The fears of the Japanese had been aroused earlier as the Jesuits made mass conversions. In 1587 Toyotomi Hideyoshi banned the Jesuits, but enforcement was minimal and Christianity spread as a craze. Christianity itself was proscribed in 1597 and there were some prosecutions, but the association of Jesuit missionary and Portuguese trader was so close as to preclude barring the one while accepting the other.

[11] Honjo. *The social and economic history . . . .* Pp. 18-20.

techniques for the manufacturing of iron and the casting of guns were copied from Dutch books.

The developments during the last decades of Tokugawa control resulted in an internal crisis at about the same time that the nations of the West approached Japan. After the visit of the American fleet under Commodore Perry in 1853, the shogunate instituted many reforms, including the end of seclusion, the curtailment of *sankin-kotai* (alternate residence in Edo), and the stimulation of industry and trade. In 1867 the *shogun* restored the governing power to the emperor. The *bakufu* organization that had begun with Minamoto Yoritomo six and one-half centuries before ended. Again the leaders of a new Japan determined to secure through imperial rescript and oligarchic guidance a life more abundant than that offered by the traditional ways of their culture. In the seventh century, they had turned to the culture of the T'ang Empire; in the nineteenth century, they turned to the science and the technology that had spread outward from Western Europe as the industrial revolution.

THE MARKET

The major economic advances in the first century or so of political consolidation under the *bakufu* were in the field of agriculture. The policies for the maintenance of armed forces on the frontier were integrated with policies for colonization. Military leaders who were given land accepted soldiers as vassals and sub-invested them with land, thus achieving the dual purposes of subsistence for the army and settlement of the land. In the Tokugawa era, peace, the spiral of conspicuous consumption, and the cityward movement of *shogun* and *daimyo* stimulated manufacturing and trade. The contacts with the West in the late Muromachi and early Tokugawa periods introduced some knowledge of European industrial arts; seclusion protected the Japanese in their fumbling attempts at production of European-type materials and permitted a significant development of native industrial arts. Handicraft industry of a highly organized type and a commercial economy developed in Japan without reference to the commercial and industrial revolutions then occurring in Europe.

Domestic handicrafts continued in the villages, but there was increasing specialization in production for the market, particularly in luxuries such as silk textiles and sake. By the beginning of the eighteenth century, products from north and central Japan were sold in Edo, Osaka, and Kyoto. These cities were the distribution centers for the bleached textiles of Nara, the cotton cloth of Kawachi, the candles of Aizu, and the seaweeds of Matsumae. The merchants of Oma and the drug peddlers of Toyama traveled throughout the country. Shrines and temples specialized in the production of particular commodities, while the luxury industries that developed in response to the demands of the nobility were centered around Kyoto. Both *shogun* and merchants attempted to regulate the developing competition among areas and products through proscriptions and production curtailment schemes.

The use of money already had a long history by early Tokugawa, but it was limited. During the period of seclusion there were developments in mining, the production of coins, and the organization of a currency system. The *daimyo* and the *samurai* used money on their trips to and from Edo and during their periods of residence there, while the wide availability of the products of industry spread the habit of transacting business with money. In fact, the inadequacy of the incomes of *daimyo* and *samurai* to meet their ever-advancing wants stimulated the further development of the handicraft and commercial segments of the economy. Common techniques for producing additional funds included the encouragement of industry and the creation of monopolies. Other means included the debasement of coins, the issuance of notes, borrowing money from the wealthy, and levying fines in money.[12]

THE PEASANT

The Tokugawa state was based on the labor of the peasant. Major emphasis was placed on the development of agriculture, with what seems to have been considerable success in the early part of the period of seclusion. Land under cultivation had been 3.7 million acres in the late sixteenth century; by 1716-1736 it reached 7.5 million acres.[13] Yields per unit of area increased as new implements were invented and ancient techniques improved. Treadmills gradually replaced older and less efficient methods for drawing water. Fish supplemented the fertilizers of the farm, while torches, lime, and whale oil were used to control insect pests. Crops were diversified and sericulture was expanded.

At the end of the sixteenth century the agricultural village was largely self-sufficient. Trade among villagers was primarily barter or interchange, locally produced rice or cloth being the medium of exchange. Only salt, metals, and medicines had to be purchased. This local economy continued in the rural areas long after it had passed in the cities, but there is considerable evidence that the money economy was spreading in the rural areas fairly early in the period of seclusion. At its simplest level, a more intensive agriculture itself required sale and purchase. If rice production was to meet tax demands, fish had to be used to fertilize the land. At a more complex level, variations in land, productive capacities, and abilities extraneous to the physical cultivation of the soil stimulated economic differentiations within the peasant society. The transfer or subdivision of land and the contraction of debts were forbidden, but the vigor of the proscriptions indicates the prevalence of the practices. Landlords, peasant proprietors, tenants, and laborers developed as recognized economic classes.

Originally the peasant surrendered to the officials approximately half his production of commodities designated as taxable, but the rate of extraction reputedly rose throughout the *bakufu* period. When the peasants attempted to escape severe taxation by growing crops not specified as taxable, taxes as high as those on rice were levied on the new crops. Thus increasing demands for taxes and increasing expenditures for production pressed the levels of living of the farmers down at the same time that the penetration of the money economy and the diffusion of knowledge of urban life pushed standards of living upward. The motivations for clearing new

[12] The advance and consolidation of the market economy are exemplified in the history of the most famous of the Tokugawa merchants, the House of Mitsui. In the early seventeenth century Mitsui Sakubei left his position as *samurai* to manufacture and trade *sake* and soy at Matsuzaka in Ise. His son served a fourteen-year apprenticeship in Edo and then returned to Ise as a money-lender. In 1673 his son, Hachirobei, took his six sons to Kyoto and established a business of silk piece goods, especially *nishijin* products. These he forwarded to Edo for sale at a branch store. He established a bank in Edo with a branch in Osaka, settling both private and governmental accounts between Osaka and Edo by bills of exchange. At his death in 1694 branch houses were founded for each of his children. *Mitsui gomei kaisha*. Tokyo, 1933. Cited: Smith, ed., *Materials* . . . . P. 169.

[13] Land under cultivation is presumed to have changed little between the early part of the eighteenth century and the opening to the West in the middle of the nineteenth century. Honjo, Eijiro. *Nihon keizai shi gaisetsu*. Part III.

land and for increasing production on land already cleared became less and less.

There was a dilemma inherent in the agricultural policies. The ruling groups desired to extract maximum quantities of commodities from the peasants in order to maintain and enrich the life of the non-agricultural people. The motivations that would stimulate the clearance of new land or increased production on old land were difficult to establish. Neither increased food, exchange commodities, nor leisure could be offered to the peasants for growing more food and turning it over to tax collectors.[14] The major approach of the shogunate to this problem of the motivation of production was restrictive. A stream of directions and proscriptions was issued to fix the peasant in his place of residence, his consumption habits, and his form of labor.

There was no basis for an economically satisfactory rate of population change within the system of Tokugawa controls. If population increased within any limited area, the amount of physical product above subsistence was likely to decrease and the burden of taxation to become more oppressive. If population decreased, the labor necessary to cultivate the land and produce the rice tax became heavier. Great famines and widespread riots of peasants indicated the dual hazards to the shogunate in the eighteenth and nineteenth centuries. Peasant mobility increased as the discontents of the countryside forced increasing numbers into vagabondage, illegal transfer of vassalage relations, or migration into cities.

The Trend of the Population

THE CENTURIES OF INCREASE

Little is known concerning the size or the rate of increase of the population during the early centuries of the *bakufu* period. Ingenious manipulations of data on size of family, numbers of towns and villages, and the amount of the rice crops suggest the following figures:[15]

Period	*Population*
1185-1333	9,750,000
1572-1591	18,000,000

If these estimates are correct, population increased substantially during the centuries of disorder and conflict. Japan does not appear to have been particularly devastated even by the wars of the sixteenth century.[16] The numbers engaged were relatively small, despite contemporary reports on the movements of hundreds of thousands of men. Direct battle fatalities cannot have been great prior to the development of modern weapons. The destruction of resources was more serious, but the rice fields and the irrigation systems were generally respected and temples were not touched. Villages and cities might be destroyed, but, except for Kyoto and a few other places, structures were easily replaced. The peasants maintained themselves in war as in peace with little dependence on outside production or transportation. Hence, the direct effects of any given period of warfare were limited to the areas that were involved in the struggle. The indirect effects were more widespread. Local famines doubtless followed military campaigns, while the moving armies carried infections throughout the countryside. The relations between war and food production are more complex. If wars encouraged crop diversification, improved techniques, land reclamation, and irrigation, the consequence of political instability may have been population increase.

The political and economic policies during the first century of the Tokugawa *bakufu* were generally favorable to population increase. Peace and order existed throughout the country, while *shogun* and *daimyo* emphasized the extension of the cultivated area, the improvement of yields, and the planting of more varied crops. The consolidation of power itself contributed to the regularity of the harvests and the storage of emergency foods, while the great roads and the coastal shipping facilities made it possible to move food to areas of distress. Indirect evidence suggests that the population increased from about 18 million at the end of the sixteenth century to perhaps 25 million at the end of the seventeenth century.[17] This increase of less than 50 per cent in a century would not be regarded as rapid in agrarian cultures where famines and epidemics are controlled and endemic diseases are limited. It was substantial indeed for a people living by ancient technologies in a region already densely settled.

The course of population growth in Tokugawa Japan tended toward the creation of numbers that were excessive in relation to levels of production and income. In fact, such an increase of population as would reduce per capita income, lessen vitality, and increase mortality was a natural correlate of the economy, the system of government, and the social structure of the *bakufu* state. However, when the population problem arose, it was as a problem of inadequate, rather than surplus, population. Definitions of population problems in terms of individual welfare were unrealistic in the hierarchical structure of medieval Japan. The population problem of the time was defined by the *shogun* in Edo and the *daimyo* of the great fiefs rather than by the people who tilled the soil. It was viewed as a shortage of manpower for the production of the commodities which, as tax levies, supported the superstructure of the regime.

THE CESSATION OF GROWTH

The report made by the *daimyo* to the Shogun Tokugawa Yoshimune in 1721 indicated that the commoner population of Japan was approximately 26 million.[18] Either the number of people or the amount of the cultivated land reported in this first survey must have been surprisingly small, for the *shogun* not only strengthened the wording of the directives for the second report, but also ordered the *daimyo* whose fiefs yielded more than 100 thousand *koku* of rice per year to report on the numbers of their people seventy or eighty years earlier. Nine lords submitted reports, presumably on the basis of surviving temple registers (Table 2). The combined population as of 1732 was 3.1 million. Average annual rates of increase were quite low, amounting to about 10 per 1,000 covered population only in the fiefs of Matsudaira

[14] The chronicles of the centuries are filled with tales of the woes of the peasants under the systematic exploitation of the agents of the *bakufu*. Unfortunately these urban commiserations on the lot of the peasant are based on descriptive materials for specific areas. Quantitative data that would permit over-all description at a certain period of time or measurement of changes over time are not available. That the lot of the peasant was difficult is obvious; whether or how much it worsened is debatable.

[15] Ishii. *Population pressure . . . .* Pp. 3-4. Also Yuzuki, Jugo, and Horie, Yasuzo. "Hompo jinko hyo." *Keizai shi kenkyu*, No. 7, pp. 188-210. May 1930. The 1185-1333 estimate was made by Yokoyama Yoshikiyo, using data on recorded size of family and number of towns and villages. The 1572-1591 estimate was made by Yoshida Togo on the basis of the rice crops in the feudal domains.

[16] Sansom. *Japan . . . .* Pp. 435-436.

[17] Yoshida, Togo. *Ishin shi hachiko*. Cited in: Ishii. *Population pressure . . . .* Pp. 3-5.

[18] Honjo, Eijiro. "The population and its problems in the Tokugawa era." *Bulletin de l'Institut international de statistique*, 25(2): 65. 1931.

TABLE 2

Population reports from the fiefs of nine *daimyo*, late seventeenth and early eighteenth centuries

Daimyo[a]	Location of fief (*Kuni*)	Year of examination	Population[b]	Average annual rate of growth
Matsudaira Kaga no Kami	Kaga, Etchu,	1720	551,754	
(Maeda)	Noto, Omi	1732	576,734	3.7
Matsudaira Mutsu no Kami	Mutsu, Hitachi,	1690	599,241	
(Date)	Shimosa, Omi	1702	617,323	2.5
		1732	647,427	1.6
Matsudaira Osumi no Kami	Osumi, Satsuma,	1698	260,961	
(Shimazu)	Hyuga	1732	339,955	7.8
Matsudaira Oki no Kami	Bizen, Bitchu,	1686	185,043	
(Ikeda)		1706	207,215	5.7
		1732	223,959	3.0
Todo Daigaku no Kami	Iga, Ise, Yamashiro,	1665	252,061	
	Yamato,	1690	284,126	4.8
	Shimosa	1732	287,242	0.3
Matsudaira Awaji no Kami	Awaji, Awa	1665	308,880	
(Hachisuga)		1688	385,751	9.7
		1732	470,512	4.5
Sakai Saemon no Jo	Dewa	1694	126,383	
		1732	131,164	1.0
Niwa Sakyo Taifu	Mutsu	1685	73,351	
		1702	76,130	2.2
		1732	70,614	−2.5
Nambu Shuri Taifu	Mutsu	1669	245,635	
		1703	306,142	6.5
		1732	322,109	1.7

[a] *Daimyo* with fiefs that yielded over 100 thousand *koku* of rice per year and that had been maintained without area changes for eighty years.

[b] The population covered was that over age 1 except in the fiefs of Matsudaira Kaga no Kami and Matsudaira Mutsu no Kami, where it was over 15, and in the fiefs of Matsudaira Oki no Kami and Matsudaira Awaji no Kami, where it was over 2.

Source: Honjo Eijiro. *Nihon jinko shi.* Pp. 44-46.

Awaji no Kami in the period from 1665 to 1688. Six fiefs reported changes in population for two time periods, roughly the last quarter of the seventeenth century and the first quarter of the eighteenth. In each of these fiefs, the rate of increase was higher in the earlier than in the later period, but change was relatively slight. However, the inference seemed justified that population increase was giving way to population decline, that conditions had been "better" in the ancient days than they were in the early eighteenth century.

THE PRESUMED STABILITY: 1726-1852

The number of commoners included in the successive reports to the *shogun* changed relatively little in the hundred and twenty-five years between the first officially accepted report, that of 1726, and the last published report, that of 1852. (TABLE 3).[19] There were 26.5 million people in 1726, 27.2 million in 1852. The low population, 24.9 million in 1792, differed from the high, 27.2 million in 1828, by less than 10 per cent. These are the types of fluctuations that might be expected in a population that had approached the limits of subsistence at the existing technical levels, a population in which changes in the food supply were reflected in fairly immediate and roughly compensatory adjustments in

[19] These reports were made in major part by compilations of data from the registers, either the *shumon nimbetsu aratame cho,* the sect register book that had been developed to enforce the proscription of Christianity, or the *koseki*, the household register book initiated with the Taika Reform. The reports were made in 1721, 1726, and at successive six-year intervals until 1852. The populations of the *kuni* survive for many of the years, often by sex; these and the detailed instructions of the *shogun* permit evaluation of completeness and relative accuracy. Coverage was somewhat inconsistent as to age, and women tended to be omitted more frequently than men. Hokkaido and the Ryukyu Islands were sometimes included, sometimes excluded. Reporting was from the place of legal domicile, so that reports on the populations of cities were understatements of the *de facto* populations. The greatest limitation of the reports, however, is the fact that they included commoners only. The imperial household and the household of the *shogun* were omitted along with the nobility, the *daimyo*, and the *samurai*, with their subordinates and their servants. The *eta, hinin,* and other people who were omitted from temple registers and *koseki* records were also excluded. For descriptions and evaluations of these Tokugawa reports, see Honjo. "The population and its problems . . . ;" Sekiyama, Naotaro. "Tokugawa jidai zenkoku jinko no saiginni." *J.m.k.,* 2(8):1-15; 4(3):1-10. August 1941 and March 1943; *Idem. Nihon jinko shi.*

TABLE 3

The number of commoners, Tokugawa reports, 1726-1852

Year	NUMBER OF PERSONS			*Males per 100 females*	*Ratio to previous report*	*Ratio to 1726*
	Total	*Male*	*Female*			
1726	26,548,998	—	—	—	—	100
1732	26,921,816	14,407,107	12,514,709	115	101	101
1744	26,153,450	—	—	—	97	98
1750	25,917,830	13,818,654	12,099,176	114	99	98
1756[a]	26,061,830	13,833,311	12,228,919	113	100	98
1762	25,921,458	13,785,400	12,136,058	114	99	98
1768	26,252,057	—	—	—	101	99
1774	25,990,451	—	—	—	99	98
1780	26,010,600	—	—	—	100	98
1786	25,086,466	13,230,656	11,855,810	112	96	94
1792	24,891,441	—	—	—	99	94
1798	25,471,033	—	—	—	102	96
1804[a]	25,621,957	13,427,149	12,194,708	110	101	96
1822	26,602,110	—	—	—	104	100
1828[a]	27,201,400	14,160,736	13,040,064	108	102	102
1834	27,063,907	14,053,455	13,010,452	108	99	102
1846	26,907,625	13,854,043	13,053,582	106	99	101
1852[a]	27,201,400	14,153,927	13,040,662	108	101	102

[a] The sum of the male and female populations does not equal the total.
Source: Honjo. *Nihon jinko shi.* P. 65. Sekiyama. *Nihon jinko shi.* Appendix. Yuzuki, Jugo, and Horie, Yasuzo. "Hompo jinko hyo." *Keizai shi kenkyu,* No. 7, pp. 188-210. May 1930.

numbers. Before accepting this interpretation of the data, it is necessary to examine the changes in the districts.

The area of Tokugawa Japan was roughly equal to that of Japan today and the distribution of the population was similar. The major concentrations of commoners were on the Pacific side, in the Kinai and the Tokaido. As early as 1750, density was 807 per square mile in the former, 417 in the latter. Southwestern Honshu, Shikoku, and Kyushu were regions of intermediate density, if total land area is considered. If data on families in agriculture per unit of cultivable land were available, these regions would appear as high density areas, for the terrain was mountainous and cities were few. Density was relatively low in the mountainous regions of central Honshu, sparse in the northeastern portion of the island. Hokkaido was almost empty, with one person per square mile.

Density of settlement was already high in Japan by the early decades of the period of seclusion. In 1750 there were 173 commoners for each square mile of total land area; if Hokkaido is excluded, the figure becomes 235. When it is remembered that about 16 per cent of the total land area is regarded as cultivable at the present time, that far less than this proportion of the land was cultivated in the eighteenth century, that techniques were simple, and that alternative employment opportunities outside agriculture were limited, the seriousness of the population-land relationship becomes apparent. This was a population highly vulnerable to interruptions in the production or distribution of food. That vulnerability extended beyond the rural areas themselves, for any interruption of the regular flow of rice made life hazardous in the great cities of the Kinai and the Tokaido.

The rates of change in the *do* (regions) reveal a slow and irregular movement somewhat comparable to that for the country as a whole (TABLE 4). If there were regular forces making for population increase or decrease within the *do*, the rates of change between any two dates should bear some relationship to elapsed time. There is little evidence of such relationship; change is slight whether the time is long or short.[20] If there were divergent changes in the various areas, then variability in population change in the *do* would be consistent with relative stability in the population of the nation. However, there are two interpretations of the behavior of the figures in reports of the *daimyo* to the *shogun.* The first is that the reports represented previous compilations adjusted more or less at random, and hence that any conclusions derived from them are based on numerical artifacts. The second is that there was some relation between the realities of the Japanese situation and the reports of the *daimyo.*

[20] The populations of the *kuni* in 1750, 1756, 1804, 1834, 1846, and 1852 are given by Yuzuki and Horie. "Hompo jinko hyo. . . ." Pp. 188-210. Populations for 1828 are given by Honjo. *Nihon jinko shi.* Pp. 63-68. Populations for 1750, 1786, 1804, 1834, 1846, 1852, and 1872 are given by Sekiyama. "Tokugawa jidai . . . ." Populations for 1750, 1804, 1834, 1846, 1852, and 1872 are available by sex. Analysis of these data for the *kuni* indicates that proportionate changes from one report to another are relatively independent of elapsed time. If the differences between the irregularly spaced reports are transformed into average annual rates of change, the rates are roughly proportionate to the briefness of the interval separating the counts. If all intercensal rates of change are treated as equivalent, the frequency distribution is roughly symmetrical. For the five intercensal periods indicated in Table 4, 30 per cent of the shifts in the populations of the *kuni* were less than ± 1 per cent; an additional 42 per cent were ± 2 to 4 per cent. In all, 72 per cent of the variations were less than 5 per cent in magnitude. In 10 per cent of the cases there were declines of 5 per cent or more, in 18 per cent increases of 5 per cent or more.

TABLE 4

The commoner population of the *do*, 1750-1852

Do[a]	1750	1756	1804	1834	1846	1852
			Population (in '000)			
Total	25,924	26,197	25,622	27,059	26,912	27,201
Hokkaido	22	23	45	68	71	65
Kinai	2,139	2,170	2,017	2,077	1,999	2,099
Tokaido	6,612	6,570	6,033	6,169	6,425	6,384
Tosando-kami	2,443	2,479	2,426	2,473	2,434	2,510
Tosando-shimo	3,237	3,180	2,878	2,974	2,899	3,002
Hokurokudo	2,160	2,213	2,308	2,641	2,534	2,598
Sanindo	1,309	1,341	1,442	1,565	1,487	1,544
Sanyodo	2,633	2,802	2,823	3,065	3,028	3,039
Nankaido	2,204	2,228	2,350	2,577	2,566	2,537
Saikaido-kami	1,323	1,324	1,293	1,366	1,366	1,341
Saikaido-shimo	1,843	1,867	2,007	2,084	2,102	2,081
			Ratio to preceding report			
Total	—	101	98	106	99	101
Hokkaido	—	104	200	149	104	92
Kinai	—	101	93	103	96	105
Tokaido	—	99	92	102	104	99
Tosando-kami	—	101	98	102	98	103
Tosando-shimo	—	98	90	103	97	104
Hokurokudo	—	102	104	114	96	102
Sanindo	—	102	108	108	95	104
Sanyodo	—	106	101	108	99	100
Nankaido	—	101	106	110	100	99
Saikaido-kami	—	100	98	106	100	98
Saikaido-shimo	—	101	107	104	101	99

[a] The *do*, named after the great roads that connected the fiefs with Edo, were located as follows: *Hokkaido*, the northern island. *Kinai*, or Inner Provinces, included Kyoto, Osaka, and the surrounding *kuni*. *Tokaido*, or Eastern Sea Road Division, extended along the coast from the Kinai to Edo and beyond the Chiba promontory. *Tosando*, or Eastern Mountain Road Division, extended eastward and northward from the Kinai through the mountainous center of Honshu to include the entire tip of northeastern Honshu. It was divided into an upper (*kami*) and a lower (*shimo*) division. *Hokurokudo*, or North Land Road Division, extended along the cold and humid western coast of Honshu, from the Kinai northeastward to the present prefecture of Yamagata. *Sanindo*, or Mountain Shade Road Division, extended from the Kinai westward along the northern coast of Honshu. *Sanyodo*, or Mountain Sunshine Road Division, extended from the Kinai westward along the southern coast of Honshu west of Kyoto. *Nankaido*, or Southern Sea Road Division, included the island of Shikoku and the *kuni* of Awaji and Kii. *Saikaido*, or Western Sea Road Division, was the island of Kyushu; it, like Tosando, was divided into an upper and a lower division.

Source: 1750-1846: Compiled from the populations of the *kuni* as given in Yuzuki and Horie. "Hompo jinko hyo . . . ." Pp. 188-210. 1852: Honjo. *Nihon jinko shi*. Pp. 63-68. The figures for 1750 to 1846 presented here differ somewhat from those given by Professor Honjo in the latter source; these in turn differ somewhat from those cited in other studies. Thus there are inconsistencies with Table 3.

This second possibility will be accepted as a hypothesis for exploration.[21]

The population changes in Tokugawa Japan are those that would be expected in a premodern population settled densely on the land and subject to high and fluctuating mortality. Growth depended on local events. Analysis of the population of small areas for limited periods of time shows sharp changes from year to year and divergent movement in various areas in the same year. As the area of analysis is extended and the time lengthened, the divergences tend to be compensatory and a fictitious stability results.

Thus in theory it is simple to explain stability in numbers in a country such as Japan in a period of seclusion and localism. In fact, the movement was from localism to ever larger areas of integration, from stagnation to development, from decline in numbers to increase. The evidence is very substantial that in Japan, as in the West, early commercial and industrial developments initiated a cycle of population increase that became pronounced after the Restoration. If we divide the century from 1750 to 1852 into two roughly equal parts, there was a transition from irregular fluctuations to a growth in population reported for the country as a whole.

[21] There is some presumptive validation of this position in the descriptive materials on the maintenance of the population registers and the techniques of counting in various regions. Furthermore, existence of a fairly general and regionally localized pattern of change within the presumably unchanging Tokugawa populations itself corroborates the deduction of approximate validity. The general concurrence between significant population decreases and the known incidence of great famines will be discussed in detail later.

The number of commoners declined 1 per cent from 1750 to 1804, increased 6 per cent from 1804 to 1852.[22]

The appearance of an unchanging balance vanishes when changes are examined for the *kuni* and for the islands, rather than for all Japan (MAP 3). Numbers increased on the southern islands of Kyushu and Shikoku throughout the century, although the rate of increase was slow and declining. Hokkaido's population increased rapidly in relative terms, although the numbers involved were small. The balance of survival was most precarious on the main island of Honshu, which included the cities of Edo (modern Tokyo), Osaka, and Kyoto. Here population decreased 3 percent between 1750 and 1804 and increased 6 per cent between 1804 and 1852.

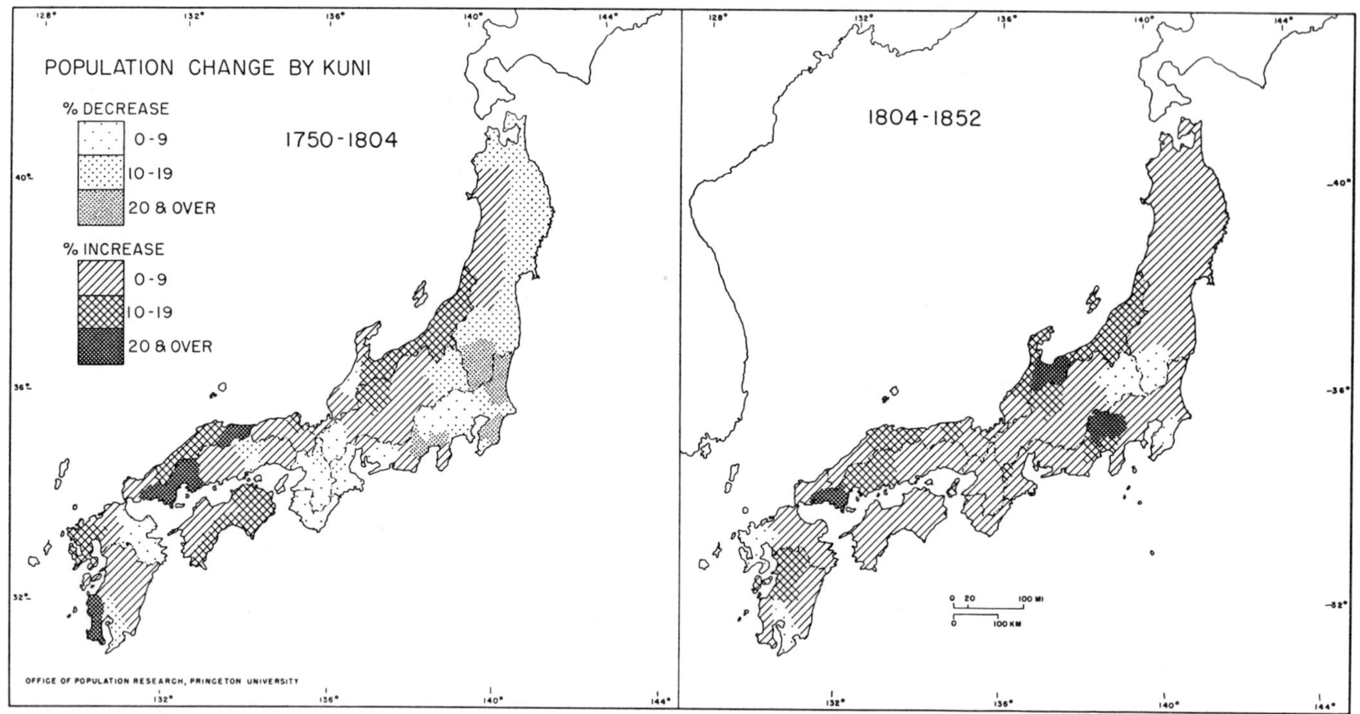

Map 3. Changes in the commoner population of the *kuni*, 1750-1804 and 1804-1852
Source: References, Table 4.

The decline in the number of commoners on Honshu between 1750 and 1804 was most apparent in Tosando-kami, the Kinai, and the Tokaido. In geographical terms, areas of decline were concentrated on the central and eastern Pacific littoral of Honshu, while major areas of growth lay beyond the mountains on the Sea of Japan, in southwestern Honshu, in Shikoku, and in most of Kyushu. In political terms, decline characterized the areas most immediately accessible to the tax-collecting officials of the *shogun*, while increase characterized the areas protected either by geographical isolation or by the localized powers of the outer *daimyo* whose capitulations to the *shogun* were somewhat nominal. In demographic terms, decline characterized the regions around Edo, Osaka, and Kyoto as well as those more remote rural areas that were centers for the rice collections that maintained the urban populations.[23]

Famines, epidemics, and other calamities caused gyrations in the numbers of the people. The most spectacular illustration is the Great Famine of 1783-1787 and its correlated catastrophes. In the summer of 1783 there was a volcanic eruption in the central mountain *kuni* of Shinano.[24] Immediate loss of life was less serious than the destruction of food, for much of the soil of several *kuni* was covered with ashes and the crops were ruined. Thousands died of famine before the lands could be cleared. The *daimyo* could not collect the rice stipends for movement to Edo. In 1782 there had been a partial crop failure in the Kinai; in 1783-1784 there was a poor crop in the Kinai and Dewa, and the crops failed in Mutsu. Since the granaries which had been a responsibility of the central government had been empty for many years, the only resources available to lessen the great catastrophe in northeastern Honshu were those of an occasional frugal *daimyo*. However, even the maximum reserves that could have been accumulated would have served only to mitigate the famine, for drought in the Kinai in 1785 led to another crop failure. In 1786 there were destructive floods on the Kanto Plain, the major granary for Edo. Again rains failed in the north, and crops were limited. By 1787 there were severe rice riots in the cities, with a destruction of rice shops that worsened the food situation. Eventually normal conditions of production

[22] The trend of the total population was generally downward to 1798, relatively unchanging to 1822, then upward to 1852, with slight recessions in 1834 and 1846. The year 1804 was prior to full recovery from the Great Famine of 1786-1792; the population was 2 per cent below that of the last pre-famine count of 1780, 2.5 per cent above the low immediate post-famine count of 1792.

[23] Professor Sekiyama arrived at this same conclusion through studying a rearrangement of the Tokugawa figures into regions comparable to those of modern Japan. As he says, "In so far as [the figures can be] believed, the stagnation in the latter half of the era can be seen in three districts—Kanto, Kinki, and Tohoku." "Tokugawa jidai . . . ." English summary.

[24] Murdoch, James. *A history of Japan*. Vol. III, "The Tokugawa epoch."

returned, but economic and demographic recovery was very slow.

The direct effects of the famines from 1783 to 1787 were concentrated in the *kuni* of Mutsu, Hitachi, and Shimotsuke. The indirect effects were widely diffused, for these *kuni* together with the great plain of the Kanto were the sources of supply for Edo. The crop failures in the Kinai resulted in the death of the peasants and spread disease and starvation into the cities. The urban people lived or died according to the grain surplus that could be moved in from the countryside. The reported commoner population for all Japan declined one million between 1780 and 1792. It failed to attain the 1780 level of 26 million until 1828, almost fifty years later.[25]

Volcanic eruptions, drought, flood, and fire continued as forces of devastation in the early nineteenth century. The Great Famine of 1836-1837 was a major factor in the national decline of 1 per cent between 1834 and 1846. On the whole, though, the trend of population was downward in the last half of the eighteenth century and upward in the first half of the nineteenth. The pattern of differences among the regions cannot be interpreted solely in terms of physical calamities and food production. The underlying factors in population change during the late *bakufu* period were social, economic, and political. The niggardliness and the caprice of nature became less and less adequate as explanations of demographic phenomena.

The Growth of Cities

The spread of the commercial economy and the differentiation of occupational classes resulted in an increase in the number and size of the castle towns.[26] In general, the importance of the town was related to the wealth and prestige of the *daimyo* (Table 5). The mobility required by the system of alternate residence was also a major factor. Most of this movement occurred on the five great highways that radiated out from the *Nihonbashi*, or Bridge of Japan, in Edo. *Shukuba-machi*, helping stations, were located each eight to twelve kilometers along these great roads.[27] Town lots were prepared along each side of the highway, the size of the lot being smaller than the usual agricultural holding but sufficient for some agriculture. Hotels for *daimyo* and *samurai* were located in the central section, as was the traffic center that handled passengers and freight. Inns for general travelers and shops were located at the peripheries. As the number of travelers and the movement of commodities increased, these *shukuba-machi* assumed more of the characteristics of towns than of villages. Moreover, as areas of production became more specialized and sub-highways were developed for transportation to the great cities, *shukuba-machi* developed along them.[28]

Table 5

The historical development of the castle towns and their status in 1950

Growth pattern[a]	Number of towns	Present status: *Shi*	Incorporated into *shi*	*Machi*	*Mura*
Total	453	103	11	174	165
1a	62	37	1	21	3
1b	45	15	0	29	1
2a	128	37	3	63	25
2b	47	2	1	15	29
3a	125	12	4	33	76
3b	46	0	2	13	31

[a] Classification as follows: 1a: Existed before 1600 and existed after 1869. 1b: Existed before 1600 but declined soon thereafter. 2a: Developed after 1600 and existed after 1869. 2b: Developed after 1600, declined soon thereafter. 3a: Ceased to function as castle towns at certain times before 1600. 3b: Ceased to function as castle towns at certain times after 1600.

Source: Fujioka. "An explanation of Japanese castle-towns. . . ." P. 18.

Thus the growth of towns was a major if unintended consequence of the requirement that *daimyo* spend alternate years of residence in Edo and maintain their families in the capital city as hostages in their absence. With peace the *samurai* became a leisure class, and they too moved to the cities. The service and distributive occupations essential to the maintenance of these sizable groups provided employment for many people even prior to the proliferating development of household industries and handicraft factories. The transportation and distribution of food brought additional people to the cities. And as transportation developed, industries became concentrated in easily accessible centers. Kyoto, Kiryu, Isezaki, Hino, and Fukushima became centers for the silk industry, while Satsuma, Iyo, Kokura, and Echigo became cotton textile centers. Nagasaki, Hakata, and Sakai became trading and industrial cities. Commercial centers included Shimonoseki, Otomari, Toda, Gifu, Matsuzaka, Toba, Yokkaichi, Otsu, Nagahama, Niigata, Sakata, Aomori, Ishinomaki, Choshi, Shimoda, Kiriu, Ashikaga, and Hachioji.[29]

The Great Cities

The great population concentrations of modern Japan were already developed in Tokugawa: Edo (Tokyo), Osaka, and Kyoto. Edo was the "city of *samurai*," Osaka the "city of merchants," Kyoto the "city of nobles, artisans, and craftsmen."[30] The maintenance of these large concentrations was one of the extraordinary achievements of the Tokugawa *bakufu*. One of the major problems was food. Three areas produced the major exportable surplus: the province of Hyuga in Kyushu; the northwestern Honshu provinces of Echizen, Echigo, Kaga, and Noto; and the northeastern prov-

[25] The regional impact of the famine can be traced in the populations of the affected *kuni* between 1756, a quarter of a century before the famine, and 1804, fifteen years after its end. Between 1756 and 1804 population decline amounted to 24 per cent in Hitachi and Shimotsuke, 11 per cent in Mutsu. Population decreased 16 percent in the *kuni* directly affected by the famine, 3 per cent in the remainder of the country.

[26] Fujioka, Kenjiro. "An explanation of Japanese castle-towns." Pp. 18-19 in: Tsujimura, Taro, Compiler. *Distribution maps on the regional geographical study of Japan.*

[27] Asaka, Yukio. "Shukuba-machi." Pp. 21-22 in: *ibid.*

[28] Although development of roads and travel facilities was necessary to the internal controls of the police state, the roads themselves were a hazard to the maintenance of a central government. Their use was, therefore, rigidly controlled. *Samurai* who were not direct retainers of the *shogun* could not move from Edo without passes from the *bakufu* officials. Barriers were scattered along the highways to prevent the importation of firearms or the escape of the hostage wives of the lords. The penalty for bypassing the barriers was crucifixion. Travel for the common people was simple, however; all they needed was a note from the village headman.

[29] Information from Tsuchiya. *An economic history . . . .*

[30] Smith, ed. *Materials . . . .* P. 37.

inces of Oshu and Dewa. Farmers in these areas baled their rice under the direct supervision of a deputy of the *shogun* and transported it first to a central official warehouse, then to the shipping port. Contractors handled the sea transportation of the rice, depositing security money, hiring private vessels, and issuing bills of lading. The ships with the Hyuga rice loaded at Kumamoto and went around north Kyushu to Osaka, a distance of less than 400 miles that in favorable weather took only twenty days. The trip from the rice areas along the Sea of Japan to Osaka took from three to six months. The ships were loaded at Niigata in the late spring. The port for the rice of the northeast was Sendai, the destination Edo.[31]

The push to escape the tax burdens and the rigorous life of the peasant was doubtless a factor in the premodern urbanization of Japan. It appears, however, that even in this early period the attractions of the cities and monetary employment were basic factors. How strong that pull must have been is illustrated in the following glowing descriptions written by Engelbert Kaempfer, a surgeon with the Dutch East India Company who resided in the Dutch settlement at Tsushima from 1690 to 1692 and made two journeys from Nagasaki to the palace of the *shogun* at Edo.[32]

Of Osaka, Kaempfer says: "Osacca is extremely populous. . . . It is the best trading town in Japan, being extraordinarily well situated for carrying on a commerce both by land and water. This is the reason why it is so well inhabited by rich merchants, artificers and manufacturers. Victuals are cheap at Osacca, notwithstanding the city is so well peopled. Even what tends to promote luxury, and to gratify all sensual pleasures, may be had at as easy a rate here as anywhere. . . . The Western Princes and Lords on this side Osacca have all their houses in this city, and their people to attend them in their passage through, and yet they are not permitted to stay longer than a night, besides that upon their departure they are obliged to follow such a road, as is entirely out of sight of the castel. . . ."[33]

And of Kyoto: "Miaco [Kyoto] is the great magazine of all Japanese manufactures and commodities, and the chief mercantile town in the Empire. There is scarce a house in this large capital, where there is not something made or sold. Here they refine copper, coin money, print books, weave the richest stuffs with gold and silver flowers. The best and scarcest dies, the most artful carvings, all sorts of musical instruments, pictures, japan'd cabinets, all sorts of things wrought in gold and other metals, particularly in steel, as the best tempered blades, and other arms are made here in the utmost perfection, as are also the richest dresses, and after the best fashion, all sorts of toys, puppets, moving their heads of themselves, and numberless other things, too many to be here mentioned. In short, there is nothing can be thought of, but what may be found at Miaco, and nothing, tho' never so neatly wrought, can be imported from abroad, but what some artist will undertake to imitate. Considering this, it is no wonder, that the manufactures of Miaco are become so famous throughout the Empire, as to be easily preferred to all others, though perhaps inferior in some particulars, only because they have the name of being made at Kio. There are but few houses in all the chief streets, where there is not something to be sold, and for my part, I could not help admiring, whence they can have customers enough for such an immense quantity of goods. 'Tis true indeed, there is scarce anybody passes through Miaco, but what buys something or other of the manufactures of this city, either for his own use, or for presents to be made to his friends and relations. . . ."[34]

With Edo, the greatest of the Tokugawa cities, Kaempfer is even more enthralled: "Of the five great trading towns, which belong to the Imperial demesnes, or crown lands, Jedo is the first and chief, the residence of the Emperor [Shogun], the capital, and by much the largest city of the Empire, by reason of the many Princes and Lords, who with their families and numerous trains swell up the Imperial Court, and the inhabitants of the city, to an incredible number. . . . Towards the sea the city hath the figure of a half-moon, and the Japanese will have it to be seven miles long, five broad and twenty in circumference. . . . The city is extreme populous, and the number of natives, foreigners, and ecclesiasticks almost incredible. . . ."[35]

Of the urban development in general: "The country is populous beyond expression, and one would scarce think it possible that, being no greater than it is, it should nevertheless maintain and support such a vast number of inhabitants. The highways are an almost continued row of villages and boroughs: You scarce come out of one but you enter another; and you may travel many miles, as it were, in one street, without knowing it to be composed of many villages, but by the differing names, that were formerly given them, and which they afterwards retain, though joined to one another. It hath many towns, the chief whereof may vie with the most considerable in the world for largeness, magnificence and the number of inhabitants. . . . Even since the Empire hath been shut up, nature, that kind mistress, taught them, and they themselves readily own it, that they can wholly subsist upon what it affords, and that they have no need of being supplied by foreigners with the necessaries of life. . . . A numerous nation, so much an enemy to idleness, as the Japanese is, and withal confined within the narrow limits of their own Country, learnt to make use of most productions of nature, which either sea or land affords, not only for the support of life, but also for its ease and pleasures . . . it is scarce credible, how much trade and commerce is carried on between the several provinces and parts of the Empire! how busy and industrious the merchants are every where! how full their ports of ships! how many rich and flourishing mercantile towns up and down the Country! There are such multitudes of people along the coasts, and near the sea-ports, such a noise of oars and sails, such numbers of ships and boats, both for use and pleasure, that one would be apt to imagine the whole nation had settled there, and all the inland parts of the Country were left quite desart and empty."[36]

THE SIZE OF THE CITIES

In 1721, when the *shogun* called on all *daimyo* for a report on the commoners in their fiefs, a population of half a million was reported for the city of Edo.[37] Population had presumably grown rapidly in the preceding century and a half when the Tokugawa were building the city as their headquarters, but in the century and a quarter after 1721 the numbers of commoners reported as resident there changed only slightly.

[31] Wigmore, H. Cited in *ibid.* Pp. 76-77.
[32] Kaempfer, Engelbert. *The history of Japan . . . 1690-92.* 3 vols.
[33] *Ibid.* Vol. III, pp. 6-7.
[34] *Ibid.* Vol. III, pp. 20-24.
[35] *Ibid.* Vol. III, pp. 71-74.
[36] *Ibid.* Vol. III, pp. 306-307, 313-317.
[37] The population data utilized here are primarily those compiled from a wide variety of sources by Yuzuki and Horie and published as "Hompo jinko hyo."

Numbers declined during the Great Famine from 1783 to 1787, increased somewhat in the early nineteenth century, decreased slightly in the 1830's and 1840's, and increased again in the last years of the *bakufu*. However, relative stability in total numbers was the outstanding characteristic.

This apparent failure of the population of Edo to increase in the last half of the period of seclusion is in sharp contradiction to the complaints as to the desertion of the countryside and the parasitic growth of the city. Perhaps the major explanation for the relatively unchanging population was the fact that the most mobile elements in the population were by definition excluded from registration and periodic reporting. The *bushi* class, with their families, retainers, and servants, spent major portions of their time in Edo, thus swelling its numbers and increasing its economic activity. Seasonal laborers came into the city in large numbers, but they retained residence in the rural areas from which they came. In addition, reports were compiled for years when the functioning of municipal administration was not disturbed by famines, epidemics, fires, or riots. The regular reports for Edo would indicate only that the "normal" and permanently resident population of commoners fluctuated relatively little in the last century and a quarter of the period of seclusion. Special "counts" made during periods of calamity indicated that the changes which occurred in the *de facto* population were substantial indeed. In October 1786, as the desolation of the Great Famine was approaching its climax, the total population was counted as the basis for the distribution of food. While the "normal" population reported in that year was 457 thousand, the persons who registered for famine relief numbered 1.3 million.

The Tokugawa reports indicate that Osaka and Kyoto had attained a considerable size. The "normal" registered population of Osaka increased from approximately 275 thousand in the early seventeenth century to 375 thousand in the early eighteenth. It reached its maximum of slightly over 400 thousand in the third quarter of the eighteenth century, then declined to approximately 300 thousand in the middle of the nineteenth. The year-to-year figures fluctuated irregularly. Population decreases in 1787, 1788, 1836, and 1837 probably reflected famine conditions, while the declines after 1848 may be related to the enforcement of the legal barriers against migratory labor. The surviving records suggest that the economic life of Kyoto was less secure than that of either Edo or Osaka. From 1634 to 1674 the registered population of the imperial capital was 350 to 400 thousand; from 1681 to 1696 it was 510 to 575 thousand; from 1711 to 1729 it was 350 to 375 thousand; and from 1732 to 1753 it was more than half a million.

Fragmentary figures as to the recorded populations of other towns abound in the literature. For instance, the castle towns of Sendai, Kanazawa, Hiroshima, and Nagoya and the commercial city of Nagasaki reputedly had commoner populations of 40 to 65 thousand, while the populations of Okayama and Tokushima reached 20 to 30 thousand.

Measurement of urbanization in Tokugawa Japan is difficult, for there is little information on the smaller commercial and industrial centers and the castle towns. Even in the *bakufu* period, however, the three great cities of Edo, Osaka, and Kyoto included 5 or 6 per cent of the total commoner population of the nation. The urbanization of the population increased in the modern period, but the great city was not a product of that period. And movements of surplus youth from the rural areas to the cities were adjustments of population to resources and employment opportunities that antedated modern industrialization by some centuries.

OTHER MOVEMENTS

The movement from the more fully utilized areas to the peripheries of settlement continued throughout the Tokugawa period. The doubling of the cultivated area during the first century and a half of the period was presumably accompanied by redistribution within the settled areas and movement outward to the frontiers. This latter movement was in part a flight from taxation, for the areas of population growth in the early nineteenth century were primarily those that were farthest removed from the tax-collectors of the *shogun*. The role of migration in the greater increase of the population living far from the great cities should not be overemphasized, however, for differential mortality may have been substantial. Those peasants who could retain a larger portion of the food they produced might suffer less from malnutrition in normal years and be less vulnerable to famine in bad ones.

Flights from calamities characterized premodern Japan, just as they do modern China. Regional famines set in motion vast outward waves that washed into the great cities. Epidemics may have acted similarly. Volcanic eruptions, earthquakes, and fires all produced local movements. Individual or family flight from intolerable circumstances was also widespread. Tokugawa law placed severe restrictions on the out-movements of *samurai*, farmers, and tradesmen, and on the in-movements of deserters, *ronin* (lordless *samurai*), and other questionable characters. The fact that in 1643 the *shogun* ordered all villages to impose more stringent punishment on farmers who left their native places to settle elsewhere indicates that the proscribed movements were occurring. Furthermore, all descriptions of the cities, the towns, and the great roads comment on the numbers of beggars and wanderers.

THE CHANGING CLASS STRUCTURE

The growth of cities and the penetration of commercial and monetary practices into peasant society imply the development of substantial mobility within the precisely defined and presumably rigid class structure of feudal society. The population reports to the *shogun* are of little value here, for the compilations excluded both the upper and the lower classes. However, many students have estimated the size of the excluded classes in order to arrive at reasonable figures for the total population of Tokugawa Japan. Professor Honjo estimates that the imperial household, the court nobility, the shogunate, the *daimyo*, the *samurai* and other military families, together with their employees and dependents, numbered from 1.2 to 1.8 million at the end of the period of seclusion. He estimates the *eta* and the *hinin*, including beggars, vagrants, prostitutes, and those without fixed domicile, at 333 thousand.[38] Professor Sekiyama, on the other hand, estimates that the excluded classes numbered from 3.8 to 4.0 million.[39]

Estimation of the size of the excluded groups at the end of the feudal period indicates little as to the class structure of the population throughout that period, for the social structure was changing and there may have been a differential

[38] Honjo. "The population and its problems . . . ." P. 66. If this excluded population of 1.5 to 2.0 million is added to the reported commoner population of 1852, 27.2 million, the total population toward the end of the period of seclusion becomes 28.7 to 29.2 million.

[39] Sekiyama. "Tokugawa jidai zenkoku . . . ." Pp. 8-10. If these estimates are accepted, the total population of the late Tokugawa period becomes something between 29.4 and 32.0 million.

natural increase for the social classes. Fragmentary local studies indicate that there were in fact appreciable differences in the composition of the population in various areas. In four *daimyo* districts, there were only slight changes between 1805 and 1851. *Samurai* constituted approximately 7 percent of the total population; *no* (farmers), 87 per cent; *ko* (handicrafts), 2 per cent; and *sho* (commerce), 3 per cent.[40] In sixteen *daimyo* districts in the year 1867, however, the variability in social structure was considerable, as the following figures indicate:[41]

Social class	*Minimum per cent*	*Maximum per cent*
Samurai	3.9	26.5
Farmers	52.4	89.6
Merchants and handicraft workers	2.5	23.4
Priests	0.8	2.5
Other	0.0	3.0

The distribution of the elite as between rural and urban areas, or as between lesser cities and great cities, cannot be determined for the Tokugawa era. In the early Meiji period, the elite lived disproportionately in the more cultured southwestern part of the country and in the smaller cities, presumably those that had been castle towns. The social and economic structures of the great cities were more multi-functional. The registration compilation of 1886 indicated that 5 per cent of the total population were nobles, *samurai*, or members of the families of these groups. At that time the upper-class groups were most prevalent in Kyushu, where they constituted 13 per cent of the total population. They made up only 3.5 per cent of the population in Honshu; within Honshu, they were least prevalent in the central region that included the great cities. In 1884 nobles, *samurai*, and their families constituted 3.3 per cent of the legally domiciled populations of Tokyo and Osaka, but 7.2 per cent of that of the 28 incorporated cities taken as a group.[42]

Agriculture remained predominant as an occupation and as a way of life throughout the pre-Restoration period. In most of the surviving records, from 80 to 90 per cent of the gainfully occupied were farmers. Their way of life was quite similar to that of the modern period. Farms were tiny and labor was intensive, but there were divisions into landowners, rich farmers, middle farmers, the poor, and the laborers. The household groups were fairly small, containing five to six people on the average, and the regional variations were comparable to those of the modern period, with larger households in northeast Honshu, smaller households in southwest Honshu and Kyushu. There was a positive association between the size of the household and its income.[43] Since the *daimyo* determined the rice stipend of the household on the basis of social status rather than need, this would indicate that either birth and death rates or migration patterns, or perhaps both, differed as between the social classes.

Birth and Death Rates

Japanese students have searched the regional and local chronicles for records of the numbers of births and deaths registered in ancient and medieval times. These ancient records, fragmentary and inaccurate as they are, yield clues as to the nature, if not the precise magnitude, of the vital balance during the period of seclusion. One of the most interesting of the surviving series of records is that for the Tsushima *han* for the years from 1687 to 1712.[44] The average annual birth rate for this *han* of some 30 thousand population was 20.8 per 1,000 total population, while the average annual death rate was 22.7. The range in birth rates was from 16.8 to 25.2, in death rates from 15.2 to 33.3. Annual fluctuations were erratic, although in fifteen of the twenty-five years deaths exceeded births. Most interesting, however, is the existence of a marked difference in the urban and rural subdivisions of the *han* in the period from 1701 to 1712. Fuchu, the present Iwahara, was the principal town, with a population of from 11 to 16 thousand. Gomura (population from 16 to 17 thousand) was rural, while Ginzan (population about 600) was a mining village with many migrant laborers. Birth rates were higher in the rural areas, while death rates were higher in the urban areas. As a result, there was a recorded natural decrease of 1 per cent per year in the urban population, a recorded natural increase of two-fifths of 1 per cent per year in the rural population. While little credence can be placed in the absolute values of the vital rates, the pattern of differences is reasonable. Cities with their predominantly male populations would have lower birth rates, while poor living conditions and greater exposure to contagion would result in higher death rates.

In a work entitled *The famine in the old Nambu han*, Mori Kahei presented vital statistics for various years between 1753 and 1798, together with information on crop conditions.[45] The Nambu *han* lived in the northeast, in Mutsukuni. The number of people declined 16 per cent during the famine years between 1753 and 1757. The recording system apparently collapsed, for in the latter year there were fewer than 10 births per 1,000 reported population, and the death rate was insignificantly above its 1753 level. Subsequently, the size of the reported population increased slowly; in 1783 it was 86 per cent of what it had been in 1753. There was another famine in 1784, and the population declined 20 per cent within the year. The birth rate changed little, but the death rate increased from 28.4 to 263.0 per 1,000 total population. Births and deaths remained about in balance throughout the later years of the Great Famine from 1783 to 1787. In 1798, the last year of record, both birth and death rates for the Nambu *han* were above 40 per 1,000 population.

Perusal of the various reports on births and deaths during the late Tokugawa period reveals birth rates that fluctuated between 20 and 30 per 1,000 total population, death rates that tended to be somewhat higher. Slow declines character-

[40] Sekiyama. *Nihon jinko shi*. P. 98.
[41] *Ibid*. P. 100.
[42] These data suggest that the functional and structural differences between the great cities and the lesser cities that have been so characteristic of modern cities may have antedated the modern period. However, the position of *daimyo* and *samurai* in the early decades of the Restoration differed greatly from that during the former regime. Moreover, the Meiji registration compilations reported people as of their place of legal domicile. Hence the abolition of the system of alternate residence and the end of the annual influx into Edo would be reflected neither in the reports of commoners of the feudal period nor in the reports of the *honseki* populations of the modern period.
[43] Sekiyama. *Nihon jinko shi*. P. 113.

[44] Sekiyamo, Naotaro. "Tokugawa jidai no shussei ritsu oyobi shibo ritsu. Sono jakkan no jirei." *J.m.k.*, 1(3):32-43. June 1940. These rates were based on a study of the *Oral testament* of Tozan Don-o in *Collections of Japanese economies*, Vol. IV, Ch. 13. [In Japanese.] Don-o was born in Tsushima in 1657, and was for many years district magistrate there. It should be noted that these data pertain to a period well before the presumed population stability of the late Tokugawa period.
[45] Sekiyama. "Tokugawa jidai no shussei . . . ." Pp. 32-43.

ized normal periods. Unfortunately for the validity of this inference from the records, both death and birth rates are so low as to be improbable. A "normal" crude death rate of 30 per 1,000 total population in Tokugawa Japan would mean that levels of mortality were as low as those achieved by such prefectures as Fukui and Ishikawa in the years from 1925 to 1930. If the assumed crude death rate of 30 was an average for healthful years and years of calamity, then normal conditions of nutrition and health would have had to be far superior to those of Fukui and Ishikawa in the period from 1925 to 1930. This does not seem probable in the light of the contemporary accounts of the deficiencies of food, the inadequacies of housing, and the other woes of the peasants, entirely aside from the prevalence of disease, the absence of doctors and medical care, and the periodicity of the great calamities. If we assume that death rates were higher than from 20 to 30 per 1,000 population, then birth rates must have been far higher than the majority of those recorded if the population of the nation was to avoid precipitant decline from the late seventeenth to the mid-nineteenth century. And there is conclusive evidence that such long-continued and rapid decline did not occur.

The surviving records of the late Tokugawa period indicate the probability of lower fertility and higher mortality in the smaller cities than in the surrounding rural areas. The statistical records of the Tokugawa period itself, the reports of travelers, and the investigations made during the early years after the opening to the West all indicate the existence of very high death rates in the great cities of Edo, Osaka, and Kyoto. Thus it would seem that rural fertility had to be quite high in order to permit the maintenance of the national population at a relatively unchanging level during the last century and a quarter of the period of seclusion.[46] A reconciliation of this conclusion concerning the nature of the balance of births and deaths in Tokugawa Japan with the widespread practice of abortion and infanticide as regulators of population change will be attempted in the next section.

Family Limitation[47]

THE CONTEMPORARY RECORDS

Contraception, abortion, and infanticide were all known to the ancient Japanese, but even in the late *bakufu* period there was no sharp differentiation among the three as biological procedures or ethical concepts. The prevention of conception appears to have been less important as a technique of limitation than abortion or infanticide. There were many recipes for contraceptives, but the formulae and the recommendations for practice indicated their base in superstition and mythology. Many medicines were sold quite openly until 1667, but they were predominantly abortificants, either *oroshi-kusuri*, "putting-down medicine," or *jiyu-gan*, "freeing capsule." Prices were high, and the persons who sold the drugs, usually women, were regarded as cruel.[48] Mechanical methods of abortion were more common than medicinal in both ancient and Tokugawa times; in fact, specialists in the procedures are reported before the Kamakura period. Women were predominant, some of them combining the practice of abortion with that of midwifery. Although some male "physicians" who performed abortions had professional status, the occupation was a despised one among women.

The procedure easily and cheaply available to the people was not abortion but *mabiki* (thinning). According to the ancient tales, when the woman in a poor family was delivered, the midwife asked the family whether to let the infant remain, *okimasu-ka*, or whether to return it, *modoshi masuka*. The midwife either cared for the infant who must be assisted to survive or managed the death of the infant for whom there was no room.

Abortion and infanticide were known throughout the society, and their utilization is reported to have been widespread. Many families of the *bushi* class had such low incomes that they had severe difficulties in obtaining food and clothing appropriate to their status. In Kyushu men were enjoined not to marry until age 30 or later, and it was regarded as somehow disgraceful to have more than three children.[49] The number of the wives who had abortions performed secretly was "countless."[50] In the cities power and wealth were in the hands of the merchants and the artisans. Among these, so it is reported, adultery was common and abortion utilized to avoid publicity and disgrace. The peasants did not resort to abortion but instead to the "inhuman" practice of infanticide. We quote: "Many of the poor peasants in the remote regions do not raise their children. Their humanity is below that of the animals. The practice [of infanticide] is beyond description, but it has become a custom and people do not think it strange. It is reported frequently that the custom [of infanticide] has penetrated even to persons of high character. This practice is most common in the Hyuga region [of Kyushu]. Here it is said that if a birth occurs to a person of high character and the decision is made to raise the child, [people] offer them congratulations. If [people] learn that the child is not to be raised they pretend ignorance; [under these circumstances] they do not offer congratulations. Generally only the first son is raised, and the others are not. If two or three sons are raised the family is ridiculed for undue attachment. This is a shocking situation."[51]

Many accounts from the late Tokugawa period show that infanticide was practiced in all classes of the population in all regions of the country. There are also impassioned condemnations by the leaders of the *bakufu* and the *han*. The documentation is illustrative and impressionistic, however, with few attempts at numerical estimation for social classes or geographic regions. Professor Honjo believes that abortion served to limit family size in Edo, Osaka, and Kyoto, but that infanticide prevailed among the peasants.[52] Citing as regions of heavy incidence the rural areas of the Tokaido lying northeast of Edo, Tosa-kuni of Shikoku Island, and

[46] Further substantiation of the hypothesis that both fertility and mortality were high during the late Tokugawa period can be derived from a backward projection of the populations of 1872 and later years to determine the levels of vital rates that must have existed to produce these populations. Since this evidence is based on manipulations of the registered populations of the early Meiji period to secure the trend of vital rates from the late pre-Restoration period to a time some decades after the Restoration, it will be presented in Chapter III.

[47] The major sources are as follows: Honjo, Eijiro. *Nihon jinko shi*. Takahashi, Bonsen. *Nihon jinko shi no kenkyu*. Honjo, Eijiro. "The population and its problems in the Tokugawa era." *Bulletin de l'Institut international de statistique*, 25(2):60-82. 1931. Droppers, Garrett. "The population of Japan in the Tokugawa period." *T.A.S.J.*, 22:253-284. 1894. Kuno, Yoshio, S. *Japanese expansion on the Asiatic continent*. Vol. II, "To the end of the seclusion period." Appendix. Ishii, Ryoichi. *Population pressure and economic life in Japan*. Chs. I and III.

[48] Takahashi. *Nihon jinko shi* . . . . Part II, Ch. 1, Section 5, pp. 333-344, "Abortion and its practitioners."

[49] Droppers. "The population of Japan . . . ." Pp. 253-284.

[50] Takahashi. *Op.cit.* Part II, Ch. 1, Section 4, pp. 332-333, "Birth limitation among the *bushi* class."

[51] *Nihon keizai daiten*. Vol. XXIII, pp. 495-496.

[52] Honjo. *Nihon jinko shi*. Pp. 116.

some areas of Kyushu, he quotes Sato Nobuhiro as follows: "Many women become pregnant, but they can not nurse their children. They murder their babies or procure abortion. By travelling around our country, I know this custom prevails. It is a very terrible fact that in a village consisting of ten houses, every year over two babies are killed. . . . This custom is most prevalent in the provinces of Ohu and Kanto. In Chugoku, Shikoku and Kyushu abortion is universal. Even in the provinces of Dewa and Oshu alone, every year about sixteen or seventeen thousand babies are killed. But no one is startled by this deplorable custom."[53]

Many of the accounts of infanticide in late Tokugawa assert that there was a greater purity in the ancient days. Illustrative of this view of the late Tokugawa period as one of decadence is the memorial that Ro-Tozan of Sendai *han* submitted to the clan authorities in 1754: "Up to fifty or sixty years ago a couple of farmers used to bring up five or six or even seven or eight children . . . but in recent years it has become a fashion among the farmers not to rear more than one or two children between a couple, though it is not clear whether this is due to the luxurious habits that prevail among them or some other causes. As soon as a baby is born, its parents put it to death. All this is ascribable to their poverty. They prefer leading as best a life as they can without encumbrances to bringing up many children to hunger and penury, and restrict the number of their children to two or three. Even rich families are contaminated by this evil custom, and deliberately restrict the number of their children. In my opinion, the prevalence of this usage is partly responsible for the waste of agricultural fields."[54]

The amount of infanticide believed to occur was very great, particularly when the area under discussion was in a remote place. The literature would indicate that in many areas of Kyushu two of each five children were killed, while in Tosa-kuni of Shikoku one boy and two girls were the maximum number allowed to survive. In Hyuga, all except the first-born were killed. In some districts nine of each ten births reported were those of boys; presumably, therefore, seven or eight of each nine girl babies were destroyed. There are reports that the *samurai* saved only the first-born.[55]

The locale of the various reports on family limitation suggests that practices of destruction were diffused throughout the islands.[56] Abortion and infanticide were believed to be so rife on *bakufu* lands and imperial estates that the cultivation of the lands, the production of rice, and hence the rice levies were jeopardized. The destruction of infants was reported from ancient times in the Kanto, while the practice was common in northeastern Honshu, not only in the peasant villages but in the towns and in the city of Sendai. Family limitation was practiced in the Chugoku region, especially in Minasaku-kuni (Okayama prefecture). In the Nankai region limitation was widespread, even among the *samurai*. Families were reported as raising two sons and one daughter; if another baby was expected, the midwife was instructed as to disposal if the sex should prove otherwise than that needed to complete the desired family.

The geographic and social-class incidence of family limitation was more complex than an urban-rural dichotomy. Abortion was associated with the elite—the Tokugawa families, the *daimyo*, the *samurai*, and the rich merchants. Infanticide was most prevalent among the peasants. Among all classes, there was presumed to be a religious differentiation, the majority of the Buddhist sects repudiating methods of limitation that involved the taking of life. In Shintoism, on the other hand, there were no taboos on interference with gestation at any time between conception and independent viability. Families limited their numbers in ways consistent with their values, their aversions, and their superstitions. Limitation applied to birth orders beyond the first or, more specifically, to conceptions or deliveries that occurred after the production of a son. In infanticide, where there was a choice, destruction was more likely for the girl baby than for the boy baby. The survival of the family through the male line was the pre-eminent value; other motivations entered only after this duty to the generations had been fulfilled. However, birth order and sex were not the only factors considered in the decision as between death and survival. "Elderly" couples in their late thirties or early forties felt it somewhat improper to have a child, especially if there was a daughter-in-law in the house. Moreover, parents were apt to decide against the continued existence of an infant born in years of unfavorable zodiacal and calendar combinations.[57]

THE MOTIVATIONS

It is often assumed that the goal of the familistic society is multiplicity of descendants. If this is so, then we have in premodern Japan a society whose members behaved in ways opposed to the basic values of their society. If the motivations for this behavior were the inexorable pressures of a poverty that precluded another mouth to feed, the co-existence of the unlimited familistic ideal and substantial infanticide would be explained. If the motivations involved aspirations for the future as well as the pressures of the present, however, the reconciliation would necessitate modification of the traditional assumptions that the supremacy of the family requires major emphasis on many children.

Analysis of the attitudes of individuals must begin with the reports of statesmen and savants. These men were divorced from and sitting in judgment on the lower echelons of the society. To the savants themselves, interpretations of the practice of infanticide by the common people presented no problem. They knew that the structure of Tokugawa society had lost its dynamism, that the land was completely occupied and the economy stagnant. Peasants were miserable, without hope for the future. Hence, they killed their young. The explanation was equally simple for the *bushi* class and the merchants. In their case, limitation of offspring signified selfishness and moral degeneration; it was symptomatic of social decay in the urban milieu.

The generations of the savants reveal the attitudes of the writers toward abortion and infanticide, but the probable attitudes of the families who practiced infanticide are seen in the factual materials they present. In a society as rigidly structured as that of Japan, interpretation must proceed separately for elite and peasant, although values and proscriptions inherent in the culture may have been common to all Japanese.

Life was difficult for the peasants. Land was scarce, production was limited, and levies were high. Poverty was omnipresent, malnutrition common, and starvation a recurrent

[53] Honjo. "The population and its problems . . . ." P. 77.
[54] *Ibid.* P. 78.
[55] *Ibid.* Pp. 78-81.
[56] The survey of incidence given here is based on materials presented in Takahashi's *Nihon jinko shi no kenkyu.*

[57] Honjo, Eijiro, "Policy of child-bearing of the Tosa clan." [In Japanese.] *Keizai ronso*, Vol. XXXVI, No. 1. January 1933. Cited in: Ishii. *Population pressure* . . . . P. 32.

threat. These economic pressures for the limitation of numbers impinged on a family structure that was exclusive rather than equalitarian. In general the eldest son succeeded the father as household head and thus had an assured future, but the possibilities for the second, third, or higher-order sons were dark. There was little place in this crowded rural society for the establishment of a branch household in a nearby area. An occasional son might be adopted by a family that lacked an heir. An appreciable number escaped the village through migration to the city, while still others secured temporary work on other fiefs or on imperial estates. In this situation where the land was filled and opportunities alternative to agriculture very limited, *mabiki* (infanticide) and *kakeochi* (escape) were the alternatives to a cumulation of people hazardous to the family and the community alike.

A family system that functioned to expel youth existing within a society that barred migration in theory, and in fact offered few opportunities to migrants, was eminently suited to the development of mores of family limitation. Such adaptability of elements cannot explain the process, however. One does not envision an unlettered peasant family deciding to preserve or destroy a newborn baby on the basis of a rational assessment of the economic opportunities available in the village or elsewhere some fifteen or twenty years in the future. It is possible that the factors of economic limitation and social structure were conducive to, or facilitated the survival of, mores of destruction; if so, they must have operated on an immediate personal level.

If the focus is shifted from the larger society to the individual family, the limitation of offspring appears as a product of the familistic system itself. The pre-eminent necessity was the continuity of the family through the male line. In an ideal world the values of living and the emphasis on the continuity of life would create a milieu in which each additional child would be welcomed. Many surviving offspring would mean prestige for the mother and honor for the father. In the real world there were conflicts between the fulfillment of the duties to the ancestors and the responsibilities for children already born. In this situation, the young couple tried to raise their first son. All the observations of the late Tokugawa and the early Meiji eras indicate that the eldest son was subject to no hazard of willed death; that, furthermore, the first two or three children were relatively secure. When the heavy infant mortality of the period is considered, this would mean that the practical decision as to life or death for a child was not required until four, five, or even six children had been born. When one further considers the hazards to the health and life of the mother, it becomes apparent that many families would not face the problem of infanticide. The decision, when it was made, would be against a background of childrearing and in a situation where father, mother, two or three surviving children, and perhaps some grandparents or other relatives were dependent for life itself on inadequate food. Infanticide might become an imperative of the familistic system for a mother whose alternative and perhaps "natural" reaction would be the preservation of the newly born at all costs. The strength of the familistic values would determine the limitation of offspring in the interests of those already born.

Motivations and attitudes among the *bushi* class are at once simpler to comprehend and more complex in derivation. They are also described more explicitly in the records. The maintenance of their accustomed way of life was difficult for *samurai* in the centuries of peace. Codes of behavior limited marriage and childbearing. According to these codes, marriage should not occur before the maintenance of a household was feasible. However, the postponement of marriage to or beyond age 30 still provided no guarantees against the production of numerous children for whom no adequate provisions could be made. The resort to abortion thus becomes comprehensible. It appears also that the response to the nuances of the culture was more rigid among the *samurai* than among the commoners. Children were less likely to be reared if they were conceived during inappropriate years or at inappropriate stages of the family cycle. Among *samurai*, as among peasants, motivations appear to have been far more complex than the simple fact of physical poverty.

THE POLICIES

Tokugawa Japan bequeathed to modern Japan both the tradition of family limitation and the tradition of positive action by the government to encourage an increase of the population. The existence of a widespread practice of family limitation is evident in the many policies that were designed to lessen it. The locale toward which the policies were directed reached from northeastern Honshu to southwestern Kyushu; the architects of the policies included the *bakufu*, the magistrates of imperial estates, the *daimyo*, and local officials. The time span of the edicts extended from the early decades of the Tokugawa shogunate until decades after the Meiji Restoration. And their provisions were surprisingly diverse and quite modern.

In the year 1667 the fourth *shogun* forbade the use of signs to indicate the availability of abortion facilities.[58] Punishment for violation was banishment from the city. This regulation pertained only to the city of Edo; elsewhere proscriptions were local or non-existent.

Moral arguments and a somewhat sympathetic approach to the problems of infanticide appeared as early as the seventeenth century. In 1663 the Lord of Aizu issued the following appeal to his people: "It is not the desire of the lord to promulgate a law the provisions of which would inflict punishment upon the mass of the people who destroy their newborn infants. His command to the government is to instruct all the people to be always sympathetic and thoughtful with regard to children. If any of you should fail to report this noble desire of our lord, and if reports of your inhuman acts thus committed should reach him, it would cause him great regret and grief. Therefore, the government hereby requests you, the mass of the people, to fulfill, immediately and strictly, the noble desire of our lord and cease to stray from the humane and righteous way."[59]

Shogun and *daimyo* used teachers, priests, and professional exhorters to rouse the people to the horrors of infanticide. This, it should be noted, was in the seventeenth century. Since the reports of commoners that presumably revealed a decline in numbers did not begin until the end of the first decade of the eighteenth century, concern over abortion and infanticide antedated concern over stability or decline in the population.

The population policies of the imperial estates were quite comprehensive. One of the magistrates developed policies that involved investigative work, stimulants to families to raise children, and punitive measures against those who de-

[58] Takahashi. *Nihon jinko shi* . . . . Part II, Ch. 1, Section 8, pp. 353-360, "*Bakufu* policy on abortion and infanticide."

[59] Honjo, Eijiro. *Jinko oyobi jinko mondai*. P. 130. Cited in: Kuno. *Japanese expansion* . . . . Vol. II, p. 373.

stroyed children. The village authorities had to report on the ability of the family to raise a newly born baby. In order to procure this information an official visited the home. If the family that was unable to raise the baby presented a receipt for the registration of the birth in the village books, an allowance was granted that extended from the month of birth to the fifteenth year of age. Hoes were given to boys and girls at age 15. These material encouragements were combined with punitive measures. All stillbirths were investigated; where stillbirths and abortions were reputed to be especially numerous, "special investigations" were made.

Peasants who were devout Buddhists were imported into areas where the destruction of life was severe. However, the numbers transferred were so small that the quantitative effects must have been negligible. For instance, peasants from Niigata were brought to one of the imperial estates. Each family was provided with food and a horse for the journey and received a house, tools, and one *cho* of land in the area of settlement. Between 1795 and 1829 some three hundred migrant households were settled on this one estate.

Many of the policies appear rather progressive today. In 1794, a new magistrate was appointed for an imperial estate of 182 villages located in the present Ibaraki prefecture. When he found that abortion and infanticide were widely practiced, while waste land and poverty were increasing, he established a system of allowances graduated according to birth order and the probability of destruction. The first child would be raised, regardless of poverty, and therefore required no allowance. The second male or female child was treated as the first in case the first had died; the same procedure applied to later birth orders. The second surviving child received allowances for three years, the third for five years, the fourth or higher order for six to seven years. Relief could be continued for ten years. Records of grants under this scheme extend from 1801 through 1843.

The population policies in the *bakufu* lands of the Kanto were similar to those on the imperial estates. There were surveys of the numbers of pregnant women, reports on deliveries, and allowances for second and higher-order children, the amount depending on the circumstances. Regulations for midwives were promulgated, and groups were moved from Buddhist areas to centers where infanticide was common. Severe regulations were sometimes issued. In Kagoshima, for instance, orders of 1832 established compulsory reporting of pregnancies and decreed the death penalty for the performance of infanticide. It is reported that even these drastic measures were not successful in suppressing customs that had existed for hundreds of years. Hence, alternative policies were tried, rice being given to families who bore third or higher-order children and permitted them to survive. Regulations of 1873 in Miyazaki prefecture likewise required reports of pregnancies and deliveries, with severe punishments for abortion, infanticide, or abandonment. It is reported that this law was ineffective in eliminating infant destruction prior to the middle of the Meiji era.

The similarities in the population policies are rather striking. Positive policies involved subsidies in rice or in money. The grants for survival were available only to children beyond the first and they were usually graduated upward in a rough relationship with the probabilities of destruction. Grants were quite inadequate for the total maintenance of the child.[60] The earliest allowances were grants of rice. In 1784 the Lord of Shirakawa ordered that one sack of rice be given annually to each family that had raised five or more children.[61] In 1787 Lord Nakamura ordered that each newborn child should receive one sack of rice a year for seven years. In 1799 comprehensive graduation was introduced. A third child was to receive two sacks the first year and one sack annually for four years; a fourth child, four sacks the first year and two sacks annually for six years; a fifth child, five sacks the first year, three sacks for two years, and two sacks for five years. Twins, in special danger of *mabiki*, were to receive twelve sacks annually for three years. In 1814 the local government of Nihon-matsu adopted a similar scheme of rice subsidy. The second child received one sack of rice; the third and the fourth, three sacks. Twins received five sacks each in the third month of the first year, and three sacks annually thereafter for four years.

[60] This summary rests on the various studies of Professor Honjo, previously cited.

Monetary subsidies co-existed with rice subsidies, gradually supplanting them in the late Tokugawa and early Meiji periods. In 1794 the Lord of Shirakawa granted a small amount of money in the first and twelfth months of the first year to each child except the first-born. In 1832 the Nihon-matsu government combined monetary subsidies with the gift of a garment annually to each child under age 10, again excepting the first-born. The Mito, Shonai, Yonezawa, Sendai, Akita, Kagoshima, and other *han* also granted subsidies of one type or another.

NUMERICAL ARGUMENTS

In almost all of the surviving records of the Tokugawa period, birth rates are far lower than those to be expected in a population where marriage occurred at early ages and there was no limitation of family size.[62] Abortion and infanticide might have reduced birth rates to the low levels reported in the surviving records, but there is an alternative explanation in underregistration. Similarly, the small number of young children evident in many of the age structures may represent only the underenumeration of young children.[63] Quantitative data on births, deaths, and age structures of the type available for feudal Japan permit no conclusions as to the extent or the degree of family limitation.

Although quantitative evaluation of the extent of the control of fertility is not possible, the outer limits to the amount of control that may have existed can be defined in general terms. Since population changed slowly in the nation as a whole, abortion and infanticide cannot have reduced effective fertility much below the level of mortality, including in the latter not only the deaths during ordinary periods but also those associated with famine and epidemic.[64] More specifically, the birth rate must have been higher than the death rate in normal years if there was relative stability in total numbers over a period of time that included both the normal years and those of severe famine or epidemic. If the expectation of life at birth were 25 years—and it probably was not much higher—a crude birth rate of approximately 40 per thousand

[61] A sack of approximately 2.5 bushels.

[62] There is evidence that marriage actually occurred at somewhat younger ages than in the rural areas of Japan in the early census period. Sekiyama, Naotaro. "Tokugawa jidai no kon'in nenrei ni kansuru ichi kosatsu." *J.m.k.*, 2(3):17-26. March 1941.

[63] Uchida, Kan'ichi. "Tokugawa jidai noson jinko no ichimen." Pp. 163-171 in: Jinko mondai kenkyu kai. *Dai-nikai jinko mondai zenkoku kyogi-kai hokokusho.* Sekiyama, Naotaro. "Baku matsu Chikugo-no-kuni ichi noson no jinko jotai ni tsuite." *J.m.k.*, 1(6): 1-13. September 1940.

[64] Effective fertility is here defined as infants born alive and permitted to survive, subject only to natural hazards.

total population would be necessary to maintain numbers. Hence, virtually all the recorded birth rates for feudal Japan are so low as to be inconceivable; they cannot be used as measures of the "normal" level of fertility. They need not reflect the prevalence of family limitation, although it is possible that they may do so. The numerical judgments of the majority of the students of infanticide are suspect also, for the destruction of all infants except the first-born, or even except the first three, would have led to precipitant decline in total population. Such decline is not reflected in the Tokugawa reports of commoners, and the Japanese students who have reported a heavy incidence of abortion and infanticide do not assert as a necessary corollary the existence of rapid decline in total population.

The fact that the fertility of the population in the period of seclusion would be considered as "high" in the modern world does not preclude a very substantial practice of abortion or infanticide. "High" is a relative term when used to assess premodern fertility, for there is cumulating evidence from many areas that levels of fertility differ widely even among peoples living in objectively comparable areas under rather similar economic conditions. As we have said previously with reference to the Japanese, fertility that was substantially below mortality over considerable periods of time would lead to precipitant decline in numbers and ultimately to extinction. But above the level of relationships between fertility and mortality that means decline in numbers, there are alternatives to the situation in which an unchanging fertility that approaches some ill-defined and probably nondefinable biological maximum creates pressures of increasing numbers on available subsistence that lead to severe malnutrition and starvation.

Fertility and mortality stand in some functional relationship to each other at whatever level or combination of levels one assumes. In pre-Restoration Japan, the limitation of offspring occurred through decisions that eliminated those for whom living conditions would have been least adequate and the chances of premature death greatest. It cannot be argued that the relationship between fertility control and mortality reduction was direct, that therefore infanticide had no influence on population change. It can be argued that infant destruction which was limited primarily to infants of middle and higher birth orders and which permitted the replacement of children who died involved substantial reductions in death rates below what they would have been otherwise. In this sense, infanticide was an adjustment to living conditions that involved severe hazards of premature death. It was quite consistent both with the survival of the individual families over the generations and with the maintenance of the national population.

DEMOGRAPHIC RELEVANCE

The numerical aspect of family limitation in premodern Japan is not the most significant factor in the evaluation of the relevance of that limitation to the population increase of the industrializing society. Folkways and traditions of fertility control are in the heritage of the modern Japanese. Older men and women living today have heard their parents or their grandparents discuss the abortion and infanticide that the ancestors practiced to limit their offspring—perhaps not the family of the mother or the grandmother, but other families in other villages or remote areas. Moreover, the government instituted policies to assist people in rearing children, and the motivations for those policies involved the health of the economy and the power of the state. It is not asserted here that declining fertility and pro-natalist population policies in the industrializing culture are primarily products of attitudes and actions in the premodern culture, but rather that the developments of the industrial culture may have been facilitated by the heritage of the older culture.

Among the Japanese there were fundamental similarities in the cultural conditioning of, and the individual motivations in, the limitation of family size in the Tokugawa and the modern worlds. The pressure of numbers on subsistence and the misery of poverty do not explain the control of fertility in the industrial society; they did not explain the abortion and the infanticide of the agrarian society. The limitation of family size proceeded in accordance with the values of the culture, and it involved positive as well as negative aspects. In the eighteenth century, as in the twentieth, the definitions of situations and the associated values varied for groups within the culture—and so did the incidence and the specific techniques of abortion and infanticide.

The similarities in the practice of family limitation in past and present are striking, but so are the differences. The modern limitation of births in the Western world involves primarily the control of conceptions; that in Japan involved primarily the elimination of the product of conception. It was *ex post facto* planning. The role of economic pressures was probably great; it is possible that it was the specific sequence of events after conception that led to the ultimate decision for destruction. Abortion and infanticide were difficult adjustments to the imperatives of survival and the values of hierarchical familism. There is little evidence of the ideal of the small family as such.

The necessary conclusion from the Japanese experience is that the role of family limitation in premodern societies may have been underestimated and the motivating factors oversimplified. Comprehensive analysis in other areas is required before conclusions can be drawn as to the typicality of the family values and reproductive mores of the Japanese during the latter half of the period of seclusion. In Japan, family limitation was not only consistent with, but occurred in the service of, the ancestor-oriented family system. It was not a fundamental deviation from the family values of the great Eastern cultures. It does not make Japanese experience irrelevant to the assessment of the probable future in other industrializing areas of the East.

Change in the Changeless State

The accumulating frictions created by demographic and economic change within a presumably changeless political and economic structure slowly undermined that structure. The complete analysis of the development of instability in the state that was to remain forever without change involves many factors other than mere numbers of people and changes in those numbers. In a superficial sense, population was a passive factor in the internal transformations of the centralized police state of the Tokugawa *bakufu*. The high and fluctuating death rates of a people subject to famine and epidemic, the elimination of later-born children, the movements of the dispossessed into the cities—these were products of the failure of economic development in a situation where such development was still possible. If inquiry is pursued into the labyrinth of factors responsible for economic inadequacy, however, the coincidence of enforced political stability and an alteration in social structure that was the product of and tended toward social mobility emerge as basic incompatibilities.

Thus far population has been considered as a dependent variable. Scrutiny of the developmental span from the *bakufu* at Kamakura in the twelfth century to that at Edo in the nineteenth century reveals the increase of population as a powerful compulsion to change. Political, social, and economic organizations impinged on the conditions under which the people lived, the commodities available for that living, and the aspirations that influenced activities in spheres of life. Mortality, fertility, and migration continually created new populations whose size, composition, distribution, and dynamics were the facts, the opportunities, and the problems of the political and social order and the economic system of production and distribution. A changeless society would require a changeless population. A changing population dictates a balance of the forces of change throughout the economy and society. If that balance does not occur or occurs in ways inconsistent with the population dynamics generated by the society and economy, population emerges as a pre-eminent problem. This is what happened in Japan in the eighteenth and early nineteenth centuries.

PART II

THE TRANSITION, 1852-1918

CHAPTER III

Increase and Redistribution

THE agricultural, commercial, and industrial revolutions in Western countries led to sustained population increase. Famines and epidemics yielded to new means of production and distribution and to the sciences of medicine and public health. The agricultural population expanded in the home countries and overseas, while rural youth moved outside agriculture. Eventually, major portions of the people labored in great cities that had become more healthful than the villages.

The growth that followed the changes in modes of production and ways of living in the Western world could not have continued indefinitely. The slowing of the growth cycle might have come through limitations to subsistence and increased mortality. Instead it came through declines in fertility. In some countries, birth rates declined earlier than death rates. But generally it was declining mortality that permitted the long period of population increase, and it was declining fertility that reduced the rate of that increase. Population growth was a phase in the movement from a rough balance of births and deaths at high level to an approximate balance or irregular increase at fairly low levels.[1]

If the critical factors in the declining rates of population growth in Western cultures were industrialization and urbanization, then the trends in Japan should have been similar to those in Western countries. If the demographic transition as it occurred among European peoples was associated with specific developments in European cultures, then that transition might not have occurred in Japan or it might have occurred in a greatly modified form.

Theoretical formulations based on Western experience indicate the plausibility of a Western-type transition in Japan; also, theoretical formulations based on the premodern experience of Japan indicate the plausibility of a specifically Japanese or a generalized Eastern type of transition. Hence, we shall examine the official statistics of Japan in the period from 1852 to 1918 to determine the relationships between industrialization and population changes. We shall approach the analysis with four statements of relationships that have been derived from Western experience.

(1) There are necessary relations between industrial development and population change.

(2) The population increase that accompanies industrialization proceeds slowly in its early stages but becomes more rapid as social and economic changes become more comprehensive.

(3) Urbanization occurs along with industrialization, and it is also a major factor in population change.

(4) Declining mortality is a major factor in population increase in the early period of modernization, growth being due to declines in famines and epidemics and to lesser mortality in normal periods. Although there may be changes in fertility in the early period, those changes are not sufficient to prevent the continuing increase of the population. Eventual declines in the rates of population increase come through declines in fertility that are more rapid than those in mortality. Substantial declines in fertility are usually manifest first in urban areas and in the upper social and economic groups.

THE MOVEMENT TO MODERNIZATION

The Japan of the middle of the nineteenth century was a backward and densely peopled country. While the leaders of a secluded Japan had struggled for tranquility without change, the countries of the West had experienced the agricultural, commercial, and industrial revolutions; the development of the nation-state and the great empire; the advance of science and its applications in technology and public health; and the struggle against the divine rights of kings and the exactions of oligarchies. Japan had retreated to seclusion in the early seventeenth century to avert internal dissension and external conflict. The attempt to legislate against change had failed, but change had been muted. Japan's commercial revolution, her monetary economy, her roads, and her cities were painfully inadequate in comparison with the factories, the exchange economies, the railroads, the ships, and the guns of the nations that sought her trade and the empires that threatened her sovereignty.

The lateness of the historic period was not the only hazard Japan faced as she sought to become the Britain of the East. Her resources were limited even when assessed by the Tokugawa statesmen. Her people had increased to some 30 million within an agricultural economy so limited that little was produced beyond subsistence. Capital accumulation had been possible mainly for merchants, and investment opportunities were limited by low productivity and inefficient economic organization. There were students of literature and the arts, philosophers and economists, but there were no engineers. And the leaders who must chart the difficult course of economic progress and political appeasement that would carry their country from the Middle Ages to the nineteenth century within a few decades were themselves the emotional and intellectual products of an isolated culture.

There were positive aspects to the balance sheet of Japanese industrial potentialities, even as viewed from the difficult first days of the Meiji Restoration. The long centuries had per-

[1] Until recently, there was little historic experience to indicate the levels at which fertility stabilizes or reverses its downward movement. Projections of future populations tended to move fertility ever downward to create situations where population decline became sustained and serious. With the upswing of births in World War II and the postwar years, the advance in methods of fertility analysis, and the improvements in the data susceptible to analysis, it has become apparent that the evaluation of the future course of fertility in low-fertility countries is not simple. Problems of the economic and psychological interrelations of fertility at or near replacement levels, and of the differentiation of short-run fluctuations in numbers of births from long-run changes in family size, may become germane for Japan in the near future.

mitted a fusion of people and culture; there were no deep schisms of race, language, or religion. There were traditions of unity and greatness—and there was a cloistered emperor, to whom even the most powerful *shogun* had gone to receive his appointment. General order and stability prevailed in local areas, despite sporadic revolts of peasants. The people were accustomed to an incessant toil that yielded little beyond subsistence and to taxation for which there was little direct return. They were disciplined to obey and to accept status within a firm hierarchy. Life was regulated by obligations and responsibilities which, skillfully manipulated, could not only sanction a political and economic milieu different from that of the past but assure its smooth functioning. Furthermore, and perhaps most important, there were groups whose social superiority bore the sanction of the centuries. Theirs were the traditions and the techniques of leadership—and in the lower *samurai* there were strong drives to build a society that would give them more adequate incomes.

The demise of the political *bakufu* occurred in the years from 1867 to 1871. Here, as in the Taika Reform of the seventh century, revolution was avoided by adjustment and compromise. And, as in Taika, the changes represented an interpenetration of the old and the new. Political changes occurred without basic changes in social structure. In return for the abrogation of their political and economic privileges, the *daimyo* received pensions equal to one-tenth the nominal income from their former fiefs, titles of nobility in a new hierarchy, and absolution from their responsibilities for retainers and debts. *Samurai* received pensions equal to half their nominal incomes, together with permission to enter business.

The economic differentiations of the former society were retained in the Restoration era. The new government acknowledged its debts to the merchants and bankers who had financed the Imperial Restoration. The illegal mortgages that the great merchants and the petty businessmen had secured on farm lands were transformed into ownership rights, thus creating classes of absentee landlords and tenants. Townspeople and farmers received the right to choose their occupations.

The struggle for political modernization and centralization continued through the 1870's and 1880's. In 1873 a Ministry of Home Affairs was placed in direct control of prefectural and city governments. A universal conscription law was passed. There were strong arguments for immediate expansion, particularly for military expeditions to Korea, but the central government pursued cautious policies. Envoys who had gone to the West in 1871 returned in 1873 with the warning that acquiescence to the demands of the West was essential until Japan increased her economic and military power.

Thus the continuity of the political and social structure was not broken in the transition from the Tokugawa agrarian to the Restoration industrial era. In fact, the advance of the state and the growth of the industrial economy were facets of a single process. Power was the goal, industrialization the prerequisite. The old interpersonal relationships, technically abolished with the *han*, persisted in the bureaucracy, in the co-operation of *samurai* and merchants, and in the adjustments that permitted social stability and industrial advance in an unfavorable economic milieu. There were pressures against individualism, industrial advances based on forced savings channeled into concentrated ownership and military production, and paternalistic attitudes carefully fostered to maintain peace in government and in industry. These were major determinants of the changing balance of births and deaths that created the population growth and the population problems of Meiji and of modern Japan.

INDUSTRIALIZATION[2]

The basis for the industrial development of Japan had been laid in the commercial developments of the eighteenth and early nineteenth centuries. The superficial transformation of a localized structure of handicraft industries into a national economy proceeded rapidly, but there were deep barriers to the achievement of substantial industrial production based on modern technologies. The labor force was largely illiterate, capital accumulation was slow and inadequate, and managerial personnel was deficient. The leaders of the Restoration were aware of the political implications of this economic unpreparedness for modern industrialization. The entrance of Western capital to utilize the manpower of Japan might well have produced an economic vassalage that would have permitted the maintenance of national sovereignty only on the sufferance of the Western powers. If this was to be avoided, Japan had to combine a political policy of appeasement and cautious advance with an economic policy of rapid development in the strategic industries.

The government assumed the role of entrepreneur in mining and in the heavy industries. Engineering, naval, and technical schools were founded and staffed by foreign instructors, and Japanese students were sent abroad to master the techniques of the West. Mining, transportation, and communication services were developed with government capital. In general, the government retained ownership and control of the strategic industries, the financial institutions, and the larger trading companies, and sold the peripheral or the less strategic industries to trusted financial oligarchs at a fraction of their cost. The aim of the state was ". . . to create the conditions which should lead the entrepreneur to direct and organize the economic resources of the country in the way believed to be desirable."[3]

One of the most serious of the problems facing the Restoration government was that of capital.[4] If munitions factories, railways, and capital equipment were to be built or purchased quickly by a country living on the margin of subsistence, emphasis would have to be placed on production rather than consumption goods. Income and capital assets would have to be increased among those individuals who could devote the major portion to savings, and decreased among the many who would dissipate the increased income in consumption. Accordingly, funds raised by taxation, primarily on land, were invested in new industries or used as subsidies for existing industries, while state credit was used to guarantee loans.

Problems of capital formation and continuing economic growth might have become simpler by the early twentieth

[2] The industrialization of Japan is not analyzed in detail here, in part because the complexities of the subject would require more space than is permissible in an analysis of the population, in part because of the magnitude and quality of the literature on the subject. Citations that constitute leads to this economic literature are included in the Bibliography. For the period under consideration here, two sources in English are particularly valuable: Lockwood, William W. *The state and economic enterprise in modern Japan, 1868-1938.* Also: Allen, G. C. "Japanese industry: Its organization and development to 1937." Pp. 477-786 in: Schumpeter, E. B., Editor. *The industrialization of Japan and Manchukuo, 1930-1940.*

[3] Allen, G. C. "The last decade in Japan." *Economic History,* 2(8):629. January 1933.

[4] Reubens, Edwin P. "Foreign capital in economic development: A case-study of Japan." *Milbank Memorial Fund Quarterly,* 27(2): 173-190. April 1950.

century had not the development of empire led to the investment of government funds in enterprises that private capital could not or would not undertake. As the rapid pace of economic development required heavy imports of capital equipment and raw materials, the government encouraged the export trade with subsidies to shipping and foreign trading companies, low railway rates on export goods, and the organization of special institutions for the development of foreign markets. Levels of living within Japan rose slowly but, in the long run, substantially.

There was a gradual transfer of the labor force from agricultural to industrial activities. Factory employment was a sensitive index; by 1904 there were half a million workers employed in factories with five or more workers, while in 1914 there were 1.5 million.[5] In 1894 there were 778 corporations engaged in manufacturing, with a total capital of 44.6 million yen. By 1914 there were over five thousand such corporations, and their capital was 834 million yen. Statistics such as these indicate the magnitude of the advance spearhead of Japanese industrialization—the more or less modern factory with at least five workers, and particularly the great corporate enterprise. However, these factories absorbed only a small portion of the manpower that had been rendered surplus in the rural areas by the changes in agriculture and the collapse of household industries. The dispossessed and underemployed peasants were the real manpower problems of the early Restoration period.

Many of the ancient industries of the countryside were ruined as the tax structure and fiscal policies of the government reduced the subsistence available from agriculture. The growth of cotton and the household production of thread and textiles collapsed with the importation of standardized products at cheap prices, while the area in sugar cane was cut three-fourths in the five years between 1877 and 1882. Imported kerosene replaced locally produced wax-tree and rapeseed oil. Paper made in factories from wood pulp replaced the handmade paper of the past. And so the story went. From the point of view of the peasant household, the situation required the development of new sources of income supplementary to agriculture. To the business leaders, the situation offered labor so cheap that the costs and risks of capital investment could be minimized. The result was the rapid development of sericulture as a source of direct agricultural income, the establishment of new types of household industries throughout the countryside, the migration of boys and young men to urban areas, and the movement of girls to the cotton-textile dormitories.

The adjustments of the increasing numbers of rural people to the new economic pressures proceeded rapidly. The percentage of all households engaged in agriculture declined from 71 per cent in 1884 (29 prefectures) to 64 per cent in 1904, 60 per cent in 1909, and 58 per cent in 1919. The proportion of agricultural households engaged in domestic or supplementary industry, including sericulture, increased fairly consistently from less than one-fourth in 1884 to more than one-third in 1919.[6]

The movement of girls to the factories was an adjustment both to the precarious balance of subsistence in the agricultural villages and to the compulsions of the new industries to reduce their labor costs to a minimum. The number of women in factories employing ten or more workers, excluding government factories, increased from 51 thousand in 1882 to 426 thousand in 1895-1900, 637 thousand in 1905-1909, and 829 thousand in 1910-1914. Women constituted 59 per cent of all factory workers in 1895-1899 and 71 per cent in 1910-1914. The preponderance of women was even greater in the textile factories. Here the number of workers increased from 76 thousand in 1899 to 90 thousand in 1909—and four-fifths were women.[7] Single girls were preferred for economic and social reasons. They could be secured cheaply, and their employment fitted in with the status structure of the family.

SOCIAL STABILITY AND SOCIAL CHANGE

A survey of the activities of the Japanese government in the early decades of political and economic transformation might seem to indicate that a mighty social revolution had accompanied the abolition of the *bakufu*. With the recognition of the legal equality of all classes of the population, the names of the *eta* and the *hinin*, the despised and outcaste lower classes, were added to household registers. Buddhism was no longer the official religion. Freedom of crop and of occupation was granted, while barriers to the alienation and partition of land were removed. Reform spread to the lesser social regularities; even the calendar was changed.

The changes in social structure were less radical than those in law. It has been said, quite aptly, that the Meiji Restoration was a *coup d'état* rather than a revolution. Freedom to sell land and to choose an occupation were granted—but agricultural retardation was preserved by low incomes, continuing heavy toil, and indoctrination in the virtues of fealty to emperor and acceptance of status. The obligations and responsibilities in personal relations and in duty to the imperial household were emphasized in the developing educational institutions. Order and conformity were maintained by the armed forces and security police.

The achievement of intellectual and technical equality with the West required education, while the preservation of the proper virtues required indoctrination. These two goals were combined in the structure of the school system in the early Meiji period. Educational officers were appointed in 1868, and a Department of Education was established in 1871. The code of education, issued in 1872, was modeled on the centralized French system. Imperial rescripts ordered that "henceforth shall education be so diffused that there shall be no ignorant family in the land, and no family with an ignorant member . . . as for higher education, it is left to the intellectual capacity of each individual; but if a child, male or female, does not attend an elementary school, the guardian shall be held responsible for the neglect."[8]

School attendance increased rapidly. The reports proudly noted that by 1878 over 40 per cent of the boys and 23 per cent of the girls of school age—roughly age 6 to 14 by Western style—were in school. By 1885 to 1890, 65 per cent of the boys and 31 per cent of the girls were attending school.

[5] Factory statistics were given in summary form in the *Nihon teikoku tokei nenkan* issued from 1882 to 1940 by Naikaku tokeikyoku.

[6] Norman, E. Herbert. *Japan's emergence as a modern state.* P. 158. Cited to: Tsuchiya, Takao, and Okazaki, Saburo. *Nihon shihon shugi hattatsu shi gaisetsu* [Outline history of the development of Japanese capitalism]. P. 42.

[7] Norman. *Op.cit.*, P. 152. Cited to: Tsuchiya and Okazaki. *Op.cit.* P. 291.

[8] This and the quotations that follow are from: Japan. Department of Education. *A general survey of education in Japan. 1937.* Data on the growth of the educational system were included annually in *Nihon teikoku tokei nenkan.* For a description of the educational system, see: U.S. Office of Strategic Services. Research and Analysis Branch. *Civil affairs handbook.* Section 15, "Education." M354-15, 1944.

Difficulties developed, however, for the tempo of educational progress and the admiration of things Western led to acceptance of thoughts and practices antithetical to the true virtues of traditional Japan. So, in October 1890, the Emperor Meiji issued a rescript on education "which definitely and once for all, established the educational policy of the country." The rescript follows: "Know ye, Our subjects: Our Imperial Ancestors have founded our Empire on a basis broad and everlasting and have deeply and firmly implanted virtue; Our subjects ever united in loyalty and filial piety have from generation to generation illustrated the beauty thereof. This is the glory of the fundamental character of Our Empire, and herein also lies the source of Our education. Ye, Our subjects, be filial to your parents, affectionate to your brothers and sisters; as husbands and wives be harmonious, as friends true; bear yourselves in modesty and moderation; extend your benevolence to all; pursue learning and cultivate arts, and thereby develop intellectual faculties and perfect moral powers; furthermore advance public good and promote common interests; always respect the Constitution and observe the laws; should emergency arise, offer yourselves courageously to the State; and thus guard and maintain the prosperity of Our Imperial Throne coeval with heaven and earth. So shall ye not only be Our good and faithful subjects, but render illustrious the best traditions of your forefathers. The Way here set forth is indeed the teaching bequeathed by Our Imperial Ancestors, to be observed alike by Their Descendants and the subjects, infallible for all ages and true in all places. It is Our wish to lay it to heart in all reverence, in common with you, Our subjects, that we may all thus attain to the same virtue."

Thus filial piety and loyalty were linked to the destiny of empire. A trained labor force and a literate population were to be secured without jeopardizing the social oligarchy or political continuity. Girls were educated to comprehend and accept their roles as wives and mothers, as the bearers of sons who would "guard and maintain the prosperity of Our Imperial Throne coeval with heaven and earth." Here was a policy that went far beyond the Tokugawa's legislation against change. This was education for economic change combined with social stability.

Population Statistics

The planned transformations of the political, social, and economic structure of Japan required a current inventory of human resources at once more extensive and more accurate than the records of the *daimyo* had been. The answer to the need for data was simple, and it was known to the Japanese—the periodic enumeration of people in a national census.[9] But this was not done. Instead, Meiji Japan turned backward to the centuries-old pattern of a household registration system as a source of information on population, occupation, migration, and vital statistics. The model was the Taika Reform of 645 to 650 A.D.; the goal was the creation of a national system of residence allocation, legal identity, and control of individuals that would facilitate the controls essential to an authoritarian state.

The law for the establishment of residence and the collection and tabulation of data on population status and population movements was the *Koseki-ho* (registration law) of April 1871. The minor civil divisions within each prefecture were grouped together into wards, and a chief of households and a deputy chief of households were appointed for each. After enumerating the people resident within his ward and compiling a register of households and occupations, the chief of households submitted a report to the regional government office. These offices in turn submitted summary tabulations, together with copies of the household reports, to the prime minister. This survey, which approached an enumerative census in the modern sense, provided the initial registers of households that constitute the primary record basis for demographic statistics in Japan.

The registration law of 1871 called for a new survey of the population each five years. If this provision had been implemented, Japan would have had in effect both a quinquennial census and a current registration system. Actually, the plan for periodic enumerations had to be abandoned, and demographic statistics were secured by manipulations of the registration data. From 1873 to 1880 annual estimates of population were made by adding births and acquisitions of domicile to the population as of the end of the previous year, then subtracting deaths and losses of domicile. The population estimates for 1881 and 1882 were made without adjustments for changes in domicile. Modifications in detailed procedures were made between 1883 and 1897, but the fundamental system remained the same: the estimate of the previous year was taken as the base, births and additions to the register were added, and deaths and losses from the register were subtracted.

A series of quinquennial summations of the registers was initiated in 1898 and continued until 1918. Changes in domicile were recorded as they occurred, but the count of the population was made directly from the household registers at the end of each fifth year. "Intercensal" estimates were made by adjusting for natural increase and domicile changes. The quinquennial summations included not only numbers of people in the prefectures and the minor civil divisions, but also age, marital status, family status, and household position. The reports of these compilations constitute the so-called "censuses" of 1898, 1903, 1908, 1913, and 1918.[10]

The difficulties which the Japanese experienced with their registration system were similar to those experienced by other countries.[11] In a stable society the addition of births to, and the subtraction of deaths from, registers that were initially correct would maintain a continuing inventory of the population of local areas and, by summation, of the country as a whole. Unfortunately, the initial registers were neither complete nor correct, and it required decades of habituation before the registration of births and deaths approached completeness. The difficulties involved in the registration of migrations were never solved. The published estimates of the total population of the country differed from one year to another not only in

[9] Sugi, Kyoji, "the father of Japanese statistics," directed a census of the Shizuoka *han* in 1869. During the 1870's and 1880's he recommended again and again that national statistics be expanded, that censuses be taken, and that a school of statistics be founded. There was discussion of Japanese participation in a world census of 1900, but this did not prove feasible. The subject of a census rose again in 1910, but the acquisition of Korea prevented serious planning. An empire census was contemplated for 1915, but the outbreak of World War I served as rationalization for further procrastination. Finally on October 1, 1920, an enumerative census was taken in Japan, Taiwan, and Karafuto; disturbances associated with the independence movement of 1918 and 1919 prevented its execution in Korea.

[10] Specific citations to these compilations are given in the Bibliography, p. 400.

[11] A valuable description of these difficulties was published by the Cabinet Bureau of Statistics in 1916 under the title: *Taisho ni'nen matsu jinko seitai chosa no kekka ni yoru teikoku jinko gaisetsu.*

the amount of the recorded natural increase of the year in question but in the balance of the delayed registration of the births, the deaths, and the migration of earlier years.

ANNUAL ESTIMATES

The survey of January 29, 1872, indicated that 33.1 million persons had *honseki*, or legal domicile, in Japan (TABLE 6).

TABLE 6

Annual changes in population, 1875-1919

	POPULATION WITH HONSEKI IN JAPAN						ESTIMATED POPULATION IN JAPAN		
		Changes per 1,000 population							
Year (December 31)	*Number (in '000)*	*Total*	*Additions to registers*	*Natural increase*	*Births*	*Deaths*	*Number (in '000)*	*Increase per 1,000 population*	*Ratio to 1872 as 100*
1875	34,338	9.9	3.7	6.2	25.3	19.1	35,555	8.9	102.2
1876	34,628	8.4	0.0	8.4	26.1	17.7	35,870	8.9	103.1
1877	34,899	7.7	0.0	7.8	25.5	17.8	36,166	8.2	103.9
1878	35,769	24.3	16.7	7.6	24.5	16.9	36,464	8.2	104.8
1879	35,925	4.5	0.1	4.3	24.4	20.1	36,649	5.1	105.3
1880	36,359	11.8	4.1	7.7	24.3	16.6	36,965	8.6	106.2
1881	36,700	9.3	2.3	7.0	25.6	18.7	37,259	7.9	107.0
1882	37,017	8.6	1.7	6.9	24.9	18.0	37,569	8.3	107.9
1883	37,452	11.6	2.8	8.8	26.8	18.1	37,962	10.5	109.1
1884	37,869	11.0	3.9	7.1	25.8	18.6	38,313	9.2	110.1
1885	38,151	7.4	3.8	3.6	26.9	23.2	38,541	5.9	110.7
1886	38,507	9.2	6.3	2.9	27.3	24.4	38,703	4.2	111.2
1887	39,070	14.4	6.6	7.8	27.1	19.3	39,029	8.4	112.1
1888	39,607	13.6	3.0	10.6	29.6	19.0	39,473	11.4	113.4
1889	40,072	11.6	1.6	10.0	30.2	20.2	39,902	10.9	114.6
1890	40,453	9.4	1.5	8.0	28.3	20.4	40,251	8.7	115.6
1891	40,719	6.5	0.8	5.7	26.7	21.0	40,508	6.4	116.4
1892	41,090	9.0	1.2	7.8	29.4	21.6	40,860	8.7	117.4
1893	41,388	7.2	1.4	5.8	28.5	22.6	41,142	6.9	118.2
1894	41,813	10.2	1.4	8.8	28.9	20.1	41,557	10.1	119.4
1895	42,271	10.8	1.5	9.3	29.5	20.2	41,992	10.5	120.6
1896	42,708	10.2	1.6	8.6	30.0	21.4	42,400	9.7	121.8
1897	43,229	12.0	1.5	10.6	30.9	20.3	42,886	11.5	123.2
1898	43,764	12.2	1.4	10.9	31.3	20.4	43,404	12.1	124.7
1899	44,270	11.4	1.2	10.2	31.4	21.1	43,847	10.2	126.0
1900	44,826	12.4	1.1	11.3	31.7	20.4	44,359	11.7	127.4
1901	45,446	13.7	1.0	12.6	33.1	20.4	44,964	13.6	129.2
1902	46,042	12.9	1.0	12.0	32.9	20.9	45,546	12.9	130.9
1903	46,732	14.8	2.8	12.0	32.0	20.0	46,135	12.9	132.5
1904	47,220	10.3	0.9	9.4	30.6	21.2	46,620	10.5	133.9
1905	47,678	9.6	1.0	8.6	30.6	21.9	47,038	9.0	135.1
1906	48,165	10.1	1.0	9.1	29.0	20.0	47,416	8.0	136.2
1907	48,820	13.4	1.2	12.2	33.2	21.0	47,965	11.6	137.8
1908	49,589	15.5	2.7	12.8	33.7	20.9	48,554	12.3	139.5
1909	50,254	13.2	1.2	12.1	33.9	21.9	49,184	13.0	141.3
1910	50,985	14.3	1.5	12.8	33.9	21.1	49,852	13.6	143.2
1911	51,754	14.9	1.1	13.7	34.1	20.4	50,577	14.6	145.3
1912	52,523	14.6	1.2	13.5	33.4	20.0	51,305	14.4	147.4
1913	53,363	15.7	1.9	13.8	33.3	19.5	52,039	14.3	149.5
1914	54,142	14.4	1.2	13.2	33.8	20.6	52,752	13.7	151.6
1915	54,936	14.4	1.4	13.1	33.2	20.2	53,496	14.1	153.7
1916	55,637	12.6	1.3	11.3	32.9	21.6	54,134	11.9	155.5
1917	56,336	12.4	1.2	11.1	32.7	21.6	54,739	11.2	157.3
1918	56,667	5.8	0.4	5.5	32.2	26.7	55,033	5.4	158.1
1919	57,234	9.9	1.0	8.9	31.6	22.8	55,473	8.0	159.4

Source: *Honseki* populations and rates of change, 1872-1913: Nihon. Naikaku tokei-kyoku. *Taisho ni'nen matsu jinko seitai chosa no kekka ni yoru teikoku jinko gaisetsu.* P. 9. 1914-1919: *Idem. Nihon teikoku tokei nenkan.* Various issues. Estimated population in Japan: *Idem. Population du Japon depuis 1872.* Pp. 4-7.

The annual estimates of the population in the succeeding years reflected the changing balance of factors of inaccuracy and error as well as actual changes in the population.[12] From 1873 to 1876 there were many acquisitions of domicile, presumably by persons who were omitted in the enumeration of 1872. In 1878 the registered population of Okinawa increased from 160 thousand to 310 thousand, making the annual rate of change for Japan as a whole many times greater than that of adjacent years. The rate of increase rose again in 1887-1889, when the registration system was being revised to include previous omissions of population in the estimation of current populations.

After the first national census was taken in 1920, the Bureau of Statistics computed a revised series of annual estimates.[13] The techniques of adjustment were straightforward. The 1920 census population, a *de facto* count, was pushed backward to 1898 by subtracting births and immigrants and adding deaths and emigrants. Then the 1872 population was projected forward to 1898 by adding births and acquisitions of domicile and subtracting deaths and losses of domicile. These computations gave two estimates of the *de facto* population as of December 1, 1898, one based on forward projection of the *honseki* population of 1872, the other based on backward projection of the *de facto* population of 1920:[14]

Type of Projection	*Population (in '000)*
Forward projection, 1872 to December 1, 1898	43,554
Backward projection, 1920 to December 1, 1898	43,219
Difference	335

The agreement between the expected and the recorded population in Japan at the end of the year 1898 is quite extraordinary. On this date the population with *honseki* in Japan numbered 43.8 million. If we remove the 85 thousand Japanese reported as abroad and the 33 thousand reported in Taiwan, the estimated population in Japan becomes 43.7 million.[15] The estimated *de facto* population was 43.4 million.

It is tempting to conclude that the registration compilations as of the 1880's and 1890's were essentially correct. Unfortunately for this argument, the components of the registration populations and the estimated populations are not independent. The agreement between the two is due in major part to the fact that the number of births and deaths reported to the *koseki* were assumed to be correct in both the original annual estimates and the revisions of those estimates. In the original series, only births and deaths reported in the year of occurrence were included; in the adjusted series, those reported in subsequent years were also added. Births and deaths that were not reported were excluded from both series. Census and registration experience throughout the world indicates that omissions of registration would be most frequent for babies who failed to survive the first few months or years of life. Hence, it is probable that there are rather large errors in the components of growth used to build the estimated populations.

AGE COMPOSITION AND VITAL RATES

By the second decade of the twentieth century, the records of the *honseki* population had achieved a rather high degree of accuracy for the nation as a whole[16] (TABLE 7). However, this relative accuracy in the age structures at the national level does not eliminate the problems involved in the measurement of fertility and mortality from the records of a continuing registration system. Relative completeness in records even for young children cannot be assumed to mean complete and immediate reporting of births and infant deaths. A completely accurate age report would be secured if the names of all babies who were born during and survived the year were added to the *koseki* on the last day of the year—but in this case babies who were born and died during the year

[12] The factors responsible for the erratic movements were manifold. Births occurring during one year and not reported until the next were classified as "additions to the register" rather than being allocated back to produce revised estimates of birth rates and rates of natural increase. Similarly, deaths whose registration was delayed were noted as "subtractions" from the registers. The names of persons discovered without registration were added to the registers; the names of those who had disappeared and were presumed dead were removed. A further source of erratic fluctuation was introduced by the timing of the reporting of losses and gains of legal domicile. The local office in an area of origin maintained a person in its *koseki* (household record book) until it received a notification of the acquisition of *honseki* (legal domicile) in another place. The result was that, for the country as a whole, acquisitions of legal domicile consistently surpassed losses of household registration, whereas if the reporting had been accurate and simultaneous, the two would have had to balance.

[13] Nihon. Naikaku tokei-kyoku. *Population du Japon depuis 1872*. The numbers of births and deaths utilized were those reported as occurring within Japan. The problem was more difficult for the years from 1872 to 1898, for then the numbers of births and deaths were available only for the *honseki* population, which included those Japanese outside Japan who maintained legal domicile within the country. However, annual estimates of the populations with *honseki* in Japan were transformed into estimates of the population physically present in the country by subtracting the number of Japanese abroad at each date. These revised computations were made somewhat more precise than the historical series by adding to the vital phenomena of a given year those events that were registered in subsequent years, applying uniform techniques of estimation throughout, and allowing for such special events as the registration of a substantial portion of the population of Okinawa in a single year.

[14] The difference was distributed in the final series of corrected estimates, the population based on the 1920 census being assumed to be correct.

[15] Nihon. Naikaku tokei-kyoku. *Résumé statistique de l'Empire du Japon*, 15e année, 1901, Table 17; 16e année, 1902, Table 18.

[16] A fairly accurate indication of the errors involved in the age and sex structures of the *honseki* populations for 1913 and 1918 can be secured by estimating the size and the age and sex composition of the populations that would have had to exist in Japan on December 31, 1913, and December 31, 1918, to produce the populations enumerated on October 1, 1920. In computing, the 1920 population was moved backward to the dates of the registration compilations on the basis of the recorded numbers of deaths by sex and age. The expected populations for 1913 and 1918 are subject to errors involved in the underenumeration of the 1920 census, the underregistration of deaths, and the net change by migration to and from Japan. These sources of error are relatively small for the comparison as of December 31, 1918, and somewhat greater for December 31, 1913.

This test of the registration compilations of 1918 and 1913 involves a comparison of *honseki* populations that included Japanese outside Japan with a *de facto* population in Japan. The registration of children under five years of age was rather complete in 1918, if it can be assumed that the *honseki* population was not inflated appreciably by the inclusion of children living outside Japan. The deficiency of children was greater in 1913, even disregarding the greater role of incompletely recorded deaths in the construction of the expected populations as of 1913. Deviations of *honseki* from expected populations in the late childhood and adult ages reflect the joint influence of errors in the *koseki* records from which the registration compilations were made and the inclusion of Japanese outside Japan in those records. The pattern of the age deviations of the *honseki* from the expected population indicates that the omitted group consisted primarily of adults, and that it was predominantly male, both characteristics of the Japanese population outside Japan at the period.

It should be noted also that people from the Empire and aliens were included in the enumeration of 1920 but excluded from *koseki* records. However, in 1920 these two groups numbered only 78 thousand in a total population of almost 56 million.

TABLE 7

Per cent deviations of population, by age, in the registration compilations from those expected on the basis of the census of 1920

Year and population	*Total*	AGE GROUPS						*Children under 5*
		0-14	*15-19*	*20-34*	*35-44*	*45-64*	*65 and over*	
1918 honseki								
Total	3.3	0.2	1.8	5.2	4.9	4.6	12.5	—0.2
Male	4.2	0.4	2.9	5.9	6.1	5.8	18.2	0.2
Female	2.4	—0.0	0.7	4.5	3.8	3.2	8.0	—0.5
1913 honseki								
Total	3.3	—0.5	3.9	5.4	4.6	4.5	12.6	—2.1
Male	4.3	0.1	5.1	6.3	5.7	5.7	18.3	—1.9
Female	2.2	—1.1	2.7	4.5	3.6	3.4	8.0	—2.3
1913 police count								
Total	—0.8	—4.3	3.3	1.0	1.9	—1.2	3.5	—8.3
Male	—0.8	—4.2	2.7	—0.8	2.0	—0.1	8.4	—8.4
Female	—0.8	—4.4	3.8	2.7	1.8	—2.3	—0.4	—8.4

Source: Nihon. Naikaku tokei-kyoku. *Taisho ku'nen kokusei chosa hokoku*, IV.A.1; *Idem. Nihon teikoku jinko seitai tokei.* 1913 and 1918. *Idem. Jinko dotai tokei.* 1913-1920.

would be excluded from the reports both of births and of deaths. Moreover, relative validation of the reports for 1913 and 1918 does not constitute validation for the reports of earlier years. In fact, the final accuracy achieved by the registration compilations is a tribute to the persevering labors of the Japanese to improve a historic registration system ill-adapted to the conditions of the period of history in which it was maintained.

Even completely accurate reporting of age at the national level would not imply accuracy with reference to the age reports for areas within the country. For analysis of the internal dynamics of population, whether migration, fertility, or mortality, we need size, age structure, migrations, and births and deaths for populations living in specific areas. *Honseki* allocations of residence give us people with familial allegiances in the areas from which they are reported.

DISTRIBUTION AND URBANIZATION

Honseki populations were properly subjects for social rather than demographic research. The urban population on a *honseki* definition included only those persons resident in urban areas who had transferred *koseki* from areas of origin to new places of residence. The rural population included those urban residents whose *koseki* had not been transferred. Measurement of the extent of the discrepancies would require knowledge of the *de facto* population of urban and rural areas, and this does not exist prior to 1920. The urban-rural distribution of the "present resident" population should have provided a more adequate measure of the extent of the urbanization that had occurred.[17] In fact, it resulted in a greatly inflated estimate of the urban population, for short-time migrants registered when they entered a city but failed to register when they left. Moreover, as migration from rural to urban areas increased, the excess of the present-resident population in the cities and the deficits in the rural areas increased both absolutely and relatively.

There is no statistical solution to the problem of the actual urban-rural distribution of the population, for neither *honseki* nor present-resident populations can be assumed to be correct. A crude index of the magnitude of the errors is given by a comparison of the populations of the registration compilation of December 31, 1918, with those of the enumerative census of October 1, 1920. These populations should differ, for the *honseki* population as of 1918 included Japanese abroad but excluded aliens; the present-resident population as of 1918 excluded both Japanese abroad and aliens; the enumerative census of October 1, 1920, was a count of the population physically present within Japan on the census date. Furthermore, the final registration compilation as of the end of 1918 and the initial enumerative census as of October 1, 1920, were separated by twenty-one months in which births and deaths, emigration and immigration influenced both the total population of the country and its internal distribution. That the problems are much more fundamental than differences in time and coverage becomes obvious if the populations of the *shi* and *gun*[18] in the most urbanized prefectures are contrasted (TABLE 8). The variations of the types of population for individual areas are quite comprehensible in the light of differences in historical growth and cultural milieu, but they preclude precise analysis of internal migration or population distribution prior to 1920.[19]

[17] Since persons who left their place of habitual residence for more than a very brief period of time were required to have a notification of such departure entered in the *koseki* at the place of habitual residence and to register as a temporary in-migrant in the area to which they went, there was direct information on migrants and hence a way to adjust the counts from the *koseki* to conform to a resident population. The Japanese made these corrections at several of the compilation dates, calling the corrected figures a "present resident" population.

[18] *Shi* are incorporated municipalities, generally with populations greater than 30 thousand. The *gun* are districts that include all territory not in *shi*.

[19] The Japanese were aware of this problem of internal allocation. They attempted to enumerate the population through cooperation with the police. This attempt to secure accurate data on the structure of the populations actually in the prefectures and the cities also failed. If the "expected" populations as estimated from the 1920 enumeration are contrasted with the populations surveyed by the police, it is evident that there was underenumeration of young children and duplicate counting of young adults in the mobile ages. Comparison of the age structures of prefectural populations as determined by *honseki* reports with those reported in the

TABLE 8

The population of the *shi* and the *gun* in the industrialized prefectures, by type of residence allocation, 1920 and 1918

Prefecture	Population (in '000)			Registered per 100 enumerated		*Present-resident population per 100* honseki *population*
	Enumerated October 1, 1920	Honseki, *December 31, 1918*	*Present-resident December 31, 1918*	Honseki	*Present-resident*	
Tokyo	3,699	2,414	3,719	65	100	154
Shi	2,212	1,463	2,390	66	108	163
Gun	1,487	951	1,329	64	89	140
Kanagawa	1,323	1,113	1,323	84	100	119
Shi	513	305	536	60	105	176
Gun	811	807	787	100	97	98
Aichi	2,090	2,067	2,140	99	102	104
Shi	534	380	543	71	102	143
Gun	1,556	1,687	1,597	108	103	95
Kyoto	1,287	1,161	1,384	90	108	119
Shi	591	437	670	74	113	153
Gun	696	724	714	104	102	99
Osaka	2,588	1,870	2,888	72	112	154
Shi	1,338	854	1,717	64	128	201
Gun	1,250	1,016	1,172	81	94	115
Hyogo	2,302	2,117	2,321	92	101	110
Shi	693	343	673	50	97	196
Gun	1,609	1,774	1,648	110	102	93

Source: Nihon. Naikaku tokei-kyoku. *Taisho ku'nen kokusei chosa hokoku.* IV.B. Table 1. *Idem. Nihon teikoku jinko seitai tokei*, 1918. Tables 1 and 4.

The registration system established in the early years of the Restoration remained the sole source for national demographic statistics until the first enumerative census was taken in 1920. For this period of almost fifty years, analysis of the population increase that accompanied urbanization and industrialization must move through the labyrinths of deficiencies and errors that characterize registration compilations. Analysis of the interrelations of population, economy, and social structure during the century from 1850 to 1950 can use the relatively accurate data of modern censuses and vital statistics for only three decades.

It has been an easy task to criticize the demographic statistics that flowed from the Tokugawa reports of commoners and the household registers of the Restoration period. To do so was not an original undertaking. The real task is not a critique of the data but their utilization to deduce the processes of growth and redistribution that occurred prior to 1920. The beginnings of the changes in population increase, age composition, migrations, and vital rates that accompanied the industrialization of Japan cannot be subjected to satisfactory quantitative analysis. To forgo analysis, however, would render the brief census period of the last three decades one for superficial description rather than meaningful interpretation with depth in time. So it is that we examine the records of the years from 1852 through 1918 for clues as to the nature and the magnitude of the transformations in the structure and dynamics of population.

police surveys indicates that the errors in both types of data were particularly great in the urban areas.

POPULATION INCREASE

Long-continued population increase accompanied the diffusion of the economic and medical technologies of the West into the densely settled agricultural areas of Monsoon Asia. Whether substantial increase also occurred in Japan during the initial decades of contact with the West is a critical problem. It is probable that population increase began in the early nineteenth century, but there is no conclusive evidence that the rate of increase quickened in the early decades after the opening to the West. The period involved extended roughly from the last Tokugawa report in 1852 to the Meiji survey of 1871-1872. The report of 1852 indicated a total population somewhere between 29.4 and 32 million, while a population of 34.8 million is suggested by the report of the year 1872. Thus the increase of population in these two decades of transition from seclusion to the modern era may have amounted to less than 10 per cent; it certainly did not reach 20 per cent.

The records of the changes in Japan between 1852 and 1872 do not permit an estimation of the rate of population increase. It is probable, however, that growth was slow and irregular during the early decades of contact with the West. The opening of the country permitted the importation of food in critical years, but it also created economic difficulties for many of the people. The old economy and the old securities were disintegrating, while the new order did not permit easy movement to new employment for those whose former occupations had vanished. Moreover, the additional mortality consequent on new and more virulent diseases may have been greater than the reductions in traditional risks achieved by the early efforts at public sanitation and mass inoculations.

The rate of growth remains problematical for many decades after the Restoration of 1868, but the fact of growth is indisputable (TABLE 9). The population, which had been 35.2 million in 1873, reached 55 million in 1918.[20] Numbers increased almost three-fifths in less than half a century. Rates of increase in the estimated actual population rose gradually from perhaps three-quarters of 1 per cent per year in the 1870's and 1880's to almost 1 per cent in the 1890's, and approached 1.5 per cent in the early decades of the twentieth century.

The increase in the numbers of the Japanese was large. There were 17 million more Japanese with legal domicile in Japan in 1918 than there had been in 1888, only three decades earlier (TABLE 10).[21] There were almost 10 million more adults aged from 15 to 64; almost 5 million of them were men who were claimants to positions in the labor force. By 1918 men entering the labor market at age 15 to 19 were over four times as numerous as those aged from 65 to 69 who had either retired or ended effective participation. The dependent youth who would be the labor cohorts of the future were increasing year by year; boys under 15 numbered less than 7 million in 1888, over 10 million in 1918. The number of women in the childbearing ages was moving sharply upward. It should be emphasized that this description of the increasing numbers of the Japanese pertains to the three decades that ended in 1918, not to the three decades that ended in 1940 or in 1950.

TABLE 9

The increase of the population, 1873-1918

Year (December 31)	POPULATION (IN '000) Honseki	Present-resident	Estimated actual	PERCENTAGE INCREASE QUINQUENNIAL Honseki	Present-resident	Estimated actual
1873	33,626	33,750	35,154	—	—	—
1878	35,769	[a]	36,464	6.4	—	3.7
1883	37,452	[a]	37,962	4.7	—	4.1
1888	39,607	40,105	39,473	5.8	—	4.0
1893	41,388	42,061	41,142	4.5	4.9	4.2
1898	43,764	45,403	43,404	5.7	7.9	5.5
1903	46,732	48,543	46,135	6.8	6.9	6.3
1908	49,589	51,742	48,554	6.1	6.6	5.2
1913	53,363	55,131	52,039	7.6	6.5	7.2
1918	56,667	58,087	55,033	6.2	5.4	5.8

[a] Not available.

Source: *Honseki* and present-resident populations, 1873-1918: Nihon. Naikaku tokei-kyoku. *Nihon teikoku jinko seitai tokei.* 1898, 1903, 1908, 1913, 1918. Estimated actual population: *Idem. Population du Japon depuis 1872.* Pp. 4-5.

REDISTRIBUTION AND URBANIZATION

The population increase that accompanied industrialization in the West was associated with a substantial redistribution of population. In its economic aspect, this redistribution involved a movement from agricultural to non-agricultural employment. In its demographic aspect, it involved a movement from rural to urban areas. There is no rationale for assuming that the movements of people that accompanied industrialization in Japan should parallel those of the West in detail, for the experiences of the Western nations indicate that the pace of population redistribution reflects the type and speed of industrialization, while the patterns of migration reflect differences in the underlying culture and in specific factors in economy, family organization, and social structure. The critical question is whether the broad pattern of a cityward movement of rural people and an urbanization of population structure occurred in Japan.

REGIONAL REDISTRIBUTION: 1852-1885

In the last century of seclusion, population appears to have increased both in the culturally advanced and economically progressive southwest and in the isolated regions beyond the mountains (TABLE 11). The direction of movement altered sharply as the new economy gained momentum. Relatively

[20] The *honseki* population was 33.1 million in 1872 and 57.9 million in 1920. The increase indicated by the difference between these figures would be excessive, for the 1872 registration count should have been 1.7 million higher, whereas the 1920 registration count should have been one million lower. The *honseki* population as of 1920 was 2.4 million above the *de facto* population as estimated from the censuses of 1920 and 1925, but some 1.4 million of this excess can be attributed to the Japanese in the colonies and abroad and to aliens and colonials in Japan. The increase in the number of Japanese wherever found would be better as a measure of population growth than increase within Japan, for movement to and from the country was a product of political and economic expansion. In 1872 there were few Japanese outside Japan, for the colonists of the late Muromachi period had amalgamated with the indigenous populations of the areas in which they lived. Some movements abroad had occurred prior to 1868, for the prohibition on migration had ended with the capitulation in the 1850's.

[21] The inadequacies of the registration system preclude comparisons for periods earlier than 1888, although age tabulations were published for these years. The problem of the accuracy of the summations as late as 1888 is a complex one. Here it may be sufficient to state that the general outline of the increase is valid, although the individual figures and the specific differences at successive time periods are not precise measurements of the facts.

TABLE 10

Changes in the *honseki* population, by sex and age, 1888-1918

Age	POPULATION (IN '000) 1888	1898	1908	1918	INCREASE (IN '000) 1888-1918	1888-1898	1898-1908	1908-1918
				Total				
Total	39,607	43,763	49,588	56,667	17,060	4,156	5,825	7,079
0-14	13,360	14,367	16,968	19,889	6,529	1,007	2,601	2,921
15-64	24,069	26,989	30,013	33,561	9,492	2,920	3,024	3,548
15-19	3,397	4,342	4,432	5,440	2,043	945	90	1,008
20-34	9,008	10,259	11,808	12,536	3,528	1,251	1,549	728
35-44	5,151	5,061	5,689	6,952	1,801	—90	628	1,263
45-64	6,513	7,327	8,084	8,634	2,121	814	757	550
65 and over	2,178	2,407	2,606	3,217	1,039	229	199	611
				Male				
Total	20,008	22,074	25,046	28,625	8,617	2,066	2,972	3,579
0-14	6,753	7,265	8,604	10,062	3,309	512	1,339	1,458
15-64	12,272	13,722	15,240	17,065	4,793	1,450	1,518	1,825
15-19	1,723	2,191	2,252	2,774	1,051	468	61	522
20-34	4,588	5,207	5,969	6,389	1,801	619	762	420
35-44	2,668	2,603	2,919	3,540	872	—65	316	621
45-64	3,292	3,721	4,101	4,363	1,071	429	380	262
65 and over	983	1,087	1,202	1,498	515	104	115	296
				Female				
Total	19,599	21,689	24,542	28,042	8,443	2,090	2,853	3,500
0-14	6,606	7,102	8,365	9,827	3,221	496	1,263	1,462
15-64	11,798	13,267	14,773	16,496	4,698	1,469	1,506	1,723
15-19	1,675	2,151	2,180	2,666	991	476	29	486
20-34	4,420	5,052	5,839	6,147	1,727	632	787	308
35-44	2,482	2,459	2,770	3,412	930	—23	311	642
45-64	3,220	3,606	3,983	4,271	1,051	386	377	288
65 and over	1,195	1,320	1,404	1,719	524	125	84	315

Source: Nihon. Naikaku tokei-kyoku. *Nihon teioku jinko seitai tokei.* 1898, 1908, 1918. *Idem. Nihon teikoku tokei nenkan.* 1892 [For 1888].

TABLE 11

The population of the regions, 1750-1852 and 1872-1885

Region	TOKUGAWA REPORTS (IN '000) 1750	1852	MEIJI COMPILATIONS (IN '000) 1872	1885	PER CENT CHANGE 1750-1852	1872-1885
Total	25,924[a]	27,201	32,634	37,502	4.9	14.9
Kinai	2,139	2,099	2,024	2,348	—1.9	16.0
Tokaido	6,612	6,384	7,392	8,585	—3.4	16.1
Tosando-kami	2,443	2,510	2,762	3,866	2.7	40.0
Tosando-shimo	3,237	3,002	3,354	3,992	—7.3	19.0
Hokurokudo	2,160	2,598	3,300	3,711	20.3	12.5
Sanindo	1,309	1,544	1,629	1,771	18.0	8.7
Sanyodo	2,633	3,039	3,532	3,944	15.4	11.7
Nankaido	2,204	2,537	3,225	3,618	15.1	12.2
Saikaido	3,165	3,422	5,138	5,463	8.1	6.3
Hokkaido	22	65	278	204	195.4	—26.7

[a] The report giving the population by sex indicated a total of 25,918 thousand. This figure appears in Table 3.

Source: Populations, 1750 and 1852: Yuzuki and Horie. "Hompo jinko hyo." *Keizai shi kenkyu*, No. 7. May 1930. Populations and areas, 1872 and 1885: Rathgen, K. "Amtliches Bevölkerungsstatistik."*Mittheilungen der Deutschen Gesellschaft für Natur- und Völkerkunde Ostasiens*, 4:324. 1876. The figures for 1750 and 1852 are reports of commoners, while the figures for 1872 and 1885 are compilations of the *honseki* populations.

large increases occurred in the less densely settled northeastern regions, in part under the stimulus of settlement programs. These regions absorbed about one-third of the population increase of the period between 1872 and 1885. However, the industries, the construction, and the service activities of the new era were concentrated in the Tokaido and the Kinai—and here people moved. The Tokaido alone absorbed about one-fourth of the increase of the early Restoration period. Southwest Honshu, Kyushu, and Shikoku, with over two-fifths of the total population in 1872, absorbed only one-fourth of the increase in the next fifteen years.

PREFECTURAL REDISTRIBUTION: 1903-1918

The establishment of a national government in Tokyo was accompanied by numerous and fairly frequent changes in the administrative areas into which the country was divided. This doubtless contributed to efficient administration, but its effects on analysis are rather disconcerting. Not until 1903 were the areas of the prefectures delineated on a relatively permanent base. From 1903 to 1918, it is possible to trace the movements of population between prefectural areas that remain constant from one five-year period to the next.

Rapid population redistribution proceeded along with the economic developments of the early decades of the twentieth century.[22] Total present-resident population, 48.5 million in 1903, increased one-fifth to reach 58.1 million in 1918 (TABLE 12). An increase of ten million people in fifteen years in crowded Japan necessitated substantial redistribution if acute overcrowding of the agrarian areas was to be avoided. That redistribution occurred, and it took two major forms. Numerically most significant were the movements to the cities of Tokyo, Yokohama, Nagoya, Osaka, Kyoto, and Kobe (MAP 4). The prefectures containing these cities absorbed 3.7 million people, almost two-fifths of the nation's total increase of 9.5 million.[23] The industrial prefecture of Fukuoka in southwestern Japan increased its population by more than one-half million. The only other prefecture with an increase of comparable magnitude was Hokkaido, and here the increase of 1.1 million was compounded of frontier expansion and urban growth. Altogether, 5.4 million people were added to the populations of the six metropolitan prefectures, Fukuoka, and Hokkaido in the brief period of fifteen years.

The thirty-nine prefectures outside the eight centers of growth included some lesser cities as well as the major agricultural areas of the country. They differed widely in physical resources, density of settlement, and extent of poverty. Considered as a totality, their increase of 1.9 million in the period from 1903 to 1918 was two-fifths that of all Japan. Rates of increase approached the national average in the economically backward regions of the northeast but virtually disappeared in the agrarian prefectures near the developing conurbations. The only prefectures of appreciable increase in the southwest were those that offered employment opportunities outside agriculture: Wakayama, Hiroshima, Nagasaki, Miyazaki, Kagoshima, and Fukuoka.[24]

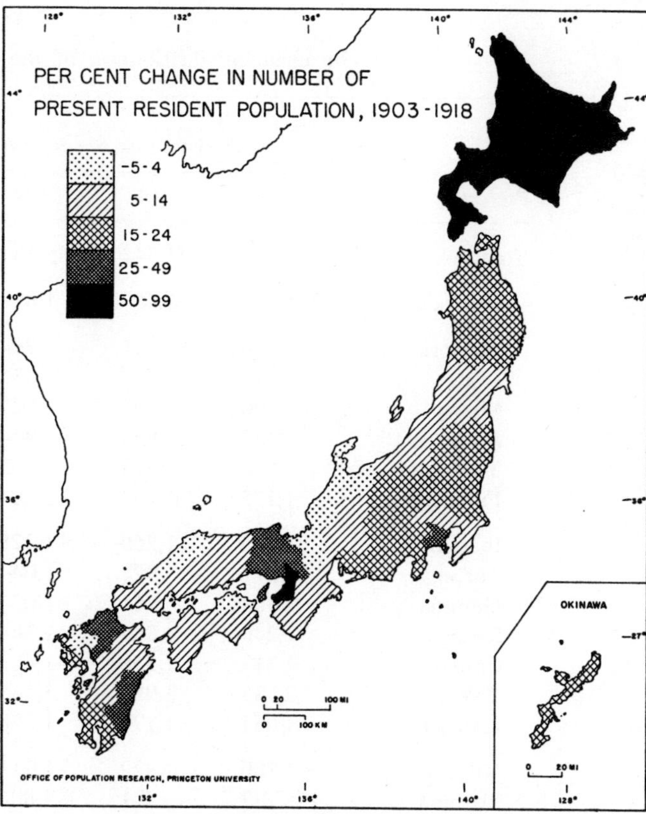

Map 4. The change in the present-resident population of the prefectures, 1903-1918
Source: Reference, Table 12.

URBANIZATION[25]

The growth of the cities in Japan was comparable to that which occurred in other countries in their early decades of industrialization, although the pace of the increase may have been greater. In Japan the spectacular aspect was the role of six cities: Tokyo, Yokohama, Nagoya, Osaka, Kyoto, and Kobe. In 1888, the 2.4 million people in these six great cities constituted 6 per cent of the total population of Japan; in 1918, the 6.1 million people in these same cities constituted 11 per cent of the total population of the country. Tokyo had grown from 1.3 million in 1888 to 2.3 million in 1918, but its rate of increase was dwarfed by that of the other five cities. Osaka grew from 443 thousand to 1.6 million, Kobe from 116 to 593 thousand.

[22] Measurement of population distribution and migration in the period from 1903 to 1918 is hampered by the plethora of difficulties involved in the allocation of people by place of *honseki* or place of present residence, but the phenomenon of differential increase was so outstanding that the deficient statistics serve only to blur the outlines of the process rather than to conceal its existence. For the years 1908 and 1913, the correlation between the percentage changes in the present-resident and in the *honseki* populations of the prefectures is .78, whereas the correlation between percentage changes in the "present-resident" and the "'corrected present-resident" populations is .96.

[23] These were the prefectures of Tokyo, Kanagawa, Aichi, Osaka, Kyoto, and Hyogo.

[24] The prefecture of Okinawa is reported with a sizable increase, but registration was seriously deficient.

[25] The measurement of urbanization involves substantial difficulties. Data were published for the *shi* (incorporated municipalities), but few cities of less than 30 thousand population were incorporated. All the area of the country outside the *shi* was included in *gun*; minor civil divisions within the *gun* were either *machi* or *mura*, terms that may be translated roughly as "towns" and "villages." If the population of the *shi* is described as urban, then the population of the *gun* must be described as rural, but *gun* with aggregated settlements of 30 thousand or more people included sizable proportions of people who were dependent on occupations other than agriculture. Moreover, the population defined as that in *shi* could increase by the creation of new *shi* or the incorporation of additional territory into existing *shi*. If these expansions in urban population occurred because the newly created *shi* or the areas newly added to existing *shi* had become economically and psychologically urban, the increase in urban population could be considered as real. An unknown portion of the increase was a statistical artifact, however, for areas rural by any criterion except the legal were sometimes incorporated in *shi*.

TABLE 12

The changing distribution of the present-resident population, 1903-1918

Prefecture	POPULATION (IN '000)				PER CENT IN COMMUNES OF LESS THAN 10,000			
	1903	*1908*	*1913*	*1918*	*1903*	*1908*	*1913*	*1918*
Total	48,543	51,742	55,131	58,087	79.3	75.1	72.4	68.1
Hokkaido	1,090	1,459	1,818	2,178	67.7	57.4	50.4	42.3
Aomori	666	721	764	798	87.0	86.0	86.4	83.5
Iwate	749	777	835	870	95.7	95.4	92.1	90.6
Miyagi	906	893	927	955	86.8	86.9	85.7	82.8
Akita	838	893	944	977	88.2	86.5	83.8	85.1
Yamagata	880	913	965	987	84.2	83.9	82.7	81.9
Fukushima	1,175	1,234	1,304	1,390	90.2	89.0	88.0	86.4
Ibaraki	1,200	1,260	1,328	1,408	91.0	90.7	90.6	88.4
Tochigi	912	977	1,044	1,103	80.7	79.6	79.1	75.0
Gumma	904	961	1,021	1,082	88.2	85.6	83.1	80.4
Saitama	1,240	1,285	1,344	1,392	96.7	94.8	92.3	89.7
Chiba	1,317	1,358	1,402	1,396	94.4	94.0	92.6	91.9
Tokyo	2,533	3,054	3,145	3,719	23.2	20.0	18.5	14.5
Kanagawa	1,051	1,178	1,228	1,323	60.4	51.6	48.8	43.7
Niigata	1,780	1,822	1,911	1,916	86.7	84.3	82.5	81.7
Toyama	777	771	806	803	81.5	81.2	80.0	78.4
Ishikawa	768	780	805	803	82.4	81.0	79.0	75.2
Fukui	636	630	652	637	85.3	84.8	82.7	83.1
Yamanashi	541	573	609	633	91.8	91.3	91.2	89.2
Nagano	1,349	1,402	1,484	1,564	89.4	89.2	88.3	85.1
Gifu	1,021	1,031	1,095	1,120	92.6	92.2	89.5	87.2
Shizuoka	1,293	1,376	1,484	1,592	88.0	86.7	83.2	79.6
Aichi	1,752	1,887	2,073	2,140	77.0	58.7	53.6	52.9
Mie	1,044	1,077	1,102	1,115	85.6	82.9	81.8	81.0
Shiga	717	694	697	704	90.0	89.2	88.9	88.5
Kyoto	1,055	1,156	1,288	1,384	62.0	57.3	52.6	43.4
Osaka	1,823	2,144	2,461	2,888	42.4	38.8	33.0	29.2
Hyogo	1,834	1,983	2,144	2,321	79.4	75.1	70.9	63.2
Nara	558	570	601	594	89.3	89.9	85.3	83.9
Wakayama	698	723	770	795	87.8	83.8	84.0	82.0
Tottori	436	441	471	465	89.2	88.2	87.3	85.4
Shimane	731	738	759	718	93.5	93.4	93.2	93.3
Okayama	1,188	1,223	1,261	1,286	88.1	87.5	86.3	84.3
Hiroshima	1,509	1,599	1,692	1,688	78.7	75.3	72.8	68.3
Yamaguchi	1,015	1,045	1,090	1,099	86.1	82.7	78.2	74.9
Tokushima	708	721	742	744	86.7	84.6	84.3	83.9
Kagawa	712	730	760	714	85.1	84.0	84.3	82.8
Ehime	1,035	1,058	1,098	1,128	92.6	92.1	92.1	89.1
Kochi	646	671	694	709	94.5	94.3	94.4	92.8
Fukuoka	1,571	1,721	1,926	2,113	84.0	73.3	67.1	53.0
Saga	655	672	694	679	92.8	91.3	91.0	83.4
Nagasaki	1,015	1,104	1,135	1,230	73.9	68.4	71.4	66.4
Kumamoto	1,198	1,236	1,303	1,311	92.7	92.7	90.7	90.0
Oita	855	880	927	921	94.3	87.0	84.7	84.1
Miyazaki	502	542	597	651	92.0	89.3	86.9	80.8
Kagoshima	1,184	1,275	1,397	1,462	51.9	43.0	37.8	39.1
Okinawa	476	502	534	581	38.5	38.8	34.0	34.6

Source: Nihon. Naikaku tokei-kyoku. *Nihon teikoku jinko seitai tokei.* 1903-1918.

Cities grew rapidly, but Japan long remained a predominantly rural country. As late as 1918 less than one-third of the Japanese lived in places of 10 thousand or more population, while only one Japanese of each six lived in a city of 50 thousand or more (TABLE 13). However, urbanization has an inherent significance that transcends the mechanical fact of a concentration of people in limited areas. The urban people were physically removed from the agrarian milieu. They were subjected to stimuli and pressures that produced change rather than stability. It was their social structure and their family system that bore the initial shocks of changing technologies and altered routines of living and working. Here the small family pattern evolved, gradually becoming more widespread and more tenaciously held within the urban groups as it spread slowly outward through the rural areas.

However "rural" is defined, there was an accumulation of people in the rural areas during the early decades of the Restoration. Increase in the rural population continued for the country as a whole from 1903 to 1918, although there were great differences in the rates of increase in the *gun* populations of the prefectures.[26] Increase was proportionately greatest in the colonization area of Hokkaido, the poor regions of the northeast, the backward areas of the far southwest, and the environs of the metropolitan centers. If we remove the rural increase in the areas of economic opportunity represented by Hokkaido, the prefectures containing the six great cities, and Fukuoka, the total rural increase of 5.5 million between 1903 and 1918 is reduced to 3 million. Over two-fifths of the increase in the population outside incorporated cities was either suburban, i.e., in areas directly related to the economy of the cities, or in the subsidized settlement area of Hokkaido. The "rural" increase adjacent to cities may be more a phenomenon of urbanization than of population pressure on the land.

The absorption of the youth of rural areas into urban centers is even more striking if the commune of 10 thousand population is taken as the dividing line between rural and urban. Whereas the total present-resident population increased one-fifth in the fifteen-year period from 1903 to 1918, communes of 10 thousand population or more increased nine-tenths, those of less than 10 thousand about one-fortieth. In

[26] A study of net movements for the precensal period is presented in the analytical report on the registration compilation of 1913. Here the problem of migration was approached in two ways: (a) the ascertainment of migration as a residual between total growth and natural increase; (b) the tabulation of the present-resident population to indicate persons resident in the prefecture with *honseki* there, persons present with *honseki* elsewhere, and persons absent with *honseki* in the prefecture. The data are so defective that few conclusions can be drawn, although there is evidence throughout that rural areas gained less than their natural increase, while towns and cities increased more. There is a rough positive relationship between the proportion of the present-resident population with *honseki* elsewhere and the proportion of the total population urban. The more highly urbanized prefectures had higher proportions of migrants in their total population. Nihon. Naikaku tokei-kyoku. *Taisho ni'nen matsu jinko seitai chosa no kekka ni yoru teikoku jinko gaisetsu.*

TABLE 13

The present-resident population, by size of commune, 1888-1918

	YEAR OF COMPILATION						
Size of commune	*1888*	*1893*	*1898*	*1903*	*1908*	*1913*	*1918*
				Number of communes			
Total	—	15,160	14,778	13,532	12,453	12,356	12,261
Under 10,000	—	14,946	14,545	13,262	12,080	11,887	11,705
10,000-49,999	110	196	212	245	344	432	510
50,000-99,999	8	12	13	16	19	26	32
100,000 and over	6	6	8	9	10	11	14
				Population (in '000)			
Total	40,106	42,060	45,403	48,543	51,742	55,132	58,087
Under 10,000	34,936	35,344	37,302	38,550	38,843	39,907	39,545
10,000-49,999	2,214	3,412	3,774	4,446	6,009	7,431	8,968
50,000-99,999	534	789	829	1,077	1,353	1,856	2,282
100,000 and over	2,422	2,515	3,498	4,470	5,537	5,938	7,292
				Per cent distribution			
Total	100.0	100.0	100.0	100.0	100.0	100.0	100.0
Under 10,000	87.1	84.0	82.2	79.4	75.1	72.4	68.1
10,000-49,999	5.5	8.1	8.3	9.2	11.6	13.5	15.4
50,000-99,999	1.3	1.9	1.8	2.2	2.6	3.4	3.9
100,000 and over	6.0	6.0	7.7	9.2	10.7	10.8	12.6
				Per cent change			
Total	—	4.9	7.9	6.9	6.6	6.6	5.4
Under 10,000	—	1.2	5.5	3.3	0.8	2.7	—0.9
10,000-49,999	—	54.1	10.6	17.8	35.2	23.7	20.8
50,000-99,999	—	47.8	5.1	29.9	25.6	37.2	23.0
100,000 and over	—	3.8	39.1	27.8	23.9	7.2	22.8

Source: Nihon. Naikaku tokei-kyoku. *Nihon teikoku jinko seitai tokei.* 1888-1908: 1908 Annex, Tables XI-XIII; 1913, Table VII; 1918, Table IX.

15 of the 47 prefectures there was a decrease in the registered population of the smaller communes. The largest decreases were in the prefectures that included large cities or were adjacent to prefectures with such cities. The largest increases, on the other hand, were in the settlement area of Hokkaido and in the poor areas of northeast Honshu.

The registration statistics of the early twentieth century thus demonstrate that the increase of people on the land was slowing. In fact, the evidence is reasonably conclusive that it was virtually eliminated in the more prosperous and the urbanized areas. However, the limitations of this analysis of changes in the distribution of the increasing population of Japan should be emphasized again. No data on the numbers of people in rural areas, however defined, can yield measures of changes in levels of living. All that can be said with surety is that the pressure of population on the land within the existing organization of Japanese agriculture and village life would have become greater if substantial urbanization had not occurred.

TABLE 14

The vital rates of the Japanese, 1875-1919

Year (December 31)	*Honseki population (in '000)*	VITAL RATES			*Children 0-4 per 1000 women aged 15-49*
		Birth rate	*Death rate*	*Rate of natural increase*	
1875-79	35,111	25.2	18.0	7.2	—
1880-84	37,079	26.3	19.5	6.7	464[a]
1885-89	39,081	28.3	21.5	6.8	485
1890-94	41,093	28.4	21.1	7.2	483
1895-99	43,248	30.6	20.7	9.9	—
1900-04	45,984	32.0	20.4	11.7	527[b]
1905-09	48,759	32.0	20.9	11.1	527[c]
1910-14	52,140	33.6	20.2	13.4	559[d]
1915-19	55,527	32.4	22.5	9.9	542[e]

[a] Ratio for 1884. [b] 1903. [c] 1908. [d] 1913. [e] 1918.
Sources: Nihon. Naikaku tokei-kyoku. *Jinko dotai tokei*. 1942. Ratios of children to women computed from age distributions in: *Idem. Nihon teikoku tokei nenkam*, 1886-1902. *Nihon teikoku jinko seitai tokei*. 1903, 1908, 1913, and 1918.

THE BALANCE OF BIRTHS AND DEATHS

The relative stability of the population of Japan in the last century and a quarter of the period of seclusion must have been due to an approximate balance of births and deaths. The increase of population that accompanied economic development and its associated changes must have been due to an excess of births over deaths. There can be no other explanation of growth or decline during these centuries, for the migration to and from Japan was negligible in the *bakufu* period and numerically slight in the early modern period.

The assumption that increasing rates of natural increase are due primarily to declines in death rates is implicit in most discussions of population increase, urbanization, and redistribution. However, rising rates of increase might equally well be produced by increases in the birth rate, or by any combination of directions and speeds of change in birth and death rates that leaves an increasing difference between the two. If abortion and infanticide were widespread in Tokugawa Japan, the lessening of such limitation may have produced an increase in the birth rate and thus have become a factor, if not the major factor, in an increasing rate of natural increase.

The official reports indicate that birth rates increased irregularly from a low of 25 per 1,000 total population in 1875-1879 to 32 in 1915-1919 (TABLE 14). Death rates also increased, though less rapidly. If these data are correct, population increase during the period from 1875 through 1919 was due more to an increase in fertility than to a decrease in mortality. This would mean that the Japanese vital transition in the first sixty years or so of the Restoration period differed from that of Western nations at rather comparable periods of industrial development and city growth. The critical question is the accuracy of the records of vital events. Early publications of the Bureau of Statistics included a warning statement that the majority of the additions to the registers were the survivors of unrecorded births of earlier years.[27] Perusal of the detailed vital records for the late nineteenth and early twentieth centuries indicates that relative completeness and accuracy in the reporting of vital events was achieved only gradually as the reporting system itself was improved and people became habituated to reporting. Thus the problem becomes that of manipulating the data yielded by an admittedly defective statistical system to determine the probable levels of birth and death rates and the direction of movements in those rates during the decades when reported changes in mortality and fertility might be statistical artifacts, actual occurrences, or some combination of the two.

MORTALITY

Some of the transformations of the early decades of contact with the West were favorable to a reduction in mortality, while others were conducive to an increase. Agricultural improvements within the country and access to external markets reduced the number and severity of the famines and hence lessened the mortality from malnutrition and disease. However, the important factor in the evaluation of trends in mortality is not the changing adequacy of the food supply but rather the changing incidence of epidemic and endemic diseases. The seclusion that had barred Japan from contact with medical and public health advances made in other countries had also isolated her people from exposure to the diseases of these other countries.

Many major diseases had long existed in Japan—some, such as dysentery, being reported in the legendary period.[28]

[27] In the early decades after the Restoration, birth and death rates were highest in the industrial and urban areas, lowest in the rural areas. In 1883, crude birth rates were over 30 per thousand total population in Tokyo, Aichi, and Osaka prefectures, but below 17 in Kochi, Kagoshima, and Okinawa. Crude death rates, above 20 in the more urban prefectures, reached low rates of 12 per 1,000 total population in Kagoshima and 9 in Okinawa. For the country as a whole, the correlation between crude birth and death rates for the years 1883-1884 was .7; for the year 1914-1915, the comparable correlation was .3.

Any analytical approach to the vital statistics of the period from 1872 on yields corroborative evidence of their inaccuracies. As late as 1913 the official reports of the Bureau of Statistics stated that infant deaths were so incompletely recorded as to be valueless for historical study. Failures to report deaths during the earlier years are evident in the accumulations of the aged in the successive reports. Projection of the age distributions of the 1920 census backward with recorded deaths indicates some underregistration of infants, although the deviations thus secured cannot be assumed to represent a correction factor for recorded births. The registration system was self-contained; infants who were born and died without registration were outside birth statistics, death statistics, and age distributions.

[28] U.S. Army. *Civil affairs handbook, Japan*. Section 13, "Public health and sanitation."

Nineteen severe epidemics of dysentery were reported between 861 A.D. and 1829. Typhoid and paratyphoid were reported in the early Tokugawa period. Fifty-six epidemics of small pox were reported between 735 and 1833. A description of the symptoms of pulmonary tuberculosis was included in the earliest Japanese medical book, written in 984. Beri-beri was described in the Kamakura period, while an epidemic of influenza was reported in 860. Malaria was an ancient and a widespread disease. However, many of these diseases were endemic in limited areas and restricted in their impact on population growth both by the barriers to migration that limited epidemics and by the low virulence of the infections. Contact with the West brought new diseases and more virulent strains of old diseases at the same time that the increasing mobility of the new society favored contagion and the generation of epidemics.

Cholera became a major hazard in the decades after its introduction in 1822.[29] Some three million persons were stricken in the great epidemic that began in 1858; between July and September of 1860 the bodies of over 250 thousand victims were cremated in Tokyo alone. Other great epidemics occurred in 1877-1878 and in 1886, but control was achieved rapidly in succeeding decades. The last major epidemic, that of 1902, produced only nine thousand deaths. Bubonic plague, another major disease introduced after the opening of the country, was so rigidly controlled that only in the year 1907 did it cause as many as five hundred deaths. Dysentery reached its peak in 1893, with 41 thousand deaths reported; in the early twentieth century only from two to four thousand deaths were reported per year. Vaccination controlled smallpox; secondary epidemics occurred in 1886, 1897, and 1908, but they were limited by extensive programs of vaccination. Typhus never became a major killer. Childhood deaths from diphtheria were reduced sharply by the early twentieth century. Typhoid fever revealed a fairly regular increase in the incidence of cases and deaths, although improved diagnosis may have been a factor.

The development of a public health program and sanitation played a major role in the improvement of health and the reduction of mortality.[30] Numbers of doctors and other medical personnel increased rapidly during the early years of the Restoration. By 1880 the government reported 36 thousand doctors, approximately one for each 1,000 population.[31] By 1898 there were 43 thousand doctors and 36 thousand registered midwives. After this early period of marked growth, the number of doctors increased less rapidly than the total population; the 42 thousand medical practitioners of 1914 provided only 8 doctors for each 10 thousand total population. Levels of medical service were quite low, however, for as late as 1920 only two-fifths of the doctors were graduates of imperial universities or other medical colleges. Three-fifths had either passed qualifying examinations, including the "old examination," or were practicing under the "old system." The situation with midwives was similar. In 1914, only 23 thousand of the 31 thousand midwives were graduates of designated schools or institutions. Half of the licensed midwives had passed the qualifying examinations; the remainder were practicing under "old systems."

The trend in general health conditions is difficult to evaluate. The great hazards of Japan remained: cities with inadequate sources of water and sewage disposal systems and an agriculture that maintained the production of the fields through the use of night soil. Increasing numbers of people resided temporarily in the cities, where overcrowding and poor working conditions increased both the chances of contagion and susceptibility. The majority of the people remained on the land, however, and here there is evidence that general levels of living increased slowly.

Manipulations of the age structures of the *honseki* populations yield reasonably conclusive evidence that mortality was declining in the decades after the Restoration.[32] The declines in this period continued into the period when the first official life table was constructed (FIGURE 1). The general picture revealed by life tables for the years between 1891-1898 and 1909-1913 is one of declining mortality, although the true magnitude of the decreases is masked by the improvements in death registration that continued throughout the period.[33]

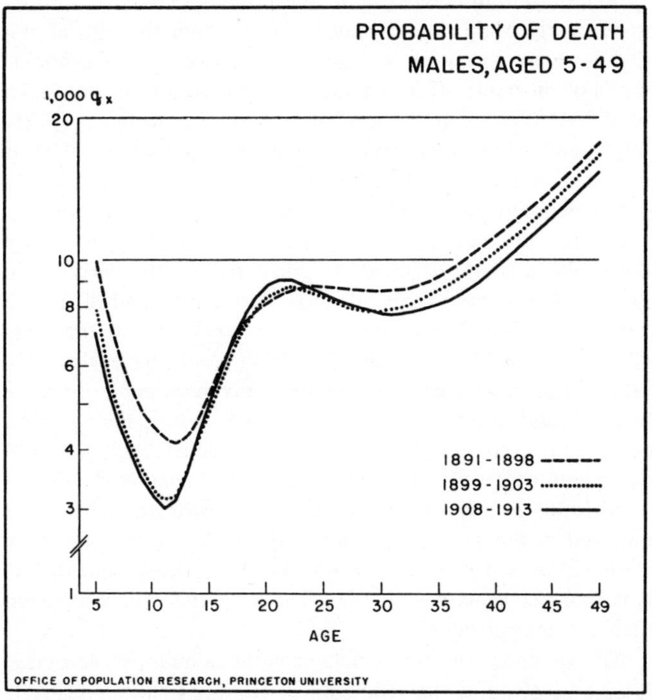

Figure 1. Probability of death, males aged from 5 to 49, registration life tables, 1891-1898, 1899-1903, and 1908-1913

Source: Nihon. Kosei-sho, daijin kambo, tokei chosa-bu. *Dai-9-kai seimei hyo.* Pp. 72-77.

[29] Nihon. Naimu-sho, eisei-kyoku. *Sanitary statistics, 1913-1924.* The inadequacies of these early data on deaths from notifiable diseases are admitted; but, since public health and medical facilities were improving throughout the Meiji period, the proportion of all deaths that were reported probably increased. If so, the decline in deaths from notifiable diseases was more rapid than the absolute numbers cited here would indicate.

[30] From 1868 to 1872 the East College of the Imperial University controlled sanitary administration and medical education, but in 1872 a medical section was established in the Department of Education. This medical section, raised to bureau status in 1873, was later transferred to the Home Department, where it was named the Sanitary Bureau. Not until 1937 was a Ministry of Health and Welfare established.

[31] More detailed health and medical statistics than those in the general statistical yearbooks were published in the following sources. Nihon. Naimu-sho, eisei-kyoku. *Eisei nempo.* And: Nihon. Naikaku tokei-kyoku. *Shiin tokei. Idem. Statistiques des causes de décès de l'Empire du Japon. . . .*

[32] Morita, Yuzo. *Jinko zoka no bunseki.* Professor Morita utilized all available materials in a quantitative reconstruction of the early populations.

[33] In the precensal life tables, incompletely recorded deaths were related to populations whose size and age structures were not accurate. The consequence was error that varied from age to age and as between the sexes. Infant mortality in 1898-1903 was at the level that characterized the Netherlands or England and Wales at the beginning of the twentieth century, whereas mortality at

FERTILITY

In the latter part of the nineteenth century, population grew at a generally increasing rate and death rates were declining. We can attach no precise figures to either the increasing rate of population growth or the declining mortality, nor can we estimate the level of mortality in the late Tokugawa period. However, the largely descriptive materials on levels of living, conditions of sanitation, and the prevalence of ill health and disease permit no inference other than that mortality was very high. Hence a relatively high fertility was required if growth was to occur—and growth did occur. Birth rates of from 25 to 30 per 1,000 total population are unlikely to have characterized the Japanese in 1852 or 1872. If the expectation of life at birth in the eighteenth and early nineteenth centuries was 25 years, then the birth rate would have had to reach 40 per 1,000 population if decline in numbers was not to occur. If the birth rate then increased substantially over time, mortality would have had to remain essentially at its original level to avoid the production of rates of natural increase more rapid than those that occurred. Thus the coincidence of slowly increasing rates of increase and a slowly declining mortality in the latter half of the nineteenth century precludes the possibility of rapidly increasing fertility during this period.

Some crude inferences as to the probable levels of fertility in the early Meiji period may be made from the official statistics on the basis of reasonable inferences as to probable levels of mortality. If it is assumed that mortality in the Japan of the 1880's was at the level that existed in Korea in 1926-1930, and if the registration age distribution as of 1891 is accepted as accurate, then the crude birth rate in 1886 could not have been much below 40 per 1,000 total population.[34]

Further and more speculative deductions may help to clarify the problem of the level of the birth rate in the early Meiji period. If the crude birth rate was between 38 and 40 in the 1880's, then the death rate implicit in mortality at the level of the Korean life table for 1926-1930 would have yielded a rate of natural increase higher than any reasonable estimate of the actual rate for the period. In other words, the age data of the 1891 compilation should be projected back to 1886 by means of an assumed mortality above that of Korea in 1926-1930. But if this is so, then the estimated birth rate required in the 1880's to produce the children of the 1890's would have had to be above 40. All this is hypothetical, but it is more consonant with the realities of the Japanese scene than are official figures.

All we know of the social, economic, and psychological factors involved in the reduction of fertility in the industrializing countries of the West and in Japan would support the inference that there had been no substantial diffusion of contraceptive practice among the Japanese prior to 1880 or 1890. This statement, it should be noted, is limited to the types of fertility controls that have been correlated historically with the development of an industrial and urban society and the diffusion of its ways of living, its pressures, and its values. It may not be relevant to the analysis of temporal changes in abortion and infanticide. And the critical question with reference to Japan is not the diffusion of contraceptive practice but the changing incidence of abortion and infanticide. Descriptive reports, local and national laws, and occasional studies of local areas all indicate that there was considerable infanticide for decades after the Restoration, but that increasing economic opportunities, rising levels of living, and increasing social mobility resulted in declining incidence.

A continuing practice of infanticide is consistent with the previous conclusions as to population increase, mortality, and fertility in the first quarter-century or so after the opening to the West. A crude birth rate of 40 or even 45 per 1,000 total population does not permit the inference that family limitation was negligible. Reproduction at the age-specific birth rates that characterized the agricultural areas of Tohoku in 1925 would have produced crude birth rates of 50 or more in the Japan of the late Tokugawa or the early Restoration period. If patterns of marriage and family life were such as to produce crude birth rates of 50 or 55 in the absence of family limitation, then a widespread practice of abortion and infanticide could have occurred without reducing crude birth rates below 40.[35]

A hypothetical curve for the evaluation of fertility from the late Tokugawa period to the third decade of the twentieth century would carry fertility upward in an irregular fashion until sometime in the 1880's or 1890's, possibly with a period of relatively unchanging high fertility in the decade or so before the turn of the century. Then sometime in the last quarter of the nineteenth century, decline would begin, so slowly as to be imperceptible at first, but increasing gradually. Unfortunately the data of the registration system do not permit the computation of accurate rates of change during this period. The age data of the registration compilations can be used for the compilation of ratios of children to women. If the basic data were accurate, these ratios would reflect the combined influence of the levels, and the changes in fertility and in childhood mortality. Since the basic data are not accurate, we must again assess the question of the period at which and the extent to which the inaccurate data can be used to estimate levels and changes in fertility.

The ratio of children under 5 to women aged from 15 to 49 increased from 490 in 1888 to 497 in 1898 and 559 in 1913.[36] Assuming the accuracy of the basic data, the type of increase in fertility ratio revealed here could be produced by increases in fertility, decreases in childhood mortality, or some combination of the two. Somewhat detailed analysis of the behavior of the ratios and their component variables indicates that increasing child-women ratios among the Japanese of the nineteenth century do not reflect changes in fertility, whether of increase or of decrease. Instead, the behavior of the ratios prior to the twentieth century is due primarily to improve-

age 10 was at the level that characterized the countries of Western and Northern Europe in the 1870's and 1880's. The existence of this type of divergent chronological relationships casts suspicion on the accuracy of the basic data for Japan; furthermore, statistics on infant mortality are officially admitted to have been deficient as late as 1913. The use of the life tables based on registration data and the later ones utilizing more accurate vital statistics and the age data of the enumerative census to establish a time series of changes in mortality is not valid.

[34] Korean life tables: Sai, Kiei. "Chosen jumin no seimei hyo." *Chosen igakkai zasshi*, 29(11):2180-2220. November 1939. Age distributions of Japanese: Nihon. Naikaku tokei-kyoku. *Nihon teikoku tokei nenkan.*

[35] No analysis of the official figures on numbers of births is presented here, since underregistration of births approached one-third in the middle of the 1880's and may have been as much as one-tenth in 1913. Analysis for the period 1898-1918 and bibliography are presented in: Teruoka, Gito. "An essay on the population problem of Japan in the light of social biology." *Reports of the Institute for Science of Labour.* Report No. 1. 1931. 18 pp.

[36] The age distributions for individual years are included in: Nihon. Naikaku tokei-kyoku. *Nihon teikoku tokei nenkan.* The age distributions for prefectural populations according to the various residence allocations are found in: *Idem. Nihon teikoku jinko seitai tokei*, 1898, 1903, 1908, 1913, and 1918.

ments in the current reporting of births and deaths and hence in the quality of the compilations used for the computation of the ratios. A specific illustration of the qualitative deficiencies of the data will suffice. The child-woman ratio as computed from the age distribution of the registration compilation of 1886 is 485. However, reported children aged from 0 to 4 in 1886 could not have produced the survivors aged from 5 to 9 in 1891. If we make the reasonable assumption that the children aged from 5 to 9 in 1891 existed, and estimate the number of children aged from 0 to 4 who must have lived in 1886 to produce the survivors of 1891, the ratio of children to women in 1886 becomes something more than 550.

If the response of the Japanese family to the development of the industrial society and the diffusion of the pressures and values associated with it was comparable to that of the families of the West, differential fertility should have been apparent by 1900 or 1910. Fertility should have declined in the urban and industrial areas, whereas there is little reason for assuming much change in the isolated rural areas. Ratios of children to women for the prefectures from the registration summations of 1903 to 1918 permit the testing of this hypothesis. There were in fact wide variations in fertility ratios among the prefectures as early as 1903,[37] and these variations are consistent with the theory that the decline in fertility began earliest and proceeded furthest in the urban areas, diffusing outward gradually into rural and remote areas (TABLE 15). Ratios were higher in the rural areas of northeastern Japan than they were in those of southwestern Japan; they were lower in the prefectures containing the cities of Tokyo, Osaka, Kobe, and Kyoto than in the prefectures containing the more recently developed concentrations of Nagoya and Yokohama. Both the Tokyo-Yokohama and the Osaka-Hyogo-Kyoto areas were fringed by prefectures with relatively low fertility ratios.

The patterns of fertility differences revealed by the ratios of children to women in the *honseki* populations are roughly similar to those in the *de facto* populations of the census period from 1920 to 1940. *Honseki* populations are a confusing basis for the determination of relationships among fertility, rurality, and urbanization, however, for persons living in cities maintained *honseki* in rural areas and registered the births of their children in *koseki* in the villages.[38] If the populations of the police counts are used instead of those of the registration compilations, the relationship between fertility and urbanization is more concise. In 1913, the ratios of children to women as computed from the police survey data were 413 for Tokyo, 432 for all cities of 50 thousand or more, excluding Tokyo, and 550 for the population of the *gun*.

Child-women ratios for the majority of the prefectures increased from 1903 to 1908 and 1913 and then decreased from 1913 to 1918. This typical change was more pronounced for the most urbanized prefectures, with the result that differences in child-women ratios were greater at the end of the period than they had been at the beginning. Although this changing areal distribution is in part a function of changing completeness of registration and of differences in childhood mortality, it supports the inference that increasing differentials in the fertility of geographic areas and social-economic classes may have been characteristic of the early decades of industrialization and urbanization.

THE DEMOGRAPHIC TRANSITION

The exploration of the defective registration statistics of the early Meiji era was not undertaken in order to reconstruct the historical development of the population of Japan as a contribution to research on that country. Rather, the purpose was a comparison of the relationships between population increase and industrialization in Japan with those that have existed elsewhere in industrialized societies. In Japan, early and sustained declines in mortality were followed by declines in fertility, with a consequent increase in the rate of population growth in the early period of modernization. Migration from rural to urban areas facilitated the development and diffusion of ways of living that lowered rates of human reproduction. It was already apparent in the second decade of the twentieth century that rates of decline in fertility were likely to surpass those in mortality at some future time.

Japanese experience supports the hypothesis that a demographic transition is a necessary correlate of industrialization and urbanization. It also indicates that changes in population during a period of industrialization are related both to the nature of the premodern culture and to the type of the economic development. It is improbable that the transitions in fertility, mortality, and natural increase that occurred in Japan could have been predicted on the basis of population facts alone. If this is so, the experience of one culture in transition cannot be used to predict the transition in another.

There are pervasive legends of uniqueness in the population balance of ancient and medieval Japan. The extent to which the mortality and fertility of the Japanese were unique in levels or in patterns of transition can be determined only after comprehensive analysis of the premodern and the transitional patterns of growth in other Asian cultures. Certain conclusions concerning the occurrences in Japan may be offered, however, for many aspects of the presumed uniqueness are conjoined products of the inaccurate statistics for Japan and ignorance of the dynamics of population in other cultures during periods of culture contact and crisis.

There is nothing in the official mortality statistics of Japan that, critically viewed, would attribute any uniqueness to the Japanese. It may be that the initial shocks of the politico-economic transformation combined with the prevalence of

[37] Direct validation of the prefectural ratios as measures of fertility is not possible for the years 1903, 1908, and 1913. However, the last registration was made as of December 31, 1918, and the first enumerative census was taken as of October 1, 1920. For 1920 the ratios of children to women were relatively accurate measures of differential fertility; these ratios, crude birth rates, and gross reproduction rates for prefectures gave similar pictures of regional differentials. Both measures as computed for 1920 were highly correlated with the ratios of children to women for the *honseki* population as of December 31, 1918. Accepting the 1920 data as correct, the ratios for 1918 were too high for the urban prefectures, too low for the rural areas. Since the general direction of the bias inherent in the data for the precensal period was to mask the extent of the rural-urban differences that existed, conclusions as to the origin and extent of urban-rural differentials based on data for *honseki* populations are conservative.

[38] In 1913 the correlation between the proportion of the present-resident population living in communes of 10 thousand population or less and the proportion of the population with *honseki* outside the prefecture was —.74, while the correlation between ratios of children to women in the police counts and the proportion of the present-resident population in communes of less than 10 thousand population was .28 in 1908 and .43 in 1913. In the latter year the correlation between the ratios of children to women in the police count and the proportion migrant in the present-resident population was —.37. Correlations of fertility ratios for *honseki* populations and rurality ratios for present-resident populations were insignificant, although always positive in sign: .23 in 1903, .02 in 1908, .13 in 1913, and .11 in 1918. The correlation of fertility ratios and rurality ratios in the enumeration of 1920 was .36, whereas correlations of gross reproduction rates and rurality ratios were .45 in 1920, .42 in 1925, .39 in 1930, and .37 in 1935.

TABLE 15

Ratios of children to women, 1903-1918 and 1920
(Children under 5 per 1,000 women aged from 15 to 49)

Prefecture	Honseki registrations 1903	1908	1913	1918	Police counts 1908	1913	Census of 1920
Total	527	527	559	542	490	531	562
Hokkaido	695	706	716	693	580	591	716
Aomori	651	630	669	624	571	626	666
Iwate	557	528	599	592	504	582	638
Miyagi	545	506	580	592	512	596	662
Akita	587	563	578	578	536	573	645
Yamagata	560	532	575	559	519	578	595
Fukushima	553	525	560	570	494	556	619
Ibaraki	479	495	525	544	461	531	606
Tochigi	541	540	575	583	513	547	636
Gumma	584	554	576	571	500	536	576
Saitama	538	523	565	560	509	577	576
Chiba	512	498	526	517	473	521	565
Tokyo	483	500	527	501	406	442	450
Kanagawa	554	521	554	543	488	521	555
Niigata	512	531	580	551	533	580	619
Toyama	582	607	649	577	593	618	619
Ishikawa	546	558	596	546	556	595	561
Fukui	545	557	593	547	548	588	576
Yamanashi	539	526	568	570	505	553	653
Nagano	533	514	548	540	514	543	528
Gifu	553	544	608	582	547	609	609
Shizuoka	586	571	613	598	516	611	622
Aichi	554	553	612	564	502	555	541
Mie	523	526	570	525	526	564	546
Shiga	504	496	532	499	473	544	536
Kyoto	497	503	526	478	448	477	454
Osaka	484	496	516	462	443	447	419
Hyogo	546	548	573	527	480	526	513
Nara	544	544	573	518	512	555	549
Wakayama	525	526	562	527	510	563	575
Tottori	479	477	535	542	475	525	559
Shimane	441	440	482	479	428	481	525
Okayama	499	497	527	486	464	486	494
Hiroshima	518	522	552	539	479	542	577
Yamaguchi	473	471	509	502	442	476	544
Tokushima	526	546	577	555	521	568	605
Kagawa	548	555	603	561	545	605	624
Ehime	532	530	560	548	496	554	586
Kochi	517	494	498	485	459	479	523
Fukuoka	553	535	541	517	496	526	527
Saga	540	547	550	528	486	528	558
Nagasaki	498	499	514	497	445	478	581
Kumamoto	463	473	484	504	440	457	558
Oita	463	472	501	503	437	476	540
Kagoshima	474	531	534	547	457	477	610
Miyazaki	515	525	551	564	444	465	604
Okinawa	402	425	415	527	460	442	574

Source: 1903-1918: Nihon. Naikaku tokei-kyoku. *Nihon teikoku jinko seitai tokei*. 1903, 1908, 1913, 1918. 1920: *Idem. Taisho ku'nen kokusei chosa hokoku*. IV.A.1.

introduced diseases to produce some increases in mortality in the first decades of contact. Since population increase was in process from the opening of the country until the Restoration, however, the increases in mortality must have been episodic rather than continuous. Their consequences were not devastating if the country as a whole is considered. Comparable increases occurred in many countries of the West when industrial employment and urban living replaced life in agricultural villages. The fundamental fact is that the expanding industrial economy and the increasing activities designed to prevent deaths resulted in substantial and continuing declines in mortality from the 1860's or 1870's onward. Declining mortality was a factor leading to population increase in an industrializing Japan, as it had been earlier in the West.

The basic question in regard to the demographic transition in Japan concerns fertility. Some techniques of family limitation doubtless exist in all cultures, but the practice of infanticide in Japan seems to have been more extensive than that in other great Asian cultures. Moreover, in Japan the initial impact of economic modernization tended toward an increase in fertility. In the Western world there were decades and even centuries in which industrial and urban development meant a wider diffusion of contraceptive practice and a further decline in fertility. In Japan, the amelioration of economic conditions, wider opportunities for employment, and the increase of social mobility presumably resulted in, or were accompanied by, a reduced incidence of family limitation. The reasons adduced for infanticide lessened as the industrial society developed. Children who were not needed to replace their parents in the villages could migrate to the developing cities, to employment outside agriculture, or to the Empire. In this situation, the existence of numerous children broadened the bases of security for the family and facilitated rather than retarded the welfare of the eldest son and heir. The same matrix of values that sanctioned abortion or infanticide now sanctioned the rates of childbearing so often presumed to be an inherent characteristic of the peasant society.

The Japanese experience supports the hypothesis that it is the transitional society that manifests the highest fertility. The high levels of fertility in some areas of the contemporary world may be transitional phenomena. In other areas, modernization may result in a substantial increase in fertility. There is also the possibility that the fertility controls of an ancient society may decline simultaneously with the increase in the controls of an industrial society. If so, there may be a considerable period in which the demographic transition involves a change in the class incidence of family limitation but not in its total amount.

PART III

THE CHANGING POPULATION, 1920-1955

CHAPTER IV

Population Changes: The Bases and the Patterns

THE 1920's and 1930's were decades of culmination and of crisis in Japan. Rapid industrialization provided employment in urban areas for the sons and daughters of the peasants; emigration to areas protected by the administrative services and the armed forces of Japan was available to all who wished the opportunity. Birth rates were declining, the rate of natural increase slowing. Projection of the trends of the past into the future indicated that population growth would cease in the late twentieth or the early twenty-first century.

The population problem became a matter of serious concern in the depressed years of the early 1930's. With the movement into China and the defense activities in Japan, the government's definition of its population problem shifted. Population growth itself was regarded as an essential strength. Optimism concerning the economic future of the Empire replaced the earlier pessimism about the crowded home islands. In the government's views, rich and strategic regions would be developed by Japan and peopled by Japanese. The internal problems that were not solved by the migration of Japanese would vanish as Japan became the industrial nucleus of a great imperial structure.

The 1920's were a decade of peace, the 1930's a decade of minor war and preparation for major war. If the pattern of the past had continued, the late 1940's and the early 1950's would have been a period of economic development and preparation for further expansion. This had been the pattern of the past, from the absorption of the Ryukyu Islands and the conquest of Taiwan to the establishment of Manchoukuo. But the pattern broke. The move into China in 1937 led through eight years of war to defeat, the liquidation of the imperial structure, and military occupation within boundaries reduced to those of the Tokugawa period.

The Japan of the 1920's and 1930's was far removed from her own agricultural past, but modernization was irregular. Hand agriculture existed alongside machine technology; historic family relations persisted in the metropolis. Peasant households supplemented limited incomes by factory employment, while urban households labored in industries under conditions of immobility almost equal to those of remote villagers. In parts of industry, the transformation to the twentieth century was telescoped into less than three-quarters of a century; in other parts of industry, in the family structure, and in the values by which the people lived, the transition was often limited and sometimes superficial.

The materials for analysis of the Japanese population became progressively more adequate. Complete censuses of the population of Japan and most of the colonial areas were taken each five years between 1920 and 1940.[1] These censuses permit detailed analysis of the increasing population of Japan at the same time that they yield materials of inestimable value on other peoples and cultures of northern and eastern Asia.

The exigencies of war and defeat increased Japan's needs for information on the size, the characteristics and the distribution of her population. The maintenance of political continuity and civil discipline throughout the war and postwar years permitted the collection of statistics to meet these needs. A special survey made early in 1944 pictured the population close to maximum concentration, for strategic bombing had not yet begun. A count in the fall of 1945 pictured the population close to the maximum dispersion that had occurred as a result of the bombing of the cities. Another survey in the spring of 1946 and a special census in 1947 pictured the absorption of the former armed forces in a civilian economy, the reception of the repatriates, and the restoration of prewar demographic patterns. The censuses of 1950 and 1955 permit analysis of population trends from the prewar into the postwar period.

THE INCREASING POPULATION

In Japan in the years from 1920 to 1955 there were many censuses, and levels of accuracy were quite high. The problem is the definition of the population that is to be subjected to analysis, for the people of post-Restoration Japan could move about without reference to the barriers imposed by the Tokugawa *shogun* in the seventeenth century. The Empire was growing in area and becoming more closely integrated, with consequent increases in the mobility of the people. After 1931 Japanese and subject peoples alike moved outside the formal structure of the Empire. In the last years of the imperial era, the swift political and military movements resulted in frequent changes of area and population in Japan and the other countries of the Empire, Manchoukuo, and the occupied areas of Asia and Oceania. With the defeat of 1945, the Empire disappeared as a political entity, and all Japanese from what had been designated as the Co-Prosperity Sphere were returned to the restricted area of the home country.

Analysis of the population present within Japan itself would be inadequate. Until 1945 Japanese manpower was utilized in imperial areas as well as in Japan itself. Moreover, manpower within Japan consisted in part of native Japanese, in part of workers from the colonial and occupied areas. At the end of the war, substantial proportions of the Koreans, the Ryukyuans, and other former colonial subjects chose repatriation to their homelands. Japanese scattered throughout the Pacific area had no choice; repatriation was compulsory. The

[1] Citations to the publications of the various censuses and surveys of the population of Japan, the Empire, and related areas are given in the Bibliography.

liquidation of imperial expansion involved the absorption of earlier migrants and their children in the broken economy of Japan itself. Hence we shall glance backward at the 1920's and 1930's before considering the population developments of the present in the area that is now Japan.

1920 to 1940

In 1920, there were 56.0 million people in Japan; in 1940, there were 73.1 million (Table 16). The significance of this increase of 17 million in the population of crowded Japan is difficult to describe in meaningful terms. Increase alone in Japan was greater than the entire population of the Philippine Islands in 1939; it was as large as the population of Korea in 1920. This increase in the population of Japan in this twenty-year period would have peopled an empty land equivalent in area to Japan itself with 114 persons for each square mile.

The magnitude of the increase in the Japanese population was great, but the rate of the increase was not high. It amounted to little more than 30 per cent in twenty years, and it was lower in the 1930's than it had been in the 1920's. But the practical import of the increase of population to economic and military development in Japan, the colonies, and the other areas of the East was not lessened particularly by the fact that the rate of increase might have been higher.

Table 16

The population of Japan and the former Empire, 1920-1940

Area	*1920*	*1925*	*1930*	*1935*	*1940*[d]
			POPULATION (IN '000)		
Total	77,729	84,279	91,421	98,934	105,226
Japan	55,963	59,737	64,450	69,254	73,114
46 prefectures	55,391	59,179	63,872	68,662	72,539
Okinawa	572	558	578	592	575
Outlying areas	21,766	24,542	26,971	29,680	32,112
Korea	17,264[a]	19,523	21,058	22,899	24,326
Taiwan	3,655	3,993	4,593	5,212	5,872
Karafuto	106	204	295	332	415
Kwantung[b]	688	766	956	1,134	1,367
Nanyo-gunto[c]	52	56	70	103	131

[a] A special survey, rather than a census, was taken in Korea in 1920.

[b] The Kwantung Leased Territory alone is included in this compilation, since the South Manchuria Railway Zone was attached to Manchoukuo in 1937.

[c] The South Sea Islands, received as a mandate from the League of Nations.

[d] The censuses of 1920-1935, inclusive, were *de facto* enumerations. In 1940 the enumeration of the general civilian population was *de facto*, but members of the armed services and persons attached thereto were allocated to the place of enumeration of the relatives who reported them in the census.

Source: Kojima, Reikichi. *Waga kuni saikin no fu ken oyobi toshi jinko, Showa jugo'nen kokusei chosa no kekka ni yoru.*

Analysis predicted on the assumption that the increase of 17 million people within Japan between 1920 and 1940 was a precise measure of population growth would ignore one of the essential characteristics of Japanese demographic development prior to 1945—its integral relation with territorial expansion. The Japan of 1920 differed greatly from the land that Perry's Black Ships had "opened" to the West in the middle of the nineteenth century. The island of Hokkaido had been occupied in a northward push that carried the Japanese up through the southern part of Saghalien Island. Hokkaido itself soon became a prefecture of Japan, while Karafuto long remained part of the Empire.[2] The early expansionism turned southward, too, the Ryukyu Islands being added to Japan as the prefecture of Okinawa, while Taiwan was added to the Empire. In the early twentieth century the drive for additional territories resulted in the acquisition of the Kwantung Leased Territory, the South Manchuria Railway Zone, and Korea. Strategic islands in Micronesia were secured after World War I as a mandate from the League of Nations and added to the Empire in fact, if not in legal right.

In 1920 Japan was the mother country of an empire of 77.7 million people. Almost 22 million lived in the colonial areas; of these, 17.3 million were in Korea and 3.7 million in Taiwan. By 1940 the Japanese boasted that the population of the Empire exceeded 100 million. Three-fifths of the twenty-year increase of 27.5 million had occurred in Japan, two-fifths of it in the colonies. In relative terms, however, the growth of the colonies surpassed that of Japan itself. The population of Korea increased two-fifths, that of Taiwan three-fifths. Increase was even more rapid in Karafuto, Kwantung, and Nanyo-gunto, for these were areas of heavy capital investment and substantial immigration. The net result of the varying rates of increase during the years from 1920 to 1940 was a phenomenon that largely canceled the delight of the Japanese in the total population of 100 million in 1940. The populations of the colonial areas were growing more rapidly than that of Japan.

The last years of the Empire witnessed the maximum expansion of the Japanese people, but in the view of the Japanese themselves the events of this period were movements toward the domination of the eastern littoral of Asia and the islands of the South Pacific. Collaboration was replacing conquest and annexation, however, and so Japanese responsibilities and Japanese migration were extended to areas outside the formal political relations of empire (Table 17).

In the first sixty years after the Restoration, the major movements outside Japan had been internal redistribution in a sense, for they were movements under the Japanese flag. As late as 1920, Japanese in the dependent areas were more numerous than Japanese in foreign countries. Migration outside the Empire increased sharply during the 1930's: by 1940 the 1.7 million civilian Japanese in the colonies were only slightly more numerous than the 1.6 million civilian Japanese abroad. Of these latter, however, 822 thousand were in Manchoukuo and 168 thousand in Occupied North China. International redistribution was minimal. The redistribution that was occurring was within the northeast Asian region and it was associated with Japanese expansion.

Whether the redistribution of the Japanese population within the northeast Asian region between 1920 and 1940 is judged to have been major or minor depends on the standard of comparison. The numbers involved were substantial if measured against other currents of migration in the 1920's and 1930's, but they were small if measured against the increase occurring within Japan or the size of the base population. Prewar Japan included 97.7 per cent of the world's Japanese in 1920, 95.6 per cent in 1940.[3]

[2] Karafuto became a prefecture of Japan in 1942. It is included with the colonies rather than the home country in Table 16.

[3] The out-movements of Japanese were compensated in part by an in-movement of colonials. Non-Japanese in Japan numbered 78 thousand in 1920, 478 thousand in 1930, and 1.3 million in 1940.

TABLE 17

The numbers of the ethnic Japanese, 1920-1940 (in '000)

Area	*1920*	*1930*	*1940*
The world	57,191	65,766	75,082
Japanese Empire[a]	56,611	65,149	73,500
Japan[b]	55,885	63,972	71,810
Outlying areas	726	1,177	1,690
Korea	377	527	708
Taiwan	164	228	312
Karafuto	103	284	395
Kwantung	79	118	198
Nanyo-gunto	3	20	77
Foreign countries[c]	580	617	1,582

[a] Excluding the South Manchuria Railway Zone.
[b] For comparability with the postwar definition of ethnic Japanese, a distinction should be made between Japanese and Ryukyuans, the latter presumably being those with *honseki* in Okinawa or some parts of Kagoshima. Prewar statistics do not permit this distinction.
[c] Including the South Manchuria Railway Zone, which had a Japanese population of 81 thousand in 1920 and 107 thousand in 1930.
Source: 1920: Nihon. Naikaku tokei-kyoku. *Taisho ku'nen kokusei chosa kijutsu hen.* Appendix. 1930: *Idem. Showa go'nen kokusei chosa saishu hokokusho.* 1940: *Idem. Census of 1940. Selected tables.* Also: Manshukoku. Kokumu-in. Somu-cho, rinji kokusei chosa jimu-kyoku. *Zai Manshukoku Nihonjin chosa kekka hyo. . . .* and: Nihon. Gaimu-sho chosa-kyoku. *Kaigai zairyu hompojin chosa kekka hyo Showa 15-nen.*

1940 TO 1955

When the census was taken on October 1, 1955, there were 89.3 million people in Japan. Fifteen years earlier, on October 1, 1940, there had been 72.5 million.[4] This increase of 16.8 million from 1940 to 1955 was almost as great as the increase that had occurred between 1920 and 1940.

Further perspective on the significance of population growth is given by a comparison of growth within the present area of Japan for the overlapping periods of 1920 to 1940 and 1935 to 1955. The earlier period was one of expansion and war-associated developments. The population grew from 55.4 million in 1920 to 72.5 million in 1940; the increase of 17 million amounted to 31 per cent of the population at the beginning of the period. The later period of twenty years, from 1935 to 1955, was one of war and defeat, exodus and repatriation, destruction and reconstruction. The population grew from 68.7 million in 1935 to 89.3 million in 1955; the increase of 21 million amounted to almost 30 per cent of the 1935 population.[5]

THE ECONOMIC TRANSFORMATION

The critical questions that must be asked about developments in modern Japan concern the relations among economic well-being, cultural advance, and population. If population is increasing more rapidly than the means available for its support, that pessimism which is labeled Malthusianism may have erred only in detail. The outlook for the long future in Japan—and, inferentially, in all the East—will be dark.

In Japan, the answer as to the relations between economic growth and population increase is clear. Whether the data be national product, capital formation, or the physical volume of production, economic growth has been more rapid than population increase.[6] Estimates of Japanese economists indicate that the average rate of growth in national income from 1878-1882 to 1938-1942 was approximately 4 per cent. During this period net savings amounted to about 16 per cent annually.[7]

Striking evidence of the greater dynamism of the economic as compared with the population factor lies in a comparison of population and production indices from 1935 to the present (FIGURE 2). If 1934-1936 is taken as the base period, the increase during the decade from 1935 to 1944 amounted to 7.9 for population, 78.8 for industrial production.[8] In mid-1946, population was 10.8 per cent above its prewar level, but industrial production was 69.3 per cent below its prewar level.

The economy was more dynamic than the population in recovery. In 1947, industrial activities as a whole were at 46.2 per cent of the 1934-1936 level; by 1955, the index of industrial activity had risen to 187.9. As compared with industrial production, population changes were relatively slight even when repatriation, declining death rates, and a baby boom combined to give Japan the most rapid rate increase in her history.

The indices of production for specific industries indicate the interrelations between economic and demographic factors in Japan. The general index of industrial production was 142 in 1938 and 179 in 1944. The index for mining reached a maximum of 147 in 1943; for chemical manufacturing, a maximum of 165 in 1939. The index for the production of machinery reached 463 in 1944. The index for textile production dropped from 100 in 1934-1936 to 86 in 1940 and 21 in 1944; non-durable manufacturing as a whole dropped to 51 in the latter year. Many of the postwar increases in industrial production have also been related to international difficulties.

It would seem that simple definitions of population prob-

[4] Populations at the various census dates within the present boundaries of Japan are given in: Nihon. Sori-fu, tokei-kyoku. *Nihon tokei nenkan, 1954.* For the population in 1955, see: *Idem. Zenkoku to do fu ken gun shi ku cho son betsu shotai oyobi jinko gaisu. Showa 30-nen 10-gatsu ichijitsu genzai.*

[5] The comparisons are for the 46 prefectures of Japan, excluding Okinawa, which is now under United States administration as the Ryukyu Islands. The Amami Islands were returned to Japan in December of 1953 and were included in the 1955 census. In the prewar years and at present they are a part of Kagoshima Prefecture.

[6] This conclusion is substantiated in several studies presented to a Conference on Economic Growth in Selected Countries, sponsored by the Social Science Research Council on April 25-27, 1952. On economic development in general: Lockwood, William W. *The state and economic enterprise in modern Japan, 1868-1938.* On capital formation: Reubens, Edwin P. *Absorption of foreign capital in Japan's economic development: The middle stages (1896-1913).* On national income: Oshima, Harry T. *Survey of various long-term estimates of Japanese national income.* See also: Kuznets, Simon, *et al. Economic growth: Brazil, India, Japan.*

[7] Yamada, Yuzo, "The income growth and the rate of saving in Japan." *The Annals of the Hitotsubashi Academy,* 4(2):79-97. April 1954. Other estimates of Professor Yamada indicate that for the years from 1920 to 1940 the average annual per cent increase was 6.2 for gross product, 5.9 for net product, and 6.9 for producers goods consumed. There was a substantial increase in net product per worker throughout major segments of the economy. In agriculture, the number of workers decreased while net product increased. In mining and manufacturing, there were increasing numbers of workers and increasing net products per worker. *Idem.* "The national income and industrial structure in Japan." *Ibid.,* 1(1):27, 30. October 1950.

[8] The index numbers are described in: Nihon. Keizai antei hombu. "Index numbers of industrial production." *Japanese Economic Statistics,* Annex 1. May 1952. The indices from 1937 through 1955 are given in *Japanese Economic Statistics,* Bulletin No. 118, Section 1, "Industrial Production." June 1956.

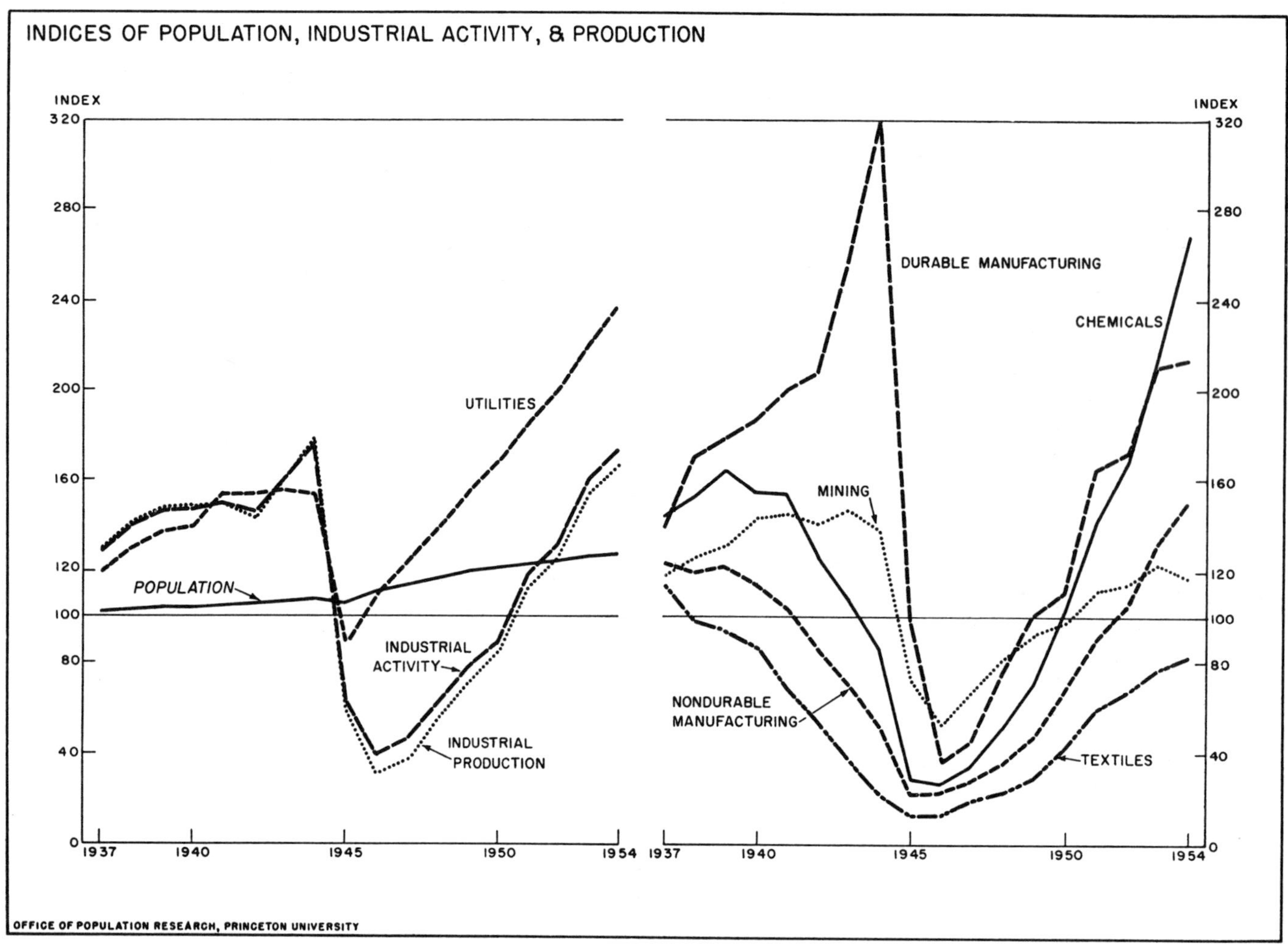

Figure 2. Annual indices of population, industrial activity, and production, 1937-1954
(Composite indices weighted by value added in base period)
Source: Nihon. Keizai antei hombu. *Japanese Economic Statistics*, Section 1, No. 106, pp. 6-7. June 1955.

lems either in terms of increases in the number of people or in terms of changes in industrial activity have little validity for the Japan of the last three decades. They do if attention is concentrated on short-run fluctuations, but in the long run the interrelations are important and complex. In the decades from 1920 to 1950, population increase was a force pushing continually upward. Growth seemed to proceed with a momentum of its own, annual changes being relatively immune to changes in resources available to the economy or levels of industrial production. Population growth was a dependent variable in the sense that it was a product of the manifold transformations that had occurred in the preceding periods. But, in another sense, the increasing population was a propulsion to change in all segments of the economy.

INDUSTRIAL STRUCTURE AND THE RESOURCES BASE

In twentieth-century Japan, ancient and modern organizations of production and distribution were related in a complex and ever-changing national pattern.[9] Along with the small shops and the establishments of medium size, there were great factories with modern equipment. These establishments did not co-exist as separate elements in a tripartite economy, for there was interpenetration in production, organization, and distribution. In some of the small household industries, production was solely for the local market; the differentiation of owner, laborer, and distributor was scarcely greater than it had been in legendary days. In others, the operations were performed in small shops but finance, allocation, and distribution were organized by commercial capitalists much as they had been in the Tokugawa period. In still other cases, small establishments were segments of vertical combinations. Establishments of medium size might be independent or they might be units in a hierarchical organization that included the great establishments which were the apex of the industrial structure. The concentration of capital, ownership, and management was personified in the *zaibatsu* groups.

The persistence of hand labor in family factories or tiny shops was related both to the existence of a redundant and ever-increasing population and to the nature of the resources base that supported Japan's industrial development.[10] Coal and iron were seriously deficient for a nation that had no choice but to maintain an increasing population through an

[9] Allen, George C. "Japanese industry: Its organization and development to 1937." Pp. 477-624 in: Schumpeter, E. B., Editor. *The industrialization of Japan and Manchoukuo.* Kamii, Yoshio. "Industrial transformation in Japan, 1929-1936." *International Labour Review*, 40(4):516-533. October 1939. The persistence of this basic industrial structure is demonstrated in the postwar establishment censuses. See: Nihon. Sori-fu, tokei-kyoku. *Jigyosha tokei chosa kekka hokoku. Showa 26-nen.*

[10] Yamanaka, Tokutaro. "The nature of small industries: A survey of the economic interpretation in Japan." *The Annals of the Hitotsubashi Academy*, 4(1):2-14. October 1953.

industrializing economy.[11] However, trees and water were major resources.[12] The forests that covered over half the land area yielded timber and related products and controlled soil erosion. Rugged topography and heavy rainfall permitted hydro-electric developments. The generation of electric power was an essential basis for the rapid development of light industry, especially in chemicals and metals. By the late 1930's hydro-electric power provided four-fifths of the energy for military production and the civilian economy.[13] Japan had become not only the leading producer of electric power in the Far East but one of the major producers in the world. In 1937 she ranked fourth among the nations in installed capacity and per capita consumption, fifth in per capita output.[14]

The position of Japan in mineral resources was less favorable than that of the majority of the industrial powers of the West. Until the middle 1930's she was relatively self-sufficient in ordinary coal, but her known reserves would have lasted less than 250 years at the 1936 rate of consumption. Anthracite and coking coal were imported. By 1936 former exportable surpluses of copper had been replaced by substantial deficits. Domestic production of petroleum met only 10 per cent of the civilian requirements. Imports constituted 88 per cent of the iron ore, 35 per cent of the pig iron, 90 per cent of the lead, and 60 per cent of the zinc and tin. Only one-third of the salt was produced locally. All the aluminum ores and nickel were imported.

The question was often raised as to whether deficiencies in chemicals and minerals within Japan barred her from moving beyond the textile-type economy of the early decades of her economic modernization. However, changing technologies altered both the definition and the utilization of resources. Synthetic gasoline, synthetic nitrates, rayon, water power, and improved techniques of utilizing basic minerals mitigated Japan's weaknesses. Military conquests brought new chemical and mineral resources within the Empire and its affiliated areas.[15] The optimism of Japan was virtually unlimited as her planners surveyed the resources of the Asian region. An official five-year plan as of 1938 envisioned self-sufficiency by 1942 in iron and steel, coal, light metals, zinc, soda, sulphate of ammonia, pulp, rolling stock, motor cars, and shipping.

The growth of the area of political economic unity, the discoveries of new resources, and the development of more effective techniques of utilization were stimulated by and contributed to visions of a new era of economic development in the Western Pacific. The system of alliances envisioned in the plans for the Co-Prosperity Sphere would have completed the Cinderella-like transformation of Japan. The rubber and the oil of Indonesia, the coal of Hainan Island, and the other resources of southern and southeastern Asia, added to those of Manchoukuo and North China, would have provided the material basis for a great industrial power. This Asian variant of what we in the United States once referred to as "manifest destiny" was to be reversed by defeat, but defeat in war was not foreseen in the decades of territorial growth.

When defeat came and the Japanese faced the problems of maintaining a high rate of industrial development without ownership of the resources of the areas they had conquered, pessimism about the industrial future became widespread. By 1955, however, all segments of the economy except trade were far more developed than they had been in the prewar years. In relation to 1934-1936 as 100, the indices were 187 for industrial production, 127 for agricultural production, and 118 for levels of consumption. The index for population was 130. Real national income per capita was 13 per cent above the 1934-1936 level; it was equal to that of 1939, the highest prewar level.[16]

AGRICULTURE AND FOOD SUPPLY

As industrialization proceeded, the society retained much of its basis in and its orientation toward the peasantry. Japan's continuing preoccupation with her food supply was understandable, for cultivable land was limited and settlement was dense. The acquisition of empty lands was difficult. To the east was the Pacific Ocean; to the west was the densely settled mainland; to the north were the frozen areas; to the far south were islands believed to be fabulously rich, but these were pre-empted by Western powers. The culture emphasized stability, order, and veneration of the ancestors. Throughout the millennia, population had tended to increase along with the food supply and to suffer decimation when a natural catastrophe or the caprice of man interfered with regularity in production. So close was the identification of food and people that the characters for "population" utilized the symbol for "mouth." And food was tantamount to rice, for which other foods were supplements or unsatisfactory substitutes.

The increase in the production of rice paralleled or surpassed the growth of population from the late nineteenth century through the first two decades of the twentieth.[17] The cultivated acreage increased substantially in the late nineteenth century, while more intensive techniques, fertilization, and improved varieties of rice resulted in increases in yields per acre. Both the increases in cultivated acreage and in yields were time-limited, however, for only 16 per cent of Japan's land was cultivable, and attainable increases in yields per unit of area tended to become progressively smaller. Population, on the other hand, continued to increase.

The Japanese examined the slowing curves of rice production and the ascending curves of population growth and drew the obvious conclusion. There were difficulties ahead if the Japanese had to subsist on the yields from their own lands. The most desirable solution appeared to be the extension of the national territory. Taiwan, acquired in 1895, was to supplement Japan's rice deficits in addition to furnishing her with subtropical products such as sugar that could be grown only at high cost and in limited quantities in the southern parts of Japan itself. Transportation, internal order, medical services, irrigation works, plant breeding, and an elaborate system of agricultural extension transformed the basically Chinese economy of the island into a rural factory for the production of exportable agricultural surpluses. Between 1900 and 1938 the acreage planted in rice increased 92 per cent, the yield per acre 118 per cent, the production of rough rice

[11] SCAP. GHQ. *Japanese natural resources.* Section III, pp. 523-527.

[12] *Ibid.* Chapter 2, "Power and fuel resources." Chapter 7, "Increased forest production."

[13] Taking production in 1934-1936 as 100, the index for electricity reached 156 in 1943 and 151 in 1944, dropped to 95 in 1945, but reached 200 in 1952. *Japanese Economic Statistics,* Bulletin No. 87-88, Section 1, p. 8. November-December 1953.

[14] U.S. Office of Strategic Services. *Civil Affairs Handbook.* Section 6, "Natural resources."

[15] Schumpeter, E. B., "The chemical resources of the Japanese Empire and Manchoukuo," and "The mineral resources of the Japanese Empire and Manchoukuo." Chapters 10 and 11 in: Schumpeter, Editor. *The industrialization. . . .*

[16] An analysis of these trends in the postwar years is given in Part 1, "General survey," of the Economic Planning Board's *Economic Survey of Japan (1955-1956).*

[17] U.S. Office of Foreign Agricultural Relations. *Civil Affairs Handbook.* Section 7, "Agriculture." Also: Penrose, E. F., *Food supply and raw materials in Japan. . . .*

356 per cent. Exports to Japan averaged 194 million pounds per year from 1902/03 to 1906/07. In 1937/38 to 1941/42 such exports averaged 1.4 billion pounds.[18]

The story in Korea was similar to that in Taiwan. After it was added to the Empire in 1910, Korea's economy was developed as a section of the imperial economy. Irrigation was extended, varieties of rice were improved, and fertilizers were imported. The Koreans, too, were numerous, but local food deficits after the removal of rice were met by the importation of millet and sorghum from Manchoukuo, where Chinese migrant labor under Japanese economic guidance produced sizable surpluses of agricultural products.[19]

Thus an equation that related population increase to food production within Japan had become quite inadequate by the early decades of the twentieth century. The tradition of a direct relation between the increase of the food produced within Japan and the increase of the population persisted. The experience of the war years intensified the Japanese belief in the necessity of self-sufficiency in agricultural production. However, population growth had made it impossible to provide cultivable land for all the sons of the peasants; industrialization made it unnecessary to do so. The basic requirement for demographic survival had become the increase of industrial production and the expansion of international trade.

Mobility and Cultural Change

In twentieth-century Japan, homogeneity has been yielding to heterogeneity, stability to instability. In the preceding sections this change was presented as it related to the increase of the population and the development of the economy. Here it will be viewed in relation to the stability and instability of the society.

Japan is peculiarly fortunate in the absence of deep ethnic or cultural schisms. Although diverse people mingled in the Japanese islands in the prehistoric period, no substantial immigrations occurred in the millennium that preceded the Restoration of 1868. This absence of ethnic intrusions that would create cultural schisms did not mean uniformity throughout Japan. The differences between peoples were appreciable, whether in physical traits and physical variability, sub-cultural characteristics, or social classes. The *suiheisha*, the water-level people, continued to exist in their separate villages, but these people beyond the pale had always existed within Japan. On the whole, their lowly status was accepted by themselves and their neighbors, or found expression in what the larger society regarded as social disorganization and criminality. There was some evidence of a slow rise of the *suiheisha* groups, proceeding both through an advance in educational achievements and levels of living and through the greater mobility that was possible in cities. The individual or the family found it difficult to escape identification with the minority group of origin, however, for the *koseki* included information on social class and arranged marriages made "passing" difficult, if not impossible. In the postwar reforms the designation of class was eliminated from the *koseki*, but peculiarities in social reactions and ways of living still make it difficult to hide the fact of origin in the disadvantaged classes.

In the days of the Shogunate, migration to and from Japan had been barred by law. The removal of the barriers created no movement into Japan in the first half-century of the modern period. Physical and linguistic differences combined with lower levels of living to retard the settlement of Western peoples in Japan, while government policies and a resistant social structure limited the inflow from mainland Asia. The early growth of the Empire did little to break the physical isolation of Japan; in 1920 there were only 78 thousand non-Japanese in the entire country.[20] The Koreans among these intruders were concentrated in the mining areas of Hokkaido and Fukuoka and in the metropolitan areas of central Honshu; the aliens lived in relative social isolation in Tokyo, Yokohama, Kobe, and Nagasaki. Surrounding these geographically concentrated and culturally isolated groups were the masses of the Japanese, for whom a "foreigner" remained a novel sight.

Economic developments outside Japan and industrialization within eventually generated movements that lessened the ethnic and cultural homogeneity. As Koreans continued to move into the mining areas and the great cities, localized situations of rather acute conflict arose. However, immigration from the colonial or affiliated areas never offered any real threat to the persistence of Japanese physical types or the preservation of Japanese culture. As late as 1940, over 98 per cent of the people in Japan were ethnically Japanese.

Linguistic homogeneity developed along with ethnic stability in Japan's isolated population. Despite regional differences in pronunciation and usage, there were no real schisms based on language. Moreover, the difficulties of the written language insulated the people from easy intellectual contacts with the outer world. Japanese students, administrators, and businessmen who wished to learn from or work efficiently with the West were forced to acquire one or more of the languages of the West. Few Westerners spent the long time necessary to learn the intricate written language of Japan. Thus linguistic differences between Japan and the West placed a heavy handicap on the acquisition of the knowledge of the West by the Japanese at the same time that it insulated Japan from the direct penetration of Western literature and thought.[21]

Religion was an integrating rather than a divisive force. In 1950, there were 110 million adherents of religious organizations in this nation whose total population was only 83.2 million, for exclusive allegiance was not required. Of the 110 million "believers" in 1950, 57.3 per cent were Shintoists, 39.9 per cent Buddhists, 0.4 per cent Christians, and 2.4 per cent members of other organizations.[22] Shintoism and Buddhism co-existed with little friction.

The continuity of the social structure and the discipline of

[18] U.S. Office of Foreign Agricultural Relations. *Civil Affairs Handbook*. Section 7, "Agriculture."

[19] During the prewar decades the trends in the production and consumption of other foods were comparable to those of rice. In most instances, the increases in production proceeded more rapidly than the increase in population, with a consequent increase in per capita consumption. In recent years, there has been a substantial diversification in production and importation, with rice assuming a less significant role in the total national diet.

[20] Nihon. Naikaku tokei-kyoku. *Taisho ku'nen kokusei chosa hokoku*. IV.A.1. Table 25.

[21] The ethnic heterogeneity developing during recent decades has done little to lessen linguistic unity among the Japanese, for most of the immigrants have been Korean nationals who were subjected to the language of Japan both in Korea and in Japan. The insularity began to break down when events thrust the Japanese outside northeastern Asia. In the areas occupied during the war, English was a necessary lingua franca.

[22] Nihon. Sori-fu, tokei-kyoku. *Nihon tokei nenkan, 1951*. Table 225. In 1952 the number of believers was only 80.4 million, owing in large part to a decline in believers in Shintoism from 62.8 million in 1950 to 34.5 million in 1952. Between 1950 and 1952 foreign missionaries increased from 1,985 to 3,589; believers in foreign faiths declined from 429 to 420 thousand. See: *Ibid. 1953*. Table 244.

the people were the strongest of the forces preserving the old Japan within the new. However, industrialization and urbanization barred the preservation of a stable culture. Changes in migration and fertility indicate that stability was yielding to instability as early as the First World War. The education of women was a necessary aspect of modernization, but such education was inconsistent with a subservient role for women. Even a carefully nurtured state Shintoism could not prevent the material values of the industrial society from becoming pervasive forces, especially in the cities. Even during the 1930's the co-existence of peasant ideologies and industrial dynamism was a tribute to the efficiency of the police state.

The outward manifestations of change are implicit in the indices of economic development already cited. Increases in per capita income indicated changes in the conditions of living as well as in types of work. Savings provided the basis for expansion in the private economy and in government activities. These developments in turn meant employment opportunities in Japan or the Empire, eventually even in Manchoukuo or the farther regions of Asia. The upper personnel of banks and business enterprises learned to know the peoples and the cities of the world, West as well as East.

The forces of the changing society differed widely from region to region and from class to class, in part because of sub-cultural variations, in part because the resistances to change were so great. The economy was a fairly rigid structure whose tiny apex rested on a broad base of scarcely differentiated poor. The records of income tax collections reveal this clearly. In the middle of the interwar decades Japan levied an income tax on all persons with net incomes of 1,200 yen or more. In 1927 this was roughly equivalent to a gross income of from $925 to $950 for a family with two dependent children.[23] Even at this low level, only one in each 45 adults paid a personal income tax during the years 1928-1930. If, somewhat more realistically, all income tax payments are attributed to men, then only one in 25 paid a tax. From 3 to 4 per cent of the men in the industrial prefecture of Tokyo, Osaka, Kyoto, and Hyogo paid personal income taxes, but only 1 per cent of the men in the northeastern prefectures of Aomori and Iwate, and less than one-half of 1 per cent in Okinawa. Moreover, whether one considers the advanced urban or the backward rural area, the concentration of income was very great even within that small proportion of men who paid the taxes.

Despite the heavy concentration of wealth and income in the hands of a few, the habits of a monetary economy spread throughout the country. In Japan thrift was a major virtue. Most of that 97.8 per cent of the people whose personal incomes were too low to be taxable saved portions of those incomes and invested them in ways that contributed to capital formation. In 1929-1931, 82.5 per cent of all persons aged 15 and over had postal savings accounts.[24] The amounts were small, 71.4 yen on the average, but the significance of this fact of widespread savings outside land and the durable expenditures that accompany land ownership cannot be overstressed. The commercialization of values was in process among the toilers on the land as well as among the workers in the cities.[25]

Geographic mobility was a product and a factor of change. If one surveys Japanese road and railway statistics from the vantage point of the West, the 125 thousand kilometers of the national and regional network of roads and the 27 thousand kilometers of main-line railroads that existed in 1940 appear unimpressive for a nation half again as populous as England.[26] But if one walks along the paths between China's rice fields and looks eastward toward the Pacific, these facilities become symbols of the movement of the Japanese away from the life of the peasant East. The reduction of the symbol to some quantitative index of social mobility or social change is difficult, for trips of equal distance on a specified rail line may differ greatly in psychological significance. A crude index is furnished by the monthly average number of passengers carried on the railroads: 104,377 thousand in 1930, 136,186 thousand in 1936, 474,167 thousand in 1951.[27]

The railway is a means of movement for all classes of the population. In the cheapest of the facilities, farmers and peddlers carry small produce to market. Urban sons and daughters go home to visit or to assist in periods of rush work; schoolchildren come in groups to visit Tokyo, Nara, or other centers of Japanese life and culture. Village and town people come in contact with distant worlds as they see the trains go by. Metropolitan or interurban trains carry people from places of work in central cities or factory areas to suburban or even town and village residences at considerable distances. Urban people go to remote parks or other scenic areas for vacations.

It is the bus rather than the train that best symbolizes the mechanical basis for social change in the once stable villages of Japan. The train facilitated movement along the fixed path of the tracks and so left the people of the hill and mountain country isolated from the new society. The bus was utilized in more dispersed areas and for a wider range of services. It brought rural children to urban schools and permitted people to live in the country. It brought rural people into the city to work. It spread knowledge of the ways of the urban areas into the most remote parts of the country. Here also figures on passengers carried may be used as a crude index of mobility. In 1952 the buses of Japan National Railway carried 105.1 million passengers, private buses carried 1.9 billion, and cars for hire carried another 376 million.[28]

[23] Nihon. Okura-sho. *The financial and economic annual of Japan, 1927*. P. 28. Data on the number of persons paying income tax and the amount of tax paid were published in the section on taxation in: Nihon. Naikaku tokei-kyoku. *Nihon teikoku tokei nenkan*.

[24] The data used here refer to persons with deposits at the end of the year. Prefectural compilations of number of persons with deposits and average size of deposits were published annually in *Nihon teikoku tokei nenkan*.

[25] The proportion of the population with deposits and the average size of deposits were larger in the relatively prosperous southwest than in the more backward northeast, larger in the urban than in the rural areas. There was one curious exception, however. Persons with postal savings exceeded the total number of persons aged 15 and over in several prefectures—and these were areas of heavy out-movements in which the emigrants might be expected to send back their savings to their home areas. This was the emigrant remittance pattern functioning internally, generally, in the situation in which the area of destination was urban, the area of origin rural.

[26] In 1951 there were 137,099 kilometers of roads 4.5 meters or more in width, 9,296 kilometers being national roads and 127,804 kilometers prefectural roads. In 1947 there were also 85,312 kilometers of city roads, of which 36,584 kilometers were passable by motor vehicle, and 654,428 kilometers of town and village roads, of which 134,999 kilometers were passable by motor vehicle. Nihon. Sori-fu, tokei-kyoku. *Nihon tokei nenkan, 1953*. Pp. 208-209. Railway statistics from: Nihon. Un'yu-sho. *Un'yu geppo*, 4(9):15. February 1953. The road and railroad statistics of the Ministry of Transportation differ somewhat from those published by the Bureau of Statistics.

[27] Nihon. Un'yu-sho. *Un'yu geppo*, 4(9):18. February 1953.

[28] Nihon. Sori-fu, tokei-kyoku. *Nihon tokei nenkan, 1953*. Pp. 216-217. In addition, private tramways carried 3.0 billion passengers in the course of 1952.

Communication by telephone, letter, newspaper, and radio is a more direct indicator of cultural change than physical mobility. The modern media of communication are widely available and frequently used in Japan. Letters and newspapers are commonplaces of life for millions of people. The cultural identification of rural people with the ways of living and thinking that characterize the cities received a tremendous stimulation through the radio. And here, in the ratio of radio subscribers to households, is the most startling single index of the modernization of Japan. The number of radio subscribers per 100 households increased from 18 in 1935 to 39 in 1940 and 50 in 1944.[29] There was a sharp drop in 1945 and 1946, but radios and radio subscriptions were apparently high on the priority lists for expenditures after the war. In 1950 there were 55 radio subscriptions per 100 households; in 1952, there were 64. The introduction of television is being met with the same enthusiasm that greeted radio.

The numerical indicators of cultural change have been cited for all Japan in order to indicate the movement of the nation as a whole toward those ways of life that are characteristically modern. Within the country, it was the upper social-economic groups and the urban dwellers who first enjoyed the new means of physical movement and cultural contact. The means of contact themselves facilitated the diffusion of the new and essentially urban customs and values into lower social-economic classes and over broader geographic areas. Always, however, the differences in productivity and income among segments of the economy and regions of the country retarded the cultural equalization theoretically made possible by modern transportation and media of communication.

In the relatively stable Japan of 1925-1935, per capita productivity was not only higher but increasing more rapidly in the more industrialized prefectures.[30] The villagers, always a disadvantaged class, were becoming more so. The proportion of men paying a personal income tax was lowest in the isolated agricultural prefectures of the far southwest and the far northeast, highest in the metropolitan prefectures that included the cities of Tokyo and Osaka. Communication by telephone, wire, or letter reflected cultural levels, income available, and previous contacts. In letters received, for instance, there was a direct relationship with urbanization, industrialization, and high per capita incomes, an inverse relation with rurality, agriculture, and poverty. Despite these differences at any given time, however, the adoption of new media was so rapid that the retardation of backward areas represented cultural lags, often of brief duration. In 1952, for instance, the proportion of households with radio subscriptions exceeded 80 per 100 in the metropolitan prefectures, but sank to only 35 or 40 per 100 in some of the prefectures of southern Kyushu.

Education

The development of the educational system has already been noted as one of the dynamic elements underlying the population changes of the Restoration period. By the second quarter of the twentieth century the Japanese were one of the most literate peoples in the world.[31] Among persons 25 years of age or older in 1950, 93.5 per cent of the men and 84.1 per cent of the women had completed four years of schooling.[32] These percentages may seem low in the light of the previous statement concerning the high degree of literacy in the Japanese population, but it must be remembered that the population 25 years of age and over in 1950 included large numbers of older people whose educational attainments were far below those of the generations that completed formal education in the late prewar and war years.

The education that became so widespread in Japan was that of the six-year elementary school; losses at the successive steps on the educational ladder were quite severe. This becomes apparent if we consider the percentages of the population who had completed specified grade levels of formal education as a cohort passing through the educational system.[33] In this hypothetical cohort, only 78.5 per cent of the boys and 65.3 per cent of the girls completing five or six years of school completed seven or eight years. And of those who completed seven or eight years, only 43.4 per cent of the boys and 44.1 per cent of the girls completed the ninth year of school. The loss of students at successive educational levels was greater for girls than for boys, and it was greater in the *gun* than in the *shi*. The most educated people in the Japanese population were the urban men, while the least educated were the rural women. In the population of 1950, 8.5 per cent of all urban men aged 25 or over had completed the years of schooling usually regarded as equivalent to graduation from a university. The comparable percentage for rural women was 0.1.

In prewar Japan formal education was designed to maintain social stability rather than to stimulate social change. The subjects in the curriculum of the elementary schools included morals, language, arithmetic, national history, geography, science, drawing, singing, sewing, and gymnastics. Two hours per week were devoted to morals, while roughly half the total time in the first three grades and one-third in the last three were devoted to language. Textbooks were issued by the Department of Education, and the use of the approved books was compulsory. When this control of the content of education through uniform curricula and texts proved insufficient to regulate the thought of the students, a Bureau of Student Control was created. When "improper" thoughts spread throughout the universities, the name of this bureau was changed to the Bureau of Thought Control.

The indoctrination of "the teaching bequeathed by Our Imperial Ancestors, to be observed alike by Their Descendants and subjects, infallible for all ages and true in all places" was a simple procedure in the decades when peasants were led forward by a benevolent oligarchy. With advancing technologies, the impersonal milieu of cities, and the extension of

[29] *Ibid.* P. 227.

[30] Tachi, Minoru. "Chiikiteki ni mitaru waga kuni seisanryoku no hatten to jinko no suseki." *J.m.k.*, 5(2):15-44. February 1946. Also: Jinko mondai kenkyu-kai. *Hompo jinko zoka no keiko oyobi suryoteki hendo ni tsuite.*

[31] By the 1930's over 99.5 per cent of all children of school age were reported as being in school. Since school age covered eight years (age 6 through 13) and elementary school was six years, this would seem to indicate either substantial retardation or a large proportion of continuation beyond elementary school. The footnotes say, however, that "children attending school" include "those who were of school age and were attending ordinary elementary schools, and also those who had completed the course of such schools but were still under fourteen years of age." See the section on education in *Nihon teikoku tokei nenkan.* A description of the organization of the education in the late prewar years is given in: Nihon. Mombu-sho. *A general survey of education in Japan, 1932.* A description and evaluation of the postwar reorganization is presented in: Japanese Education Reform Council. *Education reform in Japan. The present status and the problems involved, 1950.*

[32] Nihon. Sori-fu, tokei-kyoku. *Showa 25-nen kokusei chosa hokoku.* Vol. III, Part 1, Table 12.

[33] *Ibid.*, Table 11.

education, the shackled mind became a more difficult achievement of government. Industrial development required education—but education risked a social transformation that denied the values economy and education were designed to serve.

The rigid control of the educational process and the fiscal limitations to its extension retarded Japanese intellectual development in its upper reaches and slowed social transformations among the masses. It is difficult to escape the conclusion that the police state which limited critical analysis barred the development of both the intellectual leadership adequate to the prevention of war and the technologies essential to winning it. Again the paradox: the oligarchy that desired the education of the people in the service of national economic and political advancement feared the social consequences of education. Hence the numbers of the educated were not sufficient to meet the needs of the nation for a skilled and adaptable labor force and army. In the 1930's the extension of the upper middle school and the proliferation of technical training schools were relating education more directly to the requirements of the war situation, but emphasis was still placed on subservience.

The creation of an educational system similar to that of the United States was one of the major goals of the Allied Powers during the years of the occupation of the country. The difficulties in the implementation of such a program were substantial; evaluation of achievements would be premature. Perhaps the most significant development in recent years lies in the great increase in school attendance beyond the elementary level rather than in the specific organizational form of the school system itself. In 1950 about three-fifths of youth aged from 13 to 18 were attending school (TABLE 18). This movement of the modal educational level upward into the high school ages was occurring in all the regional and social-economic areas of the country.

Education at the college level has remained concentrated in the urban and industrial areas, although this predominance of school attendance in the resident population reflects in part the local residence of college students. The higher education of Japanese women lags behind that of men, but the increasing proportions of high school graduates among girls will be reflected in increasing college attendance in the future.

Analysis of school attendance yields clues as to the direction of social and demographic changes in the future. Analysis of educational levels portrays the population of the present and gives an objective, if somewhat indirect, measure of the changes that have occurred in the past. In the Japan of 1950, the proportion of adults who had completed less than the six years of compulsory schooling may be taken as an index of cultural backwardness. Conversely, the proportion of adults who had completed thirteen years or more of schooling may be taken as an index of cultural advance. If we use these indices and arrange the prefectures according to the proportions of the gainfully occupied in agriculture and forestry, we find a close relationship between dependence on agriculture and cultural backwardness, between dependence on industries other than agriculture and cultural advance (TABLE 19). These relationships existed for both men and women, but in all types of prefectures the educational achievements of the men were greater than those of the women. In fact, the educational levels of men in the agricultural prefectures were superior to those of the women in the metropolitan prefectures of Tokyo and Osaka. Industrial occupations, higher incomes, and better education were components of the way of living in the great cities. Agricultural and handicraft activities, low incomes, and limited education were interrelated components of the way of life in the villages.

THE DEMOGRAPHIC TRANSFORMATION

DENSITY

In no other country are the relations among numbers of people, rates of population increase, resources, and culture more apparent than in Japan. The land was densely settled in 1920, when there were 378 people per square mile of total

TABLE 18

School attendance among youth aged from 6 to 24, by sex, prefectures by industrial type, 1950
(Per cent of age group attending school)

AGE	JAPAN	PREFECTURES BY INDUSTRIAL TYPE[a]					HOKKAIDO
		Metropolitan	*Industrial*	*Intermediate industrial*	*Intermediate agricultural*	*Agricultural*	
Total, 6-24	56.0	54.2	55.3	55.6	57.4	56.5	55.0
6-12	89.1	87.5	88.8	88.8	89.6	89.4	89.7
13-18	59.5	59.4	59.8	60.5	61.8	58.5	56.4
19-24	5.9	13.4	7.3	4.3	5.3	4.4	3.4
Male, 6-24	57.7	57.2	57.2	57.0	58.3	58.2	56.6
6-12	89.2	87.5	88.8	88.8	89.7	89.5	90.1
13-18	61.5	61.7	62.6	62.0	62.9	60.6	59.3
19-24	8.5	20.8	10.3	5.7	5.1	6.3	4.8
Female, 6-24	54.3	51.1	53.5	54.3	56.5	54.9	53.4
6-12	89.0	87.4	88.7	88.8	89.6	89.4	89.2
13-18	57.5	57.0	57.1	59.0	60.6	56.4	53.5
19-24	3.4	5.4	4.4	2.9	5.4	2.6	2.0

[a] Prefectures classified by proportion of the gainfully occupied population in agriculture and forestry, 1930. Metropolitan, below 20 per cent; industrial, 20-39 per cent; intermediate industrial, 40-49 per cent; intermediate agricultural, 50-59 per cent; agricultural, 60 per cent or over.

Source: Nihon. Sori-fu, tokei-kyoku. *Showa 25-nen kokusei chosa hokoku.* Vol. III, Part 1, Table 9.

TABLE 19

Years of school completed by persons aged 25 and over, by sex, prefectures by industrial type, 1950
(Per cent of population aged 25 and over completing specified levels)

Years of school completed	JAPAN	PREFECTURES BY INDUSTRIAL TYPE					HOKKAIDO
		Metropolitan	*Industrial*	*Intermediate industrial*	*Intermediate agricultural*	*Agricultural*	
Total							
6 or less	42.9	33.3	38.8	41.3	44.2	47.1	49.5
7-12	51.4	56.2	54.6	53.7	51.1	48.4	46.5
13 or over	5.7	10.5	6.7	5.0	4.7	4.4	4.1
Male							
6 or less	33.2	25.8	30.2	33.1	34.7	35.5	39.8
7-12	56.8	56.6	58.1	57.9	56.9	56.3	53.0
13 or over	10.0	17.5	11.6	9.1	8.3	8.1	7.2
Female							
6 or less	51.6	40.3	46.5	48.5	52.5	57.2	59.1
7-12	46.6	55.7	51.2	49.9	46.0	41.5	40.0
13 or over	1.8	3.9	2.1	1.4	1.4	1.2	0.9

Source: Nihon. Sori-fu, tokei-kyoku. *Showa 25-nen kokusei chosa hokoku.* Vol. III, Part 1, Table 12.

land area. In 1940 there were almost 400 persons per square mile; in 1955 there were more than 600. Areas where the density of settlement is greater than five or six hundred per square mile of land may be cited: Java, the lower Ganges, the valley of the Nile. However, less than one-sixth of the Japanese land is cultivable. If we compute density by relating population to arable land, the figure is closer to economic realities. In 1920, in a land still predominantly peasant, there were 2,800 persons per square mile of cultivable land. In 1935 there were 3,500; in 1955 there were more than 4,500.

Agricultural and industrial people alike are concentrated in the areas best suited to intensive cultivation. In Japan today, as in Tokugawa and even earlier days, there is a broad pattern of crowded lowlands and sparsely settled uplands. The detailed pattern is intricate. It reflects variations in climate and topography, ancient differences in material culture and social institutions, and the new penetrations of urban and rural settlements. Density is greatest in the industrial regions that include the great cities: Tokyo and Yokohama, Nagoya, and Osaka, Kobe, and Kyoto.[34] It shades off from these areas of concentration toward the peripheries, the gradient of decline being sharpest toward the north and east. Low density still exists in northern Hokkaido and in the mountain regions of the other islands.

REDISTRIBUTION

Continuity in the general outlines of population distribution has been accompanied by a concentration of increasing proportions of the people within the areas already densely settled (MAP 5). The redistribution of population was related to the requirements of the industrializing society. From 1920 through 1935 the populations of the prefectures of Tokyo, Kanagawa, Aichi, Osaka, Kyoto, and Hyogo increased more rapidly than the populations of the less industrialized prefectures (TABLE 20). As war preparations advanced and war began in China, redistribution became more rapid. So great was the movement of people to the industrial areas that fourteen prefectures declined in total population between 1935 and 1940. The depopulation of the countryside became a reality, when only a decade earlier the pressure of people on the land had appeared to be a major political and economic problem.

In the last year of the war and the early years of reconstruction the historic pattern of urban growth was reversed. These processes of exodus and those of return will be traced in some detail in later chapters. The net consequence of the movements of the decade from 1940 to 1950 was a pattern of changes in prefectural populations that was related inversely to the extent of urban development and industrial employment. Hokkaido's population increased by almost one-third in this ten-year period, while that of Shikoku increased more than one-fourth. Within Honshu rates of increase were high in the prefectures of the northeast and in those of the mountainous central section of the island—and in those adjacent to or within easy reach of the great metropolitan centers. The populations of Tokyo and Osaka prefectures were below the levels of 1940. The major factor was the impact of the war and postwar developments on job opportunities rather than the extent of the direct damage during the war, for the populations of Hiroshima and Nagasaki prefectures in 1950 were substantially above the populations of these same prefectures in 1940.

The rate of population increase for all Japan did not change greatly in the three decades from 1920 to 1950. For the present area of Japan, the percentage increase was 15.3 from 1920 to 1930, 13.6 from 1930 to 1940, and 14.7 from 1940 to 1950. From 1920 to 1930 and from 1930 to 1940, however, the increasing population was redistributed in accordance with a distribution of economic opportunities regarded as desirable and progressive by the majority of the people. There was movement from rural to urban areas, from agricultural to non-agricultural occupations, from areas of lower to areas of higher average income. From 1940 to 1950

[34] An analysis of the concentration of population along the Pacific littoral of Honshu and the inland passage in Shikoku and Kyushu was presented by Lawrence A. Hoffman. "Japan: Main population concentrations." *Journal of Geography*, 46(2):62-69. February 1947.

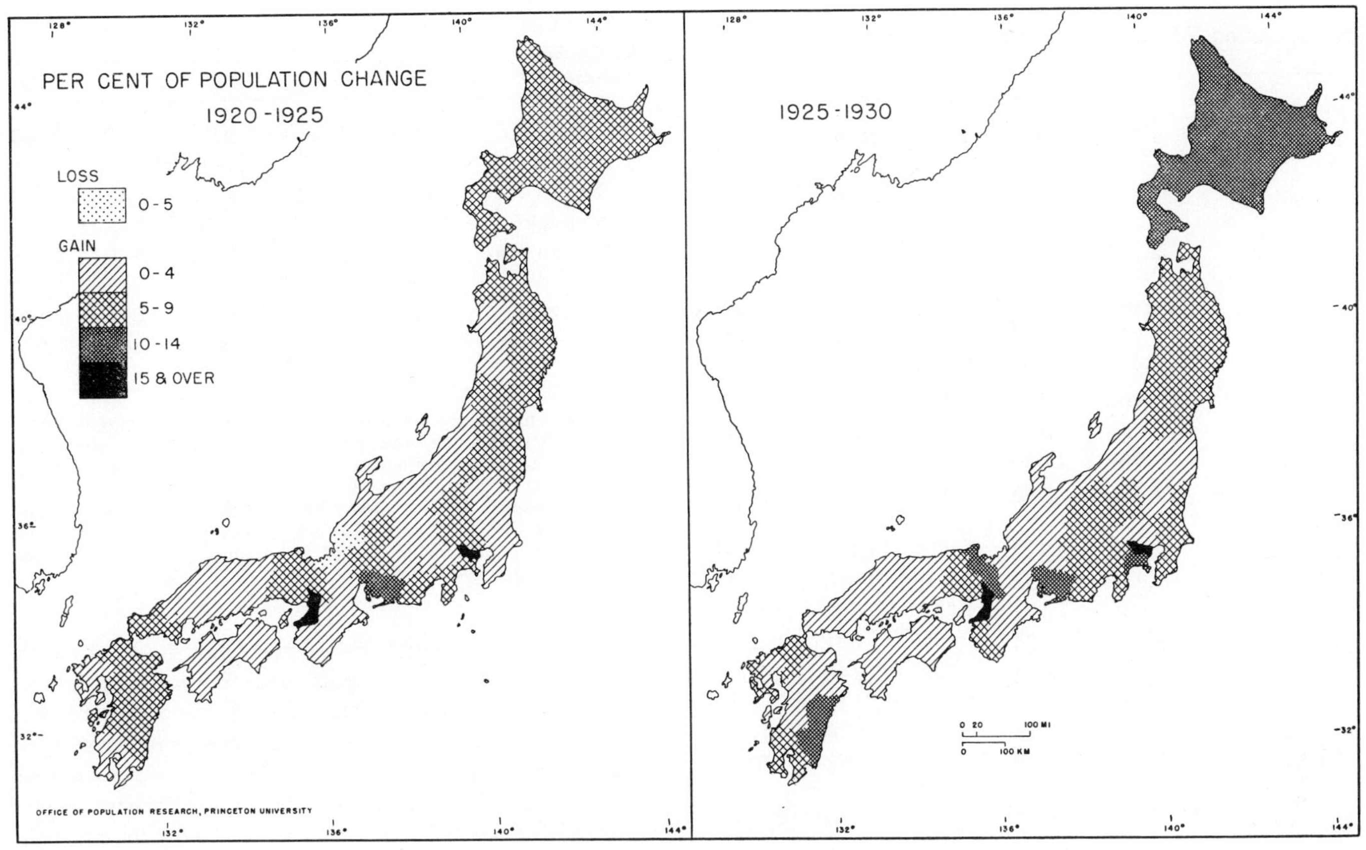

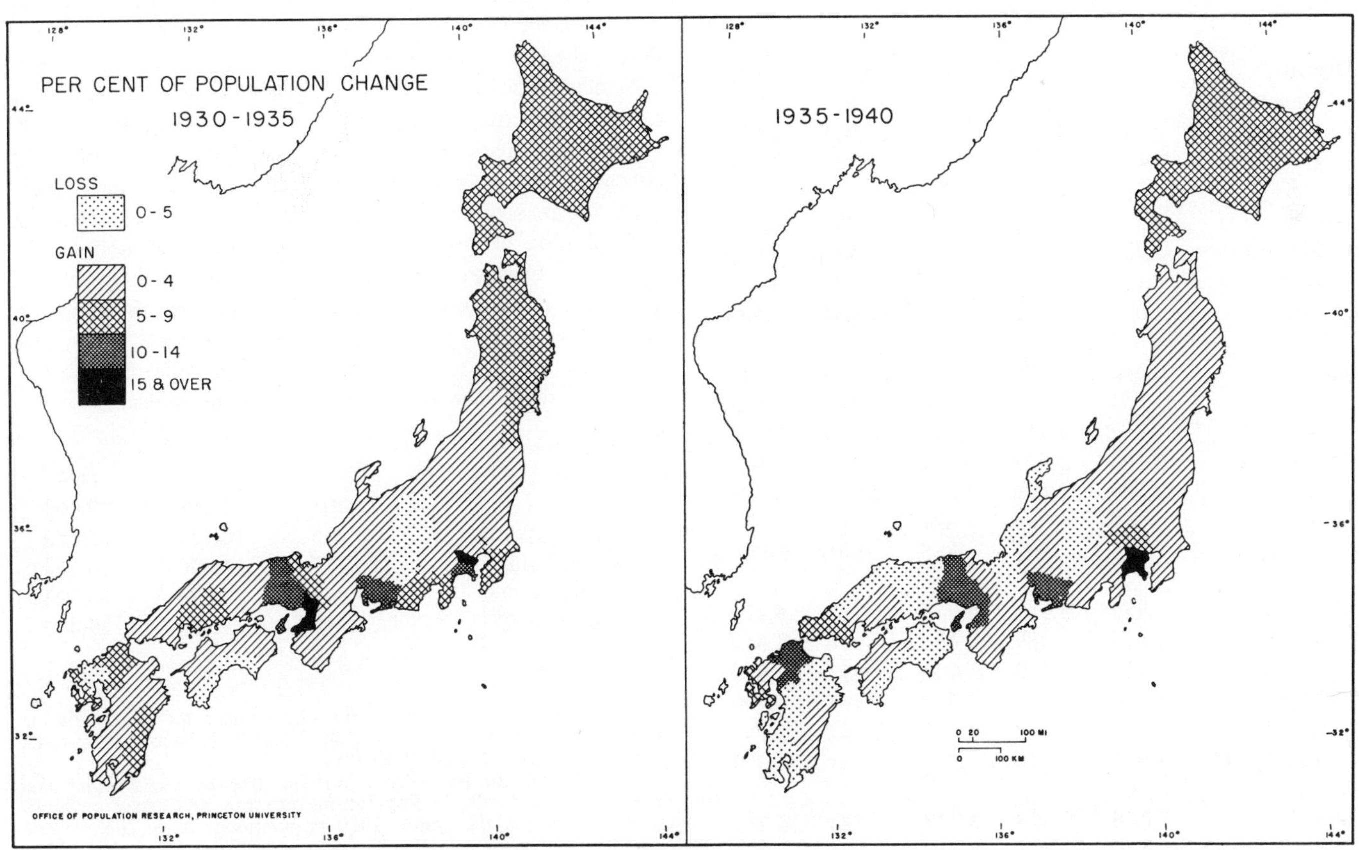

Map. 5. Population change in the prefectures in intercensal periods, 1920-1940
Source: Nihon. Sori-fu, tokei-kyoku. *Showa 25-nen kokusei chosa hokoku.* Vol. VIII, Table 3.

TABLE 20

The populations of the regions and the prefectures, 1920-1955

Region and prefecture	POPULATION (IN '000)				
	1920	*1930*	*1940*	*1950*[a]	*1955*
All Japan	55,391	63,872	72,540	83,200	89,269
Hokkaido	2,359	2,812	3,273	4,296	4,773
Tohoku	5,794	6,574	7,165	9,022	9,334
Aomori	756	880	1,001	1,283	1,382
Iwate	846	976	1,096	1,347	1,427
Miyagi	962	1,143	1,271	1,663	1,727
Akita	899	988	1,052	1,309	1,347
Yamagata	969	1,080	1,119	1,357	1,354
Fukushima	1,363	1,508	1,626	2,062	2,095
Kanto	11,128	13,772	16,866	18,242	20,645
Ibaraki	1,350	1,487	1,620	2,039	2,064
Tochigi	1,046	1,142	1,207	1,550	1,548
Gumma	1,053	1,186	1,299	1,601	1,614
Saitama	1,320	1,459	1,608	2,146	2,262
Chiba	1,336	1,470	1,588	2,139	2,205
Tokyo	3,699	5,409	7,355	6,278	8,034
Kanagawa	1,323	1,620	2,189	2,488	2,919
Hokuriku	3,847	4,087	4,289	5,179	5,215
Niigata	1,776	1,933	2,064	2,461	2,473
Toyama	724	779	823	1,009	1,021
Ishikawa	747	757	758	957	966
Fukui	599	618	644	752	754
Tosan	3,217	3,527	3,639	4,417	4,412
Yamanashi	583	631	663	811	807
Nagano	1,563	1,717	1,711	2,061	2,021
Gifu	1,070	1,178	1,265	1,545	1,584
Tokai	4,709	5,523	6,383	7,323	7,905
Shizuoka	1,550	1,798	2,018	2,471	2,650
Aichi	2,090	2,567	3,167	3,391	3,769
Mie	1,069	1,157	1,199	1,461	1,486
Kinki	8,143	9,858	11,933	11,607	12,811
Shiga	651	692	704	861	854
Kyoto	1,287	1,553	1,730	1,833	1,935
Osaka	2,588	3,540	4,793	3,857	4,618
Hyogo	2,302	2,646	3,221	3,310	3,621
Nara	565	596	621	764	777
Wakayama	750	831	865	982	1,007
Chugoku	4,970	5,341	5,718	6,797	6,992
Tottori	455	489	484	600	614
Shimane	714	740	741	913	929
Okayama	1,218	1,284	1,329	1,661	1,690
Hiroshima	1,542	1,692	1,870	2,082	2,149
Yamaguchi	1,041	1,136	1,294	1,541	1,610
Shikoku	3,066	3,310	3,337	4,220	4,245
Tokushima	670	717	719	879	878
Kagawa	678	733	730	946	944
Ehime	1,047	1,142	1,179	1,522	1,541
Kochi	671	718	709	874	882
Kyushu	8,159	9,069	9,937	12,097[a]	12,937
Fukuoka	2,188	2,527	3,094	3,530	3,860
Saga	674	692	702	945	974
Nagasaki	1,136	1,233	1,370	1,645	1,748
Kumamoto	1,233	1,354	1,368	1,828	1,896
Oita	860	946	973	1,253	1,277
Miyazaki	651	760	840	1,091	1,139
Kagoshima	1,416	1,557	1,589	1,804[a]	2,044

[a] The Amami Islands were returned to Japan in December 1953. Including these islands, the population of Japan in 1950 was 83,413 thousand. The population of Kyushu was 12,310 thousand, the population of Kagoshima prefecture 2,018 thousand.

Source: Nihon. Sori-fu, tokei-kyoku. *Showa 25-nen kokusei chosa hokoku*. Vol. I, Table 7. *Idem. Zenkoku to do fu ken gun shi ku cho son betsu shotai oyobi jinko gaisu. Showa 30-nen 10-gatsu ichijitsu genzai*. Table 2.

there was also a redistribution of population in accord with a distribution of economic opportunities, but for many of the Japanese the opportunities sought during this decade of war and reconstruction were a matter of subsistence rather than of a way of living regarded as desirable. Population increase was greatest in agricultural areas of generally low income. Population declined in the urban regions that were the symbols of economic and cultural advance. If the period from 1920 to 1950 is surveyed as a whole, regional variations in population increase seem to have little relation to the locus of social and economic opportunities as these existed prior to and even during the war of 1937-1945.[35]

Generalizations based on comparisons of populations at census dates from 1920 to 1950 are striking, but simple interpretations are difficult. The data of the census of 1940 concern a period prior to full mobilization for major war. They are reasonably accurate as a picture of the continuing redistribution of people in an industrializing economy. The data of the census of 1950 concern a period of reorganization in economy and social structure. If we compare the changing distribution of the population in the years 1947, 1950, and 1955, we see that the trend toward urban concentration has been restored.[36] The populations are in thousands:

Prefectures by industrial type	*1947*	*1950*	*1955*
All Japan	78,101	83,199	89,269
Metropolitan	8,335	10,135	12,652
Other industrial	13,316	14,550	16,104
Intermediate	24,904	25,698	26,294
Agricultural	27,694	28,520	29,447
Hokkaido	3,853	4,295	4,773

[35] The correlations between the decennial rates of population change in the prefectures were +.86 for 1920-1930 and 1930-1940, —.68 for 1930-1940 and 1940-1950.

[36] 1947 populations: Nihon. Sori-fu, tokei-kyoku. *Nihon tokei nenkan, 1950*. Table 5. Populations are not adjusted for minor island changes in the south. 1950 populations: *Idem. To, do, fu, ken jinko no suikei. Showa 27-nen oyobi 26-nen 10-gatsu ichijitsu genzai*. Table 12. 1955 populations: Reference, Table 20. In the computations of changes from 1950 to 1955, the 213 thousand population of the Amami Islands in December 1950 was added to the total population of Japan and to the population of the agricultural prefectures.

The increases in the two periods reveal a movement from agricultural to industrial areas similar to that of the prewar years. Average annual per cent changes were as follows:

Prefectures by industrial type	*1947-1950*	*1950-1955*
All Japan	2.2	1.4
Metropolitan	7.2	5.0
Other industrial	3.1	2.1
Intermediate	1.1	0.5
Agricultural	1.0	0.5
Hokkaido	4.9	2.2

In the years from 1947 to 1950 the population of the metropolitan prefectures increased at more than three times the national rate, while the agricultural prefectures increased at less than half the national rate. Hokkaido's population increased rapidly, for here there was a substantial repatriation from Karafuto and Manchoukuo in addition to national and prefectural government policies to develop this northern island.

Population trends from 1950 to 1955 were similar to those from 1947 to 1950. The metropolitan prefectures increased at a somewhat less rapid rate than they had from 1947 to 1950, as did the other industrial prefectures. The significant fact, however, is that the average annual increase for the agricultural and the intermediate prefectures was less than one-half of 1 per cent. Five prefectures had smaller populations in 1955 than they had had in 1950. Hokkaido's relative increase was less than half what it had been in the years from 1947 to 1950. The Japanese were again moving in the direction of the six great cities and the seven industrial prefectures.

URBANIZATION

The urbanization of the population of Japan is a rough measure of the impact of industrialization and social change on a people whose cultural origins and personal ties were agrarian. By 1920, Japan had moved far beyond the backwardness of the period of the Tokugawa shogunate, but the country remained essentially rural. More than four-fifths of the people lived outside the *shi*; more than two-thirds lived in communes with populations below 10 thousand.[37] Between 1920 and 1940 there was rapid increase in the number of *shi* and in the proportion of the total population resident in them. The people in the *shi* numbered 10.0 million in 1920, 15.4 million in 1930, and 27.5 million in 1940. These urban dwellers constituted 18.1 per cent of Japan's population in 1920, 24.1 per cent in 1930, and 37.9 per cent in 1940.

The increase of population in *shi* understates the urbanization of Japan, for the *shi* included few of the smaller cities and towns whose populations numbered less than 30 thousand.[38] The distribution of the population by size of commune in the decennial censuses of 1920 to 1940 was as follows, numbers being in thousands:[39]

Size of commune	*1920*	*1930*	*1940*
All Japan	55,391	63,872	72,540
1,000,000 and over	3,426	4,524	12,449
100,000-999,999	3,327	6,957	8,843
50,000-99,999	2,051	4,342	3,792
10,000-49,999	8,867	10,098	11,457
Under 10,000	37,720	37,951	35,998

Communes of 10 thousand population or more included 17.7 million people in 1920, 25.9 million in 1930, and 36.5 million in 1940. In relative terms, they included 31.9 per cent of Japan's total population in 1920, 40.6 per cent in 1930, and 50.4 per cent in 1940. The *number* of people in communes of 10 thousand population or less declined from 37.7 million in 1920 to 36.0 million in 1940; the *proportion* of the people in such communes declined from 68.1 per cent of the total in 1920 to 49.6 per cent in 1940.

The major areas of population increase were the cities of 100 thousand and over, especially the three conurbations of Tokyo-Yokohama, Nagoya, and Osaka-Kobe-Kyoto. Population increase between 1920 and 1940 amounted to 29.2 per cent for communes of from 10 to 50 thousand; 84.9 per cent for communes of from 50 to 100 thousand; 165.7 per cent for communes of from 100 thousand to 1.0 million; and 263.3 per cent for communes of 1.0 million or more.[40] The proliferation of urban areas was especially noteworthy during the 1930's. By 1940, cities of 100 thousand and over as a group included 29.4 per cent of Japan's total population.

The urbanization of the Japanese population during the decades of expansion between the two world wars was influenced both in its amount and in its characteristics by the preparations for war. In the five years between 1935 and 1940, population increase amounted to 154 per cent for Amagasaki, 94 per cent for Kawasaki, 80 per cent for Kawaguchi, 65 per cent for Muroran, and 38 per cent for Yokohama. Frictional difficulties accompanied both the "normal"

[37] Prewar areas of Japan. For the populations of minor civil divisions (*shi, machi*, and *mura*) by size groups as of the census dates from 1920 to 1950, see: Nihon. Sori-fu, tokei-kyoku. *Nihon tokei nenkan, 1949*. Table 26.

[38] The administrative distinction among *shi, machi*, and *mura* reflects the differences in the size, the density, and the characteristics of the population in these types of areas. *Shi* are definitely urban in that they are sizable concentrations of people. A *machi* will usually include a town of some size, while a *mura* includes scattered villages. To translate these terms as "city," "town," and "village" becomes meaningful only if it is realized that *machi* and *mura* are administrative areas that include virtually all the agricultural, pastoral, forest, and waste land of the country, as well as those settlements of less than 30,000 that are not incorporated. To use merely *shi* and *gun* (all areas outside the *shi*) and to equate them to city and country, to urban and rural, has a superficial similarity to Western usage, for practically all agricultural land and farming people are in the *gun*. The difficulty is that the *gun* includes considerable population that in international usage would be called urban.

The preceding limitations have concerned the validity of the classification of geographical areas as urbanization indices for specific periods of time. The difficulties are pyramided when the interest lies in changes over time. *Shi* may be formed from preexisting *machi*, often with all or parts of adjacent *mura* added. As the *shi* increases in economic function and population, it incorporates areas once peripheral. With improving transportation and communication facilities, *mura* may be combined. As a *mura* grows, it may become a *machi*.

[39] Areas of all Japan as of 1950, areas of the communes as of the respective census dates. Data from: Nihon. Sori-fu, tokei-kyoku. *Nihon tokei nenkan, 1951*. Table 9.

[40] The incorporation of new cities and the addition of previously rural areas to existing cities were major factors in the growth of the urban population. A special tabulation is available, giving the populations of the individual cities at the various census dates within the urban boundaries as of May 1, 1941. (Kojima, Reikichi, "Waga kuni. . . .") Between October 1, 1940, and May 1, 1941, fourteen new cities were incorporated. The total number of cities thus became 182; the total urban population as of the 1940 census enumeration was 28.4 million. The area included in the 182 cities had been the residence of 16.6 million people in 1920. From 1920 to 1940, the population of this "constant" area increased 71 per cent, while the urban population as defined officially increased 175 per cent. A substantial part of the urbanization was due to the formation of new cities and to incorporation. Insofar as incorporation reflects the developing functional city and the realignment of political boundaries to correspond with economic and demographic realities, it represents real rather than spurious urbanization.

urbanization of the 1920's and the "military" urbanization of the 1930's. However, urbanization itself became a matter of concern to the Japanese who studied what was happening. It looked as if the islands of Japan would become great networks of cities, dependent for their markets and their food on peoples in other areas.

Cities of 100 thousand and over were damaged severely in the last year of the war. Cities of a million or over lost more than two-thirds of their populations, while those of 100 thousand to a million lost about 30 per cent. The people who had lived in cities were adjusted to urban life, however, and the economy was irrevocably industrial. Agriculture could not provide food for all the people who lived in Japan. And so the cities grew again. The following figures trace the growth of the cities with populations of 50 thousand or more from 1940 to 1955.[41] Numbers are in thousands:

Year	*50,000 and over*	*100,000 and over*	*50,000-99,999*
1940	25,084	21,291	3,792
1945	16,411	11,014	5,397
1947	22,937	16,789	6,148
1950	27,633	21,326	6,307
1955	40,543	31,141	9,402

In the postwar years many new cities were incorporated and many old ones extended their boundaries. In the census of 1955, 50 million people, 56 per cent of the total population of Japan, were living in *shi*. More than 40 million were living in *shi* with populations of 50 thousand or more, a figure that is roughly comparable with the 28 million living in *shi* of this size in 1950. Within the area of Japan as of 1955, the percentage increases from 1950 to 1955 amounted to 39.3 for cities of one million or more, 51.4 for cities of from 100 thousand to one million, and 49.1 for cities of from 50 to 100 thousand. The population living outside cities of 50 thousand or more declined 12.6 per cent.

Population redistribution is mirrored roughly in data on communes and cities by size, for increasing population itself results in denser settlement. It might push many communes upward into larger and hence technically more urban groups. Comparisons of growth in constant areas are not yet available for 1955, but the Institute of Population Problems of the Welfare Ministry has compared the populations in 1950 with those of the same areas in 1935.[42] The results for all Japan are as follows, numbers being in thousands:

Size of commune	*1935*	*1950*	*Per cent change*
All Japan	68,459	83,200	21.2
100,000 and over	21,299	21,326	0.1
50,000-99,999	4,576	6,307	37.8
40,000-49,999	1,652	2,269	37.3
30,000-39,999	1,823	2,564	40.6
20,000-29,999	1,901	2,843	49.6
10,000-19,999	6,867	9,598	39.8
5,000-9,999	13,550	17,622	30.0
Under 5,000	16,791	20,671	23.1

About eight million people, considerably more than half the total increase of 14.5 million, were added to the populations of communes with less than 10 thousand people. Great cities of 100 thousand and over provided employment and living facilities for the same number of people in 1950, when Japan had a population of 83.2 million, that they had in 1935, when the population of the country had been 68.7 million. Prior to the defeat of 1945, the smaller communes had exported virtually their entire natural increase decade after decade. In 1950, these smaller communes provided employment or subsistence, housing, and social facilities for one-fourth more people than had resided within the same areas in 1935.

Thus in the late 1940's there were difficulties in the distribution of population in relation to economic opportunities. These difficulties extended from the great cities through the middle cities to the rural communes where the prewar pattern of stability or decline had been replaced by major increase. This blocked urbanization and its economic problems characterized Japan in 1950. In the years from 1950 to 1955 urbanization was again the major process.

THE RURAL AREAS

In the first sixty years of Japan's modernization there were few changes in the size of the rural population, but there were continuing declines in the percentages of the total population that was rural. After the movement into Manchoukuo and North China during the 1930's, the population of the *gun* declined in absolute numbers as well as in proportion of the total. The "flight from the land" of the Germans, the "depopulation of the mountains" of the Italians, had appeared in the Western Pacific region.

Analysis of the changes in the population of the *gun* in Japan as a whole throws an aura of inevitability around a process that was occurring haltingly, even painfully. In the decades from 1880 to 1940 the utilization of the land became more intensive, but there were wide differences in the rapidity of the readjustments between numbers of people and subsistence or employment opportunities.[43] Increase in population characterized the peripheral areas of the country, where isolation, poverty, and cultural backwardness coincided. Increase also occurred near the great cities, where rural people had favorable markets for their agricultural products and more abundant opportunities for employment outside agriculture. In general, however, changes in the rural population were slight relative to those occurring in the urban population.

In the preceding discussion we have assumed that rurality was a rather distinctive characteristic and that the rural population was somehow identified with the land. It would be more accurate to regard the population structure of Japan as a continuum that extended from large cities that were distinctly urban to small villages that were distinctly rural. We have approached this continuum earlier through an analysis of population distribution and changes by size of commune, disregarding the classification of the communes as *shi, machi,* or *mura*. We considered urbanization as a process that involved the movement of increasing proportions of the population to the larger communes which, if they had a population of 30 thousand or more, were generally classified as *shi*. The smaller communes, especially those with a population of 10 thousand or less, were assumed to be rural and agricultural. Size alone is a rather limited measure of rurality, however,

[41] Since the publications of the censuses of 1940, 1944, 1945, 1947, 1950, and 1955 are cited in the Bibliography, detailed citations to each specific figure are not given here. Summary tabulations for 1945, 1947, and 1955 were given in *Jinko mondai kenkyu*, No. 63. March 1956.

[42] The tabulations for Japan and the prefectures were made available in unpublished form. The classification of *shi, machi,* and *mura* by size is based on the 1950 populations. The area of Japan is that at the time of the 1950 census.

[43] Precise measurement of these differences would require analysis of the changing economic opportunities within the rural areas and their desirability relative to those available elsewhere.

for an agricultural commune of considerable area may have a population of 10 thousand or more, whereas a smaller area with some industrial or service activities may have a population below 10 thousand. The type of political organization in the smaller communes permits an approach alternative to that through size alone. In general, *machi* include larger concentrated settlements than *mura*, their people have more governmental facilities, and their employment structures are more diversified. Hence the changes in the proportions of people living in the *machi* as contrasted with the *mura* may be used as an approximate measure of urbanization within the *gun*.

Between 1920 and 1930 the total population of Japan in its prewar area increased 15 per cent; the population of the *shi*, 53 per cent; the population of the *gun*, 7 per cent.[44] But within the *gun* the population of *machi* increased 47 per cent, while that of *mura* declined 5 per cent. *Shi* and *machi* were increasing in numbers and in population, while *mura* were declining. This type of change was widespread throughout Japan, although there were some exceptions to the general pattern.[45] In Osaka and in Tottori the population of the *machi* decreased, but in Tokyo it doubled, in Nagasaki it approached a threefold increase, and in Kagoshima it quadrupled. The population of *mura* increased slightly in all the prefectures northeast of Tokyo and Chiba except Ibaragi and Aomori, where there were slight declines. Southwest of Tokyo it increased only in Toyama, Yamanashi, and Nagano. This flight from the *mura* was an approximate measure of the cultural and demographic impact of urbanization and its correlated changes on the agricultural population in the *gun*.

The Japanese land was fully utilized at existing levels of technology and social organization during the prewar decades, when numbers on the land remained relatively unchanging. Absorption of additional population would have jeopardized economic well-being, social organization, and political stability. The preservation of the status quo required the exodus of younger sons and daughters to urban areas and non-agricultural employment. In the last year of the war and the early postwar years there was an increase in the population of the *gun*. By 1955 the prewar pattern of relative stability seemed to have been replaced by one of decline.

Changes in Age Groups

Population increases must somehow be absorbed in the social and economic life of the nation. Since the population of Japan grew by 33.9 million between 1920 and 1955, it is obvious that an increasing number of people were fed, clothed, and sheltered in Japan. More than this, succeeding generations of children were educated, boys and girls found jobs, new homes were established, and the dependent youth and the aged were cared for by those in the productive middle years.

If we view population change as an increase in age groups whose demands on and contributions to the culture are equally specific, the compulsive pressures of an increasing population on institutional facilities and economic structure become apparent. The total increase of 33.9 million between 1920 and 1955 included 9.8 million children under age 15, 3.2 million youth aged from 15 to 19, 13.5 million young adults aged from 20 to 44, 5.6 million middle-aged and aging persons from 45 to 64, and 1.8 million aged (Table 21).

Figures on Japanese age trends are prosaic statements

[44] These changes in the populations of *mura* and *machi*, like those of *shi*, were due in part to population changes occurring within constant areas, in part to change in the status of areas. *Machi* could disappear or be reduced in area and population by complete or partial incorporation in *shi*, or they could become *shi*. Thus the *machi*, whose proportional increase almost equaled that of the *shi*, contributed substantially to the growth of the latter. *Machi* in their turn absorbed *mura*, while *mura* might singly or in combination change to the status of *machi*. See: Matsuda, Teijiro, and Hayashi, Keikai. *Hompo naichi tohi betsu jinko zoka ritsu no sokutei-ho, Taisho ku'nen—Showa go'nen.*

[45] Data on the population in the *machi* and the *mura* of the prefectures at the various census dates were secured by additions from the following sources: Nihon. Naikaku tokei-kyoku. *Shi, cho, son betsu jinko dotai tokei.* 1925, 1930, and 1935.

Table 21

Population and its increase by age groups, 1920-1955
(Area as of 1955)

	Population (in '000)					1920 as 100			
Age groups	*1920*	*1930*	*1940*	*1950*	*1955*	*1930*	*1940*	*1950*	*1955*
Total	55,391	63,872	71,540	83,413	89,275	115	129	150	161
0-14	20,202	23,350	26,142	29,505	29,992	116	129	146	148
0-4	7,377	8,927	9,049	11,235	9,308	121	123	152	126
5-14	12,825	14,423	17,093	18,271	20,684	112	133	142	161
15-64	32,273	37,489	41,983	49,780	54,558	116	130	154	169
15-19	5,362	6,488	7,325	8,591	8,539	121	137	160	159
20-44	18,612	21,284	23,881	28,709	32,154	114	128	154	173
Male	9,417	10,942	11,645	13,621	15,388	116	124	144	163
Female	9,194	10,343	12,235	15,088	16,766	112	133	164	182
45-64	8,299	9,717	10,777	12,480	13,865	117	130	150	167
Male	4,136	4,797	5,345	6,241	6,876	116	129	150	166
Female	4,163	4,920	5,433	6,239	6,990	118	130	149	168
65 and over	2,917	3,034	3,415	4,128	4,724	104	117	141	162

Source: Nihon. Sori-fu, tokei-kyoku. *Nihon tokei nenkan, 1951.* Table 12. The prefecture of Okinawa is excluded. *Idem. Showa 25-nen kokusei chosa hokoku.* VII. *Idem. Showa sanju-nen kokusei chosa. Ichi pasento chushutsu shukei ni yoru kekka sokuho. Zenkoku.*

unless we look at their significance in functional terms. During the ages from 20 to 44, practically all women marry, retire from employment outside the home, and devote their time to the care of husband and parents-in-law, assistance in family activities, and the bearing and rearing of children. In 1920 there were 9.2 million women in this age group; in 1955 there were 16.8 million. The increase amounted to more than four-fifths. The children for whom these women cared had increased at a somewhat less rapid rate than the women, but pre-school children were one-fourth more numerous in 1955 than in 1920, while children in school ages were three-fifths more numerous. Even if the educational level of the population had remained constant, the resources of the communities and the nation would have had to provide for a 60 per cent increase in educational facilities within a generation.

The children who finished school had to find jobs. If we glance at trends in the group aged from 15 to 19, we perceive the increase in claimants to places on farms or in the more highly developed labor markets of towns and cities. The census of 1920 enumerated 5.4 million youth aged from 15 to 19; the census of 1955 enumerated 8.5 million. The number of potential entrants into the labor force was almost 60 per cent larger in 1955 than it had been in 1920.

The men, who were the major productive element in the society, the heads of the families, and the main support for dependent children and old people, were also increasing in numbers. Men aged from 20 to 44 were three-fifths more numerous in 1955 than in 1920, despite the losses in the war of 1937-1945. Older workers, those aged from 45 to 64, were two-thirds more numerous in 1955 than in 1920. The slowest increase in any of the age groups of adults was that among those aged 65 and over, but even in this group there was an increase of three-fifths in the 35 years.

PREFECTURES BY INDUSTRIAL TYPE

The rates of increase among the age groups in the population of the country as a whole were slight if contrasted with those that occurred in the industrial regions, for the attractive force of cities was highly selective as to age (TABLE 22). The forerunners of history's great urban developments have been youth, and in the Japanese setting they were predominantly male. Soon economic opportunities became better known, and new ways of living were integrated with ancient values. Then the cities and the industrial areas became abodes for families as well as single men. The early contingents of women were young, too. They came either for independent employment or as the brides of the young men who had already moved away from agriculture. As economic structures matured in the industrial regions, the populations included higher proportions of women and children. However, the essential role of the industrial region remained that of absorbing the surplus population of other regions of the country. Continuing movements from the outside created anew the imbalances in age and sex groups that had come to be regarded as "normal" but that actually were symptoms of an economy, a society, and a population in transition.

Increases in the population in the productive ages were substantial in the metropolitan and other industrial prefectures, slight in the transitional and agricultural prefectures. The small change in the population so densely settled on the land in the agricultural prefectures was possible only because there was continuing emigration. The natural increase in the industrial prefectures combined with the absorption of immigrants from the other regions of the country and the colonial areas to create decennial increases of one-fourth to one-third or even more in the populations in the productive ages in these prefectures.

There was blockage to adequate rural-urban migration after the defeat of Japan, but movement was soon restored. The patterns of changes from 1947 to 1950 and from 1950 to 1955 were similar to those from 1935 to 1940.

POPULATION STRUCTURES AND DEMOGRAPHIC BURDENS

High dependency burdens and increasing numbers of persons in the productive ages were related aspects of the problems of economic development and labor force absorption in Japan. In the 1950's as in the 1930's, in depression as in prosperity, the burden of dependent on productive groups was greatest in those areas least able to provide for physical welfare and cultural advance. The exodus of youth to urban areas only intensified the demographic burden for those who remained behind in rural areas.

The age structure of the population in the years from 1920 to 1955 reflected the transitional status of the society and the economy (TABLE 23). The proportion of the total population under age 15 was 36.5 in 1920, 36.1 in 1940, and 33.6 in 1955. These proportions are substantially below those found in the populations of such agricultural countries as Korea, Taiwan, or India; they are substantially above those found in the populations of the advanced industrial countries of the West.

The proportions of youth in the population of Japan and the changes in those proportions over time have been similar to those that occurred earlier in Western countries. In 1871 the proportion of the total population under age 15 was 34.3 in Germany, 36.1 in England and Wales. Declines had begun earlier in France; in 1851 only 27 per cent of the population was under age 15. By 1930, however, the proportion of youth in the populations of most of Western Europe was only 23 to 25 per cent. Thus Japan's demographic structure in recent decades has been comparable to that of several Western nations half a century or so earlier. It should be noted, however, that there has been no precise parallelism in change. The processes were similar, but the rates of occurrence differed.

The proportion of persons aged 65 and over in the Japanese population has remained fairly unchanged in the last thirty years; it was 5.3 in 1920 and in 1955. If continuing declines in fertility accompany the maturing of the large cohorts of youth who now create a heavy burden of dependent on productive groups in Japan, the proportion of people who are age 65 and over must increase.

If the trends of the past continue into the future, the relations between dependent and productive groups in the Japanese population will be a balance between declining proportions of youth and increasing proportions of aged.[46] In the period from 1920 to 1950 the burden of dependent on productive groups changed little. The proportion of the total population that was either below age 15 (dependent youth) or age 65 or over (dependent aged) was 41.8 in 1920, 38.9 in 1955. It should be noted, however, that a gradual decline had occurred.

The division of the population into the three broad groups

[46] A realization of this is leading to a substantial research on the facts and the problems of aging populations in Japan. See: Tachi, Minoru. "Jinko no ronen-ka." *Nihon koshu eisei zasshi*, 1(5):33-38. July 1954. Also: Jumeigaku kenkyu-kai. *Jumeigaku kenkyu-kai nempo*. 1956. 161 pp.

TABLE 22

The populations of the prefectures by industrial type, by age, 1920-1955[a]

	POPULATION (IN '000)					PER CENT CHANGE			
Age	*1920*	*1930*	*1940*	*1950*	*1955*	*1920-1930*	*1930-1940*	*1940-1950*	*1950-1955*
					Metropolitan				
Total	6,287	8,949	12,137	10,135	12,656	42.3	35.6	−16.5	24.9
0-4	713	1,147	1,397	1,269	1,096	60.9	21.8	−9.1	−13.6
5-14	1,276	1,657	2,430	1,960	2,593	29.9	46.6	−19.4	32.3
15-19	757	1,121	1,533	1,050	1,350	48.0	36.8	−31.5	28.6
20-34	1,742	2,648	3,463	2,693	3,711	52.0	30.8	−22.2	37.8
35-49	1,067	1,401	1,972	1,837	2,167	31.3	40.8	−6.8	18.0
50-64	527	731	1,006	984	1,266	38.8	37.6	−2.2	28.7
65 and over	205	244	336	342	471	19.0	37.9	1.7	37.8
					Other industrial				
Total	9,190	10,913	13,383	14,551	16,104	18.7	22.6	8.7	10.7
0-4	1,156	1,468	1,629	1,943	1,565	27.0	10.9	19.3	−19.4
5-14	2,070	2,326	2,965	3,048	3,632	12.4	27.5	2.8	19.2
15-19	936	1,167	1,449	1,483	1,560	24.7	24.1	2.3	5.2
20-34	2,153	2,676	3,345	3,472	4,148	24.3	25.0	3.8	19.5
35-49	1,533	1,706	2,133	2,472	2,695	11.3	25.0	15.9	9.0
50-64	894	1,088	1,303	1,459	1,697	21.7	19.8	12.0	16.3
65 and over	448	482	559	673	807	7.6	16.1	20.4	20.0
					Intermediate				
Total	18,368	19,964	21,097	25,699	26,294	8.7	5.7	21.8	2.3
0-4	2,437	2,749	2,562	3,402	2,697	12.8	−6.8	32.8	−20.7
5-14	4,339	4,608	5,105	5.642	6,147	6.2	10.8	10.5	8.9
15-19	1,691	1,905	1,952	2,595	2,381	12.7	2.4	32.9	−8.2
20-34	3,703	4,217	4,473	5,668	6,193	13.9	6.1	26.7	9.2
35-49	3,079	3,067	3,335	4,166	4,248	−.4	8.7	24.9	2.0
50-64	2,014	2,287	2,453	2,742	2,988	13.5	7.2	11.8	9.0
65 and over	1,105	1,132	1,219	1,484	1,641	2.4	7.7	21.7	10.6
					Agricultural				
Total	19,187	21,234	22,612	28,733	29,448	10.7	6.5	27.1	2.5
0-4	2,695	3,117	3,002	3,957	3,366	15.7	−3.7	31.8	−14.9
5-14	4,551	5,120	5,758	6,625	7,143	12.5	12.5	15.0	7.8
15-19	1,739	1,998	2,077	3,007	2,769	14.9	3.9	44.8	−7.9
20-34	3,881	4,289	4,551	6,298	6,771	10.5	6.1	38.4	7.5
35-49	3,172	3,256	3,466	4,447	4,612	2.7	6.4	28.3	3.7
50-64	2,060	2,359	2,564	2,932	3,161	14.5	8.7	14.4	7.8
65 and over	1,089	1,095	1,194	1,469	1,624	.5	9.0	23.0	10.5
					Hokkaido				
Total	2,359	2,812	3,272	4,296	4,773	19.2	16.3	31.3	11.2
0-4	377	445	456	664	584	18.3	2.4	45.6	−12.1
5-14	589	712	831	996	1,170	20.9	16.7	19.8	17.4
15-19	239	297	354	455	478	24.1	19.4	29.1	5.1
20-34	541	643	772	1,025	1,232	18.9	20.0	32.8	20.3
35-49	368	399	471	644	716	8.2	18.3	36.7	11.2
50-64	174	234	280	350	412	34.5	19.3	25.0	17.7
65 and over	70	82	107	160	180	16.0	31.4	49.5	12.8

[a] Industrial type as determined by the proportion of the gainfully occupied population in agriculture and forestry, 1930: Metropolitan, less than 20 per cent; other industrial, 20-39 per cent; intermediate, 40-59 per cent; agricultural, 60 per cent and over. Hokkaido is considered separately because of its special economic, social, and demographic characteristics.

Source: Age distributions by sex, single year, and quinquennial are given in the prefectural volumes of the respective censuses. 1920: Nihon. Naikaku tokei-kyoku. *Taisho ku'nen kokusei chosa hokoku.* IV.B. 1930: *Idem. Showa go'nen kokusei chosa hokoku.* IV.4. 1940: *Idem. Census of 1940. Selected tables.* 1950: Nihon. Sori-fu, tokei-kyoku. *Showa 25-nen kokusei chosa hokoku.* VII. 1955: *Idem. Showa sanju-nen kokusei chosa, ichi pasento chushutse shukei ni yori kekka sokuho. Zenkoku.* Table 1. Prefectures, individual sheets. Areas as of 1955.

TABLE 23

The sex and age structure of the population, 1920-1955

Age	*1920*	*1930*	*1940*	*1950*	*1955*
	Per cent composition by age				
Total	100.	100.	100.	100.	100.
0-4	13.3	14.0	12.5	13.5	10.4
5-14	23.2	22.6	23.6	21.9	23.2
15-19	9.7	10.2	10.2	10.3	9.6
20-34	21.7	22.7	22.9	22.9	24.7
35-49	16.6	15.4	15.7	16.3	16.2
50-64	10.2	10.5	10.5	10.2	10.7
65 and over	5.3	4.7	4.7	5.0	5.3
	Sex ratios (males per 1,000 females)				
Total	1,005	1,011	1,001	962	965
0-4	1,005	1,017	1,025	1,041	1,051
5-14	1,013	1,019	1,020	1,024	1,031
15-19	1,024	1,030	1,007	1,015	1,011
20-34	1,030	1,053	1,013	889	946
35-49	1,014	1,048	1,058	951	888
50-64	982	962	955	992	995
65 and over	797	758	735	732	746

Source: References, Table 21. The computations for 1950 are based on the data of the 10 per cent sample as given in: Nihon. Sori-fu, tokei-kyoku. *Showa 25-nen kokusei chosa hokoku.* III.1. The data for 1955 are those of the 1 per cent sample.

of young, productive, and aged people gives a spurious impression of stability in demographic structure. The use of smaller age groups and consideration of the relations between the numbers of men and women show appreciable irregularities. The proportion of pre-school children mirrored the changes in birth rates in the years preceding the censuses. This proportion was low in 1940 because of the dip in births in 1938 and 1939; it was high in 1950 because of the rise in births in the early postwar years. It was reduced in 1955 because of the decline in births from 1950 to 1955. Fluctuating numbers of births and variable cohorts of pre-school children introduced waves that influenced the successive age groups in later years. The small proportion of pre-school children in the late prewar and war years resulted in a smaller proportion of school-age children in 1950. Youth aged from 15 to 19, the entrants to the productive age groups, constituted an increasing proportion of the total population each decade from 1920 to 1950, but in 1955 the proportion in this age group reflected the declines in the younger age groups in earlier years.

Between 1920 and 1950 there was a gradual increase in the predominance in the population of males under age 15. Declining childhood mortality was resulting in a larger proportionate saving of the lives of boys than of girls. At the ages of young adulthood, the ratios of the sexes were altered sharply from one period to another by migrations to and from the country and by war. External movements and military recruitment influenced the balance of the sexes among youth aged from 15 to 19, the entrants to the labor force. This is especially apparent in the decline of the sex ratio in this age group from 1,030 in 1930 to 1,007 in 1940.[47] The selective emigration of men is also apparent in the sex ratios in the ages from 20 to 34.

[47] The armed forces within Japan were included in the populations in 1920 and 1930. In 1940 all armed forces were included, whether in or outside the country.

The greatest disturbances in age and sex structures were those associated with war. In 1950, the sex ratio was 889 at age 20 to 34; in 1955, it was 946 at age 20 to 34, and 888 at age 35 to 49.

The social and economic significance of the changing age and sex structures is apparent if we consider the interrelations of age groups whose functions in the society are those of dependence and responsibility. On the whole, the burden of infant and child care was declining, although the irregularities were considerable. The numbers of the various dependent groups per 1,000 women aged from 20 to 49 indicates this tendency toward a decline in the numerical burden of dependency:

Dependent group	*1920*	*1930*	*1940*	*1950*	*1955*
Children under age 5	703	753	657	658	490
Children under age 15	1,924	1,971	1,897	1,730	1,580
Children under 15 and the aged 65 and over	2,202	2,227	2,145	1,973	1,829

The fundamental responsibility for family maintenance is that of the man. Youth under 15, women aged from 20 to 64, and those aged 65 and over may be regarded as the dependents of men aged from 20 to 64. In the years from 1920 to 1940, there were about 3,000 dependents for each 1,000 men. High postwar fertility and war losses among men combined to raise the ratio above 3,200 in 1950. Rapidly declining fertility and the maturing of age groups unscarred by war reduced the ratio to only a little over 2,600 in 1955.

The burden of dependent on productive groups was high, and it did not change greatly until recent years. Presumably the burden of the child on the adult population had been higher in the past than it was in the years from 1920 to 1940; presumably the declines from 1950 to 1955 presage further declines in the future. If the decline in the proportion of children proceeds more rapidly than the increase in the proportion of the aged, Japan may have a period in which declining numerical burdens of dependent on productive groups permit larger proportions of family and community expenditures to be devoted to qualitative improvements.

POPULATION STRUCTURE, URBANIZATION, AND INDUSTRIALIZATION

Differences in levels of fertility and patterns of internal migration operated together to reduce the ratios of non-productive to productive age groups in the cities and to increase them in the countryside (TABLE 24). From the point of view of the city, perhaps even of the total culture, the situation was favorable to rapid social change. Youth were concentrated in the areas and the occupations with higher per capita real incomes. Increasing levels of living could be achieved more rapidly because here there was a lessening of the age-old responsibilities of adults to the aged, who represented the past, and to the children, who were the future. For the rural areas, on the other hand, demographic structures were unfavorable to change. Children who had been reared in the country became productive workers in the cities; some of the aging and the aged who had been productive workers in the cities returned to the villages. The rural areas were nurseries for youth and homes for the aged.

The population of the *shi* in 1920 displayed marked concentrations in age and sex groups and structural imbalances.

TABLE 24

Age structures, by size of commune, 1930 and 1950

Age	All Japan	100,000 and over	50,000-99,999	10,000-49,999	5,000-9,999	Under 5,000
			Population (in '000)			
			1930			
All ages	63,872	11,481	4,342	10,098	12,302	25,649
0-5	10,537	1,650	685	1,695	2,129	4,378
6-14	12,813	1,885	792	2,021	2,627	5,489
15-19	6,488	1,502	536	1,091	1,168	2,191
20-64	31,001	6,129	2,200	4,903	5,751	12,018
65 and over	3,034	316	129	389	628	1,572
			1950			
All ages	83,200[a]	21,326	6,307	17,273	17,622	20,671
0-4	11,205	2,769	853	2,416	2,416	2,751
5-14	18,223	4,200	1,338	3,881	4,076	4,727
15-19	8,568	2,204	663	1,800	1,827	2,074
20-64	41,090	11,396	3,192	8,375	8,329	9,799
65 and over	4,109	756	261	799	973	1,320
			Age structure (per cent)			
			1930			
All ages	100.	100.	100.	100.	100.	100.
0-5	16.5	14.4	15.8	16.8	17.3	17.1
6-14	20.1	16.4	18.2	20.0	21.3	21.4
15-19	10.2	13.1	12.3	10.8	9.5	8.5
20-64	48.5	53.4	50.7	48.5	46.8	46.9
65 and over	4.7	2.7	3.0	3.8	5.1	6.1
			1950			
All ages	100.	100.	100.	100.	100.	100.
0-5	13.5	13.0	13.5	14.0	13.7	13.3
5-14	21.9	19.7	21.2	22.5	23.1	22.9
15-19	10.3	10.3	10.5	10.4	10.4	10.0
20-64	49.4	53.4	50.6	48.5	47.3	47.4
65 and over	4.9	3.6	4.1	4.6	5.5	6.4

[a] Including unknown ages.
Source: 1930: Based on tabulations made by the staff of Jinko mondai kenkyujo. 1950: *Jinko mondai kenkyu,* No. 63, pp. 86-89. March 1956.

The numbers of men and women were approximately equal in the total population, but in the urban population there were 87 additional men for each 1,000 women. At age 15 to 19 there were more than 200 additional men for each 1,000 women. Surpluses of men remained fairly sizable until after age 50, but then, and particularly after age 55, a curious phenomenon appeared: the feminization of the urban population. The most plausible explanation is a reverse migration of aging men, as cities offered few opportunities for self-support to men no longer employable in regular jobs. The widows, on the other hand, could assist in household tasks. There is also the possibility that elderly women came in to live with the families of their sons in the cities. There may also have been a heavier mortality among men who spent their productive lives in the cities.

The predominance of the six great cities in Japan's urban population antedated the census period. By 1920 over half the total population of the *shi* was in the cities of Tokyo, Yokohama, Nagoya, Osaka, Kyoto, and Kobe. And the distinctions between this population and the remainder of the urban population were greater than those between the rural population and the lesser cities (TABLE 25). Both the data for communes by size and those for *shi* and *gun* show the demographic subsidy from the rural areas to the cities. In the urban areas children and the aged were underrepresented, while young people in the most productive years were overrepresented. In the rural areas, on the contrary, there were disproportionate numbers of the nation's children and its aged, low proportions of its people in the productive early and middle years. These relationships among age, the balance of the sexes, and urbanization existed throughout the census period. They were less pronounced in 1950 because of the dislocations of the war, the deficits of men in the total population, and the inability of the urban economy to absorb manpower from the rural areas.

Thus far we have considered age and sex structures within the universe of demographic statistics. There has been an implicit assumption that urbanization was an index of eco-

TABLE 25

Age structures in the *shi* and the *gun*, 1920, 1930, and 1955
(Areas as of the census dates)

Age	*1920* The six large cities	*1920* Other shi	*1920* Gun	*1930* The six large cities	*1930* Other shi	*1930* Gun	*1955* The six large cities	*1955* Other shi	*1955* Gun
				Age structure (per cent)					
Total	100.	100.	100.	100.	100.	100.	100.	100.	100.
0-4	10.4	11.7	13.8	11.9	12.9	14.5	8.4	10.2	11.4
5-14	19.3	21.5	23.8	17.8	20.6	23.7	20.3	23.1	24.2
15-19	12.9	11.9	9.1	13.6	12.5	9.2	10.6	9.7	9.0
20-64	54.3	51.2	47.6	54.1	50.7	47.3	57.0	52.0	49.2
20-34	28.9	25.7	20.4	30.0	26.3	20.9	29.5	25.1	22.6
35-49	17.2	16.6	16.6	15.8	15.3	15.3	17.2	16.5	15.5
50-64	8.2	8.9	10.6	8.3	9.1	11.1	10.3	10.3	11.1
65 and over	3.0	3.8	5.7	2.6	3.4	5.3	3.7	4.9	6.2
				Urbanization of the age groups (per cent)[a]					
Total	9.8	8.2	82.0	11.8	12.2	76.0	15.9	40.4	43.7
0-4	7.7	7.2	85.1	10.1	11.2	78.7	12.8	39.4	47.8
5-14	8.2	7.7	84.1	9.3	11.1	79.6	13.9	40.4	45.7
15-19	13.1	10.1	76.8	15.8	14.9	69.3	17.6	41.4	41.0
20-64	10.9	8.7	80.4	13.2	12.7	74.1	17.6	40.8	41.6
20-34	13.0	9.8	77.2	15.6	14.2	70.2	19.0	41.1	39.9
35-49	10.1	8.2	81.7	12.1	12.1	75.8	16.9	41.3	41.8
50-64	7.9	7.2	84.9	9.3	10.6	80.1	15.3	39.2	45.6
65 and over	5.6	5.9	88.5	6.5	8.6	84.9	11.0	37.7	51.2

[a] The total population of the age group in the specific year being taken as 100.
Source: References, Table 22.

nomic transformation, and that differences by size of commune reflected differences in types of economic functioning and hence in the structure of the labor force. The direct relationships among declining proportions of youth and aged, increasing proportions in the productive ages, and the development of the industrial society are presented in TABLE 26, where the prefectures are classified by industrial type.

The proportions of pre-school and school-age children were greatest in the agricultural prefectures, least in the metropolitan prefectures of Tokyo and Osaka. Ratios of children aged from 0 to 4 to women aged from 20 to 49 indicate both the extent of the differences within Japan at any given time and the persistence of the differences over time:

Prefectures by industrial type	*1920*	*1930*	*1940*	*1950*	*1955*
All Japan	703	753	657	658	490
Metropolitan	551	621	536	552	373
Other industrial	655	701	615	633	445
Intermediate					
industrial	713	748	631	630	488
agricultural	712	761	664	656	
Agricultural	747	820	743	700	557
Hokkaido	913	931	789	804	610

The agricultural-industrial variations in proportions of children aged from 5 to 14 reveal again the basic importance of urbanization in the size and structure of regional populations. The totals of youth aged from 5 to 14 per 1,000 women aged from 20 to 49 in the various census years were as follows:

Prefectures by industrial type	*1920*	*1930*	*1940*	*1950*	*1955*
All Japan	1,924	1,971	1,897	1,730	1,090
Metropolitan	1,537	1,518	1,468	1,404	881
Other industrial	1,829	1,810	1,735	1,629	1,033
Intermediate					
industrial	1,996	2,028	1,892	1,669	1,113
agricultural	1,976	2,030	1,986	1,754	
Agricultural	2,010	2,166	2,168	1,871	1,182
Hokkaido	2,343	2,421	2,227	2,008	1,223

The responsibilities of the people in the agricultural prefectures were greater than ratios of children or youth to women would indicate, for there were relative deficits of men in the productive ages. In 1920, for instance, the number of men per 1,000 women was 972 in the agricultural prefectures but 1,103 in the metropolitan prefectures. The patterns in 1930 and 1940 were similar to those in 1920. Even in 1950,

TABLE 26

Age structures and sex ratios, prefectures by industrial type, 1920-1955

(Areas as of 1955)

Prefectural type and age	*1920*	*1930*	*1940*	*1950*	*1955*
	Age structures (per cent)				
Metropolitan	100.	100.	100.	100.	100.
0-4	11.3	12.8	11.5	12.5	8.7
5-14	20.3	18.5	20.0	19.3	20.5
15-19	12.0	12.5	12.6	10.4	10.7
20-34	27.7	29.6	28.5	26.6	29.3
35-49	17.0	15.7	16.2	18.1	17.1
50-64	8.4	8.2	8.3	9.7	10.0
65 and over	3.2	2.7	2.8	3.4	3.7
Other industrial	100.	100.	100.	100.	100.
0-4	12.6	13.5	12.2	13.4	9.7
5-14	22.5	21.3	22.2	21.0	22.6
15-19	10.2	10.7	10.8	10.2	9.7
20-34	23.4	24.5	25.0	23.8	25.8
35-49	16.7	15.6	15.9	17.0	16.7
50-64	9.7	10.0	9.7	10.0	10.5
65 and over	4.9	4.4	4.2	4.6	5.0
Intermediate	100.	100.	100.	100.	100.
0-4	13.1	13.4	11.8	13.0	10.3
5-14	23.5	22.9	23.5	21.4	23.4
15-19	9.2	9.5	9.8	10.0	9.0
20-34	20.9	22.1	22.3	22.6	23.6
35-49	16.6	15.1	15.8	16.5	16.2
50-64	10.8	11.3	11.1	10.7	11.4
65 and over	5.9	5.6	5.7	5.8	6.2
	Males per 1,000 females				
Metropolitan	1,103	1,107	1,061	1,001	1,022
0-4	1,016	1,023	1,027	1,048	1,060
5-14	1,063	1,048	1,042	1,031	1,039
15-19	1,239	1,191	1,194	1,073	1,179
20-34	1,189	1,189	1,040	952	1,052
35-49	1,142	1,197	1,171	1,005	911
50-64	1,006	998	1,004	1,072	1,044
65 and over	674	666	662	685	720
Other industrial	1,032	1,025	1,024	966	974
0-4	1,014	1,017	1,028	1,043	1,064
5-14	1,018	1,012	1,019	1,025	1,218
15-19	1,043	997	1,052	988	961
20-34	1,105	1,084	1,041	901	972
35-49	1,068	1,102	1,114	973	907
50-64	995	982	976	1,000	999
65 and over	764	736	717	726	722
Intermediate	1,015	1,020	1,005	950	944
0-4	1,018	1,019	1,029	1,052	1,036
5-14	1,030	1,024	1,020	1,019	1,019
15-19	1,067	1,052	1,022	1,000	982
20-34	1,081	1,101	1,041	883	911
35-49	996	1,037	1,051	925	862
50-64	980	952	950	976	981
65 and over	795	775	744	723	771

Source: References, Table 22.

when there was a substantial deficit of men in the total population, there was a surplus in the metropolitan prefectures.

The result of the surplus of children and aged and the deficit of men in the agricultural areas was a high burden of dependency. The numbers of children, women, and aged per 1,000 men aged from 20 to 64 show this persistent relationship between agriculture and high dependency burdens for men:

Prefectures by industrial type	*1920*	*1930*	*1940*	*1950*	*1955*
All Japan	3,087	3,058	3,045	3,207	2,626
Metropolitan	2,533	2,487	2,642	2,692	2,155
Other industrial	2,881	2,862	2,852	3,055	2,485
Intermediate					
industrial	3,087	3,034	3,016	3,197	2,738
agricultural	3,254	3,220	3,173	3,318	
Agricultural	3,307	3,353	3,345	3,428	2,866
Hokkaido	2,971	3,081	3,034	3,223	2,552

DEMOGRAPHIC DIVERSITIES

In the years from 1920 to 1940 a new heterogeneity was replacing the original homogeneity in the age and sex structures of the population. The changes were cumulative, for reduced burdens of dependent on productive groups occurred first in the great urban areas. Analysis of age structures alone yields an incomplete picture of the diversities created by economic changes, however, for the proportion of the population living in the areas of greater opportunity was increasing rapidly. Between 1920 and 1935 the increase in the number of youth under age 15 amounted to 76 per cent in Tokyo prefecture and 63 per cent in Osaka prefecture. In the agricultural prefectures around the great metropolitan centers, youth increased less rapidly than in the nation as a whole. In Toyama, Fukui, Nara, and Saga increases were less than 5 per cent; in Ishikawa there was a decrease in the number of youth. This same type of differential increase characterized the adult population. Two processes were in operation simultaneously. One was an increase in the differences between areas. The other was the movement of people to areas of greater opportunity. The result was a heavy demographic burden on the populations least able to carry it.

Recognition of the strains associated with the changes in the age structures of the groups within Japan does not mean that the age structures in these decades could have been greatly different from what they were. Internal differences in the age structures of the urban-rural and regional groups might have been reduced by lesser rates of migration from the rural areas. However, this would have meant that populations would increase in the rural areas. Blocked migration would have retarded economic development and social change to a greater extent than did the imbalances in population structures and the inequities in demographic burdens.

CHAPTER V

The Economically Active Population

CONCEPTS of the gainfully occupied population were developed in economies where the presence or absence of employment could be determined if questions were phrased precisely and enumeration procedures were adequate. These concepts are applicable only with modifications in economies such as the Japanese, where labor for subsistence is common and family enterprises are widespread. In household industries, it is difficult to segregate a laboring and a dependent population, for all family members work whenever possible at that which yields monetary remuneration to the head or food and supplies for the family. Similarly, where production and sale are carried on jointly or where the place of residence is also the place of work, all household members are likely to participate in all activities of the household and so bar a clear-cut separation of the gainfully occupied from those not laboring for gain. In an agriculture where cultivation is intensive and the main labor is done by human hands, the distinction between those in and those not in the labor force becomes arbitrary. The amount and type of work are determined by the needs of the day or season. Leisure is an interlude in a natural sequence of activities rather than a fixed period for relaxation. Moreover, in a culture that gives moral value to labor and that possesses a close-knit family system, there is not the distinction between employment and unemployment that occurs in industrial economies where employer-employee relations are contractual and specifically monetary. For many of the Japanese, the loss of a job for pay leads to labor without money wages.

Although Japanese labor practices in the decades after 1920 have retained many of the attributes of the historic culture, the ancient pattern has been changing. In the century that has passed since the opening of the country, the monetary economy has been gradually penetrating local economies. This movement toward a pecuniary society introduces major analytical difficulties, for the conception of jobs and employment has changed over time. Statistics on the gainfully occupied are not always comparable from one census to another. There is little doubt that both changing patterns of manpower utilization and changing methods of reporting employment have characterized the years since 1920.[1] Moreover, it is probable that actual changes and altered reporting practices occurred simultaneously.

[1] Other complications are added by the difficulties involved in the questions on the gainfully occupied in the 1920 census; the more sophisticated usages of the 1930 census; the virtual loss of the detailed materials in the 1940 census; and the substitution of a definition of the labor force for the one on the gainfully occupied population in the 1950 and 1955 censuses. Brief description of the procedures in the censuses of 1920 to 1940 is given in: Taeuber, Irene B., and Beal, Edwin G., Jr. *Guide to the official demographic statistics of Japan.* Part I, "Japan Proper, 1868-1945." Population Index, Vol. XII, No. 4, Supplement. October 1946. 35 pp. Also: Nihon. Sori-cho, tokei-kyoku. *Kekka hokoku tekiyo; Showa 15-nen kokusei chosa. . . . Idem. Taisho 9-nen naishi—Showa 25-nen kokusei chosa, sangyo betsu shugyosha no hikaku.*

PARTICIPATION IN GAINFUL EMPLOYMENT

In Japan, a high proportion of people are reported as gainfully occupied or in the labor force (TABLE 27). From 1920 to 1955 the changes in the economic activities of the age groups were similar to those that occurred in other industrializing countries. Practically all men who were physically able to do so sought employment throughout the central years, roughly from age 15 or 20 to age 60 or 65. From age 30 to age 44, over 95 per cent of all men were in the labor force. Movement in and out of gainful economic activity occurred mainly during the early and the late years of the productive period.

The definition of gainful employment for women is difficult, especially when agriculture, manufacturing, and distribution are often household activities. The fact that major portions of Japan's women are gainfully occupied cannot be questioned by one who has seen the cities, the towns, and the villages of Japan. Whether the reported information on the gainful activities of women is a precise picture of the true situation is a different question.

The economic activities of women are related to their family responsibilities. Since a major portion of girls are married in their late teens or early twenties, childbearing and infant care reduce gainful employment among women in their twenties and thirties. The economic activities of older women reflect both the stage of the family cycle and the possibilities for employment.

The proportion of the economically active population that was male rose in depression and declined in prosperity. In the late prewar years, older men and younger women entered employment to replace the young men in the armed forces. The advancing age at marriage for women also permitted longer periods of gainful employment.

The proportions of men and women in the labor force in 1950 were influenced both by the difficult economic conditions of the period and the war deficits of men. The high proportion of men in the labor force probably reflected both an increased preference for men and an altered structure of employment opportunities for women. Between 1950 and 1955 women entered the labor force in increasing numbers.

The changing patterns of economic activity among the Japanese were similar to those that occurred in the West. The decisions and actions of an Asian people undergoing industrialization created a labor force whose structure and whose changes were comprehensible in terms of Western experience. The economic responses to reasonably comparable economic stimuli were similar. Thus the stage was set for comparable changes in marriage patterns, familial values, the role of women, and declining fertility.

TABLE 27

The economically active population by sex, age, and military status, 1920-1955

Age	PER CENT GAINFULLY OCCUPIED						PER CENT IN THE LABOR FORCE	
	Civilian and military			*Civilian*				
	1920	*1930*	*1940*	*1920*	*1930*	*1940*	*1950*	*1955*
				Total				
Total, 10 and over	65.5	62.1	62.0	64.9	61.6	58.9	58.6	—
10-14	22.9	15.8	11.0	22.9	15.8	11.0	—	—
15 and over	72.8	69.8	71.2	72.1	69.2	67.6	65.4[a]	65.2[a]
15-19	73.0	70.3	72.0	72.8	70.0	71.0	49.9[b]	43.2[b]
20-24	76.4	73.2	75.7	72.2	69.9	57.8	77.1	78.2
25-29	76.7	72.4	71.6	76.1	71.9	64.9	69.8	73.8
30-34	77.4	74.3	73.4	77.0	74.0	71.5	71.8	72.2
35-39	77.9	75.9	75.8	77.7	75.8	75.1		
40-44	78.5	76.5	77.7	78.4	76.4	77.3	75.0	75.2
45-49	78.1	75.3	78.4	78.1	75.3	78.1		
50-54	75.8	72.9	76.4	75.7	72.9	76.2	70.5	71.2
55-59	71.8	68.0	70.7	71.8	68.0	70.7		
60 and over	49.8	45.4	48.6	49.8	45.4	48.6	44.1	44.2
				Male				
Total, 10 and over	81.6	79.5	78.0	80.4	78.5	71.9	74.4	—
10-14	20.6	14.1	10.1	20.6	14.1	10.0	—	—
15 and over	92.2	89.3	90.4	90.8	90.5	83.2	83.4[a]	82.6[a]
15-19	83.5	78.5	77.8	83.1	78.0	75.9	53.0[b]	44.9[b]
20-24	93.7	91.8	92.9	85.3	85.3	57.1	90.5	88.1
25-29	97.1	96.7	96.9	96.0	95.8	83.7	95.5	96.2
30-34	98.0	98.0	97.8	97.3	97.4	94.2	97.1	97.1
35-39	98.2	98.2	98.1	97.9	98.0	96.7		
40-44	98.2	97.9	98.0	98.0	97.7	97.3	97.0	92.2
45-49	97.9	97.0	97.4	97.8	96.9	96.9		
50-54	96.9	95.3	95.5	96.9	95.2	95.2	92.4	93.5
55-59	94.6	91.9	90.7	94.6	91.9	90.7		
60 and over	75.3	71.6	70.9	75.3	71.6	70.9	65.2	66.2
				Female				
Total, 10 and over	49.3	44.6	46.1	49.3	44.6	46.1	43.9	—
10-14	25.2	17.5	12.0	25.2	17.5	12.0	—	—
15 and over	53.4	49.1	52.2	53.4	49.1	52.2	48.6[a]	49.1[a]
15-19	62.2	61.8	66.1	62.2	61.8	66.1	46.8[b]	41.5[b]
20-24	58.9	53.9	58.5	58.9	53.9	58.5	64.0	68.2
25-29	55.3	46.7	46.0	55.3	46.7	46.0	48.3	51.8
30-34	56.2	48.9	48.2	56.2	48.9	48.2	50.0	51.3
35-39	57.5	52.0	52.5	57.5	52.0	52.4		
40-44	58.4	53.9	56.1	58.4	53.9	56.1	53.2	55.0
45-49	58.0	53.6	58.2	58.0	53.6	58.2		
50-54	54.5	50.8	56.9	54.5	50.8	56.9	48.2	48.8
55-59	49.3	45.1	51.9	49.3	45.1	51.9		
60 and over	28.2	24.3	31.0	28.2	24.3	31.0	27.2	26.3

[a] Age 14 and over
[b] Age 14-19

Source: 1920: Nihon. Naikaku tokei-kyoku. *Taisho ku'nen kokusei chosa hokoku.* VII. Tables 34 and 35. Domestic servants living in were removed from the dependent population and added to the gainfully employed, using for those aged from 15 to 60 the age distribution of the dependent population. *Idem.* Tables 26 and 27. The non-employed living on income were subtracted from the gainfully employed and added to the dependent population. Numbers in the armed forces are those given in: *Idem.* Text, p. 129. The age distribution is that of the year 1930. See also: Hasegawa, T. "Population of Japan, 1920 and 1925." *Bulletin de L'Institute international de statistique,* 25 (2):30-33. 1931. Tables XIII and XIV. 1930: Nihon. Naikaku tokei-kyoku. *Showa go'nen kokusei chosa hokoku.* IV.2. Tables 4-6. The age distribution of the armed forces is that given in: U.S. Strategic Bombing Survey. *The Japanese wartime standard of living and utilization of manpower.* Table RR. 1940: Nihon. Naikaku tokei-kyoku. *Selected tables.* Table 4. For the armed forces, by subtraction from: Nihon. Sori-cho, tokei-kyoku. *Kekka hokoku tekiyo, Showa 15-nen kokusei chosa . . .*Table 5 (total population) and Table 7 (civilian population). 1950: *Ibid. Showa 25-nen kokusei chosa hokoku.* III.2. Tables 2 and 5a. 1955: *Ibid. 1% chushutsu shukei ni yoru sokuho. Showa 30-nen kokusei chosa. Zenkoku. II.* Table 1.

The Forces of Change

POPULATION GROWTH

The influence of increasing numbers of people on the size and structure of the labor force within Japan cannot be measured directly, for population increase itself was a factor in economic and political developments. The threat that population growth presented to the traditional economic and social structure can be illustrated if we make the following assumptions. Let us suppose that rates of economic activity are fixed and that the economy is unchanging. Four limiting conditions must serve as a basis for assessing the role of population increase in the problems of a stable economy with an unchanging labor market. First, the labor force consists solely of men. Secondly, each man enters the labor force at age 15 and remains in it until death or retirement at age 65. Third, there is no escape through military service or emigration, for on October 1, 1920, all colonial people and aliens are expelled from Japan, and the country is barred from outside contacts as it was during the centuries of Tokugawa rule. Fourth, the number of jobs is fixed, and no job is relinquished except for the demographic cause assumed. Within such an isolated country, births and deaths occur at the age-specific rates that characterized the actual population of Japan from 1920 to 1940. Japan's population problem thus becomes by definition the increase of her manpower between the ages of 15 and 64, for adjustment techniques, whether economic, political, or demographic, are ruled out.[2]

In 1920 the population of Japan included 16.4 million Japanese men aged from 15 to 64. If there had been no migration, the number would have increased to 22.3 million in 1940. Under the assumptions stated above, there would have been 180 Japanese entering the labor force at age 15 to compete for each 100 jobs vacated by the death or retirement of other and generally older workers. Forty-five per cent of the annual increment to the number of men in the productive ages would have been surplus.

One hundred and eighty men competing for each 100 jobs left vacant by death or retirement, an increase of 277 thousand job claimants each year in the 1920's, 312 thousand each year in the 1930's—given the validity of the assumptions underlying the computations, this would have measured Japan's population difficulties in the years before Pearl Harbor. It is, in fact, merely the framework within which the problems developed.

CIVILIAN VERSUS IMPERIAL UTILIZATION

The structure of the civilian labor force in Japan and the movements to and from the country were influenced by political and economic expansion and war or preparation for war.[3] In 1920 the direct quantitative influence of military action was slight. The contributions of Japanese manpower in World War I were limited. The losses that occurred were almost imperceptible in the age structure of the population of 1920. However, in 1920 the armed forces of Japan governed the recently acquired Micronesian Islands and occupied the former German Concessions in China; there was also an expeditionary force in Siberia. Japan's economy was aided greatly by the acquisition of markets and shipping formerly pre-empted by the European belligerents.

The year 1930 was probably the most normal year in which Japan has ever taken a complete census. The major impact of the great depression was still to be felt; the advance into Manchuria had not begun. In 1940 the war in China had been under way for three years and something like a million men were outside the country. In 1950 the labor force was affected by the aftermath of the war of 1937-1945.

The relations among population increase, gainful employment, imperial expansion, and war were complex, and they influenced the varying age groups in different ways. The following figures on percentage changes in total and civilian gainfully occupied men by age between 1920 and 1930 and between 1930 and 1940 will serve as a basis for discussion:[4]

	Total gainfully occupied		*Civilian gainfully occupied*	
Age of men	*1920-1930*	*1930-1940*	*1920-1930*	*1930-1940*
10 and over	12.0	12.6	12.3	5.0
10-14	−24.2	−11.5	−24.2	−11.8
15-19	13.4	11.1	13.3	9.0
20-24	19.1	9.8	21.5	−27.3
25-29	23.0	14.6	23.2	0.0
30-34	18.6	15.1	18.8	11.4
35-39	8.7	21.6	8.8	20.2
40-44	2.6	17.2	2.6	16.6
45-49	12.7	8.6	12.7	8.2
50-54	23.6	3.5	23.6	3.1
55-59	15.7	12.8	15.7	12.7
60 and over	−3.5	16.3	−3.5	16.3

The declines in the numbers gainfully occupied at age 10-14 were very large, especially when it is remembered that population in this age group was increasing rapidly. However, these changes were related to economic development and social advance rather than to militarism, migration, and war. Changes in the numbers of the gainfully occupied at age 15 to 19 were influenced primarily by non-military factors except insofar as militarism altered the employment opportunities available to youth below conscript age.

The direct effect of military utilization was most severe for men aged from 20 to 24, for the conscript age was lunar age 22, which is roughly equivalent to Western age 21. Between 1920 and 1930 the relative increases in the numbers of gainfully occupied men aged from 20 to 24 and from 25 to 29 were roughly comparable to those at later ages. Neither withdrawals for military purposes nor migration from Japan had altered sharply between 1920 and 1930. Between 1930 and 1940, however, there was a decline of more than one-fourth in the number of men aged from 20 to 24 who were in civilian occupations. The withdrawal of 1.7 million men for the armed forces was the major factor in this decline, but it was not the only one. Total gainfully occupied men aged from 20 to 24, civilian and military, were only 9.8 per cent

[2] The base population from which the computations were made was that of the ethnic Japanese in Japan on October 1, 1920. Official life table values were used to move this population forward by successive five-year periods. For procedures and references to sources, see Footnote 6, this chapter.

[3] In both 1920 and 1930 the armed forces were counted at the places where they were at midnight of September 30-October 1. There are reports of movements of troops prior to the census enumeration. In the industrial classification, members of the armed forces who could be assigned to industries other than the armed forces were so assigned. Thus the numbers of individuals reported as in military service in Table 26 are those who could not be allocated to industrial categories other than the total armed forces. In other words, "civilian" labor force was defined in terms of industry rather than in terms of the civilian or military status of the persons performing the gainful activity.

[4] For source of data, see references to Table 27.

greater in 1940 than in 1930. Emigration from Japan had been substantial.

relevant additions and subtractions follow, numbers being in thousands:[6]

Age of men	Increase of ethnic Japanese: Total[7]	Resident in Japan[8]	Removed from Japan[9]	Increase in nationals of colonial areas[10]	Net increase of population in Japan[11]
15-59	5,623	4,600	1,023	474	5,074
15-19	1,013	889	124	79	968
20-24	894	649	245	92	741
25-29	1,025	740	285	89	829
30-39	1,396	1,097	299	129	1,227
40-59	1,294	1,225	69	84	1,309

The direct effects of war and migration were major factors in the economic activities of men aged from 25 to 29, though the influences were less predominant than in the ages from 20 to 24. As age advanced, population increase, industrialization, and the state of the business cycle became the critical factors.

THE RELATIONS OF THE FACTORS OF CHANGE

Population increase, migration, and economic activity were so interrelated that it is difficult to determine the influence of each specific factor. We know that the increase of the population was not a direct determinant of the increase of the labor force. Population increase continued during the 1920's and 1930's, while the gainfully occupied population was influenced in one direction by the economic difficulties of the period from 1925 to 1930, in another direction by military expansion from 1931 to 1940. It is obvious, however, that continuing population increase influenced redistribution within the country and movements from it.

Analysis of the components of population increase may enable us to separate the influences of natural increase, migration, and military recruitment on the size and composition of the labor force. We have already estimated what the population of ethnic Japanese in Japan would have been in the absence of any movement to or from the country during the years from 1920 to 1940.[5] If we subtract the actual numbers of the ethnic Japanese in Japan in 1920 from the hypothetical numbers in 1940, we have by definition the increase that would have occurred in the absence of any migration of Japanese to or from the country. The difference between the number of ethnic Japanese enumerated in Japan in 1920 and the number enumerated in Japan in 1940 is the increase in ethnic Japanese that actually occurred. A simple subtraction of this actual increase from the hypothetical increase gives us the change associated with migration.

The separation of the increase of the ethnic Japanese between 1920 and 1940 into the two component groups, those resident in and those resident outside Japan in 1940, does not take care of the entire problem of population change within Japan. Non-Japanese moved to and from Japan during this period, the major group being nationals of the colonies. The net effect of this factor on the population of Japan is simple to estimate. If we subtract the numbers of the nationals of the colonies in Japan in 1920 from the numbers of such nationals in Japan in 1940, the difference is the increase associated with the migration and natural increase of the group. With this step we have separated the increase of population within Japan into two components, the increase of the ethnic Japanese and the increase of nationals of the colonies. The

[5] See p. 82, this chapter.

The actual population aged from 15 to 59 in Japan in 1940 was 32 per cent larger than the population in the same age groups in 1920. If there had been no migration to or from Japan between 1920 and 1940, the number of ethnic Japanese aged from 15 to 49 in Japan in 1940 would have been 36 per cent greater than the number in 1920. The alternative percentage changes by age groups are as follows:

Age	Actual population including armed forces	Ethnic Japanese without migration
15-59	32.5	36.0
15-19	35.2	36.8
20-24	32.0	38.6
25-29	41.3	51.0
30-39	34.6	39.4
40-59	26.1	25.8

It may be that the critical problem of an increasing population is the absorption of the additional number of persons rather than the maintenance of the changing total number. If so, the influence of migration on the *increase* of the popula-

[6] The Japanese population in Japan on October 1, 1920, was aged to 1940, initial cohorts being added on the assumption that the fertility ratios of the actual populations were appropriate for the hypothetical populations. Differences between the Japanese present in Japan on a census date and the number estimated in the absence of migration gave the estimated number of Japanese removed from Japan. It should be noted that the figures thus secured approximate net civilian emigration plus the natural increase of the emigrants outside Japan, for the million members of the Japanese armed forces outside the country on October 1, 1940, were enumerated with the civilian population of Japan. Numbers of colonials in Japan at the census dates and hence the increase in the numbers could be secured directly from census tabulations. Some disturbance is introduced by the fact that there were some armed forces outside the country in 1920 who were returned to it prior to 1930. However, insofar as this return migration influenced the computations, it served to reduce the estimate of net emigration of Japanese. The sources for the age distributions of ethnic Japanese and people from the Empire countries in Japan were as follows: 1920: Nihon. Naikaku tokei-kyoku. *Taisho ku'nen kokusei chosa hokoku.* IV.A.1. Table 26. 1930: *Ibid. Showa go'nen kokusei chosa hokoku.* IV.I. Table 29. 1940: Nihon. Sori-cho, tokei-kyoku. *Kekka hokoku tekiyo; Showa 15-nen kokusei chosa.* . . . Table 5, p. 26. Values for the life tables of 1920-1925 and 1925-1930 are given in: Nihon. Naikaku tokei-kyoku. *Showa go'nen shichi-gatsu.* . . . For the values of the life table of 1935-36, see: *Ibid. Showa juichi'nen ichi-gatsu.*

[7] The total increase of ethnic Japanese is the increase that would have occurred if there had been no movement to or from the country.

[8] The increase in the numbers of ethnic Japanese resident in Japan is the difference between the enumerated populations of 1920 and 1940.

[9] Net removal is a residual, increase within Japan being subtracted from total increase.

[10] Nationals of the colonies enumerated in Japan in 1920 subtracted from the numbers enumerated in 1940.

[11] Increase of ethnic Japanese in Japan plus increase of nationals of the colonies.

tion may be a more accurate measure of demographic impact than the influence of migration on the size of the total population. The relations of Japanese and colonial migrations between 1920 and 1940 to the population increases that would have occurred without migration are as follows:[12]

Age of men	*Ratio of actual increase to increase that would have occurred without migration (per 100)*	*Per cent of potential increase of Japanese removed by civilian migration from Japan*	*Ratio of colonial immigrants to civilian Japanese emigrants (per 100)*
15-59	90.2	18.2	46.3
15-19	95.6	12.2	63.7
20-24	82.9	27.4	37.6
25-29	80.9	27.8	31.2
30-39	87.9	21.4	43.1
40-59	101.2	5.3	121.7

Thus far we have been considering the migrations of civilians.[13] On October 1, 1940, more than a million men in the armed forces were stationed outside the country. If they also are removed from the population of Japan as of October 1, 1940, the estimates of proportionate losses of men in the productive ages are increased greatly.

Thus there was no smooth transfer of manpower from the agricultural to the industrial economy. In the twenty years from 1920 to 1940, imperial and military migration withdrew men from the labor market of the home country. By 1950 most of the surviving migrants had been returned to Japan and the reconstruction of the economy was in process. In 1955 there was substantial migration within the country but there were no external outlets.

Industrialization and Urbanization

It has been an implicit assumption that industrialization and urbanization are the primary forces involved in the complex changes in the Japanese labor force. If this assumption is valid, then at any given time there should be differences in the economic activities of men and women in rural and urban populations, in agricultural and industrial areas. With continuing industrialization and urbanization, there should be changes in the participation rates in rural and urban populations and in agricultural and industrial occupations. The nature of these changes will be approached through an analysis of the relations between rates of participation in the labor force and the urbanization of the population.

If participation in the labor force were related solely to age, the proportion of participants should be greatest in the cities, with their concentrations of population in the productive ages, and least in the remote rural areas, with their high proportions of children and old people. Yet in Japan the general participation rate was related inversely to the size of the commune of residence. It was lowest in the metropolitan areas, highest in the *mura*. The situation in the year 1947 is illustrative.[14] In small communes with populations of 5 thousand or less, half the total population was in the labor force. The percentage declined consistently with increasing size of commune: 45.7 in communes of from 5 thousand to 10 thousand, 40.5 in communes of from 10 to 50 thousand, 36.5 in cities of from 50 to 100 thousand, and 34.7 in cities of 100 thousand and over. If we go back to the year 1930, when social and economic conditions were more stable, we secure a clue as to the causes of the low rates in great cities, whose populations were weighted with people in the productive ages. The percentages of men and women gainfully occupied in 1930 varied as follows:[15]

Size of commune	*Men*	*Women*
100,000 and over	63.6	20.0
50,000-99,999	59.0	22.2
10,000-49,999	57.3	27.8
5,000-9,999	57.3	35.6
Less than 5,000	57.7	41.0

Thus in 1930 the relationship between size of commune and prevalence of gainful employment was direct for men, inverse for women. This association between rural residence and economic participation appeared whatever the index of urbanization, and it existed throughout the country. For prefectures, the correlations between the proportions of the population gainfully occupied and the proportions of the gainfully occupied population in agriculture were $-.72$ for men, $+.65$ for women.

There are no simple regularities in the relations between the economic activities of the age and sex groups and urbanization. Some clarification of the relations appears in a comparison of the age-specific participation rates of men and women in the six great cities and the other metropolitan centers of Japan in the year 1930 (Figure 3). In general, the proportions of the gainfully occupied among men were highest in the great cities of Tokyo, Yokohama, Nagoya, Osaka, Kobe, and Kyoto, least in the other cities with populations of 100 thousand or more, intermediate in the remainder of the country. This peculiar configuration appears to be related to the characteristics of the labor migrations that built the populations of the various types of cities. The sex ratio was highest in the great cities, and the age structure was influenced heavily by an in-migration of youth. If it can be presumed that in-migrant youth who were unsuccessful in the

[12] In order to simplify presentation, the terminal dates of 1920 and 1940 have been used. It should be remembered, however, that the redistribution of men in labor force ages occurred at a generally quickening rate in the years from 1920 to 1940, the net exodus of men from Japan being substantially greater in the 1930's than in the 1920's.

[13] There is one exception—the survivors of the armed forces who were outside Japan on October 1, 1920.

[14] Special tabulations of unpublished census data by the Institute of Population Problems, Welfare Ministry. For 1947 the tabulations of labor force status were made for the total population without distribution as to age or sex. See: Tachi, Minoru, and Ueda, Masao. "A statistical study on the variation of basic demographic phenomena by the size of communities." *Nihon jinko gakkai kiyo, Archives of the Population Association of Japan*, No. 1, pp. 94-112.

[15] *Ibid.* P. 100.

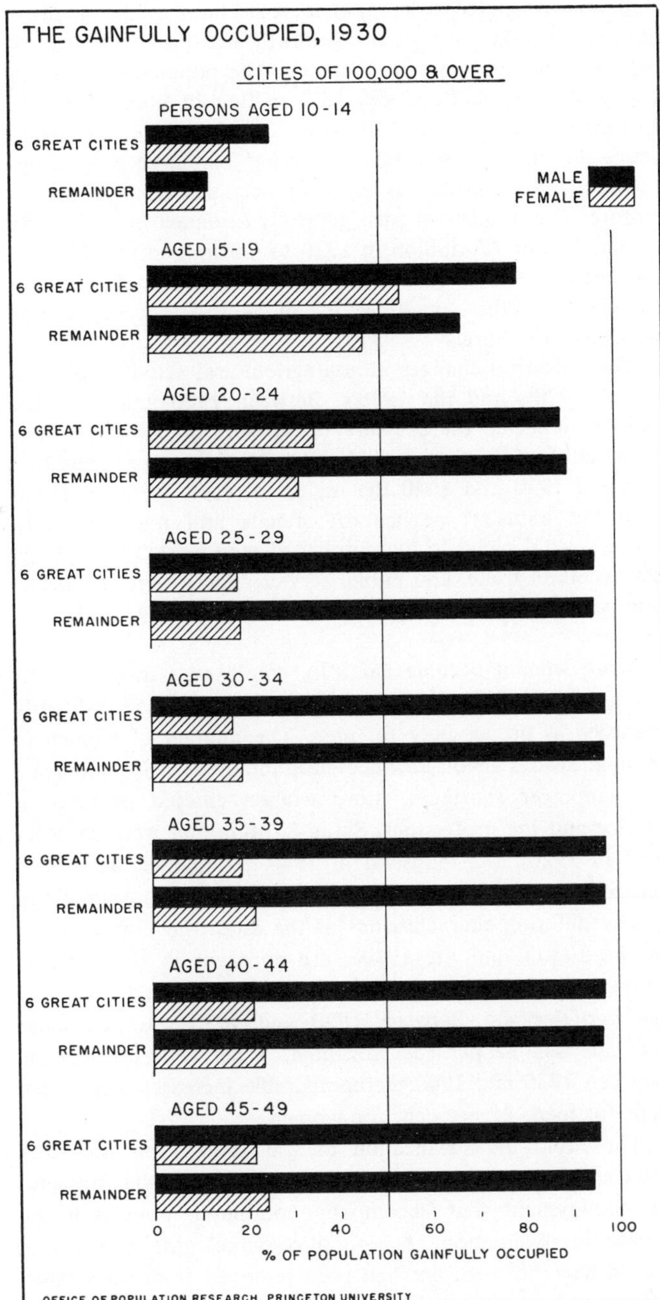

Figure 3. The gainfully occupied population, by sex and age, in the six great cities and in other cities of 100,000 and over, 1930

Source: Nihon. Naikaku tokei-kyoku. *Showa go'nen kokusei chosa hokoku.* IV.4. Tables 6 and 15.

search for jobs left the great cities, then the proportion of the gainfully occupied among those who remained and hence among the total population in the younger age groups would be high. Participation rates were also higher in the great cities for men in the middle and older ages. Here it might be assumed that those who were no longer capable of gainful employment in the great cities would be likely to move from the cities to the lesser towns or the rural areas.

Assumptions as to the relations between size of city and frequency of economic participation are hypotheses concerning the amount and the selectivity of the migration between rural and urban areas. As such, they will be considered in some detail in later sections. It is essential to note here that the possibility of gainful employment is a determining factor in the growth as well as the structure of the urban population. In a nation characterized by low levels of productivity and income, the growth of the labor force is a precondition to the growth of the so-called dependent population and hence to the normalization of the age and sex structure of the city populations. Furthermore, the persistence of gainful employment may be essential to the maintenance of urban residence. The high participation rates of men in the great cities of Japan may be characteristics of a population with major movements from rural to urban areas.

In 1930 the variations in the gainful employment of women were primarily differences between the rural and the urban segments of the economy rather than between cities of various sizes. Participation rates for girls below age 20 were much higher in the six great cities than in the other cities of 100 thousand or more; participation rates for girls aged from 20 to 24 were slightly higher. After age 25 to 29 differences by size of city were small. The high rates for women aged 25 and above occurred in areas where agriculture and household industries permitted the reconciliation of gainful employment with the proper duties of women in the home.

The participation rates for 1930 were based on a definition of gainful occupations, and they concern a period almost a generation ago. The participation rates for 1950 are based on a definition of the labor force. They concern a period when rural-urban relationships were disturbed by a heavy pressure of maturing youth on employment opportunities. Levels of living were below the standards that people regarded as adequate. The school attendance of youth had increased greatly as contrasted with 1930. Formal retirement from wage and salary jobs in large industries had been pushed down to age 55 or so to assist in the distribution of sparse jobs among a numerous people. It is understandable, therefore, that there should have been substantial changes in the participation of men and women in the labor force in urban areas. Differences between the six great cities and the other cities of 100 thousand and over had virtually disappeared. Relatively favorable employment opportunities, rapid in-migration, and high participation rates characterized several of the lesser cities of 100 thousand and over rather than the giants.

Differences in economic activities in the *shi* and the *gun* in 1950 reflected cultural as well as economic factors. Participation rates for men aged from 15 to 19 and from 20 to 24 were lower in the *shi* than in the *gun*, a difference that was probably associated with the greater prevalence of school attendance in the cities (FIGURE 4). Retirement had also entered the urban scene far more than it had the rural. There were reductions in the rural-urban differences in the economic activities of women. A variety of factors were involved, including changing industrial structures, advancing ages at marriage, and pressures on the labor market.

The economic activities of men and women in 1955 reflected both the altered condition of the economy and reduced rates of childbearing. As shown at the bottom of the next page, the percentages of participants in the labor force in cities of 50,000 and over and in the *gun* indicate sharp differences between urban and agricultural populations.

The Industrial Structure

THE NATION

The proportions of the gainfully occupied or of the labor force in agriculture, forestry, and fishing have declined since

[16] Nihon. Sori-fu, tokei-kyoku. *1% chushutsu shukei ni yoru kekka sokuho. Showa 30-nen kokusei chosa. Zenkoku.* II. Table 1.

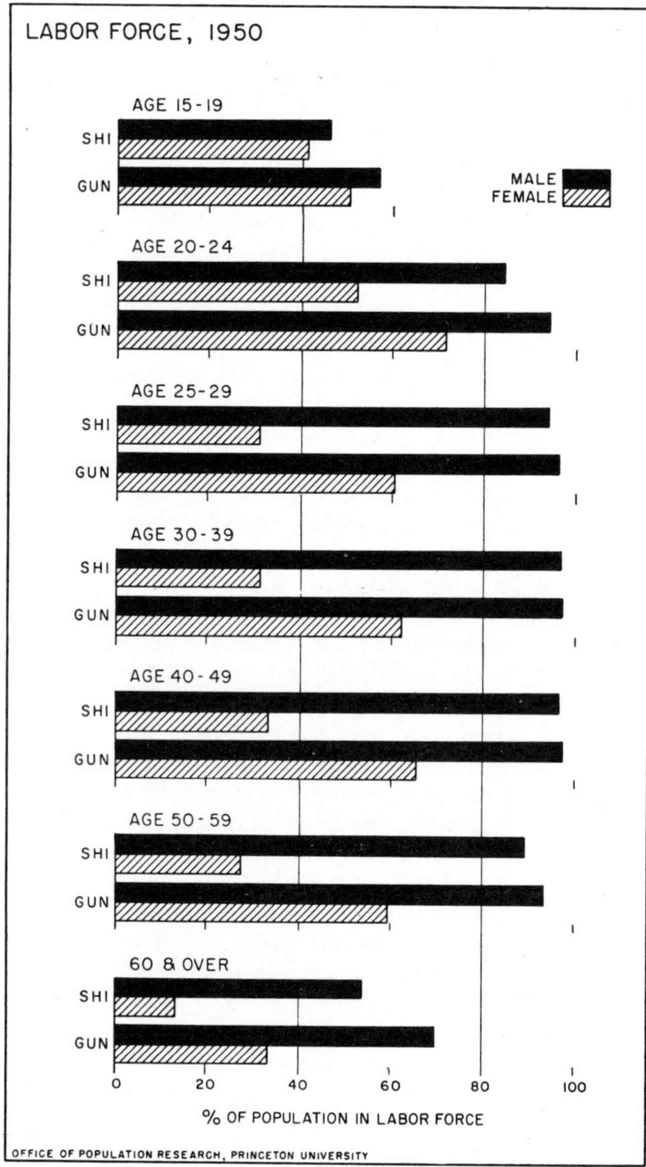

Figure 4. The labor force in the *shi* and the *gun*, by sex and age, 1950

Source: Nihon. Sori-fu, tokei-kyoku. *Showa 25-nen kokusei chosa hokoku.* III.2. Table 5.

1920, while the proportions in manufacturing, commerce, transportation, and communication have increased. From 1920 to 1940 a relatively unchanging population in agriculture was associated with rapid increase both in the numbers and in the proportion of the gainfully occupied who secured their livelihood from other sources. The population gainfully occupied in agriculture was 13.7 million in both 1920 and 1930, 13.4 million in 1940 (TABLE 28).[17] This decline understates the changes that were occurring, for large proportions of the women reported as gainfully occupied labored in agriculture. The number of men gainfully occupied in agriculture declined from 7.5 million in 1920 to 6.3 million in 1940; the proportion declined from 44.0 in 1920 to 32.0 in 1940. Thus by 1940 less than one-third of all gainfully occupied men were in agriculture.

Age	Men: Cities of 50,000 and over	Men: Gun	Women: Cities of 50,000 and over	Women: Gun
15 and over	83.7	86.9	40.3	60.7
15-19	53.0	56.0	48.3	51.4
20-24	82.8	94.2	62.0	75.0
25-29	95.2	97.1	39.8	65.8
30-34	96.5	97.4	35.2	65.6
35-39	97.1	97.6	38.9	68.9
40-44	97.3	97.6	40.8	70.5
45-49	96.7	97.5	39.1	68.7
50-54	94.7	96.3	36.4	65.1
55-59	88.8	93.2	29.7	59.2
60-64	76.6	86.9	24.0	49.6
65 and over	48.8	61.1	12.3	26.6

The industrial changes in non-agricultural activities differed in the 1920's and the 1930's. Between 1920 and 1930 the changes reflected the pressure of workers on jobs. Increases occurred mainly in unpaid labor and service activities. Between 1930 and 1940 the major increases were in manufacturing industry, particularly metals and machine tools. There were declines in the number of men working in fishing, construction, trade, and public service. There were increasing numbers of women in agriculture, manufacturing, trade, and service.

More women became gainfully employed during the war years, but few entered those occupations that were ordinarily regarded as proper only for men. The number of women in mining, always small, declined substantially. During the years of manpower shortages, more women entered government service and the professions. Some 85 thousand were so occupied in 1920, 372 thousand in 1940.[18] Nonetheless, women remained primarily in the menial and poorly paid occupations.

The differing characteristics of the industrial developments in the 1920's and the 1930's are apparent in the differing changes in the numbers of the gainfully occupied by sex in the two decades. Between 1920 and 1930 the percentage increase was 12 per cent for men, 3 per cent for women; between 1930 and 1940 the comparable increases were 4 per cent for men, 21 per cent for women.

The rapid industrialization of the 1930's and the early 1940's did not reflect a permanent solution to the problems of employment that accompany continuing population increase in a situation of limited resources. Manpower that would have been surplus had been removed from the civilian force in Japan through the migrations of civilians to the conquered areas and the growth of the armed forces. Military production made heavy requirements on the manpower left for civilian use within Japan.

The return to agriculture in the postwar years was temporary, and it was limited. In 1947, the proportion of the male labor force in agriculture was 39 per cent, greater than the 32 per cent in 1940 but approximately the same as the 40 per cent in 1930. In the years from 1947 to 1955 there was a rapid recovery of the non-agricultural sector of the

[17] Area of Japan as of the 1950 census. The Bureau of Statistics retabulated the data of the censuses of 1920, 1930, 1940, and 1947 to secure as close a comparability as possible with the categories of the labor force classification in 1950, although it was stated explicitly that the differences in the definitions of industries in 1920, 1930, and 1940 and the differences between the definitions of the gainfully occupied in 1920-1940 and the definitions of the labor force in 1947 and 1950 permitted only the broadest of comparisons. Nihon. Sori-fu, tokei-kyoku. *Sangyo betsu shugyosha no hikaku.* Pu. 1-6.

[18] These figures are based on the areas and classifications as of the census dates rather than on the retabulations presented in Table 28.

TABLE 28

The industrial structure of the economically active population, 1920-1955

Industry	NUMBER (IN '000)						PER CENT COMPOSITION					
	1920	*1930*	*1940*	*1947*	*1950*	*1955*	*1920*	*1930*	*1940*	*1947*	*1950*	*1955*
					Total							
All industries	26,966	29,341	32,231	33,329	35,575	39,154	100.	100.	100.	100.	100.	100.
Agriculture	13,727	13,742	13,363	16,622	16,132	14,856	50.9	46.8	41.5	49.9	45.3	37.9
Forestry	189	186	292	480	402	525	.7	.6	.9	1.4	1.1	1.3
Fishing	526	562	538	710	690	718	2.0	1.9	1.7	2.1	1.9	1.8
Mining	421	314	596	667	576	533	1.6	1.1	1.8	2.0	1.6	1.4
Construction	717	977	978	1,320	1,379	1,812	2.7	3.3	3.0	4.0	3.9	4.6
Manufacturing	4,438	4,702	6,845	5,440	5,646	6,968	16.5	16.0	21.2	16.3	15.9	17.8
Trade, wholesale and retail	2,650	4,113	4,083	2,115	3,835	5,403	9.8	14.0	12.7	6.3	10.8	13.8
Banking, insurance, etc.	130	194	298	251	363	608	.5	.7	.9	.8	1.0	1.6
Transportation, communication, etc.	1,133	1,289	1,516	1,709	1,806	2,207	4.2	4.4	4.7	5.1	5.1	5.2
Service	1,932	2,459	2,887	2,656	3,156	4,375	7.2	8.4	9.0	8.0	8.9	11.2
Public service	579	733	618	915	1,508	1,326	2.1	2.5	1.9	2.7	4.2	3.4
Other and unknown	524	71	217	444	82	2	1.9	.2	.7	1.3	.2	.0
					Males							
All industries	16,820	18,878	19,599	20,622	21,811	23,848	100.	100.	100.	100.	100.	100.
Agriculture	7,469	7,465	6,271	8,013	7,819	7,088	44.4	39.5	32.0	38.9	35.8	29.7
Forestry	157	156	252	418	345	403	.9	.8	1.3	2.0	1.6	1.7
Fishing	490	509	471	612	614	577	2.9	2.7	2.4	3.0	2.8	2.4
Mining	324	270	527	568	511	485	1.9	1.4	2.7	2.8	2.3	2.0
Construction	710	970	956	1,268	1,301	1,683	4.2	5.1	4.9	6.2	6.0	7.1
Manufacturing	2,892	3,276	4,959	3,981	4,025	4,838	17.2	17.4	25.3	19.3	18.5	20.3
Trade, wholesale and retail	1,831	2,904	2,608	1,433	2,343	3,191	10.9	15.4	13.3	6.9	10.7	13.4
Banking, insurance, etc.	118	175	226	167	241	408	.7	.9	1.2	.8	1.1	1.7
Transportation, communication, etc.	1,068	1,197	1,355	1,510	1,608	1,780	6.3	6.3	6.9	7.3	7.4	7.5
Service	864	1,189	1,294	1,611	1,700	2,284	5.1	6.3	6.6	7.8	7.8	9.6
Public service	564	704	527	733	1,251	1,108	3.4	3.7	2.7	3.5	5.7	4.6
Other and unknown	334	63	154	307	52	2	2.0	.3	.8	1.5	.2	.0
					Females							
All industries	10,146	10,463	12,632	12,707	13,763	15,307	100.	100.	100.	100.	100.	100.
Agriculture	6,257	6,277	7,092	8,609	8,314	7,768	61.7	60.0	56.1	67.8	60.4	50.8
Forestry	32	31	39	62	56	122	.3	.3	.3	.5	.4	.8
Fishing	37	53	67	97	76	141	.4	.5	.5	.8	.5	.9
Mining	96	45	69	100	65	48	1.0	.4	.5	.8	.5	.3
Construction	7	7	22	52	77	129	.1	.1	.2	.4	.6	.8
Manufacturing	1,547	1,426	1,887	1,459	1,621	2,130	15.2	13.6	14.9	11.5	11.8	13.9
Trade, wholesale and retail	819	1,209	1,476	681	1,492	2,212	8.1	11.6	11.7	5.4	10.8	14.5
Banking, insurance, etc.	13	18	71	84	121	200	.1	.2	.6	.7	.9	1.3
Transportation, communication, etc.	65	92	162	199	197	247	.6	.9	1.3	1.6	1.4	1.6
Service	1,068	1,270	1,593	1,046	1,456	2,091	10.5	12.1	12.6	8.2	10.6	13.7
Public service	16	30	91	182	257	218	.2	.3	.7	1.4	1.9	1.4
Other and unknown	190	7	64	137	30	0	1.9	.1	.5	1.1	.2	.0

Source: Nihon. Sori-fu tokei-kyoku. *Sangyo betsu shugyosha no hikaku.* Pp. 7, 11, and 15. The limitation of coverage to the area of Japan as of 1950 and the reclassification of the gainfully occupied in previous censuses to accord as nearly as possible with the 1950 labor force classification account for differences between the data in this table and those given in other tables based on the original publications of the censuses. 1955 data: Nihon. Sori-fu, tokei-kyoku. *1% chushutsu shukei ni yoru kekka sokuho. Showa 30-nen kokusei chosa. Zenkoku.* III.1. Table 2.

economy.[19] By 1955, less than 30 per cent of the male labor force was in agriculture.

PREFECTURES BY INDUSTRIAL TYPE

Measurement of the relative industrialization of the prefectures is difficult, whether data on industrial production or on the industrial composition of the labor force are used. It seems desirable, therefore, to base classification on the most consistently defined of all occupational-industrial categories, the gainfully occupied in agriculture.

An index of industrial type based on the proportion of the gainfully occupied population in agriculture has major analytical value. The modernization of Japanese culture was related closely to the change from a rural and an agricultural to an urban and an industrial base. Rates of population growth and changes in the age and sex structures of populations were correlated with cultural modernization and economic change in the various regions of the country. If the declining proportion of the gainfully occupied population in agriculture is an index of the basic economic and social movements in an area, the index can be used in measuring the relations of migration and vital rates to social and economic factors.

In 1930, two prefectures had less than one-fifth of their gainfully occupied population in agriculture—Tokyo and Osaka (MAP 6).[20] Five prefectures had from one-fifth to two-fifths in agriculture—Kanagawa, Aichi, Kyoto, Hyogo, and Fukuoka. Each of these five prefectures had one or more large cities within its boundaries—Yokohama in Kanagawa, Nagoya in Aichi, Kyoto in Kyoto, Kobe in Hyogo, and the cluster of cities of 100 thousand and over in Fukuoka. These five prefectures may be designated as "other industrial prefectures." In 1930 the seven industrial prefectures, including both the two metropolitan prefectures and the five other industrial prefectures, included 31 per cent of Japan's total population.

Prefectures with 60 per cent or more of their gainfully occupied population in agriculture were defined as agricultural. There were 20 prefectures in this category in 1930: Miyazaki, Oita, Kumamoto, Shimane, Tottori, Shiga, Yamanashi, Niigata, Chiba, Saitama, Tochigi, Fukushima, Yamagata, Akita, Miyagi, Iwate, Aomori, Ibaraki, Kagoshima, and Okinawa. In 1930, they included 33 per cent of Japan's total population.

In 1930, 19 of the 47 prefectures of Japan had between 40 and 59 per cent of their gainfully occupied population in agriculture. These intermediate prefectures included four with from 40 to 49 per cent thus employed: Nagasaki, Hiroshima, Wakayama, and Nara. The other 15 prefectures had from 50 to 59 per cent: Saga, Kochi, Ehime, Kagawa, Tokushima, Yamaguchi, Okayama, Mie, Shizuoka, Gifu, Nagano, Fukui, Ishikawa, Toyama, and Gumma. Together, they included 31 per cent of the total population of Japan.

If the prefecture of Hokkaido were included in the pre-

[19] The materials in *The Monthly Report on the Labor Force* differ somewhat from those of the enumerative censuses. The percentages in agriculture for men were 40 per cent in 1950, 35 per cent in 1955. The use of a labor force concept in a census taken on October 1 lessens the proportion of the population in agriculture. For the labor force materials, see: Nihon. Sori-fu, tokei-kyoku. *Rodoryoku chosa sogo hokokusho*. No. 2. Table 8. *Idem. Rodoryoku chosa hokoku*. June 1956. Table 4. Data are based on samples and were rounded independently for males and females.

[20] The industrial classification of the gainfully occupied was used. The data are given in: Nihon. Naikaku tokei-kyoku. *Showa go'nen kokusei chosa sokuho*. VIII. Table 46.

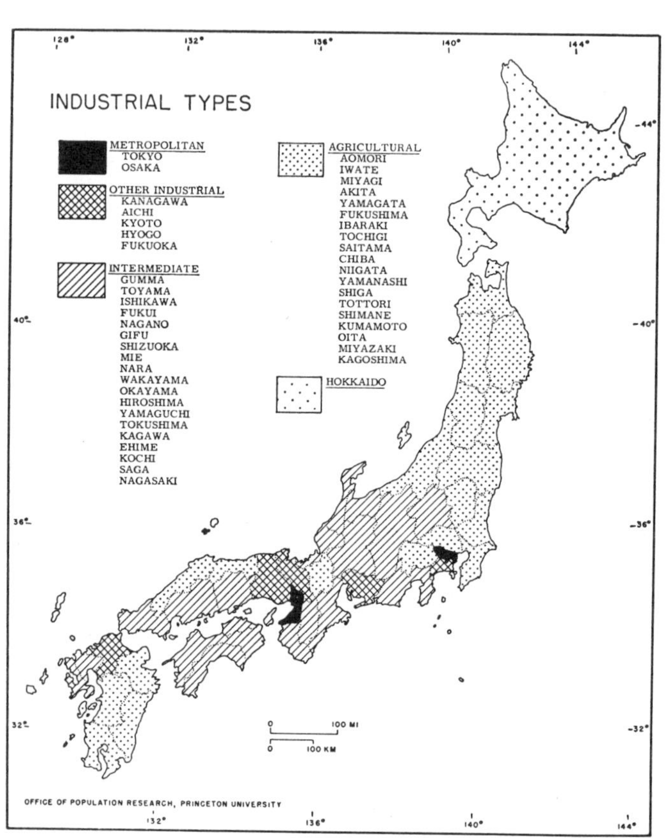

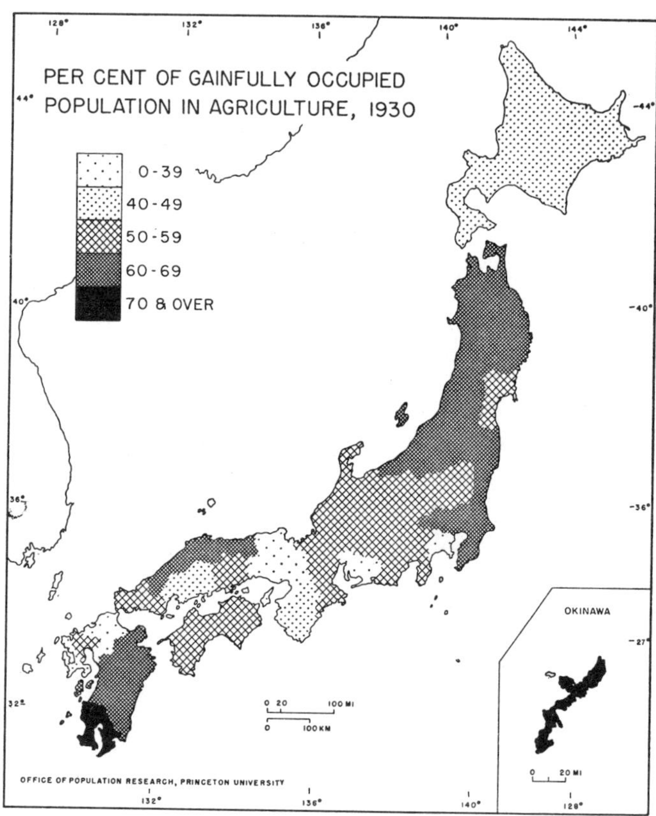

Map 6. Prefectures by industrial type; and the proportion of the gainfully occupied population in agriculture, 1930

Source: Nihon. Naikaku tokei-kyoku. Showa go'nen kokusei chosa hokoku. IV. 4. Table 17.

ceding classification of metropolitan, other industrial, intermediate, and agricultural prefectures, it would be classified as intermediate. Hokkaido should be considered separately, however, for it is comparable to a region of Japan rather than to one of the prefectures. Its settlement is recent, that of the other main islands ancient. And as contrasted with other areas of Japan, the agriculture of Hokkaido is extensive. Its climate differs greatly from that in the islands to the south, and the people are dispersed and rather isolated, in contrast with the close village life in other areas.

Since industrialization was developing throughout Japan, the differences among the prefectures at a given time might be expected to be similar to those that occurred in the national population over time. If this were so, agricultural prefectures would be nearest the characteristics of the nation at the earliest census date, while industrial prefectures would be nearest to or in advance of the characteristics of the nation at the most recent census date. Furthermore, if a classification based on the situation in 1930 yielded a delineation valid for other periods, there would be a characteristic pattern of differences among prefectures in a year remote from 1930.[21] Hence labor force participation rates are presented for the prefectures in 1950 on the basis of a classification by industrial type as of 1930 (FIGURE 5).

Theoretical anticipations are verified. For the total population of Japan, the trend was toward lesser participation of youth and the aged in the labor force. In 1950 high participation rates among youth and the aged were characteristic of the more agricultural prefectures. Participation rates declined as the proportion of the labor force in non-agricultural industries increased. In the central span of life from about age 25 to age 59, the declines in labor force participation rates from agricultural to metropolitan prefectures presumably reflected the declining proportions of women in the labor force of the industrial regions. However, there is one exception to the regularity of the changes. Labor force participation rates were lower in the agricultural prefectures (more than 60 per cent of the labor force in agriculture) than in the intermediate agricultural prefectures (from 50 to 59 per cent of the labor force in agriculture).

Labor force participation rates for men showed small differences among the prefectures when all men aged 14 and over were considered. Rates were somewhat lower in the metropolitan and other industrial prefectures, somewhat higher in the agricultural prefectures and Hokkaido. The range, however, was only from 78.1 as the low in the metropolitan prefectures to 82.8 as the high in the agricultural prefectures. Variations among the industrial types of prefectures were substantial at the younger ages, where proportions in the labor market declined progressively with industrialization, and at the upper ages, where withdrawal from the labor market was far more characteristic of industrial than of agricultural prefectures. In the central span of life, participation rates were high in all types of prefectures, though they were definitely higher in the more agricultural areas. The reconciliation of rather substantial differences at various ages with slight differences for all males aged 14 and over lies in the differences in the age structure of the male population in the various types of prefectures. The proportion of men aged 14 and over who were in the central span of life was highest in the metropolitan and industrial prefectures, lowest in the agricultural prefectures.

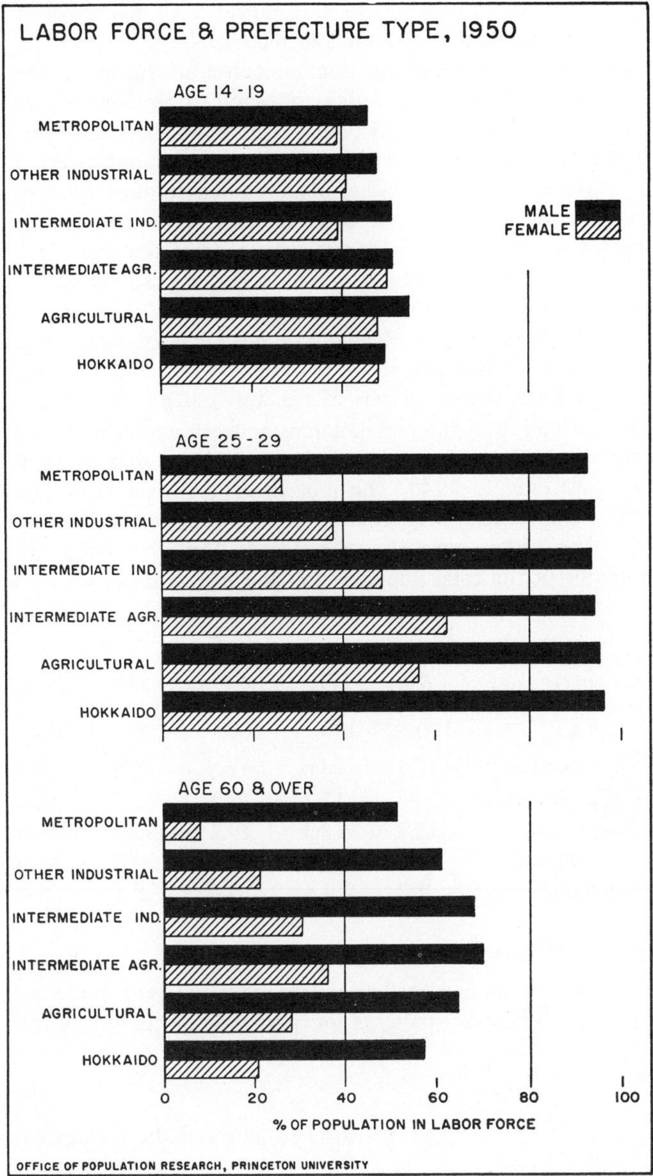

Figure 5. Labor force participation, by age and sex, prefectures by industrial type, 1950

Source: Nihon. Sori-fu, tokei-kyoku. *Showa 25-nen kokusei chosa hokoku*. III.2. Table 17.

The differences in the participation rates of women at various ages in agricultural and industrial prefectures were due to the agricultural-industrial transformation of the economy. Women preserved their ancient roles when they married; labor outside the home was not appropriate and labor within the home or the family enterprise was limited during the years of heaviest domestic responsibility. This life cycle of women was evident in their economic activity, whatever the type of prefecture. Prefectural differences at any given age reflected the availability of employment defined as

[21] The differentiations of occupational structure that existed in the year 1930 were quite similar to those that existed in the years from 1920 to 1950. As we have emphasized again and again, the normal developmental trends in Japan involved a concentration of increasing proportions of the total population in the more industrialized prefectures and the movements of population from agricultural to non-agricultural occupations in all prefectures. However, in the transformations of the decades between 1920 and 1950 the regional characteristics of Japanese culture and economy were maintained with few basic alterations. With change extending throughout a nation without sharp dislocations in regional patterns, it thus becomes possible to utilize a classification of prefectures by industrial type in 1930 to characterize the changes in constant groups of prefectures over the period from 1920 through 1954.

appropriate for women—and this meant high participation rates in agriculture and household industries.

The labor force participation rates for all Japan at any given time may be regarded as a weighted average of the participation rates in the industrial regions. In the years from 1920 to 1940, two processes were operating simultaneously to create an industrial rather than an agricultural type of structure for the country as a whole. One was the economic changes occurring within the prefectures, from the most agricultural to the most industrial. The other was an increasing movement of the population into the industrial prefectures. By 1950 the forces of change had been altered somewhat. Economic activities and social adjustments reflected a partial recovery from the conditions of the war and post-war years. The distribution of the population as between agricultural and industrial prefectures was more comparable to that in 1920 and 1930 than in 1940. The movements between 1947 and 1950 were toward a restoration of the prewar pattern. By 1955 that pattern was almost restored. The percentage distributions of the total population at the census dates were as follows:

Prefectures by industrial type	*1920*	*1930*	*1940*	*1950*	*1955*
All Japan	100.	100.	100.	100.	100.
Metropolitan	11.4	14.0	16.7	12.2	14.2
Other industrial	16.6	17.1	18.5	17.5	18.0
Intermediate	33.2	31.3	29.1	30.9	29.4
Agricultural	34.6	33.2	31.2	34.3	33.0
Hokkaido	4.2	4.4	4.5	5.1	5.4

THE RURAL-URBAN CONTINUUM

When we classified prefectures by industrial type and then found characteristic patterns of participation in economic activity by type of prefecture, primary emphasis was placed on the industrial structure of the population. The predominant type of industry was associated with prefectural differences in the structure of the labor force. It may be argued that the distinction should have been that between rural and urban populations, that differences between prefectures classified by industrial type were due to the relative proportions of rural and urban people.

Initial examination of the occupational and industrial characteristics of the gainfully occupied in the *shi* and the *gun* in 1930 reveals a seeming paradox.[22] Almost three-fourths of all men gainfully occupied in manufacturing industry lived in *gun*, only a little more than one-fourth in *shi*. No major category of economic activity was primarily urban, in the sense that the major portion of the men engaged in it lived in *shi*. However, the industrial composition of the population of the *shi* was distinctly urban. Only 4 per cent of the gainfully occupied men were in agriculture, while three-fourths were in the "urban" industries of manufacturing, commerce, and transportation. Similarly, the industrial composition of the gainfully occupied in the *gun* was appropriately rural; more than half the gainfully occupied men and three-fourths of the gainfully occupied women labored in agriculture.

The explanation for this apparent inconsistency between a continually urbanizing population structure and an economy the major portion of whose industrial workers were rural is evident in the industrial composition of the population of the communes classified by size (TABLE 29). In 1930 there was a direct association between size of place and predominance

[22] The composition of the population by sex and by age for broad, intermediate, and fine classifications of occupations and industries is available for the larger cities as well as the prefectures. Broad classifications without age are available for *shi, machi*, and *mura*. See: Nihon. Naikaku tokei-kyoku. *Showa go'nen kokusei chosa sokuho*. IV. 2; IV. 4; and VIII. The specific data cited here were secured from Vol. VIII, Table 37.

TABLE 29

The industrial structure of the gainfully occupied population, by size of commune, 1930
(Gainfully occupied, by size of commune)

Size of commune	*All industries*	*Agriculture and forestry*	*Fishing*	*Mining*	*Manufacturing*	*Trade and commerce*	*Transportation and communication*	*Public service and professional*	*Domestic*	*Other*
				Per cent distribution by size of commune						
Total	100.	100.	100.	100.	100.	100.	100.	100.	100.	100.
Under 10,000	62.3	89.0	74.6	38.6	38.8	32.8	36.1	40.4	34.4	24.3
10,000-49,999	15.0	9.4	17.4	48.4	20.1	19.8	19.0	18.2	20.2	15.7
50,000-99,999	6.1	0.7	3.6	10.6	11.2	11.4	12.0	10.9	10.3	8.9
100,000 and over	16.6	0.9	4.3	2.4	30.0	36.0	32.9	30.5	35.1	51.1
				Per cent composition within size group						
Total	100.	47.7	1.9	1.1	19.8	16.6	3.2	6.8	2.7	0.2
Under 10,000	100.	68.1	2.3	0.7	12.3	8.7	1.8	4.4	1.5	0.1
10,000-49,999	100.	29.9	2.2	3.4	26.5	21.8	4.0	8.2	3.6	0.2
50,000-99,999	100.	5.6	1.2	1.9	36.7	31.1	6.3	12.2	4.6	0.4
100,000 and over	100.	2.5	0.5	0.2	35.8	35.9	6.3	12.4	5.7	0.7

Source: Special tabulations of data from the 1930 census, published by Tachi, Minoru, and Ueda, Masao, as: "Demographic research on the differences of the fundamental population phenomena by the size of community." *The First General Meeting of the Population Association of Japan, Data Paper*, March 19, 1949. Table 6. See also: Tachi, Minoru, and Ueda, Masao. "A statistical study on the variation of basic demographic phenomena by the size of communities." Pp. 94-112 in: *Nihon jinko gakkai kiyo, Archives of the Population Association of Japan*, No. 1, 1952. The tabulations for 1950 were given in: *Jinko mondai kenkyu*. Pp. 90-91. March 1956.

of "urban" industries. However, there was no decisive break below which industrial structure could be said to be agricultural and above which it could be said to be industrial. The critical distinction between urban and rural areas, as between the majority of the small cities and the metropolitan centers, was that between agriculture combined with the handicraft production and service activities of the traditional peasant society, on the one hand, and the cluster of activities associated with modern factory production and distribution, on the other.

The peculiarities in the distribution of occupations and the characteristics of the labor force in communes classified by size are in part products of the fact that a Western industrial structure was assumed in the census enumeration and in the classification of the census data. Persons engaged in handicrafts or other household industries were returned as engaged in manufacturing industry. If the activities in homes and in small shops are eliminated, as they were in the factory statistics that included only factories having five or more workers, the relation between the city and manufacturing industry becomes clear. In 1930, one-third of all male factory operatives were to be found in the metropolitan prefectures, three-fifths in the metropolitan and the other industrial prefectures. Whatever the type of prefecture, male factory operatives were concentrated in the large cities.

A further complication was introduced in the postwar years when the *shi* annexed large areas of essentially rural territory at the same time that many small settlements incorporated as *shi*. The result of these annexations and incorporations was that the population of the cities in 1950 included larger proportions of agricultural workers than in 1930. Summary data on the percentage distribution of employed persons by major industry by size of commune in 1950 are as follows:[23]

in Western industries continued to require the traditional consumption goods and services, and so the large cities became centers for their production. It was the combination of factory industry and modern transportation and communications with the ancient ways of producing and distributing consumption goods that permitted the great concentrations in urban areas.

The Social Structure

The structure of the labor force is measured only partially by industrial categories of employment. The farms of Japan in no way resemble the wide expanse of the Kansas wheat field or the red barns and the silos of the Wisconsin dairy lands. Japanese agriculture is characterized by the clustered village, the waving green or yellow of rice fields, the cultivation of each bit of soil in a garden land whose beauty belies the poverty of a peasantry that cannot procure subsistence from the land alone. In the West, the word "industrialization" recalls the smoke of Pittsburgh, the epic of Detroit, or perhaps the mines of the Mesabi. In Japan there are the Yawata steel works and the mines of the Mitsubishi—but there are also household industries and local shops where peasants toil long hours for meager returns. Food, clothing, and considerable household equipment are produced locally by hand labor. Even in the great cities craftsmen labor long hours each day to produce the artistic products that add so much charm to Japanese life.

Japan's economic transformation is difficult to describe in numerical terms because it involved an integration of things Western and things Eastern. However, the differences in social and economic structure can be summarized by a simple index—the proportion of the labor force that consists of

Industry	*Total*	*Below 5,000*	*5,000-9,999*	*10,000-49,999*	*50,000-99,999*	*100,000 and over*
All industries	100.	100.	100.	100.	100.	100.
Primary						
Agriculture	45.2	71.6	61.6	39.2	18.8	8.0
Forestry	1.2	2.3	1.5	0.7	0.3	0.1
Fishing	1.9	1.7	2.7	2.8	1.3	0.8
Secondary						
Mining	1.7	0.5	1.1	4.1	5.0	0.6
Construction	4.3	3.0	3.4	4.4	5.7	6.4
Manufacturing	16.0	6.5	10.6	17.8	24.3	29.3
Tertiary						
Trade, wholesale and retail	11.1	4.3	6.8	11.8	17.3	21.8
Banking, insurance, etc.	1.0	0.3	0.4	0.8	1.6	2.5
Transportation, communications, etc.	5.1	2.9	3.4	5.1	7.1	8.7
Service	8.6	4.5	6.0	9.3	12.8	14.5
Public service	3.9	2.1	2.3	3.8	5.7	7.1
Other and unknown	0.1	0.1	0.1	0.1	0.1	0.2

The differentiation of rural and urban economies is blurred. Many of the manufactured products of Japan came from the villages and the smaller towns; the persistence of local production enabled the rural society to preserve its ways of living. It is true that most of the people who labored in modern factories lived in cities, but these workers were only a fraction of all the gainfully occupied of the cities. Modern workers

unpaid family workers. In 1950 more than one-third of all employed persons in Japan were in this category (Table 30). For the total employed, as for men and women considered separately, there was a direct relationship between the prevalence of unpaid family labor and the importance of agriculture in the area of residence. For men, the proportion of all the employed who labored as unpaid family workers extended from 6 per cent in the metropolitan prefectures to 24 per cent in the agricultural prefectures; the comparable range

[23] Nihon. Sori-fu, tokei-kyoku. *Showa 25-nen kokusei chosa hokoku*. VIII. *Saishu hokokusho*.

TABLE 30

Employed persons, by class of worker and sex, in the *shi* and the *gun*, prefectures by industrial type, 1950
(Per cent of employed persons)

Industrial type	TOTAL			MALE			FEMALE		
	Self-employed	*Unpaid family labor*	*Wage or salary*	*Self-employed*	*Unpaid family labor*	*Wage or salary*	*Self-employed*	*Unpaid family labor*	*Wage or salary*
				Total					
All Japan	26.1	34.4	39.5	34.8	17.5	47.7	12.2	61.3	26.4
Metropolitan	19.4	10.2	70.1	22.2	5.6	72.0	12.1	22.6	65.1
Other industrial	22.9	23.8	53.2	28.2	11.0	60.7	12.8	48.3	38.8
Intermediate	28.5	36.9	34.5	39.1	18.6	42.2	13.1	63.6	23.3
Agricultural	27.9	44.3	27.7	40.0	24.3	35.7	11.7	71.1	17.1
Hokkaido	21.4	32.8	45.8	28.0	17.0	55.0	8.6	63.5	27.9
				Shi					
All Japan	20.9	14.3	64.7	23.9	6.9	69.1	14.1	31.0	54.8
Metropolitan	18.5	8.4	72.9	20.8	4.5	74.5	12.2	18.9	68.6
Other industrial	19.0	12.8	68.2	21.0	5.7	73.1	14.0	29.6	56.3
Intermediate	24.5	18.6	56.9	29.2	9.1	61.7	15.6	36.6	47.8
Agricultural	23.5	20.3	56.2	28.1	10.0	61.9	15.0	39.3	45.6
Hokkaido	16.5	12.5	70.9	18.3	5.9	75.8	11.6	30.8	57.6
				Gun					
All Japan	28.6	44.2	27.1	41.2	23.7	35.1	11.6	72.1	16.3
Metropolitan	24.8	20.8	54.0	30.4	12.2	56.9	11.8	40.7	47.3
Other industrial	27.1	35.6	37.3	37.1	17.5	45.4	11.8	63.3	24.9
Intermediate	29.8	42.6	27.5	42.6	22.1	35.3	12.5	70.5	17.0
Agricultural	28.9	49.3	21.8	43.0	27.8	29.2	11.2	76.4	12.4
Hokkaido	23.6	41.8	34.6	33.0	22.7	44.3	7.7	73.9	18.4

Source: Nihon. Sori-fu, tokei-kyoku. *Showa 25-nen kokusei chosa hokoku*. VII. Table 14. Unknowns were not excluded prior to the computation of percentages.

for women was from 23 per cent in the metropolitan prefectures to 71 per cent in the agricultural prefectures.

The use of unpaid family labor was more prevalent in the *gun* than in the *shi*; this was true for men and for women. However, family labor was more common in *shi* located in agricultural prefectures than in *shi* located in metropolitan or industrial prefectures. A similar relationship held in the *gun*, family labor being most common in the *gun* of the agricultural prefectures, least common in the *gun* of the metropolitan prefectures. For men, the proportion of unpaid family workers in the *gun* of metropolitan prefectures was only slightly higher than the proportion of such workers in the *shi* of agricultural prefectures. The proportions of unpaid workers were higher among women than they were among men, but there were the same types of relations between the industrial characteristics of the area and residence in *shi* versus residence in *gun*. For example, the proportion of unpaid family workers in the *gun* of metropolitan prefectures was 40.7 per cent; the proportion of such workers in the *shi* of agricultural prefectures was 39.3 per cent.

The direct relationship among dependence of the regional economy on non-agricultural employment, residence in *shi* rather than in *gun*, and wages for labor would seem to indicate that labor for wages or salaries was characteristic of the new economy of the industrial areas and the cities, and that unpaid family labor, on the other hand, reflected the persistence of the customs of the old economy in the agricultural areas and the villages. In a sense this is true, for 39 per cent of the men and 87 per cent of the women who labored in agriculture in 1950 were unpaid family workers (FIGURE 6). Moreover, the proportion of unpaid family workers among men in the agricultural labor force increased with the predominance of agriculture in the industrial structure of the prefecture. There was also widespread use of family labor in wholesale and retail trade, and here, too, the proportion of the labor that was unpaid increased with the predominance of agriculture. Wage and salary incomes were much more prevalent in manufacturing industry, but here also unpaid family labor was greater in the agricultural than in the industrial regions of the country.

The persistence of an unpaid labor force appears to be due to the relations between opportunities for employment and the supply of labor. If there were opportunities alternative to unpaid utilization in the family agriculture or the family shop, there would be an exodus from the family of those who had freedom to move—men and single girls. The persistent element in the supply of unpaid family labor is the married woman. The characteristics of the agriculture, the low income derived from it, and the plethora of people on the land bar a degree of mechanization that would permit Japan's farm families to survive without the assistance given by their women as field workers.

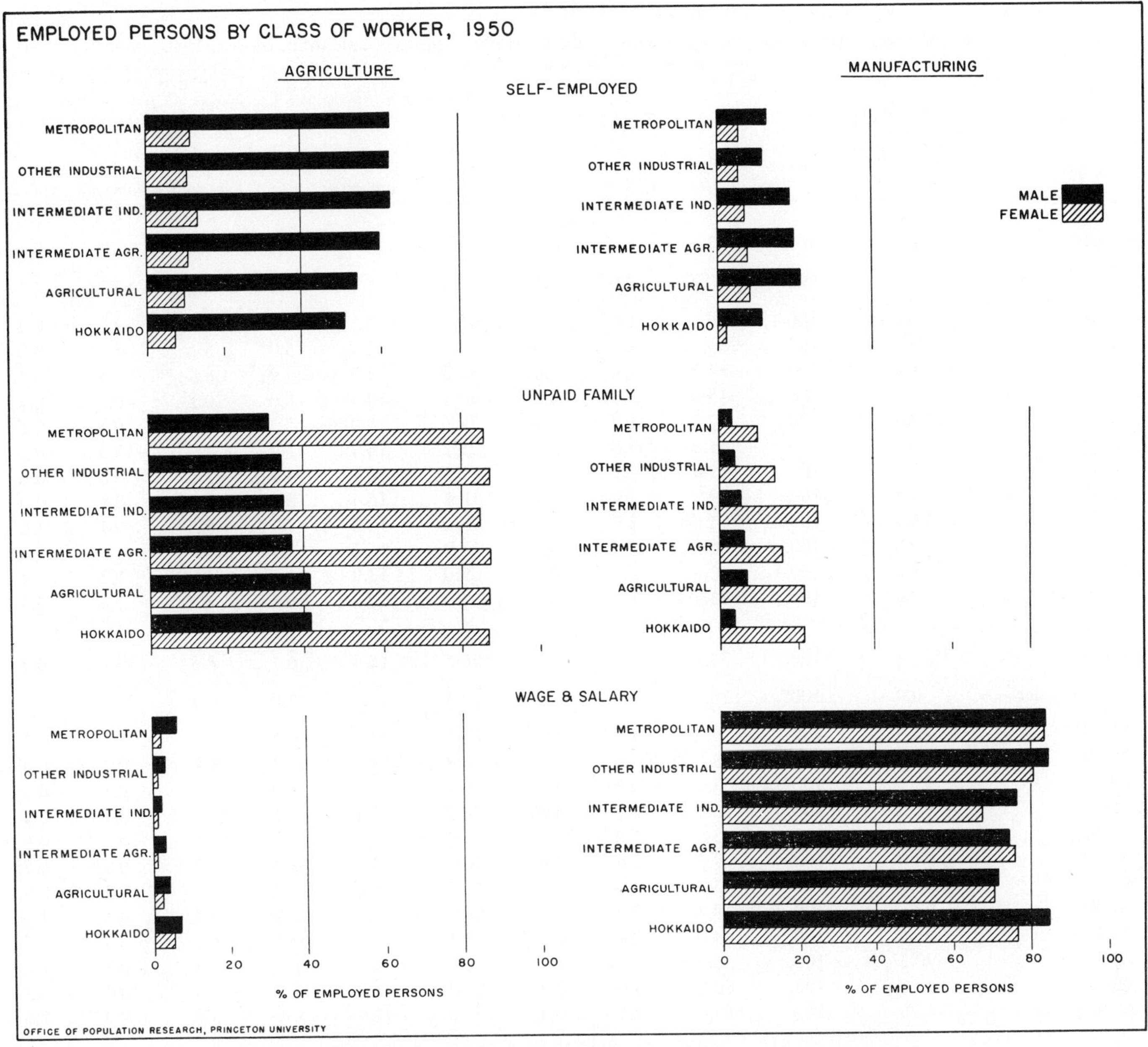

Figure 6. Employed persons by class of worker and sex, selected industry groups, prefectures by industrial type, 1950
Source: Nihon. Sori-fu, tokei-kyoku. *Showa 25-nen kokusei chosa hokoku.* III.2 Table 19.

The Demographic Structure

The differences were large in the economic roles of the age and sex groups. The importance of agriculture increased consistently with advancing age (Table 31). The aged of 1940 were almost as agricultural as the total population at the time of the Meiji Restoration. The age pattern of industrial activity differed somewhat for men and women. Men remained in non-agricultural occupations until about age 40, but thereafter there was a rapid increase in the proportions in agriculture. For women there was a direct and continuing relationship between advancing age and increasing participation in agriculture. These relations between age and industry also characterized the labor force in 1955.

Agriculture was a habitual occupation for the aging and the aged. In fishing and commerce there were few relationships between age and economic activity. In government service and the professions, the advantages of age and experience were evident in the relatively greater numbers of those in the middle and later years of productive life who engaged in these activities. It was in manufacturing industry that youth found their major opportunity. More than three-fifths of the men in manufacturing industry in 1940 were between the ages of 15 and 35, while 46 per cent of the girls were below age 20 and 65 per cent were below age 25.

Differences in the industrial composition of the gainfully occupied populations at various ages may reflect the movement of the economy over time, a movement of individuals from one industry to another as part of a life cycle of employment, or selective entrances and withdrawals from the labor market that follow characteristic age patterns. Actually, all of these factors were involved in creating the structure of the Japanese labor force. Youth entering the labor market were mobile geographically and occupationally—and so they were found in major proportions in factory employment in

TABLE 31

The industrial structure of the age groups in the gainfully occupied population, by sex, 1940

Age	Per cent of total in age group gainfully occupied	PER CENT OF THE GAINFULLY OCCUPIED POPULATION									
		All industries	Agri-culture	Fishing	Mining	Manufactur-ing	Commerce	Transpor-tation	Government and pro-fessions	Domestic	Others
					Total						
All ages	46.7	100.	42.7	1.7	1.7	24.7	14.9	4.3	7.4	2.1	0.6
10 and under	0.0	100.	10.4	2.0	0.2	10.7	11.1	0.6	2.4	62.2	0.1
11-14	13.6	100.	29.4	1.4	1.1	40.8	10.5	2.9	4.0	9.7	0.2
15-19	72.1	100.	31.1	1.5	1.6	35.1	12.9	5.7	6.1	5.7	0.3
20-24	75.2	100.	34.5	1.6	1.8	30.3	14.3	4.9	8.8	3.5	0.4
25-29	71.4	100.	35.0	1.6	2.2	30.1	14.7	5.0	10.1	0.9	0.4
30-34	73.4	100.	37.6	1.7	2.3	26.6	15.9	5.5	9.5	0.5	0.5
35-39	75.8	100.	41.8	1.8	2.2	23.2	16.7	5.2	7.9	0.5	0.7
40-44	77.7	100.	45.6	1.9	2.0	21.2	16.7	4.2	7.1	0.5	0.8
45-49	78.5	100.	49.9	1.9	1.6	18.5	16.4	3.4	6.7	0.6	0.9
50-54	76.5	100.	54.8	2.0	1.2	15.4	16.0	2.7	6.2	0.7	1.0
55-59	70.8	100.	60.9	2.0	0.8	11.9	15.2	1.7	5.4	1.0	1.1
60-64	62.6	100.	66.9	2.0	0.4	9.0	13.9	1.1	4.5	1.2	1.1
65 and over	39.8	100.	72.7	1.8	0.2	6.0	12.3	0.6	4.2	1.3	0.9
					Male						
All ages	58.3	100.	34.1	2.5	2.4	30.5	15.0	6.1	8.6	0.2	0.7
10 and under	0.0	100.	16.6	6.6	0.4	23.7	15.2	2.0	4.3	31.0	0.2
11-14	12.5	100.	29.7	2.7	1.6	42.8	13.3	4.2	4.2	1.2	0.3
15-19	77.6	100.	28.2	2.4	2.4	40.8	12.8	7.9	4.8	0.3	0.4
20-24	91.4	100.	28.2	2.3	2.5	36.7	13.2	7.0	9.4	0.1	0.5
25-29	96.5	100.	23.3	2.1	3.0	38.1	14.1	7.1	11.8	0.1	0.5
30-34	97.8	100.	25.2	2.2	3.1	34.2	15.7	7.9	11.1	0.1	0.6
35-39	98.0	100.	29.6	2.4	3.0	30.2	16.6	7.6	9.8	0.1	0.7
40-44	98.0	100.	33.5	2.6	2.7	28.1	16.8	6.3	9.0	0.1	0.9
45-49	97.4	100.	38.3	2.6	2.3	24.9	16.8	5.2	8.7	0.1	1.0
50-54	95.5	100.	44.0	2.8	1.7	21.1	16.8	4.1	8.2	0.2	1.2
55-59	90.8	100.	51.7	2.9	1.1	16.6	16.3	2.6	7.2	0.3	1.3
60-64	83.6	100.	60.2	3.0	0.7	12.2	14.9	1.7	5.8	0.4	1.3
65 and over	62.0	100.	69.4	2.5	0.3	7.6	12.7	0.9	5.2	0.4	1.0
					Female						
All ages	35.2	100.	56.8	0.5	0.5	15.1	14.7	1.2	5.4	5.3	0.5
10 and under	0.0	100.	7.8	0.1	0.2	5.2	9.4	0.1	1.6	75.5	0.1
11-14	14.8	100.	29.2	0.3	0.6	39.1	8.0	1.8	3.8	17.1	0.2
15-19	66.6	100.	34.4	0.4	0.8	28.5	13.0	3.2	7.7	11.9	0.2
20-24	59.3	100.	44.1	0.5	0.6	20.5	16.0	1.6	7.9	8.6	0.3
25-29	26.6	100.	59.0	0.6	0.6	13.6	16.0	0.8	6.6	2.6	0.4
30-34	48.7	100.	62.7	0.7	0.6	11.0	16.4	0.6	6.2	1.4	0.5
35-39	52.8	100.	65.3	0.6	0.6	9.9	16.8	0.5	4.4	1.2	0.6
40-44	56.4	100.	67.7	0.6	0.6	8.7	16.4	0.4	3.6	1.2	0.7
45-49	58.5	100.	70.2	0.6	0.5	7.3	15.7	0.3	3.3	1.3	0.8
50-54	57.2	100.	73.3	0.5	0.3	5.7	14.7	0.2	2.8	1.6	0.8
55-59	52.1	100.	76.1	0.5	0.2	4.4	13.4	0.1	2.5	2.0	0.8
60-64	43.9	100.	78.2	0.4	0.1	3.5	12.2	0.1	2.2	2.5	0.8
65 and over	23.6	100.	79.0	0.3	0.0	2.9	11.6	0.1	2.3	3.0	0.8

Source: Nihon. Sori-fu, tokei-kyoku. *Showa 15-nen kokusei chosa.* Unpublished tables.

growing industries.[24] Conversely, the gainfully occupied in recently developed manufacturing industries included high proportions of the young. With the newer industries being manned continually by the younger men of the economy, it was only natural that the data of any given census revealed a progression toward the older patterns of labor utilization with advancing age. This correlation between age and the ancient industries was especially pronounced in Japan, for here rights to jobs existed even in the great industrial groups. Moreover, age was venerated as such, and primogeniture forced the exodus to new jobs of all sons beyond the first, whenever such exodus was at all possible.

The life cycle of the individual was likely to include occupational mobility, the characteristic pattern for men being a move away from agriculture in the younger ages of gainful employment, and a return to agriculture that became apparent by age 40 to 50 and increased with advancing age. The percentage differences between the numbers gainfully occupied in agriculture at specific ages and the numbers that would be expected if all the survivors of those gainfully occupied in agriculture ten years earlier had remained in agriculture reveal this pattern:[25]

Age in terminal year	*Percentage difference, actual and expected without labor mobility or migration: men*	
	1920-1930	*1930-1940*
25 and over	−0.8	−8.3
25-59	0.3	−9.1
25-29	−17.6	−31.0
30-34	2.3	−14.9
35-39	−0.9	−8.9
40-44	3.7	−3.9
45-49	6.7	−0.3
50-54	8.3	3.5
55-59	8.4	4.4
60 and over	−5.5	−5.4

Labor mobility was correlated with the state of the economy outside agriculture and the availability of jobs in that economy. Almost one-fifth of the survivors of the agricultural labor force that was aged from 15 to 19 in 1920 had left it by 1930; the comparable exodus approached one-third in the period between 1930 and 1940.[26] These figures do not tell us where the men went—to non-agricultural occupations in Japan or to residence in the colonies or the Co-Prosperity Sphere. If they left Japan—and the selection of agricultural youth for imperial migration makes it probable that appreciable proportions did—they entered non-agricultural occupations in the areas into which they went. Conscription and military service are not involved in this computed exodus from agriculture, for youth aged from 15 to 19 in 1920 were below conscript age, while those aged from 25 to 29 in 1930 were above the major age group found in the armed services. The 1.7 million youth in the armed services in 1940 were assigned to their last civilian occupations in the 1940 census and so would not appear as emigrants from agriculture because of induction into the armed forces.

Net movements of men to and from agriculture were slight for those who were from 20 to 29 in 1920, from 30 to 39 in 1930.[27] The return to agriculture began sometime around age 40, and reached a maximum for men in their fifties. In old age it was the increasing practice of retirement rather than occupational mobility that resulted in deficits of actual below expected manpower in agriculture. For the entire age span from 25 to 59, the gainfully occupied in agriculture in 1930 differed only insignificantly from the number that would have been expected without occupational mobility. The consequence of the mobility that occurred, however, was a movement of youth toward and of the aging and the aged away from non-agricultural employment, a movement of the aging and the aged toward and of youth away from agricultural employment. Labor mobility was such as to favor the development of a young labor force and a young population in industrial and urban areas, an aging labor force and a population heavily weighted with dependents in agricultural and rural areas.

In the full employment and relative labor-shortage year of 1940, the net exodus from agriculture was substantially greater at the younger ages, and it extended upward to age 40 to 44. The return to agriculture in the late forties and the fifties was far less. This suggests that the return to agriculture was generally due to limited economic opportunities elsewhere. A comparison of the labor force in agriculture in Japan and the Ryukyus in 1950 with that expected if there had been neither labor mobility, war losses, nor international migration reveals much about the labor market in the early postwar years.[28] The percentages for men were as follows:

Age	*Percentage difference, actual and expected without labor mobility, migration or war: men*		
	1920-1930	*1930-1940*	*1940-1950*
25 and over	−0.8	−8.3	11.4
25-59	0.3	−9.1	14.2
25-39	−6.6	−19.3	4.0
40-59	6.7	−0.7	23.6
60 and over	−5.5	−5.4	1.6

Cultural adjustments and the adequacy or inadequacy of family labor were major factors in the occupational mobility of women. Practically all women were married by age 30, few women worked outside the home, and few women moved apart from families. Comparisons of the actual numbers of women gainfully occupied in agriculture with the numbers

[24] Similar relations between age and industrial structure are apparent in the data of the 1955 census. A tabulation by class of worker by industry is given by sex and five-year age groups for *shi* above and below 50 thousand and for *gun*. Nihon. Sori-fu, tokei-kyoku. *1% chushutsu shukei ni yoru kekka sokuho. Showa 30-nen kokusei chosa. Zenkoku.* 4, II. Table 1.

[25] The age composition of the populations gainfully occupied in agriculture were taken from the following sources: 1920: Nihon. Naikaku tokei-kyoku. *Taisho ku'nen kokusei chosa kijutsu hen.* VII. Tables 34 and 35. 1930: *Idem. Showa go'nen kokusei chosa saishu hokokusho.* VIII. Tables 42 and 43. 1940: *Idem. Showa 15-nen kokusei chosa. . . .* Unpublished table. The area concerned is that of the prewar period. The life tables used for aging the employed populations from one census date to the next were prepared on the basis of the mortality outside cities of 100 thousand and over in years centered on the census years.

[26] The slight increase of actual above expected at age 30 to 34 in 1930 may reflect the return to agriculture of men who at age 20 to 24 in 1920 had been in the armed forces.

[27] The slight increase of actual above expected at age 30 to 34 in 1930 may reflect the return to agriculture of men who at age 20 to 24 in 1920 had been in the armed forces within or outside Japan.

[28] The population gainfully occupied in agriculture in Japan in 1940 was aged to 1950, using survival ratios based on linear interpolation between those of 1935-1936 and 1947-1948. The age structure of the population in the agricultural labor force in the Ryukyus in 1950 was given in: U.S. Military Government, Ryukyu Islands. *Population census, 1 December 1950.*

anticipated on the basis of the survivors of the women in agriculture a decade earlier indicate that the adjustive employment of women was a major factor in the labor force:

Age	*Percentage difference, actual and expected without labor mobility or migration: women* 1920-1930	1930-1940	1940-1950
25 and over	−8.2	5.0	6.1
25-59	−4.0	7.4	14.3
25-39	−4.3	7.0	26.1
40-59	−3.6	7.8	4.2
60 and over	−34.1	−7.7	−28.1

The changes from 1920 to 1930 show that depression and a surplus of men in farm households released women from labor in the fields. Between 1930 and 1940 there was an exodus of men from agriculture, and women filled the gaps left by the departure of husbands and sons. The numbers of the gainfully occupied in agriculture in 1940 were substantially above the anticipated number up to old age. Comparison of the number of women in the labor force in agriculture in Japan and the Ryukus in 1950 with that to be expected without occupational mobility, migration, or war losses reveals the reactions of a people to a difficult economic situation. The employment of women may be related to changed patterns of childbearing, though this is unlikely. One suspects that a large number of war widows were working as unpaid family laborers in agriculture. There may have been many workers among the wives of repatriates. Whatever the explanation, a substantial increase in the employment of women in the age of major family responsibilities was evidence of crisis in the culture of rural Japan. The economic difficulties associated with increasing population seem to have led to an increase in the labor force and so to have intensified problems of employment.

Labor Force, Industrialization, and Urbanization

The empirical approach to the separation of the influence of industrialization from that of urbanization lies in a comparison of the age and sex structures of industrial groups in urban and rural areas. If the age and sex compositions of the industrial groups are similar in *shi* and *gun*, it can be assumed that industrial activity is primary. The structure of the labor force and the population in the cities could be assumed to be a by-product of the industrial structure. If the age structures of industrial groups differ widely according to the place of residence, the reverse argument holds and urbanization is the primary factor.

In 1950 the age structures of the labor force in major industrial groups were quite similar for *shi* and for *gun* (Figure 7). In both occurred the familiar pattern of a utilization in agriculture that was high among youth in their teens, low in the middle span of productive life, high among the aging and the aged. The per cent of the labor force in manufacturing industry declined consistently as age advanced, whether the area of residence was *shi* or *gun*. The difference between *shi* and *gun* lay in the industries that provided employment. The demographic structure of the city and the characteristics of its labor force were products of its industrial structure.

If the prior arguments are valid, the differences in the age structure of the labor force in prefectures classified by industrial type should reflect differences in the industrial compositions of the respective populations. Table 32 presents data for 1950 on the age composition of the agricultural and the non-agricultural labor force by sex for prefectures classified by industrial type. The hypothesis is substantiated. Major variations characterize the age structure of the agricultural and the non-agricultural groups, men and women, but not urban and rural populations *per se*. The fundamental transition in the demographic structure of the labor force involved the movement from agriculture, not the movement to the city.

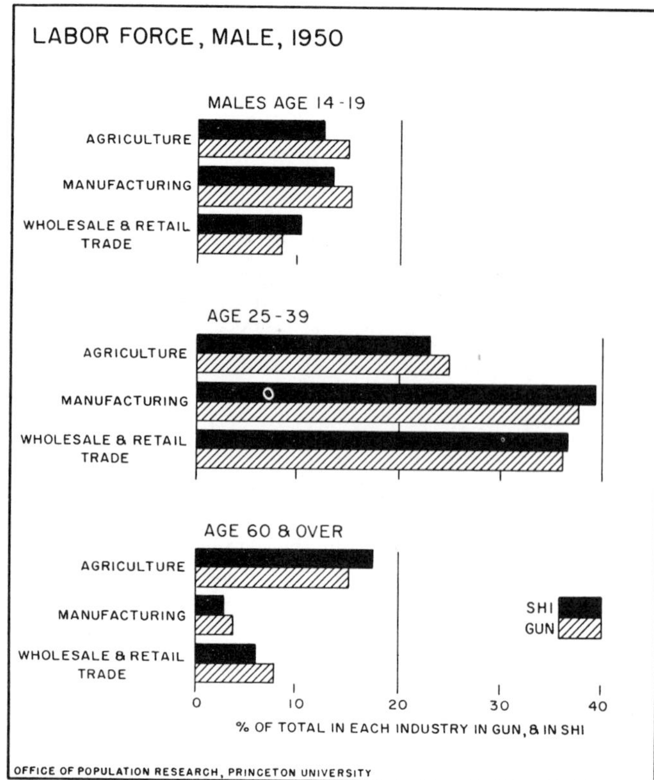

Figure 7. Age composition of the labor force in the *shi* and *gun*, males in selected industries, 1950

Source: Nihon. Sori-fu, tokei-kyoku. *Showa 25-nen kokusei chosa hokoku.* II.2. Table 16.

The Type of Industrialization

The industrial transformation of Japan involved all regions of the nation and all classes of the population, but for the rural people the involvement was often indirect. The national evolution was toward manufacturing, commercial, and professional employment rather than agricultural employment, toward life in the great cities rather than in the villages, toward income and expenditures computed in terms of money rather than the use of money as a supplement to locally produced subsistence, toward social and occupational mobility rather than stability. The agricultural people lived outside the major evolution of the culture that was being created by the sons and daughters who had left agriculture. And so there arose a dual economy, a dual society. This duality was more a product of the achievements of the culture and its limitations of physical resources than any planned strategy of industrialization. Duality was cause and consequence of the population trends of the past, and it laid the basis for the population problems of the present and the future.

The agriculture of Japan was ancient in tradition. The inventions of a long period of evolution were designed to

TABLE 32

Age composition of the labor force, by sex, agricultural and non-agricultural industries, prefectures by industrial type, 1950
(Per cent age composition, each sex)

Prefectures by industrial type	MALE					FEMALE				
	14-19	*20-24*	*25-39*	*40-59*	*60 and over*	*14-19*	*20-24*	*25-39*	*40-59*	*60 and over*
All industries	12.2	15.4	32.7	31.3	8.4	16.9	17.7	31.4	26.9	7.0
Metropolitan	10.5	15.7	37.0	32.1	4.7	22.1	24.6	30.2	20.3	2.7
Other industrial	10.9	15.7	34.1	31.7	7.5	18.1	18.8	30.6	26.3	6.2
Intermediate industrial	11.6	15.0	32.1	31.5	9.8	14.3	15.8	31.3	29.7	8.9
Intermediate agricultural	12.0	14.8	30.8	31.8	10.5	15.0	16.2	31.4	28.7	8.6
Agricultural	13.7	15.4	31.4	30.8	8.8	16.7	17.2	32.0	27.1	7.1
Hokkaido	13.2	16.9	35.3	28.4	6.2	22.4	19.8	30.2	22.8	4.7
Agriculture and forestry[a]	14.7	12.8	24.9	32.6	15.1	13.0	14.3	32.2	31.0	9.5
Metropolitan	11.7	11.7	22.8	36.5	17.3	12.0	13.9	32.4	34.3	7.4
Other industrial	12.0	11.4	22.5	35.0	19.1	9.8	13.2	32.6	34.1	10.3
Intermediate industrial	12.4	11.2	23.5	34.1	18.8	10.2	11.9	31.4	34.5	12.0
Intermediate agricultural	12.9	12.0	24.3	33.5	17.3	10.3	13.5	32.0	32.8	11.3
Agricultural	16.6	13.7	25.7	31.3	12.6	15.1	15.2	32.3	29.2	8.2
Hokkaido	18.9	14.7	27.8	28.3	10.3	20.8	16.8	31.3	25.1	6.0
Non-agricultural industry[a]	10.8	16.9	37.4	30.5	4.4	23.0	23.1	30.2	20.5	3.2
Metropolitan	10.4	16.0	38.1	31.7	3.7	23.4	25.9	30.0	18.6	2.1
Other industrial	10.6	17.0	37.6	30.8	4.0	24.5	23.0	29.0	20.4	3.1
Intermediate industrial	10.9	17.2	37.2	30.1	4.7	20.5	21.3	31.6	22.7	3.9
Intermediate agricultural	11.2	17.0	36.2	30.5	5.0	23.5	21.2	30.2	21.4	3.8
Agricultural	10.7	17.2	37.5	30.0	4.6	21.5	23.1	31.1	20.8	3.4
Hokkaido	10.8	17.9	38.8	28.5	4.0	24.8	24.8	28.7	19.1	2.6

[a] There is a category of "not classifiable and not reported," but the total number of persons aged 14 and over in the labor force, but not allocated to a specific industry, was only 82 thousand.
Source: Nihon. Sori-fu, tokei-kyoku. *Showa 25-nen kokusei chosa hokoku.* III.2. Table 17.

secure a maximum yield almost regardless of the burden of human labor. Generations had contributed to the building and the preservation of the fields until all Japan had become a garden. The surface appearance of the old Japan remained unchanged in the modern world, but the farmer who maintained the productivity of his land was enmeshed in an exchange economy and subject to the interventions of the government in all spheres of activity. Rent, taxes, and fertilizer were essential business expenditures. The unremitting toil of the family continued, but the farmer adopted procedures that increased yields.

The agriculture of Japan could not escape the heritage of population density and incessant labor. Numbers never approached an absolute limit of subsistence, but the size of the population precluded simple solutions to social and economic problems. The nation could and did import food, but the difficulties of life for the farmer were compounded as he found his costs of production high in reference to those in Taiwan, Korea, Manchoukuo, or the United States. Complex forces near and distant combined to circumscribe the economy and the lives of the people who labored in or depended on agriculture. In this situation the interrelations of land and people in an industrializing economy became a population problem.

The fundamental characteristic of Japanese agriculture was the smallness of the cultivated area in relation to the number of the people who were agriculturally employed. Large numbers of people on limited land made many technological innovations unfeasible and non-economic. Priority in both government policy and popular practice was assigned to maximum total product rather than to increased product per man-hour expended and increased levels of living among the cultivators.

The contrast between cultivated area, food production, and population in Japan and in the industrialized countries of Western Europe is striking. Japanese economists pointed out that in 1938 Japan had more than 3,000 people for each square mile of cultivated land, whereas the United Kingdom had less than 2,500. Yet Japan produced almost three-fourths of the food for her people, while the United Kingdom imported most of the food she required. In Japan there were 635 persons gainfully occupied in agriculture for each square mile of cultivated land; in England there were 85, in Belgium 130, in Italy 166.[29]

Density of settlement in the rural areas reflected both the amount and the type of cultivable land and the presence or absence of employment opportunities outside agriculture.[30] In the *gun* of sparsely settled Hokkaido, the density of settlement ranged from 13 per square mile of total land area in Nemuro to 155 in Sorachi. The number of people per square mile of cultivated land ranged from 1,761 in Oshima to 1,945

[29] Nasu, Shiroshi. *Aspects of Japanese agriculture.* P. 2.
[30] Data on population, total area, and cultivated area in the *gun,* 1920 to 1930, are given in: Nihon. Kosei-sho, jinko mondai kenkyujo. *Map of density of population in Japan.*

in Soya. In the *gun* of Honshu the number of people per square mile of cultivated land never fell below 1,000; it often exceeded 3,000 and occasionally went above 4,000. In general, rural density was less in the northeast and greater in the southwest; it was least away from the cities and greater near the cities. This was in part a reflection of the relative prevalence of opportunities for support outside agriculture, in part a reflection of the suitability of land for remunerative production.

The size of the agricultural population and the small amount of cultivable land resulted in a predominance of very small holdings. In 1935 there were 5.6 million agricultural families in Japan. Ninety per cent of these families held less than 4.9 acres of land, including the arable and the non-arable; two-thirds held less than 2.45 acres; one-third held less than 1.22 acres.[31] Tenancy was widespread, despite efforts to encourage ownership by operators. In the late prewar years the proportion of tenants who owned no land approached or exceeded 40 per cent in Miyagi, Akita, and Hokkaido. It declined gradually as the land stretched southward and westward, with one major exception—the proportion of tenants tended to be high in the vicinity of the great cities. Major portions of the farmers who owned land found the amount insufficient and so rented additional land if they were able to do so. The scarcity of land, combined with the great demand for it, forced land prices to very high levels. Absentee landlords controlled appreciable proportions of the total cultivable land; land purchase by farm operators who owned no land was extremely difficult. Even the statistics on the proportions of farmers owning land overstated the economic status of the men on the land, for owner-operators cultivated the less productive and more isolated lands, while tenants worked those that were more productive and accessible.[32]

The comprehensive land reform of the early postwar years virtually eliminated tenancy from Japanese agriculture. This did not solve the labor problems in Japanese agriculture, however, for the increased per capita income that might have resulted from the liquidation of rent payments was jeopardized, if not largely eliminated, by the fragmentation of holdings, the sharp reduction of non-agricultural employment in rural areas, the inadequacy of migration to the cities, and the substantially increased number of people on land. The percentage distribution of the regular members of farm households in 1950 by the amount of land utilized by the household for farm purposes reveals the inherent inadequacy of land redistribution as a solution to the problems of poverty in Japanese agriculture:[33]

Land utilized for farm purposes, in acres	*Percentage of regular members of farm households on farms of specified sizes*
All holdings	100.
Less than 0.735	16.4
0.735-2.44	44.7
2.45-4.89	28.3
4.90-12.24	8.7
12.25 and over	1.8

[31] Nihon. Norin daijin kambo, tokei-ka. *Norin-sho tokei hyo.* 1935. Table 5.

[32] Nihon. Norin-sho, tokei chosa-bu. *Denbata shoyu jokyo chosa.* (Survey as of 1941.)

[33] Nihon. Sori-fu, tokei-kyoku. *Nihon tokei nenkan.* 1951. Table 30.

The small amount of arable land made family support from agriculture alone impossible for a large portion of the people. The proportion of farm households in which some resident member engaged in an occupation other than agriculture was 58.1 per cent in 1941.[34] In the difficult years of 1946 and 1947 this proportion dropped to 45 or 46 per cent, but by 1950 it had increased to 50 per cent. In 28.5 per cent of the farm households in 1950, employment outside agriculture was subsidiary to the farm enterprise, but in 21.6 per cent of the farm households, labor expended and income received were predominantly non-agricultural.

The small scale of operations, the scattered holdings, the uneven terrain, and the multiplicity of people were barriers to the use of machinery in agricultural cultivation. Cultivation, sowing, and harvesting continued to be accomplished largely by hand labor. Thus there tended to be a direct relationship between cultivated acreage and household size.[35] This relationship of labor needed to labor force retained was conducive neither to economic nor to demographic equilibrium, for the labor demands of irrigated rice were highly seasonal. The size of the area that the family cultivated could not exceed the labor available to meet needs at the peak season; an agricultural enterprise manageable with family labor at the peak season could not furnish productive employment for all the members of the family throughout the year. Labor was overplentiful during most of the year, but barely adequate for transplanting, cultivating, and harvesting. Overpopulation, underpopulation, population pressure—these are conceptual terms from a world outside the rice lands. The major fact in the rice lands themselves is that the quantity of food produced is related directly to the number of laborers available at the critical periods of the crop year.

There has tended to be a functional association between the production of children and the production of rice. In the historic situation, when normal death rates were high and decimations of populations periodic, concentration on the production of children and rice may have been essential to survival. As the brakes to expansion were lifted and the once empty lands utilized, the social system remained conducive to maximum agricultural production without regard to labor costs. In the new situation, the increasing numbers of people could not find employment in agriculture. High rates of childbearing may have contributed to the welfare of the individual farm family, but they were detrimental to the economy of the industrializing nation.

The industrialization of Japan could proceed with extraordinary rapidity in part because it involved only a segment of the economy. Duality in economic structure, employment opportunities, and income distributions was a short-run stimulant to economic development. In the long run, however, the urban and industrial segment of the population could not be divorced from the demographic consequences of the maintenance of agrarian poverty within a modernizing state. The farming population was a reservoir, its human product ever ready to flow into non-agricultural occupations and force downward the incomes and the living levels achieved in other segments of the economy.

[34] *Ibid.* Table 29. Series on joint occupations in the agricultural population for prewar and postwar years are included in the various issues of the *Norin-sho tokei hyo* of the Ministry of Agriculture and Forestry.

[35] Isobe, Hidetoshi, "Labour conditions in Japanese agriculture." *Bulletin of the Utsunomiya Agricultural College*, Section B, Vol. II. No. 1. 1937.

Dualism was not a solution to the long-run problems of manpower utilization in the industrializing society of Japan. Economic solutions to manpower problems required a lessening of the pressure of an increasing agricultural labor force on employment and income outside agriculture. Demographic solutions for economic, social, and political problems required a smaller labor force and rising levels of living in agriculture. The demography of peasant life was not a separable aspect of industrialization. It was, instead, the most critical of the population aspects of economic modernization.

61177

CHAPTER VI

The Family

THE goals of the Meiji Restoration were to increase national power through an industrialization that would leave intact the central values of obedience, discipline, and loyalty. Cities grew, industries expanded, and children attended school. Moreover, at least until 1945, the sanctions of the past and the indoctrinations of the present emphasized family continuity and status-controlled relations among family members. These were intended to remain as bastions of social stability within a changing economy.

Preconceptions concerning the family system have been a barrier to research on the interrelations of family, society, and population in modern Japan. The family system, we are told by some, is a unique aspect of a genuinely Japanese culture. However, we learn from others that the family system is feudalistic, that it perpetuates a lowly position for women and high fertility, that true modernization requires a small family, similar to a Western family in composition, as well as intra-family relations and extra-family activities. In general, there are political differences between those who argue that the nature of the family system is essentially Japanese and wholly praiseworthy and those who argue that it is feudalistic and therefore deleterious.[1] The advocates of the system tend to be conservatives who resist the submergence of Japan in the culture of the West. The critics tend to be liberals who see the family system as the force that preserves the old Japan and threatens the readjustments essential to development in the world in which Japan now finds herself.

House, Family, and Household

The Japanese family system involves a complex series of relations between the institutions of the *ie*, or house, and the family. The *ie*, like the *uji* of the ancient culture, is a consanguineous or pseudo-consanguineous group whose basic function is to preserve biological and cultural continuity. It is eclectic in origin and development.[2] Veneration of the ancestors traces far back to the legendary era of Japanese culture. The Sinization of the ancient era contributed to the definition of the proper in the relations among sex, age, and kinship groups. Buddhism emphasized the other world and thus strengthened the tendency toward a veneration of the past rather than a search for happiness in the present. Shinto as an instrument of national power integrated the *ie* into the system of paternalistic values whose apex was the imperial household.

The broad search for knowledge and experience that permitted the transformation of Tokugawa Japan into a modern state included some questioning of the role of the *ie*. It was the consensus of the leaders of the Restoration, however, that the institution of the house should be extended and strengthened. Hence, while in most fields the codification of law relied heavily on Western jurisprudence, the codification of the house law represented the formulation of a legal basis for ancient institutions and procedures. The task was a difficult one that occupied several decades, the definitive prewar civil code being issued only in 1896.[3]

THE PREWAR CIVIL CODE

The civil code of the late nineteenth century was a legal statement of relations traditional in the upper classes of the society. It was at the same time a statement of the ideal relations that the leaders of the Restoration felt should be developed in the commoner population of the country, particularly in the rural areas. Hence the similarity between the code and the social reality of the period is debatable.[4] The importance of the code lay in the fact that it was a legal document. Behavior might deviate from the ideal sanctioned by the code, but legal status and enforceable rights were those specified in it. In time, the social organization outlined in the code came to pervade Japanese society, if it did not do so when the house law was formulated.

The *ie* was a network of responsibilities and obligations between head and members.[5] It was usually a biologically related group somewhat comparable in relationship structure to the parents, children, grandparents, and grandchildren of the American family of the colonial period. Like that family, it might include unmarried siblings and other relatives. However, there were differences that thwart close analogy. In

[1] The discussions in the House of Representatives of the Diet of Japan on the revision of the civil code reveal this interrelation among social status, political conservatism, and emotional attachment to the *ie*, or house. Steiner, Kurt. "The revision of the civil code of Japan: provisions affecting the family." *The Far Eastern Quarterly*, 9(2):169-175. February 1950.

[2] The reformers of Taika attempted to abolish the *uji*, but they recognized and assigned major responsibilities to the *ie*. It was the house rather than the conjugal family that was responsible for maintenance of population registers, allocation of land, and economic and military contributions to the state. It is apparent that the theoretical organization of the house as presented in the legal codes of the seventh and eighth centuries did not correspond to the realities of family structure among the people of Japan throughout the twelve hundred years that separated the Taika Reform of 650 A.D. from the Restoration of 1868.

[3] In the discussion of the civil code that preceded its final execution, there were arguments for the elimination of the institution of the house as a feudal relic. The counter-arguments stressed the family system as basic to loyalty, filial piety, and national policy. Several attempts were made to revise the books of "Relatives" and "Succession" but the last committee drafts for revision, those of 1925 and 1927, were not acted upon prior to the war of 1937-1945. Steiner. "The revision of the civil code . . . ."

[4] It is possible to argue that the family system has been decaying since the Restoration of 1868, that the Restoration itself led to the removal from the jurisdiction of the house of all matters except those of a private nature. Hozumi, Nobushige. *Ancestor worship and Japanese law*. 5th Edition. Pp. 115 and 169.

[5] The major sources for this description of the house are the laws of Japan, especially the law of registration (Law 26, March 31, 1914; revised, Law 28, 1921, and Law 20, 1924). Also: Becker, J. E. de. *Annotated civil code of Japan*. Vol. III, Book IV, "Book of relatives."

Japan, married daughters and their descendants were excluded, while sons, their wives, and their descendants might remain members of the *ie* regardless of place of residence. Co-living was nowhere a specification of the house.

Perhaps the word "specification" itself denotes the critical difference between the structure of the house in prewar Japan and the family in early America. The American family was primarily an affectional group, though congeniality as a criterion of inclusion was re-enforced by the canons of Puritan morality. The Japanese house may have been an affectional group; it almost had to be if it was to remain a viable institution. But its essential characteristic was the formal structure that dedicated the lives of individuals to the continuity and the welfare of the family group.

The head of the house possessed great authority and bore great responsibilities, but there were obligations on the part of members that made the complex pattern of relations possible. The head was bound to support the members of the house, provided they conformed to his decisions as to work, migration, and marriage. No member of a house was supposed to choose a place of residence contrary to that approved by the head. If he did so, he was subject to expulsion from the house. Defiance of the decision of the head in this or any major way abrogated the head's responsibility for support.

The primary responsibility of the head of the house was the continuation of the family line. Thus it was essential that he regulate marriage, the recognition of offspring, and divorce, and that alternative procedures be available for securing the continuity of the house if the usual biological processes of family replacement failed. The provisions of the civil code were quite specific on all these matters. No member of a house could be a participant in or sanction a marriage without the consent of the head. The marriage became a legal fact and the offspring legitimate, and therefore eligible for succession to the headship, only when the name of the wife was removed from the *koseki* of her father's house and added to that of her husband's house. The eldest son was heir presumptive to the headship and the properties of the house.

The continuity of the house and the definition of relationships within it were social as well as biological. Adoption was accomplished easily through entry of the facts about the person who was adopted in the *koseki* of the house. He then became a relative with all the rights and obligations of succession and inheritance that pertained to the position he had acquired. The social nature of the continuity of the house is further apparent in the fact that it was possible to adopt a son who would succeed to the headship in the place of a biological son who had proved incompetent or unworthy.

There were ingenious procedures for securing the continuity of the house through the male line in cases where there were no sons. If a daughter who was heiress presumptive to the head had formed an ordinary marriage, her name would have been removed from the *koseki* of her father and she and her eldest son would have lost the rights to succession. If she remained single, she could not bear a legitimate son who would be her heir and so continue the lineage. The dilemma was resolved by the adoption of a husband for the daughter. The man selected for the role had his name added to the *koseki* of the house of the heiress as the son of the present head and the husband of the daughter; he assumed the name of the house and moved into the home of his wife's family. Unless there was an agreement to the contrary at the time of the adoption and marriage, the adopted son-husband became the heir to the house.

The pressure toward conformity and the bending of legal imperatives to allow for human frailty were both components of Japanese familial functioning. Since concubinage was regarded as an antiquated and unacceptable relationship, there was no mention of it in the civil codes of the Restoration period. However, the omission in the codes which made the relationship non-existent in law did not result in its elimination. The relation retained much of the sanction of custom; the attachments of the man to the woman and the child or children were social forces that could not be denied. The child was not a *shiseiji*, a truly illegitimate offspring with registration only in the *koseki* of the mother, but it could not have a status equal to that of the legitimate offspring of the legal wife. Hence there was a special category, the *shoshi*, an illegitimate child recognized as legitimate by the father and added to his *koseki* along with his legitimate children.

The arrangements for the formation of branch houses retarded the development of gigantic multi-generational kin groups in Japan. Younger sons formed branch houses and so avoided subjugation to the elder brother when he became head of the principal house. Provisions for the formation and liquidation of branch houses seem to have been reasonably liberal except for the son who was the heir presumptive to the headship of the house.

The institution of the house was adapted easily to the changing distribution of population that accompanied industrialization and urbanization. Many people maintained house membership in the village of their origin as long as the father lived, possibly even during the life of the grandfather.[6] When the old man died, the son or grandson might establish a branch house in the city. In this case, the break with the rural community and the historic family was gradual. The family system itself continued, however, for when the branch house was established, it was subject to the same rules of the civil code as the old house in the village. The son who had been subservient to his father as the head of the house and to his elder brother as heir presumptive now became the head of a branch house, all of whose members were subservient to him.

The house is often compared with a tree, all lesser houses being branches that trace back to a principal house that is the trunk. This analogy is valuable if it is remembered that the definition of kinship delineating the branches is social rather than biological. The branching tree of the ancestors moves backward through the sons of successive generations; daughters find no place here. In other words, the branching tree includes families whose patrilineal descent unites them in a veneration of common ancestors. It excludes an approximately equal number of families whose matrilineal descent removes them from legal relationship to biological ancestors.

The *ie* was an extended family with precise regulation of exclusion as well as inclusion. The family *per se* was also a legal institution carefully described in the civil code. The head of the house was responsible for the continuation of the house and his rights as head influenced the lives of all members of the house, but those rights did not extend beyond the powers, responsibilities, and obligations appropriate to the house. The family was a less extended group, but its relations

[6] As the urban industrial society developed, the pressures of new institutions often reduced the duration or the strength of the allegiance of conjugal families to the *ie* of the husband. For instance, city authorities might require statements of residence in the area for admission to the public schools. In this case, the transfer of *koseki* would occur at the time the eldest child approached age six, if in fact the *koseki* had not been transferred earlier in anticipation of the educational requirements.

were more inclusive. Parental authority had few limitations as to sphere of life or nature of rights. Individuals could be expelled from the house, but the blood relationship of the family could not be severed.

The Japanese kinship organization was patriarchal and patrilineal. It was also patrilocal. The wife entered the home of the husband at marriage and became subject to him as the head of the family. The legal provisions that permitted the adoption of a husband for a daughter who was an heiress, or even in rare circumstances the succession of a daughter to a headship, might seem to indicate some mitigation of patriarchal authority. As a matter of fact, adoption served to transfer authority from one male to another. A truly matriarchal family seldom existed even in the case of widowship, for the widow was subordinate to the male who replaced her husband as head of the family. In the relatively few cases where the widow became head of a family, her decisions regarding economic affairs and family succession had to be submitted to the family council for approval.

The husband had both economic control and economic responsibility. Unless there was a pre-marriage contract concerning the distribution of property, the husband was responsible for all expenses arising from the marriage. He managed the wife's property and acquired the profits from it. The wife's authority to manage daily affairs was a derived authority which the head of the house could refuse to recognize in whole or in part.

Parental authority was substantial, but in the modern era it was limited by the authority of the state. Parents and children had a mutual obligation of support. A child had to reside at the place designated by the father or mother with parental power. This parent protected and educated the child and exercised disciplinary powers. Management of property was the responsibility of the parent until the child achieved majority. While migration and marriage were subject to the consent of the head of the house, decisions and arrangements were likely to be familial.

The sanctions of the house and family were overtly legal, but no institutions that were merely legal could have displayed the vitality of the Japanese kinship organization. House and family constrained the lives of individuals, but there were limited opportunities for full life outside the matrix of kinship relations. There was no defined place in Japanese society for an individual living and functioning on his own. Social participation in groups of one's peers and acceptability in the larger society both required identification with a family. In addition, the pooling of economic resources in the family lessened the insecurities of the individual in an industrializing economy where social provisions for the unfortunate or the aged were limited.

THE NEW CONSTITUTION AND THE NEW CIVIL CODE

In the West, the development of the urban industrial society was accompanied by an advance of individualism that permeated and transformed both the family and the larger society. If this transition from a familistic to an individualistic orientation of values and activities is a natural correlate of industrialization and urbanization, it should not be limited to the Western culture area. In the Japan of recent decades, widespread reactions against the family system might have been expected, particularly among educated groups in the cities. The sequence of events might have involved increasing but still socially repudiated violations of the civil code, verbal assaults on sex and family mores, eventual attacks on the *ie* and on the dictatorship of the head. There is considerable evidence that such a sequence was in process during the 1920's and early 1930's, but the indoctrination and the thought control of the 1930's and the early 1940's prevented overt opposition. An ancient civil code and a developing industrial society thus existed side by side throughout the history of Imperial Japan. The adoption of a new constitution and the revision of the civil code occurred under the direction of the Supreme Commander for the Allied Powers rather than as the result of an indigenous struggle.

The postwar constitution of Japan accorded sovereign power to the people, renounced war, and established a framework for democratic institutions.[7] Chapter III, "Rights and duties of the people," made individualism rather than familism the basic human principle in law. The articles most directly related to the family system are the following:

> Article 13. All of the people shall be respected as individuals. Their right to life, liberty, and the pursuit of happiness shall, to the extent that it does not interfere with the public welfare, be the supreme consideration in legislation and in other governmental affairs.
>
> Article 14. All of the people are equal under the law and there shall be no discrimination in political, economic or social relations because of race, creed, sex, social status or family origin.
>
> Article 24. Marriage shall be based only on the mutual consent of both sexes and it shall be maintained through mutual cooperation with the equal rights of husband and wife as a basis.
> With regard to choice of spouse, property rights, inheritance, choice of domicile, divorce and other matters pertaining to marriage and the family, laws shall be enacted from the standpoint of individual dignity and the essential equality of the sexes.

Thus the new constitution barred economic or social discrimination because of sex and placed the right of the individual to "life, liberty, and the pursuit of happiness" above the obligations to family and house.

Comprehensive revision of the civil code therefore became essential. In the revision of the "Book on relatives" and the "Book on succession" there is no direct reference to the *ie*, or house. The great powers that the head once exercised continue through custom, if at all. Parental power is lessened, and it becomes a shared responsibility of father and mother (Book IV, Ch. IV). Marriage of persons other than minor children is subject to the wishes of the individuals concerned (Article 737); a marriage is void "when there is no intention to marry common to the parties" (Article 742). Relations within the family are those of mutuality: "Husband and wife shall live together, and shall cooperate and aid each other" (Article 752). The economic status of the wife is raised by a liberalization of the provisions for her separate property (Article 762). The wife is now to receive a minimum share of one-third of the estate of her deceased spouse (Article 900, Provision 1). Illegitimate children may be recognized by either father or mother (Article 779). There is no provision in the new code whereby the wife must care for the *shoshi*, the child of her husband's concubine, as if it were her own.

Relics of the old code survive in the new, despite its adoption in conformity with a constitution that made the individual central in the society and sovereign in the nation. Marriage and other family events still become legal on registration in the *koseki*. Recognition and adoption remain critical, just as they were in the old code, in which the continuation of the

[7] "The constitution of Japan." Pp. 671-677 in: SCAP. GHQ. Government Section. *Political reorientation of Japan, September 1945 to September 1948.* For the civil code, see: Nihon. Homu-fu. Codes and statutes of Japan. No. 5. *The civil code.* Book IV, "Relatives." Book V, "Succession."

house was seen as the major purpose in the life of the individual (Book IV, Chs. II, III). The ancient virtues and the worship of ancestors are noted explicitly. Article 730 of the new civil code provides that "lineal relatives by blood and the relatives living together shall mutually cooperate." Article 897 continues the rules for succession to the performance of ancestral rites.

THE RELATIONS OF HOUSE AND FAMILY

House and family created values and status relations so pervasive that the society, the economy, and even the government have often been described as familial. The literature on the family emphasizes the extended kinship structure, its organization, its definition of roles and delineation of etiquette, and its conditioning of personalities.[8] Actually the *ie* was a temporal rather than a permanent grouping. The elite whose ancestors accompanied the descendants of the Sun Goddess from the Plains of High Heaven can trace their genealogies back through the centuries. Families in upper social strata can trace their ancestry back into Tokugawa or even earlier eras. For most of the people of Japan, however, knowledge of the *ie* goes back only a few generations.

This fact does not in itself negate the interpretation of Japanese society and culture in terms of the values and tenets of the traditional family system. However, the government that worked to consolidate and purify the family institutions in terms of the ancient past devoted major efforts to an industralization whose social consequences were antithetical to the preservation of the *ie*. In villages where main house and branch house live side by side, where personal relations appropriate to the relative status of the houses persist year after year and generation after generation, much of the contemporary structure of attitudes, values, and personality configurations may be explainable in terms of the operational kinship system. But for that majority of Japan's population who live by non-agricultural activities in *machi* and *shi*, for those whose life patterns and goals involve occupational and geographical mobility, the attitudes and values of the family system have become attenuated. Behavior tends increasingly to reflect the goals of the individual and the conjugal family as well as, or even in contradiction to, those of the extended family. It seems probable that traditional values persist as verbal and even emotional attachments, while behavioral conformity becomes less and less precise.

The major mechanism for smooth familial functioning in the rural areas during the last century of rapid population increase was the movement of younger sons outside agriculture and the villages. When land was fully utilized by a people whose family and inheritance systems were those of the *ie*, there were a fixed number of places in agriculture and hence a fixed number of households. The places that existed in the local economy were filled by fathers and then by eldest sons in a succession regarded as right and natural. There were occasional vacancies for persons outside the patrilineal succession of eldest sons, but families seldom died out in an era when such group hazards as epidemics and famines had been conquered. Moreover, adoption provided a substitute for biological heirs. The economic and social equilibrium could continue in the traditional culture because the population that would have created disequilibrium was drained off into other segments of the economy. In other words, the persistence of the behavior patterns and values of the old society required the existence of the new sectors of society as a demographic safety valve.[9]

Even in seemingly stable villages, the role of consanguineous family increased as contrasted with that of the more extended group. Private property existed alongside and often exceeded the tiny heritage of the *ie*, and this private property was subject to disposal through the legal provisions governing the economy rather than the codes governing house and family. If the second son who founded a branch house was more successful economically than the first son who inherited the headship of the main house, the elder son of this second son inherited more than the elder son of the head of the main house. With an increase in education and in the possibilities for advancement outside agriculture, the adequacy of family resources became a critical element in the future of the individual child. Parental ambitions seem to have been very strong, and these were ambitions for own children far more than for collateral kin. The consanguineous family was important even in the rural society, where the house survived more nearly intact than elsewhere in Japan.

The movement to the city occurred through the cooperation of house and family. Kin decreed and assisted in the movement from the village; other kin assisted in the adjustment to life in the city. However, the job that was secured by kin contacts was held by individual merit. Occupational advance and rising levels of living resulted primarily from the training and competence of the individual. Most marriages continued to be arranged by families and so were oriented to the house and village, but here also divergence existed. Increasing proportions of the families did not enforce decisions as to marriage if the son or daughter concerned had serious objections to the suggested mate. Many contacts of family members in the city were individual, the man in his job and his social activities, the wife in the neighborhood, the children in school and play groups. Socio-economic and other status factors not directly derivable from kin affiliation were involved in all these external relations of family members. Kin relationships themselves tended to be weakened as urban residence lessened the continuing contacts and the renewal of relations of branch with main house. For many of the younger generation in the cities, the ceremonials and the symbolisms of the ancestral *ie* became matters of description and recollection rather than of current experience.

The changes that separated the city family from its village kin group came gradually. If the family in the city lived by household industry, the growth of an individualization that was incompatible with total allegiance to the *ie* was retarded. Even in this case, however, children went to school and encountered vistas wider than those of family and kin. The day-to-day contacts in the consanguineous group became less important in the totality of contacts than they had been when family functioning was undifferentiated. The intimate family contacts themselves became an increasing proportion of the totality of all familial contacts, probably in some general relationship to the duration of residence in the city and to the socio-economic gap that separated urban residents and their rural kin.

Empirical documentation of the changing relations of the larger kinship group and the smaller group of parents and

[8] See, for instance: Kawashima, Takeyoshi. *Nihon shakai no kazokuteki kosei*. English summary: Bennett, John W., and Nagai, Michio. *Summary and analysis. . . .*

[9] The discontents of the rural areas in the era of repatriation and migration are empirical verification of this argument. See: Fukutake, Tadashi. "Waga kuni genzai ni okeru noson ryunyu jinko no jittai." *Shakaigaku kenkyu*, 1(2):134-147. December 1947.

children is handicapped by the fact that neither *ie* nor consanguineous family was subject to comprehensive statistical reporting. The *koseki* records concern the *ie*, but they are arranged with a continuous pagination for the individual house. All living members are listed, wherever they may reside, but the record is not necessarily continuous over the generations. Records destroyed by fires or other calamities were re-created through registration of present members of the *ie*. A branch house may have its records maintained in the same *koseki* office that serves the main house, or it may have them maintained elsewhere. Thus even original tabulations of data from selected *koseki* offices fail to give complete information on the interrelations of houses or the relations of houses to families.

The plasticity of the *ie* is evident in the relations between the numbers of people enumerated in specific areas and the numbers of people with *honseki* in these same areas.[10] If the ties to the extended kinship group had been all-pervasive and perpetual, people who moved to cities and industrial areas would have maintained their affiliations with the *ie* of origin by keeping their names in *koseki* there. The names of urban-born children would have been entered and maintained in the *koseki* of the grandfather, which was at the same time the *koseki* of *his* grandfather, and so on down the branching tree of the patrilineal ancestors. Actually, year after year during the census period, there has been a regular relationship between people enumerated in an urban area and people with *honseki* in that same area. In the agricultural prefectures where out-migration has been substantial for many decades, *honseki* populations are somewhat larger than enumerated populations. In the metropolitan prefectures and other industrial prefectures of heavy in-migration, people with *honseki* in the area of residence are considerably less numerous than people enumerated in the area. There is only one interpretation of the continuing similarities and the consistent differences in the enumerated and *honseki* populations of rural areas and cities, of agricultural and industrial prefectures, and that is the transfer of *koseki* from the rural area to the city. New and essentially consanguineous families have been acquiring the status of *ie*. The system of the house has been preserved, but the meaning of the system in the lives of the Japanese has been undergoing substantial modification.

THE BIOLOGICAL FAMILY

It might seem that the biological family would be the ideal familial unit with which to deal in demographic analysis. This holds true for some problems of family analysis but not for all. The longevity of parents and grandparents has a significant relation to the structure of the families that exist at any given time. Reproduction itself is a biological fact. For most aspects of family functioning, however, the social, economic, and psychological factors are more immediately relevant than the biological. The close functional and psychological bonds between parents and children are transformed with age and the dispersion of sons and daughters. In Japan, the usual limitations to the analysis of families as biological units are compounded by the prevalence of adoption. An adopted child becomes a blood-relative, not only regarded as such, but legally so. Moreover, daughters are extruded from the families of origin at marriage. Their relations are then to the family of the husband, with only a residual conditioning by the biological family in which childhood and youth were spent.

THE HOUSEHOLD

The group of related people who live together and share the experiences of that living are the unit in the measurable structure of Japanese society. This consanguineous family is part or all of an *ie*, whether main house or branch house. It is based on the biological family, although the life cycle of the family creates varying degrees of coincidence between biological family and co-living household as time advances from the marriage and the formation of the household to the death of one or both of the spouses which usually terminates it. It is the co-living household that shares a common budget and that exists at whatever level of adequacy the group income permits and by whatever standards are agreed upon by the members. Here the day-to-day adjustment occurs; here people co-operate or struggle in work and in play. Whatever the external relations with the more extended kin group, it is among the small group of people living together that relations are closest and most frequent.

The fact that the co-living household is the elementary group in the operating social organization of Japan does not mean that beliefs and values derived from this household penetrate other institutions and other relationships. Rather, it is the values of the *ie* that persist in contemporary Japan as the rationalization for forms of social, economic, and political organizations that range from labor recruitment systems to political associations. Moreover, the traditional attitudes of the extended kinship system structure the co-living household and influence its functioning, particularly as that functioning is related to the role of women.

Empirical verification of these theoretical statements concerning the interrelations of the *ie* and the co-living household is difficult, for there are no direct queries on the subject in census enumerations or special official surveys. The only approach possible at the present time is a search of census and vital statistics data to see if the structures and functions of households are consistent with the tenets of the extended kinship system. If people who form and live in households act in accordance with the ideals of the *ie* and orient their lives according to its obligations and its responsibilities, the structure of biological relations among household members should be patrilineal. There should be substantial proportions of multi-generation households, and the average household should be large. The obligations of the head of the household to offer subsistence to related individuals imply the existence of many multi-worker households, with widespread use of family labor in and outside agriculture. The position of women should be subordinate; this would apply to the structure of power within the household as well as to the occupational structure outside the household. Marriage should be almost universal, divorces few, and children numerous.

If the movement in Japan from an agricultural to an industrial society involved processes of psychological and material adjustment comparable to those that occurred in other countries, the characteristics of households that were associated with the pervasive familism of the *ie* should be most evident in the rural areas. Transformations in households should be a consistent correlate of urbanization and industrialization.

The extent of and the limitations to the conditioning of the co-living household by the values and the precepts of the *ie* are apparent in the sections that follow.

[10] For the years from 1920 through 1937, the *de facto* and the *de jure* populations of the prefectures and the cities of 100 thousand and over were published in both Japanese and French editions of the statistical yearbooks. See: Nihon. Naikaku tokeikyoku. *Résumé statistique du mouvement de la population de l'Empire du Japon*, issues published from 1922 through 1940.

Family Relations and Household Residence

THE STRUCTURE OF RELATIONS WITHIN HOUSEHOLDS

The structure of relations within the household is an index of the extent to which the values of the *ie* persist in the industrial society. Although the definitions of households in the censuses were in economic terms, the households themselves were familial institutions. In 1920, 88 per cent of all multi-person households included only relatives.[11] In households whose heads were engaged in agriculture, fishing, or mining, a non-family member was rare. Laborers, servants, and boarders entered households engaged in industry, commerce, or professional service, but even here only one household in four or five included an outsider. This familial basis of the household persisted throughout the decades of industrialization; in 1950 more than 98 per cent of all persons living in multi-person private households were related to the head.[12]

The major determinant of family residence was relationship to the head in the direct male line.[13] Such collateral relatives as were found in families were relatives of the male household members in the patrilineal succession.[14] The forces of extrusion removed the daughters of the successive generations, temporarily for labor, permanently for marriage. The forces of inclusion, insofar as they operated, brought in direct or collateral male relatives of the head for employment or in fulfillment of the obligations of maintenance. The allocation of women into households derived from the men whom they married or the sons whom they bore.

These are broad generalizations, but they are justified by detailed analysis of rural and urban populations in the various regions of the country in the censuses from 1920 to 1950. The limitation of household membership to persons in or related directly to the patrilineal succession extended from the isolated peasants of the northeastern villages to the crowded peoples of the great cities (Table 33). Collateral relatives of the household heads and lineal or collateral relatives of the spouses of the heads were excluded from the co-living family in the traditional areas of the large family, as they were in the cities where economic and social change had proceeded furthest. In the rural northeast, only 5 per cent of all family members were collateral relatives of the heads; the comparable proportion in the great cities was 4 per cent. The spouses of collateral relatives of the head numbered only one, two, or three in each 1,000 members. Relatives of the spouses of the direct male line numbered one or two in each 1,000 members.

Differences occurred primarily in the cohesion of the generations rather than in the structure of relationships (Table 34). In Japan, as in the United States, the most common household was the two-generation one of parents and children. This type of family constituted 53 per cent of all families in Japan as early as 1920, the range extending from 45 per cent in the *gun* of the northeast to 60 per cent in the great cities. Geographic and occupational differences suggest that the direction of development was toward the one- or two-generation family, away from the family of three or more generations. In the *gun* of the northeast only one in

[11] Nihon. Naikaku tokei-kyoku. *Taisho ku'nen kokusei chosa hokoku*. IV,A.3.

[12] *Ibid*. III.1. Table 15.

[13] The census schedules list the name of the head and then that of each person in the household. For each person other than the head, relationship to the head or position in the household is given in specific terms. For related persons this means such designations as son, mother, wife, brother, etc. Professor Toda utilized a one-in-one-thousand sample of the schedules of the 1920 census to tabulate relationship to the head. Toda, Teizo. *Kazoku kosei*. The word "family" is used in this section in accordance with Professor Toda's usage and means related persons living together in a household.

[14] There is considerable question here as to the biological relationships between people designated as family members and those designated as boarders, employees, or co-residents. It is probable that substantial proportions of the "outsiders" resident in households were remote relatives of the head. In fact, the permeation of the essentially economic processes of household expansion and contraction by the tentacles of familism is demonstrable in the terminology of the census schedule itself. The head of the household made the decision as to which persons in the household were relatives and which were employees, domestics, or boarders. The word for "relationship" in the census schedule was one that, precisely interpreted, means "on-going line." The reports of informants indicate that the distinction which appears so difficult to the Western analyst involved no difficulties for the Japanese who filled in the schedules. They knew whether people belonged in the status hierarchy of the family or in the rather amorphous categories of individuals attached to the family.

Table 33

The structure of relations in multi-person households, 1920

RELATION TO HEAD	ALL JAPAN	GUN			SHI	
		All gun	Gun *in the five northeastern prefectures*	Gun *in Kyoto and Osaka prefectures*	*All* shi	*The six great cities*
Total	100.	100.	100.	100.	100.	100.
Direct line of head[a]	75.8	76.1	74.3	77.0	74.1	72.1
Spouses of the direct line	20.5	20.2	20.6	20.0	22.1	23.5
Not direct line but related to head	3.3	3.3	4.6	2.7	3.3	3.7
Not direct line and not related to head	0.2	0.2	0.3	0.1	0.1	0.1
Related to spouses of the direct line	0.2	0.2	0.2	0.3	0.3	0.6

[a] Including the head.
Source: Toda, Teizo. *Kazoku kosei*. Table 15.

TABLE 34

Number of generations in multi-person households, 1920
(Per cent distribution of households)

NUMBER OF GENERATIONS	ALL JAPAN	GUN			SHI	
		All gun	Gun *in the five northeastern prefectures*	Gun *in Kyoto and Osaka prefectures*	*All* shi	*The six great cities*
			All households			
Total	100.	100.	100.	100.	100.	100.
1	17.7	15.7	8.1	15.0	25.9	27.4
2	53.2	52.2	44.8	58.7	58.9	59.5
3	27.0	29.8	39.6	25.6	14.9	12.8
4	2.1	2.5	7.2	0.8	0.3	0.3
5	0.0	0.0	0.1	0.0	0.0	0.0
			Heads in agriculture, forestry, and fishing			
Total	100.	100.	100.	100.	—	—
1	9.7	9.6	4.2	8.6	—	—
2	48.0	47.9	40.0	53.0	—	—
3	38.5	38.6	44.9	37.3	—	—
4	3.7	3.6	10.6	1.0	—	—
5	0.0	0.0	0.2	0.0	—	—

Source: Toda, Teizo. *Kazoku kosei*. Table 27.

each 12 households was limited to a single generation; in the great cities the proportion was over one in four. In the rural areas of the northeast almost two-fifths of all families included three generations; in the great cities the comparable proportion was one-eighth. Families of four generations comprised 7 per cent of those in the *gun* of the northeast, three-tenths of 1 per cent of those in the great cities. The family of five generations constituted less than one-tenth of 1 per cent of all families, even in the stronghold of Japanese familism, the villages of Tohoku.

The social and economic changes that occurred in the thirty years between 1920 and 1950 did little to modify the relationship structure of the family group living together. The following comparisons of Professor Toda's data for 1920 and tabulations for a sample of the population in 1950 reveal the persistence of relationship to the head as the major determinant of family residence:[15]

Relation to head	*1920*	*1950*
All related persons	100.	100.
Direct line	75.8	77.4
Spouses of direct line	20.5	18.7
Other related persons	3.7	3.9

The data for 1950 do not give the number of households that included three or more generations, but they do give the proportion of individuals in multi-person households who had the status of parents or grandparents of the head. Here again there is evidence of the predominance of the two-generation family, for only one in each twenty persons in a Japanese household was a parent or a grandparent of the head:

Relation to head	*Total*	Shi	Gun
All related persons	100.	100.	100.
Direct line of head			
Head	19.6	21.8	18.3
Children and grandchildren	52.6	50.8	53.7
Parents and grandparents	5.2	4.3	5.8
Spouses of the direct line			
Head	16.1	17.6	15.2
Children and grandchildren	2.6	1.6	3.1
Other related persons	3.9	3.9	3.9

In 1950 the proportion of persons living as parents or grandparents of the head was somewhat larger in the *gun* than in the *shi*; children and grandchildren were also somewhat more numerous in the *gun*. Heads and their spouses formed 33.5 per cent of the related persons in multi-person private households in the *gun*, 39.4 per cent in the *shi*. The multi-generation family was somewhat more prevalent in the rural areas, the couple with children only slightly more prevalent in the cities.

NON-FAMILY LIVING

So much attention has been focused on the role of the family in Japanese culture that there has been relative neglect of the persons who live apart from the *ie* and the consanguineous families of which they are members. The nexus of relations expected on the basis of the ideals of the kinship system was found through computations that were limited to relatives living in multi-person households. The individuals whose lives did not conform to the familistic ideal were thus

[15] Source: 1920: Toda. *Kazoku kosei*. Table 15. 1950: Nihon. Sori-fu, tokei-kyoku. *Showa 25-nen kokusei chosa hokoku*. III.1. Table 15. A similar structure of relations was indicated in a special study of family composition in Tokyo in 1934. Nihon. Tokyo shiyakusho. *Tokyo-shi kazoku tokei, Showa ku'nen chosa*. Pp. 26-37.

eliminated from analysis. Three major types of living arrangements are involved—the quasi-household, the single-person household, and residence in a multi-person household in some capacity other than that of a related member.

In prewar Japan many people lived in factory dormitories, army barracks, or the other agglomerations of the industrializing society. On October 1, 1930, 1.0 million men and 664 thousand women were enumerated in quasi-households of one type or another.[16] The largest contingents of men were in army barracks (141 thousand), although there were substantial numbers in navy units (83 thousand), hotels and commercial lodgings (198 thousand), and shops (82 thousand). Almost two-thirds of the women in quasi-households lived in factory dormitories.

In 1930, there were 694 thousand single-person households. In addition, there were 50 thousand household heads who lived with employees and servants but without related persons in the household. The 1930 census provides few data to indicate the demographic or other characteristics of the persons who lived alone or of those who lived in non-familial multi-person households.

The 1.7 million people who lived in quasi-households and the 744 thousand who lived in non-familial households were out-numbered by the 4.1 million people who lived in the households of others. Of these, 2.2 million were employees, 674 thousand domestics, and 1.2 million boarders or co-residents. The presence of unrelated persons in households was more common in urban than in rural areas. The causal relation seemed to run from occupation to family structure. Few outsiders lived in households whose heads were engaged in agriculture, fishing, mining, or communications. Here, family labor was abundant and incomes were inadequate for domestic service. Employees living with families were concentrated in households whose heads were occupied in industry and commerce, while domestic servants were most frequently found in families whose heads were in the professions and public service.

Here we are interested in non-familial living not as a phenomenon in its own right but as a reflection of the operation and vitality of the extended kin group that in theory had all-embracing responsibilities. The fact is that in 1930 some 6.5 million people, 10 per cent of the total population of the nation, lived outside the households of kin. The proportion of the 64.45 million people of Japan who had lived apart from the intimate family at some time or another during their life must have been very high.

Life away from the kin group was generally a temporary arrangement. The motivations seem to have been primarily economic. In a sense the non-familial living of family members was an adjustment of the family itself to difficult economic conditions. It seems obvious, however, that this non-familial living was conducive to social change and presaged a decline in the control of kin over the actions of the individual. Factory dormitories, boarding schools, and army barracks brought together people from different areas and cultural backgrounds. Life in the households of others was a major channel for cultural diffusion, for the majority of employees, domestic servants, and boarders came from agricultural prefectures and lived in industrial areas.

The fluidity of household membership in Japan differed from the mobility of most Western societies. Exodus and intrusion alike were conditioned by family obligations and responsibilities. The eldest son was likely to remain at home. The younger sons could leave because they had no direct responsibilities for the continuation of the family line and the veneration of the ancestors. The family head who needed additional labor for the household enterprise was apt to seek that labor among remote or collateral relatives. Youth attending school or working in the cities often boarded with relatives. Diffused familism which offered facilities for living and working in distant areas stimulated occupational re-allocation and geographical redistribution. It should be emphasized again, however, that the family system does not represent an inclusive or an adequate explanation of the formation of the industrial and urban society.

The preceding analysis of persons outside the family has emphasized conditions in 1930. This was the Japan of the conscript armies, the textile dormitories, and the low-paid labor. By 1950 there were no conscript armies.[17] Dormitory life was less common, for the reduced labor requirements of industry could be met more cheaply with local labor. There were fewer domestic servants. The barriers to migration to the cities and the passing of the Empire left households with an abundant supply of labor to conduct their enterprises, whether agricultural or industrial. Increase in the amount of education and advance in the age of entry into the labor force kept at home those youths aged from 12 or 13 to 17 or 18, many of whom had once been residents in factory dormitories or lived as non-related persons in households. Housing shortages, labor at inadequate wages, and the insecurities of the period prevented increases in the proportion of single-person households.

The net result of the economic, social, and demographic changes in Japan between 1930 and 1950 was an increase in the proportion of the people who lived as related persons in private households.[18] As a matter of fact, individuals not in this category were fewer in number in 1950, when the total population was 83.2 million, than they had been in 1930, when the total population had been 64.4 million. The persons living in quasi-households declined from 1.7 million in 1930 to 1.6 million in 1950, while non-related persons in the households of others declined from 4.1 million in 1930 to 1.4 million in 1950. The number of single-person households was 694 thousand in 1930 and 889 thousand in 1950. It was 596 thousand in 1955.

Thus the co-living family was a more pervasive aspect of Japanese culture in the early 1950's than it had been in the 1920's. The movement within Japanese culture seemed to be from an inclusive familial basis for living through a substantial dispersion of family members in the difficult decades of economic change to a new and even more inclusive basis in the consanguineous family. There was no evidence of an increase in the type of individualism that required life apart from the family group.

The Composition of Households

AVERAGE SIZE OF HOUSEHOLD

It is doubtful whether the ideal of the inclusive *ie* was ever realizable for the majority of the Japanese people. That ideal assumed multi-generational, large families surviving from the distant past into the remote future, with a mutuality in living that preserved all from the vicissitudes of existence. The deep

[16] Nihon. Naikaku tokei-kyoku. *Showa go'nen kokusei chosa hokoku.* IV.1. Table 36.

[17] Nihon. Sori-fu, tokei-kyoku. *Showa 25-nen kokusei chosa hokoku.* III.1. Tables 13-15. *Idem.* IV.1. Tables 13 and 13a.

[18] The data on persons outside households in 1930 are for the prewar area of Japan.

poverty of normal periods in densely settled areas precluded subsistence for large families, while high mortality precluded the biological development of such families. Famine and epidemic mocked the concept of the family in perpetuity. In time, increasing production and declining mortality in the modernizing economy permitted the survival of substantial portions of the children born, but this final possibility for the realization of the familistic ideal came as one facet of a ramified transformation that produced the factory, the city, public education, and declining fertility.

There is little evidence in the history of Japan that specifically Eastern cultural factors, ethical codes, or family institutions led to the development of any substantial portion of really large families. In the years from 1920 to 1950, the average number of persons per household and the variations in this number as between residential areas and occupational groups were comparable to those found in the United States a century or so ago. In Japan within its postwar area, the number of persons per ordinary household was 4.89 in 1920, 4.98 in 1930, 4.99 in 1940, and 4.97 in 1950 and 1955.[19]

The complexity of the forces determining household size is apparent in the fact that there were only slight and somewhat irregular changes in the average size of household between 1920 and 1950. Mortality had declined sharply in all areas, while fertility remained quite high in the rural areas. Population had long been increasing. Given the familistic ideal and economic abundance in village societies, the household structure might have begun to approach the five generations of legend. However, increasing longevity and economic security were products of modern science and technology, of the very forces in the new order that were incompatible with the old. Mobility, urban life, and new wants were as characteristic of the twentieth century as longer life and improved nutrition. And even science could not create the additional land that would have provided new fields for the multiplying branch houses of the second and third sons.

Differences in the average size of household as between regions and socio-economic groups are those that would be anticipated either on the basis of the previous analysis of life in Japan or on the basis of the earlier experience of Western countries.[20] In 1930 the average number of persons per ordinary household ranged from 4.7 in Osaka prefecture to 6.2 in Miyagi and Yamagata prefectures. The average was higher in agricultural than in industrial prefectures, higher in the rural prefectures of the northeast than in those of the southwest. The averages were highest in households whose heads were gainfully occupied in agriculture, lowest in households whose heads were occupied in transportation and communication, professional and public services, and manufacturing industry. Households with heads engaged in trade and commerce ranked next to agriculture in average size.

SIZE OF HOUSEHOLD, URBANIZATION, AND INDUSTRIALIZATION

The distribution of households by number of members changed slowly in the quarter-century between 1920 and 1955 (TABLE 35). Some changes did occur, but they were not in the direction of a declining household size, as might have been expected. In both *shi* and *gun* there were declines in the proportion of one- and two-person households. In the *gun* there was some increase in the proportion of households with seven or more members. The factors responsible here include the maintenance of relatively high fertility in the rural areas, the precipitant declines in death rates in infancy and childhood that permitted more of the babies born to survive and become older children and youth in families, and the inadequate economic opportunities that held youth and adults as household members engaged in relatively non-productive enterprises.

TABLE 35

Private households, by number of members, *shi* and *gun*, 1920-1950
(Per cent distribution)

Year	*All private households*	NUMBER OF MEMBERS			
		1-2	*3-4*	*5-6*	*7 or more*
1920	100.	18.3	30.5	27.2	23.9
Shi	100.	23.3	35.6	23.5	17.6
Gun	100.	17.2	29.3	28.0	25.6
1930	100.	17.3	29.9	27.2	25.7
Shi	100.	20.9	34.9	24.9	19.4
Gun	100.	16.0	28.3	27.9	27.7
1950	100.	15.5	30.7	28.4	25.3
Shi	100.	20.1	35.2	27.2	17.5
Gun	100.	12.6	27.4	29.3	30.7
1955	100.	14.3	31.1	30.7	23.9
Shi	100.	16.0	34.1	30.1	19.7
Gun	100.	11.7	26.7	31.6	29.9

Source: 1920: Nihon. Naikaku tokei-kyoku. *Taisho ku'nen kokusei chosa hokoku.* IV.A.1. Table 30. 1930: *Idem. Showa go'nen kokusei chosa hokoku.* IV.1. Table 34. 1950: Nihon. Sori-fu, tokei-kyoku. *Showa 25-nen kokusei chosa hokoku.* III.1. Table 14. 1955: *Ibid. 1% chushutsu shukei ni yoru kekka sokuho. Showa 30-nen kokusei chosa. Zenkoku.* Part 9. Table 2.

The maintenance of large households in both cities and rural areas occurred in a situation in which the differences between city and country remained appreciable. In 1950 there was a direct relationship between dependence on agriculture and the frequency of the large household, as is indicated in the following percentage distribution of households with specified numbers of persons, prefectures being classified by industrial type:[21]

Prefectures by Industrial type	*Number of persons*				
	1	*2*	*3-4*	*5-6*	*7 or more*
All Japan	5.4	10.3	30.6	28.4	25.3
Metropolitan	8.4	13.5	35.7	26.8	15.7
Other industrial	5.6	11.4	33.1	28.6	21.0
Intermediate	5.3	10.2	30.5	29.2	24.7
Agricultural	4.3	8.6	27.0	28.3	31.8
Hokkaido	3.8	8.7	29.7	27.4	30.5

[19] Nihon. Sori-fu, tokei-kyoku. *Nihon tokei nenkan, 1951.* Table 7. The figure for 1950 is computed from: *Idem. Showa 25-nen kokusei chosa hokoku.* III.1. Table 19.

[20] Nihon. Naikaku tokei-kyoku. *Showa go'nen kokusei chosa saishu hokokusho.* VIII. Tables 60-64.

[21] Nihon. Sori-fu, tokei-kyoku. *Showa 25-nen kokusei chosa hokoku.* III.1. Table 14. Computed from rounded numbers of the 10 per cent sample. Comparable analysis for the years 1920 and 1930 yields essentially similar results.

The preceding distribution of households by number of members was based on an economic rather than a family classification, for both related and non-related members of households were included. If we exclude the non-related persons, the differences in the distributions become more pronounced. The following arrangement of data pertains to the year 1950. The figures are percentages of the number of multi-person private households in the prefectures of the specified types:[22]

Prefectures by industrial type	*Number of related persons*			
	1[23]	*2-3*	*4-5*	*6 or more*
All Japan	11.2	31.7	28.9	28.2
Metropolitan	16.2	39.9	28.8	15.1
Other industrial	12.8	35.6	30.3	21.2
Intermediate	10.4	30.2	28.7	30.7
Agricultural	9.2	27.3	28.2	35.0
Hokkaido	9.5	31.6	28.5	30.3

This has been an over-all description of broad differences in the distribution of households by size for *shi* and *gun* and for prefectures by industrial type. Since the deviate households reveal many of the characteristics of the old as well as something of the development of the new, we shall pause here to examine the one-person households and the sex ratios of the populations in all households distributed by size.[24]

In 1930, 6 per cent of Japan's households were single-person establishments. There was a direct association among urbanization, industrialization, and individuals living alone; an inverse association between the small household that theoretically represents individualism and the large household that theoretically represents familism. This is simple corroboration of simple theory, but there were many relations in the Japan of 1930 that were not simple. Within the more urbanized prefectures the proportion of single-person households was related to the prevalence of such households in the major recruitment areas for migrants rather than to the size or industrial type of the prefecture of present residence.

A special tabulation of the age and marital status of persons classified as one-person households in 1950 indicated great differences in the characteristics of the men and women who lived alone.[25] The men tended to be single and young, while the women tended to be widowed and elderly. For men, living separately seemed to be either a part of the job or an alternative to dormitory or boarding house. For women, living separately must have meant the absence of a family or the existence of a family that ignored its traditional responsibilities. For both men and women, however, the number of persons living alone was small for a nation whose total population amounted to 83.2 million; individual households were maintained by only 449 thousand men and 438 thousand women.

The sex ratios of persons living in households of various sizes reveal in still another way the complex interplay of demographic factors, historic values, and economic possibilities in the structure and functioning of the Japanese family. We shall refer specifically to the year 1930, though the picture would be similar if we had used any other census year. Single-person households were predominantly male in urban areas, predominantly female in rural areas. In both urban and rural areas, there was approximately a 9 per cent deficiency in males in two-person households. Sex ratios increased progressively with size of household, reaching unity in urban areas for five-person households, in rural areas for nine-person households. Large households of from 11 to 15 persons had almost a 30 per cent excess of males in urban areas, as contrasted with a 4 per cent excess in rural areas. Households of 35 or more persons had a 50 to 100 per cent excess of males in urban areas, a deficiency of 30 per cent or more in rural areas. It is obvious that the really large households were products of the economic functioning of the society rather than natural consequences of its kinship institutions.

SIZE OF HOUSEHOLD AND INDUSTRY OF THE HEAD

In 1950, as in 1920, 1930, and 1940, the predominant factor in the determination of household size was the industry in which the head was engaged rather than the urban or rural character of the place where the family lived.[26] The percentage of all households that included from seven to ten persons was 35.7 per cent when the heads were in the agricultural labor force, 17.1 per cent when heads labored in manufacturing industry, and 15.5 per cent when heads were in government service. Forestry and fishing were comparable to agriculture, while mining, construction, trade, and transportation were comparable to manufacturing and government service. Households of 11 or more persons constituted 4.1 per cent of the households with heads in agriculture, 2.1 per cent of the households with heads in forestry, and 3.6 per cent of the households with heads in fishing. These large households numbered only one in each 100 households whose heads were in government service. Comparable relationships between household size and industry of the head existed in *shi* and *gun*, although for each type of industry the proportion of small households was less in the *gun* than in the *shi*, and the proportion of large households greater. However, the variations among different industrial groups in specific types of areas were far greater than those among comparable industrial groups in different types of areas. It was agriculture and the way of life on the farms that were perpetuating the large households in Japanese society in 1950, as in 1930 and 1920. The large household with a head engaged in manufacturing industry or trade was a transitory phenomenon. It was a product of industrialization in a milieu of poverty.

HEADS AND MEMBERS

Most of the heads of households were men,[27] but there were

[22] *Ibid.* Table 17. In considering this presentation, it should be remembered that non-related persons in households have always been least numerous in those prefectures where agriculture was the major industry and large families most numerous.

[23] Households of two or more members in which no member is related to the head.

[24] These analyses are based on the household data in the censuses of 1920 to 1950. For 1920: Nihon. Naikaku tokei-kyoku. *Taisho ku'nen kokusei chosa hokoku.* IV.A.1. Tables 30-33. For 1930: *Idem. Showa go'nen kokusei chosa hokoku.* IV.1. Tables 33-39. For 1950: Nihon. Sori-fu, tokei-kyoku. *Showa 25-nen kokusei chosa hokoku.* III.1. Tables 13-15; *Idem.* IV.1. Tables 13 and 13a.

[25] Nihon. Sori-fu, tokei-kyoku. *Showa 25-nen kokusei chosa hokoku.* III.1. Table 22. Since this tabulation is based on the 10 per cent sample, the total of 886 thousand single-person private households differs somewhat from the 889 thousand of the final tabulation as given in Vol. IV, Part 1, Table 13.

[26] *Ibid.* III.2. Tables 31-34.

[27] It is simple to formulate the theoretical structure of the *ie*, for the traditions were ancient and firm and the legal formulations for entrance and departure quite specific. The co-living household consisted primarily of persons of the direct patrilineal line, as we have seen earlier, and its structure was authoritarian. However, it lacked the legally defined rigidities of the house and so had a

substantial variations in the proportions of male heads in the industrial groups. Women were more likely to be heads of households in industries where status and income were low. Data for the year 1930 are illustrative. In that year, the heads engaged in industries requiring arduous physical labor were almost entirely men: 99 per cent in fishing, 98 per cent in mining, 99 per cent in transportation. Male heads were also predominant in the professions and public service. Women left with family responsibilities had limited possibilities for employment that would maintain themselves and their dependents. Five per cent of the heads in agriculture were women; in absolute numbers, this was the largest group of women with managerial responsibility. For the women left without land or income there were really only two possibilities—the small shop or domestic service. And in 1930, 9 per cent of all household heads in commerce were women, as were 16 per cent of all household heads in domestic service. The aged women who were widowed apparently were not always cared for by their sons, or perhaps some of them had no surviving children. In any event, 40 per cent of all heads of households without occupation were women.

For 1950 and 1955 there is information on the age and marital status of the heads of households. The results could have been deduced from a reading of the codified house laws of the old regime. A summary description for 1950 is given in TABLE 36. Among the prefectures there was a definite association between the prevalence of heads aged 60 and over and the predominance of agricultural occupations, between the prevalence of heads below age 30 and the predominance of non-agricultural occupations.

larger range of possible variation. It is reasonable to assume, though, that the great majority of the households consisted of houses or fragments of houses, and that the person who functioned as head of the household either was or would be the head of the house. Identity of house and household would not exist for substantial portions of the population at any given time, for movements in and out of the family of origin were aspects of the life cycle of individual families. In some instances, a household might consist of a conjugal family or other individuals who would later return to the family of origin, which was also the main house. In other cases, the conjugal families of sons living with the main family would leave to establish a separate household. The census schedule was filled in by the "head" of the household, not the head of the conjugal family or the house *per se*. The head of the household was the person who exercised the authority of headship. The definition does not seem to have involved difficulties in selection within the households, for authority in the household was exercised by virtue of the same traditions that had been codified in the house laws. Headship of the household, like headship of the house, was defined in terms of the structure of authority rather than in terms of economic criteria as such.

The heads of households consisted primarily of married people. In 1950, only 3.3 per cent of the heads of multi-person private households were single, while 83.7 per cent were married and 13.0 per cent widowed or divorced.[28] Single heads were somewhat more frequent in metropolitan and other industrial prefectures, as were widowed and divorced heads in intermediate and agricultural prefectures. Differences were slight, however, and they reflected primarily the differences in the proportion of men and women among household heads. Separate analysis for that 88.9 per cent of the heads of multi-person private households who were men reveals 92.0 per cent as married. The single, the widowed, and the divorced together constituted only 8 per cent of all heads. Prefectural differences were slight.

Married women living with their husbands would hardly be reported as household heads, for this was the appropriate role for the husband. If the husband were absent, and the father of the husband or some other man in a priority status were not living in the household, the census might return the married woman as the head. The majority of the female heads of households were widows, forced to maintain themselves without the assistance of husbands, fathers, or mature sons. This was true in all prefectures.

The major distinctions in the roles of the age, sex, and marital status groups in households were associated with age rather than with the type of area of residence. The average size of private households in 1955 suggests the relations between headship and the life cycles of individuals and families.[29]

Age and sex of head	*Total*	*Single*	*Married*	*Widowed*	*Divorced*
Male	5.23	3.08	5.35	4.64	2.81
Below 30	3.64	2.49	3.75	3.00	2.92
30-59	5.48	2.67	5.55	4.65	2.88
60 and over	5.29	1.76	5.45	4.65	2.46
Female	3.25	2.18	3.82	3.29	2.87
Below 30	2.62	2.26	3.09	2.96	2.61
30-59	3.50	2.14	4.00	3.56	2.96
60 and over	3.47	1.86	2.76	2.48	2.19

[28] Nihon. Sori-fu, tokei-kyoku. *Showa 25-nen kokusei chosa hokoku*. III.1. Table 19.

[29] Nihon. Sori-fu, tokei-kyoku. *1% chushutsu shukei ni yoru kekka sokuho. Showa 30-nen kokusei chosa. Zenkoku*. Part 9. Table 2.

TABLE 36

Age of heads of multi-person households, by sex, prefectures by industrial type, 1950

Prefectures by industrial type	PER CENT OF MALE HEADS			PER CENT OF FEMALE HEADS		
	Under 30	*30-59*	*60 and over*	*Under 30*	*30-59*	*60 and over*
All Japan	12.2	72.5	15.3	8.0	78.6	13.4
Metropolitan	13.7	77.0	9.4	10.6	79.2	10.2
Other industrial	13.3	72.7	14.0	9.0	78.0	13.0
Intermediate	12.2	71.6	16.2	7.7	79.2	13.0
Agricultural	11.2	72.5	16.2	6.9	79.8	13.4
Hokkaido	15.7	73.9	10.4	10.0	78.3	11.7

Source: Nihon. Sori-fu, tokei-kyoku. *Showa 25-nen kokusei chosa hokoku*. III.1. Table 20.

The role of the head of the household was critical to the determination of the education, the occupational choices, the migrations, and the marriages of youth. The headship itself represented a concentration of authority over the social, economic, and demographic processes that were transforming Japan. It may be significant, therefore, to know the proportion of persons who played this role. In 1930, almost 36 per cent of all males in multi-person private households were heads of households (TABLE 37). That 64 per cent of male household members who were related to the head included children, adults in the productive ages, and the aged who had relinquished headship. It is obvious, therefore, that headship was a common function among adult men, that most men sooner or later played the role. In numerical terms, the status of household head approached being an attribute of the men of the society. If it is objected that the powers of the head inhere in the headship of the legal house and the family but that the data used here refer to the household, we need only refer to the percentages in Table 36 on the small proportions of non-related persons in households. As a group, the heads of multi-person private households did not differ greatly from the heads of conjugal families, and the heads of conjugal families either were or were likely to become heads of main or branch houses. In addition, the numerical computations for heads of households in the different industrial groups are in accord with theoretical expectations based on the structure of responsibilities in the traditional kinship system. The male in agriculture was somewhat less likely to be a household head than the male in industrial and urban-type industries.

The role of women in Japanese society was subservience—and in 1930 only 2.7 per cent of all the females in multi-person private households were heads. Ninety-two per cent of all females—children, youth, married women, the widowed, and the divorced—lived in households as family members related to the head. The proportions reached 96.5 per cent where household heads were in agriculture; comparable figures for fishing and mining were 97.7 and 97.1 per cent. In the industry where the proportion of women heads was highest, domestic service, there was no prestige attached to the industry itself. The most common status for women living in the households of others was also that which was lowest in status, domestic service.

TABLE 37

Relation to household head of all members of multi-person households, by selected industries of heads, by sex, 1930
(Per cent of household members in membership categories, each sex)

Relation to head	Total gainfully occupied	INDUSTRY OF HEAD: Agriculture and forestry	Manufacturing	Trade and commerce	Transportation and communication	Public service and professional	Domestic	Not gainfully occupied
Males								
Total persons	100.	100.	100.	100.	100.	100.	100.	100.
Related persons	91.8	97.7	84.8	83.8	91.5	92.4	96.4	90.3
Heads	35.8	33.2	37.5	36.8	42.1	42.2	43.4	32.9
Others	56.0	64.5	47.3	47.0	49.4	50.2	53.0	57.4
Other persons	8.2	2.3	15.2	16.2	8.4	7.5	3.6	9.6
Employees	5.5	1.5	11.4	12.7	4.5	1.9	0.1	1.2
Domestics	0.1	0.1	0.1	0.1	0.0	0.3	0.1	0.5
Boarders	2.6	0.7	3.7	3.4	3.9	5.3	3.4	7.9
Females								
Total persons	100.	100.	100.	100.	100.	100.	100.	100.
Related persons	94.7	98.2	94.7	87.0	96.6	90.2	96.9	90.7
Heads	2.7	1.7	1.6	3.6	0.2	1.7	8.0	17.6
Others	92.0	96.5	93.1	83.4	96.4	88.5	88.9	73.1
Other persons	5.4	1.7	5.1	12.9	3.4	9.9	3.1	9.3
Employees	1.9	0.5	1.5	6.5	0.4	2.0	0.1	0.8
Domestics	2.1	0.6	2.0	4.4	1.4	5.3	0.8	5.1
Boarders	1.4	0.6	1.6	2.0	1.6	2.6	2.2	3.4

Source: Nihon. Naikaku tokei-kyoku. *Showa go'nen kokusei chosa hokoku.* IV.2. Pp. 552-553.

DEPENDENCY BURDENS IN HOUSEHOLDS

Average size of household and distributions of households by size have been presented as characteristic of households. The differentiation of household members as heads and as persons related to the head has been presented as a reflection of the status roles of men and women in the society of Japan. Households functioned as such, however; they were by definition groups of individuals who lived together and shared a common budget. Hence it is essential to look at the ratios of dependent to productive groups and the labor force participation rates from the focus of the household. In one sense, the dependency structures of the individual households were products of the levels of childbearing, the hazards of death, and the rates of exodus and influx in previous periods. In another sense, the dependency structures reveal the necessities that created the labor force participation rates which characterized the Japanese economy.

The simplest approach to the measurement of the demographic responsibilities of household heads is to assume that all related members other than the head are dependents of the head. These socio-biological dependency burdens on heads were associated positively with agriculture, negatively with non-agricultural industries other than such depressed and socially non-acceptable activities as domestic service. The differences between industrial groups were substantial. In 1930, there were 3.891 dependent members per 1,000 heads; the number of such dependents was 4,614 for household heads in agriculture, 3,288 for heads in public service and the professions (TABLE 38). These are types of relations that 39). The major difference was an increase in the number of related dependents per household head. Plausible explanations are many, though all are hypothetical. Extended education, advanced age at marriage, and limited employment opportunities kept youth as dependents in the parental home. It is probable that repatriation, housing shortages, and incomes below prewar levels resulted in joint living of sub-families that would have lived separately under more favorable circumstances.

The significant aspect of the comparison of 1930 and 1950 lies not so much in the increase in the dependency burdens per household head as in the failure of this burden to decline. It might appear that industrialization and urbanization were not lessening the biological dependency burdens. Closer analysis indicates that the industrial transformation was influencing households in ways that would have produced lesser dependency burdens had there been no counteracting factors. In 1930, the number of dependents per 1,000 household heads engaged in any specific industry varied widely as between the agricultural and the industrial regions of the country. In the metropolitan prefectures there were 3,100 dependents per 1,000 heads engaged in agriculture; in the agricultural prefectures there were 4,574 dependents per 1,000 heads in the same category. Similar but less extensive differences existed for heads gainfully occupied in other industries. For instance, related dependents per 1,000 heads in manufacturing industry were 3,046 in metropolitan prefectures, 3,636 in agricultural prefectures.

TABLE 38

Composition of multi-person private households, by industry of head and gainful employment of persons related to head, 1930

(Numbers per 1,000 households)

Industry	Total members	Related persons: Heads	Others: Total	Others: Gainfully occupied	Others: Not gainfully occupied	Persons not related to head
All industries	5,240	1,000	3,891	1,113	2,779	349
Agriculture	5,731	1,000	4,614	1,865	2,747	117
Fishing	5,425	1,000	4,223	1,059	3,164	201
Mining	4,733	1,000	3,556	486	3,070	176
Manufacturing	4,875	1,000	3,363	538	2,826	511
Commerce	4,981	1,000	3,256	573	2,683	725
Transportation	4,581	1,000	3,305	417	2,888	277
Service, professions	4,699	1,000	3,288	452	2,836	410
Domestic	3,979	1,000	2,847	408	2,439	132
Other or unearned income	4,263	1,000	2,993	401	2,591	271

Source: Nihon. Naikaku tokei-kyoku. *Showa go'nen kokusei chosa hokoku.* IV.2. Pp. 552-553. Single-person households and households whose heads were not gainfully occupied are excluded.

one would expect if the agricultural-industrial transformation were a movement from high to more limited fertility. Direct conclusions as to the factors involved in the positive association between high dependency burdens in households and the predominance of agriculture are difficult, for there were no tabulations on the ages of those persons in households who were related to the head. However, the existence of lower dependency burdens in the high-prestige urban occupations has no reasonable explanation other than the limitations to childbearing in the households concerned.

The difficulty with the interpretation of differences in household dependency burdens solely in terms of differences in rates of childbearing is that the dependency burdens in 1950 were quite similar to those that had existed in 1930 (TABLE

Given this pattern of relationships in 1930, a national trend toward industrialization and urbanization should have been accompanied by declining biological dependency burdens in households. The explanation for the failure of such burdens to decline between 1930 and 1950 must lie in the disturbed conditions in 1950 rather than in unique aspects of the eco-

TABLE 39

Composition of private multi-person households, by industry of head and labor force status of persons related to head, 1950

(Numbers per 1,000 households)

		Related persons				
			Others			
Industry	*Total members*	*Heads*	*Total*	*In labor force*	*Not in labor force*	*Persons not related to head*
All industries	5,295	1,000	4,201	1,281	2,921	93
Agriculture	6,059	1,000	5,008	2,227	2,782	51
Fishing	5,714	1,000	4,656	1,416	3,240	55
Forestry	5,392	1,000	4,354	1,471	2,884	37
Mining	5,081	1,000	4,057	546	3,510	24
Construction	5,063	1,000	3,959	849	3,110	104
Trade	4,919	1,000	3,726	865	2,861	192
Transportation	4,883	1,000	3,846	682	3,164	37
Manufacturing	4,809	1,000	3,701	696	3,005	109
Services	4,755	1,000	3,561	691	2,871	194
Government	4,695	1,000	3,652	716	2,936	43
Finance	4,374	1,000	3,311	573	2,738	63

Source: Nihon. Sori-fu, tokei-kyoku. *Showa 25-nen kokusei chosa hokoku.* III.2. Table 34. Single-person households and households whose heads were not in the labor force were excluded. Households with heads classified as in "other and not reported" industries were included in the totals for all industries. The computations are based on sample data.

nomic and demographic transformation of household structure in Japan.

In all households there were family members who were not in the labor force. Some of them were children, others adults. Although the available data do not permit the separation of the components, it is possible to compute a simple ratio of non-workers to workers. At the risk of some imprecision, we shall assume that the non-workers are economically dependent on the workers. Using this definition, the economic dependency ratio of non-workers to workers tends to be related inversely to the socio-biological dependency burden of related members on household heads. Increased levels of income and higher social status were accompanied by lesser participation of family members in gainful activity.

If we examine the participation of family members in the labor force in the prefectures classified by industrial type, we find a clear-cut negative relation between industrialization and the ratio of non-workers to workers among related persons living together as households. In 1930, the percentage of family members other than heads who were gainfully occupied was 15.5 in heavily industrialized prefectures, 33.8 in agricultural prefectures. For agriculture, the proportion of family members other than the head who were gainfully occupied was 31.4 in metropolitan prefectures, 41.2 in agricultural prefectures. For manufacturing industry, the comparable proportion was 12.7 in metropolitan prefectures, 19.2 in agricultural prefectures. In all types of areas, however, the gainful employment of family members in agricultural households was proportionately greater than that of family members in industrial households.

Since age and gainful activity are so closely related, it is essential to determine the role of the age structures of the various types of households in the economic activities of their members. Since young children and the aged are more prevalent in agriculture than in other industrial groups, a heavy use of the labor of children and the aged could be responsible for a substantial part of the pervasive family labor revealed in the data from the censuses of 1930 and 1950. There is direct evidence on this point in the data of the agricultural census of 1947, where family members working in the family agriculture were tabulated by age (TABLE 40). In this year, a major proportion of the family members working in the family agriculture were in the productive ages from 16 to 61—and participation rates were highest for persons aged from 26 to 60. Family labor was somewhat less prevalent in metropolitan prefectures where opportunities for outside labor were more abundant, and in agricultural prefectures where the pile-up of population on the farms was greatest.

Thus far, the labor of family members has been considered without reference to sex. The demographic implications of economic activity among members other than the head differ greatly according to whether the labor is done by men or women. In 1950 the proportion of related persons other than the head who were in the labor force was approximately equal for men and women (TABLE 41). If 30.5 per cent of all women in the household related to the head were in the labor force—and practically all women lived in households as persons related to the head—it is apparent that a substantial proportion of the spouses of household heads were in the labor force.

In the *shi* the proportion of female household members in the labor force was considerably below that of male members; in the *gun* the proportion of female members in the labor force was somewhat above that of male members. This different relationship in the *shi* and the *gun* was a result of the greater importance of agriculture in the *gun*. However, a

TABLE 40

The participation of regular members of farm households in the agriculture of the family, by age, prefectures by industrial type, 1947

(Per cent engaged in family agriculture)

Prefectures by industrial type	*Age*					
	Age 11 and over	*11-15*	*16-25*	*26-40*	*41-60*	*61 and over*
All Japan	63.0	8.6	66.5	83.4	83.7	51.1
Metropolitan	50.3	5.3	44.3	65.9	72.7	43.9
Other industrial	64.1	10.2	61.8	81.8	86.5	60.1
Intermediate	64.6	10.6	64.0	83.7	85.8	59.1
Agricultural	62.1	7.0	70.1	84.4	81.8	42.5
Hokkaido	63.5	7.0	75.3	86.9	81.9	37.6

Source: Nihon. Norin-sho, nogyo kairyo-kyoku, tokei chosa-bu. *Norin-sho tokei hyo. 1947.* Pp. 80ff.

glance at the industries other than agriculture indicates that the proportion of family members in the labor force in any given industry tended to be greater in the *gun* than in the *shi*, and that the heavier utilization of family labor in the *gun* occurred particularly among women. Thus the gainful employment of women was a product of the poverty of the rural society. The participation of the household in the modern economy of industrial occupations and urban living gave a somewhat larger proportion of women the opportunity to spend their time in household activity and child care without gainful employment.

THE ROLES OF WOMEN

The women who bear and rear the children that are both pride and problem of Japanese society are extolled for their fulfillment of the obligations of womanhood. Less obvious is their multi-functional economic role: the labor of the household, the organization of consumption, and the assistance in those activities that provide income or physical product for the family.

In the days when families and village communities were largely self-sufficient, there was an intimate relationship between household work and that labor in production which contributed to the family's maintenance. All members of the family worked together in the field or in other activities carried on by the household head. There may have been physical conflicts between the various demands on the energies of women, but there were no severe cultural conflicts. The status relationships of the family permeated the labor of the family, and the remuneration for labor was a family product.

As the monetary economy developed, work became differentiated according to whether or not it produced income. In an idealized Eastern situation, the differentiation of the labor

TABLE 41

Labor force status of related persons other than the head, by industry of the head, *shi* and *gun*, 1950

(Per cent of related persons other than the head in the labor force)

Industry of head	ALL JAPAN			SHI			GUN		
	Total	*Male*	*Female*	*Total*	*Male*	*Female*	*Total*	*Male*	*Female*
All industries	30.5	30.4	30.5	20.3	24.1	18.0	35.8	33.6	37.3
Agriculture	44.5	40.5	47.2	41.6	40.6	42.3	44.8	40.4	47.7
Fishing	30.4	35.1	27.3	—[a]	—	—	31.9	35.4	29.6
Forestry	33.8	31.8	35.1	—	—	—	34.6	32.2	36.3
Mining	13.5	18.0	10.9	—	—	—	14.0	18.1	11.5
Construction	21.4	25.4	18.9	17.2	25.1	12.2	25.0	25.6	24.6
Trade	23.2	23.1	23.3	21.1	22.2	20.5	26.1	24.3	27.2
Transportation	17.7	19.3	16.7	14.4	19.2	11.8	21.3	19.5	22.3
Manufacturing	18.8	22.3	16.7	16.3	21.7	13.1	22.5	23.2	22.1
Services	19.4	20.2	18.9	17.3	20.4	15.4	21.6	19.9	22.6
Government	19.6	20.6	19.0	15.3	19.3	12.9	24.8	22.2	26.3
Finance	17.3	19.6	15.5	15.0	19.2	12.3	—[a]	—	—

[a] Less than 1,000 households.
Source: Nihon. Sori-fu, tokei-kyoku. *Showa 25-nen kokusei chosa hokoku.* III.2. Table 34.

force would have occurred only among men, leaving the familial role of women intact. Neither the resources nor the technologies of Japan were adequate for such an ideal society, in which men labored outside the home while women were shielded within it. Japan's agriculture required much toil, while her non-agricultural activities were also based on abundant labor. Moreover, the individual family had not only traditions that barred an economic role for women outside the home but values that gave high normative status to toil. Hence the differences in the economic roles of men and women were governed not by remuneration for labor, but by the type of labor, the status relationships with other laborers, and the relationships of labor to the home.

Hypotheses concerning the changing role of women in the industrializing society of Japan can be formulated easily on the basis of Western experience. It might be assumed that the growth of remunerative employment for women would lead to conflicts between the traditional demographic position of women and their modern economic role. Any resolution of a conflict such as this would necessitate changes whose ultimate consequence would be transformations of family functions and a lessened rate of childbearing. If single women were allowed to labor outside the familial agriculture, there would be postponement of marriage, and this would alter family structure and the nexus of personal relationships within the family. If married women labored outside agriculture, there would be a discrepancy between ideals and behavior that could not be ignored. Furthermore, there would be conflicts among the requirements of the job, the recurrent pregnancies, and the continuing demands for child care.

The Japanese solution to the conflict in the economic and the demographic roles of women in the industrializing society was one of compromise. The leaders of the Restoration saw the necessity of educating women, since the women reared the sons who became the industrial workers and the soldiers. However, education for girls included indoctrination in the responsibilities of women. All this was an expressed policy of government. On a more immediate level, families had to survive economically and industry needed cheap labor. Thus women entered gainful employment, but they labored in ways consistent with the values of the culture. Single women were utilized outside the home, while married women labored within the household or the family enterprise. Single girls received wages, while married women engaged in unpaid family labor. Thus in theory the role of women could remain unchanged within a changing economy.

There was only limited success in reconciling the traditional status of women with economic activities that were increasingly Western in type. Marriage and family were influenced by the duality of education and indoctrination, the dichotomy of the wage labor of the single and the unpaid family labor of the married, and the fragmentation of family living that accompanied the labor of boys and men outside the home. On the other hand, the ancient patterns of family labor and the attitudes as to proper activities for women influenced the labor force of the industrializing economy. It is this aspect of the relationship between family and economy that we shall emphasize here.

THE ECONOMIC ROLE

The economic activities of the women of Japan have been considered before—first in Chapter V, where women were considered as a component of the labor force of the nation, and then in the present chapter, where women were considered as a component of the household. Here the relations of the family system and the marital status of women to their gainful employment will be analyzed.

In 1930, agricultural areas maintained much of the family economy of the past, while industrial areas relied heavily on the wage labor of men. High participation in economic activity characterized the women of the rural prefectures, while low participation characterized those of the urban prefectures. The proportion of women who were reported as gainfully occupied was lowest in Tokyo prefecture: less than 30 per cent of the women aged from 15 to 59, and less than 10 per cent of those aged 60 and over.[30] The highest proportion of women reported as gainfully occupied was in Nagano: 73 per cent of the women aged from 15 to 59, and 36 per cent of those aged 60 and over. Variations among the urban and the rural prefectures are rather difficult to explain simply in terms of rurality or its absence. There were differences among prefectures with relatively equal percentages of rural population, and there were differences among the industrial prefectures. These differences are striking, if the reported economic activities of women aged 60 and over are considered. In Akita prefecture in the northeast, less than one-tenth of the older women were reported as gainfully occupied; in neighboring Iwate, almost one-fourth were so reported. In Ibaragi, 43 per cent of the women aged 60 and over were reported as gainfully occupied. These differences in areas may indicate only that local factors determined the answer to the census question. They may indicate specific types of agriculture or industrial situations or differing customs with reference to the work of women.

The labor of women was largely agricultural. In 1930, there was a rough relationship between the proportions of women gainfully occupied and the proportions of the gainfully occupied in agriculture. The explanation of this association is a simple one. Gainful employment in agriculture was consistent with the family system. It involved cooperative family effort rather than departure from the household for labor.[31]

An integration of family and economy was widespread in the Japan of 1930. More than 36 per cent of all married women were gainfully occupied in agriculture.[32] The percentage exceeded 50 in Aomori, Iwate, Fukushima, and Tochigi in northeast Honshu; in Chiba adjacent to Tokyo; in Nagano, Shiga, Tottori, Shimane, and Tonushima, also in Honshu; and in Oita and Kagoshima in Kyushu. These women were assistants in the family enterprises rather than the responsible operators of establishments.

The availability of women as a subsidized labor supply conditioned the industrial as well as the agricultural development of Japan. In the early days the textile and other industries needed cheap labor. Agricultural families needed cash income, and they had daughters who were not needed on the farm. Factories were located in areas accessible to this labor supply and dormitories were constructed. Recruiting agents made contracts with the fathers that involved wage labor

[30] Nihon. Naikaku tokei-kyoku. *Showa go'nen kokusei chosa hokoku*. IV.2. Table 31.

[31] In 1930, over 4.5 million of the 6.4 million women engaged in agriculture were married, 1.1 million were single, 647 thousand were widowed, and 98 thousand were divorced. More than 71 per cent of all women gainfully occupied in agriculture were married. There was little variation in this proportion among the various prefectures. In 34 of the 47 prefectures, the proportion of all women gainfully occupied in agriculture who were married was within the limited range of 69 through 75 per cent. In only one prefecture did the proportion fall below 60, and this was Okinawa.

[32] Nihon. Naikaku tokei-kyoku. *Showa go'nen kokusei chosa hokoku*. IV.4. Table 15.

over a period of years. The fathers received the major portion of the payments. The girls became indentured laborers. In the factories they were shielded from contacts that might lead to psychological questioning and discontent. Long hours of work and supervision of their hours of leisure prevented contamination outside the factory. Thus the industries of Japan secured cheap labor, the farmers secured some cash income, the girls secured dowries—and the contracts were completed by the age then regarded as appropriate for marriage.

The number of girls who lived in factory dormitories was sufficiently large to indicate that this period of labor away from home and village may have constituted a major force of change. In 1930 there were 435.8 thousand girls in factory dormitories. Since the census of that year reported only 677.4 thousand girls aged from 12 to 20 as gainfully occupied in manufacturing industry, it is apparent that the major industrial contribution of girls in their teens came about through the dormitory system. And here, it should be noted, careful regulations saw to it that daily routines accorded with the ideals of the family.

The employment of women in factories and in industrial employment was far more extensive than the concentration of young girls in factory dormitories might indicate. In 1930 the census reported 1.4 million women as gainfully occupied in manufacturing industry. The factory statistics of the same year indicated that 911 thousand women were engaged in factories employing five or more workers.[33] If we assume that all girls in factory dormitories labored in factories with five or more workers, a simple subtraction reveals that 475 thousand of the women working in these larger factories did not live in the dormitories. In other words, even in the year 1930 slightly less than half of the women working in factories with five or more workers lived under the dormitory system that has come to be regarded as the characteristic mode of life for gainfully occupied women in Japan. If we relate the factory statistics on the total number of women employed in factories with five or more workers to the total number of women reported as gainfully occupied in manufacturing industry in the census count, we find that 519 thousand women labored in manufacturing industry in establishments that included fewer than five workers. These women were the female labor force of Japan's household and village industries.

Factories and hence factory dormitories were located with reference to the availability of natural resources and the abundance of the labor supply. There were major concentrations in the agricultural areas. One-sixth of all the girls in factory dormitories in 1930, 72.6 thousand out of a total of 435.8 thousand, were in Nagano prefecture; another 36.7 thousand were in Gumma and Saitama prefectures. Women in factory employment who lived outside dormitories were concentrated in the urban areas, particularly the metropolitan prefectures. The majority of the women who labored in the small factories with five or less workers lived in the *mura* or the smaller *machi*. These female workers in household industries comprised 2 or 3 per cent of all gainfully occupied women in the rural prefectures of northeastern Japan, and from 5 to 6 per cent of such women in the rural prefectures of southwestern Japan.

The employment of women in manufacturing industry, as in agriculture, was organized to minimize the conflict between household and economic responsibilities. Insofar as household industry was concerned, such employment was as much a part of family responsibility and functioning as the agricultural enterprise itself. The factory dormitory represented an interlude in a life cycle that in theory pursued the traditional course thereafter. And the factories tended to employ the young, and so to harmonize with the traditional pattern of life. Industry that utilized the labor of women did so in ways that minimized the impact on the role and future functioning of women.

The employment of women in manufacturing industry has been emphasized because of the possible role of such employment in changing the ways of living, expanding the social horizons, and secularizing the values of women. Commerce, and particularly retail trade, was the largest consumer of the labor of women next to agriculture. Commerce, like agriculture, could be carried on with minimum interference with household responsibilities and family status. In Japan, retail trade was usually a family undertaking. And as families moved from agricultural employment in rural areas to more remunerative employment in urban areas, engaging in commerce became a way in which women contributed to the incomes of the households while fulfilling their responsibilities as wives and mothers. In 1930 the proportion of gainfully occupied women who labored in commerce increased with general regularity from 6.9 in the *mura* below 5 thousand total population to 38.1 in the great cities of 100 thousand and over. The age structure of the group as a whole approached that of the women in agriculture rather than in industry. Marital status and employment status were intermediate between agriculture and industry.

The other two major occupations of women were quite different in their characteristics: government and the professions, on the one hand, and domestic service, on the other. The former signified the rise of women in the occupational hierarchy, while the latter signified the persistent hopelessness of the poor, the widowed, and the divorced. In 1930 there were only 352 thousand women in government service and the professions; they constituted 3.7 per cent of all gainfully occupied women. This is an overstatement of status, however, for "government service and the professions" includes a wide range of activities differing in requirements as to training, level of function, and amount of remuneration. Only 16,288 women were government officials; only 40,013 were in clerical occupations. In this nation of universal elementary education, there were only 101,887 women in education. There were 140,068 women in medical work. The types of professional activities open to women were the lesser orders; many, such as those in medical work, were semi-menial.

The total employment of women outside agriculture was as consistent a component of Japanese culture as their employment in agriculture. In agriculture, married women could be used in family enterprises without deep violation to the ways of living regarded as proper and the values accepted as natural. Where non-agricultural employment did not provide appropriate opportunities, women were not used.

MARITAL STATUS AND GAINFUL EMPLOYMENT

The relations between marital status and economic activity have permeated our discussion of the economic role of women. The fundamental fact has been stated again and again. Women were used in the monetary economy in ways consistent with their cultural and demographic role in the society. Labor outside the home was limited largely to the single. If residence was maintained in the parental home, familial supervision could be continued. If movement away

[33] Nihon. Shoko daijin kambo, tokei-ka. *Kojo tokei-hyo. 1930.*

from the home was involved, either to the factory dormitory or to the home of relatives, it occurred under conditions that permitted protection and supervision alternative to those that the father provided. The gainful employment of the married was predominantly within the home, whether it involved farm labor, piecework from factories, family production, or work in the family shop or store. The role of the widowed and the divorced was more difficult, for in the familistic society women were to be supported by their fathers, their husbands, or their sons. The widow forced to provide for herself might have an inherited position on the land or in an economic enterprise; if not, finding gainful employment with monetary wages was difficult indeed. The situation was even more difficult for the divorced woman, since she was outside the boundaries of the conventional structure of familial obligations and responsibilities.

Marital status is not an inherent attribute of individuals but a characteristic that usually changes during a lifetime. The single of one generation are subject to the propulsions and the pressures that molded the groups that preceded them. More significant in the consideration of the demographic aspects of the economic role of women is that the married women of one period have as background the experience and attitudes which they acquired as single girls. Thus the role of the single girl in the industrialization of Japan may have been a major force for population change.

The marital status of the women gainfully occupied in the major industrial groups substantiates the thesis that the obligations of the family and familistic ideals dominated the role of women in the economic sphere as elsewhere. In 1930, as in 1920, married women were predominant in agriculture, where there was a close integration of household responsibilities and gainful activity.[34] Almost half the women in commerce were married, for in retail trade household tasks, child care, and gainful activities could be sequential if not simultaneous aspects of a daily round of activities. Single women were greatly underrepresented in agriculture, for here in the unpaid labor of the family they could contribute little to household income. They constituted over 60 per cent of all women gainfully occupied in manufacturing industry and almost 60 per cent of the women in government service and the professions. They constituted 87 per cent of all women in the service category, for in Japan this meant not only work but residence away from home. The widowed and the divorced who participated in gainful employment were too few to dominate any sphere of industry.

The adjustment of women to employment is seen more clearly if the marital status groups are considered as entities. It might seem preferable to describe this situation in 1920 and 1930, particularly the latter year, for conditions in 1930 were the nearest approximation to "normal" of those in any census year in the history of Japan. However, the relationships between marital status and economic activity in 1940 were quite similar to those in 1930 and in 1920. The effects of war shortages were not sufficient to induce the Japanese to disregard the ideas of the appropriate that were the essential consequences of the family values. Hence it is the situation as of October 1, 1940, that is pictured in TABLE 42.

Even in 1940 agriculture was the most prevalent gainful employment among single girls if all ages are considered. However, 27.8 per cent of the unmarried girls who were gainfully occupied were in manufacturing industry, 15.4 per cent in commerce, and 12.7 per cent in service industries. For some unknown but sizable proportion of the two-thirds of the gainfully occupied single women who labored outside agriculture, there were opportunities for mobility and contact beyond the home. In industry it might be the factory dormitory; in commerce it might be the shop of a relative or a friend of the family in the city; in domestic service it might be a restaurant, a hotel or a home in a town or city.

The participation of married women in the labor force need not be discussed further. Eighty-seven per cent of the gainfully occupied married women of 1940 were in agriculture or commerce, mainly retail trade. The widows are an interesting group, for they had been married women and so subject to the possibilities and limitations of labor that characterized the wife. Many of them were left with dependents to maintain. They were employed in agriculture to a much smaller extent than the married women with whom they had been identified, thus indicating the probability that many of the widows of farmers were unable to maintain their agricultural establishments. Some secured employment in manufacturing industry, but their major opportunity for earning a living seems to have been through establishing or working in a store. Life was even more difficult for the divorced women. Relatively small proportions of the gainfully occupied were in agriculture, perhaps because divorce was less frequent among agricultural people, perhaps because the expulsive forces of the patriarchal family thrust out the divorced woman, while maintaining the widow if possible.

In the postwar years women entered the labor force in increasing numbers, and their activities were more diversified. The economic activities available to married women remained limited in scope, however, and the widowed and divorced were handicapped. The occupational structure of labor force participants aged from 25 to 29 in the *shi* of 50 thousand and over in 1955 illustrate the persistence of the old and the emergence of the new in the labor of women:[35]

	Single	*Married*	*Widowed*	*Divorced*
All occupations	100.	100.	100.	100.
Professional and technical	12.2	8.2	8.8	6.6
Managers and official	0.2	0.2	0.0	0.0
Clerical and related	32.7	12.1	12.8	12.3
Sales	8.8	16.6	17.6	10.9
Farmers and related workers	4.5	39.3	9.8	5.7
Workers in mines	0.1	0.1	0.0	0.3
Workers in transport	0.1	0.1	0.0	0.0
Craftsmen and laborers not otherwise classified	18.0	17.1	21.6	19.5
Service workers	23.4	6.3	29.4	44.7

The greatest advances in the occupational hierarchy had been made by the single. The married women labored in agricul-

[34] Detailed tabulations of household composition in 1920 are presented in: Nihon. Naikaku tokei-kyoku. *Taisho ku'nen kokusei chosa hokoku.* IV.A.3. In 1930 the materials on households and on employment by marital status and age were distributed in the various volumes—the national summary tabulations, the composition of the population, occupations and industries, and the prefectural volumes. See: Nihon. Naikaku tokei-kyoku. *Showa go'nen kokusei chosa hokoku.* IV.1, IV.2, IV.4, and VIII.

[35] Nihon. Sori-fu, tokei-kyoku. *1% chushutsu shukei ni yoru kekka sokuho. Showa 30-nen kokusei chosa. Zenkoku.* Part 5, I. Table 4.

TABLE 42

The industrial structure of the gainfully occupied female population, by age and marital status, 1940

Marital status	*All gainfully occupied*	*Per cent industrial structure of the gainfully occupied in the age group*						
		11-14	*15-19*	*20-24*	*25-29*	*30-34*	*45-49*	*65 and over*
All women	100.[a]	100.	100.	100.	100.	100.	100.	100.
Agriculture	56.8	29.2	34.4	44.1	59.0	62.7	70.2	79.0
Manufacturing	15.1	39.1	28.5	20.5	13.6	11.0	7.3	2.9
Commerce	14.7	8.0	13.0	16.0	16.0	16.4	15.7	11.6
Government and professions	5.4	3.8	7.7	7.9	6.6	6.2	3.3	2.3
Service	5.3	17.1	11.9	8.6	2.6	1.4	1.3	3.0
Other	2.7	2.8	4.5	2.9	2.2	2.3	2.2	1.2
Single	100.[a]	100.	100.	100.	100.	100.	100.	100.
Agriculture	31.2	29.1	33.1	30.6	23.9	19.9	35.7	45.8
Manufacturing	27.8	39.2	29.0	24.4	20.7	16.1	10.1	5.9
Commerce	15.4	8.0	13.2	18.7	26.5	31.4	24.3	11.7
Government and professions	9.0	3.8	7.9	10.5	16.0	20.5	16.4	22.0
Service	12.7	17.1	12.3	12.7	10.2	9.4	11.4	13.1
Other	3.9	2.8	4.5	3.1	2.7	2.7	2.1	1.5
Married	100.	—[b]	100.	100.	100.	100.	100.	100.
Agriculture	73.7	—	73.0	70.8	69.1	68.9	75.7	87.4
Manufacturing	8.0	—	12.5	13.0	11.3	9.6	6.0	2.0
Commerce	13.0	—	7.8	10.4	12.9	14.3	13.8	8.3
Government and professions	3.0	—	1.8	2.8	4.1	4.7	2.3	1.1
Service	0.4	—	0.9	0.6	0.4	0.3	0.3	0.4
Other	1.9	—	4.0	2.4	2.2	2.2	1.9	0.8
Widowed and divorced	100.	—[b]	100.	100.	100.	100.	100.	100.
Agriculture	57.4	—	60.9	52.4	39.5	34.8	51.1	74.3
Manufacturing	10.1	—	13.0	16.4	19.9	20.6	12.1	3.3
Commerce	19.6	—	11.7	16.8	22.7	25.2	22.5	13.7
Government and professions	5.1	—	2.6	4.4	7.9	9.7	6.1	2.7
Service	5.0	—	6.4	6.8	6.8	6.0	4.6	4.4
Other	2.8	—	5.4	3.2	3.2	3.7	3.6	1.6

[a] The small number of gainfully occupied aged 10 or below are included in "all gainfully occupied."
[b] Less than 1,000 women aged 11-14 in the marital status category.
Source: Nihon. Naikaku tokei-kyoku. *Census of population, 1940.* Unpublished tabulations.

tural and household-associated activities. More than half the widowed and more than three-fifths of the divorced served as casual labor or worked in service. In all groups, however, there were appreciable proportions in professional and technical occupations. And clerical labor was prevalent, especially among the single.

As age advanced, the proportions of the single declined, whereas the proportions of the widowed increased. The occupational structures for the women aged from 45 to 49 in 1955, again for the *shi* with populations of 50 thousand and over, are given here:

	Single	*Married*	*Widowed*	*Divorced*
All occupations	100.	100.	100.	100.
Professional and technical	29.1	3.7	7.1	6.7
Managers and official	0.8	0.7	1.6	1.0
Clerical and related	14.2	3.3	7.7	9.1
Sales	11.8	25.6	19.3	12.9
Farmers and related workers	7.9	38.2	17.2	7.7
Workers in mines	0.0	0.2	0.1	0.5
Workers in transport	0.0	0.0	0.0	0.0
Craftsmen and laborers not otherwise classified	12.6	20.5	30.0	30.6
Service workers	23.6	7.7	17.2	31.6

There is evidence of substantial upward mobility among women who remained single. Married women were limited largely to agriculture, sales, and casual labor. The middle-aged widowed and divorced women were used little even in sales. It was still casual labor and service that provided whatever employment was available. Some 7 per cent of the widowed and divorced women were in professional and technical occupations.

Rapid economic development, advancing age at marriage, and reduced childbearing exert their major influence on younger women. Hence the reorientation of the traditional economic roles of younger women in the larger cities may presage an altered role for women in the total economy.

THE DEMOGRAPHIC ROLE

The house, the family, and the household are basic institutions in the determination of demographic trends because of their relationship to marriage, fertility, and mortality. In a description of these institutions we have considered only those aspects that were tangential to our main interest. Even there we have emphasized the formal structure of households and the interrelations of household position and economic factors rather than the patterns of interaction within the family, the social roles of family members, and the ways in which the family itself becomes the intermediate force in the transition from familistic to individualistic society. This bias in the analysis of the family is more apparent than real, for population changes are evidences of family functioning. The migration that moved the youth of a peasant society cityward and sent them out from Japan was guided by family councils in rural areas. Marriage occurred in relation to the social and legal dictates of family and house. The analysis of fertility is a study of the extent to which families fulfilled their responsibilities for the continuity of the house. Hence the material that documents the existence of fundamental social and demographic changes within a family whose external structure and economic role appeared relatively unchanging is presented throughout the following chapters. There the arguments are grounded in the quantitative data of vital records, censuses, and surveys.

PART IV

MIGRATION

CHAPTER VII

Migration and Industrialization

MIGRATION has been both a product and a precondition of the development of the Japanese industrial economy. The exodus from the rural areas permitted the maintenance of a rural culture while the national population was increasing more than twofold. The influx into urban areas provided the labor force for the new economy. As migration brought increasing numbers of people into cities, age at marriage advanced and marital fertility declined, largely in response to the pressures, values, and motivations of urban life. The continuing interchange of people between city and country gave the peasants a knowledge of the new ways of life, and it kept alive the customs and values of the country in the cities.

Since migration is related so intimately both to industrialization and to changes in fertility and mortality, it is essential that the analysis of migration itself be comprehensive. A description of types of movements, of the magnitude and selectivity of each, and of the relations of one to another is essential. The major task, however, is an analysis of the interrelations of migration with other factors during the long period of population increase that accompanied the movement from an agricultural to an industrial economy. Emphasis will be placed on the contributions of the different types of migration to the reduction of demographic difficulties in a densely settled and resources-poor country.

Since neither the population available for migration nor the need for migrants was constant, it is necessary to assess the extent of the population changes associated with migration as well as the contributions of migration to the distribution of population in relation to economic opportunities. The question also arises as to how long the Japanese or any industrializing people can solve or avoid problems created by population increase in the rural areas through the absorption of that increase in ever more numerous and ever larger cities. Finally, it is necessary to consider the relations between international migration and internal economic and political problems.

It is obvious that consideration of the role of migration must enter into later analyses of fertility, mortality, and population increase. Analysis of the population problems and prospects of Japan requires investigation of movements of people and the barriers to such movements. Migrations of major scope were associated with military activities and war and these subjects will be dealt with as aspects of later analysis. In this and the following chapter, migration will be considered as a primary variable. The initial section of this chapter is a survey of internal migration in Japan comparable to that which could be presented for any country that had included questions on place of birth in its censuses. Migration is then considered from the standpoint of areas of origin as the cityward movements of peasants, from the standpoint of areas of destination as influx into urban and industrial areas. In Japan, however, internal migration produced not so much a broadly diffused urbanization as the concentration of an increasing population in large cities of 100 thousand and over. Hence Chapter VIII will take up the role of migration in the formation of cities and metropolitan areas.

MIGRATION AND MIGRANT STATUS, 1920-1950[1]

In 1920, seventy years after the *shogun* had opened Japan to the West, the country retained much of the stability of a peasant society. Population exchange within the Empire had begun, but the numbers involved were small.[2] The interchange between the regions of Japan represented an early reaction to industrialization. Net changes associated with regional movements reflected the balance between the expulsive forces of agricultural poverty and the attractive forces of industrial employment and urban life. Losses of the native-born were large for peripheral agricultural regions, slight for central industrial regions. Increments from other regions were highest in the industrial regions, lowest in the agricultural regions.[3] However, most people remained in the region in which they were born. Only in the frontier area of Hokkaido and the metropolitan regions of the Kanto and the Kinki did the proportion of the population born in the region of residence fall below 93 per cent. In six of the eleven regions it exceeded 95 per cent. As late as 1920, more than 90 per cent of the Japanese present in Japan were enumerated in their region of birth.

The appearance of stability indicated by data on interre-

[1] Questions on place of birth were asked in the censuses of 1920, 1930, and 1950, and the data for 1930 were tabulated by age. There are definite limitations to the information on historic migrations that can be secured through relating place of residence to place of birth. The Japanese absent from Japan escaped reporting, whether the absence was temporary or permanent. Since the censuses of 1920 and 1930 were *de facto*, persons resident in one area within Japan but present in another on the census date were reported as migrants. Moreover, the migrant who had spent many years in the city and then returned to the village was reported as having the same place of birth and place of enumeration and so was as stable statistically as his neighbor who had spent his life tilling the ancestral rice fields. In other words, tabulation of place of enumeration in relation to place of birth ignores the movements that have occurred between the specific points of reference.

[2] For the place-of-birth data from the 1920 census, see: Nihon. Naikaku tokei-kyoku. *Taisho ku'nen kokusei chosa hokoku.* IV. A.1, Tables 5-9; IV.B., Table 3, Tables 7-11.

[3] Okinawa may have needed emigration, but its people did not leave for other regions of Japan in appreciable numbers before 1920. If they left the Ryukyus for foreign countries, they were excluded from computations of losses based on census statistics on place of birth, for they had left the census area. Hokkaido is another exception to the general pattern of relationships. This northern island was almost empty at the time of the Meiji Restoration; in 1920, 52.9 per cent of its people were native-born. It should be noted that most of the prefectures of southern and western Kyushu sent substantial proportions of their emigrants to the colonies or to foreign countries rather than to the other prefectures of Japan.

gional movements is somewhat spurious, however, for only a small part of all migrations involved the crossing of regional boundaries. If the prefectures are used as the unit of analysis, it becomes apparent that considerable redistribution of population had already occurred by the time the first national census was taken in 1920 (TABLE 43). Eight of the 47 prefectures had lost one-fifth or more of their native-born to other prefectures, while 40 had lost more than one-tenth. There was some rough agreement between the need for migration as measured by man-land relationships in 1920 and the amount of migration that had occurred. However, the exodus of the native-born had been greatest from prefectures adjacent to or near great cities, least in the most remote prefectures. Apparently isolation barred knowledge of opportunities elsewhere at the same time that it increased the difficulties of movement.

Prefectural differences in rates of in-migration were far greater than in those of out-migration. Seven prefectures had attracted enough persons born elsewhere to account for from 20 to 50 per cent of their populations. Six of the seven were prefectures with sizable cities and considerable employment outside agriculture—the metropolitan prefectures of Tokyo and Osaka, Kanagawa with the city of Yokohama, Kyoto with the city of the same name, Hyogo with the city of Kobe, and Fukuoka with its cluster of cities. The seventh prefecture of substantial gain was Hokkaido, which had been the mecca of the north in the decades preceding 1920.

The relations of in-migration to urbanization are apparent in a comparison of the migrant status of the populations of Tokyo prefecture, the other five prefectures containing large cities, and the remainder of Japan:

of the people enumerated outside the prefecture of birth increased for the majority of the prefectures. The increase was greatest for the agricultural regions of the southwest. In this region Okinawa, Kagoshima, and Saga came within the orbits of expanding industrial areas in Kyushu and in Honshu. In such prefectures of the northeast as Aomori and Miyagi, there was a decline in the proportion of out-migrants among those born in the prefecture. The exodus of the native-born from the prefectures containing the six great cities changed only slightly. However, the influence of the cities is seen in increased exodus from prefectures adjacent to them.

The changes in influx over the decade were the converse of those in exodus. The proportions of prefectural in-migrants increased sharply in the metropolitan prefectures and declined in the agricultural prefectures of the southwest and the northeast.[5] The movements of people in industrial and agricultural areas were becoming more sharply differentiated. Out-migration increased its predominance in the agrarian prefectures, as did in-migration in the metropolitan and industrial prefectures. Since the economic and political transformation from the Restoration to the seizure of military initiative by the Kwantung Army in 1931 was evolutionary in scope and intensity, there was a gradual development of consistent relationships and trends in internal migration and population redistribution. Continuity was a major attribute of migration.[6]

The migrant status of the population of Japan in 1950 reflected changes in movements in the late prewar, war, and early postwar years. To interpret the distribution of population in 1950 is difficult, for the relations among the distribution of people, the sources of livelihood, and employment opportunities were inherently unstable.[7] The relations between

Migrant status ratios	*All Japan*	*Tokyo prefecture*	*The other five urban prefectures*	*The other 41 prefectures*
Out-migrants per 100 born in prefecture	14.9	13.6	12.8	15.3
In-migrants per 100 resident in prefecture	14.9	47.0	25.2	9.8
Net migration per 100 resident in prefecture	—	38.6	14.3	−6.5
In-migrants per 100 out-migrants	—	564.0	230.0	60.0

Developments between 1920 and 1930 produced generally consistent but relatively slight changes in the migrant status of the population as measured by statistics on place of residence in relation to place of birth.[4] However, the proportion

[4] The detailed information on migrant status in the census of 1930 is particularly valuable. The year 1930 was near the terminus of a period of economic development that was compatible with the maintenance of peace; it was also the base from which economic and demographic transformations led to war. In the census of 1930, the question on place of birth was repeated. The data were tabulated to yield the age composition of out-migrants, in-migrants, and net migrants for prefectures and cities of 100 thousand or more. Furthermore, for each prefecture it was possible to determine the place of origin of all persons enumerated in the prefecture, the place of enumeration of all persons born in the prefecture and still present within Japan proper, and the net interchange. There were no cross-tabulations of specific origin or destination by age, however. For the basic data, see: Nihon. Naikaku tokei-kyoku. *Showa go'nen kokusei chosa sokuho.* IV.1, Tables 19-25; IV.4, Tables 7-12; VIII, Tables 19-24.

[5] In-migrants and out-migrants are defined with reference to their status in a specific prefecture. The out-migrant from one of the metropolitan prefectures may be an in-migrant in another. Similarly, the out-migrant from one of the 41 rural prefectures may be an in-migrant in another. For Japan as a whole, the net in- and out-movements of the native-born are of course zero.

[6] Unchanging proportions in a specific migrant status category over time imply continuing and generally consistent movement of many factors; they do not imply geographic immobility. If migration had ceased in 1920, the numerical relation between the stable and the migrant populations would have shifted appreciably within the decade. The number of out-migrants per 100 persons born in a prefecture would have declined, for the out-migrants of 1920 would have been reduced by deaths, while the number of persons born in the prefecture would have been increased by the survivors of all the births that occurred during the decade, whether to the native-born or to immigrants of a previous period, and decreased by the deaths of the native-born resident in the prefecture in 1920. The number of in-migrants per 100 persons resident in the prefecture would have altered, too, for the number of the in-migrants of previous periods would have been depleted by deaths, whereas the resident population would have been increased by the surplus of births over deaths, whether of native-born or in-migrant population of the period prior to 1920.

It should be noted also that statistical series that represent differences between places of enumeration and places of birth are relatively insensitive to the events of the moment. The people who exist at an instant of time are the survivors of the births of many decades. Annual birth and death rates produce fairly slow changes in numbers, even if the rate of natural increase is high.

[7] These limitations to the significance of place-of-birth data may have been among the factors influencing the decision not to tabu-

TABLE 43

The prefectural interchange, place-of-birth statistics, 1920-1950

Prefectures[a]	OUT-MIGRANTS PER 100 BORN IN PREFECTURE			IN-MIGRANTS PER 100 RESIDENT IN PREFECTURE			NET MIGRATION PER 100 RESIDENT IN PREFECTURE		
	1920[b]	*1930*[b]	*1950*[c]	*1920*[b]	*1930*[b]	*1950*[c]	*1920*[b]	*1930*[b]	*1950*[c]
Hokkaido	5.6	7.1	7.1	47.1	35.1	22.9	44.0	30.1	12.8
Aomori	16.4	15.4	11.8	5.1	5.1	7.7	—13.6	—12.1	—6.3
Iwate	13.3	13.2	10.4	4.8	5.4	8.1	—9.8	—9.0	—3.6
Miyagi	19.2	18.0	14.1	7.2	8.0	12.8	—14.8	—12.3	—3.4
Akita	16.7	18.2	16.3	3.3	3.1	6.4	—16.0	—18.4	—13.2
Yamagata	13.7	15.3	16.0	3.0	2.6	6.9	—12.4	—14.9	—12.1
Fukushima	13.7	17.0	15.6	8.8	7.2	10.3	—5.7	—11.8	—7.5
Ibaraki	15.4	18.0	15.1	7.9	7.8	12.4	—8.9	—12.4	—4.0
Tochigi	16.8	20.9	18.3	10.8	9.3	12.8	—7.3	—14.7	—7.5
Gumma	14.0	16.3	14.8	12.5	11.8	13.1	—1.7	—5.3	—2.8
Saitama	18.1	19.9	15.3	7.9	9.6	18.4	—12.5	—12.9	3.0
Chiba	17.7	19.3	14.4	6.9	9.5	18.1	—13.7	—12.2	3.3
Tokyo	13.6	13.3	28.3	47.0	49.5	40.1	38.6	41.8	14.4
Kanagawa	14.9	17.3	19.0	28.9	30.8	33.7	16.5	16.2	16.5
Niigata	20.0	20.7	17.0	2.2	2.8	6.2	—22.2	—22.6	—13.8
Toyama	26.8	26.6	18.2	3.3	4.7	7.8	—32.2	—29.8	—13.8
Ishikawa	22.8	24.9	17.1	5.1	6.4	11.0	—23.0	—24.6	—8.8
Fukui	22.9	24.5	18.0	4.7	5.4	10.5	—23.6	—25.4	—10.7
Yamanashi	17.0	20.9	19.4	5.1	5.5	10.2	—14.3	—19.5	—12.5
Nagano	9.4	12.3	14.6	8.8	7.7	9.4	—0.7	—5.3	—7.3
Gifu	18.7	20.3	16.0	6.6	7.3	12.2	—14.9	—16.3	—5.6
Shizuoka	10.6	12.6	11.2	6.2	7.0	10.6	—4.9	—6.3	—1.7
Aichi	10.7	10.5	10.8	11.3	15.2	15.1	0.6	5.3	3.6
Mie	16.1	18.5	15.0	5.4	6.4	11.6	—12.8	—14.9	—5.0
Shiga	23.9	25.8	19.5	6.6	9.0	15.3	—22.9	—22.6	—6.9
Kyoto	14.8	15.8	17.0	24.1	28.1	25.3	10.9	14.6	7.9
Osaka	11.7	12.4	24.2	40.0	42.7	32.9	32.1	34.6	8.8
Hyogo	13.6	16.1	17.2	20.0	21.6	22.5	7.4	6.5	4.2
Nara	23.2	26.8	20.9	8.5	10.6	18.2	—19.2	—22.1	—4.5
Wakayama	16.1	18.0	16.9	5.9	7.6	10.8	—12.1	—12.8	—8.9
Tottori	15.6	17.6	15.0	7.5	8.1	11.9	—9.6	—11.5	—5.6
Shimane	13.3	15.6	13.1	4.5	5.2	10.2	—10.1	—12.3	—5.4
Okayama	13.6	16.4	13.0	8.0	8.4	13.8	—6.5	—9.5	—1.0
Hiroshima	16.8	18.5	16.1	9.1	10.3	13.5	—9.2	—10.0	—6.0
Yamaguchi	13.2	15.3	12.9	9.6	11.0	18.5	—4.2	—5.1	1.6
Tokushima	21.2	21.8	17.4	3.2	3.9	7.6	—22.9	—23.0	—12.7
Kagawa	23.7	24.6	18.8	4.5	5.7	11.2	—25.0	—25.0	—11.1
Ehime	17.3	18.7	14.3	4.4	5.1	9.6	—15.6	—16.7	—7.0
Kochi	12.1	14.2	11.9	3.9	4.5	8.2	—9.4	—11.3	—5.7
Fukuoka	8.1	10.4	12.5	22.7	21.7	23.8	15.8	12.6	9.1
Saga	18.9	23.0	20.1	8.0	8.2	17.8	—12.6	—19.2	—7.0
Nagasaki	9.1	12.8	13.8	15.7	14.3	17.2	7.2	1.7	0.3
Kumamoto	13.3	14.8	13.5	5.8	6.6	13.5	—8.7	—9.6	—4.2
Oita	15.9	16.9	14.9	6.5	7.9	14.6	—11.2	—10.8	—3.9
Miyazaki	7.6	9.8	9.3	11.9	11.8	14.4	4.7	2.2	2.9
Kagoshima	9.1	13.0	13.3	3.3	3.7	10.7	—6.4	—10.7	—7.2
Okinawa	1.7	7.1	—	1.6	1.3	—	—0.1	—6.2	—

[a] Okinawa was a prefecture of Japan in 1920 and 1930.

[b] The computations for 1920 and 1930 refer to the Japan-born population. Since emigrants from Japan were excluded from the census enumeration in Japan, persons born elsewhere but enumerated in Japan were also excluded. The enumeration was *de facto*.

[c] The computations for 1950 refer to the total population in Japan, since persons who had migrated outside had been repatriated and the major portion of the non-Japanese population of Japan had been returned to the place of origin. The ratios thus are not comparable to those of the 1920 and 1930 enumerations, but the migrant status situation in 1950 was not in itself comparable to that in the prewar years. Moreover, the limitation to Japan-born in 1950 would have resulted in a substantial underestimate of the migrations that had occurred.

Source: 1920: Nihon. Naikaku tokei-kyoku. *Taisho ku'nen kokusei chosa hokoku.* IV.A.1. Table 6. 1930: *Idem. Showa go'nen kokusei chosa hokoku.* IV.1. Table 19. 1950: Nihon. Sori-fu, tokei-kyoku. *Showa 25-nen kokusei chosa hokoku.* IV.1. Table 10A.

place of birth and place of residence became quite inadequate as measures of migration when the smooth patterns of the evolving society were replaced by outsurges to conquered areas, flights from bombed cities, mass repatriations of civilians, and the demobilization of millions of members of the armed forces. In 1950, economic restoration was limited, the social structure was disturbed, and the future was regarded as deeply insecure. Under all these circumstances, it is indeed significant that the patterns of relationships among the migrant status of the people and the economic, cultural, and demographic characteristics of the prefectures in 1950 were similar to those that existed in 1930 and 1920.

The Cityward Movement of the Peasant

The fundamental migration was that of the peasant to the city.[8] The labor force of the industrial areas of Japan traced its origin within one or two generations to the farming village—and that village, cohesive in value and tradition, reached out through its children and its children's children to the great cities of the home islands and the frontiers of the Empire. Changes in conditions of living and working that normally required centuries were telescoped into brief periods—for the individual migrant, even into a single journey of a few hours. There were new pressures, new opportunities, and new hesitancies. The activities of the modern day competed with the age-old responsibilities to the family and the ancestors, with consequent changes in marriage patterns and attitudes toward children. Migration as a physical movement was simple, but when it brought the peasant to the city it altered the balance of births and deaths and the population potential of the nation.

The migrant status of the populations of the prefectures was influenced both by agricultural-industrial and by rural-urban movements. Industrial prefectures contained some people working in agriculture and living in *mura*, while agricultural prefectures contained some people working outside agriculture and living in *machi* or *shi*. There was movement within, as well as movement between, prefectures. In 1920 and 1930 place of enumeration was classified in relation to place of birth in five categories: same minor civil division; another minor civil division of the same prefecture; another prefecture; the colonies; abroad. The same classification was used in 1950 except that there were no longer any Japanese colonies. Persons enumerated in the commune of birth were defined as stable. All others had been migrants.

In 1930, as in 1920 and 1950, the differences in the migrant status of the populations of the *shi* and the *gun* lay in the proportions of the stable and the migrant, not in stability or migration as absolute characteristics. In Japan as a whole, and in each prefecture, the populations of the *gun* contained larger proportions of stable individuals than did the populations of the *shi*. However, it would be inaccurate to designate the populations of the *shi* as migrant, those of the *gun* as stable. In many prefectures, most of the people in the *shi* were native-born; in the great majority, at least 40 per cent of them were. On the other hand, the populations of the *gun* included many migrants. In Hokkaido in 1930 more than one-third of the people in the *gun* reported another island of Japan as the place of birth. Migrants from other prefectures constituted almost half the people in the *gun* of Tokyo prefecture, more than one-tenth of the people in the *gun* in the other industrial prefectures of Kanagawa, Kyoto, Osaka, Hyogo, and Fukuoka.

The migrant status of the populations of *shi* and *gun* was interrelated. Prefectures with high proportions of prefectural in-migrants in the *shi* had higher proportions of such in-migrants in the *gun* than did prefectures whose *shi* populations were recruited locally.[9] Inter-prefectural migrants constituted only a small proportion of the population of the *gun* outside the frontier and metropolitan prefectures. Here, however, proportions considered apart from the absolute figures they represent are likely to lead to an unbalanced picture. In 1930, most of the people in Japan lived outside the metropolitan prefectures, and most of the people outside these areas were agricultural in occupation and rural in residence. The number of inter-prefectural migrants living in *gun* was actually greater than the number living in *shi*. Thus there was a somewhat paradoxical situation in which inter-prefectural migrants were disproportionately urban but predominantly rural.

Urbanization was a process comprehending more than the growth of cities. In fact, the growth of cities was accompanied by transformations in the population structures of adjacent rural areas.[10] The prevalence of the stable and the migrants in the Japan-born population of the *gun* in prefectures classified by the extent of the urbanization illustrates this relationship. Again the data are for the year 1930:[11]

Prefectures by per cent of population in shi	*All Japan*	*Commune of enumeration*	*Other commune, same prefecture*	*Other prefectures*
All Japan	100.	68.2	21.2	10.6
Less than 10	100.	72.9	20.6	6.5
10-19	100.	73.9	20.9	5.2
20-29	100.	58.3	19.2	22.5
30 or over	100.	55.4	23.2	21.4

late the data by age in 1950 as had been done in 1930. Cross-tabulations of place of birth by place of residence for the prefectures were published. (Nihon. Sori-fu, tokei-kyoku. *Showa 25-nen kokusei chosa hokoku*. IV.1. Table 10.) Place of birth is given by sex for the total prefecture, all *shi*, all *gun*, and the individual *shi* in the prefectural volumes. (*Idem*. VII. Table 15.)

[8] The thesis that the cityward movement of the peasant was the basic migration in Japan's period of middle industrialization may seem a platitude to those who know the story of rural-urban movement in the history of the West. However, analogical transfer of demographic generalization is hardly permissible in a study whose function is the determination of the extent to which generalizations that have evolved from Western experiences are applicable in the East. Hence it is necessary to pursue the labyrinths of Japanese statistics again, this time to document two obvious facts: (1) That migrants came predominantly from rural and agricultural areas. (2) That migrants went predominantly to cities and industrial areas. If there were cross-classifications of migrant status by industry or by the rural or urban characteristics of the area of origin, this documentation would be simple, but there are only detailed tabulations of specific variables. Field studies of migration in villages indicate the predominance of the out-movement to cities and industrial employment among men as well as the role of migration for marriage among women. See especially: Nojiri, Shigeo. *Noson jinko ido no jittai chosa*. 2nd Edition.

[9] For 1930, the correlation between the proportion of prefectural in-migrants in the populations of the *shi* and the *gun* of the prefectures was .76. The correlations were .47 for the stable, —.0 for the inter-communal migrants. The absence of correlation in the latter is due to the role of migration for marriage. See pp. 139-141.

[10] There are many factors that disturb these relationships. Prefectures differ in size and in degree of accessibility to each other. In addition, the definition of "urban" is based on the fact of incorporation. In 1930 the legal city of Tokyo included only a portion of the population of the *de facto* city. There were four *machi* of 100 thousand or more population, and in an administrative classification of 1930 these were in the *gun*.

[11] Source: Nihon. Naikaku tokei-kyoku. *Showa go'nen kokusei chosa hokoku*. IV.4. Table 7.

The relations between the migrant status of urban and that of rural populations within prefectures are also apparent if the prefectures are classified by industrial type rather than by the proportions of the population in the *shi*. In order to indicate the continuity of the patterns of migration from 1920 through 1950, the following data on the migrant status of the people in the *gun* pertain to the year 1950:[12]

Prefectures by industrial type	*All Japan*	*Commune of enumeration*	*Other commune, same prefecture*	*Other prefecture*	*Outside Japan*
All Japan	100.	68.9	19.9	9.6	1.7
Metropolitan	100.	52.8	25.4	20.0	1.9
Other industrial	100.	63.5	22.6	12.1	1.8
Intermediate	100.	70.0	19.9	8.5	1.6
Agricultural	100.	72.4	18.2	8.0	1.4
Hokkaido	100.	54.0	24.2	17.7	4.1

There was no sharp dichotomy between urban and rural areas, or between industrial and agricultural prefectures. However, migrants and new economic opportunities were concentrated in the *shi*, particularly the metropolitan centers. Outside these centers were secondary concentrations of migrants, products of the increasing opportunities in areas of diffused or incipient industrialization.

In Japan, as in the West, the amount of movement tended to be related inversely to distance (TABLE 44). The most common migration discernible in the statistics is the inter-communal—that is, from one *mura, machi*, or *shi* within a prefecture to another.[13] Migrants from considerable distances were rare throughout most of Japan. Major portions of the inter-prefectural migrants came from adjacent prefectures; only in the metropolitan prefectures and Hokkaido did remote prefectures contribute as much as one-fourth of the population. Nowhere in Japan did immigrants from the colonies constitute as much as 3 per cent of the population. Foreign migrants were few and, like the long-distance migrants within Japan and the persons born in the Empire, they were concentrated in urban and industrial regions.

Migration tended to decrease with distance, but it also tended to follow the paths of economic opportunity. The seven industrial prefectures were the centers of economic growth and employment possibilities. They drew migrants from all Japan but here, also, numbers tended to decrease with distance.

It is apparent that the most frequent move was to a place that was fairly near, but there is no direct information on specific moves. A series of short moves by many people would result in a substantial redistribution of population. The peasant in the rural village might move to non-agricultural employment in a nearby town. The youth who had grown up in this town might move to a larger town, whence in turn a migrant might go to a great city, but no one person in the series of migrants need have moved to an area remote in location or mode of life. This hypothesis is sufficiently plausible to merit exploration, for migration by stages has been characteristic of the urbanward movement in many countries. Demonstration of the presence or absence of movement by stages in Japan is significant for the interpretation of many cultural and demographic problems. Movements from familiar to unfamiliar environments by gradual stages would lessen the social adjustments and the psychological shock almost inevitable in direct transition from *buraku* to metropolis.

The predominance of local migrants in the urbanward movement is evident in the high proportions of inter-communal migrants in the *shi* of all prefectures except the metropolitan ones. In 26 of Japan's 47 prefectures, 30 per cent or more of the people in the *shi* were born in another minor civil division of the same prefecture; many of the others came from adjacent prefectures. It is apparent that the majority of the migrants to the majority of the cities moved to areas that were known directly or through personal contacts. These were generally areas of easy access for the initial movement and they were also areas in which maintenance of contacts with the family and the village was simple.

The people who moved into the smaller cities from other prefectures were predominantly short-distance migrants. The three cities of Aomori prefecture illustrate the distance factor in migration and the spurious elements involved in the use of political subdivisions as a basis for inferring distance of migration. Hirosaki-*shi* is located near the border of Akita prefecture. Aomori-*shi* is across the strait from Hokkaido, while Hachino-*shi* is on the Pacific side above Iwate prefecture. Hirosaki attracted migrants from Akita, Hachino from Iwate. Aomori-*shi* drew predominantly from Akita and Hokkaido, both easily accessible by sea routes. However, the migrants from within Aomori were twice as numerous as those from other prefectures, adjacent and distant combined.

The role of the distance factor in the exodus and redistribution of the agrarian population, the colonization of the internal frontier, the formation of cities, and the interchange within the Empire will become apparent in the more detailed analyses that follow. In all instances, relatively short-distance migration predominated over migration that involved longer distances. However, in no instance was distance alone a sufficient explanation of the facts of the migration.

DEMOGRAPHIC SELECTION AND STRUCTURAL IMPACT

Numbers of migrants considered as such permit only superficial measurement of the role of migration in the industrializing economy. Pressures and stimuli are selective, while physical requirements and capabilities circumscribe those who can move or who can capture the elusive economic opportunities that were the reason for the move. Customs and traditions act further to segregate types of people in different kinds of activity. Age, sex, physique, motivations, education, and social background influence migration. Among these characteristics, age and sex are the most objectively defined and the most often measured. They are significant as direct measures of structural change and altered replacement

[12] Source: Nihon. Sori-fu, tokei-kyoku. *Showa 25-nen kokusei chosa hokoku*. VII. Table 15.

[13] A considerable proportion of the migrants from adjacent prefectures were probably inter-communal migrants who had happened to cross a prefectural line.

TABLE 44

Per cent distribution of the populations of the prefectures, by place of birth, 1930

		IN PREFECTURE					
Prefecture	*Total*	*Same commune*	*Other commune*	*Adjacent prefecture*	*Other prefectures*	*Colonies*	*Abroad*
Hokkaido	100.	43.0	21.4	3.4	31.4	0.7	0.1
Aomori	100.	72.5	22.2	3.0	2.1	0.1	0.0
Iwate	100.	75.7	18.7	2.9	2.5	0.2	0.0
Miyagi	100.	71.4	20.3	4.5	3.4	0.3	0.1
Akita	100.	74.1	22.7	1.5	1.6	0.1	0.0
Yamagata	100.	75.1	22.1	1.4	1.2	0.1	0.0
Fukushima	100.	68.5	24.0	5.0	2.2	0.2	0.1
Ibaraki	100.	68.3	23.8	4.4	3.4	0.1	0.0
Tochigi	100.	68.3	22.3	5.0	4.2	0.1	0.0
Gumma	100.	67.2	20.8	7.7	4.1	0.2	0.0
Saitama	100.	67.3	23.0	6.3	3.2	0.1	0.0
Chiba	100.	69.0	21.3	5.5	3.9	0.2	0.0
Tokyo	100.	33.1	16.7	12.9	35.9	1.0	0.3
Kanagawa	100.	53.4	14.9	11.8	18.6	0.9	0.4
Niigata	100.	76.8	20.2	1.0	1.8	0.2	0.0
Toyama	100.	71.1	23.8	1.9	2.8	0.4	0.0
Ishikawa	100.	71.8	21.4	3.2	3.2	0.4	0.1
Fukui	100.	71.5	22.4	2.5	2.8	0.7	0.1
Yamanashi	100.	70.5	23.5	3.3	2.2	0.5	0.1
Nagano	100.	66.0	25.9	5.6	2.0	0.4	0.0
Gifu	100.	67.6	24.5	4.5	2.8	0.6	0.0
Shizuoka	100.	67.5	25.1	3.0	4.0	0.4	0.1
Aichi	100.	60.4	23.1	9.1	5.9	1.4	0.1
Mie	100.	71.2	21.7	3.3	3.0	0.7	0.1
Shiga	100.	71.7	18.5	3.9	5.1	0.6	0.2
Kyoto	100.	54.6	15.9	14.6	12.9	1.8	0.1
Osaka	100.	46.1	9.6	13.9	27.5	2.7	0.2
Hyogo	100.	56.5	20.8	9.4	11.8	1.0	0.4
Nara	100.	68.9	19.7	6.1	4.4	0.8	0.1
Wakayama	100.	68.8	22.4	4.5	3.0	0.9	0.5
Tottori	100.	68.8	22.6	5.8	2.2	0.4	0.1
Shimane	100.	69.8	24.5	2.9	2.3	0.5	0.0
Okayama	100.	64.1	26.8	5.2	3.2	0.6	0.2
Hiroshima	100.	64.4	23.9	5.6	4.5	0.8	0.7
Yamaguchi	100.	63.4	23.6	6.6	4.2	1.7	0.6
Tokushima	100.	73.5	22.4	1.9	2.0	0.2	0.0
Kagawa	100.	71.0	23.0	3.4	2.3	0.2	0.1
Ehime	100.	69.9	24.7	3.0	2.1	0.3	0.1
Kochi	100.	70.8	24.3	2.0	2.5	0.3	0.1
Fukuoka	100.	51.6	25.2	11.3	10.0	1.6	0.3
Saga	100.	68.8	22.2	4.9	3.3	0.7	0.1
Nagasaki	100.	66.4	18.4	6.7	7.4	0.7	0.3
Kumamoto	100.	70.8	21.8	4.8	1.8	0.4	0.4
Oita	100.	68.5	23.0	4.8	3.0	0.6	0.1
Miyazaki	100.	72.0	15.7	6.1	5.6	0.5	0.1
Kagoshima	100.	80.5	15.4	1.5	2.1	0.3	0.1
Okinawa	100.	86.5	11.7	0.4	0.9	0.1	0.4

Source: Nihon. Naikaku tokei-kyoku. *Showa go'nen kokusei chosa hokoku*. IV.4. Table 7.

potential and also as indirect indicators of non-demographic transformations.

The life cycles of individuals tend to impose broad regularities upon the age composition of the migrant streams in modernizing economies, and to a lesser extent in all economies. The migrations of babies and small children are secondary; the primary movements are those of adults. The dependence of the young in turn retards the movements of adults, for parents find the physical problems of movement increased at the same time that responsibilities are greater. The risks of a new life have to be considered seriously. There appears to be a life cycle of motivations related to but not identical with the cycle of family relations. As age increases, individuals establish patterns of living that increase resistances to the new at whatever levels of appeal.

Reverse migration occurs in the case of the successful who return to a satisfying life in the villages and of the failures who return for sanctuary. In either event, the reverse migrant is older than the original migrant. If this logical generalization of cultural forces and demographic relations is valid, rates of migration should increase rapidly after the age that permits independent entrance into the labor market, reach a peak in the early years of adulthood, and eventually give way in old age to a movement homeward. The data for 1930 on the migrant status of the Japan-born population by age corroborate this hypothesis. The figures are percentages of the Japan-born population:[14]

Age	*All Japan*	*Commune of enumeration*	*Other commune, same prefecture*	*Other prefecture*
Total	100.	62.7	20.9	16.4
0-9	100.	87.3	7.6	5.1
10-14	100.	77.6	13.1	9.3
15-19	100.	57.8	21.9	20.3
20-24	100.	47.0	26.6	26.4
25-29	100.	43.8	29.1	27.1
30-39	100.	44.5	29.9	25.6
40-49	100.	48.4	29.4	22.2
50-59	100.	52.9	28.7	18.4
60-69	100.	55.8	28.7	15.5
70-79	100.	59.4	28.2	12.4
80 and over	100.	61.5	28.2	10.3

Inter-prefectural and local migrations left residues of youth and the aged in the stable population. The majority of children lived in the commune of birth. The individual child thus met, played, and worked with others whose geographical habitat was similarly circumscribed. The associations of the aged were again primarily with others born in the local areas. In the ages from 20 to 50 the migrants were a majority of the total in each age group. Men in the most productive ages and women in the reproductive ages were predominant among the migrants.

Data on migrant status defined as a difference in the place of enumeration and the place of birth are not ideal for the measurement of the influence of migration on the structure of populations by sex and age. There is the general difficulty with data on place of birth—many moves are concealed and the chronology of movement is ignored. In addition, the children of former migrants are native-born inhabitants of the area of residence and so by definition belong to the stable rather than the migrant population. Many of the former migrants who return to the area of origin for the years of late maturity and old age become stable by definition of census enumeration. A query concerning only one prior period of time thus conceals the indirect contribution of the children of migrants to population redistribution and the compensatory movements that are so common in the life cycles of individuals.

The cumulative influence of migrations that were selective as to age and sex transformed the structures of the populations enumerated in the various types of prefectures (TABLE 45). Adults in areas of out-migration carried a heavy burden of dependency. The higher per capita productivity in industrial areas was correlated with lesser ratios of youth and aged per person in the productive ages. The structural differences among regions, urban and rural areas, and industrial groups cannot be attributed solely to migration. However, the movements of people, family formation, the bearing and rearing of children, the duration of life, and the frequency of death were related aspects of individual lives and group cultures. Poverty, high mortality, early marriages, and abundant child-bearing characterized areas of exodus. Greater economic opportunity, higher levels of living, lowered mortality, postponed marriages, and limited reproduction characterized areas of influx.

PREFECTURAL REDISTRIBUTION, FROM BIRTH TO 1930

EXODUS OF THE NATIVE-BORN

In the decades prior to 1930, the elementary fact in the movements of the Japanese was the transfer from agricultural to non-agricultural occupations, the movement from rural to urban area. The man-land relationships, the structure of family rights and inheritance practices, and the advancing standards of living led to regularities in the out-movements of millions of people from the agrarian society. Occasional and incidental events seem to have influenced the timing and the locale of movements rather than the origin and course of the major streams. The documentation of these statements lies in the analysis of losses of native-born from the prefectures. On the basis of the place-of-birth statistics of the 1930 census, the specific measure of loss is the ratio of persons born in a prefecture but resident outside it to persons born in the prefecture.[15]

There were fairly uniform patterns of exodus by age in the prefectures, and the levels of exodus at one age were related to those at adjacent ages. Out-migration was slight at ages under 10 and prefectural differences were not great. At age 10 to 14, out-migration was substantially higher and the prefectural differences in rates were greater. In agricultural prefectures where educational levels were low, the proportions of migrants at age 10 to 14 were at least twice those at the childhood ages. In the urban prefectures where income levels were higher, children less numerous, and educational facilities greater, the proportions of migrants among youth increased less steeply with age.

The proportion of the native-born enumerated outside the prefecture of birth tended to reach a maximum for those aged from 25 to 29, remained relatively unchanging for those in the thirties, and declined in the older age-groups (MAP 7). In the agricultural prefectures of the northeast and the southwest, almost one-third of the native-born men aged from

[14] Source: Nihon. Naikaku tokei-kyoku. *Showa go'nen kokusei chosa hokoku*. VII. Table 24.

[15] Both out-migrants from the prefecture and persons born in the prefecture exclude those individuals who left Japan.

TABLE 45

Sex and age structures of the populations of the prefectures, by industrial type, 1930

Age	All Japan	Metropolitan	Other industrial	Intermediate	Agricultural	Hokkaido
			Per cent composition			
Total	100.	100.	100.	100.	100.	100.
0-9	26.0	22.7	24.8	26.0	27.6	29.5
10-14	10.6	8.7	10.0	10.8	11.2	11.7
15-19	10.1	12.5	10.7	9.5	9.4	10.6
20-24	8.6	11.8	9.3	7.9	7.5	8.8
25-29	7.5	9.9	8.1	7.0	6.7	7.6
30-39	12.1	14.1	12.9	11.6	11.4	11.7
40-49	9.8	9.5	9.8	10.0	9.9	8.9
50-59	7.8	6.3	7.5	8.5	8.2	6.4
60-69	4.6	3.1	4.3	5.2	5.0	3.2
70-79	2.3	1.3	2.1	2.8	2.5	1.4
80 and over	.5	.2	.5	0.6	0.6	0.3
			Males per 1,000 females			
Total	1010	1107	1025	988	976	1093
0-9	1017	1022	1018	1018	1013	1018
10-14	1021	1079	1006	1010	1019	1038
15-19	1030	1191	997	973	1016	1083
20-24	1037	1178	1055	988	975	1140
25-29	1054	1182	1090	1015	981	1178
30-39	1070	1222	1125	1034	991	1201
40-49	1030	1174	1084	996	968	1184
50-59	979	1038	1006	971	940	1168
60-69	884	837	883	902	864	1102
70-79	735	620	708	778	719	903
80 and over	536	384	493	572	541	616

Source: Nihon. Naikaku tokei-kyoku. *Showa go'nen kokusei chosa hokoku.* IV.4. Table 9.

25 to 29 were enumerated outside the prefecture of birth. In the prefectures near or with easy access to the great cities, losses approached or surpassed 40 per cent. Toyama, Shiga, and Nara lost more than two of each five of their native-born men to other prefectures. Losses of women were somewhat less, but Shiga lost 38 per cent, Nara 40 per cent, Tochigi and Kagawa 36 per cent.

Something about the nature of the migrations that accomplished the redistribution of the population can be inferred from the relations among numbers of migrants at successive ages in 1930. Implicit in this argument is the assumption that the migrant status of the population by age on October 1, 1930, can be assumed to give an age pattern of rates similar to that which would have characterized a cohort passing through life. In such a cohort, migrants at one age would remain migrants at later ages by the definition implicit in place-of-birth statistics, unless they died, left Japan, or returned to the area of birth. If the population as of 1930 is regarded as a cohort, then it is apparent that until age 25 the exodus of youth from the prefectures was strong enough to create rapid increases in the proportions of the native-born who were out-migrants. After age 25 to 29 there was a slow but consistent decline in the ratio of out-migrant to native-born that continued until old age. There are alternative explanations for this phenomenon. Perhaps there was return migration to the area of origin. Perhaps older people were the survivors of the smaller number of migrants in past years when both the will to migrate and the opportunity to do so had been more limited. The causal nexus of movement and countermovement operating to produce the successive increases and decreases in proportions migrant at various ages is tantalizingly vague, and no retrospective concentration on probabilities can make it much less so.

Descriptions of the life histories of families and individuals who were migrants would make the movements of the Japanese more understandable in human terms. Migration was a structured movement. The proportions migrant at one age were related closely to the proportions migrant at the next higher age, and the proportions of males migrant at any given age were related closely to the proportions of females migrant at that same age. Migration was not a fortuitous process. In the gradually evolving world of the decades prior to 1930 it approached the predictable.

The exceptions to regularities in the age and sex structure

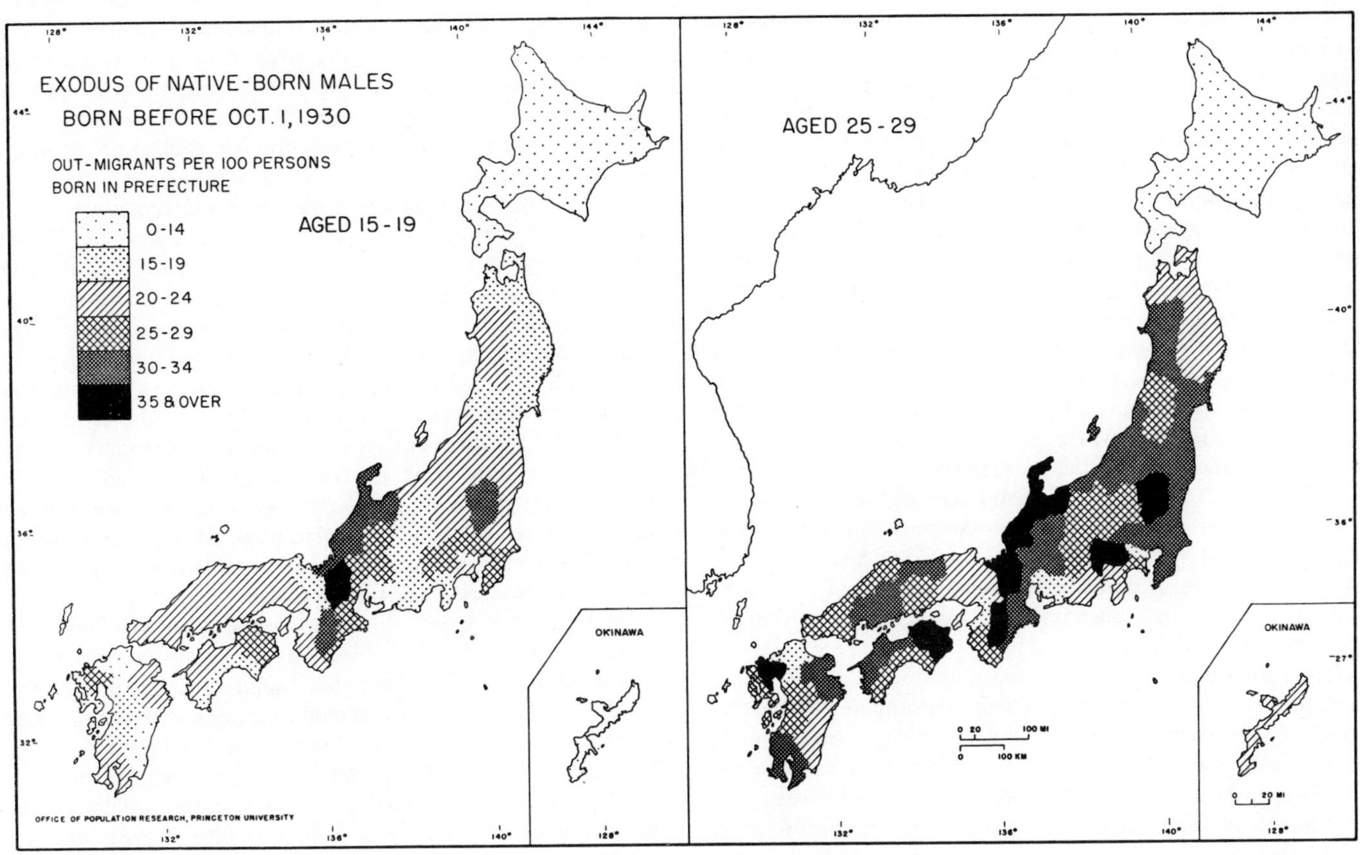

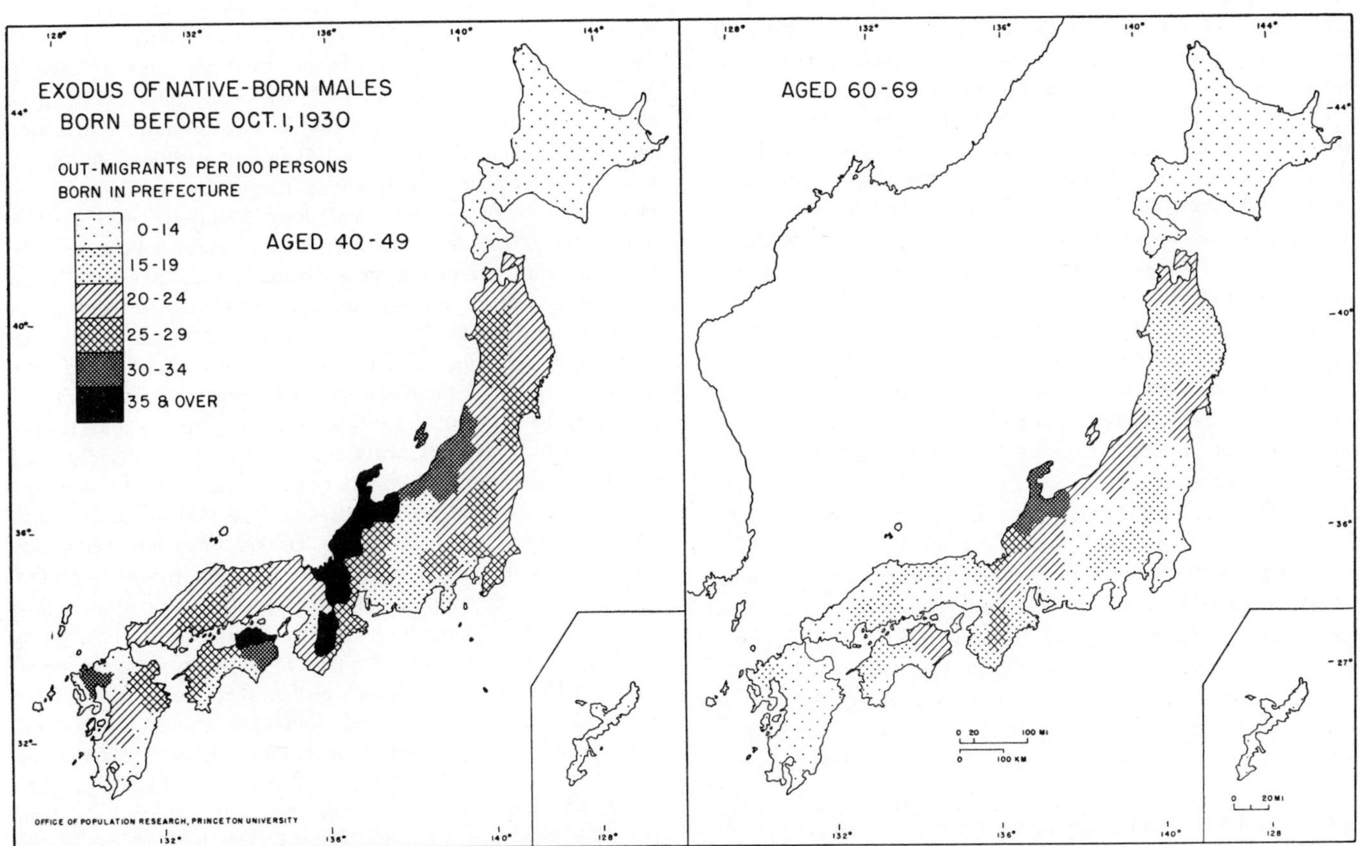

Map 7. Exodus of the native-born, from birth to October 1, 1930, males in selected ages, by prefectures
Source: References, Table 45.

of the groups of migrants from the prefectures yield further evidence of the social and economic patterning of the exodus. Migration at ages under 10 was but loosely related to migration at age 10 to 14. The former was a derived movement, while the latter was partially derived and partially independent. The relationship between the proportions migrant at age 10 to 14 and those migrant at age 15 to 19 was substantially higher.[16] From age 15 onward, the proportions migrant at one age were highly correlated with the proportions migrant at the next higher age. Out-migration was a response to forces that operated regularly or in regularly changing ways.

Regularities in the exodus from the prefectures were also apparent in the out-movements of males and females in the same or adjacent age groups. Males migrated slightly more than females as measured by the prefectural exodus of the native-born, but there was a general similarity in the levels and the age incidence of the movements.[17] Again there were exceptions. In Tokyo and Kanagawa females were a majority among the out-migrants. The out-movement of males was especially great in the prefectures along the Sea of Japan. However, these exceptions are less significant than the widespread regularity in a phenomenon as complex as movement from the area of birth.

The similarities in rates of exodus for males and females regardless of age are the product of uniform movements in childhood, somewhat divergent but finally compensating movements in the middle span of life, and comparable movements in old age. This age pattern in the relationship between the movements of males and females is comprehensible in terms of the social and economic forces of the period. At ages under 10, children moved with their families and there was a virtual identity in the exodus of the native-born among boys and girls. The slight surplus of boys was that which would be anticipated on the basis of differences in the sex ratio at birth and differential mortality in childhood.

The sphere of activities appropriate to and possible for boys and girls became differentiated between ages 10 and 25. At age 10 to 14, boys moved out for employment opportunities in neighboring or distant prefectures, whereas girls either remained at home or moved to adjacent areas where there were household industries or textile dormitories. Again there were exceptions. In several prefectures without local opportunities for girls, the exodus was quite heavy: Miyazaki, Kagoshima, Miyagi, Akita, Niigata, Toyama, and Gifu.

The divergence in the exodus of men and women in the years of late adolescence and early maturity was a consequence of their differing roles in the social structure and the differing magnitude and location of economic opportunities. The convergence of the rates was inherent in the universality of marriage, the functioning of the family system, and the inequalities in the geographical distribution of the men and women of marriageable age that had been produced by the movements of the years preceding marriage. Girls migrated as individuals during only a brief period, approximately from the age at which compulsory education was completed to the age at which marriage occurred. Men migrated independently, with or without their families, but predominantly with families if they were constituted prior to migration. Young migrants who secured jobs and minimum economic security in the cities were likely to marry girls selected by their families. To the extent that this was so, there was a migration of girls to the cities as brides. But by age 30 to 39, when virtually all Japanese were married, the proportionate exodus of the sexes was very close. It remained so in all later ages.

The exodus of Japanese from their prefectures of birth was related closely to the economic characteristics of the areas of origin (Table 46). In fact, in a land as densely settled as Japan, it was only the substantial out-movement of native-born from intermediate and agricultural prefectures that enabled declining mortality to co-exist with high fertility for decades without leading to major increases in the numbers of people attempting to secure a living from the land. And it permitted the maintenance of the ancient values at the same time that it introduced the leavens of contact and change that gradually altered the family system. The decisions of families were influential in migrations, if not determining; the influence of migrants on families ensured that something of the city reached back to the village.

In Japan the major economic pressures were in the agricultural areas, the major economic opportunities in the industrial areas. This is not the complete explanation of the exodus of the native-born, though, for almost two million of Japan's ten million prefectural out-migrants left the industrial prefecture of birth. Furthermore, exodus from one agricultural prefecture constituted influx into another. Nonetheless, the major exodus did come from agricultural areas and the major influx was in industrial and urban prefectures.

The service of out-migration in relieving pressure on the labor force in rural areas and contributing youthful workers to industry may be made somewhat more vivid by a closer view of some of the prefectures with high rates of exodus. In 1930 fifteen prefectures had lost more than one-fifth of their native-born men. These prefectures of major emigration were intermediate in industrial structure; proportions of the gainfully occupied in agriculture ranged from 40 to 59 per cent. They were all areas with long traditions of migration, and they all supplied migrants to the metropolitan centers. Saga, a small prefecture in Kyushu, lost 25 per cent of its native-born men, mainly to the adjacent prefectures of Fukuoka and Nagasaki. Kagawa and Tokushima in Shikoku and Nara and Shiga in Honshu sent from one-fifth to one-fourth or more of their men to other prefectures, the majority going to or near the cities of Osaka, Kobe, and Kyoto. Fukui, Gifu, and Ishikawa were located on the periphery of attraction for the Tokyo-Yokohama and the Osaka-Kobe-Kyoto areas. Fukui's exodus divided into two major currents, one to Tokyo and the other to Osaka. Gifu was physically barred from the Kinki region, but adjacent to Aichi prefecture with the developing city of Nagoya. Its migrants thus turned to Aichi prefecture, with a secondary current going to Tokyo. Ishikawa sent its people in approximately equal numbers to Tokyo and Osaka prefectures. The peoples from Toyama, Niigata, Tochigi, and Yamanashi moved into Tokyo. For many years, currents of migrants had moved from the poor coastal areas on the Sea of Japan to Hokkaido; as late as 1930 half the native-born who had left Toyama and Ishikawa and one-third of those who had left Niigata and Fukui were in Hokkaido.

While the exodus of the native-born from the prefectures of Japan was primarily a movement away from agriculture, the amount of the migration was proportionate neither to

[16] The coefficients of correlation for the prefectures were as follows: Ages 10-14 and 15-19, males .69, females .69; ages 15-19 and 20-24, males .90, females .91; ages 20-24 and 25-29, males .95, females .97; ages 25-29 and 30-39, males .97, females .96.

[17] Coefficients of correlation for the rates of exodus for males and females were as follows: Total, .96; age 0-9, .998; age 10-14, .77; age 15-19, .80; age 20-24, .87; age 25-29, .90; age 30-39, .93; age 40-49, .96; age 50-59, .97; age 60-69, .96.

TABLE 46

Exodus of the native-born, from birth to October 1, 1930, by sex and age, prefectures by industrial type (Out-migrants per 100 born in prefecture)

Age	*All Japan*	*Metropolitan*	*Other industrial*	*Intermediate*	*Agricultural*	*Hokkaido*
			Total			
Total	16.4	12.9	13.6	18.4	17.3	7.1
0-9	5.1	8.6	5.8	4.8	4.1	2.9
10-14	9.3	11.9	8.8	9.5	9.0	6.7
15-19	20.3	12.5	15.9	23.1	22.4	9.2
20-24	26.4	16.5	21.3	29.2	29.3	12.5
25-29	27.1	17.7	21.2	29.9	29.7	13.3
30-39	25.6	18.2	20.0	28.0	27.2	12.8
40-49	22.2	16.2	17.4	24.4	23.0	12.1
50-59	18.4	15.5	15.0	20.4	18.3	10.1
60-69	15.5	16.4	13.1	16.7	15.2	9.0
70-79	12.4	16.7	10.5	13.0	11.9	7.1
80 and over	10.3	14.9	9.3	11.1	9.5	4.8
			Male			
Total	17.3	12.5	14.1	19.6	18.2	7.2
0-9	5.1	8.6	5.8	4.8	4.1	2.9
10-14	9.1	11.7	9.1	9.5	8.6	6.6
15-19	20.7	11.9	16.9	24.4	22.1	9.3
20-24	28.6	16.4	23.1	32.3	31.5	13.2
25-29	28.5	16.6	21.8	31.9	31.4	13.5
30-39	27.3	17.4	20.9	30.3	29.1	13.1
40-49	24.1	16.6	18.5	26.7	25.0	12.2
50-59	19.5	14.7	15.4	21.7	19.6	9.6
60-69	15.9	15.6	12.8	17.1	15.9	8.2
70-79	12.1	15.9	9.9	12.5	12.1	6.4
8o and over	9.4	13.7	7.8	10.0	8.8	3.4
			Female			
Total	15.6	13.3	13.0	17.0	16.4	7.0
0-9	5.1	8.6	5.8	4.8	4.1	2.9
10-14	9.5	12.1	8.8	9.6	9.5	6.7
15-19	19.8	13.2	14.9	21.7	22.8	9.0
20-24	24.2	16.6	19.4	26.0	27.2	11.9
25-29	25.7	18.9	20.7	27.7	27.9	13.0
30-39	23.8	19.0	19.1	25.6	25.2	12.5
40-49	20.4	17.3	16.3	22.0	20.9	12.0
50-59	17.4	16.3	14.6	19.2	16.9	10.6
60-69	15.2	17.0	13.3	16.4	14.6	9.7
70-79	12.5	17.3	10.9	13.3	11.8	7.7
80 and over	10.9	15.4	10.0	11.7	9.8	5.4

Source: Nihon. Naikaku tokei-kyoku. *Showa go'nen kokusei chosa hokoku.* IV.4, Table 9; and IV.1, Table 25.

the limitations of agricultural land nor to the pressures in the local economies. The decision to migrate involved the pressures in the areas of origin, the awareness of opportunities elsewhere, the possibilities of movement, and the personal factors of qualifications, responsibilities, and motivations. In addition, movement from agriculture could occur without the crossing of prefectural boundaries. If there were developing urban centers and expanding industries within a prefecture, the adjustments among increasing people, rural pressures, and developing industries could occur in major part without inter-prefectural migration.

The exodus from the industrial prefectures differed in demographic composition and presumably in social and economic structure from the more widespread rural exodus. In Tokyo and Osaka prefectures, 35 per cent of all prefectural out-migrants were under age 15, 59 per cent were aged from 15 to 59, and 6 per cent were aged 60 or over. In the agrarian prefectures of heaviest exodus, 11 per cent of the out-migrants were under age 15, 81 per cent were between the ages of 15 and 59, and 7 per cent were aged 60 and over. The exodus of people in the central years from 15 to 59 was relatively less in industrial than in agricultural prefectures. Moreover, the out-movement from industrial prefectures was predominantly female. The explanation for the age and sex structure of out-migrants from industrial prefectures involves economic, social, and demographic selectivity. Managerial and professional men moved out from cities with their families. City-born girls went to other prefectures at the time of marriage. Many of the migrants who left the great cities after considerable periods of residence took with them children born in the cities.

The exodus from rural areas was an essential aspect of the political and economic transformation that had begun even before the opening to the West. With rates of exodus as substantial as they had been in the decades prior to 1930, accumulations of people in agricultural regions were residual, fragments of what they would have been if no migration to cities and industrial areas had occurred. Thus by 1930 the internal movements of the Japanese were the rural-urban movements of a people and a country approaching economic and demographic maturity.

INFLUX AND CONCENTRATION

If exodus involved a movement from rural to urban areas, from agricultural to industrial occupations, it follows that major portions of the Japan-born people resident outside the prefectures of birth lived in metropolitan and industrial prefectures (TABLE 47). In Tokyo and Osaka prefectures in 1930 some three-fifths of all persons in the productive ages from 20 to 49 had been born in other prefectures of Japan. In the other industrial prefectures and those moving rapidly toward industrialization, the contribution of the in-migrant to the population in the central ages amounted to one-third of the total. In the agricultural prefectures, on the other hand, in-migrants constituted less than one-tenth of the population in the productive ages.

The influx into the prefectures was as closely structured as the exodus from them. For the individual prefectures, as for groups of prefectures, the proportion of in-migrants at one age was related closely to the proportions at lower and at higher ages. The interrelations between the movements of men and women were even closer when viewed as influx than when viewed as exodus.[18] The forces of the economic transformation were operating through the mechanisms of family and community to create a new society within the old.

The changing balance of people, subsistence, and employment opportunities was achieved by redistribution rather than by exodus or influx considered separately.[19] Something of the magnitude of the redistribution achieved by 1930 may be seen through a comparison of the populations enumerated in the prefectures with the populations born there and still present somewhere within Japan (TABLE 48).[20]

Net migration is by definition the difference between out-migration and in-migration, and hence complex in derivation and composition. However, the economic organization and the social institutions of Japan had functioned with extraordinary regularity over a long period of time to create the nation-wide redistribution of population that had occurred by 1930. Net migration was almost as strongly patterned in relation to age and sex as the exodus and influx whose balance it was. The correlations between the rates of net migration for males and females were very high for youth below age 10, dropped to .89 at ages 10 to 14 and 15 to 19 when migration was individual rather than familial, then rose to .92 at age 20 to 24, .98 at age 25 to 29, and .99 at age 30 to 39 and above. The relation between net migration at one age and that at the next higher age was also close.[21]

The existence of close relationships among population movements, economic structure, and urbanization does not indicate economic determinism of migration in any precise sense. There were many types of selectivity that could have yielded the numbers of migrants involved in the redistribution of the population and the transformation of the economy. The selectivities that operated in exodus, influx, and net

[18] The correlations between proportions of prefectural in-migrants in the resident population for males and females at each age were as follows: Total, .99; age 0-9, .999; ages 10-14 and 15-19, .96; age 20-24, .94; ages 25-29, 30-39, 40-49, and 50-59, .99; age 60-69, .996.

[19] For the nation as a whole, the internal redistribution of the people produced no immediate change in population size or composition. The migrants may be considered as in-migrants or as out-migrants, but to total the in-migrants and the out-migrants would yield a meaningless figure. To subtract in-migrants from out-migrants would yield zero. And thus for the total nation there is no figure for gross or net migration that has meaning. For each area within the nation the situation is quite different, for here out-migrants and in-migrants as defined by the data on migrant status are different individuals. The sum of the migrations becomes a measure of the total impact of migration as it has operated over many decades. The difference between the movements reflects the net influence of migration on the size and composition of a population that has been transformed by the forces of birth, death, and migration from some population that might have existed without migration to the population that now exists.

[20] The population born in a prefecture and still resident in Japan on the census date is precisely that—but it is a population influenced by previous migrations that have contributed the children of the native-born to other prefectures and that have brought to this prefecture the native-born children of migrants from other prefectures. Whatever the dynamics of its creation, however, the people born within a prefecture would constitute the population of that prefecture had there been no migration among their numbers—and in this sense the native-born of the prefectures become a logical population to use as a base for the measurement of migration. This native-born population has been increased by births and immigration, depleted by deaths and emigration, to form the resident population. Thus if we relate the people actually in a prefecture on a specific date to the number born there, we have an approximate measure of the impact of migration on the native-born. This approaches a measure of the net influence of migration, but it is considered here not as net migration in a demographic sense but as indicative of the impact of migration.

[21] The correlations of net migration at ages 15 to 19 and 20 to 24 were .95 for males, .96 for females. Comparable correlations for ages 20 to 24 and 25 to 29 were .97 and .98; for ages 25 to 29 and 30 to 39, the correlations were .99 for both sexes.

TABLE 47

Influx from other prefectures, from birth to October 1, 1930, by sex and age, prefectures by industrial type
(In-migrants per 100 enumerated population)

Age	All Japan	Metropolitan	Other industrial	Intermediate	Agricultural	Hokkaido
			Total			
Total	16.2	45.9	22.0	8.0	6.4	34.8
0-9	5.0	11.5	7.4	3.6	3.0	4.5
10-14	9.2	27.7	13.9	5.5	4.6	9.6
15-19	20.0	53.2	27.1	9.7	7.3	19.8
20-24	25.9	61.2	33.3	13.1	10.2	31.5
25-29	26.7	64.7	34.1	12.4	9.8	45.9
30-39	25.3	64.3	32.8	11.5	9.3	61.6
40-49	22.1	60.6	28.6	10.0	8.3	79.8
50-59	18.4	55.7	23.7	8.4	7.1	85.2
60-69	15.5	52.5	19.8	7.1	6.3	87.8
70-79	12.4	46.3	15.4	5.7	5.4	88.8
80 and over	10.3	42.6	12.9	4.7	4.5	88.6
			Male			
Total	17.0	47.3	22.5	8.0	6.6	37.1
0-9	5.0	11.5	7.4	3.6	3.0	4.5
10-14	9.0	28.8	13.3	4.8	4.3	9.9
15-19	20.3	54.8	26.3	8.6	7.0	22.0
20-24	27.8	62.1	34.3	14.3	11.5	34.7
25-29	27.8	64.9	34.5	12.6	10.1	49.2
30-39	26.7	65.2	33.8	11.8	9.7	64.4
40-49	23.9	62.4	30.3	10.6	9.0	82.0
50-59	19.4	56.9	24.6	8.7	7.4	87.2
60-69	15.9	53.1	19.4	7.2	6.6	89.6
70-79	12.1	45.8	14.3	5.5	5.6	90.1
80 and over	9.4	39.5	11.2	4.1	4.4	90.9
			Female			
Total	15.5	44.4	21.5	7.9	6.2	32.3
0-9	5.0	11.5	7.3	3.6	3.1	4.4
10-14	9.4	26.4	14.5	6.2	4.8	9.2
15-19	19.6	51.4	27.9	10.7	7.7	17.4
20-24	24.0	60.3	32.2	11.8	8.9	27.9
25-29	25.5	64.5	33.8	12.1	9.6	42.0
30-39	23.7	63.3	31.6	11.1	8.9	58.3
40-49	20.3	58.6	26.7	9.4	7.7	77.2
50-59	17.4	54.4	22.9	8.1	6.7	82.9
60-69	15.2	52.1	20.1	7.0	6.0	85.8
70-79	12.5	46.6	16.2	5.8	5.3	87.6
80 and over	10.9	43.8	13.8	5.0	4.6	87.1

Source: References, Table 46.

Table 48

Present population in relation to population born in the prefectures, October 1, 1930, by sex and age, prefectures by industrial type

(Number enumerated in prefectures per 1,000 born in prefectures)

Age	*All Japan*	*Metropolitan*	*Other industrial*	*Intermediate*	*Agricultural*	*Hokkaido*
			Total			
Total	1009	1670	1132	895	887	1443
0-9	1007	1047	1124	994	993	1021
10-14	1010	1251	1077	968	959	1037
15-19	1014	1995	1190	862	842	1143
20-24	1019	2372	1237	828	791	1307
25-29	1017	2532	1250	813	784	1660
30-39	1013	2444	1232	823	806	2377
40-49	1005	2165	1172	843	842	4516
50-59	1002	1924	1120	869	880	6196
60-69	1001	1773	1087	897	905	7517
70-79	1000	1556	1059	923	931	8298
80 and over	1000	1485	1042	933	948	8362
			Male			
Total	1013	1745	1140	883	880	1504
0-9	1007	1047	1028	994	993	1021
10-14	1011	1279	1068	962	961	1042
15-19	1018	2127	1171	839	843	1174
20-24	1028	2536	1254	810	781	1376
25-29	1026	2686	1276	799	771	1808
30-39	1020	2602	1261	806	791	2649
40-49	1008	2302	1194	825	826	5230
50-59	1002	1996	1130	859	868	7288
60-69	1001	1809	1085	894	900	8963
70-79	1000	1557	1052	926	931	9468
80 and over	1000	1434	1039	938	954	10708
			Female			
Total	1006	1595	1124	906	894	1382
0-9	1006	1047	1028	995	993	1020
10-14	1010	1222	1085	974	957	1032
15-19	1011	1857	1210	886	840	1111
20-24	1010	2203	1220	847	802	1236
25-29	1007	2373	1220	828	799	1513
30-39	1005	2275	1202	841	822	2116
40-49	1002	2023	1149	862	857	3888
50-59	1001	1854	1111	879	891	5273
60-69	1001	1743	1088	900	909	6382
70-79	1000	1556	1065	921	931	7467
80 and over	1000	1506	1043	930	945	7367

Source: References, Table 46.

change were products of social and psychological factors deeply imbedded in the institutional structure of Japanese society. The family system was maintained and even strengthened in the modern period, its rights and responsibilities formalized by codified law and sanctioned by Imperial Rescript. The selection and rejection of migrants were aspects of the interpenetration of the most ancient of the social institutions and the most advanced of the economic developments.

Internal migrations removed people from agricultural areas and concentrated them in industrial areas (TABLE 49). As of October 1, 1930, the industrial prefectures and those in advanced transition had gained by internal migration. Agricultural prefectures and those with limited industrialization had lost by internal movements.

In the metropolitan prefectures, net gains from inter-prefectural migration extended through all age groups, though proportionate gains were greatest for those in the twenties and the thirties. Among young adults there were three in-migrants from other prefectures for each two native residents. In prefectures where from 60 to 69 per cent of the gainfully occupied labored in agriculture, there had been a net loss of some one-third of the young men through movement elsewhere in Japan.

A major concentration of population had occurred in the decades prior to 1930. Eight prefectures had gained substantially by the interchange of migrants—Tokyo, Kanagawa, Nagoya, Osaka, Hyogo, Kyoto, Fukuoka, and Hokkaido. All other prefectures contributed to the population of these eight.[22] The demographic consequences of this recruitment of millions of people were bifocal. The initial movements prevented deterioration of relations between people and economy in the villages and lesser towns. The terminal residence in the great cities and their peripheral and satellite regions created the labor force for the industrial economy. Conceptions of optimum and balance in the relations among people, resources, and developed economy are not involved here, except in the broad negative sense that the relation of people to subsistence and real income in the rural areas would have been intolerable had not migration occurred. Similarly, the importation of industrial labor and sustaining personnel was an essential aspect of economic development.

The relations between numbers of men and numbers of women in the net interchange of people demonstrate the cultural conditioning of a fundamental economic process. They also show the interrelations of many factors in the industrialization of Japan in the year 1930.

The approximate equality of boys and girls among child migrants is an interesting and not altogether expected aspect of the functioning of the Japanese family system. Given a patrilineal family system in a milieu of poverty, it might have been expected that many parents would leave daughters at home in the villages but take sons with them to the cities. If this had happened with any regularity, there would have been a predominance of boys in the balance of inter-prefectural migrants in the major areas of in-migration. There was no such preponderance. Hence we have to conclude either that families who moved did so as family groups, or that men moved and left all children at home.[23] This simple fact of a relative equality of boys and girls among migrants reveals equality in the treatment of sons and daughters. Whether this equality reflected an ancient institution or one in the process of change cannot be answered from census data on migrant status.

The relations between numbers of men and women involved in net migration at ages between 10 and 30 or 40 depended on the conflict or coincidence of the many factors involved in the creation of sex differences in exodus and influx. At age 10 to 14 the substantial differences in migration were associated with the types of labor demand in the various prefectures. Nagano, Saitama, and Gumma imported girls for labor in connection with sericulture and textiles, but they exported boys to other areas. The influence of the textile mills was still apparent in the case of girls aged from 15 to 19. However, the level of migration was higher; the major influence in net migration had become the general level of industrialization rather than a specific industry. At age 20 to 24 there was some scatter between net migratory changes for young men and young women, although in almost all prefectures the net change, whether gain or loss, was greater for males. The independent movement of women was still occurring in this age group. By age 25 to 29 ratios of net migrants to resident population for men and women were highly correlated in the gaining prefectures, though there was some scatter in the losing prefectures. From age 30 to the end of the life span, sex differences in relative change by net migration were small, although absolute gain or loss tended to be somewhat greater among men than among women. The dispersion of the sexes that had been created by an economically motivated movement of individuals was liquidated by the marital selectivity of people of similar origin implicit in the family system, with its arranged marriages.

THE MIGRANTS WITHIN THE PREFECTURES, FROM BIRTH TO 1930

The redistribution of population as between prefectures reflected both the long migrations of the industrializing society and the short migrations of the traditional society. Precise distinctions between the types of movements are difficult to make. It is reasonable to assume that the economic transformation of the country was the basic force in inter-prefectural migration, while the functioning of the traditional society was more important in movements within prefectures. If this is so, it follows that movements from agricultural to non-agricultural occupations and places of residence were more prevalent in the migrant exchanges between the prefectures, while changes in residence that involved more limited shifts in occupations or ways of living were more prevalent within prefectures. This argument involves the assumption that there was some identity of migrant status on the basis of administrative boundaries with migration on the basis of distance involved. There are factual and theoretical difficulties with simple correlations of migrant status and social processes on the basis of official statistics for administrative divisions. Prefectures differ greatly in size, topography, and economy. Insofar as distance is concerned, one needs the migrant status of the population in zones at specific distances from the defined center of movement. It

[22] The limitations of the data should be emphasized again. Exodus or influx for any given group of prefectures is the sum of the exodus or influx of the constituent prefectures and therefore includes movements between the prefectures of the group under consideration. Since age structure is not available by prefectures of origin or destination, there is no way to avoid this limitation on the analysis. The magnitude of this factor will be analyzed later for total numbers, which are available according to prefectures involved in the interchange.

[23] There is the further possibility that the marriage occurred in the city but the wife later returned to her home for the birth of the baby. But insofar as such babies were brought back to the city, there was no selection by sex.

TABLE 49

The balance of inter-prefectural migration, from birth to October 1, 1930, by sex and age, prefectures by industrial type

(Net change by migration per 100 enumerated population)

			INTERMEDIATE		AGRICULTURAL	
Age	*Metropolitan*	*Other industrial*	*Industrial*[a]	*Agricultural*[b]	*Modal*[c]	*Peripheral*[d]
			Total			
Total	39.0	10.2	6.4	−13.7	−14.0	−10.7
0-9	3.4	1.7	−0.0	−1.2	−1.3	−1.1
10-14	18.5	5.7	−1.2	−4.4	−5.4	−4.1
15-19	48.4	14.0	−4.3	−17.6	−19.5	−21.9
20-24	56.3	16.6	2.1	−25.9	−27.2	−31.6
25-29	59.4	17.6	6.2	−27.1	−29.3	−28.1
30-39	58.2	16.9	12.7	−24.9	−26.5	−18.5
40-49	53.3	13.8	21.4	−21.0	−21.0	−14.1
50-59	47.8	10.4	21.0	−16.6	−15.3	−6.3
60-69	43.4	7.7	19.2	−12.5	−11.8	−4.5
70-79	35.6	5.5	16.6	−8.9	−8.4	−2.7
80 and over	32.6	3.9	15.3	−7.8	−6.4	−1.7
			Male			
Total	41.2	10.4	8.1	−16.1	−15.3	−11.9
0-9	3.4	1.8	0.0	−1.2	−1.5	−1.1
10-14	20.1	4.9	−1.1	−5.3	−5.5	−3.8
15-19	51.1	12.2	−2.4	−22.4	−20.2	−19.8
20-24	58.5	16.6	6.9	−33.0	−29.9	−36.5
25-29	61.2	18.2	8.9	−31.4	−32.7	−33.5
30-39	60.4	17.8	14.6	−29.0	−29.7	−23.2
40-49	56.0	15.0	23.7	−24.6	−23.5	−12.8
50-59	49.7	11.1	24.0	−18.4	−17.0	−7.5
60-69	44.6	7.6	22.3	−13.2	−12.4	−4.7
70-79	35.7	4.8	19.1	−8.6	−8.4	−2.4
80 and over	30.1	3.6	17.7	−7.2	−5.8	−0.9
			Female			
Total	36.5	10.1	4.8	−11.4	−12.7	−9.5
0-9	3.4	1.7	−0.0	−1.2	−1.1	−1.1
10-14	16.8	6.5	−1.3	−4.0	−5.2	−4.5
15-19	45.1	15.9	−6.2	−13.1	−18.7	−24.0
20-24	58.1	16.6	−3.4	−19.3	−24.7	−27.2
25-29	57.3	17.1	3.4	−22.8	−25.9	−23.2
30-39	55.5	15.9	10.6	−20.8	−23.4	−14.1
40-49	50.3	12.6	18.9	−17.5	−18.5	−7.8
50-59	45.9	9.7	18.0	−14.8	−13.8	−5.1
60-69	42.4	7.9	16.2	−11.8	−11.2	−4.4
70-79	35.7	5.9	14.6	−9.1	−8.4	−3.0
80 and over	33.6	4.1	14.0	−8.2	−6.7	−2.1

[a] From 40 to 49 per cent of the gainfully occupied in agriculture. [b] From 50 to 59 per cent in agriculture. [c] From 60 to 69 per cent in agriculture. [d] Seventy per cent or more in agriculture. Hokkaido is included here as intermediate industrial in type rather than considered separately.

Source: Reference, Table 46.

would be even more meaningful if there were data on the migrant status of the people in areas outlined on the basis of ease of access.

Further difficulties with data on migrant status arise when a differentiation is made between persons born in another prefecture and those born in another minor civil division of the same prefecture. In entirely agrarian prefectures, internal movements require few changes in ways of living. In industrializing areas, however, movements within prefectures may represent either the customary mobility of the agrarian society or the newer mobility associated with urbanization.

The data on the migrant status of the population of Japan in 1930 permit clarification of some of the problems concerning movements within prefectures. While the majority of the movements in the more agricultural prefectures were correlates of the functioning of the ancient society, the drift of movement was toward non-agricultural activities and ways of living. The major recruiting areas for cities were their surrounding rural areas. However, the majority of the migrants within prefectures moved within *gun* rather than from *gun* to *shi*. The "urban" movements within prefectures were associated with industrialization and urbanization. For instance, the proportion of inter-communal migrants enumerated in *shi* was 36 per cent in the industrial prefectures, 30 per cent in the transitional prefectures, and 18 per cent in the agricultural prefectures. Within the *gun* of any given prefecture, the predominant movements were from *mura* to *machi* rather than from *mura* to *mura*.

As we examine further the variations in the numbers and the characteristics of those Japanese who had moved within the prefecture of birth, we see a major differentiation by sex. The migrant status of men was influenced primarily by economic factors, whereas that of women was mediated by the family system. The independent movements were those of men. Since families agreed upon marital selections for men, the movements of men created characteristic patterns for the movements of women. Wives tended to be somewhat younger than husbands, and they tended to come from adjacent rather than identical villages. Since the institutions of the stable society required an in-movement of wives, the demographically stable society itself tended to have appreciable proportions of men living in the commune of birth but married to women born in other communes. In the transforming society, the numbers and the characteristics of women migrants were influenced by the migrations of men, particularly by the length of the period within which the social and economic adjustments of men in their new areas of residence precluded marriage. Thus the numbers and the characteristics of the men and women who were inter-communal migrants in 1930 will be examined separately.

INTER-COMMUNAL MIGRANTS, MEN

Migrations within prefectures may be regarded either as the limited out-movements of native-born people or as intra-prefectural movements of the resident population. Since the mobility of the native-born permits us to regard the migrations within prefectures as exodus, we shall utilize this approach before proceeding to the more complex problems of the inter-communal migrant as a component of the resident population.

In 1930, 16 per cent of the men born in Japan and still resident there were enumerated in another minor civil division of the prefecture of birth. The differences among the prefectures were not great, but there was a consistent increase in the percentage with the transition from the agricultural to the industrial economy. There were also differences in exodus among the age groups, and these differences varied somewhat by type of prefecture. The following rates for selected types of prefectures are illustrative:[24]

INTER-COMMUNAL MIGRANTS PER 100 BORN IN PREFECTURES, MALES[25]

Age	*All Japan*	*Metropolitan prefectures*	*Other industrial prefectures*	*Modal agricultural prefectures*
Total	16.4	21.4	19.0	14.2
0-9	7.6	14.6	7.8	5.5
10-14	12.2	20.8	13.0	9.2
15-19	20.5	24.5	23.3	17.3
20-24	20.9	25.2	24.4	17.5
25-29	21.3	26.7	25.9	18.0
30-39	21.8	28.9	27.3	18.7
40-49	21.2	28.2	26.1	19.1
50-59	20.1	26.1	24.1	18.7
60-69	19.6	24.9	22.5	18.7
70-79	18.1	23.0	20.0	17.3
80-89	16.4	20.7	18.7	15.6

As the above data indicate, the greatest differences among the prefectures lay in the mobility of youth. After age 15 there was a general level of migrant status that persisted throughout the life span, with only slight declines in the very late ages. The differences in mobility between the prefectures of various types and the rates of mobility at the successive ages within the types of prefectures are consistent with what we know of the nature of the economy of Japan. The inter-communal migration of the native-born in the agricultural prefectures was primarily a movement from agricultural to non-agricultural employment in a *machi* or a *shi* within the prefecture. It is thus comparable to inter-prefectural movements in its low proportions of children and its sharp increase in proportions migrant at ages 10 to 14 and 15 to 19. The inter-communal migrations of the native-born in the metropolitan prefectures, on the other hand, reflected the local movements associated with the formation of the city—suburban, inter-city, and rural migration to satellite city, suburb, or central city.

The contributions of inter-communal migrants to the formation of the male populations resident in the various areas indicate that an essentially Western type of redistribution was occurring in the metropolitan prefectures. Data for selected types of prefectures are given here:[26]

INTER-COMMUNAL MIGRANTS PER 100 RESIDENT IN PREFECTURE, MALE

Age	*All Japan*	*Metropolitan prefectures*	*Other industrial prefectures*	*Modal agricultural prefectures*
Total	16.2	12.3	16.6	16.2
0-9	7.6	13.9	7.6	5.5
10-14	12.0	16.2	12.1	9.6

[24] Source: Nihon. Naikaku tokei-kyoku. *Showa go'nen kokusei chosa hokoku.* IV.4. Table 9. The tabulation is available for the total prefecture and the city of 100 thousand and over, if there was one, not for the individual minor civil divisions within the prefecture.

[25] Based on the percentage of the gainfully occupied in agriculture: metropolitan, below 20 per cent; other industrial, 20 to 39 per cent; modal agricultural, 60 to 69 per cent. Those born in the prefecture are defined as including the total enumerated anywhere in Japan.

[26] For source of data and definitions, see Footnotes 24 and 25.

15-19	20.1	11.5	19.9	20.5
20-24	20.3	9.9	19.5	22.1
25-29	20.7	10.0	20.3	23.3
30-39	21.4	11.1	21.7	24.0
40-49	21.0	12.2	21.9	23.4
50-59	20.1	13.1	21.3	21.8
60-69	19.6	13.8	20.8	21.0
70-79	18.0	14.8	19.0	18.8
80-89	16.4	14.5	18.0	16.5

Analysis of the data on place of birth in relation to age for Japan in 1930 indicates that the distinction between inter-prefectural and inter-communal migrants is quite inadequate as a basis for intensive study of the relations among industrialization, urbanization, and internal migration. However, certain broad generalizations are possible. In agricultural prefectures, where locally available labor was adequate for the maintenance of the existing economy and the developments under way, migration was primarily inter-communal. In metropolitan prefectures, the local labor supply was inadequate to meet the requirements of the growing cities and expanding industries; migrants were secured in large numbers from outside the prefecture.

INTER-COMMUNAL MIGRANTS, WOMEN

The inter-communal migrations of women were greater than those of men. The proportions migrant were comparable for boys and girls under age 15, but beginning with age 15 to 19 the proportion of short-distance migrants among women rose sharply above that for men. As the following tabulations show, this relationship held in all higher ages for all types of prefectures:[27]

INTER-COMMUNAL MIGRANTS PER 100 BORN IN THE PREFECTURES, FEMALE

Age	*Metropolitan prefectures*	*Other industrial prefectures*	*Modal agricultural prefectures*
Total	25.0	28.2	24.0
0-9	14.4	8.0	5.7
10-14	20.8	14.6	11.4
15-19	25.1	27.0	20.1
20-24	30.7	35.7	30.0
25-29	35.7	42.0	35.1
30-39	37.0	43.8	36.3
40-49	36.6	43.3	36.3
50-59	35.9	42.2	36.1
60-69	36.0	42.2	35.5
70-79	34.9	40.9	34.4
80-89	33.9	41.3	33.0

Among women there was a sharp rise in inter-communal migrants at age 10 to 14, followed by further increases at ages 15 to 19, 20 to 24, and 25 to 29. This same pattern of inter-communal migration by age existed in agricultural, transitional, and industrial prefectures; it existed in the northeastern prefectures, as in those of the southwest. The explanation must lie in a sequential influence of migration for labor and continued residence or further migration for marriage.

Since few girls aged from 10 to 14 and only small portions of those aged from 15 to 19 were married, the explanation for inter-communal migrations at these ages must lie primarily in labor migration, though in the upper social and economic classes of the more advanced prefectures there would be some migration for education. The majority of the girls employed in the textile industry, the small factories, and domestic service were from 14 to 18 years of age. Marriage occurred sometime between the late teens and the late twenties. Married women were seldom employed outside agriculture or the household industries and distributive trades that permitted the combination of work, household activities, and childbearing. Hence the relatively high proportions of women aged from 25 to 29 and over who lived outside the commune of birth must be interpreted in terms of the family rather than of the labor market. Patrilocal residence that required the movement of the bride to the home of the groom often meant transfer across the lines of *machi* or *mura*. This role of the marriage system in the creation of inter-communal migrants among women was not limited to the rural areas. Arranged marriages brought women from the *machi* and the *mura* into the *shi*, for many marriages of city men were arranged in the villages. The reverse situation occurred occasionally, the city girl being regarded as a desirable wife by the non-agricultural family in the town.

If the migrations of women were determined in major part by the place of residence of the men they married, then in areas of in-migration the proportions of migrant women in the resident populations of *shi, machi*, and *mura* should be related closely to the proportions of migrant men in the same area. If men who were inter-prefectural migrants in the great cities married women from their ancestral villages, the women also became inter-prefectural migrants. Thus the institution of the arranged marriage in the industrializing society would result in fairly small proportions of inter-communal migrants among women in the metropolitan prefectures. In the agricultural prefectures, on the other hand, the majority of the men would be stable. They cultivated family lands that passed down from eldest son to eldest son. In most instances wives would be selected from nearby areas; in many cases the *buraku* of the wife would be within the same *mura* as that of the husband. The inter-communal migrations of women would be limited. Thus an explanation of the migrations of women in terms of the family system requires that the proportion of inter-communal migrants among women in the metropolitan prefectures be similar to but slightly above that of men, that the proportion of such migrants in the agricultural prefectures be considerably above that of men. These relationships existed in the migrant status data of the 1930 census:[28]

INTER-COMMUNAL MIGRANTS PER 100 RESIDENT IN THE PREFECTURES, BY SEX

	Metropolitan prefectures		*Modal agricultural prefectures*	
Age	*Males*	*Females*	*Males*	*Females*
Total	12.3	15.7	16.2	27.0
0-9	13.9	13.8	5.5	5.7
10-14	16.2	17.0	9.6	11.9
15-19	11.5	13.5	20.5	23.8
20-24	9.9	13.9	22.1	37.2
25-29	10.0	15.0	23.3	44.0
30-39	11.1	16.3	24.0	44.7
40-49	12.2	18.1	23.4	43.0
50-59	13.1	19.4	21.8	41.1
60-69	13.8	20.6	21.0	39.5
70-79	14.8	22.4	18.8	37.3
80-89	14.5	22.5	16.5	35.2

[27] *Ibid.*

[28] *Ibid.*

Thus the proportions of inter-communal migrants among women were in part the product of a type of marital selection that removed brides to adjacent *mura*, in part that of the continued functioning of the institution of the arranged marriage in the urbanizing culture. The social institutions of the ancient order reallocated women in rough relationship to the reallocation of men.

The Stable Within the Communes, from Birth to 1930

THE RETENTION OF THE NATIVE-BORN

In 1930, seventy-five years after the opening to the West, 83 per cent of Japan's people lived in the prefecture of birth, 62 per cent in the commune of birth.[29] As contrasted with the Sinhalese of Ceylon or the Hindus of the Ganges this may be mobility, but as contrasted with the industrial populations of the West, it is stability. Only in the southern states of the United States was the retention of the native-born as high as it was in Japan in 1930.

The limitations of the tabulations of data on place of enumeration by place of birth are again apparent if we wish to define the stable population. Many Japanese move from one place to another within the minor civil division of birth. It is obvious that this type of movement would be correlated with the development of industrial areas. However, there is no alternative to a definition of the stable as those individuals who were enumerated in the commune in which they were born. If we use this definition, we are impressed by the stability that still existed in Japan in 1930. There were mobile groups and mobile areas, but in no prefecture did the mobile constitute more than 45 per cent of those who had been born in the prefecture. In 43 of the 47 prefectures, the stable constituted from 55 to 69 per cent of the people born in the prefecture and still present somewhere in Japan. The rate of mobility varied from commune to commune, from prefecture to prefecture, but the modal life was that of continued residence in or return to the prefecture and the minor civil division of birth.

Areas in which per capita incomes were relatively high and employment opportunities abundant retained high proportions of their native-born. In this case, the decision of the individual to remain in his place of birth was not an index of ignorance or backwardness; it was evidence of enlightened self-interest. Such considerations may explain the fact that more than 85 per cent of the native-born of Tokyo and Osaka had remained in the commune of birth. The retentiveness of superior economic opportunity was accompanied by an attraction for immigrants from other prefectures of Japan and the colonial areas. Thus the people who had remained in the commune of birth lived in an area that included substantial numbers of people from areas outside the prefecture. Demographic processes were favorable to the modification of ancient institutions and values.

THE NATIVE-BORN IN THE RESIDENT POPULATION

The cultural relevance of stability is related directly to the numbers and the characteristics of the mobile people who live in the community with the stable. If the people living in a disadvantaged area know of opportunities elsewhere, they are likely to move out, but there is not likely to be compensatory in-migration. The proportion of the locally born in the resident population will remain high. In this situation the selectivity of migration serves to preserve social isolation and so to perpetuate ancient structures and traditional values.

If these assumptions as to the psychological motivations and the cultural processes involved in migration are correct, there should be a relationship between high proportions of the stable in the resident population and a milieu of poverty, and between high proportions of the mobile in the resident population and a milieu of opportunity. In 1930, high proportions of the locally born in the enumerated population were correlated with rurality, dependence on agriculture, and economic backwardness. Low proportions of the locally born in the resident population were correlated with urbanization, industrialization, and higher levels of living. The locally born constituted from 90 to 95 per cent of the total population in the prefectures of northeast Honshu and the isolated areas of the southwest. In Tokyo, on the contrary, almost half the total population were born in other prefectures, more than 1 per cent outside Japan. Osaka, with 41 per cent from other prefectures and 3 per cent from abroad, ranked next to Tokyo in the mobility of its people. Below these came Kanagawa, Aichi, Kyoto, and Hyogo; Hokkaido with its pioneer fringe and its developing industrial base; Fukuoka with its heavy industries; Nagasaki; and then such developing prefectures as Hiroshima, Yamaguchi, and Miyazaki.

In 1930 there was slight relation between the proportion of the individuals born in the prefecture who were stable and the proportion that the stable constituted of the population enumerated in the prefecture. The forces influencing retention of the locally born were not related in simple fashion to the forces influencing in-migration from other areas. The data suggest that levels of stability among the locally born may be products of divergent social forces and personal attitudes. Stability in a backward area may reflect traditionalism, ignorance, or hopelessness, while stability in an advanced area may reflect technical competence, ambition, and optimism. In the in-movement from other prefectures, however, the social and psychological forces that impel individuals to move were related directly to the facts of economic expansion itself.

Since there were substantial differences between the sexes in the rates of migration within and between prefectures, there were also sex differences in the retention of individuals within the minor civil divisions of birth. These sex differences in stability and in net inter-prefectural movements are apparent if the numbers of the stable within a prefecture are related to the total population of that prefecture.[30] The proportions of the stable in the enumerated population of Nagano prefecture illustrate the factors involved. In 1930, the proportion of the population enumerated in the commune of birth was 75 per cent for men, 57 per cent for women. The majority of the migrant women had moved only short distances, however, for 34 per cent of all women enumerated in the prefecture had moved in from another minor civil division of Nagano itself. The major explanation for the lesser stability and the greater

[29] A statistical difficulty is introduced by the fact that persons born in a specific prefecture are included only if they were physically present within Japan at the time of the census. The proportion of native-born resident in the prefecture of birth is thus unduly high for such prefectures as Hokkaido, which sent migrants to Karafuto; Okinawa, which sent its people to Nanyo-gunto and outside the Empire; and Tokyo, which sent its people throughout the Empire.

[30] The stable are defined as individuals enumerated in the minor civil division of birth. They may be regarded as the residual of non-migrants among the total number of persons born in the prefecture. The total population of the prefecture consists of the stable as defined above, the inter-communal migrants within the prefecture, and the in-migrants from other prefectures or abroad. It should be noted that persons born in Japan who had left the country by October 1, 1930, were excluded from the census taken on that date.

mobility of women lay in their extensive employment in sericulture and silk-reeling. The labor demands of silk created currents of migration across the lines of *machi* and *mura* within the prefectures.

Over-all retention rates are not incisive measures of the stability of a population, for such rates combine the young who may be the children of earlier migrants, the persons in the early productive years when migration is most common, and the aged who are the survivors of a more agricultural economy in the past. In the following tabulation, the numbers of the stable are related to the total population born in the prefecture, computations being specific for age and types of prefectures:[31]

STABLE PER 100 BORN IN PREFECTURE, MALE

Age	*All Japan*	*Metropolitan prefectures*	*Other industrial prefectures*	*Modal agricultural prefectures*
Total	66.3	66.0	66.9	67.1
0-9	87.3	76.8	86.3	90.4
10-14	78.7	67.5	78.0	81.8
15-19	58.8	63.6	59.8	60.4
20-24	50.5	58.4	52.5	51.2
25-29	50.2	56.6	52.4	50.5
30-39	50.9	53.7	51.8	50.9
40-49	54.7	55.2	55.4	54.7
50-59	60.4	59.2	60.5	60.3
60-69	64.5	59.5	64.6	64.2
70-79	69.8	61.1	70.1	69.6
80 and over	74.2	65.6	73.5	74.6

Only half of the men aged from 20 to 39 were enumerated in the minor civil divisions of their birth, as contrasted with two-thirds of all men. Retention was highest in the most industrialized prefectures, where both economic opportunities and psychological advantages inhered in continued residence in the community of birth. Retention was also high in agricultural prefectures, but here inter-prefectural and inter-communal migration had removed from 40 to 49 per cent of the native-born.[32] In the intermediate prefectures where agricultural and industrial opportunities co-existed and knowledge of the modern world of the metropolis was diffused, more than half of all native-born men aged from 20 to 39 were migrants of one type or another.[33]

The relations between the stable and the mobile in the resident population indicate the position of the various areas and age groups in a modernization continuum:[34]

STABLE PER 100 ENUMERATED POPULATION, MALES

Age	*Metropolitan prefectures*	*Other industrial prefectures*	*Modal agricultural prefectures*
Total	37.8	58.7	76.5
0-9	73.4	83.9	91.0
10-14	52.8	73.0	85.3
15-19	29.9	51.1	71.6
20-24	23.0	41.9	64.8
25-29	21.1	41.0	65.3
30-39	20.6	41.1	65.2
40-49	24.0	46.4	67.0
50-59	29.6	53.6	70.4
60-69	32.9	59.6	72.1
70-79	39.3	66.6	75.4
80 and over	45.8	70.8	78.9

In the agricultural prefectures, four-fifths of all men were enumerated in the commune of birth. At the other end of the stability-mobility continuum were the prefectures of Tokyo and Osaka. Here less than two-fifths of the men resided in the minor civil division of birth. In the mobile ages, in these metropolitan prefectures only about one-fifth of the men were stable, as contrasted with the 65 to 70 per cent stable in the agricultural prefectures. Where industrialization and urbanization had developed furthest, stable men were proportionately only half as numerous as they were in the most agricultural prefectures, if total numbers are considered; only two-sevenths as numerous, if men aged from 20 to 39 are considered. This twofold increase in the mobility of the total male population, three and one-half fold increase in the mobility of males in the early productive span, is a minimum measure of the dislocations of the ancient structures associated with the development of modern Japan.

Net Migration, Prefectures, 1920-1940

The tabulations of the census data for 1930 on place of enumeration in relation to place of birth by sex and age permitted detailed descriptions of the migrant status of the population as of the date of that census. These materials concealed many of the relations between the developing culture and the increasing movements of people. They permitted only deductions as to the time sequences of migrations and the movements involved in the production of net residuals. Moreover, the situation described was a consequence of developments prior to 1930. Since there are no materials comparable in area detail or demographic precision for any date after 1930, the changes in the years from 1930 to the present are not subject to measurement on even the rough basis of migrant status by age and sex. It is possible, however, to estimate net migration across prefectural boundaries during an intercensal period. The ratio of net migrations within a period to the mid-population of that period then gives a measure of migration.[35] The measure is crude and the hazards in its use are multiple, but it has many advantages as a summary measure. All types of migrations are involved, internal and external, and the rate of net change may be contrasted for successive periods.

There was continuity in the pattern of change by migration in the four quinquennial periods from 1920 to 1940, and it mirrored the continuity in the industrialization of the economy and the urbanization of the population structure (Map 8).

[31] For source of data and definitions, see Footnotes 24 and 25.

[32] The ranks of the stable women were doubly depleted, for independent migration to seize the economic opportunities of the outer world and migration to marriage with a young man who had become immersed in the nexus of the urban economy and culture reinforced the age-old movements occasioned by the transfer to the house of the husband.

[33] The intermediate agricultural prefectures are those which had from 50 to 59 per cent of their gainfully occupied population in agriculture in 1930.

[34] For source of data, see Footnotes 24 and 25.

[35] The technique is that of adding births (adjusted for malregistration) to, and subtracting deaths occurring within the intercensal period from, the base population to secure an estimate of the population expected without migration. Subtraction of the actual population from the estimated gives net change due to migration; the ratio of such change to the mid-period population gives the rate of migration. The census populations are given in the various census volumes and in the various statistical yearbooks. Numbers of births and deaths were given annually in: Nihon. Naikaku tokei-kyoku. *Jinko dotai tokei*. For description of the adjustment of births for malregistration, see Chapter XII.

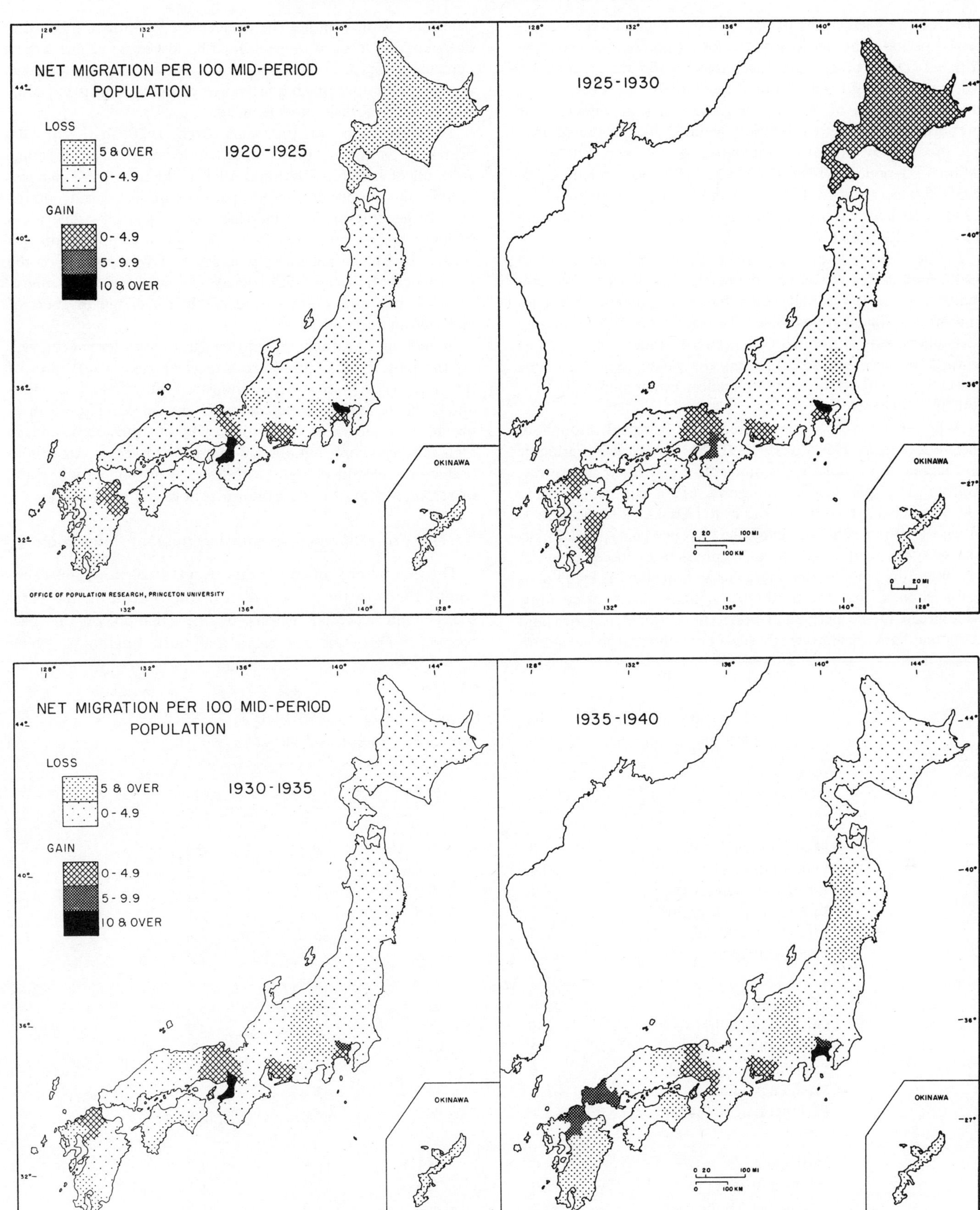

Map. 8. Net migration, prefectures, 1920-1940
Source: Populations: summary volumes, respective censuses. Births and deaths: Nihon. Naikaku tokei-kyoku. *Jinko dotai tokei.* Births adjusted for malregistration.

Most of the prefectures of Japan lost population each intercensal period. The net loss of the losing prefectures was contributed to the prefectures that included the six great cities. The process could not continue indefinitely, however, for as the conurbations of Tokyo and Osaka became larger, their proportionate gains by migration declined. Tokyo prefecture's net increase by migration amounted to 12.5 per cent of its mid-period population in 1920-1925, 10.1 per cent in 1925-1930, 8.0 per cent in 1930-1935, and 7.4 per cent in 1935-1940. The comparable percentage increases for Osaka were 10.8, 7.7, 12.4, and 4.6.

In the 1930's, and especially in the years from 1935 to 1940, prefectures whose economies were associated with light industry grew less rapidly than those with heavy industries and military installations. Since the transition of the economy was associated with the orientation of trade and transport toward the northeast Asian region, the Fukuoka area became increasingly important as a production center and a destination for migrants.

A broad pattern of internal migration persisted throughout the period from 1920 to 1940. If the twenty-year period is considered as a whole, eight prefectures gained by migration: Tokyo (31.2 per cent), Kanagawa (19.2 per cent), Aichi (11.6 per cent), Kyoto (7.8 per cent), Osaka (29.2 per cent), Hyogo (9.0 per cent), Yamaguchi (2.6 per cent), and Fukuoka (6.6 per cent). The other 39 prefectures lost population by migration. While the prefectures near the Tokyo-Yokohama conurbation lost substantially, major losses were most widespread in the peripheral prefectures, where distance and economic backwardness might have been thought to constitute deterrents to migration. The prefectures in northeast Honshu, Shikoku, and most of those in Kyushu lost heavily. The largest percentage losses were in Kagoshima and Okinawa, areas that sent migrants to Taiwan and Nanyo-gunto as well as to industrial areas in Kyushu and Honshu.

The migrations of the years from 1920 to 1940 were primarily industrial rather than agricultural. The frontiers were filled; between 1920 and 1940 Hokkaido had a net loss of migrants amounting to 8.7 per cent of its central population. In general, areas of increase were industrial, while areas of loss were agricultural (TABLE 50). Gain by migration was related to industrialization, whereas loss was related to the persistence of the agrarian society and economy. The migrations of men and women were highly correlated in areas of gain and in areas of loss.

Something of a realignment of migration patterns occurred. As the most industrialized areas reached great sizes, rates of increase rose for areas where industrialization was less developed. Increasing industrialization in intermediate prefectures provided employment opportunities within the areas, and so their historic contributions of migrants to the metropolitan prefectures declined. The withdrawals of population came increasingly from the agricultural regions of the country.

THE CONTRIBUTIONS AND LIMITATIONS OF MIGRATION

The migrations of the years from 1920 to 1940 were contributions to the preservation of the old life in the rural society and essential aspects of the creation of the new economy. This does not mean that those migrations which

TABLE 50

Net migration by sex, prefectures by industrial type, 1920-1940
(Net gain or loss per 100 mid-period population, intercensal periods)

Prefectures by industrial type[a]	*1920-25*	*1925-30*	*1930-35*	*1935-40*
	Total			
Metropolitan	11.8	9.1	9.8	6.2
Other industrial	0.7	2.6	3.2	4.5
Intermediate industrial	−4.1	−0.9	−1.2	−1.9
Intermediate agricultural	−2.7	−2.5	−3.3	−3.0
Modal agricultural	−2.7	−2.7	−3.2	−4.4
Peripheral agricultural	−5.5	−3.4	−5.4	−5.3
	Male			
Metropolitan	12.8	9.2	9.6	5.3
Other industrial	0.5	2.7	3.0	4.9
Intermediate industrial	−4.2	−0.4	−1.2	−1.9
Intermediate agricultural	−2.6	−2.7	−3.8	−3.3
Modal agricultural	−2.5	−2.7	−3.4	−5.0
Peripheral agricultural	−5.1	−3.8	−5.0	−5.8
	Female			
Metropolitan	10.6	9.1	10.0	7.2
Other industrial	1.0	2.6	3.4	4.1
Intermediate industrial	−4.1	−1.4	−1.3	−1.8
Intermediate agricultural	−2.7	−2.2	−2.9	−2.6
Modal agricultural	−2.8	−2.7	−2.9	−3.9
Peripheral agricultural	−5.9	−3.1	−5.7	−4.9

[a] Prefectural types as defined by the percentage of the gainfully occupied in agriculture, 1930: Metropolitan, less than 20 per cent; other industrial, 20-39 per cent; intermediate industrial, 40-49 per cent; intermediate agricultural, 50-59 per cent; modal agricultural, 60-69 per cent; peripheral agricultural, 70 per cent and over.

Source: References, Map. 8.

occurred were ideal for an equalization of economic opportunities and an advance in levels of living of all groups in the national population. An attempt to define an ideal structure would be rather meaningless, for migration was not an independent variable. It is possible, however, to assess something of the contributions and limitations of migration to the adjustment of population in the agricultural and industrial regions of the country.

An initial approach to the evaluation of migration is to glance at what would have happened to the population of the rural areas if there had been no out-migration. This is the postulation of an artificial situation, but it indicates the extent to which social and economic modernization in a situation of declining mortality requires migration.

The population of the *gun* in Japan was 45.9 million in 1920, 49.0 million in 1930, and 45.5 million in 1940.[36] The relative absence of increase in the population of the *gun* was associated with substantial transfers of areas from the classification of *gun* to that of *shi*, in addition to the movement of people from *gun* to *shi* within Japan or to areas outside Japan. Since incorporation of areas once rural into cities was primarily a product of the urbanization and industrialization that were occurring, it may be justifiable to assume that a condition in which there was no movement away from rural areas would be one in which there was no incorporation of parts of *gun* into *shi*. The increase in the population of the *gun* in the absence of migration from 1920 to 1940 then becomes the increase that would have occurred in the *gun* areas as of 1920 if fertility and mortality had changed as they did in the actual populations but there had been neither out-migration nor loss of area by incorporation.[37]

In the absence of migration, the rural population that numbered 45.9 million in 1920 would have reached 53.1 million in 1930 and 62.6 million in 1940. The actual *gun* population declined 0.7 per cent between 1920 and 1940. Without migration the increase during this period would have amounted to 36.4 per cent. In absolute terms, the actual population declined 336 thousand between 1920 and 1940. Under the assumed conditions of natural increase in a constant area, without migration, the population would have increased 16.7 million.

Direct migration and urbanization through incorporation were insufficient to prevent increase in the rural population during the 1920's. Specific percentage changes in the functional age groups are given here in comparison with those during the 1930's:

	Per cent change, actual populations of gun		
Age	*1920-1930*	*1930-1940*	*1920-1940*
Total	6.8	−7.1	−0.7
0-4	11.8	−16.5	−6.7
5-14	6.4	−1.3	5.0
15-19	8.8	−11.0	−3.1
20-64	6.1	−7.0	−1.3
20-34	9.2	−9.2	−0.8
35-49	−1.1	−6.7	−7.7
50-64	11.4	−3.3	7.7
65 and over	−0.1	−1.0	−1.1

[36] Nihon. Sori-fu, tokei-kyoku. *Nihon tokei nenkan*. 1950. Pp. 18-19. Okinawa is excluded.

[37] The *gun* population was aged from one quinquennial period to the next, using survival ratios from life tables for each census period for the Japanese population of Japan, excluding the six great cities of Tokyo, Yokohama, Nagoya, Osaka, Kobe, and Kyoto. The ratio of children to women at each quinquennial period in the projected population was assumed to be the same as that in the enumerated population of the *gun* at the same period.

Declines in the manpower available for employment in the *gun* came only in the 1930's, when the normal processes of the industrializing economy were re-enforced by military production, conscription, and emigration to the Co-Prosperity Sphere.

The increases of the populations of the *gun* in the 1920's were slight as contrasted with those that would have occurred if there had been no migration. Under our assumptions, death rates declined even though the population increase was occurring within a crowded rural society. The increasing population meant not only more laborers but more parents. Numbers of births and hence numbers of children increased rapidly. The aged increased also, for major portions of those who did not migrate at younger ages survived to become aged in the rural areas. The hypothetical increases in the various age groups during the decades of the 1920's and 1930's and for the period as a whole were as follows:

	Per cent increase, hypothetical populations of gun		
Age	*1920-1930*	*1930-1940*	*1920-1940*
Total	15.7	17.9	36.4
0-4	22.4	11.4	36.3
5-14	13.0	23.8	39.9
15-19	33.1	13.4	51.0
20-64	13.6	18.9	35.0
20-34	22.5	27.1	55.8
35-49	1.8	13.2	15.2
50-64	14.6	9.9	26.0
65 and over	1.6	9.1	10.9

Thus the exodus from the rural areas contributed to the reduction of the problems of the *gun* insofar as these problems were based on demographic factors. The rural areas and the agricultural population were only a segment of the total population of Japan, however, and neither were measured in more than approximate fashion by the population in the *gun*. The *gun* included settlements of appreciable size that were definitely urban, and they included large numbers of people who were gainfully occupied outside agriculture. An approach to the measurement of the role of internal migration in the redistribution of the national population may be secured on the basis of the classification of the prefectures by industrial type. Using the same techniques as hitherto, we can estimate what the populations would have been if there had been no net movement between prefectures of the different industrial types.[38] Given these expected populations, the differences between actual and expected populations may be assigned to net migration. And net migration, related to the expected population, yields rough measures of the differential influences of migration on the populations of the agricultural, intermediate, and industrial prefectures. The results concerning the migrations of men aged 15 and over are given at the top of the next page. The computations are limited to the relatively normal developmental period from 1920 to 1935.

Another approach to the measurement of the influence of internal migration may be derived from the relation of net migration to natural increase. There is little basis for questioning the assumption that Japanese agriculture should not

[38] These computations are approximations secured by using survival ratios based on the 1926-1930 life table for all types of prefectures. Since mortality was higher in the *shi* at the earlier part of the period, higher in the *gun* in the later part, the errors tend to be compensating. For the 1926-1930 life table values, see: Nihon. Naikaku tokei-kyoku. *Showa go'nen shichi-gatsu. Dai-yonkai seimei hyo*.

Prefectures by industrial type	Net change per 100 expected population, male					
	15 and over	15-19	20-34	35-49	50-64	65 and over
All Japan	−0.7	−0.6	−2.8	1.1	1.0	−0.4
Metropolitan	44.2	115.9	76.0	8.4	0.5	−1.7
Other industrial	7.1	14.8	13.7	−0.2	−0.5	0.8
Intermediate	−10.1	−20.4	−19.4	−0.1	2.5	1.5
Agricultural	−11.3	−19.8	−21.9	1.0	2.0	−2.8
Hokkaido	−4.7	−4.1	−0.4	−9.4	−10.5	2.7

have absorbed more people than were dependent on it in the 1920's and the 1930's and that the population dependent on non-agricultural employment in agricultural areas was over-abundant. If this is so, then economic adjustment would be facilitated if the net migration from agricultural prefectures was equivalent to more than the natural increase. Net changes by migration in relation to natural increase in the quinquennial periods from 1920 to 1940 indicate progress toward but not the achievement of this goal of stability or decline in the populations of the agricultural regions. Changes in prefectures classified by industrial type were as follows:[39]

Prefectures by industrial type	Net change by migration per 100 natural increase			
	1920-1925	1925-1930	1930-1935	1935-1940
Metropolitan	184	116	128	93
Other industrial	11	37	46	75
Intermediate industrial	−47	−11	−16	−30
Intermediate agricultural	−40	−36	−53	−62
Modal agricultural	−35	−34	−41	−70
Peripheral agricultural	−65	−40	−64	−80

Migration removed substantial proportions of the natural increase from the peripheral agricultural prefectures, but only in Okinawa did it virtually eliminate population increase over the twenty-year period from 1920 to 1940. In the modal agricultural prefectures, net out-migration was equal to little more than one-third of the natural increase during the 1920's and only two-fifths in the years from 1930 to 1935. In the years that followed the outbreak of the China War, out-migration was probably greater than natural increase. This was hardly a situation that could continue indefinitely, whatever its services as palliative for problems of population increase in rural areas.

It seems evident that migration even of the magnitude of that occurring in Japan in the decades from 1920 to 1940 was not a solution to the problems of an increasing agricultural population.

War: Reversal and Restoration

With the destructions and dislocations in the industrial economy that took place during the late years of the war, there were flights and return migrations to the rural areas. The metropolitan prefectures were left with only fractions of the populations they had had before the war and during its early and more successful phases.[40] Between 1920 and 1935, people moved out of agricultural and intermediate areas, into industrial and metropolitan areas. Migration maintained a relatively stable if not a declining population in the agrarian sections of the country. It allocated the major portion of the natural increase of the agrarian segment to the industrial segment. The over-all changes for the period from 1935 to 1950 seem to show the effects of industrialization in reverse:[41]

Prefectures by industrial type	Net change per 100 expected population, male			
	15 and over	15-19	20-34	35-49
All Japan	−6.4	−0.0	−13.4	−6.1
Metropolitan	−25.1	−10.1	−17.7	−37.9
Other industrial	−6.1	0.4	−7.0	−10.6
Intermediate	−1.9	1.8	−14.3	5.0
Agricultural	−2.0	1.7	−15.6	9.2
Hokkaido	1.1	4.2	−2.2	0.4

The differences between actual and expected populations in 1950 indicate major influences from military mortality and repatriation as well as internal migration. Within this framework of an unstable national population, net internal migration left the population more concentrated in the agricultural areas in 1950 than it had been in 1935.

It is difficult to segregate the influence of an altered pattern of internal migration from the influence of international movements and military mortality insofar as the male population is concerned. From 1920 to 1935 the patterns of internal migration were quite similar for men and women. If we assume that the patterns of migration would have been similar from 1935 to 1950 had not the ranks of the men suffered the losses of war, we can assess the extent of the reversals in migration that were the end product of the years of continental expansion, war, defeat, and limited restoration. The relations of the actual populations of women in 1950 to those expected if there had been no migration after 1935 are as follows:

Prefectures by industrial type	Net change per 100 expected population, female			
	15 and over	15-19	20-34	35-49
All Japan	0.1	0.8	−1.2	0.1
Metropolitan	−18.1	−13.7	−6.0	−30.6
Other industrial	0.5	4.0	2.5	−4.4
Intermediate	4.2	3.4	−1.8	10.5
Agricultural	4.0	2.0	−1.4	12.1
Hokkaido	5.9	6.0	5.0	4.5

[39] Basic data were secured from the summary volumes of the respective censuses from 1920 to 1940 and the vital statistics as reported in: Nihon. Naikaku tokei-kyoku. *Jinko dotai tokei.* Births were adjusted for malregistration.

[40] See particularly Chapter XVI. The restoration of migration to the six great cities, the metropolitan areas, and the lesser cities is noted in Chapter VIII.

[41] It should be noted that the major exodus of Japanese to imperial areas and the Co-Prosperity Sphere and the major mobilization of the armed forces occurred after 1935. The population of 1950 had been increased by the repatriation of civilians and the return of the demobilized army; it had been decreased by the mortality of the war itself and the associated excess mortality of civilian Japanese within Japan and in the imperial and occupied areas. For reference to procedures, see Footnote 38. The survival ratios utilized here were secured by interpolation between those of 1935-1936 and 1947-1948. See: Nihon. Naikaku tokei-kyoku. *Showa juroku'nen ichi-gatsu. Dai-rokkai seimei hyo.* And: Nihon. Kosei-sho, daijin kambo, tokei chosa-bu. *Dai-hachikai seimei hyo.*

Losses through excess mortality and gains through repatriation had been roughly compensatory for women aged 15 and over as a group, though there were age displacements. For the prefectures, however, there was substantial loss in the metropolitan prefectures, virtually no change in the other industrial prefectures, and substantial increase in the intermediate and agricultural prefectures and in Hokkaido. It appeared that net migration which had been leading to the concentration of increasing proportions of the population in the industrial areas was now leading to a reconcentration of population in the agricultural areas.

The distribution of the population in 1950 was that which would have been created by a rather consistent reversal of the currents of migration from 1935 to 1950. The underlying forces which had led toward industrialization had not been reversed, however. The net movement from agricultural to industrial areas had continued as long as the industrial development itself endured. When the industries were destroyed, there was a destruction of the economic basis for the pattern of population distribution. As industries were restored and cities reconstructed, the internal movements normal to the industrializing society reappeared—net exodus from the agricultural regions, net influx into the industrial regions. In 1947, the populations of the metropolitan and other industrial regions were depleted, while those of the intermediate and agricultural regions had been increased by evacuees, repatriates, and family workers. The internal migrations from 1947 to the present have been greater than those of the so-called normal years before the move into Manchuria and the beginnings of the war in China.

Estimates of net migration can be made for the three-year periods from 1947 to 1950 and from 1950 to 1953. For the earlier period there are two census counts and recorded vital events; migration is a residual.[42] For the later period there are direct reports of vital events and of migrations that involve changes of residence, population estimates themselves being secured by the addition of the components of change to the 1950 census populations.[43] The estimated rates of migration are as follows:

Prefectures by industrial type	*Net migration per 100 mid-population, annual*	
	1947-1950	*1950-1953*
All Japan	0.1	0.0
Metropolitan	4.6	3.8
Other industrial	0.9	1.0
Intermediate	−0.9	−0.8
Agricultural	−1.1	−1.2
Hokkaido	1.0	0.1

The urbanward movement from 1950 to 1955 was greater than in any previous intercensal period. Net migration per 100 mid-period population is given here for prefectures by industrial type for the prewar periods and for the years from 1950 to 1955:[44]

Prefectures by industrial type	*1920-1925*	*1925-1930*	*1930-1935*	*1935-1940*	*1950-1955*
Metropolitan	11.8	9.1	9.8	6.2	16.1
Other industrial	0.7	2.6	3.2	4.5	3.8
Intermediate	−2.7	−2.4	−2.8	−2.7	−3.9
Agricultural	−3.2	−2.8	−3.5	−4.6	−5.0
Hokkaido	−6.2	0.8	−1.6	−2.1	1.0

The patterns of net migration and their relations to the agricultural-industrial transformation of the country in the years from 1947 to 1955 were similar to those of the period from 1920 to 1940. These continuing migrations did not eliminate the problems of increasing populations in the agricultural areas of Japan. In fact, a century of out-migration had served primarily to prevent the rural population from increasing sharply. This was a major achievement, but it did not represent a sufficient adjustment in the industrializing society that had to attain some balance between population increase and economic opportunities within its own territory.

[42] Populations: 1947: Nihon. Sori-fu, tokei-kyoku. *Population census of Japan, 1 October 1947. Summary report.* 1950: *Ibid. Showa 25-nen kokusei chosa hokoku.* I. Vital statistics: Nihon. Kosei-sho, eisei tokei-bu. *Jinko dotai tokei.* 1947, 1948, 1949, and 1950. Part 1, each year.

[43] For reference to the 1950 census population and the vital statistics through 1950, see Footnote 42. Vital events and migrations for the years 1950-1951, 1951-1952, and 1952-1953 are given for the individual prefectures in: Nihon. Sori-fu, tokei-kyoku. *To, do, fu, ken jinko no suikei. Showa 27-nen oyobi 26-nen 10-gatsu ichijitsu genzai.* And: *Ibid. To, do, fu, ken jinko no suikei. Showa 28-nen 10-gatsu ichijitsu genzai.*

[44] For references to the census of 1950 and the vital statistics through 1953, see Footnotes 42 and 43. 1955 census: Nihon. Sori-fu, tokei-kyoku. *Showa 30-nen kokusei chosa hokoku. Dai-ikkan. Jinko sosu.* Vital statistics, 1954 and 1955: Nihon. Kosei-sho, eisei tokei-bu. *Jinko dotai tokei maigetsu gaisu. Showa 29-nen. Ibid. Showa 30-nen.*

CHAPTER VIII

Cities and Metropolitan Areas

In Japan pressure on the land, widening horizons, industrial opportunities and the lure of faraway places channeled migration from rural to urban areas. The changes in geographical distribution and occupational structure were basically economic, but the influences on the attitudes and actions of individuals extended beyond the economic sphere. People who had lived in the familistic and largely subsistence world of the *buraku* became residents of great cities.

The relevance of urbanization to social and demographic change presumably depends on the size and characteristics of the urban agglomerations that receive the migrants. Migrations from village to village, town to town, or city to city may involve reallocation without consequences other than those that inhere in movement itself or in a correlated occupational mobility. Movements between settlements of differing sizes constitute an adjustment continuum. In a culture with agglomerated rural settlement, movement from one *buraku* to another involves minimal economic and social adjustment, whereas movement from *buraku* to metropolis requires maximum accommodation. The experience of Japan suggests that this theoretical formulation of the social aspects of urbanization is a reasonable approximation to the historical relationships, and that the demographic correlates of urbanization were not products of urban life *per se* but of a way of living that departed sharply from familial and communal functioning in the *buraku*. It is for this reason that special attention is given to the cities of 100 thousand or more and, within this group, to the six great cities of Tokyo, Yokohama, Nagoyo, Osaka, Kobe, and Kyoto.

The Metropolitan Areas

The status of Japanese statistics is such that analysis of the metropolis must pertain primarily to 1930.[1] By this time the rapid growth of large cities was in process. In 1930, the 32 communes with populations of 100 thousand and over included 11.5 million people, almost 18 per cent of Japan's total population. In 1955, the cities of 100 thousand and over included 31.1 million people, almost two-fifths of Japan's total population.

The number of cities of 100 thousand and over changed in numbers over time. Smaller cities pushed up into higher categories; occasionally a city lost population. The growth that altered size classification came about in part through population increase in the old area of the city, in part through the incorporation of new areas.[2] The history of the 28 *shi*[3] of 100 thousand and over in 1930 reveals the role of area changes in the urbanization of the population, but it also suggests that the growth of cities within expanding areas reflected the reality of urbanization rather closely. Within their areas as of the respective census dates, 1930's metropolitan cities had a population of 7.7 million in 1920, 11.0 million in 1930, and 19.1 million in 1940, an increase of almost one and one-half times in a twenty-year period. A comparison of the populations of these same 28 cities within their municipal boundaries as of 1941 reduces the estimated growth to four-fifths in the period from 1920 to 1940.

It may be that trends of growth within the changing boundaries of incorporated *shi* exaggerate growth, whereas trends of increase within constant areas measure growth more precisely. Certainly the growth of population within specific areas over time is a more concise concept. Whether or not it is also more realistic appears doubtful in the light of the characteristics of urban growth in Japan. At any given time there was a substantial population adjacent to but not within the incorporated limits of *shi*. Some of the people who would soon become metropolitan residents through the fact of incorporation were living in satellite cities, while others lived in *machi* or *mura*. Similar processes of urban concentration were also occurring around lesser *shi*. This growth of populations around *shi* was one aspect of the redistribution of population generated by industrial development.

Although the numbers involved in the urban fringes and the outer sections of metropolitan areas cannot be estimated with precision, numbers in specific prefectures and economic regions were probably proportionate to the size of the populations in cities of 100 thousand and over, but with concentrations around the great cities.[4] If so, the metropolitan population indicated by the location of the *shi* of 100 thousand and over is an underestimate of the urban concentration that existed at any given time. The percentage distributions, as given at the top of the next page, allocate the population of all Japan and that of *shi* above 100 thousand, *shi* below 100 thousand, and *gun* to prefectures classified by industrial type. The data refer to the year 1930.[5]

In 1930, more than three-fourths of the metropolitan people lived in the industrial prefectures of Tokyo, Kanagawa, Aichi, Osaka, Kobe, Kyoto, and Fukuoka. It should be noted,

[1] The migrant status of the population of the individual cities of 100 thousand and over was given by place of birth within Japan by sex and age, but without place of origin in the separate prefectural volumes of the 1930 census. Nihon. Naikaku tokei-kyoku. *Showa go'nen kokusei chosa hokoku.* IV.4. Tables 7-9. The tabulations by age were presented in: *Ibid.* Table 9.

[2] The populations of the cities at the various census dates within the areas as of the period and within the areas as of 1941 are given in: Kojima, Reikichi. *Waga kuni saikin no fu ken oyobi toshi jinko, Showa jugo'nen kokusei chosa no kekka ni yoru.*

[3] Four of the communes of 100 thousand and over in 1930 were technically classified as *machi*. All were in Tokyo prefecture, and by 1935 all had been incorporated into Greater Tokyo.

[4] The standard metropolitan areas established on the basis of the enumeration of the population in 1950 support this conclusion. See: Nihon. Sori-fu, tokei hyojun-bu, "Establishment of standard metropolitan areas . . . ." *Statistical Notes of Japan*, No. 3, pp. 26-31. April 1954.

[5] Source: Nihon. Naikaku tokei-kyoku. *Showa go'nen kokusei chosa hokoku.* IV.4. Table 7, Individual prefectures.

Population group	All Japan	Industrial	Intermediate	Agricultural
All Japan	100.	30.6	35.4	34.0
Shi, 100,000 and over	100.	76.1	18.1	5.7
Shi, below 100,000	100.	22.7	45.1	32.2
Gun	100.	21.3	38.3	40.4

though, that almost one-fifth of the residents of great cities were living in prefectures whose economies were intermediate in type. The non-metropolitan urban population was concentrated outside the industrial regions of the country; more than three-fourths lived in intermediate and agricultural prefectures. This is a picture of the distribution of cities at an instant of time, however, and urbanization is a process of change over time. As industry developed in areas once agricultural, some of the cities that were local centers in 1930 attained metropolitan stature. Residential and industrial satellites of metropolitan centers increased in population and extended into prefectures adjacent to the industrial prefectures. The regional concentrations remained essentially as they had been, with slight realignments but without extensive convergence.

THE MIGRANTS IN THE METROPOLIS

The metropolitan centers were the destinations of the major movements of the Japanese. In 1930 the cities of 100 thousand and over included 4.4 million inter-prefectural migrants as contrasted with the 1.8 million they would have had if the distribution throughout the prefectures had been proportionate to the size of the existing populations. As the manpower needs of the great centers continued and even increased, local sources of supply became depleted and recruitment proceeded outward in eddies from the focal centers. The percentage distributions of the populations in the *shi* of various sizes and in the *gun* by place of birth illustrate the relations between size and recruitment areas. Again data refer to the year 1930:[6]

Population group	In Japan	Commune of enumeration	Another commune, same prefecture	Another prefecture
Shi				
1,000,000 and over	100.	42.0	4.7	53.2
500,000-999,999	100.	46.8	15.2	38.0
100,000-499,999	100.	44.2	27.6	28.2
Below 100,000	100.	47.4	32.5	20.1
Gun	100.	68.2	21.2	10.6

Urban growth through migration creates age structures that distinguish city populations from those of rural areas.[7] There are major differences among the age structures of various cities, however, for cities have characteristic developments associated with growth and maturity. A hypothetical cycle appropriate to the Japanese scene would be somewhat as follows. In a city long stable but currently undergoing rapid industrialization, most of the migrants consist of youth in their teens and workers in their most productive years. It is probable that males predominate among the migrants. As the growth of the city continues, the earlier migrants marry girls from their home villages and so create new migrant flows that tend to balance the sex composition of the population. The children of the migrant parents are native-born. Continuing accretions of migrants at younger ages are accompanied by an aging of the earlier migrants and an increase in the native-born population of the city itself. Eventually the maturing youth of the city are able to meet most of the labor needs. Migration declines; migrants become a less and less significant proportion of the total population. There is an approach to the normal age and sex structures implicit in the levels of fertility and mortality of the urban population.

The cities of Japan in 1930 were far removed from a stabilization of numbers and structures. Migration was occurring at an increasing rather than a decreasing rate. In this situation the proportion of urban people who were born in the city in which they lived tended to be related inversely to the size of the city (TABLE 51). In 1930, the stable were less common in the city of 100 thousand and over than in the lesser cities or the *gun*, less common in the city of a million or more than in the city of from 100 thousand to 500 thousand. There were some deviations in the relationship between size of city and the stability of population, however, for the proportion of the population born in the city of residence was greater in the cities of from 500 thousand to 1.0 million than in the cities of from 100 thousand to 500 thousand. The antiquity of individual cities and the degree of maturity in their economic structures were correlated with migrant history—and migrant history in turn was related to the increase of a native-born urban population.

The proportions of the urban populations born in other communes of the prefecture of residence depended on the demand for migrants in relation to the population available within the prefecture. Great cities could meet only small portions of their total needs for migrants from within the prefecture. Recruitment had to spread into adjoining or more remote prefectures.

Thus the migrant status of the populations of large cities reflected the interplay of historical development, achieved size, location with reference to labor supply and competing demands for that supply, and the social processes that structured migration. The native-born predominated among youth and declined in proportion to other groups as age advanced, only to increase in prevalence again in old age. Migrants from within prefectures were relatively few among youth, relatively constant in proportion throughout adult life. Inter-prefectural migrants were few among youth, increased sharply in the late teens and the early twenties, then stabilized in the major pro-

[6] Populations born in the colonies or abroad were excluded before the computation of percentages. For the source of data, see Footnote 5.

[7] The age structures of the various types of areas within Japan were described in Chapter IV, pp. 73-79. See also Chapter VII, pp. 127-129.

TABLE 51

Migrant status of the population in and outside cities of 100 thousand and over, males, by selected ages, 1930

(Number in specific migrant status group per 100 enumerated population)

Type of area	All ages	Selected ages 0-9	15-19	20-24	30-39	50-59
		Born in commune of residence				
Cities of 100,000 and over	41.4	82.4	34.1	25.4	22.8	27.3
1,000,000 and over	38.7	83.1	30.3	24.1	21.3	26.1
500,000-999,999	44.6	83.7	38.3	30.9	24.9	28.7
100,000-499,999	42.2	80.3	36.6	23.0	22.9	27.7
Outside cities of 100,000 and over	70.7	87.5	65.2	57.4	56.8	60.9
		Born in another commune, same prefecture				
Cities of 100,000 and over	13.6	5.4	15.5	14.5	16.7	18.8
1,000,000 and over	4.3	3.4	4.3	3.8	4.3	6.5
500,000-999,999	14.3	3.7	16.0	15.6	18.6	22.6
100,000-499,999	25.6	9.2	34.1	29.2	33.0	31.3
Outside cities of 100,000 and over	16.8	7.9	21.6	22.4	22.6	20.3
		Born in another prefecture				
Cities of 100,000 and over	42.2	10.9	46.0	55.4	56.8	53.1
1,000,000 and over	53.7	12.0	60.9	66.4	70.3	66.8
500,000-999,999	38.0	11.3	41.9	47.7	52.0	47.8
100,000-499,999	30.3	9.2	26.9	45.3	41.6	40.4
Outside cities of 100,000 and over	11.6	4.0	12.1	18.1	19.0	18.7

Source: Nihon. Naikaku tokei-kyoku. *Showa go'nen kokusei chosa hokoku*. IV.4. Table 9.

ductive ages of the thirties through the forties and even into the fifties.

STABLE AND MIGRANT CITIES

The demographic interchange between a metropolis and other areas cannot be subsumed completely under any simple theory of relationship among size of city, proportion of migrants, and areas of recruitment. Topography, cultural history, the specificity of labor demands, and military activities were basic factors. The complex demographic formations that resulted from the interaction of these factors may be illustrated by comparing the three most stable and the three most migrant of Japan's cities in the size range from 100 thousand to 200 thousand population as of 1930 (TABLE 52). The stable cities were Niigata, Shizuoka, and Sendai; the boom cities were Yokosuka, Yawata, and Sasebo. The slowly increasing cities typified the old Japan, with its service activities, its small industries, and its concern with local cultures. The highly migrant cities were associated directly with military activities either as bases or as production and procurement centers.

The three stable cities were quite similar in migrant status, for they were selected on the basis of the low proportions of inter-prefectural migrants in their populations. In the differences of their areas and types of recruitment, however, we see something of the demographic forces that perpetuated urban individuality and historic localisms.

Niigata prefecture lies along the Sea of Japan. Inaccessibility and low levels of income make it unattractive to people from other prefectures; dense population, poor land, and a difficult climate make out-movement attractive to those who live within it. There were two major alternatives open to people in the rural areas who wished another way of life. One led through the mountains across central Honshu to Tokyo; the other led to the city of Niigata within the prefecture itself. The migrant status of the population of the city of Niigata reflected both the unfavorable conditions in the prefecture and the economic limitations of the city. In 1930 the population was 125 thousand. Only 56 thousand were in-migrants, and of these only nine thousand were born outside Niigata prefecture. If we inspect the place of origin of the nine thousand in-migrants into a city regarded as uncultured in a prefecture regarded as backward, we find that the largest contingent, almost 1,400, reported the prefecture of Tokyo as the place of birth. Although the official statistics cannot document the fact, it is probable that the majority of these in-migrants from Tokyo were the children of earlier Niigata emigrants who had lived temporarily in Tokyo. The second largest contingent of those born out of the prefecture were 928 persons born in Hokkaido. Again there is a plausible explanation in terms of a return of earlier emigrants from Niigata rather than in terms of an attraction of the prefecture and the city to those whose cultural roots were elsewhere. Hokkaido was the historic region for agricultural settlement from Niigata as well as from other prefectures along the Sea of Japan. Presumably the parents of Niigata's in-migrants from Hokkaido were Niigata-born.

The movements from other prefectures into Shizuoka, like those into Niigata, were largely an aftermath of earlier out-migrations. The largest group consisted of persons born in

TABLE 52

Migrant status of the male population in migrant and stable cities, by selected ages, 1930

(Number in specific migrant status group per 100 enumerated population)

		Selected ages				
Cities	*All ages*	*0-9*	*15-19*	*20-24*	*30-39*	*50-59*
		Born in commune of residence				
Stable cities:						
Sendai	51.1	84.1	44.2	28.2	33.9	39.4
Niigata	54.9	85.6	52.5	45.2	34.1	35.3
Shizuoka	55.6	86.0	44.8	38.7	38.4	46.9
Boom cities:						
Yokosuka	25.5	79.9	24.8	6.3	10.3	9.7
Sasebo	28.7	78.7	27.1	8.4	10.3	9.0
Yawata	28.8	75.8	24.7	11.2	3.8	6.6
		Born in another commune, same prefecture				
Stable cities:						
Sendai	22.0	5.6	25.8	28.0	33.2	30.4
Niigata	36.4	9.2	39.7	43.0	53.7	57.4
Shizuoka	31.2	8.3	42.8	46.3	42.3	36.4
Boom cities:						
Yokosuka	11.0	4.6	11.5	6.2	16.7	26.4
Sasebo	14.2	5.9	18.9	12.1	19.7	21.9
Yawata	23.0	9.3	26.0	26.8	29.0	30.2
		Born in another prefecture				
Stable cities:						
Sendai	26.0	9.5	28.6	42.6	32.3	30.1
Niigata	8.3	5.0	7.3	11.0	11.6	7.2
Shizuoka	12.7	5.2	12.0	14.2	18.8	16.7
Boom cities:						
Yokosuka	62.6	14.7	62.8	87.0	71.1	63.5
Sasebo	56.1	14.1	52.8	78.9	69.1	69.0
Yawata	45.5	13.4	45.5	56.7	63.5	62.7

Source: Nihon. Naikaku tokei-kyoku. *Showa go'nen kokusei chosa hokoku.* IV.4. Table 9, Prefectural volumes.

the metropolitan prefectures of Tokyo, Kanagawa, and Aichi. Few migrants had come in from nearby agricultural prefectures; such rural migrants went to the great conurbations from which Shizuoka itself received back some of the children of its earlier migrants.

The migrants in the city of Sendai alone conform to customary views concerning the relation of distance to the size of migrant streams. Approximately one-fourth of the total population of the city of Sendai came from other areas within Miyagi prefecture, almost one-fourth from other areas of Japan. Major areas of recruitment were the adjacent prefectures, although there were lesser contributions from more distant prefectures.

The booming industrial-military cities of Yokosuka, Yawata, and Sasebo tapped the nearest reservoirs of manpower suitable for their needs. Knowledge of the existence of employment opportunities in such cities was widespread, and wages tended to be high. However, differences in the assignment of military manpower, variations in the types of civilian labor demanded, and the nearness of competing areas of attraction led to divergent patterns of recruitment among the three cities.

Yokosuka's migrants came from a great area that included Tokyo, the prefectures across central Honshu and on the Sea of Japan, and the prefectures of northeastern Honshu. Influx from the southwest was minimal. Sasebo and Yawata were located on the island of Kyushu. Here an overabundant rural population with inadequate outlets permitted heavy influx from nearby areas. Some 80 per cent of Sasebo's migrants came from the other prefectures of Kyushu, with a particularly heavy influx from adjacent Saga. Yawata was less favorably located for Kyushu recruitment and adjacent cities were also growing rapidly. The major areas of recruitment for Yawata were the neighboring prefectures of Oita and Kumamoto; Saga, Yamaguchi, and Hiroshima prefectures constituted secondary ones. Neither Yawata nor Sasebo recruited substantial numbers of people from the prefectures of Shikoku, and neither competed with the expanding orbits of the great cities of central Honshu.

METROPOLIS AND PREFECTURAL HINTERLAND

Urban expansion, suburbanization, and economic development created relationships between the migrant status of the people within a great city and those immediately outside it.

The convergence between the non-metropolitan and the metropolitan populations was related both to the size of the great city population and to the industrial characteristics of the prefecture, these two factors being interconnected (TABLE 53). Metropolitan centers in agricultural or transitional prefectures included high proportions of the locally born and small proportions of inter-prefectural migrants. In their prefectural hinterlands, from 75 to 85 per cent of all the people were locally born, while only from 3 to 5 per cent were inter-prefectural migrants.

The metropolitan centers in industrial prefectures were concentrated in central Honshu and in northwest Kyushu. Here two or more great cities in the same or adjacent prefectures were the vanguards of regional industrial developments that were also creating new cities. In the metropolis the locally born were relatively few, while the inter-prefectural migrants were numerous, if not predominant. The stable were far more numerous in the hinterlands than in the central cities; even in the periods of maximum migration the stable constituted absolute majorities of the total non-metropolitan populations in such industrial prefectures as Kanagawa, Aichi, and Hyogo. If the metropolitan hinterlands in industrial prefectures are compared with those in intermediate or agricultural prefectures, striking differences appear. Inter-prefectural migrants were proportionately more numerous in the non-metropolitan populations of industrial prefectures than in the metropolitan populations of agricultural prefectures. The formation of a metropolis was the terminus of a regional development.

Only limited inferences can be drawn as to the extension of urban ways of living, working, and thinking into the countryside on the basis of data on the migrant-status of the non-metropolitan populations of prefectures. The convergence of metropolitan and hinterland populations represents a lessening of the differences between the two groups, but that lessening is associated not only with the diffusion of urban patterns among the peasantry, but with the intrusion of rural patterns among city groups. In contemporary Western thinking, metropolitan and hinterland life are assumed to differ sharply as a conditioning milieu for the development of the individual, the formation of the family, and adherence to the ancient mores. Many students of the Japanese scene question whether the differentiation is as great in Japan as it is in Western cultures.

The extent of the coincidence between place of residence and place of work within the large cities substantiates the hypothesis that peasant and urban living were less differentiated in Japan than in many other industrial cultures. Major portions of the rural Japanese who migrated to the city found there a daily stability almost as great as that of the village. Even in Tokyo, 45 per cent of the men gainfully employed within the city reported their place of work as their own home (TABLE 54).[8] In rapidly growing industrial cities such

TABLE 53

Migrant status of the male population outside cities of 100 thousand and over in prefectures including cities of 100 thousand and over, prefectures by industrial type, selected ages, 1930

(Number in specific migrant status group per 100 enumerated population)

	PLACE OF BIRTH								
	Commune of enumeration			*Another commune, same prefecture*			*Another prefecture*		
Cities by type of prefecture	*All ages*	*15-19*	*30-39*	*All ages*	*15-19*	*30-39*	*All ages*	*15-19*	*30-39*
Industrial:									
Tokyo	28.6	19.4	11.8	22.0	24.5	17.8	47.3	53.3	68.5
Osaka	65.1	64.6	51.1	15.9	15.6	18.4	16.9	17.0	27.5
Kanagawa	71.7	65.6	57.6	14.2	18.6	20.0	13.0	14.9	20.3
Kyoto	65.1	59.4	51.0	16.5	19.8	20.8	16.0	17.9	23.5
Hyogo	71.3	65.8	57.8	15.5	19.5	20.8	12.1	13.4	19.4
Aichi	74.3	66.1	63.0	17.8	22.6	25.2	6.4	9.0	9.2
Fukuoka	58.3	53.7	41.2	20.8	25.1	25.6	18.6	18.5	29.7
Intermediate:									
Nagasaki	76.1	69.9	62.9	13.7	20.4	18.4	9.0	8.2	16.4
Hiroshima	78.2	72.2	68.9	15.4	19.8	21.8	4.9	6.0	7.5
Ishikawa	83.0	78.9	75.3	12.5	17.3	19.4	3.0	3.4	4.2
Hokkaido	42.6	45.8	13.3	19.8	32.6	19.0	36.6	21.0	64.9
Wakayama	75.8	70.4	65.2	16.3	20.8	23.3	6.4	7.2	9.2
Shizuoka	76.8	71.8	64.4	16.8	22.1	25.3	5.9	5.5	9.2
Okayama	77.2	75.4	67.4	16.1	17.2	23.0	5.8	6.2	8.1
Agricultural:									
Miyagi	79.6	77.7	67.7	14.7	15.9	23.9	5.3	6.0	7.9
Kumamoto	78.2	72.6	68.8	15.6	20.4	22.4	5.3	5.4	8.1
Kagoshima	85.0	80.1	77.6	11.4	16.5	17.1	3.2	2.9	5.0
Niigata	82.8	79.8	74.1	14.3	17.3	21.3	2.6	2.6	4.0

Source: References, Table 51.

[8] The figure of 45 per cent given here refers to the proportion of the total number of men gainfully occupied in Tokyo who

TABLE 54

Stability and mobility, male population of cities of 100 thousand and over, 1930

Cities by size	Per cent of men aged 25-29 born in city[a]	Per cent of occupied men working in own home[b]	Daily movement[c]			Ratio of day to night population[d]	Place of work or school[e]				Index of school attendance[f]
			Out	In	Net		Home	Elsewhere in city	Outside city	Irregular	
1,000,000 or more											
Tokyo	22.5	59.7[h]	19.9	48.3	28.4	123.0[i]	50.1	26.4	19.9	3.6	122.4
Osaka	22.2	45.9	21.4	26.7	5.3	104.1	39.7	33.9	21.4	5.0	100.7
500,000-999,999											
Kobe	20.4	32.5	2.9	3.5	0.6	100.5	27.1	65.0	2.9	5.0	108.3
Yokohama	25.5	42.7	14.9	12.8	−2.1	98.4	35.5	45.3	14.9	4.3	105.7
Nagoya	30.4	47.0	14.4	17.4	2.9	102.2	38.3	44.6	14.4	2.6	105.3
Kyoto	32.9	61.5	14.0	18.4	4.4	103.5	49.6	34.4	14.0	2.0	121.7
200,000-499,999											
Fukuoka	28.0	42.8	3.1	6.3	3.2	102.4	33.1	59.6	3.1	4.2	125.7
Nagasaki	28.3	34.9	0.4	2.6	2.2	101.6	26.3	66.1	0.4	7.2	117.9
Hiroshima	34.7	39.9	0.8	5.5	4.6	103.6	30.5	62.7	0.8	5.9	130.5
100,000-199,999[g]											
Yawata	5.9	20.2	4.6	3.8	−0.7	99.5	16.7	73.2	4.6	5.5	101.0
Yokosuka	9.5	18.3	4.6	6.4	1.8	101.5	16.2	78.2	4.6	0.9	107.2
Sasebo	10.8	19.2	0.4	2.7	2.3	101.8	16.2	80.5	0.4	2.8	108.5
Kawasaki	12.6	34.1	12.6	12.8	0.3	100.2	28.7	55.8	12.6	2.9	98.4
Moji	14.2	27.2	2.7	4.9	2.2	101.7	22.7	65.6	2.7	9.0	105.8
Sapporo	17.3	44.4	2.1	8.2	6.0	104.4	31.4	64.4	2.1	2.1	129.1
Otaru	19.2	38.7	1.2	2.9	1.7	101.3	29.2	63.1	1.2	6.4	117.4
Hamamatsu	20.2	52.2	2.4	12.8	10.4	107.8	41.4	52.4	2.4	3.8	107.7
Hakodate	22.4	34.0	0.9	1.3	0.4	100.3	26.7	67.6	0.9	4.8	109.5
Okayama	22.5	42.0	1.6	12.5	10.8	108.4	32.8	61.4	1.6	4.1	132.9
Kure	22.6	18.0	1.7	4.5	2.8	102.2	14.9	80.1	1.7	3.3	107.7
Kagoshima	26.5	43.0	1.2	8.2	7.1	105.3	29.5	61.9	1.2	7.4	138.1
Sakai	32.6	38.2	9.6	10.7	1.1	100.8	32.1	53.6	9.6	4.8	98.6
Sendai	33.9	45.2	0.9	4.0	3.1	102.4	32.2	64.8	0.9	2.0	137.6
Wakayama	34.1	50.5	5.4	15.7	10.3	107.8	40.5	51.3	5.4	2.7	111.7
Kumamoto	35.6	45.0	1.3	8.5	7.2	105.4	33.2	62.1	1.3	3.4	138.4
Kanazawa	36.2	46.3	3.4	5.5	2.1	101.7	35.6	59.7	3.4	1.3	126.5
Niigata	37.1	39.4	1.1	3.7	2.6	101.9	30.1	66.4	1.1	2.4	113.0
Shizuoka	39.9	56.6	2.3	6.1	3.8	102.9	44.0	51.2	2.3	2.5	111.4

[a] The per cent of males aged from 25 to 29 born in the city is an index of relative stability in migrant status as among the various cities.
[b] The per cent of the occupied men working in their own homes is an index of stability within the metropolitan center itself.
[c] Daily out, in, and net movements are related to the numbers of the night population who are either gainfully occupied or attending school.
[d] The day population includes the net balance of daily movements. The night population is the enumerated population as of the census data, which were *de facto* by place of enumeration as of 12:01 A.M., October 1.
[e] Place of work or school attendance is related to the total number of males gainfully occupied or attending school in the city, regardless of whether enumerated in or outside the incorporated limits of the city.
[f] The number of the night population attending school was secured by subtracting the number gainfully occupied (industrial statistics) from the number gainfully occupied or attending school. This was expressed as a ratio to the number of youth aged 6 to 13 in the night population, these ages being roughly equivalent to the ages of compulsory school attendance.
[g] Cities are ranked according to the percentage of men aged from 25 to 29 born within the city.
[h] The percentage for Tokyo is very high, since it related stable workers to the night population within an area of heavy net daily inflow. If home workers are related to the gainfully occupied plus the net balance of work and school movements, the percentage is reduced to 44.6. See Footnote 8, this chapter.
[i] This ratio for the 35 *ku* included in Tokyo in 1935 approached the ratios characteristic of the other large cities. In 1930 some one-half of the economic city was outside the incorporated city.
Sources: Nihon. Naikaku tokei-kyoku. *Showa go'nen kokusei chosa hokoku.* Place of birth: *Ibid.* IV.4. Table 9. Place of work, daily movements, day and night populations, and school attendance: *Ibid.* IV.3. Vol. I.

---

reported place of work and place of residence as the same. In other words, persons who lived outside the incorporated limits of Tokyo but worked inside the incorporated city were included in the denominator. In Table 53, on the other hand, the figure of 59.7 per cent of occupied males working in their own homes refers to the night population of the city. Persons living outside but working within the city are excluded from the denominator. For detailed data and definitions, see: Nihon. Naikaku tokei-kyoku. *Showa go'nen kokusei chosa hokoku. Jugyo no basho.* Vol. I.

as Yokosuka, Yawata, and Sasebo and in ports such as Kobe and Nagasaki, from one-fifth to one-third of the male labor force worked in their homes. And, in all cities, from 60 to 90 per cent of the women who reported a gainful occupation worked within the home. Thus for substantial portions of the urban people the familism of peasant life continued as the familism of the metropolis—the man, his wife, his children, and other relatives working together. Such concepts as the industrial labor force or the urban proletariat were not applicable to substantial portions of the Japanese who lived in metropolitan centers. The cultural stimuli of the city were limited indeed for the people for whom metropolitan life meant the persistence of economic familism.

transformations associated with metropolitan growth and the diffusion of urban values throughout the countryside. Analysis of these factors will be postponed for later and more detailed consideration.

The Great Cities

The population history of prewar Japan was in major part the history of six cities and their tributary areas: Tokyo, Yokohama, Nagoya, Osaka, Kobe, and Kyoto. The populations of the individual cities at the successive census dates between 1920 and 1940 were as follows, areas being constant as of 1941 and population being in thousands:[9]

City	*1920*	*1925*	*1930*	*1935*	*1940*
The six cities	7,673	9,134	10,811	12,785	14,384
Tokyo	3,359	4,110	4,987	5,896	6,779
Yokohama	579	595	704	797	968
Nagoya	620	784	926	1,110	1,328
Osaka	1,768	2,115	2,454	2,989	3,252
Kobe	644	704	788	912	967
Kyoto	702	826	952	1,081	1,090

The urban milieu became fully operative for the children of the migrants, however, if not for the migrants themselves. Children moved daily to school even when the activities of other family members were centered in the household. The wider contacts and broadening horizons of the children and the indirect identification of the family with the activities of the children diffused a leaven from the schools throughout all age groups. This acculturation through education occurred in remote *buraku* as in the *ku* of the great cities, but schooling of children was more complete in the cities and it extended over longer periods of time for larger segments of youth. Moreover, the stimuli associated with physical movement and social participation were more frequent and more intense in the city. The acculturation of the children of the peasant to the life and values of the metropolis in Japan merits comparison with that of the children of immigrants in the cities of the United States. It may be that the process was more efficient in Japan, because there were few barriers of language and culture between urban dwellers and peasant in-migrants.

In the smaller metropolitan centers in 1930, the incorporated city and the area of labor mobility were virtually identical. Bits of the country might be incorporated within the city, but there was little daily movement of laborers between suburban areas and central cities. As transportation developed and neighboring cities grew to become almost as one, commuting and inter-urban movements advanced. The localism of the smaller cities in 1930 was not a characteristic inherent in Japanese industrial development but rather a consequence of a technical lag in transportation that was associated with deep poverty, limited capital, and an abundant labor supply. Whenever physical facilities permitted, the flux of daily movements between central area and adjoining areas appeared in Japan.

The interactions between the peoples of the metropolis and the hinterland re-enforced the contacts associated with the migrations of people from the rural areas into the cities. The return of former migrants to the rural areas contributed further to cultural interaction between various groups of the Japanese population. The trends in age at marriage and in rates of childbearing are the most objective of the measures of the approximate extent of the cultural and psychological

Tokyo was pre-eminent among the cities. It was the center of government, industry, commerce, and culture; it was also the symbol of the aspirations and achievements of a nation. The residents of Tokyo were an urban elite to whom all other areas, even fabled Kyoto, seemed provincial. There were other symbolic cities in the East—Shanghai, Hong Kong, Singapore, Jakarta, and Calcutta—but no other had the diversity of functions and the concentration of interests that characterized Tokyo.

Yokohama was a small village of some 350 people when the last *shogun* of the Tokugawa *bakufu* designated it as an open port.[10] It grew rapidly as a trade and transport center for Tokyo, the Kanto region, and northeastern Honshu, and a major center for trans-Pacific movements. Its population reached 423 thousand by 1920 and jumped to 968 thousand by 1940, as industrial and military activities provided employment opportunities within the old city and in the industrial areas growing up on its periphery.

Nagoya, now the metropolis of the Ise Bay region, developed as a trading post on the Tokaido between Edo and Kyoto. Its modern expansion was associated with trade and service for its hinterland, the traditional textile and pottery industries, Asian trade, and strategic war industries.

Osaka has always produced substantial portions of Japan's manufacturing output, whether the handicraft articles of Tokugawa or the industrial products of the 1930's. Kobe grew as a port for Osaka, only sixteen miles away. Kobe was a center for iron and steel production, machine tools and heavy industry in general, including ship-building, motor and locomotive plants, and airplane production. By the 1940's, fringe developments and satellite cities had made Osaka and Kobe the nuclei of a conurbation that included such new cities as Amagasaki and Nishinomiya.

Kyoto symbolized the cultural and religious values of the past. Here the legendary memories of an ancient era had a reality lacking in Tokyo and Osaka. The production of

[9] Kojima, Reikichi. *Waga kuni saikin no fu ken oyobi toshi jinko, Showa jugo'nen kokusei chosa no kekka ni yoru.*

[10] Descriptions of the history, development, and prewar status of the individual cities are given by Glenn T. Trewartha in: *Japan, a physical, cultural, and regional geography.*

lacquer, porcelain, and brocades and other arts flourished in the twentieth century as in the sixteenth.

As political and economic activities in Japan became oriented toward expansion on the Asian continent, the emphasis on capital investment, plant construction, and military production shifted toward heavy industries rather than light consumers' goods. The most favored location for urban concentrations altered. New nuclei arose in the southwest, particularly along the Fukuoka-Yamaguchi passage into the Inland Sea. Here mining, iron and steel works, military production, and other heavy industries created a new conurbation. Six separately incorporated but contiguous cities developed in Fukuoka prefecture: Yawata, Kokura, Moji, Wakamatsu, Nogata, and Tobata. Their combined populations, 308 thousand in 1920, increased more than one and one-half times to reach 794 thousand by 1940. In Yamaguchi prefecture, across the narrow strait from this Fukuoka conurbation, Shimonoseki grew from 72 thousand in 1920 to 196 thousand in 1940.[11] This contiguous cluster of cities in Fukuoka and Yamaguchi prefectures lacked only ten thousand of reaching a population of a million by 1940 and surpassed it soon thereafter.[12]

THE IN-MIGRANTS

There were substantial differences in migrant status among the six great cities and among the great cities as a group, the satellite cities, and the prefectural hinterlands (TABLE 55). In the conurbations, as in the lesser metropolitan centers, the primary factors influencing the proportions of the stable and the migrant in the resident population were not only the size of the city, but its antiquity and the rapidity of its growth. Antiquity of growth influenced the extent to which labor force requirements were met by the native-born children of earlier

TABLE 55

Migrant status of the male population in the great cities, other cities of 100 thousand and over, and remainder of prefecture, by selected ages, 1930

(Number in specific migrant status group per 100 enumerated population)

Prefectures and cities	*Born in commune of enumeration*			*Born in another commune, same prefecture*			*Born in another prefecture*			*Born in Empire or abroad*		
	All ages	*15-19*	*30-39*	*All ages*	*15-19*	*30-39*	*All ages*	*15-19*	*30-39*	*All ages*	*15-19*	*30-39*
Tokyo	32.5	24.8	15.7	15.1	14.5	12.6	50.7	58.3	69.8	1.7	2.4	1.9
Tokyo	38.3	30.1	22.7	4.2	4.7	3.2	55.9	63.3	72.1	1.6	1.9	2.0
Remainder	28.6	19.4	11.8	22.0	24.5	17.8	47.3	53.3	68.5	2.1	2.8	1.9
Kanagawa	55.1	51.3	35.0	11.3	13.8	15.0	31.8	33.4	46.6	1.8	1.5	3.4
Yokohama	44.3	44.5	21.4	8.2	9.0	11.1	44.8	44.2	62.8	2.8	2.3	4.7
Yokosuka	25.5	24.8	10.3	11.0	11.5	16.7	62.6	62.8	71.1	0.9	0.8	1.9
Kawasaki	34.8	26.8	13.0	8.3	11.6	9.3	54.7	60.2	73.6	2.2	1.4	4.1
Remainder	71.7	65.6	57.6	14.2	18.7	20.0	13.0	14.9	19.7	1.1	0.9	2.1
Aichi	65.1	55.2	49.3	18.6	23.0	26.0	14.4	19.1	21.5	1.9	2.7	3.2
Nagoya	49.0	41.5	29.3	20.1	23.4	27.2	28.3	31.8	39.5	2.6	3.2	4.0
Remainder	74.3	66.1	63.0	17.8	22.6	25.2	6.4	9.0	9.2	1.5	2.3	2.6
Osaka	46.1	38.0	28.0	7.9	6.7	8.8	42.1	49.1	58.3	3.9	6.2	4.9
Osaka	39.1	30.5	20.4	4.4	3.9	5.2	51.9	58.4	69.0	4.6	7.1	5.5
Sakai	47.7	45.9	30.8	18.9	18.8	21.5	30.1	30.8	43.5	3.3	4.5	4.2
Remainder	65.1	64.6	51.1	15.9	15.6	18.4	16.9	17.0	27.5	2.1	2.8	3.0
Hyogo	60.9	54.7	42.6	16.2	19.1	21.3	21.0	23.8	33.0	1.9	2.4	3.1
Kobe	37.3	34.6	15.7	17.5	18.3	22.0	41.3	42.7	57.0	3.9	4.4	5.3
Remainder	71.3	65.8	57.8	15.5	19.5	20.8	12.1	13.4	19.4	1.1	1.3	2.0
Kyoto	56.2	43.5	42.4	12.7	14.0	16.0	28.3	38.4	37.3	2.8	4.1	4.3
Kyoto	47.3	34.3	34.0	9.1	10.6	11.2	40.5	50.2	50.8	3.2	4.9	3.9
Remainder	65.1	59.4	51.0	16.5	19.8	20.8	16.0	17.9	23.5	2.4	2.9	4.7
Fukuoka	53.9	48.3	35.2	21.1	25.8	26.0	22.6	22.9	35.2	2.4	3.0	3.6
Fukuoka	44.3	33.6	29.6	26.1	33.5	31.7	27.2	29.5	36.5	2.4	3.5	2.2
Yawata	28.8	24.7	3.8	23.0	26.0	29.0	45.5	45.5	63.5	2.8	3.8	3.7
Moji	32.9	34.0	9.6	13.0	14.3	15.6	49.3	45.5	67.7	4.8	6.3	7.1
Remainder	58.3	53.7	41.2	20.8	25.1	25.6	18.6	18.5	29.7	2.3	2.7	3.5

Source: Nihon. Naikaku tokei-kyoku. *Showa go'nen kokusei chosa hokoku.* IV.4. Table 9.

[11] Kojima, Reikichi. *Op.cit.*

[12] There were satellite and related industrial areas in both prefectures. The total urban population of Fukuoka prefecture was 1.4 million in 1940. Using constant areas as of 1941, the urban population of the combined prefectures equaled 1.9 million. Increase between 1920 and 1940 had amounted to almost three-fourths for the urban population, over one-fifth for the rural, and two-fifths for the total population of the prefectures.

migrants; rapidity of growth was a product of the size and nature of the demands for labor. In each of the six great cities, migrants were more numerous than native-born. Industrial growth had been most rapid in the satellite cities, however, and here the proportions of migrants reached very high levels. In Yokohama and Kawasaki migrants constituted from 85 to 90 per cent of all men aged from 20 to 29. Similar concentrations of migrants occurred in the rapidly developing cities of the Fukuoka conurbation, especially Yawata and Moji.

Short-distance migrants, particularly that measurable segment born within the prefecture, were predominant as long as the supply could meet the requirements of the expanding metropolis. Long-distance migrants met the deficits when that supply was exhausted. The proportion of the population drawn from other prefectures was directly proportionate to the size of the city and inversely proportionate to the size of the reservoir within the prefecture, both of these relationships being modified by the chronology of past growth, the presence or absence of competitors for the local supply, the specificity of the labor demand, and the traditional routes of migration. In 1930, Tokyo *shi* had drawn only one twenty-fifth of its male population from elsewhere in Tokyo prefecture. Nagoya, smaller, located in a larger prefecture, and without substantial competition, had drawn one-fifth of its migrants from its own prefecture.

The variations among the great cities, the lesser cities, and the non-metropolitan areas of the seven industrial prefectures were great, but all were more broadly comparable to each other than to the remainder of Japan. The growth of the six great cities and the Fukuoka conurbation was a process of geographical and occupational redistribution seldom paralleled in the history of other industrializing societies.

There is no direct information on the social and economic background of the in-migrants to the great cities. The most fruitful approach to the problem lies in classification of migrants by the characteristics of their prefectures of origin. The interchange between great cities or between industrial prefectures may be assumed to involve minimum adjustments on the part of the migrants, whereas the movements from peasant villages to great cities may be assumed to involve maximum adjustments. If these assumptions are granted, it is apparent that the extent of the interchange between the great cities and the industrial prefectures has great social and economic significance.

Substantial interchange of migrants within and between the industrial prefectures had already occurred by 1930. In no instance, however, was the inter-urban migration sufficient to cast doubt on the thesis that the agrarian-industrial transition was the major motif of internal migration (TABLE 56). Less than one-fifth of the inter-prefectural migrants in the great cities or the industrial prefectures were born in another of the industrial prefectures. Contiguity was the major factor involved in the specific interchanges that occurred. Tokyo and Yokohama stood in close relationship to each other, as did Osaka and Kobe. Yokohama's contingent of Tokyo-born was larger than that from any other prefecture; Kobe's contingent from Osaka was surpassed only by those from Okayama and Hiroshima. In both the Kanto and the Kinki, the port cities had drawn more heavily on the great metropolis than had the metropolis on its satellite city.

As late as 1930 people born outside the industrial prefectures were the major migrant influence in the greatest of Japan's cities. Such persons constituted more than four-fifths of the inter-prefectural migrants in the six great cities and their prefectures. Even in Yokohama and Kobe, where the interchange within the urbanized areas reached its maximum, three-fourths of all inter-prefectural migrants came from outside the urbanized region.

As the metropolis of the nation, Tokyo drew its migrants from all over Japan, but in both 1930 and 1935 some three-fifths of its non-metropolitan migrants reported a place of birth in one of the ten prefectures of central Honshu: Fukushima, Ibaraki, Tochigi, Gumma, Saitama, Chiba, Niigata, Yamanashi, Nagano, and Shizuoka.[13] Tokyo was the major outlet for the migrants from these prefectures. It absorbed 40 per cent or more of all prefectural out-migrants; in Chiba and Saitama the proportion went above 70 per cent. Outside this central core of absorption there were bands of prefectures that contributed one-fourth of their exodus to Tokyo. One migrant in each ten from the prefectures of Kyushu and the islands of Okinawa was enumerated in Tokyo. One-third of Hokkaido's emigrants were in Tokyo, one-seventh of Aomori's. Thus, while Tokyo's population was drawn from the nation rather than a region, the greatest relative contributions came from a belt of prefectures between central Honshu and the Sea of Japan and from the prefectures of the northeastern part of the country. The migrants from the more favored southwestern regions of the country were underrepresented in Tokyo's population.

The Tokyo-Yokohama area was a functioning industrial region insofar as internal migration was concerned. The largest group of inter-prefectural migrants in Yokohama were born in Tokyo. The primary and secondary recruitment areas for Yokohama were almost identical with those for Tokyo. However, both in Yokohama city and in Kanagawa prefecture there were appreciable numbers of migrants from Fukuoka, Nagasaki, and Kagoshima. The various prefectures of central and northeastern Honshu gave from 5 to 10 per cent of their native-born emigrants to Kanagawa. It is evident that the human materials for the great industrial region in the Kanto came disproportionately from the poorer and more overcrowded prefectures of Japan.

The cities of the Kinki grew primarily by migrations from southwestern Japan. In fact, a line drawn along the southwestern boundaries of Niigata, Nagano, and Shizuoka prefectures separates the drainage basins of the Kinki from those of the Kanto. Osaka drew substantial numbers of migrants from the prefectures of Kyushu and Shikoku, where the transportation routes of the Inland Sea facilitated movement. Kobe's area of recruitment was similar to that of Osaka except that its primary area was limited to the prefectures along the Inland Sea route: Fukuoka, Yamaguchi, Hiroshima, Okayama, Kagawa, and Tokushima. Kyoto's role as a cultural center failed to attract migrants from afar in appreciable numbers. Her major recruitment area included Fukui, Ishikawa, and Tochigi along the Sea of Japan. A secondary stream of people flowed in from the southwestern Honshu provinces that lay beyond the orbit of Fukuoka.

Nagoya was peopled primarily by migrants from Aichi itself and the adjacent prefectures. Gifu sent 43 per cent of its inter-prefectural migrants to Aichi, while Mie sent 26 per cent and Shizuoka 17 per cent. The prefectures that would have beeen primary and secondary recruiting areas

[13] The results of the special analysis on the place of birth of the population in Tokyo in 1935 are presented later, pp. 161-166, this chapter. See: Tokyo-shi. Rinji kokusei chosa-bu. *Kokusei chosa futai chosa tokeisho, Showa ju'nen.*

TABLE 56

The prefectural interchange among the great cities and their prefectures, 1930

Cities and prefectures	PER CENT OF INTER-PREFECTURAL MIGRANTS BORN IN		PLACE OF BIRTH OF INTER-PREFECTURAL MIGRANTS (NUMBERS IN '000)						
	The six prefectures	*The remainder of Japan*	*The six prefectures*	*Tokyo*	*Kanagawa*	*Aichi*	*Osaka*	*Hyogo*	*Kyoto*
The six cities	18.4	81.6	643	97	74	83	75	217	97
Tokyo	12.1	87.9	133	—	57	35	16	13	12
Yokohama	24.1	75.9	65	45	—	10	3	5	2
Nagoya	11.9	88.1	30	11	3	—	7	5	5
Osaka	23.2	76.8	290	26	6	24	—	167	67
Kobe	18.1	81.9	58	8	6	5	27	—	11
Kyoto	22.5	77.5	68	7	1	10	22	27	—
The six prefectures	18.1	81.9	1,079	166	174	135	163	294	148
Tokyo	12.0	88.0	317	—	151	71	36	32	26
Kanagawa	24.6	75.4	121	91	—	15	5	7	4
Aichi	11.2	88.8	43	16	5	—	10	7	6
Osaka	23.5	76.5	345	32	7	28	—	195	83
Hyogo	24.7	75.3	139	16	8	9	77	—	29
Kyoto	26.8	73.2	115	11	2	12	36	53	—

Source: References, Table 55.

for Aichi, had she needed additional migrants, were the major areas of flow to the conurbations of the Kinki and the Kanto.

Fukuoka was a new industrial area situated in an agricultural region far removed from the urban clusters in central Honshu. Thus the cities that developed in Fukuoka could absorb migrants in a manner more in accord with the geographic principles of migration that are based on Western materials. Migrants came primarily from adjacent prefectures in Kyushu and along the Inland Sea passage.

THE DISPERSION OF THE NATIVE-BORN

The exodus from the great cities and their prefectures involved primarily the redistribution of people within the industrial segment of the economy. Over three-fourths of the people born in Kanagawa, Hyogo, and Kyoto prefectures and enumerated elsewhere in Japan were reported in one of the other industrial prefectures. The comparable proportions were three-fifths for Osaka, one-half for Aichi, and one-third for Fukuoka. If we limit comparison to the six great cities and their prefectural hinterlands, we find that three-fifths of the out-migrants from the cities were enumerated elsewhere in the industrial prefectures.

The two-fifths of the out-movement from industrial prefectures which did not involve other industrial prefectures was in part a selective exodus of upper social and economic groups to administrative, professional, and technical positions in the less-developed areas of the country. In part, however, the out-migrants from great cities were children whose parents had failed in adjustment to the city. As a result of the play of these forces, the influx from the industrial prefectures into any given hinterland prefecture was roughly proportionate to the extent of the exodus from that prefecture to the great cities or the industrial prefectures.[14]

The influence of the mobile people from the great cities was limited by many aspects of the Japanese culture of the prewar years. The numbers of the returned urbanites were not great; substantial portions of them were the dispossessed of the metropolitan regions; the movement was more regional than national; and children returned in infancy could hardly be called urban in any meaningful sense of the term. Nonetheless, here was a process that contributed to the introduction of cultural leavens throughout Japan—even to far Okinawa, where three of each ten immigrants from the main islands had been born in the industrial centers of the Kinki and the Kanto.[15]

NET MIGRATIONS, 1925-1935

We have considered the migrant status of the populations of the great cities and their prefectural hinterlands on the basis of place of enumeration on October 1, 1930, in relation to place of birth. The analysis of the net results of these lifetime movements revealed much concerning the selectivity in migration and the relations of migration to social institutions and economic opportunities. Deductions from the migrant status of the population at a specific date concerning the course of migration and the characteristics of migrants are limited. There is no information on moves between birth and the date of enumeration other than the one simple fact of the coincidence or divergence of place of enumeration and place of birth. Hence it is essential to make some estimate of numbers and characteristics of current migrations. If we assume

[14] In general, a hinterland prefecture received in-migrants primarily from the conurbation nearest it. Northeast and central Honshu received from and gave to the Tokyo-Kanagawa area; southwestern Honshu and Shikoku interchanged peoples with the Osaka-Kobe-Kyoto conurbation of the Kinki; and Kyushu received from and sent to the developing centers of Fukuoka.

[15] In the area of Honshu below Chiba and Niigata and above Shimane, from one-fourth to one-half of all prefectural in-migrants had been born in one or the other of the six industrial prefectures of central Honshu.

that the people of a given prefecture or group of prefectures remained settled or did not cross prefectural boundaries in any moves they made, and that no people moved in, we can estimate the population expected at the time of the next census and attribute the difference between this population and that enumerated to net migration in the intercensal period. Computations of this type are presented here for the years 1925-1930 and 1930-1935.[16]

THE PREFECTURES OF THE GREAT CITIES

The net migration in the years from 1925 to 1930 and 1930 to 1935 involved the redistribution of the population of Japan between the prefectures of the great cities and the remainder of the country (TABLE 57). The seven prefectures—Tokyo, Kanagawa, Aichi, Osaka, Kyoto, Hyogo, and Fukuoka—were all areas of absorption. The net migration differed sharply from prefecture to prefecture, however, and it differed for the same prefecture from one period to another. Tokyo and Osaka were metropolitan prefectures in a rigid definition of the term. In each case a multi-million nucleus was surrounded by lesser cities. The needs for migrants were great, and local sources were limited. Influx was high; exodus, although substantial in relation to the native-born population, was slight in relation to the size of the in-migrant population. The rate of gain through net interchange moved upward sharply in young adult ages, tapered gradually in the middle and older ages, and remained high even in old age. Kanagawa and Kyoto prefectures were intermediate in the interchanges of the metropolitan prefectures and the lesser interchanges of the more diversified prefectures of Fukuoka, Hyogo, and Aichi. The magnitude of the cumulation was less and the age of maximum cumulation was lower, but the general patterns and relationships were comparable.

The patterns of net gain or loss through migration in the five years preceding the census of 1930 indicate that the great age of migrant cumulation was from 15 to 19. After age 25 out-migrants and in-migrants were relatively balanced, but there was some cumulation in most age groups. Variations as between prefectures followed the general typology established for the lifetime cumulations. In Tokyo, Osaka, and Kyoto

TABLE 57

Net gain or loss by migration, prefectures of the great cities and the remainder of Japan, 1925-1930 and 1930-1935

(Net migrants per 100 population expected without migration)

Ages	*1925-1930*		*1930-1935*	
	The seven prefectures[a]	*Other prefectures*	*The seven prefectures*[a]	*Other prefectures*
All ages	5.4	−2.2	6.3	−3.2
0-4	1.4	−0.4	1.4	−1.7
5-9	1.7	−0.1	1.5	−0.2
10-14	8.2	−2.9	9.3	−2.9
15-19	27.6	−10.5	38.0	−14.0
20-24	9.3	−6.8	11.5	−10.4
25-29	3.1	−1.5	2.9	−3.0
30-34	1.0	−0.5	0.5	−0.6
35-39	1.3	0.3	0.5	−0.4
40-44	0.5	−0.3	−0.3	−0.9
45-49	0.7	−0.1	0.6	−0.4
50-54	0.8	−0.6	0.9	−0.5
55-59	1.4	−0.2	1.8	−0.3
60-64	1.8	−0.0	1.6	−0.1
65 and over	3.4	0.7	3.6	0.4

[a] Tokyo, Kanagawa, Aichi, Osaka, Kyoto, Hyogo, Fukuoka. These seven prefectures are the same as the industrial prefectures defined as those with less than 40 per cent of the gainfully occupied population in agriculture.

Source: Age distributions: 1925. Nihon. Naikaku tokei-kyoku. *Taisho juyo'nen kokusei chosa hokoku.* II.4. Tables 4 and 6. 1930. *Ibid. Showa go'nen kokusei chosa hokoku.* IV.4. Tables 5 and 6. 1935. *Ibid. Showa ju'nen kokusei chosa hokoku.* II.2. Tables 5 and 6. Life tables: 1925-1930. *Ibid. Showa go'nen shichi-gatsu. Dai-yonkai seimei hyo.* 1935-1936. *Ibid. Showa juichi'nen ichi-gatsu. Dai-gokai seimei hyo.* Numbers of births and deaths: *Ibid. Jinko dotai tokei.* Appropriate years.

[16] The enumerated population in 1925 was moved forward by five-year age groups separately for each sex, utilizing the official life table of 1925-1930. Children under five were obtained on the basis of recorded births and deaths. The population thus procured for 1930 was the population expected at the census of 1930 in the absence of any internal redistribution. Differences between actual and expected would measure net migratory change if the age distributions and the recorded vital events were complete and precise. Comparable procedures were used for the period from 1930 to 1935. It should be noted that this type of estimate is not strictly comparable with the net migration based on place-of-birth statistics. The net intercensal population movement includes the total population, whether Japanese-born or not, and it includes accretions or depletions through inter-Empire or international movements. Since in the period from 1925 to 1930 in- and out-movement virtually balanced in both magnitude and composition, however, crude comparison is permissible.

the age patterns of the net migration from 1925 to 1930 reflect situations in which migrants were major constituents of labor forces developing within diversified and expanding economies. In the other prefectures, special factors disturbed the regularities of age and sex relationships in migration. Military forces stationed at Yokosuka and other areas in Kanagawa prefecture appeared as an in-migration of males aged from 20 to 24; Hyogo had a very small net gain in this specific group but a sharp increase at age 25 to 29, when military service was completed. Fukuoka's general pattern of increase was less sharply delineated by age, presumably because the factors of selection were different for mining and heavy industries. Aichi's recruitment for the textile mills and related enterprises drew girls aged from 15 to 19 into the prefectures for temporary employment, but failed to hold sufficient proportions of them to prevent a migrant loss at age 20 to 24, when contracts had been terminated and girls were returning home to marry.

The patterns of net migration between 1930 and 1935 were generally comparable to those of the preceding five-year period, although the rates were substantially higher.

THE GREAT CITIES

The net interchange between the prefectures of the great cities and other prefectures masks a greater mobility in the populations of the great cities themselves. Prefectures include industrial and agricultural areas, cities and villages, areas of absorption and areas of dispersion. Hence an estimation of net migration for the great cities themselves becomes essential, whatever the hazards lying in such estimation and whatever the artificialities involved in accepting the boundaries of incorporation as the limits beyond which movement becomes migration.[17]

All cities drew sizable net increments from migration at age 10 to 19 (TABLE 58). This was the basic peopling of the cities. Net movements at age 20 to 24 were influenced greatly by the military conscription of young men and the marriages of young women. Centers of heavy industry, ports, naval bases, and armament areas gained through the interchange of men in the conscript ages of 20 to 24, while other areas lost. Females in this age group continued to move into the diversified industrial areas and those where industrial employment for men was abundant and relatively remunerative; net increase was particularly high in Yokohama and Kobe. In the cities of traditional industry such as Nagoya and Kyoto, girls aged from 20 to 24 were returning to areas of origin in sufficient numbers to compensate for the in-movement of other girls for marriage.

[17] This aging of the populations of the great cities from one census period to the next to secure estimates of net migration was possible only for 1925-1930, when age distributions of the Japanese and appropriate life tables were available and areas could be made comparable.

TABLE 58

Net migration of Japanese aged from 10 to 64, six cities, 1925-1930, by sex

(Net migrants per 100 population expected without migration)

Sex and age	*Tokyo*	*Yokohama*	*Nagoya*	*Osaka*	*Kobe*	*Kyoto*
Males						
10-14	20.6	15.0	16.9	19.6	17.3	25.2
15-19	80.8	34.5	45.8	65.7	54.7	60.5
20-24	0.2	13.9	0.9	−1.6	11.0	−4.7
25-29	−23.2	18.5	5.6	2.3	19.6	−6.9
30-34	−22.2	5.4	2.8	−3.2	5.8	−5.6
35-39	−17.8	3.4	2.7	−4.4	3.2	5.2
40-44	−15.0	1.5	4.7	−1.6	3.7	−6.0
45-49	−15.1	0.2	1.9	−3.4	1.7	−1.4
50-54	−14.0	0.8	−7.1	−2.1	2.2	0.0
55-59	−14.4	1.8	2.4	−2.8	3.3	0.7
60-64	−16.1	2.8	1.4	−3.0	2.0	0.4
Females						
10-14	5.4	10.8	17.6	11.9	15.1	15.6
15-19	56.6	30.9	33.4	50.8	55.7	55.6
20-24	8.0	30.1	0.8	11.8	22.9	−2.0
25-29	−16.1	19.2	2.6	0.9	10.6	−5.9
30-34	−14.6	9.6	3.7	−2.1	5.8	−3.3
35-39	−13.0	5.8	4.3	−0.8	6.5	−2.4
40-44	−12.2	2.4	3.0	−0.5	4.3	0.6
45-49	−11.9	0.6	2.6	−0.7	5.3	0.7
50-54	−10.3	4.3	10.3	−0.0	12.7	1.1
55-59	−10.5	6.8	−2.2	1.7	8.0	1.7
60-64	−11.8	10.7	12.4	1.3	9.4	−0.7

Source: Life tables: Mizushima, Haruo, and Taniguchi, Yoshinori. "Roku dai-toshi, Tokyo, Osaka, Kyoto, Nagoya, Yokohama, Kobe jumin no seimei hyo." *Nihon minzoku eisei kyokai shi*, Vol. VIII, No. 1. 1940. Age distribution of the ethnic Japanese are included in this study.

Rates of net migration at ages above 25 reveal a widespread exodus from the central cities. A substantial part of this outmovement involved suburbanization and the growth of satellite cities rather than a return to the villages and agricultural occupations. In Tokyo, where losses were heavy and continuing, the area of the city at the time of the 1930 census was but the central concentration. Men who moved in each day for work or school were almost half as numerous as men who lived in Tokyo and worked or went to school there. One in each four of the men who lived in Tokyo moved outside daily for work or school. Hence Tokyo's migrant "losses" at age 25 and over may have reflected residential redistribution more than return migration to areas of origin. Irregular gains or even losses appear also in Osaka and Kyoto, but their magnitude is less. Since industrial development was concentrated in the inner cities of Yokohama and Kobe, net immigration continued in the middle and upper years.

The net gains or losses of central city and other areas within the prefecture were related closely to each other.[18] Tokyo prefecture outside Tokyo city gained substantially during the young migrant ages, although at a far lesser rate than the central city itself (TABLE 59). However, increase continued outside the city when the balance of movement within it became negative. The same age pattern of net movement existed in Osaka, although the growth outside the central city was less pronounced. In these prefectures, industrial areas outside the cities drew their own migrants from outside the prefecture at the same time that the inter-urban and rural-urban movements and return movements were redistributing people within the prefecture. Here the basic relationship between great city and the remainder of the prefecture was that of an urbanizing region.

In Kyoto, the areas outside the great city lost migrants in the ages when the central city was gaining them in greatest numbers, then gained migrants in the ages when the central city was losing them. Here the relationship of hinterland to great city was the rural-urban one of traditional Japanese society. In Aichi prefecture, the predominantly agricultural areas outside the great city contributed youth aged from 10 to 20 to the city of Nagoya. After age 25 both central city and prefectural areas continued to gain by the migrant interchange, although the rate of gain was lower in the prefectural areas in early adult ages and approached balance after age 35.

The migrations of women in Aichi illustrate the complexities of the economic-demographic forces that influence movement within an industrializing economy that retains its ancient social structures and its traditional industries. The population of the prefectural areas outside Nagoya contributed migrants to Nagoya at age 10 to 19, but these prefectural areas in turn gained by migration. The movements involved were those of young girls from adjacent prefectures into the textile mills.

TOKYO: CITY OF MIGRANTS

If Tokyo were but a large city in Japan, further detailed analysis could contribute little more to comparative demography than has already been presented. Tokyo, however, is both the greatest of the cities of Japan and a world metropolis. The experiences of Tokyo may furnish clues as to the outlines of the future in other regions of Japan, for Tokyo has led the demographic transformation of the nation. The role of migration to Tokyo in the industrialization of Japan may also be a portent of what will happen elsewhere as Asian peoples become integrated into industrializing cultures.

In Japan, as elsewhere, the growth of a gigantic city created problems of political administration and social welfare. National, prefectural, and municipal governments made many special studies of the population of Tokyo and the movements that created the city. The census of 1930 included materials on place of birth by area and by age; on place of work in relation to place of residence; on day population and night population; on daily movements by the occupations of the out-going night population and the in-coming day population. In 1935 the national census was a simplified one, but the city of Tokyo added two questions to its schedule, one on place of birth, the other on date of last movement into the city.[19] These data were published in great detail by streets and districts, and for the city as a whole.

A complete treatise on migration to and from Tokyo obviously cannot be presented in a study of many aspects of the demography of Japan. Instead, segments of the materials for Tokyo will be presented to clarify certain aspects of the patterns and selectivity of migration that are subject only to conjecture on the basis of the data available for other cities.

GROWTH AND REDISTRIBUTION WITHIN THE CITY

In the fifteen years between 1920 and 1935 Greater Tokyo increased its population 75 per cent, from 3.4 to 5.9 million. The rate of increase slowed, but the amount of the growth increased consistently, from 749 thousand in 1920-1925 to 905 thousand in 1930-1935.[20] Growth involved both the absorption of new migrants and the natural increase of the population within the metropolis. By 1935 the age and sex structure and the population composition were becoming those of a mature urban population. Increasing proportions of the people were living in ordinary households rather than in factory dormitories or other non-familial housing, and women were approaching numerical equality with men.[21]

The impression that urban populations are developed smoothly vanishes if one examines population movements within and around Tokyo. The Kanto earthquake of the early 1920's was a temporary deterrent to growth, but the trend toward a concentration of the nation's economic, political, and educational facilities in the Tokyo area was soon restored. The building of a modern transportation system stimulated the specialization of areas. Residential areas grew where previously there had been non-urban utilization of the land. The sex ratios of the populations of the individual *ku* mirror this progressive differentiation in the functions of areas within the city. The government, commercial, and industrial sections of the old city were heavily male; adjacent residential areas tended to approach a balance of the sexes, but the prevalence

[18] Since the number and the age composition of the population of the prefectures are not available by ethnic allegiance for 1925, it was not possible to carry through computations for the prefectures comparable to those for the cities as given in Table 58. However, total populations of the prefectures and the central cities are available by age for both 1925 and 1930, and for four of the cities there were no changes in incorporated boundaries throughout the period. Hence we are discussing here the net migration of the total population, Japanese and other, for the four great cities and their prefectures: Tokyo, Nagoya, Osaka, and Kyoto.

[19] The question asked "the date of last movement to live in the city." Tokyo-shi. Rinji kokusei chosa-bu. *Kokusei chosa futai chosa tokeisho, Showa ju'nen.* Special volumes for the individual *ku* of the old city: *Ibid. Kokusei chosa futai chosa ku hen, kyushi-bu, Showa ju'nen.* Special volumes for the *ku* of the new city section: *Ibid. Kokusei chosa futai chosa ku hen, shin shi-bu, Showa ju'nen.*

[20] Tokyo-fu. *Tokyo-fu tokeisho, dai-ippen: Tochi, jinko, sonota.* A comparable volume was issued annually.

[21] The sex ratio of Greater Tokyo was 1134 in 1920, 1153 in 1925, 1128 in 1930, and 1099 in 1935. *Ibid.*

TABLE 59

Net migration by age, four great cities and the prefectural areas outside them, 1925-1930
(Net migrants per 100 population expected without migration)

	TOKYO		AICHI		OSAKA		KYOTO	
Age	*Tokyo shi*	*Remainder of prefecture*	*Nagoya shi*	*Remainder of prefecture*	*Osaka shi*	*Remainder of prefecture*	*Kyoto shi*	*Remainder of prefecture*
Males								
10-14	20.8	19.9	17.4	−2.9	21.6	3.2	26.5	−2.1
15-19	82.5	55.9	49.2	−12.4	74.5	5.5	66.0	−7.4
20-24	1.7	41.2	2.6	−.1	3.2	9.9	−1.2	14.0
25-29	−22.7	21.5	7.9	4.2	4.2	18.6	−5.5	1.8
30-34	−21.9	16.5	5.8	3.2	−1.8	10.6	−4.5	5.5
35-39	−17.2	12.5	4.8	1.3	−2.1	8.4	−1.7	5.0
40-44	−15.2	11.7	4.2	.7	−2.3	6.3	−2.2	3.1
45-49	−14.8	12.8	2.7	.1	−2.4	5.8	−0.8	0.8
50-54	−14.2	13.9	2.7	.1	−2.7	5.7	−0.4	1.1
55-59	−14.3	15.0	2.5	−.1	−2.5	5.4	0.8	1.1
60-64	−16.1	16.3	1.3	.0	−3.0	7.9	0.4	1.0
Females								
10-14	5.4	19.7	17.8	9.2	12.2	7.3	15.9	1.6
15-19	56.9	47.9	34.5	1.2	52.8	15.1	56.6	1.6
20-24	8.4	38.4	1.9	−11.4	13.9	10.0	−0.9	8.8
25-29	−14.9	24.2	3.2	−2.3	1.8	5.5	−5.6	4.0
30-34	−14.5	14.3	4.2	.7	−1.2	6.0	−2.8	5.1
35-39	−12.8	13.9	5.0	1.1	.3	7.5	−1.8	4.5
40-44	−12.3	13.7	3.0	.4	−.5	4.8	0.5	2.9
45-49	−11.9	16.3	2.9	.4	−.1	5.8	0.9	1.5
50-54	−10.3	17.7	10.4	−3.2	.2	5.4	1.1	1.4
55-59	−10.4	19.1	−2.1	1.8	2.0	6.2	1.8	2.1
60-64	−11.8	21.3	12.6	−1.9	1.5	6.5	−0.7	2.2

Source: Life tables: References, Table 58. Age distributions, 1930: Nihon. Naikaku tokei-kyoku. *Showa go'nen kokusei chosa hokoku.* IV.4. Table 6. 1925: *Ibid. Taisho juyo'nen kokusei chosa hokoku.* II.4. Table 6.

of boarders and non-familial households meant continuing surpluses of men. Factory areas were heavily male in their early stages, but the proportion of women gradually increased until there was an approach to a biological relationship between numbers of men and women. Suburban residential areas contained a greater proportion of women than the total population.

MIGRANT SELECTION

In 1930, one in each 25 persons born in a prefecture of Japan other than Tokyo was enumerated in Tokyo. The movement toward Tokyo increased between 1930 and 1935 but the areas of recruitment changed little.[22] The primary recruitment area included all the prefectures in Honshu from Niigata and Fukushima to Nagano and Shizuoka. Secondary recruitment areas lay in northeast Honshu and in the prefectures between the Kanto and the Kinki; elsewhere the urbanizing prefectures and those on sea routes contributed substantially to Tokyo.

Since the physical and cultural life of Tokyo was so different from that elsewhere in Japan, adjustments would have been eased if the migration had been greatest where the social-economic distance was least. In the Japanese setting, however, the limitations of economic opportunities and the compulsions of the family system dictated heavier migration from the rural areas than from the cities. In 1935, the majority of the migrants in Tokyo were persons who had been born in *gun*.[23] In fact, in 1935 45 per cent of the total population of Tokyo had been born in the *gun* of other prefectures. It should be noted further that the majority of the migrants from *gun* came from the economically backward and culturally retarded regions of the country—northeast Honshu, the inner mountain areas, and along the Sea of Japan.

The migrants from various regions differed in age at migration and in duration of residence in Tokyo. They also came from regions that differed in social, economic, and demographic characteristics.[24] All migrant groups, whatever their origin, had the age structures characteristic of inter-prefectural migrants in Japan; few children, rapidly increasing numbers in the early productive ages, relative stability in the ages of maturity, slow declines as old age approached. However, the proportion of children was higher among the immigrants from urban and industrial prefectures than among those from rural and agricultural prefectures, regardless of the distance factor.

[22] The comparisons here involve Tokyo prefecture in 1930 and Tokyo city in 1935. Since all except a small portion of the total population of the prefecture had been absorbed into Greater Tokyo by 1935, the lack of comparability is not serious.

[23] Tokyo-shi. Rinji kokusei chosa-bu. *Kokusei chosa futai chosa tokeisho, Showa ju'nen.* Table 11.

[24] *Ibid.* Table 67.

Migration was selective of young adults in almost direct relationship to distance plus the socio-economic diversity of the areas of in- and out-migration. The proportion of the migrants in Tokyo who were in the late teens and the twenties was higher for the more distant prefectures, lower for the nearer prefectures. If we compare prefectures at a distance, however, we find concentration of the young greatest in immigrants from industrializing areas, least in immigrants from agricultural areas. Among the migrants from near prefectures, too, the young are somewhat more predominant among those from industrial areas. This would suggest that the old pattern of movement had been from agricultural to industrial prefectures, but that there was an increasing interchange among industrial areas.

The forces of expulsion, the hazards of migration, and the lure of Tokyo were not identical for men and women. Thus characteristic patterns of relationships between numbers of men and women occur in the sex ratios at successive ages for immigrants from specific prefectures. Rural immigration and that from a distance were more selective of men; urban immigration and that from adjacent areas were more selective of women. The sex ratios among migrants from the adjacent prefectures of Kanagawa and Saitama and the distant prefectures of Hokkaido and Oita illustrate the interaction of these factors, for Kanagawa and Hokkaido were industrializing areas, while Saitama and Oita were agricultural:[25]

	Adjacent prefectures		*Distant prefectures*	
Age	*Saitama*	*Kanagawa*	*Oita*	*Hokkaido*
15-19	1281	1080	1805	1173
20-24	931	774	2053	1146
25-29	951	872	1673	1048
30-34	971	918	1750	1050
35-39	1025	937	1715	1110
40-44	1058	918	1639	1027
45-49	1042	923	1677	922
50-54	972	874	1562	724
55-59	960	752	1411	802
60-64	848	710	1146	607

AGE AT MIGRATION AND LENGTH OF RESIDENCE

The migrants in Greater Tokyo in 1935 had come into the city at relatively young ages; 53.4 per cent of the men and 49.4 per cent of the women had been below age 20, while 83.6 per cent of the men and 82.6 per cent of the women had been below age 30.[26] Moreover, most migrants had been in Tokyo brief periods of time (TABLE 60). Migrants at ages up to 25 had arrived in major part within the preceding five or ten years; the modal age at arrival was the attained age. From age 25 on, the modal age at arrival was age 20 to 24, with subsidiary concentrations at ages 15 to 19 and 25 to 29. This concentration at the modal ages of migration decreased with increasing age; major portions of the migrants aged 60 and over had come into the city at age 45 to 49 or above.

A more precise picture is given by manipulation of the data on present age and age at migration to yield the age distributions at migration of the persons who had come into Tokyo during each of the five years preceding the census of 1935 and had remained in the city until the date of that census (TABLE 61). The largest migrant group each year was aged from 15 to 19; the major ages of migration, more carefully defined, were those from from 12 to 24. The range was somewhat narrower for women than for men, but the age pattern was similar.

Previous analysis of the numbers of the in-migrants in relation to the numbers of the native-born indicated the magnitude of the problems of economic adaptation and social adjustment involved in a situation where the migrants outnumbered the native-born. The data for Tokyo on the length of residence of the migrants in the city indicate that measurement of the difficulties of acculturation on the basis of migrants present in a city at a given time is superficial. One-sixth of Tokyo's migrants had been in the city less than a year; two-fifths had been there less than five years. Less than one-fourth had been in Tokyo fifteen years or more.

We will attempt later to follow the movements of the migrants after they have entered the great city. Now it is necessary to approach directly the problem of return migration, or, in broader terms, the extent of the population flux whose residue is the migrant population at the instant of an enumerative census.

MIGRANTS AND MIGRANT RESIDUES

The out-movement of earlier migrants from Tokyo was substantial indeed.[27] The survivors of the in-migrant group of 1930 present in 1935 were only two-thirds the number expected if death had been the only factor involved in removal (TABLE 62). One-third of the expected migrants had been removed by net out-migration. Out-migration was highly selective as to age, however, and the selection was comparable to that in immigration, except that the group of maximum movement was slightly older. Both the contribution of the migrants to the urban population of 1930 and the proportionate losses of such migrants by 1935 were greatest in the age groups from 15 to 30. For both men and women, the cumulation of a migrant population involved a very substantial replacement of individual migrants by other migrants.

The magnitude of the movements involved in the continuing formation of the Tokyo population is far greater than that indicated by net losses of earlier migrants during a five-year period. Almost 600 thousand of the 1.3 million migrants gained between 1930 and 1935 had entered the city during the year preceding the census. It is not possible to multiply this figure of 600 thousand by five and conclude that 3.0 million separate migrants had entered the city to produce the net residue of 1.2 million migrants who had last entered it sometime within the preceding five years. Some entered the city more than once, while others entered after 1930 and left before 1935, thus failing to be recorded in either census.[28] It is plain, though, that the movements involved in the development of a city are far more numerous than those measured in the population at a given time.

THE MIGRANT IN THE CITY

The move to the city was often an intermediate rather than a terminal migration. Subsequent moves within the city are concealed in most statistics, for cities are considered as units. For Tokyo, however, there is information on migrants in each

[25] References, footnote 19.

[26] *Ibid.* Table 68. This tabulation of immigrants by age of arrival includes the returned native-born.

[27] Since we know the number of migrants in Tokyo in 1935 who had last entered the city more than five years before, the estimation of migrant losses from the 1930 in-migrants involves only the computation of expected deaths in the period from 1930 to 1935.

[28] See: Toyoura, Senkichi. "Tokyo-shi ni okeru jinko koshin no ryo to shitsu." *Shakai seisaku jiho*, No. 223, pp. 48-65; No. 224, pp. 69-82; No. 225, pp. 41-64. April, May, and June, 1939.

TABLE 60

In-migrants in Greater Tokyo in 1935, by present age and age at arrival, age 0 to 44

Age in 1935	*Total*	*Age at Arrival* 0-4	5-9	10-14	15-19	20-24	25-29	30-34	35-39	40-44
					Number (in '000)					
Total	3,074	229	153	441	755	656	328	177	108	72
0-4	49	49								
5-9	84	56	28							
10-14	171	50	36	86						
15-19	450	27	28	146	249					
20-24	496	16	19	69	191	201				
25-29	410	10	12	44	107	148	88			
30-34	351	8	9	30	74	110	75	45		
35-39	278	4	7	22	43	73	60	42	26	
40-44	212	3	4	16	31	41	38	34	27	18
45-49	175	2	3	10	24	32	24	22	23	20
50-54	135	2	2	7	14	23	18	13	13	15
55-59	105	1	2	5	10	13	14	10	8	9
60-64	69	1	1	3	5	7	6	7	5	5
65-69	45	0	1	1	4	4	3	3	3	3
70-74	25	0	0	1	1	2	2	1	1	2
75-79	12	0	0	0	1	1	1	1	1	0
80 and over	7	0	0	0	0	0	0	0	0	0
					Per cent					
Total	100.	7.4	5.0	14.4	24.6	21.4	10.7	5.8	3.5	2.3
0-4	100.	100.0								
5-9	100.	66.5	33.5							
10-14	100.	29.0	20.9	50.1						
15-19	100.	5.9	6.2	32.5	55.4					
20-24	100.	3.3	3.8	13.9	38.4	40.6				
25-29	100.	2.5	3.0	10.7	26.1	36.2	21.5			
30-34	100.	2.2	2.7	8.6	21.1	31.3	21.4	12.7		
35-39	100.	1.5	2.5	8.1	15.5	26.3	21.4	15.3	9.4	
40-44	100.	1.3	1.8	7.7	14.9	19.4	18.1	15.9	12.6	8.3
45-49	100.	1.3	1.7	5.7	13.9	18.5	13.6	12.7	13.1	11.4
50-54	100.	1.4	1.8	5.2	10.3	17.2	13.2	9.8	9.9	11.2
55-59	100.	1.0	2.1	4.4	8.9	12.3	12.9	9.4	8.0	8.6
60-64	100.	1.4	1.6	4.4	7.9	10.0	8.3	9.6	7.6	7.0
65-69	100.	1.0	1.6	3.0	8.7	8.9	6.9	6.0	7.3	6.5
70-74	100.	.4	1.4	2.8	6.0	9.7	6.5	5.3	4.8	6.3
75-79	100.	.3	.7	2.7	5.7	6.4	7.3	4.7	4.2	4.0
80 and over	100.	.4	.4	1.6	5.1	6.4	5.0	5.2	3.9	3.6

Source: Tokyo-shi. Rinji kokusei chosa-bu. *Kokusei chosa futai chosa tokeisho, Showa ju'nen.* Table 18. Return migrants (individuals born in Tokyo and returning to it) are excluded from this tabulation.

of the 35 *ku* that composed the greater city in 1935.[29] And the tabulations of place of residence by place of birth are carried one step further downward than elsewhere in Japan; there is information on *ku* of residence by *ku* of birth for those born in the city.

Most of the relationships among migrant status, sex, and age structures that characterized the 47 prefectures also applied to the 35 *ku* of Tokyo. Stable populations, defined as those living within the *ku* of birth, were weighted with children. Women were more migratory than men within the city, for marriage involved movement to the house of the husband and hence frequently a crossing of the boundaries of a *ku*. While the migrants dominated the demographic structure of all *ku* in the city, they were most prevalent in the central business and industrial areas, least prevalent in the agricultural periphery of the city. People born in the city remained in the *ku* in which they were born if that *ku* possessed generally high income levels; they left the *ku* of birth if it were characterized by low income, agricultural and

[29] The descriptions that follow are based primarily on analysis of the data on the migrant status of the populations of the *ku* in: Tokyo-shi. Rinji kokusei chosa-bu. *Kokusei chosa futai chosa tokeisho, Showa ju'nen.*

TABLE 61

Age at last migration in relation to present age, selected ages at migration, Tokyo, 1935, by sex

Age at migration	RELATION OF AGE AT MIGRATION TO AGE IN 1935				
	Same age	*One year less*	*Two years less*	*Three years less*	*Four years less*
			Males		
Total	174,475	185,663	129,025	105,919	83,341
0-4	6,937	8,657	7,120	6,421	5,732
5-9	4,053	5,746	4,672	4,300	3,810
10-14	25,865	35,817	24,833	21,045	16,917
15-19	47,839	49,721	35,490	27,550	20,877
20-24	42,923	38,579	23,913	18,356	13,188
25-29	20,581	18,895	12,338	10,096	7,843
30-34	9,407	9,886	7,204	6,095	4,802
35-39	5,402	5,752	4,271	3,664	3,165
40-44	3,389	3,778	2,767	2,668	2,297
45-49	2,608	2,818	2,111	1,919	1,669
50-54	1,749	2,037	1,502	1,474	1,221
55-59	1,471	1,619	1,198	1,048	806
60-64	955	1,063	732	654	523
65-69	628	714	478	374	306
70-74	412	345	233	166	119
75-79	172	177	122	69	58
80-84	68	49	39	17	8
85 and over	16	10	2	3	—
			Females		
Total	148,251	161,904	109,653	89,121	72,908
0-4	6,952	8,555	6,903	6,183	5,556
5-9	4,086	5,516	4,469	4,183	3,594
10-14	16,398	20,675	12,680	9,671	7,247
15-19	49,821	51,080	32,050	24,372	18,657
20-24	35,737	36,864	24,723	19,905	16,945
25-29	12,305	13,744	9,777	8,223	6,788
30-34	5,969	6,760	5,164	4,490	3,834
35-39	3,390	4,141	3,322	2,867	2,458
40-44	2,514	2,924	2,331	2,227	1,909
45-49	2,351	2,663	1,967	1,770	1,585
50-54	2,156	2,573	1,846	1,693	1,454
55-59	2,251	2,301	1,637	1,377	1,170
60-64	1,778	1,694	1,221	1,035	791
65-69	1,329	1,251	849	582	512
70-74	693	641	385	304	253
75-79	320	350	237	181	115
80-84	144	141	77	49	32
85 and over	57	31	15	9	8

Source: References, Table 60.

manual occupations, and other attributes of backwardness. Forty per cent or more of the men aged from 15 to 59 who had been born in commercial and industrial *ku* remained in the *ku* of birth, while in the areas of household production only one-fifth or so of the native-born of the *ku* remained there. But in the congested slums of the Old City and the agricultural areas of the Outer City, from 50 to 60 per cent of men aged from 15 to 59 remained in the *ku* in which they had been born. Stability or migration based on knowledge of opportunity and ability to take advantage of it characterized the native-born of the more prosperous *ku* and those intermediate in the economic structure. The stability of poverty characterized the *ku* of the city where need was greatest, just as it did the most isolated of the prefectures.

The movements of the native-born among the *ku* corroborate the evidence from migrant status that internal movements involved a selective redistribution rather comparable to that occurring in Western cities. In the period prior to 1935 there

TABLE 62

Inter-prefectural migrants as of 1930, enumerated in Tokyo in 1935

Age	Number in 1930[a]	NUMBER IN 1935		NET LOSS BY MIGRATION 1930-1935		FACTORS IN IMMIGRANT DISAPPEARANCE (PER CENT)		
		Expected	Enumerated[a]	Number	Per cent of expected	Total	Death	Net migration
				Male				
Total	1,496	1,405	939	−466	−33.2	100.	16.3	83.7
0-4	30	—	—	—	—	—	—	—
5-9	50	28	16	−12	−44.2	100.	12.4	87.6
10-14	80	49	34	−15	−30.8	100.	4.9	95.1
15-19	227	78	48	−30	−38.3	100.	5.4	94.6
20-24	253	220	102	−118	−53.7	100.	6.1	93.9
25-29	212	245	126	−118	−48.1	100.	6.6	93.4
30-34	164	206	141	−65	−31.5	100.	9.4	90.6
35-39	133	158	125	−34	−21.2	100.	14.6	85.4
40-44	102	127	99	−28	−22.0	100.	17.2	82.8
45-49	84	96	82	−13	−14.0	100.	32.2	67.8
50-54	59	76	62	−15	−19.3	100.	34.4	65.6
55-59	45	51	46	−6	−11.5	100.	57.3	42.7
60-64	27	36	28	−8	−22.2	100.	50.2	49.8
65 and over	30	35	30	−5	−13.3	100.	82.6	17.4
				Female				
Total	1,217	1,143	807	−336	−29.4	100.	18.0	82.0
0-4	29	—	—	—	—	—	—	—
5-9	49	27	15	−12	−44.7	100.	12.4	87.6
10-14	66	48	32	−15	−32.0	100.	5.9	94.1
15-19	168	65	37	−27	−42.3	100.	5.9	94.1
20-24	189	162	69	−94	−57.6	100.	5.9	94.1
25-29	170	182	112	−70	−38.4	100.	8.9	91.1
30-34	130	164	127	−37	−22.7	100.	14.8	85.2
35-39	100	125	104	−21	−16.8	100.	20.4	79.6
40-44	80	96	80	−16	−16.6	100.	22.0	78.0
45-49	68	76	67	−9	−12.3	100.	29.7	70.3
50-54	52	64	53	−11	−16.8	100.	28.3	71.7
55-59	43	47	42	−6	−12.3	100.	42.3	57.7
60-64	29	38	28	−10	−26.2	100.	32.3	67.7
65 and over	44	49	41	−8	−16.9	100.	73.5	26.5

[a] This comparison involves inter-prefectural migrants in Tokyo prefecture in 1930 and Japan-born in-migrants in Greater Tokyo in 1935. The error is not large, for in 1935 only 59 thousand of Tokyo's in-migrants were born in Tokyo prefecture outside Greater Tokyo. It may be assumed that these would be approximately balanced by the inter-prefectural migrants in Tokyo prefecture outside Tokyo city in 1935 and so eliminated from the census of the city.

Source: References, Table 60, for migrant status and migrant survivors in 1935. 1930 population by migrant status: Nihon. Naikaku tokei-kyoku. *Showa go'nen kokusei chosa hokoku.* IV.4. Volume for Tokyo, Table 9. Life table: Mizushima, Haruo, *et al.* "Fu ken betsu seimei hyo, dai-nikai." *Chosen igakkai zasshi,* 29(9):1767-1803. September 1939.

was heavy movement outward from the central city, and the favored direction of movement for those with resources adequate to permit choice was to the western *ku* of the new city. The central governmental *ku* of Kojimachi retained only 30 per cent of its native-born who remained in Tokyo; out-migrants went primarily to residential areas, some in the western section of the old city, others in the western section of the new city. Other *ku* in the central area sent out comparable proportions of their native-born, but the movements were more diffused. Each of the business *ku* sent some 15 per cent of its native-born out-migrants to the prestige residential *ku* in the western areas, but the major concentration of the emigrants was in factory and residential areas adjacent to the *ku* of origin. In general, short-distance migration predominated in the movements within the city as in those within the nation.

The out-movements from the *ku* outside the central area were also highly selective. The amusement *ku* of Asakusa sent its migrants to the low-income family-factory areas to the north and east. The higher-income residential *ku* of Suginami retained 78 per cent of its native-born; those who left were scattered through the western areas, with small numbers in the low-income residential and factory areas of the city. The factory *ku* east and north of the central city sent their native-born into the northeastern *ku* that had once been agricultural. The native-born of the agricultural *ku* migrated in relatively small numbers; those who did so moved outward to the adjacent factory areas. The out-movements from Katsushika *ku* may be cited as illustrative. Only one-fourth of the native-born who remained in Tokyo lived outside the *ku* of birth. Half of these migrants were in adjacent agricultural *ku*, and one-fifth were in adjacent factory *ku*, but one-twentieth were in the fashionable western *ku*.

The internal redistribution of the native-born and the migrant within Tokyo could be examined in more detail and at greater depth. The major conclusion becomes more firmly documented as additional analysis is made. The people within Tokyo moved from areas of lower to areas of higher income, from areas of crowding and poverty to areas where the conditions of living were superior and the prestige of the address was greater. Most moves involved steps in an upward movement rather than broad jumps from slums to prestige areas. This is a Western type of city formation and a Western type of internal redistribution. Comparability is valid only on a rather broad level, however, for migration is defined on the basis of the relationship between place and date of birth and present residence or between place and date of last migration into the city and present residence. There are no clues here as to the pattern of life in the great city and the extent to which it differed from that in the lesser cities or the villages. Since these are the critical aspects of the urban movement insofar as demographic consequences are concerned, it is fortunate indeed that the city of Tokyo has been interested in the daily movements of its people.[30] Hence we can assess not only mobility but the stability of the peasant society that permeated the social and economic structure of the greatest of Japan's cities.

DAILY MOVEMENTS

The essential difference between the dense agglomeration of individuals that is rural and the dense agglomeration that is urban lies in the occupational differentiation of the labor force and the functional specialization of geographic areas. This heterogeneity involves the dependent population as well as the gainfully occupied; it involves ways of living as well as ways of working. Specialization and localization can co-exist only if there is substantial daily movement of individuals. This mobility removes the worker from the family, alters the routines and responsibilities of women, and influences parent-child relations. If the labor in the city is that of the household industry or the small shop, the urban environment has many of the characteristics of the rural area. The days are passed with limited contacts; husband, wife, and children labor together much as they might in a village.

The industrial composition of the gainfully occupied populations of the various *ku* of Tokyo indicates substantial specialization. The central *ku* of Kojimachi and Nihonbashi were the trade and fiscal centers of the city. There were gradients of specialization out from the central area of the city but the lines were blurred. Workers in commerce, transportation, public service and the professions, and domestic service showed slight concentrations. It should be noted, however, that these are characteristics of the night populations of the *ku*. Allocation to place of enumeration at midnight means place of sleep rather than place of work. For analysis of the economic specialization of areas we need the numbers and the characteristics of the people who work in specific areas, and we need a measure of movement between place of residence and place of work. These are available for Tokyo.[31]

In 1930 occupational specialization was highly developed in the daytime populations of the *ku* of Tokyo. One-fourth of the day population of Kojimachi was engaged in public service and the professions. Almost half the population of Nihonbashi was in commerce. The outer *ku* tended to be less specialized. The net daily movement of the gainfully occupied was inward toward the central city.[32] In Kojimachi there were 438 gainfully occupied during the day for each 100 who remained there at night. The surplus of day population amounted to only 60 per cent in the other business *ku*. All the *ku* of Outer Tokyo contributed to this inward movement, but the contributions differed widely from one area to another. The residential *ku* of Suginami sent out persons in the public services and the professions, as well as those in industry and commerce. The factory *ku* of Ebara sent out workers in industry, commerce, and transportation. In all areas the mobility was selective as to industry and sex. The gainfully occupied in transportation, public service, and the professions were most mobile, while domestic servants were least mobile. For any given industry, women were less mobile than men.

If we view the population as a whole, it is stability rather than mobility that emerges as the predominant aspect of daily living in Tokyo. Four-fifths or more of the night population in each of the 35 *ku* of Greater Tokyo remained there during the day. Stability was particularly characteristic of the low-income areas, where household industries flourished. Out-movement of the night population, whether measured in terms of the total population or the gainfully occupied, was most characteristic of the more Westernized segments of the economy and the more prosperous sections of the community.

Stability may be defined rather rigidly for that segment of the population who live and work within the same *ku*. Here stability may signify living and working in the same house, whereas mobility may mean working elsewhere in the same *ku*. Only one-fourth to one-fifth of the people who remained in the *ku* left the home daily for work or for school. From three-fourths to four-fifths remained at home, either as gainfully occupied persons or as persons without occupation.

A mingling of a Western type of mobility and the traditional stabilities was occurring in Tokyo. Family labor existed in the greatest of Japan's cities as in her most remote rural areas. At the same time, patterns of city formation and internal redistribution comparable to those in the West were occurring; there was specialization of individual functioning, localization of types of economic activity, and daily movement between place of residence and place of work. However, these were movements of a minor portion of the gainfully occupied population; the majority remained at home while they labored.

This pervasiveness of household labor in the great city cannot be taken as indicating the failure of psychological urbanization, although the process was slowed. There was movement of the native-born within Tokyo, and there was a distribution of in-migrants among the *ku* that suggests movement within the city after the initial entrance. The proportion of migrants paying income tax and the average payment in-

[30] Tokyo shiyakusho. *Tokyo-shi chukan ido jinko.*

[31] In addition to the volume for 1930 cited in Footnote 29, special tabulations of day and night population were published for the censuses of 1940 and 1948.

[32] These, like all previous measures of movement, are net figures. An interchange of persons in the same occupation will not be revealed as a difference in the occupational structure of the day and night populations of either *ku*. Some of the cross-movements will be compensatory, others not.

creased quite regularly with increasing duration of residence in the city.[33] Advancing age at marriage and limitation of fertility within marriage furnish the most conclusive evidence of very extensive social and psychological transformations among those in Tokyo who followed a daily round of activities almost as stable as those in the villages.

Great Cities, 1940-1955

Urbanization was the human aspect of economic development in Japan in its decades of middle industrialization. The exodus of the children of the peasants to the cities had become essential if Japan was to preserve her culture and maintain her increasing people. Continuing growth of cities would not have made Japan an England of the Pacific, for the total number of people who cultivated the land remained relatively unchanged. But the increase of the population in great cities was altering the social and political balance of the nation and jeopardizing the ancient culture even in the rural areas. Deceleration of the urbanward movement appeared highly improbable in the 1920's and 1930's, for industrialization was proceeding with apparently irreversible momentum. The metropolitan centers were symbols of Japan's solution to the problems of manpower utilization in an industrializing Asian land. Few in Japan or elsewhere saw them as portents of the hazards that lay ahead if the rate of industrialization should slacken. No one visualized the destruction of the urban economy and the return of the people to the towns and the villages which had contributed them or their parents to the urban vortex. But fewer still who witnessed this destruction of the cities in 1944 and 1945 realized the depth of the urbanization that had occurred and foretold the restoration of the cities within a few years. The population movements from 1940 to 1955 illustrate in more telling form than any other series of data the extent to which the Japanese have moved irrevocably away from the village life of the peasant East.

A comparison of population change in the six great cities, the other *shi*, and the *gun* between 1940 and 1945 with those of the period from 1920 to 1940 illustrates the complex modifications of the historic migrations to the great cities.[34] From 1920 to 1940, as we have said many times before, the migration to the cities was the human correlate of industrialization, the technique whereby a densely settled nation, poor in natural resources, maintained its rural areas without increasing pressure and provided the manpower for industrial and other non-agricultural developments. Great cities and lesser cities alike participated in this absorption of migrants. In wartime, however, the fate of the six great cities was differentiated sharply from that of Japan's other cities considered as a group. The population of the six cities on November 1, 1945, was only 44 per cent what it had been in 1940. The movements of the years from 1944 to 1946 were in major part flight and return rather than resettlement. The migrations of the industrializing state had been interrupted; they had not been reversed. The people who fled the cities did not flee to the land and remain with lineal relatives in villages. People who had lived in Tokyo would not willingly till the soil as unpaid agricultural laborers. Most of the refugees who reached the homes of relatives remained briefly as guests and then returned to the cities.

The return migration had reached major proportions by the time the census of 1947 was taken; by 1950 the prewar patterns of differential change were in evidence. The return to the six great cities occurred most rapidly, but the return to lesser cities was also swift. By 1955 the population of the six great cities totaled 14.2 million. Tokyo's population was 7.0 million, while Osaka's was 2.5 million. Yokohama, Nagoya, and Kyoto each had a population of more than a million.

Problems of Acculturation in the Cities

In the rural areas of Japan prior to 1930, individual adjustments and technical skills were much as they had been in the distant past. The economy was a household and family affair, and living was largely non-pecuniary. Labor was mainly accomplished by human hands, while social participation was familial and communal. Youth who had matured in this agricultural segment of the culture moved into the modern industrial segment—and in that fact inhered enormous problems of individual maladjustment, social retardation, and economic inefficiency. Japan used youth from her ancient past, culturally and psychologically speaking, and transformed them into the labor force that created industrial economy, armed forces, and an empire.

The changes in social and economic environment between youth and maturity were practically as great for women as for men. The wife who maintained a household and bore children in a metropolitan area had as a pattern the experience of her mother and her mother's neighbors a generation earlier in the countryside. In the village failure to marry meant disgrace, while social acceptability demanded acquiescence to the wishes of the husband. Babies arrived and status was enhanced, particularly if the babies were male and there were many of them. Midwives were local and well known; child care was taught by the mother-in-law, mother, or neighbors. As a child matured, it could assist in the care of succeeding children—and if babies died, that, too, was one of the burdens that life imposed. This was the life the girl knew—but now, married and living in the great city, the reproductive patterns of the village produced severe personal and family difficulties. The economy of the city was a monetary one. Each additional mouth meant a roughly proportionate increase in expenditure. Limited space and city streets compounded the physical problems of child care, while economic return from child labor was postponed. The ambition of the husband, the comparison of levels of living that induced both striving and discontent, and the other components of urbanization complicated the problems. These adjustments, more serious for women than for men because of woman's traditional domestic immobilization, were not "social problems" of a minority of the population of the industrial areas. Rather, they were the day-to-day compulsions that transformed the behavior of the peasant girls who had become the young married women of the great cities.

The magnitude of the family transformations involved in this peopling of the industrial regions with immigrants from the *machi* and the *mura* is difficult to estimate in the absence of life histories of individual migrants. Even if we eliminated the inter-prefectural migrations of the native-born in the industrial regions, the true provincials remained numerous. For a substantial but unknown proportion, the transition from ancient to modern life was lessened by birth or intermediate residence in a town or a smaller city. For a fortunate few,

[33] Tokyo shiyakusho. *Tokyo-shi nozei jinko chosa, shotokuzei hen, Showa ju'nen.*

[34] The internal redistribution of the war and postwar years will be considered in detail in Chapter XVI. Here the résumé is oriented toward the continuity of migration as an aspect of urbanization.

education beyond the compulsory six years of elementary school provided additional skills and a more sophisticated knowledge of the requirements for successful living in the urban world. But even if allowances are made for these minimizing factors, the creation of urban Japan through the internal movement of the Japanese was a gigantic experiment in the plasticity of the individual.

In 1930 the migrants were less predominant among the aging and the aged than among the young and those in the prime of productive life. This was a somewhat transitory condition, for as age groups matured and migration slowed, the predominance of the migrant would increase in the older groups and decrease in young adulthood. Thus there would be an approach to an even distribution over the life span. If the industrial areas became demographically mature and produced youth abundant enough to meet their own labor needs, migrants might come to predominate in the older age groups while youth were native-born.[35]

The time when inter-prefectural migration would serve predominantly to redistribute the natural increase of a uniformly developed economy with generally low fertility was still remote in 1930. The beginnings of a normalization of demographic structure through changing patterns of migration and a lessened role of migration were apparent in the 1930 place-of-birth statistics. Women were almost as numerous as men among the inter-prefectural migrants, thus producing an approach to biological sex ratios in the resident population of the prefecture, whether urban or rural. Men were still predominant in developing areas, but the degree of the predominance was minimal as contrasted to regions such as Manchoukuo. The adjustments required by migration might be severe, but they were predominantly the shared adjustments of family groups rather than the wrench experienced by single men in the urban areas and single women in the rural areas, or by married men in the cities with wives and children at home in the country.

The normalization of the demographic structure is seen most clearly in the predominance of the native-born among children in 1930. In the major industrial areas, over three-fifths of the adult migrants were in the productive span from 20 to 59; one-tenth of the migrants were children under age 10. This is not to minimize the role of the migrant, but rather to emphasize it. If we assume that most migrants married at the age that was usual for the area in which they lived and bore children at no higher a rate than the total population of the area of residence, then migrants must have contributed half of that 89 per cent of the children under age 10 who were native-born. The settled migrant was creating the biological replacements that lessened the need for the drastic adjustment involved in rural-urban migration.

Internal migration became a primary force for social change. The extent of that force was related to the prevalence of the migrant in the total population into which he merged and the extent of the divergence of that environment from the one to which he was accustomed. The major accommodation, that of the migrant in the metropolitan prefectures of Tokyo and Osaka, involved almost 40 per cent of the total number of inter-prefectural migrants; the lesser accommodation, that of the migrants in Kanagawa, Aichi, Hyogo, Kyoto, and Fukuoka prefectures, involved another 20 per cent of the inter-prefectural migrants. Twenty-five per cent moved into transitional prefectures, 13 per cent into agricultural prefectures. Thus, although there was a continuum of adjustment in migration, the majority of the migrants were concentrated in the more industrialized areas, where the divergences between past and present were greatest.

The increasing tendency of the immigrants and their children to identify themselves with the urban areas into which they had moved is revealed in the widespread transfers of *koseki* from rural to urban areas. In 1940, Tokyo prefecture's 7.2 million people included 3.8 million with *honseki* in the prefecture.[36] It could be argued that the 53 per cent of Tokyo's people who did not have *honseki* in Tokyo indicated a failure of acculturation. It must be remembered, however, that the existence of *honseki* elsewhere does not necessarily mean firm attachment to the area of origin. Attenuated relations with *mura, machi*, or *shi* in another area would be ended when the grandfather or the great-grandfather died.

The problems of acculturation were greatest in Tokyo and Osaka, but they extended throughout the country. Even in the far Ryukyus 1.5 per cent of the Japanese had *honseki* elsewhere. In the agricultural prefectures of Kyushu, Shikoku, and Honshu the internal strangers made up from 2 to 6 per cent of the resident population. In Fukuoka, Hyogo, and Kyoto prefectures one-fourth of the people had *honseki* elsewhere; the proportion exceeded one-third in Kanagawa and it reached almost one-half in Tokyo prefecture. These are high figures, but when it is remembered that 49.5 per cent of the people enumerated in Tokyo prefecture in 1930 were in-migrants and that perhaps another third of the population were the children of in-migrants, it is apparent that identification with the city had occurred in a substantial proportion of migrant families. The house, with its central values of continuity over the generations, was yielding to the great cities those members who were not in the direct line of continuity of the house. The time required for the transfer might be decades rather than years; it might be in major part a phenomenon of the second generation. The significant fact is that it was occurring.

Conclusions

The migrations that accompanied industrialization were primarily from rural to urban areas, from agricultural to non-agricultural employment. This was not a simple reallocation without economic frictions and social tensions, however, for it required departure from the cultural integrations of the old society. In Japan, as in the West, there was only a general relationship between the intensity of the population pressure in the rural society and the amount of the out-migration. Poverty, cultural backwardness, and geographical isolation combined to produce lesser rates of out-movement from many areas where objective measures would have indicated great need for it. The people with higher levels of living, greater educational achievements, and accessibility to urban and industrial areas moved with greater ease and adjusted to a new milieu more quickly. And so in Japan as in the West the situation became complex. In some areas there was severe population pressure, while in others depopulation of the countryside occurred.

The labor requirements of developing industrial areas were specific rather than general; they differed among areas and in any one area they changed over time. The characteristics of in-migrants differed in approximate relationship to the labor demands of the area. For instance, mining, the heavy indus-

[35] This actually happened in Hokkaido.

[36] Nihon. Sori-cho, tokei-kyoku. *Kekka hokoku tekiyo, Showa 15-nen kokusei chosa, Showa 19-nen jinko chosa, Showa 20-nen jinko chosa, Showa 21-nen jinko chosa.* Data for 1940 on *honseki* population by present residence for the prefectures.

tries, and the armed forces required men; the textile industry employed many women. However, migrations were always in process, with no possibility of completion except in some remote period when the requirements of the economy and the manpower available in the population would be in balance in local areas. The growth of new industrial areas created young migrant populations, while depressed conditions in old industrial areas produced populations with high proportions of the aging and the aged among migrant and sedentary population groups.

The basic shift of migration that occurred as the industrial economy and the urban society matured was the increase in the interchange of people within the industrialized and urbanized segments of the country. The major movements, however, have continued to involve the cityward migration of the peasant.

The selectivity of migrants from the total population of the areas of origin and the molding of these migrants and their children into the indigenous populations of the cities of Japan were also rather comparable to the experience of the industrializing cultures of the West. Migrants were predominantly youth, whatever their area of origin or of destination. This was true for men as for women. Comparative generalizations beyond this elementary one require more precise statement, for migration was in major part a dependent variable in a situation in which the economic system was the independent variable and the social system the factor of stability and continuity. Migrants from a distance tended to be predominantly male, the extent of the predominance increasing with distance. Migrants from near areas tended to include lesser excesses of males among the primary migrants, and the excesses that existed initially were soon lessened, if not eliminated, by the in-movement of dependents. The migration to developing industrial areas was heavily male in its initial stages, but normalization of sex ratios among both in-coming migrants and migrant groups occurred rapidly.

The migration which was transforming the occupational structure and the rural-urban composition of the nation involved great movements whose residues were fairly small in relation to the total numbers that had been involved. At any given time the majority of the migrants had been living within the areas of current residence for fairly brief periods of time. There was a cumulation of people once migrant who became the settled population of the new area, however, and this settled group became an increasing proportion of the total population of the area as the period of economic development lengthened. The appearance of flux yielded by perusal of the numbers of people moving to and from given areas was as spurious in Japan as it was in the West. The short-time movements and the interchanges were the product of economic and cultural factors as were the direct moves that resulted in permanent additions to the populations of the areas of destination.

The migrations in Japan led to adjustment to the new society rather than to episodic participation in it. After age 30 or 35 there was little net movement in or out of the industrial regions. The increasing urban and metropolitan populations became more nearly biological in their sex and age structures; generations of youth grew up in the new milieu. Differentiations in conditions of living and working arose in what had once been a relatively homogeneous rural population.

Limited natural resources, dense settlement on utilized land, a disciplined people, a familistic society, and the institution of primogeniture in the responsibilities and obligations of house and family characterized the old Japan. These were not separable factors but aspects of an integrated life. In the earlier centuries, the social, economic, and biological equilibrium of the village or the larger rural community had been achieved through the maintenance of relatively slow changes in numbers. Family and sons were pre-eminent values in the culture; indeed, they were essential to the achievement of the desirable life for the individual and the perpetuation of the family. The acceptance of human reproduction as an inherent good remained a central value even when limitation of famine and epidemic and control of disease permitted more children to mature than could obtain subsistence in the village. The older son succeeded to the headship of the house and the family land. He was required to remain agricultural and rural, while younger sons migrated. As elder sons became heads of agricultural and village households and reared the families appropriate to their values and their way of life, the need for migration rose again. Continuing migration was not a permanent solution of the problem of the son who succeeded and the other children for whom there were few opportunities.

The production of surplus youth in the rural areas has been characteristic of other industrializing cultures where old lands were densely settled and new lands were limited. In Japan, the surplus group was designated as such; it included all children beyond the eldest sons and the women married to them. The procurement of subsistence or gainful employment for younger children was the responsibility of the father and would be the responsibility of the elder brother when he succeeded to the headship. Economic compulsions as well as the sense of obligation led each family to assist its members to become self-supporting. In the majority of instances, the achievement of that self-support on any basis other than unpaid labor in the family enterprise involved migration.

The inheritance structure of the Japanese household, the control of migration and marriage by the head of the house, and the extent and intensity of the familistic basis of social and economic relationships not only made the industrialization of Japan feasible but structured the migrations basic to the formation of the industrial labor force. The resources of the family sent youth to the cities, where family members or villagers who had preceded them assisted in the matter of employment and living arrangements and supplied knowledge about how one lived in the new environment. The family resources in turn were increased by proceeds from the widely prevalent contracts that sent girls to the factory dormitories, domestic service, or prostitution for a period of years.

Marriage remained a concern of the family. Mate selection was not a major problem for a young man, even though he lived in an urban area where eligible girls were few. The family arranged a marriage. The institutions of the rural society sent girls into cities for marriage and so contributed to a rather balanced population growth in a rapidly urbanizing society. Familial arrangements sent girls to protected dormitories for factory employment and then secured husbands for them, so that the accepted role of the wife and mother could remain relatively undisturbed. Thus functioning familism continued in the industrializing state.

The family sent migrants to industrial employment and urban living, arranged their marriages, and received them back again if they became unemployed or ill. It is difficult to see how the rapid urbanization of Japan could have occurred otherwise, for the poverty of the masses of the Japanese people was far deeper than that which had characterized the nations of the West.

Japan's industrialization evolved from and rested on the manual labor of peasants. The technical and intellectual development and the emotional plasticity required for the direct movement of youth from agricultural villages to metropolitan centers might be expected to have barred a development such as that which occurred in Japan. But only a segment of industrial production involved the large factory and intricate power machinery. The commodities required for daily living remained what they had always been. Most of them were produced locally or regionally in a decentralized organization of production comparable to that of the Tokugawa period. Housing, household equipment, clothing, and food remained in a handicraft stage of production, while great factories and massive machines produced for the industrialized segments of the civilian economy, the export trade, and war. Small factories, household industries, and subcontracting permeated the cities as they did the rural areas. Daily distribution of food from neighborhood shops and use of human labor as motive force for tasks that could have been done by machine had not labor been so cheap were among the many factors that permitted great numbers of workers to live in the cities and engage in labor comparable to that of the villages. Not only migration but industrialization itself was adjusted to the underlying culture, the difficult resources situation, and the increasing population.

PART V

EXPANSION

CHAPTER IX

Frontiers of Settlement and Utilization

INDUSTRIALIZATION and urbanization within Japan were the major forces determining the redistribution of the Japanese. The movement from rural to urban areas left a relatively unchanging population in agriculture and created the labor force of an industrializing economy. An uninterrupted expansion in non-agricultural employment was essential to economic welfare and political stability. Moreover, additional numbers of people required additional quantities of food which could not be produced within the country. Increased imports in turn required increased industrial production to balance international accounts. The migration of Japanese to wider areas and the integration of these areas into an expanding national territory became accepted as demographic necessity.

At the time of the Restoration, the Japanese occupied only the three main islands of Honshu, Kyushu, and Shikoku. The major lands settled by Japanese people between 1872 and 1945 were Hokkaido, an integral part of Japan; Karafuto, the southern part of Sakhalin Island, a colony until 1943; and Nanyo-gunto, the Micronesian Islands administered as a mandate from the League of Nations. Hokkaido was developed into a semi-industrial area of net exodus within three-quarters of a century. Here the natural history of the population of a frontier can be studied, uncomplicated by ethnic or political factors. Karafuto was an experiment in agricultural and industrial development in the far north. The occupation of Nanyo-gunto involved the movement of Japanese as agriculturalists to the far south, and at the same time, it represented an organized technological development intended to exploit the resources of the tropics.

The first of the territorial additions to Japan proper was not a relatively empty land but the poor and already densely peopled Ryukyu Islands.[1] They were absorbed into the political structure of Japan in 1879, and retained the status of prefecture until 1945.

The movements of Japanese to the chilly islands of the north or the tropical islands of the south were but a preface to the great migrations of the Japanese to the crowded lands of Asia. This was movement to the frontier of economic development, even to the outer margins of culture, as the Japanese defined it. But it was no movement of "the man with the calloused hand" such as that which settled America north of the Rio Grande. Rather, this was the movement of the soldier, the businessman, the engineer, and the agriculturalist to lands where profits lay in industrial and agricultural undertakings and labor was provided by indigenous peoples.

Taiwan became part of the Japanese Empire in 1895, Kwantung and the South Manchuria Railway Zone in 1906, Korea in 1910. This was colonialism in the pattern so well known in the great Asian region where only China, Japan, and Thailand escaped dependent political status. Evolutions within Japan and the course of development in the colonies created a momentum toward further expansion of the imperial territory and increased out-movements of the people. The economic and military advances in Kwantung and the South Manchuria Railway Zone stimulated the drive to control China's Three Northeastern Provinces. After success there and the formation of the associated state of Manchoukuo, the focus was enlarged to include North China. This final imperial expansion, which began in 1937, initiated the events that led through eight years of war to the loss of all the colonial areas and the repatriation of all Japanese from the Western Pacific region.

HOKKAIDO[2]

Geographic isolation, mountainous terrain, and a severe continental climate retarded the occupation of Hokkaido.[3] Its climate is rather similar to that of New England, with cool summers and cold winters. Traditional Japanese agricultural practices were ill-adapted to the short growing seasons; the Japanese style of housing furnished inadequate protection during the long winters. However, the coastal areas had long been occupied by the Japanese, particularly as bases for fishing, and trading accommodations were made with the Ainu. Throughout the early part of the Tokugawa period, the Princes of Matsumae exercised nominal control over most of the island. However, when the Russians occupied Sakhalin Island and some of the Kuriles in the middle of the eighteenth century, strategic considerations re-enforced economic motivations for development.[4] Plans for military colonization were formulated and some slight success was achieved. By 1860 there were reported to be 60 thousand Japanese in Hokkaido.

The Meiji government established a Colonial Office to develop the agricultural and other resources of Hokkaido and to populate the island.[5] The expansion of the settled areas by spontaneous movements of families was to be replaced by planned regional development.[6] Emphasis was placed on rail-

[1] The history of the relations between Japan and the Ryukyu Islands is given, p. 179, this chapter.

[2] The analysis of Hokkaido presented here is limited to its role in the expansion of the Japanese in the period prior to 1940. Since Hokkaido was one of the prefectures of Japan, detailed analysis is presented in the substantive chapters. The migrations of the war and postwar years are considered in relation to those of the total Japanese population as an aspect of the demography of war and reconstruction.

[3] For a brief description of the landscape and a history of the settlement, see: Trewartha, Glenn T. *Japan. A physical, cultural, and regional geography*.

[4] Yoshida, Togo. "Genroku-chu Matsumae han no Karafuto ni okeru hanto." *Chigaku zasshi*, 17(200):538-550; 17(201):838-646. August and September 1905.

[5] A rather comprehensive analysis of the settlement is presented in: Scheinpflug, Alfons. "Die japanische Kolonisation in Hokkaido." *Mitteilungen der Gesellschaft für Erdkunde zu Leipzig*, 53:5-132. 1935. A bibliography of sources in Japanese and Western languages is appended.

[6] Japan. Office of Commissioner and Adviser of the Kaitakusi. *Reports and official letters to the Kaitakusi by Horace Capron, Commissioner and Adviser, and his foreign assistants.* The influ-

roads, canals, ports, communication facilities, and industries. Agricultural experiment stations were established and work begun on varieties of crops and techniques of production appropriate to the northern climate. Land was available for colonization, and in addition there were jobs for migrants in fishing, forestry, mining, and industries. The population increased from 67 thousand in 1870 to 427 thousand in 1890 and 1.6 million in 1910. It was 2.4 million in 1920, 2.8 million in 1930, and 3.3 million in 1940. The increase continued during the war and postwar years. The population reached 3.5 million in 1945, 3.9 million in 1947, and 4.3 million in 1950. In 1955 it was 4.8 million.

The northward movement of the Japanese, like the westward movement of the Americans, involved rather substantial and continuing increases in numbers. The following figures for the period from 1890-1894 to 1905-1909 understate the amount of flux involved in the settlement, for the official records are limited to individuals who intended to remain in Hokkaido for a considerable period of time:[7]

Period	*In*	*Out*	*Net*
1890-1894	178,145	22,571	155,574
1895-1899	283,398	49,554	233,844
1900-1904	236,677	45,364	191,313
1905-1909	349,180	63,321	285,859

Some people came north as fishermen or temporary laborers, while others entered Hokkaido intending to stay there but were unable to secure employment. Still others failed to adjust to the cultural and physical conditions of life in the cold north.[8] In general, people who acquired and developed land remained in Hokkaido; former agriculturalists who failed to secure holdings labored for a period and then returned south.

Hokkaido's population increase of 2.4 million between 1868 and 1920 amounted to 11.3 per cent of the total increase of 21 million that occurred within Japan. To assume that this over-all rate of absorption measures the contribution of the northern frontier to the solution of the demographic difficulties of an industrializing Japan would be erroneous, however, for Hokkaido was settled in major part by migrants from agricultural areas (MAP 9). Nine-tenths of the 916 thousand persons born in other prefectures but enumerated in Hokkaido in 1920 came from the Tohoku region of northeastern Honshu or the prefectures along the Japan Sea side of central Honshu.[9] The primary recruitment area was northeastern Honshu—the prefectures of Aomori, Iwate, Miyagi, Akita, Yamagata, and Fukushima. Here economies were predominantly agricultural and people were poor. The sons seeking jobs were numerous and the local opportunities were limited. Hokkaido was near and the industrial areas lay far to the southwest in central Honshu. The paths of movement were soon established. Moreover, the severe climate of Hokkaido was a lesser deterrent to people already habituated to life in northeastern Honshu.

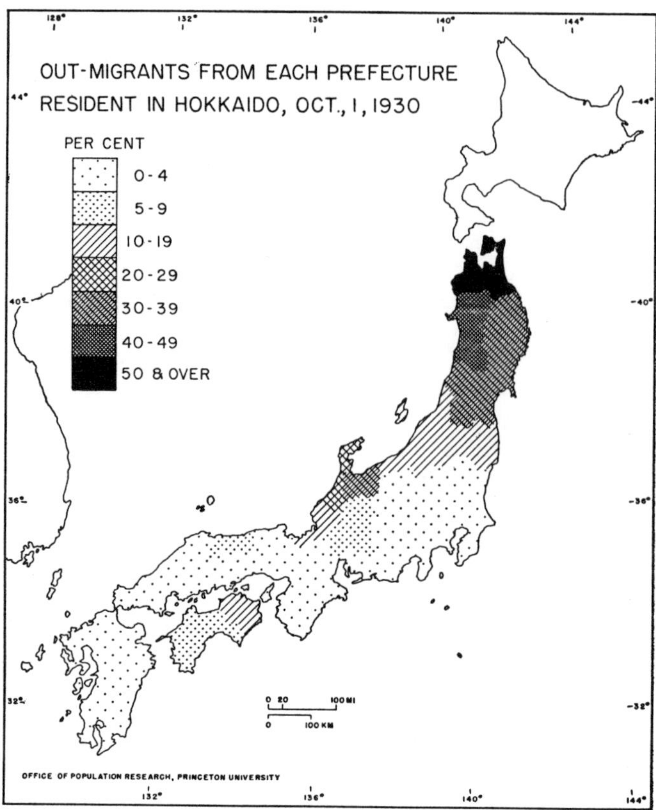

Map 9. Out-migrants from each prefecture resident in Hokkaido, by place-of-birth data, census of 1930
Source: Nihon. Naikaku tokei-kyoku. *Showa go'nen kokusei chosa hokoku.* IV.1. Table 21; IV.4. Hokkaido. Table 7.

The secondary recruitment area for Hokkaido was a cluster of prefectures along the Japan Sea in central Honshu—Niigata, Toyama, Ishikawa, Fukui, and Gifu. By 1920 these prefectures as a group had lost more than one-fifth of their total native-born population, and 27 per cent of these emigrants were enumerated in Hokkaido. A mountainous terrain, limited cultivable lands, severe climate, and social and economic backwardness had combined with high natural increase to make people move northward in the early period. But with the development of transportation facilities and the availability of employment in the great industrial nucleus of the Tokyo-Yokohama area, fewer turned to the north.

The island of Shikoku was a tertiary area for contributions to Hokkaido. In 1920 more than 13 per cent of the native-born out-migrants from Shikoku were enumerated in Hokkaido. The explanation was similar to that for the regions near the Japan Sea: poverty, economic retardation, high natural increase, and subsidized settlement.

The movements reflected in the place-of-birth statistics of the 1920 census suggest the contributions of Hokkaido to population adjustments during the late nineteenth and early twentieth centuries. The number of in-migrants from other prefectures in Hokkaido declined in absolute numbers between

ence of the advisers from the United States is quite apparent in Hokkaido today, whether one looks at the city plan of Sapporo, the scattered homesteads in the rural areas, or specific techniques utilized in agriculture.

[7] Nihon. Naikaku tokei-kyoku. *Résumé statistique de l'Empire du Japon.* In the early years there was an annual table entitled: "Statistique de la migration de Hokkaido."

[8] In all years, from 45 to 55 per cent of the heads of immigrant households reported their occupation prior to immigration as agriculture. Fishermen declined irregularly from about one-sixth of the total in the nineteenth century to less than one-tenth before World War I. General conclusions about the occupational composition of the in-migrant stream are difficult to draw because of an "other and unknown" occupational category that includes one-fourth of all households. Only one-fourth of the household heads leaving Hokkaido reported themselves as agriculturalists.

[9] Nihon. Naikaku tokei-kyoku. *Taisho ku'nen kokusei chosa hokoku.* IV.B., Hokkaido. Table 3. In 1920, over 48 per cent of the 996 thousand native-born of the northeastern prefectures who had left the prefecture of birth were enumerated in Hokkaido. Almost three-fourths of Aomori's emigrants and three-fifths of Akita's were in Hokkaido. Iwate, Miyagi, and Yamagata had sent from 45 to 50 per cent of their native-born emigrants to Hokkaido.

1920 and 1930.[10] This did not reflect a stabilization of population within the areas that had once sent large numbers of migrants to Hokkaido, for in all these areas the proportions of the native-born enumerated outside the prefecture of birth increased between 1920 and 1930. What was happening was the replacement of the agricultural by the metropolitan frontier. By 1930 the proportion of out-migrants located in Hokkaido had shrunk from 31 to 23 per cent for all Japan; from 48 to 37 per cent for the prefectures of northeastern Honshu; from 27 to 20 per cent for the prefectures on the Japan Sea side of central Honshu; from 13 to 9 per cent for the prefectures of Shikoku.

As the land frontier became a historic rather than a contemporary mecca, the maturing youth of what had once been a frontier moved toward urban and industrial areas. By 1930 the prefectures that included the six great cities had received 56 per cent of Hokkaido's surviving prefectural emigrants. Tokyo prefecture alone had received 37 per cent. The three areas of primary recruitment that had contributed 82 per cent of Hokkaido's prefectural in-migrants received only 30 per cent of her native-born out-migrants to other prefectures. Computations of the net balance of lifetime movements as of 1930 still revealed a substantial inward movement; net migration between birth and the census date amounted to 30 per cent of the enumerated population.

The age structures of the migrant groups in Hokkaido in 1930 corroborate the evidence from historical sources that the major settlement of the frontier by immigrants from the agricultural regions of Honshu and Shikoku occurred in the early decades of economic modernization. The proportion of Hokkaido's people who reported their place of birth as another prefecture of Japan increased consistently with age, reaching a maximum of 90 per cent at age 60 and over (TABLE 63). The proportion born in Hokkaido, on the other hand, exceeded 95 per cent at ages under 10.

The maturing of the frontier and the death or return migration of the earlier immigrants are apparent in the age structures of the different migrant status groups. In 1930 more than 60 per cent of the Hokkaido-born males were under age 15, whereas only 6.5 per cent of the males born in other prefectures were under age 15. Four per cent of the Hokkaido-born males were aged 40 or over, whereas 47 per cent of the males born in other prefectures were in this age group. The prefectural immigrants in Hokkaido, like the foreign-born in the United States, were an aging and a diminishing group in the total population.

The contrast between frontier migration and the rural-urban migration of an industrializing economy diminished as industrialization and urbanization transformed the economic structure and the population distribution within Hokkaido. In 1888 the combined population of the cities of Hakodate, Asahigawa, and Otaru was 105 thousand. In 1920, 22 per cent of Hokkaido's 2.4 million people lived in cities of 50 thousand or more, while 15 per cent lived in cities of 100 thousand or more. Between 1920 and 1940 the rural population increased 32 per cent, the urban population 60 per cent. During these two decades Hokkaido's net loss by migration amounted to more than two-fifths of her natural increase.[11]

Theoretical possibilities for the absorption of immigrants remained, but the alternative opportunities in the industrializing urban prefectures of central Honshu were far more attractive.

KARAFUTO

Karafuto was much more valuable to the Japanese because of its strategic location and its natural resources than because of its ability to absorb peasant settlers.[12] Fish, timber, coal, and oil and associated processing, manufacturing, and transporting activities maintained a population that increased gradually but never reached substantial size. The total population was 12 thousand in 1906 and 415 thousand in 1940. The migrations of the Japanese that contributed to this increase were small in relation to the population increase occurring in Japan. They merit analysis, however, for Karafuto was a microcosm where movements were so closely tabulated as to reveal many of the intricacies of migration that are concealed in the cruder data for Japan itself. There is also a broader significance to Japanese settlement in Karafuto, for it represented northern settlement by a people whose material and cultural adjustments were sub-tropical. Furthermore, the historical evolution of Hokkaido and Karafuto demonstrates the relations between successive frontiers.

Dreams of agricultural colonization permeate much of the literature on Karafuto, but the Japanese of an industrializing society would not move freely to the poor soils of a remote and sub-Arctic region. Subsidies were tried, small amounts of money being given to immigrants who settled on the land within six months of arrival. Subsidized settlers numbered from 1.0 thousand to 1.3 thousand families a year from 1925 to 1934, then declined to six hundred in 1937 and to only a little more than two hundred in 1938. There was continuing emigration from farms, however, for the number of farm families on the island decreased year by year during the 1930's. Farm population in 1939 was only four-fifths as large as it had been in 1933.[13]

The in-migrants in Karafuto in 1930 labored predominantly in manufacturing, commerce, and transportation (TABLE 64). Less than two-fifths of the gainfully occupied in-migrants found employment in agriculture, forestry, fishing, and mining. Almost one-fourth engaged in manufacturing; more than another fourth were in commerce, transportation, and communication. The industrial structure of the gainfully occupied in-migrants by year of arrival shows something of the historical evolution of the economic structure. The migrants of earlier periods who remained in Karafuto in 1930 were more heavily concentrated in agriculture and fishing, whereas the more recent migrants were found disproportionately in manufacturing industry and transportation.

[10] Nihon. Naikaku tokei-kyoku. *Showa go'nen kokusei chosa hokoku.* IV.1. Table 21; IV.4. Hokkaido. Table 7.

[11] There was a net loss by migration of 152 thousand between 1920 and 1925, a net gain of 23 thousand between 1925 and 1930, a substantial net loss from 1930 to 1935. In both 1925-1930 and 1930-1935 there were net losses among men and women at all ages over 40, net gains or lesser losses at ages below 40. In both intercensal periods, women gained less or lost more than men at ages under 40, but lost relatively less at ages over 40. A redistribution of youth and a return migration of the mature and the aged produced these complex patterns.

[12] For a description of Sakhalin Island, see: Berg, Lev S. *Natural regions of the U.S.S.R.* Ch. XVIII. The Russians occupied the entire island from 1875 to 1905, utilizing it as a penal colony. The Treaty of Portsmouth provided for a division at the 50th parallel, Russia retaining the northern part and Japan the southern.

[13] Karafuto-cho. *Karafuto-cho, tokeisho.* Various issues. The increasing activities in Karafuto were mainly extractive or industrial rather than agricultural. Almost half the total area was primeval forest. Timber, fagots, charcoal, and by-products yielded over half the revenue of the government and supported many people directly, more indirectly through the pulp and paper mills. In addition the island possessed coal and oil. In 1937 three-fifths of the total value of production accrued from manufacturing, including rayon pulp and paper, while a further one-sixth came from forest products.

TABLE 63

Migrant status of the male population of Hokkaido, 1930

(Per cent composition of age groups by place of birth)

		Born in Hokkaido				
Age	*Enumerated population*	*Total*	*Commune of residence*	*Another commune in prefecture*	*Born in another prefecture*	*Born in colonies or abroad*
			All Hokkaido			
Total	100.	61.7	41.7	20.0	37.1	1.2
0-9	100.	95.0	80.3	14.7	4.5	0.5
10-14	100.	89.6	62.4	27.2	9.9	0.5
15-19	100.	77.3	43.3	34.0	22.0	0.7
20-24	100.	63.1	28.9	34.2	34.7	2.2
25-29	100.	47.8	21.0	26.8	49.2	3.0
30-39	100.	32.8	13.5	19.3	64.4	2.8
40-49	100.	16.8	7.2	9.6	82.0	1.2
50-59	100.	12.4	5.7	6.7	87.2	0.4
60-69	100.	10.2	4.9	5.3	89.6	0.2
70-79	100.	9.9	4.8	5.1	90.1	0.0
80 and over	100.	9.0	4.7	4.3	90.9	0.1
			Cities of 100,000 and over			
Total	100.	58.7	37.5	21.2	39.6	1.7
0-9	100.	93.2	80.8	12.4	6.0	0.8
10-14	100.	86.2	56.7	29.5	12.7	1.1
15-19	100.	72.9	34.5	38.4	25.5	1.6
20-24	100.	57.9	25.2	32.7	39.3	2.8
25-29	100.	46.2	20.0	26.2	50.8	3.0
30-39	100.	34.9	14.4	20.5	62.1	3.0
40-49	100.	20.0	8.5	11.5	77.9	2.1
50-59	100.	13.9	5.6	8.3	85.1	1.0
60-69	100.	10.5	3.5	7.0	89.2	0.3
70-79	100.	10.0	3.3	6.7	89.8	0.2
80 and over	100.	10.2	1.9	8.3	89.5	0.3
			Remainder of prefecture			
Total	100.	62.4	42.6	19.8	36.6	1.0
0-9	100.	95.4	80.2	15.2	4.2	0.4
10-14	100.	90.2	63.4	26.8	9.4	0.4
15-19	100.	78.4	45.8	32.6	21.0	0.6
20-24	100.	64.4	29.9	34.5	33.5	2.1
25-29	100.	48.2	21.3	26.9	48.7	3.1
30-39	100.	32.3	13.3	19.0	64.9	2.8
40-49	100.	16.0	6.9	9.1	82.9	1.1
50-59	100.	12.1	5.7	6.4	87.7	0.2
60-69	100.	10.2	5.2	5.0	89.7	0.1
70-79	100.	9.8	5.0	4.8	90.1	0.1
80 and over	100.	8.9	5.0	3.9	91.0	0.1

Source: Nihon. Naikaku tokei-kyoku. *Showa go'nen kokusei chosa hokoku.* IV.4. Hokkaido, Table 9.

TABLE 64

The industrial composition of the in-migrant population of Karafuto, by year of arrival, 1930

(Per cent industrial structure of gainfully occupied in-migrants of specified years of arrival)

		YEARS OF ARRIVAL					
Industry	*All migrants*	*1930*	*1925-1929*	*1920-1924*	*1915-1919*	*1910-1914*	*Before 1910*
All gainfully occupied migrants	100.	100.	100.	100.	100.	100.	100.
Agriculture and forestry	26.4	14.6	25.4	34.4	27.6	31.0	21.3
Fishing	10.6	12.0	7.4	7.1	13.8	20.4	23.6
Mining	2.4	1.1	3.2	2.5	2.5	1.3	0.6
Manufacturing	24.6	23.7	28.8	22.7	23.9	18.0	17.4
Commerce	14.2	11.5	14.3	13.5	14.2	14.3	22.8
Transportation and communication	13.2	30.3	10.9	11.1	9.1	8.1	7.1
Professions and public service	7.6	6.0	8.8	7.4	7.7	6.1	6.4
Domestic	1.0	0.7	1.1	1.3	1.0	0.8	0.7
Other	0.1	0.0	0.1	0.1	0.1	0.1	0.1

Source: Karafuto-cho. *Kokusei chosa kekka hyo, Showa go'nen.* Table 29.

The increase in the population of Karafuto indicates that this northernmost island was as much a land of the migrant as were the metropolitan regions of Japan itself.[14] The total population was 106 thousand in 1920, 295 thousand in 1930, and 415 thousand in 1940. Intercensal increases amounted to 92 per cent from 1920 to 1925, 45 per cent from 1925 to 1930, 12 per cent from 1930 to 1935, and 25 per cent from 1935 to 1940. The order of magnitude of the migrations required to produce rates of increase such as these may be illustrated by some estimates for the period from 1925 to 1930. In these five years total population increase amounted to 45 per cent. In 1930 the male population was 25.4 per cent larger than it would have been had there been no net migration since 1925; the female population was 32.7 per cent larger.[15] Although increases through migration were greatest among youth aged from 15 to 24, there had been substantial net migration even among children. Economic absorption did not continue at these high rates, however, for the opportunities for employment in Karafuto became less as those in Manchoukuo increased. In the five years from 1930 to 1935 net migration added only one-fifth to the expected number of men aged from 15 to 24. There was net out-movement among men and women at all ages over 30.

At any given time, the majority of Karafuto's migrants were recent arrivals. In 1930, 10 per cent of the Japan-born in-migrants had entered the country for the first time in the nine months preceding the census; 54 per cent had entered in the period between January 1, 1925, and October 1, 1930. Only 12 per cent had arrived in the colony more than fifteen years earlier.

If we examine the age structures of the migrant groups within Karafuto by place of origin, the history of a frontier emerges clearly (TABLE 65). The native-born of this area of recent settlement were children; in 1930, more than 90 per cent were under age 15. The people in Hokkaido were acclimatized to a cold region and acculturated to frontier life. Hokkaido-born in-migrants in Karafuto had tended to come in family groups; they included substantial proportions of children and a more balanced sex ratio in adult ages than other groups. In general, the proportions of children among in-migrants decreased with increasing distances from Karafuto. Tokyo again constituted an exception. Her migrants, probably disproportionately represented in the public service and professional groups, included 30 per cent under 15 and 20 per cent over age 40.[16]

The interchanges of population among the main islands of Japan, Hokkaido, and Karafuto led to a major extension northward of the area of Japanese ethnic settlement. Movement occurred quickly. Farms were carved from unoccupied areas and industries placed in production within a few years, or at most a decade or so. The growth of a people who identified themselves with the new areas required a generation or more. In 1930, more than 89 thousand of the 295 thousand people in Karafuto had *honseki* in Hokkaido (TABLE 66). Three-fifths of those people whose names were still entered in *koseki* in Hokkaido had been born there, but one-fifth were born in Karafuto itself. Presumably these were the children of in-migrants from Hokkaido. The other one-fifth of the Karafuto residents who had their *honseki* in Hokkaido reported their place of birth as other prefectures of Japan, primarily those that had contributed heavily to the settlement of Hokkaido in the late nineteenth century. Thus, for many of

[14] Karafuto-cho. *Kokusei chosa kekka hyo, Showa go'nen.*

[15] Age distributions: 1925. Nihon. Naikaku tokei-kyoku. *Taisho juyo'nen kokusei chosa hokoku. Kijutsu hen.* II.1.P.68. 1930: Karafuto-cho. *Kokusei chosa kekka hyo, Showa go'nen.* Table 7. 1935. Naikaku tokei-kyoku. *Nihon teikoku tokei nenkan.* 1935, P.16. Vital statistics: 1925-1933. Karafuto-cho. *Karafuto-cho, tokeisho.* 1934-1935: Nihon. Naikaku tokei-kyoku. *Jinko dotai tokei.* Life tables for Hokkaido were used for aging the population of Karafuto.

[16] There were many complexities in the movements and countermovements that characterized the redistribution in Karafuto. Almost 3 per cent of the total population were born abroad, most of them Koreans who had been brought in to work in the mines. Of the 8.3 thousand Koreans of 1930, 559 were born in Karafuto, 79 in Japan. One-sixth of the aborigines of Karafuto were Japan-born, presumably in Hokkaido.

TABLE 65

Age structure of migrant status groups in Karafuto, by place of birth, 1930

(Per cent composition by age)

		Age								
Place of birth	*Total*	*0-9*	*10-14*	*15-19*	*20-24*	*25-29*	*30-39*	*40-49*	*50-59*	*60 and over*
Karafuto	100.	76.4	13.4	7.1	2.1	0.3	0.3	0.2	0.2	0.1
Resident in commune of birth	100.	80.0	12.3	5.7	1.4	0.2	0.2	0.1	0.1	0.1
Resident in another commune	100.	62.4	17.7	12.5	4.9	0.7	0.7	0.6	0.4	0.3
Japan	100.	10.5	7.8	9.4	11.8	14.3	21.8	13.6	7.2	3.6
Hokkaido	100.	18.0	14.5	13.6	13.7	14.0	16.2	6.2	2.6	1.1
Tohoku	100.	6.2	4.2	7.6	11.5	15.1	25.0	16.9	8.9	4.7
Japan Sea prefectures	100.	3.5	2.7	5.7	8.8	12.4	24.4	21.9	13.6	7.0
Shikoku	100.	3.0	3.2	5.4	7.5	12.3	26.9	21.9	12.4	7.5
Elsewhere	100.	7.2	3.7	6.2	10.9	15.3	26.3	17.1	9.2	4.4

Source: Karafuto-cho. *Kokusei chosa kekka hyo, Showa go'nen.* Table 10.

TABLE 66

Place of *honseki* of the Japanese population of Karafuto, by place of birth, 1930

		PLACE OF BIRTH				
			Japan			
Place of honseki	*Total population*	*Karafuto*	*Total*	*Hokkaido*	*Tohoku*	*Other*
Total[a]	284,198	70,359	213,356	80,548	74,571	58,237
Karafuto	65,316	24,885	40,361	18,094	12,496	9,771
Japan	218,882	45,474	172,995	62,454	62,075	48,466
Hokkaido	89,360	17,476	71,788	52,688	9,372	9,728
Tohoku	74,326	16,552	57,664	5,389	51,318	957
Other prefectures[a]	55,196	11,446	43,543	4,377	1,385	37,781

[a] Since Japanese born outside Karafuto or Japan (prewar area) are omitted, the components do not equal the total.
Source: Karafuto-cho. *Kokusei chosa kekka hyo, Showa go'nen.* Table 26.

those who finally achieved identification with the new area, the process of acculturation had involved two generations.

We have emphasized the fact that *honseki* were maintained in the villages of origin, that adjustment to and acceptance of permanency of residence in the north were a slow process. We should also stress the fact that acculturation did occur finally for the majority of those who settled permanently in the new area. Persistence of historic allegiances might seem to be indicated by the fact that 65 per cent of the Hokkaido-born immigrants in Karafuto maintained *honseki* in Hokkaido, while less than one-fourth had transferred *honseki* from Hokkaido to Karafuto. Actually, this fact indicates the changeability of allegiances, for persons with *honseki* in Hokkaido were the children or grandchildren of people born in the southern islands—and only 15 per cent of the total number of Hokkaido-born in Karafuto had *honseki* in a prefecture south of Hokkaido.

Evaluation of the numerical significance of the movement of the Japanese to Karafuto depends on whether the focus is Karafuto itself or Japan. If we regard Karafuto as a settlement frontier, the conclusion is obvious. Economic development and ethnic occupation were swift. The net changes by migration per 100 expected population by sex and age for the decades of the 1920's and 1930's indicate something as to the rates at which migrants were being absorbed:[17]

[17] Age distributions in addition to those cited in Footnote 14: 1920: Karafuto-cho. *Taisho ku'nen jugatsu ichijitsu genzai, dai-ikkai kokusei chosa kekka hyo.* 1940: Nihon. Kosei-sho, daijin kambo, tokei chosa-bu. *Dai-hachi kai.* Data section. The life tables used were those for Japan outside the cities of 100 thousand and over at each of the census dates.

Age	1920-1930		1930-1940	
	Male	Female	Male	Female
15-59	139.4	134.0	23.5	16.9
15-19	130.6	117.8	27.6	24.3
20-24	229.0	207.6	39.2	38.6
25-29	264.2	229.7	67.2	37.1
30-34	197.3	159.6	47.5	17.8
35-39	121.4	114.4	12.0	−0.7
40-44	93.4	80.0	10.0	1.8
45-49	66.6	63.8	6.9	−3.2
50-54	55.5	65.4	−4.0	0.6
55-59	45.9	67.0	−13.0	1.1

If Karafuto is regarded as an outlet for the increasing population of Japan, its contribution seems insignificant. Karafuto's own population was 106 thousand in 1920 and 415 thousand in 1940, an increase of little more than 300 thousand in twenty years. During this same period the population within Japan increased more than 17 million. However, migration to Karafuto furnished a demographic outlet for Hokkaido, just as in earlier decades Hokkaido had been an outlet for the Tohoku region. The major contribution of Karafuto to the solution of the population problems of the industrializing state did not lie in the migrations of people, but in the economic development of the northern island as a source of supply and an outpost of empire. For the achievement of these goals, migration was essential and that which occurred was adequate.

Okinawa

The Ryukyus are among the strategic islands along the Pacific littoral of the Asian continent.[18] They begin some eighty miles south of Kyushu and reach within seventy miles of Taiwan. Fairly dense populations had developed even prior to the annexation by Japan. Land for cultivation was generally poor and limited, while the resources for activities other than agriculture and fishing were sparse. After the annexation, Okinawa was a remote prefecture geographically and a marginal area economically. The location of the islands delayed educational and other social advances for the indigenous population. Cultural differences between the Ryukyuans and the Japanese furthered discrimination. With an already adequate or more than adequate population, high rates of natural increase, negligible industrialization, and limited urbanization within the islands, the propulsions to out-migration were great.

The economic limitations and the increasing population of the Ryukyu Islands might have created a tragic situation had Okinawa been a contained area. However, the fact of population increase itself is sufficient evidence of the integration of Okinawa into the larger and more economically developed society of Japan. The population increase was associated with a reduction of death rates; this in turn was associated with an extension of health activities, increased and regularized food supplies, an increase of commercial production, and disaster relief. The integration with Japan also gave access to employment opportunities outside the islands. In other words, Okinawa was an agricultural region with free movement to an industrializing area of higher income levels and more abundant social and cultural opportunities. As in so many similar situations elsewhere, its people, and particularly its youth, became one of its major export commodities. Their remittances became one of the major sources of income for a substantial portion of the families who remained on the Islands.

In the year 1920, when the first census was taken, Okinawa had a total population of 571 thousand. The population was 577 thousand in 1930 and 573 thousand in 1940, an increase of only 0.4 per cent in twenty years. Here alone, among the 47 prefectures of prewar Japan, out-migration had been sufficient to remove almost the entire natural increase.

In the absence of migration, population increase would have been rapid, and it would have quickened over time. The percentage increases in the 1920's and the 1930's in the absence of migration would have been as follows:[19]

Age	1920-1930	1930-1940
15-59	15.9	20.9
15-19	16.0	39.9
20-34	24.2	37.2
35-49	6.5	3.4
50-59	13.5	−3.0

The extent of the migration that occurred each decade is indicated by the deviations of the actual populations from those expected without migration. Percentage losses were as follows, the decades being considered separately:

Age	1920-1930	1930-1940
15-59	−19.0	−22.5
15-19	−21.2	−38.3
20-34	−28.4	−32.9
35-49	−11.6	−4.5
50-59	−3.2	−1.2

A comparison of the changes expected without migration and the migrations that occurred indicates a rough correspondence between population increase and out-migration only insofar as total numbers were concerned. Emigrants from Okinawa came primarily from the younger productive ages; here migration led to declining numbers. Children increased in numbers until the emigration of youth became a major factor in reducing family formation and hence numbers of births in the island population. The aged were increased in numbers both by the aging of larger cohorts subject to lesser depletion by migration in the past and by return migration.

[18] The southward movement of the Japanese was heralded by the early occupation of the Ryukyu Islands. The Islands did not become colonies, however, for they were organized and administered as the prefecture of Okinawa and as Oshima *gun* of Kagoshima prefecture. From 1920 to 1940, Okinawa was the most agricultural of the prefectures of Japan. Both the structure of the population and the rates of out-migration were appropriate to this status. In 1945 Okinawa was removed from the jurisdiction of Japan. The analysis of the demography of the agricultural prefectures of Japan in 1950 does not cover it. In 1952 a few small islands were returned to Japan; in December 1953, Amami *gun* reverted to Japan.

Since Okinawa was a prefecture of Japan from 1920 through 1945, the analysis of population growth and distribution, economic change and educational advance, urbanization and family formation, fertility and mortality, and war losses and dislocations need not be repeated here. And since Okinawa prefecture was removed from Japan in 1945, analysis of the postwar developments in the islands is not appropriate to a study of the demography of Japan.

[19] Based on the ratio of the population expected without migration to the population at the beginning of the decade. Sources of data: 1920: Nihon. Naikaku tokei-kyoku. *Taisho ku'nen kokusei chosa hokoku.* IV.B. Table 10. 1925: *Ibid. Taisho juyo'nen kokusei chosa hokoku.* II.4 Table 6 (Number of aliens estimated). 1930: *Ibid. Showa go'nen kokusei chosa hokoku.* IV.4. Tables 6 and 11. 1935: *Ibid. Showa ju'nen kokusei chosa hokoku.* II.2. Table V (Number of aliens estimated). 1940: *Ibid. Census of 1940. Selected tables.* Table 2. The life tables used were those for Japan outside the cities of 100 thousand and over at each of the census dates.

A comparison of the population in 1940 with that in 1920 reveals the disturbed age structure that follows migration such as that occurring in Okinawa in the 1920's and the 1930's:

	POPULATION		
Age	*1920*	*1940*	*Per cent change*
Total	571,092	573,476	0.4
Under 15	213,857	233,581	9.2
0-4	80,472	81,610	1.4
5-14	133,385	151,971	13.9
15-59	317,300	279,292	−12.0
15-19	56,599	44,659	−21.1
20-34	120,873	98,958	−18.1
35-49	94,142	87,548	−7.0
50-59	45,686	48,127	5.3
60 and over	39,935	60,603	51.8

The people from Okinawa moved northward into Japan and outward into colonial areas or to areas where the movements of Japanese were being subsidized. In 1940, 80 thousand Japanese with *honseki* in Okinawa were enumerated elsewhere in Japan. The majority of them lived in the prefectures containing the six great cities.[20] The numbers of persons having *honseki* in Okinawa but enumerated in a metropolitan prefecture were as follows: Osaka, 42 thousand; Hyogo, 11 thousand; Tokyo, 7 thousand; Kanagawa, 6 thousand; Aichi, 3 thousand; and Kyoto, 1 thousand. The majority of the laborers on the sugar plantations of Nanyo-gunto were immigrants from Okinawa. Here they went to rural communities rather than to or near great cities as they had done in Japan.[21] Outside Japan, the Empire, and Manchoukuo there were 57 thousand Japanese with *honseki* in Okinawa.[22] Major concentrations were as follows, numbers being in thousands:

Middle and South America—30 (Brazil—16)
North America—14 (Hawaii—13)
Asia—13 (Philippines—10)

Thus the first of Japan's territorial additions became a source of migrants to the crowded islands of Japan, the colonial areas she had acquired, and the overseas areas where Japanese labor received subsidized passage. Here is a clear demonstration of the insufficiency of the interpretation of expansion in terms of population pressures within Japan.

NANYO-GUNTO[23]

The northern islands were outlets for part of the population increase of Japan, especially during the earlier decades of economic modernization. Agricultural difficulties in northeastern and west central Honshu stimulated movements to lands that would have been regarded as unsuitable had alternative opportunities been available. As the national economy developed, migrants were attracted to non-agricultural employment and urban residence. By the 1930's there was an exodus of people from the rural areas in Hokkaido and in Karafuto. The growth which was still occurring in total population was associated with industrialization and urbanization within the former frontier areas.

[20] Nihon. Sori-cho, tokei-kyoku. *Kekka hokoku tekiyo, Showa 15-nen kokusei chosa* . . . .

[21] See page 181, this chapter, on the Japanese in Nanyo-gunto.

[22] The year is 1940. Nihon. Gaimu-sho chosa-kyoku. *Kaigai zairyu hompojin chosa kekka hyo, Showa 15-nen.*

[23] Nanyo-gunto, literally translated, means "Islands of the South Seas."

The conception of a southward movement developed along with that of a northern colonization. In the southern areas of the Pacific were sparsely settled lands and abundant raw materials. Japanese culture was sub-tropical in many of its major adaptations; Japanese agriculture was suitable for production under tropical conditions; physiological acclimatization in the south was less difficult than in the north. The areas that would permit major settlement lay far to the south, however, and they were pre-empted by European colonial powers or occupied by European peoples as sovereign states. It is difficult to determine when the vision of colonization in Sumatra, Borneo, New Guinea, and the "empty lands" of Australia first appeared. At any rate, the locus of the initial southern move became the tiny islands formerly held by Germany rather than the great islands of the Indies then under the sovereignty of the Netherlands. Micronesia permitted experiment in tropical settlement and development. Thus it, like Karafuto, achieved a significance far beyond its limited service as a demographic frontier.

Micronesia is an apt name for the series of volcanic islands and coral atolls scattered throughout the southwest Pacific east of the Philippines and Taiwan, north of New Guinea and Melanesia, west of Polynesia, and south of the Bonin Islands.[24] The former German islands mandated to Japan by the League of Nations included the Marianas (except Guam), the Carolines, and the Marshalls. Within the vast expanse of the Pacific, many of these bits of land were long "undiscovered," or, once "discovered" were largely ignored during the early period of Pacific expansion. Some of them became ports of call for trading vessels and whaling ships that required food and water. During the course of the nineteenth century, the islands became more and more intermeshed in the political and economic maneuvers of the imperial powers. With the defeat of Spain at the end of the century, those that did not pass to the United States were sold to Germany and were ruled, together with her other Micronesian areas, as adjuncts to New Guinea. Imperial Germany lost the islands in 1914, before the conquest of the air had created new potentialities for the pinpoints of land that dotted the Pacific from San Francisco to Manila and from Sydney to Tokyo. Imperial Japan received the islands as a mandate from the League of Nations and, after a period of indecision in the 1920's, moved rapidly forward during the 1930's with the program of militarization that was to etch in the history of the Pacific such names as Kwajalein, Eniwetok, Saipan, and Tinian.[25]

[24] References to historical and contemporary sources on the demography of the Micronesian Islands and related factors are given in the Bibliography, p. 445.

[25] The economic and the strategic history of the islands of Micronesia is predominantly that of the aliens who have utilized their resources, converted their peoples, and struggled for the lands and waters whose possession is essential to the hegemony of the eastern and southeastern Asian region. The Micronesians have been pawns in the "history" that surged around them—in general, impediments to the occupying powers or the contending military forces. In fact, the history of Micronesia might have been less complicated if there had been no Micronesians, or if all the people of the atolls had succumbed to the warfare, the diseases, and the famines that accompanied civilization. Natives existed, however, and they became subject in succession to Germany and Japan. The documentation is profuse. The Germans counted people and sent scholars to write tomes on the islands and their inhabitants. Japan established a record system for current inventory, collected vital statistics, and conducted five enumerative censuses. The 1930 census alone was published in four large volumes, giving for each unit the numbers, age, sex, marital status, place of birth, and occupation of the people of the major ethnic groups. Japan too sent her anthropologists and her archaeologists, and she added technical assessments oriented toward economic development and strategic utilization.

To both the Spaniards and the Germans, the islands of Micronesia were tangential to more important areas. Spain's focus of interest in the Pacific was the Philippines, while Germany emphasized New Guinea. Japan's demographic difficulties were so great that any land and any resources were desirable. A redundant labor supply invited the subordination of fiscal considerations to production possibilities.

The drive for the development of a Japanese population and culture in Micronesia was muted in part because of the publicity of annual reports to the League of Nations, in part because it was realized that procedures must be related to native capabilities. Public health and sanitation activities were expanded. Schools were started for native children, with a four-year course that placed heavy emphasis on "morals" and conversational Japanese.

The major population changes in Nanyo-gunto were by-products of the utilization of the limited lands of the Marianas by Japanese laborers engaged in the production and processing of sugar cane. The migration of the Japanese was not a movement of individual peasant families to a frontier where land was cleared from the jungle and homes built from the felled trees—or from coral. Rather, a subsidized corporation, the South Sea Development Company, cared for its employees and its share tenants in the traditional paternalistic fashion. The Company received state lands without rent, monopoly rights, subsidies, and tax exemptions. Laborers and tenants paid their own transportation from Japan but they received housing, medical service, and accident protection. Wage rates were about half those in Tokyo.

Although the early economic development of the southern islands emphasized the production of sugar, other types of agricultural production and more intensive utilization of the resources of the sea were contemplated. In the 1930's Japanese were moving into Ponape in the east Carolines for the production of manioc. Agricultural research was conducted in the adaptation of rice, coffee, pineapples, bananas, and potatoes to the peculiar conditions of the islands. The fishing industry was regarded as having the greatest possibilities for increases in food production and for the absorption of Japanese labor.

The production of sugar required the use of agricultural labor at low levels of remuneration, while the administration of the islands and the planning of expanded activities required professional, managerial, and technical personnel. There is evidence in the *honseki* maintained by the Japanese in Nanyo-gunto that two groups of people had been recruited from quite different segments of the Japanese home population. The following data are suggestive:

Place of HONSEKI	*1930*[26]	*1935*[27]	*1939*[28]
Japan	19,629	50,299	75,238
Tokyo	2,190	4,053	4,484
Okinawa	10,176	28,972	45,701

The only areas other than Okinawa that sent any appreciable number of migrants to the sugar plantations and related activities in Micronesia were northeastern Honshu and southern Kyushu.

The demographic evolution of the in-migrant Japanese population of Nanyo-gunto was comparable to that in Japan and the other colonies (TABLE 67). The early movement was predominantly male, but the proportion of women increased rapidly as family workers replaced labor battalions. Soon children born in the South Seas contributed to the normalization of the age and sex structure of the population. The sex ratio of the total Japanese population decreased from 5,395 males per 1,000 females in 1920 to 1,619 in 1930 and 1,363 in 1940. The Japanese were becoming a settled population in Micronesia—and Micronesia was becoming a Japanese land. Japanese constituted 7 per cent of the total population in 1920, 28 per cent in 1930, and 61 per cent in 1940. Natural increase was contributing to this rapid growth, for crude birth rates were from 49 to 51 per 1,000 total population and death rates were from 12 to 17. In the 1930's rates of natural increase approached or surpassed 3.5 per cent per year.

The impact of the Japanese on the economy, culture, and people of Micronesia was limited by their occupational and geographic concentration. As of 1930, some 16 thousand of the 20 thousand Japanese were in Saipan District, while more than 2 thousand were in Palau District. There were fewer than 750 Japanese in Truk and Ponape Districts respectively, less than 500 in Jaluit District, only 241 in Yap District. In the area of dense settlement, Saipan, 53 per cent of the gainfully occupied Japanese men and 67 per cent of the gainfully occupied women engaged in agriculture. The influence Japanese agriculturalists might have had on the practices of the Micronesians was limited by this concentration in limited areas of specialized production. In the Carolines and the Marshalls the Japanese were occupied predominantly in industry, commerce, and government service, but here also they were so concentrated in area and in type of economic activity that their direct influence on native life was limited.

The economic development of Nanyo-gunto, with its threatened inundation by Japanese, was not in the tradition of the dual economies of the East Asian tropics. Here there was small use of native labor in specialized agricultural production. Some Micronesians produced copra for the export trade, and about five hundred Micronesians labored in the phosphate mines of Angaur Island. Native production for exchange was limited indeed in relation to the production by imported laborers whose ethnic origin was the same as that of the administering power. The explanation inhered in part in the "primitive" condition of the Micronesians who reputedly "did not like to work," in part in factors extraneous to Micronesia. Japan's own demographic position differed sharply from that of European colonial powers, for she had abundant and culturally retarded labor within her own country. The internal colonials of the Ryukyu Islands created a segregated microcosm of rural Japan in Micronesia. It was in some ways comparable to the Japanese movement into Hokkaido and Karafuto, or to American expansion westward across the continent, however, for the Kanakas of Micronesia, like the Ainu of Hokkaido and Karafuto and the Indians of the United States, could not compete with the numerically superior and technically advanced immigrants. Nanyo-gunto was becoming a Japanese ethnic area.

TAIWAN

Japan's first major venture in imperial expansion involved the island of Taiwan. Fourteen thousand square miles with potentialities for development and colonization were enticing, but in addition they occupied a strategic location. Taiwan is scarcely a hundred miles from the shores of South China.

[26] Nanyo-gunto. Nanyo-cho. *Showa go'nen Nanyo-gunto tosei chosa sho. III. Hojin gaikokujin hen.* Table 25, pp. 452-453.

[27] Nanyo-gunto. Nanyo-cho. *Showa ju'nen Nanyo-gunto chosa sho, dai-ikkan, tokei hyo.* 1. Part II, Table 4, pp. 138-141.

[28] Nanyo-gunto. Nanyo-cho. *Nanyo-cho tokei nenkan, 1939.* Secret Edition. Table 8, pp. 8-9.

TABLE 67

The population of Nanyo-gunto, by ethnic group, 1920-1940

Ethnic group	*1920*	*1925*	*1930*	*1935*	*1940*[a]
Total	52,222	56,294	69,626	102,537	131,258
Japanese[b]	3,671	7,430	19,835	51,861[c]	80,490[d]
Micronesians	48,505	48,798	49,695	50,573	50,648
Aliens	46	66	96	103	120
Males	28,010	30,100	37,929	57,333	72,641
Japanese	3,097	5,074	12,262	31,158	46,434[e]
Micronesians	24,877	24,964	25,596	26,107	26,146
Aliens	36	62	71	68	61
Females	24,212	26,194	31,697	45,204	58,617
Japanese	574	2,356	7,573	20,703	34,056[f]
Micronesians	23,628	23,834	24,099	24,466	24,502
Aliens	10	4	25	35	59

[a] In 1940 all armed forces and persons attached thereto were allocated to the place of enumeration of the relatives who reported them in Japan proper.
[b] Japanese include nationals of the colonies other than South Sea Islanders.
[c] Including 546 Koreans and 6 Taiwanese.
[d] Including 3,472 Koreans and 7 Taiwanese.
[e] Including 2,284 Koreans and 7 Taiwanese males.
[f] Including 1,188 Korean females.
Source: 1920-1925: Japanese Government. *Annual report to the League of Nations on the administration of the South Sea Islands under Japanese Mandate.* Various issues. 1926-1931: Nihon. Naikaku tokei-kyoku. *Nihon tokei nenkan.* Various issues. 1930: Nanyo-gunto. Nanyo-cho. *Showa go'nen Nanyo-gunto tosei chosa sho.* I. *Sokatsu hen.* 1935: *Ibid. Showa ju'nen Nanyo-gunto tosei chosa sho, dai-ikkan, tokei hyo.* I. 1940: Nihon. Naikaku tokei-kyoku. *Census of 1940. Selected tables.* Table 1.

Luzon lies two hundred miles to the south, while northward lie the Ryukyus and Kyushu. The land and the people of Taiwan have long been involved in the struggles for control of the Pacific area.

Taiwan was a settled and somewhat developed land before the Japanese came. The Polynesian people who had moved into the virgin island in the long distant past possessed neither the art of political organization nor a knowledge of rice culture, but their techniques of aggression and attrition were sufficient to bar major migrations from the crowded mainland. The Portuguese visited Taiwan in the sixteenth century and gave it the name of Ilha Formosa, but they did not occupy it. It was a Dutch fleet from Java that first brought the culture and the economy of the West to the island. The Dutch ruled the western plain and other sections of the island from 1624 to 1661. These were days of crisis in China. As the Manchus moved from the north toward the centers of resistance in the south, soldiers and civilians alike fled across the narrow waters to Taiwan. Aborigines were pushed back toward the mountains and the Dutch fortresses were captured. From 1683 to 1895 Taiwan was ruled by a bureaucracy from China. Migrants came as settlers, first primarily Haklos from Fukien, then Hakkas from Kwantung. As the plains along the south were filled, settlement moved northward until the entire western plain was occupied. Increasing quantities of rice, sugar, camphor, oil cake, and other tropical products were sent to China and, after the British-Chinese Treaty of 1860, abroad. Japan secured Taiwan at the conclusion of the Sino-Japanese War of 1894-1895, and moved quickly to subjugate the people, preparatory to developing the resources of the island.[29]

The Japanese who first struggled with the problems of Taiwan knew little about long-run difficulties of economic and political development, particularly those aspects that involved population increase.[30] Their technicians and politicians estimated that 1.75 million acres could be added to the cultivated area of Taiwan, and that yields could be improved on areas already under cultivation. Half a century would be required for this agricultural development, they believed, and they saw the deficiencies of the native labor force as a major deterrent to rapid progress. Patterns of work were quite different from those in Japan, as none but the Hakka women worked in the fields. Natural increase seemed to offer few possibilities for an increase in the labor force, for recorded births were few and recorded deaths were numerous. The Japanese estimated that it would take more than a century for the population to reach six million. The importation of Chinese labor in the pattern of the plantation agriculture of southeast Asia and the islands of Oceania seemed the only feasible solution to the economic problems created by inadequacies of manpower.

The course of social and economic development in Taiwan during the twentieth century demonstrated the demographic naïveté of the Japanese officials. The early legends of Western travelers and the impressions of the Japanese as to the low fertility of the Chinese people in Taiwan were fallacious. As high mortality yielded to public health services and more

[29] A brief history is given in: Grajdanzev, Andrew J. *Formosa today.* Ch. II. For a detailed analysis of the demography of the Taiwanese population of Taiwan, see: Barclay, George W. *Colonial development and population in Taiwan.*

[30] References to demography and related aspects of life in Taiwan are given in the Bibliography, pp. 443-445.

adequate nutrition, the island of presumed depopulation demonstrated the reproductive power of Chinese people under favorable environmental conditions.

ECONOMIC DEVELOPMENT AND POPULATION INCREASE

Taiwan was an ideal site for the development of an agricultural economy supplementary to that of Japan. Its tropical climate permitted double and triple cropping, and the sugar and the fruits that Japan lacked could be grown in relative abundance. The cultivated area was extended, simple technical improvements introduced, more efficient varieties of rice and sugar developed, and cultivation practices improved. Agricultural experiment stations carried out research, while extension agents supervised production from the preparation of the soil to the marketing of the crop. The development corporations combined Japanese capital, management, and skills with Taiwanese land and labor. The government stimulated and protected capital formation and managerial control at the same time that its police and health policies stimulated the growth of a relatively healthy and quiescent labor force. The Taiwanese had only to contribute their labor and to give of their limited incomes to pay taxes, rents, and production expenses such as those for fertilizers.

The balance sheet of colonialism in Taiwan was generally satisfactory for the Japanese.[31] The initial capital came from Japan. Conditions were favorable enough to compensate for the hazards associated with fluctuating prices. Resources were underdeveloped at Japanese technical levels, and a benevolent government contributed protection, subsidies, and compulsion as needed. The developmental enterprises were so profitable as a whole that net income permitted expansion and diversification within Taiwan along with a flow of capital to Japan. While agricultural processing underwent development there was little industrialization in the sense of an economic transformation that removed major portions of the maturing youth of the peasant families from agriculture and village life. The industrialization that involved a labor force in urban areas began in the 1930's with the development and utilization of the mineral and hydro-electric resources of Taiwan as supplements for deficiencies in Japan. In time, Taiwan became a bastion for further economic and political penetration into those areas of Asia and Oceania that lay to the south.

The increasing product of Taiwanese agriculture sustained an increasing number of people at slowly advancing levels of living.[32] The total population increased 93 per cent between 1905 and 1940 (TABLE 68).[33] Improvements in sanitary, health, and nutritional conditions resulted in continuing declines in death rates, whereas whatever impact industrialization and urbanization might eventually have had on fertility was barely discernible by the late 1930's.

Throughout the Japanese period, the culture of Taiwan remained predominantly agricultural, rural, and insular. The cultivation of the land and the moving of the products of the land—sacking, rudimentary processing, and manufacturing of the jute gunny-sack—were the ways in which the Taiwanese earned their living. The procurement of food, clothing, and shelter involved some purchases from the outer money market, but the household and local industrial structures of the traditional society remained the major bulwark beyond immediate subsistence production. The resources, the capital, and the labor supply for industrialization of a Japanese type were available, but comprehensive industrialization did not occur.

Both the stability and the movement in the economy and the society of Taiwan were reflected in the growth of the cities and the characteristics of their populations. As late as 1940 more than four-fifths of the total population remained in the *gun*, and in the population of the *shu* (cities) there was an intermingling of urban and rural occupations. The real movement toward industrialism became apparent in the years from 1935 to 1940, when the normal momentum of an industrializing economy was re-enforced by the push toward imperial autarchy and military strength. New cities were created, old cities extended their areas, and population increased within the former boundaries of the cities. However, even urbanization of the magnitude of that occurring in this last quinquennial period was not sufficient to terminate the increase of the population in the *gun*. The total intercensal increase was 660 thousand; *shu* absorbed 44 per cent of this increase, *gun* 56 per cent. The Taiwan of 1935-1940 was less developed demographically than the Japan of the late nineteenth and early twentieth centuries.

THE ROLE OF THE JAPANESE

In theory, the administration and development of Taiwan were based on *kodo seishin*, the Spirit of the Imperial Way, the endless and indefatigable love of the mother for her children.[34] In fact, the Taiwanese were the laborers on the land and in the shops, while the Japanese were the administrators, entrepreneurs, professional personnel, and technicians (TABLE 69). The Taiwanese were rural and lowly; the Japanese were urban and generally advanced in social status. In 1930, 41 per cent of the Japanese were engaged in the professions and public service, 20 per cent in commerce, 16 per cent in industry, 10 per cent in transportation and communications, and only 5 per cent in agriculture and forestry. Among the Taiwanese, on the other hand, 71 per cent of the gainfully occupied were in agriculture, 8 per cent in commerce, and 9 per cent in industry. The Japanese, who constituted slightly less than 5 per cent of the total population, furnished 0.4 per cent of those occupied in agriculture, 3 per cent in mining, 9 per cent in industry, 10 per cent in commerce, and 17 per cent in transportation and communications, but 42 per cent of those in professional and public service. Taiwanese who entered industries other than agriculture usually held the unskilled and lower clerical positions.

The Japanese remained relatively few in number, despite the expansion and diversification of their role in the political and economic structure of Taiwan. Their proportion in the total population increased slowly from 3.9 per cent in 1915 to 5.0 per cent in 1930 and 5.4 per cent in 1940. Non-natives other than Japanese remained few: 9 thousand in 1905, 57

[31] This thesis is developed in some detail by George W. Barclay in: *Colonial development and population in Taiwan.*

[32] There is no reliable information as to the size of the population at the time of the conquest. The Japanese reported the population as 2.6 million in 1896 and 3.1 million in 1905, a highly improbable increase of more than one-fifth during the nine years that included the pacification of the island and the establishment of government.

[33] There are some artificialities in the reputed increase, for there were extensions of the area of coverage and a more inclusive coverage within areas that included "tamed" or "partially tamed" aborigines. The "untamed" aborigines were reputedly enumerated in 1930, but the number assumed to exist in that year is not known. Some 150 thousand were enumerated in 1935. These are included here as Taiwanese. The migrations of Taiwanese were slight. The migrations of Japanese were substantial, but they were not the major factor in the increase of 2.8 million between 1905 and 1940.

[34] See the explicit statement on page 21 of: *Taiwan. A unique colonial record.* 1937-38 Edition.

TABLE 68

The population of Taiwan, by ethnic group, 1905-1940

Year	*Total*	*Japanese*[a]	*Taiwanese*[b]	*Other*[c]
		Number (in '000)		
1905	3,040	57	2,973	9
1915	3,480	135	3,326	19
1920	3,655	165	3,467	24
1925	3,993	184	3,775	34
1930	4,593	229	4,314	50
1935	5,212	272	4,883	57
1940[d]	5,872	315	5,510	47
		Per cent change		
1905-15	14.5	136.2	11.8	105.3
1915-20	5.0	21.4	4.2	30.4
1920-25	9.2	12.0	8.9	39.4
1925-30	15.0	24.5	14.3	45.7
1930-35	13.5	18.8	13.2	14.4
1935-40	12.7	15.6	12.8	−17.2
		Per cent composition		
1905	100.	1.9	97.8	0.3
1915	100.	3.9	95.6	0.5
1920	100.	4.5	94.8	0.7
1925	100.	4.6	94.5	0.8
1930	100.	5.0	93.9	1.1
1935	100.	5.2	93.7	1.1
1940	100.	5.4	93.8	0.8

[a] Including Koreans and, in 1940, one male from Nanyo-gunto. Koreans numbered 6 in 1915, 69 in 1920, 297 in 1925, 898 in 1930, 1,474 in 1935, and 2,376 in 1940.

[b] Including those aborigines that were included in the specific enumerations.

[c] Others are "foreigners," mainly Chinese.

[d] Censuses from 1905 through 1935 included armed forces present in Taiwan. In 1940, members of the armed forces and persons attached thereto were reported by their families or other responsible persons and allocated to the residence of the person reporting them. Hence Japanese armed forces in Taiwan were allocated in major part to Japan.

Source: 1905. Taiwan. Rinji Taiwan koko chosa-bu. *Rinji Taiwan koko chosa shukei gempyo, zento no bu, Meiji 38-nen.* 1915: Taiwan. Sotoku kambo rinji koko chosa-bu. *Dai-niji rinji Taiwan koko chosa kekka hyo, Taisho yo'nen.* 1920: Taiwan. Sotoku kambo, rinji kokusei chosa-bu. *Dai-ikkai Taiwan kokusei chosa, dai-sanji rinji Taiwan koko chosa, shukei gempyo, zento no bu, Taisho ku'nen.* 1925: *Ibid. Kokusei chosa kekka hyo, Taisho juyo'nen.* 1930: *Ibid. Kokusei chosa kekka hyo, zento hen, Showa go'nen.* 1935: *Ibid. Kokusei chosa kekka hyo, Showa ju'nen.* 1940: Taiwan. Sotoku kambo, bunsho-ka. *Fuho,* No. 4170, pp. 130-131. 1941.

thousand in 1935, 47 thousand in 1940. Knowledge of the outer world and stimulants to change reached the Taiwanese through the Japanese, if at all. Similarly, it was the Japanese who gave to the outer world whatever knowledge it possessed of the island, its products, and its peoples.

The migrations and the socio-economic activities that create elites are manifest in the history of the Japanese in Taiwan. The earliest Japanese migrants were the soldiers of the conquest, but other groups came as civilian employees of government or as private workers. In 1905, ten years after the acquisition of the island, the sex ratios and age structures of the Japanese were those of a highly migrant population.[35] The sex ratio of 1,500 men for each 1,000 women was transitional, however, for migratory labor was being replaced by settled workers. Families had come, and Taiwan-born children were growing up on the island. The sex ratio for young children was a biological one, undisturbed by migration. In the ages from 16 to 25, however, there were marked deficiencies of men; the sex ratios were 780 for age 16 to 20 and 650 for age 21 to 25. Girls in these groups were moving to the island to marry men somewhat older than themselves. In the major productive ages from 21 to 40 there were 1,600 men for each 1,000 women. People over age 40 were the survivors of earlier migrants; they were few in number and there were 3,000 men for each 1,000 women.

The censuses of 1915, 1920, and 1925 show the continuing movement of a migrant population toward a stable population that was never achieved. The maturing of Japanese children

[35] Taiwan. Rinji Taiwan koko chosa-bu. *Rinji Taiwan koko chosa kekka hyo, Meiji 38-nen.* Pp. 26-27.

TABLE 69

The industrial composition of the gainfully occupied population of Taiwan, by ethnic group, *shu*, and *gun*, 1930

(Per cent composition of ethnic and residence categories)

	TOTAL			JAPANESE[a]			TAIWANESE[b]			ALIEN[c]		
Industry	*Total*	*Shu*	*Gun*	*Total*	*Shu*	*Gun*	*Total*	*Shu*	*Gun*	*Total*	*Shu*	*Gun*
						Total						
Total	100.	100.	100.	100.	100.	100.	100.	100.	100.	100.	100.	100.
Agriculture	67.2	9.7	74.2	5.0	0.9	11.4	71.1	13.9	76.1	3.4	0.2	7.4
Fishing	1.7	1.6	1.7	1.8	1.8	1.7	1.7	1.7	1.7	0.5	0.3	0.7
Mining	1.0	1.3	0.9	0.5	0.2	0.9	1.0	1.8	0.9	3.2	1.1	5.8
Industry	10.1	26.5	8.1	16.4	16.5	16.0	9.2	28.1	7.6	43.5	44.8	41.7
Commerce	9.1	26.6	7.0	20.3	25.2	12.9	8.2	26.9	6.7	29.0	27.5	30.9
Transportation and communications	3.2	11.2	2.2	9.9	9.3	10.9	2.8	11.2	2.0	13.4	17.9	7.9
Professions and public service	3.7	14.0	2.5	41.2	40.1	42.9	2.0	5.8	1.6	3.0	3.2	2.8
Domestic	0.5	1.8	0.3	1.7	2.4	0.6	0.4	1.6	0.3	0.9	1.0	0.8
Other	3.5	7.3	3.1	3.2	3.6	2.7	3.6	9.0	3.1	3.1	4.0	2.0
						Male						
Total	100.	100.	100.	100.	100.	100.	100.	100.	100.	100.	100.	100.
Agriculture	64.0	9.4	71.7	4.7	0.9	10.0	68.6	13.6	74.0	3.0	0.2	6.5
Fishing	2.2	2.0	2.3	2.1	2.2	2.0	2.3	2.1	2.3	0.5	0.3	0.7
Mining	1.2	1.5	1.2	0.5	0.2	1.0	1.2	2.0	1.1	3.4	1.1	6.1
Industry	8.6	23.4	6.5	18.2	18.5	17.6	7.4	22.5	5.9	43.2	44.0	42.3
Commerce	10.5	26.8	8.2	14.9	19.8	8.1	9.8	29.1	7.9	29.2	27.8	31.0
Transportation and communications	4.3	13.1	3.0	11.0	10.1	12.1	3.7	13.5	2.8	14.2	19.0	8.5
Professions and public service	4.7	15.2	3.2	45.2	44.3	46.4	2.5	6.4	2.1	3.0	3.2	2.7
Domestic	0.1	0.2	0.1	0.0	0.1	0.0	0.1	0.3	0.1	0.3	0.3	2.0
Other	4.4	8.4	3.8	3.4	3.9	2.8	4.4	10.5	3.8	3.2	4.1	2.0
						Female						
Total	100.	100.	100.	100.	100.	100.	100.	100.	100.	100.	100.	100.
Agriculture	75.5	11.0	80.7	6.8	0.5	21.2	77.8	15.2	81.3	10.0	0.9	19.7
Fishing	0.3	0.0	0.3	0.0	0.0	0.0	0.3	0.0	0.3	0.1	—	0.2
Mining	0.3	0.4	0.2	0.0	—	0.2	0.3	0.6	0.2	0.6	0.2	1.1
Industry	14.1	40.9	12.0	7.0	8.0	4.7	14.2	52.6	12.0	46.5	58.3	33.6
Commerce	5.4	25.7	3.9	48.1	48.8	46.3	4.1	16.9	3.4	25.9	22.0	30.2
Transportation and communications	0.4	2.3	0.2	4.7	5.6	2.7	0.2	1.2	0.2	0.4	0.5	0.3
Professions and public service	1.2	8.3	0.6	21.0	22.3	18.1	0.6	3.4	0.5	3.7	4.1	3.3
Domestic	1.5	9.1	0.9	10.2	12.5	4.9	1.2	7.8	0.9	10.9	12.4	9.3
Other	1.3	2.3	1.2	2.2	2.3	1.9	1.3	2.3	1.2	1.9	1.6	2.3

[a] Including Koreans.
[b] Including enumerated aborigines.
[c] Primarily immigrants from China.
Source: Taiwan. Sotoku kambo, rinji kokusei chosa-bu. *Kokusei chosa kekka hyo, zento hen, Showa go'nen.* Table 93.

in Taiwan combined with the ever-changing currents of migration to adapt population to political and economic requirements. Men continued predominant in the migration, as they were in the urbanward movement in Japan itself, but their predominance became less as migration came to involve essentially the choice of a place and a way of life rather than a hazardous venture to an unknown area. The age structures of the Japanese and the Taiwanese populations in 1930 picture the changes that had occurred in both populations during thirty-five years of symbiotic development. At the time, the proportion of the total population under age 15 was 34.7 per cent for the Japanese, 41.2 per cent for the Taiwanese.[36]

Any detailed analysis of the migrations of the Japanese in 1930 and the preceding years is hardly merited, for the period is long past and the numbers of people involved were few. Instead, we shall seek answers to three problems, each answer having a relevance that extends beyond the island world of Taiwan or even the Empire of that time. The first is the selectivity of the in-migration, the nature of the raw materials from which the elite of a rapidly developing empire was formed. The second is the relation among the in-migration of the governing people, internal migration, the growth of the indigenous population, and the preservation of the migrant status of the ruling group. The third is the contribution of the in-migration to demographic adjustment and the alleviation of the population problem in the home country. The results of this search for selectivity and upward mobility will be presented in integrated form rather than as answers to the specific queries.

The migrations to Taiwan were more diverse than those to agricultural frontiers. As early as 1905 there was bimodality in the *honseki* of the Japanese. The rural areas of Japan that were located near Taiwan contributed substantially, particularly Kagoshima and Kumamoto, but few had come from the adjacent Ryukyu Islands. Numbers tended to decrease with distance from Taiwan, with one significant exception: the great urbanized prefectures of Hyogo, Osaka, and Tokyo. Fifteen years later, in 1920, the *honseki* of Japanese in Taiwan show an increased preponderance of people from Kyushu but an extension of the area of recruitment upward around the shores of the Inland Sea. After the passage of another fifteen years, in 1935, there were 271 thousand Japanese in Taiwan. More than half of them maintained *honseki* in Okinawa, Kyushu, and the Honshu prefectures of Yamaguchi and Hiroshima. All the other prefectures had contributed to Taiwan, but the bimodality that reflected the major contributions of the great cities had disappeared.

The early movements to Taiwan had included soldiers, administrators, and business groups, but they had also included laborers and peasants. It was this bimodality in occupational structure and social status that was reflected in the distribution of the Japanese by *honseki* in 1905. Major portions of the men functioning on professional and managerial levels were in Taiwan on assignment from governmental or private organizations. These groups contained disproportionate representation from the metropolitan prefectures, particularly Tokyo. The laborers of the occupation came primarily from the southern prefectures, particularly Kagoshima and Kumamoto. These immigrants were less exacting in the life they demanded in Taiwan, for their areas of origin in Japan were poor and their opportunities through migration to cities in Japan rather limited. People of lower economic status who moved to Taiwan faced substantial financial problems if they decided that they wished to return to Japan, and thus were apt to remain as permanent settlers.

The differences in the initial reactions of immigrants conditioned later migrations. Professional people and business groups might find life in early Taiwan less attractive than that at home and report this fact to their friends. People from the rural areas whose home status was far below that of the residents of Kyoto or Tokyo might enjoy the status of an elite group in Taiwan. They would be more likely to send home glowing reports of the new life. Thus not only selective retention of original migrants but selective recruiting of future migrants would occur. These hypotheses are speculative, but they are consistent with detailed data on the interrelations and trends in the *honseki* of the Japanese in Taiwan. They also account for the increase in the numbers of Japanese with *honseki* in the agricultural regions and the relative stability in the numbers of Japanese with *honseki* in Tokyo, Osaka, and Hyogo prefectures.

A high selectivity in migration, or substantial upward economic mobility, or a combination of the two, was necessary to create the Japanese population in Taiwan from the people of the agricultural prefectures of southwest Japan. In 1930, the industrial composition of the gainfully occupied male population in Taiwan differed little according to place of *honseki* in Japan. Half of the gainfully occupied men from Kagoshima were classified in the professions and public service, less than 5 per cent in agriculture.

The development of an elite from persons of diverse but predominantly agrarian backgrounds had occurred within a single generation. Again in 1930, 94 per cent of the gainfully occupied Japanese in Taiwan were Japan-born, and this figure differed little from one industrial group to another. Some industrial groups were more mobile than others, if mobility is expressed in terms of the proportion of a given group that had been in Taiwan for varying numbers of years. On this criterion, persons in public service and the professions were most mobile, agriculturalists least mobile. However, a residentially stable group had developed among those who had migrated from Japan. In 1930, over one-third of all the gainfully occupied Japanese men in Taiwan had been there for more than fifteen years.

The demographic processes that were forming an ethnic minority from a migrant group were apparent in the age structures of the migrant status groups, although the length of the period was too brief to have created the native-born elite inherent in the situation. In 1930, more than four-fifths of the Japanese under age 10 were born in Taiwan.[37] This proportion dropped to two-thirds at age 10 to 14, two-fifths at age 15 to 19, and one-tenth at age 20 to 24. The native-born Japanese were not residentially stable within Taiwan, however, for the proportion of men living outside the province of birth increased sharply with age. There were two processes operative: one, the evolution of an indigenous population; the other, internal redistribution.

Korea

In 1592 the Japanese had invaded Korea as a step toward the conquest of China. After seven years of war the Japanese forces were withdrawn and Japan herself moved toward

[36] Taiwan. Sotoku kambo, rinji kokusei chosa-bu. *Kokusei chosa kekka hyo, zento hen, Showa go'nen.* Table 14.

[37] Taiwan. Sotoku kambo, rinji kokusei chosa-bu. *Dai ikkai Taiwan kokusei chosa, dai-sanji rinji Taiwan koko chosa, yoran hyo.* Table 10. 1930: *Ibid. Kokusei chosa kekka hyo, zento hen, Showa go'nen.* Table 55.

seclusion. Soon Korea accepted the suzerainty of the Manchu. Then from the seventeenth to the nineteenth century she also withdrew into seclusion. In Japan, the centuries of comparative isolation from external contacts involved the maintenance of peace, the extension of agriculture and, during the early period, rapid population increase. There was a growth of great cities and a development of production to supply the necessities and luxuries of an urban population. A commercial revolution involving both a substantial merchant class and a pecuniary economy was well advanced by the time of the opening to the West. The leaders of the Restoration turned toward the West to learn its techniques of industry and power, and they guided Japan cautiously along paths that ensured economic and military power in conjunction with political independence and social stability. In Korea, the last decades of isolation involved dynastic friction, social disorganization, and a deepening poverty. Here there was no great development of cities and no rising merchant class. Instead a landed aristocracy retained authority and limited even handicraft industries. During the early decades of contact with Western peoples there was vacillation on policy, with continuing reliance on China and a general procrastination in political and economic modernization. This reaction against the encroaching culture of the West had occurred in Japan also, but in Korea delay was longer and more serious. By the final quarter of the nineteenth century, Japan's major political orientation was toward the mainland of Asia, and Russia was extending her influence in the Far East. The imperial struggles led to the annexation of Korea by Japan in 1910.

Japanese rule changed the balance of births and deaths that had kept the numbers of the Koreans relatively constant, altered the occupational and residential distribution of the population, and stimulated both internal and external migration. Efficient economic utilization required the establishment of political order and the development of transportation and communication facilities, public health and sanitation, agricultural improvements, and eventually limited industrialization. The products of the economic development were diverted from local consumption into export channels. Thus death rates declined sharply, but a predominantly agrarian and illiterate people, living according to ancient ways, preserved the early age of marriage and the abundant childbearing that had enabled their ancestors to survive in the hazardous past. The consequence was a rate of population increase that jeopardized the social and economic welfare of the Korean people.

THE INCREASE OF THE KOREANS

In 1910, the year of the annexation, the Japanese instructed their police to make a complete count of the number of "natives" in Korea. The official report was 13.1 million.[38] The Government General stated that 200 thousand Koreans lived across the Yalu River in the Chientao area of China's northeastern region. The number in Japan was small. In 1940 there were 23.5 million Koreans in Korea, 1.4 in Manchoukuo, and 1.2 million in Japan. Within this thirty-year period the number of Koreans within Korea had increased by four-fifths, whereas the number in the northeast Asian region as a whole had almost doubled.

The increase of the Korean people during the colonial period is comparable to that of other peoples in and outside Asia who were subjected to supervised development (TABLE 70). Here, as elsewhere, increase was due primarily to a reduction of death rates under social and economic conditions that left fertility almost untouched. The Japanese deplored and feared the increase of the Koreans, but the continuation of population growth was a necessary correlate of the material, social, and economic conditions of the time. In 1930, four-fifths of the gainfully occupied men were in agriculture, and less than 6 per cent of the people lived in cities. In 1940, 69 per cent of the gainfully occupied men were in agriculture, and 10 per cent of the people lived in cities.

There were fundamental incompatibilities between the goals of the Japanese in Korea and the increase of the Korean population. The high rate of increase induced by the preservation of the agricultural society could not continue without reducing agricultural surpluses. The development of employ-

[38] Chosen. Government General. *Annual report on administration of Chosen, 1907-* . See especially: *The second-third annual report . . . 1910/1911.* Also: Chosen. Kosei kyokai. *Chosen ni okeru jinko ni kansuru shotokei.*

TABLE 70

The population of Korea, by ethnic group, *shi* and *gun*, 1925-1940

Population	*Numbers (in thousands)*				*Per cent change*		
	1925	*1930*	*1935*	*1940*	*1925-1929*	*1930-1934*	*1935-1939*
Total	19,523	21,058	22,899	24,326	7.9	8.7	6.2
Shi	850	1,190	1,606	2,821	40.0	35.0	75.7
Gun	18,673	19,868	21,293	21,506	6.4	7.2	1.0
Japanese	443	527	619	707	19.0	17.5	14.2
Shi	221	268	334	435	21.3	24.6	30.2
Gun	222	259	285	272	16.7	10.0	−4.6
Koreans	19,020	20,438	22,208	23,547	7.5	8.7	6.0
Shi	608	890	1,245	2,377	46.4	40.0	91.0
Gun	18,412	19,549	20,963	21,170	6.2	7.2	1.0

Source: 1925: Chosen. Sotoku-fu. *Kan'i kokusei chosa kekka hyo, Taisho juyo'nen.* Pp. 492-576. 1930: *Ibid. Chosen kokusei chosa hokoku, Showa go'nen.* 1935: *Ibid. Chosen kokusei chosa hokoku, Showa ju'nen, do hen.* 1940: *Ibid. Chosen kokusei chosa kekka yoyaku, Showa jugo'nen.* Table 7.

ment opportunities alternative to agriculture required major capital investments, and it necessitated social and educational opportunities for Koreans. An industrializing Korean economy competed for the markets and the raw materials desired by Japan herself.

A demographic crisis in Korea was averted by the increased and more diversified employment opportunities that accompanied Japanese military and industrial developments in the northeast Asian region. Koreans moved into Japan for employment in menial occupations for which Japanese labor had by now proved inadequate. They moved northward and westward to take advantage of the agricultural and industrial opportunities that accompanied Japanese developments in Manchoukuo. These external safety valves permitted major flows of Koreans from their crowded country. Between 1925 and 1940 the number of Koreans within Korea increased by 4.5 million. If there had been no migration of Koreans to or from the country, the increase would have been over 6 million. Migration had removed one-fourth of the population growth that would otherwise have occurred in Korea. The contributions of this out-movement to the achievement of a manpower-employment balance within Korea were larger than these over-all figures indicate, for the Korean migrants were predominantly men in working ages. In the absence of migration, the number of Korean men aged from 15 to 59 would have grown from 5.3 million in 1925 to almost 7 million in 1940, an increase of 30 per cent within a fifteen-year period. The actual increase was 16 per cent.

The utilization of Korean labor in the industrialization of Japan and Manchoukuo lessened but did not eliminate the increase of the Korean people within Korea. Numbers increased 24 per cent between 1925 and 1940. The absorption of this growth in the population within the limited economy of Korea was difficult. The accumulation of people in the rural areas continued in the 1925-1930 period, but between 1930 and 1940 there was considerable economic development within the country.[39] In this decade the total male population of Korea, including the Japanese, increased 13.5 per cent, but the number of persons engaged in agriculture declined almost 10 per cent and the number in industry increased 44 per cent. By 1940, 28 per cent of all gainfully occupied Korean men reported an occupation other than agriculture, and 10 per cent of the Koreans lived in cities. Redistribution within the country had been accelerating as the youth of the rural areas moved cityward and the crowded southern people moved northward for employment in the growing industrial centers, particularly those along the Yalu. In the five years between 1935 and 1940 the total population of Kyonggi-do (Keiki-do), including Seoul (Keijo), increased 17 per cent, while that of strategic Hamkyong-pukto (Kankyo-hokudo) increased 29 per cent. Four rural provinces lost in total population: Ch'ungch'ong-namdo (Chusei-nando), Cholla-namdo (Zenra-nando), Kyongsang-namdo (Keisho-nando), and Kangwon-do (Kogen-do).[40] By 1940, 9 per cent of all Koreans were living in a province other than that in which they were born; this proportion rose to 13 per cent for the migrant ages between 20 and 34.

If the growth of the Japanese economic and military system had continued without war or depression, the movement of Koreans outside Korea and the growth of cities within the country might have ended the period in which population growth augmented the problems of man-land relations in Korea. Eighty per cent of the increase of 3.2 million Koreans within Korea between 1925 and 1935 was absorbed in the rural areas. Between 1935 and 1940, on the other hand, 85 per cent of the increase of 1.3 million was absorbed in urban areas. Three facts are basic to assessment of this achievement, however. First, in the period between 1935 and 1940 the total natural increase of the Koreans in Korea was 2.4 million. Over 900 thousand migrated, leaving only 1.4 million of the 2.4 million increase within the country. Cities absorbed 85 per cent of the natural increase that remained within Korea—but only 48 per cent of the total natural increase. Second, both emigration and urbanization were by-products of Japanese activities rather than indigenous developments. Third, this first rough approximation to adequate utilization of the increasing people generated by economic developments of a colonial type occurred sixty-five years after Korea signed the first trade treaty with Japan, thirty years after Japan achieved effective control of the peninsula. In Japan, where economic development was indigenous, the rural population remained relatively unchanged from the Meiji Restoration to 1930 and declined thereafter. The entire natural increase was absorbed in the cities and in non-agricultural employment and, prior to 1930, there was little net loss through movements from the country.

THE ROLE OF THE JAPANESE

Japan supplied the managerial, professional, and technical groups responsible for the transformation of the economy of old Korea into one that maintained a greatly increased population and yielded export surpluses. The Japanese who moved to Korea in the early days were diversified; they included administrators, businessmen, laborers, and adventurers. They came predominantly from nearby areas of Japan where pressures of poverty were great.[41]

A strictly demographic assessment would indicate the relatively minor role played by these Japanese immigrants either in the alleviation of the population problem in Japan or in the increase in the rate of population growth in Korea. But here, as in Taiwan, Japanese movement to Korea was an aspect of political and economic movements that altered the relations of people to resources, the conditions of living, the internal migrations, and the balance of births and deaths in the areas of origin and of destination. The numbers of Japanese in Korea were important because they were a directive minority. In 1940 over one-fourth of the gainfully occupied Japanese men in Korea were in public service and the professions, only one-twentieth in agriculture.[42] Among the Koreans, on the other hand, over seven-tenths of the gainfully occupied men were in agriculture and only one-twentieth in public service and the professions. In 1944, one-fifth of the gainfully occupied Japanese men were in public service and professional occupations, excluding the armed services, while 37 per cent were in clerical and technical occupations.[43] Among Koreans, 95 per cent of the gainfully occupied men and 99 per cent of the gainfully occupied women were laborers.

Educational opportunities and educational achievements were commensurate with the role of the ethnic groups within

[39] Chosen. Sotoku-fu. *Chosen kokusei chosa kekka yoyaku, Showa jugo'nen.*

[40] Provincial names are given in Korean, with the Japanese names in parentheses.

[41] Chosen. Sotoku-fu. *Chosen kokusei chosa hokoku, Showa go'nen. Zensen hen, kekka hyo.*

[42] Chosen. Sotoku-fu. *Chosen kokusei chosa kekka yoyaku, Showa jugo'nen.*

[43] Chosen. Sotoku-fu. *Jinko chosa kekka hokoku, Showa juku-'nen go-gatsu ichijitsu.*

the economy of Korea. In 1944 the 3 per cent of the civilian men in Korea who were Japanese included half the college graduates of the country and over two-fifths of those who had some education beyond the elementary school level. In this same year, two-thirds of the Korean men aged 15 and over reported that they had never attended school. Less than 3 per cent had attended middle school; one-tenth of 1 per cent had attended a college or university. Education was being extended during this period, though, for more than two-fifths of the Korean boys aged from 15 to 19 had either completed elementary school or were attending school. Of Korean men aged from 20 to 24, 54 per cent had never attended school. Three-fourths of the Korean men who had been boys of school age when the Japanese annexed Korea in 1910 had never attended a school of any type.

THE MIGRANT INTERCHANGES

The exodus of the Koreans was greater than the influx of Japanese. Almost 500 thousand Koreans left Korea between 1925 and 1935; 900 thousand left between 1935 and 1940. On October 1, 1940, there were 707 thousand civilian Japanese in Korea, 1.2 million Koreans in Japan. In addition, there were 1.4 million Koreans in Manchoukuo. These 2.7 million Koreans in Japan and Manchoukuo constituted over 10 per cent of the total number of Koreans in the northeast Asian region.[44] (FIGURE 8). Their removal had resulted in an appreciable diminution of the pressure of an increasing agrarian people on the developing industrial and urban components of the Korean economy.

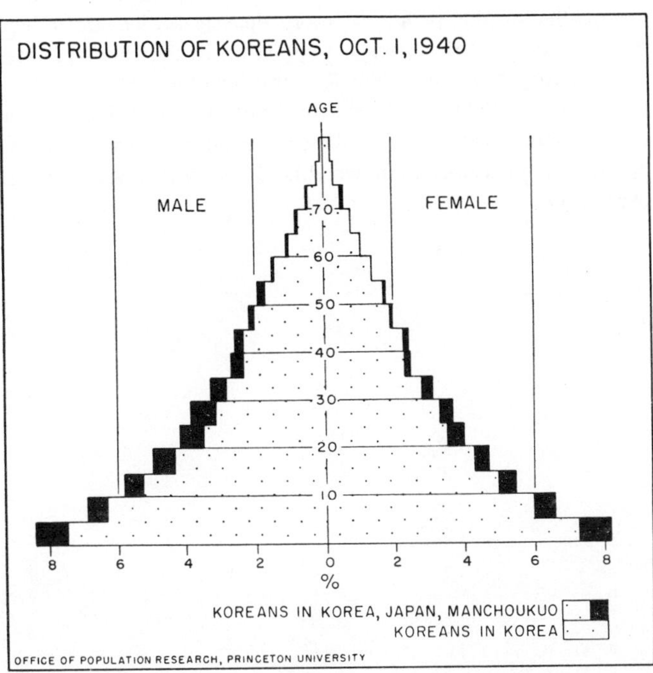

Figure 8. Per cent distribution of the Korean population in northeast Asia, by sex and age, October 1, 1940
Source: Chosen. Sotoku-fu. *Chosen kokusei chosa kekka yoyaku, Showa jugo'nen.* Manshukoku. Kokumu-in, somu-cho. [Population by ethnic groups and age, census of 1940.] *Seifu koho,* various issues, 1941-1942. Nihon. Naikaku tokei-kyoku. *Census of 1940. Selected tables.* Table 2.

[44] In the 1940 censuses of Japan, Korea, and Manchoukuo, 10 per cent of the total number of Korean children under 5 years of age and 15 per cent of the total number of men aged from 15 to 44 were enumerated outside Korea.

The migrations that removed 2.7 million Koreans from their crowded homeland represented both a continuation of the ancient processes of agricultural outflow on the peripheries of settlement and an introduction into mainland Asia of the complex movements and counter-movements that accompany modern industrialization. The 1.4 million Koreans in Manchoukuo in 1940 included 616 thousand in Chientao Province, where the northward push of Korean agricultural peoples had created an ethnically homogeneous Korean area within a Chinese region.[45] Within Manchoukuo, the Koreans were moving outward from Chientao, for they were more adept at northern rice cultivation than the Chinese. Industrial opportunities in urban areas multiplied as industrial developments in Manchoukuo were added to those in Kwantung and the South Manchuria Railway Zone. By 1940 there were more than 800 thousand Koreans in Manchoukuo in addition to those in Chientao Province. The greatest concentrations were in provinces adjacent to Korea where industrial developments were substantial; 500 thousand were enumerated in Kirin, Fengtien, Mutankiang, and Tunghua Provinces. In industrial Manchoukuo the Koreans were intermediate in the occupational hierarchy, with the Japanese above them and the Chinese below.[46]

The Koreans who moved to Japan came mainly from southern Korea, and they went principally to the industrial and urban regions of Japan. Fukuoka, Osaka, Tokyo, Kanagawa, Aichi, Kyoto, and Hyogo prefectures included two-thirds of the Koreans in Japan in 1940.[47] Within these metropolitan prefectures the Koreans were predominantly urban residents. Osaka, with its 215 thousand Koreans, contained the third largest number of Koreans of any city in the northeast Asian region, surpassed only by Seoul and Pyongyang.

THE ASSESSMENT

A note about the mythologies of migration may precede the demographic conclusions. There have been a number of widely accepted beliefs concerning the mobility of the Japanese. They were, it was held, a sedentary people who would not leave their crowded islands. As partial explanation, it was argued that Japan's culture was semi-tropical and hence that the Japanese would not move into cold climates. Students who have noted the course of Japan's mainland empire were prone to make two further generalizations: one, that the industrializing Japanase would not move to an agricultural frontier; the other, that the relatively higher levels of living of the Japanese people precluded substantial movements into areas inhabited by Asians of lower levels of living. The movements to Hokkaido, Karafuto, and Nanyo-gunto dispose of all these arguments except the last, and the movements to Taiwan and Korea dispose of it. Japanese moved to the frigid north and to the humid tropics; they moved into agriculture and into industry. They did not move to areas where economic opportunities were less desirable than those in Japan. Neither did they move into areas where they faced substantial discrimination as aliens. In positive terms, they moved toward greater economic opportunities in areas where political sta-

[45] Manshukoku. Kokumu-in, somu-cho. [Population by ethnic groups and age, census of 1940.] *Seifu koho,* various issues, 1941 and 1942. Also: Manshukoku. Kokumu-in, somu-cho, *Rinji kokusei chosa jimukyoku. Zai Manshukoku Nihonjin chosa kekka hyo. Kotoku shichi'nen rinji kokusei chosa, zenkoku hen.* Table 3.

[46] Koyama, Eizo. "Manshu ni okeru ido jinko: Rodoryoku to shite no coolie." *J.m.k.,* 1(3):1-31; (4):1-38. June and July, 1940.

[47] Nihon. Naikaku, tokei-kyoku. *Census of 1940. Selected tables.* Tables 1-2.

bility was ensured by the government and the armed forces of Japan and where the Japanese themselves were a superior group.

LIMITS OF LAND SETTLEMENT

Hokkaido, Karafuto, and Nanyo-gunto exemplify almost perfectly the limitations of pioneer settlement, whether agricultural or industrial, as a solution to problems of population pressure in densely settled regions. The migrants were recruited from the backward agrarian regions of Japan and they transferred the fertility of those regions to the areas into which they moved. In 1920, Hokkaido's gross reproduction rate of 3.3 was surpassed only by that of 3.4 in Aomori; its gross reproduction rate of 2.7 in 1935 was surpassed only by those of the four northeastern Honshu provinces. Fertility was related to the particular characteristics of residence and occupation on the frontier, and it was subject to the same depressant forces that operated elsewhere in Japan. In the more industrialized frontier of Karafuto, the gross reproduction rate was 2.7 in both 1930 and 1935. In Nanyo-gunto the birth rates of the migrants from the Ryukyus and the other agrarian areas of southwest Japan remained near 50 per 1,000 total population throughout the interwar decades. In Hokkaido, where there was a substantial movement to cities and non-agricultural employment throughout the 1920's and 1930's, fertility declined consistently and rather rapidly. However, at the rate of decline that characterized this period, it would have taken many decades to reduce the net reproduction rate to unity, even if mortality had remained at the somewhat high levels of the period.

While migrants and the children of migrants were settling the frontiers in the far north and the far south, other migrants were moving to the great cities and the industrializing regions. Tokyo grew primarily through the continuing in-migration of the surplus youth of the agricultural areas of northern and eastern Japan, the same regions that had peopled the northern islands. In Tokyo, however, the rural migrants modified the marriage pattern and the reproductive mores of their areas of origin and adopted those of the urban area into which they had moved. The gross reproduction rate of Tokyo was 2.2 in 1920 and 1.7 in 1935.

The out-movement of the surplus population of the rural areas reduced the pressure of people on the land, whatever the destination of the migrants. In the short run, the productive use of the labor of rural migrants in both the large cities and the frontier regions contributed to an increasing national income and an improving balance between people and resources for the nation as a whole. The critical problem for long-run assessment is the extent of the reduction in fertility and hence in potential labor force that accompanied agricultural versus industrial migration. In Japan, the contribution of frontier migration to the reduction of national fertility was limited. The migrants to the expanding frontiers in the north and in the south retained intact the high fertility patterns of the rural areas from which they came. There was a secular drift downward, since the peoples of the maturing frontier were also subject to the economic pressures and the cultural changes of the industrializing society.

Land settlement and frontier expansion were demographic palliatives during a period of rapid economic development. Once occupied, the frontiers became areas of potential population pressure unless further outlets were found, either in the cities or in still other frontier areas that could in their turn absorb the surplus people of more densely settled areas. The development of the Japanese population in the three-quarters of a century after the Meiji Restoration indicates that industrialization and the spread of urban patterns and values among the peasants were more efficient techniques for reducing population pressures than were land settlement and frontier expansion.

CHAPTER X

Imperial Expansion

THE early out-movements of the Japanese were limited ventures. No area was immediately available to accommodate any large proportion of the increasing population of Japan, and none provided major supplements to the land and other resources of Japan. But Manchuria offered promise of land for food production, minerals for industry, and a location strategic for consolidation or advance. The movement toward the greater Empire began with the conquest of Kwantung and the South Manchuria Railway Zone. It developed through the creation of the Empire of Manchoukuo and the establishment of a subservient government in the occupied areas of China. It involved episodic war and sporadic difficulties in 1931 and later years; limited war from 1937 to 1941; major war from 1941 to 1945. It led through the greatest extension of power in the history of Japan to the only total defeat and military occupation in that history.

The migrations of the Japanese to Kwantung, the South Manchuria Railway Zone, Manchoukuo, and Occupied China were comparable to those that had occurred earlier to Taiwan, Korea, and Nanyo-gunto. However, the numbers involved were greater, the developments were more rapid, and the association with the armed forces and military action was closer. Manchuria was neither an island of few possibilities nor a poor and overcrowded country. Rather, it was a vast area with potentialities for development as the nucleus of an industrializing northeast Asian region. The fundamental goals of the Japanese were industrial rather than agricultural, and the techniques used to achieve these goals were more complex than those of the late nineteenth and early twentieth centuries. While the annexation of Taiwan and Korea was in the pattern of the colonialism of earlier centuries and other countries, that of Manchoukuo was the precursor of indirect imperialism.

The consideration of the demographic aspects of Japanese imperial expansion into the northeast Asian region will be limited. The emphasis is placed on the Japanese, for this study concerns the demography of industrialization in Japan and among the Japanese people. Thus it touches only lightly upon the major demographic correlates and consequences of Japanese expansion—the transformation of Manchuria into a Chinese land through one of the greatest migrations of the twentieth century, the development of an industrial economy and its associated urban structures on the Asian mainland, the training of Chinese as an industrial labor force, and the building of a model of economic-demographic development even now being reconstructed by the Chinese Communists.

The migrations of the Japanese are difficult to summarize because of the scope and the rapidity of the movements. Manchuria will be considered first, including the early movements into Kwantung and the South Manchuria Railway Zone, as well as the later movements into Manchoukuo. Then follows a survey of events in Occupied China. The changing distribution of the Japanese in the world will be traced for the decades from 1920 to 1940, with emphasis on numbers and characteristics in the year 1940. Finally, we will undertake a summary consideration of the geographical expansion of the Japanese in relation to the industrialization in Japan.

MANCHURIA

Manchuria prior to the late nineteenth and early twentieth centuries was a frontier, never effectively peopled despite the pressure of population south of the Great Wall. The reasons lie in part in the remoteness of Manchuria's central plains and their agricultural and climatic conditions, in part in the characteristics of Chinese culture.

The traditional culture of China was efficient in that its agricultural techniques, family mores, and country-city relations enabled a great number of people to live in a limited area. However, it did not develop techniques that permitted the Chinese to adjust efficiently to geographic and climatic regions unfitted for the ancient ways of agricultural cultivation and rural life. And so Manchuria remained relatively empty. It has been estimated that less than two million Chinese were living in the northeast Asian region beyond the Great Wall when the Manchus conquered China in the seventeenth century. Under the Ching dynasty, Manchuria was preserved as a source of replenishment for Manchu life and culture rather than utilized for Chinese settlement. Some clandestine movements occurred, but cultural inertia, the hazards of pioneer life, and inadequate agricultural techniques barred any movement such as those that sent pioneers from Europe across the Atlantic Ocean and the American continent.

Manchuria's location made the area relatively immune to Western penetration from the sea during the early centuries of European expansion, but the Russians were advancing overland to the Pacific by the middle of the seventeenth century. Russian fortifications along the Amur were countered by Manchu programs for the defensive colonization of the northern frontier, but the difficulties were insurmountable in the pre-railroad period. Chinese estimates placed the population of all north Manchuria at less than two million people as late as the end of the nineteenth century.

The modern phase of development began with Russia's decision to build a railroad cutting across central Manchuria to Vladivostok. The railroad was completed in 1903, and Japan attacked Russia. By the terms of the Treaty of Portsmouth of 1905, Japan received the Kwantung Leased Area in the Liaotung peninsula and the portions of the former Russian Railway that ran from Harbin to Dairen and Port Arthur, together with sovereignty over the narrow strip of the Railway Zone itself. From 1905 to 1931 Japanese penetration of Manchuria was based on this limited but highly urbanized and economically developed area. After 1931 the entire region of the Three Northeastern Provinces and Jehol, together with Kwantung, were subject to economic development as a region in close relation to Korea and Japan. The population increase in the region was substantial, though estimates must substitute for precise figures. When Japan began her modern career of expansion on the mainland in 1905, there are said to have been from 16 to 22 million people in the Three Eastern Provinces of China and 410 thousand in Kwantung. The Research Department of the South Manchuria Railway Company estimated the population of Manchoukuo and the South Manchuria Railway Zone as 30 million in 1932. In addition, there were 961 thousand persons in Kwantung. The population enumerated on October 1, 1940, numbered 43.2 million in Manchoukuo and 1.4 million in Kwantung.[1]

The distribution of the population in 1940 illustrates the interrelated influences of topography, strategic factors, railroads, other economic activities, and historic settlement patterns in its growth (Map 10). Kwantung, the political, economic, and military base for Japanese domination, had an average density of 395 persons per square kilometer, over three times that of any province of Manchoukuo except Fengtien. The region of dense settlement within Manchoukuo was a wedge in the center, based on the provinces of Fengtien, Chinchow, and Antung, and extending upward through Kirin Province to the junction of the SMR[2] with the former Chinese Eastern Railway in Pinkiang Province. These five provinces, including the special municipality of Hsinking, contained 22.6 per cent of the area of Manchoukuo and 63.7 per cent of its population.[3] They possessed a disproportionately large share of the population engaged in industrial and commercial occupations, and they were also the major areas for rural settlement and agricultural production.[4] The mountainous peripheral country was sparsely peopled, especially the Hsingan provinces and Heiho. Strategic colonization, military transportation facilities, mining, and war-oriented industries produced intermediate densities of from 10 to 25 persons per square kilometer in the northeastern provinces adjoining the Soviet Far East. Continuing Korean immigration produced an over-all density of 28 persons per square kilometer in mountainous Chientao Province.

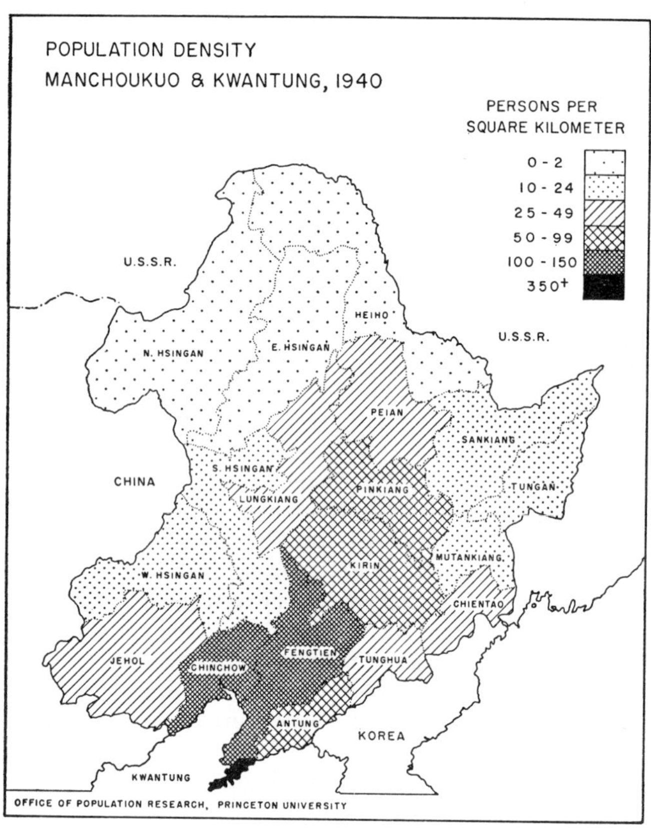

Map. 10. Density of population, Manchoukuo and Kwantung, October 1, 1940

Source: Manchoukuo: References, Footnote 1. Kwantung: Kanto-kyoku. "Kanto-shu kokusei chosa no kekka ni yoru jinko oyobi shotai, Showa jugo'nen." *Kanto-kyoku kyokuho*, No. 858, Supplement, pp. 1-4. April 19, 1941.

The rapidity of the industrial development of the northeast region is apparent in the growth of its cities. In 1940, the 4.4 million people resident in cities of 100 thousand and over constituted 10 per cent of the total population of Manchoukuo. The broad urban-rural patterns of settlement for the region as a whole remained those of a predominantly agricultural population. Twelve of the fifteen large cities were concentrated in the five south central provinces. This region included 4.0 of the 4.4 million people enumerated in cities of 100 thousand or more. In it lay Mukden (population 1.14 million), Harbin (662 thousand), and Hsinking (554 thousand). There were only two cities with a population of 50 thousand or more in the eleven mountainous provinces girdling Manchoukuo, and these two, Chiamussu and Mutankiang, owed their growth to the same type of industrial and military activity that had led to the growth of the cities of the central plains.

CHINESE

The building of the railroads and associated economic developments initiated a migration of Chinese labor that made Manchuria ethnically Chinese. By 1940, 36.8 million of the total population of 43.2 million were Chinese, as compared with only 2.7 million Manchus and 1.1 million Mongols (Table 71). There is little precise knowledge of the movements prior to 1923, when the Research Department of the South Manchuria Railway Company began publication of an annual series of estimates on migration to and from Manchuria, including Kwantung and the SMR Zone.[5] According to this series, there were 6.7 million Chinese immigrants in the decade from 1925 to 1935, but there was a return migration of 3.0 million, amounting to 45 per cent of the number of immigrants. The total migration between 1925 and the end of the first quarter of 1943 amounted to 14 million, but

[1] 1940: Manshukoku. Kokumu-in, somu-cho. [Population by ethnic groups and age, census of 1940.] All Manchoukuo: *Seifu koho*, No. 2503, pp. 256-258. September 22, 1941. Provinces and *hsien: Ibid.*, nos. 2108, 2122, 2136, 2189, 2212, 2236, 2278, 2343, 2407-2411, 2413, 2439, 2483, 2492, and 2503. Various dates, 1941-1942. For the earlier years, see the South Manchuria Railway Company's *Report on progress in Manchuria. . . .* If both the estimate as of December 31, 1932, and the census as of October 1, 1940, are correct, the total population of Manchoukuo and Kwantung increased 13.7 million in a period of less than eight years. Subtracting the net balance of Chinese coolie migration, 1.5 million, and an estimated net migration of 1.4 million Japanese and Koreans, the natural increase for the eight-year period would have had to amount to over 3 per cent per year to produce this total population increase. Since this rate of natural increase is not probable, it would seem that population estimates, migration figures, or both were in error.

[2] The South Manchuria Railway Company.

[3] Data on the populations and areas of the provinces and *hsien* were translated by Edwin G. Beal, Jr. and published in connection with his article, "The 1940 census of Manchuria." *The Far Eastern Quarterly*, 4(3):243-262. May 1945.

[4] Manshukoku. Chian-bu keimu-shi. *Manshu teikoku genju jinko tokei. Kotoku roku'nen jugatsu ichijitsu genzai, shokugyo betsu jinko tokei hen.*

[5] South Manchuria Railway Company. *Report on progress in Manchuria . . . .* Various issues. Also: Toyo keizai shimpo-sha. *Toyo keizai nenkan . . . .* Various issues.

TABLE 71

The population of the provinces of Manchoukuo, by ethnic group, 1940

(Numbers in '000)

		JAPANESE EMPIRE			"MANCHURIANS"						
Province	*Total*	*Japanese*	*Koreans*	*Other*	*Chinese*	*Manchu*	*Mongol*	*Moslem*	*Other*	*Nationals of third powers*	*Without nationality*
Total	43,203	818	1,450	1	36,873	2,677	1,066	194	50	4	65
Hsinking	555	110	16	0	411	8	1	6	1	0	1
Kirin	5,609	43	168	0	5,163	182	21	31	1	0	1
Lunkiang	2,094	24	8	0	1,880	65	100	8	8	0	0
Peian	2,319	30	28	0	2,164	90	2	4	0	0	0
Heiho	150	9	2	0	123	11	1	1	2	—	1
Sankiang	1,416	40	35	0	1,259	75	0	3	2	0	0
Tungan	512	29	33	—	418	31	0	0	0	0	0
Mutankiang	688	47	118	0	453	63	0	3	1	0	4
Pinkiang	4,234	71	66	0	3,735	298	7	12	3	2	39
Chientao	848	20	616	0	174	32	0	1	6	0	0
Tunghua	982	10	95	0	832	40	0	4	0	0	0
Antung	2,232	28	66	0	1,910	213	4	10	0	0	0
Ssuping	3,005	23	45	0	2,690	234	4	8	1	0	0
Fengtien	7,566	272	116	0	6,255	848	9	50	14	1	1
Chinchow	4,318	36	23	0	3,774	325	133	17	10	0	0
Jehol	4,553	9	1	0	4,244	136	135	27	1	0	0
West Hsingan	764	1	1	0	612	1	144	4	0	—	0
South Hsingan	1,027	3	9	0	549	12	450	3	0	0	0
East Hsingan	200	4	2	0	156	11	24	0	0	0	0
North Hsingan	132	9	1	0	71	1	31	1	0	0	18

Source: References, Footnote 1.

the net gain by migration amounted to only about 5 million. These figures on net Chinese immigration are believed to be understatements.

The annual fluctuations in the SMR migration series reveal the pattern of Chinese migration, even though they measure its magnitude only in crude approximation. Although the migration was a consequence of the development of railroads and job opportunities within Manchuria, the annual volume of movement reflected economic and political conditions in the area of origin, whether China or Manchuria. Immigration increased sharply after periods of famine or revolution within North China, and return migration increased in periods of war or political insecurity within Manchuria. In general, movement flowed from regions of disorder to regions of greater order.

Selectivity in the migration resembled that in comparable labor movements within Western culture. Before the war, 96 per cent of the Chinese migrants came from the densely settled and neighboring provinces of Shantung and Hopei, only 4 per cent from other provinces of China. Within Manchuria, the recent migrants remained predominantly in the south, while the settlement and the seasonal labor in the more open regions of the north were undertaken by earlier migrants or by the native-born. Systems of labor recruitment and utilization became increasingly complicated as Manchoukuo embarked on its Five Year Plans and the problem became one of a scarcity rather than a surplus of labor. At all times, however, migrants came from low economic levels within their villages of origin in North China and they held the more poorly paid jobs in Manchuria. This was true even in the earlier period, when practically all migrants except those to the SMR Zone were agricultural workers. It remained true when the majority of the seasonal laborers were used in Japanese-sponsored construction, mining, and industrial developments.[6]

THE KOREANS

The Korean migration into Manchoukuo was second to that of the Chinese. In 1940 there were 1.45 million Koreans in Manchoukuo itself—616 thousand in Chientao, 118 thousand in Mutankiang, 116 thousand in Fengtien, and 168 thousand in Kirin. The movements of the Koreans were noted earlier as correlates or consequences of Japanese policies in Korea. By the 1930's some of the Koreans in Manchoukuo had developed into a group intermediate between the administrative, executive, and professional people, who were Japanese, and the farmers and laborers, who were Chinese. However, the data of the annual police surveys made by the central government indicate that the majority of the Koreans were also agricultural and rural.

As late as 1939, the data compiled from the Manchoukuo

[6] Migration was highly seasonal. Chinese men left in February or March after the Chinese New Year and returned in November or December. This fluctuating labor supply was adapted to utilization during the agricultural season, but it retarded the development of either a stable or a semi-skilled labor supply within Manchuria. In the later years an increasing proportion of the migrants were accompanied by dependents and so presumably were more likely to remain within the country.

registers indicate that 73.3 per cent of the gainfully occupied Korean men were in agriculture.[7] According to the more accurate data of the census of 1940, 70.7 per cent of the gainfully occupied Korean men and 93.5 per cent of the gainfully occupied Korean women were so employed.[8] However, the industrial structure of the Koreans shows that they were a population in early economic transition from agricultural to industrial employment. Gainful employment outside agriculture was more common for men than for women, more common for youth than for the middle-aged and the aging. The following data on the percentages of the gainfully occupied in each age group who reported agriculture as their major industry reveals an age and sex pattern rather similar to that in the intermediate agricultural prefectures of Japan:

Age	*Male*	*Female*
16 and over	70.4	93.5
16-20	66.7	88.3
21-25	60.3	89.5
26-30	62.2	95.0
31-35	66.3	95.9
36-40	71.6	96.1
41-45	77.1	96.3
46-50	80.6	96.7
51-55	84.6	97.1
56-60	88.1	97.7
61-65	90.4	93.6
66-70	92.7	95.6
71 and over	95.8	94.4

The relations between Japanese imperial developments and Korean migrations are apparent in the relative proportions of migrants in the various age groups of Koreans in Manchoukuo. In 1940, only 30.1 per cent of Manchoukuo's 1.45 million Koreans had been born there. The proportion of immigrants increased quite sharply in the younger ages—from 34.0 per cent for those aged 10 or less, to 51.6 per cent at age 11 to 15, 67.5 per cent at age 16 to 20, 82.9 per cent at age 21 to 25, and 89.0 per cent at age 26 to 30. At age 51 and over, 97 or 98 per cent of Korean men and women in Manchoukuo were Korean-born. If we distribute the migrants by period of arrival in Manchoukuo, we see a rather complex pattern. In numerical terms, 309 thousand of the 1.0 million Korean immigrants had arrived in Manchoukuo prior to 1930; 155 thousand in the years from 1931 to 1935; 549 thousand in the years from 1936 to 1940.

The years in which Koreans of the various ages arrived in Manchoukuo reflect two historic movements. The earlier movement occurred while the Three Northeastern Provinces were part of China. It was primarily an agricultural settlement. The later movement occurred during the Japanese control of Manchoukuo, and it was both agricultural and industrial. The percentage distribution of the migrants in the various age groups by period of arrival for males appears at the top of the next column.[9]

The recency of the migration is indicated by the proportions who had come in during the year preceding the census; the percentages were 24.2 at age 16 to 20, 27.4 at age 21 to 25, and 22.0 at age 26 to 30. The high proportions of the

	Period of arrival			
Age	*1936-1940*	*1931-1935*	*1926-1930*	*Before 1926*
Total	56.1	14.8	7.2	21.9
10 and under	87.7	12.3	—	—
11-15	66.4	25.1	8.5	—
16-20	64.8	16.9	10.7	7.6
21-25	65.2	12.5	8.0	14.2
26-30	59.7	14.4	6.6	19.3
31-40	50.1	15.2	6.7	28.0
41-50	40.3	14.5	8.5	36.7
51 and over	29.5	12.4	9.0	49.1

older migrants who had been in Manchoukuo fifteen years or more indicate that many of these migrants who arrived for temporary jobs may have remained rather than return to the poor agricultural areas of North Korea from which most of them came.

The women migrants were less numerous than the men at all ages, and they had migrated somewhat more recently at all ages. It is probable that many came to marry Korean men already established in Manchoukuo. The industrial statistics suggest that most of them married Korean men gainfully occupied in agriculture. The participation of these women in gainful employment was very high, almost 70 per cent at age 21 to 30, 75 to 80 per cent at age 36 to 55. And, as we said earlier, 95 per cent or more of the gainfully occupied women aged 26 and over labored in agriculture. The total picture of the Koreans in Manchoukuo is rather comparable to that of the Koreans in Japan; they were a migrant group in transition to minority status.

THE JAPANESE

The third largest migration was that of the Japanese, who became bureaucrats, technicians, and administrative and supervisory personnel, first within the orbit of Kwantung and the South Manchuria Railway Zone, and later throughout Manchoukuo. On October 1, 1940, there were 820 thousand civilian Japanese in Manchoukuo. The rationalization for Japanese interest included the familiar motif of the need for agricultural settlement to relieve the overpopulation of the home country. The *de facto* acquisition of Manchuria in 1931 was followed by announcements of great colonization schemes that were to secure the settlement of a million Japanese families on the land within twenty years. Information on plans, organizations, and operational techniques was freely available from official and unofficial sources, in journals, broadcasts, and SMR publications. These colonization schemes were failures insofar as settlement is concerned, though figures on numbers of Japanese agricultural colonists differ. They appear to have numbered less than 85 thousand by the outbreak of the Pacific War in 1941.

The Japanese enumerated in Manchoukuo in 1940 were civilians, for Japanese armed forces were reported through military channels and allocated primarily to Japan. The relations between the movements of military personnel and civilians were so close, however, that the distinction between the two is somewhat arbitrary. One-third of the "civilian" Japanese men enumerated by Manchoukuo in 1940 had an army or a navy "service relationship," even though they were not at the time in or attached to the armed forces.[10] Men aged from 21 to 25, the conscript ages, were less than 70 per cent

[7] Manshukoku. Chian-bu keimu-shi. *Manshu teikoku genju jinko tokei. Kotoku roku'nen jugatsu ichijitsu genzai, shokugyo betsu jinko tokei hen.*

[8] Manshukoku. Kokumu-in-somu-cho, rinji kokusei chosa jimukyoku. *Zai Manshukoku Nihonjin chosa kekka hyo. Kotoku shichi'nen rinji kokusei chosa, zenkoku hen.* Table 3.

[9] *Ibid.* Table 4. [10] *Ibid.* Table 1.

as numerous as the preceding or the following age groups, and of this group who had escaped military service two-fifths had "service relationships." The proportions of the gainfully occupied men with such relationships increased to 66.1 per cent at age 26 to 30 and then declined to 62.2 per cent at age 31 to 35 and 31.7 per cent at age 36 to 40; it dropped to 7.9 per cent at age 41 to 45 and to even smaller percentages thereafter.

The proportions of the gainfully occupied among Japanese civilians in Manchoukuo were similar to those of urban populations in Japan. Among men, the percentage gainfully occupied increased from 54.2 at age 16 to 20 to 88.6 at age 21 to 25 and 97.9 at age 26 to 30, then remained at this high figure until the usual declines of late middle and old age.[11] Most of the men were recent migrants; 74.0 per cent had arrived between 1936 and 1940, 18.7 per cent between 1931 and 1935, 2.4 per cent between 1926 and 1930, 4.8 per cent before 1926. The proportions who had arrived after the beginning of the China War suggest the interrelations among civilian migration, military recruitment, and war production more clearly than any other data available for the Empire:[12]

	Per cent of migrants arriving in:			
Age	*1940*	*1939*	*1938*	*1937*
Total	25.1	21.4	15.8	6.9
10 and under	32.7	26.0	15.7	7.6
11-15	33.1	16.2	11.0	6.3
16-20	36.7	32.4	21.4	2.6
21-25	26.9	23.6	22.6	9.5
26-30	19.9	19.0	15.0	10.4
31-40	17.9	17.2	12.8	6.8
41-50	18.6	14.3	10.4	5.2
51 and over	19.1	10.9	7.2	4.3

The migrations mirrored in the tabulations of the census of 1940 were recent, but the migrants had generally high economic status. Moreover, substantial numbers had moved with their families. The proportions of the men who were married were rather similar to those of the urban groups in Japan: 55.8 per cent at age 26 to 30, 87.0 per cent at age 31 to 36, 91.9 per cent at age 36 to 40. Only 5.3 per cent were single at age 36 to 40, only 3.1 to 3.6 per cent at ages over 40. The possibility that major portions of the married men had left their families at home in Japan is ruled out by the fact that in 1940 there were 189 thousand married men and 151 thousand married women in Manchoukuo.

The migrations of Japanese women highlight both the class structure of the Japanese group in Manchoukuo and the presumed permanence of the relationship of Japan to the Manchoukuo regime. The women were recent migrants, as were the men, but the majority of the migrations had been for marriage rather than for jobs. The relationships among recency of migration, gainful employment, and marital status were as follows:

	Age		
Variable	*16-20*	*21-25*	*26-30*
Per cent migrant	92.7	98.3	99.3
Per cent of migrants arriving:			
1940	39.0	31.9	20.4
1939	26.4	25.6	19.4
1938	13.1	15.5	14.5
1937	5.1	8.1	9.4
Per cent gainfully occupied	61.4	38.3	19.9
Per cent single	90.0	38.4	13.9

[11] *Ibid.* Table 2. [12] *Ibid.* Table 4.

Almost two-thirds of the 37 thousand Japanese girls aged from 16 to 20 had arrived in 1939 or 1940, and most of them were single. It is probable that most of those who labored outside the entertainment and related fields had come with their families. More than three-fifths were gainfully occupied and, since few Japanese in Manchoukuo were gainfully occupied in agriculture, it is obvious that most of the girls labored outside agriculture. There were 58 thousand women aged from 21 to 25; most of them were recent migrants. More than three-fifths were married, while less than two-fifths were gainfully occupied. Presumably, many of these women had migrated for marriage. The 54 thousand women aged from 26 to 30 were older migrants, and most of them were married. Less than one-fifth were gainfully occupied. Thus we see in Manchoukuo, as in Japan, the role of marriage in the migrations of women and the preservation of the traditional status of women in the family through their withdrawal from the labor market outside the home after marriage. In broad outline and in detail, the migrations of Japanese women to the cities and the industrial areas of Manchoukuo were similar to the migrations of Japanese women to the great cities and the industrial areas within Japan itself.

THE INTERRELATED ROLES

The activities of the Chinese, the Koreans, and the Japanese were related to each other and to the activities of Manchus, Mongols, Russians, and other groups. The distribution of the gainfully occupied population of all Manchoukuo by ethnic group indicates the differentiations and the overlappings in the roles of the various groups.[13] At the end of 1939 the proportion of gainfully occupied men in agriculture and forestry was 74.0 for Manchurians (Chinese, Manchus, and Mongols combined), 73.3 for Koreans, and 10.3 for Japanese. The proportions in the three categories of manufacturing industry, commerce, and transportation were 13.7 per cent for Manchurians, 13.0 per cent for Koreans, and 44.8 per cent for Japanese. The proportions in public service and the professions were 4.4 per cent for Manchurians, 5.9 per cent for Koreans, and 26.2 per cent for Japanese. Members of the armed forces were not included in the civilian registers from which these data were abstracted.

Differences in the extent, the recency, and the selectivity of the migrations combined with differences in levels of fertility and mortality to create contrasting age and sex structures among the ethnic groups. The age structures of the indigenous peoples were similar to those of the indigenous peoples in the other colonial areas; the age structures of the migrant groups were similar to those of migrants elsewhere in the Empire. The migrant groups were weighted with young men, the extent of the weight being proportionate to the geographic and social-economic distance traversed in the movement. In Manchoukuo, as in the cities of Japan and among the migrant ethnic groups elsewhere in the Empire, in-migrant groups were yielding to native-born minority groups.

[13] Manshukoku. Chian-bu keimu-shi. *Manshu teikoku genju jinko tokei. Kotoku roku'nen jugatsu ichijitsu genzai, shokugyo betsu jinko tokei hen.*

The extent and the selectivity of migration were not the only factors responsible for the differences in age and sex structures among the peoples of Manchoukuo. Cultural values and practices associated with marriage and family created substantial differences in fertility, while ways of living, types of labor, income levels, and accessibility to health facilities and medical services were responsible for equally great differences in mortality. By 1940, however, death rates had been reduced far below birth rates among practically all ethnic groups. Population increase was appreciable among Manchus and Mongols, as among Chinese. Ratios of children to women were lower among the primarily urban Japanese than among any of the other groups, but they were not low in any absolute sense among the Japanese. Ratios were very high among Koreans, Chinese, Manchus, Moslems, and Mongols. Death rates, while high by Japanese standards, were far below those in North China.

The data are defective, but the evidence is cumulative and quite conclusive that the developments carried out by the Japanese initiated a sequence of events similar to those that had produced rapidly increasing populations throughout the dependent areas of Monsoon Asia. Increase and regularization of the food supply combined with famine relief and epidemic control to reduce mortality. The social and economic developments were not yet sufficient to reduce birth rates substantially below those traditional in the cultures. Thus the conditions in the new area were favorable to population growth both among indigenous peoples and among the immigrant Chinese and Koreans. By 1940 natural increase within Manchoukuo was leading toward the growth of a labor force that eventually would meet the needs of the region without massive in-migration from the densely settled areas of China and Korea.

INTERNAL REDISTRIBUTION

Internal migration, agricultural colonization, and urbanization were all aspects of the growth and redistribution of the population of Manchoukuo. The influence of migration from the outside is apparent in the sex ratio of 124 for the entire country, but the influence of internal migrations is apparent in the variations in the sex and age composition of the populations of the provinces, the cities, and the *hsien* (subdivisions of provinces).[14] Sex ratios for provinces were approximately equal to or below the national average in the central region, higher toward the periphery of the country. Ratios of less than 110 males per 100 females occurred only in Fengtien, Chinchow, and Antung, where Chinese migrants were more likely to consist of family groups, and where a dense agricultural population within the province sent male migrants to the developing cities. Ratios of over 175 occurred in North Hsingan, Heiho, Tungan, and Mutankiang—all active centers of war preparation, and all so sparsely settled that labor had to be imported from China, Korea, or southern Manchoukuo.

The greatest imbalance in the numerical relationship of the sexes, and thus presumably the heaviest concentration of in-migrants, were found in the cities. In 1940, the range among the fifteen cities of 100 thousand and over was from 128 in Liaoyang and 138 in Antung, both old cities, to 200 in Mutankiang and 259 in Penhsifu, both war-boom cities. The median ratio was that of 166 for Hsinking, the capital. These high sex ratios in cities were due in part to the prevalence of international migrations, in part to movements from rural areas to the cities. In Fengtien Province, for instance, the sex ratio was 167 in the cities, 109 in the *hsien*. However, only three of the twenty *hsien* had ratios of under 100, while four had ratios of 130 or over. In general, the predominance of males was least in the non-industrial *hsien* adjacent to large cities and in those with old and dense agricultural populations; it was greatest in agricultural, industrial, or strategic areas located in the sparsely settled frontier regions.

The predominance of men throughout Manchuria created social and demographic imbalances more severe than would be indicated by the sex ratios for total populations. The numerical relations of the sexes in childhood were those normal for a sedentary population, but beginning with early adolescence the male population was increased disproportionately by migration until in the central working ages of 15 to 50 men outnumbered women two or three to one.

The marital status of individuals is a crude reflection of the extent to which the migration of Chinese peasants disturbed the traditional pattern of Chinese family life. In 1940 in Mukden, for instance, there were 494 thousand men between the ages of 16 and 51, as contrasted with 235 thousand women. If the proportion of married women in Mukden was the same as that in the Manchurian population of Kwantung in 1935, and each married woman in Mukden was married to a man resident in Mukden, there were 175 thousand married couples in the city. If this estimate is correct, then two-thirds of the men aged from 16 to 51 were single or living apart from their families. Major disruptions in the traditional familial basis of living and working were associated with the absorption of Chinese into the diffusing industrial activities of the Japanese in Kwantung, the SMR Zone, and Manchoukuo.

There were major differences in the ratios of dependent to productive groups in the rural and the urban areas. Among the Koreans of Chientao Province in 1940, 40 per cent of the population was under age 16, 6 per cent was age 61 or over. Only 54 per cent of this predominantly agricultural and rural population was in the central span of productive life from age 16 to age 60. The burden of dependents per male worker in the productive ages was high indeed. In the cities of Mukden and Harbin, by contrast, one-fourth of the total population was under 16, 4 per cent was age 61 or over; from 70 to 75 per cent of the people were in the productive ages. Ratios of persons in the dependent ages to males in the productive ages were quite low. It cannot be assumed that age ratios in the cities of Manchoukuo reflect the actual burden of dependency on the men laboring in those cities, however, for dependents in the places of origin were major forces stimulating the movements of men in search of employment. Emigrant remittances to North China furnish strong corroboration of this fact. Low dependency ratios among the Chinese in the cities of Manchoukuo in 1940 reflected in part the geographical segregation of the worker from his dependents, in part the severity of the economic conditions that operated against the establishment of new families within the cities. They indicated economic pressure rather than the adoption of the small-family pattern as a part of the process of modernization.

[14] A high or low sex ratio for an area cannot be assumed to indicate the amount of internal migration unless movements are highly selective as to sex. However, Chinese coolie migration, recent Japanese and Korean migration, industrial and agricultural seasonal migration within the country, and movements into the cities for employment were all predominantly male. Hence a sex ratio above the national average of 124 can be assumed to reflect a concentration of migrants, even though the amount of the migration cannot be assumed to be proportionate to the extent of the excess.

DEMOGRAPHIC IMPLICATIONS

The geographical migrations, the occupational mobility, and the demographic transformation among Chinese were comparable to those among Japanese, just as those among Japanese were comparable to those among Western Peoples. However, it cannot be concluded from these similarities in migration and the evolution of a native-born population that the demographic significance of Manchuria for Asian peoples was similar to that of the American frontier for European peoples. Manchuria's potential contribution to the development of the Far East lay in some form of industrialization that would serve as the vanguard of the economic development of all China. She did not and could not serve as a major demographic safety-valve that would secure a more adequate relation of people to land in the densely settled areas of China itself. Moreover, the population growth occurring within Manchoukuo would have created serious economic problems if the type of economic and demographic developments that characterized the first half of the twentieth century had continued. The basis for these conclusions will become quite apparent as we consider the demographic service of Manchuria to the three areas that had contributed most to the migrations: Japan, Korea, and China.

In the decades when Japan was consolidating her position in Kwantung and developing the agricultural and industrial resources of Manchuria, there was a major emphasis on the contributions of Manchuria to the relief of rural overpopulation in Japan. The migration of millions of Japanese as agricultural colonists was an attractive prospect; it would increase the welfare of the people in Japan and secure a loyal population in Manchuria. But the vision of vast plains in a faraway land dotted with replicas of Japanese villages never became a reality. The levels of living of Japan's farmers seemed low to the urban Japanese, but they were far above those of Chinese peasants. Since that mass settlement which alone could have contributed greatly to the resolution of Japan's population problems would have entailed the direct competition of Japanese and Chinese in subsistence and in production for the market, mass settlement did not occur. Japanese moved to the cities and to non-agricultural employment, but here also factors of competition were critical. Manchurian industry needed laborers, but Japanese would not compete with either Koreans or Chinese. Japanese would move onto the mainland of Asia only as an upper social and economic group, and here the absorptive capacity of Manchuria was limited. The migrations of Japanese did not solve the population problem of Japan through the reduction of internal population pressures. Japanese did not occupy any appreciable proportion of the lands of Manchuria. However, the contributions of Japanese migration to the demographic evolution of Manchoukuo and Japan were not less because they were indirect. The Japanese immigrants contributed direction and supervision to the developing economy of Manchoukuo. For Japan, the emigrants to Manchoukuo were the entrepreneurs of a mainland industrialization that carried implicit within it a solution to Japan's problems of access to agricultural and other raw materials and markets for finished goods. Theories of migrations as safety-valves for accumulating population pressures are hardly sufficient explanations for migrations such as those occurring in the northeastern Asian region.

The permanent contributions of the movement into Manchuria to the economic adjustments of the Korean people were limited. In 1940 there were 23.5 million Koreans in Korea, 1.45 million in Manchoukuo. To assume that Manchoukuo could have continued to absorb her own ever-increasing Korean population, plus the 450 thousand to 500 thousand annual increase of the Koreans in Korea, would be naïve indeed. However, Manchoukuo became an urban and industrial frontier for the Koreans rather than a sparsely settled area where land could be cultivated. Koreans moved increasingly as laborers in industrial enterprises, as dwellers in the cities rather than in the rural areas. Manchoukuo's fundamental significance to Korea, as to Japan, lay in industrial development rather than in the existence of a frontier that relieved the pressure of overpopulation.

The fact that Manchuria was a relatively sparsely settled land adjacent to the densely settled "famine provinces" of North China led many students to assume that a flow of population would lessen the pressure in North China and develop the immense potentialities of Manchuria. Actually, Manchuria could serve only as the most limited of direct frontiers for a people as numerous as the Chinese. The analogy with the service of the American frontier to an industrializing Europe is hardly valid. The Manchoukuo of the 1930's was densely settled as compared with the America of the colonial period, and its limited area was adjacent to a China that was beginning its economic modernization with somewhere between 500 and 600 million people.

A few crude computations illustrate the difficulties involved in alleviating population pressure in China through agricultural settlement in any frontier regions. The population-carrying capacity of Manchuria has been estimated on the assumption that all potential agricultural resources were utilized according to existing techniques.[15] If the amount of cultivated land per capita in Manchuria reached that characteristic of south Manchuria in 1936, the total population would be about 82 million. If the per capita cultivated acreage were reduced still further to that of Hopei and Shantung provinces of China, the population would be 137 million. If we accept this estimate and further assume that the rate of natural increase within Manchuria was 1.5 per cent per year,[16] and that there was an annual net immigration of one million persons, density of settlement in all Manchuria would reach that characteristic of south Manchuria by 1960, that characteristic of Shantung and Hopei by 1980. The total population would reach 200 million by the year 2000. These specific computations are conjectural. It is quite possible, however, that migration might have continued until the population pressures north and south of the Great Wall were equalized. If this had occurred within a matrix of hand agriculture, low levels of living, and intact fertility, the ultimate consequences of the economic development of the northeast region would have been the equalization of poverty.

Occupied China

The out-migrations of civilian Japanese proceeded rapidly as Japan's armies conquered Chinese areas below the Three Northeastern Provinces. The addition of the conquered areas

[15] Moyer, Raymond T. "The agricultural potentialities of Manchuria." *Foreign Agriculture*, 8(8):171-191. August 1944.

[16] An approximation to the rate of natural increase within Manchoukuo and Kwantung was secured by assuming that the age structures and fertility of East Hsingan and Chientao were representative of the rural areas, and that those of Mukden and Harbin were representative of the urban areas. A population with the sex ratio and the degree of urbanization of Manchoukuo and Kwantung in 1940, and subject to mortality at the level characteristic of Korea during the period from 1925 to 1930, would have a crude birth rate of from 40 to 45 per 1,000 total population and a crude death rate of from 20 to 25. Hence it is quite conservative to estimate the rate of natural increase as 1.5 per cent per year.

of China to the Japanese imperial structure was intended as a permanent relationship in a great Co-Prosperity Sphere that would unite the industrial capacities of Japan with the agricultural resources of mainland Asia. The cities of North and Central China became new meccas for the administrators of government, the technicians and managers of industry, and the less reputable groups who follow conquering armies into alien lands. By October 1, 1940, more than 355 thousand civilians with *honseki* in the Japanese Empire were resident in China—284 thousand Japanese, 54 thousand Koreans, and 17 thousand Taiwanese.[17] Here finally appeared to be the solution to Japan's problems. The demands for Japanese manpower in China seemed to be insatiable, the supply deficient.

The Japanese in China were recruited widely from within Japan itself and from parts of the Empire. The places of *honseki* indicate two major sources for migrants. One was the Inland Sea prefectures of Okayama and Hiroshima; the other was the prefectures of Kyushu. Nagasaki led all other prefectures with 20,302 persons. Fukuoka came second with 19,710. Over 13 thousand of Kagoshima's citizens were in China, but only 883 of Okinawa's. Here, as in the other migrations of the Japanese, migrants were recruited primarily from the nearest geographical areas with suitable people who were inadequately utilized locally. And, as in the other migrations, there was an exception to all the principles of geographical selectivity in the contributions of Tokyo prefecture. Tokyo's 16 thousand civilian citizens in China ranked her third in all Japan as a source of migrants, surpassed only by Nagasaki and Fukuoka.

The migrations that had brought the Japanese to China were diverse in type. A comparison of the number of migrants born in the prefectures of Japan with the number of migrants having *honseki* in these prefectures reveals small but sizable deficits of the native-born in all prefectures. Moreover, 35 thousand persons with *honseki* in Japan were born outside Japan, 9 thousand in Empire areas, 26 thousand in China itself. Thus two of the typical processes of imperial growth could be discerned within three years after the military movement into China. The first was the interrelation of the frontiers—the movement from Hokkaido to Manchoukuo to North China, from Fukushima to Tokyo to China, from Kagoshima to Fukuoka to Manchuria to China. The second was the formation of a native-born group of Japanese in the new area, the beginning of an elite for whom the imperial area might have become home had the political structure of the period survived.

The Japanese in China in 1940 appear to have been a more highly selected group than any of the earlier pioneers of political and economic penetration. There were few youth and few aged, the concentrations being young men in their twenties and thirties. Only 1,211 of the total of 130,371 gainfully occupied men were in agriculture. College graduates were very plentiful for a Japanese population—7 thousand. Almost all children of the appropriate ages were in elementary or middle school, and large proportions of the boys were going on to high school and college either in China or in Japan. Many of the women were middle school graduates.

The civilian Japanese were associated closely with an army that held and developed local areas while it continued military actions. Migration was controlled to prevent an undue exodus either of skilled personnel or of moral undesirables from Japan. In these circumstances, the movements were predominantly male. Sex ratios were quite high in the age group over 40, where men outnumbered women two or three to one. These older men apparently left their families at home in Japan or the Empire while they accepted foreign assignments. Something of this sort occurred among men in their thirties, for in this age group there were 1,957 men for each 1,000 women. For youth in their twenties, however, there were 1,166 men for each 1,000 women. The presence of children in almost normal numbers for an urban population of upper social-economic status suggests that the Japanese who were moving to North and Central China regarded the move as an economic opportunity. In 1940, 22.8 per cent of all the Japanese were under age 15; the proportions were 19.9 per cent for men and 26.7 per cent for women. There were almost 900 children under age 15 for each 1,000 women aged from 20 to 49.

Plausible arguments can be given for disregarding this last demographic spillway of Imperial Japan. However, the conquests in China illustrate the conditions under which an industrializing people will migrate and the types of migration that can be solutions to population problems such as those of Japan. Here, as in Manchoukuo, Japanese found social and economic opportunities superior to those at home. Moreover, they moved as a racially and culturally superior people, not as a racially suspect and culturally backward people tolerated because they would develop difficult and isolated areas from forest into productive fields. The number of civilian Japanese in China alone after three years of military occupation was almost 60 per cent of the number in the world outside the colonies, Manchoukuo, and China. It is difficult to escape the conclusion that the successful migrations of the Japanese have been correlates of war rather than of peace, products of the ambition of the educated people of the modern society and the pursuit of profits by the great companies, rather than of the despair of tenant farmers and the welfare schemes of governments.

Other Areas

In 1940, more than three-quarters of a century after the theoretical opening of new portions of the world to Japanese emigrants, the Foreign Ministry of Japan reported that less than half a million people with *honseki* in Japan lived outside Japan, the colonies, Manchoukuo and Occupied China.[18] The distribution by continents was as follows:

Continent	*People with* honseki *in Japan*
Total	475,821
Asia (outside Japanese-occupied areas) and Oceania	40,502
North America, including Hawaii	206,871
Latin America	226,847
Europe	1,429
Africa	172

[17] Nihon. Gaimu-sho chosa-kyoku. *Kaigai zairyu hompojin chosa kekka hyo, Showa 15-nen.* Table 1.

[18] Reports to the Japanese consulates or embassies were tabulated annually to provide data on Japanese abroad. Each census year there was a detailed reporting and summation. In 1940, when there were censuses in Japan, the colonies, and Manchoukuo, especially detailed reports were required for all areas outside the imperial structure. The survey utilized required information on name, date of birth, place of birth, place of *honseki*, year of last in-migration, gainful employment and industry, and highest grade of school completed. The major publication was: Nihon. Gaimu-sho chosa-kyoku. *Kaigai zairyu hompojin chosa kekka hyo, Showa 15-nen.*

Distribution was more concentrated than these continental totals imply. Only six countries outside the area of imperial rule had as many as 10 thousand Japanese with *honseki* in Japan. The numbers in the individual countries in 1940 were as follows:

Country	*Persons with* honseki *in Japan*
Philippines	19,233
Hawaii	92,097
Canada	20,043
United States	94,731
Peru	20,056
Brazil	193,156

These figures on Japanese abroad are compilations of registrations with the consulates in the various countries and regions of the world. There are major omissions, particularly of isolated groups and of young children. There may also be duplications and errors. For instance, there was often substantial delay in the removal of the names of the dead from the consular lists. Since the Japanese do not recognize the acquisition of citizenship by Japanese born abroad, many of the individuals reported as Japanese were also citizens of other countries. Presumably the consular reports were most complete and accurate for such areas as Mindanao in the Philippines and the region of concentrated settlement in Brazil where recent Japanese immigrants were living as Japanese, least complete and most inaccurate in areas such as the United States where assimilation was in process. Problems involving intermarriage of Japanese with other ethnic groups did not arise except in a few areas where assimilation was occurring.

If migration is viewed solely as a technique of draining off population from a country regarded as overpopulated, then these migrations of the Japanese outside the sphere of Japanese control were insignificant. If it is viewed in terms of its demographic, economic, social, and political interrelations, then we cannot cast aside the migrations of the Japanese so casually. Migration was believed to have been a significant factor in population adjustment; perhaps the belief itself was a factor in adjustment, regardless of its truth or falsity in the light of statistical analysis. There may be situations in which other Asian peoples in process of industrialization will flow into still other areas in major numbers. Hence the trickle of migration of Japanese from the central area of Japanese power merits consideration on practical as well as on theoretical grounds.

In historical terms, the Asian migrations of the Japanese were recent, the North American migrations old, the Latin American migrations intermediate or continuing. In 1940, the proportion of Japanese who had been residents in the areas of enumeration less than five years were 77.0 per cent for Asia and Oceania (including China), 5.9 per cent for North America, and 19.8 per cent for Latin America.[19] Conversely, the proportions resident ten years or more were 12.9 per cent for Asia and Oceania (including China), 87.6 per cent for North America, and 45.1 per cent for Latin America. The Japanese in most areas of the world represented either "old" or "new" migrations. Only in the Philippines and Brazil were there continuing movements from the 1920's through the 1930's. And in the case of both these countries, the migrations of the Japanese were centrally planned, heavily subsidized, and politically oriented.

The earlier migrations of the Japanese had been in the tradition of the contract labor system. Men were moved in groups for specified tasks. In 1940, the sex ratios for Japanese aged 60 and over were above 5,000 in the Philippines and the United States, above 4,000 in Canada. The more recent migrations were also predominantly male, but the excess of men was markedly less. In 1940 in Brazil the sex ratio for Japanese aged 60 and over was less than 1,200. However, in no area of the world external to Japan did the sex ratio of the Japanese group as a whole indicate normality in age and sex structures. The continuing interchanges between Japan and other areas were such as to maintain imbalances in sex and age structures. There were losses of Japanese youth in the return of the sons to Japan for education; there were increases through the in-migration of brides. The normal aging of the population was retarded by the return of aging and aged to Japan—a migration itself doubtless selective as to sex, marital status, and the presence or absence of children in the land of residence.

The status of the Japanese abroad was related to the economic and cultural conditions, the income levels, the social mobility, and the political philosophy of the society into which they had moved. In the Philippines, as in Brazil, the Japanese were agricultural people living under conditions reminiscent of those in Japan. In Hawaii, Canada, and the United States, most Japanese were employed in industries other than agriculture, and many of them lived in cities. In the agricultural settlements of Asia and Latin America, educational levels were lower than those in Japan itself. In the United States, the total Japanese population had achieved educational levels almost equivalent to those of the elite and highly selected group in Occupied China (TABLE 72). It is interesting to note that the proportion of the Japanese women in the United States who had graduated from college was greater than that of Japanese men who had secured college degrees in any area except the United States and China.

The age structures of the overseas Japanese suggest the existence of differential fertility similar to that found within Japan. Ratios of children under 5 per 1,000 women aged from 20 to 49 were very high in the Philippines and Brazil, low in Hawaii and the United States, intermediate in China. The number of youth under age 15 per 1,000 women aged from 20 to 49 was 972 in Asia (including China), 726 in North America, 1,968 in Latin America. In the Philippines the ratio was 2,471; in Sao Paulo, Brazil, it was 1,930. The ratios were 703 in the United States and 605 in Hawaii.

Selective recruitment within Japan contributed to the differences among the Japanese abroad. The predominant places of *honseki* for Japanese in the United States were the prefectures along the Honshu side of the Inland Sea—Wakayama, Okayama, Hiroshima, and Yamaguchi in Honshu, together with Fukuoka and Kumamoto in Kyushu. These were on the whole the more well-developed areas of the old Japan. Migrants to Hawaii came in major portions from Yamaguchi, Fukuoka, Kumamoto, and Okinawa, with Niigata and Fukushima as a secondary area of origin. These areas were more feudal in social organization and less well-developed in economy. The agricultural settlers in the Philippines and Brazil come from the lower economic groups and the more isolated areas, particularly Okinawa and southern Kyushu.

19 Presumably native-born children were given the duration of residence of the father, since the tabulations on duration of residence include the total Japanese population and the numbers are such that children under five cannot all be included in the "less than five years" resident category. See: *Ibid.*

TABLE 72

Educational status of Japanese with *honseki* in Japan but resident outside Japan, the Empire, or Manchoukuo, 1940

Selected continents and countries	Per cent persons of school age or over but never attending	Per cent of those who had attended school, by highest school of graduation: Elementary	Middle	Higher	College
			Males		
World	2.2	56.4	20.0	4.4	3.1
Asia	0.5	49.4	26.8	7.8	5.0
China	0.2	45.9	29.0	8.2	5.3
Philippines	0.8	89.3	6.0	0.6	0.4
North America	3.3	53.5	20.1	1.5	2.3
Hawaii	5.3	59.4	14.7	0.4	0.9
Canada	1.5	69.8	13.2	0.5	0.7
United States	1.8	45.5	25.9	2.7	3.8
Latin America	3.9	73.3	7.1	1.0	0.4
Peru	1.7	87.5	6.9	0.6	0.2
Brazil	4.3	72.1	6.4	0.8	0.3
			Females		
World	5.1	61.0	22.4	0.9	0.3
Asia	2.1	59.6	31.3	1.4	0.1
China	1.7	58.6	32.2	1.4	0.1
Philippines	1.5	95.0	2.5	0.2	0.1
North America	6.6	51.8	24.4	1.0	0.7
Hawaii	10.9	58.6	16.0	0.4	0.0
Canada	2.6	69.6	16.4	0.4	0.1
United States	2.4	41.2	34.4	1.7	1.4
Latin America	7.9	73.7	5.4	0.2	0.0
Peru	3.0	87.1	7.8	0.2	0.0
Brazil	8.6	74.0	4.7	0.1	0.0

Source: Nihon. Gaimu-sho chosa-kyoku. *Kaigai zairyu hompojin chosa kekka hyo, Showa 15-nen.*

Ten thousand of the 19 thousand Japanese in the Philippines had *honseki* in Okinawa. The recruitment for Brazil was more nearly nation-wide than any other of the external migrations, but even here there was considerable selectivity. Hokkaido, Hiroshima, and Fukuoka each contributed from 10 to 15 thousand people, while Fukuoka and Okinawa contributed from 15 to 20 thousand. More than 21 thousand of the 51 thousand Japanese with *honseki* in Kumamoto were in Brazil. However, a few thousand migrants from each of the prefectures of Tohoku, the Japan Sea side of central Honshu, and the intermountain areas of heavy population pressure were found in Brazil in 1940.

In Japan the decisions as to migration were made by the heads of houses or family councils rather than by individuals or consanguineous families. There, as in the West, the general principles as to the role of geographic-economic nearness remained valid. Migrants came in major numbers from the nearest accessible areas where people found the prospects of life abroad more attractive than the realities of life at home. Migrants who went beyond the sphere of Japanese control originated in the main in the lower social and economic levels of Japanese society and entered the lower levels of the countries where they settled. The migrants were predominantly of agricultural rather than industrial origin, from *mura* rather than *shi.* Their education had been received in elementary schools rather than in colleges. The history of the migrants after they had settled in new countries depended on the channels of upward mobility open to them. If economic opportunities for men and educational opportunities for children were superior to those in Japan, the controls of the old society of Japan were gradually loosened. Assimilation proceeded for the Japanese in these special circumstances as it had in similar situations for immigrants from European countries. In the United States, acculturation occurred for the Japanese despite the gulf of culture and ethnic origin, and amalgamation was in process even before World War II.[20] In Hawaii the Japanese were components of the multi-racial and multicultural society. In both the United States and Hawaii, physical type responded to the altered environment and the changed patterns of marital selection. In the Philippines and Brazil, on the other hand, agricultural migrants transplanted their own closed society into agricultural regions.

The processes of migration and migrant adjustment presented a dilemma to Japan. The demographic justification for emigration lay in the relief of population pressures, but emigration was also a means of imperial expansion. The demographic contributions of migration would have been maximized if Japanese could have entered freely into an area

[20] Sabagh, George, and Thomas, Dorothy S. "Changing patterns of fertility and survival among the Japanese-Americans on the Pacific coast." *American Sociological Review,* 10(5):651-658. October 1945.

such as the United States and been assimilated rapidly into its industrial and urban culture. The political contributions of migration would have been maximized if Japanese had moved freely into strategic areas and remained firmly Japanese in culture and in loyalties. The movements of the Japanese to low-income agricultural areas were successful in that the Japanese remained Japanese, their loyalties to house and emperor largely intact. However, the development of large colonies abroad was difficult. The movement of poor people to undeveloped land was an expensive activity. Thus the type of migration that maintained and even increased the number of loyal Japanese in the world contributed little to the solution of the population problem of Japan because the numbers involved were relatively small and the costs great. Migration of peasants to still more retarded peasant areas maintained the fertility of the migrant groups at levels appreciably above those current in the rural areas of Japan in the period after the migrants left.

The Dispersions of Two Decades: 1920-1940

Within three-quarters of a century after the Meiji Restoration, Japan had secured a great imperial area—Taiwan, Korea, Nanyo-gunto, Karafuto, and Kwantung within the Empire, Manchoukuo and Occupied China within the Co-Prosperity Sphere. In 1940, however, only 2.9 million of the 75.2 million Japanese in the world were living in these areas (Table 73). The Japanese had shown that they could develop an industrial region far to the north of the homeland to which their people and culture were adjusted, but less than 400 thousand Japanese were living in Karafuto. Taiwan and Nanyo-gunto had demonstrated the contributions Japan might make to the development of the tropical lands of southeastern Asia, but only 389 thousand Japanese were living in these areas. The drive for hegemony over northeast Asia had begun in the early Restoration period. To secure domination of the great regions which they controlled in 1940, the Japanese had hazarded the Russo-Japanese War, the Manchurian conquest, and the invasion of China south of the Great Wall. Yet in 1940 only 2.1 million Japanese were living in this mainland area of the Empire and affiliated states. Less than half a million Japanese were living in foreign areas. In fact, some 71.8 million of the 75.2 million Japanese in the world were living in the 47 prefectures of Japan itself.[21]

Comparison of the numbers of Japanese in Japan, in the areas of hegemony, and in other regions leads to a facile but somewhat spurious repudiation of migration as a major factor in the demographic adjustments to Japanese industrialization. Migration was not a demographic panacea, but it was a palliative. Practically all the currents of emigration removed young men who would otherwise have been contenders in the labor markets of the home country. In 1940 there were 8 per cent fewer Japanese men aged from 20 to 34 in Japan as civilians than there would have been without migration and war-associated mortality between 1920 and 1940.[22] In addition, one million men were outside Japan as members of the armed forces.

Although imperialism, militarism, and their associated movements were significant factors in the balance of people and resources within Japan and in the areas dominated by Japanese, the fundamental determinants of the size and distribution of the Japanese population remained natural increase and internal redistribution within Japan itself (Table 74). The population increments that produced such rapid rates of increase among Japanese in the colonial and occupied areas were relatively small in terms of the size of the base population of Japanese in Japan and the rate at which this population was increasing. The percentage deficiencies and surpluses in numbers of men in relation to those expected without migration or war losses serve as illustration:[23]

	Japan		*Empire*	
Age	*1920-1930*	*1930-1940*	*1920-1930*	*1930-1940*
15-59	−1.2	−3.8	39.6	33.2
10-19	−1.3	−3.4	50.5	48.7
20-24	−4.2	−7.6	204.6	72.5
25-29	−2.9	−8.0	129.5	116.0
30-44	0.1	−2.2	11.7	22.3
45-49	0.2	−0.9	−5.4	−0.3

Relatively small decrements among Japanese in Japan were sufficient to produce rapid increase in the Japanese populations of the colonial and related regions. In each occupied area, rates of increase were high in the early period of occupation, low as the agricultural economy became organized, high again with the transition to industrial and military utilization in the 1930's. Throughout there was a process of turnover among migrants that diffused the influence of the external areas throughout Japan. In the decade from 1920 to 1930, the number of Japanese increased more rapidly in the colonies than in areas outside the Empire, more rapidly in Karafuto and Nanyo-gunto than in Taiwan and Korea. In the decade from 1930 to 1940, the greatest increases were in the northeast Asian mainland and, within it, in the newly affiliated areas of Manchoukuo and Occupied China.

With the dispersion of the Japanese came new concentrations, for in all areas to which they went major portions lived in the larger cities. The wider physical distribution did not involve assimilation into the culture of the areas into which the Japanese went, even for the native-born children of the migrants. Amalgamation was slight. The movements into the colonies were comparable to those of Western peoples ruling native peoples in colonial territories. The movements into the wider areas of the Asian mainland were comparable to those of the German migrants who regarded themselves as ethnically superior to other groups in Eastern Europe or in Latin America. The cultural integration that would have permitted Japanese to live in other Asian areas without imperial protection did not develop. Thus the continued contributions of Japanese to the economic development and urban growth in the areas where they resided were dependent on the continuation of the political *status quo* or further extension of Japanese rule.

[21] Since members of the armed forces were allocated to the residence of their nearest of kin, the populations given for the various areas outside Japan are reasonably close to civilian populations.

[22] These computations were made on the assumption that there was no migration of Japanese to or from Japan between October 1, 1920, and October 1, 1940, but that births and deaths in this fictitiously secluded population occurred at the rates which characterized the actual Japanese population of Japan in the successive intercensal periods between 1920 and 1940. Since armed forces were included in the 1940 population utilized for Japan proper, and the life tables of civilian deaths in normal periods were used, this is essentially a picture of what the civilian migrations of the Japanese would have been without war mortality.

[23] See Footnote 22 concerning the aging of the Japanese population of Japan. The populations of the colonial areas were aged to 1930 and 1940, the life tables of Japanese in Japan being used for the 1920-1930 period, interpolations between the life tables of 1935-1936 and 1947-1948 being used for the 1930-1940 period.

TABLE 73

Distribution of the Japanese in the world, by sex and age, 1940

		JAPAN			COLONIAL AND IMPERIAL AREAS					FOREIGN AREAS			
Age	*World*	*Total*	*The 46 prefectures*	*Okinawa*	*Total*	*North (Karafuto)*	*South (Taiwan and Nanyo-gunto)*	*Northeast Asia. (Korea, Kwantung, Manchou-kuo)*	*Occu-pied China*	*Total*	*Asia and Oceania, excluding China*	*North Amer-ica*	*Latin Amer-ica*
					Total								
Total	75,198	71,810	71,236	574	2,912	399	389	1,840	284	474	41	207	227
Under 15	26,917	25,896	25,662	234	891	144	134	548	65	129	11	34	84
15-59	42,517	40,253	39,974	279	1,943	241	243	1,243	216	319	28	153	138
15-19	7,650	7,269	7,224	45	323	41	38	222	22	58	2	31	25
20-29	12,241	11,450	11,382	68	700	69	79	461	91	90	9	41	40
30-39	9,751	9,175	9,114	61	512	63	68	315	66	65	9	24	32
40-59	12,875	12,359	12,254	105	409	69	59	245	36	107	9	57	41
60 and over	5,764	5,661	5,600	61	78	14	12	49	3	25	1	19	5
					Male								
Total	37,656	35,778	35,508	270	1,611	221	206	1,021	163	265	27	114	124
Under 15	13,599	13,081	12,962	119	452	73	67	279	33	66	7	18	42
15-59	21,498	20,194	20,067	127	1,120	141	132	718	129	182	21	82	79
15-19	3,852	3,632	3,610	23	188	21	20	137	10	30	1	16	13
20-29	6,115	5,693	5,661	31	371	37	40	245	49	51	6	22	23
30-39	4,979	4,631	4,605	26	312	39	39	190	44	36	6	12	18
40-59	6,552	6,238	6,191	47	250	44	34	146	26	64	7	32	25
60 and over	2,560	2,503	2,479	24	40	8	6	24	2	18	1	15	3
					Female								
Total	37,541	36,032	35,728	304	1,300	177	183	819	121	209	14	92	103
Under 15	13,317	12,815	12,700	115	438	71	66	269	32	64	6	17	41
15-59	21,020	20,059	19,906	152	823	100	111	525	87	138	8	71	59
15-19	3,798	3,637	3,615	22	135	20	18	85	12	28	1	15	12
20-29	6,127	5,757	5,720	37	329	32	39	216	42	41	3	20	18
30-39	4,772	4,543	4,508	35	200	24	29	125	22	28	2	12	14
40-59	6,323	6,121	6,063	58	158	24	25	99	10	42	2	25	16
60 and over	3,204	3,158	3,121	37	39	6	6	25	2	7	0	5	2

Source: Japan and Okinawa: Nihon. Naikaku, tokei-kyoku. *Census of 1940. Selected tables.* Table 2. Karafuto: Nihon. Kosei-sho, daijin kambo, tokei chosa-bu. *Dai-hachi kai seimei hyo.* Data section. Nanyo-gunto: Age distribution as of 1939 as given in Nanyo-gunto. Nanyo-cho. *Nanyo-cho tokei nenkan.* 1939, secret edition. Taiwan: Taiwan. Provincial Government. Bureau of Accounting and Statistics. *Results of the seventh population census of Taiwan, 1940. . . .* Korea: Chosen. Sotoku-fu. *Chosen kokusei chosa kekka yoyaku, Showa jugo'nen.* Kwantung: Kwantung, Kanto-kyoku. "Kanto-shu kokusei chosa no kekka ni yoru jinko oyobi shotai, Showa jugo'nen." *Kanto-kyoku kyokuho,* No. 858, Supplement, pp. 1-4. April 19, 1941. Ages estimated. Manchoukuo: Manshukoku. Kokumu-in, somu-cho, rinji kokusei chosa jimukyoku. *Zai Manshukoku Nihonjin chosa kekka hyo. Kotoku shichi'nen rinji kokusei chosa, zenkoku hen.* Other areas: Nihon. Gaimu-sho chosa kyoku. *Kaigai zairyu hompojin chosa kekka hyo, Showa 15-nen.*

TABLE 74

World distribution of Japanese aged from 15-59, 1920-1940

Area and year	*Age 15-59*	AGES				
		15-19	*20-24*	*25-29*	*30-44*	*45-59*
World						
1920	31,742	5,506	4,756	4,049	10,595	6,835
1930	36,863	6,630	5,641	4,934	11,384	8,275
1940[a]	42,517	7,650	6,309	5,932	13,713	8,913
Japan (47 prefectures)						
1920	30,884	5,409	4,591	3,909	10,245	6,729
1930	35,717	6,478	5,440	4,759	10,965	8,076
1940[a]	40,253	7,269	5,944	5,506	12,947	8,588
Empire						
1920[b]	547	66	109	92	212	67
1930[b]	815	111	154	132	287	131
1940[a]	1,131	182	167	192	401	189
Abroad						
1920	311	31	57	47	137	38
1930	331	40	47	44	132	68
1940[a]	1,132	199	199	234	365	136

[a] Armed forces allocated to residence of kin reporting them.
[b] Excluding the South Manchuria Railway Zone and including armed forces wherever stationed.
Source: 1920: Nihon. Naikaku tokei-kyoku. *Taisho ku'nen kokusei chosa kijutsu hen.* 1930: *Ibid. Showa go'nen kokusei chosa saishu hokokusho.* 1940: References, Table 72.

The Mobility of the Industrializing Region

The economic development of the colonial areas as segments of the Japanese imperial system increased mobility in the populations of the affiliated areas. The usual emphasis in analyses of the populations of the individual Asian areas has been on stability, for quantitative materials have been limited largely to the period from World War I to 1930 or 1931. Actually, all migrations increased in frequency throughout the last quarter-century of the Empire. The stable life was characteristic of agriculture; the mobile life was a product of non-agricultural activities and city growth.

The building of the Empire in the classic agricultural pattern required the movements of Japanese as administrative, professional, and managerial personnel. It did not generate interchanges of any magnitude. Japanese became the labor force of Karafuto and Nanyo-gunto, but cultural differences, distances, and limited numbers barred external movements of the Ainu and the Micronesians. The Taiwanese increased rapidly throughout the Japanese period, but the agriculture of the area was relatively prosperous, the distance to Japan was great, and the culture not conducive to exodus. In 1940, only 20 thousand Taiwanese were living in Japan, less than 1,000 elsewhere in the Empire. The movement of Koreans into Japan was a counter-current to the exodus of the Japanese. As we have seen earlier, Korea was an area of pressure on limited and generally poor land. There was land access to Manchuria to the west and north, sea access to Japan in the east. In 1920, ten years after the formal annexation of Korea by Japan, there were 42 thousand people from the colonies in Japan, virtually all of them Koreans. In 1930, the number had increased to 424 thousand; in 1940 it was 1.2 million. In demographic structure, as in numbers, this influx of Koreans into Japan was largely compensatory to the Japanese exodus prior to the movement into Manchoukuo and Occupied China. Korean migrants, like Japanese, were young, and men outnumbered women. As the migration developed, however, proportions of women increased, families were established, and children were born in a land not their own among people of an alien culture. A Japanese minority was developing in Korea, a Korean minority in Japan.

The economic roles of the emigrant Japanese and the immigrant Koreans were complementary, each group filling a vacuum in the society of the other. The vacuum in Korea was in groups skilled in the procedures and techniques of modern production and distribution, while the vacuum in Japan was in the groups whose occupations were menial and remuneration low. Japanese from the more rural and somewhat backward prefectures of Japan who had secured education and industrial or governmental experience found in Korea a path to upward mobility in the industrial society. Koreans from the agricultural areas of south Korea moved as unskilled laborers to or on the peripheries of Japanese cities. Here they too found a path to higher income.

As the pace of migration quickened in the late 1930's, the exodus of Japanese exceeded the influx of Koreans, with the result that for the first time international migration was reducing not merely the Japanese population of Japan but the total population of the country. Korean movements had become substantial, however, for the increase in the number of Koreans in Japan amounted to some 800 thousand between 1930 and 1940, to about 350 thousand between 1940 and

1945. At the time of Japan's surrender there were 1.6 million Koreans in Japan.

The movements that involved the crossing of territorial lines were minor among those being generated by Japanese industrial and military activities. Urbanization and regional redistribution were occurring in once lethargic peasant societies. The analysis of these migrations and their implications for the various areas is not appropriate to a study of the Japanese, for they were the somewhat accidental carriers of the industrial culture of the West to other societies of the East. The Japanese repatriation of the postwar years disentangled the various imperial and colonial peoples, leaving only the substantial Korean minorities in Japan and Manchuria as ethnic heritages of the period of intra-Empire and imperial mobility. The return of the Japanese and their absorption in the economy of Japan will be considered later as one of the demographic consequences of expansionism and war, as one of the population problems of reconstruction and development. The disentanglement of the population with changes of empire in Karafuto, Taiwan, Nanyo-gunto, Korea, Kwantung, China, and Southeast Asia is a subject for separate study.

PART VI

NATURAL MOVEMENTS

CHAPTER XI

Marriage

MARRIAGE among the Japanese is a folk ritual. Its historical evolution and present form alike reflect the merging of traditions from the peoples and cultures that moved into Japan in the ancient days. Among the common people co-operative and easy relationships once prevailed, with boys' and girls' clubs, sleeping houses, and group-arranged marriages.[1] Among the elite, on the other hand, the principles governing marriage were Confucian. The sex practices and reproductive institutions of the common people were derived in major portion from the southern intrusions, while those of the elite trace to China.

The codified laws of the Great Reform of the seventh and later centuries prescribed family domination and individual submission in the selection of marriage partners, the behavior of wives, and the dissolution of marriages. Over the centuries marriage and family patterns became highly developed for the *bushi.* Regulations concerning marriage, separation, and remarriage were detailed. The peasants were influenced by the norms and practices of the upper groups, but they responded more directly to changes in the economic and political structure. The major evolutionary forces appear to have been those of the society itself operating within the culturally intermingled patterns of the past. The political instability of the period of the *shoen* strengthened the role of the male and the cohesion of the family group. Political, social, and ethical forces re-enforced the economic compulsions toward the subordination of the individual to the family which maintained continuity between past and future. The villages were densely settled, land was limited, and cultivation intensive. Adequate production required abundant family labor, but as mouths to feed this labor threatened the family's survival. Specific marital and family practices may not have been determined by this economic and cultural background, but they represented adjustments to it. Primogeniture retarded the fragmentation of holdings and the cumulation of people on tiny plots. Endogamy was also suitable to the external situations in which families found themselves. Marriages within villages involved a reallocation of the labor supply but no additional burden of labor or of maintenance for the village as a whole. Marriages outside the village involved readjustments in day-to-day family relations. They also altered labor relations and created tensions as to ownership and cultivation rights.

In the premodern period, marriage patterns differed in various regions of the country.[2] With the Restoration the statesmen selected as the models for the nation the codes of the *bushi* class and the Confucian-based family system.[3] The problem was that of transforming the divergent and often permissive social controls of sexual behavior, marriage, and divorce into a monolithic familism. The individual life was to become subordinate to that of the *ie*, or house. The *ie* was to be the essential institution in a way of life that would maintain the social structure and the values of the agrarian past in the industrializing present. The marital provisions of the civil code were the most critical of all the control devices of the old Japan. They were intended to serve as an impenetrable barrier to any individualization of values that would destroy the family system and the imperial institution.

CIVIL CODES AND STATISTICS

The regulations of legal marriage in the civil code were reasoned specifications rather than simple assertions of male prerogatives.[4] If the head of the house was to be responsible for the veneration of ancestors, the continuity of the house, and the preservation of property, he had to control the marital selection of the son who was the heir and to guard against the dissipation of property or the disgrace of name by his other children. Hence the head of the house had the authority to refuse *koseki* entry to any marriage of which he did not approve.[5] Responsibility rather than personal wishes, duty rather than happiness, were the critical factors in decisions concerning marriage. This had been true for the head of the house when he was young, for the mother-in-law when she was a bride. It had to remain true so long as the patrilineal and patriarchal familism institutionalized in the *ie* was the dominant regulator of individual life.

When the Western analysts in the offices of the Supreme Commander for the Allied Powers surveyed the Japanese scene, they found in the marriage system and its correlated status of women the basic causes of "feudalism" in the society. Hence the new constitution and the revisions of the civil code ". . . uprooted the centuries-old semi-feudal 'house system,' founded upon Confucian principles, and replaced them by a code premised upon a respect for the dignity of the individual and equality of the sexes."[6] Article 24 of the new constitution read as follows:

> Marriage shall be based only on the mutual consent of both sexes and it shall be maintained through mutual cooperation with the equal rights of husband and wife as a basis.

[1] Kawashima, Takeyoshi. *Nihon shakai no kazokuteki kosei.* Ariga, Kizaemon. *Nihon kon'in shi ron.* Part 1. Also: Chiba, Masashi. "Wakamono gumi no ichi ruikei-sonraku kozo ni kanren shite." *Ho shakaigaku,* No. 3, pp. 50-64. 1953. Fueto, Toshio. "No gyoson ni okeru. . . ." *Ho shakaigaku,* No. 4, pp. 102-110. 1953. And: Yanagida, Kunio, Editor. *Sanson seikatsu no kenkyu. Ibid. Kaison seikatsu no kenkyu.*

[2] Chiba, Masashi. "Wakamono gumi no ichi ruikei—sonraku kozo ni kanrei shite." *Ho shakaigaku,* No. 3, pp. 50-51. 1953.

[3] Kawashima, Takeyoshi. *Nihon shakai* . . . . Pp. 7-15.

[4] English translations of the prewar civil code: Becker, J. E. de. *Annotated civil code of Japan.* Vol. III. Sebald, W. J. *The civil code of Japan.*

[5] It should be repeated here that any vital event became official only when it was entered in the *koseki.* Legal marriage was the entry in the *koseki. De facto* marriage by whatever ritual and/or ceremony left no record for legal or statistical purposes. There were and are no marriage licenses; there were and are no legal provisions requiring registration. On the other hand, *koseki* entry constitutes legal marriage without any ceremony, religious or civil.

[6] SCAP. GHQ. Government Section. *Political reorientation of Japan.* . . . P. 215.

With regard to choice of spouse, property rights, inheritance, choice of domicile, divorce and other matters pertaining to marriage and the family, laws shall be enacted from the standpoint of individual dignity and the essential equality of the sexes.[7]

The revisions of the civil code abrogated the powers of the head of the *ie*, replacing them with the powers of co-equal parents according to Western democratic concepts.[8] Parental control of marriage and the selection of marriage partners remained permissible only in the case of minors. Young married couples could establish new registrations in the *koseki* without reference to male parent or head of the ancestral house. Marital difficulties were to be adjusted in a Court of Domestic Relations rather than by decision of the head of the house or the family council. Grounds for divorce became identical for men and women, and equitable property settlements were obligatory in legal separation or divorce. In 1947 and 1948 the Japanese were given constitutional provisions and statutes more equalitarian than those in force in many American states.

Thus many of the continuities and the changes in the marriage and divorce laws of Japan are products of legal and political decisions. Official statistics on marriage and divorce are by-products of the implementation of the laws for legal rather than statistical purposes. It is therefore difficult to relate the marriage habits of the people to the demographic and social changes of the period of industrialization. In Imperial Japan the codes pushed beneath the surface of recorded statistics the major manifestations of whatever individualistic forces were operative in the society. In contemporary Japan, the codes affirm an equality of the sex and age groups and a hedonistic orientation of values that is patently far from the realities of Japanese life. This does not mean that no relationship exists between legal codes and behavioral trends, for social changes may lag behind legal codes in some phases of human behavior at the same time that social realities are far in advance of legal codes in other phases. It may be that the altered family law itself is or will become a major force for change. The sense of responsibility and obligation inculcated under the Confucian-oriented familistic society may become a sense of social responsibility to laws premised on the value of the individual rather than the family. If this occurs, the existence of constitutional safeguarads to freedom and sex equality in marriage and divorce may facilitate a movement of Japanese marriage customs toward those of other industrial societies. On the other hand, there are deep relations among the legal structure of the house, its control of marriage, and the future of the society. Hence there may be movements toward the restoration of the legal status of the house and the legal authority of its head. The question of the future of marriage thus becomes part of the larger question of the direction of change in the Japanese political and social structure. The regulated marriage with its subordination of the individual was an indispensable basis for the house, the closely disciplined people, the oligarchic society, and the police state. The marriage based on the choices and the decisions of the individuals concerned would represent the transfer of social dominance from the older to the younger generation and thus give a far greater influence in societal evolution to the more liberalized and "Westernized" segments of the population.

The prewar legal codes were mechanisms for making rigid and constant practices that were already in the folkways of a substantial portion of the population. The relative smoothness of their functioning was due in part to the fact that pre-marital sex relations, marriage rituals, and separations occurred without reference to the laws on the formation and dissolution of marriage. The rigid proscriptions and imperatives of the code governed only those marriages that were entered in *koseki*. The laws regulated primarily those marriages that had already achieved some degree of stability.

In theory, and probably in fact in most instances, the decision to arrange a marriage was that of the head of the family or the house rather than of the individual concerned. Arrangements were made through a go-between. Sometimes the family itself decided what other family was to be approached; in other cases the go-between suggested candidates from whom selection could be made. The operations seem to have been quite flexible, particularly in large cities. Friends might consider the problem and suggest a possible candidate. Marriage bureaus functioned in the cities. Increasingly, too, the couple were allowed to meet with apparent casualness before the betrothal became definite. More and more families permitted a veto of the candidate by the son or daughter. The betrothal and marriage ceremonials traced to folk Shinto rather than to Buddhism. After the marriage ceremony occurred the couple were joined in a socially acceptable union. No license was required prior to the performance of the ceremony and no report was required after it. Since there were neither licenses nor reports, there were no entries in the *koseki* and hence no sources from which statistics could be procured.

Socially accepted marriage was not legal marriage, for legality involved an entry in the *koseki* and the final acceptance of the bride into the house of the husband.[9] In many if not most rural and traditional families, this final step was postponed until the bride had demonstrated two essential qualifications for a daughter-in-law. She had to be acceptable to the mother-in-law, and she had to demonstrate through pregnancy that she could continue the family line. The bride who failed in either of these tests could be rejected. Definitive status in the husband's family was secured when the marriage was entered in the *koseki* of the husband. Only then were children legitimate. Divorce of the wife remained simple, however, until the passing of the years integrated the wife into the husband's family. Divorce was no longer appropriate after the wife had mourned for her parents-in-law and had aided her husband in developing his property. Nevertheless, it remained a threat, for it was realizable at the wish of the husband. Divorce left the wife without property or means of support unless her family of origin received her back or her husband's family provided for her. Neither had any legal obligation to do so.

The ideal life cycle of the girl in the rural areas involved marriage before age 18, pregnancy, the recording of the marriage, and then a long period during which children were born and raised and the paternal family cared for in the manner appropriate to a daughter-in-law. Eventually the children married, the mother became a mother-in-law, and the frustrations of her own earlier years were compensated in the ritualistic subservience and labor of her daughters-in-law. The ideal life cycle of the boy is more difficult to summarize, for here there was expected non-conformity that seldom received the scholarly attention given the conventional lives of women. Prostitu-

[7] *Ibid.* Reproduction of *The constitution of Japan.* Ch. III, "Rights and duties of the people," Article 24.

[8] See the discussion in Chapter VI, "The Family."

[9] The deviate forms of marriage in which the husband entered the house of the wife will be considered later.

tion was accepted as necessary and normal, while institutionalized but extra-legal concubinage permitted relations outside the legal marriage and family. Whatever the role of extra-marital sex relationships in the ideal life cycle of the male, however, conformity to and responsibility for family, house, and ancestors were the major duties. Status in the community was related to the respectability of the legally established family. In middle and old age a man was expected to have sons whose characters and activities gained the approval of the larger family and community. Thus the husband could fulfill his ideal role only if the wife had been faithful to her duties of propriety and fertility. If she was lacking in either respect, the husband and the family of the husband were shamed not only while the marriage endured but into the next generation.

The marriage system of the Japanese permitted the coexistence of conformity and deviation. Conformity pertained to the formation and maintenance of families legally recognized by the *ie* through *koseki* recording. Deviations in sex relations did not involve the legal wife or touch the ancestral functions of the *ie*. The marriage patterns and the extramarital sex practices thus operated to conceal the influence of industrialization and urbanization. Changes could occur without reflections in the statistics of those marriages and divorces which had been recorded in *koseki* with the permission of the heads of *ie*.

Changes occurred in legal marriage and divorce under the old constitution and the old civil code, but they came gradually as the relations between husbands and wives, parents and children, were influenced by social and economic changes. The heads of houses whose role as decision-makers was preeminent in the preservation of the society without change were themselves products of a society in transition. Here, as in so many aspects of Japanese society, evolutionary changes occurred within a legal and a social system that in theory had created an unchanging structure.

The statistics that mirror the changing marriage and divorce patterns of the Japanese are as complex as the social realities and the legal codes that they reflect. The ceremonies that precede the establishment of a home are marriage by a *de facto* definition but, as we said earlier, this ceremony is private and involves no requirements of license or registration. Statistical data are by-products of the *koseki* registration that brings the bride into the house of the husband, or of the *koseki* erasure that removes the wife from the husband's house. Hence a terminology that appears comparable in Japan and the West differs in critical respects. Japanese legal definitions of our standard Western terms are as follows:

Single—Persons not recorded as married, widowed, or divorced in a *koseki*.

Marriage—The recording in the appropriate *koseki* of the relevant facts concerning the individuals concerned.

Married—Persons entered in *koseki* as married.

Widow or widower—The surviving individual from a recorded marriage broken by a recorded death. Both the marriage of the couple and the death of the spouse have been entered in *koseki*.

Divorce—The legal dissolution of a legal marriage through *koseki* changes.

The difficulties involved in the utilization of data from *koseki* on marriage and marital status have been known to the Japanese for many decades, but satisfactory solutions were difficult to find. From 1872 until 1918 the official data on population, marriage, and marital status were summations of entries in the *koseki*. When rates of marriage, divorce, or remarriage were computed, marriages and divorces as currently recorded were related to populations of specified marital status as legally determined by prior recordings. Internally consistent series were available to indicate trends in the frequency of marriage and divorce, and in the proportions of the single, married, widowed, and separated in the population. The only difficulty was the question of the relevance of the trends or the differentials as thus established to the changing frequency of family formation and dissolution.

As enumerative censuses were planned and finally taken, they provided an alternative source to the *koseki* for information on marriage and marital status. Here emphasis was placed on *de facto* situations without reference to *koseki* records. The single were defined as those living without mates, the married as those living with mates. The widowed were those who had been married, with no specifications as to the legal status of the marital relationship. The divorced and separated were those who had lived as married persons but whose marital relationship had ceased for some cause other than the death of the spouse.

Thus the analysis of family formation and dissolution presents major analytical problems. The *de facto* marital status is available for October 1 in the census years. Comparisons of these cross-sections of the population at separated periods of time are valuable, but the processes involved in the formation and dissolution of marriages appear as blurred residues of complex events. Detailed tabulations are available annually on the numbers of marriages and divorces recorded in *koseki* during the year and on the characteristics of the persons who participated in them. However, there are no base populations of individuals classified by legal rather than *de facto* marital status. For instance, legal first marriages are those recorded in *koseki* by persons without previous marriages so recorded. The single population of the census consists of persons who were not living as married persons at the time of the census and had not done so in the past. Thus we are presented with four alternatives if we wish to compute marriage rates. In the first, we can remain within the census system and consider changes in *de facto* marital status at specific points of time, generally five years apart. In the second, we can relate numbers of marriages or divorces by type and characteristics of the participating individuals to the total population enumerated in the census without reference to marital status. In the third, we can attempt to adjust the census populations with their marital status defined in *de facto* terms to the requirements of the legal definitions of marital status. In the fourth, we can attempt to derive vital rates directly from the marital status data of the census. We shall explore all of these approaches.

It should be noted that the incongruities between census data and vital statistics reports are themselves valuable data for the analysis of the functioning of the marriage and family systems of the Japanese. Here in the contrast of the systems we see the ways in which the most intimate relationships of an agrarian familistic society respond when individuals are subjected to the separations, the economic pressures, and the hedonistic if not individualistic aspirations of an urbanizing society.

The Postponement of Marriage

The major familial adjustment of the Japanese to industrialization and urbanization was the postponement of marriage. The early transition from Tokugawa to modern Japan is not open to analysis, for the registration compilations of the late nineteenth and early twentieth centuries reveal an increase in the practice of marriage registration rather than a change in marital habits. The earliest national data on the *de facto* marital status of the population pertain to the year 1920, more than half a century after the Meiji Restoration. By 1920 and 1925 the transition from early marriage appears far advanced in the cities, if only cities and rural areas are compared. If comparisons are made between different types of agricultural and non-agricultural prefectures, it becomes obvious that the theory of a direct transition from early to late marriages that was proportionate to the transition from an agricultural to an industrial economy is not a complete explanation of what occurred in Japan. The following data on the percentages of the married among girls aged from 15 to 29 pertain to the year 1925:[10]

	Age		
Prefecture	*15-19*	*20-24*	*25-29*
Iwate	34.1	82.6	91.4
Akita	31.2	82.1	91.7
Gumma	4.0	48.3	84.9
Saitama	5.5	53.8	86.2
Tokyo	9.8	59.4	85.1
Osaka	11.2	63.5	85.4
Kagoshima	9.6	59.6	81.9
Okinawa	13.8	64.3	82.4

The differences in proportions married at the younger ages in 1925 reveal the persistence of a pre-modern regional culture during a period when the influence of the industrial society was diffusing throughout the nation. In such northeastern agricultural prefectures as Iwate and Akita, approximately one-third of the girls aged from 15 to 19 were married. Thus one might argue that in isolated agricultural prefectures there remained some substantial degree of conformity to the traditional ideal of marriage before age 18. However, Kagoshima and Okinawa in the far southwest also depended heavily on agriculture, and they too were isolated from the main currents of change. Here the proportions of girls married in their teens were quite low. In fact, the marital status of young girls in these areas regarded as backward in the Japan of the period was comparable to that of young girls in the industrial prefectures of Tokyo and Osaka. The lowest proportions did not occur in the great cities but in prefectures such as Gumma and Saitama, where numbers of single girls in the young ages were inflated by in-migrants who lived in the textile dormitories. In the total national picture in 1925, however, there was a general association between relatively high proportions married at the younger ages and the extent of the dependence of the prefecture on agriculture, between relatively low proportions married at the younger ages and the transition of the prefectures to industrial occupations and urban residence. Both the regional differences and the diversities between agricultural and industrial prefectures persisted among women aged from 20 to 24 and 25 to 29, although the magnitude of the differences declined sharply. By age 25 to 29 major portions of all the women in all the prefectures either were or had been married.

If we focus attention on the changes between 1920 and 1955 rather than on the areal differences in levels in 1925, we see immediately that the major transition in the marital status of the Japanese was an increase in the proportions of the single at the younger ages (TABLE 75). Changes were irregular between 1920 and 1925, perhaps because of difficulties with the census question as to *de facto* marital status when it was first asked in 1920. From 1925 to 1940 the proportion of the single increased consistently for both men and women. This trend was apparent again in 1955, after deviations for the men in the early postwar years. The increase in the proportions of single women at the younger ages represented postponement rather than avoidance of marriage, however, for the proportions of those never married at age 35 and over were 3 per cent or less from 1920 to 1940. The proportions of the single among women aged 30 and over were increasing in 1950 and 1955, however, for the deaths of young men in the war years precluded marriage for many of the girls.

Perhaps the most extraordinary aspect of these data on the number of Japanese girls remaining single is the relatively slight evidence of the impact of imperial migration, the Manchurian and China wars, and World War II. The absence of the armed forces and the military dead of the Manchurian War would have had their primary influence on the marital status of women aged from 20 to 29 in 1935, 25 to 34 in 1940, and 35 to 44 in 1950. The major impact of the China War would have been apparent in the marital status of women aged from 20 to 29 in 1940 and 30 to 39 in 1950, while the major impact of World War II would be apparent in the proportions of single women aged from 25 to 34 in 1950. While there have been some increases in the single among the older ages of women, the increases in the single among all women do not appear to be proportionate to the losses of men either in or associated with the war of 1937-1945. Perhaps there were compensatory adjustments in the marriages of men that prevented the cumulation of a sizable population of never-married women.

Postponement of marriage occurred among men as well as among women, and with almost as great regularity, in the years from 1925 to 1935. There were increases in the single between 1935 and 1940, for in the latter year more than a million and a half men were in the armed forces. In Japanese culture the wisdom or the legal controls of the elders tended to prevail; conscription and war service resulted in postponement of marriage. In 1950 there were major deficits of men and hence theoretical surpluses of women. The demographic readjustment to this situation occurred through a greater frequency of marriage among men, and particularly a decline in the age at which single men married. In 1950, the proportion of men under 30 who were single had declined to the levels of 1935. This downward movement in the age of men at marriage combined with higher rates of remarriage among the widowed and divorced to minimize the increases in the proportions of the single among women. By 1955, however, the prewar trends toward increasing proportions of the single were again evident.

The downward trend in proportions married among men and women in the early years of adult life occurred in both *shi* and *gun*, although at each census date the proportions of the single were substantially higher in the *shi* than in the *gun* (TABLE 76). This is the type of relationship that would be expected if the postponement of marriage were a product or correlate of the development of the industrial economy and the urban culture.

Differences in the proportions married at the younger ages

[10] Nihon. Naikaku tokei-kyoku. *Taisho juyo'nen kokusei chosa hokoku.* II.2.

TABLE 75

The proportions of the single by sex and age, 1920-1955

Age	*1920*	*1925*	*1930*	*1935*	*1940*	*1950*[a]	*1955*[a]
				Men			
15-19	97.2	98.2	99.0	99.4	99.6	99.5	99.9
20-24	70.9	72.4	79.6	84.0	90.0	82.9	90.2
25-29	25.7	25.0	28.7	34.8	42.0	34.5	40.7
30-34	8.2	7.1	8.1	8.9	10.3	8.0	9.2
35-39	4.1	3.4	3.9	4.0	4.4	3.2	3.0
40-44	2.8	2.3	2.4	2.4	2.7	1.9	1.7
45-49	2.3	1.9	1.8	1.8	2.0	1.5	1.2
				Women			
15-19	82.3	85.9	89.3	92.5	95.7	96.6	98.2
20-24	31.4	29.6	37.7	44.9	53.5	55.3	66.1
25-29	9.2	7.8	8.5	11.1	13.5	15.2	20.2
30-34	4.1	3.5	3.7	4.0	5.3	5.7	8.0
35-39	2.7	2.3	2.4	2.4	2.9	3.0	4.0
40-44	2.1	1.9	1.8	1.8	2.0	2.0	2.4
45-49	1.9	1.8	1.6	1.5	1.6	1.5	1.7

[a] The 46 prefectures of postwar Japan.

Source: 1920: Nihon. Naikaku tokei-kyoku. *Taisho ku'nen kokusei chosa hokoku.* IV.A.1. Prefectures, IV.B. 1925: *Ibid. Taisho juyo'nen kokusei chosa hokoku.* II.2. Prefectures, II.4. 1930: *Ibid. Showa go'nen kokusei chosa hokoku.* IV.1. Prefectures, IV.4. 1935: *Ibid. Showa ju'nen kokusei chosa hokoku.* II.1. Prefectures, II.2. 1940: *Ibid. Census of 1940. Selected tables.* Table 3. Also: Nihon. Sori-cho, tokei-kyoku. *Kekka hokoku tekiyo, Showa 15-nen kokusei chosa. . . .* 1950: *Ibid. Showa 25-nen kokusei chosa hokoku.* IV. Prefectures, VII. 1955: *Ibid. 1% chushutsu shukei ni yoru kekka sokuho. Showa 30-nen kokusei chosa. Zenkoku.* I. Table 2.

TABLE 76

The single in the *shi* and the *gun*, by sex and age, 1920-1955

(Per cent single)

	MEN						WOMEN					
Age	*1920*	*1925*	*1930*	*1935*	*1950*	*1955*[a]	*1920*	*1925*	*1930*	*1935*	*1950*	*1955*[a]
							Shi					
15-19	98.9	99.0	99.5	99.7	99.7	99.9	86.5	89.6	92.0	94.3	97.1	98.4
20-24	82.7	81.6	86.4	89.3	87.7	93.0	39.4	36.6	44.9	51.6	59.5	69.9
25-29	38.2	33.9	37.3	42.9	42.5	47.5	13.7	11.2	11.9	14.5	18.0	23.6
30-34	13.1	10.3	11.3	11.8	10.2	11.9	6.5	5.1	5.5	5.5	7.0	9.9
35-39	6.3	4.8	5.4	5.1	3.8	3.4	4.2	3.2	3.5	3.2	3.8	4.5
40-44	4.1	2.8	3.2	2.9	2.0	1.7	3.3	2.5	2.6	2.3	2.5	2.8
45-49	3.2	2.3	2.3	2.1	1.6	1.2	3.0	2.3	2.1	1.9	1.8	2.0
							Gun					
15-19	96.6	97.9	98.7	99.2	99.4	99.8	81.1	84.5	88.1	91.3	96.2	98.0
20-24	66.5	68.3	76.1	79.8	79.4	87.1	29.1	27.0	34.6	40.2	52.5	61.3
25-29	21.9	21.5	24.9	29.1	28.7	33.6	8.0	6.7	7.1	8.9	13.2	16.2
30-34	6.7	6.0	6.8	7.1	6.3	6.4	3.5	3.0	3.1	3.2	4.7	5.9
35-39	3.6	3.0	3.4	3.4	2.7	2.8	2.3	2.0	2.1	2.0	2.5	3.5
40-44	2.5	2.1	2.2	2.2	1.8	1.8	1.9	1.7	1.6	1.6	1.7	1.9
45-49	2.1	1.8	1.7	1.7	1.5	1.3	1.7	1.7	1.4	1.3	1.3	1.4

[a] In 1955, many small places had been incorporated as *shi*. The marital status given here is that for *shi* with populations of 50 thousand or over.

Source: References, Table 75.

in the sub-cultures of rural Japan were related to differences in institutional structures and in the availability of land and other resources for the establishment of branch families. As the modern society developed and all the cultivable land was utilized, most of the sons except the eldest had to leave the village. The eldest son succeeded to the land, and so his need for wife and children as labor re-enforced his obligations of procreation under the family system. Thus the eldest sons in the agricultural population married at younger ages than other youth in rural areas—and areas peopled predominantly by agricultural households revealed substantially higher proportions of men married at the younger ages. The marital status of women was a derivative of the forces impinging on men.

The exodus from agriculture led to delayed marriage among the boys and girls who left. Since few of the younger sons had special training or appreciable wealth, they entered non-agricultural occupations at low levels of remuneration, security, and status. In the Japanese setting, this out-migration and labor at small wages necessitated a postponement of marriage; it was not considered proper for a man to establish a family until he was able to provide adequately for wife and children. Conscription and military service introduced further delays in marriage arrangements.

The delay in marriage on the part of men was a harmonious element in the preservation of the traditional social structure within the world for which in theory it was so ill adapted. Girls could fill positions as lowly paid labor in the industrializing economy without jeopardizing their later role as wives dependent on the incomes of husbands. Before World War II most of the village youth completed their formal education at age 12 or 13. The years of adolescence and early maturity might be occupied with assistance in agricultural activities or local small-scale industries. Increasingly, however, girls moved to factory dormitories in adjacent areas or to nearby cities and metropolitan areas for employment. The positions that these girls could secure were temporary, lasting a few years at most, and pay was barely enough for subsistence apart from family or dormitory life. The conditions of living and working were not conducive to the development of attitudes of independence that would have led to defiance of parental authority and refusal to accept an arranged marriage. Whether the marriage that was eventually arranged brought the girl back to a rural village, moved her from a rural area to a city, or kept her in her place of residence, the employment of girls in their teens and early twenties led to a sharp divergence between the ideal age of marriage in the historic culture and the actual age of marriage in the modern society. It was a deviation arranged and controlled by the family, however, and so in the tradition of the old society. Increasing age at marriage had no necessary relationship to changes in individual values.

The postponement of marriage in the cities, as in the rural areas, was a product of the interaction of premodern cultural factors and modern economic and political forces. In general, there were larger proportions of the single among girls and young women in cities than in rural areas. However, the extent of the postponement of marriage was not proportionate to the size of the city. In fact, the single were relatively fewer in the great cities than in the smaller ones. In the individual cities in any size group, however, the age at which marriage occurred was related to the industrial structure and the amount and type of employment opportunities. Proportions of single girls were high in cities whose economic bases were in long-established local industries that used the labor of women and had low wages for men. The married men and women at the younger ages were relatively most numerous in cities where there had been a rapid growth of heavy industry, for in these cities jobs for men were plentiful and wages were relatively high. It would appear that men married as soon as they could afford to do so. The marital status of men appeared to be the independent variable.

The relative proportions of the single in cities were associated both with the prevalence of migrations that were selective of sex and marital status and with the marital habits of the urban population itself. The interrelations among industrial structure, selective in-migration, selective out-migration, and migrant replacements may be illustrated by the cases of the boom cities of Yawata, Yokosuka, and Sasebo in the year 1930 (FIGURE 9).[11] The relations were complicated in the case of men by the presence of armed forces in Sasebo and Yokosuka.[12] In Yawata, a city of civilian industry, the proportion of single men was low at age 20 to 24; this was also true of the other boom cities if civilian men alone were considered. The young migrants in boom cities came directly from rural areas where people had a firm belief in early marriage. Incomes in the cities were relatively high. Deficiencies in the numbers of girls of the requisite ages in the cities were not deterrents to marriage, for arranged marriages brought brides from rural areas into cities. Out-migration from the boom cities seems to have been selective of the married, while the influx of migrants at older ages brought single men into the cities.

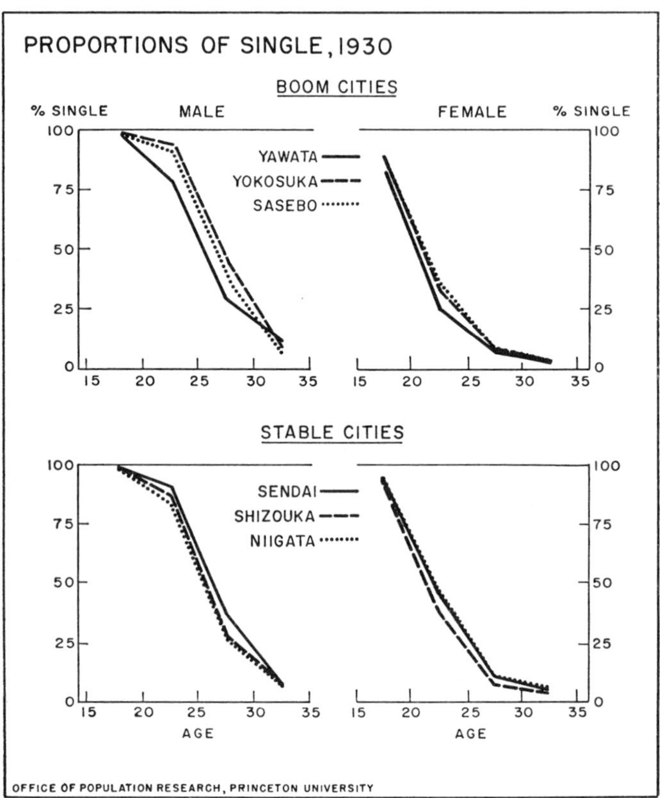

Figure 9. The proportions of the single in selected boom and stable cities, by sex and age, 1930
Source: References, Table 75.

[11] Three stable and three boom cities were selected on the basis of the place-of-birth data of the census of 1930. The migrant status of the populations of the cities was considered in Chapter VIII, pp. 150-151.

[12] Sasebo and Yokosuka were naval bases.

The economic opportunities and the marriage habits in the stable cities of Shizuoka, Sendai, and Niigata might be assumed to be characteristic of the old Japan rather than the new. If so, it must be argued that the postponement of marriage in the cities of feudal and early modern Japan was great indeed. In 1930, the youth who resided in these cities of stable and traditional economies had difficulty in finding employment, and wages were low. Large portions of the young men had grown up in an urban environment that stimulated wants not realizable at the levels of income current at the time. Economic, social, and demographic factors were all involved in the postponement of marriage among men. Marriages among women in these cities were dependent on decisions made by men and hence the marriages of native-born girls were postponed by the factors barring men from establishing homes at early ages. The number of girls who moved in for marriage was also reduced by the postponement of marriage among men.

The consequence of industrialization of a modern factory type was an age at marriage substantially above that in agricultural villages but substantially below that in cities whose industrialization was of a small-factory or household type. Within prosperous boom cities, the release of economic pressures was conducive to marriage at relatively young ages. There is a suggestion here that the widespread and continuous postponement of marriage in Japan may be a product of pressures that prevent the realization of desires rather than of changes in ideals and a new way of life.

The variations in age at marriage in rural areas and in cities, in types of economic areas and in regions of the country, indicate that there was no automatic and proportionate relationship among industrialization, urbanization, and the postponement of marriage. It is necessary, therefore, to re-emphasize the major fact, the postponement of marriage in the national population. We may debate what might have occurred in Japan had the family system, the structure of industrialization, and the levels of income been different from what they were, but we cannot debate what actually happened between 1920 and 1955. The pressures and the aspirations of the transforming economy and society produced a great increase in the proportions of the single in ages long regarded as appropriate for marriage in the cultures of the East. The postponements extended throughout the country, from the greatest of the cities to the most remote of the rural areas, and they increased over time. The adjustments of family formation occurred at the beginning of adult life. There was postponement rather than rejection of marriage.

The Married

The major transition in the marital status of the Japanese may be viewed either as the relative increase of the single at the younger ages or as the relative decline of the married at these ages (Table 77). Marriage remained the status toward which practically all Japanese moved. By age 35 to 39 more than 90 per cent of all men were currently married and less than 5 per cent were single. Maximum proportions of married women came somewhat earlier; by age 30 to 34 more than 90 per cent were or had been married, while only 4 or 5 per cent remained single.

The dominance of the married was transitory, for their proportions started to decline at age 35 to 39 for women, age 45 to 49 for men. From these ages onward the proportions of the married declined, slowly at first, then more rapidly.

Table 77

The proportions of the married, by sex and age, 1920-1955

Age	*1920*	*1925*	*1930*	*1935*	*1940*	*1950*	*1955*
			Men				
15-19	2.6	1.7	1.0	0.5	0.4	0.4	0.1
20-24	27.4	26.0	19.6	15.4	8.9	16.6	9.6
25-29	70.6	71.7	68.7	63.0	56.7	64.0	58.2
30-34	87.6	89.0	88.5	87.8	87.2	90.1	88.8
35-39	90.9	92.0	92.0	91.8	92.0	94.7	94.9
40-44	91.0	91.7	92.1	92.1	92.3	95.0	95.7
45-49	89.5	89.9	90.3	90.6	91.0	93.4	95.1
			Women				
15-19	16.6	13.2	10.3	7.3	4.2	3.3	1.7
20-24	64.9	67.1	60.1	53.3	45.2	42.7	33.0
25-29	85.7	87.6	87.6	85.0	82.8	79.1	76.5
30-34	89.4	90.4	90.7	90.1	88.8	83.3	84.9
35-39	88.1	88.9	89.2	89.2	88.5	82.6	83.5
40-44	84.5	84.9	85.4	85.5	85.5	82.1	80.4
45-49	79.1	79.0	79.3	79.7	79.8	78.5	78.4

Source: References, Table 75.

The status to which the surviving people were moving was that of the widowed and the separated (Table 78). In the successive census enumerations from 1920 to 1940, each hundred men aged from 35 to 44 included 90 or 91 married men, 3 or 4 single men, and 4 or 5 widowed or separated men. By age 60 to 64 one man in each five was widowed or separated.[13] By age 80 over three-fifths were widowed or

Table 78

The proportions of the widowed and separated, by sex and age, 1920-1955

Age	*1920*	*1925*	*1930*	*1935*	*1940*	*1950*	*1955*
			Men				
15-19	0.2	0.1	0.0	0.0	0.0	0.0	0.0
20-24	1.7	1.5	0.8	0.6	0.2	0.6	0.2
25-29	3.7	3.3	2.5	2.1	1.3	1.5	1.1
30-34	4.2	3.9	3.4	3.4	2.5	1.9	2.0
35-39	4.9	4.5	4.1	4.2	3.6	2.1	2.0
40-44	6.2	6.0	5.4	5.4	5.0	3.0	2.6
45-49	8.2	8.1	7.9	7.6	7.0	5.2	3.6
			Women				
15-19	1.1	0.9	0.4	0.2	0.1	0.1	0.0
20-24	3.7	3.3	2.3	1.8	1.3	2.0	0.9
25-29	5.1	4.6	4.0	3.9	3.7	5.7	3.3
30-34	6.4	6.0	5.5	5.8	5.9	11.0	7.0
35-39	9.2	8.7	8.3	8.4	8.6	14.4	12.5
40-44	13.3	13.2	12.8	12.7	12.5	15.9	17.3
45-49	19.0	19.3	19.2	18.8	18.6	20.1	19.9

Source: References, Table 75.

[13] The discussion here is limited to the relatively "normal" decades from 1920 to 1940. The situation in 1950 is considered in the next section on the relations between the marital status of the population and the industrial structure of the prefectures.

separated, less than two-fifths married. The transition was comparable for women, although magnitudes differed sharply. For each 100 women in their thirties, 89 or 90 were married, 3 or 4 single, 6 or 8 widowed or separated. By age 45 to 49, the age at which childbearing ends, less than four-fifths of the women were married, while almost one-fifth were widowed or separated.

The dynamics of marital status are far more intricate than those indicated in a generalized statement of the emergence of the married from the single and the transformation of the married into the widowed and the separated. The folkways and mores of the traditional culture with reference to divorce, separation, and remarriage, the selectivity of migration, the pressures and opportunities in the agricultural and the industrial segments of the economy, the differential and declining mortality were all involved in creating the generally regular differences and changes in marital status from 1920 to 1955.

THE MARITAL STATUS OF MEN AND WOMEN

The roles of women from adolescence to death were associated directly with marital status. Compulsions to marriage, restrictions of widowhood, and mores hostile to remarriage could not be violated with impunity. For men, on the other hand, marriage was a part of the socially proper and individually satisfactory life, but there was a considerable sphere of social participation and economic activity not dominated directly by marital status.

We have shown previously that the proportion of women single at the younger ages was related to the transition from village to city, from an agricultural to an industrial economy. In addition we indicated that within agriculture the eldest sons and hence their brides married at younger ages than those who moved elsewhere for job and residence, that within cities the proportions of women married at the younger ages were related to the types of jobs at which men labored. These were illustrations of the factors making for the postponement of marriage among men and its impact on the women a few years younger, who were the major age group from which brides were recruited.

Sex differences in marital status remained substantial after the ages at which practically all men and women were married. From age 30 to 34 onward the proportion of men married was substantially higher than the proportion of women. From 1920 through 1940 there was a very slight upward movement in the proportions of the married among men aged from 30 to 34 and over, a change that might be taken to reflect the slowly declining death rates of women that left fewer men as widowers. There were small upward movements in the proportions of the married among women aged from 25 to 29 and over between 1920 and 1930. There was virtually no change between 1930 and 1935, when activities in Manchuria and rapid industrialization in Japan were influencing the deaths of men. Then there were appreciable declines between 1935 and 1940, when the China War and rapid imperial development were leading to the out-movements of large numbers of men.

The effects of war, exodus, and repatriation on the marital status of men and women in 1950 indicate the significance of factors other than difference in age at marriage and normal mortality in creating the deficiencies of the married and the surpluses of the widowed and the separated among women. Between 1940 and 1950 the proportion of the married increased at all ages among men, decreased at all ages among women. Among the widowed and separated, the reverse relationship held, the proportion at age 30 to 34 and over declining from its already low levels for men, the proportion at age 25 to 29 and over increasing from its already substantial levels for women. Higher rates of remarriage of the widowed and the separated among men are the only factors that could produce relationships in change such as those found in Japan in the last three decades.

The marriage system of the Japanese would have involved an unstable equilibrium indeed were it not for the prevalence of remarriage among men. The population was increasing rapidly throughout the modern period, so that practically every age group was larger than the one immediately above it, smaller than the one immediately following it. Since grooms were a few years older than brides, rigorous monogamy without remarriage would have necessitated that some girls remain single—yet marriage was almost universal for girls, as for men. Concubinage would have been a solution, but concubinage was declared illegal in the modern period and in fact seems to have been rather infrequent in the form of an acknowledged maintenance of two wives at the same time. In the prewar decades, higher rates of remarriage among the separated and widowed men served to provide husbands for girls. The evidence from the 1950 census indicates an approach to an equilibrium of sorts through the same process, widows being left in their status while widowers married single girls. It seems probable, however, that some appreciable portions of those who remained single at ages 25 to 29 and 30 to 34 in 1950 will remain single, the men available for husbands selecting brides from the girls in the younger age groups.

MARITAL STATUS AND INDUSTRIALIZATION

The postponement of marriage occurred among youth. It was young people who left the old ways of living, moved to cities, got new and unfamiliar jobs, and eventually secured higher status and more adequate incomes. Once marriage occurred, however, the major regulators of conduct were the rules of the traditional society rather than the forces of the industrial society. Among women there was a somewhat lesser frequency of the married in the metropolitan and other industrial prefectures than in the transitional and agricultural prefectures, but after age 30 these differences were slight (TABLE 79). The major change was not in marriage as a normal aspect of the life cycle but in the age at which marriage occurred.

The striking aspect of a comparison of the proportions of women married in agricultural, intermediate, and industrial areas during a period of almost kaleidoscopic changes in ways of living is the regularity of the differences among areas at a given time and the similarities in the changes in all types of areas over time. The levels and changes in the proportions married were products of many factors—the marriage customs in rural and urban areas, the internal movements to the cities, the emigration of men to the colonial and associated areas, the declining mortality that reduced the chances of widowhood, and the changing frequencies of divorce and remarriage. The way of life seems to have remained relatively stable in a period that would be assumed to be conducive to instability.

In 1950 the marital status of the population had been influenced by the losses of war, the repatriation of Japanese from the East Asian region to the home islands, and the complex social, psychological, and economic readjustments of the first five postwar years. The pattern of differences as among metro-

TABLE 79

Proportions married among women aged from 15 to 49, prefectures by industrial type, 1925-1950

Prefectures by industrial type	*Age 15-49*	*Ages*						
		15-19	*20-24*	*25-29*	*30-34*	*35-39*	*40-44*	*45-49*
				1925				
Metropolitan	63.8	10.4	61.1	85.2	88.9	87.5	82.9	75.1
Other industrial	66.6	11.0	66.0	87.4	90.2	88.8	84.9	78.6
Intermediate	68.6	13.7	68.3	88.0	90.6	89.0	85.0	79.5
Agricultural	69.5	14.7	68.3	88.0	90.6	89.0	85.1	79.4
Hokkaido	71.9	18.3	76.9	91.3	93.2	92.1	88.4	82.4
				1930				
Metropolitan	61.6	7.8	52.6	85.0	89.2	87.8	83.5	75.8
Other industrial	65.0	8.9	58.8	87.4	90.5	89.1	85.2	78.8
Intermediate	66.7	10.8	61.9	88.2	90.9	89.3	85.6	79.8
Agricultural	67.3	11.5	62.0	88.1	91.1	89.5	85.8	79.8
Hokkaido	68.5	13.1	69.9	90.7	93.0	91.8	88.2	82.5
				1940				
Metropolitan	57.4	3.3	39.0	79.0	86.5	86.7	83.3	76.4
Other industrial	61.0	3.8	45.3	83.4	88.8	88.2	84.9	79.4
Intermediate	63.1	4.6	48.9	84.4	89.4	88.7	85.6	80.3
Agricultural	62.4	4.7	45.5	83.1	89.4	89.1	86.3	80.9
Hokkaido	62.0	4.4	51.3	87.0	91.1	90.4	87.8	81.6
				1950				
Metropolitan	56.7	2.4	34.3	73.2	81.8	82.6	81.2	76.3
Other industrial	58.4	3.1	41.3	78.4	83.1	82.6	81.6	77.4
Intermediate	59.2	3.6	45.5	80.1	82.7	81.8	81.7	78.7
Agricultural	58.6	3.5	43.9	80.1	83.8	82.8	82.6	79.4
Hokkaido	60.2	2.6	44.4	85.1	88.7	87.4	85.2	80.5

Source: References, Table 75.

politan, other industrial, intermediate, and agricultural prefectures remained similar to that of the 1920's and the 1930's, though the scars of war are plainly discernible, especially among women (FIGURE 10). For Japan as a whole, 55.4 per cent of all women aged from 20 to 24 and 15.2 per cent of those aged from 25 to 29 were single. These were the women in age groups that would have married men of the ages of those who suffered the heaviest mortality of the war years. There was a concentration of single women in the metropolitan and other industrial prefectures. Here it may be presumed that employment opportunities were more abundant and life apart from the married state more feasible. Given the deficiencies of men, it would seem that proportions of single women in the upper age groups would be substantially larger in the future than they have been in the past. As of 1955, however, the proportion of women who had never married was only 4.0 per cent at age 35 to 39, 2.4 per cent at age 40 to 44, and even less at age 45 and over.

In 1955 more than 9 per cent of the women aged from 35 to 39 were widowed. These women had been aged from 20 to 24 in 1940 and so participants in the war marriages of that period. There were 14.4 per cent widowed in the group aged from 40 to 44 in 1955—the survivors of the women who were in the central marriageable ages at the time when war began in China in 1937. The percentages of the widowed were highest in the cities of 50,000 and over, lowest in the *gun*.

MARITAL STATUS AND ECONOMIC ACTIVITY

The persistent relations between the rural-urban or agricultural-industrial character of the areas of residence and the marital status of the population indicate a close association between marital status and the economic activities of individuals. The direction of the causality is difficult to determine and it is probable that interaction occurred. For men, early marriage meant early employment and hence the absence of higher education or training. However, there were low rates of employment among men who remained single until an advanced age. In 1940, the proportions of gainfully occupied among men in the various age groups differed greatly according to marital status:[14]

[14] Nihon. Naikaku tokei-kyoku. The data used here and in the following pages on economic activity by marital status, age, and sex are based on unpublished tabulations of the 1940 census materials.

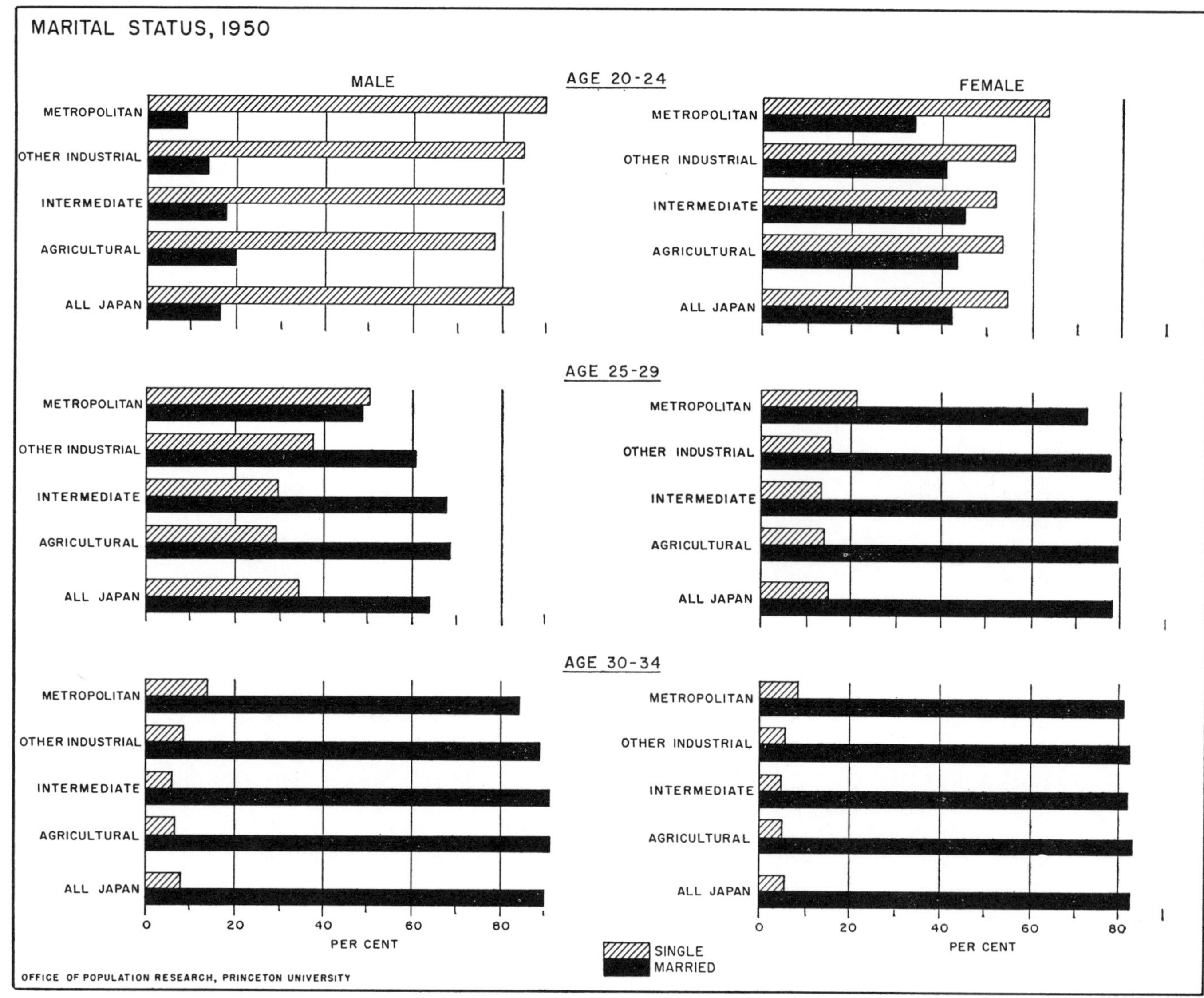

Figure 10. Marital status, by sex and age, prefectures by industrial type, 1950
Source: References, Table 75.

Age	*Single*	*Married*	*Widowed and separated*
15-19	77.5	97.1	—
20-24	90.7	97.9	93.7
25-29	93.5	98.7	93.8
30-34	89.8	98.9	92.9
45-49	82.5	98.0	93.6
65 and over	57.0	68.7	49.6

It could be argued that the married, with their heavier economic responsibilities, felt pressures to increase their earnings and therefore had higher participation rates in gainful employment; that the single, the widowed, and the separated had fewer responsibilities and therefore more freedom of choice as to whether or not to seek gainful employment. While this type of relation between marital status and economic activity is plausible, it is hardly an adequate explanation of the observed facts. Since marriages were arranged largely by families, who took due consideration of economic factors, it is not likely that the sequence ran from marriage to the necessity to secure employment. There is an alternative approach to the explanation of the higher rates of economic activity among married men. It may be presumed that the physically and mentally incompetent remained disproportionately among the single. It may also be presumed that remarriage was more likely to occur among men physically and mentally able to secure and hold jobs. If so, the sequence ran primarily from the characteristics of individuals to gainful employment and then to marital status.

This speculative interpretation rests on the data for all Japan in 1940, a year when industry and manpower alike were being mobilized for a more extensive war than that in which Japan was then engaged. The structure of the economy and the general patterns of labor force participation had altered greatly by 1955, but the relations between economic activity and marital status remained similar to those in 1940. The following labor force participation rates are based on the 1 per cent sample tabulation of the data of the census of 1955:[15]

[15] Nihon. Sori-fu, tokei-kyoku. *1% chushutsu shukei ni yoru kekka sokuho. Showa 30-nen kokusei chosa. Zenkoku.* Part 5(1), Table 4.

Age	Single	Married	Widowed	Divorced
12-19	52.1	85.0	—	—
20-24	84.1	96.2	100.0	79.4
25-29	89.6	97.2	88.9	83.2
30-34	79.7	97.0	81.5	78.9
45-49	69.0	96.2	88.3	83.4
65 and over	46.4	62.8	42.2	46.1

The relations between rates of gainful employment and marital status were less direct among women than among men.[16] The participation rates for Japanese women in 1940 picture these relations by age:

Age	Single	Married	Widowed and separated
11-14	14.8	—	—
15-19	67.4	49.9	—
20-24	72.9	43.1	65.1
25-29	66.0	42.6	64.6
30-34	63.5	46.5	68.8
45-49	59.0	57.6	62.2
65 and over	33.5	37.6	18.9

Almost three-fourths of the single women aged from 20 to 24 were gainfully occupied. Gainful employment does not seem to have been a motivating force in decisions to remain single, however, for as age advanced the proportion of the gainfully occupied declined. It should be noted that at all ages the proportions of the gainfully occupied among the single were less for women than for men.

The codes of the house made the care of the widow the responsibility of the family of the deceased husband, but the data from the 1940 census suggest that the widowed and the separated were even more dependent on their own labors than were the single. There is a distinct pattern by age, however. Young widowed and separated women, those under age 45, carried the burden of maintenance for themselves and their children, or at least labored to carry part of that burden. Participation rates for the widowed and the separated were higher than those for either the married or the single women. In the older ages the widowed and the separated women were represented to a lesser degree in gainful employment than the married or the single. This was particularly true for widows aged 60 and over. High status and a sheltered life for the widow apparently came only when her sons were old enough to care for her. It did not occur when the labor and sacrifice of the care would have had to be provided by the father or the brothers of the deceased husband.

Again the data from the census of 1955 corroborate those from the wartime census of 1940. The information on economic activity by marital status in cities and rural areas indicates the close association between the economic activities of married women and agriculture. It also suggests the economic factors that may be involved in the postponement of marriage in the cities. The participation rates are given here for married women in selected age groups in the cities of 50 thousand and over and in the *gun*; data are from the 1 per cent sample tabulation of the 1955 census:[17]

Age	All Japan	Shi, 50,000 and over	Gun
15-19	50.0	30.7	65.4
20-24	48.1	27.5	65.9
25-29	44.5	26.4	63.2
30-34	44.9	26.6	64.1
45-49	50.2	31.9	66.9
65 and over	30.1	17.6	37.3

The society which in the superficial view provided jobs as an alternative to marriage for its girls tended to bar continuity in employment in those jobs that might have been genuine alternatives to marriage. Girls who remained single beyond age 25 or so labored in menial or lower clerical positions. If they worked in manufacturing industry, it was in the small shop rather than the large factory. The distribution of the gainfully occupied single girls in age groups by major industry shows the changing employment practices with reference to women. Again, the data pertain to the Japanese in Japan in 1940:

Industry	AGE 11-14	15-19	20-24	25-29
Total	100.	100.	100.	100.
Agriculture	29.1	33.1	30.6	23.9
Manufacturing	39.2	29.0	24.4	20.7
Commerce	8.0	13.2	18.7	26.5
Professional and public service	3.8	7.9	10.5	16.0
Domestic service	17.1	12.3	12.7	10.2
Other	2.8	4.5	3.1	2.7

The labor of married women was one aspect of the habits of continuing labor so prevalent in the culture. It occurred in almost complete conformity to the role of the married woman as wife and mother. The industrial composition of the gainfully occupied population of married women age by age shows great regularity—agriculture, household industry, household distribution activities, with a gradual increase in the predominance of agriculture. The data for selected ages in 1940 were as follows:

Industry	20-24	35-39	45-49
Total	100.	100.	100.
Agriculture	70.8	70.8	75.7
Manufacturing	13.0	8.5	6.0
Commerce	10.4	15.0	13.8
Other	5.8	5.7	4.5

The widowed and the separated were the disadvantaged classes of this society in transition, as they probably had been in the original society. A girl who married into a house whose roots were in agriculture had strong claims to the resources of that house only if the man she married was the heir and she produced a son to maintain the family line. Otherwise, at widowhood she became a burden. Duty required that she be provided for, but tradition decreed that in turn she labor in the household activities without remuneration. If the girl who married into an urban family was left a widow at a relatively young age, her situation was even more difficult. The male relatives of the dead husband might find it impossible to care for her financially, whatever their conceptions of their obligations. Thus the rate of gainful employment of widowed, divorced, and separated women was very high. Adult sons

[16] The economic role of women in the Japanese family was discussed in Chapter VI, "The Family," pp. 115-119.

[17] Nihon. Sori-fu, tokei-kyoku. *Op.cit.* Part 5(1), Table 4. All the materials on labor force participation by age and marital status in 1955 are based on the 1 per cent sample tabulations.

apparently assumed the burden of caring for widowed mothers.

The situation was difficult indeed for young widows who had to secure gainful employment, and many of them had to do so. They were not hired by the factories using female labor, for the widow would be a permanent member of the labor force and so require paternalistic provisions for current welfare and old age security. The widows of Japan could not cultivate land as so many widows have done in the history of America, for land was a precious commodity not freely available for rent or purchase. The activities of the gainfully occupied widows in 1940 show their disadvantages in a year of relative prosperity. The percentage occupational structures are given for selected age groups:

Industry	*25-29*	*35-39*	*45-49*
Total	100.	100.	100.
Agriculture	39.5	36.8	51.1
Manufacturing	19.9	19.3	12.1
Commerce	22.7	25.9	22.5
Service	6.8	5.7	4.6
Other	11.1	12.3	9.7

If the Japanese society of 1940 is viewed as a whole, the major contribution of women remained the unpaid toil of the married women who assisted their husbands in field, shop, or house. Economic activity and social role were products of marital status rather than determinants of it.

The married women in the labor force in October 1955 were concentrated in those occupations that could be pursued without leaving the home. The activities of the single, the widowed, and the divorced were more differentiated, and the patterns were those to be anticipated on the basis of the historic Western experience for the single, and on the ancient Japanese experience for the widowed and the divorced. The percentage occupational composition of the marital status group is given here for women aged from 30 to 34:

Occupation	*All women*	*Single*	*Married*	*Widowed*	*Divorced*
Total	100.	100.	100.	100.	100.
Professional	5.2	14.6	3.6	6.1	7.1
Clerical	5.4	22.4	2.4	7.9	9.1
Sales	11.2	7.3	11.6	13.3	11.2
Laborers, primary industrial	56.0	16.0	66.2	30.2	20.8
Skilled laborers and not classified	13.7	16.7	12.0	23.9	21.8
Service workers	8.2	22.8	3.9	17.8	28.9
All others	0.3	0.2	0.3	0.9	1.0

The traditional patterns of labor force participation for women prevailed in the cities of Japan in 1955. For single women, the major occupations had become those classified as clerical, lesser professional, and service other than domestic. The percentage occupational composition of the marital status groups is given here for women aged from 30 to 34:

Occupation	*All women*	*Single*	*Married*	*Widowed*	*Divorced*
Total	100.	100.	100.	100.	100.
Professional	8.0	15.2	6.0	6.1	7.7
Clerical	11.8	29.8	6.1	11.6	12.7
Sales	17.2	7.9	20.9	16.0	13.1
Laborers, primary industrial	26.7	4.6	38.1	13.2	6.0
Skilled laborers and not classified	20.5	17.0	20.8	26.2	21.8
Service workers	15.1	25.2	7.7	25.0	37.3
All others	0.6	0.3	0.4	1.9	1.4

Changes in rates of participation in economic activity and diversification of that participation were both chiefly characteristic of single women in the urban areas. The participation rates by age and marital status, the advancing age at marriage, and the postponement and reduced rates of childbearing all suggest that there were pressures on the ancient barriers against the employment of married women outside the home. Definitive evaluation of these trends must await the detailed labor force and fertility data for the great cities in 1955.

Unrecorded Marriages

The census enumerators made no distinctions between the recorded and the unrecorded marriage, between the legally divorced and the factually separated. Moreover, census data collected each five years concealed much of the processes of marriage formation and dissolution. We must turn to direct analysis of the registration data. This requires some consideration of the unreported marriages and the extent of the delays between the occurrence and the reporting of marriages.

The Prevalence of Unreported Marriages

A theoretical course for marriage reporting is simple to formulate for anyone who knows the history of our own marriage system. Once a legal system was established, a transfer of the sanctions of marriage from a folk to a legal basis would be anticipated. In Japan, knowledge of the legal requirements for recording was diffused widely by 1920. Such knowledge must have been nation-wide by 1940. The *koseki* system had functioned throughout the country for many decades, and educational status was fairly high. Hence it might be assumed that the differences in the promptness and the frequency of registration would reflect differences in the integration of the people into an economy that made legitimacy and inheritance matters of legal importance. It might also be assumed that those more sensitive to the social pressures for conformity would be less tolerant of informal marriages, and particularly that families of somewhat assured status would hesitate to accept the role of non-legal wife for a daughter. Hence it could be argued that geographic or social nearness to urban centers would lead to the disappearance of the informal marriage in other than a concubinal relationship. Conversely, it could be argued on theoretical grounds that geographic and social isolation would be accompanied by high proportions of unrecorded marriages.

These speculations are broadly consistent with the fragments of information we possess on the frequency of unrecorded marriages in the population as a whole.[18] The proportions of married men and women whose unions were unrecorded was highest in the younger age groups and declined rapidly until the early thirties (TABLE 80). By the late thirties or early forties there was a relative plateau that corresponded to the proportion of marriages that would remain unrecorded. This characteristic age pattern existed in 1920 and in 1940, but between 1920 and 1940 the proportion of marriages which were unrecorded declined rapidly in all sex and age groups. A comparison of the proportions of the informally married in 1940 among the survivors of the various groups of 1920 indicates that less than 5 per cent of the surviving unions remained unrecorded twenty years or more after their occurrence.[19]

The role of economic factors in lessening the lag between the occurrence of marriage and the recording of the fact of marriage is seen in striking form in the comparative frequency of marriages among the armed forces and civilian men in 1940. At this time military allowances and benefits could be allocated only to wives with legal status, i.e., recorded marriages. The over-all proportions of unrecorded marriages were quite similar: 7.0 per cent for civilians, and 6.6 per cent for the armed forces. However, the military men were a young group. The proportions of unrecorded marriages among the armed forces were less than half those among civilians of comparable ages.[20]

TABLE 80

Proportions of married Japanese whose marriages were not recorded in *koseki*, by sex and age, 1920 and 1940

Age	MALES: 1920[a] (Estimated)	MALES: 1940[b] Civilians	MALES: 1940[b] Armed forces	FEMALES: 1920[a] (Estimated)	FEMALES: 1940[b]
15-19	69.2	46.5	—	57.7	38.6
20-24	44.5	29.4	14.5	30.4	18.5
25-29	27.2	15.3	7.2	18.2	8.0
30-34	18.5	7.2	2.9	14.9	5.4
35-39	15.4	5.2	2.3	13.8	5.1
40-44	14.4	5.0	2.0	12.7	5.2
45-49	13.5	5.1	1.8	11.9	5.3
50-54	12.9	5.2	4.1	9.4	5.2
55-59	13.1	5.4	—	8.7	5.2
60-64	12.2	5.5	—	5.8	5.1

[a] Estimated by assuming that the proportion of legally single in each age was the same in the enumerative census of October 1, 1920, as in the registration compilation of December 31, 1918.

[b] Responses to a question as to whether or not the marriage was recorded. Japanese with *honseki* in Japan only.

Source: 1920: Marital status, compilation of 1918: Nihon. Naikaku tokei-kyoku. *Nihon teikoku jinko seitai tokei, 1918.* Census of 1920: *Ibid. Taisho ku'nen kokusei chosa hokoku.* IV.A.1. 1940: Nihon. Sori-cho, tokei-kyoku. *Kekka hokoku tekiyo, Showa 15-nen kokusei chosa.* Also: Nihon. Naikaku, tokei-kyoku. *Census of 1940. Selected tables.* Table 3.

[18] The only direct information on whether marriages were recorded or not was secured in the 1940 census, and Japanese demographers question the accuracy of response. The mobilization of the army had produced widespread national debate over government policies with reference to the granting of allowances and insurance benefits to wives whose marriages were not recorded. Major reliance is placed on these data for 1940, however, since they are the only national materials available. Estimates are possible for 1920 through the application of the proportions of the legally married in the registration population of 1918 to the population enumerated in 1920. It is then assumed that the differences between the *de facto* married and the estimated legally married represent the unrecorded marriages.

[19] The decline in the proportion of strictly illegitimate births from 4.8 per cent of all births in 1920 to 2.0 per cent in 1930 substantiates the hypothesis of a decline in informal unions, for the offspring of such unions are registered as illegitimate births unless the marriage is recorded prior to or simultaneous with the recording of the birth.

[20] It is recognized that the trend toward a decline in unrecorded marriages has been demonstrated for the married population only. As long as both husband and wife survive, a record can be made at anytime. If either dies or if the marriage is broken by separation, the relationship that existed previously will remain permanently outside the *koseki*. No information on the non-reported status of the widowed and the divorced has been located for Japan, though such data exist for Taiwan. There in the year 1920 the proportion whose status was extra-legal, in the sense that it was unreported, was substantially higher among the widowed than among the married. It was highest for the separated, for here the non-recorded separations of the legally married were added to the

THE DELAY IN RECORDING

The evidence is limited, but it indicates that the unrecorded marriage has been decreasing in frequency as a lifelong adjustment. Whether the delay between the marriage ceremony and the recording of the marriage has also been diminishing is more conjectural, although there is some evidence of earlier registration. In 1947 and later years, the marriage statistics included a tabulation of the marriages recorded during the year by the year in which the ceremonies occurred.[21] Summary data for the years from 1947 to 1950 are as follows:

Marriages	*1947*	*1948*	*1949*	*1950*
Reported in year	934,170	953,999	842,170	715,081
Year of occurrence:				
1950	—	—	—	346,044
1949	—	—	404,445	275,374
1948	—	443,255	320,739	47,091
1947	484,434	387,810	59,876	13,666
1946	366,279	66,807	18,568	8,287
1945	40,897	16,234	8,914	
1944	12,459	7,658	4,517	
1943	7,548	5,631	3,722	12,093 (1941-1945)
1942	3,866	3,346	2,428	
1941	3,085	3,223	2,339	
1936-1940	7,360	8,818	7,084	4,576
1931-1935	3,085	4,426	3,607	2,571
1926-1930	2,171	3,194	2,629	4,353 (1930 or earlier)
1925 or earlier	2,442	2,924	2,457	
Unknown	544	673	845	1,026

The proportion of marriages reported immediately after occurrence was quite small. In 1947 some 10 per cent of the marriages occurred less than a month prior to recording in the *koseki*; almost 30 per cent occurred within the three months preceding the report. Over half of the marriages reported in 1947 had occurred within a year; over nine-tenths had occurred within two years. However, a delay of five years or more between occurrence and reporting took place for 2 per cent of the marriages reported.

Data on the time of occurrence of marriages reported within a year give no direct basis for estimating the number of marriages that occurred but were not reported in the year in question. The distribution of the numbers of marriages in the years from 1947 to 1950 by year of occurrence suggests that there were definite regularities in the delay. With the accumulation of data for additional years, cohort analysis will become possible.

UNRECORDED MARRIAGES AND THE INDUSTRIAL TRANSITION

Clues as to the nature of the unrecorded unions in Japan may be secured by comparing the proportions of the marriages that were unreported in the prefectures classified by industrial type. There is little agreement between the data for 1940 and the conception of the unrecorded marriage as a survival of the folk society in the urbanizing world. The proportions of married women whose unions were not recorded varied inversely with dependence on agriculture. In fact, for women aged from 15 to 49 as a group and for each quinquennial age class of women within this group, there was a direct relationship between the prevalence of unrecorded marriages and the industrialization of the economic structure (TABLE 81).[22]

If the unrecorded marriages are products of the modern as well as the ancient society, or of the impact of the modern on the ancient society, then the frequency of unrecorded marriages should furnish clues as to those sex and age groups and those segments of the society in which familial living violated the codes of the house. A series of hypotheses may permit exploration of the relationships among unrecorded marriages where unions are socially sanctioned, casual or temporary unions that are more feasible in the cities than in the villages, unions that accord with traditional concubinage, and liaisons between the elderly.

In the ages when marriage occurred with great frequency, the delays of the traditional society combined with the deviations of the new society to produce high proportions of unrecorded marriages. The rapid declines in the proportions of unrecorded marriages as age advanced reflected the practices of the ancient order in recording the marriage after pregnancy occurred, possibly even at the time when the birth of the child was reported.

Since men may be assumed to have made the primary decisions as to whatever types of unions existed, we may glance first at the prevalence of unrecorded marriages among men in various types of employment (TABLE 82). At all ages,

---

separations of the married whose marriages had not been recorded. Taiwan. Sotoku kambo, rinji kokusei chosa-bu. *Dai-ikkai Taiwan kokusei chosa, dai-sanji rinji Taiwan koko chosa, shukei gempyo, zento no bu, Taisho ku'nen.*

[21] Detailed tabulations are available for months of the year as well as for the year as a whole. Nihon. Kosei-sho, eisei tokei-bu. *Jinko dotai tokei.* 1947—.

[22] For women aged from 15 to 49 as a whole and for all age groups of women except those from 15 to 24, the proportion of all women (single, married, and widowed or separated) living in unrecorded unions varied directly with the departure from the agricultural base. At ages 15 to 19 and 20 to 24 the frequency of the single was so much greater in the metropolitan prefectures that the proportion of all women with unrecorded marriages decreased somewhat. However, above age 15 to 24 the excess in the proportions of marriages that were not recorded more than compensated for the difference in the proportions of all women married.

TABLE 81

The unrecorded marriages among women, by age, prefectures by industrial types, 1940

Prefectures by industrial type	*Ages 15-49*	AGE GROUPS *15-19*	*20-24*	*25-29*	*30-34*	*35-39*	*40-44*	*45-49*
				Per cent of married women				
All Japan	8.0	38.6	18.5	8.0	5.4	5.1	5.2	5.3
Metropolitan	10.7	43.7	22.8	11.1	7.4	6.9	7.2	7.5
Other industrial	9.0	40.9	20.2	9.0	6.3	5.8	5.6	6.1
Intermediate	7.6	40.4	18.4	7.1	4.9	4.8	5.0	4.6
Agricultural	6.2	34.7	15.3	6.0	4.0	3.8	4.0	4.3
Hokkaido	8.5	33.6	15.5	7.0	5.8	6.3	6.7	8.7
				Per cent of all women				
All Japan	4.9	1.6	8.4	6.6	4.8	4.5	4.4	4.2
Metropolitan	6.1	1.4	8.9	8.8	6.4	6.0	6.0	5.7
Other industrial	5.5	1.6	9.2	7.6	5.6	5.2	4.7	4.8
Intermediate	4.8	1.8	9.0	6.0	4.4	4.2	4.3	3.7
Agricultural	3.9	1.6	7.0	5.0	3.6	3.4	3.5	3.4
Hokkaido	5.3	1.5	7.9	6.1	5.3	5.7	5.9	7.1

Source: Nihon. Naikaku tokei-kyoku. Tabulations, 1940 census.

TABLE 82

The proportion of unrecorded marriages, by sex, economic status, and major economic activity, 1940

	PER CENT OF THE MARRIED						PER CENT OF THE TOTAL					
		ECONOMIC STATUS		GAINFULLY OCCUPIED				ECONOMIC STATUS		GAINFULLY OCCUPIED		
Sex and age	*Total*	*Not gainfully occupied*	*Gainfully occupied*	*Agri-culture*	*Manufac-turing*	*Com-merce*	*Total*	*Not gainfully occupied*	*Gainfully occupied*	*Agri-culture*	*Manufac-turing*	*Com-merce*
					Men							
15-19	44.1	44.2	44.1	46.0	48.3	43.7	0.2	0.05	0.2	0.5	0.1	0.1
20-24	26.3	31.8	26.2	21.1	30.9	29.2	2.4	0.7	2.5	2.7	2.6	2.0
25-29	14.5	22.0	14.4	10.0	17.4	16.1	8.3	4.4	8.4	6.7	9.8	8.6
30-34	7.0	14.8	6.9	3.7	8.9	8.2	6.0	6.5	6.1	3.4	7.7	7.2
35-39	5.1	12.6	5.0	2.5	6.7	6.4	4.8	6.9	4.7	2.3	6.1	5.9
40-44	5.0	11.9	4.9	2.5	6.4	6.5	4.6	7.5	4.6	2.3	5.8	6.1
45-49	5.0	9.9	4.9	2.5	6.6	7.0	4.6	6.8	4.5	2.4	6.0	6.5
50-54	5.2	7.8	5.1	2.8	7.1	7.7	4.6	5.7	4.6	2.4	6.3	7.0
55-59	5.4	6.4	5.3	2.9	7.8	8.2	4.6	4.7	4.5	2.5	6.6	7.2
60-64	5.5	5.9	5.4	3.1	8.8	9.6	4.3	4.1	4.4	2.5	7.0	8.0
65 and over	5.3	5.2	5.4	3.2	10.4	10.9	3.4	2.7	3.9	2.3	7.3	8.1
					Women							
15-19	38.6	38.3	38.8	36.0	48.6	44.1	1.6	2.5	1.3	2.4	0.7	0.8
20-24	18.5	19.0	17.7	14.1	30.1	22.6	8.3	12.0	5.8	7.5	6.3	4.8
25-29	8.0	8.9	6.7	3.9	15.1	11.5	6.6	8.0	5.0	3.4	9.5	7.0
30-34	5.4	6.3	4.4	2.2	9.6	9.1	4.8	5.9	3.7	2.1	7.1	6.7
35-39	5.1	6.1	4.1	2.1	8.3	8.8	4.5	5.7	3.5	2.0	6.0	6.7
40-44	5.2	6.4	4.1	2.3	8.1	9.1	4.5	5.7	3.4	2.0	5.6	6.7
45-49	5.3	6.8	4.2	2.5	8.3	9.4	4.2	5.5	3.3	2.1	5.4	6.6
50-54	5.2	6.8	4.1	2.6	8.9	9.4	3.8	4.7	3.0	2.1	5.3	5.9
55-59	5.2	6.6	4.1	2.8	8.7	10.2	3.2	3.7	2.7	2.0	4.5	5.5
60-64	5.1	6.0	4.2	2.9	9.9	11.1	2.5	2.6	2.3	1.8	4.1	4.9
65 and over	5.1	5.5	4.4	3.2	11.3	12.6	1.2	1.1	1.7	1.3	3.1	3.5

Source: Nihon. Naikaku tokei-kyoku. Tabulations, 1940 census.

the proportion of married men living in unrecorded unions was higher among those not gainfully occupied than it was among the gainfully occupied. And among the latter, the proportion of unrecorded unions was higher for men employed in manufacturing industry and commerce than it was for those in agriculture.

The proportions of unrecorded marriages were lower among the gainfully occupied women than among those not gainfully occupied. Among the former, however, great and persistent differences in the legality of the marital status were associated with the type of industry in which the women labored. Women gainfully employed in agriculture married earlier, and their marriages were recorded with less delay. Proportions of unrecorded unions were high among women engaged in manufacturing and commerce. The residual 5 per cent of unrecorded marriages that characterized all the women of Japan in 1940 did not represent a minimum proportion of socially acceptable marriages that were not recorded for some reason associated with the family system. Rather, the proportion of unrecorded marriages for the nation as a whole was the average of widely differing rates of extra-legal unions in the various social and economic groups.

If the preceding interpretations of the proportions of unreported marriages are correct, the major forces creating the marriages with extra-legal status were non-conformist, even disruptive. They did not represent trial marriage in a rigid familistic society. If we regard the legally married, the married living in unreported unions, and the widowed and the separated as distinct groups with different economic roles, we find a substantial concentration of the legally married in agriculture (TABLE 83). The women living in unrecorded unions, like the widowed and the separated, were overrepresented in manufacturing industry and in commerce. If we examine the situation for men, we see that men living in unreported unions were the least agricultural of any marital status group. Viewed from the standpoint of the area of residence, the unreported marriages were more a phenomenon of the cities than of the rural areas. From the standpoint of the occupational structure, the unreported marriages were concentrated in production and service activities outside agriculture. And the women living in unreported unions took their place along with the widowed and the separated women as the disadvantaged classes in Japanese society.

IMPLICATIONS

Conclusions derived from analysis of the responses to a question as to the legality of marital status must be drawn with caution. This is particularly true when the question was

TABLE 83

Economic activities of the Japanese, total married, unrecorded unions, and widowed or separated, by sex and age, 1940

	PER CENT GAINFULLY OCCUPIED			PER CENT OF THE GAINFULLY OCCUPIED: AGRICULTURE			MANUFACTURING			COMMERCE		
Sex and age	*All married*	*Unrecorded unions*	*Widowed and separated*	*All married*	*Unrecorded unions*	*Widowed and separated*	*All married*	*Unrecorded unions*	*Widowed and separated*	*All married*	*Unrecorded unions*	*Widowed and separated*
						Men						
15-19	97.1	97.1	—	51.5	51.2	—	23.6	24.6	—	6.6	6.3	—
20-24	97.9	97.4	93.7	38.1	30.7	42.2	31.6	37.3	28.1	9.7	10.8	8.5
25-29	98.7	98.1	93.8	27.1	18.7	26.6	36.8	44.5	37.4	13.0	14.5	12.5
30-34	98.9	97.6	92.9	26.1	14.1	21.9	33.7	43.3	37.7	15.5	18.5	15.1
35-39	98.8	97.1	93.0	30.1	14.6	24.7	29.7	39.4	35.3	16.7	21.2	15.9
40-44	98.6	96.7	93.7	33.9	17.1	29.8	27.7	36.4	32.4	16.9	22.7	15.4
45-49	98.0	96.2	93.6	38.6	19.9	36.5	24.6	33.0	27.8	17.0	24.2	15.1
50-54	96.3	94.5	91.1	44.1	23.7	43.0	20.8	28.8	23.2	17.0	25.7	14.9
55-59	92.0	90.5	85.1	51.9	29.0	51.1	16.3	24.1	18.1	16.7	26.1	14.3
60-64	85.8	84.7	76.3	60.5	34.7	59.5	11.9	19.4	13.2	15.3	27.0	13.3
65 and over	68.7	69.6	49.6	69.2	40.7	70.4	7.6	14.6	7.8	13.3	26.9	11.2
						Women						
15-19	49.9	50.2	67.4	73.0	67.4	60.9	12.5	15.6	13.0	7.8	8.8	11.7
20-24	43.1	41.4	65.1	70.8	56.3	52.4	13.0	22.0	16.4	10.4	13.2	16.8
25-29	42.6	35.8	64.6	69.1	39.9	39.5	11.3	25.6	19.9	12.9	22.3	22.7
30-34	46.5	37.5	68.8	68.9	35.3	34.8	9.6	21.2	20.6	14.3	29.7	25.2
35-39	50.8	40.6	70.5	70.8	37.0	36.8	8.5	17.3	19.3	15.0	32.5	25.9
40-44	54.7	43.6	67.8	73.1	41.2	43.1	7.3	14.3	16.1	14.6	32.1	24.7
45-49	57.6	45.6	62.2	75.7	44.9	51.1	6.0	11.9	12.1	13.8	31.0	22.5
50-54	58.2	45.6	54.6	79.0	50.0	58.9	4.6	9.9	8.6	12.6	29.2	20.3
55-59	55.7	44.2	46.2	82.3	56.0	65.1	3.5	7.4	6.1	11.1	27.3	17.9
60-64	50.7	41.5	37.2	85.3	59.5	69.9	2.6	6.2	4.5	9.5	25.4	15.7
65 and over	37.6	32.6	18.9	87.4	63.6	74.3	2.0	5.2	3.3	8.3	23.7	13.7

Source: Nihon. Naikaku tokei-kyoku. Tabulations, 1940 census.

asked at only one census, and that during a war year when the advisability of giving soldiers allowances to wives in informal marriages was being debated. Nonetheless, it is difficult to see how either the hesitancies of normal periods or the motivations of a war period could have produced biases that would have created systematic differences between sex and age groups in types of areas and in industrial groups.

The traditional marriage system of Japan involved a delay between the celebration of marriage and the recording of the marriage. That delay meant that at any given time appreciable proportions of the married were living in unrecorded unions. This delay was generally brief, a year or so at most. It occurred for most men sometime between age 26 and age 32, for most women sometime between age 22 and age 28. Some small portions of the unrecorded marriages at any given time might never be recorded. For instance, if the father of the husband refused *koseki* registration, the marriage could not be made legal. But on the whole, only 1 or 2 per cent of the population aged from 30 to 35 and over would, at a given time, be living in unrecorded marriages that were consistent with the mores of the family system.

In the rural areas among people occupied in agriculture there were few permanent deviations from the behavior sanctioned by the *ie*. Presumably there were a few marriages that could not be recorded, and there was some concubinage. On the whole, however, the traditional marriage system prevailed. Practically all people married and practically all marriages were recorded in *koseki* if they endured and the functions of biological replacement were fulfilled. In the industrial regions and in non-agricultural occupations, on the other hand, there were many relations that were not sanctioned by the practices of the village societies. A virtual disappearance of unrecorded unions failed to materialize even among older men and women. Presumably the widowed and the separated formed new unions without benefit of legality. Married men maintained extra-legal families while they lived and labored away from the residence of the legal wife and children. Some of the women in unrecorded unions approached the status of concubines; for them, gainful employment was less prevalent than for legally married or widowed women. In general, the women living in unreported unions held no assured status in the society and their economic level seems to have been low. They labored in disproportionate numbers in the amusement industries and domestic service.

The legal marriages of the Japanese reflected the persistent familism which was the proper adjustment between the sexes in the interests of the continuation of house, people, and nation. The official statistics, which are limited to the recorded marriages, place the beginning of marriage at the date of acceptance of the bride by house and family. They thus exclude that initial period of adjustment in which the rejection of the bride is a simple matter in the hands of the family. The official vital statistics also exclude those forms of unions which were not considered proper by the society. They are thus eminently suited for the analysis of the accepted marital patterns in Japanese society, but their use in the analysis of human reproduction is limited.

MARRIAGE RATES

The number of marriages recorded per 1,000 total population changed little in Japan from the beginning of the twentieth century to the beginning of the war of 1937-1945 (TABLE 84).[23] There were episodic fluctuations but no long-time trends. Marriage rates rose somewhat after the Sino-Japanese and Russo-Japanese wars. The upward thrust after World War I reached its height in 1920, when there were 9.8 registered marriages per 1,000 total population. The years of depression brought rates downward, the rate of 7.2 in 1933 being the lowest so far recorded in the twentieth century. The involvement in China brought sharp gyrations: an upward movement accompanying mobilization in 1937, followed by a severe dip as economic conditions deteriorated in 1938 and 1939. Rates were high from 1941 through 1943, for major mobilization entailed military allowances for wives and a strong pro-natalist policy on the part of the government. There are only limited records for the years from 1944 through 1946. A postwar boom occurred in 1947, 1948, and 1949 as the armed forces were demobilized, repatriates settled, families united, and the tasks of redevelopment attacked. The rate of 12.0 per 1,000 total population in 1947 is the highest in the vital records. Decline continued until the rate reached approximately 7.9 in the period from 1951 through 1954.

TABLE 84

Rates of marriage and divorce, Japanese in Japan, 1900-1955

(Per 1,000 total population)

Period	*Marriage*	*Divorce*
1900-1904[a]	8.2	1.4
1905-1909	8.4	1.2
1910-1914	8.4	1.1
1915-1919	8.3	1.0
1920-1924	9.0	0.9
1925-1929	8.2	0.8
1930-1934	7.6	0.8
1935-1939	8.1	0.6
1940	9.2	0.7
1941	10.8	0.7
1942	9.1	0.6
1943	10.0	0.7
1947[b]	12.0	1.0
1948	11.9	1.0
1949	10.3	1.0
1950	8.6	1.0
1951	7.9	1.0
1952	7.9	0.9
1953	7.8	0.9
1954	7.9	0.9
1955	8.0	0.8

[a] Japan including Okinawa, 1900-1943.
[b] Area of the period.
Sources: 1912-1942: Nihon. Naikaku tokei-kyoku. *Jinko dotai tokei, 1942,* Summary table. 1943-1949: Nihon. Sori-fu, tokei-kyoku. *Nihon tokei nenkan, 1953.* Table 15. 1950-1954: Nihon. Kosei tokei kyokai. *Kokumin eisei no doko, Showa 28-nen. Kosei no shihyo* 1(7):54. 1954. 1955: Nihon. Kosei-sho, eisei tokei-bu. *Jinko dotai tokei maigetsu gaisu. Showa 30-nen nenkei-bun.* No. 117, pp. 42-43.

[23] The basic data are the numbers of marriages and divorces of Japanese in Japan recorded in *koseki* in Japan during the individual years. These numbers are related to the total population of the country. Koreans, other people from the colonies, and aliens are included in the population base, but their marriages and divorces are not included in the vital reports.

Divorce rates, in contrast to marriage rates, revealed a generally consistent downward trend. The rate per 1,000 total population was 1.4 in 1900-1904, 0.9 in 1920-1924, 0.6 in 1935-1939. There was a slight increase during the years of war, a somewhat greater increase to 1.02 in 1947. Divorces remained at this level until 1950, but rates declined slightly to less than 1 per 1,000 population from 1952 through 1955.

Crude rates of marriage and divorce are difficult to interpret. The previous analysis of census data on marital status indicated the existence of a long-time downward trend in the proportions married at the younger ages.[24] Numbers of recorded divorces per 1,000 total population without standardization for age or marital status are not a firm basis for a conclusion as far-reaching as the one apparently indicated by the crude data, i.e., that divorce rates declined with industrialization and urbanization. Analysis must involve the changing characteristics of the married and the divorced as well as the changing types of marriage and divorce. We will approach the problem through a consideration of first marriages. After this we will turn to remarriage, the characteristics of persons marrying and remarrying, and, finally, the dissolution of marriages and the characteristics of the divorced.

FIRST MARRIAGES

The analysis of marriage statistics is more difficult than that of fertility and mortality statistics, for while births and deaths are non-repeatable events in the life of an individual, the possibilities for marriage, divorce, separation, and widowhood are multiple. However, the basic demographic analysis of marriage concerns the first marriage. This is by definition the non-repeatable event.[25]

In Japan from 1919-1921 to 1934-1936, the movement in the number of first marriages per 1,000 population was sharply downward in the younger ages, rather irregular in the intermediate ages, and slight in the upper ages (TABLE 85). Since the proportion of marriages that were recorded in *koseki* was increasing and the length of the delay between celebration and recording was decreasing, the downward trend in recorded marriages in the younger ages understates the decline that was occurring in all marriages.[26]

The over-all stability or slow declines in rates of formal marriage at later ages would be anticipated in a population in which marriage at the younger ages was almost universal. Thus the evidence from age-specific rates of first marriages corroborates that from the census data on marital status. There was a really substantial postponement of marriage among the Japanese.

Marriage rates per 1,000 total population do not yield the probabilities of marriage at the various ages. Neither do they indicate the changing relations between recorded and actual marriages. The disappearance of the single in the successive census enumerations may be used as an approximation of the pattern of marriage rates by age and the trends in that pattern over time.[27] Two major deficiencies of this approach must be emphasized. The first is the lack of stability in marriage rates themselves. In a population with a sharp upward trend in age at marriage, each age group will have been subjected to higher rates of marriage in the past than those that characterize the age groups younger than itself. The second deficiency is that associated with migration. The single may disappear from a closed population by marriage or by death. In an open population, they may also disappear by migration, and on this there are no data and no reasonable basis for estimation. If migrations were non-selective as to marital status they could be ignored, but the migrations to and from Japan were highly selective as to age and sex and presumably also as to marital status. Nonetheless, the rates of disappearance of the single in the census enumerations are illuminating. Something of the magnitude of the error will be noted later.

Among men, the rates of disappearances of the single were at their maximum at age 25 to 29 throughout the period from 1920 to 1940. There was a continuing decline in rates of disappearance at ages under 24, a continuing increase in rates of disappearance at age 30 to 34. The disappearances per 1,000 single as estimated for men in the census years of the prewar period were as follows:[28]

Year	*15-19*	*20-24*	*25-29*	*30-34*
1920	25.3	148.1	244.5	183.7
1925	18.9	151.9	275.4	172.7
1930	12.2	124.5	286.0	171.9
1935	7.2	105.7	274.4	203.4
1940	5.0	52.3	278.3	210.8

The rate of disappearance per 1,000 single men aged from 15 to 34 was 93.3 in 1920 and 94.2 in 1925. It then declined to 86.5 in 1930, 84.3 in 1935, and 75.3 in 1940.

The rates of disappearance for single women aged from 15 to 34 declined more sharply than those for single men. These approximate marriage rates per 1,000 single women were 161 in 1920 and 163 in 1925; they declined to 147 in 1930, 135 in 1935, and 116 in 1940. The factors responsible were the strong declines in marriage probabilities at ages 15 to 19 and 20 to 24. The rates for five-year age groups were as follows:

Year	*15-19*	*20-24*	*25-29*	*30-34*
1920	127.7	259.2	188.1	122.3
1925	119.4	296.6	195.2	97.3
1930	93.7	284.1	228.6	101.8
1935	67.4	267.6	222.0	134.0
1940	46.5	236.6	251.9	120.9

[24] There are many factors involved here. A coincidence of a decreasing lag between occurrence and registration and an increasing proportion of registrations combined with an advancing age at marriage could produce compensating changes that would give an illusion of stability. The changing age composition of the population is also a factor. For nuptiality tables, see: Tachi, Minoru. "Kekkon no seimei hyo." Pp. 51-78 in: Nihon. Kosei-sho, jinko mondai kenkyujo. *Chosa kenkyu shuyo kekka. 1952.* Also: Tachi, Minoru, and Kawakami, Mitsuo. *Marriage table of Japan and life table by marital status, 1935.* Data Paper, Twentieth Annual Meeting, Japan Statistical Society, 1952.

[25] Almost unsurmountable difficulties are inherent in those aspects of the Japanese legal and social structure that pertain to marriage. First marriages are reported as such, and the tabulations of the characteristics of the participants include age. These are the events recorded in the *koseki*, however, and the population to which they relate consists of the total number of persons who have not had a previous marriage recorded in the *koseki*. Since that population is not obtainable for any year after 1918, the only procedure that does not involve hazardous assumptions as a basis for estimates is the computation of rates of first marriage per 1,000 total population. The total population at any given age, however, is not the population subject to the risks of a first marriage.

[26] In the postwar years, marriage by previous marital status is tabulated only for marriages occurring and reported in a given year. Because of selectivities in the delays in reporting, these tabulations are not comparable with those for prewar years.

[27] The technique used here is that of Giorgio Mortara. See pp. 17-39 in: United Nations. Department of Social Affairs. *Methods of using census statistics . . . .* Population Studies No. 7. Lake Success, N.Y., 1949. 60 pp.

[28] All computations were made by single years of age, with consolidations for convenience of presentation.

TABLE 85

First marriages of the Japanese, by sex and age, from 1919-1920 to 1934-1936

	PER 1,000 TOTAL POPULATION				PER 1,000 JAPANESE	
Age	*1919-1921*	*1925-1926*	*1929-1931*	*1934-1936*	*1920-1921*	*1930-1931*
			Male			
15-19	7.1	4.5	2.8	1.6	7.2	2.9
20-24	64.9	62.2	50.2	42.9	65.4	51.5
25-29	80.4	78.3	78.5	87.4	80.9	80.5
30-34	30.9	27.0	25.3	28.0	31.1	25.9
35-39	11.7	9.8	8.5	8.8	11.8	8.6
40-44	6.1	4.7	4.0	4.1	6.1	4.1
45-49	3.6	2.8	2.3	2.4	3.6	2.3
50-54	2.2	1.8	1.5	1.5	2.2	1.5
55-59	1.3	1.1	1.0	1.0	1.3	1.0
60-64	0.7	0.7	0.7	0.7	0.7	0.7
			Female			
15-19	49.3	42.3	31.9	23.1	49.3	32.1
20-24	95.8	96.2	93.6	95.9	95.9	94.4
25-29	34.7	31.7	28.5	36.1	34.7	28.6
30-34	13.0	10.8	9.3	9.3	13.0	9.4
35-39	6.3	5.1	4.3	4.4	6.5	4.3
40-44	3.4	2.8	2.4	2.5	3.4	2.4
45-49	1.9	1.7	1.4	1.5	1.9	1.5
50-54	1.0	1.0	0.9	0.9	1.0	0.9
55-59	0.5	0.1	0.2	0.6	0.5	0.5
60-64	0.2	0.5	0.2	0.3	0.2	0.2

Source: Nihon. Naikaku tokei-kyoku. *Jinko dotai tokei.* Various years.

If the numbers of first marriages as estimated from census data are related to the total population rather than to the single, there is corroborative evidence of substantial delays in the registration of marriages. The data for the years from 1920 to 1935 are presented here, the rates being first marriages per 1,000 women:

Age	*Recorded 1919-1921*	*Estimated 1920*	*Recorded 1934-1936*	*Estimated 1935*
15-19	49.3	105.0	24.7	62.4
20-24	95.8	81.2	32.1	120.1
25-29	34.7	17.2	94.4	24.6
30-34	13.0	5.0	28.6	5.4

If the estimated rates were approximately correct, it would be possible to estimate the delays in registration and the ages at which *de facto* marriages occur. Unfortunately, the rates that measure the disappearance of the single overestimate the marriage rate. There is a crude test available. At the estimated rates of disappearance of the single, the proportions of a cohort of girls aged 15 who should have survived and remained single at age 34 can be computed and compared with the actual proportions single at the various census dates. As the following data indicate, the amount of the overestimation of marriage is not great:

	Estimated per cent single			*Actual per cent single*		
Age	*1920*	*1930*	*1940*	*1920*	*1930*	*1940*
15	100.	100.	100.	97.1	99.1	99.7
20	47.2	56.6	74.5	48.4	58.8	77.5
25	11.9	12.0	19.5	13.0	13.1	21.3
30	4.6	3.9	5.7	5.3	4.5	6.5
34	2.7	2.5	3.0	3.2	3.0	4.3

Changes in marriage have occurred so rapidly that a cohort approach would be valuable if the data permitted it. The girls who postponed marriage at one age married a few years later. In this situation, a rapidly declining rate of marriage at one age necessitated compensatory increases in the succeeding ages. To assume that any group of Japanese women went through life subject to the age-specific legal or actual marriage rates of a specific time period would be unrealistic indeed. The cohort of 1920 is cited, utilizing the estimated number of marriages per 1,000 single:[29]

Age	*Cohort of 1920*	*Year 1920*	*Year 1935*
15-19	127.7	127.7	67.4
20-24	296.6	259.2	267.6
25-29	228.6	188.1	222.0
30-34	134.0	122.3	134.0

The advance in age at marriage and the continued prevalence of marriage as an almost universal way of living are demonstrated both in the rates of recorded marriages and in the rates of total marriages estimated from the census age distributions. The critical difference between the two series is not the fact of marriage but the date at which it occurred. Definite analysis must await the collection of data on the occurrence of marriage for a sufficiently long time to permit a cohort approach to the problem. In the meantime, caution is necessary in any discussion of the age at marriage or the rates of marriage in Japan.

[29] The "cohort of 1920" had the marriage rates of 1920 at age 15 to 19, of 1925 at age 20 to 24, of 1930 at age 25 to 29, of 1935 at age 30 to 34.

REMARRIAGE

The frequencies of recorded marriages by age and the changes in such frequencies over time were rather comparable, whether all marriages or first marriage alone were considered. The word "rather" in this statement requires emphasis, however. Rates for first marriage and for total marriages were quite similar at the early ages, but the divergences increased with age until they became substantial in middle and old age (TABLE 86). Over 95 per cent of all marriages under age 25 were first marriages. This was true for both men and women. As death removed spouses and marriages were terminated by divorce, the numbers eligible for remarriage increased sharply. By age 40 to 44 for men and age 45 to 49 for women, remarriages surpassed first marriages.

TABLE 86

Marriages of the widowed and the separated per 100 marriages of the single, by sex, from 1919-1921 to 1934-1936

	MALE				FEMALE			
Age	*1919-1921*	*1924-1926*	*1929-1931*	*1934-1936*	*1919-1921*	*1924-1926*	*1929-1931*	*1934-1936*
15-64	19.9	17.0	15.5	14.3	11.5	9.6	8.8	8.0
15-19	1.3	1.1	0.7	0.5	1.1	0.8	0.6	0.4
20-24	3.1	2.4	1.7	1.3	4.4	3.3	2.4	1.7
25-29	9.4	7.4	6.0	4.2	19.2	16.1	15.2	10.4
30-34	33.5	30.8	27.1	23.3	42.7	42.3	41.7	38.4
35-39	81.1	80.0	78.4	71.7	68.6	67.6	70.9	65.5
40-44	122.3	137.4	136.3	135.2	92.4	92.7	95.5	95.4
45-49	160.7	174.0	189.4	184.8	124.9	118.2	124.2	122.5
50-54	199.6	206.8	210.8	231.9	170.0	151.2	143.9	149.8
55-59	246.2	254.8	238.7	245.8	214.2	199.4	172.9	162.3
60-64	285.9	277.5	280.6	272.1	264.0	220.3	230.9	178.4

Source: Nihon. Naikaku tokei-kyoku. *Jinko dotai tokei.* Respective years. Also: Nihon. Kosei-sho, kenkyujo, jinko minzoku-bu. *Jinko tokei soran.*

The ratios of remarriages to first marriages have showed a general tendency toward decline in all sex and age groups throughout the development of the industrial society of modern Japan. This phenomenon of decline is shown for age groups by sex for the years from 1919-1921 to 1934-1936 in Table 86. It had existed for decades before the first census was taken in 1920. The previous marital status of the men and women participating in recorded marriages between 1900 and 1934 reveals this decline clearly. The proportionate distribution of men by previous marital status is cited:

Years	*Single*	*Widowed*	*Divorced*	*Separated*
1900-1904	80.8	7.5	10.4	1.2
1905-1909	82.0	7.7	9.0	1.4
1910-1914	83.5	7.6	8.2	0.6
1915-1919	83.8	7.7	8.0	0.5
1920-1924	84.0	8.8	7.1	0.1
1925-1929	85.7	7.7	6.3	0.1
1930-1934	86.6	7.5	5.8	0.1

In a society where death rates were declining, there would be a declining proportion of men who were widowed and therefore available for remarriage. This obvious explanation is hardly valid for Japan, however, for the proportion of all marriages that involved widowers remained fairly constant at 7.5 to 8.8 per cent. The real decline came in the proportion of marriages in which the man had been divorced. The increasing stability of recorded marriages again emerges as a fact in twentieth-century Japan.

The problems of reconciling the theoretical formulation of the Japanese family system with the facts recorded in the *koseki* are difficult indeed. The percentage distributions of women marrying by previous marital status have changed as follows:

Years	*Single*	*Widowed*	*Divorced*	*Separated*
1900-1904	83.4	2.7	9.6	4.3
1905-1909	84.0	2.7	8.0	5.3
1910-1914	88.7	2.8	7.9	0.6
1915-1919	89.2	2.7	7.5	0.6
1920-1924	90.3	3.2	6.4	0.2
1925-1929	91.5	2.9	5.6	0.1
1930-1934	92.2	2.6	5.1	0.1

There are alternative theoretical explanations that will rationalize some of the facts as to levels and trends in remarriage. We might assume that remarriage itself was controlled by the family system in the interests of the continuity of the generations in the male line. The discarding of spouses could occur only in ways formalized by the family system and without disruption of that system. The difficulty with this theory is that rates of remarriage declined with industrialization and urbanization. In other words, the rates of remarriage declined as the family itself was undergoing the readjustments involved in an increase in geographical mobility and occupational diversification. A second explanation of remarriage among the Japanese would proceed on the assumption that remarriage was a product of the loosening of the ties of the old family system, and of the penetration of Western culture. A theory involving the impact of urbanization, secularization, and educational advance on the cohesive family structure of an agrarian society is enticing. It is quite consistent with historical experience in many of the industrializing cultures of the West. But again there are difficulties, since the facts are not consistent with the theory. Rates of remarriage declined most sharply in the younger ages, where the adjustments to urban life and industrial technology were presumably most advanced. Hence there must be a third theoretical formulation which proceeds from the assumption that there actually was a stabilization of marriage during the decades when a general solidification of the social structure and an integration of the political order took place.

The Stabilization of Marriage

DEVIATE TYPES OF MARRIAGE

The integration of marriage and house laws suggests that the milieu of the house may have been the paramount factor in the stability of marriage. The modal marriage was that of the patriarchal society, in which residence, responsibilities, and obligations moved directly down male lines. In this type of marriage, the wife moved to the residence of the husband, assumed his name, and became a part of the living and working group that constituted his house. In other cases, marriage involved deviant procedures that permitted the maintenance of the name of the wife and the procurement of heirs for her house. In *nyufu kon'in* the husband played the subservient role. His name was added to the *koseki* of the wife's family, he moved to her home, and he assumed the name of her house. The *muko yoshi kon'in* permitted the acquisition of a son-in-law by a family desiring an heir, but it involved a higher social status for the man. The son-in-law was adopted at or before marriage to the daughter, thus becoming son as well as son-in-law. If the wife were the eldest daughter and had no brothers, this adopted son-in-law had inheritance rights to the headship of the house of his wife.

These three types of marriages represented divergent social status for the husband within the family. The ordinary marriage, where the wife's identity was merged in that of her husband's family, was the norm; it included 91.4 per cent of all marriages in 1919-1921, and 92.6 per cent in 1934-1936. The least acceptable of any of the marriage types was that of the *nyufu kon'in*, where the man gave up name and status to secure economic advantages in the family of his wife. These marriages constituted only 2.5 per cent of all marriages. The *muko yoshi kon'in* involved much higher status for the husband, for he had inheritance rights in the family into which he was adopted. Over 5 per cent of all marriages were of this type, which showed some tendency to decline with urbanization. However, the *nyufu kon'in* and the *muko yoshi kon'in* were deviant forms of marriage throughout the post-Restoration period. The relatively small decline in their frequency cannot have been a major factor in the stabilization of marriage relationships.

EARLY MARRIAGES

The changing prevalence of marriages at ages that deviate from those appropriate to the culture may also be a factor in the duration of the marriages, the frequency of dissolution, and the extent of remarriage. In this argument it is assumed that the modal age at marriage reflects the type of cultural adjustments making for permanency in the family. It is further assumed that the dispersion of age relationships around modal patterns and changes in such dispersion reflect the changing efficiency of the pressures to conformity in the culture.

The very early marriages that might be expected to be unstable because of the age factor alone were not prevalent in Japan even in the late nineteenth century, when the *koseki* records first became relatively complete and accurate. In 1910 the average age at recorded first marriage was 23 for women and 27 for men. In 1935 the comparable averages were 24 for women and 28 for men.

A relatively high and generally increasing average age at first marriage for Japan as a whole could conceal the presence of substantial areas in which marriage occurred at much younger ages. However, the average ages at the time of recorded marriage for the various prefectures over the years from the 1890's to the present would not be regarded as low in other agrarian societies of the East. An analysis of the variations among the prefectures in the average age at recorded marriage in 1915 indicated a positive association among age at marriage, the development of the non-agricultural economy, and the growth of cities. Average ages were lowest in agricultural prefectures, highest in metropolitan prefectures. The range was substantial at a given time, and the changes were appreciable over time. In 1915, the average age at first marriage for women was 20 in Aomori and Iwate, but 25 in Tokyo and Osaka. In 1935, the average age for women was 22 in Aomori and 21 in Iwate; in Tokyo and Osaka it was over 25.

THE AGES OF HUSBANDS AND WIVES

The Japanese ideal required that the husband be a few years older than the wife. Migration, with its disruptions of village life and its incentives to advancement in the great cities, operated to increase the difference between the age of husband and wife. A comparable effect was produced by the limitations to economic opportunity in the villages. Relatively prosperous agricultural life, combined with substantial industrial opportunities, tended to decrease the difference between the ages of the spouses. As a consequence, differences in average ages of husbands and wives at recorded marriages were high both in the agrarian and in the industrial prefectures, low in the prefectures with intermediate economies. The average difference for the nation as a whole remained quite stable at about four years.

The major change over time was a lessening in the proportion of marriages that deviated from the normal age difference between husband and wife rather than any change in that average difference (Table 87). The proportion of marriages in which either husband or wife was very young declined, and the decline was particularly great in the proportion in which both were very young. The proportion of women marrying at age 15 to 19 was cut in half between 1904-1906 and 1934-1936. In 1904-1906 half of all the marriages in which the husband was below age 25 involved women under age 20. In 1934-1936 over three-fifths of men marrying before age 25 were married to women aged from 20 to 24.

As age advanced, deviations from the modal age difference became less frequent. Deviant types persisted, however. Marriages of women to men younger than themselves were found in limited numbers; one suspects that these young husbands were poor boys rising in economic status through marriage.

Both declining frequencies of marriage among the very young and declining proportions of marriages with substantial differences between the ages of husbands and wives were conducive to the stability of marriage. Before we draw further conclusions from these limited phenomena, however, we should analyze the direct index of family stability or instability, the prevalence of divorce.

TABLE 87

Age of wives at recording of marriage, by age of husbands, age 15 to 39, 1904-1934

(Per cent of wives in specified ages, all wives taken as 100 per cent)

Age of husband	AGE OF WIFE *15-19*	*20-24*	*25-29*	*30-34*	*35-39*
Total					
1904-1906	28.2	41.2	18.0	6.7	2.9
1914-1916	27.4	42.0	16.0	7.0	3.7
1924-1926	24.2	48.2	15.4	5.4	2.8
1934-1936	14.2	54.9	19.0	5.4	2.7
20-24					
1904-1906	49.7	43.1	6.3	0.7	0.1
1914-1916	48.9	45.3	5.1	0.6	0.1
1924-1926	43.3	51.5	4.6	0.5	0.1
1934-1936	30.4	63.7	5.4	0.4	0.1
25-29					
1904-1906	23.4	52.1	20.4	3.4	0.6
1914-1916	25.1	54.0	17.2	2.9	0.6
1924-1926	21.1	60.9	15.6	1.9	0.3
1934-1936	12.6	67.8	18.0	1.3	0.2
30-34					
1904-1906	10.2	39.3	34.3	12.6	2.7
1914-1916	10.1	39.4	32.2	13.7	3.7
1924-1926	8.0	44.3	33.6	10.7	2.6
1934-1936	4.2	43.2	40.0	10.1	2.0
35-39					
1904-1906	3.8	23.1	35.7	23.9	9.9
1914-1916	3.8	21.1	31.8	26.0	13.1
1924-1926	3.2	23.0	36.5	23.0	10.8
1934-1936	1.7	18.6	39.0	26.2	10.9

Source: Nihon. Naikaku tokei-kyoku. *Jinko dotai tokei*. Various years.

DIVORCE

In Japan, as in the West, divorce was and is a legal act. There is thus a statistical record that permits some measurement. Unfortunately, analysis contributes little to knowledge of the social and psychological correlates and the demographic consequences of marital separations in the society of Japan. The codified law included a rather long list of legal justifications for the dissolution of marriages. Much study has been devoted to this list, and much effort has been expended in getting it modified to accord with changing ideas of the proper. Most divorces did not involve court action, however, but merely an agreement to remove the name of the offending member from the *koseki*.[30] In the most common instance, the wife's name was removed from the *koseki* of her husband's house, the wife herself returning to her own family or establishing a house of her own. If the marriage had involved the procurement of a son-in-law, divorce involved the removal of the name of the husband from the *koseki* of the house of the wife. Most curious to the non-Japanese is the type of divorce where both husband and wife continued to reside in the same house after the divorce.

Something as to the factors involved in legal divorce can be deduced from the statistics on divorce by type of marriage.[31] Annual divorces per 100 marriages amounted to four or five for marriages in which the husband had lived with the family of the wife, as contrasted with three for marriages in which the wife had lived with the family of the husband. This is an understandable differentiation, for the role of the man in the wife's family cannot have been an easy one, and internal difficulties were compounded by lesser status in the community. However, the type of marriage cannot be a complete or even a major explanation of divorce, for instances in which the husband left the home of the wife constituted only 10 per cent of all divorces.

The hazards of divorce were greatest in the second year of marriage rather than the first. Some five-sixths or more of the recorded divorces occurred within five years or less of the recorded marriage. However, the average time between marriage and divorce increased rather than decreased during the 1920's and 1930's.

The ages of husbands and wives securing divorces, and the relationships of the two, indicate that divorce was most prevalent in the ages of early maturity and maximum nuptiality. Almost half of the divorced men were aged from 25 to 34; over half of divorced women were aged from 20 to 29.

The number of divorces per 1,000 population aged from 15 to 64 declined consistently for both men and women between 1919-1921 and 1939-1940 (TABLE 88). This over-all change was due primarily to a decline in the frequency of legal divorce among younger adults. For men aged from 25 to 29, the number of divorces per 1,000 total population was 7.6 in 1919-1921, 4.5 in 1939-1940. For women aged from 20-24, the number of divorces per 1,000 total population was 7.7 in 1919-1921, 3.7 in 1939-1940. Relating divorces to Japanese ethnic population does not alter the pattern of decline. Relating recorded divorces to current recorded marriages does not lessen it. Thus it seems that the frequency of recorded divorce declined with industrialization and urbanization.

The remarriage of the divorced furnishes clues as to factors operative in the disruption of first marriages and the formation of new ones (TABLE 89). The population of the divorced was dynamic, depletions through remarriage and death amounting to a substantial portion of the total created by divorce in the younger ages, far exceeding it in the upper ages.[32] Divorce was related to the possibilities for remarriage and the characteristics of the husband, but whether the selection was related to the family responsibilities of the old order or the individualism of the new is debatable. It should be noted that the childlessness of wives may account for the divorces and the remarriages of men, but it cannot explain the remarriages of divorced women.

A decline in rates of recorded divorces does not necessarily mean a stabilization of the family. The initial marriage experience of most couples and the complete experience of some occurred prior to the recording of marriage in the *koseki*. Insofar as delayed recording of a marriage made it in

[30] In the prewar years, only 400 of the approximately 50 thousand divorces occurring annually involved court action. The others took place by mutual consent and left no legal or statistical record beyond the mere change in the *koseki*.

[31] Divorce statistics, like those on marriage, were procured from the following sources: Prewar: Nihon. Naikaku tokei-kyoku. *Jinko dotai tokei*. Postwar: Nihon. Kosei-sho, eisei tokei-bu. *Jinko dotai tokei*.

[32] And hence the marital status defined as "divorced" at an instant of time is an understatement of the magnitude of divorce in the population.

TABLE 88

Divorces in relation to total population and to marriages, by age, 1920-1940

	MALE					FEMALE				
Age	*1919-1921*	*1924-1926*	*1929-1931*	*1934-1936*	*1939-1940*	*1919-1921*	*1924-1926*	*1929-1931*	*1934-1936*	*1939-1940*
	Divorces per 1,000 total population									
15-19	0.3	0.2	0.1	0.0	0.0	2.3	1.5	1.0	0.6	0.4
20-24	4.0	3.1	2.1	1.4	1.1	7.7	6.5	5.4	4.2	3.7
25-29	7.6	6.3	5.6	4.7	4.5	6.5	5.7	5.3	5.0	4.8
30-34	6.0	5.2	4.9	4.6	4.5	4.3	3.9	3.8	3.5	3.4
35-39	4.1	3.7	3.8	3.3	3.2	2.8	2.6	2.7	2.5	2.2
40-44	2.8	2.6	2.7	2.5	2.3	1.8	1.7	1.9	1.7	1.6
45-49	2.0	1.9	2.1	1.8	1.7	1.2	1.2	1.3	1.1	1.1
50-54	1.4	1.4	1.5	1.4	1.2	0.7	0.7	0.8	0.7	0.7
50-59	1.0	1.0	1.1	1.0	0.9	0.4	0.4	0.5	0.4	0.4
60-64	0.7	0.7	0.8	0.7	0.7	0.2	0.2	0.3	0.2	0.2
	Divorces per 1,000 marriages									
15-19	51	45	36	34	32	47	36	32	27	26
20-24	60	49	43	34	36	77	66	57	44	37
25-29	87	76	58	52	44	158	156	164	127	98
30-34	146	149	154	134	101	231	254	292	270	200
35-39	194	212	250	223	174	264	305	371	338	251
40-44	210	239	280	265	191	283	322	412	360	252
45-49	218	247	310	273	193	279	319	407	342	238
50-54	221	258	322	278	185	277	311	375	327	366
55-59	230	261	324	285	197	300	315	386	311	222
60-64	260	262	329	275	203	320	312	378	327	210

Source: Nihon. Naikaku tokei-kyoku. *Jinko dotai tokei.* Various years.

fact a trial marriage, the trial involved familial suitability and reproduction performance rather than personal happiness. If this were indeed the role of the informal marriage, then divorce after marriage should have been rare, particularly during the early decades when registration of marriage was long delayed. However, divorces were most frequent when and where unrecorded marriages were most prevalent, and divorce rates declined along with increasing conformity to the requirements for the recording of marriage.[33]

CONCLUSIONS

The theory that industrialization and urbanization are accompanied by an increasing instability of marriage is not substantiated in Japan either by the statistics on marriage from the *koseki* records or by the statistics on marital status from the census enumerations. Divorce rates declined throughout the period of *koseki* records. They declined not only in relation to total population but in relation to recorded marriages, though here the decline in divorces was greatest and most consistent in the younger ages, somewhat erratic and even replaced by increases in some of the upper ages. The proportions of the divorced and the separated in the enumerative censuses declined quite consistently from one census to the next. The only logical explanation of these relationships is a relatively high stability of the unrecorded marriages as well as of those that were formally registered.

The conclusion that the Japanese family became more stable in the period of economic development and urbanization is consistent both with the transition in the patterns of recorded and unrecorded marriage among the Japanese and with the changing economy and society of Japan. Deviate marriages that would involve adjustment difficulties within the family and in the community decreased both absolutely and proportionately to all marriages. Marriages of the very young decreased in frequency, while there was greater and greater concentration of the age at marriage around that age which was modal for the area and the time period. The education of girls, their economic experience, and their more advanced age may have altered the types of marital arrangements that were acceptable to their families. Certainly girls who were literate and had some knowledge of the larger society and the monetary economy had roles within the family different from those of their forebears in the more completely peasant society. The future status of the modern girls as wives became no less certain; their tenure in that status became more secure.

The urban monetary economy itself was conducive to a stabilization of the family, in the formal sense that the family continued to exist without dissolution by separation or divorce. The family remained central in way of life and of work in the cities and the industrial areas. The alternatives to familial living were few; in general they were not attractive at the normal income levels of the Japanese. It may also be that

[33] The usual assumption would be that the stability of unions would be greatest among the upper social-economic and the more educated groups. If this were so, then in the absence of other changes divorce rates should have been least frequent in the early period of more limited and more delayed registration, and should have become more frequent as the peoples of more isolated areas, with lower income and less education, registered the fact of marriage. This hypothetical historical sequence did not occur.

TABLE 89

Divorces and the disappearance of the divorced, by sex and age, from 1919-1921 and 1934-1936

(Per 1,000 total population)

	1919-1921				*1934-1936*			
		DISAPPEARANCE OF DIVORCED				DISAPPEARANCE OF DIVORCED		
Age	*Divorced*	*Marriage*	*Death*	*Net change*	*Divorced*	*Marriage*	*Death*	*Net change*
				Men				
15-64	3.3	2.3	0.4	0.6	2.2	1.4	0.3	0.5
15-19	0.3	0.1	0.0	0.2	0.0	0.0	0.0	0.0
20-24	4.0	1.5	0.1	2.4	1.4	0.4	0.0	1.0
25-29	7.6	4.6	0.2	2.8	4.7	2.3	0.1	2.3
30-34	6.0	4.8	0.4	0.8	4.6	3.2	0.2	1.2
35-39	4.1	3.7	0.4	0.0	3.3	2.5	0.3	0.5
40-44	2.8	2.7	0.5	−0.4	2.5	2.0	0.4	0.1
45-49	2.0	2.0	0.6	−0.6	1.8	1.5	0.5	−0.2
50-54	1.4	1.5	0.7	−0.8	1.4	1.2	0.6	−0.4
55-59	1.0	1.1	0.9	−1.0	1.0	0.9	0.8	−0.7
60-64	0.7	0.7	1.2	−1.2	0.7	0.6	1.1	−1.0
				Women				
15-64	3.4	2.2	0.4	0.8	2.3	1.3	0.3	0.7
15-19	2.3	0.4	0.0	1.9	0.6	0.1	0.0	0.5
20-24	7.7	3.1	0.3	4.3	4.2	1.3	0.1	2.8
25-29	6.5	4.6	0.5	1.4	5.0	2.6	0.3	2.1
30-34	4.3	3.7	0.4	0.2	3.5	2.4	0.3	0.8
35-39	2.8	2.8	0.4	−0.4	2.5	1.9	0.3	0.3
40-44	1.8	2.0	0.4	−0.6	1.7	1.4	0.3	0.0
45-49	1.2	1.5	0.5	−0.8	1.1	1.1	0.4	−0.4
50-54	0.7	1.0	0.6	−0.9	0.7	0.8	0.5	−0.6
55-59	0.4	0.6	0.7	−0.9	0.4	0.5	0.6	−0.7
60-64	0.2	0.3	0.8	−0.9	0.2	0.3	0.8	−0.9

Source: Nihon. Naikaku tokei-kyoku. *Jinko dotai tokei.* Various years.

families in a commercial or partially commercialized economy were less willing than peasant families to receive daughters back after the dissolution of marriages. If the girl banished from her husband's family had to maintain herself, her opportunities for adequate employment as a divorcee were slight. Thus while social developments enhanced the role of women, economic factors forced women to accept whatever conditions were necessary to the maintenance of status in a family. It is quite understandable that marital separations decreased in frequency.

Marriage in Japan has been in transition during the twentieth century, but the magnitude and the direction of many of the changes are difficult to determine. The reason inheres in part in the continuation of the *koseki* records as a basis for the data on population movements in a modernizing state. There are deeper reasons, for the social institutions of an ancient culture have also been in transition. Individuals whose attitudes and values concerning marriage and family derive from the peasant state live in an industrializing and urbanizing world. The society of Japan remains familial; only thus could individuals and the society as a whole move on to the achievement of ever more industrialization and ever greater cities. The age at marriage has advanced, but marriage remains the accepted pattern of living and it is achieved eventually by almost all Japanese. The family, once formed, appears to be more stable than it was in the early Restoration period.

CHAPTER XII

Fertility

IN the decades after the First World War, place of residence, living conditions, and patterns of personal relations were altered for major portions of the Japanese. In the changes in family formation, as in urbanization and external migration, there were broad similarities between the developments in the industrializing cultures of the West and those in this first industrializing culture of the East. There were also differences. Some reflected the period at which the changes occurred and others reflected factors in the Japanese situation—sparse resources, economic pressures, the institutions of the folk society, and the values of the elders. Were changes in fertility also broadly comparable to those that occurred in Western cultures, however much they differed in detail? If so, are the past trends among the Japanese relevant to an assessment of the prospects for other Asian peoples in their periods of industrialization and urbanization?

At any given time during the decades when the new Japan was evolving from the old society of the Tokugawa *bakufu*, the rate at which new life was being produced seemed a minor factor in the totality of the nation's problems. A few students realized the importance of research on fertility, and occasionally special data were collected by the Cabinet Bureau of Statistics.[1] In 1925 and 1930 numbers of births were tabulated by age of father and mother for the prefectures and larger cities; tabulations by age of mother are available for the nation as a whole for the years from 1937 through 1943. Beginning with 1947, numbers of births were tabulated by age of mother and by birth order. In 1950 there was a census question on the number of children ever born to married women, but only summary data have been published for areas within the country.

Analysis of the changing fertility of the Japanese is complicated by the fact that vital statistics are a by-product of the *koseki* system. Since only Japanese are included in *koseki*, the official statistics on births refer only to Japanese. Chief among the peoples who have been omitted are the Koreans, who form a substantial minority even in postwar Japan. Furthermore, many practical difficulties are involved in the utilization of a purely administrative system for data collection. Until recently, the reports of births to Japanese in any specific year were not the births that occurred within the year, but the births that occurred within and were reported during the year.[2] Another problem concerns the relations between the populations enumerated in an area at successive dates and the births reported as having occurred within that area in the intercensal period. In a society as mobile as that of the Japanese, a baby born within an area may not be the child of anyone present in that area at the preceding census date or of anyone present at the following census date. Averaging of the two populations to secure an applicable population is hazardous. The difficulties are compounded by the fact that young wives often go home to have the first baby, thus resulting in a disproportionate occurrence of births in rural rather than in urban areas.

The problems inherent in the contradictions between vital records and census enumerations are serious. Enumerated children under age 1 were used to derive correction factors for numbers of recorded births.[3] The reasons for this procedure lie in specific characteristics of the official statistics and the culture of the period. Analysis of the age data of the censuses from 1920 to 1940 indicated that infants were enumerated with remarkable completeness. They included those whose parents were Japanese, people from the colonies, and aliens, and their numbers were thus comparable with those of women enumerated in the census. Moreover, the use of infants below age 1 avoided the problems involved in relating reported births to enumerated populations in a migrant society.[4] Since most of the babies were nursed by their mothers, baby and mother were enumerated in the same minor civil division. If the mother had moved into the city soon after the birth of the child, then the child was also considered a migrant.

TRENDS IN NATIONAL FERTILITY

In stable peasant societies of the East where life continued in the routine of the seasons and the years, where food was adequate for the maintenance of life and epidemics were limited, fertility changed little from one period to another. Persistently high birth rates characterized the populations of Taiwan, Korea, and Kwantung. They have not characterized modern Japan. Crude birth rates moved generally downward during the years of the First World War and the influenza epidemic, but then shot upward to reach in 1920 the highest levels ever recorded in Japan. They declined quite regularly from 1921 through 1937 (TABLE 90). The economic and military difficulties of the early period of the China War brought the birth rates down to 27 per 1,000 total population in 1938 and 1939, but the full employment and military successes of the early years of what was believed to be a vic-

[1] Major published materials are cited in the Bibliography.

[2] At present, vital events that are reported in January, February, and March of the following year are included in the final tabulations of the events for the year in question. However, births to Koreans are still excluded.

[3] The numbers of infant deaths that were recorded have to be utilized to secure estimates of numbers of births from numbers of recorded children below one year of age, but possible errors in the completeness and residence allocations of infant deaths could not result in major errors in estimates of births at the levels of infant mortality which existed in Japan during the period under analysis.

[4] Strictly speaking, the use of enumerated children to estimate births yields measures of the reproductive performance of the women enumerated in areas rather than the reproduction of the population present in the areas during the time periods in question. In practice, the relative differences between recorded and estimated births at census years were utilized as correction factors for recorded births. These factors were logical in geographic and social-economic patterns at any given census period and were highly correlated over time.

TABLE 90

Annual fertility, 1920-1955

Year	BIRTHS TO JAPANESE IN JAPAN		Female births per 1,000 women Aged 15-49[b]	Gross reproduction rate[c]
	Number (in '000)	Per 1,000 population[a]		
1920	2,012	36.1	77.6	2.7
1921	1,976	35.0	75.6	2.6
1922	1,954	34.1	74.0	2.5
1923	2,029	34.1	75.7	2.6
1924	1,984	33.7	73.2	2.5
1925	2,072	34.8	75.7	2.6
1926	2,089	34.7	74.6	2.6
1927	2,046	33.5	72.8	2.5
1928	2,120	34.2	74.2	2.6
1929	2,062	32.8	71.3	2.4
1930	2,071	32.4	70.2	2.4
1931	2,089	32.2	70.3	2.4
1932	2,168	32.9	71.9	2.4
1933	2,106	31.5	69.0	2.3
1934	2,028	30.0	66.1	2.2
1935	2,174	31.7	69.3	2.3
1936	2,086	30.0	65.4	2.2
1937	2,165	30.8	66.7	2.2
1938	1,912	27.1	57.7	1.9
1939	1,886	26.6	56.2	1.9
1940	2,100	29.4	61.4	2.1
1941	2,260	31.1	65.2	2.2
1942	2,216	30.2	62.9	2.2
1943	2,235	30.2	62.7	2.2
1944	—	—	—	—
1945	—	—	—	—
1946	—	—	—	—
1947	2,679	34.3	64.9	2.2
1948	2,682	33.5	63.6	2.1
1949	2,697	33.0	63.3	2.1
1950	2,338	28.1	53.6	1.8
1951	2,138	25.3	48.3	1.6
1952	2,005	23.4	44.4	1.5
1953	1,868	21.5	40.6	1.3
1954	1,770	20.0	37.5	1.2
1955	1,707	19.3	36.4	1.2

[a] Official rates, unadjusted. Okinawa Prefecture excluded, 1920-1943.

[b] Numbers of births adjusted for underreporting, 1920-1943, with age distributions based on intercensal interpolations and projections. 1947-1955, births related to Japanese women.

[c] Indirect technique of computation for all years except 1925, 1930, 1937-1943, and 1947-1953.

Source: Populations and age distributions, censuses of the respective years, cited in Bibliography. Intercensal data by interpolation. For 1951 and later years: Nihon. Sori-fu, tokei-kyoku. *Zenkoku nenrei betsu jinko no suikei. . . .* Series were not revised to accord with the official estimates from 1920 to 1950. *Ibid. Zenkoku nenrei betsu jinko no suikei. Taisho 9-nen—Showa 15-nen oyobi Showa 22-nen—Showa 25-nen.*

Numbers of births: 1920-1925: Nihon. Sori-fu, tokei-kyoku. *Nihon tokei nenken, 1949.* Table 44, excluding Okinawa. 1926-1947: *Idem. 1951.* Table 14. 1948-1955: *Idem. Tokei geppo,* no. 83. November 1956. Schedule reports for 1955 adjusted on the basis of the ratios of preliminary to final numbers in 1953 and 1954. Births by age of mother: References, Table 93.

torious war were accompanied by substantial recoveries in fertility. Birth rates dropped sharply in the years of bombing, flight, and defeat, but the bombs that leveled the cities destroyed the *koseki* that might have documented the human losses of the period. When vital reporting was restored on a national basis in 1947, the crude birth rate was 34.3, roughly the level of the mid-1920's. Decline was apparent by 1949 and it soon became rapid—from 33 in 1949 to 28 in 1950, 23 in 1952, and 19 in 1955.

Description of changes in fertility will be undertaken for three time periods. During the first, from 1915 to 1919, recorded births and base populations were secured from the registration system. Here determination of the accuracy of the observed trend must precede any interpretation of its significance. In the second, from 1920 to 1943, there was a period of years—1920 through 1937—that merits special attention because it was the only approximation to "normality" in modern Japan. The third, from 1947 through 1955, includes a postwar rise in fertility, a few years of quite high fertility, and then very rapid decline.

WORLD WAR I, 1915-1919

The official statistics of the Japanese indicate that the birth rate declined from 34 per 1,000 total population in 1914 to 32 in 1919, then rose to 36 in 1920 and did not again reach a rate as low as that of 1919 until the depression year of 1933.[5] Since analogy with experience elsewhere would lead to an anticipation of declining fertility with increasing industrialization, it is puzzling to find the birth rates in the 1920's above those of the preceding decade.

It is possible that the shift in the birth rate and the resumption of decline from a higher level are artifacts of the change from rates computed on the basis of registration compilations to rates computed on the basis of enumerative censuses. However, if we take the survivors of the cohorts of the years prior to and immediately after 1920 and follow them through the enumerative censuses, we find bulges in the age pyramids that correspond to the survivors of the birth cohorts of 1920 and the succeeding years. Conversely, there are indentations in the pyramids that represent the survivors of the birth cohorts of the years from 1915 through 1919. Thus the age distributions of the censuses corroborate the evidence from the contemporary vital statistics that there was a shift in fertility or in infant and childhood mortality between 1915-1919 and 1920-1924.[6] In fact, the annual variations in estimated fertility derived from the census age distributions are quite consistent with those in recorded birth rates. Estimated births per 1,000 women aged from 15 to 49 and gross reproduction rates for the last precensal and the early censal years are as follows:[7]

[5] The rates for the years 1914-1920 cited here are for the area of prewar Japan. Nihon. Sori-fu, tokei-kyoku. *Nihon tokei nenkan, 1949.* Table 44.

[6] The irregularities in age structures could have been produced by increases in fertility, decreases in mortality, or some combination of the two.

[7] The enumerated population as of October 1, 1920, was moved backward year by year, using the recorded numbers of deaths by age and sex. If corrections had been made for the underreporting of deaths in the period prior to 1920, a substantial portion of the differences in estimated female live births between the late precensal and the early censal years would have been eliminated. However, there was no objective basis for estimating the extent of the underreporting of deaths.

Year	*Estimated female live births per 1,000 women aged 15-49*	*Gross repro-duction rate*
1914	74.3	2.5
1915	72.7	2.4
1916	72.6	2.5
1917	70.6	2.4
1918	68.9	2.4
1919	69.3	2.4
1920	77.6	2.7
1921	75.6	2.6
1922	74.0	2.5
1923	75.7	2.6

There are *a priori* grounds for expecting some reduction in fertility in the years from 1915 through 1919, for the events during and immediately following World War I moved men from civilian life into the armed forces and withdrew youth from the farms to the cities.[8] Japan's participation in World War I was slight compared with that of nations whose armies fought on the Western front, but she had armed forces in the South Seas, the China ports and, later, Siberia. The removal of European ships and European products from Asian and African markets was a major stimulus to Japanese production and trade, and the movements of labor to industrial centers and employment in shipping separated families already formed and postponed the marriages of youth. The marriage rate declined sharply in 1916 and 1917, increased somewhat in 1918-1919, shot upward in 1920 and 1921. Moreover, the influenza epidemic of 1918-1919 may have led to reduced conceptions.

YEARS OF EMPIRE, 1920-1943

In the early 1920's, the fertility of the Japanese was already far below that characteristic of the peoples who tilled the soil of Mainland Asia. The highest birth rate in the years after World War I was 36 in 1920; the rate then fell with general regularity year after year to 30 in 1936 and 31 in 1937. There were reflections of the Manchurian involvement and the depression of the early 1930's, but on the whole this was a period in which the underlying forces of change operated with only superficial disturbances. The war that began in 1937 developed quite differently from the limited actions in which Japan had engaged previously. Military and economic dislocations combined to send birth rates downward to 27 in 1938 and 1939. With the economic recovery if not prosperity of the war years, altered military regulations on marriage and home leave, and pro-natalist population policies, the birth rate recovered to something over 30 per 1,000 total population in 1941-1943. Defeat in the field, the bombing of the cities, food deficiencies, and disease brought the demographic consequences of war to Japan in 1944 and 1945. The delayed effect was apparent in reduced birth rates from late 1944 to the middle of 1946.[9]

The question may be raised as to whether the apparent decline in fertility in Japan was not an artifact of the statistical system. The *koseki* was an institution of the rural society. Perhaps its functioning became less accurate as individuals moved away from the control of the family in the village community. The increasing numbers of Koreans in Japan resulted in discrepancies between the numbers of births that occurred within the country and the number that were registered in *koseki* within Japan. However, the use of estimated numbers of births that include those to non-Japanese and that make other adjustments for malreporting does not result in any substantial change in any of the measures of fertility. The adjusted birth rates for the intercensal years from 1920 to 1940 are as follows:[10]

Intercensal periods, October 1 to October 1	*Average annual birth rate*
1920-1925	36.7
1925-1930	34.7
1930-1935	32.6
1935-1940	29.3

Changes in birth rates demonstrate the fact of decline in fertility but they tell little of the factors involved. It could be argued that in an Eastern culture influenced by the institutions and attitudes of Confucianism the decisions as to marriage and childbearing would be made by men. If so, major emphasis should be placed on the relations of births to the characteristics of the fathers. This is a theoretical rather than an empirical proposition, for the data do not permit analysis of the fertility of men. If the age data of the censuses and the numbers of births recorded in *koseki* are to be used to analyze fertility, the biology of reproduction dictates that major emphasis be placed on the fertility of women. Mothers are physically present at the place where their babies are born; fathers need not be. Neither reported births nor births estimated from enumerated children can be related to the men physically present within an area on the assumption that the infants and fathers reside in the same area.[11] Hence both for statistical and for biological reasons it is necessary to follow conventional procedures and relate births to women.

Persistent decline in the rates at which women bear children has been characteristic of Japan since 1920.[12] Female

[8] In 1916 the Bureau of Statistics made a special survey of births by age of mother in Hokkaido and 15 other prefectures. The data were quite defective; proportions of mothers of unknown ages were high. Moreover, there were no appropriate age distributions for the women who had produced the reported births. These 1916 data on births were related to the *de facto* populations of women from the 1913 police count and the average *honseki* populations of 1913 and 1918. In all instances, the gross reproduction rates as thus estimated were lower than those for the same prefectures in 1920. However, this is not independent verification of the validity of the lower fertility prior to the census of 1920, for all computations lie within the self-contained universe of the registration system. The 1916 data were published in the 1925 analytical report: Nihon. Naikaku, tokei-kyoku. *Fubo no nenrei to shussei to no kankei.*

[9] The *koseki* were maintained throughout the war years in some prefectures, but these were regions relatively unaffected by the war. Hence they permit few inferences as to fertility in the nation as a whole.

[10] Estimated numbers of births were secured by deriving corrective factors from relating enumerated children under age 1 plus appropriate allowances for infant deaths to reported births and then applying these factors to births for other years.

[11] In theory, the extent of the error introduced by this assumption would vary with the extent and the characteristics of the mobility in the society. In Japan in the 1920's and 1930's there were excesses of married men in the urban and industrial areas, excesses of married women in the rural and agricultural areas.

[12] The birth rate per 1,000 total population makes no allowances for differences in the age and sex composition of populations. In theory, declining proportions of the total population consisting of women in the childbearing ages could result in declining birth rates, even though the rates at which women bore children remained unchanged. That this was not a major factor in the decline of the birth rate in Japan is indicated by the fact that trends in female or in total births to women aged from 15 to 49 are similar to those in birth rates. In fact, the picture of trends and of varia-

births per 1,000 women aged from 15 to 49 numbered 77 in 1920, 70 in 1930, and 61 in 1940. In the years from 1920 to 1937 there were only slight deviations of annual values around a straight-line downward trend. In 1938 and 1939, however, there was a sharp drop below the trend line. The recovery in the years from 1940 through 1943 restored fertility ratios approximately to their trend-line values.

The period of childbearing lasts approximately from age 15 to age 49, but the rates of childbearing differ greatly throughout this span of some thirty-five years (TABLE 91). At its beginning few women are married and exposed to the risk of childbearing. As the thirties approach practically all women are married, and most of them are capable of having children. During the thirties and forties, there are increases both in sterility and in widowhood. Cultural and biological factors are intermingled in the changing relations of fertility to age, and both are changing over time. In Japan after World War I, age at marriage was advancing and the rates at which husbands died were declining. Marital fertility was becoming subject to varying degrees of control in the different social-economic groups. The results of the changes are shown in the average annual rates of decline in fertility from 1925 to 1937:

Age	*Female births per 1,000 women* 1925	1937	*Average annual per cent change, 1925-1937*
15-49	75.7	66.7	−1.0
15-19	24.0	10.8	−6.4
20-24	116.8	90.6	−3.1

tions in fertility are virtually identical, whichever of the two measures is used. For the year 1950, the correlation between the birth rate and the ratio of female births to women aged from 15 to 49 in the 46 prefectures of Japan was .99.

Age	*Female births per 1,000 women* 1952	1937	*Average annual per cent change, 1925-1937*
25-29	131.2	123.9	−0.5
30-34	115.5	105.2	−0.9
35-39	88.8	78.4	−1.0
40-44	38.4	34.1	−1.0
45-49	6.5	5.1	−3.0

During these thirteen years, the decline in births was most rapid for women below age 25, least for women aged from 25 to 34, and higher again for women aged 35 and over. Relative declines in childbearing were substantial among older women, but the numerical impact was slight. Moreover, as we shall see later, different causal forces were operating at the younger and the older ages.

Description of variations and changes in the fertility of Japanese women requires measures that take account of the changing rates of reproduction at the various ages. The summary measure that is commonly used and easily computed from data that can be secured for Japan is the gross reproduction rate. This rate is a construct based on the reproductive performance of a given group of women in a specific period. It is given demographic relevance by the assumption that a cohort of women passing through life might behave as did the women of the period in question. In more precise terms, the gross reproduction rate is the summation of age-specific fertility rates expressed in terms of female births per 1,000 women. It is thus a measure of the extent to which women would replace themselves with girl babies if there were no hazards of death prior to age 50 and if childbearing at each age occurred at the rate which characterized the specific time period. Despite its age-standardization, its behavior over time and its variations as among geographic areas are very similar

TABLE 91

Female births per 1,000 women, 1925-1954

Year	AGE GROUPS *15-49*	*15-19*[a]	*20-24*	*25-29*	*30-34*	*35-39*	*40-44*	*45-49*[b]
1925[c]	75.7	24.0	116.8	131.2	115.5	88.8	38.4	6.5
1930	70.2	17.7	103.5	125.4	109.6	82.7	36.4	5.6
1937	66.7	10.8	90.6	123.9	105.2	78.4	34.1	5.1
1938	57.7	9.0	77.7	106.8	91.6	69.5	31.1	4.5
1939	56.2	7.6	72.0	106.9	92.8	68.8	30.2	4.5
1940	61.4	7.3	75.1	120.6	105.1	74.1	31.9	4.9
1942	62.9	7.0	77.7	121.9	108.5	78.5	34.5	4.7
1943	62.7	6.2	74.0	121.8	110.6	82.3	34.7	4.8
1947[d]	64.9	7.2	81.6	131.0	114.2	76.6	27.9	3.4
1948	63.6	8.5	88.8	125.6	102.8	72.1	28.6	2.4
1949	63.3	7.9	88.7	131.1	104.3	65.9	23.8	1.7
1950	53.6	6.5	78.2	115.4	85.4	51.0	17.5	1.2
1951	48.3	5.2	69.1	106.2	79.1	44.0	14.0	0.9
1952	44.4	4.3	63.8	100.6	72.4	37.7	11.1	0.7
1953	40.6	3.6	59.3	94.0	64.5	32.0	8.9	0.6
1954	37.5	3.1	55.3	88.1	57.8	27.4	7.2	0.5

[a] Including female births to girls under age 15.
[b] Including female births to women aged 50 and over.
[c] 1925-1943. Prewar area of Japan, with corrections for underreporting.
[d] 1947-1953. Postwar area of Japan, without corrections for underreporting. Reported births are related to Japanese women only.
Source: Prewar: Nihon. Naikaku tokei-kyoku. *Jinko dotai tokei.* Respective years. Postwar: Nihon. Kosei-sho, eisei tokei-bu. *Jinko dotai tokei.* 1947-1954.

to those of crude birth rates.[13] In the seventeen years from 1920 to 1937, annual gross reproduction rates, like crude birth rates, showed only irregular fluctuations around a straight-line downward trend. There were reactions to the Siberian expedition, the Kanto earthquake, the great depression, and the movement into Manchuria, but they were slight. The reaction to the Chinese War was severe in 1938 and 1939, but by 1941 the gross reproduction rate had recovered to a position slightly above its trend-line level.

Interpretation of the gross reproduction rate is difficult in situations such as that of Japan, where the economy is dynamic, mortality is declining rapidly, and there are cyclical fluctuations in rates of childbearing. The artificiality of the assumption that a generation of women would follow the experience of a specific year may be illustrated by some comparisons for the women who were aged from 15 to 19 in 1925 and from 40 to 44 in 1950:

Female births per 1,000 women

Age	*Cohort of 1925*	*Year 1925*	*Year 1930*	*Year 1940*	*Year 1950*
15-19	24.0	24.0	17.7	7.3	6.5
20-24	103.5	116.8	103.5	75.1	78.2
25-29	—	131.2	125.4	120.6	115.4
30-34	105.1	115.5	109.6	105.1	85.4
35-39	—	88.8	82.7	74.1	51.0
40-44	17.5	38.4	36.4	31.9	17.5

Further examination of the fertility of this cohort of women who were aged from 15 to 19 in 1925 gives some clues as to the interpretation of gross reproduction rates in the period of Japanese demographic history with which we are concerned. The gross reproduction rate for this generation of women was approximately 2.2.[14] The major period of childbearing occurred during the years from 1930 to 1944, with a midpoint at approximately 1937. The gross reproduction rate for the year 1937 was 2.2. Was a gross reproduction rate of 2.2 in 1937 then approximately representative of the childbearing of the women who were aged from 15 to 19 in 1925, and from 40 to 44 in 1950? In 1950 there is information on the number of children ever born to women of specified ages—and the women aged from 40 to 44 in that year reported 4.4 children per woman.[15] Estimates based on the female births to all Japanese women in the year 1937 and on the completed fertility of women aged from 15 to 19 in 1925 show 4.5 children per woman. Thus there is some evidence that in prewar Japan gross reproduction rates were rough measures of the total childbearing of the group of women then in the central years of the reproductive period.

The decline in the gross reproduction rate between 1920 and 1937 would have required an annual decline of 1.27 per cent per year if it had occurred regularly throughout the period. The gross reproduction rate in 1940 was almost one-fourth less than it had been in 1920. This is a substantial decline, but it was not sufficient to produce a decrease in the annual number of births. It is obvious that numbers of births are a product not only of the frequency of births to women in specific age groups but of the number of women in those age groups. In 1920 in the prewar area of Japan there were 13.3 million women aged from 15 to 49; in 1940 there were 17.4 million women in this age group. This increase in numbers of women was a heritage of the movement from higher to lower levels of fertility and mortality. In the past that lay back of 1920, as in the period from 1920 to 1940, the rate at which women bore children was less than the rate at which their mothers had borne children. However, the mortality of each generation of women was less than the mortality of their mothers' generation. These two propositions may be phrased in more general terms. In a population where fertility is declining, the on-coming cohorts of women are increased beyond the size implicit in current fertility by the higher fertility of the past. And in a population where mortality is declining, the on-coming cohorts of women are increased beyond the size implicit in the vital balance that existed at the time of their birth by the continuing decline in mortality.

The role of declining fertility in reducing the annual increments to the population was great, even though it was not sufficient to create declining numbers of births year by year during the prewar period. The magnitude of the contribution may be illustrated if we make the simple assumption that during each year between 1925 and 1940 women reproduced at the same age-specific rates as had the women of 1925. The reduction of births below those expected at 1925 age-specific birth rates was 9.8 per cent in 1930, 15.5 per cent in 1935, and 22.4 per cent in 1940. The loss in births through declining fertility was 586 thousand in the intercensal period 1925-1930, 1.6 million in 1930-1935, and 2.6 million in 1935-1940. By summation we see that the persistence of the age-specific fertility of the year 1925 to the year 1940 would have added 4.8 millions to the number of births that occurred in Japan.

POSTWAR YEARS, 1947-1955[16]

When the functioning of the vital reporting system was restored on a national level in 1947, the crude birth rate of the Japanese in Japan was 34 per 1,000 total population, the ratio of female births to women aged 15-49 was 65, and the gross reproduction rate was 2.2. Alarm concerning the high birth rate was widespread within and outside Japan. Actually this birth rate of the year 1947 reflected a postwar readjustment rather than a major deviation from the long-run downward trend of fertility. The birth rate of 34 in 1947 was the highest since the middle 1920's, but the gross reproduction rate for this year was the same as that in the middle 1930's. The ratio of female births to women in the reproductive ages was only slightly above the value derived from a projection of the 1920-1937 trend line.

The story of the fertility of the Japanese from 1947 through 1955 is one of decline. The year-to-year values are reproduced here from Table 90:

Year	*Crude birth rate*	*Female births per 1,000 women 15-49*	*Gross reproduction rate*
1947	34.3	64.9	2.2
1948	33.5	63.6	2.1
1949	33.0	63.3	2.1
1950	28.1	53.6	1.8
1951	25.3	48.3	1.6
1952	23.4	44.4	1.5
1953	21.5	40.6	1.3
1954	20.0	37.5	1.2
1955	19.3	36.4	1.2

[13] The correlation of crude birth rates and gross reproduction rates for the prefectures was .98 in 1950. Relations were equally close in the earlier census years.

[14] On the assumption that female births per 1,000 women were 125 at age 25-29, 70 at age 35-39, and 1 at age 45-49. The assumption as to a war deficit of births is minimal. See the age schedules of the national population, Table 91.

[15] Nihon. Sori-fu, tokei-kyoku. *Showa 25-nen kokusei chosa hokoku.* III.1. Table 28.

[16] The behavior of fertility and infant mortality during the war and early postwar years is considered in Chapter XVI.

In 1949 the ratio of female births to women in the reproductive ages was still above the projected value based on the experience of 1920-1937; in 1950 the ratio was somewhat below the one projected; in 1955 the actual value was less than three-fourths of the projected value. The gross reproduction rate declined from 2.2 in 1947 to 1.2 in 1954 and 1955. In the light of this decline in fertility in the postwar years, the decline of the prewar years seems limited indeed.

The extraordinary nature of the recent declines in Japanese fertility is seen in a comparison of prewar and postwar levels of crude birth rates and gross reproduction rates. The crude birth rate was 33 in 1930-1935, 19 in 1955. The gross reproduction rate was 2.6 in 1925, 1.2 in 1955. The rate in 1955 was thus less than half that in 1925.

The annual changes in age-specific fertility in recent years indicate something of the factors involved in the rapid declines. A comparison of the rates of childbearing in 1947 with those in 1943 shows an appreciable increase in births to women in those age groups in which marriage was customary in Japan, i.e., ages 20 to 24 and 25 to 29. There were only slight increases in births to women below and above these modal marriage ages, i.e., 15 to 19 and 30 to 34. Among women aged from 35 to 39 and over, there were substantial declines. A comparison of age-specific rates in 1948 with those for 1947 shows increases among women aged from 15 to 24, and declines thereafter except for a slight increase among women aged from 40 to 44. Between 1948 and 1949 the only substantial change was an increase in the fertility of women aged from 25 to 29. In 1950, and again in 1951 and 1952, declines were general in all age groups, although the rates of decline were most notable for women aged from 35 to 39 and 40 to 44. By 1951 and 1952 it was apparent that childbearing was being concentrated increasingly in the fifteen-year span from age 20 to age 34, and within this span in the five-year period from age 25 through age 29.

The changes in fertility in recent years doubtless reflected the economic, social, and psychological factors of the period. However, many postponed marriages had occurred in the early years of peace as the army was demobilized and people living abroad were repatriated. Couples separated by the military or civilian service of the husband or the displacements of the years of flight were reunited. There was also permissive legislation for fertility limitation. In late 1948 contraception, abortion, and sterilization were made legal. In 1949 the economic factor was recognized as a justification for abortion and sterilization. In 1952 there were major liberalizations of the law. The influence of deficiencies of men and the planned limitation of fertility by means of contraception, abortion, and sterilization will be considered in Chapter XIII. Here they are mentioned only as essential background information.

The upsurge in marriages in the early postwar years was clearly a major factor in the increase of first births in 1947 and 1948 and of second births in 1949 and 1950 (Table 92).

Table 92

Number of live births per 1,000 women, by age of women and orders of birth, 1947-1954

Order by year	*Women 15-49*	Ages of women						
		15-19	*20-24*	*25-29*	*30-34*	*35-39*	*40-44*	*45-49*
All births								
1947	133.3	15.0	167.9	270.3	234.8	156.9	56.7	6.3
1948	130.9	17.6	182.9	258.3	211.7	148.2	58.6	5.0
1949	129.6	16.1	181.3	268.3	214.0	134.7	49.0	3.5
1950	109.8	13.3	161.4	237.6	175.5	104.8	31.6	2.3
1951	99.0	10.7	141.8	217.6	162.1	89.9	28.8	1.6
1952	91.2	8.8	130.8	206.1	149.0	77.3	23.0	1.4
1953	83.4	7.4	121.4	192.8	132.7	65.5	18.3	1.2
1954	77.2	6.4	114.0	181.6	119.1	56.6	14.9	0.9
First births								
1947	38.1	14.2	117.5	71.5	16.1	4.5	1.1	0.3
1948	42.1	16.4	128.9	77.8	17.3	4.9	1.1	0.2
1949	35.9	14.4	109.8	64.3	15.0	4.3	0.9	0.1
1950	29.9	11.7	92.8	53.1	13.0	3.6	0.7	0.0
1951	24.6	9.3	77.6	42.2	10.8	3.0	0.5	0.0
1952	23.9	7.7	74.9	42.6	10.5	3.0	0.5	0.0
1953	23.5	6.5	73.5	43.6	9.6	2.6	0.4	0.0
1954	23.9	5.8	73.5	47.1	9.7	2.6	0.4	0.0
Second births								
1947	27.0	0.7	40.0	92.4	31.9	7.4	1.5	0.3
1948	25.4	1.2	42.7	80.6	27.9	7.1	1.5	0.2
1949	31.6	1.7	59.4	97.1	30.1	7.2	1.4	0.1
1950	30.9	1.6	56.8	96.4	29.9	6.9	1.1	0.1
1951	27.5	1.3	49.8	84.8	27.8	6.2	1.0	0.0
1952	24.3	1.1	41.9	74.8	25.9	5.9	0.9	0.1
1953	21.3	0.8	35.7	66.4	22.4	5.1	0.8	0.1
1954	19.7	0.6	31.1	62.6	21.0	4.9	0.7	0.0

Order by year	Women 15-49	AGES OF WOMEN 15-19	20-24	25-29	30-34	35-39	40-44	45-49
Third births								
1947	20.3	0.0	8.4	64.4	51.3	13.2	2.3	0.3
1948	19.2	0.0	9.4	61.1	45.3	13.0	2.4	0.2
1949	20.7	0.1	10.2	67.6	48.5	12.2	2.1	0.1
1950	18.2	0.1	10.2	57.5	42.2	10.9	1.7	0.1
1951	19.0	0.1	12.7	61.6	40.9	9.8	1.4	0.1
1952	19.2	0.1	12.2	62.0	41.7	9.7	1.3	0.1
1953	17.8	0.1	10.4	56.7	39.4	9.0	1.1	0.1
1954	15.7	0.0	8.1	48.6	36.0	8.5	1.0	0.0
Fourth births								
1947	15.2	0.0	1.6	28.8	54.6	21.0	3.5	0.3
1948	14.1	0.0	1.6	27.2	49.3	20.2	3.7	0.3
1949	14.3	0.0	1.5	28.2	51.9	19.2	3.2	0.2
1950	11.7	0.0	1.2	22.5	41.8	16.3	2.6	0.1
1951	11.0	0.0	1.4	21.8	39.3	14.5	2.0	0.1
1952	10.2	0.0	1.6	20.5	35.5	13.3	1.9	0.1
1953	9.8	0.0	1.6	20.6	32.6	12.1	1.7	0.1
1954	9.0	0.0	1.2	18.7	29.6	11.1	1.6	0.1
Fifth births								
1947	11.3	0.0	0.3	9.6	41.3	27.6	5.3	0.5
1948	10.2	0.0	0.3	8.7	36.4	25.9	5.5	0.4
1949	9.7	0.0	0.3	8.4	36.4	24.3	4.9	0.2
1950	7.5	0.0	0.2	6.2	27.1	19.3	3.7	0.2
1951	6.6	0.0	0.2	5.5	24.8	16.7	3.1	0.1
1952	5.7	0.0	0.2	4.9	20.9	14.6	2.6	0.1
1953	5.6	0.0	0.2	4.5	17.6	12.6	2.3	0.1
1954	4.2	—	0.1	3.8	14.6	10.8	1.9	0.1
Sixth to ninth births								
1947	19.4	—	0.0	3.6	39.1	77.2	33.0	2.9
1948	18.0	—	0.0	3.1	35.0	71.7	34.3	2.5
1949	15.8	—	0.0	2.7	31.9	63.2	28.7	1.7
1950	10.7	—	0.0	1.8	21.3	44.9	16.5	1.1
1951	9.3	—	0.0	1.6	18.4	37.5	16.7	0.8
1952	7.2	—	0.0	1.3	14.3	29.2	12.9	0.7
1953	5.6	—	0.0	1.1	10.9	23.0	9.9	0.5
1954	4.3	—	0.0	0.8	8.2	17.9	7.8	0.5
Tenth or higher births								
1947	2.0	—	—	0.0	0.5	6.0	10.1	1.7
1948	1.9	—	—	0.0	0.4	5.5	9.9	1.4
1949	1.5	—	—	0.0	0.3	4.3	7.9	1.0
1950	1.0	—	—	0.0	0.2	2.9	5.3	0.6
1951	0.8	—	—	0.0	0.2	2.2	4.2	0.4
1952	0.6	—	—	0.0	0.1	1.6	2.9	0.4
1953	0.4	—	—	0.0	0.1	1.1	2.1	0.3
1954	0.3	—	—	0.0	0.0	0.7	1.4	0.2

Source: Births: Nihon. Kosei-sho, eisei tokei-bu. *Jinko dotai tokei*, 1947-1954. Population estimates: 1948-1950. *Ibid. Vital and health statistics in Japan.* Part II, Table I-1. 1951-1953: Nihon. Sori-fu, tokei-kyoku. *Zenkoku nenrei betsu jinko no suikei.* 1951, 1952, and 1953. 1954: *Idem. Nihon Tokei nenkan*, 1955/56, p. 40.

If natural dynamics were all that was involved in fertility, the postwar marriages should have sent waves of births upward through the higher births orders and the older ages of women. The years from 1947 through 1953 are a brief period for the exploration of a phenomenon such as this, but the data suggest barriers to the occurrence of births of even relatively low orders in the years after 1949.

From 1947 to 1951 declines were proceeding more rapidly in upper than in lower-order births. First-, second-, and third-order births together constituted 64 per cent of all births in 1947, 72 per cent in 1951, 77 per cent in 1954. From 1949 onwards, however, the major absolute declines occurred in the lower-order births. These changes in fertility cannot be attributed to changes in marital status, for roughly similar proportions of single and widowed women existed throughout the years from 1947 to 1954. Rather, the explanation must be sought in the changing rates of reproduction in a mature and largely married population of women.

Consistently declining fertility characterized all age groups of women from age 30-34 to the end of the reproductive years. In general, the rates of decline were greater for higher-order births to older women. For no age group of women were sixth- to ninth-order births half as numerous in 1953 as they had been in 1947; tenth- and higher-order births per 1,000 women were less than one-third as numerous in 1953 as they had been in 1947. The age-specific birth rates summarize the continuity more concisely than a verbal description can:

	Females births per 1,000 women			
Age of women	*1925*	*1937*	*1947*	*1954*
15-49	75.7	66.7	64.9	37.5
15-19	24.0	10.8	7.2	3.1
20-24	116.8	90.6	81.6	55.3
25-29	131.2	123.9	131.0	88.1
30-34	115.5	105.2	114.2	57.8
35-39	88.8	78.4	76.6	27.4
40-44	38.4	34.1	27.0	7.2
45-49	6.5	5.1	3.4	0.5

Thus the declines of recent years are new only in their magnitude. It may be presumed, therefore, that they reflect the continued operation of those social and economic forces that have been transforming the fertility of the Japanese throughout the period of industrialization.

Fertility in the Prefectures

The interrelations of culture, economy, social change, and fertility can be seen more clearly in the experience of groups within Japan than in that of the nation as a whole. There are elements of uniformity in Japanese society—the integrated culture, the incessant toil, the shared poverty. But there are also diversities among the areas of Japan and the segments of Japanese society. To avoid journeys down the byways of local situations, analysis of uniformities and variations in the fertility of the population of the prefectures will be oriented toward three specific questions. The first is the regional variation in fertility at the beginning of the census period. The second is the direction and the magnitude of the changes over time.[17] The third is the relationship between differences in fertility at a given time and changes over time.

Levels of fertility, 1920-1925

There are widespread and persistent geographic and socio-economic differences in the fertility of the Japanese. Fertility is highest in the northeast and it shades off to the south and west in Honshu, only to rise again in Kyushu and Okinawa (Map 11). As early as 1920-1925, however, birth rates that

[17] Since numbers of births by age of mother were available for the prefectures only for the years 1925, 1930, and 1947, gross reproduction rates for other years were computed by indirect techniques. Hypothetical schedules of fertility for given ratios of female births to women aged from 15 to 49 were constructed on the basis of the prefectural and city schedules available for the year 1930. The regressions of age-specific on general fertility had no predictive value insofar as the downward course of fertility was concerned. However, comparisons of indirectly computed gross reproduction rates for 1925, 1930, and 1947 with the rates computed directly indicate a high degree of agreement.

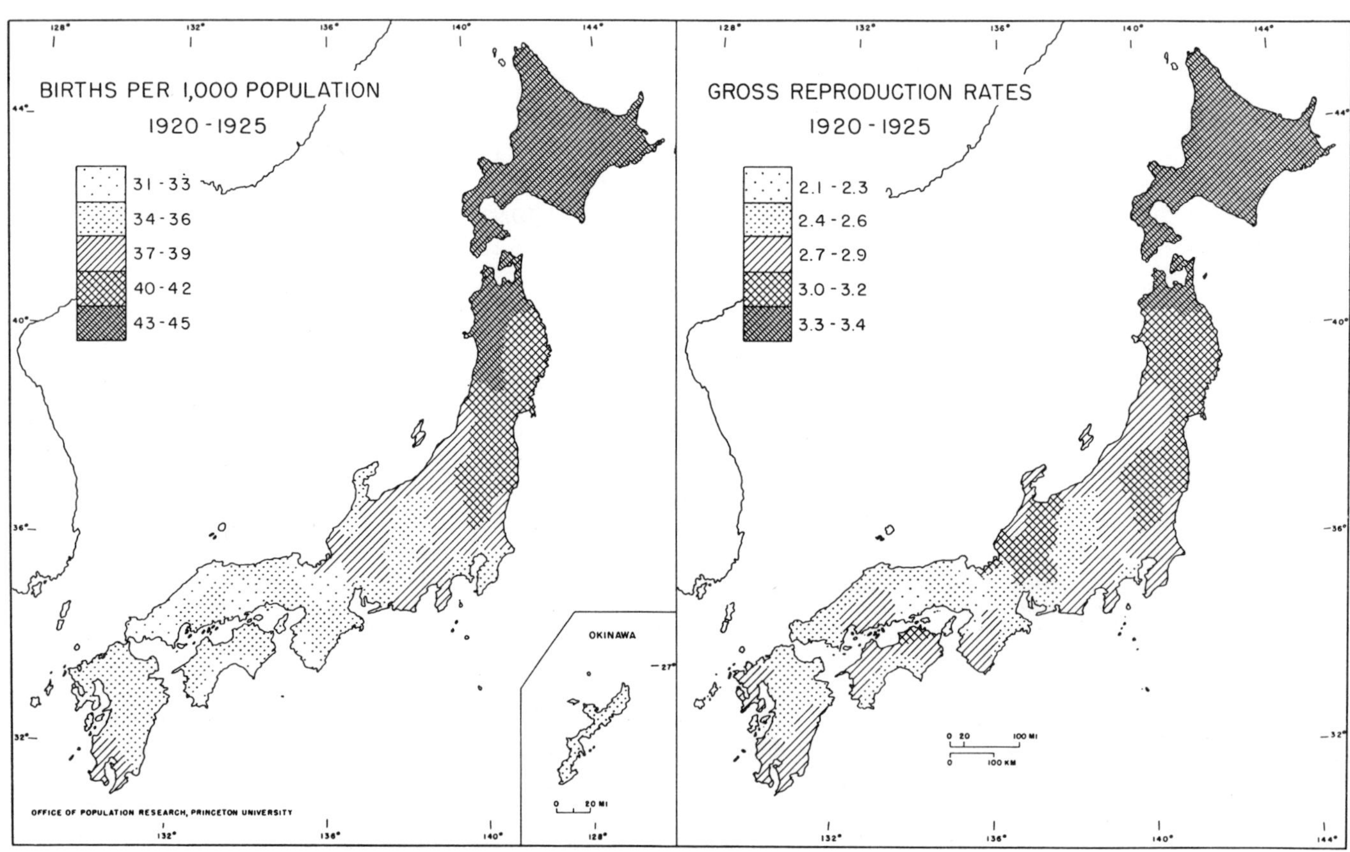

Map 11. Birth rates and gross reproduction rates, by prefectures, 1920-1925
Source: References, birth rates, Table 93; gross reproduction rates, Footnote 18.

would merit the use of the adjective "high" in the Asian setting existed only in Hokkaido and the prefectures of northeast Honshu. The highest rate was that of 45 per 1,000 total population in Aomori. Enclaves of low birth rates in the Kanto and the Kinki show that there were major deterrents to human reproduction in the period immediately after World War I. Rates were somewhat higher along the Japan Sea and in the peripheral regions of the far southwest. The differences in birth rates in the agricultural regions of the southwest and in those of the northeast indicate a cultural conditioning of fertility within the rural society.

The geographic pattern of gross reproduction rates in 1920-1925 was comparable to that for crude birth rates. Rates were highest in the northeast; here gross reproduction rates of 3.0 and over were widespread. Rates were lower in southwestern Honshu, an area regarded by the Japanese as possessing a higher culture. Rates were lower in the prefectures facing the Pacific than in those along the Japan Sea. They were lower in the center of the country, where the chief metropolitan areas were located; higher in the peripheries of the country, where agriculture predominated.

These crude birth rates and gross reproduction rates for the prefectures of Japan permit a rather obvious generalization. If there was a level of fertility characteristic of the premodern culture of the East in general or of that of the Japanese in particular, it was not apparent in the fertility of the Japanese in the early 1920's. There was variability within regions of physical and economic homogeneity; there were also similarities between areas widely separated in space and divergent in topography, climate, and economy. There were differences among the great conurbations, the surrounding areas, and the remainder of the country. There were also differences among the conurbations. The relations of social, economic, and demographic factors to fertility will be examined in detail later. Here it is necessary only to emphasize the fact that considerable heterogeneity existed within a broad pattern of regional localization in Japan at the beginning of the census period. Uniformity in reproductive behavior had disappeared from the Japanese scene by 1920, if indeed it had ever existed.

VARIATIONS AND CHANGES, 1925-1930

The numbers of births occurring to parents of various ages are available for each of the 47 prefectures for 1925 and 1930.[18] This is a limited time period, but it is one quite appropriate for an analysis of the changing fertility of an industrializing society. In the late 1920's the living conditions and the aspirations of the people were relatively free of the pressures and dislocations that came later with militarism and war. The behavior of birth rates during this brief period of "normality" in the old Japan may be more relevant to the evaluation of future experience in other areas undergoing economic development than the experience of Japan in the later years of more mature industrialization.

Detailed materials on age-specific fertility for a variety of local areas in Japan in 1925 and 1930 also permit a testing of the hypothesis that geographic differences in fertility at specific time periods may be taken as stages in a process of transition. If this hypothesis is valid, it would be possible to reconstruct the history of past declines in fertility in Japan and to estimate the declines that will occur in the future. The past for all Japan would have been comparable to levels of reproduction in the high fertility areas of 1925 or 1930; the future for all Japan could be estimated from those levels characteristic of the low fertility areas in this same period. A specific instance may illustrate the facts and the possibilities. In 1925, the highest ratio of female births to women aged from 15 to 49 was that of 95 in Aomori, while the lowest was that of 59 in Osaka. The hypothesis for investigation is whether differences such as these represent a time sequence as well as a geographic difference, and, if so, the length of the time lags that were involved.

The approach to this problem of prefectural differences as possible reflections of time trends lies in a detailed examination of the situation in 1925 and in 1930 considered as entities and then in relation to each other. The year 1925 is selected for detailed discussion (MAP 12). As the previous analyses of crude birth rates and gross reproduction rates have indicated, there were sizable differences in fertility among the prefectures. Total fertility was higher in the peripheries of the country, lower in the areas of the great conurbations in central Honshu. Higher and lower are vague terms, however, for the fertility of the northeast was far higher than that of any other peripheral region of the country, including the equally agrarian areas of the southwest. Fertility was higher in the metropolitan centers of the Kanto than in those of the Kinki.

Regional variations in fertility were greatest among the very young women and became progressively less with advancing age until they were negligible for women aged from 45 to 49. For women aged from 15 to 19, female births per 1,000 women ranged from 9 to 62, although there was a clustering of 33 of the 47 prefectures at rates between 15 and 34. There was a major concentration of high rates in northeast Honshu, with a secondary concentration in the prefectures of central Honshu on the Sea of Japan. Rates were low in the central Honshu urban regions and in the historic cultural centers of the southwest such as Nagasaki, Hiroshima, and Okayama. Unfortunately for uniformities and hypotheses of recapitulation, the lowest rates were in Gumma and Nagano prefectures. Here there were concentrations of young girls in textile factories.

The general distribution pattern of the fertility of the women aged from 20 to 24 is comparable to that of women aged from 15 to 19, but a disturbing variability appears within regions. There is a constricted range of variation among the prefectures of southwest Honshu, Kyushu, and Shikoku, but there are sharp variations among the prefectures in northeastern and central Honshu. The age-specific fertility of the women of Nagano is as low as that of the women of Tokyo, whereas that of the women of Kanagawa exceeds that of the women of Tokyo. Many other illustrations of such geographic incongruities could be cited. It appears that age-specific fertility rates and the relationships among them are associated in part with regional characteristics, in part with characteristics that are specific to individual areas. Simple projection backward to the past or forward to the future is obviously hazardous.

The detailed pattern of change in the fertility of the populations of the prefectures can be traced for the years from 1925 to 1930. In this period, declines in total fertility were greatest in the developing northeast prefecture of Miyagi, the Tokyo-Yokohama area, the prefectures along the Sea of Japan in central Honshu, and the prefectures of Tottori, Hiroshima, and Kochi. Intermediate declines occurred in the great band of prefectures surrounding the Tokyo-Kanagawa area, in southwest Honshu, and in northeast Kyushu. Slow declines

[18] For 1925: Nihon. Naikaku tokei-kyoku. *Fubo no nenrei betsu shussei tokei. Taisho 14-nen.* For 1930: *Ibid. Fubo no nenrei betsu shussei oyobi shisan tokei, Showa go'nen.*

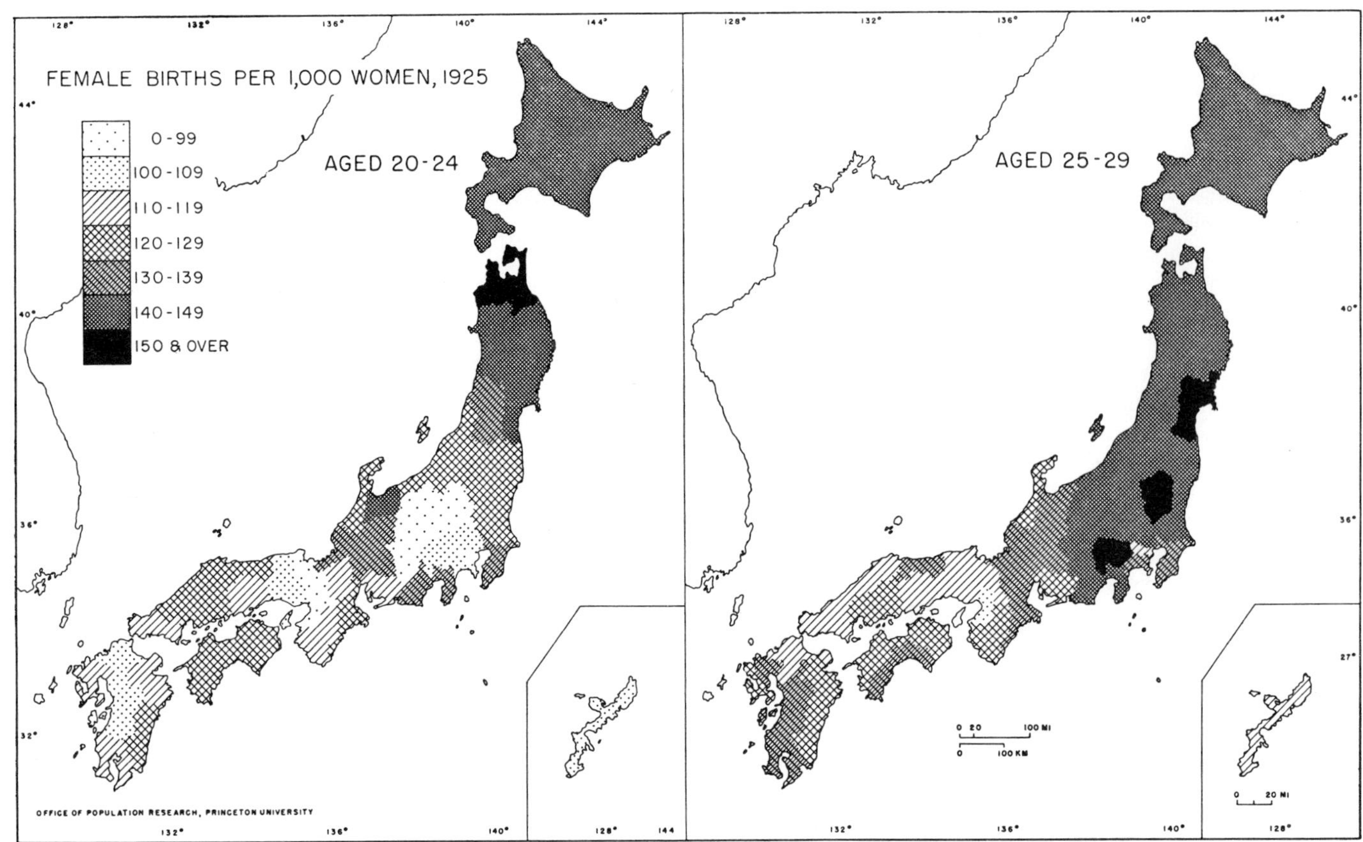

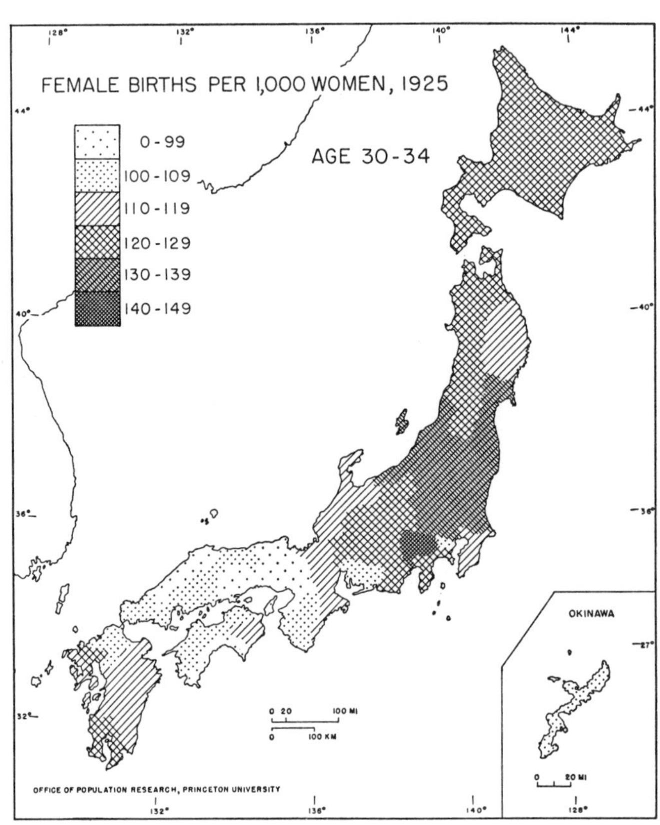

Map 12. Female births per 1,000 women, selected ages, by prefectures, 1925
Source: References, Footnote 18.

characterized the high fertility prefectures of Tohoku, south Kyushu, and Shikoku. Two broad conclusions are possible. First, decline was general. It occurred in virtually all age groups in almost all the prefectures, whatever their location and whatever their cultural, social, economic, or demographic characteristics. Second, decline was not a mechanical process related solely to location or to the pre-existing levels of fertility.

Clues as to the pattern of changes in fertility are given by the geographic patterns of the declines in births to younger women. Declines in births to women aged from 15 to 19 were greatest in the high fertility areas of the northeast, along the coast of the Sea of Japan in central Honshu, and in the far southwest of Honshu. Declines were least in the Tokyo-Yokohama and the Osaka-Kobe-Kyoto areas. For the 47 prefectures as a whole, there was a clear-cut relation between the level of childbearing at this age in 1925 and the amount of the decline between 1925 and 1930.[19] The relation was less close between the level of fertility in 1925 and the percentage decline between 1925 and 1930.

The distribution of the declines in fertility at age 20 to 24 was quite different from that at age 15 to 19. For the older age group, declines were slight in the high fertility areas of the northeast, but they were substantial in the high fertility areas along the Sea of Japan and in the peripheral prefectures that were accessible to metropolitan centers. There was little relation between the level of childbearing in 1925 and either the amount or the rate of decline between 1925 and 1930.

Between age 25 to 29 and age 40 to 44 there were no significant relations between levels of childbearing in 1925 and absolute or relative declines during the period from 1925 to 1930. At age 45 to 49 there was some tendency for fertility to decline more in prefectures where the level was high.

A decline in fertility that extends throughout a nation in the younger ages and is widespread in the upper ages must be the product of basic changes, yet the patterns of decline in Japan bear no simple relation to geographic factors or to the level of fertility itself.[20] Before concluding that the decline is associated with forces impinging on individuals without reference to the milieu or the area in which they live, it may be desirable to approach the problem in a somewhat different form. It is probable that the reproductive behavior of an age group of women alive at an instant of time reflects the totality of the experience of the women. Women aged from 15 to 19 in 1925 were born in 1905-1909, entered school in 1911 to 1915, and began work about 1920. Women aged from 35 to 39 in 1925 were born in 1880 to 1884, entered school, if they attended at all, in 1886 to 1891, and began work about 1895 to 1899. What is needed is an analysis of the reproductive performance of groups of women as they move through the years from age 15 to age 44 or 49. Childbearing at one age could then be related to that at the next age. The differences in levels of fertility would measure the impact of forces developing over time. The absence of the necessary data prevents a comprehensive analysis of the fertility of cohorts of women. A limited approach is possible, however, for we have age-specific fertility for each of the prefectures in 1925 and in 1930.

There were relations between the fertility of women at one age and that at the next higher age, but they were complex. There was a close relation between the fertility of women aged from 15 to 19 in 1925 and the fertility of the same women at age 20 to 24 in 1930.[21] There was only a slight relation between the fertility of the women aged from 20 to 24 in 1925 and the fertility of this same group of women at age 25 to 29 in 1930. There was again a close relation between the fertility at one age in 1925 and the fertility at the next higher age in 1930 for women aged from 25 to 29 or over in 1925. Thus there appears to have been one constellation of factors influencing fertility during the ages at which marriage occurred, and another constellation influencing fertility during the ages at which virtually all women either were or had been married.

TRANSITION, 1920-1955

The downward movement of fertility that characterized Japan in the period from 1920 through 1940 extended from the most remote regions to the heart of the economy and Empire in central Honshu (TABLE 93). Decline was continuous in all prefectures in all intercensal periods from 1920 to 1940. There was one exception to the downward drift that characterized the 1920's and the 1930's. The gross reproduction rates in Tokyo and Kanagawa prefectures increased slightly between 1920 and 1925.

Total declines in fertility during the twenty years from 1920 to 1940 were substantial. In the prefectures in central Honshu along the Sea of Japan, gross reproduction rates declined a third or more during these two decades. Comparable declines occurred in Hyogo, Nara, and Wakayama prefectures, in Hiroshima and in Kagawa. Somewhat lesser declines occurred in the majority of the prefectures on the peripheries of the country, whether northeast or southwest. These declines appear to have been responses to changes both in individual motivations and in the structure of economic opportunities within and outside Japan. The regularities in rates of decline were not such as to permit predictive generalizations. In the 1920's and the 1930's there were only slight relations between the levels of gross reproduction rates at the beginning of a period and the amount or the rate of decline over the decade.[22]

The variations in the rates of decline in fertility in the decades of the 1920's and 1930's were not sufficient to alter the basic differences in the levels of fertility that characterized the prefectures. The correlations between gross reproduction rates in the successive census years were high.[23] The persist-

[19] The correlations between the level of fertility in 1925 and the amount of the change during 1925-1930 were as follows: age 15-19, +.83; age 20-24, —.02; age 25-29, —.05; age 30-34, —.12; age 35-39, —.22; age 40-44, —.07; age 45-49, +.38. The amount of decline was considered as a positive number.

[20] There were definite relations between the fertility of successive age groups, thus indicating the existence of general forces, but not whether they were geographic, social-economic, or individual. The correlations at the successive ages in 1925 were as follows: 15-19 with 20-24, .76; 20-24 with 25-29, .36; 25-29 with 30-34, .92; 30-34 with 35-39, .95; 35-39 with 40-44, .91; 40-44 with 45-49, .63.

[21] The correlations were as follows: 15-19 in 1925, 20-24 in 1930, .79; 20-24 with 25-29, .33; 25-29 with 30-34, .90; 30-34 with 35-39, .95; 35-39 with 40-44, .84; 40-44 with 45-49, .50.

[22] Correlation coefficients between the levels of the gross reproduction rate and the per cent declines in the 47 prefectures were —.08 in the earlier period, +.02 in the later. Correlations between the levels of the gross reproduction rate and the amounts of the decline were .16 in the earlier period, .46 in the later. In these correlations, the amount or the per cent of decline was used as a positive value. Hence a positive correlation signifies that higher values of the measure of fertility were associated with greater absolute or relative declines in that value.

[23] The correlations between gross reproduction rates in successive census years were as follows: 1920 and 1925, .93; 1925 and 1930, .96; 1930 and 1935, .97; and 1935 and 1940, .95. The correlations refer to the 46 prefectures of postwar Japan.

TABLE 93

Birth rates in the prefectures, 1920-1955

	INTERCENSAL RATES[a]					ANNUAL RATES[b]			
Prefectures	*1920-1925*	*1925-1930*	*1930-1935*	*1935-1940*	*1950-1955*[b]	*1947*[c]	*1950*[c]	*1952*[c]	*1955*[d]
All Japan	36.7	34.7	32.6	29.3	22.4	34.3	28.1	23.4	19.4
Hokkaido	43.3	40.2	37.5	33.6	27.0	36.8	34.2	28.9	21.7
Aomori	44.8	43.0	40.9	35.9	29.4	41.5	36.0	31.0	25.5
Iwate	42.1	40.2	38.2	35.4	28.2	36.5	33.9	30.1	24.3
Miyagi	41.6	39.4	36.9	33.5	25.8	35.4	32.0	27.4	22.4
Akita	43.4	41.9	39.3	34.8	26.1	38.0	32.6	27.9	22.6
Yamagata	40.5	38.8	35.8	32.6	23.4	32.8	30.0	25.4	20.2
Fukushima	40.3	38.5	35.7	32.6	26.7	35.7	32.8	28.6	23.5
Ibaraki	38.8	36.9	34.4	31.1	24.3	34.3	29.3	25.2	21.7
Tochigi	40.7	38.0	35.3	31.6	24.2	35.7	30.2	25.2	21.7
Gumma	38.3	35.9	33.2	30.6	22.3	34.7	28.0	23.5	20.1
Saitama	38.5	35.8	33.5	30.8	23.3	36.8	29.1	24.4	21.0
Chiba	35.5	34.2	32.7	29.3	22.0	34.8	26.9	23.0	19.8
Tokyo	34.4	33.4	30.6	27.1	18.7	31.7	23.6	18.8	15.9
Kanagawa	36.6	35.4	32.3	29.2	20.8	33.9	26.4	21.1	17.6
Niigata	38.2	36.1	34.3	31.6	23.4	35.4	29.3	25.1	20.9
Toyama	38.9	36.5	33.7	29.7	20.8	42.2	27.6	21.8	18.1
Ishikawa	35.6	32.9	30.7	27.0	20.9	40.1	27.4	21.4	18.8
Fukui	37.4	34.0	31.5	28.4	22.1	34.9	28.2	23.5	19.7
Yamanashi	37.6	35.2	34.1	31.5	22.0	32.6	26.3	22.8	19.5
Nagano	34.6	33.2	30.7	28.2	19.1	30.0	24.3	19.7	17.7
Gifu	37.9	36.1	33.5	30.8	21.4	34.3	26.8	22.3	18.6
Shizuoka	39.2	37.2	34.4	30.0	23.1	34.6	28.4	24.1	20.5
Aichi	36.5	35.0	32.7	30.1	20.2	33.4	25.9	20.7	17.3
Mie	35.9	34.5	31.6	28.1	19.9	32.6	25.5	20.7	17.1
Shiga	33.7	31.4	29.1	26.0	19.8	30.1	24.9	20.7	17.6
Kyoto	32.0	29.9	28.1	25.2	17.0	31.0	22.5	17.5	14.5
Osaka	34.0	31.7	29.6	27.5	19.2	31.2	24.3	19.3	16.0
Hyogo	34.9	32.1	29.9	26.6	20.2	32.0	24.7	20.4	17.2
Nara	34.9	31.9	29.6	25.5	20.0	30.8	24.3	21.2	16.7
Wakayama	33.9	31.6	29.5	25.6	19.5	32.0	24.2	19.9	17.3
Tottori	34.2	31.7	29.4	26.6	22.1	32.8	26.8	22.8	19.4
Shimane	32.6	30.9	30.1	27.4	21.8	36.4	28.3	22.7	18.5
Okayama	31.0	29.5	28.3	25.1	19.3	33.0	24.3	19.6	16.9
Hiroshima	34.6	31.7	29.3	25.9	19.9	33.7	25.4	20.4	17.5
Yamaguchi	32.3	29.8	29.4	25.0	21.4	33.3	27.8	21.9	17.8
Tokushima	35.3	34.0	32.3	29.3	23.0	37.0	29.0	23.8	20.5
Kagawa	36.6	33.6	31.6	27.5	20.4	37.3	26.0	21.7	17.7
Ehime	35.3	33.8	31.9	28.9	23.2	36.3	29.9	24.6	19.9
Kochi	33.8	31.9	29.0	24.7	20.4	33.8	26.4	21.4	18.2
Fukuoka	36.2	34.1	32.8	30.0	24.2	34.1	30.9	24.6	19.8
Saga	36.5	34.5	33.3	29.8	26.1	34.7	31.7	27.1	22.9
Nagasaki	35.4	33.9	32.9	30.7	28.6	34.6	33.2	29.6	24.7
Kumamoto	34.8	34.0	32.3	28.7	25.2	34.6	30.3	26.5	22.3
Oita	35.3	33.8	32.0	28.9	23.4	34.3	29.3	24.5	20.7
Miyazaki	36.6	36.1	35.6	31.7	27.0	37.6	32.4	28.8	23.5
Kagoshima	37.2	35.4	35.0	31.0	25.1	33.6	30.5	28.4	24.8
Okinawa	34.5	33.9	33.0	31.2	—	—	—	—	—

Notes and references are on p. 243.

ence of prefectural levels reflected the integrated character of developments in Japan.

When the consistency of the changes external to population was replaced by the more heterogeneous changes of the war and postwar years, diversities in rates of reproduction became greater. Changes in the geographic pattern of fertility were not great between 1940 and 1943; the correlation of the gross reproduction rates for the two years was .90. The increases in fertility between 1943 and 1947 were appreciable, and the factors influencing fertility did not operate uniformly throughout the country. In general, gross reproduction rates declined somewhat in the high fertility areas of the northeast, but remained unchanged or increased slightly in the southwest where fertility had been lower in the prewar years. The largest increases occurred in the metropolitan regions of central Honshu. The correlation between the gross reproduction rates of the prefectures in 1943 and in 1947 was .69. By 1950, decline was again the pre-eminent force. Aomori alone of all the prefectures had a fertility in 1950 as high as it had had in 1940. The correlation between the gross reproduction rates in 1947 and in 1950 was .65. To some extent, though, the lowered correlations of prefectural rates in the successive periods of the war and postwar years reflected departures from and returns to a pattern of relations inherent in the Japanese society and economy. If the thirty-year period from 1920 to 1950 is divided into two equal periods, there is an obvious continuity in the distribution of levels of fertility. The correlations of the gross reproduction rates were .80 for 1920-1935 and .90 for 1935-1950.

Perusal of the measures of fertility for the postwar years and analysis of the changes in fertility between the prewar and the postwar years show only limited regularities in change (TABLE 94). The correlations of gross reproduction rates in 1947 with the amount of change during 1947 to 1950 amounted to .31; a comparable correlation with the percentage of change was .16. The correlation of crude birth rates in 1947 with the amount of change from 1947 to 1950 was .25; a comparable correlation with the percentage of change was .02.

There is a suggestive and perhaps significant relation between the levels of birth rates and their changes in the years of rapid decline from 1950 to 1953. The correlation between the levels of the birth rates in 1950 and the amounts of the declines from 1950 to 1953 was .31. There was thus a slight relation between high birth rates and larger absolute declines. However, the correlation between the levels of the birth rates in 1950 and the percentage declines from 1950 to 1953 was —.43. Neither of these relations is close.

If 1925 is taken as a base line and the span from 1925 to 1947 is considered, there are indications of relations between the level of the gross reproduction rate and both the amount and the per cent of decline. The correlation with the amount of decline was .66; with the per cent of decline, .50. If the period is extended from 1925 to 1950, however, the indications are reduced. The correlations of declines from 1925 to 1950 with levels in 1925 were .53 for the absolute and .07 for the relative decline. The same change in the pattern of diffusion occurs if crude birth rates are considered. The correlations of levels in 1930-1935 with the decline to 1947 were .55 for the amount of decline, .57 for the per cent of decline. The correlations of levels in 1930-1935 with the declines to 1953 were .27 for the absolute and —.24 for the relative decline. The new forces inducing decline in recent years differed in their incidence from the old forces of the "naturally" declining fertility as it existed prior to the rapid diffusion of abortion, sterilization, and contraception.

It is possible that the generality and crudeness of the available measures of fertility obscure the relations that exist between the earlier extent of the childbearing and the rapidity of change. The decline in national fertility occurred first and predominantly among younger women, those aged 15-19 and 20-24. In the later prewar years there were substantial declines in the fertility of women in the central years of the reproductive period. In the recent period of decline in total fertility, there have been major declines in the rates of childbearing among women aged 35 and over. This national pattern of change from 1920 to 1955 permits the inference that lesser rates of childbearing were associated with factors that impinged most directly on youth, and that decline moved upward in the age span of the reproductive period.

Age-specific birth rates for the prefectures are available for the year 1947, almost a quarter of a century after 1925. Economic conditions were still difficult in 1947. The cities were not yet fully restored and repatriates were coming home. New marriages were yielding increased numbers of first births. Babies born to reunited couples were raising fertility rates for all durations of marriage and all birth orders. In the interval between 1925 and 1947 the country had undergone industrialization and urbanization, and experienced the destruction of total war; it had made great progress in education, and had acquired the knowledge if not the physical possessions of the modern world. Fertility in 1947 was far below the fertility of 1925. In fact, if the women of Japan in 1947 had reproduced at the age-specific rates of 1925, female births would have been 80 per cent more numerous than they actually were. The declines that occurred over the quarter-century were greatest where fertility had been highest. The correlations between the numbers of female births per 1,000 women in the specific age groups in the prefectures of 1925 and the decline in numbers between 1925 and 1947 were as follows:

Age	*Correlation*
15-19	.97
20-24	.24
25-29	.67
30-34	.72
35-39	.45
40-44	.43
45-49	.96

Notes to Table 93

[a] Adjusted for malreporting. [b] Not adjusted for malreporting.
[c] Final tabulations, including returns that came in January-March of the following year.
[d] Estimated final returns, correction factor (based on data for 1953 and 1954) applied to data of monthly schedule reports.

Source: Populations of the respective years: Censuses, cited in the Bibliography, and for 1952, the official estimates. Nihon. Sori-fu, tokei-kyoku. *To, do, fu, ken jinko no suikei. Showa 27-nen oyobi 26-nen 10-gatsu ichijitsu genzai.*
Numbers of births: 1920-1940: Nihon. Naikaku tokei-kyoku. *Jinko dotai tokei.* 1947-1953: Nihon. Kosei-sho, eisei tokei-bu. *Jinko dotai tokei.* 1954-1955: *Ibid. Jinko dotai tokei maigetsu gaisu. Showa 29-nen nenkei-bun. Ibid. Showa 30-nen.*

TABLE 94

Gross reproduction rates in the prefectures, 1920-1955

Prefectures	*1920*[a]	*1925*[b]	*1930*[b]	*1935*[a]	*1940*[a]	*1943*[a]	*1947*[b]	*1950*[c]	*1955*[c]
Hokkaido	3.32	3.17	2.95	2.71	2.35	2.37	2.35	2.31	1.38
Aomori	3.39	3.24	3.05	2.92	2.44	2.60	2.63	2.43	1.56
Iwate	3.19	3.04	2.93	2.84	2.56	2.56	2.58	2.23	1.51
Miyagi	3.16	3.11	2.87	2.76	2.47	2.54	2.15	2.14	1.38
Akita	3.21	3.15	3.01	2.81	2.44	2.44	2.45	2.17	1.40
Yamagata	2.96	2.92	2.76	2.57	2.36	2.24	2.06	1.93	1.25
Fukushima	3.00	2.96	2.76	2.66	2.49	2.40	2.19	2.23	1.52
Ibaraki	2.99	2.89	2.74	2.70	2.41	2.27	2.17	2.01	1.40
Tochigi	3.03	3.01	2.86	2.71	2.40	2.31	2.28	2.07	1.39
Gumma	2.86	2.64	2.48	2.35	2.24	2.26	2.22	1.90	1.30
Saitama	2.90	2.73	2.56	2.52	2.21	2.29	2.30	1.96	1.35
Chiba	2.73	2.68	2.53	2.44	2.08	2.10	2.24	1.82	1.28
Tokyo	2.12	2.16	1.90	1.74	1.60	1.91	1.80	1.45	0.86
Kanagawa	2.58	2.64	2.28	2.11	1.93	2.08	2.35	1.68	0.99
Niigata	2.97	2.85	2.68	2.48	2.21	2.25	2.24	2.04	1.37
Toyama	3.16	2.94	2.51	2.19	2.08	2.19	2.65	1.82	1.10
Ishikawa	2.86	2.65	2.30	2.03	1.83	2.10	2.47	1.79	1.19
Fukui	3.03	2.79	2.48	2.15	1.99	2.19	2.10	1.90	1.29
Yamanashi	2.97	2.86	2.61	2.54	2.32	2.30	2.09	1.89	1.28
Nagano	2.52	2.48	2.29	2.19	2.08	2.01	1.83	1.61	1.10
Gifu	3.01	2.83	2.64	2.42	2.30	2.23	2.09	1.82	1.13
Shizuoka	2.91	2.86	2.62	2.40	2.18	2.13	2.10	1.90	1.27
Aichi	2.66	2.53	2.31	2.12	2.03	2.05	2.05	1.70	1.04
Mie	2.67	2.62	2.42	2.21	2.06	2.00	1.96	1.69	1.05
Shiga	2.61	2.50	2.25	2.06	1.93	2.00	1.88	1.67	1.11
Kyoto	2.29	2.12	1.88	1.70	1.60	1.78	1.88	1.47	0.87
Osaka	2.21	2.00	1.79	1.70	1.62	1.85	1.93	1.52	0.89
Hyogo	2.53	2.24	2.02	1.87	1.66	1.90	1.99	1.61	1.02
Nara	2.76	2.43	2.15	1.96	1.76	1.75	1.82	1.55	1.01
Wakayama	2.71	2.42	2.20	2.01	1.68	1.83	1.87	1.58	1.04
Tottori	2.59	2.55	2.26	2.13	1.86	1.99	1.67	1.77	1.19
Shimane	2.51	2.50	2.31	2.31	2.02	2.18	2.30	1.96	1.23
Okayama	2.38	2.21	2.05	1.95	1.69	2.01	2.10	1.61	1.05
Hiroshima	2.71	2.56	2.25	2.11	1.81	1.98	2.12	1.61	1.02
Yamaguchi	2.54	2.43	2.23	2.14	1.75	2.10	2.21	1.86	1.09
Tokushima	2.98	2.70	2.63	2.40	2.15	2.16	2.30	1.98	1.31
Kagawa	3.08	2.63	2.47	2.29	1.94	2.01	2.31	1.71	1.12
Ehime	2.70	2.65	2.51	2.39	2.18	2.24	2.33	1.99	1.28
Kochi	2.52	2.40	2.19	2.04	1.79	1.88	2.11	1.66	1.09
Fukuoka	2.55	2.41	2.23	2.17	2.02	2.06	2.17	1.98	1.18
Saga	2.73	2.63	2.45	2.36	2.20	2.21	2.18	2.13	1.50
Nagasaki	2.71	2.61	2.50	2.46	2.28	2.19	2.25	2.22	1.64
Kumamoto	2.61	2.60	2.50	2.37	2.12	2.17	2.18	2.02	1.42
Oita	2.66	2.66	2.46	2.37	2.07	2.21	2.19	1.94	1.31
Miyazaki	2.82	2.70	2.71	2.63	2.24	2.26	2.39	2.17	1.52
Kagoshima	2.76	2.74	2.69	2.65	2.30	2.15	2.09	2.12	1.64

[a] Estimated age schedules of fertility were secured on the basis of the linear relations between general and age-specific fertility in all the age schedules of fertility that were available for the year 1930. The discrepancies between the rates as thus computed and those based on the schedules for the prefectures in the years 1925 and 1947 were slight.

[b] Age-specific schedules of fertility for the prefectures.

[c] Estimated age schedules of fertility based on the actual schedules for the year 1949.

Source: Populations, age distributions, and numbers of births: References, Table 93. Births for all years except 1955 are adjusted for malreporting on the basis of children under age 1 enumerated in the censuses. Age schedules of fertility: 1925: Nihon. Naikaku tokei-kyoku. *Fubo no nenrei betsu shussei tokei. Taisho 14-nen.* 1930: *Ibid. Fubo no nenrei betsu shussei oyobi shisan tokei, Showa go'nen.* 1947 and 1949: unpublished tabulations.

Thus in the younger and in the older childbearing ages, the sharpest reductions in fertility occurred in those prefectures where it had been highest. There was also an appreciable correlation between initially high rates of childbearing in the ages of maximum reproduction, those from 25 to 34, and the extent of the decline in fertility. There thus was a major diffusion of limitations in marital fertility between 1925 and 1947, a diffusion that proceeded in some relation to the level of fertility in 1925.[24]

Industrialization and Fertility

In the ancient world, the increase of the population of Japan depended on the balance of births and deaths in the countryside. As the modern world evolved, increasing proportions of the people lived in cities. The relations among industrialization, urbanization, and fertility became critical in the determination of levels and trends in fertility for the nation.

Economic development and the downward movement of fertility have been interrelated aspects of the modernization of Japan. These relations were apparent in the data of the registration compilations of the early twentieth century.[25] They emerge in clear form in the data on fertility secured in the census of 1950. In that year the number of children ever born per 1,000 women aged 45 and over increased with the dependence of the population on agriculture as major industry (Table 95). This general relationship between high fertility and predominance of agriculture held for women of all ages with one exception: at ages under 25, fertility was slightly higher in the intermediate than in the agricultural prefectures.

The age-specific fertility of the women of 1925, 1930, and 1947 shows persistent associations between agriculture and fertility (Table 96). The greater rates of childbearing in agricultural as compared with intermediate or industrial prefectures characterized not only all women in the reproductive ages but women at each age. Between 1925 and 1930 fertility moved downward for each age group of women within each group of prefectures in all industrial areas. By 1947 fertility had moved sharply downward in all areas for women who were aged 25 or less or 35 and over. In metropolitan, other industrial, and intermediate prefectures, births to women who were between the ages of 25 and 34 were relatively more numerous in 1947 than they had been in 1930. Even here, though, the movement of fertility was downward in the agricultural prefectures and in Hokkaido.

The differences among agricultural, intermediate, and industrial prefectures have persisted in the recent years of rapidly declining fertility. The crude birth rates for the years 1947, 1950, 1952, and 1955 show the declines in the period since the passage of the Eugenics Protection Law and the spread of practices of birth limitation.[26]

Areas	*1947*	*1950*	*1952*	*1955*
All Japan	34.3	28.1	23.3	19.4
Metropolitan	31.3	23.9	18.5	15.9
Other industrial	32.9	26.5	21.0	17.6
Intermediate	34.4	27.3	22.6	19.1
Agricultural	35.4	30.2	26.1	21.8
Hokkaido	36.7	34.2	28.8	21.7

[24] Widowhood may be a factor in these correlations between level and amount of decline in the prefectures only to the extent to which such widowhood tended to be more prevalent in the prefectures with higher fertility. Since data on marital status are not available for the prefectures in 1947, it is not possible to compare marital fertility in 1925 with declines in marital fertility from 1925 to 1947. However, the selective impact of war widowhood on fertility cannot have been sufficient to account for more than a small part of the differential reduction in the fertility of women. Widowhood was concentrated among women under age 35 and so could not influence the correlations at ages 35 and over. Insofar as there was a heavier decline in normal widowhood in the prefectures of high fertility, this would be a factor tending to buoy fertility and so to obscure the relations between original levels and amounts of decline.

[25] The correlations between ratios of children under 5 per 1,000 women aged from 15 to 49 and the proportion of the population of the prefectures living in minor civil divisions of 10 thousand population or less were .3 in 1908, .4 in 1913, and .4 in 1920; comparable correlations using gross reproduction rates were .4 in 1920, 1925, 1930, and 1935. For the census period more accurate measures of rurality were available than the relative predominance of communes of 10 thousand population or less, and the relations between high fertility and rurality, between low fertility and urbanization, become much clearer. In 1930 the correlation between the gross reproduction rate and the proportion of the gainfully occupied population in agriculture was .7; the correlation between the gross reproduction rate and the proportion of the population living in cities was —.6. It should be noted that the correlation between the per cent of the population urban and the per cent of the gainfully occupied population in agriculture was —0.9.

[26] Source: References, Table 93.

Table 95

Number of children ever born per 1,000 women, by age, prefectures by industrial type, 1950

		PREFECTURES BY INDUSTRIAL TYPE				
Age of women[a]	*All Japan*	*Metropolitan*	*Other industrial*	*Intermediate*	*Agricultural*	*Hokkaido*
15 and over	2,634	2,085	2,455	2,689	2,825	2,991
15-19	17	14	15	20	17	18
20-24	416	296	389	452	443	458
25-29	1,423	1,170	1,329	1,466	1,490	1,754
30-34	2,588	2,134	2,468	2,589	2,746	3,176
35-39	3,641	2,960	3,374	3,630	3,949	4,434
40-44	4,388	3,411	4,044	4,336	4,857	5,396
45 and over	4,632	3,864	4,355	4,563	4,928	5,774

[a] Since the question as to number of children ever born was asked only of married women, the illegitimate births to single women who had remained single until the date of the census were excluded.

Source: Nihon. Sori-fu, tokei-kyoku. *Showa 25-nen kokusei chosa hokoku.* III.1. Table 28.

TABLE 96

Female births per 1,000 women, by age, prefectures by industrial type, 1925, 1930, and 1947

Prefectures by industrial type	*Age 15-49*	*Quinquennial ages* 15-19	20-24	25-29	30-34	35-39	40-44	45-49
1925								
All Japan	75.7	24.0	116.8	131.2	115.5	88.8	38.4	6.5
Metropolitan	63.1	15.2	89.0	110.4	96.1	71.6	30.0	5.3
Other industrial	69.1	18.5	107.5	121.1	105.5	80.5	34.1	5.7
Intermediate	73.7	24.3	119.3	129.8	113.1	82.5	36.6	5.6
Agricultural	80.7	27.2	125.7	140.9	123.7	94.8	41.2	7.4
Hokkaido	92.5	36.5	146.8	146.3	129.0	103.4	50.1	9.6
1930								
All Japan	70.2	17.7	103.5	125.4	109.6	82.7	36.4	5.6
Metropolitan	57.1	10.6	76.7	103.9	88.5	62.7	26.0	4.4
Other industrial	63.2	13.6	93.0	114.4	98.0	72.6	31.7	4.8
Intermediate	68.5	18.3	104.8	124.2	106.8	80.0	34.9	4.9
Agricultural	76.6	20.4	113.7	137.7	121.6	92.6	41.1	6.3
Hokkaido	86.8	26.3	135.7	144.1	126.4	97.6	47.4	7.8
1947								
All Japan	64.5	7.2	80.8	130.0	113.4	76.2	27.8	3.4
Metropolitan	53.6	4.4	58.7	112.0	99.5	60.5	19.2	2.1
Other industrial	59.4	5.6	72.4	121.2	106.4	68.3	23.1	2.7
Intermediate	63.4	7.5	84.3	128.9	109.9	73.3	26.3	2.6
Agricultural	66.7	7.3	81.2	133.2	119.2	83.8	32.1	3.9
Hokkaido	69.8	5.6	88.8	139.1	116.0	82.9	35.3	4.8

Source: Reference, Tables 93 and 94.

The gross reproduction rates for the prefectures by industrial type substantiate the evidence of the crude birth rates as to the rapidity of the declines in recent years. The rates presented here include those for the prewar and the postwar periods in order to illustrate the increase in the speed of decline:[27]

Areas	*1925*	*1930*	*1947*	*1950*	*1955*
All Japan	2.6	2.4	2.2	1.8	1.2
Metropolitan	2.1	1.9	1.8	1.5	0.9
Other industrial	2.4	2.1	2.0	1.7	1.0
Intermediate	2.6	2.4	2.2	1.8	1.2
Agricultural	2.8	2.7	2.3	2.0	1.4
Hokkaido	3.1	2.9	2.4	2.3	1.4

The question as to whether there is convergence or divergence in the fertility of the regional populations is a difficult one to answer. There was evidence of increasing divergence in the 1920's and the 1930's, but the changes between 1930 or 1935 and 1947 suggest convergence. The ratios of measures of fertility in the agricultural prefectures to those in the metropolitan prefectures indicate the same types of differentials in 1950 as in earlier years. In the years from 1950 to 1955, the absolute amount of the decline in fertility was greater in agricultural than in industrial prefectures. The percentage declines were greatest in the metropolitan and other industrial prefectures.[28]

The age distributions that permit the computation of ratios of children under 5 to women in the reproductive ages are more widely available than either recorded births or enumerated children under one year of age. TABLE 97 presents ratios of children to women for the prewar, war, and postwar years.[29] There is some evidence here, as in the gross repro-

[27] Source: References, Table 94.

[28] Gross reproduction rates based on recorded births indicate some widening of the differentials, but the discrepancies between enumerated infants and reported births in the metropolitan prefectures indicate that the maldistributions of the prewar years have survived to the present, though apparently in lesser degree. Gross reproduction rates utilizing births for 1950 estimated on the basis of enumerated children under age 1 and recorded infant deaths do not corroborate the suggestions of convergence in the 1947 data. The declines in crude birth rates from 1950 to 1953 were relatively more rapid in the prefectures with low birth rates and hence suggest increasing divergence. Without age standardization, such evidence is suggestive only.

[29] There are difficulties in the interpretation of ratios of children to women as measures of levels or changes in Japan that preclude their general use for such measurement. Infant and childhood mortality has been declining rapidly. A ratio of children to women includes a substantial influence of childhood mortality in the early years, particularly in 1920, when children aged from 0 to 4 were survivors of the births of 1916 to 1920. In the critical years of the war, ratios of children to women in later census enumerations are virtually the only measure of fertility available. Yet here, in the years from 1944 through 1946, childhood mortality may again have been a major factor in reducing levels of fertility and altering differentials between geographic areas if the measure of fertility that is used is a ratio of children to women. In any period, the use of a child-women ratio smooths the annual changes in fertility,

TABLE 97

Female children under 5 (Western) or under 6 (lunar) per 1,000 women aged from 20 to 49 (Western) or 21 to 50 (lunar), 1920-1955
(1950 area)

		PREFECTURES BY INDUSTRIAL TYPE				
Type of age and year[a]	*All Japan*	*Metropolitan*	*Other industrial*	*Intermediate*	*Agricultural*	*Hokkaido*
Western ages						
1920	349	273	325	353	372	453
1930	374	307	347	376	407	462
1940	324	264	303	324	368	391
Lunar ages						
1944[b]	284	255	275	283	302	336
1945[c]	304	234	287	305	323	357
1946[d]	251	205	237	250	266	304
Western ages						
1947	296	249	293	293	312	360
1950	322	269	310	319	343	394
1955	239	181	216	240	313	304

[a] Ratios based on Western ages are comparable in the different censuses, for children aged from 0 to 4 are the enumerated survivors of the births of the five years preceding the census date. Ratios based on lunar age are not comparable, and the lack of comparability is greatest at lunar age 1. Children aged 1 are the survivors of the births after the preceding January 1 to the census date; children aged 2 are the survivors of the calendar year preceding the calendar year of the census, etc.
[b] Survivors of births, January 1, 1940, to February 22, 1944.
[c] Survivors of births, January 1, 1941, to November 1, 1945.
[d] Survivors of births, January 1, 1942, to April 26, 1946.

Source: References to the censuses of the respective years are given in the Bibliography.

duction rates and the crude birth rates, that fertility was declining more rapidly in the industrial than in the agricultural prefectures before the war, that the differentials among areas were lessened during the late war and early postwar years, but that the declines in fertility in recent years have been accompanied by a restoration of the prewar differentials. There is no evidence of any convergence of fertility in relative terms, although the amount of the differentials has decreased.

The relations between industrialization and fertility also existed among the Japanese in areas that are now foreign. The ratio used here is total children aged from 0 to 4 per 1,000 women aged from 20 to 44:[30]

Areas	*1920*	*1930*	*1940*
Japan, 46 prefectures	802	863	732
"Urban" areas			
Taiwan	641	746	677
Korea	644	717	665
Kwantung	527	675	665
South Manchuria Railway Zone	582	744	—
"Settlement" area			
Karafuto	870	923	783
"Rural" areas			
Okinawa	832	904	929
Nanyo-gunto	581	883	755

Japanese in the colonial areas of Taiwan, Korea, Kwantung, and the South Manchuria Railway Zone lived primarily in cities and engaged in non-agricultural occupations. Their fertility was substantially below that of the general population of Japan. In Karafuto and Nanyo-gunto there was an extension of the area of settlement of the ethnic Japanese. In these peripheral areas, where agricultural or pioneer conditions predominated, fertility was appreciably higher than that in the general population of Japan.[31]

URBANIZATION AND FERTILITY

The relation between the industrial characteristics of an area and the fertility of its people need not imply that the causal relations run from economic activity *per se* to fertility, for different types of economic activity imply differences in places of living as well as in types of work. The majority but not all of the Japanese women in metropolitan prefectures lived in cities; the majority but not all of the women in agricultural prefectures lived in towns and villages. Some of the women in industrial prefectures lived in *mura*, while some of the women in agricultural prefectures lived in *shi*. Thus it is possible to determine the relation between fertility and the industrial characteristics of the prefectures, holding constant the size of the communes in which the women live. This type of tabulation is given in TABLE 98, the measure of fertility being the number of children under age 1 for each

which is one of the factors that is of major concern in the recent years of precipitant change.

[30] References to the censuses of the different areas in 1920, 1930, and 1940 are given in the Bibliography.

[31] The ratio of children to women in Nanyo-gunto in 1920 is the apparent exception, but the population count in that year was taken by the military government and the occupation was in its initial stages.

TABLE 98

Children under one year of age per 1,000 women aged from 15 to 44, by size of commune, all Japan and prefectures by industrial type, 1930

		SIZE OF COMMUNE				
Prefectures by industrial type	*Total population*	*100,000 and over*	*50,000-99,999*	*10,000-49,999*	*5,000-9,999*	*Below 5,000*
All Japan	142.8	111.7	120.2	137.9	156.3	160.8
Metropolitan	117.8	105.8	133.1[a]	133.6[a]	135.4	138.5
Other industrial	129.9	115.9	110.2	129.3	141.9	151.9
Intermediate	143.5	113.0	107.6	123.6	147.4	158.3
Agricultural	158.2	117.7	120.5	144.3	165.1	166.7
Hokkaido	177.2	132.9	161.9	188.0	195.7	195.3

[a] These communes are in Tokyo prefecture and are functionally suburban to Tokyo-*shi* rather than independent cities.

Source: Nihon. Kosei-sho, jinko mondai kenkyujo. Tabulations from the data sheets of the 1930 census.

1,000 women aged from 15 to 44. The data refer to the year 1930. In general, fertility declined as the size of the commune of enumeration increased. Moreover, the fertility of the women enumerated in communes of any given size increased with the predominance of agriculture in the industrial structure of the prefecture.[32] Maximum fertility occurred in the small *mura* of the most agricultural prefectures; minimum fertility occurred in the great cities of the metropolitan prefectures. The influence of milieu on fertility was great; the fertility of women in the cities of 100 thousand and over in Hokkaido was comparable to that of the women in the *mura* of Tokyo and Osaka prefectures.

DIFFERENCES, SHI AND GUN

The balance of the forces of change and conservatism has been such as to produce declines in rates of childbearing throughout the *gun* from Tohoku to southern Kyushu, throughout the *shi* from the small centers of the northeast and the southwest to the great conurbations of central Honshu (MAP 13). Moreover, there has never been one level of fertility that was urban and another that was rural. The fertility of an area, including its villages, its towns, and its cities, was associated negatively with the general levels of industrialization and urbanization of the area, positively with the persistence of agriculture and rurality. Over and beyond this relationship of fertility, economy, and distribution pattern, though, there was a geographical relationship. The highest fertility was in the northeast, with a downward drift toward the southwest. The per cent in *shi* and the gross reproduction rates for the populations of the regions in 1930 illustrate this phenomenon:[33]

Region	*Per cent in* shi	*Gross reproduction rate*
Hokkaido	24.9	3.0
Tohoku	11.6	2.9
Kanto	24.8	2.2
Hokuriku	13.8	2.5
Tosan	11.0	2.5
Tokai	30.0	2.4
Kinki	46.5	2.0
Chugoku	19.4	2.2
Shikoku	14.1	2.4
Kyushu	19.7	2.4

There were close relations between levels of fertility in *shi* and *gun*. Correlations between gross reproduction rates of *shi* and *gun* in the prefectures were .7 or higher at each census date from 1920 through 1950. This relation existed without reference to the size of the *shi* or the proportion of the prefectural populations resident in *gun*. Levels of fertility were related to aspects of culture other than industrialization and urbanization.

From 1920 to 1935 the gap between the fertility of *shi* and *gun* changed slightly; the average annual per cent decline in gross reproduction rates was 0.9 for the *gun*, 1.1 for the *shi*. The gross reproduction rate for the *shi* was 72 per cent that of the *gun* at the beginning of the fifteen-year period, 70 per cent at the end. In the early postwar years, the relative gap between the fertility of *shi* and *gun* seemed to have narrowed.[34] Ratios of children under 5 to women aged from 20 to 49 in the *shi* and the *gun* in the period from 1920 to 1947 or 1950 also suggest convergence. However, the declines in the years from 1950 to 1955 produced greater divergences among the areas. The ratio of fertility in the *gun* to that in

[32] There are some deviations from the regularity of the dual relationship of fertility to the industrial structure of the area and to the size of the place of residence. The forces reducing fertility were intensified in some transitional situations, whether the transition involved an industrial structure intermediate between the agricultural area and the metropolis or a size of city intermediate between the *mura* or the small *shi* and the great city. For large *machi* and small *shi*, fertility tended to be lower in transitional than in agricultural prefectures or in industrial prefectures other than the metropolitan ones. In the lesser industrial and transitional prefectures *shi* of 50 to 100 thousand population tended to have lower fertility than *shi* of 100 thousand and above.

[33] Per cent in *shi*: Nihon. Naikaku tokei-kyoku. *Showa gonen kokusei chosa sokuho*. IV.4. Table 1. Fertility data: References, Tables 93 and 94.

[34] A lessening of the gap in crude and standardized birth rates in 1947 as compared with 1920, 1930, and 1935 has been demonstrated. Ueda, Masao. "Some recent tendencies on urban and rural population." *The Third General Meeting of the Population Association of Japan. Data Paper.* November 13, 1949. Tables. It is difficult to use recorded births without adjustment, for incorporation was proceeding rapidly and recorded vital events pertained to the changing areas of the *shi, machi*, or *mura*. However, with a census taken on October 1 the births allocated to the populations of the *shi* would be expected to be too few, those allocated to the population of the *gun* too numerous. If this is a valid assumption, actual convergence would be greater than the convergence indicated by uncorrected data.

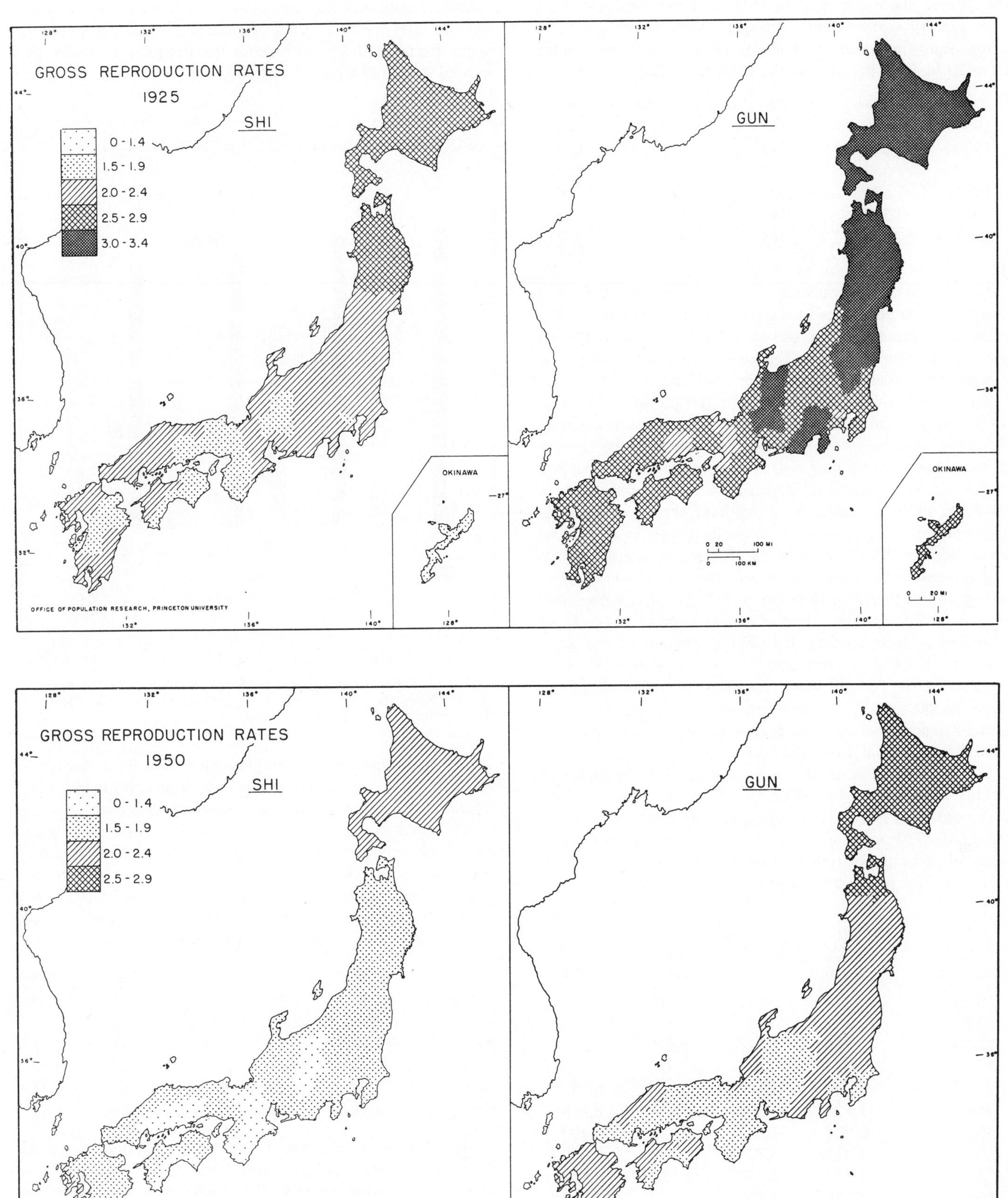

Map 13. Gross reproduction rates in the *shi* and the *gun* of the prefectures, 1925 and 1950

Source: Numbers of births: References, Table 93. Births by age of mother: References, Table 94.

the *shi* was about the same in 1955 as it had been a quarter of a century earlier. These changing relations are apparent in the following ratios of children under 5 to women aged from 20 to 49 in the *shi* and the *gun* from 1920 to 1955:[35]

Year	*Total*	*Six great cities*	*Other* shi	Gun
1920	535	497	583	744
1930	611	575	648	804
1940	554	533	579	732
1947	539	493	564	636
1950	592	546	619	703
1955	490	361	464	572

The ratios of *shi* to *gun* in 1920 were below those in 1930, a relationship to be expected because infant and childhood mortality were far higher in the *shi* than in the *gun* in the five years that preceded the census of 1920. The ratio in the *shi* was 76 per cent of that in the *gun* in 1930 and 1940. The comparable percentages were 85 in 1947 and 76 in 1955.

The changing relations between the fertility of the populations in urban and in rural areas have no simple explanation. Since the cities have incorporated rural territory, the fertility of the *shi* as a group may reflect this change in the structure of the urban population. Industries were still depressed in 1947 and 1950, so youth who would have been in urban areas under prewar conditions were forced to remain in *machi* and *mura*. Perhaps this stoppage of the channels of internal migration retained a low-fertility group in the *gun*, depressing fertility there, at the same time that it left the cities with somewhat older populations containing more married couples and so increased their fertility. By 1955 migrations to the cities had exceeded even prewar numbers. Whether any true convergence of the fertility of urban-industrial and rural-agricultural populations was occurring thus remains debatable. Certainly, definitive answers cannot be secured for a period as disturbed as that from 1947 to 1955.

The significance of trends in rural-urban differentiations in fertility in Japan may be subject to debate, but differentiations have occurred. As final illustration, we may cite data from the census of 1950 on numbers of children ever born per 1,000 women in four populations: all *shi* and the *ku* area of Tokyo Prefecture, all *gun* and the *gun* in Aomori Prefecture:[36]

Age of mothers	*All* shi	*Tokyo-to,* ku *area*	*All* gun	Gun *in Aomori prefecture*
15 and over	2,246	1,989	2,875	3,065
15-19	14	12	19	28
20-24	352	270	459	766
25-29	1,280	1,124	1,525	1,848
30-34	2,313	2,095	2,782	3,279
35-39	3,184	2,860	3,947	4,743
40-44	3,730	3,308	4,814	5,618
45-49	3,991	3,636	5,122	5,400
50-54	4,021	3,623	5,130	5,609
55-59	4,087	3,750	5,020	5,684
60 and over	4,186	3,923	4,697	5,186

VARIATIONS AMONG SHI

The inverse relation between size of city and level of fertility has been somewhat blurred in Japan.[37] Gross reproduction rates for cities grouped according to size in the census years from 1920 to 1935 show the irregular relations that existed during this period (FIGURE 11). The persistent difference was that between the six great cities and the lesser cities, whatever their size. It may be that differences in the industrial structures of the *shi* and the correlated differences in the numbers and characteristics of the migrants modify the operation of whatever factors are inherent in size *per se*. The interrelations of size, industrial structure, and cultural role are apparent in the rather substantial differences that existed among the six great cities themselves. Gross reproduction rates are given here for the years from 1920 to 1940:

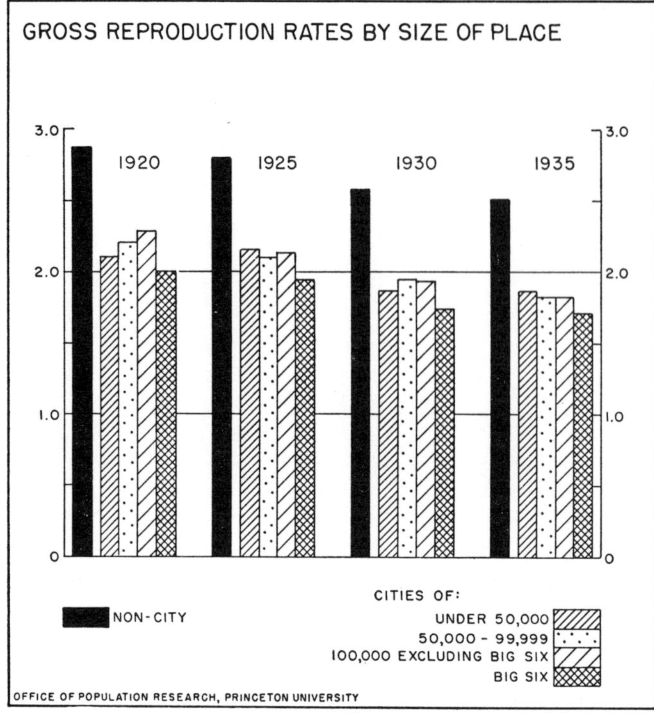

Figure 11. Gross reproduction rates, by size of place, 1920-1935

Source: Populations by age: prefectural volumes of the censuses of the respective years. Numbers of births: References, Table 93. Births adjusted for maldistribution.

City	*1920*	*1925*	*1930*	*1935*	*1940*
Tokyo	1.93	1.85	1.57	1.70	1.57
Yokohama	2.09	2.31	2.02	1.86	1.82
Nagoya	2.30	2.29	2.10	1.96	1.91
Osaka	1.91	1.89	1.73	1.66	1.58
Kobe	2.07	1.85	1.71	1.66	1.51
Kyoto	1.99	1.82	1.64	1.56	1.51

The fertility in the great cities was lower initially, and in the relatively normal years from 1920 to 1935 decline was more rapid. Gross reproduction rates show an increasing divergence of *shi* and *gun*, of greater and lesser *shi*:

[35] 1920-1940, prewar area; 1947-1955, postwar area. Ratios for 1950 are based on the age distributions of the 10 per cent sample tabulation; those for 1955 on the age distributions of the 1 per cent sample tabulations.

[36] Nihon. Sori-fu, tokei-kyoku. *Showa 25-nen kokusei chosa hokoku*. III.1. Table 28.

[37] The inconsistency between this conclusion and the deductions concerning fertility by size of commune in 1930 presented in Table 100 is more apparent than real. The communes of 100 thousand and over in Table 100 are dominated by the six great cities rather than the cities of 100 thousand and over, excluding the great cities. Furthermore, Table 100 refers to communes with a population of from 10,000 to 49,999, and thus includes many *machi* along with the small *shi*. In addition, there is some influence of differential infant mortality in the ratio of children under age 1 to women aged 15-44.

Shi	*1920*	*1935*	*Ratio of 1935 to 1920*	*Average annual per cent change*
All Japan	2.7	2.3	.87	0.9
Shi	2.1	1.8	.84	1.1
Under 50,000	2.1	1.8	.88	0.8
50,000-99,999	2.2	1.8	.83	1.3
From 100,000 to the six cities	2.3	1.8	.79	1.5
The six cities	2.0	1.7	.86	1.2
Gun	2.9	2.3	.87	0.9

The age-specific fertility of women in *shi* is available only for cities of 100 thousand and over in 1925 and 1930.[38] In these years the lower general fertility of women in the cities of 100 thousand and over as contrasted with that of women in lesser *shi* and *gun* resulted from lower fertility among all age groups of women (TABLE 99). Rates of decline at the various ages were greater in the cities of 100 thousand and over than in the remainder of the country, except for women aged from 25 to 29. The failure of metropolitan fertility to decline rapidly in this age group was probably associated with a retardment of age at marriage, which meant that larger proportions of women were having first and second births after, rather than before, they had passed their twenty-fifth birthday. The average annual rates of change for the period from 1925 to 1930 were as follows:

Age	Shi *of 100,000 and over*	*Remainder of country*
Age 15-49	—1.0	—0.9
15-19	—7.4	—5.7
20-24	—2.4	—1.7
25-29	0.0	—0.5
30-34	—1.0	—0.5
35-39	—1.0	—0.9
40-44	—1.8	—0.6
45-49	—2.9	—1.8

The differences in the rates of childbearing among the cities were great, and they followed no obvious pattern (TABLE 100). Some differences appeared to be related to size of city, industrial structure, and regional culture, but these general patterns were modified by factors specific to the individual cities. In the northeastern cities of Hakodate, Sapporo, Otaru, and Sendai, fertility was relatively high among younger women. This was presumably a reflection of the family structure and reproductive mores of the Tohoku region. However, the younger women of such centers of heavy industry as Kure and Yawata also had relatively high fertility. Rapid immigration of girls from the surrounding rural areas seems to have been conducive to high rates of reproduction, but the decline in fertility in the individual cities of rapid growth indicated that girls from rural regions did not maintain the levels of reproduction characteristic of the areas in which they had spent their youth.

The preceding analysis of the differences in the fertility of women in cities of varying sizes and characteristics has emphasized the situation in the relatively peaceful years between the two great wars. By 1947, there was a substantial

[38] The differentiation between the fertility of the metropolitan centers and of the lesser *shi* was recognized implicitly in the vital statistics published by the government of Japan. In 1925 and 1930 there were special tabulations of births by age of father and mother for each city that had had a population of 100 thousand or more at the previous census; in 1937 and later years, births by age of parents were published annually for the nation and the cities of 100 thousand and over as a group. There are difficulties with the data for 1937 and later years, for there are no age distributions of potential parents from actual enumerations, and migration was occurring so rapidly as to preclude estimation. Data for individual *machi* are far less adequate than those for smaller *shi*. No tabulations of births by age of mother in the *shi* either separately or as a group are available for the postwar years.

There is no evidence that the validity of the general or the age-specific birth rates of women as measures of levels and trends in reproduction in the metropolis were influenced in any consistent way by the peculiar and changing composition of the group of cities. In 1920 there were 16 cities of 100 thousand and over in Japan; this is the group of cities for which births by age of parents are available in 1925. The cities of Fukuoka, Kumamoto, Okayama, Niigata, and Sakai reached 100 thousand between 1920 and 1925; they are included in the non-metropolitan rather than the metropolitan population of 1925. In 1925 there were 21 cities of 100 thousand and over; these are the cities for which special fertility data are available in 1930. Between 1925 and 1930 the cities of Kawasaki, Moji, Hamamatsu, Yokosuka, Wakayama, and Shizuoka passed the 100 thousand mark but they are included in non-metropolitan population in the special tabulations for 1930. Average levels of fertility were not influenced by these deletions, for there was little relationship between size of city and level of fertility *per se*.

TABLE 99

Age-specific fertility of women in *shi* of 100 thousand and over and in the remainder of the country, 1925 and 1930

(Female births per 1,000 women)

Year and size group	AGES *Age 15-49*	*15-19*	*20-24*	*25-29*	*30-34*	*35-39*	*40-44*	*45-49*
1925								
Total	75.7	24.0	116.8	131.2	115.5	88.8	38.4	6.5
Shi 100,000 and over[a]	59.1	16.0	88.6	104.1	88.0	64.8	26.1	5.1
Remainder of country	77.3	25.0	120.9	133.7	118.2	91.3	39.7	6.6
1930								
Total	70.2	17.7	103.5	125.4	109.6	82.7	36.4	5.6
Shi 100,000 and over[a]	53.6	11.0	76.6	99.0	82.1	57.4	23.2	4.1
Remainder of country	72.6	19.0	108.2	129.5	113.3	86.1	38.2	5.7

[a] *Shi* of 100,000 and over are those *shi* classified as such on the basis of the previous census.

Source: Nihon. Naikaku tokei-kyoku. *Fubo no nenrei betsu shussei oyobi shisan tokei*. 1925. *Ibid*. 1930.

TABLE 100

Age-specific fertility of women in the *shi* of 100 thousand and over, 1925 and 1930

Shi	Year	Population (in '000)	Gross reproduction rate	FEMALE BIRTHS PER 1,000 WOMEN							
				15-49	15-19	20-24	25-29	30-34	35-39	40-44	45-49
Kure	1925	139	2.2	70.5	35.0	107.6	104.2	91.5	67.6	31.0	8.8
	1930	190	2.0	64.3	23.1	102.9	107.1	80.1	62.6	24.4	5.4
Sendai	1925	143	2.4	66.6	13.5	105.7	128.4	107.7	78.7	32.8	3.9
	1930	190	2.1	60.7	9.7	88.1	116.3	102.2	73.8	29.4	6.5
Sapporo	1925	145	2.4	70.1	19.9	112.9	125.2	102.2	74.2	35.3	6.2
	1930	169	2.2	64.8	11.8	100.7	120.7	93.3	69.3	30.1	5.1
Yawata	1925	118	2.2	72.6	27.7	102.5	109.6	96.4	66.1	32.4	7.7
	1930	168	2.0	67.3	22.6	95.4	103.3	91.8	64.3	25.3	6.1
Kumamoto[a]	1925	147	—	—	—	—	—	—	—	—	—
	1930	164	1.8	48.4	6.2	56.8	95.3	90.8	61.0	30.2	9.2
Kanagawa	1925	147	2.0	54.2	16.7	93.1	101.4	87.1	62.9	26.2	1.9
	1930	157	1.6	46.7	10.0	81.1	90.3	71.3	54.6	19.3	2.0
Otaru	1925	134	2.4	70.6	21.2	112.1	122.2	98.5	78.9	29.0	7.3
	1930	145	2.1	63.8	11.2	98.6	119.7	99.5	62.2	29.2	7.3
Okayama[a]	1925	125	—	—	—	—	—	—	—	—	—
	1930	139	1.5	45.2	10.8	77.0	88.0	61.8	46.0	14.5	6.4
Kagoshima	1925	125	2.2	57.7	6.0	69.0	112.1	115.5	86.1	42.5	13.9
	1930	137	1.9	51.4	5.2	59.4	96.0	101.7	74.6	39.1	7.3
Niigata[a]	1925	109	—	—	—	—	—	—	—	—	—
	1930	125	2.2	66.2	14.8	91.0	132.2	99.9	74.9	24.6	3.9
Sakai[a]	1925	105	—	—	—	—	—	—	—	—	—
	1930	120	1.7	50.7	10.6	70.5	97.6	81.1	49.8	20.4	4.7
Osaka	1925	2,115	1.8	56.8	16.1	87.3	98.6	81.9	58.0	22.0	3.9
	1930	2,454	1.7	53.4	11.3	76.0	97.0	78.7	52.7	19.7	3.5
Tokyo	1925	1,995	1.9	55.2	12.2	75.2	102.2	87.4	64.2	24.8	5.0
	1930	2,071	1.6	46.6	7.7	60.9	91.3	78.5	55.3	22.8	3.5
Nagoya	1925	769	2.2	66.5	18.8	107.0	117.5	97.8	75.3	29.4	3.7
	1930	907	2.0	61.9	15.3	96.3	112.7	90.7	64.0	26.3	3.1
Kobe	1925	644	1.8	56.6	17.2	92.2	93.3	76.8	53.2	21.3	5.0
	1930	788	1.7	53.3	12.5	78.9	94.6	76.0	49.3	20.7	3.7
Kyoto	1925	680	1.8	51.8	12.5	80.6	97.2	83.6	59.6	22.2	3.8
	1930	765	1.6	47.6	9.2	69.1	93.9	75.2	51.8	19.5	2.8
Yokohama	1925	406	2.3	71.9	17.9	95.7	125.6	105.8	77.3	34.8	7.7
	1930	620	2.0	62.7	11.4	87.2	109.7	94.4	67.5	28.2	6.0
Hiroshima	1925	196	1.9	55.9	19.2	93.7	99.0	80.8	58.3	25.0	8.0
	1930	270	1.7	50.5	13.5	86.0	89.1	73.4	49.0	19.4	5.3
Fukuoka[a]	1925	146	—	—	—	—	—	—	—	—	—
	1930	228	1.7	49.8	9.0	66.7	95.0	82.0	60.1	25.2	7.1
Nagasaki	1925	189	2.2	64.0	17.1	93.5	110.2	102.7	75.5	32.6	6.3
	1930	205	1.9	56.2	15.8	76.9	96.1	88.0	68.1	32.3	5.2
Hakodate	1925	164	2.4	71.8	23.7	115.0	121.8	104.1	71.0	33.2	7.2
	1930	197	2.1	65.6	15.7	103.4	112.5	98.2	66.3	28.8	3.5

[a] Cities of less than 100,000 population in 1920 and so excluded from the special compilations of births by age of mother in 1925.

Source: References, Table 102.

reduction in the differences between lesser cities and the six great cities. The differences among the great cities themselves were almost eliminated. Gross reproduction rates were 1.8 in Tokyo, Nagoya, Kobe, and Kyoto, 2.0 in Yokohama and Osaka. Differences were developing again by 1950, however, as the cities restored the industrial and cultural life which distinguished them from each other. In 1950 as in 1930, however, neither size of city nor industrialization of the prefecture was adequate as an explanation of the level of fertility. As the following gross reproduction rates indicate, fertility in the *shi* was everywhere lower than fertility in the *gun*, but fertility in *shi* and *gun* alike advanced with the increasing dependence of the area of residence on agriculture:

Area	*Total*	Shi	Gun
All Japan	1.8	1.6	2.0
Metropolitan	1.5	1.4	1.7
Other industrial	1.7	1.6	1.9
Intermediate	1.8	1.6	1.9
Agricultural	2.0	1.7	2.2
Hokkaido	2.3	2.0	2.5

VARIATIONS WITHIN SHI

If the lesser fertility of urban women is a response to altered ways of living and associated changes in values and aspirations, there should be heterogeneity in the reproductive performance of women in the different areas and social-economic classes of the city. This was indeed the fact as early as 1930. In that year the fertility of women in the *ku* (districts) of the great cities extended from levels far below those characteristic of any total urban population to levels comparable to those of women living in the villages of Tohoku (TABLE 101). The differences in levels of fertility were related to ways of living in the cities, the occupations and income levels of husbands, and presumably the educational status and cultural aspirations of the couple or the larger family. In Tokyo the fertility of women was lowest in the business and residential areas in the center of the city. Women who lived in the belts of residential *ku* surrounding this central area had relatively low fertility. Gradations of fertility outward from the center were rather comparable to those that would have been anticipated on the basis of the ecology of United States cities. Fertility rates substantially higher than those in the central city and the inner belt of *ku* occurred in the residential and factory areas to the southeast. Fertility was relatively low in the elite Western residential areas. The rates of reproduction among the women who lived in the low income areas of the north were comparable to those of the peasant society. In these areas lying within one of the world's largest cities, family factories and agriculture permitted life in the city to possess a degree of family integration and residential stability almost as great as that in remote *mura*.

VARIATIONS AMONG GUN

In the three decades from 1920 to 1950 there were major differences in fertility among cities, and there were major variations within them. Levels of fertility at given times and changes over time mirrored the diverse influences of the developing industrial society on the institutions and values associated with marriage, family, and childbearing. Hence substantial variations in the fertility of women in the *gun* would be expected. In fact, one might anticipate a rough continuum from the low fertility of *gun* populations in close association with urban industrial life to the high fertility of *gun* populations living by subsistence agriculture and insulated from contacts with the modernizing society and economy.

The crude birth rates for *gun* in 1925, 1930, and 1935 indicate that variations comparable to those among the rural areas of the different prefectures existed among the *gun* (MAP 14).[39] The range within any given prefecture was associated with the modal level of fertility characteristic of that prefecture; it was limited, if considered in terms of the high and the low in fertility found within the minor civil divisions of a diversified society such as that of the United States.

The national picture of variations in fertility within the *gun* reflected both the homogeneity of the Japanese rural culture and economy and the limitations of the community life, agricultural techniques, and reproductive mores. However, the

[39] In 1925, 1930, and 1935 there were special tabulations of vital statistics for minor civil divisions within the prefectures. Nihon. Naikaku tokei-kyoku. *Shi, cho, son betsu jinko dotai tokei. Taisho juyo'nen. Ibid. Showa go'nen. Ibid. Showa ju'nen.*

TABLE 101

Fertility of women in the *ku* of the six great cities, 1930 and 1935
(Children age 0 per 1,000 women aged from 15 to 49)

	1930			*1935*		
City	*Total city*	*Low* ku	*High* ku	*Total city*	*Low* ku	*High* ku
Tokyo[a]	89.3	60.0	117.1	103.9	56.0	142.5
Yokohama	117.0	105.6	141.8	109.8	100.5	128.9
Nagoya	116.0	108.2	133.3	115.4	109.0	131.7
Osaka[b]	100.7	65.4	119.0	101.0	63.0	117.5
Kyoto[c]	87.5	74.9	93.6	93.0	75.8	120.7
Kobe[d]	99.7	—	—	100.4	68.1	116.7

[a] Old City, 1930; Greater Tokyo, 1935.
[b] *Ku* boundaries as in 1930.
[c] Five *ku* in 1930; two *ku* added in 1935.
[d] No *ku* divisions in 1930.

Source: Nihon. Naikaku tokei-kyoku. *Showa go'nen kokusei chosa hokoku.* IV.4. *Fu ken hen. Tokyo, Kanagawa, Aichi, Osaka, Kyoto, Hyogo.* Table 4. *Ibid. Showa ju'nen kokusei chosa hokoku.* II.2. *Fu ken hen.* Table 3.

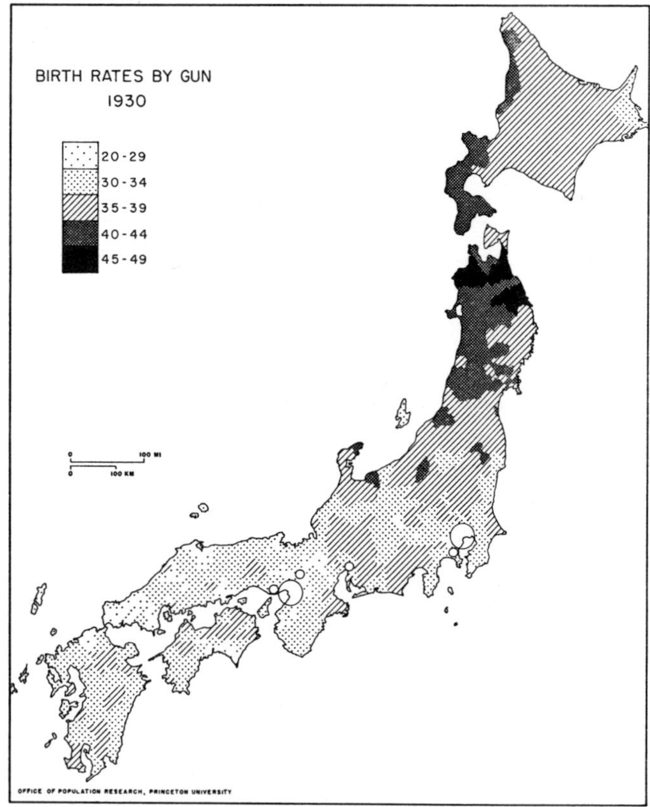

Map 14. Birth rates in the *gun*, 1930
Source: References, Footnote 35.

variations among the *gun* were associated with the same factors that created the differentiations between *shi* and *gun*. High fertility in the *gun* was associated with geographic isolation, economic retardation, and low levels of living. Low fertility in the *gun* was associated with nearness to cities, the presence of economic activities other than agriculture, and higher levels of living. These relationships existed in developed form in 1925 and thus presumably antedated the census period. In 1925, the crude birth rates of the *gun* in Aomori prefecture extended from a low of 40 to a high of 50; the comparable range in Iwate was 37 to 48. In Hokkaido, where areas settled by migrants from the high fertility areas of Tohoku existed along with developing metropolitan centers, the range in the crude birth rates of the *gun* was from 31 to 44. In Kyoto prefecture the average birth rate in the *gun* was 30, a rate below that for any individual *gun* within Hokkaido or the prefectures of Tohoku. The low birth rate among the *gun* of Kyoto prefecture was 27, while the high was 35.

These types of differences in birth rates within and among the rural areas of Japan existed in 1930 and 1935, as in 1925. The impact of the industrial society appeared to be felt throughout the countryside, however, for the downward movement so characteristic of the fertility of the *shi* and *gun* populations of the prefectures was prevalent in the *gun*. From 1925 to 1930 and from 1930 to 1935 there were irregularities, and in general the declines were slight. However, very high birth rates, such as those that existed in the Tohoku region in 1925, were disappearing from the Japanese scene. Crude birth rates that approached 50 per 1,000 total population were not to be found among the *gun* in 1935.

The relations among lower fertility, proximity to cities, dependence on commercialized agriculture, and more adequate transportation suggest that the differentiation of fertility was correlated with economic development within the rural population.[40] The assumption that differences in the levels of fertility among the *gun* reflect the impact of the industrial society may be tested empirically for the year 1930, for here we have not only the age distributions of the census, which permit a more accurate measurement of fertility, but the occupational characteristics and the migrant status of the people enumerated in the individual *gun*.

In 1930 there was some positive association between fertility and dependence on agriculture in the *gun*. The ratio of female children under age 1 to women aged from 20 to 44 was taken as a measure of fertility.[41] The proportion of all gainfully occupied men reporting agriculture as a major industry was assumed to be a measure of family dependence on agriculture. Coefficients of contingency were then computed for the *gun* within the separate regions. The results were as follows:

Region	*Coefficient of contingency*
All Japan except Hokkaido and Okinawa	.49
Tohoku	.39
Kanto	.46
Hokuriku	.54
Tosan	.30
Tokai	.22
Kinki	.60
Chugoku	.34
Shikoku	.45
Kyushu	.32

The differences in the closeness of the relation between the level of human reproduction and the prevalence of agricultural life are perhaps more striking than the prevalence of a relationship between the two variables in all regions. The explanation for these divergences in the extent of association is somewhat speculative, but it is consistent with the results of many studies of local areas and with the known characteristics of economic transformation in Japan. In the peripheral regions of the country, practically all men who labored in any segment of the industrial structure utilized ancient techniques, and they and their families lived in an agricultural milieu. Fishing, household industry, and trade were almost as integral segments of village life as agriculture itself. In some areas the proportion of the gainfully occupied men who were engaged in agriculture reflected the occupational differentiations of the old order. In others, the presence of substantial nonagricultural employment indicated a different way of life and an altered structure of family relations.

[40] The prevalent malregistration of births in relation to the place of enumeration of children casts suspicion on rates based on reported births. Since populations of *gun* differ in the relative proportions of men and women and the age composition of women, some age and sex standardization is necessary. It is possible to evaluate these sources of error through estimating the number of births in the *gun* on the basis of enumerated children aged 0 and then relating these births to the number of women aged from 15 to 44 rather than to the total population. This was done, and it was found that the ratios of female births to women in the reproductive ages as based on the age distributions of the census of October 1, 1930, were highly correlated with the crude birth rates for the calendar year 1930. Variations among the *gun* within the regions occurred around a modal fertility whose geographical distribution was that of the crude birth rates. The types of errors that might have vitiated the reliability of the crude birth rates of the *gun* as a measure of fertility did not in fact do so.

[41] The data were secured from Tables 3 and 17 in the prefectural volumes of the 1930 census. Nihon. Naikaku tokei-kyoku. *Showa go'nen kokusei chosa hokoku.* IV.4. *Fu, ken hen.*

The penetration of the new industrial economy had effects that differed according to the type of industry, the specific characteristics of the impact, and perhaps the nature of the sub-culture. The development of mining might introduce fairly advanced technologies, but the ways of life in the mining villages preserved the high fertility of the agrarian culture. In the Tosan and Tokai regions, industrialization in the *gun* might signify household industry, which was compatible with high fertility. On the other hand, it might mean factory dormitories, where large numbers of single girls served to lower the fertility of the total female population. In the industrial centers of the Kanto and the Kinki, there was a close relation between the predominance of agriculture and fertility in the populations of the *gun*. Here non-agricultural employment indicated urban contacts and integration with the money economy. There was also a rather high association between fertility and agricultural employment along the Sea of Japan. Here perhaps the direct access and established migrations to the Kanto and the Kinki had resulted in an adoption of the more urban values.

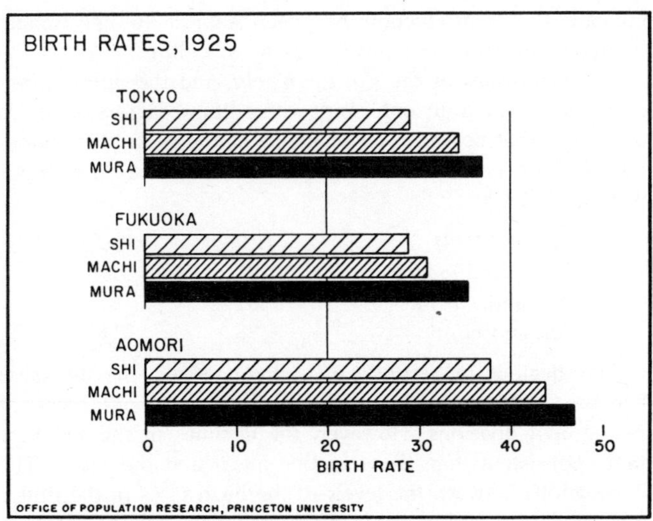

Figure 12. Birth rates in *shi, machi,* and *mura* of selected prefectures, 1925

Source: References, Footnote 35.

VARIATIONS AMONG MACHI AND MURA

The critical questions throughout the peasant East concern the fertility of the peasant and the conditions under which that fertility changes. Data that pertain to the *gun* are not adequate for the measurement of the reproduction of the peasant, for *gun* include agricultural hamlets, larger villages, towns, and small cities up to 30 thousand or more in population. Differences in fertility among *gun* may reflect rural-urban differences in fertility at the village-town level; changes in the fertility of *gun* may reflect urbanization proceeding below the level of the incorporated city. The only feasible approach to the measurement of fertility in rural areas more homogeneous with respect to rurality or its absence than the *gun* is to utilize the *mura* and the *machi* for this purpose. The *mura* is agrarian in demographic structure and economic characteristics; it is unlikely to include a town with major employment opportunities divorced from agriculture and related activities. The *machi* is more diversified in economic structure, more "urban" in the facilities and services available to its residents. The available statistics corroborate the general impression that the areas of concentrated settlement in the *machi* approach Western definitions of an urban population in towns of from 10 thousand to 30 thousand population. However, the *machi* that include towns that we would define as urban also include villages that are strictly agricultural in occupational structure and ways of living.

In Japan as a whole, as in each prefecture, birth rates were lowest for the *shi*, intermediate for the *machi*, and highest for the *mura* (FIGURE 12). This was true in 1925, 1930, and 1935. The existence of higher crude birth rates in *mura* than in *machi* seems incontrovertible. The problem is the interpretation of the observed differences. Perhaps the lower fertility of the *machi* is the product of a malregistration of births similar to that which occurred in the *shi*. However, the validity of the trends in the birth rates for *machi* and *mura* derives considerable support from the consistency of the rates from one time period to another. Birth rates are not capricious variables; in subsistence agricultural societies they reflect the stable institutional framework and the deep-rooted values of the family system and the village community. If the birth rates for minor civil divisions at successive time periods are reasonably consistent measures of the reproductive performance of the population, there should be high correlations in rates for comparable areas at successive time intervals. Using the prefectures as the units of analysis, the correlations between unadjusted birth rates in 1930 and 1935 were .96 for the total population, .93 for the *shi*, .94 for the *machi*, and .95 for the *mura*.[42]

The crude birth rates for the *mura* are the nearest approximation to the fertility of the peasant that is possible through utilization of the censuses and vital statistics of Japan. An examination of the ratios for the *mura* of the prefectures in 1925 indicates considerable variation in fertility from one region of Japan to another. The range of birth rates among the populations of the *mura* was also wide. Perhaps the most significant aspect of the birth rates of the *mura* in 1925 were the enclaves of very high fertility. In that year the birth rate for the *mura* in Aomori prefecture as a whole was 47 per 1,000 total population; in two of the *gun* the birth rates were over 50. While these high birth rates cannot be assumed to represent maximum fertility for a Japanese population under favorable biological, environmental, and cultural conditions, birth rates of from 40 to 44 per 1,000 total population do

[42] The problem of validating the differences in levels between *machi* and *mura* is more difficult. Age structures of the *machi* would be more conducive to high crude birth rates than those of the *mura*. Tests of malregistration are difficult, for only total populations and numbers of birth are available for analysis. However, the analysis of prefectures, *shi*, and *gun* indicated that the malregistration of births was a major factor only in the large cities. It would not be likely to assume major proportions in the relatively stable populations of *machi* and *mura*.

There are difficulties of area comparability also. Total populations refer to the areas enumerated at the time of the census. Numbers of births are those reported for the area as defined throughout the year, without adjustments for area comparability with the census. Area changes occur most frequently at times close to a census date. Most of the area changes involve the incorporation of territory from adjacent *machi* or *mura* into *shi*. There are other types of changes that influence the allocation of births to *machi* or *mura*. Two or more *mura* may consolidate to become *machi*, and *machi* become *shi*. Since *mura* are often subject to loss of area but seldom to gain, area changes would tend to inflate the birth rates of *mura* and so contribute to the observed high birth rates. Since *machi* gain from *mura* and lose to *shi*, the birth rates of their populations are subject to increase or to decrease by incorporation. If area changes were major factors, however, they would introduce capricious changes into the levels of fertility in *mura* at successive census dates. And, as we have indicated, the correlations at successive dates are very high, especially for the *mura*, where the theoretical problem is the greatest.

indicate that reproduction has been subject to appreciable limitation by factors of physiology or of culture.

The birth rates of the *shi*, the *machi*, and the *mura* within prefectures varied in conformity with cultural factors or forces of change that pervaded all segments of the prefectural populations. The correlations among the unadjusted birth rates were as follows:

Types of areas	*1930*	*1935*
Mura and *machi*	.91	.88
Shi and *machi*	.81	.75
Shi and *mura*	.78	.74

The decline in fertility that characterized the Japanese between 1925 and 1935 extended throughout all types of minor civil divisions. However, the declines in the *shi* were more consistent than those in the *machi* and the *mura*. The correlations between the levels of the birth rates in the minor civil divisions within prefectures in 1930 and the declines from 1930 to 1935 were as follows:

Area	*Amount of change*	*Per cent of change*
Prefectures	.44	.36
Shi	.64	.63
Machi	.40	.38
Mura	.47	.42

These relations between birth rates and changes in birth rates in *mura, machi,* and *shi* in 1930 and 1935 are factual, but the conclusion that fertility was declining somewhat more rapidly in *mura* with high fertility than in those with lower fertility is not necessarily valid. Urbanization operates to leave areas of higher fertility in contracting agricultural regions. Between 1930 and 1935, for instance, the population of *mura* was increasing in the high fertility regions of Tohoku, whereas the population of *mura* was decreasing in the lower fertility regions of central and southwest Japan. In view of the relation between contiguity to cities and incorporation and the correlated relation between nearness to cities and fertility, it is probable that *mura* with low fertility were more likely to be absorbed within *machi* or *shi* than were *mura* of higher fertility. Thus the greater selective disappearance of low fertility *mura* could create a spurious correlation between level and decline in birth rates in *mura*. Somewhat similar processes of selective absorption and transformation existed for *machi*. For *shi*, on the other hand, the decline in fertility was so great that it overrode the frequent absorption of once-rural people, whether through in-migration or incorporation.

The behavior of birth rates for *mura* and *machi* considered separately demonstrate the role in fertility decline of the transformation of the characteristics of areas as opposed to the altered behavior of individuals who remain in constant and comparable areas. In the period studied, declines in the birth rates of *machi* and *mura* were slight for the nation as a whole, yet the birth rates of *gun* which consisted of *machi* and *mura* were moving downward. The major process responsible was the differential increase of the population of the *machi* and the *mura* within the *gun*. The decline of the birth rate in the *gun* of Japan was associated with an urbanization of the population of the *gun*.

Migration, Urbanization, and Fertility

MIGRATION

Migration was the adjustment process whereby the rural areas maintained their traditional culture and the cities secured both their labor force and their cultural vitality. Low proportions of prefectural in-migrants in the resident population were associated with heavy dependence on agriculture and high fertility, whereas high proportions of prefectural in-migrants were associated with urbanization and low fertility.[43] This negative association between the predominance of the migrant and the level of fertility existed among the *gun* of the regions of Japan in the year 1930:

Region	*Coefficient of contingency*
All Japan minus Hokkaido and Okinawa	.49
Tohoku	.30
Kanto	.60
Hokuriku	.43
Tosan	.72
Tokai	.59
Kinki	.65
Chugoku	.38
Shikoku	.22
Kyushu	.33

Again, there were substantial differences in the closeness of the association in the various regions. Dependence on agriculture and stability were interrelated variables, as were dependence on industry or commerce and mobility. The causal factors involved in residential stability were not identical with those involved in the predominance of agriculture, however, and so the relations between these two variables and fertility were not constant. In general, the proportion of in-migrants in the population bore little relation to fertility or to dependence on agriculture when the proportion of in-migrants was low. High proportions of in-migrants were associated with low fertility, except where migrants were engaged in mining or other occupations that preserved the physical conditions, institutions, and values of the old society.

URBANIZATION

Urbanization had a dual influence on national fertility. Lesser rates of childbearing in urban areas influenced national fertility through declines in the fertility of those who were and remained urban. In addition, the urban proportion of the total population was increasing rapidly, so that the lower fertility rates for urban women applied to increasing portions of the total population. In the period prior to the China War, the major influence of urbanization on fertility occurred through the increasing proportions of the population residing in urban areas, rather than through declines in the fertility of a constant urban population. Between 1920 and 1935 the average annual increase in the number of women aged from 15 to 49 amounted to 1.4 per cent for Japan as a whole. This national figure was the result of an average annual increase of 5.6 per cent in the number of women in reproductive ages in the *shi*, a decrease of one-fifth of 1 per cent in the number of women in these ages in the *gun*. Within cities grouped according to size, the average annual percentage change was −0.3 for cities of less than 50 thousand, 5.0 for cities of from 50 thousand to 100 thousand, 9.5 for cities of 100 thousand and over (excluding the six great cities), and 5.9 for the six great cities.

The influence of urbanization on national fertility may be

[43] Place of birth for minor civil divisions, 1930: Nihon. Naikaku tokei-kyoku. *Showa go'nen kokusei chosa hokoku.* IV.4. *Fu, ken hen.* Tables 7, 8.

illustrated by three hypothetical assumptions. The initial one involves an unchanging situation with reference to fertility and the size of the urban population in the twenty years between 1920 and 1940.[44] The number of women living in *shi* remains the same in 1920, 1930, and 1940, the entire national increase being absorbed in *gun*. There are no changes in the age-specific fertility of women in either *shi* or *gun*, these two remaining constant at 1920 levels. Under these conditions of stability, the national gross reproduction rate would increase slightly, from 2.70 in 1920 to 2.74 in 1940.[45] By assumption, all the natural increase of the nation would have accumulated in the *gun* and the proportion of all women reproducing at the levels of the *gun* would have been increased. In this hypothetical situation of unchanging fertility in *shi* and *gun* combined with the absence of any increase in the population of the *shi*, the number of births in 1940 would have been 40 per cent higher than the number in 1920.

In the second assumed situation, fertility declines in *shi* and in *gun*, but the populations of *shi* remain constant from 1920 to 1935.[46] Here, there is an assumption of declining fertility without migration to the cities. Under these conditions, the gross reproduction rates for Japan as a whole would be 2.70 in 1920, 2.61 in 1925, 2.43 in 1930, and 2.37 in 1935. The decline in national fertility would be blunted, in contrast to reality, where declining fertility and migration operated concurrently to reduce the fertility of the total population.

In the third situation, fertility in *shi* and *gun* remains unchanged at 1920 levels but the relative population of the *shi* increases as it actually did. There is an assumption of unchanging fertility in *shi* and *gun* under conditions of rapid urban growth. In this case, the gross reproduction rates for the nation would have been 2.70 in 1920, 2.67 in 1925, 2.64 in 1930, and 2.56 in 1935.

A comparison of these hypothetical gross reproduction rates permits a rough allocation of numerical significance to declining age-specific reproductive performance in *shi* and *gun* as contrasted with urbanization, defined solely as increase in the population living in *shi*. In the first estimates, there was neither declining fertility nor urbanization. In the second estimates, there was declining fertility but not urbanization. In the third estimates, there was urbanization but not declining fertility. In the years from 1920 to 1935, almost one-third of the decline in the fertility of the population of Japan was associated with an increase in the proportion of the women living in *shi* rather than with changes in the rates of child-bearing among women in *shi* and *gun*.

THE INTERRELATIONS

The declining fertility that accompanied industrialization and urbanization was not a uniform response of people to impersonal forces of transformation. Fertility declined insofar as the new forces altered the living conditions, the institutions, and the attitudes and values of the people. If the ways of living and thinking continued as of old, declines in fertility were slight. In the late years of Imperial Japan, the ancient culture with its mores of abundant reproduction survived not only among peasants in remote villages, but in the slums of great cities where former peasants worked as family units and preserved the status structures and values of the historic culture in the physical surroundings of "urban" life.

The rapidity of the decline in fertility was related to the extent of the economic and cultural changes that influenced individuals and families. Industrial employment and urban residence that left cultural milieu and values untouched had little influence on fertility. As industrialization and urbanization developed, increasing proportions of the population were influenced directly or indirectly by them. Economic inadequacy, cultural stability, intellectual quiescence, and high fertility became an associated complex of life and values among ever more limited groups. The economic and cultural changes were not confined to geographic area, occupation, or social structure. It is in this sense that the experience of Japan suggests that declining fertility is a necessary correlate of industrialization and urbanization.

[44] These computations assume mortality at the changing levels which characterized the total Japanese population of Japan during the period.

[45] It should be noted that the national gross reproduction rates presented here are based on age schedules of fertility that are the sum of urban and rural births as separately estimated. This sum differs somewhat from the more precise national estimates utilized for the computation of the rates used in previous sections of this chapter.

[46] This hypothesis is limited to the period from 1920 to 1935 because the allocation procedures for the armed forces in the 1940 census altered the urban population through the allocation to their rural areas of origin of many rural in-migrants who were inducted in cities.

CHAPTER XIII

The Control of Fertility

THE facts concerning declining fertility of the Japanese were considered in the preceding chapter. Emphasis was placed on levels of fertility at the beginning of the census period and declines between 1920 and 1955. In 1920 the fertility of Japan was far below that of the still agrarian peoples of the Asian mainland and the major islands of the Western Pacific and Southeast Asia. Differences in fertility within the country were great, and they were those to be expected on the basis of Western experience. Fertility was highest in the agricultural areas, where the old society persisted in a nearly intact form; it was lowest in the upper social and economic groups in large cities. As industrialization and urbanization proceeded in the years after 1920, there were changes in the culture, in the milieu, and presumably in the psychological reactions of the Japanese. These changes were conducive to declining fertility.

The matter of limitations to fertility within a society is far broader than the specific practices designed to permit coitus without conception or to eliminate the embryo at some time between conception and extra-uterine viability. Major deterrents lie in the nature of the definitions of acceptable relations between men and women and in the extent of the deviations of behavior from stated codes. In the social structure of Japan, adherence to the codes of propriety removes the single, the widowed, the separated, and the divorced from the reproductive population. The absence of husbands removes married women from the category of those who can properly bear children. Hence any changes in the relative proportions of the marital status groups in the population alters the reproductive performance of the population as a whole, provided all other factors remain constant. Any separations of husbands and wives lessen the births to married women in rather direct relationship to the ages of the wives and the duration of the separation, again on the assumption that all other factors remain constant.

There were widespread discrepancies in Japan between actual behavior and actions that were consistent with the ideals of the family system. Some of the sex relations outside the family were sanctioned by the rules of the old society, while others occurred in defiance of those rules. There was non-conformity to the familistic ideal that was disapproved by members of both the old and the new society. Again, assuming that all other conditions remained unchanged, altered frequencies of relations between the sexes outside marriage resulted in roughly proportionate changes in the numbers of children resulting from such relations.

At no period of Japanese history has reproductive performance corresponded precisely to that anticipated on the basis of a direct relation between sex activities and reproductive performance. In the late Tokugawa *bakufu* and the early Restoration period there was widespread infanticide and abortion. The differences in the fertility of residential and occupational groups within Japan a quarter of a century ago imply family limitation among broad segments of the married population. The continuing declines in fertility suggest that increasing proportions of couples were taking increasingly effective actions of some sort to break the ancient associations between family life and childbearing. There may have been an increasing practice of complete or periodic abstinence, but it is difficult to accept this as an adequate explanation. It is necessary to assume an increasing prevalence of what may be designated as overt practice of limitation, whether contraception, abortion, or sterilization.

It is reasonable to assume that all factors of decline were interrelated. The culture was an integrated one, and the sex behavior of individuals formed patterns that tended to persist through adult life.

The analysis of the limitation of fertility presented in this chapter is quite formal. Emphasis is placed on the measurable factors associated with the declines in fertility that were occurring. The first step is a consideration of the role of the changing marital status of women and the increasing deficits of men in the reduction of fertility. Then follows a separate study of fertility outside marriage and the fertility of the married. Against this background of the structural transformations and their demographic correlates in live births, an analysis is made of the means used by the Japanese to secure the desired goals of birth limitation. Contraception, abortion, and sterilization are considered separately, and then as they operated in interrelation to reduce fertility to its present relatively low levels.

THE FACTORS IN DECLINE

CHANGING MARITAL STATUS

In 1920 and 1925 the regional distribution of fertility rates indicated higher levels of human reproduction in those areas where the agrarian order persisted without major modification, lower levels in those areas where urban residence and industrial employment signalized the development of the new culture and the new economy. Marriage postponement followed the same pattern. The marriage of girls at young ages was most frequent in the agricultural enclaves of Tohoku, where birth rates were highest. Postponement of marriage to the early or even the middle twenties was most frequent in the large urban centers, where birth rates were lowest.

Inspection of the proportions of women ever married in 1950 by age for prefectures classified by industrial type and for *shi* and *gun* will serve to recall the marriage habits of the Japanese (TABLE 102). The primary change between 1920 and 1950 was an advance in age at marriage rather than avoidance of marriage. For women below age 30, differences in fertility among regions at a given time and changes in fertility over time might be associated with differences in the proportions married. For women aged 30 and over, differential fertility could not be interpreted in terms of differences in

TABLE 102

Per cent of Japanese women ever married, prefectures by industrial type, *shi* and *gun*, 1950

		PREFECTURES BY INDUSTRIAL TYPE					TYPE OF AREA	
Ages	*All Japan*	*Metro-politan*	*Other industrial*	*Inter-mediate*	*Agricul-tural*	*Hokkaido*	*Shi*	*Gun*
15 and over	74.1	70.7	73.9	75.7	74.1	73.0	72.2	75.3
15-19	3.5	2.4	3.6	3.7	3.7	3.2	2.9	3.9
20-24	44.5	35.2	43.2	47.3	45.9	46.8	40.2	47.4
25-29	84.1	78.3	81.2	86.0	84.9	90.1	81.5	86.0
30-34	94.3	91.2	94.7	94.7	94.4	96.5	92.6	95.4
35-39	96.8	94.9	95.9	97.3	96.9	97.5	95.9	97.4
40-44	97.7	95.7	98.0	97.8	98.0	99.0	96.8	98.3
45 and over	98.4	97.7	98.7	98.2	98.2	99.4	98.0	98.5

Source: Nihon. Sori-fu, tokei-kyoku. *Showa 25-nen kokusei chosa hokoku.* III.1. Table 28.

marriage frequencies. The single women had virtually disappeared by age 30, but the loss of husbands through death was becoming frequent enough to depress fertility.

If differences in marital status were involved in the differences in fertility among the prefectures, there should be a positive relation between proportions married at ages under 25 and age-specific fertility, a negative relation between proportions widowed or separated at ages 30 or 35 and over and age-specific fertility. Changes in fertility over time should reflect the divergent influences of the changing proportions of the single at the younger ages and the changing proportions of the widowed in the middle and upper ages. These anticipated relations existed in 1930. In that year the fertility of women in prefectures and in cities was related rather directly to the prevalence of the single in the early years of the reproductive period, more remotely to the prevalence of widowhood and separation in the later years of the period. The relations between fertility and marital status were slight in the years of maximum reproduction, roughly from age 25 to age 34.[1]

The relation between age-specific fertility and marital status should be most direct in a population without planned limitation of fertility. As family planning becomes more widespread and the techniques used more effective, the closeness of the associations should decrease. Moreover, in a population subject to rapidly declining mortality, widowhood should become less and less of a factor in the levels of childbearing achieved by older women. In the published statistics of Japan there are few possibilities for direct testing of these hypotheses. Numbers of births by age of mothers in the prefectures have been published for 1925 and 1930. The marital status of women in the prefectures has been published for the censuses from 1920 through 1940 and for 1950, but not for the intermediate censuses of 1944, 1945, 1946, and 1947. The measurement of declines in fertility and their associations with marital status thus requires an indirect approach. One might assume a maximum level of fertility that would exist among married women if they lived continuously with their husbands and made no efforts to limit conceptions or to avert the consequences of conceptions in later live births. However, premodern fertility in Japan did not approach maximal levels. Since the primary interest lies in the further limitation of births that occurred with modernization, measures of absolute limitation are not essential.

The difficulties of measurement are avoided if the problem is defined as the measurement of the declines in fertility that occurred in the last quarter-century or so. Data are available on legitimate and illegitimate births by age of father and mother in the prefectures and large cities in 1925. Thus it is possible to compare the number of births in later years with those that would have occurred if reproduction had continued at the levels of 1925.[2] Subtraction of the actual number of births from the hypothetical number gives the deficit of births associated with the increasing dispersion or intensity of the factors operating to reduce fertility.[3] The ratio of the deficit as thus determined to the number expected at 1925 levels of fertility gives a measure of relative decline. The over-all figures on deficits of births for the years from 1930 through 1955 are as follows:[4]

	DEFICITS TO WOMEN		DEFICITS TO MEN	
Year	*Number (in '000)*	*Per 100 expected births*	*Number (in '000)*	*Per 100 expected births*
1930	235	9.8	161	6.9
1935	405	15.5	308	12.2
1940	621	22.4	456	17.5
1947	560	17.3	46	1.7

[1] Correlations between age-specific fertility and proportions single in the prefecture were as follows: 15-19, —.97; 20-24, —.86; 25-29, —.08; 30-34, —.19; 35-39, —.11. Comparable correlations for cities of 100 thousand and over were of less magnitude but persisted to higher ages: —.85 at age 15-19; —.77 at age 20-24; —.34 at age 25-29. Correlations between age-specific fertility and the proportions married were positive: .85 at 20-24; .20 at 25-29; .38 at 30-34; .40 at 35-39; .39 at 40-44; .14 at 45-49.

[2] This is not a precise statement, for the persistence of the age-specific birth rates of 1925 would have led to increasing numbers of girls aged 15 by 1940 and from that time onward to rapidly increasing numbers of women in the ages that were being subjected to the high fertility rates of the year 1925. In our illustration, the rates of the year 1925 are applied to the enumerated or estimated population of women in the year in question, without allowances for the cumulative impact of the maintenance of high fertility on numbers of women.

[3] The detailed data for 1925 are given in: Nihon. Naikaku tokei-kyoku. *Fubo no nenrei betsu shussei tokei. Taisho 14-nen.*

[4] Expected numbers of births were secured by applying the age-specific rates as of 1925 for women in quinquennial ages from 15 to 49 and for men in quinquennial ages from 20 to 59. The age distributions used were those of the respective censuses and, for the postcensal years, the official estimates of the Bureau of Statistics. Numbers of births from the schedule reports for 1955 were increased by the ratio of schedule to final reports for 1953 and 1954.

	DEFICITS TO WOMEN		DEFICITS TO MEN	
Year	*Number (in '000)*	*Per 100 expected births*	*Number (in '000)*	*Per 100 expected births*
1950	1,086	31.7	479	17.0
1951	1,364	39.0	749	26.0
1952	1,559	43.9	946	31.9
1953	1,773	48.9	1,168	38.3
1954	1,962	52.6	1,347	43.3
1955	2,057	54.3	1,492	46.3

If the women of Japan had continued to live in a culture without deficits of men, had married, separated, and become widowed in the same proportions as the women alive in 1925, and had maintained the same age-specific fertility—both legitimate and illegitimate—as the women of 1925, live births in 1955 would have been more than twice as numerous as they were. Changes in the relative numbers of men and women, in the marital status of women, in the rates of conception in and outside marriage, and in the incidence of abortions had reduced live births to little more than half the number that would have occurred if no additional factors or forces of limitation had entered the population after 1925.

The relation of deficits of men to the marital status and the fertility of women is apparent in the fact that the ratios of actual births to those expected at 1925 levels of fertility were much higher for men than for women. In 1955, for instance, the hypothetical deficit amounted to 54 per cent for women, 46 per cent for men. In the years from 1930 to 1935 there was some migration outside Japan; by 1935 there had been some losses of men in military action. In these years, however, the separation of the sexes and excessive death rates among men were relatively minor factors. Even in 1940, disturbances in the balance of the sexes in Japan were not the major factor depressing marital relationships and rates of childbearing among women. In that year the hypothetical deficit in births to men was 78 per cent that in births to women. In the postwar years there were appreciable surpluses of women, some of them widowed, some of them single, who had to remain so because of the paucity of men in the population. In 1947, when first births to the newly married and additional births to reunited families might have been expected to produce maximal reproduction in the married population, deficits of births to men were slight, less than 2 per 100 expected births. For women, on the other hand, births were 17.3 per cent below the expected levels. In the years after 1947 there were compensatory movements in the marriage rates for men and women, the marriage ages for men being reduced and a high proportion of the widowed and the separated men marrying again. With the increase in contraceptive practices, abortion, and sterilization, numbers of births fell sharply below the levels expected at the age-specific fertility of 1925. By 1950 the deficits to men were more than half as great as those to women; in 1951, deficits to men were two-thirds those to women. In 1955 the deficits of births to men were 72 per cent as great as those to women, a relation quite comparable to that of the years from 1930 to 1940. Deficits of men were responsible for a minor part of the declines in fertility that occurred between 1925 and 1955.

Something as to the relative incidence of the declines in fertility associated with the postponement of marriage and the limitation of fertility within marriage can be deduced from the changes in the levels of reproduction to women of various ages. Increasing proportions of the single among younger women would lead to declining numbers of births to all women in the younger ages. Births to women in the twenties would be influenced by the changing age at marriage, with its correlated changes in the age at which first births occurred. In the ages at which all women were or had been married, however, declines in numbers of births would indicate limitation of fertility among the married, unless widowhood and separations removed increasing numbers of women from the childbearing population.[5] In the following tabulation, percentage differences between actual births and those expected at the age-specific levels of 1925 are given for each age group of women for 1947, 1950, and 1954:

Age of women	*1947*	*1950*	*1954*
15-49	−17.3	−31.7	−52.6
15-19	−70.0	−73.2	−87.0
20-24	−30.8	−33.2	−52.6
25-29	−0.9	−12.5	−32.7
30-34	−1.8	−26.5	−50.0
35-39	−14.1	−42.9	−69.0
40-44	−27.6	−54.6	−81.1
45-49	−47.7	−80.7	−93.0

The greatest declines in fertility have occurred among the youngest and the oldest of the age groups of women in the reproductive ages. Reproduction has become increasingly a function of women in the central span of the reproductive period, roughly from age 25 to 34. In these years in Japan most women are married. It is particularly significant, therefore, that in 1950 and later years major declines in fertility were occurring among women aged from 25 to 29 and from 30 to 34. As between the two groups, the major declines occurred in births to women aged from 30 to 34.

Thus far the analysis of hypothetical declines in fertility below 1925 levels has been in terms of relative changes in births to women of various ages. The numerical significance of relative declines depends on the magnitude of the childbearing that existed among the age groups of women. As early as 1925, childbearing at the younger ages was limited by the widespread postponement of marriage to the late teens and the early twenties. Childbearing at the older ages was limited both by the changing physiological capacities of the women and by the attitude that women over forty should not have children. In the prewar years, the proportionate declines in fertility were greatest in the ages at which rates of reproduction were least. In the years from 1947 through 1954, rates of decline were increasing among those age groups of women where childbearing was highest. As early as 1951, three-tenths of the deficit in births to all women was a deficit to women aged from 25 to 34. The percentage of the total birth deficits that occurred to mothers in specific ages illustrates the increasing numerical impact of the declines on women aged from 25 to 34:

Year	*All ages*	*Under 25*	*25-34*	*35 and over*
1947	100.	74.5	3.5	22.1
1948	100.	56.7	18.8	24.5
1949	100.	55.5	12.1	32.4

[5] If all other factors remained equal, one would expect an increase in fertility above 1925 levels among the older women. Declining mortality among men would reduce the proportion of widows, while declining proportions of separated and divorced among women would increase the proportion of the women exposed to the risk of conception.

Year	*All ages*	*Under 25*	*25-34*	*35 and over*
1950	100.	42.7	27.0	30.3
1951	100.	41.0	29.9	29.1
1952	100.	39.5	31.8	28.7
1953	100.	37.6	34.5	27.9
1954	100.	36.1	36.7	27.2

Advancing age at marriage, the losses of men during the war, and the limitation of fertility by the married were all involved in varying proportions in the fertility of women in the ages from 25 to 34 in the postwar years. The obvious next step is the measurement of declines in the fertility of married women below the levels expected on the basis of the reproductive performance of married women in 1925. The difficulty is that the marital status of the population of Japan is not available for any year between 1940 and 1950. Births to married women in 1940 were less than 5 per cent below those expected if the 1925 levels and age-patterns had persisted. By 1950 the deficit in births had increased to 21 per cent. Deficits were negligible for married women below age 25. There was a heavy concentration of the deficits among women aged 35 and over, although, as in total births to all women, an increasing proportion of the deficit could be attributed to women aged from 25 to 34.

In recent years, the fertility of Japanese women has not been normal in the sense that it reflected the orderly functioning of forces of stability and change. Fertility was depressed by major war losses among the young men who would have been in the ages of maximum fertility had they survived. Fertility was inflated by the heavy childbearing of recently established families and those reunited after the separations that accompanied war and defeat. However, the changing fertility of the years from 1947 to 1955 cannot be explained entirely in terms of changes in the marital status or the age and sex structure of the population. Rapidly declining fertility among women aged 35 or over cannot be explained in terms of changes in marital status during the years under study. The losses of the war cannot have been of major significance in a decline in births to women aged from 25 to 34 in the years from 1950 to 1955, for the war deaths occurred from 1937 to 1945. The most significant of the recent changes is the decline in total and in marital fertility to women aged from 25 to 34. Limitation has become a modal rather than a peripheral characteristic of reproduction.

Fertility Outside Marriage

There was an underlying assumption in the preceding section that a rather direct relation existed between marital status and fertility, that increasing proportions either of the single or of the widowed meant corresponding reductions in the proportion of the population participating in reproduction. In a broad approach the neglect of illegitimacy is valid. Whatever the patterns of sex relations in the remote past, the socially sanctioned relations of a monogamous family have been the nucleus of human reproduction in the modern period of Japan. Illegitimacy occurred, however, and as late as 1920 it accounted for 8 per cent of all live births. Demographic interpretation of this figure is difficult, for illegitimate births resulted from unions whose respective positions in the structure of Japanese society differed widely. The institution of the *ie* provided for its own preservation through implicit sanction of illegitimacy to yield heirs when familial reproduction was inadequate or lacking. Non-conformity to the codes of the family also occurred. Some of the forms of non-conformity were structured within the context of the *ie*, while others represented deviate behavior. Insofar as the familistic codes remained guides to action, some portion of the births that were technically illegitimate were in reality familial reproduction.

The decline in the proportion of births classified as illegitimate indicates an increasing conformity to the legal codes of the greater society. The proportions of illegitimate among all births declined as follows:[6]

Year	*Total*	*Recognized illegitimate*[7]	*Strictly illegitimate*[7]
1920	8.2	3.4	4.8
1925	7.3	3.9	3.4
1930	6.4	3.9	2.6
1935	5.7	3.7	2.0
1940	4.1	2.7	1.4
1947	3.8	2.2	1.6
1948	3.2	—	—
1949	2.7	—	—
1950	2.5	—	—
1951	2.2	—	—
1952	2.0	—	—
1953	1.9	—	—
1954	1.7	—	—

Declining proportions of illegitimate births conform to simple interpretations if the purview is broad. Difficulties arise with analysis of the separate trends for recognized and strictly illegitimate births. The recognized illegitimate births resulted from unions where marriage did not occur but where the father assumed legal responsibility for the child, often rearing it in his legal family. The child so recognized had many of the prerogatives of legitimacy, and bore few of the stigma of illegitimacy. In some instances the mother was a concubine; marriage could not occur because the father had a legitimate wife. In other instances marriage was not desired by the father or his family, but responsibility dictated recognition of the child. In either case, the statistical enigma is the mother of the illegitimate child recognized as legitimate by the father. No information concerning her was entered in the *koseki* of the father of the child, and no information concerning the paternity of the child was entered in the *koseki* of the family of the mother.

Illegitimate births recognized by the father constituted 3.4 per cent of all reported live births in 1920. This percentage increased slowly to 4.0 in 1927 and declined slowly to 3.8 in 1934. Declines then became sharper. In 1940 recognized illegitimate births were 2.7 per cent of all births. In 1947 there was again a classification of illegitimate births according to the regulations for the *koseki* and the status of the child. In that year, 2.2 per cent of all births were illegitimate but recognized. During this period the civil code was revised. It was thought that the "recognized" classification of illegitimate births implied a recognition of concubinage and thus was a symbol of the degradation of wives. The separation of illegiti-

[6] Source: 1920-1935: Nihon. Naikaku tokei-kyoku. *Résumé statistique du mouvement de la population de l'Empire du Japon.* 1936-1943: *Ibid. Jinko dotai tokei.* 1947—: Nihon. Kosei-sho, eisei tokei-bu. *Jinko dotai tokei.*

[7] A recognized illegitimate birth is one recognized by the father and entered in the *koseki* of his *ie*; the strictly illegitimate birth is not recognized by the father and is either entered in the *koseki* of the *ie* of the mother or in a new *koseki* established by the mother for herself and the child. See the discussions of the family system (Chapter VI) and marriage (Chapter XI).

mate births by type according to recognition was not mentioned in the new civil code. Thereafter births in Japan, as in the United States, were divided into the simple dichotomy of the legitimate and the illegitimate.

The changing prevalence of behavior regarded as proper and of that assumed to reflect immorality is also evident in the levels and trends of the strictly illegitimate births. The illegitimate birth might occur in a socially sanctioned union where the marriage had not been recorded in the *koseki*. In this case, illegitimacy was an artifact of the requirements for and the attitudes toward registration. On the other hand, the illegitimate birth might result from illicit relations defined as such in the social situation. In 1920, almost 5 per cent of all births were strictly illegitimate. From 1920 to 1947 decline was continuous and rapid. The proportion of strictly illegitimate births in relation to total births was cut in half between 1920 and 1932. The proportion in 1932 was reduced more than one-third by 1942. There was some increase in the early postwar years, but the number of illegitimate births per 100 total births was only 1.6 in 1947 as compared with 1.4 in 1940. Here, as in the case of the recognized illegitimate births, the assignment of priorities to the factors involved in the decline is difficult. The increasing prevalence of early registration of marriages would result in a substantial reduction of technically illegitimate births to informally married couples. The wider knowledge of contraceptive practices and the availability of abortions might result in lesser rates of childbearing among the unmarried. Even in the prewar period, abortions may have become more frequent as the development of the urban and industrial society intensified the social stigma that attached to the unmarried mother and the illegitimate child. These explanations are speculative, but the fact of decline is not. Birth rates have declined far below the levels of the early 1920's, and a greatly reduced proportion of those births are illegitimate by either the modern or the ancient definition of the term.

The relative prevalence of illegitimacy in great cities and in the remainder of the country corroborates the impression gained from national trends that the institutional forces of the old society were not the sole regulators of extra-marital conduct. The extent of individual conformity or departure from accepted mores of sex behavior seems to account for many of the variations and trends in illegitimacy (TABLE 103). In the early 1920's, illegitimacy was more prevalent in the great cities than in the remainder of the country, but as the cities became a normal part of the life of the industrializing society, the percentages of births that were illegitimate dropped at a more rapid rate in the great cities than outside them. It should be noted, however, that the greatest decline in the large cities was in the strictly illegitimate births. In this sphere of reproductive behavior, great cities and other areas had achieved a relative equality of proportions by the early 1930's. It was the recognized illegitimate birth, which presumably reflected the survival of ancient institutional forms in the modern world, that maintained its relative numerical superiority in the large cities.

The relations between reproduction within and outside the legal family seem reasonable if we examine the situations in which the Japanese found themselves during these decades. The custom of postponing the registration of marriage until pregnancy or childbirth introduced hazards that were especially great for girls in the large cities. In villages the status of the family and the public opinion of the community tended to ensure ethical treatment of the pregnant girl by the man involved. In the anonymity of large cities such protection was greatly reduced, if not lacking entirely. The village habits persisted, however, the sequence of behavior moving from the unrecorded marriage to the pregnancy of the wife and then the decision as to whether or not to register the marriage. If the man or his family did not wish to conform to the requirements of the situation, the position of the girl was very difficult. Since the values of the *ie* dictated that she be repudiated, return to the village was not always possible. Moreover, the disgrace of an illegitimate conception stimulated a movement of pregnant girls to the cities, either with or without the connivance of their families. There was a fairly high incidence of illegitimacy in the great cities in the 1920's and the early 1930's. As conditions developed that should have been conducive to increases in illegitimacy in the cities, admitted illegitimacy declined far more rapidly than it did outside the great cities, until in the years after 1935 the differences were slight. Perhaps another process of urbanization was operative here. The development of the great city may have generated leavens of tolerance that were missing in the villages. A more diffused humanitarianism plus concepts of public welfare and legal assignments of responsibilities may have led to a wider practice of recognition of the illegitimate child by the father. It may be significant that the proportion of all births which were illegitimate yet recognized by the father remained relatively unchanged at from 3.1 to 3.7 per cent of all births from 1923 through 1938. In the great cities, on the other hand, recognized illegitimate births declined from more than 5 per cent of all births in the years prior to 1930 to 3.8 per cent in 1937 and 3.6 per cent in 1938.

Since the values of the Japanese gave priority to boy babies, it may be worth while to examine the sex ratio of legitimate, recognized illegitimate, and strictly illegitimate births for clues as to the processes involved in the changing frequencies. It was possible to postpone the recording of a marriage until the baby was born and then to record marriage and birth simultaneously without jeopardy to the legitimacy status of the child. It might be argued, therefore, that marriage would be more likely to occur in cases in which the baby was a boy. If such a selective process was operative, it was not of sufficient magnitude to be apparent in the sex ratios of legitimate live births. It can also be argued on theoretical grounds that the baby would be more likely to be recognized by the father if it were a son. If this were so, the sex ratio of recognized illegitimate births should favor males more than that of all live births, whereas the sex ratio of the strictly illegitimate births should indicate a predominance of females. These relations existed in Japan in the years prior to the Pacific War. However, the deviations of sex ratios in recognized illegitimate and legitimate births are so small as to suggest that the sex of the live-born offspring was not the determining factor in marriage or recognition.

The hazards to the status of women and children inherent in the social structure of Japan are apparent in the numbers of strictly illegitimate per 100 legitimate live births by ages of mothers in 1930:[8]

Age of mother	*All Japan*	*Communes of 100,000 and over*	*Remainder of country*
15-19	11.0	13.3	10.7
20-24	3.5	4.5	3.3

[8] Source: Nihon. Naikaku tokei-kyoku. *Fubo no nenrei betsu shussei oyobi shisan tokei, Showa go'nen.*

TABLE 103

Illegitimacy status of live births, by type, large cities and remainder of the country, 1923-1938
(Illegitimate births per 100 live births)

	COMMUNES, 100,000 AND OVER			REMAINDER OF THE COUNTRY		
Year	*Total*	*Recognized*	*Other*	*Total*	*Recognized*	*Other*
1923	10.7	5.3	5.4	7.4	3.7	3.7
1924	10.2	5.4	4.8	7.3	3.7	3.6
1925	10.2	5.5	4.6	6.9	3.6	3.3
1926	10.0	5.7	4.3	6.7	3.7	3.0
1927	9.7	5.7	4.0	6.6	3.7	2.9
1928	9.1	5.4	3.6	6.4	3.7	2.7
1929	8.8	5.4	3.5	6.3	3.7	2.6
1930	8.6	5.3	3.3	6.1	3.6	2.5
1931	7.9	5.0	2.9	6.1	3.7	2.4
1932	7.7	5.0	2.7	5.8	3.4	2.3
1933	7.0	4.6	2.4	5.9	3.6	2.3
1934	6.8	4.5	2.3	5.8	3.6	2.2
1935	6.3	4.3	2.0	5.6	3.5	2.1
1936	6.1	4.1	2.0	5.4	3.4	2.0
1937	5.5	3.8	1.8	5.0	3.2	1.8
1938	5.3	3.6	1.7	4.8	3.1	1.7

Source: Nihon. Naikaku tokei-kyoku. *Jinko dotai tokei.* 1920-1938. Also: *Ibid. Resume statistique du mouvement de la population de l'Empire du Japon.* 1920-1938.

Age of mother	*All Japan*	*Communes of 100,000 and over*	*Remainder of country*
25-29	1.9	2.6	1.7
30-34	1.8	2.3	1.7
35-39	2.1	2.8	2.0
40-44	2.5	3.6	2.4
45-49	6.2	7.6	6.0

Illegitimacy was more prevalent in communes of 100 thousand and over than in the remainder of the country at all ages. However, the age concentration of the incidence of illegitimacy is much more striking than the city-country differences. Illegitimacy was particularly high among mothers under age 20. There was a sharp decline at age 20 to 24, a further slow decline until age 30 to 34, a slow increase to age 40 to 44, and then a sharp increase at age 45 to 49. The high rates in the younger ages would be expected if illegitimate births occurred to mothers whose marriages were not registered; they would also be expected if illegitimate births represented violations of the mores. The increased rates of illegitimacy at the older ages imply deviate relations by widowed and separated women. It may be that illegitimacy involves a continuation of ancient practices into a milieu in which they are no longer appropriate. There is no doubt but that it also involves violations of the codes of the *ie*.

The prevalence of recognized illegitimate births to very young and quite old fathers is even more striking than the inequalities in the distribution of the strictly illegitimate births to the very young and quite old mothers. In 1930, the numbers of recognized illegitimate births per 100 legitimate births were as follows:

Age of father	*All Japan*	*Communes of 100,000 and over*	*Remainder of country*
15-19	17.2	39.2	16.3
20-24	7.6	12.3	7.1
25-29	4.4	6.2	4.1
30-34	3.3	4.6	3.1
35-39	3.0	4.3	2.8
40-44	3.2	4.6	3.0
45-49	4.4	6.4	4.1
50-54	7.9	10.9	7.5
55-59	15.1	21.8	14.2

This is not the age distribution of fathers that would characterize recognized illegitimacy if the phenomenon represented traditional concubinage. Neither is it the age incidence that would be expected if substantial proportions of the men who labored in cities left legal families in the villages and had children by concubines in the cities. Recognized illegitimacy was most widespread among births to very young fathers whose resources were inadequate for the responsibilities of marriage. It was high again among births to fathers aged 50 or over. Recognized illegitimacy, like strict illegitimacy, reflected in major part deviate behavior in an urbanizing society.

Data on the legitimacy status of births support the conclusion that the limitation of illegitimate births proceeded more rapidly than the limitation of legitimate births. There are two possible explanations: one in terms of a more rigid channeling of sex relations within marriage; the other in terms of a breaking of the association between sex relations and fertility among the unmarried and the widowed. As a basis for the selection of the correct alternative, we present the number of illegitimate births per 100 total births, by age of mother, for 1947, 1950, and 1954:

Age of women	*1947*	*1950*	*1954*
15-49	3.8	2.5	1.7
15-19	12.9	9.0	6.9
20-24	5.1	2.6	1.7
25-29	3.3	2.0	1.3
30-34	2.8	2.3	1.7
35-39	2.9	2.5	2.6
40-44	3.2	2.6	3.0
45-49	5.5	3.3	3.8

These figures suggest that illegitimacy is associated primarily with forces other than conformity to the institutional arrangements of the old society. In the years from 1947 to 1954 there was an extraordinary decline in the number of illegitimate births per 1,000 total women. The magnitude and the age characteristics of this decline were similar to those in total fertility, but they were more rapid. The extension of the practice of contraception and abortion seems to have been a factor in the limitation of fertility outside marriage as well as within it.

If contraception and abortion postpone the premarital conception or birth which is the stimulus to legal marriage, it is possible that they are also factors in the advance in the age of marriage which has been so characteristic a feature of demographic evolution in Japan. While the availability of modern means of limitation may have contributed to the decline of illegitimate births in recent years, it does not appear probable that such availability would be a major element in the postponement of marriage among the vast majority of the people. It does seem probable that the factors conducive to postponement of marriage and those conducive to effective limitation of fertility within marriage are similar. If so, any distinction between the forces involved in the postponement of marriage and those involved in the reduction of the fertility of the married is artificial.

The Fertility of the Married

In a pure type of ancestor-oriented familism there would be few volitional deterrents to the fertility of married women. Fertility would be responsive to factors that lessened the frequency of relations between the sexes, reduced conceptions, or increased fetal and neonatal mortality. There would be few variations according to the social and economic characteristics of the areas of residence. In more specific terms, if Japanese patriarchal familism were in fact what it should be in theory, the fertility of married women would have few relations to industrialization or urbanization.

AGE-SPECIFIC MARITAL FERTILITY, 1925-1950

Whatever the relations between marital fertility and environmental factors may have been in the nineteenth century, by 1925 and 1930 the primary variations in the fertility of married women within Japan were associated with economic and social rather than with physiological factors. For each age of women, marital fertility was less in cities of 100 thousand and over than in the remainder of the country. And for each age of women in cities of 100 thousand and over and outside such cities, fertility was lower in 1930 than it had been in 1925. The numbers of legitimate female births per 1,000 married women were as follows:[9]

	ALL JAPAN		CITIES OF 100,000 AND OVER	
Age	*1925*	*1930*	*1925*	*1930*
15-49	105.6	101.2	94.2	85.3
15-19	157.1	146.7	147.9	117.4
20-24	164.8	161.4	144.8	137.2
25-29	145.5	137.9	124.4	115.0
30-34	124.2	116.1	101.0	90.9
35-39	95.7	88.6	74.6	64.2
40-44	42.7	40.6	31.6	27.1
45-49	7.6	6.4	6.8	5.2

The differences in the legitimate fertility of married women, like the differences in the total fertility of all women, were associated closely with the transition from the agricultural to the industrial economy and society (Table 104). The differences in marital fertility among metropolitan, other industrial, intermediate, and agricultural prefectures were substantial indeed, and they characterized married women in all ages of the reproductive period. It should be emphasized that these relations existed a quarter of a century ago.

The critical question raised by the inverse relation between industrialization and marital fertility is that of the prevalence of family limitation. It is difficult to explain the situation if one discards the assumption that there were widespread practices of limitation among the married as early as 1925, and that these practices increaesed along with the movement from the agricultural to the industrial society, from the rural area to the city.

It should be noted that postponement of marriage and limitations of fertility within marriage have emerged again as interrelated aspects of social and economic change. Areas with the lowest proportions of the married at the younger ages had the lowest fertility among the married at these ages, whereas areas that had preserved the habit of early marriage maintained high fertility among the married.

The age-specific marital fertility in the prefectures and large cities in 1925 and 1930 corroborates the broad picture secured by grouping the prefectures along an agricultural-industrial continuum. There were positive associations between the proportions married at the successive ages and the fertility of the married at those ages. Marital fertility was high in those prefectures with large proportions of the population resident in communes of 10 thousand or less. It was relatively low in prefectures where the proportions of in-migrants were low. These differences in the fertility of married women existed despite the fact that there were surpluses of men in the in-migrant areas and deficits of men in the out-migrant areas.

[9] The numbers of legitimate and strictly illegitimate births by ages of mothers for prefectures and cities of 100 thousand and over were published in the following sources: Nihon. Naikaku tokei-kyoku. *Fubo no nenrei betsu shussei tokei, Taisho 14-nen. Ibid. Fubo no nenrei betsu shussei oyobi shisan tokei, Showa go'nen.* The married women in the census data are the *de facto* married, whereas the legitimate births of the vital statistics include only those registered in *koseki*. The recognized illegitimate births were excluded, since the fact that the father recognized the child without marrying the mother is presumptive evidence that these births were illegitimate in the demographic sense that they were not the children of the wife of the man who made the recognition. The strictly illegitimate births were attributed to the married women, although a portion of them would be socially illegitimate in a Western definition rather than the children of socially sanctioned but non-registered unions. In the adjustments of the data on registered births for consistency with the numbers of births estimated from enumerated children, the malregistered births in each prefecture and city were assumed to be legitimate and to be comparable to legitimate births in distribution by age of mother. It should also be noted that the cities of 100 thousand and over were more numerous in 1930 than in 1925. However, the differences in age-specific marital fertility are not altered appreciably if the rates for 1930 are limited to the cities as of 1925.

TABLE 104

Legitimate female births per 1,000 married women, by age, prefectures by industrial type, 1925 and 1930

Prefectures by industrial type	*Ages 15-49*	QUINQUENNIAL AGES *15-19*	*20-24*	*25-29*	*30-34*	*35-39*	*40-44*	*45-49*
				1925				
Metropolitan	94.1	124.8	137.7	124.9	104.5	78.8	34.2	6.4
Other industrial	99.5	145.2	154.8	134.5	113.7	87.7	38.5	6.7
Intermediate	103.2	156.3	170.0	143.4	121.6	93.0	41.4	6.6
Agricultural	113.3	171.0	178.8	157.3	134.4	104.5	47.3	9.0
Hokkaido	120.1	169.0	177.1	152.5	131.5	105.8	52.9	10.7
				1930				
Metropolitan	88.6	116.2	137.5	118.4	96.3	69.0	29.9	5.3
Other industrial	93.3	129.3	149.9	127.1	105.4	78.8	35.6	5.7
Intermediate	98.6	146.6	161.0	137.0	114.5	86.9	39.2	5.6
Agricultural	110.6	161.6	177.1	153.3	131.0	101.3	46.8	7.4
Hokkaido	119.0	167.0	180.9	151.8	130.1	100.9	50.3	8.2

Source: Births: Nihon. Naikaku tokei-kyoku. *Fubo no nenrei betsu shussei tokei, Taisho 14-nen. Ibid. Fubo no nenrei betsu shussei oyobi shisan tokei, Showa go'nen.* Age distributions of married women: *Ibid. Taisho juyo'nen kokusei chosa hokoku. Fu ken hen.* Table 6. *Ibid. Showa go'nen kokusei chosa hokoku. Fu ken hen.* Table 6.

Within the cities of Japan the variations of fertility among the *ku* suggest that limitations to reproduction among the married were responses to a life regarded as offering opportunities rather than reactions to the pressures of poverty. In 1930 and 1935, for instance, marital fertility in Tokyo was low in the central residential *ku*, intermediate in the *ku* surrounding this central area, and high in the more prosperous residential *ku* to the south and west.[10] Ratios of 200 or more children below age 1 per 1,000 married women aged from 15 to 49 were found only in the low-income *ku* to the north and east, where families subsisted by household industry or by agriculture. The reactions of the families in the *ku* of Tokyo to differences in social and economic milieu were quite comparable to those of people in New York or Chicago, Birmingham or San Francisco.[11] Lower marital fertility, like lower total fertility, reflected distance from the household-oriented familism of the traditional culture rather than the pressures of economic poverty *per se*. Positive motivations rather than pressures were the important factors in the limitation of marital fertility.

These early limitations to marital fertility among the Japanese were responses to the new society, for they were associated positively with its manifestations in occupational transformation and residential relocation. There were major differences in marital fertility among the people in the agricultural prefectures, however, and these presumably reflected practices of limitation that had persisted from the old society.

The movement of age-specific rates of marital fertility in the last quarter of a century has been downward, very slowly in the years from 1925 to 1943, very rapidly in the years from 1947 to the present. The numbers of legitimate female births per 1,000 married women in selected years from 1925 to 1950 were as follows:[12]

Age of married women	*1925*	*1930*	*1940*	*1950*
15-49	105.6	101.2	98.6	81.5
15-19	157.1	146.7	151.0	145.8
20-24	164.8	161.4	161.9	158.8
25-29	145.5	137.9	145.5	135.8
30-34	124.2	116.1	117.4	93.7
35-39	95.7	88.6	82.8	52.1
40-44	42.7	40.6	36.5	17.3
45-49	7.6	6.4	5.8	1.0

In the nation as a whole there was relatively unchanging fertility of the married at ages under 25, decline at age 35 and over. In the postwar years there has been decline at age 25 to 34.

THE REPRODUCTIVE HISTORIES OF THE WOMEN OF 1950[13]

The information included in the 1950 census on numbers of children ever born to married women suggests that differential fertility has long characterized this population. Num-

[10] In the prefectural volumes of the various censuses there is a tabulation of the population in special ages, including those under age 1. In the prefectures with cities organized in *ku*, these age distributions are given for the *ku*. Marital status of women was available in quinquennial ages. For Tokyo, Kanagawa, Aichi, Hyogo, Osaka, and Kyoto prefectures, see: Nihon. Naikaku tokei-kyoku. *Showa go'nen kokusei chosa hokoku. Fu ken hen. Ibid. Showa ju'nen kokusei chosa hokoku. Fu ken hen.*

[11] The relationships between the socio-economic characteristics of the area of residence and marital fertility that existed in Tokyo characterized the different areas within the other great cities. In 1930 and in 1935 in each of the great cities there was a high degree of association between the level of general fertility and the level of marital fertility in the *ku*. Within the cities, high fertility was associated with the predominance of Western-type rather than of traditional industry.

[12] Rates are given only for years when there was census data on marital status.

[13] Nihon. Sori-fu, tokei-kyoku. *Showa 25-nen kokusei chosa hokoku.* III.1. *10% chushutsu shukei kekka, sono ichi. Danjo betsu, nenrei, haigu kankei, kokuseki mata wa shusshin-chi, kyoiku,*

bers of children born per 1,000 ever-married Japanese women in the various age groups were as follows:

Age of women	*All Japan*	Shi	Gun
15-19	493	500	490
20-24	936	876	970
25-29	1,691	1,571	1,773
30-34	2,745	2,498	2,916
35-39	3,762	3,321	4,054
40-44	4,491	3,855	4,896
45-49	4,764	4,076	5,200
50-54	4,785	4,094	5,195
55-59	4,762	4,165	5,083
60 and over	4,622	4,280	4,775

Several significant facts are revealed by this simple summary compilation from the first nation-wide census data on fertility. For the nation as a whole, the average number of children ever born per ever-married women was below 5 for the cohort of women who had reached age 15 in the year 1905. There is no evidence here that Japanese fertility in the twentieth century has been as high as that which now characterizes the agricultural societies of Asia or Latin America.

The limitation of fertility among married women had not occurred in the early years of married life, for here numbers of children ever born differed little in *shi* and in *gun*. Differences in the fertility of the women in the various types of areas became greater as the age of the women advanced. This age pattern of differences occurred among the prefectures classified by industrial type as well as among the *shi* and the *gun* (FIGURE 13).

The regional and the social-economic differences in fertility are blurred by broad combinations of *shi* and *gun*, or of all prefectures by industrial type. The extent of the contrast that has existed in recent decades is indicated by a comparison of the agricultural region of Tohoku and the urban agglomeration of the Kanto. Numbers of children ever born per 1,000 ever-married women in Aomori and Tokyo-to may be cited:

Age of women	*Aomori*	*Tokyo-to*
15-19	333	500
20-24	1,225	811
25-29	2,180	1,478
30-34	3,615	2,348
35-39	4,882	3,129
40-44	5,788	3,618
45-49	5,625	3,845
50-54	5,864	3,864
55-59	5,684	4,011
60 and over	5,575	4,141

It may be argued that the differences in average numbers of children ever born to ever-married women reflect differences in the proportions of the childless in the various areas rather than differences in rates of childbearing among those who are able to bear children. An initial approach to this and related questions as to the factors responsible for the differences in past reproductive performance lies in comparisons of mothers rather than of ever-married women. When this is done, the pattern of differences is not changed substantially. FIGURE 14 pictures the data for prefectures by industrial type; a comparison of number of children ever born per 1,000 Japanese mothers of specified ages in the *shi* and the *gun* is given here:

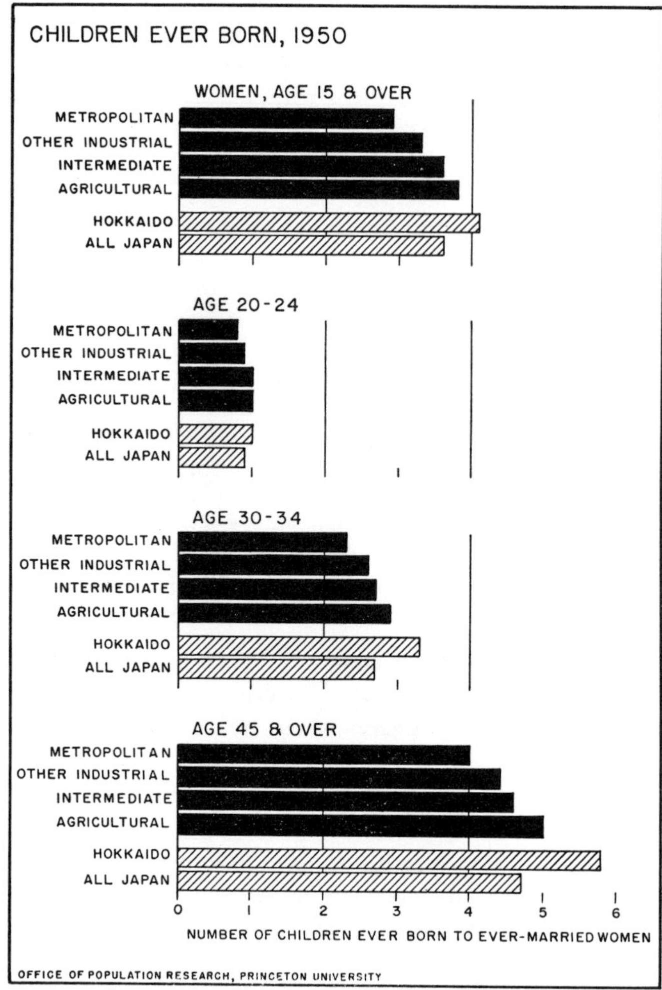

Figure 13. Number of children ever born to ever-married women of specified ages, prefectures by industrial type, 1950
Source: References, Footnote 13.

Age of women	*All Japan*	Shi	Gun
15-19	1,237	1,278	1,220
20-24	1,388	1,341	1,415
25-29	1,990	1,908	2,045
30-34	3,064	2,859	3,199
35-39	4,140	3,747	4,390
40-44	4,938	4,349	5,299
45-49	5,280	4,621	5,678
50-54	5,356	4,690	5,733
55-59	5,422	4,864	5,717
60 and over	5,297	4,979	5,434

The changing probabilities of widowhood may also be related to the changes in numbers of children ever born to women who were or had been married in 1950. The following

shotai, jutaku, shussanryoku. The tables on number of children ever born to married Japanese women are as follows: 28: Number of children ever born per 1,000 Japanese women 15 years old and over, by age, for all Japan, all *shi*, all *gun*, prefectures, and the six largest cities. 29: Japanese women 15 years old and over who are or have been married, by number of children ever born by age, marital status of women, for all Japan, all *shi* and all *gun*. 30: Japanese women married once, 15 years old and over, by number of children ever born, by age and duration of marriage of women, for all Japan, all *shi* and all *gun*. 31: Japanese women married once, 15 years old and over, by number of children ever born, by duration of marriage of women, for all Japan, all *shi* and all *gun*. The data were tabulated only for the 10 per cent sample. No data are included in the prefectural volumes.

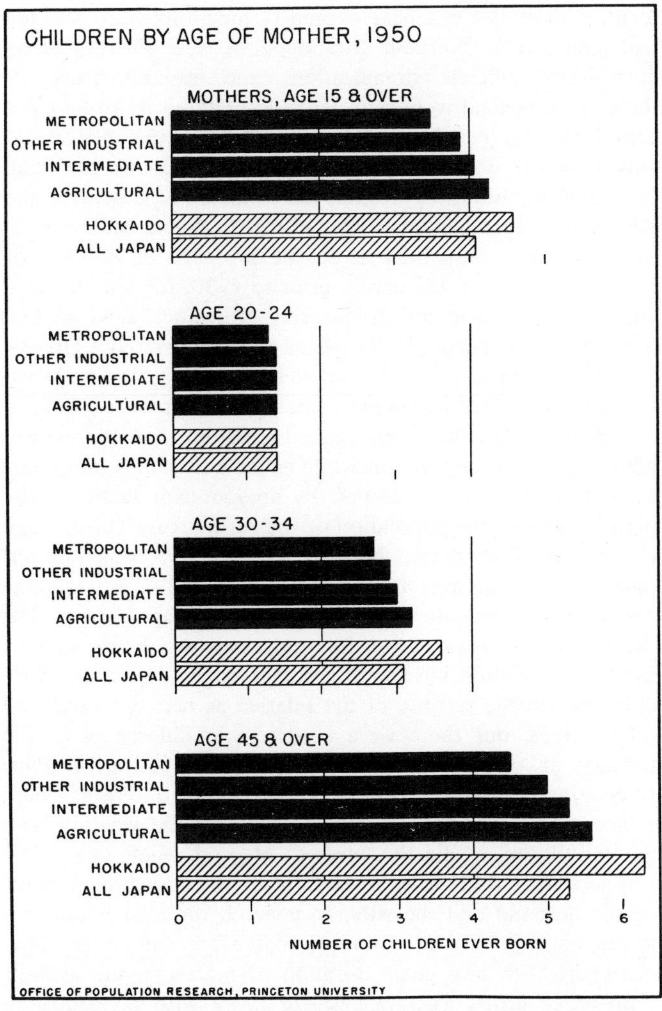

Figure 14. Number of children ever born to mothers of specified ages, prefectures by industrial type, 1950
Source: References, Footnote 13.

computations give the average number of children ever born by the age and marital status of the women in 1950:

	MARRIED		WIDOWED AND DIVORCED	
Age of women	Shi	Gun	Shi	Gun
15-19	0.5	0.5	1.0	0.8
20-24	0.9	1.0	0.8	0.7
25-29	1.6	1.8	1.0	1.1
30-34	2.6	3.0	1.6	1.9
35-39	3.5	4.3	2.3	2.9
40-44	4.0	5.1	3.0	3.8
45-49	4.3	5.4	3.5	4.3
50-54	4.3	5.4	3.7	4.6
55-59	4.4	5.4	3.9	4.6
60 and over	4.5	5.1	4.2	4.6

In the Japan of 1950, the women who were or had been married were characterized both by a rather surprising degree of childlessness and a rather high prevalence of upper-order births. If we take all women who were or had been married and limit ourselves to the women aged from 45 to 49, we find that 9 per cent had never borne a child alive, whereas 17 per cent had borne only one or two children.[14] One fourth of these women whose major period of childbearing had occurred in the late 1920's and the 1930's had had two children or less. Thirty-two per cent had borne three, four, or five children, while 30 per cent had borne six, seven, or eight. Almost 12 per cent had borne nine or more. If we take only the currently married women aged from 45 to 49, we find 8.7 per cent childless, 15 per cent with one or two births, 31 per cent with three to five births, 32 per cent with six to eight, and 13 per cent with nine or more.

The women of the *shi* included larger proportions of the childless, larger proportions with one or two births, and smaller proportions with six or more. The women of the *gun* included far larger proportions with six to eight or more births. Summary percentage distributions for women married once by numbers of children born indicate this difference between *shi* and *gun* to be of major magnitude:[15]

Number of children ever born	*All Japan*	Shi	Gun
0	7.3	8.8	6.4
1	7.9	10.8	6.0
2	8.0	10.5	6.5
3-5	32.8	36.6	30.5
6-8	31.5	25.3	35.2
9 and over	12.5	7.9	15.3

The completed fertility of married women is influenced by age at marriage, duration of marriage, medical and physiological deterrents to conception and gestation, limitation practices, and other factors. Some of these can be studied on the basis of censuses and survey data, while others require medical research. The question as to the factors responsible for differential childbearing among the women who had been married only once can be approached by an analysis of the proportions of the childless and of those with numerous offspring in relation to the duration of marriage. We give here by duration of marriage the percentage of the women aged from 40 to 44 in the *shi* and the *gun* who were either childless or had borne nine or more children:[16]

	CHILDLESS		NINE OR MORE BIRTHS	
Duration of marriage in years	Shi	Gun	Shi	Gun
0-4	43.8	37.5	0.0	0.0
5-9	22.6	16.7	0.0	0.0
10-14	17.4	11.6	0.0	0.0
15-19	9.8	7.2	1.0	2.0
20-24	5.8	4.5	5.8	12.1
25-29	4.3	3.3	9.2	18.1

It is immediately obvious that the differences between the women of the *shi* and the *gun* lie primarily in the proportions who have had many children rather than in the proportions with no children. The proportion childless among women aged from 40 to 44 is very high for marriages of brief duration, quite low for marriages of long duration.[17] These durations of

[14] Nihon. Sori-fu, tokei-kyoku. *Showa 25-nen kokusei chosa hokoku.* III.1. Table 29.

[15] *Ibid.* Table 30. The data for women married once included the reproductive experience of the widowed but excluded that of the remarried. Since the widowed and separated were more prevalent in the *gun* than in the *shi*, this factor would tend to reduce the differences in the fertility of the married in *gun* and *shi*.

[16] Age 40 to 44 is used instead of 45 to 49, or 45 and over, to avoid the addition of a five-year period of the reproductive span in which childbearing is limited sharply by physiological factors.

[17] There would also be a selection of the less fertile among those whose marriages were broken by divorce or desertion. However, the high proportions of the childless also appear in sample data for 1940 dealing with the fertility of couples in which the wife was aged 45 or over.

marriages may be translated into age at marriage. None of the women aged from 40 to 44 who had been married less than five years had married earlier than age 35. All of the women aged from 40 to 44 who had been married from 25 to 29 years had been married prior to age 20.

Perspective on the relations between duration of marriage and childlessness is given by the fact that low durations of marriage among older women are deviant patterns involving small proportions of all women. In the *gun* in 1950 only 16 thousand women aged from 40 to 44 had been married less than five years. Some 436 thousand had been married from 20 to 24 years, while 359 thousand had been married from 25 to 29 years. If we take the modal durations of marriage for these women aged from 40 to 44 in the *gun* in 1950, we find the following percentage distributions of numbers of children ever born:

Number of children ever born	DURATION OF MARRIAGE IN YEARS		
	15-19	*20-24*	*25-29*
0	7.2	4.5	3.3
1	6.8	4.6	3.9
2	7.6	5.5	5.0
3-5	45.4	32.5	28.2
6-8	30.9	40.8	41.5
9 or over	2.0	12.1	18.1

In these modal durations of marriage among the women of the *gun* who had completed the major portion of their childbearing by 1950, the major consequence of an increased duration of marriage was an increase in the number of births of higher orders, although there was also a decrease in childlessness.

In assessing the broader relevance of the reproductive histories of the women of 1950, it is essential to stress the interrelations of the changes in fertility rather than the separate factors. Later marriage and limitation of fertility within marriage were consistent rather than divergent facts. Social motivations re-enforced biological deterrents in creating relations among age at marriage, duration of marriage, and numbers of children born. All processes of change converged toward a lessening of the proportion of upper-order births.

It is possible to discuss, but not to evaluate, the existence of persistent childlessness in a familistic society. It is not reasonable to assume that any large proportion of Japanese families would choose to remain childless. If childlessness is not voluntary, the interpretation of incidence is difficult. Perhaps venereal disease and induced abortions were responsible in part for the high rates of childlessness among women of whatever age. However, it is not reasonable to assume that physiological differences account for a phenomenon that varies as among *shi* and *gun* and among the prefectures classified along an agricultural-industrial continuum.

FERTILITY BY SOCIAL-ECONOMIC STATUS

Studies of the current fertility or the reproductive histories of the women in specific areas of Japan are numerous in the demographic literature.[18] In 1940 the Institute of Population Problems of the Welfare Ministry conducted a nation-wide fertility study.[19] Certain areas and occupations were selected and almost 137 thousand questionnaires were distributed by government officials, organizations, and business firms. Of these, 81 thousand were returned, and of these in turn 11 per cent were eliminated as erroneous. The selective factors involved in the distribution and return of schedules are such that interpretations of results are difficult.[20] However, the differential reproduction of the women aged 45 and over in 1940 indicates something as to the presence or absence of family limitation in the period prior to 1930, for the marriage and years of maximum childbearing of women aged 45 and over in 1940 occurred in the years centered around 1920.

In the Japan of the early twentieth century, as in the West, fertility was higher for women whose husbands were gainfully occupied in agriculture and related activities than for women whose husbands engaged in white-collar and professional pursuits. Rurality *per se* was not the predominant factor in the high fertility of the population of the rural areas. The average number of children ever born to farmers, 4.98, was substantially above that ever born to fishermen, 4.04. Rural wage earners had a fertility above that of urban wage earners, but the fertility of businessmen in rural areas was below that of small and medium businessmen in the cities. There was little difference in the fertility of the salaried as between rural and urban areas, but there were considerable differences in the fertility of the salaried according to specific occupations. Interestingly enough, primary teachers were a fertile group, policemen an infertile group. The wives of the wealthy bore many children, as did the wives of men on relief.

There were differences in fertility by the educational status of the husband and the wife. In general, the associations between educational status and fertility were similar to those elsewhere. For any given duration of marriage, the average number of births was smallest for those with no education and generally low for those who had not completed primary school. People without education in a society where education was almost universal were deviates. Aside from this disadvantaged group, there was a negative association between the education of husbands or of wives and fertility. Maximum fertility occurred among those whose education had ended with the completion of primary school. From primary school graduates to college graduates there was a slight but generally consistent decline in fertility.

A second major survey of the fertility of the Japanese was made by the Institute of Population Problems of the Ministry of Welfare as of July 1952.[21] Since the initial analysis was

[18] A special family study was undertaken in Tokyo in connection with the censuses of 1935, but its results as to fertility were limited. The selection from schoolchildren eliminated sterile couples as well as those without surviving children. Tokyo shiyakusho. *Tokyo-shi kazoku tokei, Showa ku'nen chosa.*

[19] The major report seems to be the following: Okazaki, Ayanori. "Shussanryoku chosa kekka no gaisetsu." *J.m.k.*, 1(7):1-95. October 1940. A series of modifications and elaborations have been published in later years, including the following: "Fufu kankei jizoku kikan to shussanryoku." *J.m.k.*, 5(2):1-14. February 1946. "Nokosha no shissanryoku ni kansura tokeiteki kansatsu." *J.m.k.*, 7(2):1-18. September 1951.

[20] For instance, the rural areas for the study were secured through the selection of 80 villages from among low, medium, and high birth-rate areas in 1938, chosen presumably according to some criterion of typicality or accessibility. The categories of the poor or of those on relief were selected in Tokyo on the basis of classification by the city government. In all areas the coverage was limited to couples living together. There was also a moral criterion. Schedules were eliminated if a live birth had occurred within seven months after *de facto* marriage or a stillbirth within four months.

[21] Summary results were published in English: Okazaki, Ayanori. *A fertility survey in Japan of 1952.* A re-analysis was made to determine the interrelations of fertility, duration of marriage, and social-economic variables—particular emphasis being placed on changes in the years immediately prior to 1952. A preliminary report has been published: Honda, Tatsuo. *An analysis of postwar fertility in Japan. Renewed tabulations of results of the fer-*

made primarily on the basis of couples in which the wife was 45 years of age or over, the conclusions pertain in major part to the differentials in fertility that existed in the years prior to the Second World War rather than to the changes in the incidence and extent of differentials in the period of fertility decline during which the survey was made. The results corroborate the evidence from the prewar census and vital statistics as well as those of the fertility survey of 1940. Socio-economic differentials in the fertility of women by husband's occupation, educational status, and monthly cash expenditure reveal the expected inverse relationships among socio-economic status, education, income, and fertility.[22]

The Planned Limitation of Fertility

The legal barriers to family limitation in Japan did not differ greatly from those in most Western countries prior to 1948. Infanticide was defined as murder, while abortion was only permitted for therapeutic or eugenic reasons or to preserve the life of the mother. Fertility, as we have seen, varied in accordance with the realities of socio-economic differentials. It bore little immediate relation to the detailed provisions of the law, the volatile public press, the adjurations of publicists, or even the presumed vigilance of government in the enforcement of the law.

THE EUGENIC PROTECTION LAW

In September 1948 the Diet of Japan passed a rather comprehensive modification of the National Eugenic Law of 1940. The stated objective of this law of 1948, which became effective as of January 1949, was to prevent the increase of inferior descendants and to protect women for whom pregnancy would involve severe health hazards.[23] Overtly, it was not a measure to reduce population growth, although some members of the Diet thought it might operate in that way. The stated justifications for the law were eugenic and medical, not demographic.[24] The three provisions of the law relating to fertility permitted an extension of contraceptive facilities, the performance of abortions by private physicians for reasons of maternal health, and sterilization for reasons of excessive childbearing as measured by health criteria. The far-reaching consequences of a law designed for eugenic protection were determined by the demographic situation and the attitudes of the people toward that situation as it influenced their personal lives. An amendment in 1949 that included economic factors as contra-indications for pregnancy among women who already had many children was medical realism. It does not appear to have represented a devious route by which the government could sponsor abortions as a means of "solving" the population problem.

The first provision of the Eugenic Protection Law concerned voluntary and in some cases compulsory sterilization. The list of legal reasons included hereditary disease or deformity, infectious leprosy in either spouse, or danger to the life of the mother from pregnancy or delivery. Then another reason was added. If the mother already had several children, each delivery having weakened her health, sterilization could be performed after investigation and affirmation. Successive revisions made sterilization available to a woman if her health would be endangered by conception or delivery, the decision to be made by the physician.[25] The only consent required was that of the individual concerned and the spouse.[26]

The second provision of the Eugenic Protection Law of 1948 relative to fertility legalized interruptions of pregnancy by physicians designated for that purpose.[27] Originally some abortions could be performed at the discretion of a physician, but the majority required investigation and prior approval by a Eugenic Protection Committee.[28] In the revision of the law in April 1952, a designated physician was allowed to perform the operation without consultation, the only requirement being the consent of the person in question or the spouse. There had to be nominal justification under the broad legal requirement that the operation could be performed only "if the health of mother is endangered by the continuation of pregnancy or the delivery due to physical or economical reasons."[29]

The third provision of the Eugenic Protection Law concerned "practical guidance in adjustment of conception." In the original law, there were provisions for the establishment of Eugenic Protection Consultation Offices in association with the Health Centers or by private associations. The major trend here has been toward a greater emphasis on the provision of facilities for contraceptive advice, with particular reference to the training of personnel licensed to provide such services.[30]

---

tility survey of 1952. The Institute of Population Problems, Research Data A—No. 18, 1956. 17 pp.

[22] The studies that indicate the probable characteristics of the differences produced by the population trends of the postwar years are those oriented toward the extent and influence of the practice of family limitation within marriage. These will be summarized later.

[23] Eugenic Protection Law. Law No. 156 of 1948. The contents of the law were made available in English form for the WHO-UN Western Pacific Regional Seminar in Vital Statistics by Dr. Yoshio Koya. See: Nihon. Kosei-sho, koshu hoken-kyoku. Ministry of Welfare. Public Health Bureau. *Summary of program to promote conception control*. Tokyo, 1952. 17 pp. See also: Mainichi shimbun-sha. Jinko mondai chosa-kai. *Some facts about family planning in Japan*. By Minoru Muramatsu.

[24] Chapter 1, Article 1. "The object of this Law is to prevent the increase of the inferior descendants from the standpoint of eugenic protection and to protect the life and health of the mother as well."

[25] Status as of August 1954: Article 3. "Eugenic operation subject to judgment of the physician. The physician may exercise the eugenic operation on a person who comes under any of the following items, with the consent of the person in question and the spouse (including a person under the same conditions as getting married though not notified to the authorities concerned, hereafter the same interpretation being followed) . . . ." Provision 4. "If the life of the mother is endangered by conception or by delivery." Article 5. "If the mother has several children and her condition of health seems such that she gets weakened in a marked degree with each occasion of delivery."

[26] "For purposes of the content prescribed . . . the sole consent of the person in question shall be sufficient, if the spouse is unknown or cannot express his intention."

[27] Eugenic Protection Law, 1952 and 1954, Chapter 3, Article 14. "The physician designated by the Medical Association which is a corporate juristic person established in the prefectural district as a unit (hereinafter referred to as the designated physician) may perform the artificial interruption of pregnancy. . . ."

[28] In the law of 1948 there were detailed provisions for Eugenic Protection Committees that would determine the permissibility of the operation, and in most prefectures most of the operations were performed with authorization from Committees. The Committees were eliminated in the revision of April 1952. As the law stood in 1954, Chapter 3, Article 14 states that the abortion requires "the consent of the person in question and the spouse," but "where the spouse is unknown or is incapable of expressing his will or where the spouse has ceased to exist for the person in question after the conception has taken place, the consent of the person in question alone shall be sufficient for purposes of the consent as mentioned in the preceding paragraph."

[29] The status of 1954 as given in Chapter 3, Article 14, provision 4: "If it is feared that the health of the mother may be affected in a marked degree for physical or economic reasons by the continuation of pregnancy or by delivery."

[30] Article 15, status as of 1954. "Practical guidance of a female by the employment of contraceptive instruments designated by the Minister of Welfare shall not be given as a matter of profession, except by the physician and those who have received designations of the Prefectural Governor. However, the act of inserting a contraceptive instrument into the hollow of the uterus shall not be done as a matter of profession except by the physician. Those who

The legalization of abortion and sterilization under the auspices of private physicians for health reasons that included economic factors gave all Japanese women from the fishing villages of Hokkaido to the suburbs of the great cities access to medical facilities for post-conception control of fertility. The allocation of responsibility for giving contraceptive advice to Eugenic Protection Consultation Offices associated with Health Centers made it lawful for public health doctors and, later, licensed midwives and nurses to give women information, advice, and assistance in contraception. Here indeed was an experimental situation.

Congruence between legislative acts and reproductive behavior cannot be assumed *a priori*, nor can it be established easily by opinion polls or reporting systems. The legalization of activities once prohibited may alter the answers people give to inquiring reporters and stimulate new series of government statistics. The problem of measuring the influence of an altered legal situation is made even more difficult by the fact that congruence in change need not mean causality. Practice may alter with or without a change in law and with or without an admission of the altered practice. In a society that reveres ancestors and orients the present toward the future, real attitudes toward the limitation of fertility may be concealed even though there are no overt prohibitions in ethics or religion. Moreover, where young wives live subject to mothers-in-law, the lack of congruence between practice and admission of the practice may be great.

Cultural taboos, social-psychological resistances, and moral judgments are involved in the movement of any people from the mores of abundant reproduction to the values and practices of planned parenthood.

EVIDENCES OF LIMITATION PRACTICES, 1920-1940

The one long series of data relevant to birth limitation that has been collected on a national basis and published in the detail that permits analysis is that on stillbirths. Hence it may be appropriate to supplement the earlier analysis of live births and precede the discussion of specific practices of limitation with an analysis of stillbirth statistics for the 1920's and 1930's.

The interpretation of statistics on stillbirths is always difficult, for willed destruction and natural loss are combined in some proportion in the reports on pregnancy wastage and neonatal mortality. A brief résumé of historical change in Japan poses the problem. The number of reported stillbirths per 1,000 live births declined somewhat irregularly from 104 in 1901 and 1902 to 92 in 1910, 71 in 1920, 60 in 1925, 56 in 1930, and 53 in 1935. Deaths of the live-born under one month of age per 1,000 live births also decreased, from 77 in 1901 and 1902 to 69 in 1920, 50 in 1930, and 45 in 1935.[31] Stillbirths and deaths within a month of birth were 18 per cent as numerous as live births in 1901; the percentage declined to 14 in 1920 and 11 in 1935. Three major aspects of these figures should be noted. The first is the high level of the losses, even in the middle 1930's. The second is the great decline in the rates of wastage. The third is the difference in rates of decline among the types of wastage. Mortality in the first month after birth declined more rapidly than mortality in the later months of the first year; fetal mortality declined more rapidly than mortality in the first month after birth. These are curious changes if they represent natural processes. That mortality which presumably was related directly to the prevalence of environmental hazards declined less rapidly than the neonatal mortality and the pregnancy wastage which presumably were related more directly to physiological hazards.

If the hypothesis that direct action was involved in the levels of fetal and early infant mortality is correct, the relative proportions of fetal deaths among legitimate and illegitimate births in larger cities and rural areas should provide clues. The illegitimate pregnancy posed problems of economic hardship and social ostracism if the mother remained unmarried after the birth of the child. Both the economic difficulties before delivery and the problems of support after delivery were greater in the cities. The recognition of fetus and infant by the father reduced the difficulties. The family of the father assumed responsibility for the baby; presumably the father contributed to the maintenance of the mother.[32] The recorded data substantiate the expected relations between stillbirth ratios and legitimacy status (TABLE 105). The ratio of stillbirths to live births was very high among illegitimate gestations and births, even though it is recognized that illegitimate conceptions that were aborted remained in the illegitimate category, whereas some portion of those carried to term dis-

TABLE 105

Stillbirths per 1,000 live births, by legitimacy status, cities of 100 thousand and over and remainder of the country, 1923-1935[a]

	LEGITIMATE		RECOGNIZED ILLEGITIMATE		STRICTLY ILLEGITIMATE	
Year	*Large cities*	*Outside*	*Large cities*	*Outside*	*Large cities*	*Outside*
1923	36	41	13	30	239	218
1924	34	40	10	29	260	210
1925	33	38	12	31	262	203
1926	34	37	11	33	270	203
1927	31	36	10	33	276	196
1928	32	35	12	33	306	206
1929	32	35	12	35	304	200
1930	33	34	9	37	319	201
1931	32	34	13	38	357	204
1932	32	33	15	39	366	204
1933	31	32	20	38	369	199
1934	32	33	20	41	392	206
1935	31	31	18	39	421	201

[a] Stillbirths of seven months' gestation or more.
Source: Nihon. Naikaku tokei-kyoku. *Jinko dotai tokei.* 1923-1935.

may receive designations of the Prefectural Governor as mentioned in the preceding paragraph shall be limited to the midwives, health nurses, and nurses who have finished a lecture course approved by the Prefectural Governor in accordance with the standard established by the Minister of Welfare."

[31] Stillbirths by duration of gestation and infant deaths by days and weeks of the first month and the months of the first year of life were given annually in: Nihon. Naikaku tokei-kyoku. *Jinko dotai tokei.* Summary data were given in the *Resume statistique du mouvement de la population de l'Empire du Japon.*

[32] There are selective factors in the situation that make analysis difficult. If an illegitimate conception is carried through to birth, the birth may be made legitimate by marriage or recognized as legitimate. A higher proportion of male births among the recognized illegitimate indicates that there is some sex-selective recognition, though the sex ratios in the births of the legitimacy types indicate that many factors other than sex of offspring were involved in the decision as to recognition. Stillbirths would be more likely to remain strictly illegitimate. The civil code forbade the recognition of a stillborn child except under rare circumstances, but analysis of the age composition of deaths from the seventh through the tenth months of gestation indicates almost the same distribution for illegitimate and recognized illegitimate stillbirths.

appeared into the categories of the recognized illegitimate and the legitimate. It should be noted, furthermore, that the trend of the illegitimate stillbirth ratio was sharply upward in the large cities.

Ratios of stillbirths to live births by age of mother by legitimacy status suggest an interpenetration of cultural and biological factors even more clearly than do over-all ratios. The ratio of legitimate stillbirths to legitimate live births increased quite consistently with age, the ratio being appreciably lower at all ages outside the great cities than within them. Among the illegitimate, on the other hand, ratios were much higher in the great cities and the pattern of change with age was one of decline. The following ratios of stillbirths per 1,000 live births pertain to the year 1930; stillbirths of all gestations are included:

	LEGITIMATE		ILLEGITIMATE	
Age of mother	*Large cities*	*Other*	*Large cities*	*Other*
15-44	53	48	558	314
15-19	46	33	745	366
20-24	43	35	672	391
25-29	45	40	458	284
30-34	58	51	442	226
35-39	74	67	372	230
40-44	95	90	352	223

It may be argued that the stillbirth ratios cited here only document the fact that the civil code bars the recognition of a stillbirth by the father, and that therefore live births disappear from the illegitimacy category whereas stillbirths remain within it. However, if stillbirths cannot be recognized, there should be no stillbirths classified as recognized illegitimate. There are such stillbirths. In 1930, recognized illegitimate stillbirths per 1,000 recognized illegitimate live births were 16 in large cities and 56 outside such cities.[33] The stillbirth ratios in the areas outside great cities were highest for fathers below age 35, the period when biological hazards to the fetus were lowest and recognized illegitimate live births most frequent.

The decline in stillbirth ratios for illegitimate births from 1939 to 1943 is conclusive demonstration that factors other than physiological ones were involved in the prevalence of stillbirths. In the legitimate category, stillbirths per 1,000 live births declined from 45 in 1939 to 38 in 1943. The decline was slow and quite regular among the age groups of mothers (TABLE 106). It is possible that such a decline could be interpreted in terms of the facilities for prenatal care that were associated with the population policies of the war years. In the illegitimate category, on the other hand, there were major declines, particularly in the case of mothers below 35 years of age. The explanations can hardly lie in improved prenatal care, for the decline began before the new policies were initiated. If the explanation lies in a change of attitude toward the illegitimate baby or in new laws for the payment of soldiers' allowances, then the influence of such factors on stillbirths ratios shows that the prevalence of stillbirths was determined by social as well as physiological factors.

TABLE 106

Stillbirths by legitimacy status, by age of mother, 1930 and 1939-1943 (Stillbirths per 1,000 live births)

Age of mother	*1930*	*1939*	*1940*	*1941*	*1942*	*1943*
			Legitimate			
15-49	48	45	43	41	39	38
15-19	34	40	43	43	42	43
20-24	36	35	35	35	33	33
25-29	41	37	35	34	32	31
30-34	52	46	42	39	38	37
35-39	68	62	58	53	52	49
40-44	91	81	76	69	69	65
45-49	79	79	70	67	64	63
			Illegitimate			
15-49	353	429	400	361	249	208
15-19	415	515	472	417	284	232
20-24	442	573	532	464	302	249
25-29	317	434	398	385	248	203
30-34	260	295	282	273	202	167
35-39	249	265	258	245	180	162
40-44	239	240	223	216	200	165
45-49	116	120	125	121	82	124

Source: 1930: Nihon. Naikaku tokei-kyoku. *Fubo no nenrei betsu shussei oyobi shisan tokei, Showa go'nen.* 1939-1942: *Ibid. Jinko dotai tokei.* 1943: Unpublished tabulations.

The mortality by days within the first months of life according to legitimacy status is also suggestive of factors of neglect, if not of more positive action. Deaths per 1,000 live births in the years 1924 and 1925 indicate the handicap of illegitimacy among deliveries reported as live births:

Age in days	*Legitimate*	*Recognized illegitimate*	*Strictly illegitimate*
0-30	55.8	77.7	168.1
0-4	21.0	26.2	71.8
5-9	12.4	20.6	46.6
10-14	7.6	14.3	25.2
15-30	14.7	16.6	24.5

The greater hazards to life for the illegitimate continued throughout the first year of life, although the extent of the excess lessened with time. Again in 1924 and 1925, deaths of infants under age 1 per 1,000 live births were 144 for legitimate births, 163 for recognized illegitimate births, and 277 for strictly illegitimate births. In cities of 100 thousand and over, the comparable rates were 149 for legitimate births, 122 for recognized illegitimate births, and 341 for strictly illegitimate births.

The relative influence of inherent hazards, differential care, and deliberate action on prenatal and early postnatal mortality cannot be determined on the basis of official reports on live births and stillbirths. Occasional studies demonstrate the major role of deliberate action in the early mortality in specific areas. In 1940 and 1941 public health doctors con-

[33] The distribution of legitimate stillbirths by age of father was similar to that by age of mother. The number of stillbirths per 1,000 live births increased consistently with age of father. For recognized illegitimate stillbirths, on the other hand, the ratio of stillbirths to live births tended to decline with advancing age of father. The outstanding fact was the height of the ratio of stillbirths to live births outside the cities of 100,000 and over. Here, stillbirths were actually more frequent among the recognized illegitimate than among the legitimate births to fathers under age 35.

ducted an intensive study of a village in the southeastern part of Ibaraki-ken and five other villages on Lake Kasumigaura.[34] In these villages birth rates were relatively low, the relations of farmers to land were quite favorable, and stillbirth and infant mortality rates were high. The conclusion of the doctors who made the study was that stillbirth and infant death rates were related, and that the high rates in this region were based not on medico-biological factors but on social circumstances. In other words, abortion and infanticide were contemporary practices in these communities.

The Means of Limitation

Distinctions between the prevention of conception and interference with the developing embryo are critical in the ethics and religions of the West. Among increasing proportions of Protestants, the control of conception in the interests of the responsibilities of parenthood is not only permitted but approved. Among Catholics the only contraception permitted is that defined as natural—that is, coitus during the period when the ovum is not fertilizable. Induced abortion is considered murder, except in those special circumstances where the induction of fetal death is essential to preserve the life or perhaps the health of the mother. The attitudes of Protestant groups to sterilization are more difficult to categorize simply. In general, it is approved if further childbearing would endanger the health or the life of the mother, and it is frowned upon if its sole purpose is contraception.

The distinctions between means of achieving reduced fertility that lie so deep in the ethic of the West are blurred in Japanese thinking. In the early postwar days, the printed character commonly used to signify "birth limitation" in the advertisements in the mass-circulation women's magazines included both "contraception" and "abortion." What this lack of precise differentiation in the minds of the Japanese people has meant in the results of field surveys of attitudes and opinions is rather disquieting to contemplate. Toward the end of the Occupation a carefully conducted public opinion poll on population included a specific question as to the meaning of the character for "contraception" in contrast to the character for "birth limitation" as a general term, including abortion.[35] Five per cent of the national sample of respondents gave a nearly correct answer; 48 per cent said that they did not know; 47 per cent gave answers indicating a vague belief that there were differences between the two.

CONTRACEPTION

The studies on attitudes toward contraception and on contraceptive practices that have been made in Japan are hard to summarize without overgeneralization.[36] Their results are suggestive rather than definitive, for difficulties in response were great and the groups surveyed often represented fortuitous selection. The early postwar studies indicated that a majority of the people "favored" birth control, and this majority became preponderant if married women with few children and those beyond the age of conception were excluded from the samples. Approximately one in five married couples admitted the practice of contraception at some time; the number sank to one in ten, or even twenty, in agricultural villages. The extent of contraceptive practice was correlated with urban residence, degree of education, and upper social-economic status. It appeared to decline with distance from the great urban centers. The techniques employed by the married couples who were practicing contraception were those traditional in the culture. One-third or more used the condom; another one-fourth or more relied on periodic abstinence, and one-tenth used *coitus interruptus*. These three methods together accounted for some three-fourths of the contraceptive experience reported. Studies on the efficiency of contraceptive practice were so limited that generalization seems unwise.[37]

The demographic statistics of prewar Japan permit the inference that there was a widespread limitation of fertility among the married as early as 1925, and that practices of limitation increased rather consistently from 1925 to the end of the war. The inference of a widespread planned limitation of marital fertility received further support from the data on past fertility secured in the 1950 census of population. The vital statistics for the years from 1947 to 1953 demonstrated the existence of declines in marital fertility for the nation as a whole. Six recent studies permit us to sketch the extent and the characterisitcs of the spread of contraceptive practice through a period of rapidly declining fertility. The Population Problems Research Council of the Mainichi Newspapers conducted a nation-wide survey in April 1950.[38] The Institute of Population Problems of the Welfare Ministry made a series of studies of contraceptive practice in thirteen of the more rural prefectures in 1949 and 1950.[39] The Mainichi Council made a second national survey in May 1952, with emphasis on the spread of contraception in the two years since the first study.[40] As of July 1, 1952, the Institute of Population Problems included a questionnaire on contraception as part of a national sample study of fertility.[41] As of April 1, 1954, the Statistical Division of the Ministry of Welfare attached a survey of contraceptive practice to its annual administrative survey of health and welfare activities, and in May of 1955 the Mainichi Council made a third survey.[42]

The practice of contraception was spreading rapidly throughout Japan in the years from 1950 to 1955 (Table 107). Practice was most widespread in the great cities, but between 1952 and 1955 the rate of increase was more rapid in the *gun* than in the great cities. By 1952 more than one in each five couples in the *gun* reported current contraceptive practice, while an additional one-third reported some practice either at present or at some time in the past. In 1955 almost one-third of the couples in the *gun* said that they were practicing contraception, while more than one-half said that they had practiced contraception at some time.

[34] Saito, K., and Homma, H. "Nyuyoji shibo o shiheisuru inshi ni kansuru kenkyu. Ibaraki-kenka noson ni okeru chosa kenkyu, Dai-ippo, jumbi chosa to sono seiseki no kento." *Koshu eisei*, 4(1):76-88, 6(1-2):6-10. January 1943 and September 1947.

[35] Nihon. Kokuritsu yoron chosa kenkyujo. National Public Opinion Research Institute. *Public opinion research on population*. Research No. A-10. Tokyo, 1950, II, 47 pp.

[36] Citations to individual studies are given in the Bibliography. A summary of the results of various polls and surveys is given in: Nihon. Kosei-sho, jinko mondai kenkyujo. *Saikin no jinko ni kansuru tokei shiryo*. 7th Edition. Report No. 92. Pp. 63-65.

[37] Aoki, Hisao. "Chiho ni okeru jutai chosetsu no jikko koka ni tsuite-Yamagata-ken jugo shi, cho, son no moderu chosa." *J.m.k.*, 7(2):19-28. September 1951.

[38] Mainichi shimbun-sha. Jinko mondai chosa-kai. *A survey of public opinion in Japan on the readjustment of overpopulation*.

[39] Shinozaki, Nobuo. "Present conditions of spread of birth control in Japan. . . ." *Archives of the Population Association of Japan*, No. 1. 1952. Pp. 50-57.

[40] Mainichi shimbun-sha. Jinko mondai chosa-kai. *Public opinion survey on birth control in Japan*.

[41] Honda, Tatsuo. *A survey of spread of birth control*.

[42] Nihon. Kosei-sho. [Survey of prevalence of contraceptive practice in Japan . . . . April 1, 1954.] *Kosei no shihyo*, Vol. I, No. 12. October 1954. Mainichi shimbun-sha. Jinko mondai chosa-kai. *Third public opinion survey on birth control in Japan*.

TABLE 107

The practice of contraception, 1950, 1952, and 1955

Area	PER CENT REPORTING PRACTICE			INCREASE, 1950-1955			
				Amount		*Per cent*	
	1950	*1952*	*1955*	*1950-1952*	*1952-1955*	*1950-1952*	*1952-1955*
				Present practice			
All Japan	19.5	26.3	33.6	6.8	7.3	34.9	27.8
Six cities	23.7	34.8	37.7	11.1	2.9	46.8	8.3
Other *shi*	23.6	31.1	34.0	7.5	2.9	31.8	9.3
Gun	17.4	22.1	31.9	4.6	9.8	38.5	44.3
				Ever practiced			
All Japan	29.1	40.2	52.5	11.1	12.3	38.1	30.6
Six cities	35.7	52.0	56.6	16.3	4.6	45.7	8.8
Other *shi*	32.9	46.0	52.9	13.1	6.9	39.8	15.0
Gun	26.6	34.6	50.8	8.0	16.2	30.1	46.8

Source: Mainichi shimbun-sha. Jinko mondai chosa-kai. *Public opinion survey on birth control in Japan.* Pp. 30-31. Also: *Third public opinion survey on birth control in Japan.* Pp. 23-24.

The critical question with reference to the diffusion of contraceptive practice concerns the families who live in *mura* and labor in agriculture, lumbering, or fishing. It is among these people that the traditional family system remains most nearly intact, and it is here that resistances have been greatest. Earlier studies of contraceptive practice made under the auspices of the Institute of Population Problems indicated percentages of practice as follows: *shi*, 23.8; *machi*, 18.3; farming villages, 10.9; mountain villages, 9.8; fishing villages, 6.9.[43] Occupational rates of practice were 4.9 per cent for fishermen, 8.9 per cent for farmers, 7.2 per cent for laborers, 15.3 per cent for tradesmen, 17.6 per cent for people in other professions, 18.1 per cent for industrialists, and 23.8 per cent for salaried men. In general, contraceptive practice increased according to the urban character of the place of residence, the extent of the education of the couple, and the pecuniary and upper social-economic status of the place of the occupation. Rates of practice were minimal among people who lived in the *mura*, were limited in educational background to the elementary school level, and labored in agriculture. Rates were high among salaried and professional families who lived in large cities and had relatively high levels both of education and income.

By 1955 occupational differences in rates of contraceptive practice had been reduced substantially. The percentages of men reporting practice in the third national survey of the Mainichi Press were as follows:

Occupations of men	*Ever practiced*	*Present practice*	*Past practice*
Farmers and fishermen	44.5	25.4	19.1
Laborers	47.6	35.8	11.8
Commercial and industrial proprietors	55.3	37.4	17.9
Salaried workers	64.9	39.7	25.2
Professional workers	67.8	41.0	26.8
Other	34.6	19.7	14.9

[43] Shinozaki, Nobuo. "Present conditions of spread of birth control in Japan."

The attitudes toward children appropriate to the traditional society were yielding to the realities of a life that included no additional land, limited opportunities for children, major expenditures for the rearing of children, and increased responsibilities for the conjugal family. In 1955, only one-fifth of the men in the six great cities, 14.0 per cent of those with some college education, and 22.2 per cent of the salaried workers reported that they expected to depend on their children in their old age. Children were still regarded as old-age insurance in rural areas (51.8 per cent), among farmers and fishermen (63.1 per cent), and among those with less than nine years of education (48.6).[44]

The ideal of the planned small family was widespread.[45] In 1955, 43.5 per cent of the couples with two children wanted no more, while 28.4 per cent wanted only one more. In 1952, only one couple in five had expressed a desire for four or more children. At this time the proportions desiring no more than the two children they already had were greatest among women from 35 to 49 years of age in the great cities, among salaried and professional men, and among those with some college education. Almost two-thirds of the people favored contraception (65.0 per cent); the proportions favoring it were 64.0 per cent among men and 58.9 per cent among women in rural areas, 57.5 per cent among farmers and fishermen, and 60.6 per cent among those with less than nine years of education. The trends in fertility from 1952 to 1955 are consistent with these expressions of opinion.

The ideal of the small family and intellectual approval of contraception were clearly more widespread than the efficient practice of contraception. The reasons for this situation were manifold. To many, contraception was a word for something known and practiced elsewhere. Newspapers, press, and radio were the great sources of information in urban and rural areas, and for all social classes.[46] In 1955, 16 per cent of the women questioned had learned something from the Health Center and the Eugenic Marriage Bureau, 10.1 per cent from a practicing doctor; 12.9 per cent from a midwife, 11.1 per

[44] Mainichi shimbun-sha. Jinko mondai chosa-kai. *Third public opinion survey on birth control in Japan.* Pp. 4-5.

[45] *Ibid.* Pp. 11-15. [46] *Ibid.* P. 22.

cent from a lecture, and 2.3 per cent from a private birth control clinic. Although there is some duplication of sources in these figures, it is clear that public health activities in the field of contraceptive service were reaching substantial proportions of Japanese women at the informational level at least. At the same time, it should be emphasized that 58.1 per cent of the women reported magazines as a source of knowledge about contraception.

The practice of contraception was spreading as a folk adjustment to the situation in which the people found themselves, and means of contraception were accepted or rejected in the light of experience and values in this situation. Among most groups the use of contraception began after the birth of children, not before.[47] Among 30.6 per cent of the women below age 25, however, contraception had begun with marriage; this was true also for 11.6 per cent of the salaried men. In all areas and among most social-economic and educational groups, the most frequent period at which contraception practice began was after the birth of the second child.

The means of contraception utilized in 1955 remained those long known in the culture: condom, abstinence, *coitus interruptus*. Tablets that were easily usable and inexpensive were the major "new" method utilized, but their use was reported in only 8.7 per cent of the cases, as compared with 56.8 per cent for condoms. The tablets were used more widely in the rural areas and among the poorly educated, while periodic abstinence was more widely practiced among the better-educated in the cities.

The barriers to a wider use of contraception did not lie in an absence of general motivation for family limitation. The low levels of effectiveness of many of the techniques seem to have produced disillusionment and frustration rather than decisions to practice more effectively. The Japanese compulsions to effective use were rather different from those in other countries where people faced similar problems at comparable levels of motivation for fertility control; in Japan, abortions were available, they were relatively safe, and they were cheap. It is particularly significant, therefore, that a rapid increase in contraceptive practice was correlated with the nation-wide resort to induced abortion.

As we noted earlier, there have been two government surveys of contraceptive practice based on samples of the national population. One was made by the Institute of Population Problems of the Welfare Ministry as of July 1, 1952, the other by the Statistical Division of the Welfare Ministry as of April 1, 1954.[48] In 1952 and in 1954 information on contraceptive practice was secured from couples living together in which the wife was below 50 years of age. The percentage of couples answering the question who admitted the practice of contraception was 21.7 in 1952 and 35.9 in 1954. The practice in *shi* and *gun* is indicated by the following percentages:

Area	*1952 (Per cent of couples answering the question)*	*1954*[49] *(Per cent of couples returning a questionnaire)*
All Japan	21.7	33.2
Shi	28.1	37.2
Gun	17.6	30.4

The most rapid increase in this period of 21 months was that for women in the *gun*. This suggests that contraceptive practice was increasing among women whose resistances to it had been assumed to be very high. The percentages of married women admitting practice give further evidence of a rapid diffusion of contraceptive practice among groups hitherto rather impervious to it:

Age of wives	*Per cent currently practicing 1952*	*1954*[50]
20-24	28.8	33.9
25-29	24.3	41.0
30-34	33.8	44.2
35-39	22.7	41.3
40-44	12.1	26.9
45-49	4.3	11.4

The motivations to restrict births seem to have been associated more closely with numbers of children already born than with the age of the husband or the wife *per se*. In 1952, the percentages admitting present contraceptive practice by number of living children were as follows:

Number of children	*All Japan*	Shi	Gun
0	7.8	9.0	6.9
1	25.3	31.5	20.9
2	27.4	34.0	22.5
3	27.8	36.9	22.0
4	27.3	34.5	22.7
5	14.9	19.4	12.5
6 or over	9.4	15.5	6.9

Between 1952 and 1954 there was a rapid increase in the population of the *shi*, with corresponding changes in the population of the *gun*. In 1952 the percentages are a proportion of those answering the question as to contraceptive practice; in 1954 the percentages are a proportion of the total returning questionnaires. Both the movements to the cities and the inclusion of unknowns in the base for the percentages reduced the percentages practicing contraception in the *gun*. Hence the true figures on the percentage of practice in 1954 would be larger than the percentages that are cited here:

[47] Analysis of the data on first births by age of women by duration of marriage for the year 1951 corroborates this information from the national surveys.

[48] The studies are cited in Footnotes 41 and 42. There are major problems of comparability between the two studies. In 1952 the study of contraceptive practice was a segment of a broader study of fertility. The fertility questionnaire itself was given by the regular enumerators of the Bureau of Statistics to the national sample used for the monthly survey of the labor force. The questionnaire on limitation was given to that third of the sample which would be dropped in the current month in order to avoid later resistances in the labor force survey itself. Thus the sample was very small. In 1954 the questionnaire was distributed to all households in the Welfare Ministry's sample of 1 in 100 households. It was associated with an annual survey of health and welfare activities. In both instances the returns on limitation practices were anonymous. In 1952 the returns were mailed by the respondents; in 1954 the enumerator called the following day to collect a sealed envelope. Detailed data are not yet sufficient for analysis of the biases in the studies. There is no evidence of systematic factors that would create divergent biases in the two studies and therefore invalidate the use of the data for approximate evaluation of changes that occurred in the period from July 1, 1952, to April 1, 1954.

[49] The per cent of couples failing to answer was 7.5 per cent, but no separate figures are available for *shi* and *gun*. However, the computation of the 1954 percentages to eliminate the unknowns would increase the percentage practicing and thus increase the rate of diffusion between 1952 and 1954.

[50] These percentages have been recomputed as a percentage of those answering the specific question in order to secure comparability with the 1952 percentages.

Number of children	All Japan	Shi	Gun
0	11.5	14.4	8.9
1	30.6	33.6	28.0
2	42.2	47.5	38.1
3	41.8	46.7	38.5
4	37.9	41.8	35.5
5	30.5	32.8	29.3
6	24.2	26.8	23.1
7 or over	16.8	18.9	16.1

Thus it appears that rates of contraceptive practice by married women already having one or more living children almost doubled between 1952 and 1954. By 1954 the differences between *shi* and *gun* were small for women who already had two or more children. Moreover, women in *shi* and *gun* were using the techniques available to them without medical assistance. The percentages of the couples reporting use of the various techniques are given on the basis of the 1954 survey:[51]

Technique	All Japan	Shi	Gun
Condom	39.0	41.3	37.1
Periodic abstinence	30.9	29.9	31.7
Chemicals	12.3	12.0	12.6
Vaginal diaphragm	5.1	4.2	5.9
Other	12.6	12.6	12.6

Discussion of the relation of this rapid diffusion of contraceptive practices in the *gun* to the rapid diffusion of other means of limitation will be postponed until the available materials on abortion and sterilization have been presented. The question raised here is that of the role of government activities in the increasing practice of contraception. While no causation can be established, there is a coincidence between the activities of the Institute of Public Health in the fields of research and education and the incidence of contraceptive practice among the groups that the Institute was trying to reach.[52] Dr. Koya and his associates have made long-time experimental studies in agricultural and mining villages to discover the requirements for the adoption of contraceptive practice in villages.[53] There have been field studies of the social and economic backgrounds, the attitudes, the correlated factors, the medical aspects, and the health consequences of abortions.[54] A similar field study has been made of women who were sterilized under the provisions of the Eugenic Protection Law, and of the interrelations among contraceptive practice, induced abortion, and the decision for sterilization.[55] Many studies have been made by prefectural governments and individual doctors.

The legislation of 1948 was permissive insofar as contraception, abortion, and sterilization were concerned. There was no authorization for the Welfare Ministry to stimulate family planning in general or to advocate the adoption of one method as against another. However, by 1952 the health effects of induced abortions led to an authorization of the Institute of Public Health to undertake such educational and training activities as would lead those desiring to limit family size to choose contraception rather than abortion. Educational meetings were held and training courses were given for midwives and nurses. Any quantitative measurement of effects is difficult. By 1953, however, there were 673 Eugenic Protection Consultation Offices attached to Health Centers, 19 to other public offices, and 55 private ones, yielding a total of 747.[56] Individual consultations for contraceptive advice numbered 23 thousand in 1950 and 44 thousand in 1951. There were 99 thousand such consultations in the last six months of 1952 and 62 thousand in the first six months of 1953. In the last half of 1952 there were 4,408 mass education meetings that reached an estimated 630 thousand people. In the first half of 1953, 8,556 meetings reached an estimated 692 thousand people. By the end of 1953 more than 31 thousand contraceptive workers had been trained, and of these 16 thousand had been reported as licensed. By September 25, 1954, there were 36 thousand trained workers in the prefectures, and 28 thousand of them were licensed.

Figures on numbers trained are impressive, but they are not a complete measure of the extension of contraceptive services. Such activities influence some people directly, but they influence many more through conversations, newspaper reports, radio presentations, etc. There is a further intangible aspect. Government activities have been accepted as meaning that the government approved of contraception but disapproved of abortion. It is not possible to say more than that the research and educational activities of the Welfare Ministry may be a significant factor in the rapid extension of contraceptive practice.

ABORTION

Resort to abortion is doubtless common in all countries where strong motivations to limit fertility exist without a wide knowledge and availability of acceptable and effective techniques of contraception. Abortions are also prevalent in many stable societies where the sanctions are those of the ancient culture. In most societies, however, abortion is a subject seldom discussed openly and infrequently subjected to attempts at data-collection and analysis. In Japan the combination of a comprehensive habit of data-collecting with a legalized system of abortions has produced official data on abortions reported as performed in accordance with legal provisions. The total numbers of induced abortions reported are as follows:[57]

[51] These are percentages of methods used, not of a combination of methods used by individuals. For the nation as a whole, 68.1 per cent of those answering the question used a single method, while 27.4 per cent used a combination of methods. Among those using a single method, condom accounted for 42.6 per cent; periodic abstinence, 24.9 per cent; and vaginal diaphragm, only 3.7 per cent. Of those using two methods, 48.7 per cent used condom plus periodic abstinence.

[52] Some of the prefectural Health Departments have also been very active.

[53] For a general summary statement, see: Koya, Yoshio. *Present situation of family planning among farmers and coal mine workers in Japan.* United Nations World Population Conference. Research reports are cited in the Bibliography.

[54] Koya, Yoshio, and Muramatsu, Minoru. "A study of health and demographic aspects of induced abortion in Japan." Special reports 1-3. *Bulletin of the Institute of Public Health,* June 1953, December 1953, and September 1954.

[55] Koya, Yoshio, Muramatsu, Minoru, Agata, Sakito, and Suzuki, Naruo. "A study of health and demographic aspects of female sterilization in four health centers of Shizuoka Prefecture, Japan." *Milbank Memorial Fund Quarterly,* 33(4):368-392. October 1955.

[56] These and other materials on government activities or activities reported to the government are taken from the last report of the Welfare Ministry. Nihon. Kosei-sho, koshu hoken-kyoku. *Activities under the Eugenic Protection Law for the year 1953.*

[57] Unless specifically noted otherwise, the official data on abortions and sterilizations are taken from the report of the Welfare Ministry for the year 1953. Nihon. Kosei-sho, koshu hoken-kyoku. *Activities under the Eugenics Protection Law for the year 1953.* In case of conflicting figures, the preferred ones are those used by Dr. Muramatsu in: Mainichi shimbun-sha. Jinko mondai chosakai. *Some facts about family planning in Japan.*

Year	Total	At the discretion of an authorized physician[58]	With approval of a committee[58]
1949	246,104	145,021	101,083
1950	489,111	168,961	320,150
1951	638,350	179,593	458,757
1952	798,193	—	—
1953	1,068,066	—	—
1954	1,143,059	—	—
1955	1,170,143	—	—

The extent of the wastage between conception and live birth is evident if numbers of stillbirths between the fourth month and the completion of pregnancy are added to the numbers of abortions induced within the first three months of pregnancy. The incidence of reported induced abortions in relation to reported conceptions is given here for all Japan and for selected prefectures for the year 1953:

Area	Induced abortions within 3 months	Live births plus stillbirths	Total reported conceptions	Total induced abortions	Induced abortions per 100 reported conceptions
All Japan	962,281	2,055,464	3,017,745	1,068,066	35.4
Kyoto	28,692	33,545	62,237	31,040	49.8
Osaka	49,292	87,971	137,263	54,910	40.0
Tokyo	57,306	133,790	191,096	61,539	32.2
Aomori	17,912	42,099	60,011	19,893	33.1
Iwate	16,332	42,224	58,556	18,533	31.6
Ibaraki	13,067	53,918	66,985	14,835	22.1
Oita	12,400	32,278	44,678	14,512	32.4
Miyazaki	16,900	32,084	48,984	19,888	40.6
Kagoshima	13,065	50,618	63,683	15,450	24.2
Chiba	9,869	50,058	59,927	11,386	18.9
Nara	3,461	16,156	19,617	3,874	19.7

In 1953 the highest incidence of reported induced abortions was in the metropolitan prefectures, and the lowest incidence was in such prefectures as Chiba and Nara that were adjacent to the great metropolitan prefectures. Rates were also high in the rural prefectures of Tohoku, where fertility had been very high, and in the rural prefectures of Kyushu, where fertility had been somewhat lower. Reported abortions alone were sufficient to have produced major reductions in birth rates in all the prefectures of Japan.

The initial question concerns the accuracy of the reported numbers. These numbers are minimal. There are many reasons for concealment but there is nothing in the operational procedures for reporting that would lead to duplication of reports. The abortions performed in accordance with Article 13 of the early law, those authorized by local Eugenic Protection Committees, were reported, but abortions performed at the discretion of the designated physicians were substantially underreported. The reasons inhere both in factors personal to physicians and in the characteristics of the abortions. A reported abortion entails a public record of income that may be used for tax purposes. There is thus a financial deterrent to complete reporting by physicians. If abortions are performed for frail women with many children, reporting may be a mere formality, perhaps disregarded in the pressure of time but certainly not handled cautiously because of legal danger to the physician. If an abortion is performed for a young woman in excellent health and having only one child, discretion might indicate silence. The same thing would apply to induced abortions where the pregnancy was illegitimate. There have been many attempts to estimate the frequency of non-reported abortions. Some have used the confidential reports of designated physicians, but since these physicians are the authors of the incomplete returns under investigation their reports of underreporting are somewhat suspect. A recent estimate places the number that occurred in 1953 at from 1.8 to 2.3 million instead of the reported 1.1 million.[59]

Evaluation of abortion as a means of population control is not the province of the demographer as such, for the religious proscriptions, the ethical standards, and the social values that surround the relations of the sexes and the replacement of the generation are major factors in ultimate decisions as to the acceptability of abortion by any people. The availability of an operation to induce abortion is one of the major facts in the demographic situation of contemporary Japan, however, and it is related directly to the rapid reduction of the rate of population increase. Here alone among all the Asian and African countries have the developments of modern science and technology found practical applications in the reduction of births as well as in the reduction of deaths. The course of events in Japan merits objective analysis insofar as that analysis is possible.

In theory, the Eugenic Protection Law made abortions available to those women whose health would be endangered by the bearing of the child. The danger might arise from physical factors *per se*, or from a poverty that entailed overwork, poor nutrition, and associated difficulties. If health hazards were the criteria of the physicians, abortions should

[58] In the revision of 1952, the procedures were liberalized so that the designated physician could decide to perform an abortion without authorization or consultation. In 1952 and 1953 committees continued to function for cases of eugenic sterilization or ones in which rape was involved. They approved about 2,500 abortions per year, about half for rape and half for unspecified causes.

[59] Muramatsu, Minoru, and Ogino, Hiroshi. "Estimation of the total numbers of induced abortions as well as of sterilization operations for females in Japan for years of 1952 and 1953." *Bulletin of the Institute of Public Health*, 4(1-2):1-2. September 1954.

have been most frequent among women aged 35 and over. They should have been rare indeed among women aged from 15 to 19, and scarce among women aged from 20 to 24, for a negligible number of the former and many of the latter were single. Pregnancies that did occur among those who were married would be predominantly first- or second-order and hence hardly within any reasonable definition of excessive childbearing. The discrepancy between the purposes of the act and the facts for that segment of abortions that are reported is striking (TABLE 108). Numbers of induced abortions

TABLE 108

The incidence of reported induced abortions, by age of women, 1950-1954

Age of women	*1950*	*1951*	*1952*[a]	*1953*	*1954*
		Abortions per 1,000 women			
All women[b]	23.1	29.6	36.3	47.7	49.8
15-19	4.0	4.7	3.8	3.9	3.7
20-24	28.3	37.5	33.3	42.6	43.4
25-29			57.2	76.9	80.7
30-34	39.4	49.7	65.9	88.0	92.1
35-39			59.2	76.7	81.3
40-44	20.3	14.5	32.5	41.4	42.2
45-49			4.2	5.7	5.7
		Abortions per 1,000 live births			
All women	209	299	398	572	646
15-19	302	441	432	525	571
20-24	144	212	254	351	381
25-29			278	399	445
30-34	279	391	443	663	773
35-39			765	1,172	1,437
40-44	592	879	1,411	2,259	2,826
45-49			3,149	4,877	5,984

[a] Percentage distribution for July-December applied to the total number reported for the year.
[b] All abortions related to numbers of women aged 15-49.
Source: Mainichi shimbun-sha, jinko mondai chosa-kai. *Some facts about family planning in Japan.* Pp. 26-27.

per 1,000 women aged from 15 to 49 increased from 23.1 in 1950 to 49.8 in 1954; the number of induced abortions per 1,000 live births increased from 209 in 1950 to 646 in 1954. The incidence of abortions by age suggests that abortions were a modal means of fertility control rather than an aberrant practice. Proportionate reductions in fertility through abortion were greatest at the youngest and the oldest ages of childbearing. In absolute terms, however, abortions were most frequent at the ages of maximum childbearing. In all years from 1950 through 1954, more than 85 per cent of the women having induced abortions reported as such were in their twenties and thirties. More than 40 per cent of the reported abortions were secured by women in their twenties; the proportion of all induced abortions performed on women aged from 25 to 29 increased from 25.6 in 1952 to 26.7 in 1954. Numbers of abortions per 1,000 women or per 1,000 live births to women in this age group were moving sharply upward.

Most of the abortions reported were performed prior to the end of the third month of the pregnancy. In 1953, 962 thousand of the 1.1 million abortions were performed during this period, which is regarded as most appropriate by medical people.[60] Practically all were performed ostensibly for reasons of maternal health, with the economic factor stated as the major reason. In most cases the operation was performed in the doctor's office, the woman returning home the same day. Conditions were generally aseptic, the doctors had been trained in the technique, and there was routine use of penicillin.

The effects of the abortions on maternal mortality and maternal health are difficult to evaluate. Early studies on the effects of abortion indicate that maternal deaths were associated with poor techniques and unskilled practicians. Many abortions were delayed until the later months of pregnancy. As the practice has continued, the designated physicians have received further training and gained experience. The women have learned that the operation should be performed in the early months of pregnancy. Studies of the Institute of Public Health on women who had operations with the approval of Eugenics Protection Committees reveal some ill effects, particularly generalized complaints, but these women cannot be assumed to represent a national sample.[61] Major health problems are believed to surround the repetition of abortions. However, evidence is accumulating that the strong motivations which lead to repeated induced abortions lead ultimately to attempts at contraceptive practice and perhaps finally to sterilization.

The trends in the mortality of women in the reproductive ages or of women from causes designated as puerperal will be considered later in the analysis of mortality. Here it should be noted only that the mortality of women has not increased. The argument against abortions from the standpoint of mortality has to involve the thesis that mortality would have declined more rapidly if there had been no abortions. This type of argument is difficult to substantiate. It might be assumed that all women who wished to limit births practiced contraception effectively. If so, the mortality of women in the childbearing ages would have been reduced. On the other hand, it might be assumed that contraception practice remained limited and ineffective, and that no women had abortions. In this case, the pregnancies would have been carried to term and delivered by midwives in the home without aseptic conditions or penicillin. The women would have had to care for the new babies in addition to fulfilling responsibilities toward the rest of the family, household duties, and family work activities. In this case, the answer might be that the legalization of induced abortions had been associated with reductions in maternal mortality.

The fiscal aspects of a system of abortions performed by specially trained physicians might seem prohibitive. At first impression they seem so in Japan; fees of 1,000 to 2,000 yen ($3.00 to $6.00) are substantial sums to Japanese families. However, most Japanese families receive health services, whether from a private company, a government industry, the government acting as an employer, or a co-operative health

[60] A major medical problem remained, however, for the numbers performed later than the third month were as follows: 4th, 37 thousand; 5th, 34 thousand; 6th, 25 thousand; 7th, 9 thousand. In 1954, 1,042 thousand of a total of 1,142 thousand were performed in the second and third months of pregnancy, 68 thousand in the fourth and fifth months, 32 thousand in the sixth and later months.

[61] Koya, Yoshio, *et al.* "Preliminary report on a survey of health and demographic aspects of induced abortion in Japan." *Archives of the Population Association of Japan*, No. 2, pp. 1-9. 1953. Detailed analytical materials are being published currently in the *Bulletin of the Institute of Public Health.*

organization. Most of the health services operated by industries or government offer virtually free medical service to employees, including abortions to women employees. Services are furnished at half-cost to the dependents of employees. Since the usual cost of a unit of service is 600 yen and an abortion is a unit of service, the cost at half price is about 300 yen—in terms of U.S. currency, less than one dollar. In some places the cost is substantially less; the lowest price known to the writer is the 15 yen charge made by the health services of a mining company in Hokkaido.

Many facts about abortions have been presented. Abortions are legal on the basis of eugenic and health reasons; more than 1.1 million were reported in 1954; a prevalence of physicians using modern techniques and antibiotics seems to make the operation more acceptable to many families than the alternatives of childbirth or consistent and careful contraception; the hazards of illness or death are not sufficient to serve as major deterrents; the inclusion of abortions in health insurance services lessens the economic barrier. The critical questions involve the motivations that lead to abortions rather than to contraception, the relations of abortion to fertility, and the direction in which this means of birth limitation is leading the culture. It is easy to project a future in which live births will be inadequate to maintain the population and decline will ensue. It is also simple to envision a situation in which all the repressive measures of the state will be turned against abortions, which will have again been made illegal. It is difficult to evaluate the past or assess the future. There are no official records, no field studies, and no historic experience elsewhere in the East that can offer parallels. The only approach to explanations more satisfactory than conjecture lies in whatever analysis of the demography of abortions is possible. Such analysis is possible primarily for that segment of abortions that were included in the official reports on stillbirths.

STILLBIRTHS, ABORTION, AND INFANTICIDE

It is improbable that the resort to abortion in Japan could have attained its present magnitude without a cultural base in which post-conception limitation of fertility was accepted and practiced. The previous analysis of the incidence of stillbirths by age of mother and legitimacy status and the changes in stillbirth ratios over time indicates that such a cultural base did exist. The change in reported stillbirths in the years from 1947 to the present is consistent with the assumptions that substantial numbers of induced abortions have always been included in the stillbirth statistics, and that fluctuations in the ratio of stillbirths to live births continue to reflect changes in induced abortions (TABLE 109). During these years when abortion had been made legal under specified conditions and the incidence was known to be increasing rapidly, the number of reported stillbirths of gestations in the third month and beyond increased from 46.2 per 1,000 live births in 1947 to 92.8 in 1950, 100.8 in 1951, 101.9 in 1952, and 102.9 in 1953.[62] Ratios of stillbirths to live births increased for all ages of mothers, but the spectacular increases were on the peripheries of the childbearing ages, for mothers under age 20 and those aged 40 and over. In 1950 it is possible to distinguish spontaneous and induced stillbirths. Here the great increase in stillbirths was in the induced abortions to women in the early and in the terminal years of childbearing. In fact, the frequency of spontaneous abortions per 1,000 live births in 1950 was quite similar both in general level and in age incidence to the frequency of all stillbirths in 1947.

The data on stillbirths taken in conjunction with those on live births yield some evidence concerning infanticide. The statistical data for most peoples of the world and practically all the special studies are consistent with the assumption that the sex ratio at conception is very high, but that selective mortality of the male reduces the ratio throughout the period of gestation. Purely as a biological phenomenon, the sex ratio at expulsion would be expected to decline with increase in the duration of gestation. The prevalence of induced abortions as such would not exercise a major influence on the sex ratio of stillbirths, for the sex of the fetus would not be known prior to the induction of the abortion. In a culture that places a high valuation on sons, major deviations in the masculinity of stillbirths would suggest planned interference with pregnancy at a period when the sex of the fetus was known—that is, after parturition. This by definition would be infanticide. In 1950, the sex ratios among spontaneous and induced stillbirths by month of occurrence yield no substantial evidence of such postnatal elimination. In fact, induced stillbirths in the tenth and eleventh lunar months of gestation are more predominantly male than spontaneous stillbirths. At earlier months

[62] Computed from annual series in: Nihon. Kosei-sho, jinko mondai kenkyujo. *Saikin no jinko ni kansuru tokei shiryo.* Pp. 48-49.

TABLE 109

Reported stillbirths per 1,000 live births, by age of mother, 1947-1950[a]

Age of mother	*1947*	*1948*	*1949*	1950 *Total*	1950 *Spontaneous*	1950 *Induced*
15-49	46.2	53.7	71.4	92.8	45.6	47.2
15-19	71.0	84.4	138.9	207.4	73.7	132.1
20-24	48.0	53.8	69.0	89.0	46.6	42.3
25-29	38.9	45.2	56.9	70.3	39.2	31.1
30-34	40.5	47.9	64.3	85.3	42.0	43.2
35-39	53.0	60.7	88.3	121.0	51.8	69.2
40-44	77.4	88.3	135.8	220.2	74.4	118.8
45-49	94.7	138.2	231.6	386.4	117.2	262.2

[a] Total reported stillbirths, 4th month and beyond.
Source: Nihon. Kosei-sho, eisei tokei-bu. *Jinko dotai tokei.* 1947-1950.

of gestation the induced abortions are less male than the spontaneous abortions, a relationship consistent with the assumption that the male fetus is less viable and that therefore prenatal death serves as a mechanism securing an approach toward equality in the numbers of the sexes at birth.

Official data on reported abortions cannot yield a definitive answer to the question of postnatal limitation of offspring, however, for planned elimination after birth would not be reported as such under the provisions of the Stillbirth Registration or the Eugenic Protection Act. However, if it is assumed that the probability of postnatal elimination is greater for female than male babies, it is possible to estimate a minimum frequency of infanticide that is associated with selective elimination of the girl baby. All that is required is analysis of sex ratios for recorded live births by birth order and by age of mother. For the years from 1947 through 1949, the number of males per 1,000 females in the terminal birth orders increased as the birth order increased and the age of mother advanced.[63] The sex ratios are as follows:

Birth orders and ages of women	*Males per 1,000 females, live births*
7th order, women aged 25-29	1091
10th order, women aged 30-34	1156
12th and higher orders:	
Total	1647
Women aged 35-39	1535
Women aged 40 and over	1688

If terminal birth orders are included, the sex ratio of all live births declines from 1059 where mothers were below age 20, to 1050 where mothers were aged from 30 to 34, and then increases to 1061 where mothers were aged 40 and over. If the terminal births are eliminated, the decline in the sex ratio is continuous.

The conclusion from analysis of sex ratios in stillbirths and in live births is that there is some infanticide in modern Japan, but that it constitutes a very small proportion of the total regulation in the society.

The prevalence of stillbirths has been considered in relation to that of live births, and emphasis has been placed on legitimacy status. Stillbirths were found to be more prevalent among illegitimate than legitimate births. Ratios of stillbirths to live births were high in the initial and the terminal years of the reproductive period. In general, stillbirths were more frequent in the marginal categories of legitimacy status and among women in the ages marginal for reproduction. The picture of incidence shifts if numbers of reported stillbirths by age of the women are related to the numbers of women in the age groups, without reference to the legitimacy status of the stillbirth or the marital status of the woman (TABLE 110).

In the years from 1947 to 1950, stillbirths were concentrated among women in the ages when childbearing was prevalent rather than in the marginal ages. This incidence differed greatly from that to be expected if the purpose of the Eugenics Protection Act were being achieved. A frequency of induced stillbirths that differed little from age 20 to age 39 could hardly reflect the biological hazards of childbirth. Such a frequency would be difficult to interpret in terms of the hardships that were the overt concern of legalized abortion.

Definitive evaluation of the divergences between the purposes of the legalization of abortions and the resort of Japanese women to abortion would require that abortions be related to married women rather than to all women, for certainly the resort to abortion by the single, the separated, and the widowed would represent a violation of the mores of the familistic culture. Unfortunately, data on stillbirths by age of women and the marital status of women are available only for the census year 1950. For that year, the number of reported stillbirths per 1,000 married women were as follows:

Age of women	*All stillbirths*	*Spontaneous*	*Induced*
15-49	17.4	8.6	8.9
15-19	84.6	30.3	54.3
20-24	33.4	17.5	15.9
25-29	21.1	11.8	9.3
30-34	17.9	8.8	9.1
35-39	15.3	6.5	8.7
40-44	8.5	3.3	5.2
45-49	1.0	0.3	0.7

Thus the frequency of induced stillbirths to married women declined consistently with advancing age of women, as did the number of spontaneous stillbirths. Additional light is shed on this relationship, so indicative of a resort to induced abortion on the part of the single and the married with few children, by an inspection of the frequency of stillbirths to women

[63] Maruoka, Hikoo. "Seihi ni kansuru kenkyu. Dai-2 hen. Shussei no seihi." *Igaku kenkyu*, 22(3):87-100. March 1952.

TABLE 110

Stillbirths per 1,000 total women, by age, 1947-1950

Age of women	*1947*	*1948*	*1949*	1950[a] *Total*	*Spontaneous*	*Induced*
15-49	6.1	6.8	9.2	10.2	5.0	5.2
15-19	1.0	0.6	2.2	1.7	1.0	1.7
20-24	8.0	9.5	12.5	14.3	7.5	6.8
25-29	10.4	11.0	15.4	16.6	9.3	7.4
30-34	9.4	9.9	13.4	14.9	7.3	7.6
35-39	8.3	8.7	11.9	12.6	5.4	7.2
40-44	3.0	4.8	6.6	7.0	2.7	4.3
45-49	0.5	0.6	0.8	0.8	0.2	0.6

[a] The age distributions used for 1950 are those of the 10 per cent sample tabulation.
Source: Reference, Table 108.

of specified age by the order of pregnancy involved. These ratios relating stillbirths to women regardless of marital status are given in TABLE 111 for the period from 1947 through 1950.[64]

Stillbirths increased for all ages of women and all pregnancy orders from 1947 through 1950, though in all years the highest incidence occurred among first and second pregnancies to women aged from 20 to 29. Lesser peaks occurred for sixth to ninth pregnancies among women aged from 35 to 39.

[64] For 1951 the data on stillbirths by order of gestation by age of mother pertain only to those at 28 weeks or over. The trends by order by age of woman are similar to those for the years from 1947 to 1950.

If stillbirths by order of pregnancy are related to live births by order of live birth, bimodality is quite apparent.[65] The number of induced abortions by order in relation to births by order was very high for first pregnancies or births to women aged from 15 to 19, and for sixth- or higher-order pregnancies or births to women aged 40 and over. For any order of pregnancy or birth, the frequency of stillbirths was highest at the first age of mothers at which the pregnancy-birth order appeared, dropped at the next age of mothers, and then increased at each successive age. The ratio of first-order stillbirths to first-order

[65] Prior to 1951, stillbirths were given only by pregnancy order, live births only by order of live birth.

TABLE 111

Reported stillbirths per 1,000 women, by order of gestation and age of mother, 1947-1950

Age of mother	All gestations	ORDER OF GESTATION 1	2	3	4	5	6-9	10 or above
				1947				
15-49	6.2	2.1	1.0	0.7	0.6	0.5	1.1	0.2
15-19	1.1	1.0	0.1	0.0	0.0	—	—	—
20-24	8.1	5.8	1.7	0.5	0.1	0.0	0.0	—
25-29	10.5	3.9	2.7	2.1	1.1	0.5	0.2	0.0
30-34	9.5	1.3	1.2	1.6	1.8	1.6	2.0	0.1
35-39	8.3	0.5	0.5	0.6	1.0	1.2	4.0	0.5
40-44	4.4	0.2	0.1	0.2	0.2	0.4	2.4	0.9
45-49	0.6	0.0	0.0	0.0	0.0	0.0	0.3	0.1
				1948				
15-49	7.0	2.5	1.1	0.8	0.6	0.5	1.2	0.2
15-19	1.5	1.3	0.1	0.0	—	—	—	—
20-24	9.8	6.9	2.2	0.6	0.1	0.0	0.0	—
25-29	11.7	4.4	3.0	2.3	1.2	0.5	0.2	0.0
30-34	10.1	1.4	1.3	1.7	2.0	1.7	2.0	0.1
35-39	9.0	0.6	0.5	0.7	1.0	1.3	4.5	0.5
40-44	5.2	0.2	0.1	0.2	0.3	0.5	2.9	1.0
45-49	0.7	0.0	0.0	0.0	0.0	0.0	0.4	0.2
				1949				
15-49	9.2	2.8	1.7	1.1	0.9	0.8	1.7	0.2
15-19	2.2	2.0	0.3	0.0	0.0	0.0	0.0	—
20-24	12.5	7.8	3.5	0.9	0.2	0.0	0.0	0.0
25-29	15.3	4.6	4.4	3.3	1.9	0.8	0.4	0.0
30-34	13.8	1.5	1.6	2.3	2.8	2.5	3.0	0.1
35-39	11.9	0.6	0.5	0.9	1.3	1.8	6.1	0.7
40-44	6.6	0.2	0.1	0.2	0.4	0.6	3.9	1.3
45-49	0.8	0.0	0.0	0.0	0.0	0.0	0.4	0.2
				1950				
15-49	10.2	3.1	1.9	1.4	1.0	0.8	1.7	0.2
15-19	2.8	2.5	0.3	0.0	0.0	0.0	0.0	—
20-24	14.4	8.8	4.1	1.2	0.2	0.0	0.0	0.0
25-29	16.7	4.5	5.0	3.9	2.1	0.8	0.3	0.0
30-34	15.0	1.5	1.8	2.7	3.2	2.7	3.0	0.1
35-39	12.7	0.7	0.6	1.0	1.5	2.1	6.3	0.6
40-44	7.0	0.2	0.2	0.2	0.4	0.6	4.1	1.3
45-49	0.9	0.0	0.0	0.0	0.0	0.0	0.5	0.3

Source: Reference, Table 108.

pregnancies or live births was high for young women. This ratio dropped sharply for the second order of stillbirths and live births, but increased as order of pregnancy or birth increased. Reported stillbirths are comparable to abortion and contraception in the early stages of diffusion, with substantial frequencies among the unmarried or the newly married at the younger ages and among the older women who have had many pregnancies or live births. This suggested pattern of post-conception limitation of fertility by age and marital status is contrary both to the purposes of the legal act permitting abortions and to the familial values of Japanese culture. The implementation of the act as intended would lead to high ratios of induced abortions among later-order pregnancies or births to older women. The familial values of Japanese culture would preclude abortion until there were one or two live births.

Insofar as reported stillbirths indicate the prevalence of abortions at all stages of gestation, it is evident that induced abortions occur in substantial proportions among unmarried youth and among older women. The resort to abortion seems to be occurring among unmarried girls, married women for whom pregnancy and birth are inappropriate, and widows.

The intermingling of that which is defined as moral and that which is defined as immoral is quite apparent in some of the reports on stillbirths for local areas. The following data refer to the city of Kyoto for the year 1951:[66]

Age of women	*Stillbirths per 1,000 live births*	ILLEGITIMATE PER 1,000 LEGITIMATE	
		Live births	*Stillbirths*
15-49	124	46	408
15-19	375	239	5,409
20-24	137	47	769
25-29	94	37	298
30-34	100	41	253
35-39	169	49	101
40-44	223	78	180
45-49	667	333	273

It is difficult to assess the relations between the incidence of those abortions reported as stillbirths and the much greater number reported only in the data of the Welfare Ministry. Reported stillbirths pertain only to abortions that occur in the fourth and later months of pregnancy, whereas most induced abortions occur in the second and third months. The distribution of reported induced abortions for the last six months of 1952 and the first six months of 1953 reveal high proportions among women aged from 25 to 39.[67] The evidence from abortions reported by the designated physicians cannot be taken as definitive, however, for physicians would be most likely to report those abortions performed in full conformity with the specifications and the intent of the law. In addition, the answers to the questions of enumerators bent on securing data for special studies would be most complete for those women whose abortions were legally justified.

Whatever the intricacies of the interrelations between induced abortions reported as such and that segment of such abortions reported as stillbirths, some general conclusions seem valid. Stillbirth statistics reflect the changing frequency of induced abortions among the Japanese. Infanticide has survived in some areas and among some classes, as has conscious neglect of the infant after birth, but they cannot have been a major determinant of levels or trends in fertility in the period under study. Induced abortions occurring in the fourth and later months were relatively most frequent among the young, where they served to terminate undesired pregnancies, and among the aged, where they served to terminate pregnancies that had occurred at a time of life when childbirth was not considered proper. In absolute terms, stillbirths and presumably induced abortions as a whole were most frequent among younger married women desiring to postpone or to limit first and second births and among older married women with many children. The frequency of stillbirths, and presumably also of induced abortions as a whole, was associated positively with industrialization and urbanization, negatively with dependence on agriculture and rural life. Whatever the intent of the law, a major contribution of the greater ease in securing abortions was a further reduction of fertility among those educated and urban groups who presumably knew and practiced contraception to the greatest extent. In all regions of the country, however, there was a regular increase in the ratio of stillbirths to livebirths over the years from 1947 through 1953. The following figures illustrating this relationship are stillbirths of all durations per 1,000 live births:[68]

Prefectures by industrial type	*1947*	*1950*	*1951*	*1952*	*1953*
All Japan	46.2	92.8	100.8	101.9	103.7
Metropolitan	51.0	98.0	107.2	112.7	120.9
Other industrial	46.6	100.6	108.7	112.1	113.9
Intermediate	44.9	93.0	100.8	100.0	100.3
Agricultural	46.4	90.1	97.4	96.8	97.7
Hokkaido	42.9	77.9	89.5	96.7	99.8

STERILIZATION

Sterilizations performed under the Eugenic Protection Law have been reported as follows by the Welfare Ministry:[69]

Year	*Total*	*Male*	*Female*
1949	5,752	68	5,684
1950	11,403	130	11,273
1951	16,233	239	15,994
1952	22,424	389	22,035
1953	32,422	585	31,911
1954	—	—	37,099
1955	—	—	41,727

How many sterilizations have actually been performed is a subject almost as speculative as the real number of induced abortions. One estimate places the number in 1953 as from 134 to 172 thousand;[70] the general assumption is that from five to ten are performed for each one reported.

[66] Kyoto-shi. Eisei-kyoku. *Kyoto-shi eisei tokei nempo, 1951.* Pp. 22, 23, and 75. Stillbirths include those in and beyond the fourth month of gestation.

[67] Data for July-December 1952: Nihon. Kosei-sho, eisei tokei-bu. *Vital and health statistics in Japan.* Part II, Table VI, A.s. Data for January-June, 1953: *Nihon sanji keikaku joho, The Japan Planned Parenthood Quarterly* 4(3-4):53. July-December 1953.

[68] Source: 1947-1950. Nihon. Kosei-sho, eisei tokei-bu. *Jinko dotai tokei.* 1951: Nihon. Kosei-sho, daijin kambo, tokei chosa-bu. *Jinko dotai tokei maigetsu gaisu, Showa 26-nen kei.* Table 1. 1952: *Ibid. Showa 27-nen nenkei bun.* Table 1. 1953: *Ibid. Kokumin eisei no doko. Kosei no shihyo,* Vol. I, No. 1, p. 55.

[69] Data on sterilizations are taken from the Welfare Ministry's report for 1953: Nihon. Kosei-sho, koshu hoken-kyoku. *Activities under the Eugenic Protection Law for the year 1953.* Later figures, courtesy of Dr. Minoru Muramatsu.

[70] Muramatsu, Minoru, and Ogino, Hiroshi. "Estimation of the total numbers of induced abortions as well as of sterilization operations for females in Japan for the years of 1952 and 1953." *Bulletin of the Institute of Public Health,* 4(1-2):1-2. September 1954.

The rapid increase in sterilizations bears little relation to the eugenic goals for which the law was passed, for all but a negligible number of the operations are performed for reasons of mother's health. And here, as in the case of induced abortions, "mother's health" is the acceptable rationalization for family limitation. In demographic terms, the sterilizations already performed represent a substantial contribution to the limitation of fertility.

The future role of sterilization in the limitation of fertility is related closely to the spread and the efficiency of contraceptive practice. The increase in sterilization permits the inference that if present types of contraceptives remain the sole means available to the Japanese, the incidence of sterilizations will increase.

CONTRACEPTION, ABORTION, AND STERILIZATION

The psychological processes that lead to contraceptive practice are presumed to be associated with urbanization, individualistic motivations, and secular attitudes toward life. Abortion, on the other hand, is explained in terms of economic pressures by the Japanese who have been interviewed on the question. If this dichotomy in the cultural, material, and attitudinal basis for contraception and abortion exists in fact as in theory, it would be reasonable to expect reduced numbers of induced abortions with the restoration of a viable economy and the achievement of higher levels of employment at more adequate levels of income. Moreover, induced abortions would be expected to have been most frequent in the poor agricultural regions of the country, where women bear many children while participating in the work of home and field. Both these anticipations are contrary to fact. On the national level, the rate of induced abortion rose sharply during a period of economic reconstruction when levels of living were moving upward. Field studies in local areas indicated that induced abortions were more frequent among the middle and upper social-economic classes in urban areas than among the poor of the cities or the farmers of the rural areas. In Tokyo and its surrounding areas, the proportion of pregnancies terminated by induced abortions was substantially higher in the *shi* than in the *machi*, and substantially higher in the *machi* than in the *mura*. This was true not only for total pregnancies, but for each specific pregnancy order from the first to the eighth.[71] In the national survey conducted by the Population Problems Research Council of the Mainichi Newspaper Company in 1952, the incidence of abortions was found to be correlated positively with the education of wives.[72] In fact, if one took most of the studies on the incidence of induced abortions in Japan and substituted the word "contraception" for the word "abortion," the results would appear quite similar to those from studies of incidence in other countries.

The close interrelations between contraception and abortion are immediately apparent when the experience of individual women with abortion is related to the experience of these same women with contraception. In the Mainichi study of 1952 the proportion of wives who had had abortions was low among those who had never practiced contraception.[73] It was high among wives practicing contraception, advancing from 20 per cent for those under age 25 to 45.5 for those aged from 35 to 49. In the study made in 1952 by the Institute of Population Problems, a special tabulation was made of the type of pregnancy termination for pregnancies resulting from contraceptive failure. The percentage distributions were as follows:[74]

Type of termination	*All Japan*	*Urban areas*	*Rural areas*
Live birth	42.7	37.9	47.2
Stillbirth (spontaneous)	7.3	5.8	8.7
Abortion (induced)	50.0	56.3	44.1
Total	100.	100.	100.

If abortions are procured for pregnancies that have resulted from contraceptive failure, it would seem that more careful use of more adequate contraceptives would lessen the need for and hence the frequency of abortions. This may account for a somewhat lesser rate of abortions among women practicing contraception in great cities than in urban areas. The resort to abortion after contraceptive failure cannot be the total explanation for abortions, however, for the Mainichi study of 1952 revealed high rates of abortions among a group designated as past contraceptors, i.e., those who had once practiced contraception but no longer did so. Here it may be that contraception was tried and given up, perhaps as esthetically or emotionally unsatisfactory in use, perhaps as affording inadequate protection.

If contraception and abortion are viewed in relation to Japanese culture itself, without reference to Western conceptions of the desirable, the acceptable, and the expected, the present situation is quite comprehensible. The attitudes of the people toward control are not highly specific as to means. In the Mainichi study of 1952, most men and women expressed verbal approval of abortion. Only 3.2 per cent of the men and 3.1 per cent of the women opposed it for religious reasons. Seven per cent of both men and women opposed it because it was harmful to the health of the mother; another 7 per cent opposed it because they believed its effects to be demoralizing. With these prevalent attitudes toward abortion, the basic question for families was the adoption of family limitation practices of any type. The selection of limitation as between contraception and abortion became one of means to a far larger extent than is true among peoples whose ethical system has a Christian basis.

Sterilization is the answer of increasing numbers of Japanese women to the dilemma of choice between successive abortions or unsatisfactory contraceptive practice. Abortions involve a pain cost, physical inconvenience, the social unpleasantness of concealment, and apparently a widespread feeling of having done something that is not quite proper. If continued, there may be hazards to health. Contraception is an alternative, but it does not appear to be popular. There are timidities about the purchase of supplies, their use is inconvenient and undesirable, and pregnancy is likely to occur anyway. As we have noted earlier, there are two established sequences in the limitation practices of Japanese women, and there may be a third as well. In the first, there is contraceptive practice with abortion used to terminate an unplanned pregnancy. In the second, abortion precedes contraceptive practice. In the third, there is a series of abortions

[71] Shinozaki, Nobuo. [*Sexual life of the Japanese.*] Translated: "Spontaneous and induced abortions." *Nihon sanji keikaku joho, The Japan Planned Parenthood Quarterly*, 4(3-4):54. July-December 1953.

[72] Mainichi shimbun-sha. Jinko mondai chosa-kai. Population Problems Research Council. *Public opinion survey on birth control in Japan.* Pp. 48-49.

[73] *Ibid.* Pp. 50-51.

[74] Honda, Tatsuo. *A survey of spread of birth control.*

without interludes of contraceptive practice. None of these is satisfactory as a continuing solution to the problems of family limitation. If the numbers of children desired are already secured, sterilization seems a solution. The economic barriers are not great, for the health insurance facilities provide sterilization at greatly reduced costs. In the studies of the Institute of Public Health, there were few evidences of psychological difficulties among women who had been sterilized. On the contrary, there was personal relaxation at having achieved a definitive solution to a hitherto recurrent problem, since there was no need for further efforts to avoid conception and no fear that conception would occur.

Conclusion

The existence of a widespread limitation of fertility that was willed is apparent in the differentials and the trends in the marital fertility of the Japanese. Age at marriage, widowhood, childlessness—these and other formal factors can explain some part of the variations in the fertility of married women at given periods of time and some part of the decline in such fertility over time, but they cannot explain all the variations at any given time or the sharp variations from year to year. Planned limitation existed in the population of Japan in 1920. In the decades after 1920, practices of limitation were diffused over broader geographic areas and accepted by increasing numbers of people in ever-wider ranges of social groups.

In the years before World War II a major portion of the increasing limitation of fertility among the Japanese was associated with the postponement of age at marriage and the separation of couples by the military service or migration of the husband. The process of fertility decline was continuous, but slow. In the middle 1930's the fertility of the Japanese was far below that of the peasant peoples of the East, but it remained high enough to produce a rather large population increase. In this connection it is useful to recall the reproductive experience of the women who were completing their childbearing period in 1950. If the focus is Japan itself, it is significant that almost one-fourth of all women who were or had been married were either childless or had had the one or two births that would be regarded as low fertility even in the West. If the focus is the future of other Asian areas, it is significant that a century after the opening to the West and the beginning of a process of comprehensive modernization, 45 per cent of all married Japanese women who had survived the childbearing period had had six or more children.

In the postwar years there has been a rapid spread of contraceptive practice and a nation-wide resort to abortions. There is increasing acceptance of sterilization. The decline in marital fertility has been rapid, and it has extended from Tokyo to the villages of Hokkaido in the northeast and Kyushu in the southwest. This is not the response of an agrarian society in the initial period of its social and economic modernization. It is the response of a literate people who have radios and electric lights, who live in a country with a network of transportation and communication facilities, and who work in major part in activities other than agriculture. The formal facts of changing levels of reproductive behavior, of contraceptive products manufactured and induced abortions performed, and of the diffusion of the various means of limitation singly or in combination contribute little enough to any real knowledge of the changing attitudes and values of the Japanese in the realm of fertility control. They offer even less basis for estimating under what circumstances or with what speed contraception or other types of birth restriction might develop in other Asian populations.

The distinctive cultural and political milieu of modern Japan has predisposed toward high or low fertility, toward relatively unrestricted or rigidly restricted fertility, depending on the situation of the period. Underlying this factor of the central society are the values of ancestor-oriented familism, the reproductive mores of peasants who live in adjustment to the land and cultivate it with their hands, the disruptive forces of rapid industrialization and urbanization, the compelling aspirations of youth in a transforming society, and the shocks of the war and defeat. Whether Japanese experience is or is not typical of that to be anticipated elsewhere in Asian nations undergoing industrialization is a question that must remain unanswered until other Asian peoples have become industrial and urban. In the meantime, it must always be remembered that the Japanese entered the modern world with a tradition of family limitation; that they maintained close identification with the soil, their unique culture, and their imperial institutions; and that the high fertility of the late nineteenth and early twentieth centuries was in part a product of the planned creation of appropriate values by a central group who controlled education, press, and police. It must also be remembered that the essential aspect of modernization in all segments of the economy and the society has been movement from the traditional values and behavior of the peasant society toward behavior, if not values, similar in broad outline to those in other urban and industrial societies.

CHAPTER XIV

Mortality

FROM death rates not too dissimilar to those of European countries in the early days of the Industrial Revolution, Japan has moved rapidly to rates that are only slightly behind those of other modern industrial nations. The distinctive aspect of this development in Japan is that it has not been a close correlate of an advance to high levels of income and nutrition. At any given time during the past several decades, Japanese mortality has been considerably lower than might be expected on the basis of general relations between death rates and per capita national income or the caloric value of food. Japan gave the first major demonstration that reduced and even low mortality could be achieved in somewhat unfavorable environmental conditions.

Even today a general survey of the Japanese scene would not lead to an expectation of low death rates. Japan's people live close to each other, whether in rural villages or in the residential areas of cities. Although there are appreciable differences in levels of living in various regions and among social and economic classes, the predominant fact is the simplicity, if not the poverty, of living conditions. Japan has steel mills, hydro-electric works, newspapers and books, radios and television, but housing and way of life remain traditional in form. Nutrition is inadequate; proteins, fats, minerals, and vitamins are deficient. Fuel is used sparingly for cooking and for heating houses, shops, and factories. Family living is crowded, with consequent hazards of contagion. Hours of work are long, conditions of work are poor, and relaxation is limited, especially for women.

Japanese agriculture is intensive, as we have said before, and the land requires fertilizer that the farmers are ill-prepared to buy in sufficient quantities. Domestic animals are so scarce that animal manure cannot contribute much to the soil. Thus the use of human waste continues. Hand-drawn carts are used to collect the waste from the houses, and distribution to farmers often requires transportation for some distances.

Rapid urbanization, crowded living conditions, inadequate nutrition, minimal plumbing and sewerage installations,[1] and the direct use of night soil imply severe hazards to health. That such hazards exist will be demonstrated later when the major causes of death are examined. There are counteracting folkways, however, and government emphasis on sanitation is firm. Cleanliness and the bath are entrenched in the Japanese way of life. Annual cleaning of house and premises is both customary and compulsory. And as cities grew, the provision of purified water was recognized as an essential municipal function.[2]

Japan's acceptance of the life-saving techniques of modern science has been partial—necessarily so, for the poverty of the people and the limitations to government facilities precluded the adoption of preventive or curative measures that required changes in ways of living, special diets, expensive drugs, rest, or institutional care. Vaccination and external procedures that reduced the hazards of specific diseases were adopted quickly by the government and seized upon avidly by the people. The downward course of mortality in Japan was related broadly to advances in educational and cultural levels among the people. It was related directly to developments in public health services and advances in science which banished the diseases that had been the great killers. Thus the subject of mortality is introduced with a consideration of the public health services and the training of medical personnel.

PUBIC HEALTH AND MEDICAL CARE[3]

Western customs and practices were the initial models in the fields of public health and medical service, but there were progressive modifications to adapt procedures to the Japanese scene. Emphasis was placed on the training of large numbers of medical and health personnel rather than on the development of high levels of competence in lesser numbers. Home remained the appropriate place for illness and death; familism tended to structure medical-care facilities and circumscribe the achievements of physicians. The substitute for the great Western hospital was a small institution where the family moved in with the patient and furnished not only food and nursing service but emotional support. However, the general discipline of the population and its respect for the dictates of government permitted an efficient use of laws and police regulations in health and sanitary activities that would be difficult to find equaled elsewhere.

In prewar Japan health preservation, communicable disease control, chronic disease prevention, and medical affairs were responsibilities of the Sanitary Bureau of the Ministry of Home Affairs. Authority was given to civilian rather than medical personnel. Administration was highly centralized, but there was a sanitary bureau or office in each *shi*, *machi*, and *mura*. There was a gradual development from sole concern with sanitary inspection and communicable disease control to consideration of the more fundamental aspects of problems of public health. Health guidance centers were established in many areas as early as 1930, and a law establishing Health

[1] In Japan in 1937 there were 17,877 water closets with purification arrangements, 68,817 connected directly to the mains. Of these latter, 55,221 were in Tokyo, 13,277 in Nagoya. See: Nihon. Kosei-sho, eisei-kyoku. *Eisei nempo, 1937*. Pp. 124-125.

[2] In 1937 there were 652 waterworks approved, and 603 were established. Twenty-six per cent of all the houses in Japan were supplied, although the variations among the prefectures were great. Waterworks were a function of cities; in general, the proportion of the population supplied from the works increased with the proportion of the population of the prefecture that was urban. In Tokyo and Osaka prefectures the percentage of households supplied was above 70; it was 60 in Kanagawa, 47 in Kyoto, 41 in Hyogo, 36 in Aichi, 29 in Fukuoka. The percentage was less than 5 per cent in agricultural prefectures without large cities. *Ibid.* Pp. 122-123.

[3] This summary of health and medical facilities relies heavily on the knowledge of Dr. Marshall C. Balfour.

Centers became effective in 1937.[4] By 1944 there were 306 Health Centers; in 1945, when all governmental public health institutions were integrated into the system, there were 770 centers. During the 1930's, the facilities of these centers and the training of their personnel were limited, if compared either with the ideals of the Japanese doctors of the period or with the facilities and personnel available after the war. However, these prewar developments formed the basis for a great expansion of health facilities in the postwar period. Health Centers numbered 689 in 1950, 724 in 1951, and 772 in 1954.

The responsibilities of the Health Centers were comprehensive. According to the law of 1947, the following functions were assigned to them: (1) health education; (2) vital statistics; (3) improvement of nutrition and health sanitation; (4) environmental sanitation; (5) public health nursing; (6) medical social service; (7) maternal and child hygiene; (8) dental hygiene; (9) laboratory tests and examination services; (10) prevention of tuberculosis and other communicable diseases; and (11) other programs for the improvement and promotion of public health at the local level.

The centers emphasized mass diagnosis and treatment. In 1953 the following activities were reported: health consultations, 5.6 million; mass examinations, 18.1 million; patients treated, 1.8 million; person receiving immunization, 9.7 million; x-ray examinations, 16.6 million. The emphasis on service is indicated by the characteristics of the 5.6 million health consultations. More than 2.4 million concerned tuberculosis, while 769 thousand concerned venereal disease. Only 510 thousand were classified as maternity cases, 630 thousand as infants, and 283 thousand as pre-school children. Of the mass examinations, 14.2 million were for tuberculosis and 784 thousand for venereal disease, while 124 thousand were maternity cases, 640 thousand were infants, and 257 thousand were pre-school children. Part of the explanation for the concentration of effort lies in the limitation of facilities. The services outlined above were provided by staffs that in total numbered only 4,846 physicians, 7,576 public health nurses, and 26,549 other personnel.

The programs of inoculation were far more extensive than the activities of the Health Centers. By 1953 almost 30 million persons, more than a third of the total population, had received preventive inoculation against tuberculosis.[5] Vaccinations totalled 10.4 million in 1952 and 7.1 million in 1953. Total immunizations in 1952 were 41 million. Immunizations other than those against tuberculosis included 4.5 million smallpox, 31.0 million typhoid and paratyphoid, 3.8 million diphtheria, 1.6 million whooping cough, and 270 thousand epidemic typhus.

Medical care was private, with physicians organized in a network of small hospitals and clinics. Patients paid for their services and their medicines either directly or through the health services of the organization for which they worked. In the prewar period, physicians were generally ill-trained by Western standards, but they were relatively plentiful and they were widely distributed over the country. In 1935 there were 8.4 physicians and 2.9 dentists per 10,000 population; by 1941 there were 9.3 doctors, 3.4 dentists, 8.6 midwives, and 20.6 nurses. Losses among medical personnel were heavy during the war and training was retarded. After the war the dissolution of the armed forces and the repatriation of civilians returned many doctors to civilian activities in Japan. However, normal processes of attrition were operative, training facilities were still limited, and the population was increasing rapidly. By 1952 the medical personnel per 10,000 population included 9.9 physicians, 3.4 dentists, 5.8 pharmacists, 3.5 public health nurses, 11.6 midwives, and 24.1 clinical nurses.

The relative emphasis on public and private activities in the broad field of medical care is perhaps indicated by the fact that in 1952 less than five thousand physicians were listed among the personnel of Health Centers, whereas there were 85 thousand physicians in Japan.

The outlook for health and the reduction of disease and premature death appeared dark in the early postwar years. The reduction of death rates to prewar levels and progress beyond this required new preventive and therapeutic measures and techniques. However, the new inventions had been discovered and the techniques of production and use developed while Japan was isolated by the war. As the Japanese learned of the new chemicals, the antibiotics, the inoculations and the vaccinations, the health services and the private practitioners developed procedures for their use. Soon Japanese industry was producing the chemicals and drugs at prices suitable to wide use in Japan and export to Asia.

The Japanese drive for the achievement of health and the postponement of death utilized and extended much of the knowledge of the West, but the developments within Japan were selective adaptations to local needs and possibilities. Thus the experience of the Japanese may offer some basis for assessing the probable future in other countries where mortality is still relatively high.

Mortality in the Nation, 1920-1955

PROBLEMS OF DATA

Demonstration of the fact of declining mortality is difficult for the decades prior to 1920. Improvements in *koseki* records in the late nineteenth and early twentieth centuries resulted in continuing and probably spurious increases in death rates as computed from official statistics. In the early 1920's registration procedures were modernized and legal regulations became more comprehensive. In addition, increasing health and medical services led to a wider public knowledge of the legal requirements for the reporting of deaths. Regulations concerning burial or cremation permits gave further impetus to death reporting. The commercialization of the economy and the development of individual property rights created familial reasons for removing the names of the dead from the *koseki*. Finally, the enumerative census of 1920 provided an accurate inventory of the population by sex and age and broke the circular relationship between mortality and population that had existed throughout the period when *koseki* records were the sole source of national demographic statistics.

The mortality reporting of the years from 1920 to 1925 was rather good, if judged against the background of the historic statistics for Japan or the contemporary statistics in other areas of the Western Pacific. If comparisons are made with the mortality reporting of the countries of the West where levels of living and educational standards were higher, doctors numerous and well-trained, and public health systems more adequately financed, Japan's mortality data seem relatively inaccurate. Reported deaths were those of Japanese

[4] Nihon. Kosei-sho. *A brief report on public health administration in Japan, 1954.* P. 5.

[5] For a description of the programs, see: Nihon. Kosei-sho. *A brief report on tuberculosis control program in Japan, 1953.* The statistics given here are from: *A brief report on public health administration in Japan,* issued by the Kosei-sho in 1954.

only, whereas census counts included colonials and aliens.[6] Stillbirth reporting was deficient, and infant deaths were underreported in many regions of the country. Cause-of-death reporting was inadequate, for many, if not most, deaths occurred without medical attendance. The proportions of all deaths reported as due to unspecified causes or to senility were high.

The difficulties with death records in Japan are mentioned as a prelude to the consideration of mortality because, contrary to the situation in fertility, there is no way to measure the error in numbers or in areal distribution. However, the deficiencies should not be overstressed. The statistical services of Japan have provided the most comprehensive and reasonably accurate mortality data available for any Asian area.[7] Internal consistency in death rates from age to age and between males and females, and regularities in changes over time, indicate that the course of death rates can be traced with fair precision. The experience of Japan permits a study of the social and economic interrelationships and the cultural conditioning of mortality within an industrializing society.

CHANGES, 1920-1954

Since 1920, the course of the death rate has been downward for the total population and for most of its component sex and age groups in virtually all regions and practically all social-economic classes (Table 112). The movement was

[6] The national life tables pertain to the Japanese only, but rates for areas within the country generally relate the deaths of Japanese to the total population. This introduces a factor of differential accuracy as between areas and an artificial factor of decline over time.

[7] If it is argued that Taiwan is an exception, it need only be indicated that the statistical sources for Taiwan were developed by Japan. Moreover, the mortality data for Taiwan are primarily those for an agricultural economy without major urbanization, and they refer only to a period of colonial dependence.

TABLE 112

Mortality in Japan, 1920-1955

	DEATHS PER 1,000 POPULATION				
Year	*Crude*	*Standardized*[a]	*Infant deaths per 1,000 live births*	*Neonatal deaths per 1,000 live births*	*Stillbirths per 1,000 total births (live and still)*
1920	25.4	25.2	166.2	69.0	66.8
1921	22.8	22.5	169.2	68.5	65.4
1922	22.5	22.1	167.2	67.5	63.4
1923	23.0	22.5	164.2	66.3	61.9
1924	21.4	20.8	156.9	63.2	59.6
1925	20.3	19.9	142.8	58.1	56.6
1926	19.1	18.7	138.0	56.9	56.0
1927	19.7	19.3	142.3	56.4	54.1
1928	19.8	19.3	138.2	54.2	53.6
1929	19.9	19.4	142.6	55.4	53.7
1930	18.2	17.8	124.5	49.9	53.8
1931	19.0	18.8	132.0	51.7	52.8
1932	17.7	17.6	117.9	47.9	52.3
1933	17.7	17.7	121.7	48.5	51.4
1934	18.1	18.0	125.3	50.6	52.8
1935	16.8	16.8	107.1	44.7	50.5
1936	17.5	17.5	117.2	48.1	50.5
1937	17.0	17.0	106.2	43.8	49.0
1938	17.7	17.6	115.0	46.2	49.5
1939	17.7	18.1	106.7	44.3	49.6
1940	16.4	16.7	90.4	38.7	46.3
1941	15.7	16.1	84.4	34.2	43.7
1942	15.8	16.1	85.8	34.1	41.3
1943	16.3	16.7	87.0	33.8	39.9
1947	14.6	15.0	76.7	32.3	44.2
1948	11.9	12.0	61.7	28.2	50.9
1949	11.6	11.6	62.5	27.6	66.7
1950	10.9	10.8	60.1	27.4	84.9
1951	9.9	—	57.5	27.5	92.2
1952	8.9	—	49.5	25.5	92.5
1953	8.9	—	49.1	25.5	94.0
1954	8.2	—	44.7	—	95.8
1955	7.8	—	39.8	—	95.9

[a] Standardized to 1935 sex and age distribution.

Source: 1920-1952: Nihon. Kosei-sho, eisei tokei-bu. *Vital and health statistics in Japan....* 1953: Nihon. Kosei-sho. *A brief report on public health administration in Japan.* 1954 and 1955: Nihon. Kosei-sho, eisei tokei-bu. *Jinko dotai tokei maigetsu gaisu.* 1954, Table I, pp. 30-31. 1955, Table I, pp. 42-43.

generally rapid, and it continued with appreciable regularity except for the late war and early prewar period. The crude death rate for the entire country was 22.2 in the intercensal years from 1920 to 1925, 17.3 in the years from 1935 to 1940. The state of civilian health was maintained without severe deterioration through 1943. Deaths increased sharply in 1944, 1945, and 1946, but the collapse of the registration system in the severely affected areas permits only rough estimates of the increase in mortality, its chronological history, or its incidence by sex, age, and area. By 1947 the prewar health facilities had been restored and the crude death rate was approximately at the level that would have been expected in the absence of military losses or civilian casualties.

The new public health and medical facilities introduced into Japan after the war produced a revolutionary shift in the level of mortality, its incidence by sex and age, and its relations to types of work and conditions of living. Such chemicals as DDT and the antibiotics were used widely. Preventive immunization against tuberculosis was a national program. The crude death rate dropped from 14.6 in 1947 to 8.9 in 1952 and 7.8 in 1955. The extent of the declines in mortality are indicated by the following percentage changes from 1920-1925 to 1947, 1952, and 1955:[8]

Rate	*1947*	*1952*	*1955*
Deaths per 1,000 population	−36.6	−61.3	−66.1
Infant deaths per 1,000 live births	−53.4	−69.9	−75.8
Neonatal deaths per 1,000 live births	−51.7	−61.9	—
Stillbirths per 1,000 total births	−30.3	+45.9	+51.3

Thus the crude death rate of 1952 was only two-fifths the rate of the years 1920-1925. The infant death rate of 1952 was less than one-third what the rate had been in 1920-1925. Stillbirths alone revealed a substantial increase, but this upward movement of prenatal mortality was the product of actions taken to limit live births rather than of deteriorating conditions in nutrition, health, or vitality.

The evidence of crude death rates as to changes in mortality may be questioned on a variety of grounds. Changing rates of fertility and mortality in combination with changing rates and types of migration were altering the sex and age structure of the population. All deaths of non-Japanese and the deaths of Japanese that were reported late were excluded from currently reported statistics, while non-Japanese were included in the populations that were the denominators in the computation of rates. These and other factors associated with war and the movements of people present difficulties in precise analysis. In numerical terms, however, the combined influence of all the sources of error and inaccuracy was slight in relation to the extent of the declines. Examination of the time trends in the expectation of life as presented in TABLE 113 indicates the accuracy of these statements, for the values of the life tables are independent of changes in the age composition of the population, and they relate the deaths of Japanese in Japan to the Japanese population of Japan, with appropriate adjustments for delayed registrations.[9]

In the intercensal period from October 1, 1920, to September 30, 1925, the expectation of life at birth was 42.1 years for males and 43.2 years for females. These values would be appropriate to a premodern economy. In 1954-1955 the expectation of life at birth was 62.8 years for males and 66.8 years for females. The expectation had increased almost one-half within two decades.

Changes in the expectation of life at a specific age summarize anticipated experience throughout that part of life which remains after the specific age. The probabilities of dying give a more concise picture of the characteristics of the decline in mortality from the prewar to the postwar years (FIGURE 15). In the prewar years the declines were occurring primarily among infants and young children. Declines among youth aged from 5 to 14 and adults aged from 20 to 49 were slight, whether viewed in absolute or in relative terms. In the postwar years the largest declines occurred among young children, but rates of decline were greater at the higher ages. The amounts and per cents of decline in the probabilities of death per 1,000 population are given here for males for the two periods 1920-1925 to 1935-1936 and 1947-1948 to 1952-1953:[10]

	AMOUNT OF DECLINE		PER CENT OF DECLINE	
Age	*1920-1925 to 1935-1936*	*1947-1948 to 1952-1953*	*1920-1925 to 1935-1936*	*1947-1948 to 1952-1953*
0	49.0	26.5	30.2	34.6
1	11.4	22.7	23.6	72.3
2	5.7	8.1	21.8	52.9
3	3.1	4.5	18.7	44.6
4	1.4	3.0	13.3	44.1
5	0.5	2.0	7.1	41.7
10	0.8	0.9	25.0	50.0
15	1.2	1.4	20.0	53.8
20	0.8	4.7	7.4	67.1
25	0.3	5.9	3.2	64.8
30	0.5	4.6	6.1	56.8
35	1.1	4.2	12.6	52.5
40	1.6	4.1	15.2	46.6
50	1.4	4.2	7.5	29.4
60	3.7	7.3	9.4	22.7
70	8.1	10.8	9.6	15.1
80	16.5	6.4	9.0	4.2

The cumulative effect of thirty years of generally declining mortality was a series of death rates in 1952-1953 that were far below those immediately after World War I. The ratios of life-table death rates in 1952-1953 to those in 1920-1925 were as follows:

Age	*Male*	*Female*
0	.310	.307
1	.180	.181
2	.276	.274
3	.337	.304
4	.362	.330
5	.400	.359
10	.281	.189
15	.200	.122
20	.213	.157

[8] Nihon. Kosei-sho, eisei tokei-bu. *Vital and health statistics in Japan. . . .*

[9] The national life tables are reproduced in summary form in: Nihon. Kosei-sho, daijin kambo, tokei chosa-bu. *Dai-hachikai seimei hyo.*

[10] Two series of life tables are currently published—one by the Division of Health and Welfare Statistics of the Welfare Ministry (Kosei-sho, eisei tokei-bu), the other by the Institute of Population Problems of the Welfare Ministry (Kosei-sho, jinko mondai kenkyujo). The series used here is that of the Institute of Population Problems.

Age	Male	Female
25	.337	.250
30	.427	.317
35	.437	.336
40	.448	.372
50	.543	.558
60	.633	.655
70	.715	.709
80	.807	.736

DECLINES BY CAUSE

Early in Japan's modern history, quarantine and vaccination eliminated the irregularities characteristic of the mortality of premodern populations. Deaths from cholera, plague, and smallpox became small in number. Gradually the contagious diseases of childhood were brought under control. Between 1920 and 1943 scarlet fever, whooping cough, measles, diphtheria, and epidemic meningitis together were responsible for only from 2 to 2.5 per cent of all deaths (TABLE 114). In

TABLE 113

Expectation of life, by selected ages, 1920-1925 to 1954-1955

	OFFICIAL LIFE TABLES				ABRIDGED TABLES, JINKO MONDAI KENKYUJO				
Age	*1920-1925*	*1925-1930*	*1935-1936*	*1947*	*1950-1951*	*1951-1952*	*1952-1953*	*1953-1954*	*1954-1955*
				Male					
0	42.06	44.82	46.92	50.06	57.91	60.03	61.30	62.15	62.80
1	49.14	51.07	51.95	53.74	60.60	62.49	63.56	64.38	64.73
2	50.62	52.35	52.92	54.57	60.44	62.23	63.08	63.90	64.17
3	50.96	52.54	53.02	54.63	60.02	61.77	62.53	63.30	63.52
4	50.81	52.33	52.74	54.23	59.45	61.19	61.88	62.62	62.80
5	50.35	51.85	52.22	53.61	58.73	60.46	61.12	61.86	62.01
10	46.53	47.93	48.25	49.49	54.21	56.04	56.64	57.35	57.47
15	42.31	53.58	43.85	44.93	49.52	51.32	51.88	52.59	52.69
20	39.10	40.18	40.41	40.89	45.10	46.81	47.28	47.97	48.07
25	36.06	37.01	37.35	37.60	41.11	42.61	42.89	43.57	48.67
30	32.59	33.43	33.89	34.23	37.19	38.46	38.58	39.25	39.36
35	28.87	29.61	30.10	30.62	33.10	34.23	34.23	34.88	35.00
40	25.13	25.74	26.22	26.88	28.99	30.00	29.88	30.51	30.63
50	18.02	18.49	18.85	19.44	21.00	21.92	21.56	22.15	22.27
60	11.87	12.23	12.55	12.83	13.87	14.77	14.28	14.88	14.94
70	7.11	7.43	7.62	7.93	8.60	9.30	8.52	9.07	9.10
80	3.87	4.15	4.20	4.62	4.87	5.33	4.45	4.90	4.88
				Female					
0	43.20	46.54	49.63	53.96	61.09	62.23	64.67	65.66	66.79
1	49.42	52.10	54.07	57.40	63.53	65.40	66.65	67.63	68.51
2	50.86	53.37	55.02	58.30	63.42	65.18	66.23	67.18	67.96
3	51.22	53.59	55.13	58.42	63.02	64.76	65.70	66.60	67.32
4	51.12	53.43	54.89	58.06	62.47	64.19	65.05	65.94	66.61
5	50.71	53.00	54.40	57.45	61.75	63.48	64.27	65.18	65.83
10	47.00	49.18	50.47	53.31	57.20	59.03	59.77	60.64	61.24
15	43.12	45.11	46.33	48.81	52.54	54.33	55.00	55.84	56.42
20	40.38	42.12	43.22	44.87	48.19	49.80	50.37	51.17	51.73
25	37.72	39.23	40.23	41.48	44.15	45.55	45.93	46.69	47.22
30	34.69	35.98	36.88	37.95	40.19	41.38	41.59	42.32	42.80
35	31.44	32.53	33.30	34.24	36.10	37.18	37.26	37.94	38.38
40	28.09	29.01	29.65	30.39	31.97	32.95	32.93	33.56	33.98
50	20.95	21.67	22.15	22.64	23.80	24.66	24.47	25.01	25.38
60	14.12	14.68	15.07	15.39	16.21	17.00	16.71	17.19	17.48
70	8.44	8.88	9.04	9.41	10.03	10.72	10.26	10.68	10.87
80	4.41	4.73	4.67	5.09	5.51	6.04	5.52	5.84	5.95

Source: 1920-1925 to 1947, national life tables: Nihon. Kosei-sho, daijin kambo, tokei chosa-bu. *Dai-hachikai, seimei hyo.* Pp. 4-5 and 84-89. 1947-1954: Nihon. Kosei-sho, jinko mondai kenkyujo. *Dai-yonkai kansoku seishi jinko hyo seimei hyo. . . .Dai-7-kai kansoku seishi jinko hyo, seimei hyo.* 1954-1955: *Idem. Dai-8-kai kansoku seishi jinko hyo, seimei hyo. Showa 29-nen 4-gatsu 1-jitsu—Showa 30-nen 3-gatsu 31-nichi.*

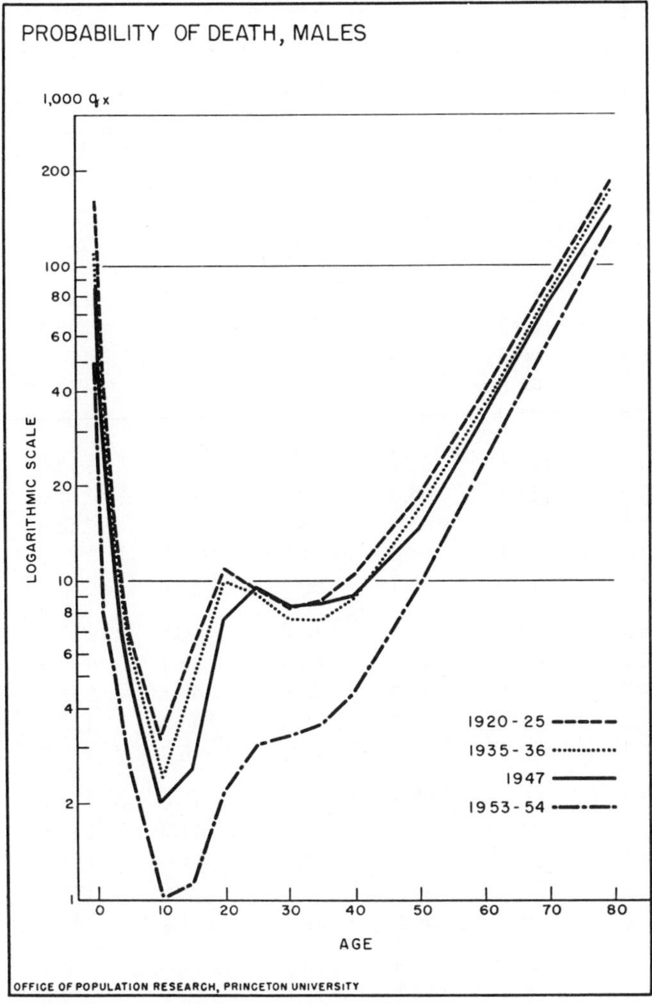

Figure 15. The probability of death, males, 1920-1925, 1935-1936, 1947, and 1953-1954
Source: References, Table 115.

fact, deaths from suicide and accident were more numerous than deaths from the common diseases of children. Deaths from starvation also became rare, though malnutrition remained a major factor in susceptibility to many diseases. In the years from 1920 to 1925, the number of deaths from beri-beri had amounted to 36 per 100 thousand population. Improving knowledge of nutrition and generally increasing levels of income reduced the incidence by 75 per cent in the next two decades.[11]

Lack of sanitation and living conditions that facilitated contagion were causal or associated factors in the respiratory diseases that were the major causes of death among the Japanese. The death rates from tuberculosis per 100 thousand population declined slightly from 210 in 1920-1924 to 186 in 1930-1934 and then increased to reach 218 in 1942. Death rates from influenza were episodic, while those from pneumonia and bronchitis declined slowly. From 1920 to 1924, however, one-fourth or more of all deaths were diagnosed as respiratory.

A major portion of the deaths that occurred in Japan from 1920 to 1942 could have been postponed by improved sanitary practices, more balanced diets, and better medical care. The application of available knowledge would have lessened the incidence of and deaths from the respiratory diseases, diarrhea, dysentary, typhoid, and beri-beri. This group of diseases that might have been reduced to small proportions was responsible for about two-fifths of all deaths from 1920 to 1942. This does not mean that some control was not achieved, for death rates from preventable diseases considered as a unit were declining at about the same rate as all deaths. Within the preventable diseases, however, there was duality in change. There was decline in mortality from diseases subject to environmental control or influenced by direct medical action. Diarrhea and enteritis yielded somewhat to improving sanitation; pneumonia and bronchitis, to medical care. Deaths from diseases whose incidence reflected poor living and working conditions decreased little or even increased. The major one of these was tuberculosis.

The conquest of causes of death hitherto impregnable to public health attack was the major factor in the decline in mortality in the years from 1947 to 1953. The ratios of death rates from specific causes in successive time periods indicate both the altered pattern of the saving of lives in the postwar as contrasted with the prewar period and the extent of the achievements in recent years:

	RATIOS		
Cause of death	*1935 to 1925*	*1947 to 1935*	*1953 to 1947*
Tuberculosis	.983	.983	.355
Pneumonia	.703	.858	.412
Bronchitis	.586	1.281	.396
Diarrhea, etc.	.679	.806	.355
Nephritis	.806	.713	.403
Intracranial lesions of vascular origin	1.026	.778	1.034
Heart disease	.860	1.078	1.064
Cancer	1.016	.954	1.211
Accidents	.993	1.185	.795
Senility	.976	.885	.766

Mortality in the Prefectures

Base line: mortality in the early 1920's

The analysis of decline presupposes a base line from which decline is measured. The selection of this line for mortality analysis poses difficult problems, for the years of the late precensal period were quite abnormal. Major migrations into the cities had occurred as Japan secured shipping and foreign markets, and conditions in the cities of the time were not conducive to health or longevity. Military expeditions to Siberia, China, and the South Seas returned diseased and disabled men to die as civilians in Japan. Finally, the Kanto earthquake of 1923 resulted in great destruction and a major loss of life. The influenza epidemic contributed its toll, crude death rates rising to 26.9 per 1,000 total population in 1918 and 25.4 in 1920. The distortions of the events surrounding the year 1920 are minimized if the intercensal period from 1920 to 1925 is selected as a basis. The major deaths of the influenza epidemic had occurred by the fourth quarter of 1920; the excess deaths that remained were compensated in part by a lesser mortality in the following years. The losses of the Kanto earthquake were not a major influence in the deaths of a five-year period.

In the years from 1920 to 1925 the death rate in Japan

[11] The numerical data cited here are from the following sources: Nihon. Kosei-sho, eisei tokei-bu. *Vital and health statistics in Japan. 1953.* Nihon. Kosei-sho. *A brief report on public health administration in Japan. 1954.*

TABLE 114

The ten leading causes of death, 1920-1953

(Deaths per 100,000 population)

Year	*Tuberculosis, all forms*	*Pneumonia*	*Bronchitis*	*Diarrhea, enteritis, and ulceration of the intestines*	*Nephritis*	*Intracranial lesions of vascular origin*	*Heart disease*	*Cancer*	*Accidents*	*Senility*
1920	223.8	312.8	94.4	256.3	99.2	158.6	63.9	72.4	46.8	131.1
1921	213.0	200.6	92.3	272.9	105.7	160.7	66.4	71.9	43.4	133.5
1922	218.8	196.5	90.6	267.4	106.3	160.3	65.4	71.4	44.6	132.3
1923	203.4	205.7	62.5	284.4	107.8	163.8	73.0	72.3	123.9	131.6
1924	193.7	209.8	61.0	257.5	105.8	175.7	69.4	70.4	44.1	125.5
1925	193.7	215.5	59.6	237.2	100.3	162.1	67.1	70.1	41.9	117.0
1926	185.7	177.9	51.6	231.8	98.2	163.4	62.8	70.3	42.2	111.0
1927	193.3	194.6	54.1	242.5	97.5	165.8	63.5	69.8	47.6	120.8
1928	190.8	201.0	52.2	233.6	100.6	165.3	64.0	71.3	43.0	123.3
1929	194.2	190.5	50.2	246.3	103.2	171.6	65.7	69.1	42.0	124.5
1930	185.3	156.7	43.4	220.7	98.5	163.7	64.1	70.0	40.8	118.6
1931	186.1	198.0	46.5	213.5	98.4	165.0	64.3	68.4	38.7	130.8
1932	179.4	169.7	41.6	206.3	92.6	162.5	58.9	68.4	40.3	116.6
1933	187.9	157.5	37.7	193.4	89.1	165.4	59.7	69.8	44.5	123.4
1934	192.5	181.7	39.6	186.7	87.3	168.7	62.5	70.5	46.7	127.9
1935	190.4	151.6	34.9	161.1	80.8	166.4	57.7	71.2	41.6	114.2
1936	206.7	159.6	37.1	171.5	82.3	169.3	61.3	70.4	42.9	130.8
1937	203.8	152.3	33.8	168.4	79.4	168.4	60.5	71.7	41.6	119.4
1938	209.2	166.0	36.6	163.6	87.2	179.3	66.9	71.1	43.5	138.7
1939	216.0	183.6	35.0	156.8	82.2	184.0	66.5	71.8	39.8	133.2
1940	212.5	153.2	31.2	149.4	75.7	178.3	63.3	70.8	39.4	124.4
1941	210.7	141.7	30.0	131.1	67.9	171.5	58.1	71.0	38.1	122.8
1942	218.4	143.1	30.2	130.2	68.9	170.2	58.9	71.7	42.0	129.9
1947	187.2	130.1	44.7	129.9	57.6	129.4	62.2	67.9	49.3	101.1
1948	179.9	66.2	32.4	104.1	45.7	117.9	61.3	69.6	48.7	80.1
1949	168.8	68.7	31.3	87.5	41.2	122.6	64.5	71.8	41.9	80.9
1950	146.4	65.1	28.1	82.4	32.4	127.1	65.0	77.4	40.0	70.2
1951	110.3	59.8	22.4	90.2	29.2	125.1	64.5	78.4	37.8	70.7
1952	82.1	49.9	17.1	53.0	25.7	128.4	62.4	80.8	36.3	69.2
1953	66.4	53.6	17.7	46.1	23.2	133.7	66.2	82.2	39.2	77.5

Source: 1920-1952: Nihon. Kosei-sho, eisei tokei-bu. *Vital and health statistics in Japan, 1953.* Part II, *Tables* II.D.5. 1953: Nihon. Kosei-sho. *A brief report on public health administration in Japan, 1954.* Pp. 14-15.

averaged 23 per 1,000 total population.[12] Death rates below 20 occurred only in Miyazaki, Kagoshima, and Okinawa, all prefectures where the infant deaths and stillbirths reported suggest underreporting (MAP 15). In the industrial prefectures, crude death rates were 21 or 22 per 1,000 total population. In the Tohoku region of the northeast there were prefectural death rates as high as 26. The highest mortality occurred in the prefectures across the mountains of central Honshu on the Sea of Japan. Here, three-quarters of a century after the opening to the West, death rates were 27 or more per 1,000 total population.[13]

The picture of geographical variations in mortality yielded by crude death rates is corroborated both by age-standardized death rates and by the values of life tables.[14] The expectation of life at birth for males in Japan from October 1, 1920, to September 30, 1924, was 42.1 years. For 30 of the 47 prefectures, the expectation was from 40 to 44 years. It was above 45 years for seven prefectures, below 40 for ten prefectures. In general, the expectation of life at birth was low in the agricultural prefectures along the Sea of Japan and in Tohoku and in the predominantly industrial prefectures. The expectations for males were 35.9 in Toyama, 36.6 in Ishikawa, and 38.0 in Fukui, all prefectures along the Sea of Japan; 37.3 in Iwate and 38.8 in Aomori, both prefectures of the Tohoku region. Expectations were similarly low in the indus-

[12] Without adjustments for underreporting or for the exclusion of the deaths of the people from the colonies.

[13] Intercensal rates per 1,000 mid-period population were 27.0 in Toyama, 27.4 in Kukui, and 27.9 in Ishikawa.

[14] Standardized death rates: Tachi, Minoru, and Ueda, Masao. "Taisho ku'nen, Taisho juyo'nen, Showa go'nen, Showa ju'nen. Do, fu, ken betsu, shi, gun betsu hyojunka shussei ritsu, shibo ritsu oyobi shizen zoka ritsu." *J.m.k.*, 1(1):21-28. April 1940. Life tables by Dr. Haruo Mizushima.

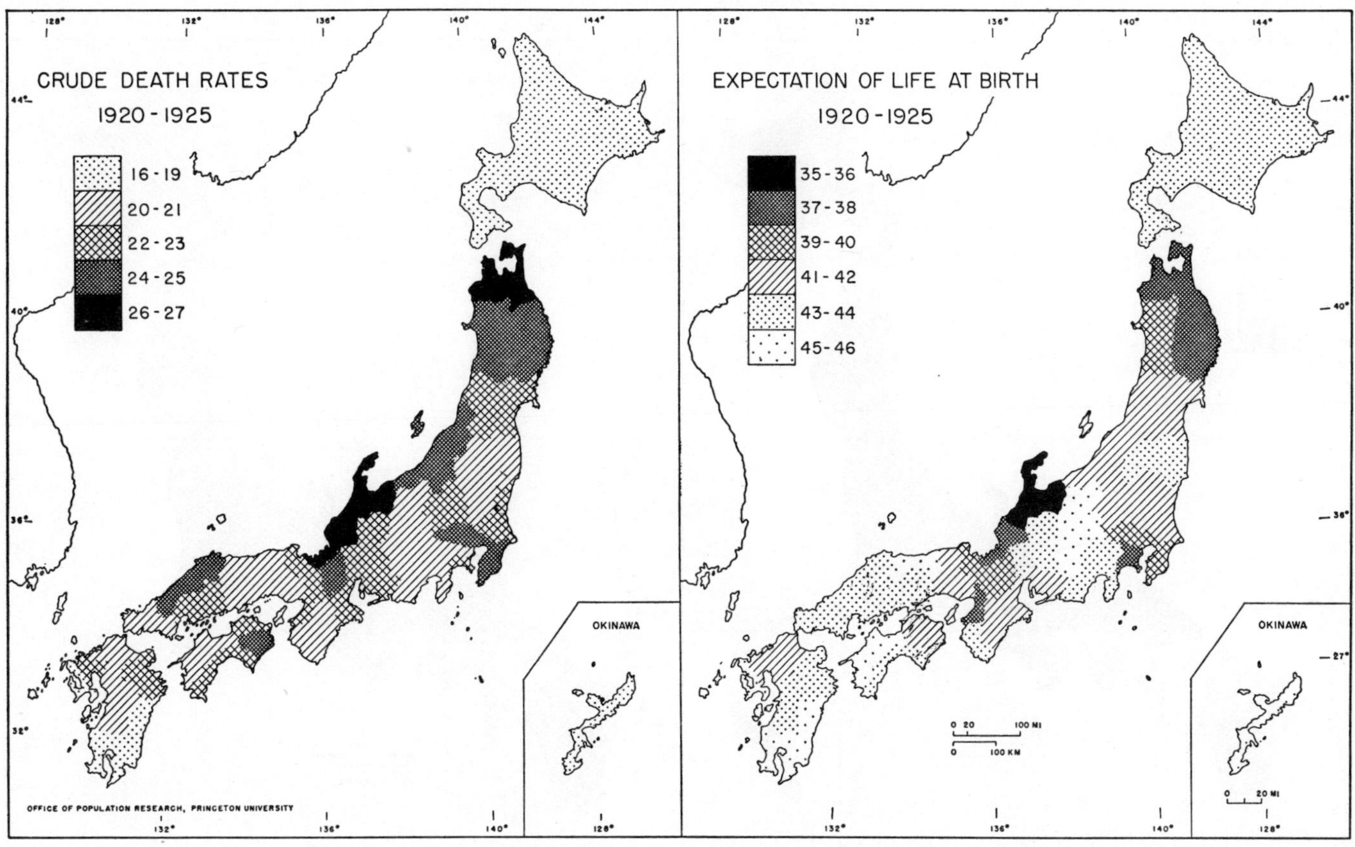

Map 15. Death rates and expectation of life at birth, prefectures, 1920-1925
Source: Death rates: Nihon. Naikaku tokei-kyoku. *Jinko dotai tokei.* Expectation of life: Reference, Table 115.

trial prefectures—38.1 in Osaka and 38.6 in Tokyo. Each industrial prefecture was the center of an area with low expectations.

In the early 1920's the mortality of the Japanese was higher than that of the industrial populations of the West, lower than that of the agricultural populations of the East.[15] There were variations among areas, high death rates occurring where the agrarian culture survived in less modified form and also where modern industry and great cities were concentrated. Death rates were lowest in those areas where increased agricultural production, raised educational levels, and developing industry attested the penetration of the skills and technologies of the West. Here many of the advantages of the economic transformation were felt, without the health hazards of urban concentrations.

CHANGE IN THE PREFECTURES

The regional variations in mortality were substantial. They were associated with physical and climatic hazards, occupational activities, health facilities, and living levels. The changes influencing mortality were nation-wide, however, and the pursuit of health characterized all socio-economic groups and sub-cultures. Declines in mortality tended to be proportionate to the feasibility of securing such declines. In quantitative terms, mortality tended to decline most rapidly where it had previously been highest, with a consequent coincidence of rapid downward movements and convergence in prefectural rates.

[15] It should be noted that by 1920 death rates changed little from year to year. The episodic mortality of famine, epidemics, and other catastrophes had been eliminated as major factors in mortality.

The downward movement between 1920-1925 and 1953 was so rapid that there was a complete absence of overlap in prefectural death rates at the beginning and the end of the period (MAP 16). The modal range of the death rate in 1920-1925, that which existed for 36 of the 46 prefectures (Okinawa excluded), was from 20 to 24; in 1953 the modal rate was below 10, and it characterized 34 of the 46 prefectures. The prefectural clustering in death rates and the downward movement of this clustering are so striking that they are presented here:[16]

	NUMBER OF PREFECTURES				
Death rate	*1920-1925*	*1930-1935*	*1947*	*1950*	*1953*
7-9	—	—	—	5	34
10-14	—	1	19	40	12
15-19	4	34	27	1	—
20-24	36	11	—	—	—
25-29	6	—	—	—	—

The series of life tables for the prefectures of Japan computed by Professor Haruo Mizushima and his colleagues shows a distribution of the expectation of life at birth in 1920-

[16] Crude death rates were influenced both by internal redistribution and by changing age structures. However, the comparison of death rates standardized to the sex and age composition of the population of October 1, 1925, yields a picture of differentials and trends similar to that of crude rates. In general, the use of crude death rates masked the decline in areas of heavy in-migration and rapid fertility decline. For standardized death rates for the prefectures, see: 1920-1935: Tachi and Ueda. *Op.cit.* 1947: *Ibid. 1947-nen no shi-bu gun-bu betsu oyobi to do fu ken betsu hyojunka shussei ritsu shibo ritsu oyobi shizen zoka ritsu.* 1949-1950: Nihon. Kosei-sho, jinko mondai kenkyujo. *Saikin no jinko ni kansuru tokei shiryo.*

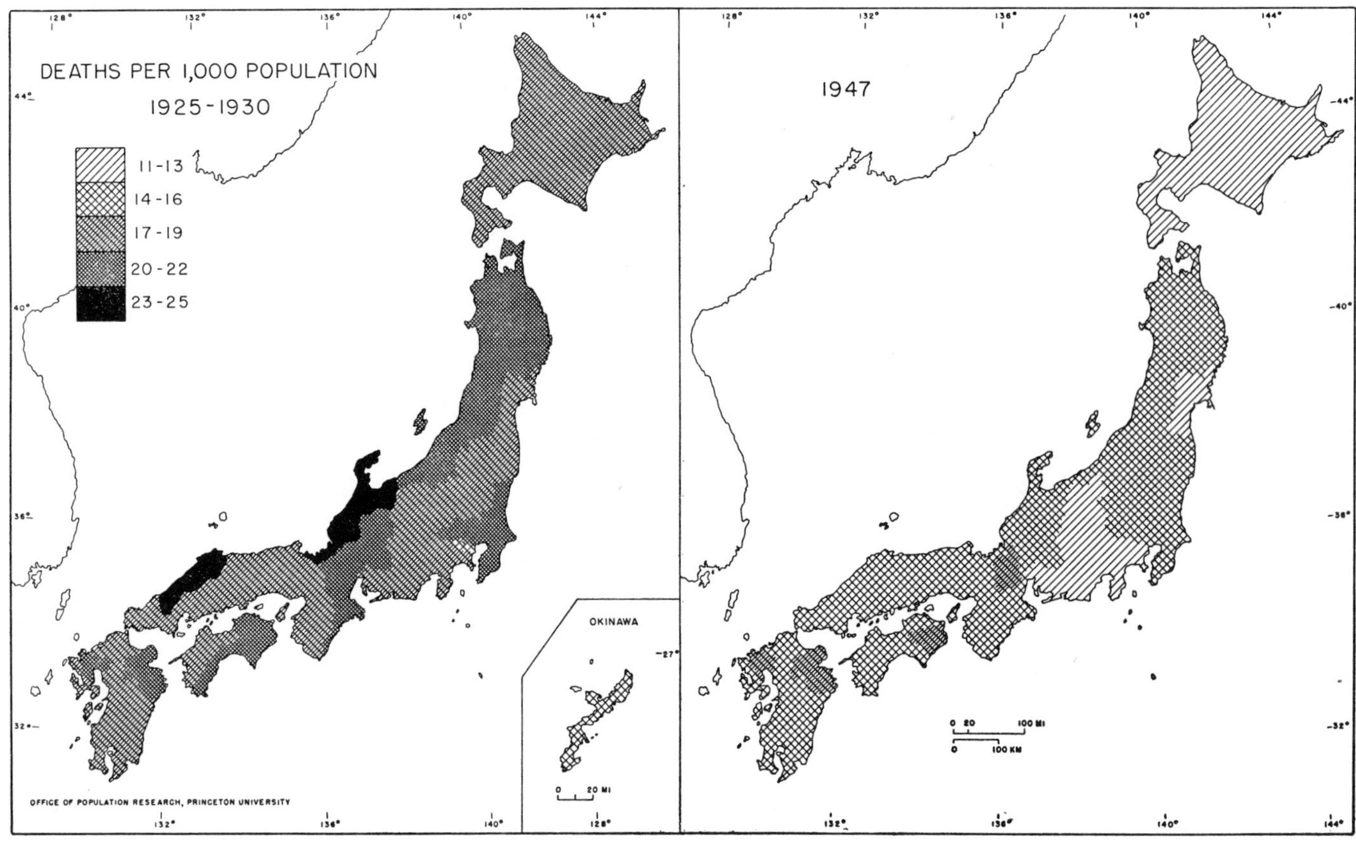

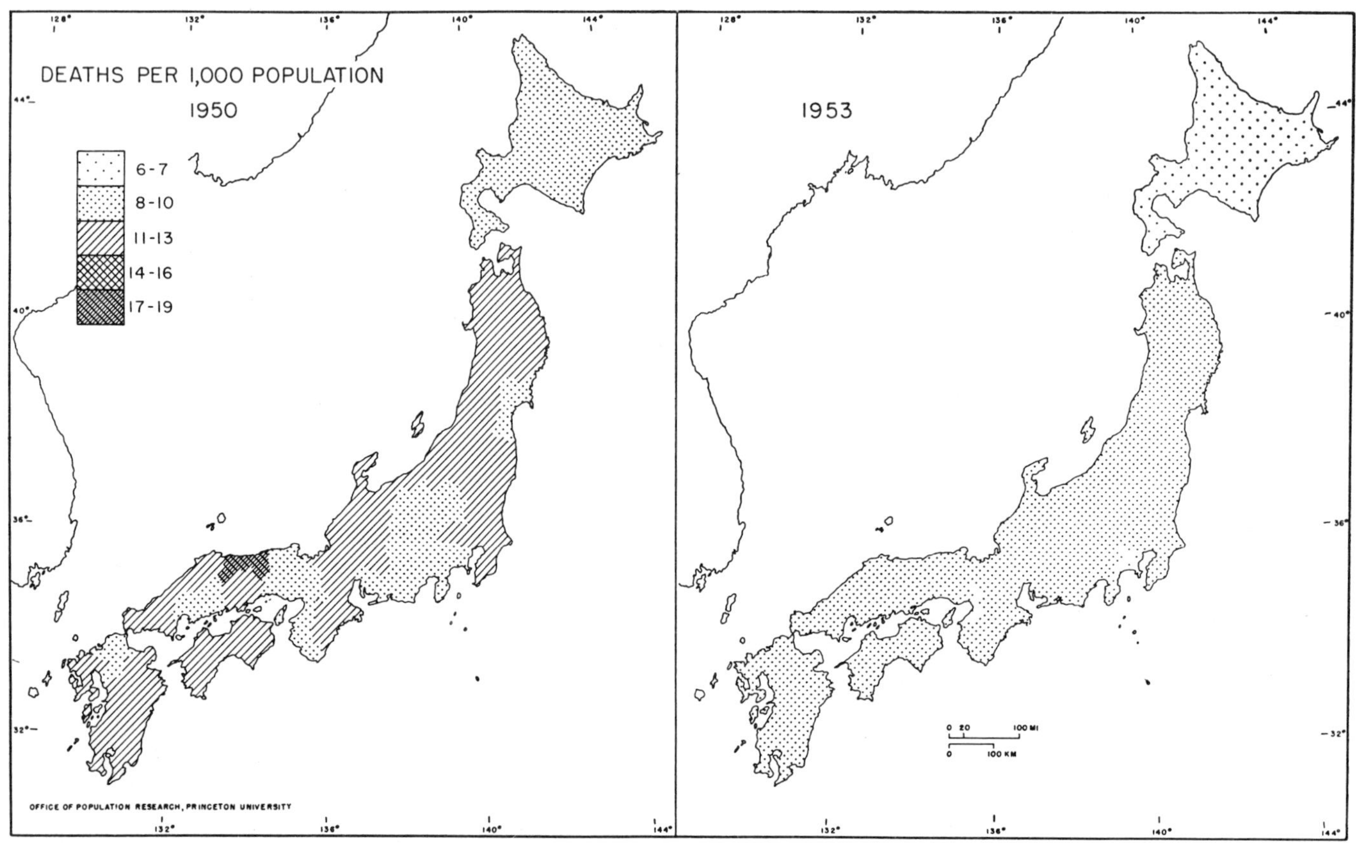

Map 16. Death rates, prefectures, 1925-1930, 1947, 1950, and 1953
Source: Nihon. Naikaku tokei-kyoku. *Jinko dotai tokei.* Also: Nihon. Kosei-sho, eisei tokei-bu. *Jinko dotai tokei.*

1925 and a pattern of decline from that period to 1950 quite similar to the variations and rates of decline in crude death rates (TABLE 115). There was a marked convergence in rates among the prefectures, but that convergence was a complex and changing phenomenon. In the prewar years the tendency toward a positive association between high mortality and substantial decline was limited to the years of infancy and childhood. From age 12 through age 52, the association between level of mortality and the amount or the percentage of decline was slight. Correlations between the life-table death rates in 1925-1930 and the amount and per cent of decline between 1925-1930 and 1930-1935 were as follows:

	LEVEL IN 1925-1930 AND AMOUNT OF DECLINE TO 1930-1935		LEVEL IN 1925-1930 AND PER CENT OF DECLINE TO 1930-1935	
q_x	*Male*	*Female*	*Male*	*Female*
q_0	.55	.59	.31	.22
q_5	.68	.51	.31	.46
q_{12}	.14	.44	.11	.19
q_{22}	−.27	.05	−.03	.00
q_{32}	−.05	−.05	.03	−.13
q_{52}	.29	.34	.21	.23

There was a positive association between the level of mortality in the prewar period and the amount or the percentage of decline from the prewar to the postwar years. The correlations extended from birth through the productive years. The fact that correlations were higher and more regular for women than for men suggests persistent factors influencing the mortality of the sexes unequally. The correlations were as follows:

	LEVEL IN 1930-1935 AND AMOUNT OF DECLINE TO 1947-1948		LEVEL IN 1930-1935 AND PER CENT OF DECLINE TO 1947-1948	
	Male	*Female*	*Male*	*Female*
q_0	.80	.84	.39	.43
q_5	.76	.88	.63	.77
q_{12}	.86	.96	.64	.77
q_{22}	.85	.87	.73	.65
q_{32}	.57	.81	.58	.66
q_{52}	.59	.44	.45	.35

The regional and prefectural distributions of crude death rates remained similar from year to year, although there was a tendency toward convergence in rates.[17] Decline was occurring throughout the country, with a somewhat more rapid decline in the prefectures where rates were high. This was true whether decline was measured in absolute or relative terms. The correlations were as follows:

Variables	*Amount of change*	*Per cent of change*
Level in 1930-1935 with change to 1947	.78	.60
Level in 1947 with change to 1950	.33	.61
Level in 1950 with change to 1953	.75	.54
Level in 1930-1935 with change to 1953	.90	.36

[17] The correlations of the crude death rates in the prefectures were as follows: 1930-1935 with 1947, .73; 1947 with 1950, .61; 1950 with 1953, .72. There were also high correlations between the different measures of mortality at a given time. For the period for which comparisons are possible, the crude death rates yielded results similar to those based on more refined rates. The correlation between the level of the crude death rate in 1930-1935 and the amount of the change in that rate from 1930-1935 to 1947 for the 46 prefectures was .78. The correlation between the amount of decline in crude rates and the amount of decline in intrinsic rates for the same period was .72.

The altered ways of living and techniques of life-saving that radiated out from the great cities and the government in Tokyo involved some changes conducive to increased longevity and other changes inimical to it. Some techniques for reducing mortality could be used without changes in social structure, income distribution, or consumption and saving patterns. Others would have required a reorganization of economy and society. In addition, the acceptance of practices that led to reduced mortality varied greatly according to the values that were affected. The continuity of the family, the predominant role of the eldest son, the dedication to work, and the ambition to advance involved tenacious values. To have or not to have a vaccination against smallpox or an inoculation against tuberculosis was an easy choice. The decision was explicit and the goal of increased longevity was unquestioned. To concentrate family resources on one or two children rather than to distribute lesser opportunities among many children was not recognized as a choice that altered the possibilities of death. Families did not analyze the statistics on tuberculosis before they sent a daughter to a textile dormitory.

Decisions that influenced the rate of savings and the structure of investment influenced death rates. Lower income meant low levels of nutrition, while priorities in government spending left limited funds for health and welfare activities. Thus the direction of the economic development of Japan was related to the causes of death and the frequency of death.

Generalizations concerning the relations of death rates to culture, society, and economy have been given as facts. Actually they are hypotheses for verification or disproof through the analysis of the recorded data on deaths. Three relations only will be pursued here: the relation of mortality, industrialization, and urbanization; the mortality of women and children; and the imprint of the social structure on death rates by sex and age.

Industrialization, Urbanization, and Mortality

The mortality of the Japanese declined in proportion to the increase in industrialization and urbanization. This relationship at the national level over time indicates little concerning interrelations within the nation, nor does it permit hypotheses as to what relations could have existed. As the culture of the West developed, industrialization and urbanization were associated with increasing per capita product, more adequate nutrition, public health, and preventive medicine. These social and economic changes influenced practically all peoples within the culture, rural as well as urban. This was also true in Japan, but there were counteracting factors. Incomes were lower in the villages, ignorance was greater, and medical facilities were less adequate. Labor was chiefly carried on outdoors, however, and the work routines were less compelling than those in the cities. The numbers of contacts were less, while the area of intense contact was circumscribed. The disposal of waste was a hazard to health in almost direct ratio to the density of settlement.

Many conditions in the cities retarded the reductions in mortality that might have been associated with higher incomes, advanced educational levels, and more plentiful medical services. The city-dwellers lived in crowded areas and labor was likely to be carried on within the home, in small factories exempt from minimum labor standards, or in factories where ventilation, sanitation, and safety provisions were inadequate. Hours of work were long, days of rest were few, and pro-

TABLE 115

Expectation of life at birth in the prefectures, 1920-1925 to 1950

	MALES					FEMALES				
Prefectures	*1920-1925*	*1925-1930*	*1930-1935*	*1947-1948*	*1950*	*1920-1925*	*1925-1930*	*1930-1935*	*1947-1948*	*1950*
All Japan	42.1	44.8	—[a]	51.5	57.5	43.2	46.5	—[a]	55.3	60.7
Hokkaido	43.6	44.5	45.8	51.1	57.9	45.3	46.6	48.2	55.6	60.9
Aomori	38.8	41.4	43.3	48.5	53.2	39.9	43.2	46.3	51.1	55.7
Iwate	37.3	44.3	44.5	50.0	54.2	42.1	45.9	46.4	52.7	55.6
Miyagi	42.5	45.4	47.2	52.3	57.7	44.6	47.4	50.0	56.3	60.2
Akita	39.7	42.6	44.3	47.4	53.9	40.7	44.0	46.3	50.3	56.2
Yamagata	42.0	43.4	44.9	49.5	55.8	43.3	45.5	47.4	52.7	59.3
Fukushima	43.2	45.6	47.0	51.8	56.8	45.0	47.9	49.7	54.9	59.2
Ibaraki	42.6	45.8	47.2	53.0	56.6	44.6	48.7	50.3	56.5	59.5
Tochigi	42.0	46.3	46.9	53.6	56.4	46.2	48.6	49.8	57.1	59.2
Gumma	42.2	45.2	47.3	52.5	57.9	43.1	46.4	49.0	55.4	60.5
Saitama	40.7	44.0	44.9	52.8	58.8	41.9	46.3	46.8	55.4	58.6
Chiba	39.9	43.4	45.2	52.1	56.8	42.2	46.5	49.1	57.7	60.2
Tokyo	38.6	44.9	47.5	55.5	59.6	39.4	46.8	50.2	59.0	63.0
Kanagawa	38.6	45.2	46.6	54.7	59.5	39.8	47.8	49.9	59.1	63.5
Niigata	41.0	43.7	45.1	50.5	56.4	42.3	45.6	47.2	54.2	59.8
Toyama	35.9	39.9	40.7	49.7	55.5	37.8	41.2	42.6	52.9	57.5
Ishikawa	36.6	38.8	39.2	50.5	55.0	36.6	39.4	40.7	54.8	58.4
Fukui	38.0	40.5	40.4	50.0	56.6	37.1	39.7	40.7	53.1	59.0
Yamanashi	44.7	48.2	48.6	54.6	58.9	45.2	49.2	51.0	58.4	62.6
Nagano	45.4	48.2	49.5	53.7	59.9	46.7	50.1	51.8	57.6	62.6
Gifu	43.4	45.2	45.8	52.6	58.4	42.0	44.6	45.8	54.4	60.4
Shizuoka	44.3	47.0	47.7	54.2	59.2	45.4	48.7	50.5	58.0	63.2
Aichi	41.2	44.0	45.8	54.1	58.5	41.8	45.0	47.9	58.0	61.8
Mie	42.0	45.0	45.2	50.8	58.2	43.0	46.6	47.3	54.4	61.9
Shiga	40.9	44.5	44.7	49.5	57.6	42.1	46.6	47.3	53.0	61.2
Kyoto	40.5	43.8	45.6	51.3	59.0	41.5	45.3	48.1	55.3	63.3
Osaka	38.1	43.0	44.5	50.1	57.8	39.0	44.7	47.4	54.6	62.0
Hyogo	41.8	44.7	45.8	51.4	58.3	42.7	46.8	48.8	55.4	62.1
Nara	42.7	45.0	43.9	51.3	57.7	43.7	46.8	46.9	55.6	61.3
Wakayama	44.4	47.2	47.2	52.8	59.1	46.3	49.4	50.3	57.2	62.8
Tottori	45.2	46.6	47.4	50.5	58.7	46.8	49.7	50.7	54.7	62.9
Shimane	43.0	44.2	45.5	52.4	58.0	43.0	44.0	46.0	55.9	60.5
Okayama	44.7	46.7	47.7	51.2	58.5	45.8	48.4	50.2	55.8	62.5
Hiroshima	44.8	46.7	47.7	52.5	59.4	43.2	47.5	49.6	56.4	62.8
Yamaguchi	44.2	46.0	46.8	51.5	58.1	44.4	46.8	48.5	54.6	61.7
Tokushima	42.6	45.7	45.7	50.6	55.9	42.2	46.4	47.4	53.6	58.3
Kagawa	42.6	45.7	46.6	53.8	57.7	43.3	46.1	48.5	57.3	61.3
Ehime	45.1	47.0	48.3	53.2	59.1	45.4	48.5	50.2	56.3	62.6
Kochi	44.3	45.9	47.7	53.5	58.6	45.9	47.8	50.0	57.6	62.2
Fukuoka	42.1	43.3	44.8	50.3	57.7	43.6	45.3	47.6	54.8	61.2
Saga	42.5	43.5	44.3	47.8	56.2	43.6	45.8	47.5	53.0	60.0
Nagasaki	45.4	46.4	46.8	50.8	56.3	47.9	48.8	49.7	54.5	60.2
Kumamoto	44.7	46.9	48.1	51.9	58.2	46.6	48.5	50.2	56.2	61.3
Oita	43.2	44.6	45.1	49.7	56.4	43.9	45.4	46.7	53.4	59.0
Miyazaki	47.9	49.1	49.2	52.5	56.6	48.7	49.6	50.9	55.3	60.5
Kagoshima	45.6	47.2	47.9	50.4	56.6	47.7	50.1	51.2	54.6	60.6
Okinawa	46.3	46.0	47.2	—	—	50.5	50.5	51.8	—	—

Notes and references are on p. 295.

tective foods were lacking. It was in the cities, though, that the medical and sanitary services had their initial and eventually their greatest effect. Water supplies, public sanitation, and police inspections lessened infection from the diseases often associated with great human density.

In theory, the existence of multiple hypotheses concerning the relations among industrialization, urbanization, and death rates presents few difficulties. All that is required is manipulation of the numbers and characteristics of the populations and the deaths in geographic areas classified by degree of urbanization and industrialization. In fact, there is an underlying biological fallacy in this approach. Many causes of death involve deterioration that is related to the history of the individual. Other causes appear on superficial observation as direct consequences of the environment of the individual at or immediately preceding the time of death, but resistances and vitality are related to the individual's background. The environmental factors involved in length of life are those of a period of time. In a society without geographic, social, or economic mobility, the place of death and the characteristics of the individual at the time of death reflect his life history. In this case, comparisons between the numbers and the characteristics of those dying in various areas permit deductions as to the role of geographic, economic, and social factors in mortality. However, the people of an industrializing economy are characterized by geographic, social, and economic mobility. Lowered vitality or disease acquired in one place may be associated with migration that leads to death in another place. Analysis of rural-urban or agricultural-industrial differences in death rates requires caution in the interpretations as to causation or association.

THE GENERAL INTERRELATIONS

If industrialization was the primary force in the reduction of Japanese death rates, it might be assumed that at any given time mortality would be highest in agricultural areas and would decline with the increasing prevalence of industrial activities. In 1930, there was some negative relationship between the proportion of the gainfully occupied population in agriculture and the expectation of life at birth in most of the intermediate and agricultural prefectures. This relationship within the middle ranges held at neither extreme, however. In the metropolitan and other industrial prefectures, expectations of life at birth were intermediate rather than high, as they should have been if the level of mortality were a function of the departure from agriculture. In the isolated prefectures on the Sea of Japan, intermediate dependence on agriculture was associated with low expectations of life at birth.

In recent years, when the diffusion of new discoveries for disease prevention or control led to marked reductions in death rates, the innovations seem to have been most readily available and most frequently used in the industrial regions. However, variation among the regions remained at this new low level of total mortality. The following figures are deaths per 1,000 total population:

Type of prefecture	*1947*	*1950*	*1952*	*1955*
All Japan	14.6	10.9	8.9	7.8
Metropolitan	12.8	8.6	7.0	6.0
Other industrial	14.1	9.9	8.2	7.2
Intermediate	15.1	11.3	9.3	8.3
Agricultural	15.0	11.9	9.8	8.5
Hokkaido	13.4	10.0	7.9	6.9

Crude death rates dropped rapidly in all types of prefectures, but they remained low in the metropolitan prefectures and high in the agricultural prefectures.[18] Hokkaido, with its combination of cities and agricultural areas and its active Health Department, occupied an intermediate position.

The analysis of death rates for prefectures classified by industrial type suggests that the relations between mortality and the transition to industry were neither simple nor unidirectional. Age-specific death rates in the prefectures show wide variations. Some seem reasonable in the light of the economic differences among the prefectures, while others seem to be associated with climatic or cultural factors. A more detailed inspection of the levels and the age patterns of mortality in limited areas seems indicated. An external selection of the areas suitable for such inspection is available. In their analysis of the patterns of mortality in the prefectures of Japan in 1925-1930, Dr. Mizushima and his colleagues were interested in the curves of mortality by age. They found six types in the prefectures. One, found only in Okinawa, may be discarded because of atypicality and the probable inadequacies of the data. Five prefectures were selected by Dr. Mizushima and his colleagues as illustrative of the types of mortality curves. If Osaka is added to the five, there are two agricultural prefectures (Aomori and Miyazaki), two intermediate (Ishikawa and Okayama), and two industrial (Tokyo and Osaka). Comparisons of these paired prefectures, similar in industrial status but divergent in mortality type, corroborate the hypothesis that changes in mortality are not simple products of industrial development (FIGURE 16).

Aomori and Miyazaki were primarily agricultural prefectures, one in northeast Honshu, the other in Kyushu. In Aomori, as in the Tohoku region generally, death rates were very high at age 0 and age 1. The crest and trough so characteristic of the age pattern of mortality in Japan in 1925-1930 were present; the crest at age 22 was pronounced and the trough at age 32 was deep. The expectation of life at birth for males was 41.4 years, 3.4 years less than that for the nation as a whole.

[18] An examination of standardized death rates for the prefectures in 1950 indicates that these differences would be likely to persist with age standardization. See: Nihon. Kosei-sho, jinko mondai kenkyujo. *Saikin no jinko ni kansuru tokei shiryo.* 7th Edition. P. 56.

Notes to Table 115

[a] No national life tables were computed for the intercensal period because of the problem of deaths associated with the Manchurian military activities. Expectation of life at birth for 1935-1936 was 46.9 for males and 49.6 for females.

Source: All Japan—1920-1925 through 1947-1948: References, Table 112. 1950: Mizushima, Haruo; Kusukawa, Akira; and Matsuura, Koichi. "1950-nen, 1951-nen, 1952-nen kanzen seimei hyo. 1953-nen, 1954-nen, 1955-nen kanryaku seimei hyo." *Igaku kenkyu,* 26(11):2821-2847. 1956. Prefectures—1920-1925: Mizushima, Haruo, *et al.* Unpublished life tables. 1925-1930: *Ibid.* "Fu ken betsu seimei hyo, dai-ikkai." *Chosen igakkai zasshi,* 28(8):1136-1175. 1938. 1930-1935: *Ibid.* "Fu ken betsu seimei hyo, dai-nikai." *Chosen igakkai zasshi,* 29(9):1767-1803. 1939. 1947-1948: *Ibid.* "Dai-3-kai fu ken betsu seimei hyo, Showa 22-nen 4-gatsu—Showa 23-nen 3-gatsu." *Eisei tokei,* 4(1):14-29. 1951. 1950: Majima, Yujiro. "1950-nen fu ken betsu seimei hyo." *Igaku kenkyu,* 26(1):1-23. 1956. Life tables are also available for 1948-1949: Mizushima, Haruo, *et al.* "Dai-4-kai fu ken betsu seimei hyo, 1948-1949." *Eisei tokei,* 5(2):1-17. 1952.

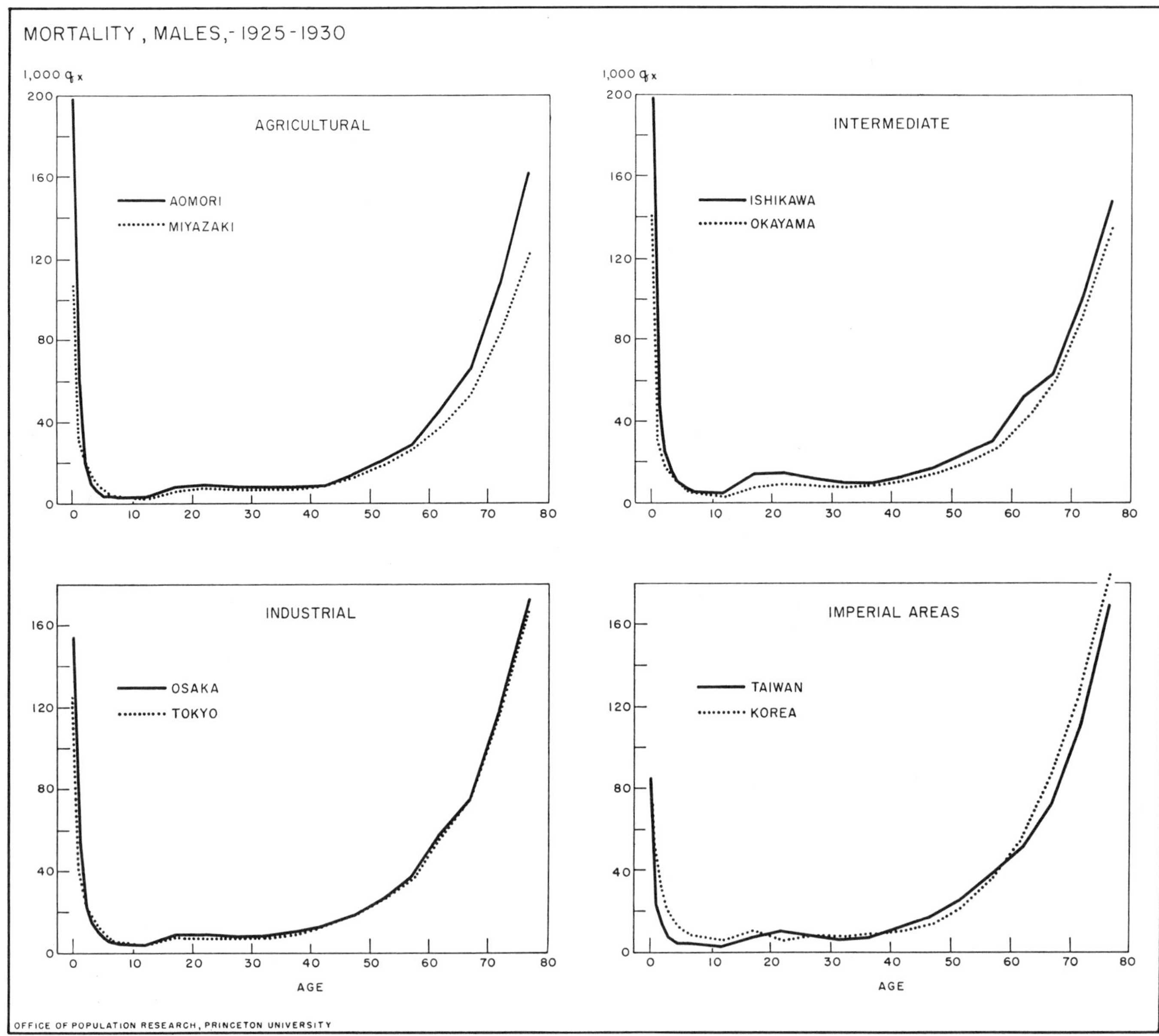

Figure 16. Age patterns in the mortality of Japanese males, selected prefectures by industrial type, and imperial areas, 1925-1930
Source: References, Table 115.

Miyazaki was an agricultural prefecture with a mountainous topography. In 1925-1930 death rates at ages 0 and 1 were low in comparison with those in Aomori. Death rates in the young productive ages were conspicuously below those in Aomori, and rates remained low in the older ages. The expectation of life at birth was 49.1 years, 7.7 years more than that in Aomori, 4.3 years more than that in the nation as a whole.

The widest variations in mortality occurred in prefectures with intermediate economies, areas where agriculture and industry, city and country, existed together. In 1925-1930, the expectation of life at birth for males was 38.8 years in Ishikawa but 46.7 in Okayama. The age structure of mortality in Ishikawa was similar to that in other prefectures along the Sea of Japan, where winters were cold and damp. Mortality in infancy and childhood was heavy. The crest at ages 17 and 22 was high, the trough at age 32 low in relation to the height of the crest. At most ages, death rates were above those in the agricultural prefectures of the Tohoku. Okayama's economy was also intermediate, and it, like Ishikawa, included a metropolitan center. Here, however, death rates were substantially below those in all Japan. The crest and trough of young adulthood were blunted rather than accentuated as in Ishikawa.

The patterns of mortality in the industrial prefectures were less variable than those in either agricultural or intermediate prefectures. Industrialization and urbanization at their greatest development in Tokyo and Osaka prefectures were accompanied by limited mortality in the very young, high mortality in the pre-school and school-age children, increased but relatively low mortality in the early productive ages, decreased and still relatively low mortality in the late twenties and early thirties, and quite high mortality from the thirties to the end of the life span.

There were substantial divergences in the age patterns of mortality for Japanese in Taiwan and Korea. These Japanese were non-agricultural in occupation, urban in residence, and mainly middle and upper in social-economic status. The expectation of life at birth for males in Taiwan was 3.7 years above that for all Japanese in Japan, while that in Korea was 0.3 years lower. The favorable milieu of an urban elite had not produced substantially lowered mortality even in Taiwan. The pattern of mortality by age in Taiwan was similar to that in Tokyo prefecture, although death rates of infants and young children in Taiwan were below those in Tokyo, while death rates of young adults were higher. In Korea, on the other hand, the death rates of the Japanese were very high during childhood and adolescence.

It is plausible to argue that the primary factor influencing mortality would be the size and characteristics of the place of residence rather than occupation. Hence, it is necessary to examine the differences in death rates in *shi, machi,* and *mura,* and in the cities by size.

DEATH RATES IN SHI, MACHI, AND MURA[19]

In 1925, differences in crude death rates for *shi, machi,* and *mura* were slight, and the direction of the differences was not consistent (TABLE 116). The death rates of the *shi* were generally somewhat below those of the *mura,* with the *machi* sometimes above and sometimes below the *shi,* sometimes above and sometimes below the *mura.* From 1925 to 1935 the direction of movement was downward in the majority of the prefectures, with a differentiation of death rates as among the types of communes. There were underlying forces that influenced all the people living in a prefecture, however, and so the death rates of the *shi, machi,* and *mura* within the prefectures were correlated.

	1930	*1935*
Shi and *machi*	.74	.72
Machi and *mura*	.78	.70
Shi and *mura*	.67	.44

Death rates for *mura,* as for *machi* and *shi,* tended to be higher in northeastern Honshu and along the Sea of Japan and lower in southwestern Honshu and in Kyushu, although the regional transition from northeast to southwest was less pronounced in mortality than in fertility. There was consistency in these geographic variations in death rates.[20] The differences in age structures may have been a factor in the persistent differences in death rates among *shi, machi,* and *mura.*[21] However, the crude death rate is related to actual changes that occur in the population of the area. Moreover, the crude rate measures the prevalence of death, with its psychological and material adjustments. The frequency of death, the age structures of the populations, and the economic, social, and cultural factors in health are an interrelated complex.

An analysis of the changes in crude death rates over time yields some suggestive results.[22] There was an association between the levels of the death rates in 1930 and the absolute and relative declines between 1930 and 1935. These associations were greater for *machi* and *mura* than for *shi.*[23] Decline in death rates in the rural areas may have been due primarily to changes in the economy and the society. In the cities, on the other hand, declines in mortality reflected specific actions of the administrative authorities in the fields of health and sanitation, particularly the provision of pure water for drinking and household use, the inspection of foods, and the disposal of waste.[24]

MORTALITY IN AND OUTSIDE THE METROPOLISES

Economic development of a modern type was concentrated in the large cities, where education was most accessible and most widespread. Here also the public health and medical facilities of the nation were concentrated. The cities were the instigators of change in virtually all aspects of life, and change moved out from them, in paths that were influenced by geographic, economic, and social proximity as well as physical distance.

The downward movement in mortality between 1925-1926 and 1935-1936 characterized both the populations of the cities of 100 thousand and over and the populations outside such cities. The expectation of life at birth for males in the large cities increased from 41.8 in 1925-1926 to 47.0 in 1935-1936 (TABLE 117).[25] The comparable expectations for females were 43.6 and 50.0 The major postponements of death for men occurred at ages under 5; from age 5 to the end of life, the increase in expectation of life seldom reached one year. For women also, the major increases in expectation of life occurred in childhood, but the increases in the upper ages were larger and they were persistent.

The significance of the changing expectations of life in the cities of 100 thousand and over are visualized more easily if phrased in terms of the disappearances of an original cohort. In 1925-1926 half of an original cohort of men would have been alive at age 51; in 1930-1931 half would have reached age 52; in 1935-1936 half would have reached age 55. The improvements in the rates of survival were greater for women.

[19] The relations between size of commune and level of crude death rates at given times have been somewhat irregular, rates tending to be highest for the smallest communes and lowest for the great cities of 100 thousand and over. With age standardization the differences became irregular or disappeared. See: Tachi, Minoru, and Ueda, Masao. "A statistical study on the variation of basic demographic phenomena by the size of communities." Pp. 107 and 110 in: *Archives of the Population Association of Japan,* No. 1. Tokyo, 1952. 102 and 130 pp. Also: *Ibid.* "Chiiki shakai no okisa to jinko gensho." *J.m.k.,* 8(2):10-72. October 1952.

[20] The correlation of the crude death rates in 1930 with those in 1935 was .84 for *shi,* .87 for *machi,* .88 for *mura.*

[21] For analyses based on standardized rates, see: Tachi, Minoru, and Ueda, Masao. "Showa ju'nen naichi 127 shi hyojunka shussei ritsu, shibo ritsu, oyobi shizen zoka ritsu, yono." *J.m.k.,* 1(5): 20-27. August 1940. Ueda, Masao, *et al.* "To do fu ken kaku shi kaku gun betsu. Jinko mitsudo—Jinko zoka wariai." Pp. 243-366 in: Nihon. Jinko mondai kenkyujo. *Chosa kenkyu shuyo kekka,* 1952.

[22] Actually the declines in mortality in Japan were so great that changes in age structures cannot have been the primary factors in the declines.

[23] The correlations between levels in 1930 and the amount of decline during 1930-1935 were .37 for *shi,* .58 for *machi,* .55 for *mura.* Correlations between levels in 1930 and percentage declines were .25 for *shi,* .50 for *machi,* and .47 for *mura.*

[24] These hypotheses are consistent with the analysis of those standardized death rates that are available. The major problem in comparisons of death rates for *shi, machi,* and *mura* remains, after age standardization, that of the influence of selective migration for death.

[25] Life tables were computed by the Office of Population Research for the six great cities; the cities of 100 thousand and over as a group; the cities of 100 thousand and over, excluding the great cities; and the respective populations outside the cities as variously defined for 1920-1921, 1925-1926, 1930-1931, 1935-1936, and 1940-1941. (Life tables for males in 1940-1941 were not used for comparative analysis because of the influence of the war.) The work was directed by Dr. George Stolnitz, using Reed-Merrell techniques modified at the lower and upper ages. Age distributions were secured by summations from the prefectural census volumes. People from the colonies and aliens were excluded, in 1925 and 1935, by estimations. Recorded deaths were used despite the errors introduced by incorporations, but the use of a two-year period roughly centered on the census date compensated in part for this deficiency. The great incorporation of territory into Tokyo in 1932 was not involved. The major problems were the movements prior to death and the possibility of erroneous allocations of deaths somewhat comparable to those that occurred for births. However, these factors would be more significant for men than for women and children.

TABLE 116

Death rates in *shi, machi,* and *mura,* 1925-1935
(Deaths per 1,000 population)

	1925			1930			1935		
Prefectures	Shi	Machi	Mura	Shi	Machi	Mura	Shi	Machi	Mura
Hokkaido	21.5	19.7	17.9	19.4	18.2	16.0	17.6	16.4	14.8
Aomori	22.8	23.2	23.3	21.1	22.0	22.6	19.6	19.2	18.5
Iwate	21.8	21.3	23.0	17.9	20.3	21.1	18.1	18.3	18.4
Miyagi	19.2	20.5	20.1	18.4	18.4	18.5	16.7	17.2	16.4
Akita	21.1	22.9	23.2	19.1	20.0	20.8	17.3	18.8	19.0
Yamagata	19.3	20.5	22.2	18.9	19.3	20.8	17.7	18.0	18.4
Fukushima	18.7	19.4	26.0	17.2	18.1	18.4	16.8	16.6	16.7
Ibaragi	19.5	23.5	21.6	17.0	17.0	18.9	14.8	16.2	18.3
Tochigi	17.4	20.4	20.2	15.0	17.7	17.9	13.7	16.2	17.0
Gumma	19.8	20.4	21.5	16.7	17.2	17.8	14.6	16.0	17.1
Saitama	21.9	19.6	23.3	18.9	17.5	19.8	15.3	16.8	19.4
Chiba	24.7	22.0	22.5	22.2	19.2	20.8	18.1	18.5	19.1
Tokyo	16.6	18.1	19.4	13.1	14.5	17.3	12.7	12.3	16.9
Kanagawa	18.5	19.7	19.8	15.2	16.1	16.7	14.5	15.8	16.3
Niigata	20.4	20.9	27.6	17.7	19.5	20.0	16.5	18.0	18.6
Toyama	23.6	24.3	23.8	20.4	22.2	22.7	19.7	20.5	22.1
Ishikawa	22.7	25.2	26.3	22.3	24.1	23.7	21.8	22.5	23.7
Fukui	23.2	26.2	25.5	23.0	22.7	24.4	20.4	19.8	22.1
Yamanashi	19.0	19.8	27.8	16.3	18.8	17.1	16.4	16.6	17.4
Nagano	19.1	17.6	19.3	15.8	15.8	17.2	15.4	15.6	16.2
Gifu	19.9	21.0	22.2	17.9	19.6	20.8	16.2	17.4	19.3
Shizuoka	19.7	20.0	20.3	16.9	17.8	18.1	15.0	16.7	17.0
Aichi	19.2	21.4	21.4	16.7	18.2	19.2	14.3	16.2	18.0
Mie	21.3	22.0	23.4	17.3	18.3	19.7	17.0	18.1	18.9
Shiga	24.7	23.0	22.5	20.3	17.4	20.3	16.6	16.5	19.1
Kyoto	18.9	18.6	21.6	16.2	17.1	20.0	13.9	15.8	19.2
Osaka	19.2	20.3	20.9	15.5	16.7	18.5	14.0	15.5	17.9
Hyogo	18.9	20.2	20.1	16.6	17.6	18.2	14.7	17.1	17.6
Nara	20.2	21.7	20.8	16.0	19.4	18.6	16.3	19.9	18.9
Wakayama	20.8	19.6	18.5	16.7	17.6	17.2	18.5	16.8	17.5
Tottori	20.5	21.6	19.5	20.8	20.5	18.6	18.9	17.9	17.8
Shimane	19.9	23.0	22.9	20.6	23.2	23.4	15.6	19.3	20.4
Okayama	16.9	18.2	19.6	16.3	16.8	18.5	15.6	16.8	18.4
Hiroshima	18.2	19.5	21.8	15.5	18.0	19.3	14.0	17.0	18.2
Yamaguchi	17.4	18.9	19.9	17.9	19.1	20.2	16.2	18.1	19.2
Tokushima	23.6	21.2	21.8	19.8	19.2	19.3	19.3	20.3	19.2
Kagawa	19.0	19.2	20.1	17.3	18.2	19.2	17.1	16.8	17.9
Ehime	21.1	24.0	21.5	19.4	18.8	17.9	18.8	16.6	17.0
Kochi	24.9	21.2	20.2	21.4	19.0	17.5	21.4	18.9	16.8
Fukuoka	19.0	19.6	19.7	18.0	18.9	19.3	16.5	17.2	17.2
Saga	20.7	18.7	20.6	19.9	21.2	21.6	18.8	17.5	18.5
Nagasaki	15.9	17.6	18.4	17.0	20.2	18.7	15.3	17.8	17.6
Kamamoto	19.4	18.8	18.8	17.5	19.1	18.8	16.4	16.9	17.3
Oita	17.2	20.0	20.5	19.1	19.4	20.6	17.5	19.3	19.6
Miyazaki	15.8	17.9	17.3	16.7	17.1	16.9	15.6	16.9	16.5
Kagoshima	15.2	19.4	18.0	16.5	18.3	17.5	15.7	16.9	16.9
Okinawa	16.2	18.3	19.9	15.6	11.7	16.9	15.5	13.0	16.7

Source: Nihon. Naikaku tokei-kyoku. *Shi, cho, son betsu jinko dotai tokei. Taisho juyo'nen. Ibid. Showa go'nen. Ibid. Showa ju'nen.*

TABLE 117

Expectation of life at selected ages, by cities of 100 thousand and over and areas outside such cities, 1925-1926, 1930-1931, and 1935-1936

	MALES			FEMALES		
Age	*1925-1926*	*1930-1931*	*1935-1936*	*1925-1926*	*1930-1931*	*1935-1936*
			Cities 100,000 and over			
0	41.84	43.55	46.96	43.61	46.11	50.02
1-4	48.24	48.95	50.93	49.14	50.86	53.40
5	49.53	49.28	50.74	50.62	51.36	53.30
10	45.77	45.56	46.89	47.10	47.76	49.50
15	41.64	41.37	42.65	43.42	43.98	45.64
20	38.21	37.91	39.12	40.42	40.84	42.41
25	34.33	34.48	35.63	37.34	37.79	39.16
30	30.84	30.74	31.93	34.19	34.53	35.75
35	26.98	26.94	28.03	30.86	31.16	32.19
40	23.16	23.21	24.14	27.47	27.74	28.58
45	19.61	19.63	20.43	23.98	24.23	24.90
50	16.26	16.33	17.00	20.44	20.69	21.31
55	13.26	13.37	13.91	17.13	17.26	17.80
60	10.63	10.74	11.15	13.92	14.04	14.43
			Outside cities			
0	44.70	45.71	46.62	46.45	47.93	49.35
1-4	51.65	52.06	52.37	52.48	53.51	54.47
5	52.37	52.31	52.44	53.32	53.81	54.61
10	48.44	48.34	48.41	49.48	49.93	50.61
15	44.07	43.93	43.98	45.38	45.77	46.41
20	40.64	40.49	40.58	42.47	42.69	43.40
25	37.48	37.46	37.74	39.62	39.85	40.56
30	33.91	33.94	34.40	36.39	36.57	37.27
35	30.09	30.11	30.64	32.97	33.09	33.70
40	26.22	26.23	26.75	29.49	29.56	30.05
45	22.47	22.45	22.92	25.87	25.90	26.33
50	18.89	18.87	19.26	22.15	22.16	22.54
55	15.56	15.53	15.87	18.58	18.56	18.91
60	12.56	12.55	12.81	15.20	15.16	15.45

Source: Age distributions: prefectural volumes of the various censuses by summation. Numbers of deaths: annual vital statistics publications. See Footnote 25.

In 1925-1926 half of an original cohort of 100 thousand girl babies would have disappeared by age 50, one year earlier than for men. In 1930-1931 half of the cohort of girls would have disappeared by age 54, two years beyond the comparable midway point of disappearance for men. By 1935-1936 the advantage of the women had increased to four years; their number would have been reduced 50 per cent by age 59, as contrasted with age 55 for men.

Declines in mortality generally comparable to those within the cities of 100 thousand and over were occurring outside the cities, but the levels from which the declines began were somewhat lower and the declines were less rapid. Throughout this period, the mortality in the cities of 100 thousand and over remained substantially higher than that outside the cities. The gap between the metropolitan centers and the remainder of the country was decreasing, however, so that a projection into the future indicated a period not far distant when the expectation of life in the great cities would be higher than that outside such cities.

The major portion of the population in cities of 100 thousand and over in all Japan lived in the six great cities. Both census enumerations and death reports are available for each of these cities from 1920 through 1940. In 1920-1921 the expectation of life in the great cities was substantially below that in the remainder of the country. At birth the expectation for males was 37.0 years in the cities, 39.8 years outside them. The comparable expectations for females were 37.2 and 40.8. By 1930-1931 the expectations at birth had converged; for males they were 44.9 in the great cities and 45.4 outside; for females they were 47.4 in the great cities and 47.7 outside. In the middle of the 1930's the favorable situation of the great cities continued until age 20 to 24 for males, age 25 to 29 for females. Above these ages, the average future lifetime at each specific age was still greater without than inside the cities.

IMPLICATIONS

Major diversities in mortality were associated with overtly comparable economic situations. There were substantial differences in levels of mortality within industrializing and urbanizing areas and between rural areas and cities. These areal differences in the early years after World War I cannot be assumed to be those of the premodern period, for this was almost three-quarters of a century after the opening to the West. However, the differences are difficult to explain except in terms of the influence of climatic and cultural factors during a period of industrialization and urbanization. This interpenetration implies that there was no uniform level of mortality in premodern Japan.

In the modernization of Japan, many types of changes influenced ways of living and rates of dying that were initially diverse. Economic development and social change produced a downward drift of mortality, but age-specific death rates did not move consistently downward at comparable rates.

There was a general relation between levels and declines in mortality in the rural areas. Death rates that were high declined more rapidly than those that were low, whether decline was measured in absolute or in relative terms. This leveling of differences appeared to be associated with the diffusion of many aspects of the new society rather than with specific health and medical activities. Declining mortality also occurred in the cities, particularly in the metropolitan centers and the great cities. Here, the role of specific activities was quite apparent. More adequate water supplies, sanitary inspection, slum clearance, and direct public health activities created sharp differences in the timing and the rates of decline in mortality in the individual cities.

The result of the coincidence of differing levels of mortality and differing rates of decline was an initial lessening of the differences between mortality in the great cities and that in the remainder of the country, and then a reversal of the direction of the differences. In the early 1920's the mortality in cities was above that in the rural areas. By the early 1930's the differences were slight. By the middle of the 1930's mortality in the great cities was below that in the remainder of the country. Since the further improvements that can be achieved in mortality are related to the lowness of the level already achieved, continued decline in the pattern of the years from 1920 to 1935 would have resulted in slower declines in the great urban areas and more rapid declines in the towns and villages. This would have led to an equalization of levels of mortality throughout the country. The differential mortality of the middle decades of industrialization and urbanization was a temporary product of economic development, medical progress, and social change.

Death and the Production of Life

THE MORTALITY OF WOMEN

The mortality of young girls was not influenced by reproductive hazards except insofar as the fertility of the mothers influenced conditions in the home and the need to labor outside it. In 1920-1921 the death rates of girls aged from 5 to 9 were far higher in the six great cities than in the remainder of the country, but declines in the great cities reduced mortality to the level of that in the remainder of the country by 1940-1941. Similar initial relationships and trends characterized the death rates of girls aged from 10 to 14, but mortality in the great cities remained above that outside them as late as 1940-1941 (Table 118). In general, life outside the great cities was more conducive to survival than that in the cities, but improvements were occurring more rapidly in the cities.

The relations between mortality in and outside the six cities

Table 118

The mortality of women aged from 10 to 34, six cities and remainder of the country, 1920-1921 to 1940-1941

($_nq_x$ per 100,000)

Ages	*1920-1921*	*1925-1926*	*1930-1931*	*1935-1936*	*1940-1941*
10-14					
Six cities	4,437	2,715	2,462	2,290	1,878
Outside	2,559	1,937	1,800	1,711	1,539
15-19					
Six cities	6,394	4,259	3,990	3,637	3,546
Outside	5,927	4,724	4,312	4,394	4,095
20-24					
Six cities	7,059	4,307	4,365	3,835	3,279
Outside	7,130	5,172	5,187	5,049	4,844
25-29					
Six cities	7,293	4,647	4,312	3,903	3,313
Outside	6,802	4,623	4,461	4,365	4,317
30-34					
Six cities	7,031	4,676	4,561	3,850	3,517
Outside	6,323	4,528	4,345	4,028	3,937

Source: References, Table 117 and Footnote 25.

altered as girls reached the age of marriage and childbearing.[26] As early as 1925-1926, the mortality of girls aged from 15 to 19 was lower in the cities than in the remainder of the country, and the differences persisted over time. Major declines in mortality were apparent at age 20 to 24; death rates for young women in this age group in 1940-1941 were less than half what the rates for the comparable age group had been two decades earlier. Outside the great cities, on the other hand, there was little decline in mortality at this age between 1925-1926 and 1940-1941.

Since marriage and childbearing were more common among women aged from 20 to 24 outside than in the great cities, it is plausible to argue an association among advancing age at marriage, lessened rates of childbearing, and lowered mortality. The relationship is most convincing for women aged from 25 to 29, for this was the age of most frequent childbearing. In the great cities, the death rates for women in this age group declined almost one-third between 1925-1926 and 1940-1941. There were declines in death rates outside the great cities, but they were much less.

Since few Japanese women remained single after age 30, the differences in the death rates of women aged 30 and over in and outside the great cities were responsive primarily to conditions associated with the family. Prior to 1930 the age-specific death rates for women in their thirties and forties were appreciably higher in the great cities than outside them. Sometime after 1930-1931, the more rapidly declining death rates of women in the great cities crossed the more slowly

[26] Migration to the rural areas for childbirth or a selective out-migration of those with many children may concentrate the deaths at childbirth and the deaths associated with child-rearing outside the great cities. However, there is no basis for assuming such a continuing increase in selective exodus as would be required to explain any major portion of the observed differences or trends in the probabilities of dying throughout the reproductive ages.

declining rates for women in the remainder of the country. By 1940-1941 the death rates throughout the reproductive period from age 20 to age 44 were less within than outside the great cities.

Maternal deaths registered as such have never accounted for more than a small portion of the deaths of women in the reproductive ages. The number of maternal deaths per 1,000 live births declined gradually from 3.5 in 1920 to 2.1 in 1942 and 1.6 in 1947.[27] The rate has remained rather stable in recent years, whether regarded as a percentage of all deaths of women in the reproductive ages or as a rate per 1,000 live births. Deaths reported as due to puerperal causes have remained slightly less than 1.0 per cent of all deaths of women. The proportions to women of various ages were similar in the prewar and postwar periods, as the following data indicate:[28]

Age of women	PER CENT OF DEATHS OF WOMEN REPORTED AS PUERPERAL		
	1924-1925	*1934-1935*	*1950*
15-19	1.4	0.8	1.1
20-24	4.7	3.6	4.0
25-29	5.7	5.3	5.9
30-34	7.2	7.0	6.5
35-39	7.7	7.5	6.3
40-44	4.4	4.5	3.3
45-49	0.6	0.4	0.3

The relative absence of change in maternal mortality does not indicate the absence of associations between fertility and the mortality of women. The apparent stability was associated with divergent trends in maternal deaths by cause, changing frequencies of births, and many other medical and demographic factors. However, neither the earlier high fertility of women nor the prevalent abortions of recent years have been accompanied by major excess mortality that can be attributed directly to the hazards of pregnancy or abortion.

The preceding discussion of the mortality of women in the reproductive ages involves the implicit assumption of concurrence among high fertility, heavy responsibilities of child care, and mortality. If this concurrence exists, one might expect negative relations between gross reproduction rates and some of the measures of mortality in the prefectures.[29] Such relations were slight both in 1925-1930 and in 1930-1935. This is not conclusive evidence of the absence of relations between high fertility and high mortality, for both were influenced by migration and occupational mobility. Levels of fertility were highly correlated with the industrial and urban character of the prefecture, the association being negative. In the period from 1925 to 1935 the associations between industrialization and mortality differed at the various ages, and they were changing over time. Hence the associations between fertility and mortality that would have been expected in a stable society may have been obscured.

There is another aspect of the relation between the production of life and mortality: the relation between fertility and the deaths of infants. It can be argued that fertility, the mortality of women in the reproductive ages, and infant mortality should be associated. It can also be argued that relations between fertility and infant mortality should be more direct than those between fertility and the mortality of women in the reproductive ages. The external variables are fewer and the length of time in which they influence the probabilities of dying is shorter. These again are plausible arguments, but the data do not support them. In 1925-1930 and in 1930-1935, the relations between gross reproduction rates in the prefectures and the probabilities of dying at age 0 or age 1 were insignificant. By 1930-1935 there was an association between low fertility and low infant mortality in the industrial prefectures, but elsewhere the association was slight. High fertility *per se* was not the predominant hazard to the survival of women and infants. Conversely, high proportions of survivors among infants born had not led to reductions in numbers of children born.

THE MORTALITY OF INFANTS

In the industrializing countries of the West it was the mortality of infants that was most responsive to changes in economic and social conditions. Hence analysis of the course of infant mortality in Japan may permit some assessment of the role of the changing environment in the levels and trends in mortality at later ages.

From 1900 to 1915 the number of infant deaths per 1,000 live births was somewhere between 150 and 160 in practically all years. It then moved rapidly upward to a peak of 189 per 1,000 live births in the influenza year of 1918. After 1918 the trend was downward, with episodic interruptions such as those of 1938 and 1939 that reflected the difficult conditions of particular years. The rate was 169 in 1919-1920, 133 in 1929-1930, and 84 in 1941.[30] The infant death rate had been cut in half within twenty years. Until 1926 one-fourth or more of all deaths reported in Japan were those of infants under one year of age. By 1934 the proportion was down to one-fifth; by 1940 it was less than one-sixth. The extraordinary declines in infant mortality were resulting in very substantial saving of life at its beginning, a decline that was not matched by proportionate savings at any higher ages.

The declines in infant mortality were nation-wide, and they continued in each prefecture year after year (TABLE 119). In 1919-1920 infant death rates were 200 or more in Aomori and Akita in the northeast, in Fukui and Ishikawa on the Sea of Japan, in Ibaraki on the Pacific, and in Osaka, while rates of from 175 to 199 occurred in the surrounding prefectures. If the country is viewed as a whole, the high rates of Hokkaido and northeastern Honshu shaded into an area of lesser mortality in Niigata, Fukushima, Tochigi, and Gumma, and then into what was very low infant mortality for the period—rates of less than 150 in Nagano and Yamanashi. Infant death rates above 175 occurred in the metropolitan prefectures and their surrounding areas. Then, below Hyogo, there was a lessening of infant death rates, with especially low levels in Kyushu. Even with allowances for the probable underreporting of live births and infant deaths, the variations are striking. The pattern was in part a consequence of location and climate, in part a function of the concentration of people in non-agricultural employment and urban living, and in part a correlate of cultural differences that antedate the modern period.

27 Kasama, Naotake. "Hompo bosei shibo no tokeiteki kansatsu." *J.m.k.*, 2(11):49-87. November 1941.

28 Sources: 1924-1925 and 1934-1935: Nihon. Naikaku tokeikyoku. *Jinko dotai tokei.* 1950: Nihon. Kosei-sho, eisei tokei-bu. *Jinko dotai tokei.*

29 Professor Mizushima has made major analytical use of the ratios of individuals surviving from one age to another as indexes of levels of mortality and their associations with external factors. See especially: Mizushima, Haruo, *et al.* "Seison-hi yori mitaru kenko-do no chiriteki bumpu." *Chosen igakkai zasshi*, 29: 2137-2152. 1939. And: "Geographic variations of longevity in Japan and their recent changes." *Archives of the Population Association of Japan*, No. 1, pp. 30-36. 1952.

30 Infant death rates for the years from 1920 to 1953 are given in Table 112.

TABLE 119

Infant mortality in the prefectures, 1919-1920 to 1953 (Infant deaths per 1,000 live births, by place of occurrence)

Prefectures	*1919-1920*	*1929-1930*	*1939-1940*	*1950*	*1955*
All Japan	169	133	98	60	40
Hokkaido	175	134	103	56	39
Aomori	221	197	144	95	58
Iwate	192	152	137	90	65
Miyagi	178	137	107	59	41
Akita	203	171	139	80	53
Yamagata	196	152	122	68	47
Fukushima	167	129	100	63	49
Ibaraki	201	152	116	69	47
Tochigi	167	119	93	56	40
Gumma	160	112	90	54	38
Saitama	186	134	109	66	48
Chiba	196	162	118	67	46
Tokyo	168	114	68	44	27
Kanagawa	164	120	76	41	30
Niigata	163	138	101	58	39
Toyama	196	180	139	83	52
Ishikawa	200	186	137	83	52
Fukui	201	179	137	77	48
Yamanashi	146	108	87	53	28
Nagano	145	105	80	49	33
Gifu	167	132	105	64	42
Shizuoka	151	126	92	58	37
Aichi	169	140	97	59	40
Mie	177	142	111	67	42
Shiga	169	143	111	65	46
Kyoto	185	138	89	51	32
Osaka	222	148	96	55	35
Hyogo	180	133	96	56	36
Nara	183	153	120	67	48
Wakayama	142	124	97	59	38
Tottori	153	135	103	61	37
Shimane	153	149	115	64	41
Okayama	152	131	105	62	39
Hiroshima	145	113	93	53	41
Yamaguchi	122	116	89	51	36
Tokushima	162	122	108	76	48
Kagawa	170	136	109	68	51
Ehime	143	116	92	57	41
Kochi	167	137	92	62	40
Fukuoka	174	140	96	53	33
Saga	156	150	112	64	38
Nagasaki	136	119	94	60	36
Kumamoto	124	106	80	54	34
Oita	142	130	106	67	45
Miyazaki	115	109	88	61	40
Kagoshima	105	97	82	60	34
Okinawa	79	60	46	—	—

Source: To 1943: Nihon. Naikaku tokei-kyoku. *Jinko dotai tokei.* 1950: Nihon. Kosei-sho, eisei tokei-bu. *Jinko dotai tokei.* 1955: *Ibid. Jinko dotai tokei maigetsu gaisu. Showa 30-nen.* Pp. 42-43.

By 1924-1925 no prefecture in Japan except Aomori had an infant death rate of 200 or over. The areas of heavy mortality remained generally similar to those of 1919-1920, but very high rates were now above 175 instead of 200 or more. The declines in infant mortality proceeded throughout the country from quinquennium to quinquennium. By 1939-1940 no prefecture in Japan had an infant death rate above 150, and Tokyo's rate had dropped below 70.

The rates of decline, like the levels, were reactions to many factors. The ratio of the life-table death rates for female infants in 1935 to those in 1930 for prefectures may be cited as illustrative. In this five-year period there were two areas in which mortality at age 0 was declining rapidly: the agricultural prefectures of northeastern Honshu, where mortality was high, and the metropolitan prefectures of central Honshu, where mortality was already relatively low in terms of the general level in Japan. In the prefectures of central Honshu along the Sea of Japan, infant mortality was high and declines were slight. Among the prefectures in other than these three regions, there was a tendency for higher rates to decline more rapidly than lower rates.

INFANT DEATHS IN THE METROPOLISES

Life in the great cities of Japan was hazardous indeed for infants as late as the second and third decades of this century. In the early years of the First World War, when Japan was economically prosperous and at peace, one in each four or five babies born in the great cities of the Kinki died within a year of birth. In the year 1915 the infant death rate was 258 in Osaka, 211 in Kobe, and 208 in Kyoto. It was 147 in Nagoya, 199 in Yokohama, and 147 in Tokyo.

Infant mortality in the great cities remained at very high levels during and immediately after the First World War, but in the years from 1922 to 1924 a decline began that proceeded with great rapidity in the next two decades. In Tokyo and Yokohama the infant death rate rose in 1923 as a consequence of the great earthquake, but reconstruction and modernization following the catastrophe initiated substantial declines. Tokyo's infant death rate, 179 in 1923, was reduced to 123 in 1925. Yokohama's rate, 200 in 1923, dropped to 144 in 1925. Almost equally great declines occurred in the other great cities. By 1930 Tokyo's rate had dropped to 90, Yokohama's to 111, and the rates in the cities of the Kinki were one-fourth to one-third lower than they had been in 1925. The year 1935 was the first in which infant death rates dropped below 100 in Yokohama, Nagoya, Kyoto, and Kobe. Decline continued in the late prewar and early war years. By 1942 the infant death rate had declined to 68 in Tokyo. It was below 75 in Yokohama, Kyoto, and Kobe; 85 in Nagoyo; and 84 in Osaka. In each of the six great cities, the infant mortality rate in 1942 was less than half what it had been two decades earlier. "Eastern" infant mortality rates had been reduced to "Western" rates within twenty years.

The declines of infant mortality in the six great cities and the other metropolitan cities of 100 thousand and over were more rapid than those that occurred outside such cities. In 1923 the infant death rate was 199 in the great cities; 174 in the cities of 100 thousand and over, excluding the six cities; and 160 in the remainder of the country. By 1935 the infant death rates were 89 in the six great cities; 98 in the cities of 100 thousand and over, excluding the six cities; and 111 in the remainder of the country. Within these twelve years the rank order of great city, lesser metropolis, and non-metropolitan population had been reversed.

Some Social Aspects of the Changing Mortality

THE CURVES OF MORTALITY BY AGE

By the 1890's Japan's economic transformation was well under way. Youth were migrating to the cities, and non-agricultural employment was developing rapidly. It was during this decade that the Sino-Japanese War occurred and the Japanese started the development of Taiwan. In the life table for the *honseki* population of 1891-1898, there was a trough in the curve of mortality for Japanese males at age 10 to 12, a steep rise to age 25, a very slight decline from age 25 to age 29, and then persistent increase (Figure 17).[31] In 1898-1903 there was a trough at ages 11 and 12, rapid increase to a crest at age 21, decline to age 30, and then continued increase until the highest ages. This, the typical curve of mortality rates among the Japanese in the 1920's and 1930's, was already apparent at the turn of the century. As compared with the late prewar years, however, the trough between ages 10 and 14 was not so low, the crest was not so high, and the post-crest dip was slight.

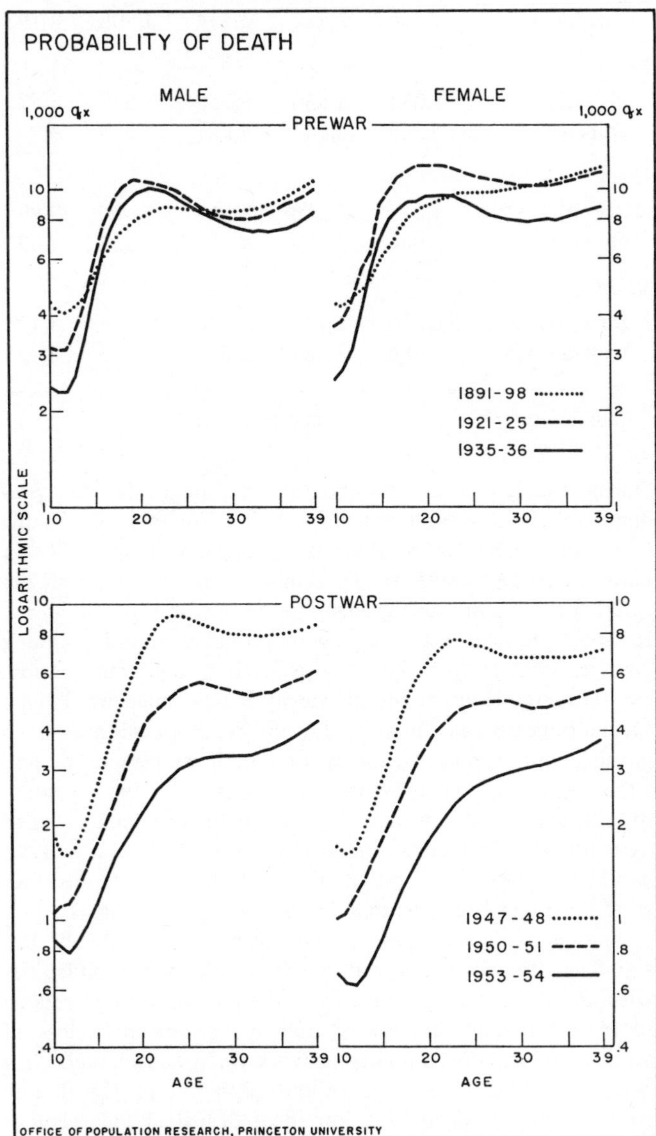

Figure 17. Changes in the probability of dying, ages 10-39, by sex, selected periods, 1891-1898 to 1953-1954
Source: References, Table 113.

The curves of mortality for men in the years from 1920 onward are derived from recorded deaths and the age data of censuses. The curve of the years 1921-1925 is noteworthy for the depth of the trough, the height of the crest, and the magnitude of the post-crest decline. The death rate for boys, 317 per 100 thousand at age 10, declined to 307 at age 11, then rose to 1,083 at age 19. The decline that followed carried the rate to 822 per 100 thousand population at age 32, one-fourth below the rate at age 19. Regularly increasing mortality began at age 32 and continued throughout the upper ages. The trough prior to the age of migration and of labor, the crest at the ages of maximum migration and urban residence, and the depression at about age 30 persisted in 1926-1930 and 1935, with the peak of the crest and the bottom of the dip moving toward higher ages.

The characteristic age changes in the death rates of men were apparent in 1947. If the mortality at age 10 is taken as 100, mortality declined to 87 at age 12, increased to 490 at age 25, declined to 431 at ages 30 and 31, and then began an upward movement. The characteristic age curve of trough, crest, and dip did not appear in the official life table for 1950-1952, and it was absent from the life tables of later years.[32] The curves of mortality for women were at once comparable to and significantly different from those for men. In 1891-1898 the peak was low and there was no post-crest decline in mortality. By 1909-1913 the peak was pronounced and the dip was perceptible, although the curve was relatively broad and smooth. In the period from 1920-1925 to 1935-1936 there was declining mortality at all ages, but the characteristic changes by age persisted. As contrasted with men, the curve of mortality rose sharply from age 10 or 11 onward. The crest occurred in the late teens and the early twenties and it was more gradual and prolonged than that for men. The post-crest dip was a long slow decline, and there was some indication of a secondary declivity in the early forties. In 1947 the crest occurred at age 24 and the decline continued until ages 34 and 35. In 1950-1951 the irregularities were slight, though there was a dip in mortality from ages 27 and 28 to ages 31 and 32. By 1951-1952 the irregularities had disappeared.

The evolution, maturity, and disappearance of the trough, the crest, and the dip in the curve of mortality give in synoptic form the history of the limitation of death in Japan. In a superficial sense the history of the irregularities in the mortality curve is the history of tuberculosis, bronchitis, and pneumonia, modified by that of diarrhea and other digestive infections. In a deeper sense, the regularization of the mortality curve is a symbol of the adjustment of the people to life in an industrial and urban society.

The interpretation of the characteristic age pattern of mortality lies in the nature of the changes influencing mortality in the years from the late nineteenth century to the present.[33]

[31] There have been eight official life tables: 1891-1898, 1898-1903, 1909-1913, 1921-1925, 1926-1930, 1935-1936, 1947, and 1950-1952. The first three were based on registered deaths and the compilations of the populations listed in the registers; the last five were based on registered deaths and the enumerated population of Japanese within Japan. Deficiencies in the registration life tables have been noted in earlier sections; those deficiencies were especially great among children and the aged. Here we shall assume that rough comparisons between the successive registration and census life tables are possible for the migrant years and thus secure a time span from 1891-1898 to 1953-1954.

[32] Mizushima, Haruo; Kusukawa, Akira; and Matsuura, Koichi. "1950-nen, 1951-nen, 1952-nen kanzen seimei hyo. 1953-nen, 1954-nen, 1955-nen kanryaku seimei hyo." *Igaku kenkyu*, 26(11): 2821-2847. 1956.

[33] The changes in place of residence, education, occupation, and migration and their relations with sex and age have been described in detail in the previous chapters. The implicit assumption is made

The protection of family, community, and school gave to the very young the advantages of material modernization without the disadvantages that accrued to adults. The break in the nature and the magnitude of life hazards occurred for the great majority of Japanese youth at the completion of the period of compulsory schooling. At this time the protected life of youth was replaced by gainful employment and migration. Life in the villages, attending school and assisting in family activities, yielded to life in full employment, often and increasingly in the cities. Long hours of work, inadequate sanitation, and low income meant sharply increased chances of death. In these associations between age and the nature of livelihood we have an explanation of the rise in mortality at age 12 or 13 and during the subsequent years. We can also derive an explanation of the dip in mortality in the late twenties or early thirties, for individuals who survived to adjust in cities had higher incomes, established families of their own, secured more adequate housing, and improved their conditions of living. Since upward mobility is so intimately correlated with age in Japanese society, advancing age may have meant less hazardous occupations and better conditions of work. Gradually, however, the physiological processes of aging predominated and mortality increased regularly with advancing age. The trough and the crest in the mortality of early adulthood were products of industrialization and urbanization.

The simple interpretation that explains trends in the curves of mortality for all Japan is quite insufficient to explain the difference in the curves for urban and rural areas within the country. At the critical ages of physical migration and occupational mobility, death rates were lower in the six great cities that were the epitome of industrialization and urbanization than they were either in all cities of 100 thousand and over or in the non-metropolitan population of Japan (TABLE 120). Prior to the great waves of migration among youth in their late teens and early twenties, death rates were higher in the six great cities than outside them. From ages 15 or 20 to age 35, death rates were least in the great cities, whose hazards in theory should have produced sharp increases in death rates. Yet this general inverse relationship between the massive urban agglomeration and the death rate held for women as for men.

The distribution of life hazards within Japan seems to have been a function of the interaction of health status and migration rather than of the inherent hazards of life in specific areas. The death rates in the life-table populations are not those of a cohort moving from birth to extinction. Neither are they the death rates for indigenous metropolitan and non-metropolitan or urban and rural populations. The death rates for the populations of geographic areas are based on the deaths recorded in the individual areas related to the populations enumerated in those areas. Migration that is selective as to physical condition influences both the composition of the population subject to the risk of death and the geographical distribution of the deaths that occur.

The age patterns of migration and of mortality are consistent with the theory of a causal interrelationship. The populations below age 10 were predominantly native-born in all areas of Japan and migrants remained scarce among those aged from 10 to 14. This was true in *shi*, as in *machi* and *mura*. Thus death rates at ages below 15 reflected the social, economic, and health conditions of the area of residence.

here that the coincidence between death rates and social and economic factors or changes implies causal association.

TABLE 120

The mortality of men aged from 10 to 34, six cities and remainder of the country, 1920-1921 to 1940-1941

($_nq_x$ per 100,000)

Age	*1920-1921*	*1925-1926*	*1930-1931*	*1935-1936*	*1940-1941*
10-14					
Six cities	2,540	1,829	1,746	1,603	1,317
Outside	1,765	1,396	1,317	1,282	1,228
15-19					
Six cities	5,044	3,541	3,459	3,265	3,153
Outside	4,714	3,734	3,734	3,806	4,192
20-24					
Six cities	5,034	3,430	3,758	3,579	3,579
Outside	6,210	4,643	4,987	5,320	4,982
25-29					
Six cities	4,877	3,216	3,367	3,420	2,998
Outside	5,666	3,999	4,115	4,537	4,590
30-34					
Six cities	5,330	3,434	3,676	3,308	3,177
Outside	5,486	3,681	3,671	3,816	4,033

Source: References, Table 117 and Footnote 25.

During the late teens and the twenties, migrants were predominant in the labor force of the cities. The selection of this migration influenced rural-urban differences in mortality in quite predictable ways. In the familistic society of Japan the eldest son remained as successor to the headship of the house. In this, physical selectivity was probably minor. Among younger sons, on the other hand, selectivity was highly probable. Although some of the physically handicapped were given special opportunities, there was a positive association between physical and mental adequacy and both movement to and adjustment in the cities. With these selective factors operating to differentiate the physical status of non-agricultural and agricultural populations, the death rates of the rural areas would have been higher than those of the cities if all other conditions had been identical in the two types of areas.

The physical selection of in-migrants was probably less significant than selective out-migration. Economic difficulties with an associated departure from the city were often related to ill-health. Such diseases as tuberculosis meant a loss of vitality and a reduced ability to work for a considerable time prior to death. Thus selective out-migration of the ill and those for whom death was imminent disturbed the relations between the health hazards of areas and the mortality of their populations. In general, selective out-migration reduced death rates in the cities and increased death rates in the rural areas. Migration had indirect effects also, for in diseases such as tuberculosis secondary foci of infection developed in the rural areas that received migrants back from the areas that were the primary foci.

The mortality of the people in an area at a given date need not measure the hazards to health or the probabilities of dying implicit in the conditions of that area. However, the social process that produced migration for death was not fortuitous. The family absorbed the unemployed or the ill in time of need. The acceptance of responsibilities such as these was another contribution of the peasants to the rapid growth of the cities.

THE DIFFERENTIAL MORTALITY OF THE SEXES

In all societies, cultural factors play a pervasive role in mortality. Differential mortality is a necessary consequence of differential social and economic roles. Quantitative verification of this thesis is difficult, for adequate data on mortality over periods of time have been limited largely to peoples of Western culture. Here there are similarities in the social, economic, and demographic roles of women, in the secular trends toward the lessening of discriminations or privileges based on sex, and in the individualization of the status of children. The study of the sex differences in mortality that were associated with diversities in the cultures of primitive groups might seem academic. It is quite otherwise with the mortality of the Japanese, for their experience in the past may be relevant to the experience in the future of the multitudinous peoples of the great cultures of mainland Asia.

The familism of Japan produced differences in the material conditions of life and the pressures of living for men and for women. The society assigned the performance of household duties and the care of youth and the aged to women, at the same time that it accepted, if it did not require, their participation in the work of the fields. The mode of living was favorable to the survival of the male, especially in the centuries of peace. With the opening to the West and the industrial transformation, there were elements of change in the relation of the sexes, but the preferential position remained that of the male. There was a more concentrated care of the boy baby, and boys were given priority when food was insufficient. The transitional culture should have produced an excess mortality of girls in infancy and childhood roughly proportionate to the intensity of the familistic tradition and behavior. It is more difficult to argue *a priori* as to what should have happened to the differential mortality of the sexes during early maturity. Here the familism that had retarded health and vitality among young girls barred married women from factory and marketplace. Life among the aging and the aged should have been favorable to longevity among women and men, for past selection had been intensive and age itself dictated privilege in food, work assignments, and rest.

This has been a statement of the expectation as to differential mortality in a particular society that can be characterized as familistic. The intent was to emphasize the importance of the Japanese data. In Japan it is possible to determine the course of change as an agrarian society was transformed into a less familistic and a more industrial society. Japanese mortality experience during the last century is not that of the traditional familistic order. It is, instead, the differential mortality of a family system, a society, and an economy undergoing change.

The hypothesis that the priorities accorded to sons would result in a surplus mortality of female babies roughly proportionate to the intensity of the familistic tradition is not substantiated by Japanese experience. The death rates of infants declined rapidly over time, but there were only slight changes in the ratio of the mortality of girl babies to that of boy babies (FIGURE 18). It is possible that differences in maternal care were involved in the relative levels of mortality for girl and boy babies, but it does not seem probable. The ratios of female to male mortality were quite similar in the great cities and the remainder of the country, and these ratios

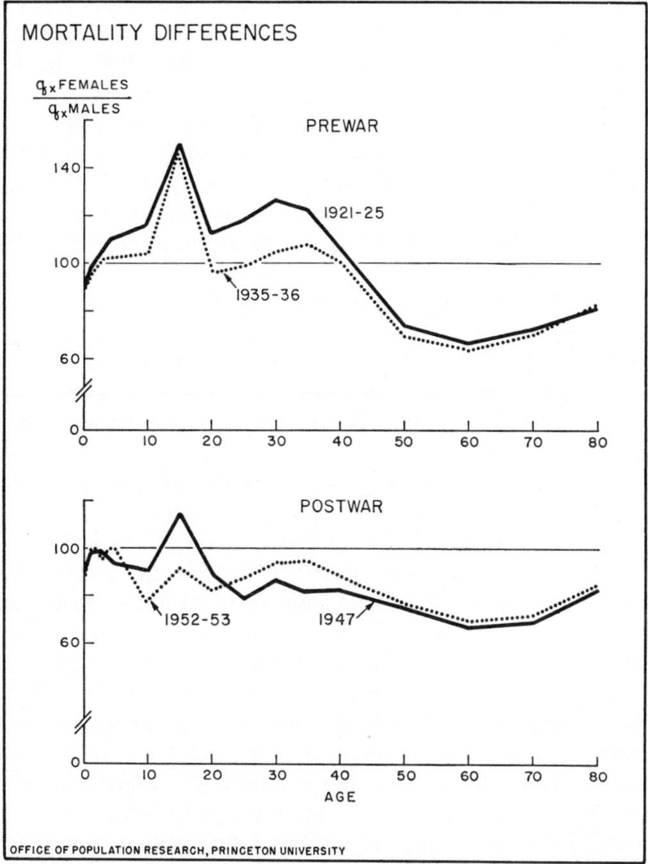

Figure 18. The declining excess in the mortality of females, 1921-1925, 1935-1936, 1947, and 1952-1953 (Ratio of q_x for females to q_x for males)
Source: References, Table 113.

changed slowly during a period of rapid transition. Virtually the same conclusion follows from an examination of sex differentials in mortality at ages 1 through 4. Excesses in death rates for girls aged from 1 to 4 over those for boys of the same age were somewhat greater in the large cities than outside them. However, there were slow declines in the excess deaths of girls. By 1935-1936 the death rates for girls aged from 1 to 4 were actually less than those for boys. This change from excess to deficit of mortality for girls occurred outside the great cities earlier than within them. Familial preferences for sons may have been involved, but the priority accorded boys does not appear to be a complete explanation of differences within the country.

Children aged from 5 to 9 are subjected to the external environment of community and school; in addition, little girls begin to assume responsibilities for assistance in home activities. In 1920-1925 and 1925-1930 the excess female mortality at this age was substantially greater than that during infancy and the pre-school ages. In the great cities in 1925-1926, the death rates for girls aged from 5 to 9 were almost 20 per cent above those for boys of the same age. By 1935-1936 the excess had declined to only 1 per cent in the great cities, and death rates for girls were actually below those for boys in the country as a whole. It is difficult to find an interpretation of these trends that does not involve at least an implicit assumption of an improvement in the status of girls with reference to that of boys.

One is tempted to a degree of speculation concerning the impact of familism on the mortality of children that is not justified by the data under consideration. In Japan during the interwar decades there was poverty and malnutrition, but the problems of physical survival were neither immediate nor acute for most families. The women who nursed their babies may have suffered a loss of vitality, but most babies received nutrition sufficient for survival. Infanticide and exposure were not common. The preferential treatment of the son seems to have become more important after infancy. If the mother had another baby, the older child might be relegated to a secondary position. It should be remembered, though, that the care devoted to a child may be related both to the sex and to the birth order of that child. The older sister who cares for a younger brother is highly valued by Japanese parents. It seems clear that the excess mortality of little girls was an unintended consequence of ways of living that differed for little girls and little boys. It was not the result of a planned neglect of little girls.

The greatest excesses in the mortality of girls were the products of their economic role in youth rather than of their roles as less-valued babies or, later, as neglected and overworked daughters-in-law. In 1925-1926 in the great cities, the death rates for girls aged from 10 to 14 were almost half again as high as those for boys; the excess declined from 48 per cent in 1925-1926 to 43 per cent in 1935-1936. The excess outside the great cities was 39 per cent in 1925-1926 and 34 per cent in 1935-1936. These were the ages when girls completed elementary school and entered the employments traditional for them: the factory dormitories, domestic service, and prostitution. It was the distribution of these employments outside the great cities and industrial areas that produced the surplus in the mortality of girls in the rural areas. And here, where fiscal returns to families were involved, the lessening of the disabilities of girls was slight.

Industrialization and urbanization in a milieu of low income, long hours of work, and generally unsanitary conditions placed severe penalties on men. The curve of deaths by age has been described previously. Death rates increased steeply from age 10-14 to ages 15-19 and 20-24, declined slightly at ages 25-29 and 30-34, rose slightly at age 35-39 and increased greatly at age 40-44. These changes may be regarded as the human cost of economic development for the men of Japan. If so, the costs were equally great, if not greater, for the women who were, in the main, homemakers and assistants in family labor. In 1925-1926 the death rates for women were far above those for men at each age from 15 through 39. The excess hazards of women were in part associated with childbearing, but the greatest excesses occurred at age 15 to 19, when only a few were married. It may be significant, however, that declines in the excess deaths of women came primarily at age 20 to 34. Part of this reduction in the excess mortality of women was associated with the lessened rates of childbearing. However, declines in fertility during these ages were insufficient to explain the declines in the mortality of women relative to that of men. Improvement in the status of women seems to be a necessary assumption.

During the years of maximum human reproduction, from age 20 to 34, the excess mortality of women was far larger in the great cities than outside them. It is not possible to conclude from this that factors other than childbearing and child care were critical in the excess mortality of women. The death rates for men aged from 20 to 34 were lowered in the great cities, and raised outside them, by the selective out-migration of the physically and mentally handicapped and the ill. Women aged from 20 to 34 were less subject to selective out-migration, for they were married women whose out-migration depended on that of their husbands. The family system dictated the return of the man to the familial home when he was ill. If the woman became ill, she continued to reside in the city. The departure from her family at marriage was irrevocable for a woman.

At all ages beyond the forties, the death rates for men were above those for women. This dividing line did not change in the 1920's and 1930's, but the advantages of women as compared with men increased throughout the period. Prior to recent years, the chances for survival among women improved with reference to those among men at all ages beyond infancy. At ages where there were excesses of deaths among women, the excesses became less or even vanished at some of the younger ages. At ages where there were deficits in the deaths of women, the deficits became larger. The relative weights to be assigned to familistic versus more specific social and economic factors may be debatable. It is in a major sense an artificial problem. Familism, with its emphasis on the reproductive and household responsibilities of women and its containment of the lives of all its members, pervaded the society and the economy. The result of all the factors influencing the production and maintenance of life was a severe disadvantage for women during childhood, adolescence, and the major childbearing ages. The consequences of the social and economic changes of the interwar decades were a rapid decline in these disadvantages of women, with correlated declines in their mortality that were more rapid than those for men.

The rapid declines in mortality in the postwar years were accompanied by a virtual disappearance of the types of excess mortality of women that had been so characteristic of Japan. This, again, has been due to the overriding influence of medical products that permit the saving of life without changes in social institutions or the economic structure. The argument cannot be continued from the prewar into the postwar period that changes in the differential mortality of women reflect changes in their roles in the society. Their change in status may be continuing, but the use of mortality statistics to document it is no longer valid. Several points are worth noting, however. The employment situation is reducing the jobs available to women, while social welfare and labor legislation preclude employment under the conditions hat once existed. In the years since 1948-1949, the death rates of girls aged from 15 to 19 and from 20 to 24 have declined at a more rapid rate than those of boys the same age. It may be that the changed conditions of employment and the continued postponement of marriage are both involved. At age 25 to 40, however, there has been an increase in the ratio of the death rates of women to those of men. Here, the decline in the age-specific mortality of women has been less than that of men. Far more detailed mortality statistics than those now available would be required to corroborate the hint that the abortions now so frequent among women aged from 25 to 40 may have retarded the reduction in the death rates of women.

CHANGING HAZARDS AND LIFE CYCLES

In a sense, death rates permit a critique of the material success of a culture. The extent of the postponement of death toward a terminus that is ultimately unavoidable measures the adequacy of physical levels of living and the achievements in utilizing knowledge and discipline to manipulate the environment and control the activities of individuals. We shall attempt to portray these human aspects of the changing mortality of the Japanese through considering the experiences of cohorts moving through life at the rates of mortality that existed from the 1920's to the 1940's. Perhaps we should extend the consideration to the social and economic significance of the low levels of mortality that now exist in Japan. However, the elements of conjecture here would be so great as to render assessment of human significance speculative rather than analytical.

The great advances in health and the postponement of death in Imperial Japan occurred in infancy and early childhood. The achievements of the Japanese for their children were substantial indeed, whether viewed against the background of their own past, or in contrast to the levels of mortality characteristic of the indigenous peoples of the colonies, or in comparison with the probable situation in China. In 1925-1930 the proportion of boy babies surviving to age 5 was 61 per cent among the Koreans in Korea and 73 per cent among the Taiwanese in Taiwan, as compared with 78 per cent among the Japanese in Japan. No single prefecture in Japan had the degree of wastage among its children that characterized all the Koreans, and only Aomori in the far northeast of Honshu and the three prefectures of Toyama, Ishikawa, and Fukui on the Sea of Japan had a wastage as high as that of the Taiwanese in Taiwan. Declining death rates among infants and young children had already lessened the age-old tragedies of parents in the cultures of the Orient. The achievement of reduced mortality in Japan had not been a particularly expensive process. The factors responsible were a diffusion of some simple principles of sanitation and nutrition plus a relatively small amount of public health and medical care. Uncontaminated water supplies and sanitary inspection in the great cities required small per capita investments. Neither the reorganization of society nor undue restrictions on economic practices were involved. The measures enforced were in accord with the desires of the people. The Japanese accepted the role of government, they loved their children, they sought health, and they had faith in inoculations. Thus public health and medical personnel worked in accord with the values of the culture as they struggled to reduce infant and childhood mortality.

The effects of the declining death rates in infancy were not limited to the psychological, for the increasing numbers of living children became powerful forces of change in family and village life. The high valuation of children may have been a concomitant rather than a consequence of high mortality. Whatever the facts as to their remote origins, high fertility and high mortality in combination produced a small average size of family. The declines in the mortality of the young during the period of early and middle industrialization permitted the realization of the large-family ideal.

The mortality of school-age youth was low and the regional variations were slight. In 1925-1930 from 97 to 99 per cent of the boys and girls who reached age 6 survived to age 12. These were the years of compulsory education. The hazards of work in farm, factory, or shop lay ahead. Vaccinations, quarantines, and other factors reduced deaths from the major epidemic diseases and the contagious diseases of childhood.

The Japanese social system was generally favorable to the reduction of mortality in infancy, childhood, and school ages. For youth, taken here as age 17 to 32, the problem was quite different. Conflicting values and alternative uses of major capital resources were involved in the policy decisions that would have been essential to substantial reductions in mortality. At 1925-1930 levels of mortality, 88 per cent of the men alive at age 17 would have survived to age 32; in 1930-1935 only 87 per cent would have survived this span of youth. Mortality had increased rather than decreased. An inspection of survivorship ratios from age 17 to age 32 for the prefectures indicates high proportions surviving in northeastern, eastern, and central Honshu and in eastern Kyushu; low proportions along the Sea of Japan; average or below average proportions in southwest Japan. The distribution pattern is similar for women, but the percentage of those alive at age 17 who survived to age 32 increased from 1925-1930 to 1930-1935 instead of decreasing, as it did for men. The increase was slight, however, the precise percentage of survivors from age 17 to age 32 being 86.1 in 1925-1930 and 86.7 in 1930-1935.

The ages from 17 to 32 included the period of entry into the labor market, as well as that of migration from country to city. This was also the stage of life at which marriage occurred and families were established. The major cause of death associated with the relatively high and increasing mortality among men was tuberculosis. Tuberculosis was also a factor in the persistent high death rates among women.

The direct associations among tuberculosis mortality, industrialization, and urbanization were disturbed by the fact that the area where tuberculosis was acquired was not necessarily the area where death occurred. In fact, neither in 1925-1930 nor in 1930-1935 was there any clear-cut relation between the general level of mortality aside from tuberculosis and the mortality from tuberculosis. In 1925-1930 the expectation of life for males at age 12 in the absence of deaths from tuberculosis showed a high belt extending along the Sea of Japan from Akita down to Kyoto.[34] Osaka prefecture was an extension of this belt of high expectation. There was also high expectation in eastern Kyushu. Chiba prefecture alone among the prefectures on the Pacific side was in the upper brackets of general mortality. There was quite a different geographical distribution of the number of years that would have been added to the expectation of life at age 12 if deaths from tuberculosis had been removed. The areas of high tuberculosis mortality were Hokkaido, central Honshu in a semicircle from Tokyo around through Ishikawa and down through Hyogo, the eastern Shikoku prefectures, the prefectures on the southwest tip of Honshu, and the central line of prefectures through Kyushu. The explanation of these distribution patterns of general and tuberculosis mortality involve medical, epidemiological, and demographic factors. Before pursuing them, we should attempt to determine whether and how the incidence of mortality from tuberculosis was related to the economic transformation of the country.

A grouping of the prefectures by the proportion of the population gainfully occupied in agriculture indicated a somewhat higher incidence of deaths from tuberculosis in the industrial prefectures, but the range within any type of prefecture was great. Tuberculosis mortality was relatively high in the industrial prefectures, relatively low in the agricultural prefectures of northeast Honshu. Aside from these prefectures, there appeared to be no direct association between the extent of the employment outside agriculture and the increase in tuberculosis mortality. Part of the distribution pattern may have been climatic. The high incidence along the Sea of Japan may have been associated with the long and wet winters, while the high incidence in Hokkaido may have been a product of

[34] Taniguchi, Yoshinori. "Hompo ni okeru kekkaku shibo ni yoru heikin yomei tanshuku no chiriteki bumpu." *Chosen igakkai zasshi*, 29:2153-2170. 1939.

the transfer into the north of modes of housing and ways of living adapted to the southern islands. The major answer to the puzzle is found in migration. The great concentrations of tuberculosis deaths were not in the industrial prefectures themselves, but in those prefectures whose youth had been drained off as migrants into the industrial areas.

The limitation of the mortality from tuberculosis prior to the availability of inoculation would have imposed great constraints on Japanese industry, and it would have involved great extensions of hospital and welfare facilities. Even in "rural" areas adolescents labored under crowded conditions at very low wages. Many lived in the textile dormitories or other accommodations for group living. Long hours of labor, poor conditions of work, crowded housing conditions, and diets low in protective foods contributed to lowered resistances. Once infection occurred, there were few governmental facilities for care and isolation. The individual with active tuberculosis lived in intimate association with his family or friends in the city. When maintenance and care became essential, he returned to his family in the country, thus exposing them to the risks of infection. If the wife acquired tuberculosis the return home was less likely, but the possibilities of infection for the immediate family were major. To have lessened this particular human cost of industrialization would have required later entrance into the labor market, shorter hours of work, codes for space and sanitation in shops and factories, and allowances for illness. It would also have required wages adequate for better housing and nutrition among laborers and their families. In addition to all these, public provisions for the segregation and care of the infected would have had to replace the familial care of the diseased. The death rates from tuberculosis are perhaps the clearest measure of the human costs of an industrial transformation based on the utilization of labor at minimum direct costs in current wages. These rates also reveal the limits of the familistic society as a substitute for the welfare facilities of the state.

The high mortality of the early productive years was associated with the hazards of tuberculosis and other respiratory diseases. There were other hazards in these ages, partially related to the tuberculosis-industrialization-urbanization nexus of factors, partially independent. Military conscription and the increasing utilization of the armed forces did not lead to any high risks of death in military action prior to 1937, or even to 1941. The direct military deaths that occurred were not reported in the vital statistics of Japan, but the disabled and ill among military personnel and civilian migrants were returned to Japan. In the years from 1931 on, militarism and imperial expansion were leading to increasing hazards of death for men. Among women, on the other hand, the historic hazards of death through childbirth and child care were lessening. The building-up of the armed forces and the military activities outside the country may have been factors in the increasing age at marriage and the lessening rates of childbearing. If so, there may have been a causal relationship between the increasing mortality of men and the declining mortality of women in the years during which Japan moved toward World War II.

The hazards of the industrializing society were not over for those who survived the late teens and the twenties. The proportions of those who survived the mature productive years—roughly, age 32 to 62—were least in the areas recently agricultural but undergoing current industrial development. Here the risks to health and life resulting from industrial and urban development were superimposed on the risks of the agricultural society. In most instances there was little lessening of mortality through the out-migration of the ill, for the majority of the migrants came from within the prefectures. Selective migration involved primarily a reallocation of urban and rural deaths within the prefectures.

CONCLUSIONS

In the early years after World War I there were substantial differences in the mortality of the populations in rural areas and in cities. As urbanization and industrialization developed, there were decreases in the diversities that had existed in the earliest period of measurement. Death rates that were high declined more rapidly than those that were low, whether decline was measured in absolute or in relative terms. In the villages, the leveling of differences was associated with the general changes of the new society rather than with specific health or medical activities in local areas. Declining mortality also occurred in the cities, particularly in the metropolitan centers and the great cities, and over time there was a lessening of differences. Here the role of specific factors was quite apparent, and there were sharp differences in the timing and the rate of decline in mortality in individual cities.

The result of the coincidence of initially differing levels of mortality and differing rates of decline was a reduction in the differences between mortality in the great cities and in the remainder of the country, followed by a reversal of the direction of those differences. In the early 1920's the mortality in the great cities was far above that in the remainder of the country. By the early 1930's the differences were slight. By the late 1930's mortality in the great cities was below that in the remainder of the country. Since the further improvements that could be made in mortality were related to the lowness of the level already achieved, the continuation of the mortality trends of the prewar period would have resulted in slower declines in mortality in the cities, more rapid declines in mortality in the villages, and an equalization of levels of mortality throughout the country.

The mortality of the Japanese has long been below the levels that would be expected in a country with a per capita national income, levels of living, and nutritive standards such as those that exist in Japan. The discipline of the people, the protective health services of the government, the broadly based and low-cost facilities for private medical care, and many personal and institutional factors were involved in a partial divorce of mortality from economic conditions. The major reductions in mortality were those in the early ages. Beyond these, there was virtual elimination of deaths that could be prevented by quarantine or inoculation.

The trends in death by cause and by sex and age for areas and for social-economic groups permit some broad generalizations as to the achievement and the limitations of the Japanese in the reduction of mortality. Some of the achievements were by-products of the modernization of the economy, while others were due directly to health and medical activities. In many, if not most, reductions in mortality there was an interplay of the general forces of social and economic development and the specific advances in the sciences and the technologies of health and medical practices. A regularized food supply for the nation as a whole and its constituent areas was a product of modern economic development. Modern transportation was essential to the reduction of deaths from natural catastrophe and their ancient correlates of flight and starvation. The integration of the people within an advancing economy combined with formal education to replace superstitious practices with ways of child care that lessened the chances of illness and death. Public health services and private medical care were powerful, if not separately measureable, factors in improving the health and nutritive practices of the people.

The behavior of mortality in the postwar years has been a reasonable extension of that in the prewar years, given the changes in the scientific knowledge and the technologies applicable in the fields of health, medical care, and sanitation. In the prewar years the major achievements were those that reduced mortality in infancy and childhood. In the postwar years there were great new advances that permitted the limitation of tuberculosis and the other respiratory and infectious diseases. There was an increase in the number of diseases that could be controlled without changes in the resources situation, the levels of income, or the ways of living. The differences in mortality in various geographic areas, occupations, and social-economic classes may have widened somewhat as the new limitations to death were introduced, but the rapid declines in national mortality and the patterns of decline in death rates show a movement of all groups within the nation toward very low mortality. The great problems remaining in Japan, as in the West, are those associated with mortality in the middle and late years.

CHAPTER XV

Natural Increase

THERE is no evidence that the rate of natural increase of the Japanese has ever been high by modern standards.[1] A birth rate of 45 per 1,000 total population combined with a death rate of 20 yields an increase of 2.5 per cent per year. This was the prewar situation in Taiwan. A birth rate of from 40 to 45 combined with a death rate of from 12 to 14 yields an increase of from 2.6 to 3.3 per cent per year. Rates such as these occur today in many areas where the high fertility of the peasant society co-exists with the low mortality made possible by modern public health activities. The highest rate of natural increase recorded in the history of Imperial Japan was that of 15.6 per 1,000 population in 1926.

Rates of natural increase in Japan have therefore been relatively low and fluctuations have not been great. In the modern statistical record, there are no sharp changes such as those that occur in a population living close to subsistence level. There were declines in 1905-1906, 1918-1919, and 1938-1939, but there was always an excess of births over deaths. Even in 1918, when the recorded death rate was 26.8 per 1,000, there was a recorded natural increase of 5.4. Growth was expected and was natural; its rates fluctuated within the relatively narrow limits of from 0.5 to 1.6 per cent per year throughout the first forty-four years of the twentieth century. During thirty-seven of these years, the rate was somewhere between 1.0 and 1.5 per cent per year.[2] There is a suggestion that rates of natural increase changed little during almost half a century of rapid industrialization and urbanization. Earlier analysis of the trends in the growth of the population from the middle of the nineteenth century to 1918 supports this generalization.

INCREASE OF THE NATIONAL POPULATION

In the analysis of levels, trends, and differentials in natural increase in the years since 1920, it is necessary to divide the period into two segments. During the 1920's and the 1930's change occurred along an established path. In recent years vital events have reflected evolutionary forces, economic reorientations, and psychological reappraisals.

CRUDE RATES, 1920-1940

Rates of natural increase adjusted for the incompleteness of birth registration and consolidated into five-year averages indicate a peak of increase in the years from 1925 to 1930 and slow decline thereafter. The rates for the intercensal periods are as follows:[3]

Period	*Rate*
1920-1925	14.5
1925-1930	15.2
1930-1935	14.6
1935-1940	12.0

Perusal of the annual figures indicates that the decline after 1925-1930 was produced by episodic fluctuations (TABLE 121). The rates for the years 1936, 1937, and 1940 were close to those expected on the basis of trends from 1920 to 1935. It was the rates for the years 1938 and 1939 that carried the average for 1935-1939 substantially below those for the other intercensal periods.[4]

The maximum annual rates of natural increase in prewar Japan were about 1.5 per cent per year. These are not high rates of increase if viewed in a global perspective. However, 1.5 per cent per year in the Japan of the 1920's and 1930's yielded large absolute increases. It was the size of the annual additions to the population rather than the rate of the increase that attracted the attention of Japanese and foreigners alike. In 1920, the year of the first census, natural increase amounted to 602 thousand. Annual additions mounted steadily to 872 thousand in 1925 and 938 thousand in 1926. Numbers then fluctuated somewhat, but population increase became a dramatic fact when the additions to the population in the depression year of 1932 exceeded one million. Even in the "low increase" years of 1938 and 1939, natural increase amounted to over 625 thousand a year. In the war years of 1941, 1942, and 1943, the annual excess of births over civilian deaths amounted to more than a million a year. Most of the increase in Japan's population from 55.4 million in 1920 to 73.3 million in 1943 was due to the excess of births over deaths.[5] It is understandable, therefore, that the increase should have been regarded as rapid even though, in comparative terms, the rate of increase was not high.

CRUDE RATES, 1947-1955

The relatively low rates of natural increase in the 1920's and 1930's were eclipsed by the higher rates of the early postwar years. Mortality declined rapidly under the combined

[1] The reconstruction of trends in natural increase prior to 1920 relies on the data of a deficient but generally improving registration system. Analysis of trends in mortality and fertility and hence in relations between the two cannot be carried back of 1920. Thus, thirty-five years of experience are available, but these years include only brief periods that were normal in the sense that they were not influenced by depression, expansion, war, or occupation.

[2] The rates cited here refer to the *honseki* population for the years prior to 1920, to the *de facto* population and the natural increase of ethnic Japanese in Japan for the years from 1920 to 1943. The area is that of prewar Japan.

[3] Numbers of births were adjusted for underreporting and the exclusion of non-Japanese, while numbers of deaths were not adjusted.

[4] The total population was used as the base for the computation of rates, although the exclusion of military and related deaths introduced inaccuracies.

[5] In order to maintain consistency with the data given in Table 121, the figures cited here refer to the area of postwar Japan, excluding Amami Oshima in Kagoshima prefecture. For the area of the period from 1920 to 1945, the population and the natural increase of Okinawa prefecture would have to be added.

TABLE 121

Natural increase of the Japanese in Japan, 1920-1955

Year	NUMBERS (IN '000)[a]			RATES PER 1,000 POPULATION		
	Births	*Deaths*	*Natural increase*	*Births*	*Deaths*	*Natural increase*
1920	2,012	1,409	602	36.1	25.4	10.7
1921	1,976	1,279	697	35.0	22.8	12.2
1922	1,954	1,278	675	34.1	22.5	11.6
1923	2,029	1,324	705	34.1	23.0	11.1
1924	1,984	1,245	739	33.7	21.4	12.3
1925	2,072	1,200	872	34.8	20.3	14.5
1926	2,089	1,151	938	34.7	19.1	15.6
1927	2,046	1,205	841	33.5	19.7	13.8
1928	2,120	1,228	893	34.2	19.8	14.4
1929	2,062	1,251	811	32.8	19.9	12.9
1930	2,071	1,162	909	32.4	18.2	14.2
1931	2,089	1,231	857	32.2	19.0	13.2
1932	2,168	1,166	1,002	32.9	17.7	15.2
1933	2,106	1,185	922	31.5	17.7	13.8
1934	2,028	1,225	803	30.0	18.1	11.9
1935	2,174	1,152	1,022	31.7	16.8	14.9
1936	2,086	1,220	866	30.0	17.5	12.4
1937	2,165	1,198	967	30.8	17.0	13.8
1938	1,912	1,250	662	27.1	17.7	9.4
1939	1,886	1,259	627	26.6	17.7	8.9
1940	2,100	1,177	924	29.4	16.4	13.0
1941	2,260	1,140	1,120	31.1	15.7	15.4
1942	2,216	1,158	1,058	30.2	15.8	14.4
1943	2,235	1,205	1,031	30.2	16.3	13.9
1944	—	—	—	—	—	—
1945	—	—	—	—	—	—
1946	—	—	—	—	—	—
1947	2,679	1,138	1,541	34.3	14.6	19.7
1948	2,681	951	1,731	33.5	11.9	21.6
1949	2,697	945	1,751	33.0	11.6	21.4
1950	2,338	905	1,433	28.1	10.9	17.2
1951	2,138	839	1,299	25.3	9.9	15.4
1952	2,005	765	1,240	23.4	8.9	14.4
1953	1,868	773	1,095	21.5	8.9	12.6
1954	1,770	721	1,048	20.0	8.2	11.9
1955[b]	1,727	693	1,034	19.3	7.8	11.6

[a] Japan minus Okinawa for the years 1920-1944.
[b] Preliminary.

Source: References, Chapter XII, Table 90, and Chapter XIV, Table 112.

impetus of Japanese activities and massive pressures from the Public Health and Welfare Section, General Headquarters, Supreme Commander for the Allied Powers. At the same time the increase in the number of newly married couples and the reunion of older married couples led to substantial increases in numbers of births. The result of this coincidence of declining mortality and temporarily high fertility was a natural increase of 1.5 million in 1947, 1.7 million in 1948, and 1.8 million in 1949. The natural increase in these three years alone exceeded the total civilian repatriation that followed the end of the war. It was also larger than the emigration from Japan in all the years of conquest and imperial expansion.

The annual excess of births over deaths began to decline in 1950, but even in 1955 it exceeded one million. The persistence of increase in a population with rapidly declining fertility is illustrated here in striking form. Whereas the natural increase in prewar Japan had reached a maximum of 1.1 million in 1941, in postwar Japan it did not decline to 1.0 million until 1954. For the nine years from 1947 to 1955 natural increase amounted to more than 12 million.

The behavior of birth, death, and natural increase rates from 1947 through 1950 does not deviate sharply from that to be expected on the basis of prewar trends. Birth and death rates alike were declining. Natural increase declined slightly, from 19.7 in 1947 to 17.2 in 1950. Departures from the prewar situation were already apparent, for mortality was below its prewar trend line by 1947, whereas fertility crossed its prewar trend line in 1950. Precipitant declines in fertility and continuing declines in mortality characterized the years from 1950 to 1955. A comparison of the vital rates for 1955 with those for 1950 shows a decline of 8.8 per 1,000 total population in the birth rate, 3.1 in the death rate, and 5.6 in the rate of natural increase. The levels of birth and death rates are now such that relatively large declines can still occur in birth rates, whereas only small declines can occur in death rates. Continuations of declines in birth and death rates similar to those that have been occurring since 1950 will lead to major reductions in the rate of natural increase.

NET REPRODUCTION RATES

Numbers of births and deaths are recorded facts. The difference between the two sets of figures is not only real but simple to understand; it is the increase in the size of the population.[6] No hypotheses or contingencies are involved in interpretation. However, a precise description of population increase must take account of the fact that numbers of births and deaths are influenced by the sex and age composition of the population as well as its total size. The age distributions that influence present birth and death rates are products of numbers of births and deaths in the past; the present numbers of births and deaths are creating the age distributions of the future. A measure of fertility used in earlier chapters to obviate the problem of differences in the age structures of populations was the gross reproduction rate.[7] This represents for a given age-specific schedule of fertility the average number of daughters that would be borne by a cohort of females, all of whom had lived to the end of the childbearing period. A measure that reflects the combined influence of fertility and mortality on population increase is the net reproduction rate. The basic estimate involves the number of daughters that would be borne by the survivors to successive ages of a cohort of newly born girl babies, provided the survivors at each age reproduced at the rates of the given age-specific fertility schedule. The net reproduction rate is the ratio of the number of daughters as thus estimated to the number of newly born girls in the original cohort. The gross and net reproduction rates for Japanese in Japan are as follows:[8]

Year	*Gross reproduction rate*	*Net reproduction rate*	*Ratio of net to gross rate*
1920-1921	2.6	1.5	.58
1925-1926	2.6	1.7	.66
1930-1931	2.4	1.6	.68
1935-1936	2.3	1.6	.70
1940-1941	2.1	1.6	.73
1947	2.2	1.7	.78
1948	2.1	1.8	.82
1949	2.1	1.8	.82
1950	1.8	1.5	.85
1951	1.6	1.4	.87
1952	1.5	1.3	.88
1953	1.3	1.2	.89
1954	1.2	1.1	.90
1955	1.2	1.1	.91

The balance of declining fertility and mortality produced slow changes in net reproduction rates from 1920-1921 to 1940-1941. In the years from 1920 to 1925 declines in mortality were greater than those in fertility, but in the fifteen years from 1925 to 1940 fertility declined more rapidly than mortality. In 1925-1926 the net rate was less than two-thirds the gross rate. In 1940-1941 the net rate was almost three-fourths the gross rate.

In 1947, the first postwar year for which measurement is possible, fertility was buoyed by the abundant childbearing of newly formed marriages and recently re-united families.[9] Mortality, on the other hand, had been reduced substantially below the rather high levels of the late war and early postwar years. The net reproduction rate was 1.7, approximately the same as the rate in 1925-1926. In 1948 and 1949 fertility remained high but mortality dropped rapidly. The net reproduction rates of 1.8 for these two years were the highest achieved by the Japanese. By 1950, resort to abortion was becoming more widespread and contraceptive practice was increasing. Fertility dropped sharply and consistently. By 1955 the net reproduction rate was only a little above unity.

Reproduction rates limited to the female population have major deficiencies as measures of the trend of reproduction in Japan. In the years prior to the war, increasing numbers of men had gone to the cities of the homeland, the armed forces, the colonies, or the Co-Prosperity Sphere. In the postwar years there were the deficits of men produced by war. There were substantial proportions of the single and the widowed among women. The estimates of the reproductive performance of men in the years from 1925 to 1950 therefore assume a particular significance in any assessment of the factors that were involved in the changing gross and net reproduction rates for women. The rates given here are from the Institute of Population Problems:[10]

[6] On the assumption that there is no net balance of migration to or from the area under consideration.

[7] See Chapter XII, pp. 234-235.

[8] For the years from 1920 through 1941 the numbers of births are adjusted for underreporting and exclusions. Age schedules of fertility for 1920-1921 and 1935-1936 are estimated from the regression of age-specific on general fertility for prefectures and cities in 1930. Age schedules of fertility as of 1925 were used for 1925-1926. Appropriate age schedules of fertility were available for 1940 and 1941. Although these were war years, the mortality of women alone is involved in these computations and the influence of war was relatively slight. Age schedules of fertility were available for the years from 1947 through 1951; schedules were estimated for 1952 and 1953 on the assumption of a continuation of the downward movements of 1950 and 1951. Life tables used for the years from 1920-1921 through 1940-1941 were those computed by the Office of Population Research, while those for the years from 1947 through 1954 were prepared by Jinko mondai kenkyujo. The life table for 1955 is that computed by Professor Mizushima. Mizushima, Haruo, *et al.* "1950-nen, 1951-nen, 1952-nen kanzen seimai hyo. 1953-nen, 1954-nen, 1955-nen kanryaku seimei hyo." *Igaku kenkyu*, 26(11):2821-2847. 1956.

Most of the life tables refer to the periods from July 1 to June 30, whereas fertility schedules refer to calendar years.

[9] Interpretation of the net reproduction rates as indicative of the future increase of the population of Japan is invalid. Projective interpretation would involve the assumption that the experience of women at a given time could be taken as indicative of lifetime experience. This assumption was not valid for Japan even in the relatively stable years of the 1920's and the early 1930's. Even if the historic data of Japan were such as to give us the reproductive and mortality histories of cohorts of women, we could project the experience of the past into the future only with the most serious reservations. After the mid-1930's, relative stability in patterns of marriage and marital relations was replaced by the deviations of war, defeat, and re-adjustment. In the postwar years the facilities for and the attitudes toward the limitation of births changed greatly, as did the probabilities of death prior to or during the reproductive period.

[10] Rates for women: Nihon. Kosei-sho, jinko mondai kenkyujo.

Year	GROSS REPRODUCTION RATES		NET REPRODUCTION RATES	
	Men	*Women*	*Men*	*Women*
1925	2.8	2.5	1.7	1.6
1930	2.6	2.3	1.6	1.5
1937	2.4	2.1	1.6	1.5
1947	3.0	2.2	2.1	1.7
1950	2.5	1.8	2.0	1.5

The gross and net reproduction rates for the women overestimate the declines in fertility, particularly in the postwar as contrasted with the prewar years. However, deficits of men were responsible for only a fraction of the declines in fertility from 1947 to 1955.

The gross and net reproduction rates for men cannot be taken as alternative and "true" measures of reproduction as contrasted with biased measures for women. In the postwar years, the age at marriage for men declined and the remarriage of the widowed and the divorced occurred more frequently and more quickly. These compensatory adjustments in marital status reduced the birth deficits that otherwise would have occurred in the postwar period.

INTRINSIC RATES

If perchance a population should continue to develop over time subject to given age-specific birth and death rates, it would develop a characteristic sex and age structure that was stable.[11] The birth rate, the death rate, and the rate of natural increase of this stable population are "true" in the sense that they are not influenced by the past age structures; they are intrinsic in the sense that their appearance as actual rates is implicit in the continuation of the age-specific vital rates of the specific period until such time as the stable population is achieved. Or, if we wish to avoid the assumption of actual evolution, we may say that the intrinsic birth, death, and natural increase rates are those that would characterize a population with the sex and age structure that would be produced by the continuation of the age-specific fertility and mortality of the time periods.

The interpretation of intrinsic rates for a population changing as rapidly as that of modern Japan requires considerable caution. In 1925 all intrinsic rates were above the crude rates. In 1937 and later years intrinsic birth rates and intrinsic rates of natural increase were below the crude rates. The intrinsic rates for the years for which direct computation is possible are as follows:[12]

Year	*Type of rate*	*Births*	*Deaths*	*Natural increase*
	Crude	35.0	20.3	14.7
1925	Intrinsic	35.9	21.1	14.8
	Crude	32.4	18.2	14.2
1930	Intrinsic	33.3	19.1	14.2
	Crude	30.9	17.1	13.8
1937	Intrinsic	30.8	17.6	13.2
	Crude	34.3	14.6	19.7
1947	Intrinsic	32.1	14.9	17.2
	Crude	28.1	10.9	17.2
1950	Intrinsic	26.4	12.2	14.2

Retrospective or projective interpretations of intrinsic vital rates are not valid theoretically, and they have no empirical justification in Japan's own past. The intrinsic rates for the Japanese population demonstrate conclusively that the declining vital rates of the Japanese were not products of the changing age composition of the population. Instead, the actual rate of natural increase of the early 1920's was below that inherent in the age-specific fertility and mortality of the period. However, the actual rates of natural increase in the late 1940's and the early 1950's were above those inherent in the age-specific fertility and mortality of the period. The differences between crude birth and death rates underestimate the "true" declines that were occurring.

THE TREND OF THE INCREASE

It was both the time period and the nature of Japanese industrialization that permitted Japan to move through a transition in fertility and mortality without passing through a long period when annual rates of increase were very high. By the 1920's fertility had been reduced considerably below the level of the 1880's, if not indeed below the level of the late feudal period. The death rate had been reduced far below the level of the middle of the nineteenth century, but it remained high by Western standards. The Japanese had struggled to raise the health of their nation and achieve the postponement of death, and the knowledge, the training, and the research institutions of the West had been available to them. However, in the first century of Japan's transformation there was no means whereby mortality could be reduced quickly without fundamental changes in ways of living.

The slow decline of mortality occurred within an industrializing and urbanizing society. The movement from rural to urban life was conducive to an advancing age at marriage and limitation of childbearing among the married. The interpenetration of city and country, industry and agriculture, slowed the diffusion of new familial and reproductive mores from city to country. The coincidence of slow declines in mortality and delayed declines in fertility meant that natural increase long remained substantial but never reached the high levels that now characterize many agrarian societies. In recent years precipitant declines characterized fertility and mortality alike, but congruence in movements limited changes in rates of natural increase.

VARIATIONS AND TRENDS IN THE PREFECTURES

The rate of increase of the population of Japan is a meaningful figure, for it is the rate that has characterized a nation whose economy and people were changing from village residents to city dwellers. It is a complex figure, for it is a weighted average of the rates of increase in geographic areas and among social and economic groups. Hence once again we turn to a description of variations and trends in the prefectures.

CRUDE RATES

In the years from 1920 to 1925 the average annual rate of natural increase was 14.5 per 1,000 total population. The highest rates of natural increase occurred in the northeast; Hokkaido's rate was 23.9, while the rates in the Tohoku region ranged from 17.0 to 19.0 (TABLE 122). Rates were low in the

---

Saikin no jinko ni kansuru tokei shiryo. 7th Edition. Table 53. Rates for men: Courtesy of Jinko mondai kenkyujo. The rates for females as computed by the Institute differ from ours for several reasons: (1) Adjustments for incomplete reporting of births differ. (2) The years of reference are different. (3) The life tables differ.

[11] Lotka, A. J. "The geographic distribution of intrinsic natural increase in the United States, and an examination between several measures of net reproductivity." *Journal of the American Statistical Association*, 31(194):273-294. June 1936.

[12] Takagi, Naofumi, and Takayasu, Hiroshi. "Senzen sengo ni okeru antei jinko dotai ritsu ni kansuru ichi shisan." *J.m.k.*, No. 63, p. 69. 1956. Crude rates differ slightly from those in Table 121 for prewar years.

TABLE 122

Rates of natural increase in the prefectures, 1920-1955
(Natural increase per 1,000 total population)

	INTERCENSAL PERIODS					CALENDAR YEARS		
Prefectures	*1920-1925*	*1925-1930*	*1930-1935*	*1935-1940*	*1950-1955*	*1947*	*1950*	*1955*
All Japan	14.5	15.2	14.6	12.0	13.5	19.6	17.2	11.6
Hokkaido	23.9	22.1	20.7	17.1	19.0	23.3	24.3	14.8
Aomori	18.6	20.1	20.5	15.7	19.6	26.1	22.9	17.4
Iwate	17.2	18.7	17.7	15.4	17.9	20.9	20.9	15.6
Miyagi	19.1	20.0	19.5	16.8	17.2	22.0	21.6	15.0
Akita	17.7	19.6	19.4	15.3	16.4	22.0	20.4	14.2
Yamagata	17.1	17.4	16.3	14.0	13.6	17.1	18.6	11.6
Fukushima	18.4	19.1	17.9	15.3	17.1	21.3	21.3	14.8
Ibaraki	15.6	16.7	15.8	13.1	14.0	20.1	17.1	12.6
Tochigi	19.7	19.2	17.5	14.3	14.5	21.7	18.3	13.2
Gumma	16.3	16.5	15.7	13.3	13.3	20.7	17.1	12.1
Saitama	14.5	14.6	13.7	11.8	13.4	22.3	16.9	12.6
Chiba	10.2	12.5	12.9	10.3	11.9	20.7	14.8	11.0
Tokyo	13.4	17.2	16.5	14.0	12.1	19.4	15.4	10.2
Kanagawa	13.5	17.7	16.3	14.4	13.5	21.6	17.6	11.2
Niigata	13.8	14.8	14.4	12.7	13.9	20.2	17.5	12.3
Toyama	11.9	12.4	10.7	7.5	11.0	25.5	15.0	9.8
Ishikawa	7.7	7.6	6.4	3.3	10.5	23.6	14.2	9.7
Fukui	10.0	9.1	7.5	5.8	11.8	18.2	15.7	10.8
Yamanashi	16.6	17.0	16.9	15.0	13.3	18.8	16.0	11.6
Nagano	14.6	15.5	14.1	11.7	10.1	16.4	13.8	9.3
Gifu	14.8	15.0	13.5	11.6	12.1	19.4	15.6	10.6
Shizuoka	18.1	18.6	17.1	13.5	14.8	21.5	18.5	13.0
Aichi	13.9	15.1	14.9	13.6	11.9	19.5	15.8	10.1
Mie	12.9	14.0	11.8	9.0	10.8	16.8	14.4	9.0
Shiga	9.4	10.4	8.8	6.8	10.0	12.9	13.2	8.8
Kyoto	9.7	10.7	10.8	9.0	8.8	16.1	12.8	7.2
Osaka	11.9	13.7	13.7	12.7	11.5	16.4	15.1	9.3
Hyogo	13.1	13.2	12.5	10.2	11.8	17.1	14.7	9.8
Nara	13.1	12.1	10.0	7.1	10.4	14.9	13.1	7.9
Wakayama	13.7	13.5	11.9	8.8	10.2	17.4	13.5	9.0
Tottori	13.0	12.1	10.6	7.7	12.7	17.1	15.8	11.0
Shimane	8.5	7.9	8.5	6.1	11.5	19.7	15.5	9.5
Okayama	9.5	10.0	9.9	6.6	10.0	17.0	13.0	8.7
Hiroshima	12.1	12.4	11.6	8.2	10.8	18.4	14.7	9.4
Yamaguchi	10.4	10.5	10.7	6.4	12.0	16.9	16.6	9.5
Tokushima	11.1	12.8	11.7	9.2	12.7	19.7	15.7	11.2
Kagawa	13.5	13.4	12.5	8.7	10.6	21.9	14.4	9.0
Ehime	13.9	14.5	13.7	11.1	14.1	20.9	18.9	11.7
Kochi	11.7	11.7	10.4	6.8	10.6	18.2	14.4	9.2
Fukuoka	15.2	14.5	14.9	12.4	15.5	18.7	20.5	12.3
Saga	14.2	13.5	13.2	10.5	16.0	17.5	19.8	14.1
Nagasaki	15.8	15.3	14.9	12.5	18.8	18.6	21.3	16.5
Kumamoto	13.9	14.7	14.1	10.8	15.4	19.5	18.8	14.0
Oita	12.5	12.4	11.4	8.6	12.8	17.0	16.6	11.7
Miyazaki	18.0	18.6	18.6	14.7	17.3	22.5	20.8	15.3
Kagoshima	18.3	15.8	17.9	13.3	16.1	18.0	18.7	16.2
Okinawa	17.6	17.0	16.9	14.2	—	—	—	—

Source: Populations of the respective years: Censuses, cited in the Bibliography. Numbers of births and deaths: 1920-1940: Nihon. Naikaku tokei-kyoku. *Jinko dotai tokei.* 1947-1953: Nihon. Kosei-sho, eisei tokei-bu. *Jinko dotai tokei.* 1954-1955: *Ibid. Jinko dotai tokei maigetsu gaisu. Showa 29-nen. Ibid. Showa 30-nen.* For adjustments in reported numbers of births, see Chapter XII, Table 93.

prefectures along the Sea of Japan, where death rates were high; in the industrial prefectures, where birth rates were low; and in southwest Honshu, where average death rates coincided with relatively low birth rates. Changes were irregular and generally upward between 1920-1925 and 1925-1930. In the latter period, Aomori and Miyagi joined Hokkaido with rates of natural increase that exceeded 2 per cent per year. From 1925-1930 to 1935-1940 declining rates of natural increase characterized most of the prefectures of Japan. The sharp downward movement for the period from 1935 to 1940 reflected primarily the dislocations of the military and industrial mobilization of 1938 and 1939.

Changes in rates of natural increase were more complex than those of birth or death rates considered separately. Changes in fertility were primarily reflections of the influence of industrialization and urbanization on the agrarian society, and the direction of change was downward. The changes in mortality also reflected the influence of industrialization and urbanization, but rates increased in some prefectures, declined in others. The absence of close associations between levels or changes in fertility and mortality introduced variations into the relations between natural increase and geographic, social, or economic factors. The changes in rates of natural increase from 1930 to 1935 indicate the difficulties in interpretation. The rate of natural increase for the whole country was 14.2 in 1930, 14.6 in 1935. The rates of natural increase in the prefectures were closely associated in the two years; the correlation was .93. Rates increased in some prefectures, decreased in others. There was no significant relationship between the levels of the rates in 1930 and the amount or per cent of change from 1930 to 1935.

In the long run there was persistent decline in birth and death rates and hence a pattern of change in natural increase. Simple correlations of the variables for the prefectures for the years from 1920-1925 to 1952 indicate the nature of the change:

Year	*Birth and death rates*	*Natural increase and Death rate*	*Natural increase and Birth rate*
1920-1925	.25	−.44	.74
1925-1930	.17	−.42	.84
1930-1935	.05	−.54	.81
1935-1940	.05	−.51	.76
1947	.21	−.26	.89
1950	.32	−.13	.90
1952	.37	.10	.96

Relations between birth and death rates, always slight, almost disappeared in the 1930's. In the postwar years of rapid decline in fertility and mortality, there was an increasing association between birth and death rates. As mortality declined, it became less and less significant as a factor in natural increase. By 1952 the correlation between the crude birth rate and the crude rate of natural increase was .96.

NET, INTRINSIC, AND STANDARDIZED RATES

Crude rates of natural increase for prefectures are influenced both by differences in age-specific fertility and mortality and by differences in the sex and age structures of the population. A typically rural age structure, with its concentrations of children and aged, will have relatively high crude death rates and relatively low crude birth rates. Typically urban areas, on the other hand, will have relatively high crude birth rates and relatively low crude death rates. Thus the characteristic differences in the age structures of populations may mask whatever real differences exist in rates of natural increase between urban and rural areas. TABLE 123 presents various refined measures of natural increase in the prefectures of Japan: net reproduction rates for 1925-1930, 1930-1935, 1947, and 1950; intrinsic rates of natural increase for 1930, 1930-1935, and 1947; and rates standardized for sex and age, 1920, 1934-1936, and 1950.

In the years from 1925 to 1930 net reproduction rates were 2.0 or over in three prefectures in the northeast, and they approached 2.0 in the other prefectures of the Tohoku region. Net rates were higher in the agricultural than in the industrial areas but within this broad socio-economic pattern, they were higher in the northeast than in the southwest. However, the lowest rates were found in two quite different types of areas: the great metropolitan prefectures of central Honshu, and the backward agricultural prefectures along the Sea of Japan.

The net reproduction rate for Japan as a whole declined from 1.7 in 1920-1925 to 1.6 in 1925-1930. This small change concealed diversities in the changes in the prefectures. Net reproduction rates declined more rapidly in the northeast than in the southwest. Sharp declines occurred both in the great industrial prefectures of the Kanto and the Kinki and in the agricultural prefectures along the Sea of Japan. In 1930-1935, though, fertility was still quite high. The net reproduction rate was over 2.0 in Miyagi; it approached 2.0 in other northeastern prefectures. The lowest rate was that of 1.2 in Osaka.

In 1947 the net reproduction rate for Japan as a whole was 1.7. The over-all figure for the nation differed little from that for the years from 1925 to 1935. Internal variations were less than they had been in the earlier years, though the persistence of the dislocations of war may be as responsible for the lessening of prefectural differences as a true convergence in levels of fertility and mortality. By 1950 the net rate had declined to 1.5 for the nation, and there had been declines in most of the prefectures except those in Kyushu.

The picture of changes yielded by intrinsic rates of natural increase is quite similar to that yielded by net reproduction rates. In 1930 there was a great range in rates, from 25.4 in Akita, where the intrinsic birth rate was 45.1, to 3.4 for Osaka, where the intrinsic birth rate was 25.0 and the intrinsic death rate 21.6.[13] Between 1930 and 1947 there was a substantial lessening of the differences among the prefectures. By the latter year, increase was dependent in major part on fertility, the correlation of the intrinsic rate of natural increase with the intrinsic birth rate being .9, that with the intrinsic death rate −.4. There was no correlation between intrinsic birth and death rates.

The patterns of geographic variations and temporal changes were similar, whether intrinsic or crude vital rates were used as the basis of measurement. In 1930 the correlation between intrinsic and crude rates of natural increase for the prefectures was .8. The correlations of changes in crude rates from 1930-1935 to 1947 with those in intrinsic rates for the same period were .7 for death rates, .8 for birth rates, and .9 for rates of natural increase.

The refined measures of natural increase that have been presented here refer only to the female population. No allowances were made for regional differences or changes in the numbers or the characteristics of men. Moreover, births were

[13] Mizushima, Haruo. "Geographic variations in true increase rate of population in Japan." *Nihon jinko gakkai kiyo*, No. 1, pp. 22-29. 1952.

TABLE 123

Net reproduction rates, intrinsic and standardized rates of natural increase, prefectures, various dates, 1925-1950

	NET REPRODUCTION RATES				INTRINSIC RATES OF NATURAL INCREASE			STANDARDIZED RATES OF NATURAL INCREASE		
Prefectures	*1925-1930*	*1930-1935*	*1947*	*1950*	*1930*	*1930-1935*	*1947*	*1920*	*1934-1936*	*1950*
All Japan	1.7	1.6	1.7	1.5	15.4	16.0	18.3	10.5	14.7	20.1
Hokkaido	2.0	1.9	1.9	1.9	22.3	21.0	21.4	14.1	18.9	26.6
Aomori	2.0	2.0	2.0	1.9	23.8	24.7	23.9	12.9	17.6	23.9
Iwate	2.0	1.9	1.9	1.8	22.3	22.2	21.7	13.0	17.7	21.7
Miyagi	2.1	2.0	1.9	1.8	24.1	24.2	21.1	14.6	22.2	24.0
Akita	2.0	2.0	1.9	1.8	25.4	24.8	21.9	11.3	17.6	21.4
Yamagata	1.9	1.8	1.6	1.6	22.7	21.3	16.6	12.8	19.8	21.1
Fukushima	2.0	1.9	1.9	1.8	23.1	23.4	21.0	11.8	21.0	25.1
Ibaraki	2.0	1.9	1.8	1.7	22.0	23.6	20.1	13.2	20.8	21.5
Tochigi	2.0	1.9	1.9	1.7	23.2	23.1	21.3	15.8	22.4	23.5
Gumma	1.7	1.7	1.8	1.6	18.5	18.7	19.7	18.4	22.3	22.5
Saitama	1.7	1.7	1.9	1.6	17.8	19.7	21.0	15.4	20.7	22.2
Chiba	1.7	1.7	1.8	1.5	17.2	19.0	20.6	10.6	17.4	18.8
Tokyo	1.4	1.3	1.6	1.3	6.9	8.0	13.6	0.5	10.9	16.3
Kanagawa	1.7	1.6	1.7	1.5	13.5	13.6	18.5	8.3	13.9	19.6
Niigata	1.8	1.8	1.8	1.7	20.7	19.8	19.6	13.5	20.3	22.1
Toyama	1.6	1.4	2.0	1.5	14.5	12.1	23.9	9.4	9.0	14.3
Ishikawa	1.4	1.3	1.9	1.5	9.3	7.1	22.7	9.9	6.9	15.5
Fukui	1.4	1.3	1.6	1.5	11.7	8.9	16.9	12.3	9.2	17.5
Yamanashi	1.8	1.8	1.8	1.6	20.6	21.0	19.8	17.7	24.8	24.0
Nagano	1.7	1.6	1.7	1.4	18.2	17.3	17.7	16.4	20.5	20.0
Gifu	1.7	1.6	1.7	1.5	17.8	16.2	18.6	16.4	17.0	18.9
Shizuoka	1.9	1.8	1.8	1.6	19.2	19.3	20.2	13.1	19.4	23.0
Aichi	1.6	1.5	1.7	1.4	12.1	12.0	17.4	11.8	13.9	18.1
Mie	1.7	1.5	1.6	1.4	16.2	15.2	16.7	3.0	16.0	18.0
Shiga	1.6	1.4	1.5	1.4	14.7	13.4	13.2	12.9	14.3	18.0
Kyoto	1.3	1.2	1.4	1.3	5.5	4.9	12.4	4.0	8.0	15.3
Osaka	1.2	1.2	1.4	1.3	3.4	2.8	11.5	3.0	4.7	15.4
Hyogo	1.4	1.3	1.5	1.4	9.6	8.5	14.1	3.7	8.9	15.9
Nara	1.6	1.4	1.4	1.3	13.7	11.2	12.8	11.9	10.5	15.5
Wakayama	1.6	1.5	1.5	1.4	15.3	12.6	16.6	16.2	12.3	16.9
Tottori	1.7	1.6	1.5	1.5	16.4	15.5	14.3	12.7	14.8	18.8
Shimane	1.5	1.5	1.8	1.7	13.4	16.6	21.2	9.4	14.5	20.6
Okayama	1.5	1.4	1.7	1.4	13.5	13.0	18.0	9.0	11.0	15.3
Hiroshima	1.6	1.5	1.7	1.4	14.5	14.2	17.6	10.2	11.9	16.5
Yamaguchi	1.6	1.5	1.7	1.6	12.8	13.5	17.5	8.9	11.0	18.9
Tokushima	1.8	1.7	1.8	1.6	19.2	18.9	21.4	13.8	17.0	20.4
Kagawa	1.7	1.6	1.9	1.4	18.0	20.0	21.9	16.8	15.2	17.0
Ehime	1.8	1.7	1.9	1.7	19.3	20.0	21.9	14.2	18.2	23.4
Kochi	1.6	1.5	1.7	1.5	14.1	15.1	18.9	9.5	11.4	17.3
Fukuoka	1.5	1.5	1.6	1.7	11.2	13.4	17.0	3.3	11.1	21.9
Saga	1.7	1.7	1.7	1.8	16.1	17.9	18.3	12.8	17.6	24.2
Nagasaki	1.8	1.8	1.7	1.9	17.4	18.0	18.7	12.4	17.7	25.6
Kumamoto	1.8	1.7	1.8	1.7	18.0	18.8	19.5	15.1	19.7	23.8
Oita	1.7	1.6	1.7	1.6	15.9	17.6	18.1	11.2	15.6	20.6
Miyazaki	1.9	2.0	2.0	1.8	22.6	22.8	24.1	15.1	20.0	25.8
Kagoshima	1.9	2.0	1.7	1.8	19.8	21.9	18.2	17.7	23.6	26.7
Okinawa	1.8	1.8	—	—	16.7	21.7	—	—	—	—

Source: Net reproduction rates: 1925-1930 and 1930-1935, computed from fertility data cited in Table 94, using the following life tables: Mizushima, Haruo, *et al.* "Fu ken betsu seimei hyo, dai-ikkai." *Chosen igakkai* (continued, bottom of p. 317.)

related to all women in the reproductive ages rather than merely to married women. It may be desirable, therefore, to present one more series of rates of natural increase, this time rates standardized not only as to the age structures but as to the marital status of women in 1925.[14]

Standardization of the age and marital status of women removed much of the decline in birth rates from 1920 to 1950, while standardization of age alone retained the major portion of the decline in death rates. Thus standardization rates of natural increase were very high in 1950. Hokkaido's rate was 26.6 per 1,000 population, while Kagoshima's was 26.7. Twenty-five of Japan's prefectures had standardized rates of natural increase of 20.0 or more.

The major conclusions derived from analysis of net reproduction rates and intrinsic rates of natural increase for the prefectures of Japan are similar to those derived from the crude rates. The birth rate was the major factor in the level of the rate of natural increase in the prewar years. Its role became even more predominant in the postwar years, when mortality was reduced to such low levels that prefectural variability became slight in absolute terms.

A century of modernization left all Japan's prefectures with appreciable rates of population increase. Major declines in fertility had carried birth rates far below the levels of the peasant cultures of the East. Declines in mortality had carried death rates to levels similar to those in Western nations where industrialization was far more advanced and levels of living considerably higher. The coincidence of declining fertility and declining mortality long preserved rates of natural increase that changed only slightly and rather inconsistently as among the various prefectures. Eventually, however, decline in mortality had to become quantitatively small, if for no other reason than that there are limits below which death rates cannot fall if men remain mortal. With fertility, on the other hand, the forces creating decline were becoming more compulsive and the range within which decline was possible remained rather large. In the years after 1950, decline in the rate of natural increase occurred with considerable rapidity.

Industrialization, Urbanization, and Natural Increase

The changes in rates of natural increase in single countries over time and the variations among countries at a given time have been associated with the movements away from agriculture and village life. It might be assumed, therefore, that the rates of natural increase among the prefectures of Japan would be associated inversely with industrialization. Average annual rates of natural increase among the prefectures indicate that such a relationship existed, but that it was slight in the years from 1920 to 1940:[15]

Prefectures by industrial type	*1920-1925*	*1925-1930*	*1930-1935*	*1935-1940*	*1950-1955*
Metropolitan	12.8	15.8	15.4	13.5	11.9
Other industrial	13.4	14.2	14.0	12.0	12.6
Intermediate	13.3	13.6	12.5	9.6	12.3
Agricultural	15.5	16.2	15.7	12.8	14.8[16]
Hokkaido	24.0	22.1	20.7	17.1	19.0

In groups of prefectures classified by industrial type, as in the individual prefectures, there is some evidence of convergence in rates of natural increase between 1920 and 1940. The regularities in change in fertility, mortality, and natural increase were disturbed in the early postwar years, however, and in 1947 differences in rates of natural increase were slight. By 1950 the prewar differences in levels of natural increase were quite apparent, owing primarily to the rapid decline of birth rates in great cities and industrial areas. In the years after 1950, natural increase has declined sharply in all types of prefectures, but the inverse relations between industrialization and natural increase have persisted. Annual rates per 1,000 total population are given here for 1947, 1950, 1953, and 1955:

Prefectures by industrial type	*1947*	*1950*	*1953*	*1955*
All Japan	19.7	17.2	14.4	11.6
Metropolitan	18.5	15.3	11.5	9.9
Other industrial	18.8	16.6	12.8	10.4
Intermediate	19.3	16.0	13.3	12.3
Agricultural	20.4	18.3	16.3	14.8
Hokkaido	23.3	24.2	20.9	19.0

The differences in rates of natural increase among the prefectures are blunted by the heterogeneity of occupations and residence. A more accurate picture can be secured by analysis of the *gun*. In general, rates of natural increase in *gun* were very high in the northeastern part of the country. In the *gun* of Hokkaido, for instance, the natural increase was 2.0 per cent in 1925, and 2.2 per cent in 1930 and 1935. In the *gun* of Aomori, the annual increase was 2.2 per cent in 1925, 2.3 per cent in 1930, and 2.6 per cent in 1935. These *gun* were located in a region whose sub-culture generated very high fertility. Education was at low levels, and earnings came from farming, forestry, or fishing. In the *gun* in the industrial region of the Kinki, on the other hand, the fertility of the sub-culture was low, the economy was diversified, and educational levels were higher. As early as the 1920's, average annual rates of natural increase were less than 1 per cent per year.

The picture of regional variations in the natural increase of the population living in the *gun* is not altered appreciably if the analysis is based on replacement ratios rather than on crude rates of natural increase.[17] There were substantial varia-

[14] Series of standardized rates have been computed in the Institute of Population Problems for prefectures and cities at various time periods. Specific references to the standardized rates discussed here are given in Table 123. References to other series are included in the Bibliography.

[15] Source: References, Table 122.

[16] The population of Amami Oshima was included in the population of the agricultural prefectures in 1950.

[17] A simple measure of *gun* fertility that involves some age standardization is the ratio of female births to women aged from

Table 123 (continued)

zasshi, 28(8):1136-1175. August 1938. *Ibid.* "Fu ken betsu seimei hyo, dai-nikai." *Chosen igakkai zasshi*, 29(9):1767-1803. September 1939. 1947: Mizushima, Haruo. "Geographic variations in true increase rate of population in Japan." *Nihon jinko gakkai kiyo*, No. 1, p. 24. 1950: Life tables: 1950: Majima, Yujiro. "1950-nen fu ken betsu seimei hyo." *Igaku kenkyu*, 26(1):1-23. 1956. Intrinsic rates of natural increase: Mizushima, Haruo. *Op.cit.*, pp. 23-24. Differences in life tables and adjustment techniques account for the differences between the total rates for all Japan and those given on p. 313. Standardized rates of natural increase: 1920: Tachi, Minoru, and Ueda, Masao. "Taisho ku'nen, Taisho juyo'nen, Showa go'nen, Showa ju'nen. Do fu ken betsu, shi gun betsu hyo junka shussei ritsu, shibo ritsu oyobi shizen zoka ritsu." *J.m.k.*, 1(1):21-28. 1940. 1934-1936 and 1950: Nihon. Kosei-sho, jinko mondai kenkyujo. *Saikin no jinko ni kansuru tokei shiryo.* 7th Edition. P. 56.

tions in ratios as among the *gun* within the prefectures in 1930, although these variations tended to cluster around the replacement level of the prefecture (MAP 17). In Hokkaido,

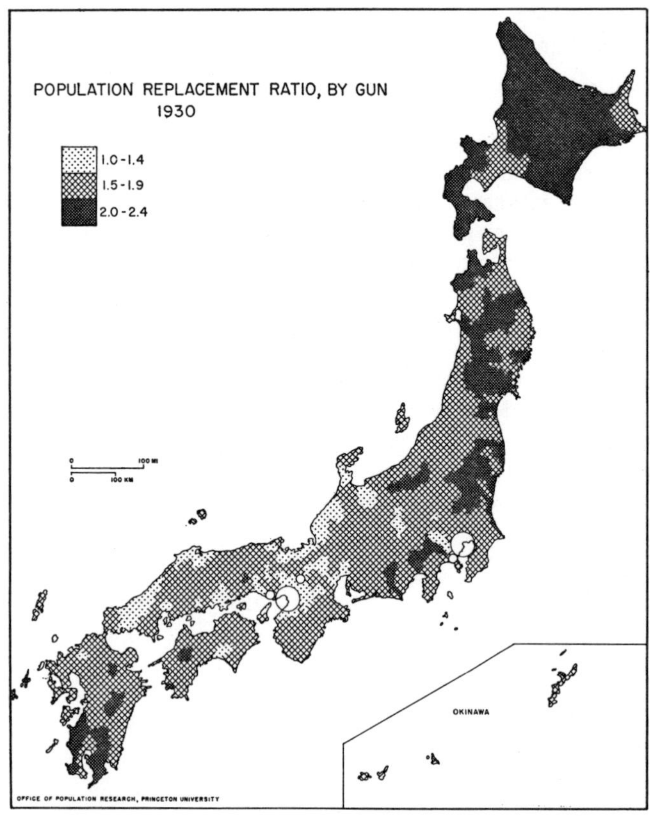

Map. 17. Population replacement ratios in the *gun*, 1930
Source: Populations: Nihon. Naikaku tokei-kyoku. *Showa go'nen kokusei chosa hokoku.* IV.4., Table 3. Life tables, prefectures: Mizushima, Haruo, *et al.* "Fu ken betsu seimei hyo, dai-ikkai." *Chosen igakkai zasshi*, 28(8):1136-1175. August 1938

eleven of the fourteen *gun* had replacement ratios of 2.0 or over; the lowest replacement ratio was 1.9, the highest 2.3. Very high replacement ratios occurred frequently throughout northeastern Honshu. In Tokyo prefectures, replacement ratios in the majority of the *gun* ranged from 1.6 to 1.9; in Kanagawa they ranged from 1.7 to 2.0. The people in the *gun* of the industrial prefectures had replacement ratios rather comparable to those of the agricultural areas from which they drew their migrants. Replacement ratios were lower among the *gun* of the southwest, whether in rural regions or industrial centers. In none of the *gun* of Osaka, Kyoto, and Hyogo prefectures, however, did replacement ratios go below unity. In the far southwest, where populations were predominantly isolated and agricultural, there were again *gun* with replacement ratios of 2.0 or over.

The widespread and consistent differences in rates of natural increase for areas within Japan are even more apparent if *machi, mura,* and *shi* are considered. These relations are shown for selected prefectures in FIGURE 19. In Japan as a

15 to 49. This measure as computed for the year 1930 was presented in Chapter XII. For each prefecture, the prefectural life tables for 1925-1930 can be utilized to determine the number of births required to replace women aged from 15 to 49 in the life-table population. The ratio of the actual fertility ratio to the life-table ratio is a rough measure of the relation between existing levels of fertility and mortality and those necessary for replacement. There are deficiencies in this procedure, since it assumes that the age structure of the actual population is that of the life-table population.

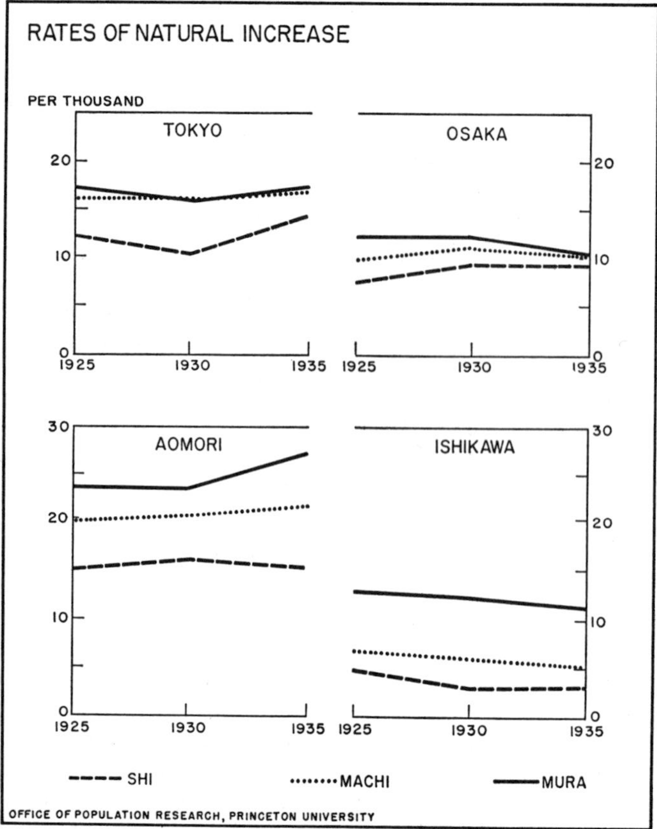

Figure 19. Rates of natural increase in *shi, machi,* and *mura,* selected prefectures, 1925-1935
Source: Nihon. Naikaku tokei-kyoku. *Shi, cho, son betsu jinko dotai tokei.* Taisho juyo'nen. Also: *Ibid. Showa go'nen. Ibid. Showa ju'nen.*

whole and in all prefectures, rates of natural increase were highest in the *mura* of remote agricultural areas and lowest in the *shi* of industrial areas. However, rates of natural increase were highly correlated for the *shi*, the *machi*, and the *mura* of the prefectures, and for each type of area the differences persisted over time.[18] The correlations between rates of natural increase by types of commune within prefectures were as follows:

Types of communes	*1930*	*1935*
Shi-machi	.74	.68
Machi-mura	.90	.89
Shi-mura	.71	.58

[18] Although the comparisons for *shi, machi*, and *mura* are based on crude vital rates, it should be noted that differences in age distribution tend to mask the differences in rates of natural increase between urban and rural areas. The populations of *mura* were weighted with children and the aged, while the populations of *shi* were weighted with young adults. *Machi* occupied an intermediate position. Standardization of birth and death rates would increase birth rates, decrease death rates, and thus increase the rate of natural increase in the *mura*. Comparable standardization would reduce the rate of natural increase in the *shi*. The maldistribution of births in the metropolitan and other industrial prefectures would reduce rates of natural increase in these prefectures below the true level. Comparable but less extreme malregistrations may occur elsewhere. It is this problem of the allocation of births to the place of occurrence or of habitual residence that constitutes the major hazard in the analysis of rates of natural increase for minor civil divisions, not the problem of differences in age distribution *per se*. Net reproduction rates and intrinsic rates would be subject to the same problems of validation as crude rates.

The correlations between rates of natural increase in 1930 and 1935 were as follows: total prefectures, .93; *shi*, .86; *machi*, .91; and *mura*, .92.

Crude rates of natural increase suggest that differences comparable to those among *mura, machi,* and *shi* exist within cities.[19] In Tokyo in 1935 natural increase was 14.5 per 1,000 total population. Rates were low in the central industrial areas, intermediate in the residential and commercial factory areas, high in the slum, household industry, and agricultural areas. Rates of from 1.8 to 2.0 per cent per year characterized the *ku* of Tokyo where people lived and worked in subsistence and household activities.

The Saving of Life and the Growth of Population

The demographic, social, and economic aspects of changes in fertility and mortality such as those that have occurred in Japan are not fully apparent in rates of increase, whether crude or refined. The changes in the numbers and the characteristics of people are the facts essential to the evaluation of the cultural significance of given vital rates. Even the absolute amount of the increase is inadequate as a measure of social relevance, for the sex and age characteristics of a net increment to a total population are influenced by fertility and mortality in their joint impact on a population already in existence.

MORTALITY DECLINES AND GROWTH

The influence of declines in age-specific mortality on the generation of the population increase of the Japanese may be estimated by assuming that the mortality of 1920-1925 remained in effect throughout the twenty years from 1920 to 1940.[20] The difference between the population as it would have existed in 1940 with actual fertility and mortality but without migration, and the population that would have existed with actual fertility but the 1920-1925 level of mortality, is a measure of the saving of life associated with mortality declines between 1920-1925 and 1940. The saving of life for ethnic Japanese in this fifteen-year period was as follows, numbers being in thousands:

Age	*Total*	*Male*	*Female*
All Japanese	3,380	1,550	1,830
0-4	901	466	435
5-9	763	385	378
10-14	492	239	252
15-19	165	66	98
20-44	644	209	435
45-64	270	128	142
65 and over	147	56	91

If these savings of life from reduced mortality are expressed in percentage terms, the results are as follows:

Age	*Total*	*Male*	*Female*
All Japanese	100.	100.	100.
0-4	26.6	30.0	23.8
5-9	22.6	24.9	20.6
10-14	14.5	15.5	13.8
15-19	4.9	4.3	5.4
20-44	19.0	13.5	23.7
45-64	8.0	8.2	7.8
65 and over	4.3	3.6	5.0

It is apparent that the declines in mortality between 1920 and 1940 were equivalent in some part to a lesser rate of decline in fertility. The evolution of population increments at older ages is evident in the hypothetical savings of life at ages 5 to 9 and 10 to 14. Moreover, reduced mortality in the years from 1920 to 1940 led to substantial savings of the lives of women in the childbearing ages.

The conclusion that declining mortality exercised its major influence in infancy and childhood is valid only if attention is focused on population growth in a brief period of a decade or so. Declining mortality which resulted in major savings of the lives of the very young had characterized the Japanese in the early twentieth century as well as in the years from 1920 to 1940. The lives that were saved at the younger ages led eventually to increases in population at later ages. And cohorts of women increased in size by the lower mortality to which they had been subjected in childhood yielded larger numbers of births at any given level of fertility. Thus the reduction of mortality in infancy and childhood not only led to greater increases in the population in the productive ages but created the demographic basis for an increased number of births. The relations between the infant death rates of one generation and the numbers of live births in the next generation were fairly direct and far from inconsequential in magnitude.

This somewhat theoretical discussion and hypothetical measurement of the influence of the age-pattern of mortality decline on population growth in general and on the numbers of births in particular becomes concrete if we examine the trends in the numbers of women in the reproductive ages in Japan from 1920 to 1955. Numbers of women are in thousands:

Age	*1920*	*1935*	*1950*	*1955*
15-49	13,139	16,126	21,274	23,227
15-19	2,642	3,265	4,243	4,246
20-34	5,921	7,797	10,093	11,333
35-49	4,576	5,064	6,938	7,649

Thus numbers of women aged from 15 to 49 increased 77 per cent from 1920 to 1955. Changes differed sharply from one

[19] If the forces altering vital rates were industrialization and urbanization, it would seem essential to analyze the net reproduction of the urban population. Many such attempts have been made, but interpretations are difficult. Births occurring to women in the cities can be estimated on the basis of babies enumerated in the cities. In mortality rates there were disturbances associated with urbanization, particularly the selectivity of the ill and the physically unfit in out-migration, but there is no feasible technique for adjustment. Measures of net reproduction would involve relations between urban fertility adjusted for malregistration and migration and urban mortality accepted as reported.

[20] The Japanese population of Japan as of October 1, 1920, was aged through the successive five-year periods to 1940 on the assumption that this population of ethnic Japanese, uninfluenced by migrations to or from the country, was subject to the fertility of the actual population and to the mortality of the life tables of 1920-1925, 1925-1930, and 1935-1936. The populations thus secured for each census date constituted the expected populations. The 1920 population of ethnic Japanese was then aged through the successive five-year periods to 1940 on the assumption that it was subject to the fertility of the actual population but remained subject to the mortality of the 1920-1925 life table. The increase in population associated with declines in mortality was secured by subtracting the population aged at 1920-1925 levels of mortality from the population that would have existed with changing mortality and without migration. The sources of data are as follows: 1920 Japanese population: Nihon. Naikaku tokei-kyoku. *Taisho ku'nen kokusei chosa hokoku.* IV.A.1. Table 26. Life tables: *Ibid. Showa juroku'nen ichi-gatsu. Dai-rokkai seimei hyo.*

period to another.[21] For instance, numbers of girls aged from 15 to 19 increased 623 thousand between 1920 and 1935, 978 thousand between 1935 and 1950. There was practically no increase between 1950 and 1955. The girls aged from 15 to 19 in 1935 were the survivors of the reduced birth cohorts of the years from 1915 to 1919, and they had been subjected to the high infant mortality of those years and the high childhood mortality of the early 1920's. The girls aged from 15 to 19 in 1950 were the survivors of the large birth cohorts of the years from 1930 to 1934, and here reduced infant and childhood mortality had done much to compensate for whatever reductions in fertility had occurred by 1930-1934. These girls aged from 15 to 19 in 1950 are moving upward into the ages of reproduction at a time when death rates in adult life have been reduced to a fraction of their former levels.

The cumulative effect of earlier high fertility and sharply reduced infant and childhood mortality with later sharp declines in adult mortality will be a major force of growth in the Japanese population for many years in the future. The infants born in the years from 1925 to 1940 will reach age 20 between 1945 and 1960; they will pass age 35 between 1965 and 1980. The high birth cohorts of 1947 to 1950 will become age 20 between 1967 and 1970; they will pass age 35 between 1982 and 1985. Eventually the aging of smaller birth cohorts will lessen the increase in the numbers of women in the reproductive years, but the survivors of the births of 1955 will not reach age 45 until the end of the century. The relations between annual births and deaths and the size of the next generation are stubborn facts that thwart easy manipulation of population size or composition.

Internal Redistribution and Growth

The influence of changes in mortality on the size of the population and the rates of increase in the age groups has been emphasized. The relation of fertility to growth is so obvious that it has not been elaborated. Not so obvious but of great long-run significance is the internal migration that alters the numbers of women subject to the fertility and mortality levels of the various regions of the country. The movement of peasants to urban and industrial areas between 1920 and 1935 resulted in a concentration of women in the reproductive ages in the metropolitan and industrial areas, with a substantial influence on the natural increase of the nation (Figure 20). The difficulties of the postwar years prior to 1950 practically obliterated this transformation that was so apparent in 1935; between 1935 and 1950 women aged from 20 to 34 had increased almost as much in the agricultural prefectures, with their higher rates of natural increase, as in the industrial prefectures, with their lower rates. By 1955 the prewar pattern was restored. Increasing numbers and proportions of women were again subjected to the lower rates of reproduction that characterize urban and industrial populations. This, too, is a factor in the reduction in rates of increase in the nation in recent years.

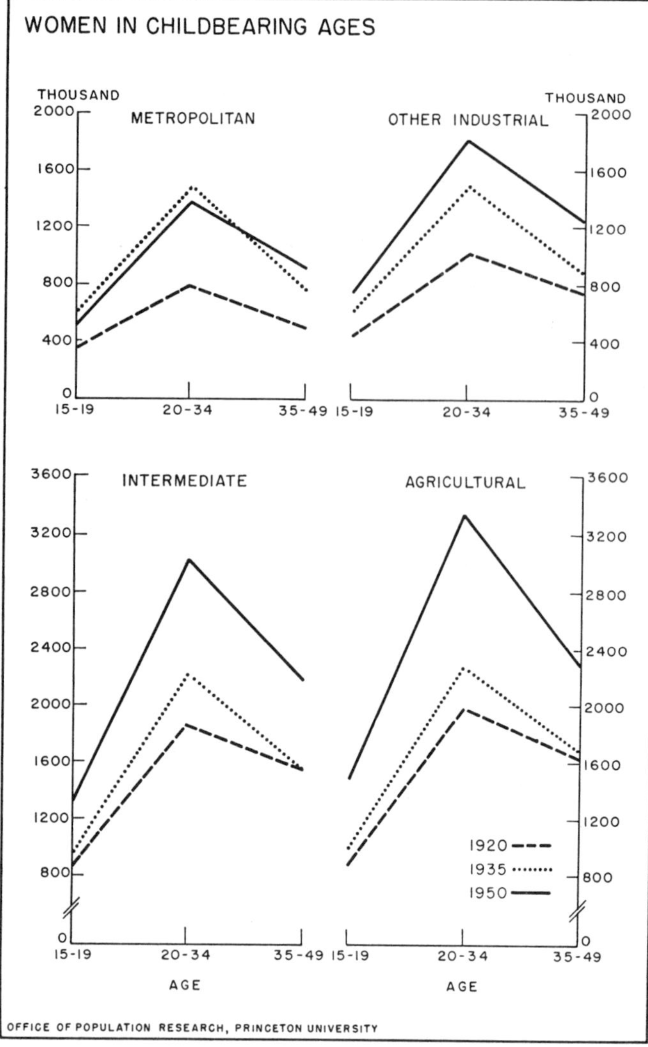

Figure 20. Number of women in the childbearing ages, prefectures by industrial type, 1920, 1935, and 1950

Source: Prefectural volumes, censuses of 1920, 1935, and 1950.

Natural Increase and the Structure of the Population

alternative paths, 1920-1950

The chronological relations of the declines in fertility and mortality gave modern Japan a population that approached the minimum that could have been expected in an industrializing population. If we add to this coincidental relationship in the components of natural increase the fact of the losses of a prolonged and major war, we have to conclude that Japan's present population is smaller than the one that would be anticipated in another population undergoing a comparable industrial evolution.

The illustrations selected to relate levels of fertility and mortality to the amount and the structure of population growth are simple ones, derived directly from the experience of Japan. In 1920-1925 and 1925-1930, the mortality of the life table is assumed to coincide with the fertility implicit in the child-woman ratios of the census at the beginning of the respective years; basically, fertility lags five years behind mortality. Similar lags are produced by assuming the coincidence of the fertility of 1930-1935 and the mortality of 1935-1936, the fertility of 1942-1947 and the mortality of 1947-1948, and the fertility of 1945-1950 and the mortality of 1950-1951.[22]

[21] These numbers are influenced somewhat by civilian migration, but this factor is minimal if comparisons are made between 1920 and 1950. Most emigrants left Japan after 1920 and, if they survived, were repatriated prior to 1950. Sources of data for the national and prefectural populations: 1920: Nihon. Naikaku tōkei kyoku. *Taisho ku'nen kokusei chosa hokoku.* IV.B. 1935: *Ibid. Showa ju'nen kokusei chosa hokoku.* II.2. 1950: Nihon. Sori-fu, tokei-kyoku. *Showa 25-nen kokusei chosa hokoku.* III.1. (10 per cen sample tabulations.)

[22] The age distributions were secured from the censuses of Japan and the colonial areas for the respective years and from the surveys of the Foreign Ministry. Life tables are the official ones ex-

The population selected for manipulation is that of Japanese in the world. The reason for using this group rather than Japanese in Japan or the total population of Japan is that these latter groups were both subject to major migrations in the period under study. Japanese in the world were subject only to increase by birth and decrease by death. Naturalization and assimilation were negligible factors except in continental United States, Hawaii, and Canada, and here Japanese survey definitions were based on ethnic rather than nationality criteria.

The enumerated or surveyed population of Japanese in the world in 1920, 1930, 1940, and 1950 and the numbers that would have existed with alternative combinations of mortality and fertility in the later years are as follows, numbers being in millions:

Assumed vital rates	*Enumerated 1920*	*Hypothetical* *1930*	*1940*	*1950*
As enumerated	57.1	65.8	75.2	84.2
Fertility, 1942-1947 Mortality, 1947-1948	57.1	64.3	73.5	83.6
Fertility, 1915-1920 Mortality, 1920-1925	57.1	65.5	75.6	87.7
Fertility, 1930-1935 Mortality, 1935-1936	57.1	66.2	77.2	90.3
Fertility, 1920-1925 Mortality, 1925-1930	57.1	66.7	78.2	92.2
Fertility, 1945-1950 Mortality, 1950-1951	57.1	67.4	80.4	95.8

The number of Japanese in the world increased from 57.1 million in 1920 to 84.2 million in 1950, an increase of 27.1 million in thirty years. There are two combinations of fertility and mortality in other periods that would have yielded roughly comparable populations in the year 1950. One, that of 83.6 million, would have been secured if fertility in the years from 1920 to 1950 had been at the level of the war-deficit years of 1942 to 1947 and mortality had been at the 1947-1948 level. The other, that of 87.7 million, would have been attained if fertility had remained at the level of 1915-1920 and mortality at the level of 1920-1925.

The differences in the sex and age structures of the populations that evolved from the various combinations of fertility and mortality were not only significant factors in determining the future cohorts of births in these populations, but also matters of some import for social and economic functioning (FIGURE 21). The assumptions involving higher fertility and mortality generate populations with disproportionate increases among children and youth, whereas the assumptions involving lower fertility and mortality yield populations whose greatest proportionate increases occur in the productive ages. The following percentage relations of hypothetical to actual in 1950 are limited to women in order to avoid any major influence of the war losses of the 1937-1945 period on the age structure of the population in 1950:

Assumptions	*Total*	SELECTED AGES *0-4*	*20-34*	*35-44*
Enumerated	100.	100.	100.	100.
Fertility, 1942-1947 Mortality, 1947-1948	97.9	90.6	93.6	108.5
Fertility, 1915-1920 Mortality, 1920-1925	101.4	111.6	96.3	96.0
Fertility, 1930-1935 Mortality, 1935-1936	105.0	111.0	99.8	102.0
Fertility, 1920-1925 Mortality, 1925-1930	106.8	118.5	101.4	100.3
Fertility, 1945-1950 Mortality, 1950-1951	111.0	109.4	106.4	115.7

cept that for 1950-1951, which was computed by Jinko mondai kenkyujo. Detailed citations to all sources are given in the Bibliography.

The proportion of youth increased if higher fertility was assumed, whereas the proportion of adults increased if lower fertility was assumed along with decreased mortality. Since lowered mortality involved primarily reductions in deaths among infants and young children, the combinations of fertility and mortality that involved higher fertility also involved greater losses of children by death. The influence of the compensatory changes in fertility and mortality in minimizing changes in the age structure of the population is apparent in comparisons of the age composition of the increase in population between 1920 and 1950, as given at the top of the next page.

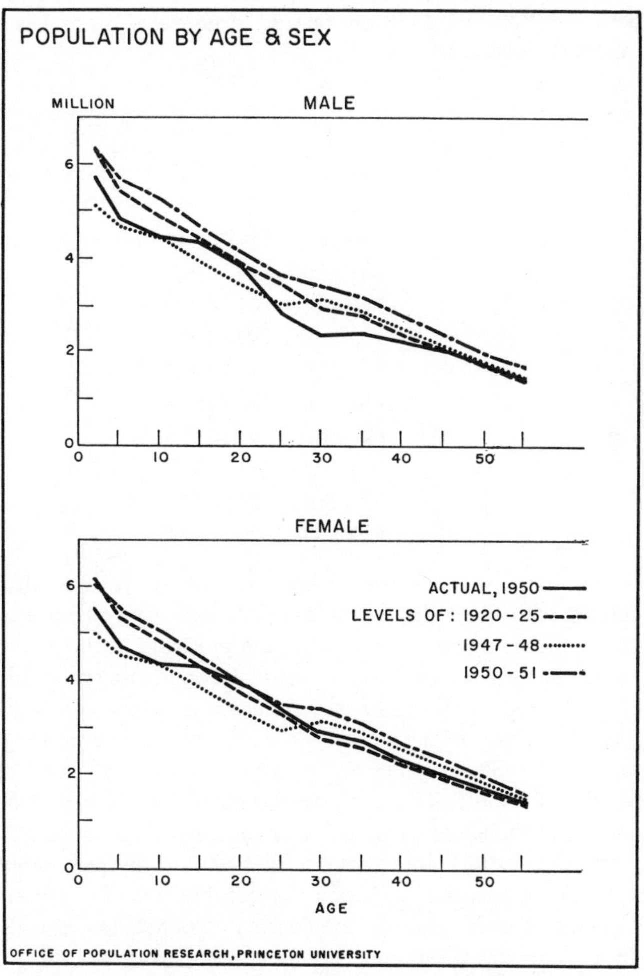

Figure 21. Japanese population in the world in 1950, by sex and age, on various assumptions as to fertility and mortality, 1920-1950
Source: References, Footnote 22.

The composition of the population by sex was influenced by the character of the declines in mortality and their relation to the levels of fertility that were assumed. The sex ratio of

Assumptions	Total	PERCENTAGE AGE COMPOSITION OF INCREASE Under 15	15-19	20-44	45-59	60 and over
Enumerated	100.	33.4	11.6	35.1	12.7	7.2
Fertility, 1942-1947 Mortality, 1947-1948	100.	28.3	8.8	40.0	15.2	7.7
Fertility, 1915-1920 Mortality, 1920-1925	100.	39.8	10.5	34.9	10.6	4.3
Fertility, 1930-1935 Mortality, 1935-1936	100.	37.9	10.1	35.2	11.3	5.5
Fertility, 1920-1925 Mortality, 1925-1930	100.	40.4	10.5	34.2	10.2	4.6
Fertility, 1945-1950 Mortality, 1950-1951	100.	34.0	9.4	36.9	12.8	6.9

live births changed little in the decades from 1920 to 1950, but the relation of the sex ratio at birth to the sex ratio of the total population was influenced both by the numbers of births added to the existing population each year and by the relative mortality of males and females in each age group. These relations among the levels of fertility and mortality, the death rates of males and females at successive ages, and the structure of population increase by sex are quite apparent in the sex ratios of the population increase that would have occurred between 1920 and 1950 on varying assumptions as to levels of fertility and mortality:

Assumptions	Total	MALES PER 1,000 FEMALES IN POPULATION INCREASE Under 15	15-19	20-44	45-59	60 and over
Enumerated	861	1,054	985	667	1,002	697
Fertility, 1942-1947 Mortality, 1947-1948	950	1,044	1,017	951	933	708
Fertility, 1915-1920 Mortality, 1920-1925	1,030	1,006	1,025	1,096	1,063	724
Fertility, 1930-1935 Mortality, 1935-1936	996	1,011	1,024	1,031	967	727
Fertility, 1920-1925 Mortality, 1925-1930	1,016	1,014	1,024	1,062	1,022	720
Fertility, 1945-1950 Mortality, 1950-1951	1,017	1,071	1,053	1,004	972	883

The similarities of the actual populations, decade after decade, with those that would have resulted from the coincidence of the relatively low fertility and mortality of the period of the 1947 census, or the relatively high fertility and mortality of the period of the 1920 census, illustrate in almost classic form the fallacy of attributing social, economic, or even long-run demographic significance to gross amounts or rates of fertility and mortality *per se*. At the same time, it should be noted that the existence of either of these hypothetical combinations of fertility and mortality in 1920 and its persistence to 1950 represents a highly improbable relation among economy, society, and the components of population growth. To assume the persistence of the fertility of 1942-1947, a period that included the late war and early postwar years, is contrary to knowledge of the behavior of birth rates. Persistence of the rates of the period after World War I is inconsistent with knowledge of the interrelations of developments. Continuation of high birth and death rates would imply limited industrialization and urbanization and little advance in public health. Thus the conditions that would maintain high birth and death rates would preclude the economic developments that permitted an increasing population to be fed, clothed, and provided with amenities.

Any brief lag of fertility behind mortality other than that of the periods after the two great wars would have generated populations substantially larger than those that existed in 1930, 1940, and 1950. It would be quite possible to compute a lesser increase of the Japanese. For instance, the fertility of 1955 could be assumed to exist alongside the mortality of 1920-1925. The combination of the reduced fertility that was largely the product of industrialization and urbanization, and their associated social-psychological changes, with the high mortality of an early period would yield computations without empirical relevance.

As mortality declined in Japan, there were increases in the excess of males under age 15, declines in the excess of males at age 20 to 44, and lesser deficits of males at age 60 and over. These, it should be noted, reflect the differences in the rates of decline in mortality for men as contrasted with women, rather than the amount of the decline *per se*. The differences in the sex ratio of the total increase in the population during the thirty-year period from 1920 to 1950 depend not only on the differential mortality by sex in the individual age groups but on the size of the entering cohorts in relation to the size and age structure of the existing population. Here also the level of fertility emerges as a significant factor influencing the sex ratio of the population subject to changing levels of fertility and mortality.

Thus even in the relatively brief period of three decades, the sex and age structures of the population were influenced significantly by the nature of the balance of births and deaths that yielded given rates of increase. Declining fertility and mortality produced changes in age structures that altered the numbers of births and deaths at given schedules of fertility and mortality. The nature of social and economic opportunities for populations with high proportions in the productive ages were conducive to changes that induced further declines in fertility.

STABLE POPULATIONS

The changing relations of fertility, mortality, and migration created the sex and age structures of the populations enumerated in the censuses. The maintenance of the age-specific levels of fertility and mortality at any given period would create a characteristic age structure that was stable.[23] In the years before the China War, fertility and mortality were changing regularly, and the patterns of the declines were compensatory. For instance, birth rates were declining, but smaller proportions of infants born died in the early years. Thus, the age structures of the enumerated populations were similar to those of the stable populations. The numbers of persons in each age group per 10,000 in the enumerated and the stable populations of 1925 and 1937 demonstrate the slow changes in the structures of the enumerated populations, the similarities of enumerated and stable populations, and the greater sensitivity in the age structures of the stable population:[24]

	ENUMERATED		STABLE	
Age	*1925*	*1937*	*1925*	*1937*
Total	10,000	10,000	10,000	10,000
Under 15	3,668	3,686	3,727	3,481
0-4	1,383	1,346	1,417	1,295
5-14	2,285	2,340	2,310	2,186
15-64	5,825	5,851	5,857	6,000
15-19	986	960	982	956
20-34	2,206	2,306	2,310	2,303
35-44	1,117	1,077	1,126	1,170
45-64	1,516	1,508	1,439	1,577
65 and over	507	465	413	516

The changes in annual rates of fertility and mortality, the losses of war, and repatriation produced major irregularities in the age structures of the enumerated populations in postwar Japan. The altered trends in fertility and mortality produced major differences in the age structures of the stable populations implicit in the vital rates of the prewar and the postwar years. Moreover, the rapidity of the declines in vital rates produced appreciable changes in the age structures of the populations implicit in the continuation of the vital rates of successive years. The numbers of persons in each age group per 10,000 total population in the enumerated and estimated populations of 1950 and 1965 and in the stable populations generated by the vital rates of these years are given here:[25]

Age	*Enumerated 1950*	*Estimated 1965*	*Stable 1950*	*Stable 1965*
Total	10,000	10,000	10,000	10,000
Under 15	3,538	2,373	3,256	1,569
0-4	1,347	684	1,184	502
5-14	2,191	1,689	2,072	1,067
15-64	5,968	6,995	6,121	6,581
15-19	1,030	1,131	920	570
20-34	2,297	2,727	2,305	1,855
35-44	1,146	1,387	1,204	1,357
45-64	1,495	1,750	1,692	2,799
65 and over	494	631	626	1,852

In the enumerated population of 1950, sharp irregularities had disturbed the smooth progression of the sex and age groups so characteristic of the population of prewar Japan. The stable population of 1950 showed none of these irregularities, for it was one that would have been produced by the unchanging age-specific fertility and mortality of 1950. Moreover, the stable population of 1950 showed a continuation of the types of structural changes that had characterized prewar populations. As compared with 1937, the proportions of youth were reduced, while the proportions of adults had increased. This fortuitous continuity in stable populations was due to the fact that fertility in 1950 did not deviate greatly from the level implicit in the continuation of the downward trend of the prewar years.

In the years after 1950, age-specific schedules of fertility and mortality were far below those implicit in the prewar trends. The influence of these declines was apparent in the enumerated populations of 1955. If the declines continue for another decade, the actual population of Japan will have greatly reduced proportions of youth, but the proportions of the aged will still be fairly small. However, the stable population produced by the hypothetical fertility and mortality of 1965 will differ greatly from the estimated population of 1965 and from any previous enumerated or stable population in Japan. In the stable population of 1937, persons 65 and over were 15 per cent as numerous as those below age 15. In the stable population produced by the estimated vital rates for 1965, persons 65 and over will be more numerous than those below age 15.[26]

The sex ratios of the age groups and the age structures of the male and female populations enumerated in the censuses were influenced both by the patterns of mortality and by the sex-selective migrations and deaths associated with imperial expansion. The changing pattern of mortality is a primary factor influencing the sex ratios of the age groups within the stable population. The numbers of males per 1,000 females

[23] See p. 313 for consideration of intrinsic vital rates.

[24] Takagi, Naofumi, and Takayasu, Hiroshi. "Senzen sengo ni okeru antei jinko dotai ritsu ni kansuru ichi shisan." *J.m.k.*, No. 63:68-75. March 1956. On the structure of populations, see also: Lorimer, Frank. "Dynamic aspects of the relation of population to economic development." *Bulletin of the International Statistical Institute*, 33(4):243-254. 1954. Coale, Ansley J. "The effects of changes in mortality and fertility on age composition." *Milbank Memorial Fund Quarterly*, 34(1):79-114. January 1956. Stolnitz, George J. "Mortality declines and age distribution." *Ibid.*, 34(2): 178-215. April 1956.

[25] The estimated population is that which would exist if fertility declined to a schedule of age-specific rates that yielded a total fertility of 1,600 births per 1,000 women and mortality declined to a schedule that yielded an expectation of life at birth of 66.47 years for men and 70.89 years for women. Takagi, Naobumi. "Suikei shorai jinko. Showa 25-nen—Showa 40-nen." *J.m.k.*, No. 62:80-90. December 1955.

[26] Studies of the aging and of the manifold problems raised by an aging population are included in the publications of the Gerontological Association of Japan. Jumeigaku kenkyu-kai. *Jumeigaku kenkyu-kai nempo*. 1956. 161 pp.

are given here for the stable populations of 1925, 1937, 1950, and 1965:

Age	*1925*	*1937*	*1950*	*1965*
Total	1,034	1,012	1,013	966
0-4	1,030	1,033	1,045	1,041
5-14	1,032	1,032	1,041	1,040
15-19	1,046	1,040	1,040	1,039
20-34	1,062	1,041	1,038	1,034
35-44	1,089	1,044	1,030	1,028
45-64	1,032	987	992	982
65 and over	777	735	788	774

The reduction in the excess mortality of females was a major aspect of the declining mortality of the Japanese.[27] This reduction occurred in a period of rapidly declining mortality at all ages. Since the sex ratio at birth included an excess of males, the reductions in infant deaths involved a greater saving of males. Thus there was an increase in the sex ratios of the younger age groups of the stable populations. The more rapid reductions in the mortality of women created lesser excesses and eventually deficits of men in the middle and upper ages. Thus the effect of reduced mortality was a reduction in the excess of males in the total population so characteristic of the enumerated and the stable populations of the Japanese. The sharp reduction in fertility accentuated the trend toward an excess of females by changes in the age structures that gave increasing weight to the middle and upper ages where females are most predominant at any level of mortality.

Growth Potential in the 1930's

The intrinsic birth and death rates generate a population with an unchanging age structure that grows at the intrinsic rate of natural increase. The age structure of the stable population is a constant characteristic. It is growth itself that is the fundamental characteristic in so far as the social and economic implications of the realization of the stable population are concerned. The age structures and the vital rates of prewar Japan were similar to those of the stable populations that would have been generated by the age-specific fertility and mortality of that period. Hence it is possible to select a date and estimate the size of the stable population that would have been produced by a continuation of the vital rates of that period. The census population selected is that of 1935, while the vital rates are those of 1934-1936.[28]

In 1935 the population of Japan was 69 million. Growth at the intrinsic rate of natural increase of 1934-1936, 1.34 per cent per year, would have yielded a population of 90 million in 1955 and 110 million in 1970 (Figure 22). By the latter year there would have been 38.4 million youth under age 15, 66.0 million adults aged from 15 to 64, and 5.2 million persons aged 65 and over. The political and economic implications of a population growth such as this may be illustrated by examining the hypothetical trends in the number of men. The numbers for 1940, 1955, and 1970 are in thousands:

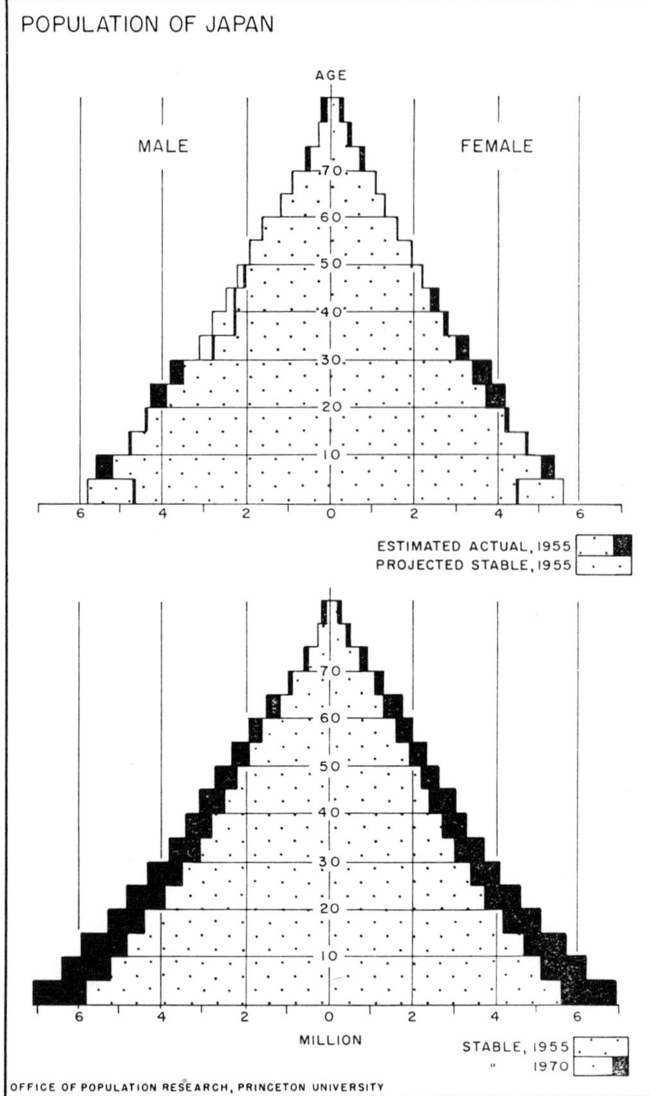

Figure 22. The sex and age composition of the population of Japan in 1955 and 1970, assuming growth at the rates of the stable population of 1934-1936

Age	NUMBER OF MALES *1940*	*1955*	*1970*
Total	36,820	45,014	55,019
0-4	4,770	5,830	7,120
5-14	8,270	10,100	12,350
15-19	3,610	4,410	5,390
20-34	8,660	10,590	12,950
35-44	4,390	5,380	6,570
45-64	5,660	6,920	8,460
65 and over	1,460	1,784	2,179

The stable population as of 1934-1936 could be projected further and further into the future. Its rate of increase and its age structure would remain the same, but its annual increments would become larger and larger. For a period of some unknown length, increases in levels of living might have continued, but it would have been a treadmill situation. By

[27] See Chapter XIV, "Mortality," pp. 305-306.

[28] In 1935, the percentage of males was 50.22 in the stable population, 50.15 in the enumerated population. Intrinsic vital rates were 31.5 for births, 18.1 for deaths, and 13.4 for natural increase. Crude vital rates for 1943-1936 were 30.7 for births, 17.4 for deaths, and 13.3 for natural increase. In the stable population, 36.89 per cent of the total were under age 15, while 4.65 per cent were aged 65 or over. In the enumerated population, 35.02 per cent were under age 15, while 4.75 per cent were aged 65 or over. The mean length of female generation was 29.94.

assumption, neither fertility nor mortality was changing, and so increase was perpetual.

The projection of the stable population as of 1934-1936 into the future illustrates the potentialities for growth inherent in the vital situation of Japan in the mid-1930's. It indicates in numerical form the size of the population increase that results as time passes without retardation in rates of growth. We have been considering a nation that began its economic and social modernization with some 30 to 35 million people. If we had been concerned with a China that was beginning the transition with more than half a billion people, the numbers secured through projection would have become large indeed.

A EUROPEAN-TYPE DEVELOPMENT

The broad patterns of decline in fertility and mortality in Japan were similar to those in European countries. In the latter, industrialization began at varying dates, assumed different forms, and moved at unequal speeds within and between countries. In the period from the end of the First World War to 1935, fertility and mortality were declining in all countries. In general, the rates of decline were related to the heights of the levels that had been achieved. Thus it was possible to utilize the relationships that existed for the various countries at a given time to develop techniques for projecting levels of fertility and mortality in the individual countries into the future on assumption of comparability of change throughout the Continent. Such projections were made by the Office of Population Research of Princeton University.[29] We are not concerned here with the results of the projections or their validity as predictions, but rather with the fact that this is a general model of population change in European countries in the interwar decades. If the same model is used to project the population of Japan, it provides a numerical illustration of the potential of the Japanese population in the middle 1930's on the assumption that its development was similar to the generalized type occurring in Europe during the period.

The model of interwar Europe yielded coincident and rapid declines in fertility and mortality for Japan. The following populations would have been produced in 1955 and 1970, numbers being in thousands:[30]

Age	*1940*	*1955*	*1970*
All ages	72,700	84,707	94,585
0-4	9,110	8,760	7,940
5-14	17,040	16,890	16,500
15-19	7,300	8,380	8,270
20-34	16,950	22,060	23,380
35-44	8,140	10,750	14,310
45-64	10,790	13,530	18,510
65 and over	3,370	4,337	5,675

In this situation growth would have been slowed by 1970, but it would not have ceased. The quinquennial increase would have been 3.9 million between 1950 and 1955, and 2.8 million between 1965 and 1970. Men in productive ages who had numbered 21.8 million in 1940 would have numbered 32.6 million in 1970, an increase of 50 per cent within a generation.

Any close agreement between the population projected for 1955 on a European model and the actual one would be fortuitous. The development of the population of Japan from 1935 to 1955 was not a smooth unfolding of the potentialities of the population of 1935. The nation underwent war, repatriation, and major deviations in the regularities of a changing vital balance. Projection on a European model indicated a population of 80.3 million for the present area of Japan in 1955. The population enumerated in 1955 was 89.3 million. Comparison of the age groups in the two populations shows marked excesses of youth in the actual population (FIGURE 23). Until 1949 fertility declined far less rapidly than would

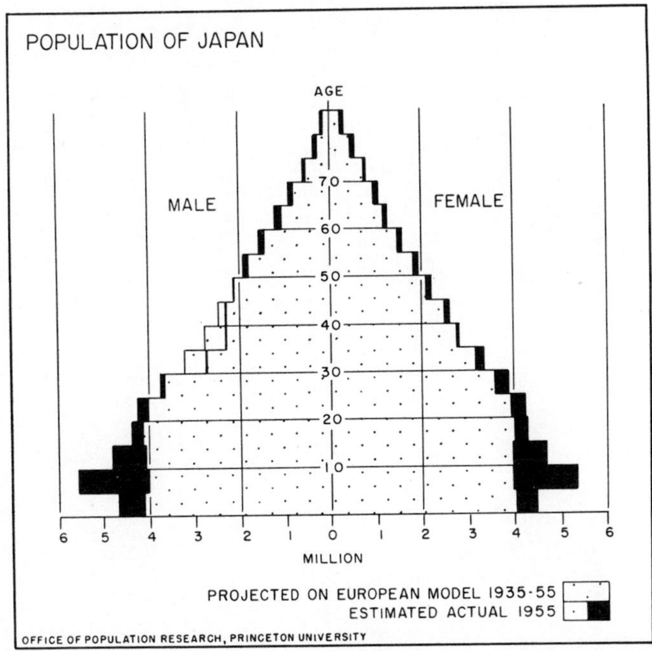

Figure 23. The population of Japan, estimated actual, 1955; and projected on a European model, 1935-1955

have been expected on the basis of the European model. On the other hand, declines in fertility and in mortality from 1947 to 1955 were far more rapid than those implicit in the European model or in the experience of Japan's own past.

The problem of estimating future populations in the light of the altered trends in fertility and mortality of the postwar years will be considered in the final chapter on the prospects for Japan's population. Prior to this, it is necessary to consider the demographic aspects of war and the relations between vital rates and policies designed to influence those rates.

[29] Notestein, Frank W., *et al. The future population of Europe and the Soviet Union.* See especially Chapter 1, "The approach to the problem," and Appendix 1, "Methodological notes."

[30] The base population is that of Japan proper in 1935, i.e., the 47 prefectures, including Okinawa.

PART VII

DEMOGRAPHY IN PEACE AND WAR

CHAPTER XVI

The Demography of War

THE study of the direct demography of war is a relatively simple undertaking, even though indirect techniques and estimates have to substitute for much of the more exact analysis that would be possible if the statistical services of peace survived through war. However, war is seldom a single event or series of events with a specific beginning and a specific end. Whether military action ends in victory or defeat, repercussions are felt throughout the nation and continue to affect its demography. When a major war terminates an expansionist policy that has been pursued for three-quarters of a century, as it did in Japan, analysis of the demographic correlates and consequences of militarism becomes difficult, yet unavoidable in a study such as this.

The early developments in Japanese militarism and expansionism were shaped by the values and the social structure of the old society.[1] The common soldier was not held in particular esteem; persons of high status or preferred familial position were excused from conscript service. Once created, the functions of the defensive army gradually merged into those of an offensive army of strategic expansionism. Demographic and political aims became integrated, first internally, then externally. The subjugation and settlement of Hokkaido were motivated by both demographic and military considerations. Demographically they were an outlet for population surpluses from other areas. Militarily they represented defensive settlement rather than offensive expansion. Since the Ryukyu Islands were an area associated historically with Japan, their annexation was not regarded as the conquest of an alien land. The annexation of Taiwan was justified by the Japanese primarily on the grounds of political and economic necessity. It was argued that no nation could afford to remain in a position where access to the basic requirements of life for its people could be barred by the trade policies of another country. The Japanese saw in Taiwan possibilities for labor migrations. They believed that Taiwan itself had labor deficits and would continue to have them because of the slow growth of the native population. They knew that Japan had an overabundance of people in agriculture. Thus the planned emigration of Japanese would provide a needed labor supply in Taiwan and at the same time relieve population pressure in the overcrowded rural areas of the home country.

Japan achieved recognition as a military power through the defeat of Russia in 1904-1905. The arguments for expansion remained defensive, but increasing emphasis was placed on offensive action. Demographic factors were cited to bolster claims to resources held by other peoples. And so the growth of the population that was deplored on economic grounds became a rationalization for conquests that forged a great imperial structure.

The series of national censuses that began in 1920 permit a quantitative analysis of the role of war in the development of the population of Japan. The age pyramid of the population in 1920 is a revealing one (FIGURE 24a). Here would be

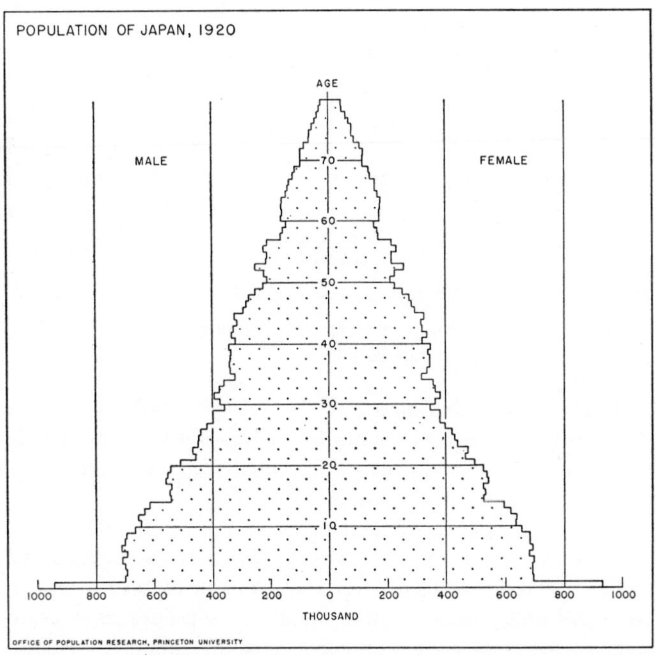

Figure 24a. The population of Japan by single years of age, 1920

Source: Nihon. Naikaku tokei-kyoku. *Taisho ku'nen kokusei chosa hokoku.* IV.1 Table 15. *Ibid. Showa ju'nen kokusei chosa hokoku. Zenkoku hen.* II.1. Table 13.

recorded whatever scars had been left by the wars of the late nineteenth and early twentieth centuries. People aged 25 in 1920 were the survivors of the babies born in the year that Taiwan was added to the Empire. Young people aged 15 and 16 were the survivors of the births of the years of the Russo-Japanese War. Children aged from 3 to 5 were the survivors of babies born during Japan's years of nominal participation in World War I. It is possible similarly to determine the location of the deficits of men that would have been created by substantial military mortality had it existed in any of the wars of the past. Actually there were no major irregularities in the age and sex structure of the population of Japan in the year 1920 that could be associated directly with the mobilization of armies and military actions. There was a slight gash in the birth cohort of 1906—but this was a consequence of the disastrous zodiacal combination of the year rather than of the Russo-Japanese War. There was no major deficit of births during World War I similar to those that occurred in the belligerent populations of Europe. There were no perceptible gashes to indicate the military deaths of 1895, 1904-1905, or 1915-1918. The age pyramid of the population in 1935 shows no deficits of men or shortages of children that might have been produced by the movement into Manchuria in 1931

[1] Ogawa, Gotaro. *Conscription system in Japan.*

(FIGURE 24b). The conclusion is obvious. A substantial empire had been achieved without appreciable human costs.

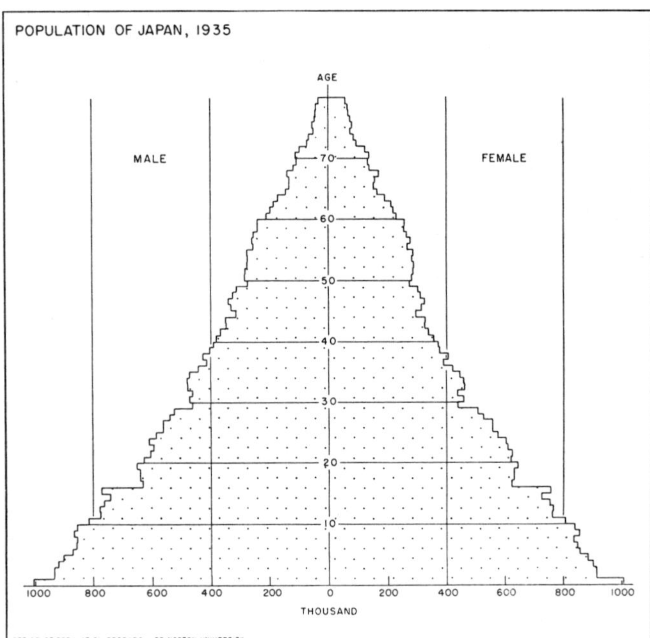

Figure 24b. The population of Japan by single years of age, 1935
Source: References, Figure 24a.

Until the move into China in 1937, the disturbed registration of births that occurred in inauspicious years were more significant than wars as creators of irregularities in the age structure of the Japanese population.

In 1920 Japan was still involved in the aftermath of war and colonial expansion. The Micronesian Islands, surrendered to her by Germany soon after the outbreak of World War I, were still under military rule. Japanese armed forces were in some of the former German concessions in China. An expeditionary force was in Siberia, and Korea was so disturbed after the uprising of 1918 that no census of others than Japanese could be taken there. In 1930 the Manchurian intervention occurred. Presumably comprehensive preparations for this move had been under way for some time. Despite the difficulties that were associated with past and contemplated expansionist activities, the 1920's were the nearest approximation to a decade of peace in the history of Japan from the late nineteenth century to the middle of the twentieth.

From 1931 to 1937 Japanese armed forces, civilian administrators, and technicians led in the expulsion of the forces of the Republic of China from the Three Northeastern Provinces and Jehol, and the establishment of the Empire of Manchoukuo. The industrial wedge of the South Manchuria Railway Zone was merged into this new nation. Plans were made for the industrialization of the economy in close relation with that of Japan. The land was to be colonized by millions of Japanese families who moved in from Japan itself. There is little information on the numbers of the armed forces stationed in Manchoukuo, but there are no evidences of substantial military mortality. Perhaps the fact that the Japanese published a national life table for the census year of 1935-1936 rather than for the quinquennial period of 1930-1935 indicates excess deaths associated with their activities in Manchoukuo.

In 1937 war began in China. By 1940 the involvement was substantial. Individual victories were auguries of surrenders that never occurred. The Japanese recognized the difficult population and manpower problems that they faced. They needed the data of a national census. They realized, though, that information on the numbers, distribution, and characteristics of their armed forces and their productive manpower had to be concealed. As we have noted earlier, the members of the armed forces were allocated to the place of residence of their nearest responsible kinsmen and their last civilian occupations were given. These procedures were followed for the benefit of outsiders. For official use, there were special tabulations of the "population behind the front," i.e., persons neither in nor attached to the armed forces and hence available for military production and civilian activities. Censuses of population were taken in all the colonies and in Manchoukuo. Special efforts were made to secure completeness and accuracy in a broadened survey of the Japanese outside the Empire and Manchoukuo, particularly in China. Thus during the year before Pearl Harbor an inventory of the human resources of Japan, the colonies, and Manchoukuo was combined with an inventory of other Japanese in the Co-Prosperity Sphere.

The normal statistical activities of the government continued through 1943, but interpretation of the data collected becomes increasingly difficult. Armed forces were increased sharply in numbers, while disabled and ill men were returned from the armed forces to the civilian population. Deaths occurring outside Japan were excluded from the vital statistics that pertained to persons present within Japan. Deaths of men in the armed forces were excluded if they occurred in Japan; deaths of demobilized men were excluded if the statement of cause of death indicated that it was associated with war.[2] Thus there is no knowledge of total deaths to relate to a total population, no knowledge of a civilian population to which recorded deaths that were mainly civilian can be related. Ignorance as to the precise numbers and the regional movements of the armed forces hinders any except the most general of interpretations of levels of fertility.

By 1943 it was evident that skilled labor and technical personnel were in short supply and that planning for the dispersion of plants, workers, and dependent groups in the civilian population could not be based on the outmoded data of the census of 1940. Thus a national survey was conducted in 1944 in Japan, Taiwan, Korea, and Kwantung.[3] Enumeration was limited to civilians and military personnel living outside camps or installations, and emphasis was placed on industrial skills. The date of the census, February 22, 1944, enables us to form a picture of the distribution and characteristics of the population close to the point of maximum geographic and economic concentration for war.

Long-range bomber attacks on Japan itself were initiated from the Marianas in November of 1944. Major attacks on the cities began in March of 1945. The destruction of the buildings that housed *koseki* records and the dispersion of the population eliminated complete or meaningful vital reporting in the industrial areas. Collection of national vital statistics ceased after 1943.

The war ended with surrender in August of 1945. The government was intact, and there was little break in civilian discipline. Then there occurred an extraordinary phenomenon—the co-operation of the Japanese and the personnel of

[2] Information from coding clerks in the Division of Health and Welfare Statistics, Ministry of Welfare, who had worked with the reports for this period.

[3] Karafuto had been added to Japan as a prefecture in 1942 and thus was included in the survey of Japan proper.

the powers who had conquered them in the improvement of the statistical activities of the government of Japan. An emergency count of the population was made as of November 1, 1945. A fairly comprehensive national survey was made on April 26, 1946. By the latter half of 1946, national vital statistics reporting was restored. In 1947 annual vital statistics were compiled that were more comprehensive in some respects than those published before the war. On October 1, 1947, there was a complete national census. The regular decennial enumeration was conducted as of October 1, 1950, and a simplified census was taken as of October 1, 1955.

The demography of war and reconstruction was abundantly documented in the censuses, but analysis was limited. The reasons are as understandable as they are regrettable. The staff of General Headquarters, Supreme Commander for the Allied Powers, was concerned with operating problems and the achievement of thte goals of the Occupation. Research was not one of those goals. So rapid were the redistribution and reconstruction of the economy that the data of one census became antiquated before the tabulations were completed. And thus data of major value for research on the demography of war and the demographic behavior of people in crises were laid aside while another count of the population was made. A Japanese analysis of the course of the war and the developments of the postwar years awaited the restoration of national sovereignty. By the time this occurred in 1952, the population problems were so acute and so intimately related to the economic and political problems of government that understaffed organizations could not devote major effort to what had become historical research. Moreover, the rapid declines in mortality and fertility in recent years offered exciting new fields for research.

The survey of the demography of militarism, war, and restoration presented here is broad in scope but limited in depth. The direct demography of war is considered first—the numbers and the fate of the armed forces. Consideration of the "population behind the front" follows logically, including not only numbers and characteristics but internal redistribution. There is then a summary description of exodus, influx, and repatriation, of the return of the peoples who had moved out from Japan throughout the course of empire. The process of repatriation was linked with the restoration of the economy and the distribution pattern, which is the next topic considered. Finally there is a summary consideration of the demographic balance for the decade from 1940 to 1950.

The Armed Forces

Universal conscription was introduced in Japan by the law of 1873.[4] It remained in force until 1945, with successive modifications that tended toward greater inclusiveness of participation and more rigor in specifications. Originally all men aged from 17 to 40 registered for service, but those of social, economic, or political stature were exempted, as were those essential to the line of succession in the family. The commoners not exempted by these regulations were selected by lot for active service in the numbers needed. A national organization of manpower into regular army, first and second reserves, and national militia existed without major disturbances of social institutions or the civilian labor force. In 1873 the standing army consisted of only 32 thousand men, although there were an additional 21 thousand men in each of the reserves.

[4] Ogawa. *Op.cit.*

Arguments about the nature of military service and the adequacy of the provisions for internal defense and international responsibilities continued throughout the formative period of the armed forces. In the *bakufu* era, the state had been a military dictatorship with an elite warrior class. This feudal attitude persisted in the modern era and many argued that the common people were poor physical and intellectual material on which to base the security of the state and the fate of the nation. As it developed, the conscript service gave the soldier low prestige. Men who could be spared by government, community, society, and family became members of the armed forces, while responsible men were exempted. Gradually, however, the internal position of the government was consolidated and the *bushi* class no longer constituted a threat to the national government. Military thinking was oriented toward external expansion rather than internal security, and the realities of military power became known to the leaders in Japan. By 1889 privileges given to the upper social classes and exemptions designed to protect the family system had been eliminated. Gradually the size of the regular army was increased and periods of service in active units and in reserves were lengthened. A brief description of the system as it existed at the time of the China War will indicate something of the probable nature and the changing magnitude of the influence of conscription on the structure and growth of the population.

The conscription law required that all men aged from 17 to 40 serve in the armed forces. The army itself consisted of the standing army, the conscript reserves, and the national army. Medical examinations were given at age 20. Active service was for two years; on its completion the men went into the first reserve for 17 years and four months, and then were enrolled in the national army until they reached age 40. Men in only fair physical condition and those in good physical condition who were not needed for the active army went into the first conscript reserve. Here they were subject to a six months' training period with troops and to additional periods of 50 days as needed. At the end of a period of 17 years and four months, they too were enrolled in the national army until they reached age 40. Men of still poorer physical condition were placed in the second conscript reserve, where the requirements were similar to those in the first conscript reserve. Men of definitely inferior physical condition were in the national army from age 20 to age 40. Boys aged from 17 to 20 were in the national army and subject to service in case of general mobilization.

The military records that would permit assessments of the demographic characteristics of the armed forces and the demographic interrelations of military and civilian life are singularly deficient. The census records furnish a partial substitute, for they give the numbers and the characteristics of those in active service at the successive census dates. There are problems here, however, for the numbers and the location of the armed forces were facts of strategic significance, and thus were subject to concealment.

The census provisions for the years from 1920 to 1935 gave clues as to the location of installations. Accordingly, in 1940 members of the armed forces were enumerated as if they were members of the civilian population. The specific census instructions concerned military personnel in active service, mobilized personnel, members of crews of ships of the army and navy, "and those who being outside of the territorial limits of the Empire, have gone to the front as civilian employees in the military service, as members of the information services, as Shinto ritualists, Shinto priests, and religionists."[5] These individuals were to be entered on the household forms according to their family or house relationships as follows: (1) A person who is married, including the informally married, with the family in whose house his wife is residing. (2) A single person, with the family in whose house his father is residing, or, if he has no father, his mother. (3) A person without wife, father, or mother, with the family in whose house his eldest son is residing. (4) A person without wife, parents, children, with the family in whose house his grandfather is residing, or, if he has no grandfather, his grandmother. (5) A person who has no wife, parents, children, or grandparents, with the family in whose house his eldest brother or sister is residing. (6) A person who has no wife, parents, children, grandparents, brothers, or sisters, with the family in whose house the individual who informed him of his military status is living.

The data from the censuses combined with information supplied by the Demobilization Board permit annual estimates of the size of the armed forces, the location of troops within or outside Japan, and the numbers of military deaths.[6] This series extends over the period from 1935 to 1945 only. Prior to this time, the source materials for military demography apparently consist only of the census data. The returns from the census enumerations show that there were 234 thousand members of the armed forces in Japan in 1920. In 1930 there were 223 thousand members in Japan and 35 thousand members outside. When it is remembered that the census of October 1, 1930, was taken somewhat less than a year prior to the invasion of Manchuria, the figure for armed forces outside Japan seems far too low. Examination of the detailed data and the explanatory notes in the 1930 census confirms this suspicion. Troops were enumerated by the military command. The regulations of the army for the census of 1930 provided that troops, offices, schools, and institutes under the control of the army were to be investigated by the army (Article 2). However, Army Command No. 3527 of August 30, 1930, provided that those who lived in official residences, meadow quarters, and battery quarters which were not in the army census area should not be enumerated in the army census. The areas thus excluded were to be covered by the *shi*, *machi*, or *mura* in which they were located. In addition, "On the precise day of the census, those who are out of the barracks shall be enumerated by the *shi, machi*, or *mura* where they are, though they usually live in barracks." The probability of a movement of troops on a census date is obvious.

The industrial and occupational data of the census offer an approach to the question of the size and distribution of the armed forces. In the detailed industrial classifications we find the following information:[7]

Industrial classifications	*Industry*	*Number of gainfully occupied (in '000)*
249	Army	179
250	Navy	101

The total of 280 thousand persons gainfully occupied in the army and the navy is admittedly incomplete, for there were specific instructions that classifications 249 and 250 were to be used only for those men who could not be classified elsewhere. The occupational classifications and the numbers enumerated were as follows:[8]

Occupational classifications	*Occupation*	*Number of gainfully occupied (in '000)*
324	Army officers	15
325	Non-commissioned officers and soldiers	143
326	Navy officers	8
327	Non-commissioned officers and sailors	78

The men in military occupations, 243 thousand, were 37 thousand fewer than those in the military industries.

Obviously incomplete and generally inconsistent numbers characterize the materials on military and naval personnel in the local areas that are known to have been military centers.

The census of Japan included only troops stationed within Japan. The Army Department's regulations for the army census of 1930 provided in Article 13 that the regulations should not be applied for troops stationed in Korea, Taiwan, Karafuto, or territories that were not part of the Japanese Empire.[9] Search of the occupational and industrial data for the various colonies and related areas in 1930 yields the following results as to members of the Japanese armed forces:

Area	*Occupational classifications 324-327*	*Industrial classifications 249-250*
Taiwan[10]	6,987	7,635
Korea[11]	20,623	—
Kwantung[12]	1,652	10,866
South Manchuria Railway Zone[13]	8,652	8,743
Karafuto[14]	9	29

Even the detailed rules for excluding all who could be classified elsewhere are hardly adequate as an explanation of these figures. There was an additional mandate in the army's regulations for the 1930 census. Under date of June 10, 1930, it was ordered that army-dispatched troops were to be excluded from the number of Japanese reported by the Foreign Affairs Department. For instance, troops who were moved outside the legal boundary of the South Manchuria Railway Zone disappeared from official Japanese statistics.

This perusal of the census data on military manpower as of 1930 shows that the data do not represent a complete report on the number of Japanese in the armed forces. The exclusions within and outside Japan being what they were, it follows that information on the demographic and economic composition of the admitted military forces cannot be taken as a basis for

[5] Instructions on the back of the census schedule. The census form and the instructions were published in: Nihon. Naikaku. *Genko horei shuran*. Section 6, Subsection 4, pp. 242/1-242/2. December 15, 1940.

[6] Nihon. Sori-fu, tokei-kyoku. *Taisho 9-nen—Showa 25-nen, waga kuni nenji betsu jinko no suikei*.

[7] Nihon. Naikaku tokei-kyoku. *Showa go'nen kokusei chosa saishu hokokusho*. P. 352.

[8] *Ibid*. P. 184.

[9] Kwantung and the South Manchuria Railway Zone were leased areas, while Nanyo-gunto was a mandate from the League of Nations.

[10] Taiwan. Sotoku kambo, rinji kokusei chosa-bu. *Kokusei chosa kekka hyo, zento hen, Showa go'nen*. Pp. 126 and 244.

[11] Chosen. Sotoku-fu. *Chosen kokusei chosa hokoku, Showa go'nen. Zensen hen, kekka hyo*. P. 176.

[12] Kwantung. Kanto chokan kambo, chosa-ka. *Kanto-cho kokusei chosa kekka hyo, dai-sankan, sono ichi, shokugyo, sangyo oyobi shitsugyo, Showa go'nen*. Pp. 26 and 624.

[13] *Ibid*. Pp. 135 and 744.

[14] Karafuto-cho. *Kokusei chosa kekka hyo, Showa go'nen*. Pp. 178 and 244.

analysis of the demography of the armed forces. Moreover, there was an intermingling of civilian and military personnel in the civilian population reported as such. And, finally, there were armed forces that were shielded from any reporting by Japanese authorities, whether the Statistics Bureau or the Foreign Ministry.[15] The general conclusion is obvious. Analysis of the demography of conscription or of the military system is not possible for 1930 or any earlier year.

In 1935 there were reported to be 287 thousand men in the armed forces within Japan and 220 thousand outside the country. Presumably some mobilization had occurred in connection with military hazards and actual military activities in Manchuria. Presumably some Japanese had been killed in combat or in guerrilla actions. The usual official life table for the quinquennial period was not computed for the years from 1930 to 1935, but instead a life table was computed for a single year centered on the census date of October 1, 1935.

The build-up of the military forces was continuous after 1935, but the increments to the army and navy indicated preparations for limited rather than total war (TABLE 124). By October 1, 1937, the armed forces had passed the million mark, with more than three-quarters of a million men outside Japan. By October 1, 1940, war had been in process in China for some three years. The involvement with the United States was only a little more than a year in the future. There were 1.7 million men in the armed forces.[16] The numbers in the ages of major concentration and the extent of mobilization in these ages were as follows, numbers being in thousands:[17]

Age	*Total male population*	*Armed forces*[18]	*Per cent in the armed forces*
20-24	3,040	1,093	35.9
25-29	2,823	375	13.3
30-34	2,494	93	3.7
35-39	2,247	31	1.4

Thus, there was a heavy concentration of the armed forces in the initial conscript ages. Almost two-thirds—64.6 per cent, to be precise—were in the age group 20-24, while an addi-

[15] Corroborative evidence is found in a comparison of Japanese males in the world in 1930 with the number expected on the basis of a projection from 1920 to 1930. In 1930, some 86 thousand men were missing from the age groups from 15 to 29, 40 thousand of them in the age group 20-24. However, there were 19 thousand men aged from 30 to 34 in addition to the number expected. If we return to the 1920 census, we find the statement that the census excluded 39 thousand troops in Siberia and 2,400 in Tsintao. See: Nihon. Naikaku tokei-kyoku *Taisho ku'nen kokusei chosa kijutsu hen.* P. 34.

[16] Since armed forces were reported by relatives, military personnel inducted in imperial areas might be reported as from Japan, whereas personnel inducted in Japan might be reported from an imperial area. The geographic distribution of armed forces personnel either at the census date or at the time of induction is hopelessly confused by the reporting procedure. Despite all these difficulties, the information on the demographic characteristics of the armed forces and the extent of the military mobilization in 1940 is valuable as the only reasonably firm picture of the military forces in the history of Japan.

[17] Nihon. Sori-cho, tokei-kyoku. *Kekka hokoku tekiyo, Showa 15-nen kokusei chosa. . . .* The total male population here includes Koreans and other colonial men in Japan, Okinawa being excluded. The armed forces are the total for all Japan, including Okinawa.

[18] The population designated as armed forces for linguistic simplicity included members of the armed forces and persons attached thereto. It apparently also included individuals in military installations. Hence there are a small number of children and a few women reported in the military population. The subtraction of the military population as thus defined from the total population gave a population designated by the Japanese as the "population behind the guns."

TABLE 124

The armed forces of Imperial Japan, 1935-1945

(Numbers in '000)

	LOCATION[a]			NET CHANGE BY LOCATION			NET CHANGE BY CAUSE		
Year	*Total*	*In Japan*	*Outside Japan*	*Total*	*In Japan*	*Outside Japan*	*Deaths*	*Emigration from Japan*	*Withdrawals from civilian population*
1935, Oct. 1	507	287	220	—	—	—	—	—	—
1936, Oct. 1	564	291	273	57	4	53	0	53	57
1937, Oct. 1	1,078	302	776	514	11	503	12	515	527
1938, Oct. 1	1,289	327	962	211	25	186	49	235	260
1939, Oct. 1	1,419	343	1,076	130	16	114	42	156	172
1940, Oct. 1	1,683[b]	510	1,172	264	167	96	33	129	206
1941, Oct. 1	2,391	533	1,858	709	23	686	29	714	737
1942, Oct. 1	2,809	494	2,315	417	−40	457	66	523	483
1943, Oct. 1	3,375	1,017	2,358	566	524	43	100	143	666
1944, Feb. 22	3,732	1,349	2,383	357	332	25	69	94	426
1944, Oct. 1	5,039	2,160	2,878	1,306	811	495	146	641	1,452
1945, Aug. 15	6,963	3,458	3,505	1,925	1,298	627	1,127	1,754	3,053
1945, Nov. 1	3,492	87	3,404	−3,472	−3,371	−101	—	—	−3,472

[a] Okinawa and Karafuto are classified as outside Japan.
[b] Census data.
Source: Nihon. Sori-fu, tokei-kyoku. *Taisho 9-nen—Showa 25-nen, waga kuni nenji betsu jinko no suikei.* Tables 9 and 10.

tional 22.2 per cent were in the age group 25-29. More than 92 per cent were in the ages from 20 to 34. Within these general ages of concentration, there was major concentration at ages 21, 22, and 23. If we relate armed forces to the Japanese population of Japan, we find that inductions had amounted to 15.3 per cent at age 20, 59.3 per cent at age 21, 55.2 per cent at age 22, 38.3 per cent at age 23, and 22.7 per cent at age 24. From the strategic standpoint this was a recently recruited service, and it was the service of a country that had not been subjected to major pressures on available manpower. It appears also as a military force in process of expansion. From a demographic standpoint, this is not an army whose recruitment would have any major direct effects on marriages and births within Japan. Most of the men were below the customary age for marriage, more than two-thirds being below age 25.

The military mortality in the China War prior to October 1, 1940, was relatively slight, if it is viewed in relation to the extent of the conflict. It involved technological warfare in which the advantages of skill, mobility, and matériel were clearly with the armed forces of Japan. The First Demobilization Board of the Japanese government reported 144 thousand deaths in the Japanese armed forces from January 1937 through December 1940—75 thousand in 1937 and 1938, 39 thousand in 1939, and 30 thousand in 1940.[19] A crude estimate of total excess mortality secured by projecting the 1930 population to 1940 on the assumption of normal mortality reveals 200 thousand men missing in the ages from 20 to 29 and a further 57 thousand missing in the ages from 30 to 34. Combining these census-derived estimates of losses, we find a total of 257 thousand Japanese men missing from the population enumerated in the Co-Prosperity Sphere in 1940. This is a rough measure of the deaths of members of the armed forces associated with the war in Manchuria and China. In the perspective of total war, these losses were slight. In the perspective of the military history of Japan, they were far larger than the nation had suffered in any of its earlier wars. And in 1940 victory was not won. The conflict in China gave promise of continuing indefinitely as a war of attrition.

The Japanese armed forces were increased rapidly as the military situation became more acute. By October 1, 1941, there were 2.4 million men in the armed forces. In the year from October 1, 1940, to October 1, 1941, some 737 thousand men were withdrawn from the civilian population and 714 thousand additional men were sent overseas. War remained limited, however, and casualties were slight. The great territorial expansions during 1942 and 1943 involved only 166 thousand deaths. Japan was losing her technical superiority, however, her relative position vis-à-vis the United States being the reverse of that with China and the other Asian countries. By February 22, 1944, there were 3.7 million men under arms, but the military situation continued to deteriorate and major military actions threatened. Total mobilization began. The number of men in the armed forces mounted to 5.0 million on October 1, 1944, and 7.0 million on August 15, 1945.

The official reports of deaths among the armed forces of Japan outside the country are as follows:

Period	*Deaths (in '000)*
Oct. 1, 1935-Sept. 30, 1940	136
Oct. 1, 1940-Feb. 21, 1944	263
Feb. 22, 1944-Sept. 30, 1944	146
Oct. 1, 1944-Aug. 15, 1945	1,127
Total, Oct. 1, 1935-Aug. 15, 1945	1,672

[19] It should be emphasized that all data on military mortality refer to deaths of members of the armed forces rather than to deaths that can be ascribed to military action.

Interpretation of these losses in terms of military campaigns poses major problems. It is obvious that the military dead cannot be in major part men who died in battle, for land actions were limited and only two million of Japan's seven million armed forces were ever in action. The distribution of deaths by the military theaters in which they occurred indicates that the major losses were associated with military risks other than actual combat. The summary of deaths by theaters which follows is that of the General Staff of the War Department of the United States, and it is limited to the period of conflict with the United States, i.e., from December 7, 1941, to August 15, 1945:[20]

Theater	*Deaths (in '000)*
South Pacific	684
Central Pacific	273
India-Burma	128
China	126
Aleutian	8

The total dead in this computation is 1.2 million, as contrasted with the Japanese figure of 1.5 million for the same period. It should be noted that the major military mortality occurred in the South rather than in the Central Pacific area. The battles in the Philippines and Okinawa occurred in the late period of the war and accounted for only about one-fifth of the military dead, instead of the three-fifths or more suggested by the official chronologies. If we turn to the reports made in 1947 by the First Demobilization Board of the Government of Japan, we can make the following tabulation of deaths in the armed forces:[21]

	Deaths (in '000)		
Period	*Total*	*Army*	*Navy*
Total	2,095	1,749	347
Reported deaths	1,675	1,329	347
Jan. 1937-Dec. 1941	147	144	3
Jan. 1942-Dec. 1943	325	230	95
Jan. 1944-Aug. 1945	1,203	955	248
Deaths not reported	420	420	—

In the explanations of this material, the Demobilization Board notes that navy deaths were reported incompletely in 1944 owing to the breakdown in communications, and that the figures for army deaths in late 1944 and 1945 include deaths that occurred prior to 1945 but were deported in 1945 or later years. In addition to the 1.7 million confirmed deaths in the army reported here, there were 420 thousand presumed dead. Total dead for Japan plus Okinawa thus amounted to about 2.1 million. A subtraction of numbers of men aged from

[20] U.S. War Department. General Staff. *Biennial report of the Chief of Staff of the United States Army July 1, 1943 to June 30 1945 to the Secretary of War.* Washington, D.C., Infantry Journal Press, 1946.

[21] Report to the Economic and Scientific Section, GHQ, SCAP, by the General Affairs Section of the First Demobilization Board of the Government of Japan, 1947.

20 to 44 in Japan *and* Okinawa in 1950 from the number expected in this same area *with* repatriation but without war indicates a deficit of 2.0 million men.

The military records that would have permitted the reconstruction of the military mortality of the war years were burned by the Japanese soon after the surrender. Even allocations of deaths as "killed in action" and "other" is impossible. The U.S. Strategic Bombing Survey presented information from Japanese army medical records indicating that 459 thousand Japanese were killed in action in the course of the Pacific War.[22] The proportion of deaths in relation to the numbers deployed was 47.3 in the island areas—the Solomons, New Guinea, the Marshalls, Gilberts, Carolines, and Marianas; the Philippines; Iwo Jimo; and Okinawa. Deaths amounted to 18.2 per cent of the numbers deployed in the Burma theater and 9.4 per cent in China. For the three areas considered together, the 459 thousand battle deaths amounted to 23.1 per cent of the 2.0 million troops deployed.

The data from the Japanese army suggest that perhaps three-fourths of the deaths in the armed forces were due to factors other than battle. The nature of these factors will be discussed in more detail later when we attempt a human balance sheet of the 1940's. Here we need only note the difficulty of the situations faced by the armed forces of Japan throughout the course of the war. Japanese troops, acclimatized to the relatively mild and temperate lands of Japan itself, were sent in major numbers either southward to the tropics or northward to Korea and Manchuria. Supply lines, when they functioned, carried limited provisions. Troops were supposed to rely in major part on the resources of the areas where they were stationed and to arrange for the production of much of their own food. In many areas, such as Java, production in the indigenous economy declined below its prewar levels. In areas such as the atolls, local production or procurement was impossible. Life itself depended on maintenance of the sea connections with the homeland. Disease and malnutrition existed in varying degree in all theaters. As Japan lost control of the sea and garrison after garrison was isolated, starvation became paramount as a cause of death. For many soldiers who survived the war, repatriation was delayed, and that delay also entailed insufficient food, health protection, or medical care. Even the knowledge of heroic deaths in defense of the homeland was denied to major portions of the Japanese families whose sons did not return from the Asian war.

The Population Behind the Front

As we have emphasized again and again, Japan's modern development involved the integration of a largely ancient society into a segmented modern industrial structure. In agriculture and major fields of domestic production, human hands did the work that might have been done by machines. Self-sufficiency had been lost long ago, however. A major portion of the nation's food had to be imported, as did fertilizer, the raw materials for industrial production, and coal and oil for internal transportation and the movements of ships and planes. Japan was ill-equipped for a long war against opponents with advanced industrial economies. Her military technology was advanced by Asian standards, and so she won a series of wars quickly and at slight human or economic cost. In war with Western powers, the limitations of Japan's industrial development became increasingly critical. Her long years of planning and great investments in construction for defense and offense were based on scientific and psychological illusions. Islands that had been made into fortresses impregnable from the sea were not defensible against air attacks, while mobile warfare mocked the presumed impenetrability of defensive perimeters. Temporary victories consequent on an enemy's lack of preparation did not lead to negotiated peace but instead stiffened the will to resist.

The achievements of the Japanese in their era of victory were of overwhelming importance to the evolving nationalism of Asian peoples; their role as legends influencing Japanese decisions in the future is a major question. The armed forces raised a flag of the Rising Sun in the Aleutians, the Philippines, and Indonesia, while their battleships carried it into the Indian Ocean. The armies of Western powers surrendered to Japanese generals; detailed terms were arranged and papers signed in the citadels of the Western colonial structure. A Co-Prosperity Sphere was established in the Far East, and "Asia for the Asians" became the slogan of a new Asian imperialism. The Co-Prosperity Sphere was short-lived, however, and the war did not follow the course that the Japanese had expected. The Soviet Union repelled the German armies, Britain survived, and victory was won by the Allied Powers in Europe. The democracy of the United States proved capable of incisive and sustained military action. Scientific advances, applied technology, industrial know-how, and strategic planning permitted effective war across the thousands of miles of the Pacific. The Japanese fleet was sunk or immobilized, the air force was liquidated, and the waters that had been defensive protection became barriers that prevented the movements of men or matériel. Surrender preceded invasion.

Japan's manpower was superabundant for peace, but her industrial potential was insufficient for modern war. Demographic forces were involved both in the early victories and in the later defeats, but their operations were indirect. Population was one element among a number of social and economic factors that were related to the political decision to initiate war and to the course of the war once the decision had been made. Given the national psychology, the social structure, the scientific and technical levels, and the industrial limitations of Japan, it does not seem that the outcome of the war would have been affected greatly had the population been either much greater or far smaller than it was. Some of the demographic reasoning that lies back of this conclusion will become apparent as we trace the vicissitudes of the "population behind the front" in the years from 1940 to 1945.

October 1, 1940-February 22, 1944

The years from 1940 through 1943 were thought by the people of Japan to be a period of continuing victories. The extension of the war with China to include the United States came on December 7, 1941, and during the following months the conquests were great, the costs minimal. The maximum expansion perimeter was reached early in 1942, and was held almost unchanged until November 1943. The demographic health of Japan remained excellent. In the three years and almost five months between the census of October 1, 1940, and the survey of February 22, 1944, there were 7.7 million births and 4.0 million deaths, yielding a natural increase of 3.7 million. The size of the armed forces was being increased, however, and major portions of the newly drafted were being sent overseas to bolster defenses at points where it was believed attacks might come. Some 2.3 million men were withdrawn from the civilian population, 2.0 million being net

[22] U.S. Strategic Bombing Survey. *Summary report (Pacific War).* Washington, D.C., 1946.

additions to the military forces, while 264 thousand were replacements for men who had died. Civilian in-migration amounted to 204 thousand, military out-migration to 1.5 million, leaving a net migration loss of 1.3 million. The population within Japan increased from 71.4 million on October 1, 1940, to 73.8 million on February 22, 1944;[23] the "population behind the front" increased from 70.8 million to 72.5 million during this same period.[24] Mobilization for war produced major disturbances in the sex and age structures of the civilian population. The excess of women in this population increased from 1.7 million in 1940 to 3.8 million in 1944. In a society whose institutional structure and economic functioning were geared to an excess of males, this excess of females was serious indeed. Its impact becomes more vivid if we examine the incidence by age (TABLE 125). In the population behind the front in 1940 there were 954 males for each 1,000 females; by 1944 this ratio had declined to 902.[25] The sex ratios of civilians in the ages from 15 to 44 show something of the influence of the war on families and economic activities:

[23] The population within Japan is the *de facto* population of the country, including the armed forces. Japan is defined as excluding Okinawa.

[24] The "population behind the front" is the *de facto* civilian population of the country, excluding the armed forces. Precise estimates with various adjustment factors have been made by the Bureau of Statistics of the Prime Minister's Office. The estimates used here, like those of the Bureau of Statistics, are for the area of Japan as of 1950, but in order to obtain consistent series by sex and age as well as total numbers, the population within the 1950 area is taken as the area of 1940 minus Okinawa or the area of 1944 minus Okinawa and Karafuto. The difference between the more careful and the approximate estimate is not great—70,857 thousand for the former, 70,808 for the latter.

[25] This sex ratio is not a precise measure of the sex ratio in the civilian population, for in 1944 officers and others living outside armed forces installations were reported as in the civilian population.

TABLE 125

The population behind the front, 1940-1945
(Japan, excluding Okinawa and Karafuto)

Age	NUMBERS (IN '000) *Total*	*Male*	*Female*	*Excess of females*	*Males per 1,000 females*
			October 1, 1940[a]		
All Japan	70,809	34,578	36,231	1,652	954
Under 15	26,134	13,205	12,928	−277	1,021
15-19	7,293	3,624	3,670	46	987
20-34	15,044	6,796	8,248	1,451	824
35-49	11,323	5,795	5,528	−268	1,048
50-64	7,600	3,711	3,889	179	954
65 and over	3,415	1,447	1,968	521	735
			February 22, 1944[b]		
All Japan	72,474	34,359	38,114	3,755	902
Under 16	25,968	13,141	12,827	−314	1,024
16-20	7,804	3,807	3,997	190	952
21-35	14,503	5,616	8,887	3,271	632
36-50	12,240	6,140	6,099	−41	1,007
51-65	7,895	3,923	3,973	50	988
66 and over	4,064	1,732	2,332	599	743
			November 1, 1945[c]		
All Japan	71,998	33,894	38,104	4,210	890
Under 16	26,477	13,388	13,089	−298	1,023
16-20	7,821	3,849	3,971	122	969
21-35	14,327	5,433	8,894	3,460	611
36-50	11,985	5,859	6,125	266	957
51-65	7,688	3,801	3,888	87	978
66 and over	3,700	1,563	2,137	573	732

[a] Western ages.

[b] Lunar ages. Age 1 at the census date included the survivors of the births from January 1 to February 21, 1944.

[c] Lunar ages. Age 1 at the census date included the survivors of births from January 1 to October 31, 1945.

Source: 1940: Nihon. Naikaku tokei-kyoku. *Census of 1940. Selected tables.* Table 2. 1944: Nihon. Sori-fu, tokei-kyoku. *Kekka hokoku tekiyo. . . . Showa 19-nen jinko chosa. . . .* 1945: *Ibid. Kekka hokoku tekiyo. . . . Showa 20-nen jinko chosa.*

Age[26]	Males per 1,000 females 1940	1944
15-19 (16-20)	987	952
20-24 (21-25)	643	516
25-29 (26-30)	875	652
30-34 (31-35)	991	761
35-39 (36-40)	1,033	943
40-44 (41-45)	1,059	1,031

In 1940 the deficits of men were slight at ages under 20 and over 29. The majority of the men in the armed forces were youth aged from 20 to 24. In social and economic terms, this meant that youth leaving school could migrate and enter employment in the usual sequence of events that followed school graduation. Army service was concentrated in the years prior to marriage, as conscription had always been, and so the delays in marriage and family formation did not assume major proportions. There had been some downward movement in the age of military service by 1944, but there was still no evidence of substantial pressures upon the available supply of manpower for military purposes. Few of the youth aged 18 and 19 were in military service. At age 20 to 24, however, almost half the men were missing from the civilian population. The deficit of men as contrasted with women was one-third at age 25 to 29 and one-fourth at age 30 to 34. Conscriptions at earlier ages were being continued in the military service and the mobilization of the reserves had assumed substantial proportions.

At the same time that military mobilization removed men from the civilian labor force, there were increasing demands for labor for war production, military transport, and essential defense activities. There was some increase in the employment of women, though the major readjustments seem to have occurred through a more intensive utilization of the labor of men and the extension of the period of employment downward into the ages below conscription and upward into the ages beyond retirement. The proportions of the civilian population reported as gainfully occupied in 1944 were as follows:[27]

Age (lunar)	*Men*	*Women*
16-20	88.2	60.1
21-25	95.4	68.8
26-30	96.4	47.0
31-35	97.5	45.9
36-40	97.9	49.6
41-45	98.2	53.7
46-50	97.8	56.6
51-55	96.6	56.9
56-60	93.7	53.6
61 and over	68.2	30.8

Relatively high proportions of women were gainfully occupied in 1944, but it is significant that the proportions were not higher. The traditional ideas of appropriate activity for women remained economic deterrents throughout the war years. Then, too, women did not have the competence to undertake tasks previously barred to them. Japan's wartime economy functioned primarily by drawing on individuals of both sexes below and above those ages where the major role lay—military service for men, marriage and reproduction for women. The percentage age structures of the gainfully occupied by sex in 1944 illustrate this relationship:

Age (lunar)	*Men*	*Women*
Total gainfully occupied	100.	100.
11-15	2.2	3.1
16-20	16.9	22.7
21-25	8.5	16.4
26-30	8.8	9.0
31-35	10.0	8.4
36-40	10.7	7.8
41-45	10.5	7.6
46-50	9.1	6.8
51-55	7.4	5.6
56-60	6.2	4.9
61 and over	9.6	7.5

The industrial readjustments were those to be anticipated in a war situation: declining proportions in agriculture and fishing, a sharp curtailment in commerce and transportation, a small absolute but large proportionate decline in the service industries.[28] There were relative increases in mining, industry and construction, and government and professional service. The proportions of the gainfully occupied in agriculture and forestry in 1940 were 33.4 for men and 56.6 for women; the corresponding percentages for 1944 were 27.9 for men and 57.2 for women. The percentage of gainfully occupied men in industry and construction increased from 31.0 in 1940 to 41.4 in 1944; the comparable percentages for women were 15.3 in 1940 and 18.0 in 1944.

As the withdrawals from the civilian population increased and the war effort continued, there were major problems in food production, large deficits in consumers' goods, and sharp declines in levels of living. Until early 1944, the broad changes in geographic distribution and industrial allocation were similar to those of previous decades. Industrial mobility was from agricultural to industrial activities, while geographic mobility was from agricultural to intermediate and industrial prefectures.

The changes in the concentration of the female population are shown in TABLE 126. Inductions into the armed forces and civilian movements to and from Japan had been so great that

[26] The age data of the 1940 census were tabulated in Western ages, those of the censuses of 1944 and 1945 in lunar ages.

[27] Computed from data in: Nihon. Naikaku tokei-kyoku. *Special survey of 1944. Selected tables.* Table 6. The survey of 1944 did not follow the same procedures as the regular census. Ages were lunar rather than Western. In addition, the survey was taken as of February 22 rather than October 1. Even though the questions concerned usual occupation and industry, it is probable that appreciable proportions of the people who would have reported themselves as gainfully occupied in agriculture and other seasonal activities on October 1 reported themselves as not gainfully occupied on February 22. This would apply particularly to women.

[28] For a detailed analysis of the changes in manpower utilization in the war years, see: U.S. Strategic Bombing Survey. *The Japanese wartime standard of living and utilization of manpower.* Part III, "The wartime utilization of manpower," devotes a special section to the developments during the period from December 1941 to February 1944. The analysis presented here is based on the following sources: 1940: Nihon. Sori-fu, tokei-kyoku. *Nihon tokei nenkan.* Table 37, pp. 68-70. The figures on the gainfully occupied refer to the total population, including the armed forces. However, the proportionate industrial composition of the armed forces prior to induction differed but slightly from that of the general male population. Hence the industrial composition of the civilian population, expressed in proportionate terms, is quite similar to that given here for the total population. 1944: *Ibid.* Table 36, pp. 66-67. The population is *de facto* civilian, except that military personnel living outside military installations were included.

TABLE 126

The female population of the prefectures: years of concentration

Age	NUMBERS (IN '000) Oct. 1, 1930[a]	Oct. 1, 1940[a]	Feb. 22, 1944[b]	RATIO TO 1920 AS 100 Oct. 1, 1930	Oct. 1, 1940	Feb. 22, 1944
		All Japan				
Total	31,755	36,231	38,114	115	131	138
0-4	4,426	4,468	4,260	121	122	—
5-14	7,145	8,460	8,567	113	134	135
15-19	3,196	3,670	3,997	121	139	151
20-34	7,050	8,248	8,887	119	139	150
35-49	4,799	5,528	6,099	105	121	133
50-64	3,414	3,889	3,973	119	136	139
65 and over	1,726	1,968	2,332	106	121	144
		Metropolitan				
Total	4,248	5,888	6,086	142	197	204
0-4	567	689	704	160	195	—
5-14	809	1,190	1,189	131	192	192
15-19	511	699	661	151	207	196
20-34	1,210	1,698	1,717	152	213	216
35-49	638	908	1,041	128	182	209
50-64	366	502	531	139	191	202
65 and over	146	202	243	120	166	199
		Industrial				
Total	5,390	6,610	6,981	119	146	154
0-4	728	803	795	127	140	—
5-14	1,156	1,468	1,481	113	143	144
15-19	584	706	746	128	154	163
20-34	1,284	1,639	1,756	126	160	172
35-49	812	1,009	1,134	110	136	153
50-64	549	659	682	122	147	152
65 and over	277	325	386	109	128	152
		Intermediate				
Total	10,041	10,672	11,281	108	115	122
0-4	1,362	1,264	1,211	113	105	—
5-14	2,288	2,534	2,545	106	118	118
15-19	966	1,021	1,160	113	119	135
20-34	2,098	2,252	2,476	112	121	132
35-49	1,526	1,650	1,807	98	106	116
50-64	1,168	1,259	1,267	115	124	124
65 and over	633	691	814	104	114	134
		Agricultural				
Total	10,733	11,483	12,119	110	118	124
0-4	1,548	1,486	1,338	115	111	—
5-14	2,541	2,856	2,935	113	127	130
15-19	992	1,072	1,247	113	123	143
20-34	2,160	2,295	2,546	109	116	128
35-49	1,643	1,746	1,878	101	108	116
50-64	1,222	1,336	1,356	116	127	129
65 and over	627	692	819	104	114	136

TABLE 126 (continued)
The female population of the prefectures: years of concentration

Age	NUMBERS (IN '000)			RATIO TO 1920 AS 100		
	Oct. 1, 1930[a]	*Oct. 1, 1940*[a]	*Feb. 22, 1944*[b]	*Oct. 1, 1930*	*Oct. 1, 1940*	*Feb. 22, 1944*
			Hokkaido			
Total	1,344	1,577	1,648	120	141	148
0-4	221	226	212	118	121	—
5-14	351	411	417	121	142	144
15-19	142	172	183	126	152	161
20-34	297	363	392	120	146	158
35-49	181	215	239	111	132	146
50-64	108	133	136	141	173	176
65 and over	42	56	69	119	158	194

[a] Western ages.
[b] Lunar ages. Children in age 0-4 were actually those in lunar age 1-5 and were the survivors of the births of the period from February 22, 1940, to February 21, 1944.
Source: 1930: Nihon. Naikaku, tokei-kyoku. *Showa go'nen kokusei chosa hokoku.* IV.1. 1940 and 1944: References, Table 125.

changes in the male population would not indicate industrial transformations and altered civilian functioning. The changing residential allocation of women was largely free from such disturbances. Women were not taken into the armed forces nor, in this period, were they moving abroad to newly conquered areas.

Between 1940 and 1944 the numbers of girls aged from 15 to 19 declined in the metropolitan prefectures and increased only slightly in the industrial prefectures. The major increases came in intermediate and agricultural prefectures. This same pattern of differential increase occurred for girls aged from 20 to 24. The explanation is somewhat speculative. Unmarried girls probably remained home to substitute for absent brothers in work on the farms and in other rural activities.

If it could be assumed that the movements of married women and children remained correlated with those of their husbands as in previous years, the movements of women would reflect the population dynamics of the period. This assumption of continuity in the relations of the migrations of men and women is plausible, but it is not valid for the wartime migrations of the Japanese. Many marriages that would have been accompanied by the movement of the bride to the city if the nation had been at peace were not so accompanied during war. Mobilized men with families often sent those families home, and home was likely to be outside the metropolitan prefectures. The role of women remained familial. Adjurations, proscriptions, and threats did not persuade major portions of the women to fill roles inappropriate for them. This was particularly true for married women.

The general process of population redistribution between 1940 and 1944 was one of continued industrialization and urbanization, though incorporation was proceeding so rapidly that measurements of the changes are difficult. Practically all existing cities extended their boundaries, and 41 new *shi* were created.[29] The total population of *shi* amounted to 37.7 per cent of the national population in 1940 and 41.3 per cent in 1944. There were great differences in changes by type and size of city. Population increased rapidly in smaller cities where strategic industries were located, but there was stability or decline in the large cities whose major industrial bases lay in consumers' goods and general distribution. Tokyo, Osaka, Kyoto, and Kobe lost in population, while there were slight increases in Yokohama and Nagoya. Rapid increases occurred in the secondary concentrations in the Tokyo and Nagoya areas, where plains offered sites for aircraft factories and related industries. Substantial increases occurred in the Hiroshima and Nagasaki areas, in Hiroshima because of the naval base at Kure, in Nagasaki because of the port and shipbuilding facilities of the city itself and the requirements for the naval base at Sasebo. Illustrative of the speed of the movements are the percentage increases in selected cities: Tachikawa in Tokyo-to, 62.9 per cent; Toyokawa in Aichi, 145.8 per cent; Kawasaki in Kanagawa, 26.8 per cent; Yokosuka in Kanagawa, 26.5 per cent; Handa in Aichi, 23.5 per cent; Kure in Hiroshima, 22.9 per cent; and Omura in Nagasaki, 97.3 per cent.

[29] Further incorporations of *shi* were forbidden in the middle of the year 1944.

The populations of the *shi* increased more rapidly than those of the *gun* in almost all prefectures, so that the urbanization of the population structure of the nation continued. This increase of the *shi* occurred in prefectures losing in total population as well as in those gaining. The manpower demands for the armed forces and military industries alike were focused on the populations of the *gun*, and particularly on their agricultural components. As labor declined in quantity and deteriorated in quality, the amount of the uncultivated land increased and the yields from cultivated lands declined. Food became scarce in the cities. As of February 22, 1944, however, the major air attacks had not occurred, civilian deprivation was not serious, and the nature of the external military situation was not realized by the majority of the people.

FEBRUARY 22, 1944-NOVEMBER 1, 1945

The penetration of the Japanese perimeter began before the survey of February 22, 1944, was taken, but military action had been limited and had occurred far away from the home islands. The early moves included attacks on Attu in the Aleutians in May 1943, the conquest of Bougainville in November 1943, and the assault on the Gilbert Islands in the

Central Pacific, also in November 1943.[30] One prong of the major amphibious attack on Japan itself went to the Philippines, while the other prong went through the Marshalls to the Marianas and then to Okinawa. Quoting the United States Strategic Bombing Survey: "By March, 1945, prior to heavy direct air attack on the Japanese home islands, the Japanese air forces had been reduced to Kamikaze forces, her fleet had been sunk or immobilized, her merchant marine decimated, large portions of her ground forces isolated, and the strangulation of her economy well begun."[31]

The Japanese military response to the approaching crisis was a heavy build-up of the armed forces. They were increased from 3.7 million on February 22, 1944, to 5.0 million on October 1, 1944, and 7.0 million on August 15, 1945. Between February 22, 1944, and the surrender on August 15, 1945, almost 2.5 million members of the armed forces left Japan, 1.3 million of them to replace the dead, 1.1 million to increase the military manpower available. The great increase of the armed forces came within Japan, from 1.3 million on February 22, 1944, to 2.2 million on October 1, 1944, and 3.5 million on August 15, 1945. Military mobilization and civilian depletion of this order exerted major pressures on the population remaining in civil life. Natural increase slowed and then became negative as births declined precipitantly and civilian deaths from non-military causes and air bombardments shot upward. From February 22, 1944, to September 30, 1944, there was a natural increase of more than half a million, but between October 1, 1944, and August 15, 1945, there was a natural decrease of 178 thousand. The population resident as civilians within Japan declined from 73.8 million on February 22, 1944, to 72.1 million on August 15, 1945. The population behind the front, 72.5 million on February 22, 1944, declined to 68.7 million by August 15, 1945.

Massive concentrations of population in war production centers continued to be effected through a combination of voluntary enticements and compulsive recruitments. The result was a cumulative decline in the agricultural labor force, further reduction in cultivated acreage, decreased yields on land cultivated, and a seriously deteriorated food situation. By early 1944 the majority of the farm workers consisted of women, children, and older men. There were only 4.2 million men aged from 16 to 60 for the 5.6 million agricultural households.[32] Changes in farm labor between February of 1944 and February of 1945 were estimated by the Ministry of Forestry and Agriculture as follows:[33]

Change	*Total*	*Men*	*Women*
Net decrease	868,860	701,199	167,661
Loss			
Total	1,250,711	923,050	327,661
Deaths	358,991	108,010	250,981
Net out-migration	168,460	91,780	76,680
Conscription	723,260	723,260	0
Gain			
Total	381,851	221,851	160,000
Demobilization	61,851	61,851	0
National school graduates	320,000	160,000	160,000

[30] U.S. Strategic Bombing Survey. Pacific War. *Summary report (Pacific War)*. P. 7.

[31] *Ibid.* P. 9.

[32] U.S. Strategic Bombing Survey. Pacific War. *Japanese wartime standard of living and utilization of manpower*. P. 9.

[33] *Ibid.* P. 19.

The Ministry of Agriculture estimated that the number of able-bodied men in agriculture decreased by another half million between February and August of 1945. By the latter date, less than two-thirds of the agricultural households included an able-bodied male worker.

The strains placed on industrial labor in the final months of the war were similar to those in agriculture. There were attempts to increase student participation in the labor force, and there were major drives to induce contributions of additional labor from all civilians. There was discussion of a labor draft for women but such a draft was never undertaken. Registrations of single women aged from 20 to 44 were made in February and November of 1944. The number of such women gainfully occupied increased from 4.8 to 5.2 million during this period, while the number not gainfully occupied decreased from 592 to 486 thousand. Plans were made to import additional workers and some 300 thousand were brought in during 1944, but Japan needed skilled rather than unskilled labor and workers were becoming scarce in Korean agriculture.[34] Prisoners of war and convicts were used; theaters and other non-essential establishments were closed to obtain manpower for more essential purposes. But the great reservoir of married women was neither registered nor conscripted.

Strategic air attacks on Japan itself began from the Marianas in November of 1944 as preparation for a planned invasion of Japan in November of 1945.[35] Incendiary raids on cities began on March 9, 1945, with a saturation bombing of Tokyo in which fifteen square miles of the most densely settled parts of the city were burned. On March 11, Nagoya was bombed. By March 19, Osaka and Kobe had also been bombed. Raids increased in numbers and in tonnage, especially after the Eighth Air Force was activated on Okinawa. In all, 66 cities were attacked and 40 per cent of the built-up areas destroyed. On August 6 an atomic bomb was dropped on Hiroshima; on August 9 an atomic bomb was dropped on Nagasaki. On August 15, 1945, Japan surrendered.

The structure and distribution of the population of Japan at the time of the surrender are not known, but the simplified survey of November 1, 1945, shows the people close to this lowest point in their national history. Total population is variously reported as 72.0 or 72.2 million; taking the lower figure, 33.9 million were men, 38.1 million women. The excess of women was 4.2 million. On August 15, 1945, the total population in Japan had been estimated at 72.1 million. Between August 15 and October 31 there was a net in-migration of 86 thousand which about balanced the natural decrease of 67 thousand. However, in this period 3.4 million members of the armed forces had been demobilized. This means at the end of the war, the civilian population included only about 30.5 million men, as contrasted with 38.1 million women. The number of men per 1,000 women was approximately 800.

The excesses of women and the sex ratios in the age groups as recorded in the survey on November 15, 1945, were as follows:

Age	*Excesses of women (in '000)*	*Males per 1,000 females*
Total	4,210	890
Under 16	−298	1,023
16-20	122	969
21-25	1,416	588

[34] U.S. Strategic Bombing Survey. Pacific War. *Summary report (Pacific War)*. P. 76.

[35] *Ibid.* P. 16.

Age	*Excesses of women (in '000)*	*Males per 1,000 females*
26-30	1,208	570
31-35	836	684
36-50	266	957
51-65	87	978
66 and over	573	732

In this population of November 15, 1945, the sex ratio in the age group from 16 through 35 was 611. If we assume that all members of the armed forces stationed within Japan on August 15, 1945, were somewhere in the age span from 16 to 35, we find the sex ratio in the civilian population in this age group to be only 229. By the time the war ended, the number of men aged from 16 to 35 in the civilian population was less than one-fifth the number of women.

The population physically present in Japan, excluding Okinawa, was 71.4 million on October 1, 1940. It was 72.2 million on November 15, 1945. There was a net increase of 780 thousand in the population present within the country. However, during these five years 3.9 million members of the armed forces had left Japan, and on November 15, 1945, some 3.5 million members of the armed forces were outside Japan awaiting transportation home. If these surviving members of the armed forces are added to the 72.2 million people within the country, the population becomes 75.7 million. In the absence of any repatriation or exchange of minorities, this 75.7 million, rather than the 72.2 million of the census, is the population that would have formed the basis for future population growth. It may also be noted that natural increase between October 1, 1940, and November 1, 1945, amounted to 4.0 million, deaths of the armed forces outside Japan to 1.5 million. Net natural increase during the five years and one month of the period that included the entire Pacific War was 2.5 million. Military defeat had not involved the extermination of military manpower. There were no losses that precluded rapid recovery if the birth and death rates of the prewar years could be restored.

From the demographic point of view, the major development of the last months of the war was the desertion of the cities and the areas of danger, the flight to safety in smaller *shi*, in *machi*, and in *mura*. Again the female population is considered in order to avoid the influence of changes in the size of the armed forces outside the country and the movements of the recently demobilized armed forces within the country. Detailed age changes are given in TABLE 127, but total population changes tell the story of the flights of the last months of war, figures being in thousands:

TABLE 127

The female population of the prefectures: years of dispersion and early return

	NUMBERS (IN '000)			RATIO TO 1944 AS 100	
Ages	*Feb. 22, 1944*[a]	*Nov. 1, 1945*[a]	*April 26, 1946*[a]	*Nov. 1, 1945*	*April 26, 1946*
		All Japan			
Total	38,114	38,104	38,209	100	100
1-5	4,260	4,568	3,882	107[a]	91[a]
6-15	8,567	8,522	8,625	100	101
16-20	3,997	3,971	4,032	99	101
21-35	8,887	8,894	9,142	100	103
36-50	6,099	6,125	6,327	100	104
51-65	3,973	3,887	3,967	98	100
66 and over	2,332	2,137	2,234	92	96
		Metropolitan			
Total	6,086	3,147	3,597	52	59
1-5	704	334	340	48[a]	48[a]
6-15	1,189	590	707	50	60
16-20	661	350	382	53	58
21-35	1,717	819	967	48	56
36-50	1,041	607	694	58	67
51-65	531	320	360	60	68
66 and over	243	127	147	52	61
		Industrial			
Total	6,981	6,214	6,352	89	91
1-5	795	731	634	92[a]	80[a]
6-15	1,481	1,326	1,372	90	93
16-20	746	638	659	86	88
21-35	1,756	1,490	1,571	85	90
36-50	1,134	1,058	1,106	93	98

TABLE 127 (continued)

The female population of the prefectures: years of dispersion and early return

Ages	NUMBERS (IN '000)			RATIO TO 1944 AS 100	
	Feb. 22, 1944[a]	*Nov. 1, 1945*[a]	*April 26, 1946*[a]	*Nov. 1, 1945*	*April 26, 1946*
51-65	682	636	657	93	96
66 and over	386	335	352	87	91
		Intermediate			
Total	11,281	12,791	12,537	113	111
1-5	1,211	1,521	1,251	126[a]	103[a]
6-15	2,545	2,842	2,800	112	110
16-20	1,160	1,306	1,304	113	112
21-35	2,476	2,937	2,940	119	119
36-50	1,807	2,044	2,070	113	114
51-65	1,267	1,342	1,347	106	106
66 and over	814	799	825	98	101
		Agriculture			
Total	12,119	14,172	13,948	117	115
1-5	1,338	1,736	1,443	130[a]	108[a]
6-15	2,935	3,326	3,303	113	112
16-20	1,247	1,480	1,488	119	119
21-35	2,546	3,219	3,229	126	127
36-50	1,877	2,159	2,192	115	117
51-65	1,356	1,446	1,457	107	107
66 and over	819	805	835	98	102
		Hokkaido			
Total	1,648	1,780	1,775	108	108
1-5	212	245	213	116[a]	100[a]
6-15	417	437	442	105	106
16-20	183	198	200	108	109
21-35	392	428	434	109	111
36-50	239	258	266	108	111
51-65	136	143	145	105	107
66 and over	69	71	75	103	109

[a] The age group 1-5 on February 22, 1944, consisted of the survivors of the births from January 1, 1940, to February 21, 1944, a period of four years, one month, and 21 days. The group aged 1-5 on November 1, 1945, consisted of the survivors of births between January 1, 1941, and October 31, 1945, a period of four years and ten months. The group aged 1-5 on April 26, 1946, consisted of the survivors of births between January 1, 1942, and April 25, 1946, a period of four years, three months, and 25 days.

Source: 1944 and 1945: References, Table 125. 1946: Nihon. Sori-cho, tokei-kyoku. *Kekka hokoku tekiyo. . . . Showa 21-nen jinko chosa.*

Prefectures by industrial type	*Feb. 22, 1944*	*Nov. 1, 1945*	*Ratio of Nov. 1, 1945, to Feb. 22, 1944, as 100*
All Japan	38,114	38,104	100.
Metropolitan	6,086	3,147	51.7
Other industrial	6,981	6,214	89.0
Intermediate	11,281	12,791	113.4
Agricultural	12,119	14,172	116.9
Hokkaido	1,648	1,780	108.0

Women had fled the industrial areas; they had moved in major numbers to intermediate and agricultural prefectures. There is some evidence of selective migration in the changes by age, but such selectivity was not great. The out-migrations were flights rather than carefully planned moves. The destination of those fleeing the industrial areas was determined in major part by accessibility rather than by location of kin. If it is suggested that the situation requiring flight was too urgent to permit a choice of destination, it need only be pointed out that by November 1, 1945, the war had been over almost three months. Those who were moving on to their place of origin from a transitory refuge would already have done so. In fact, many had already returned to the cities from which they had fled and had started trying to rebuild residences and restore an economic basis for livelihood.

The behavior of the people when the industrial economy collapsed reveals more clearly than any other single episode the pervasive nature of the changes that had been occurring as the urban milieu replaced the primary contacts of the village. In theory, the urban people should have returned to the families of origin in the villages. The head of the *ie* had the obligation of support. The ties of kin were strong. The ritualistic behavior of family members should have minimized the frictions that arise as families live together. This is ancient theory, but it had been outmoded by the urbanization of children and grandchildren. Those who had migrated had become more prosperous than those who had remained behind. In the years of their economic success and upward mobility they had regarded brothers and sisters, nephews and nieces, in the village as "country cousins." They had looked down upon village life as dull and crude, and they had spurned the toil of the fields. In the immediate crisis of the bombings and the flights, the rural family fulfilled its obligations, but it was ill-prepared economically or psychologically to continue to house and feed relatives whose kinship, though genuine, had seldom been manifested. Tensions developed in the group living in crowded quarters. The problems were comparable to those of Cincinnati families returned to the Kentucky hills, of Birmingham factory workers returned to share-cropping in the Alabama back country.

Urbanization had become more than a matter of urban residence; it involved the habits and the aspirations of the people. This acculturation had also occurred among those who had lived as civilians in the colonies, Manchoukuo, or China. The soldiers who were returned to their places of *honseki* were no longer adjusted members of the village communities. The final confirmation of the deep transformations wrought by urban living and non-agricultural labor is the refusal of substantial proportions of the Koreans in Japan to accept repatriation to their homes in the villages of Korea.

Before we consider the restoration of the industrial society and the urban economy, it is necessary to note briefly the population movements that accompanied the liquidation of the Japanese Empire and its associated political structure in the occupied and affiliated areas of the Co-Prosperity Sphere.

Exodus and Return

In earlier chapters we described the outward movements of the Japanese in the period prior to 1940.[36] Five more years remained before the surrender of Imperial Japan and the final trek homeward. In the movements of this period there were divergences over time and between areas.[37] A major exodus from Japan had occurred as Manchoukuo and North China were subjected to Japanese political and economic control. To the Japanese of the 1930's and the early 1940's opportunities for personal advancement and upward family mobility seemed to lie in migration, and this continued for a decade in the case of Manchoukuo, for five years in that of Occupied China, for lesser durations in other conquered areas.

If the China War had ended with a new affiliated state in the Japanese imperial structure, it is probable that the movements that were so substantial in the 1930's would have quickened in the 1940's.[38] Almost a quarter of a million Japanese did go to "foreign areas" in 1940-1941, most of them to China, but economic development and civil administration had to yield priority to military production and military action after the war was extended to the entire Western Pacific area late in 1941 (Table 128). In 1941-1942, 91 thousand Japanese went to occupied areas. By 1943 those in responsible positions knew that almost any sector of the Co-Prosperity Sphere might become a military theater. Civilians were evacuated from strategic areas in Nanyo-gunto, Okinawa, and Karafuto. Many people returned to Japan. At the time of the surrender, however, there were many more civilians abroad than there had been in 1940. A comparison of the geographic distribution in 1940 and 1945 follows, numbers being in thousands:[39]

Areas	*Enumerated Oct. 1, 1940 (Persons with honseki in Okinawa included)*	*Estimated as of Aug. 15, 1945 (Ryukyuans excluded)*
Total	3,033	3,119
Colonies	1,808	1,553
Karafuto	399	277
Taiwan	312	322
Nanyo-gunto	77	28
Korea	707	711
Kwantung	313	215
Other occupied areas	1,225	1,566
Manchoukuo	820	1,004
Other China	364	464
Other Asia	41	99

Many Japanese in the colonies identified themselves with land they regarded as inalienably Japanese. These people either remained where they were or moved to adjacent areas that they believed were safer. In Taiwan and Korea there were some individual movements but no mass retreat "homeward" to Japan. Many of the islands of Micronesia were evacuated. People from Karafuto moved down into Hokkaido. In Manchoukuo and North China the story was different. The Japanese in these areas were recent migrants, and most of them were associated with the activities of armed forces and military governments. Physical factors barred movement, however, for overland distances were great and sea transport was inadequate. In August of 1945, 1.5 million civilian Japanese, half of all those abroad, became aliens in countries that the

[36] Chapter IX and X.

[37] The existence of censuses in 1930, 1935, and 1940 dictates a chronology of analyses that differs widely from the chronological developments that motivated or retarded migration.

[38] The annual movements of the Japanese are difficult to trace statistically because of the definition of "Japanese" that was adopted by the Allied Powers and the changed boundaries of the postwar years. Prior to its conquest, Okinawa was a prefecture of Japan, its people inseparable in the statistics from those of other prefectures. Ryukyu was a historic culture studied by Japanese as by other anthropologists; the Ryukyuans were recognized as having distinctive characteristics. However, the natives of the Ryukyus were citizens of Japan rather than of the colonies. After the war the former prefecture of Okinawa plus part of Kagoshima prefecture remained under United States occupation as a strategic area. Some small islands and Amami Oshima have reverted to Japan. Thus, individuals who had migrated to Japan prior to 1945 and had been enumerated in censuses as Japanese were defined as foreigners in 1945. In the postwar reconstruction of prewar statistics, it became necessary to record interchanges between Okinawa and the rest of Japan as movement between Japan and a colonial area. And "Japanese" repatriated from such areas as Nanyo-gunto included "Japanese" returned to one of the 46 prefectures of postwar Japan, as well as "Ryukyuans" returned to areas that formerly had been included in Okinawa or Kagoshima prefectures but that now were foreign.

[39] Estimated by SCAP, GHQ, Economic and Scientific Section.

TABLE 128

Net civilian movements to and from Japan (46 prefectures), 1920-1945

Period	Total	JAPANESE Total[a]	To foreign countries[a]	To territories[a]	Non-Japanese
Oct. 1, 1920-Sept. 30, 1925	52,487	−147,570	2,653	−150,223	200,057[b]
Oct. 1, 1925-Sept. 30, 1930	8,073	−191,984	−60,149	−131,835	200,057[b]
Oct. 1, 1930-Sept. 30, 1935	13,269	−399,475	−300,719	−98,756	412,744[c]
Oct. 1, 1935-Sept. 30, 1940	−309,573	−722,317	−558,473	−163,844	412,744[c]
Oct. 1, 1940-Aug. 15, 1945	550,239	192,808	−129,942	322,750	357,431
Oct. 1940-Sept. 1941	−98,183	−170,881	−234,477	63,596	72,698[d]
Oct. 1941-Sept. 1942	47,997	−24,701	−91,291	66,590	75,698[d]
Oct. 1942-Sept. 1943	158,772	86,074	16,351	69,723	72,698[d]
Oct. 1943-Feb. 1944	95,656	65,366	38,389	26,977	30,290
March 1944-Sept. 1944	139,592	97,185	59,904	37,281	42,407
Oct. 1944-Aug. 1945	206,405	139,765	81,182	58,583	66,640
Sept. 1945-Oct. 1945[e]	85,608	272,508	—	—	−186,900

[a] Movements to and from Okinawa and Karafuto are included as movements to and from territories.
[b] Based on censuses of October 1, 1930.
[c] Based on censuses of October 1, 1940.
[d] Based on censuses of February 22, 1944.
[e] This total includes the balance of movements from August 15, to October 30, 1945.

Source: Nihon. Sori-fu, tokei kyoku. *Taisho 9-nen—Showa 25-nen, waga kuni nenji betsu jinko no suikei*. P. 22.

Japanese had been fighting for periods ranging from eight to fourteen years.

The decision of the Allied Powers to effect compulsory repatriation of Japanese meant that 3.1 million civilians had to be moved back to a Japan that was now defined to exclude the Ryukyu Islands. The unconditional surrender of Imperial Japan left 3.5 million members of the armed forces abroad. In all, 6.6 million Japanese were abroad in the Co-Prosperity Sphere when Japan surrendered.

The liquidation of the Empire was a gigantic undertaking. All Japanese were to be returned to Japan, and all non-Japanese were to be offered repatriation. At the surrender, there were 1.6 million nationals of the former colonies in Japan, 1,241 thousand of them Koreans. There were also 65 thousand foreigners. In addition, there were people who had moved from the poor and crowded lands of the Ryukyu Islands to secure jobs in the more industrialized economies of Kyushu and Honshu. People from the colonies were scattered widely in other territories and occupied areas (TABLE 129). There are no accurate records of the citizens of the colonies and the Ryukyus who served with the Japanese armed forces, but reports on their activities in the various areas suggest that the numbers were considerable.

Many other peoples had moved as a result of the wars that began in Manchuria in 1931. Large numbers of Koreans had moved to industrial employment in the northern part of their own country and in Manchoukuo. There were millions of refugees in China. There had been substantial movements of laborers and refugees in Southeast Asia. Natives of island areas had been transferred to other areas to vacate land for military activities. Westerners had fled the East before the victorious armies of Japan or, failing to flee, spent the war years in internment camps. And there were, of course, the armies of the Allied Powers, Western and Asian.

In some areas living conditions were relatively good and the Japanese maintained amicable relations with the peoples they governed. Here repatriation went smoothly. In other areas there were great difficulties. In Java the Indonesians and the Japanese Army of Occupation alike were hungry and ill. In most areas Japanese troops were held together and moved as groups, some of them after long periods of waiting. Civilians were collected in groups and sent to embarkation points. For many, this meant going through areas where the hostility of residents was as understandable as it was bitter. There is a large literature on repatriation, but quantitative data are limited and inaccurate.

The Japanese returning home were loaded on ships of whatever types were available, moved to the nearest reception port, processed with health checks and DDT dustings, and given minimum clothing and supplies. The chronology of the movement is given in TABLE 130, the areas from which repatriation occurred in TABLE 131. As of January 1, 1950, there were 377 thousand Japanese reported as not repatriated, 237 thousand of them in Siberia, 79 thousand in Karafuto and the Kuriles, and 60 thousand in Manchuria. A report by the Japanese government to a special Committee of the United Nations on Prisoners of War gave a summary of the information on these missing people as of May 1, 1952:[40]

[40] Statement of Mr. Nishimura, Chief of the Treaty-Bureau, Foreign Ministry, Japanese Government, on Aug. 27, 1952. A more recent statement is that issued by the Embassy of Japan in the United States in *Japan Report*, Vol. I, No. 1, pp. 2-8. According to a statement by Mr. Sonoda, Parliamentary Vice-Minister for Foreign Affairs, there were 2.73 million Japanese nationals in Manchuria, North Korea, South Sakhalin, and the Kurile Islands at the end of the war. The U.S.S.R. transferred 575 thousand of them to camps in Siberia, Outer Mongolia, Central Asia, and other areas. Later a considerable number were moved to Manchuria and North Korea. Only 472 thousand Japanese were repatriated. Information secured from families by the Japanese indicated that those known to be alive and in the U.S.S.R., Sakhalin, or the

TABLE 129

Non-Japanese civilians repatriated from areas of the Co-Prosperity Sphere other than Japan

Area from which repatriated	*Total*	NATIONALITY				
		Koreans	*Taiwanese*	*Ryukyuans*	*South Sea Islanders*	*Chinese*
Total	199,057[a]	105,343	40,194	45,812	6	7,702
Ryukyu	1,778	1,757	21	—	—	—
Karafuto, Kuriles	55	55	—	—	—	—
Korea, South	1,924	—	91	274	—	1,559
Korea, North	54	—	12	42	—	—
Manchuria	11,609	11,609	—	—	—	—
Manchuria, Dairen	4	2	—	—	—	2
U.S.S.R., Siberia	154	150	4	—	—	—
China	58,924	58,924	—	—	—	—
Hong Kong	3,102	302	2,800	—	—	—
Hawaii	4,996	2,647	25	2,322	—	2
Taiwan	20,497	3,449	—	17,048	—	—
Pacific Ocean Islands	40,742	14,014	578	26,004	—	146
Philippines	19,399	1,408	11,998	—	—	5,993
Dutch Indonesia	542	454	82	—	6	—
Indo-China, Northern	135	120	15	—	—	—
Southeast Asia	25,507	7,401	17,984	122	—	—
Australian Army Zone	9,635	3,051	6,584	—	—	—

[a] The total was given as 199,066.
Source: Nihon. Hikiage engo-cho. *Hikiage engo no kiroku.* Pp. 84-85.

Area	*Number on Aug. 15, 1945*	*Living*	*Dead or unknown*
Total	346,397	81,288	245,427
Siberia and other U.S.S.R.	59,873	17,230	42,643
Karafuto and the Kuriles	11,168	2,622	7,612
North Korea	36,897	2,408	33,484
China	238,459	59,028	161,688

Between August 15, 1945, and the fall of 1950, repatriation contributed a net increase of 5 million people to Japan. Some 6.3 million Japanese were returned to Japan, while 1.2 million non-Japanese left Japan. Few Japanese remained abroad in the areas that had been the Co-Prosperity Sphere. As of 1952, perhaps 70 or 80 thousand Japanese who had been in the Japanese army survived in the prison camps of the Soviet Union. Japan itself retained substantial ethnic minorities, however, for the repatriation of Koreans was only partial and many who left Japan came back as illegal entrants. In 1950, 99.2 per cent of the total population of Japan were Japanese with *honseki* in Japan.[41] The other eight-tenths of 1 per cent included 467 thousand persons with *honseki* in Korea, 41 thousand with *honseki* in Karafuto, and 40 thousand Chinese. Many Ryukyuans had either failed to leave Japan at the end of the war or had returned, for 61 thousand people with *honseki* in Okinawa were enumerated in Japan in 1950. Other ethnic groups included only 23 thousand people.

Kuriles on May 1, 1955, numbered 12,642. In addition, there were known to be more than seven thousand Japanese nationals held in China.

[41] Nihon. Sori-fu, tokei-kyoku. *Showa 25-nen kokusei chosa hokoku.* III.1. Table 6.

Koreans were as numerous in Japan in 1950 as they had been in 1935. And in 1950, as in 1935, they were primarily a marginal economic group in industrial areas, particularly the great conurbations. In 1950 they constituted 1.2 per cent of the population in the metropolitan and other industrial prefectures, 0.8 per cent in the intermediate prefectures, 0.4 per cent in the agricultural prefectures, and 0.2 per cent in Hokkaido.

The major problems of the repatriates were similar to those of the general population of Japan, particularly of the refugees from the cities. Special factors which complicated life for them will be discussed separately for the military and the civilian repatriates.

About half the armed forces were outside Japan at the time of the surrender. These men became repatriates, but their problems of adjustment were those of the demobilized army and navy. Since the major groups in the armed forces were youth in their twenties, most of the ex-soldiers had families to which they could return. The literature includes many stories of the places that were held for absent sons and of the tragedy when the sons did not return. In the later years of the war many men were mobilized. Most of these men had families of their own, and again places were held for them. The women who tilled the fields and ran the shops presumably included many whose sons and husbands were in the armed forces.

Many of the men returned from the armed forces to find that their families had fled from destroyed urban areas. Economic problems were great, and there were no pensions or welfare benefits. In late 1945 and 1946 return to the large cities was forbidden. When return became possible, jobs were few and wages low. Adjustments were difficult for men who had been officers. The civilian positions they had left vanished

TABLE 130

Repatriation, civilian and military, October 1945-September 1950 (Numbers in '000)

Period	Net	To Japan[a]	From Japan[b]
Total	5,055	6,249	1,194
Oct. 1945-Sept. 1946	3,556	4,593	1,038
Oct. 1945	86	272	187
Nov. 1945-April 1946	1,546	2,308	762
May 1946-Sept. 1946	1,925	2,013	88
Oct. 1946-Sept. 1947	1,001	1,136	135
Oct. 1947-Sept. 1948	318	329	11
Oct. 1948-Sept. 1949	149	156	7
Oct. 1949-Sept. 1950	31	34	3

[a] Including Japanese from Okinawa, Karafuto, and other island areas removed from the jurisdiction of the government of Japan.
[b] Including Ryukyuans returning to the Ryukyu Islands (formerly Okinawa and part of Kagoshima).
Source: Nihon. Sori-fu, tokei-kyoku. *Taisho 9-nen—Showa 25-nen, waga kuni nenji betsu jinko no suikei.* P. 23. Data from SCAP, GHQ, Economic and Scientific Section.

with the defeat, and so readjustments began under difficult circumstances. The Health Centers secured physicians at low government salaries from among the men released from the medical corps of the armed forces, but other professional groups were not so fortunate.

Adjustments for some of the civilian repatriates were comparable to those of the demobilized soldiers. If men had gone abroad for temporary service in connection with the war, they might have retained places in the society and labor force in Japan. However, most of the civilian repatriates had thought that they were migrating permanently or for a long period of time. Many had been born in the colonial areas. All were adjusted to life in the upper classes of highly stratified societies. The men were trained for professional, executive, or managerial positions, not for labor. The women were trained for the life appropriate to the family status, not for the toil of the fields, the shops, or the factories. All of these people were returned to Japan with only what luggage they could carry. The assets they had accumulated in the area in which they had lived vanished with the defeat. On landing, they were sent to their place of *honseki* in Japan. Here there were no lands or jobs awaiting them, perhaps not even a lineal relative whose familial responsibilities included the provision of subsistence. There were no jobs in the cities. There was no land for sale or for rent, and practically none to reclaim on a squatter basis.

TABLE 131

Repatriated population, by military status and region, 1945-1952

Region	TO END OF 1952					PERIOD OF REPATRIATION		
			Armed forces					
	Total	Civilian	Total	Army	Navy	To end of 1946	1947-1950	1951-1952
Total[a]	6,251,439	3,152,752	3,098,687	2,843,061	255,626	5,096,323	1,153,585	1,531
U.S.S.R. Zone	1,311,472	806,803	504,669	499,702	4,967	321,208	990,245	19
Siberia	470,364	17,985	452,379	448,142	4,237	5,000	465,356	8
Karafuto, Kuriles	292,591	276,606	15,985	15,959	26	5,613	286,977	1
Dairen	225,962	215,045	10,917	10,449	468	6,126	219,833	3
North Korea	322,555	297,167	25,388	25,152	236	304,469	18,079	7
Manchuria	1,045,696	1,003,767	41,929	41,663	266	1,010,837	34,697	162
Mainland China	1,501,695	463,946	1,037,749	992,735	45,014	1,492,397	9,008	290
Hong Kong	19,242	4,981	14,261	9,784	4,477	19,050	173	19
South Korea	596,012	414,790	181,222	173,741	7,481	591,765	3,875	372
Taiwan	479,469	322,083	157,386	147,970	9,416	473,316	6,105	48
Islands near Japan	62,389	2,382	60,007	55,148	4,859	62,389	0	0
Ryukyu Islands	69,413	12,051	57,362	48,254	9,108	64,396	5,014	3
Indonesia	15,695	1,483	14,212	12,803	1,409	0	15,619	76
North Indochina	32,117	3,451	28,666	28,518	148	31,583	480	54
Pacific Islands	130,951	27,505	103,446	73,765	29,681	130,795	115	41
Philippines	132,966	24,207	108,759	94,941	13,818	132,303	627	36
Southeast Asia	711,120	56,137	654,983	561,307	93,676	623,909	86,916	295
Hawaii	3,667	318	3,349	3,309	40	3,411	185	71
Australia	138,738	8,442	130,296	99,198	31,098	138,167	526	45
New Zealand	797	406	391	223	168	797	0	0

[a] Repatriates from the United States, Canada, and South America are not included.
Source: Repatriation Section, Relief Bureau, Repatriation Relief Agency. Compiled and published in: Nihon. Sori-fu, tokei-kyoku. *Nihon tokei nenkan.* 1953. Pp. 50-51. Also, to end of 1949: Nihon. Hikiage engo-cho. *Hikiage engo no kiroku.*

The national government, prefectures, and minor civil divisions did what they could to alleviate the desperate situation. Army barracks became places of residence—for limited periods of time, it was hoped, but often they served this purpose for years. There was some resettlement in Hokkaido. There were community projects to facilitate the search for jobs, but the labor market of Japan was not able to absorb all the repatriates. Many of them who had been in the upper strata of Imperial Japan became marginal workers in postwar Japan.

In 1950 the census included a question on repatriate status, and the answers were tabulated for a 10 per cent sample of the population. These queries were asked during the military occupation of the country and apparently aroused suspicion as to the intended use of the data. Comparisons of known repatriates and reported repatriates are as follows, numbers being in thousands:[42]

Repatriates	*Total*	*Civilian*	*Military*
Transported	6,249	3,150	3,099
Enumerated in 1950	4,824	2,617	2,120
Difference	1,425	533	979

It is evident that the reports of repatriates in the 1950 census were incomplete, especially for former members of the armed forces.

The labor force status of the repatriates by occupation and industry is suggestive, but the repatriate groups differed so sharply from each other and from the general population in sex and age composition that conclusions must be tentative. Comparisons in the industrial composition of the labor force among all Japanese and among the repatriates are given here for *shi* and for *gun* in 1950:[43]

	SHI		GUN	
Industry	*All Japan*	*Repatriates*	*All Japan*	*Repatriates*
Total	100.	100.	100.	100.
Agriculture	12.8	6.8	61.3	41.5
Forestry and logging	0.2	0.3	1.6	2.4
Fisheries and aqua-culture	1.0	1.1	2.4	3.3
Mining	1.2	2.1	1.8	4.2
Construction	5.2	7.1	3.2	5.2
Manufacturing	27.7	25.6	10.1	13.4
Wholesale and retail trade	19.7	18.8	6.4	9.3
Finance, insurance, etc.	2.2	2.4	0.4	0.7
Transportation, communication, and other public utilities	8.1	10.8	3.6	6.3
Services	14.4	13.2	6.1	7.6
Government	7.3	11.2	2.7	5.8
Not classifiable and not reported	0.3	0.3	0.2	0.3

The repatriates were engaged in agriculture to a lesser extent than the general population, but the marked deficits of women would contribute toward this difference. The higher proportions of repatriates in construction and government may be due to the fact that men predominated in the repatriate labor force. On the whole, the data on labor-force participation, occupations, and industries of the repatriates in 1950 indicate that they were reabsorbed into the national economy in rough proportion to the structural divisions of that economy. If we remember the general upper-class social-economic composition of the civilian repatriates, this congruence with the general population confirms one's impressions that readjustment of the civilian repatriates involved major downward mobility.

There were major problems of adjustment among the repatriates. Some remained in barracks and subsisted on relief allowances or occasional labor for years after the end of the war. Most of them found some niche in the society and participated in reconstruction. As participants, the repatriates are part of the population that is considered in the following sections on reconstruction and the population balance of the decade from 1940 to 1950.

Restoration

In the late period of the war and the early period of the peace, the outlines of Japan's near future took shape. The U.S.S.R. occupied Karafuto and some of the Kuriles, together with Korea north of 38°. The United States retained the Ryukyu Islands. Japan was limited to the four main islands of Kyushu, Shikoku, Honshu, and Hokkaido. To these islands all the ethnic Japanese in Asia and Oceania were returned. In the view of those who had fought a militant Japan, it was essential to ensure that Japan should not again become a threat to other nations. She was to be denied industries that could form the basis for rearmament. The economy and the society of the mid-1930's were the target for the restoration. There were to be increases in crop yields and in cultivated land. There were plans for a population of 10 million in Hokkaido. Japan was to remain a semi-industrialized economy, characterized by widespread land ownership and by competition among small units in production and distribution.

The new order was signalized in the Imperial Rescript of

[42] Data on repatriates: Nihon. Sori-fu, tokei-kyoku. *Hikiage shin-kokusha su.* P. 3. The distinction is between "kyoryumin," those who resided overseas prior to the termination of the war, and military personnel plus civilians attached thereto.

[43] Data on age and on labor force status, occupation, and industry are published in broad age groups but the class intervals differ and interpolation in the age categories of the repatriates is hardly permissible in the absence of information as to expected age structures. Sources of data were as follows: All Japan: Nihon. Sori-fu, tokei-kyoku. *Showa 25-nen kokusei chosa hokoku.* III.2. Table 16. Repatriates: Nihon. Sori-fu, tokei-kyoku. *Hikiage shin-kokusha su.* P. 11.

January 1, 1946, in which the emperor denied his divinity and the inherent superiority of his people. In this same rescript, however, the emperor reaffirmed the charter-oath of the Emperor Meiji as the basis for the reconstruction of the "new" Japan. The five provisions of this oath merit restating in the light of subsequent developments:[44]

(1) Deliberative assemblies shall be established and all measures of government decided in accordance with public opinion.

(2) All classes, high and low, shall unite in vigorously carrying on the affairs of State.

(3) All common people, no less than the civil and military officials, shall be allowed to fulfill their just desires so that there may not be any discontent among them.

(4) All the absurd usages of old shall be broken through, and equity and justice to be found in the workings of nature shall serve as the basis of action.

(5) Wisdom and knowledge shall be sought throughout the world for the purpose of promoting the welfare of the Empire.

The most urgent problem in the latter part of 1945 and 1946 was to ensure the survival of the people. The situation has been described as one of incipient chaos. Nutrition was at the starvation level. There had been severe health deterioration. Cholera, plague, and other diseases were introduced with the repatriates. Damage to wealth was estimated by the Economic Stabilization Board as 25 per cent for general national wealth and 22 per cent for personal wealth.[45] Damage had been one-fourth for public buildings, one-third for machinery and equipment for industry, and four-fifths for shipping vessels. Damage to furniture and household belongings amounted to one-fifth. The percentage of housing units destroyed was 46 in Tokyo, 33 in Yokohama, 24 in Shizuoka, 27 in Aichi, 32 in Osaka, 28 in Hyogo, 23 in Hiroshima, 11 in Nagasaki, and 19 in Kagoshima.[46] The collapse in production between 1944 and 1945-1946 has already been noted.[47]

The story of the rapid restoration and extraordinary development of the Japanese physical plant and economic activity need not be retold here. The period from 1945 through 1947 was one of restoration and reform: the conquest of malnutrition by the importation of food and the rationing of an increasing local production; the control of disease and the improvement of health and medical facilities and practices; the change of institutional structures to form a democratic and equalitarian society. The great companies, the famous *zaibatsu*, were liquidated. There was comprehensive land reform. The new constitution provided for universal franchise, preservation of human rights, and repudiation of war. From 1948 through 1950 emphasis was placed on economic rehabilitation *per se* as the objective of the Occupation.[48] After the Korean War began in June 1950, there was a re-orientation to economic development in the industrial sector. In April 1952 the Occupation ended.

The restoration of the prewar patterns of population growth and distribution proceeded swiftly in the years from 1945 to 1950. Estimates of population change between 1945 and 1950 will be considered first. These numbers are only approximate, for numbers of registered vital events and reported repatriates were subject to considerable error, particularly in 1945 and 1946. There were omissions in the 1945 count, and there were many illegal entries, particularly of Koreans. The following estimates are in thousands:[49]

Population, November 1, 1945, adjusted			72,150
Natural change			
Births	12,075		
Deaths	−5,376		
Net addition			6,699
Migration			
Return of armed forces		3,099	
Civilian repatriation		3,150	
Movements from Japan		−1,194	
Movements in Oct. 1945		−86	
Net addition			4,969
Adjustment, errors in components			−616
Population, October 1, 1950			83,200

The net increase in population in the five years after the end of the war amounted to 11,050 thousand. In view of the amount of attention that has been paid to repatriation as a factor of increase, further inspection of the components of growth is justified. If there had been no civilian repatriation, only the armed forces would have been returned to Japan. In this case, the population growth would have been somewhat as follows, numbers being in thousands:

Population, November 1, 1945, adjusted	72,150
Natural increase	6,699[50]
Return of armed forces	3,099
Adjustment, errors in components	−616[51]
Population, October 1, 1950	81,330

The actual population of Japan on October 1, 1950, was 82.3 million. Without the repatriation of civilians, the population would have been 81.3 million. Two million of the total increase of 11 million, less than one-fifth of the total, was due to the net balance of civilian repatriation. Three million, almost three-tenths, of the total increase was due to the return of the men who had been in the armed forces.

The repatriated civilian Japanese were somewhat less balanced in sex and age composition than the home population, but somewhat more balanced than the Korean population repatriated from Japan to Korea. The three million or more members of the armed forces returned from abroad plus the 3.5 million demobilized in Japan contributed greatly to the restoration of a fairly normal balance in age composition and sex ratios in the civilian population of Japan. In TABLE 132 the age structures are presented in summary form from the censuses of 1945, 1946, 1947, and 1950.

The sex ratio for the civilian population in Japan on February 22, 1944, was 902. On November 1, 1945, after the de-

[44] SCAP, GHQ. *Summation. . . . Non-military activities in Japan and Korea. . . .* No. 4, January 1946. Pp. 20-21.
[45] Nihon. Sori-fu, tokei-kyoku. *Nihon tokei nenkan,* 1949. Section XXVII.
[46] SCAP, GHQ. *Summation. . . . Non-military Activities in Japan.* No. 11, August 1946. P. 90.
[47] See Chapter IV, pp. 61-63.
[48] See Chapter V, and especially Table 30. For a summary, see: Fine, Sherwood M. *Japan's postwar industrial recovery.*

[49] Source: Nihon. Sori-fu, tokei-kyoku. *Taisho 9-nen—Showa 25-nen, wagakuni nenji betsu jinko no suikei.* Table 5.
[50] If there had been no civilian repatriation, the net natural increase would have been somewhat smaller than this figure.
[51] Again, under the assumed altered conditions, the errors in official statistics would have been somewhat different.

TABLE 132

The population of postwar Japan, by sex and age, 1945-1950

Age	Total	Male	Female	Excess of females	Males per 1,000 females
	NUMBER (IN '000)				
			November 1, 1945[a]		
All Japan	71,998	33,894	38,104	4,210	890
Under 16	26,477	13,388	13,089	−298	1,023
16-20	7,821	3,849	3,971	122	969
21-35	14,327	5,433	8,894	3,460	611
36-50	11,985	5,859	6,125	266	957
51-65	7,688	3,801	3,888	87	978
66 and over	3,700	1,563	2,137	573	732
			April 26, 1946[a]		
All Japan	73,114	34,905	38,209	3,305	914
Under 16	25,284	12,777	12,507	−271	1,022
16-20	8,010	3,977	4,033	55	986
21-35	15,734	6,592	9,142	2,550	721
36-50	12,346	6,019	6,327	308	951
51-65	7,864	3,898	3,967	69	983
66 and over	3,876	1,641	2,234	593	735
			October 1, 1947[b]		
All Japan	78,101	38,129	39,972	1,843	954
Under 15	27,573	13,945	13,629	−316	1,023
15-19	8,264	4,145	4,119	−25	1,006
20-34	17,701	8,154	9,547	1,393	854
35-49	12,933	6,404	6,528	124	981
50-64	7,886	3,913	3,973	59	985
65 and over	3,745	1,568	2,176	608	721
			October 1, 1950[b]		
All Japan	83,200	40,812	42,388	1,576	963
Under 15	29,428	14,944	14,484	−461	1,032
15-19	8,568	4,318	4,250	−67	1,016
20-34	19,113	9,018	10,095	1,077	893
35-49	13,536	6,594	6,942	348	950
50-64	8,442	4,208	4,234	27	994
65 and over	4,114	1,731	2,383	653	726

[a] Lunar ages.
[b] Western ages.
Source: 1945 and 1946: Nihon. Sori-fu, tokei-kyoku. *Kekka hokoku tekiyo, . . . Showa 20-nen jinko chosa, Showa 21-nen jinko chosa.* 1947: *Ibid. Showa 22-nen rinji kokusei chosa kekka hokoku.* No. 7. 1950: *Ibid. Showa 25-nen kokusei chosa hokoku.* III.1.

mobilization of the armed forces, the sex ratio was only 890. With the return of men from abroad there was an upward movement—to 914 on April 26, 1946, 954 on October 1, 1947, and 963 on October 1, 1950. By the latter date practically all men who would be returned were present in Japan. The deficits of men in 1950 were scars that could be erased only by the aging of the population and its replacement by new cohorts untouched by the mortality of war.

The scars of the Pacific War and the upward movement of the cohorts depleted by war are seen in the sex ratios of the age groups from 1944 to 1950. By the latter date practically all ethnic Japanese in the former Co-Prosperity Sphere had been returned to Japan. The following ratios are those of males per 1,000 females.[52]

[52] Source: References, Tables 127 and 132. The ages for 1944, 1945, and 1946 are in lunar form.

Age	*1944*	*1945*	*1946*	*1947*	*1950*
15-19	952	969	986	1,006	1,016
20-34	632	611	721	854	893
20-24	516	588	783	909	986
25-29	652	570	622	782	839
30-34	761	684	747	860	830
35-49	1,007	957	951	981	950

At the end of the war, civilians in Japan were dispersed in accordance with the patterns of their flight from the bombing targets or their exodus prior to the bombings. Their return began quickly and continued despite SCAP's prohibition of movement into cities of 100 thousand and over. The movements of women between 1945 and 1946 have already been given in summary form in Table 127. In TABLE 133 redistribution is summarized for the decade from 1940 to 1950, through a comparison of 1947 and 1950 with 1940, and then a comparison of 1950 with 1947. All ages are in Western reckoning; all censuses were relatively complete and accurate. The limitation to women largely eliminates the influence of demobilization and lessens the influence of civilian repatriation and war mortality. The data need not be described or interpreted in detail, for this restoration of the Japanese urbanization was analyzed in Chapter VII.

THE BALANCE OF THE DECADE

The analysis of the demography of the decade of the 1940's has been segmented by subject and by time period. Consideration was given first to the armed forces and the population behind the front in the years from 1940 to 1945, then to exodus and repatriation as civilian and military movements, and finally to the restoration from 1945 to 1950. The changes in natural increase and migration from 1940 to 1950 are summarized in TABLE 134, the basic distinction being that between the five years of war and the five years of peace. Summary for the decade as a whole yields the following balance of changes, the areas being those of 1950 and the numbers in thousands:

Components of change	*1940-1945*	*1945-1950*	*1940-1950*
Births	10,899	12,075	22,974
Deaths	6,891	5,376	12,267
Natural increase	4,008	6,699	10,707
Net emigration	−3,233	—	—
Net immigration	—	4,969	1,736
Adjustment	5	−616	−611
Net change	780	11,052	11,832

For both the years of war and those of peace, natural increase was very substantial. The major difference between the two periods was the exodus of armed forces and civilians in the war years, the return of armed forces and civilians in the years of peace. The major population increases in the postwar as contrasted with the prewar years were associated with the continuation of high levels of fertility, the limited mortality of the war years, and the rapidly declining mortality of the postwar years.

The war was a disturbance to the Japanese population rather than a catastrophe. If there were changes in the trends toward urbanization, declining fertility, and declining mortality, they were not apparent during the late 1940's and they are not yet apparent in the 1950's.

In these final sections, the balances of the decade will be surveyed as they relate to urbanization, natural increase, and changes in the population in the productive ages.

URBANIZATION

The growth of cities during the prewar and early war years, the flights of the late war years, and the returns after the war have been noted earlier as aspects of the concentration, dispersion, and restoration of the distribution pattern of the 1940's. The major analysis was based on a classification of prefectures by industrial type, however, and so pertained more directly to industrialization than to urbanization. In FIGURE 25 the distribution of the population is given by size of commune at each census from 1920 to 1950, together with the intercensal changes and the percentage compositions. The limitations are obvious, for incorporations alter the status of areas with or without changes in the characteristics of the areas. Increasing population pushes communes into classes of higher size without changes in the area distribution of the population. The broad picture is a striking one, however, especially for those who anticipated that the great Japanese cities would never again achieve their prewar size.

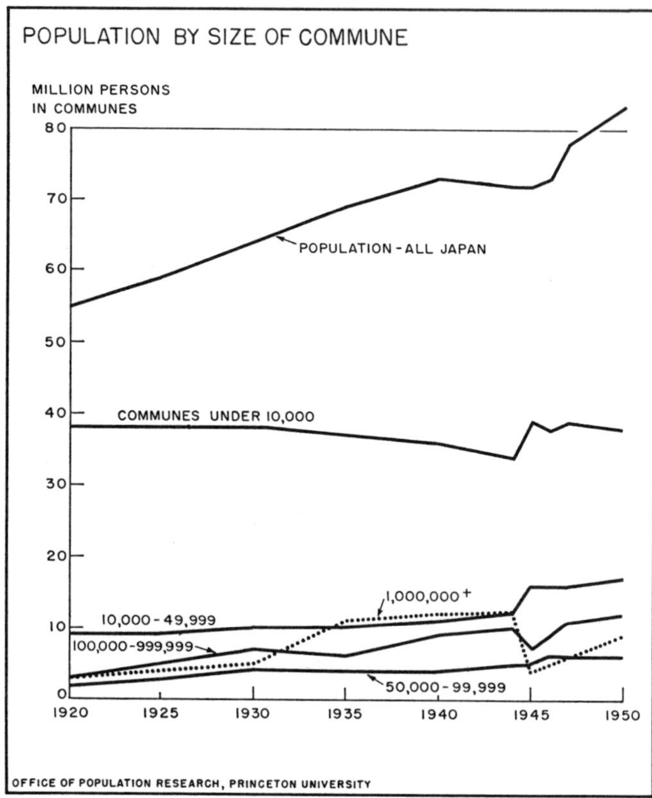

Figure 25. Population by size of commune, 46 prefectures, 1920-1950

Source: Nihon. Sori-fu, tokei-kyoku. *Showa 25-nen kokusei chosa hokoku.* I. Table 6.

In the prewar years, communes below 10 thousand in population retained relatively constant populations or declined. Growth occurred in the cities, especially those of 100 thousand and over. From 1940 to 1944 the growth of the larger communes continued. but there was decline at the peripheries of the size distribution, in the rural communes below 10 thousand and in the great cities above 1 million. There was rapid increase in medium-sized cities, those of from 50 to 99 thousand. In this category were the satellite cities that were

TABLE 133

The female population of the prefectures: years of restoration

Age	NUMBERS (IN '000) Oct. 1, 1940	Oct. 1, 1947	Oct. 1, 1950	RATIO TO 1940 AS 100 Oct. 1, 1947	Oct. 1, 1950	RATIO TO 1947 AS 100 Oct. 1, 1950
All Japan						
Total	36,231	39,972	42,409	110	117	106
0-4	4,468	4,764	5,488	107	123	115
5-14	8,460	8,865	9,019	105	107	102
15-19	3,670	4,119	4,243	112	116	103
20-34	8,248	9,547	10,093	116	122	106
35-49	5,528	6,528	6,938	118	127	106
50-64	3,889	3,973	4,238	102	109	107
65 and over	1,968	2,176	2,393	111	122	110
Metropolitan						
Total	5,888	4,135	5,065	70	86	122
0-4	689	469	619	68	90	132
5-14	1,190	808	964	68	81	119
15-19	699	426	506	61	72	119
20-34	1,698	1,116	1,382	66	81	124
35-49	908	769	916	85	101	119
50-64	502	389	475	78	95	122
65 and over	202	158	203	78	100	128
Other industrial						
Total	6,610	6,758	7,393	102	112	109
0-4	803	810	950	101	118	117
5-14	1,468	1,441	1,510	98	103	105
15-19	706	682	744	97	105	109
20-34	1,639	1,664	1,819	102	111	109
35-49	1,009	1,152	1,249	114	124	108
50-64	659	663	730	101	111	110
65 and over	325	345	391	106	120	113
Intermediate						
Total	10,672	12,859	13,201	120	124	103
0-4	1,264	1,494	1,662	118	132	111
5-14	2,534	2,826	2,799	112	110	99
15-19	1,021	1,315	1,291	129	126	98
20-34	2,252	2,993	3,026	133	134	101
35-49	1,650	2,102	2,185	127	132	104
50-64	1,259	1,333	1,386	106	110	104
65 and over	691	795	852	115	123	107
Agricultural						
Total	11,483	14,300	14,620	124	127	102
0-4	1,486	1,726	1,930	116	130	112
5-14	2,856	3,324	3,253	116	114	98
15-19	1,072	1,488	1,479	139	138	99
20-34	2,295	3,305	3,346	144	146	101
35-49	1,746	2,220	2,277	127	130	103
50-64	1,336	1,437	1,478	108	111	103
65 and over	692	801	861	116	124	107

TABLE 133 (continued)

The female population of the prefectures: years of restoration

Age	NUMBERS (IN '000) Oct. 1, 1940	Oct. 1, 1947	Oct. 1, 1950	RATIO TO 1940 AS 100 Oct. 1, 1947	Oct. 1, 1950	RATIO TO 1947 AS 100 Oct. 1, 1950
			Hokkaido			
Total	1,577	1,919	2,129	122	135	111
0-4	226	264	327	117	145	124
5-14	411	466	493	113	120	106
15-19	172	209	223	122	130	107
20-34	363	469	520	129	143	111
35-49	215	285	311	133	145	109
50-64	133	150	169	113	127	112
65 and over	56	76	86	136	154	113

Source: References, Tables 125 and 132.

TABLE 134

Changes in population in Japan, 46 prefectures, October 1, 1940-September 30, 1950 (Numbers in '000)

Period	Total population (beginning of period)	NATURAL INCREASE Births	Deaths	Natural increase	MIGRATION Civilian	Armed forces	Total	Adjustment	Net change
OCT. 1, 1940-OCT. 31, 1945	—	(10,899)	(6,891)	(4,008)	(550)	(−3,869)	(−3,233)	(5)	(780)
Oct. 1, 1940-Feb. 21, 1944	—	(7,715)	(3,971)	(3,744)	(204)	(−1,473)	(−1,269)	(−19)	(2,455)
Oct. 1, 1940-Sept. 30, 1941	71,400	2,239	1,139	1,099	−98	−714	−813	−6	281
Oct. 1, 1941-Sept. 30, 1942	71,600	2,296	1,157	1,140	48	−523	−475	−6	659
Oct. 1, 1942-Sept. 30, 1943	72,300	2,201	1,198	1,003	159	−143	16	−6	1,014
Oct. 1, 1943-Feb. 21, 1944	73,300	979	477	502	96	−94	2	−2	501
Feb. 22, 1944-Oct. 31, 1945	—	(3,185)	(2,920)	(265)	(346)	(−2,395)	(−1,964)	(24)	(−1,676)
Feb. 22, 1944-Sept. 30, 1944	73,800	1,282	773	509	140	−641	−502	8	16
Oct. 1, 1944-Aug. 14, 1945	73,800	1,544	1,722	−178	206	−1,754	−1,548	13	−1,712
Aug. 15, 1945-Oct. 31, 1945	72,100	358	425	−67	—	—	86	2	21
NOV. 1, 1945-SEPT. 30, 1950	—	(12,075)	(5,376)	(6,699)	—	—	(4,969)	(−616)	(11,052)
Nov. 1, 1945-April 25, 1946	72,150	757	751	6	—	—	1,546	−30	1,522
April 26, 1946-Sept. 30, 1947	—	(3,443)	(1,782)	(1,661)	—	—	(2,926)	(−154)	(4,432)
April 26, 1946-Sept. 30, 1946	73,670	819	618	201	—	—	1,925	−45	2,081
Oct. 1, 1946-Sept. 30, 1947	75,750	2,623	1,164	1,460	—	—	1,001	−109	2,352
Oct. 1, 1947-Sept. 30, 1950	—	(7,876)	(2,844)	(5,032)	—	—	(498)	(−432)	(5,098)
Oct. 1, 1947-Sept. 30, 1948	78,101	2,718	986	1,732	—	—	318	−144	1,905
Oct. 1, 1948-Sept. 30, 1949	80,010	2,711	943	1,768	—	—	149	−144	1,773
Oct. 1, 1949-Sept. 30, 1950	81,780	2,447	915	1,532	—	—	31	−144	1,419
Oct. 1, 1950	83,200	—	—	—	—	—	—	—	—

Source: Nihon. Sori-fu, tokei-kyoku. *Taisho 9-nen—Showa 25-nen, wagakuni nenji betsu jinko no suikei.* P. 19.

centers of war production and the nearby cities that were areas for dispersion. Between 1944 and 1945 it was the great cities from which people fled. Cities of a million and over had only one-third the population on November 1, 1945, that they had had on February 22, 1944. Cities of from 100 thousand to 999 thousand lost almost three-tenths of their total population in this brief period. From 1945 onward, however, there was a restoration and even an intensification of the prewar and early war trend. The largest relative increases occurred in the great cities of a million and more; the next largest increases occurred in cities of 100 thousand and over. The population in communes of 10 thousand and less declined, though the rate of the out-movement was small in relation to the increases that had occurred between 1944 and 1946.

In the prewar years, the movements of people were so massive that smaller and smaller proportions of the total population lived in the communes below 10 thousand, while ever-increasing proportions lived in the communes of 100 thousand and over. Even the wartime exodus from the cities was not sufficient to recreate an agrarian Japan. The proportion of the population in communes of 10 thousand or less was 54.8 on November 1, 1945; it had been 59.4 on October 1, 1930. After 1945 the percentage in the small communes declined rapidly until in 1950 it was 46.1. In absolute terms, however, the exodus from the communes of 10 thousand and below was not sufficient to drain off the very rapid natural increase and compensate for the refugees and repatriates who came in during 1944 and later years. In 1950, cities of 100 thousand and over had not recovered the numbers they had had in the period from 1935 to 1944, despite the rapidity of the return migrations. Relative increase had occurred in the number of people in the smaller communes, those with a population of from 10 to 100 thousand.

The role of the smaller *shi* in the absorption of refugees and repatriates is even more apparent in a classification of areas as *gun* and *shi*, with the six great cities segregated from the other *shi* (TABLE 135). In the years of flight, the lesser *shi* changed little in total numbers, since they received refugees from the great cities and contributed young people to the armed forces and war industries. The great cities lost, the *gun* gained. From 1946 to 1947 the great cities gained 2.7 million, the lesser cities 3.2 million, the *gun* only 268 thousand. In

TABLE 135

The population of the six great cities, other *shi*, and *gun*, 46 prefectures, 1940-1950

Age	SIX GREAT CITIES				OTHER SHI				GUN			
	1940	*1945*	*1947*	*1950*	*1940*	*1945*	*1947*	*1950*	*1940*	*1945*	*1947*	*1950*
	Population (in '000)											
Total	14,359	6,348	9,017	11,188	13,102	13,674	16,841	20,015	45,039	51,976	52,244	51,998
0-4	1,652	639	1,015	1,393	1,547	1,691	2,073	2,695	5,848	6,920	6,573	7,115
5-14	2,849	1,155	1,742	2,128	2,924	3,068	3,620	4,185	11,316	13,004	12,549	11,943
15-19	1,818	779	959	1,161	1,553	1,558	1,846	2,081	3,994	5,484	5,459	5,307
20-34	4,123	1,496	2,391	3,001	3,267	2,912	4,118	4,905	9,214	9,919	11,193	11,163
35-49	2,340	1,353	1,745	2,033	2,094	2,440	2,933	3,404	6,942	8,192	8,255	8,099
50-64	1,189	725	896	1,104	1,231	1,421	1,597	1,911	5,186	5,543	5,393	5,429
65 and over	388	202	268	368	487	585	654	834	2,540	2,912	2,823	2,942
	Amount of change (in '000)											
Total	—	−8,011	2,668	2,171	—	572	3,167	3,174	—	6,937	268	−246
0-4	—	−1,012	376	378	—	144	382	622	—	1,072	−347	542
5-14	—	−1,694	587	386	—	144	553	565	—	1,689	−455	−606
15-19	—	−1,039	181	202	—	5	288	235	—	1,490	−25	−152
20-34	—	−2,628	895	610	—	−355	1,206	787	—	706	1,273	−30
35-49	—	−987	392	288	—	345	493	471	—	1,250	62	−156
50-64	—	−464	172	208	—	190	176	314	—	357	−150	36
65 and over	—	−185	65	100	—	99	69	180	—	372	−90	119
	Per cent change											
Total	—	−55.8	42.0	24.1	—	4.4	23.2	18.8	—	15.4	.5	−.5
0.4	—	−61.3	58.9	37.2	—	9.3	22.6	30.0	—	18.3	−5.0	8.2
5-14	—	−59.5	50.9	22.2	—	4.9	18.0	15.6	—	14.9	−3.5	−4.8
15-19	—	−57.2	23.2	21.1	—	.3	18.5	12.7	—	37.3	−.5	−2.8
20-34	—	−63.7	59.8	25.5	—	−10.9	41.4	19.1	—	7.6	12.8	−.3
35-49	—	−42.2	29.0	16.5	—	16.5	20.2	16.0	—	18.0	.8	−1.9
50-64	—	−39.0	23.7	23.2	—	15.4	12.4	19.7	—	6.9	−2.7	.7
65 and over	—	−47.7	32.2	37.4	—	20.3	11.8	27.5	—	14.6	−3.1	4.2

Source: References, Tables 125 and 132.

relative terms, the great cities gained 42 per cent, the lesser cities 23.2 per cent, the *gun* 0.5 per cent. From 1947 to 1950 the *gun* lost almost a quarter of a million people, while the great cities gained 2.2 million, the lesser cities 3.2 million.

The rearrangements of the years from 1945 to 1947 were products of the emergency moves of those who had left dangerous areas or had been returned to the country. The changes from 1947 to 1950 occurred during a period of industrial growth; they indicated the directions in which people moved when they had an opportunity to choose.

The differences between the population enumerated in 1935 and the population expected in that year without migration after 1920 give a picture of the "normal" structure of migration in Japan. In the following data, these differences between enumerated and expected populations are expressed as percentages of the expected population. Males only are considered:

Prefectures by industrial type	*Age in 1935*				
	15 and over	*15-19*	*20-34*	*35-49*	*50-64*
Metropolitan	44.2	115.9	76.0	8.4	0.5
Other industrial	7.1	14.8	13.7	−0.2	−0.5
Intermediate	−10.1	−20.4	−19.4	−0.1	2.5
Agricultural	−11.3	−19.8	−21.9	1.0	2.0
Hokkaido	−4.7	−4.1	−0.4	−9.4	−10.5

If urbanization had continued as a normal aspect of an industrializing economy from 1935 to 1950, the distribution and structure of the populations in 1950 would have differed greatly from the ones which actually existed in that year. The following figures are comparisons of the enumerated population of men in 1950 with the numbers expected in the absence of migration or war. Differences are again expressed as percentages of the expected populations:

Prefectures by industrial type	*Age in 1950*				
	15 and over	*15-19*	*20-34*	*35-49*	*50-64*
Metropolitan	−25.1	−10.1	−17.7	−37.9	−27.1
Other industrial	−6.1	−7.0	−10.6	−4.9	1.9
Intermediate	−1.9	1.8	−14.3	5.0	8.8
Agricultural	−2.0	1.7	−15.6	9.2	9.3
Hokkaido	1.1	4.2	−2.2	0.4	1.5

The differences between enumerated and expected populations for men reflect the combined influences of war mortality, repatriation, and retarded urbanization. In order to illustrate the cessation of internal movements that had occurred in the decade of the 1940's, summary data are presented for women. Again the figures are the differences between enumerated and expected populations in 1950 expressed as percentages of the expected populations:

Prefectures by industrial type	*All women aged 15 and over*		*Women aged 15-19*	
	1920-1935	*1935-1950*	*1920-1935*	*1935-1950*
Metropolitan	42.8	−18.1	87.7	−13.7
Other industrial	8.2	0.5	21.0	4.0
Intermediate	−9.0	4.2	−13.9	3.4
Agricultural	−9.9	4.0	−18.5	2.0
Hokkaido	−6.6	5.9	−7.9	6.0

NATURAL INCREASE IN JAPAN[53]

The increased separation of the sexes, the deterioration in living conditions, the exodus of families under difficult living and housing conditions, and the growing apathy as war continued all contributed to declines in fertility. Since these declines became manifest in reported live births by mid-1944, they reflected lessened conceptions and increased pregnancy wastage in the period from late 1943 onward. Deaths were increasing in late 1944 also, especially those associated with malnutrition. In 1945 there were major civilian fatalities from the military actions of the Allied Powers, particularly in the strategic industrial areas and the great cities of Japan itself. For the areas that reported, the ratios of deaths to births by months in the years from 1943 through 1946 are given in FIGURE 26. Ratios for the year 1937 are included for comparative purposes.[54]

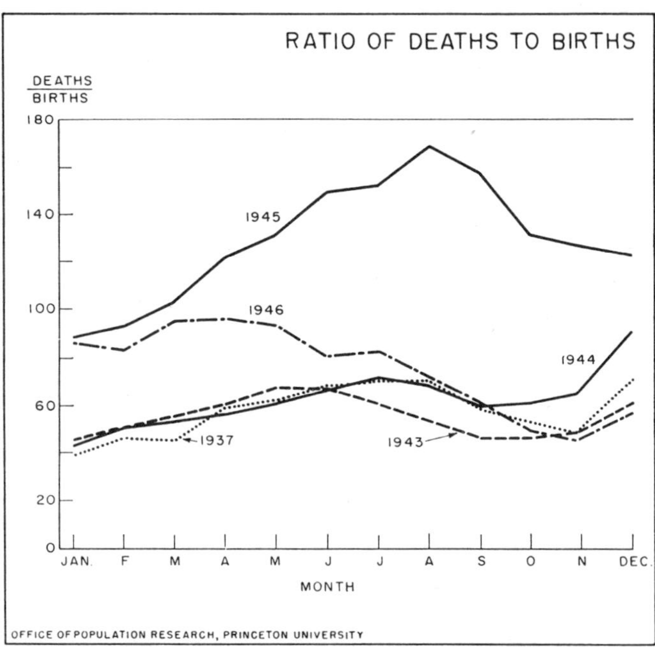

Figure 26. Ratio of deaths to births by months in the war period
Source: Nihon. Kosei-sho, eisei tokei-bu. *Jinko dotai tokei*. 1946. Part 1. Tables 2 and 3 and Appendix 2.

[53] The *koseki* system remained largely intact within Japan and reporting procedures operated as usual throughout most of the year 1944 and even in the spring of 1945. The data for the year 1943 were collected and tabulated in 1944. The bombings of 1945 destroyed major portions of the records of urban areas for the year 1944, and the national statistical system was largely ineffective in 1945. National reporting was resumed in sufficient detail to enable summations to be published for the third and fourth quarters of 1946. Annual reports were resumed in 1947. The task here is limited. It involves the reconstruction of the levels of fertility and mortality in the years from 1944 to 1946. Then there is the question of the deaths of Japanese in the war years, whether within or outside Japan, whether from military or non-military causes. Finally, there is the question of the balance of the decade from 1940 to 1950.

[54] The Cabinet Bureau of Statistics issued a report on June 4, 1946, giving the available data for the period from 1944 through 1945. An analysis of these and other materials is presented in: Tachi, Minoru. *Nihon jinko no shorai*. Pp. 30-35. The number of prefectures reporting varied from one month to another. For December 1945, only 12 prefectures were included: Miyagi, Yamagata, Fukushima, Gumma, Fukui, Nagano, Hyogo, Tottori, Yamaguchi, Kochi, Saga, and Miyazaki. These were primarily rural prefectures, and ones in which bomb damage and direct war destruction were minimal. Moreover, they were not the prefectures into whose ports returning soldiers and civilians were re-introducing the diseases of the region that had long been under control within the country. The ratios of deaths to births given here for 1945 and the first six months of 1946 are computed from data re-

On an annual basis, the ratio of deaths to births was 53.9 in 1943, slightly below the ratio of 55.4 in 1937. There was some deterioration in the early months of 1944; after the middle of 1944 there was continuing deterioration. By March 1945 deaths of civilians exceeded births even in the rural prefectures; if Tokyo had been included in this month when 90 thousand people died, the ratio would have been far higher. By August 1945 the ratio had risen to 154 for the rural prefectures and 168 for all prefectures. Food importation and emergency medical services resulted in rapid improvements after the Occupation began. By December 1945 the death-birth ratio was down to about the level of April 1945. By August 1946 the ratio was roughly "normal." By December 1946 it was considerably below the level for the same month either in 1937 or in 1943.

Ratios of deaths to births give only a rough picture of the effects of the war in its climatic years. The population surveys help little, for enumeration in 1945 or 1946 did not attain the level of accuracy characteristic of the regular censuses. The numbers of survivors to specified ages does not permit a separation of the effects of lowered fertility and increased mortality. However, Japan did not experience declines in fertility such as those that produced the smaller cohorts of the European nations in World War I. Sharply lowered numbers of births and greatly increased rates of infant mortality characterized a period lasting two years at most. Numbers of survivors by single years of age in 1950 show this clearly:[55]

Age on Oct. 1, 1950	*Survivors of births during*	*Number (in '000)*	*Per 1,000 total population*
0	Oct. 1, 1949-Sept. 30, 1950	2,316	27.8
1	Oct. 1, 1948-Sept. 30, 1949	2,523	30.3
2	Oct. 1, 1947-Sept. 30, 1948	2,480	29.8
3	Oct. 1, 1946-Sept. 30, 1947	2,347	28.2
4	Oct. 1, 1945-Sept. 30, 1946	1,540	18.5
5	Oct. 1, 1944-Sept. 30, 1945	1,640	19.7
6	Oct. 1, 1943-Sept. 30, 1944	1,991	23.9
7	Oct. 1, 1942-Sept. 30, 1943	1,934	23.2
8	Oct. 1, 1941-Sept. 30, 1942	1,987	23.9

The Division of Health and Welfare Statistics of the Welfare Ministry collected all available information on deaths in the years 1945 and 1946 and computed life tables.[56] It is obvious that mortality at the levels of these years would not characterize a cohort passing through life. However, the results state the costs of the last year of the war and the first year of the peace in striking form.[57] In 1945 the expectation of life at birth was 23.9 for males, 37.5 for females. The comparable expectations for 1946 were 42.6 and 51.1. Life table death rates per 1,000 population were as follows:

	Males		*Females*	
Age	*1945*	*1946*	*1945*	*1946*
0	198.7	124.7	156.9	96.5
1	56.6	29.9	42.8	24.4
2	29.5	19.5	22.2	16.1
3	22.8	13.0	17.2	10.7
4	14.2	8.5	10.6	7.1
5-9	60.8	22.2	45.0	18.3
10-14	50.7	12.9	39.3	12.4
15-19	115.9	32.1	72.9	27.2
20-24	280.9	69.1	80.1	42.6
25-29	255.1	72.7	72.2	43.1
30-34	196.2	65.7	69.5	41.1
35-39	166.3	64.8	76.0	43.5
40-44	134.4	69.0	79.2	45.9

There is no estimate of the numbers of the armed forces who died as a result of the raids on Japan, but there are estimates of the number of civilians who died in Japan as a result of "military action." In 1949 the Bureau of Statistics reported the total number as 289 thousand.[58] Major areas of death were Tokyo (97,031), Kanagawa (6,637), Shizuoka (6,473), Aichi (11,324), Osaka (11,089), Hyogo (11,246), Hiroshima (86, 141), and Nagasaki (26,238).

Analysis of the births and deaths within Japan from 1940 to 1950 indicates that increased births and reduced deaths from 1947 to 1950 compensated for the reduced births and the increased deaths from 1943 to 1946.[59] The annual recorded or estimated births and civilian deaths are as follows, numbers being in thousands:[60]

Date	*Births*	*Civilian deaths*	*Natural increase*
Oct. 1, 1940-Sept. 30, 1941	2,239	1,139	1,099
Oct. 1, 1941-Sept. 30, 1942	2,296	1,157	1,140
Oct. 1, 1942-Sept. 30, 1943	2,201	1,198	1,003
Oct. 1, 1943-Sept. 30, 1944	2,261	1,250	1,011
Oct. 1, 1943-Feb. 21, 1944	979	477	502
Feb. 22, 1944-Sept. 30, 1944	1,282	773	509
Oct. 1, 1944-Oct. 31, 1945	1,902	2,147	−245
Oct. 1, 1944-Aug. 14, 1945	1,544	1,722	−178
Aug. 15, 1945-Oct. 31, 1945	358	425	−67
Nov. 1, 1945-Sept. 30, 1946	1,576	1,369	207

ported by the Department of Health Statistics of the Ministry of Welfare. Nihon. Kosei-sho, eisei tokei-bu. *Jinko dotai tokei. 1946.* Part 1. Tables 2 and 3 and Appendix 2. See Footnote 57 for an explanation of 1945 and 1946 vital statistics.

[55] Nihon. Sori-fu, tokei-kyoku. *Showa 25-nen kokusei chosa hokoku.* IV.

[56] Nihon. Kosei-sho, eisei tokei-bu. *The abridged life tables 1948.* Appendix.

[57] The figures for January-June 1945 include births of previous years and abandoned children. Deaths of the previous years, disappearances, war deaths, deaths from injuries, and illnesses are all included in the reports on deaths. Births to and deaths of Japanese outside Japan are included, as well as those few events reported for colonials and foreigners within Japan. The vital events for the last half of 1945 are those reported by the heads of *shi, machi,* and *mura* to the prefectural governors; reported events were included regardless of specific time or place of occurrence. The same regulations governed the collection of vital statistics in the first half of 1946. Hence the data of the life tables include all military deaths that were reported in Japan, though the deaths may have occurred at earlier periods, and outside Japan. For a detailed explanation of procedures, see: Nihon. Kosei-sho, eisei tokei-bu. *Jinko dotai tokei.* Part 1, Introduction.

[58] Nihon. Sori-fu, tokei-kyoku. *Jinko tokei nenkan. 1949.* Table 607. A sample survey conducted by the Morale Division of the Strategic Bombing Survey, using Japanese sources, estimated 333 thousand dead. See: U.S. Strategic Bombing Survey. *The effects of atomic bombing on health and medical services in Hiroshima and Nagasaki.* Pp. 1-2. The estimate of the Bureau of Statistics included civilians only, and since Hiroshima was a staging area, military dead from the atomic blast may have been substantial.

[59] The mortality of the armed forces and of the repatriates prior to repatriation are excluded from the data on which this generalization is based.

[60] Nihon. Sori-fu, tokei-kyoku. *Taisho 9-nen—Showa 25-nen, wagakuni nenji betsu jinko no suikei.* P. 19.

Date	Births	Civilian deaths	Natural increase
Nov. 1, 1945-April 25, 1946	757	751	6
April 26, 1946-Sept. 30, 1946	819	618	201
Oct. 1, 1946-Sept. 30, 1947	2,623	1,164	1,460
Oct. 1, 1947-Sept. 30, 1948	2,718	986	1,732
Oct. 1, 1948-Sept. 30, 1949	2,711	943	1,768
Oct. 1, 1949-Sept. 30, 1950	2,447	915	1,532
Total, Oct. 1, 1940-Sept. 30, 1950	22,974	12,267	10,707

A straight line fitted to the female fertility ratios from 1920 to 1937 and projected to 1953 indicates the compensatory nature of the deviations in fertility (FIGURE 27).[61] Fertility

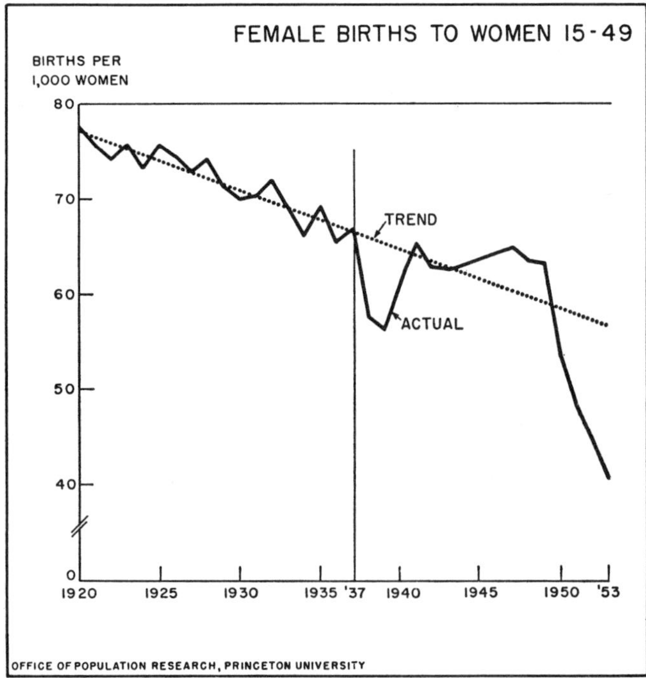

Figure 27. The deviations of fertility from prewar trends, 1920-1953 (Female births per 1,000 women aged 15-49)
Source: References, Table 90.

was below the trend line in 1938 and 1939, roughly at trend values from 1941 to 1943, and then substantially below those values in 1944 and 1945. In 1947 and 1948 actual fertility was far above trend values, but by 1950 it was below expected values on the basis of the prewar downward movement.

The balances of births and deaths and the currents of movement were such that the reproductive performances of the women in the prefectures maintained similar geographic patterns in the prewar and the postwar years (MAP 18). The ratios of girls to women remained highest in the rural areas of the northeast, lowest in the industrial areas of central Honshu. The ratios for the prefectures suggest a widening of prefectural differences in the years of flight, a narrowing in the early postwar years. The number of girls under 5 per 1,000 women aged from 20 to 49 were as follows, the prefectures being classified by industrial type:[62]

[61] This trend for the years from 1920 to 1937 and its projection into the postwar years has been used previously in the analysis of the regularity of the decline from 1920 to 1937 and the rapidity of the decline from 1947 to 1955.

[62] References to sources of data are given in Tables 125 and 132.

Prefectures by industrial type	*1940*	*1944 (lunar)*	*1945 (lunar)*	*1946 (lunar)*	*1947*	*1950*
All Japan	324	284	304	251	296	322
Metropolitan	264	255	234	205	249	269
Other industrial	303	275	287	237	288	310
Intermediate	324	283	305	250	293	319
Agricultural	368	302	323	266	312	343
Hokkaido	391	336	357	304	351	394

The comparability of the ratios from one period to another is disturbed by the use of lunar and Western ages. The pattern of change is clearer if the girl-women ratios in the prefectures are related to the national ratio for the year as 100:

Prefectures by industrial type	*1940*	*1944*	*1945*	*1946*	*1947*	*1950*
All Japan	100	100	100	100	100	100
Metropolitan	82	90	77	82	84	84
Other industrial	94	97	94	94	97	96
Intermediate	100	100	100	100	99	99
Agricultural	113	106	106	106	105	106
Hokkaido	120	118	118	121	118	122

A comparable analysis for the six great cities, the other *shi*, and the *gun* from 1930 to 1950 suggests that fertility was influenced in differing ways in cities of various sizes. If the girl-women ratios are again expressed in relation to the ratios for all Japan as 100, the results are as follows:

Year	*All Japan*	*Six great cities*	*Other shi*	*Gun*
1930	100	76	86	107
1940	100	81	88	111
1945	100	72	92	106
1947	100	82	94	106
1950	100	82	94	107

The disturbances of the 1940's were not sufficient to alter the regular progressions so characteristic of the declining fertility of the Japanese. At any given time, whether 1940, 1945, or 1950, girl-women ratios were lowest in the metropolitan prefectures, highest in the agricultural prefectures and Hokkaido. And at any given time they were lowest in the six great cities, higher in the lesser *shi*, and highest in the *gun*.

DEATHS IN THE ADULT AGES

In the difficult and almost chaotic situation of a plethora of data but no consistent series, the estimation of the losses of adult lives associated with war, demobilization, and repatriation must be made for the decade from 1940 to 1950. The measurement of the losses of life requires an estimate of the number of people who would have been alive in 1950 if there had been no war. This in turn necessitates an estimate of what the place-time death rates would have been. It can be assumed that the declines would have continued, but the speed of the decline would have been related to conditions in Japan and the extent of the adoption of public health and medical advances. The assumptions as to hypothetical trends can lead to substantial differences in numbers of survivors expected in 1950. Three assumptions were explored in the light of Japan's own record and the events in the world of health external to Japan: (A) That mortality declined from 1935-1936 to 1950 according to the pattern of decline that had occurred in Eu-

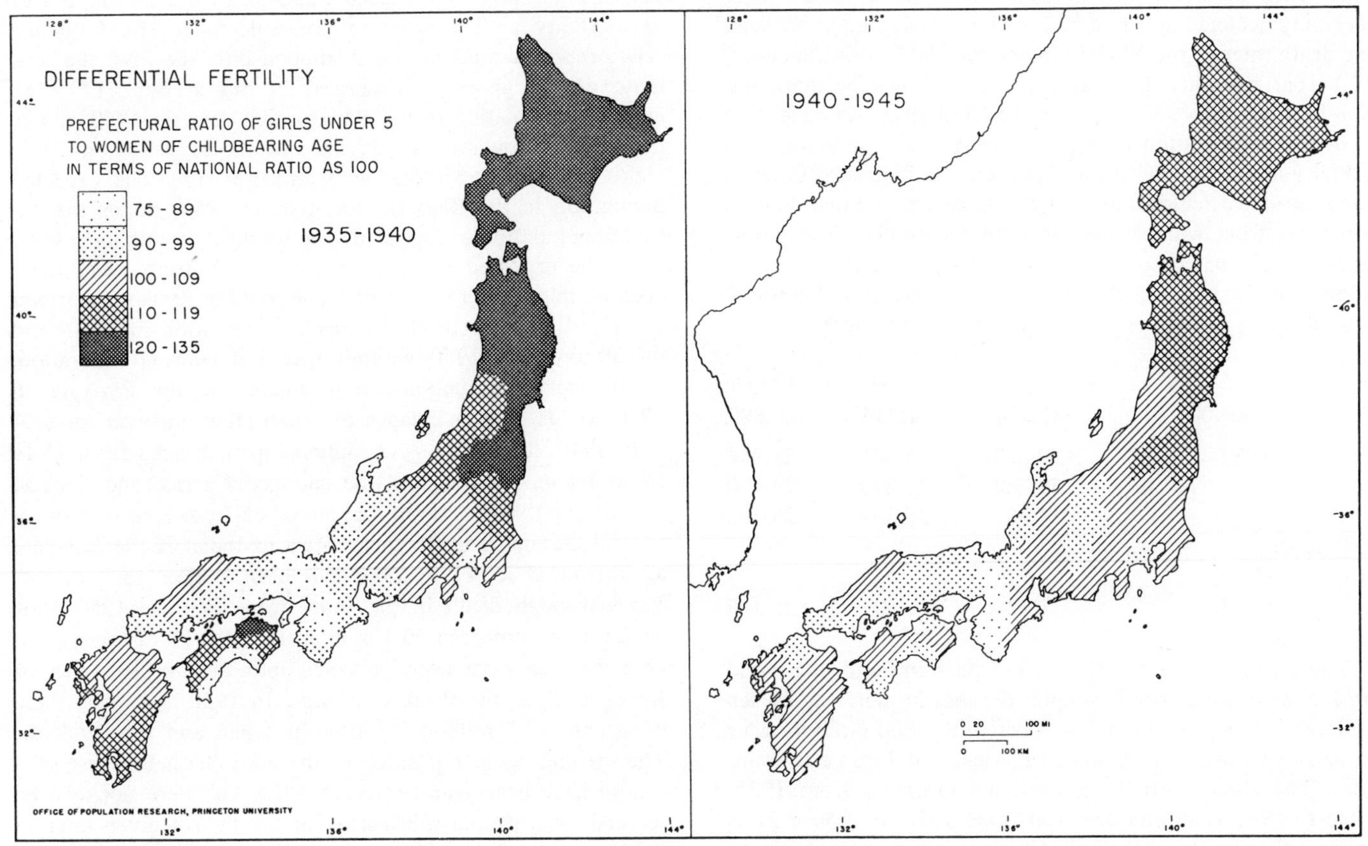

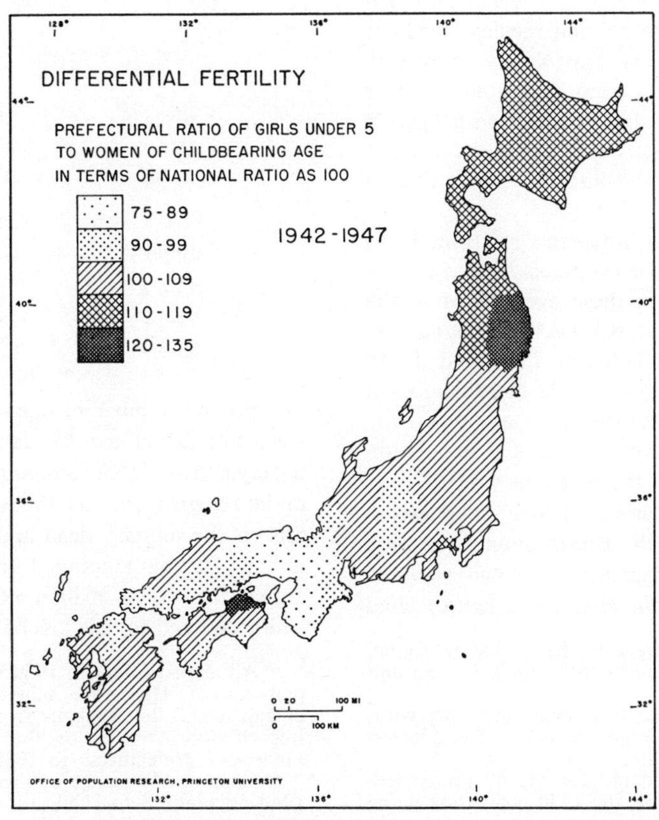

Map. 18. Differential fertility in the war years. Ratios of girls to women, 1935-1940, 1940-1945, and 1942-1947
Source: References, Tables 125 and 132.

rope when mortality was at comparable levels.[63] (B) That mortality declined at a rate indicated by interpolation between the death rates of the 1935-1936 and the 1947-1948 life tables. (C) That mortality declined at a rate indicated by interpolation between the 1935-1936 and the 1950-1951 life tables.

In the computation of expected numbers of survivors, the primary interest is not in the Japanese who happened to be in Japan at a particular date, but the Japanese in Japan and in the areas from which Japanese were repatriated. The differences in anticipated numbers of adult Japanese in this Repatriation Area in 1950 on the three assumptions as to "normal" mortality are as follows, numbers being in thousands:

		Total	*Male*	*Female*
1940		42,224	21,335	20,889
1950	A	50,328	25,421	24,908
	B	50,280	25,290	24,990
	C	51,304	25,899	25,405
Difference:				
C—A		975	478	497
C—B		1,024	609	415

The choice between a European-type trend and one based on Japanese experience is simple: declines in mortality by sex and age between the prewar and postwar period did *not* occur in accord with the generalized experience of European countries. The choice between a projected mortality from 1935-1936 to 1947-1948 and one from 1935-1936 to 1950-1951 is more difficult. On the whole, it seems most reasonable to select the decline from 1935-1936 to 1947-1948 as one "expected" without war. Major investments and technical assistance went into Japanese public health and medical facilities during the period of the Occupation; Japan's own drives to reduce mortality in the early 1940's were associated with her war goals, her manpower needs, and her population policies.[64] Whether the Japanese effort could or would have been as great without the stimulus of war and the financial and technical contributions of SCAP is doubtful.

In 1940, there were 40.3 million Japanese aged from 15 to 59 in the 47 prefectures that then constituted Japan, and an additional 1.97 million Japanese in these age groups in the Western Pacific and Southeast Asian regions.[65] Assuming normal mortality and no migration between 1940 and 1950. Japanese aged from 15 to 59 in 1950 would have numbered 48.1 million in Japan and the Ryukyus, 50.3 million in the Repatriation Area (TABLE 136). The enumerated population aged from 15 to 59 in Japan and the Ryukyus in 1950 was 47.5 million. The military agreements and their implementation provided that all Japanese in the Repatriation Area were to be returned to Japan. Most Japanese who had survived were returned by October 1, 1950. Hence the figures cited permit estimates of the expected balance of the decade insofar as mortality and repatriation are concerned. The following relationships should be noted, though only the first, the estimate of net losses, is discussed in this section: (1) The expected population in the Repatriation Area in 1950, minus the actual population of Japan and the Ryukyus in 1950, yields an estimate of the net war losses. (2) The expected population in the Repatriation Area in 1950, minus the expected population in Japan and the Ryukyus in this same year, gives the expected number of civilian repatriates had there been no migration to or from Japan and the Ryukyus between 1940 and 1950.[66] (3) The expected population in Japan and the Ryukyus in 1950 without war and with no migration, minus the actual population in Japan and the Ryukyus in 1950, yields the net balance of repatriation and war losses.[67]

In 1940, there were 42.2 million Japanese aged from 15 to 59 in Japan, the colonies, the conquered areas, and the rest of that great Asian region that stretched from Karafuto down around Oceania and Southeast Asia to India. If the Japanese aged from 5 to 49 in 1940 had been subject to "normal" losses through death in the years from 1940 to 1950, they would have numbered 50.3 million. By 1950 all of these Japanese were to have been collected into the postwar area of Japan itself or the Ryukyu Islands. In 1950, however, there were only 47.5 million Japanese in Japan and the Ryukyus. The sex and age composition of the 2.8 million Japanese who should have been enumerated in 1950, but were not, can be secured by a simple subtraction of the figures given later in Table 137. It was as follows, numbers being in thousands:

Age	*Total*	*Male*	*Female*
Total	2,819	2,285	534
15-19	123	90	34
20-24	382	277	105
25-29	830	698	131
30-34	570	498	73
35-39	382	346	36
40-44	234	186	48
45-49	153	98	55
50-54	94	59	35
55-59	51	33	18

Thus the number of Japanese in the productive ages who were not accounted for in the censuses of Japan and the Ryukyus as of 1950 amounted to 2.8 million; of these, 2.28 million were men, 534 thousand women. Since in the official reports the military dead and the civilians dead as a result of military action amounted to only 1.8 million, it might be argued that excess civilian mortality due to non-military causes had accounted for the loss of a million adults in the productive

[63] Notestein, Frank W.; Taeuber, Irene B.; Kirk, Dudley; Coale, Ansley; and Kiser, Louise. *The future population of Europe and the Soviet Union.*

[64] The acceptance of a lesser expected decline in mortality without war avoids the derivation of maximum estimates of war losses. It is therefore a conservative procedure.

[65] These computations were carried out for the 47 prefectures of prewar Japan for three reasons. One, the 1940 population living in the area of Japan as of 1950 is known exactly only in total numbers, not in ethnic affiliation or in sex and age composition. Since a census was taken in Japan on October 1, 1950, and in the Ryukyus on December 1, 1950, the 1950 population of the prewar area is known in close approximation. Two, residual sovereignty of the Ryukyus is retained by Japan. Three, persons with *honseki* in the Ryukyus were included in the armed forces of Japan and subject to the mortality of those armed forces.

[66] All armed forces in 1940 were enumerated as if in Japan (47 prefectures). Hence the subtraction of the estimated populations of Japan and the Ryukyus from the estimated populations of the Repatriation Area yields the survivors of the civilians outside Japan (47 prefectures) in 1940.

[67] Comparable agings of the 1920 populations to 1930 and the 1930 populations to 1940, using life tables that represented or approximated actual mortality levels for the Japanese in the respective areas, permitted comparisons of estimated with actual populations at succeeding census dates. The agreement between expected and enumerated for the Repatriation Area and the world as a whole was extraordinary. In fact, these agings yielded estimates of the returned soldiers in 1930 and the military dead in 1940 that were close to the official figures for the groups concerned.

TABLE 136

The numbers of the Japanese enumerated in 1940 and in 1950, and the numbers "expected" in 1950, ages 15-59, by sex
(Numbers in '000)

Ages	ENUMERATED IN 1940		ENUMERATED IN 1950	EXPECTED IN 1950	
	Japan and Ryukyus	*Repatriation area*	*Japan and Ryukyus*	*Japan and Ryukyus*	*Repatriation area*
			Total		
Total 15-59	40,253	42,224	47,461	48,103	50,280
15-19	7,269	7,593	8,599	8,437	8,722
20-24	5,944	6,271	7,737	7,895	8,119
25-29	5,506	5,889	6,183	6,713	7,012
30-34	4,832	5,133	5,199	5,469	5,770
35-39	4,343	4,562	5,057	5,086	5,439
40-44	3,772	3,930	4,498	4,455	4,732
45-49	3,174	3,289	4,011	3,964	4,164
50-54	2,865	2,949	3,413	3,366	3,507
55-59	2,548	2,608	2,763	2,717	2,814
			Male		
Total 15-59	20,194	21,335	23,006	24,076	25,290
15-19	3,632	3,822	4,329	4,273	4,418
20-24	2,953	3,112	3,818	3,981	4,095
25-29	2,739	2,958	2,813	3,337	3,511
30-34	2,428	2,612	2,347	2,699	2,844
35-39	2,203	2,337	2,370	2,515	2,716
40-44	1,933	2,032	2,207	2,224	2,393
45-49	1,627	1,699	2,015	1,993	2,113
50-54	1,443	1,494	1,726	1,698	1,785
55-59	1,235	1,270	1,381	1,355	1,415
			Female		
Total 15-59	20,059	20,889	24,456	24,027	24,990
15-19	3,637	3,771	4,270	4,164	4,304
20-24	2,991	3,159	3,919	3,914	4,024
25-29	2,766	2,930	3,370	3,376	3,501
30-34	2,404	2,522	2,853	2,770	2,925
35-39	2,139	2,225	2,687	2,571	2,723
40-44	1,839	1,899	2,291	2,231	2,340
45-49	1,547	1,591	1,996	1,971	2,050
50-54	1,422	1,455	1,687	1,668	1,722
55-59	1,313	1,338	1,382	1,362	1,400

Source and procedures: The distributions of the populations by sex and age were secured for the 46 prefectures of Japan, Okinawa, the individual colonial areas, Manchoukuo, and the occupied and other parts of the Repatriation Area. Detailed citations to sources are given in the Bibliography. Straight-line interpolations between the L values of the life tables of 1935-1936 and 1947-1948 yielded expected values centered at the middle of the 1940-1945 and 1945-1950 intercensal periods. Aging was carried out for five-year age groups by sex separately for the individual areas and for the two intercensal periods involved. The populations enumerated in 1950 were secured from the census publications of Japan and the Ryukyus, also cited in the Bibliography.

years of life. Examination of the distribution of the deficits in population by sex and age makes this assumption of general excess civilian mortality suspect. The deficits of males are concentrated in the conscript ages, particularly among those who reached age 22 after 1937. Only 182 thousand of the 2.3 million deficit consists of youth too young to have been in the armed forces by 1945 or of mature men who were 45 or over when the war ended. It would appear, then, that the deficits of men primarily represented military deaths or Japanese still missing from Japan. A careful perusal of the official data indicates a total of the reported dead and missing as follows, numbers again being in thousands:

Military dead after October 1, 1940[68]	1,536
Presumed dead outside area of U.S.S.R.[69]	400
In Siberia but not repatriated[70]	200
Expected deficit	2,136

Since our total deficit is 2,285 thousand, the official deficit of 2,136 thousand fails to account for 150 thousand men.[71]

Our deficit of 534 thousand women aged from 15 to 49 suggests that the official estimate of 289 thousand civilian dead from military action may be an understatement. Some, but not many, of these half of a million missing women may have been among the Japanese in the Kuriles, Karafuto, China, and the U.S.S.R. who had not yet been repatriated on October 1, 1950. However, the age composition of the deficits indicates a heavy concentration at age 20 to 29 in 1950. These were girls aged from 15 to 24 in 1945. During the late years of the war, they had taken jobs in industrial areas and filled many of the places vacated by men in cities. As such, they were subject to high risk in the air attacks. They were also the group of women most subject to the risks of tuberculosis and other respiratory diseases.

A minor portion of Japan's war dead were lost in military action, and few died as a result of diseases among the armed forces or in the civilian population. There were small proportions of deaths among the Japanese who fought victoriously against Asian nations or, in the early period, the Western powers. The Allied strategic plans involved few engagements between masses of men; in those that occurred, the Japanese lost heavily. The strategic bombing of cities might have been accompanied by heavy mortality as a result of the actions themselves and correlated breakdowns of sanitary services and food distribution. Japanese discipline was maintained, however, and the Allied Powers gave warnings of attacks in advance. Evacuations lessened direct deaths, while some modicum of health service was maintained, and food was secured somehow. Malnutrition was widespread but famine was averted and there were no great epidemics.

Demographic factors, institutional structures, and familial values influenced both the numbers and the characteristics of the fatalities. Manpower was plentiful, so the armed forces in the early years of the war consisted primarily of youth aged from 22 to 24 or 25. As the war continued and its intensity increased, men of younger and older ages were inducted. However, the size of the population and the number of men in the armed forces were factors almost irrelevant to the final decision of the war. Japanese military manpower was not exhausted; when Japan surrendered, five of the seven million men under arms had never been in action.

The assumption that air warfare, and particularly atomic bombing, would destroy whole families rather than just individuals was not validated by the Japanese experience. In Hiroshima, major numbers of deaths occurred in the central city. Loss of life was heaviest among workers and those on the streets, and both groups included large portions of youth. The troops who were in the staging area in Hiroshima presumably included many youth. In Nagasaki the bomb brought heavy deaths in munitions and aircraft works. Here also deaths were selective of individuals rather than family groups.

The major mortality of war among the Japanese was an unplanned consequence of the technological character of the war. When the Allies by-passed areas, they left Japanese men isolated in places where they could not survive without access to the technical and scientific culture to which they belonged. Troops far from home found themselves unable to produce the necessary food or to organize the native societies so that the food would be produced in sufficient quantities. As control of the air and the sea lanes was lost, there were few imports of food or medical supplies. Men left on the coral atolls and the volcanic islands died. The troops in areas such as Java were reduced to starvation diets and subject to the malaria of a tropical area without drugs. With the surrender the sanitary controls collapsed in many areas. Diseases long eliminated from Japan became rampant among her defeated armies abroad.

The conquest of the Co-Prosperity Sphere had been made possible by Japan's mastery of many of the techniques of applied science and her development of an industrial economy. The deaths of the imperial armed forces in the areas they occupied and in their return homeward after defeat are a striking illustration of what can happen to modern men when the supports of a complex industrial society are withdrawn.

THE LIQUIDATION OF THE CO-PROSPERITY SPHERE

On October 1, 1940, almost three-quarters of a century after the Meiji Restoration and almost half a century after the conquest of Taiwan, there were 2 million Japanese civilians aged from 15 to 59 outside Japan itself but in the area designated by the Japanese as the Co-Prosperity Sphere. If there had been no war and no further migration, and the Japanese had followed only the peaceful pursuits that were leading to gradually declining mortality, there would have been 2.2 million Japanese civilians aged from 15 to 59 in these same areas in 1950. Their composition by sex and age would have been as follows, numbers being in thousands:

Age	*Total*	*Male*	*Female*
15-59	2,177	1,214	963
15-19	285	145	141
20-24	224	114	110
25-29	299	174	125
30-34	301	145	156
35-39	353	201	152
40-44	277	168	109

[68] Nihon. Sori-fu, tokei-kyoku. *Taisho 9-nen—Showa 25-nen, waga kuni nenji betsu jinko no suikei.*

[69] Report to the Economic and Scientific Section, GHQ, SCAP, by the General Affairs Section of the First Demobilization Board of the Government of Japan, 1947.

[70] There were 237 thousand reported as in Siberia and not repatriated. It may be assumed that at least 200 thousand of these were men.

[71] The actual expected deficit would be somewhat larger, for some of the dead and the missing would have died during the decade had they been subject only to the usual hazards of civilian life.

Age	*Total*	*Male*	*Female*
45-49	199	121	79
50-54	141	87	54
55-59	98	60	38

These 2.2 million expected survivors are not identical with the Japanese aged from 15 to 49 in 1950 who had been moved home as repatriates. There was flux in the movements of the Japanese in the early years of victory. In the last years of war, the return migrations exceeded the new out-migrations by an estimated 193 thousand.[72] These movements of the war years were selective as to sex and age. Out-migrants were men, while return migrants included many women and children. It may be argued that the survivors of the ethnic Japanese outside Japan in 1940 measure the effects of the liquidation of the imperial structure in more accurate form than do the numbers of those who were moved home by Allied orders.

The Japanese who went out to the colonial and imperial areas had been youth in their prime. They had been or had become highly selected as to upper social and economic status, educational levels, and income. As Japanese became settled minority groups in the areas of control, generations of Japanese children matured in the occupied areas themselves. By 1950 appreciable proportions of the men who had been in the migrant ages in 1940 and the preceding years were now older workers, men who would find readjustment difficult. However, there were relatively high proportions of youth aged from 15 to 19 and 20 to 24 among the expected repatriates of 1950. For these young men, any work experience they might have had prior to 1945 was outside Japan itself. "Return" for them was return to the land of their fathers and mothers, not to a land in which they had grown up.

In the days of her expansion, Japan exported the young and the skilled and thus decreased the pressures on the labor markets of the home country. Since her trained and ambitious people had opportunities abroad, problems of unemployment among the well-educated classes such as haunted prewar Europe did not concern her. These very selectivities in out-migration complicated the social, economic, and political problems of the homeward trek and the ensuing re-allocation and re-adjustment. Older workers came back from urban areas and non-agricultural occupations to a country whose urban areas were destroyed and whose industrial, technical, and professional opportunities were limited. The refugees of the Empire added additional numbers to fields already greatly overcrowded. Failing to find suitable employment, they moved downward in the social-economic scale or remained dependent residents of the army barracks and other repatriate relief facilities. The youth who returned contributed to the great annual increase in new workers seeking jobs.

The problems of repatriate absorption would have been difficult even if the home economy had been functioning at high levels. In postwar Japan, solutions satisfactory both to the repatriates and to the home population were impossible. Internal economic re-absorption left men who had been engineers or administrators in Manchoukuo trying to till newly cleared fields in Hokkaido or run tiny shops in *machi* and *shi*. A new migration of Japanese technical, managerial, and professional people to the agrarian nations of the Pacific region might have contributed to restoration and economic development in these areas, but such migration was barred by nations that remembered the Japanese expansion and the war against Japan. The few opportunities for migration to agricultural hinterlands in Latin America did not attract these people who had been living abroad as a governing race under the protection of their own country and its armed forces.

THE BALANCE OF WAR AND REPATRIATION

In Japan and the Ryukyus considered together, the population aged from 15 to 59 in 1950 was 600 thousand less than would have been expected had there been neither war deaths nor migrations of Japanese between 1940 and 1950. In other words, Japan's population in 1950 was less than would have been expected in the absence of war. However, the balance of changes in the sex and age groups had distorted the symmetry that formerly characterized the age structure of the Japanese population.

The difference between the enumerated population of Japan and the Ryukyus in 1950 and the population expected in this same area without war or repatriation was as follows, numbers being in thousands:

Age	*Total*	*Male*	*Female*
15-59	−642	−1,070	429
15-19	161	55	107
20-24	−158	−163	5
25-29	−530	−524	−6
30-34	−270	−353	83
35-39	−29	−145	116
40-44	43	−18	61
45-49	47	23	24
50-54	47	28	19
55-59	46	26	20

Repatriation lacked a million of compensating for the war losses among men, but it resulted in a net increase of more than 400 thousand in the female population. The large net increase associated with the war came in the age group 15-19, the age of entrance to the labor force. There was also a net increase of people aged 40 and over. The losses were concentrated among men in the most productive years; the increases were concentrated at the margins of the productive years and among women. The high proportions of the widowed and the increase of the single among women have been noted earlier, as has the reduction in fertility associated with the deficits of men. Thus severe frictional problems were introduced into a population that had hitherto approached symmetry in the relations of its sex and age groups.

[72] The estimated numbers of repatriates aged from 15 to 59 in Japan and the Ryukyus are reasonably consistent with the official figures on total civilian repatriates. If we assume that total survivors had the same sex and age structure as the survivors of the Co-Prosperity Sphere residents enumerated in the 1950 census, the estimated total number becomes 3.1 million. Allowance for the survivors of the 193 thousand who had already returned reduces the expected number to a little less than 3 million. Numbers of "civilians" reported as repatriated indicate a probable 3 million surviving to the census of 1950. However, the 377 thousand not repatriated at the date of the census may have included something like 200 thousand civilians. Considering the complexity of the movements of Japanese prior to the surrender of 1945, the difficult conditions that barred adequate record-keeping during the early months of rapid repatriation, the transfers from civilian to military status, and the uncertainties as to numbers of survivors of non-repatriated persons, the general agreement is supporting evidence for the official reconstruction of numbers of civilian repatriates. It should be recalled that enumeration of civilian refugees was deficient in the census of 1950. Numbers of Japanese abroad at the termination of hostilities were estimates.

Population Increase and War

The relations among population increase, industrial development, peace, and war will be a major motif in the later consideration of the population problems and policies of Japan. Here the focus is on the direct relations between war and population increase in a single decade. There is no consideration of the evolution of the population with which that decade began, for this evolution has been subject to detailed analysis in the preceding chapters. There is no projection beyond 1950, for that will be undertaken in future chapters.

The course of fertility and civilian mortality in the 1940's involved compensatory movements. Fertility was buoyed by government policies, economic conditions, and psychological forces in the early part of the decade. In the middle 1940's there were sharp declines associated with the absence of men, the disruption of normal life by the evacuations, the deteriorated conditions of health and nutrition, and the increased resort to abortion. In the late 1940's there were sharp increases in births as postponed marriages occurred, families were reunited, and the economy and society functioned nearer subsistence agrarian levels than it had for many years. By 1950, industrial and urban restoration were far advanced. Fertility in 1940 and in 1950 deviated little from that anticipated on the basis of a projection of the observed trend of decline from 1920 to 1937. There were great annual fluctuations in numbers of births, but it is doubtful whether they represented any major net gain or loss.

The health and medical developments of the decade combined with the policies of the Japanese government and those of SCAP to compensate in major part for the excess civilian deaths of the war and early postwar years. On the conservative assumption that the level of mortality measured in the life table of 1947-1948 would have been reached in the absence of war, there was an approximate balance of the forces tending to increase and to decrease mortality for the decade as a whole. However, there were major differences in the factors influencing mortality in the specific sex and age groups. In mortality, as in fertility, the war produced major irregularities in annual rates. Basically, however, the mortality controls of the industrial society were maintained and even increased throughout all but a brief part of the decade. There was no lapse into premodern conditions that might have decimated the population.

There were major war losses among the Japanese; our estimates for the productive ages from 15 to 59 alone indicated 2.3 million men and 534 thousand women missing in the censuses of 1950. A very small number of these were repatriated after October 1, 1950; a few may still be alive as prisoners in the U.S.S.R. or Mainland China. The repatriation of practically all surviving Japanese to Japan lacked 642 thousand of compensating for the war losses in the group that was from 15 to 59 years of age in 1950. For the Japanese as a people, however, repatriation involved a territorial redistribution and not a compensation. The measurement of the human tragedy of the war lies in the total of almost three million adults who should have been alive in 1950 if the war had not been fought.

In the non-human terms of demographic balance sheets, Japan's losses of men and women in the productive ages were not sufficient to prevent major increases in these age groups. Growth in manpower between 1940 and 1950 was substantially less than it would have been without war, but the defeated and occupied Japan and Ryukyus of 1950 had 5.2 million more men and women in the ages from 15 to 59 than they had had in 1940.

A measure of loss requires that deficits in population in 1950 be related to the expected population in the Repatriation Area, rather than simply in Japan itself. TABLE 137 gives the

TABLE 137

The war losses among Japanese aged from 15 to 59 in the Repatriation Area, 1940-1950
(Numbers in '000)

Population by sex	*15-59*	*15-19*	*20-24*	*25-29*	*30-34*	*35-39*	*40-44*	*45-49*	*50-54*	*55-59*
Expected population, 1950	50,280	8,722	8,119	7,012	5,770	5,439	4,732	4,164	3,507	2,814
Male	25,290	4,418	4,095	3,511	2,844	2,716	2,393	2,113	1,785	1,415
Female	24,990	4,304	4,024	3,501	2,925	2,723	2,340	2,050	1,722	1,400
Expected increase, 1940-1950	8,056	1,129	1,848	1,124	636	878	802	874	558	207
Male	3,955	596	983	553	233	379	361	415	291	145
Female	4,101	533	865	571	404	499	441	460	267	62
Deficit in expected population	2,819	123	382	830	570	382	234	153	94	51
Male	2,285	90	277	698	498	346	186	98	59	33
Female	534	34	105	131	73	36	48	55	35	18
Per cent deficit in expected population	5.6	1.4	4.8	11.8	9.9	7.0	4.9	3.7	2.7	1.8
Male	9.0	2.0	6.8	19.9	17.5	12.7	7.8	4.6	3.3	2.3
Female	2.1	0.8	2.6	3.7	2.5	1.3	2.1	2.7	2.0	1.3
Deficit as per cent of expected increase	35.0	10.8	20.7	73.9	89.6	43.5	29.2	17.5	16.8	24.6
Male	57.8	15.1	28.2	126.2	213.7	91.3	51.5	23.6	20.3	22.8
Female	13.0	6.4	12.1	22.9	18.1	7.2	10.9	12.0	13.1	29.0

Source and procedures: Note, Table 136.

population expected in 1950 without war, the increase expected between 1940 and 1950 without war, and the war losses, the latter being related both to the size of the expected population and to the amount of the expected increase.

The population increase of the Japanese was lessened by war. However, the frictional difficulties of imbalances between the sexes and irregularities in the age groups outweighed any hypothetical release of pressure from a reduced number of people. Furthermore, the destruction of resources, organization, and markets so far surpassed the losses of life that the population problem became more rather than less severe. War losses adequate to prevent population increase could have been produced only by an economic destruction and a social disorganization so great that the population problem would have been far more acute than it was with the losses that occurred.

In another and rather cynical approach to the demography of war, the dynamics of a population are analyzed with reference to the ability of that population to sustain war and to recuperate from the losses suffered in war. In this respect, Japan remained in a "favorable" position. Fertility was still sufficiently high to permit large numbers of births throughout most of the war and postwar years. The cohorts of youth were large; they have already or will soon replace the age groups deeply scarred by war with numbers adequate for labor force needs and family formation.

The direct losses of the war to the Japanese people were less significant for the future of the population than the reactions of the people to the war, the defeat, and the problems of life under the conditions that remained possible to them in the postwar years. These questions that involve demography in peace as in war are considered in the next chapter.

CHAPTER XVII

Problems, Projections, and Policies

Most students in Japan and elsewhere have viewed the population problem of Japan with pessimism. There has been general agreement on the need for reduced rates of population growth, but there has been little agreement as to how the reductions were to be secured. Some have advocated government policies to encourage contraceptive practices, while others have pleaded for a movement of millions of people or a redistribution of the world's resources. Still others have argued that there should be no direct policies. In this view, declining rates of population growth are by-products of industrialization and urbanization; the solutions to population problems are seen to lie in economic development, in a further application of scientific knowledge to food production, and in an expansion of regional and world trade. Reorganization of the social structure, redistribution of income, and extension of internal markets have also been considered in relation to the problems of population growth and living levels.

It would be possible to limit the discussion of the Japanese population problem to an analysis of numerical prospects. The projection of past trends in fertility, mortality, and migration into the future would permit an estimation of the size and composition of the population in future years. The projected populations could be discussed without reference to problems of social structure, family values, economic organization, or political forces. However, there is a fundamental difficulty with this or any other approach that is limited to an analysis of population statistics. Projections of the population into the future would have to be based on an assumption of continuity in the forces of change. As such, they would be illustrations of hypothetical demographic changes, but their relevance to the prospects for growth would be questionable.

The population of Japan has been projected into the future many times and under many assumptions. Some projections have been made for use in government planning, while others have been made in connection with questions of policy. Still others have been demographic studies, made without reference to population problems or policies. These population projections of the past are valuable data for research. They permit objective analysis of the relations among the facts of the population situation, the interpretations of those facts, and government attitudes toward policy. It is possible that study of the reactions of the Japanese to difficult population situations in the past may offer clues as to developments in the future.

The relations between population growth and the economic, fiscal, and military policies of Japan cannot be ignored. The growth of an already numerous people was always available as a rationalization for production and market policy, territorial expansion, or military action. One cannot casually deny that a relation existed between internal population pressures and the external actions that led to the acquisitions of colonies and the attempt to create the Co-Prosperity Sphere. The fact that official or scholarly arguments possessed flaws or ignored critical aspects need not mean that the men who propounded them were consciously specious or that the institutions which implemented decisions acted in conscious hypocrisy. An illustration will emphasize the point. In earlier chapters it was shown that the Japanese moved out into colonial areas and Manchoukuo as the governmental, professional, and managerial elite of an occupying power rather than as peasants on the land.[1] But these demographic facts do not gainsay the sincerity of the scholars and statesmen who advocated the mass emigration of peasants for the relief of population pressure within Japan.

The definition of population problems and the formulation of solutions to them were more than abstract intellectual activities. Men were immersed in the physical, cultural, and intellectual climate of the era in which they lived. The milieu that influenced scientists included the objective facts of existing relations among people, technology, and resources. Moreover, interpretations of presumably objective facts changed as the political and economic situation changed. The definition of the future accepted as a basis for research altered many times. Students who were quite rational in each existing situation developed the bases for policies that were contradictory if viewed chronologically. New studies and new policies were integrated with economic changes and altered climates of opinion that, in their turn, influenced demographic behavior. The interplay between demographic factors and economic, social, and political situations underlay the changing definitions of population problems and population policies.

The Formative Decades

During the late *bakufu* and the early modern periods, the population problem appeared as a simple relation between the number of the people and the subsistence available to them. There were government actions that concerned population, but there was no population policy as such. The moves against infanticide and abortion were motivated by the beliefs of the upper classes that these practices were barbarian. The planned settlement of Hokkaido was undertaken in order to relieve population pressure in overcrowded areas of Honshu and Shikoku, but it also served to ensure Hokkaido against foreign encroachment. The motives in planned migration were generally mixed, whether in the movement from Tohoku to Hokkaido or in that from Japan to Brazil.

In the early years of the Meiji Restoration, as during the late Tokugawa *bakufu*, growth was taken as an index of national vitality. It was proof of the rejuvenation of the people after the torpor of the feudal era. It was argued that, while great power could be achieved by a nation of only 50 million or so in the nineteenth century, Japan needed 80 to 100 million

[1] Chapters IX and X.

people if she was to achieve the status of a great power in the twentieth century.

Japan's visions of imperial status were immensely enhanced by victory in the Russo-Japanese War. World War I brought about territorial additions without human cost, an entrance into European-dominated markets by Japanese ships carrying goods made in Japan, and advances in industrialization. In the 1920's pessimism replaced the exuberance of the years of swift advance in economic structure and political suzerainty. Many events contributed to the shift; fiscal deflation and the termination of shipbuilding after the Washington Conference may be mentioned specifically. Disillusion with imperialism became widespread as the armed forces of Japan returned without additional territory or the *élan* of decisive victories. The increasing price of food, the scarcity of rice, and rice riots intensified the fears that existed in this food-deficient nation. The heavy human and material losses of the Kanto earthquake contributed to its economic difficulties. The Japanese were forced to realize their political and economic vulnerabilities.

These years of reorientation, if not of crisis, were the early 1920's. The great newspapers used news space and editorial columns to point out that the population problem was a matter of national concern. By one of the ironical coincidences that have plagued modern Japanese history, the early 1920's was also the period when the United States Immigration Act barred Japanese from migration to the United States.

In the years after World War I there was a widespread interest in population in many areas of the world other than Japan. Events within Japan were influenced by this interest and its correlated developments in research. Japan herself had taken her first national population census in 1920. Her students returning from abroad brought knowledge of statistical activities and research techniques with them.

Thus in the 1920's many factors were conducive to the formulation of explicit population policies. There was a grave economic situation for which the increasing numbers of people and the growing labor force seemed to be responsible. There was a spectacular increase in population, in part a heritage of the long-time trends of past growth, in part a consequence of the sharp reductions in death rates that were then occurring. There was research that indicated the magnitude of the population increase that lay ahead as well as the contemporary relations among poverty, the persistence of the old values, high fertility, and the wastage of infant life. Finally, there was the shock of exclusion, with its generation of claustrophobia on the one hand and of militant defense reactions on the other.

Estimates of the future population of Japan and concern over the economic aspects of population increase did not arise *de novo* with the population crises of the late 1920's and the early 1930's. The majority of the early estimates, whether Japanese or Western, had involved projections of rates of increase into the future. Sir George Knibbs accepted as fact the reported average annual rate of increase of 1.08 per cent in 1906-1911 and indicated that a population growing at this rate would double each 64.2 years.[2] H. L. Wilkinson made different computations and estimated that the population of Japan in the year 2000 might be from 120 to 170 million.[3] An official study of the problem of the supply of rice included estimates of future populations made by projecting the 1909-1913 average annual rate of increase of 1.417 per cent. According to these computations, the population would increase from 56 million in the year 1917 to 129 million in the year 2017.[4] In 1927 the Cabinet Bureau of Statistics projected the trend of the increase over the period from 1872 to 1925.[5] According to this estimate, the population would increase more than 50 per cent in the 33 years from 1926 to 1959, to reaching 90 million in the latter year. The population in 1959 would be more than two and one-half times what it had been at the time of the Meiji Restoration.

The reports of commoners by the Tokugawa Shogun, the registration compilations in the years from 1872 to 1918, and the censuses were tempting data for those who wished to consider the curve of change over a long period. Raymond Pearl had included Japan in his series of studies.[6] Professor Mizushima, former director of the Biometrics Institute at the Imperial University of Keijo, distinguished between an ancient cycle of growth under the Tokugawa *bakufu* and a new cycle in the modern era.[7] The logistic as thus computed indicated a population of 79 million in 1950 and 104 million at the end of the century. The upper asymptote of 110 million was approached soon after the year 2050.[8]

Professor Soda was apparently first among the Japanese to utilize age-specific fertility and mortality as a basis for estimating future populations. He assumed that fertility as of 1925 and mortality as of 1921-1925 would continue in force.[9] The annual numbers of births would increase from 2.2 million in 1931 to 3.2 million in 1960. Total population would reach 90.4 million in 1960.

The most widely known early estimates are those made by Professor Ueda. The problem of allowing for an increasing number of women in the reproductive ages and declining age-specific fertility was solved by assuming that the annual number of births would remain at 2.1 million.[10] It was assumed that death rates would continue at the level of 1920-1925. There was no allowance for migration. Under these assumptions, the total population, 56.0 million in 1920, would reach 87.7 million in 1970. The numbers in broad age groups were as follows, numbers being in thousands:

Age	*1930*	*1950*	*1970*
Total	64,062	78,360	87,746
0-14	23,502	25,829	25,829
15-59	35,823	45,963	53,395
60 and over	4,737	6,568	8,522

Professor Ueda emphasized that the assumptions in his projections were unrealistic. This was indeed true. His estimate for all Japan in 1960 was almost reached by the 46 prefectures remaining to Japan in 1950; his estimate for 1970 was surpassed by 1955. However, Professor Ueda stated that reduc-

[2] Knibbs, Sir George H. *The shadow of the world's future*. P. 47.

[3] Wilkinson, H. L. *The world's population problem and a white Australia*. P. 198.

[4] Nihon. Norin-sho. *Kome jukyu no genzai oyobi shorai*. P. 3. Cited in Ishii, Ryoichi. *Population pressure. . . .* P. 227. There was a typographical error in the figure for the year 2017.

[5] Cited in Ishii, *op.cit.* Published in: Nihon. Jinko shokuryo mondai chosa-kai. *Jinko mondai ni kansuru chosa komoku oyobi kore ni taisuru hosaku no sankoan.*

[6] Pearl, Raymond. *Studies in human biology*.

[7] Mizushima, Haruo. "Growth and structure of population." Reprinted from: *The Keijo Journal of Medicine*, 5(2):122-139. June 30, 1934.

[8] *Ibid.* P. 126.

[9] Soda, Takeo. "Jinko zoka no suitei." Pp. 76-110 in: Ueda, Teijiro, Editor. *Nihon jinko mondai kenkyu*. Vol. I.

[10] Professor Ueda revised his estimates several times. The definitive publication is: Ueda, Teijiro, Editor. *Nihon jinko seisaku*. The figures used here are cited from: *Ibid.* "Bevolkerunsfrage und Wirtschaft in heutigen Japan." *Weltwirtschaftliches Archiv*, 46(1): 93-117. July 1937.

tions in current fertility could not solve immediate problems of population. He was concerned with the increase in manpower in the productive ages. He pointed out that unemployment in the cities and underemployment in the villages constituted dangers for the future unless there were rapid increases in employment opportunities. His policy conclusions included further industrialization and urbanization, together with a spread of contraceptive practices.

Professor Ueda regarded population increase and declining rates of growth as natural processes. He cited the similarity of Japanese developments and those in Germany. He stressed his belief that population itself was not a problem, that the economic situation rather than the number of people made for over- or under-population.

Population and Food: The Commission

Population projections and other demographic studies were only parts of the great national debate on the population problems of Japan. The search for panaceas was widespread. Some medical men and some lay leaders advocated the encouragement of contraceptive practices. More politically oriented groups stressed the need for further industrialization and increased emigration. When the Tanaka Cabinet came into power in July of 1927, it emphasized the fact that the nation had to be founded on industry. Population was recognized as a problem, however, and two positive steps were taken as initial moves in the search for a solution. A Department of Overseas Affairs was created to encourage emigration and colonization, and a Commission for the Study of the Problems of Population and Food Supply was organized.

The Commission on Population and Food was thus appointed in a period of inchoate and often contradictory national reflection on the population problem. In his opening address to the Commission, Premier Tanaka stressed his belief that population was a symbol of expanding national strength. In the government draft placed before the Commission, it was stated that ". . . in Japan, which is not blessed by Heaven in unlimited natural resources, and where industry is not yet fully developed, the intensification of the density of population disturbs the balance of the supply and demand of labour, and results in unrest in our national life. . . ."[11]

The Commission on Population and Food included experts and national leaders in various fields. Its assessments of the problem stimulated widespread deliberation. Eight outline reports were submitted to the government between 1927 and 1930 on the following subjects: (1) internal and external colonization; (2) adjustment of the labor supply; (3) population policy in the colonies; (4) population control; (5) promotion of industry; (6) improvement of the distribution and consumption of the national wealth; and (7) establishment of a social department in the government. Recommendations provided for a "reasonable" diffusion of birth control and almost revolutionary changes in methods of distribution and manner of consumption of the national income. These economic recommendations included social and unemployment insurance, limitation of corporate dividends, taxation of unearned incomes, and government supervision of monopolies.

The Commission for the Study of the Problems of Population and Food Supply functioned in the years from 1927 to 1930. It made recommendations to the government of Japan. The government disregarded them. However, there were some fragmentary results. In 1932 men who had been members of the Commission and leaders in related sections of the government established an institute to conduct scientific research on the population question.

It is interesting to speculate concerning the course of events if the government had accepted the comprehensive recommendations of the 1930 Commission on Population and Food. The climate of the period was favorable to the extension of planned parenthood. If the resources of the government had been mobilized to implement the policies proposed by the Commission, the natural decline of the birth rate might have been stimulated. As events developed, the duties, responsibilities, and recommendations of the Population Commission of 1948 were similar to those of the Commission of 1930.

Increase for the Co-Prosperity Sphere

The economic and military developments of the 1930's provided increasing employment opportunities outside agriculture and withdrew youth from the civilian labor market of Japan, whether as members of the armed forces or as civilian emigrants to industrial and strategic frontiers. Internal and intra-Asian developments alike intensified the forces that reduced rates of population growth, but a government facing the immediate problems of war long ignored developments in the population field. There was no interference with contraceptive supplies or the operations of contraceptive clinics. The courts were lenient in their enforcement of the penalties for abortion, and arguments for the legalization of abortion and sterilization were heard. Economic development, urban concentration, and public thinking were all favorable to a rapid decline of the birth rate. Expansionist activities and adjurations to patriotism failed, in the absence of a pro-natalist policy, to halt the downward drift. In fact, the industrialization and urbanization that accompanied militarization led to sharp declines in fertility. Japan seemed to be escaping the treadmill of economic development and population increase. If fertility continued to decline, however, she would lose the abundant manpower that provided both material and excuse for political expansion.

And so once again the population problem became a subject of acute national concern, but this time deficiencies of manpower constituted the problem. Slowing rates of natural increase presaged a future time when, it was held, manpower would be inadequate for its manifold responsibilities.[12] Official projections of the population indicated that maintenance of the fertility rate of 1937 and the mortality rate of 1935-1936 would not produce a population of 100 million by 1960. If fertility and mortality continued to decline as they had between 1925 and 1937, the population would reach its maximum size of 123 million in the year 2000. "After that it will begin gradually to decline, and the Japanese people will enter upon the path that leads to self-extinction."[13]

The projections that lay back of this fear for the future were based on the assumption that the rates of decline in fertility and in mortality in the years from 1925 to 1937 would persist beyond the end of the twentieth century. The future

[11] Translated by Ryoichi Ishii from: *Jinkobu toshin setsumei.* [Reports of the Population Section, Commission on Population and Food, 1930.] See Ch. III, "Development of population policies since the early Meiji period," in Ishii, Ryoichi. *Population pressure.*

[12] Nihon. Kosei-sho, jinko mondai kenkyujo. "Jihen-ka no jinko mondai." *Shuho*, December 18, 1940. Pp. 9-17.

[13] Nihon. Naikaku, kikaku-in. "Jinko mondai o do sura ka?" *Shuho*, February 12, 1941. P. 30.

populations thus generated would be as follows, numbers being in thousands:[14]

Age	*1935*	*1965*	*1995*
Total	69,254	101,609	122,328
0-4	9,329	10,590	9,139
5-14	16,217	20,155	18,719
15-19	6,641	9,334	9,507
20-34	15,944	24,247	27,945
35-44	7,452	13,797	17,797
45-64	10,447	17,462	27,353
65 and over	3,225	6,024	11,868

The decline in national population was in the distant future, even in the highly unlikely event that these projections were realized. Omens of the future would appear sooner, however, for the number of children aged from 5 to 14 would decline by 1995, and youth of conscript age would decline soon thereafter. Moreover, while rates of increase were declining in the younger ages, they would become higher in the upper ages. As the staff of the Institute of Population Problems pointed out, the transition would be similar to that undergone by European countries. Attention was called to the fate that had befallen France. The predictions of the future of European populations were cited. The basis for the fear of the future in Japan is evident in the ratios of the populations in specific ages at thirty-year intervals, the population in the earlier year being taken as 100:

Age	*1965 to 1935*	*1995 to 1965*
Total	146.7	120.4
0-4	113.5	86.3
5-14	124.3	92.9
15-19	140.6	101.8
20-34	152.1	115.2
35-44	185.2	129.0
45-64	167.1	156.6
65 and over	186.8	197.0

Problems of race and quality also concerned the demographers. In the old order of the nineteenth century, the white race had dominated. Even in 1940, "In East Asia, outside Japan and Manchoukuo, there is no nation or race which is not in reality under the subjugation of the white race."[15] A new order had begun to appear when the Japanese "crushed" the Russian Empire and established a new prestige for the colonial races. With the Pacific War the new order emerged and industrial progress that normally would have required from twenty to thirty years had come about within two or three years. Deficits of industrial labor had become acute problems. Moreover: "It is really necessary to have a great number of superior people in order to cultivate the soil and develop the culture of this great region cooperatively with the other races of the continent. In addition to the pioneers in Manchoukuo there must be manufacturers, merchants, and people of superior intellect and skill to labor in Manchoukuo, North China, Central China, South China, and the South Seas for the sake of the natural resources of East Asia, of creating resources and of developing them, for a great reconstruction will strain the capacity and the number of the people. If we think of the distant future of mutual prosperity in all Asia, and if we give heed to the glorious mission of the Japanese race, the one thing of which we can never have enough is the number of superior people belonging to the Imperial nation."[16]

Since declining fertility had occurred among those of "superior" stock while the rate of increase of the "inferior" had remained high, genetic deterioration was believed to be in process. It was argued that the high birth rate essential for the development of the Co-Prosperity Sphere would eliminate dysgenic trends and improve the quality of the race.

Further impetus was given to the formulation of pro-natalist policies in Japan by the clear realization that the economic development and public health of the new order would stimulate a vast increase of the Chinese population.

The outline for the establishment of population policy was decided upon at a conference of the Cabinet on January 22, 1941.[17] Here the political and cultural objectives were stated, as well as more general demographic ones, and the procedural lines were indicated. Population policy was to be developed as an essential basis for Japan's fulfillment of her mission ". . . to establish the East Asia Co-Prosperity Sphere and to plan for its healthy development and permanence." There were four specific goals of policy: (1) to ensure the perpetual growth of the population; (2) to surpass the rate of increase and the quality of the populations of other nations; (3) to ensure the armed forces and the labor for a high degree of national security; and (4) to redistribute the Japanese population in order to ensure guidance for the peoples of East Asia. These were stated as goals. If they were to be achieved, the Cabinet held that they must have proper spiritual bases. Four specific psychological beliefs were recognized as preconditions to the success of policy: (1) to be conscious that the highest values lay in the permanent progress of the Japanese race; (2) to reject an individualistic world outlook and to found life on the family (*ie*) and the race (people, or nation); (3) to be conscious of duty and to take pride in leadership and development of the East Asia Co-Prosperity Sphere; and (4) to recognize that the basic conditions for the national accomplishment of duty were the higher development, quantitatively and qualitatively, of the population of Japan itself.

The plans for population increase emphasized the need for a concurrent increase in births and decrease in deaths. The plans for birth increase involved a decline in the age at marriage and an increase in the number of children per married woman. Eleven specific recommendations were made. It is interesting to note that the eleventh and final recommendation was to ". . . prevent and prohibit contraception and abortion as means of birth control and eliminate venereal disease." The first and fundamental recommendation was psychological and cultural, i.e., "to strive for the exclusion of unhealthy thoughts and to strengthen the family system." The nine intermediate recommendations concerned measures to lessen the economic costs of children and to give rewards to

[14] Nakagawa, Tomonaga. "Shorai jinko no keisan ni tsuite." *J.m.k.*, 1(2):1-13. May 1940.

[15] Nihon. Kosei-sho, jinko mondai kenkyujo. "Jihen-ka no jinko mondai." *Shuho*, December 18, 1940. Pp. 9-17.

[16] *Ibid.* P. 11.

[17] These decisions are reproduced in many of the books on population written during the early 1940's. The one used here, entitled "Jinko seisaku kakuritsu yoko," and attributed to the Naikaku (Cabinet), was published as an appendix in: Nihon. Jinko mondai kenkyu-kai. *Jinko seisaku to kokudo keikaku.* See also: Nihon. Naikaku, kikaku-in. "Jinko mondai o do suru ka." *Shuho*, February 12 and 19, 1941. Pp. 23-31 and 36-45.

those with children. Specific policies included a system of marriage loans; a reform of the school system, especially through stimulating recognition of the national duty of motherhood; restraint of gainful employment among women over age 20; differential taxation of the married and the single; family allowances, with suggestions for a Family Burden Adjustment Treasury System; and preferential rationing and public recognition by appropriate means for families with many children.

The plans for reduction of mortality concentrated on attacks on infant mortality and tuberculosis. For the former, emphasis was placed on guidance activities in the Health Centers and an increase in public health nurses. The campaign against tuberculosis was envisioned in broad terms that included not only early discovery and more sanitaria but health insurance, improved housing, lesser hours of labor, and more adequate nutrition.

Plans for improvement in the quality of the population were placed on a co-ordinate status with those for an increase in numbers. The goal of the policies on quality was defined as ". . . increase in the spiritual and physical nature necessary for work and national defense." Quality here was conceived in social as well as genetic terms; the goals were not only the prevention of the reproduction of the unfit but the creation of ways of living believed to be conducive to the preservation of physical strength and the perpetuation of the values of Japanese culture. Seven specific policies were outlined: (1) rationalization of the distribution and structure of the population, with special reference to the dispersion of the population in metropolitan areas; (2) the preservation of the source of superior military and civilian manpower through working for a combination that maintained a fixed agricultural population in Japan and ensured that 40 per cent of all ethnic Japanese were in agriculture, whether in Japan, Manchoukuo, or China; (3) a reform of school courses, an alteration in methods of training, and an extension of provisions for physical education in order to further the spiritual and physical as well as the intellectual training of youth; (4) an emphasis on the training of urban youth in order that the cities of an urbanizing nation might also serve as a source of supply for superior manpower, military and civilian; (5) provision of a compulsory system of group training for fixed periods in order to ensure diligent training of mind and body among young men; (6) establishment of a healthy and simple style of living for the people; and (7) planning the promotion of eugenic thoughts and thoroughly strengthening the national eugenic laws.

When the Planning Board of the Cabinet issued its statement on policy, it deleted the seventh recommendation, but added two additional ones: To endeavor to spread superior thought, and to increase the self-consciousness of the Japanese people.[18] And then the Planning Board concluded: "The goal of population policy cannot be attained with specific plans alone. . . . We must abandon our individualistic outlook on the world. . . . We also must realize our pride and responsibility as leaders in the establishment and development of the sphere of co-prosperity in East Asia, and at the same time we must recognize and understand the fact that to accomplish such a responsibility the Japanese population should make a remarkable advance in numbers and in quality. The self-consciousness of the Japanese themselves is the fundamental premise of progress of the Japanese people. Without this, it is virtually impossible to attain the goal of our population program, no matter what plans are set up to that end. For this reason the present population program places racial consciousness at its foundation."[19]

Thus, as Japan attempted through force to attain the political, economic, and cultural leadership of Eastern Asia, she adopted population policies designed to ensure manpower adequate in quantity and in quality for the role. There were honors and awards to mothers of many children, marriage loans, advance notices to army inductees, furloughs, family allowances, and special privileges for pregnant women and those with young children.

It is difficult to measure the influence of these policies on the population trends of the war years and impossible to assess what their effect might have been, had the future envisioned by Imperial Japan become a reality. The facts are that fertility rose above its low levels of 1938 and 1939 to slightly above where it would have been expected to be if the prewar downward movement had continued.[20] With the transfer of armed forces to overseas theaters and the further separations consquent on labor mobility, the maintenance of levels expected in the absence of war might be taken as a major achievement. However, there are two points that bar acceptance of this failure of fertility to drop precipitantly as indicative of successful population policies. In the first place, the comprehensive population activities were initiated in a period characterized by high levels of employment, an intact civilian economy, and either military success or unawareness of military reverses. Thus both economic and psychological factors predisposed toward continuing family formation and childbearing. In the second place, the policies designed to secure high levels of fertility did not eliminate the practices of limitation prevalent in the society. Fertility in urban and industrial areas increased somewhat between 1940 and 1943, but fertility in most rural areas continued its downward course. However, urban-rural and industrial-agricultural differentials persisted in 1943, as in 1940 or 1935. Reported stillbirths declined, but field studies indicated the persistence of abortion and infanticide.

The population policies of the war years favored a family-oriented life. Prestige was accorded to the wife and mother rather than to the women who strove for status in the world defined as belonging to men. Policies designed to reduce infant mortality were quite successful. Clinics for the care of babies, rewards for the mothers of many children, and a heightened community interest in young children were tangible aspects of policies that continued into the postwar years. The intensive campaigns against tuberculosis achieved spectacular successes in the postwar years, but the basis for them had been laid during the war. BCG vaccination, for instance, was introduced experimentally during the war years.

The population policies developed in 1940 and 1941 were accepted by the Cabinet and implemented by executive agencies of the government. Acceptance of the goals and the basic principles of implementation was almost universal in the press and in the demographic literature. However, the thought control of the war years was such that current policies could not have been questioned with impunity.

Contrary to the reaction to the reports of the Commission on Population and Food in 1930, in the early 1940's there

[18] Nihon. Naikaku, kikaku-in. "Jinko mondai o do sura ka?" *Shuho*, February 19, 1941. Pp. 36-45.

[19] *Ibid*. P. 45.

[20] See Chapter XVI, pp. 350-359.

was government planning for action, action itself, and wide public participation in the development of opinion. The policies were reasonably effective. It should be noted, however, that they were consistent with the familial values and the ethnocentrism of the culture. They strengthened indoctrinated expansionist sentiments through positive appeals to responsibilities that also involved individual and family opportunities for advancement. The demographic action was deeply flattering. It was designed to arrest the diffusion of the "pernicious" values of urban life and Western individualism. It was not action requiring modification of historic values.

SCAP: Policies, Actions, and Evaluations

The Allied Powers were aware of the population situation of Japan even before they assumed the responsibilities of the Occupation. They also knew the role that population had played as a rationalization for expansion over the decades when the Empire and the Co-Prosperity Sphere were being forged. The Allied strategy of the war had been predicated on the assumption that Japan could be defeated through the destruction of industry rather than by the attrition of manpower. The planning for the immediate problems of the Occupation was based on the assumption that the population would survive the war relatively intact, with some gashes among men of military ages and some deficits of births, but without substantial impairment of its potential for future growth. Longer-run planning even before the end of the war assumed a restoration of the prewar trends toward decline both in fertility and in mortality. The population on October 1, 1945, was estimated as about 71 million, the future population in 1950 as about 83 million.[21]

Knowledge of the economic and political problems of population and employment in postwar Japan did not lead to advance planning for the introduction and implementation of policies designed to influence the rate of population growth. Population policy *per se* was in ill repute. The policies developed in the late 1920's and early 1930's had been of a type acceptable to American thinking, but they had been ignored by government and leadership groups within Japan. The relations among militarism, racialism, and population policy in the late 1930's and early 1940's were well known. Moreover, the changing demographic and political implications deduced from population research had led to distrust of demography and demographers.

There were elements in American culture and aspects of conflict in American life that would have precluded effective population policy on the part of the Occupation even if it had been regarded as essential from the standpoint of Japan and the Japanese. Overt governmental policy in the field of fertility control had no basis in American experience; it was not in accord with American traditions with reference either to the family or to the proper role of government. Moreover, while there was agreement as to the existence of a severe population problem in Japan, there was and could be no agreement as to the desirable approach to a solution. And, finally, there were awkward questions as to the spheres of life appropriate for policy formulation by an army of occupation.

With the surrender of Japan, the immediate tasks of the Allied Powers were those of ensuring the demobilization of the armed forces and the destruction of war matériel. To the military government, the restoration of transportation and distribution channels, the relief of destitution, and the prevention of epidemics were tasks as gigantic as they were critical. Armed forces and repatriates were pouring into the ports of the country, many of them from areas where typhus, plague, and cholera were prevalent. Koreans were moving toward ports to secure passage home. Homeless evacuees from bombed-out cities numbered millions. In Hiroshima and Nagasaki there was the aftermath of history's first experience with atomic bombs.

The gradual restoration of prewar trends in mortality, fertility, and migration has been described in previous chapters. In a sense, this was the restoration of normalcy, but the differences in achieved levels and rates of change in the separate demographic variables created a demographic situation that was basically new.

The reduction in mortality came quickly. The general goals of the Occupation, the humanitarianism and efficiency of the Public Health and Welfare Section of SCAP; the hopes and fears of the Japanese—all these were favorable to an extension of health activities. By 1947 death rates had been reduced to somewhere near the levels that would have been anticipated on the basis of prewar rates of decline. It was already apparent that tuberculosis could be brought under control and that further progress could be made in the limitation of deaths from a variety of causes. Death rates hitherto characteristic of the West were being attained in a culture whose levels of income were far below those of any of the advanced industrial Western cultures.

Fertility increased sharply in the early years of the Occupation, despite the losses of young men in the early marriageable ages and the persistence of practices of control in many sections of the population. The people had been indoctrinated for many years with the virtues of abundant reproduction. The performance of abortions had been subject to severe punishment in the war years, and contraceptive supplies were not available. There were many new families having the first or second child. There may have been many families having babies to replace the children who had died in the war years. The birth rates were actually not high in comparison with what would have been expected in an agrarian culture, but they appeared very high after the declining fertility of the late 1930's. In addition, the population had increased so greatly that annual numbers of births were very large. The differences between relatively high birth rates and sharply reduced death rates produced the highest rates of natural increase in Japan's history.

The reactions to the high natural increase were intensified by the return of some seven million Japanese who had been abroad. Admittedly, three and a half million of these were members of the armed forces, people whose homes were in Japan. The other three and a half million were Japanese whose exodus from their homeland had contributed substantially to the reduction of pressure on the labor market in Japan in the 1920's and the 1930's. However, there were no vacant places in agriculture or in industry for repatriates. There were no new places for youth maturing within Japan. The initial movements of the demobilized armies and the civilian repatriates were primarily to their places of *honseki* in Japan. Thus in the immediate postwar period another vast group of people once predominantly urban joined the evacuees still in the rural areas. The return to the cities began soon, but the early returnees con-

[21] U.S. Office of Strategic Services. Research and Analysis Branch. *Population and migration in Japan.* Report No. 2450. Washington, September 8, 1945. (Classification canceled by authority of Order Sec. Army, by TAG. 8L 103.)

sisted disproportionately of the mature who had fled. Normal migration within the demographic and social setting of Japan could have occurred only if all the evacuees, the refugees, the repatriates, and the demobilized armed forces other than first sons had been able to move out into non-agricultural occupations. Migration would have had to continue swiftly enough to prevent increase of the people in agricultural occupations and in villages. This rate of migration had occurred in the 1930's when war-associated industrialization, movements to the developing centers of the Empire and affiliated and occupied areas, and conscription had reinforced the normal labor force requirements of an industrializing economy.

The original economic plans for Japan had envisioned a return to the levels of living of the mid-1930's in a country without either military equipment or the capacity to produce such equipment. As knowledge of the intensity of the agriculture, the paucity of the resources, the limitations of markets, and the institutional adjustments to abundant labor grew more definite, the depth of the problem of developing a viable economy became apparent. The quantitative documentation of the existing problem and the requirements for the future in terms of trade and markets became known at about the time the population increase reached toward and then exceeded 2 per cent per year.

Projections of the future population made in the Economic and Scientific Section of SCAP contributed to the realization of the magnitude of the economic difficulties that lay ahead. Three series of estimates were made. All assumed that the age-specific mortality as of 1948 continued to 1970. Fertility decline from 1948 to 1953 was assumed to occur at three different rates; after 1953 there was assumed to be a uniform amount of decline in the ratio of births to women aged from 20 to 44. In the minimum estimate as of 1970, fertility would be at about the level reached in the United States in 1940. Total populations estimated in specific future years were as follows, numbers being in thousands:[22]

Year (Jan.)	*Minimum*	*Medium*	*Maximum*
1948	79,129	79,129	79,129
1950	82,495	82,811	83,097
1955	87,255	89,002	90,531
1960	91,683	94,953	98,037
1965	95,820	100,772	105,518
1970	99,558	106,244	112,670

In its analysis of the implications of the population increase in Japan, the Economic and Scientific Section of SCAP placed major emphasis on the increasing labor force. It pointed out that, assuming a continuation of age-specific labor force participation rates as of 1949, Japan's labor force would increase by more than one-third in the twenty years from 1950 to 1970, and that this increase was almost unavoidable. Some reductions could be made by later entrance and earlier retirement; if the structure of the Japanese economy was altered and incomes were much higher, married women could cease to labor as unpaid family workers. However, it was emphasized that the hard core of the problem consisted of the increase in the numbers of men in the productive ages. Analysis of the structure of the labor force indicated that no additional employment would come in agriculture, but that agriculture would contribute workers to the more industrial segments of the economy. The absorption of the total increase of the labor force in non-agricultural employment would require a level of industrial employment in 1970 that was from 50 to 70 per cent above that of 1940.[23]

The analysts of the Natural Resources Section of SCAP also understood the land-resources-people relation in Japan. Demographic consultants were added to the staff, and they served to focus public discussion on the population problem.[24] The Natural Resources Section prepared an analysis of the natural resources of Japan. In this study the projections of the Economic and Scientific Section were used as a basis for the assessment of future resources requirements. There were also references to the relation among population increase, resources requirements, and resources use. In the conclusion it was stated that the population problem was part of the resources problem, and that the problem created by reduced death rates could hardly be solved humanely except through reduced birth rates.[25]

The Catholic Women's Club of the Tokyo-Yokohama area protested this publication as a violation of the following statement by General MacArthur: ". . . The Supreme Commander wishes it understood that he is not engaged in any study or consideration of the problem of Japanese population control. Such matter does not fall within the prescribed scope of the Occupation, and decisions thereon rest entirely with the Japanese themselves. . . . Birth control, with its social, economic and theological sides, is, in final analysis, for individual judgment and decision. The more basic problem of population is long range and world-wide and certainly not within the purview of prescribed allied policy or the defined scope of the Supreme Commander's executive responsibility or authority."[26]

SCAP recalled the copies of *Japan's Natural Resources* that had already been issued, ordered the offending sentences deleted, and turned the book over to a private concern for publication.[27]

In the spring of 1949 the Public Opinion and Sociological Research Unit of the Civil Information and Education Section planned a survey of attitudes toward the population problem. The schedules were designed and pre-tested in Tokyo and surrounding prefectures. Interviewers were hired from the various universities, and field locations were determined for a national sample. In June of 1949 the survey was ordered canceled.[28]

The absence of research on the population problem or population policy by SCAP does not mean that other policies of SCAP failed to have a major impact on the population problem of Japan, or that the actions and policies of SCAP were not significant factors in the attempts to formulate policy on the part of the Japanese. It was SCAP that preserved the Japanese population as a relatively intact biological group.

[22] SCAP. GHQ. Economic and Scientific Section. "Future population of Japan, 1950-1970." *Japanese Economic Statistics, Bulletin*, No. 32, pp. 142, 147. April 1949. *Bulletin*, No. 33, pp. 221-224. May 1949.

[23] SCAP. GHQ. Economic and Scientific Section. "Japan's future labor force." *Japanese Economic Statistics, Bulletin*, No. 40, Section IV, pp. 23-25. See also: *Ibid.* Section III, pp. 5-8. December 1949.

[24] Dr. Warren Thompson spent three months in Japan early in 1949 as consultant to the Natural Resources Section, GHQ, SCAP. He was followed by Mr. P. K. Whelpton.

[25] Also in 1949, SCAP refused a military permit to enter Japan to Mrs. Margaret Sanger with the explanation that her visit would be used for political purposes.

[26] *Nippon Times*, July 2, 1949. Statement issued June 6, 1949.

[27] United Press dispatch of February 7, 1950, reproduced in *New York Herald Tribune*, February 8, 1950.

[28] Seki, Keigo. P. 70 in: "CIE ni okeru shakai chosa no tenkai." Pp. 68-80 in: Nihon minzokugaku kyokai. *Shakai chosa, Minzokugaku kenkyu*, Vol. XVII, No. 1. February 1953.

It was SCAP that contributed so greatly to the reduction of death rates and, through this, to the increase of the population.

Many of the early policies of SCAP were conducive to high birth rates. The economy was to function at its 1934-1936 levels, with emphasis on employment in agriculture and small industries. The economic pressures in the villages were to be eased through a land redistribution program that would make Japan a country of operator-owners in the American tradition. On the other hand, some policies of SCAP were conducive to a reduction in fertility. There was to be equality in inheritance, with no primogeniture for boys and no disinheritance for girls. There was to be equality of opportunity for all social classes and for women as for men. Education was to be emphasized, and media of mass communication were to serve the democratic process.

On the whole, the indirect influence of SCAP and the period of the Occupation seems to have been favorable to declining fertility. The people who were to be restored to the living levels of 1934-1936 saw Americans and their ways of life, and they saw American movies. Many Japanese visited America, and American publications were brought to Japan. Aspirations rose rapidly, until for many urban groups they approached those of the Americans. Perhaps deeper than all these were the reactions to defeat and the pervasive feeling of hopelessness. Land reform tied people to land from which they could not secure a living. The abolition of primogeniture barred the ancient securities for the eldest sons, while the absence of economic opportunities in the industrial and urban economy spread pessimism about the chances of second and third sons. SCAP policies barred American action in the population field, but the numerous controversies on the subject awakened Japanese to the inconsistencies between SCAP policies in Japan and the limitation practices of the American people. Moreover, birth control became and remained a widely publicized topic.[29]

A definitive evaluation of the relation of the Occupation to population trends in Japan and the population policies of the Japanese would require a type of analysis not possible here. Two final points should be noted. First, the adoption of population policies by a conquering army might well have furthered the already strong identification of population policy with militarism and war rather than with peace and welfare. Second, the advocacy of family limitation among the Japanese by an army of occupation that was predominantly American would have permitted the accusation of genocide. However, the extent to which SCAP policies or their absence were responsible for the national resort to abortion is an unanswerable question.

Japanese Moves Toward Policy: 1946-1949

In the last months of the war and the early months of the Occupation there was widespread distress, an obviously high mortality, and an economic and social order or lack of it that seemed to presage the end of the historic Japan. There were reports that deaths would exceed births by a million or so in 1946, and that Japan's population could be expected to shrink to 60 million within a decade. The pessimism of the Bureau of Statistics, with its estimate of 60 million, was exceeded by that of the Ministry of Public Welfare, which reputedly estimated that the population would decline to 50 million within a decade or two.

The restoration of the statistical system and the analyses of demographers soon revealed that fears of decline were groundless, that in fact the population was then increasing and presumably would continue to do so. Estimates for the years from 1946 to 1950 were made by a Subcommittee on Population for the Statistics Committee of the Economic Stabilization Board.[30] It was assumed that fertility would move in relation to prewar Japanese trends, but with a postwar behavior comparable to that of Germany after World War I. In specific terms, the birth rate, 28.0 per 1,000 total population in 1946, would rise to 30.5 in 1947 and decline either to 26.5 or 24.0 in 1950, the two assumptions being carried through as Estimates I and II respectively. The death rate was assumed to be 26 in 1946; mortality was assumed in Estimate I to decline to the level of the 1935-1936 life tables by 1950, and in Estimate II to decline to the level of the 1920-1925 life tables.[31] Repatriation was assumed to be completed in 1946. The resultant total populations were as follows, numbers being in thousands:[32]

Year	*Estimate I*	*Estimate II*
April 26, 1946	73,734	73,734
October 1, 1946	75,810	75,810
October 1, 1947	77,899	77,802
October 1, 1948	78,502	78,164
October 1, 1949	79,238	78,511
October 1, 1950	80,088	78,833

Proposals for Policy

Thus it was demonstrated that on any reasonable assumption as to a functioning economy not subject to natural or man-made catastrophe, population increase of major magnitude would continue. The Institute of Population Problems (Jinko mondai kenkyujo) analyzed the results of the projections insofar as rates of increase and changing sex and age structures were concerned, but the function of the Institute was limited to research. Policy problems were obviously critical, however, if rapid natural increase was to occur within the constricted area and economy of postwar Japan. On January 30, 1946, a round-table conference on the population problem was held by the Ministry of Welfare. As a result of the discussions, a Population Planning Committee was appointed by the Foundation Institute for Research on Population Problems.[33] The Committee reported on November 20, 1946, with a "Proposal on the fundamental course and aim of population policy."[34] It began its report with the statement that the balance between population and carrying capacity had been destroyed, that unparalleled surplus population was now an un-

[29] It should be noted that the Occupation authorities permitted the importation of sheet rubber and other materials that could be used in the manufacture of contraceptive supplies.

[30] Nihon. Keizai antei hombu, tokei kenkyu-kai, jinko bunka-kai. *Shorai jinko no suikei ni kansuru hokoku. Showa 21-nen 8-gatsu.*

[31] The q_x values of the fourth life table yielded a death rate of 20 in 1946. Accordingly the q_x values were raised to give a death rate of 26 and then used as the base line for the projected age-specific death rates.

[32] Tachi, Minoru; Ueda, Masao; Kubota, Yoshiaki; and Takagi, Naobumi. "Showa nijugo 'nen made no suikei jinko no bunseki." *J.m.k.*, 5(3-4-5-6). March-April 1947. *Ibid.* "Showa nijugo'nen made no suikei shorai jinko no kaisan." *J.m.k.*, 5(7-8-9). July-September 1947.

[33] The Institute for Research on Population Problems (Jinko mondai kenkyu-kai) was reorganized as the Foundation Institute for Research on Population Problems (Jinko mondai kenkyu-kai, zaidan hojin).

[34] Jinko mondai kenkyu-kai, zaidan hojin, jinko taisaku iinkai. Foundation Institute for Research on Population Problems, Population Planning Committee. *Proposal on the fundamental course and aim of population policy*. Tokyo, November 30, 1946. Typescript.

deniable fact. Two countermeasures had to be explored: one, an increase of the capacity for supporting population; the other, the regulation of population itself. As to the first, the increase of capacity, the Foundation Institute was pessimistic. It pointed out high production costs in agriculture, scarcity of raw materials, limitation of markets, and the prospective industrialization of neighboring countries. Its members feared that surplus population would continue, that there might be ". . . no way left except requesting the sympathetic co-operation of foreign countries concerning peaceful emigration."

The questions concerning quality and the regulation of population presented many difficulties. With reference to quality, the Committee believed that the National Eugenic Law should be transferred from a voluntary to a compulsory basis. Recommendations for expanded activities to reduce mortality were agreed upon by all members of the Association; there were no conflicts of values concerning the desirability of saving the lives of infants and the tubercular. The recommendation of the diffusion of contraceptive practices was recognized as inevitable, but as a difficult matter. In the belief of the Institute, "birth control is liable to weaken the sense of responsibility for marriage, and to lead to the decline of sex morality." Moreover, with contraception, there was believed to be a counter-selection of the unfit. In a minority dissent, strong opposition to contraception was combined with an advocacy of solutions through economic development, distribution control, and emigration.

After 1946 the anticipated increase in births occurred, and deaths declined far more rapidly than had been expected. The government and the public alike became concerned over the future of the country if the numbers of people continued to increase so rapidly. At a conference on April 15, 1949, the Cabinet decided to establish a Population Problem Council ". . . to make investigation and deliberation concerning the population of our country in meeting the inquiry of the Prime Minister." The Council was organized in two sub-committees, one on population capacity, the other on population control. On November 29, 1949, the Council made interim recommendations to the government.[35] Its general conclusion was as follows: "The solution of our problems demands not only the suppression of population expansion through birth control but also emigration overseas coupled with the rehabilitation of domestic industry and restoration of foreign trade for enhancing the country's population supporting capacity."[36]

The report of the Council presented the facts as to population increase and potential growth. It also indicated the limited contributions of birth control to the reduction of population growth in the short run. The relations of family planning to family economies and public health were indicated as critical benefits. Abortions were condemned severely, as was the projected revision of the Eugenics Protection Law.

In practical terms, the Population Council realized that Japan's freedom of action to implement its recommendations in the economic field or with reference to emigration were limited severely. With reference to conception control, it made four specific recommendations: (1) Immediate improvement of health centers, eugenic marriage consultation offices, and similar organizations to train personnel and provide nation-wide public health education on the population problem, family planning, eugenic protection, and techniques of contraception. (2) Special efforts to diffuse contraception among lower social-economic groups, with revision of the Livelihood Protection Law to provide materials free of charge. (3) The establishment of a government office to administer population affairs, including guidance in family planning, and the strengthening of the Population Problems Institute and the Institute of Public Health. (4) "It is essential to exercise precaution not to harm the retention of good social customs and popular morals when information on conception control is furnished and when efforts are made to popularize this control."[37]

No actions were taken on any of the recommendations. The Council lapsed in March 1950.[38]

ACTION FOR BIRTH LIMITATION

While the Cabinet's Population Commission was deliberating on the intricate economic, social, and moral aspects of the population problem, a revision of the Eugenics Protection Law of 1940 was placed before the Diet. The bill appeared innocuous, but its major advocates were those who favored the diffusion of contraception.[39] As approved on September 10, 1948, the bill had as its stated object ". . . to prevent the increase of the inferior descendants from the standpoint of eugenic protection and to protect the life and health of the mother as well." Sterilization was permitted not only for eugenic reasons but if the life of the mother was endangered by conception or delivery, or "if the mother has several children and her health conditions seem to be remarkably weakened by each occasion of delivery" (Ch. II, Article 3.5). Induced abortions for strictly eugenic reasons could be performed at the discretion of the physician. For other reasons, listed below, the physician, with the consent of the person in question and the spouse, was to apply to a District Eugenic Protection Commission for investigation and permission: (1) If a female had any one of a specified list of diseases. (2) "If a mother has again conceived within a period of one year after delivery, and seems remarkably injurious for her health by delivery." (3) If a mother with several children had again conceived and would have her health injured seriously by delivery. (4) If a woman had conceived under conditions of threat or violence.

Eugenic Marriage Consultation Offices were to be established, and they were to be attached to Health Centers. In the bill as originally passed, consultation on contraception techniques was solely for eugenic protection (Article 20).

A series of amendments liberalized the provisions of the Eugenic Protection Law as passed in 1948. In 1949, economic factors became permissible reasons for sterilization, induced abortion, and contraceptive advice.[40] In 1952 a comprehensive revision abolished the Eugenic Protection Committees, whose duty it had been, under Article 13, to investigate requests for abortions. The requirement for consultation with another physician was abolished. Moreover, the reporting procedure was changed so that reports went through the medical associations.

Thus while SCAP refused to consider population problems as within the purview of the Occupation and the Cabinet of

[35] Nihon. Jinko mondai shingi-kai. Population Problem Council. *Recommendations of the Population Problem Council in the Cabinet, Japanese Government, Nov. 29, 1949*. Tokyo, 1949. 20 pp.

[36] *Ibid*. P. 2.

[37] *Ibid*. P. 12.

[38] *J.m.k.*, 9(3-4):55-56. March 1954.

[39] The detailed provisions of the law as originally passed and in its successive amendments have been noted in Chapter XIII, "The Control of Fertility," pp. 269-270, and 276.

[40] For a discussion of diverse points of view at this time, see: Ryokufu-kai. "Zadankai: Jinko mondai o megutte." *Ryokufu bunko*, 1(1):32-59. October 1949.

Japan ignored recommendations made to it by a Population Commission it had appointed, the Diet of Japan legalized sterilization and abortion and placed contraceptive services in Health Centers. Initially limitations were severe and control of operations stringent. Increasingly, however, there was liberalization of reasons justifying these practices to include broadly defined economic factors and liberalization of controls over the designated physicians.

In this same period, while policy *per se* was being denied, the government of Japan again permitted the open sale of contraceptives and SCAP permitted the importation of materials.[41]

CONTRACEPTION FOR MATERNAL HEALTH

With the government decision to avoid the field of policy, the general public disillusionment with unsatisfactory and inefficient contraceptives, and the legalization of sterilization and abortions for the preservation of the health of mothers, the demographers and the public health, religious, and civic leaders of Japan were presented with a peculiar dilemma. The government that denied policy now permitted abortions at the discretion of physicians and placed contraceptive services in its Health Centers. The people might therefore be correct in assuming that government favored the limitation of births. This was not admitted; the activities permitted by government were presented as health policies, not as solutions to or alleviations of the population problem. There was general agreement among public health and medical people that abortions were an inefficient means of family limitation, and that a series of abortions might involve health hazards for the mother.

The Institute of Public Health was the organ of the Japanese government with official responsibilities for action with reference to the health hazard of abortions. A demographic section was established in the Institute and field studies of abortion and sterilization were undertaken. These studies covered incidence, social and economic correlates, psychological motivations and consequences, costs, and health hazards.[42] Experimental studies were made in three agricultural villages to determine the extent of existing practices of limitation, the receptivity to planned parenthood, and the response to general education and specific instructions in contraceptive techniques.[43] More recent studies extended the same experimental research approach to mining villages.[44]

The studies in the villages demonstrated that highly trained public health personnel working continuously with peasant or mining families over periods of years could conduct the public education and give the medical instruction that would lead to a major, consistent, and quite effective practice of contraception. However, the per capita investment of funds and personnel in these experimental villages could not be duplicated in all the local areas of Japan. Hence the Institute undertook more general educational programs, held institutes for the training of physicians, and then developed a program for training and licensing midwives.

The major role played by the Institute of Public Health was neither requested nor implemented as population policy. This was a public health activity, a program to lessen the harm presumably caused by abortions whose performance was presumably permitted to protect health.

RESEARCH, PUBLICATION, AND DECLINE OF FERTILITY

There was quiescence in the field of population policy in the years after 1949. The injunctions of General MacArthur barred activity by the technical staffs of the Allied Powers. The disregard of the recommendations of the Population Council of 1949 by the Japanese government furnished presumptive evidence that here, too, there were barriers against the consideration of policy. The public discussion created by these various controversies contributed to a still more widespread focusing of public attention and public debate on population and the population problem. Arguments over the Eugenic Protection Act of 1948 and its successive revisions made people conscious of population needs and spread the information that abortion and sterilization could be secured. Advertisements, shop displays, and other paraphernalia of distribution called attention to contraceptives.

The continuing increase of the population, the persistence of inadequate employment opportunities, and the recurrent statistical reports of the government were perhaps the most important of the forces educating people to the fact that a population problem existed. In 1947, 1948, and 1949 the country was told month by month and season by season of the high number of births, the reduced number of deaths, and the increase of the population. Monthly the Statistics Bureau of the Prime Minister's Office announced the size of the population and the size of the labor force, together with its occupational and industrial composition. The results of the censuses placed in sharp focus not only the growth of the population but the high densities throughout rural areas and cities. Economic reports contributed nothing to optimistic evaluations of the present or the future. People who had once been urban but now were displaced, youth for whom there were no jobs in distant cities, repatriates who remembered the years of the Co-Prosperity Sphere as a happy interlude, college graduates for whom the professions had no openings—these and many other groups began to think in terms of demographic solutions. It was their decisions as to their own families that led to sharp declines in national fertility and altered the population prospects for the nation.

The Institute for Research on Population Problems (Jinko mondai kenkyujo) continued its researches and its services to government agencies dealing with population or population statistics. Series of projections reflected the attempt to maintain statistical cognizance of developments occurring with such rapidity that specific projections were outmoded prior to publication. Analyses of the course of fertility and mortality were continuing. Initially there were field studies of contraceptive practice in limited areas. These were extended in scope until the pattern of regional and social-economic differentials in contraceptive practice and the speed of its diffusion began to emerge. In 1952 the Institute cooperated in a project whereby information on fertility, contraceptive practices, and abortion were secured by regular enumerators from a subsample of the national sample in current use by the Bureau

[41] The Pharmaceutical Law was revised in July 1947 and contraceptives could be sold openly as of May 1949.

[42] Detailed citations of the published results of these studies are given in the Bibliography. For English summaries, see: Koya, Yoshio. "A study of induced abortion in Japan and its significance." *The Milbank Memorial Fund Quarterly*, 32(3):282-293. July 1954. Also: Koya, Yoshio; Muramatsu, Minoru; Agata, Sakito; and Suzuki, Naruo. "A survey of health and demographic aspects of reported female sterilizations in four health centers of Shizuoka Prefecture, Japan." *The Milbank Memorial Fund Quarterly*, 33(4):368-392. October 1955.

[43] Koya, Yoshio, *et al. Research on population health, especially test studies in three rural villages.* Published on behalf of The Japan Association of Public Health.

[44] Koya, Yoshio. *Present situation of family planning among farmers and coal mine workers in Japan.* United Nations World Population Conference E/Conf./3/50.

of Statistics. Life tables were computed each year so that trends in the components of growth could be followed separately and combined in refined measures of reproduction.

The studies of the Institute for Research on Population Problems were not limited to formal demography removed from an economic and social context. There were studies of the distribution of the population, economic structure and occupational mobility in special groups in limited areas and, within a larger context, the population-carrying capacity of rural areas and the population potential of the cities. It is difficult to assess the influence of this research. The studies were used in government action and planning. The members of the Institute's professional staff spoke and wrote on population subjects. The senior members of the staff participated in the official, quasi-official, and unofficial committees concerned with population problems.

A major role in stimulating public concern and public thinking outside the government was taken by the Mainichi Press. In 1949 the editorial bureau of the Mainichi Newspapers established a Population Problems Research Council. The secretariat was furnished by the newspaper, and the membership consisted of citizens from various fields of specialization. The Mainichi conducted surveys and public opinion polls on population. National surveys of attitudes toward and practices of family limitation were conducted in 1950, 1952, and 1955. Other surveys concerned economic and social aspects of the population problem and alternative solutions—invisible unemployment in agricultural villages, the family system and population in rural communities, the influence of emigrants on their home villages. Materials from these studies were published in the Japanese and English editions of the Mainichi Newspapers. The studies were published in full in Japanese, and summary reports were issued in English. The Population Problems Research Council published books on the population problem and sponsored lectures and discussion meetings.[45]

The Foundation Institute for Research on Population Problems (Jinko mondai kenkyu-kai) seems to have undergone a period of relative inactivity after its early policy recommendations in 1946. In 1951 it issued a bulletin called *A white paper on Japanese population.*[46] This was a factual report on the trend of the population, its industrial structure in relation to fertility, the problem of food, and the spread of birth control and legal abortion. This report was presented as the first of an "enlightenment series." At this time, Jinko mondai kenkyu-kai had defined its function as a twofold one: (1) to carry out surveys and research on the population problem; and (2) to arrange and improve facilities that could contribute to a solution of the problem, operating co-operatively with other groups whose goals were similar.

The research and the public educational activities carried out by or associated with the demographers had broad similarities, whatever the time period and whatever the sponsoring group. Everywhere the dichotomy between increase of the economic base and decrease of the birth rate existed, along with a recognition that policy movements in both directions were essential. There was acceptance of the basic elements of SCAP reforms, but there was also a continuity in the desire for emigration and a recognition that an increase in productive capacity was a more attractive goal than a restriction of births for the negative reason that economic poverty or health dangers required it. Finally, all research and policy groups opposed induced abortion.

The economic aspects of population research and the general statements of the economic requirements of the increasing population were not a basis for operational decisions by government. They could not have been expected to become such. There is the obvious fact that Japan was a country under military occupation in the period prior to 1952, and even thereafter major decisions as to desirable international fiscal and trade policies could not be implemented unilaterally by the Japanese. Economic activities and economic policies involved two major requirements that took priority over demographic and labor force requirements in the short run. The first was the maintenance of imports to meet the requirements of the people and to restore the physical plant of the country. The second was the maintenance of fiscal solvency with a reasonable balance between external trade and fiscal balances and internal inflation or deflation. Rates of capital formation and production indexes had direct and major relevance to the present. Rates of population increase were slow-moving variables in these postwar years. Moreover, manipulation of current birth rates would influence the population in the productive ages substantially only after two more decades had passed. There was still another difficulty. The formulation of population policy was in major part an activity of or associated with the Welfare Ministry. Population research and public health were allocated to this ministry in the structure of the Japanese government. The powerful economic ministries and the Cabinet remained remote both from research and from the turmoil of public debate.

This does not mean that economic developments and economic policies were not factors in the formation of public opinion and the trend of events in the demographic field in these early postwar years. The population problem was defined in economic terms: "population pressure" economically measured, latent unemployment, imbalances in the geographic and economic distribution of youth and productive workers, the cumulation of people in the rural areas, the influx into the cities. Whatever the relations might be in the long run, at any specific time the economic factors were the independent variables, while the population policies and the demographic evaluations were the dependent variables.

Ancient economic practices and current economic decisions were forces both in the preservation of high fertility and in the stimulation of practices of limitation. A duality in the relations of labor practices to levels of fertility was a heritage of the economic and population policies of the war years. Familistic relations between companies and employees were conducive to the preservation of the old ways of life as long as the economy was expanding. The oldest son of the employee had a job with the company; often younger sons could be absorbed in the company either in Japan or in a branch or an affiliated company overseas. In the days when national concern was focused on the permeation of "artificial values" among the people and policies were designed to ensure the continuation of large families, systems of family wages were instituted. In the postwar period the companies could offer no employment to younger sons, and the former employees returning from abroad could not be absorbed in Japan. An

[45] Mrs. Margaret Sanger visited Japan in the fall of 1952 at the invitation of the Population Problems Research Council of the Mainichi Newspapers. Her activities in Japan are described in: Mainichi shimbun-sha, jinko mondai chosa-kai. Mainichi Newspaper. The Population Problems Research Council. *Family planning movement in Japan.* Population Problems Series, No. 9, Tokyo, 1953.

[46] Jinko mondai kenkyu-kai. Association for the Research of Population Problems. *White paper on Japanese population.* Population Research Series, No. 1. Tokyo, 1951. 37 pp.

assured future for the children was gone. In many cases, the future of the worker himself was insecure. Family wages persisted, though financial equalization was largely wiped out by inflation. Even at a minimum level, however, the system of family wages stimulated the reduction of fertility. New employment or the maintenance of old employment tended to be selective with reference to family size. Labor practices moved from the ancient status relations toward the "temporary" worker and the productivity wage. More specifically, abortions were added to the health services subsidized by the companies, in part to avoid the long-time payment of even small allowances. Contraceptive supplies were sold at wholesale prices or subsidized cost, and in some instances there were active educational activities to spread contraceptive practices.

The demographic developments in the years of the Occupation indicate slight relations among the reports of learned commissions, the studies of scholars, and the decisions of representative groups of national leaders as to what the people should do in the field of family planning. Political realities, the lethargies and hesitancies associated with the proper role of women in the culture, the structure of medical care, the absence of indigenous crusades for birth control, and the retarded state of research on human conception and gestation and on sex practices and attitudes all contributed to a schism between what the leaders said or recommended and what the people did. These various factors may be noted briefly, since most of them have been discussed in detail in connection with one or another of our substantative analyses.

The interrelation of political factors, population trends, and population policies is probably the most neglected of all fields of research, and yet the relations here are fundamental. The government of Japan, like SCAP, reacted against the population research and the population policies of the past by taking the firm position that the regulation of family size was a matter for decision by individual families. Moreover, it may be seriously questioned whether or not the Cabinet was convinced that the permanent policy of the government had to be based on an anti-natalist policy. Economists and statesmen alike had seen that the population problem was not an independently definable problem, that it appeared and vanished with changes in the political and economic situation of the country. They realized that whether or not the population of the present was to be a problem or asset in the future depended on economic and political events still to occur. The technical validity of the assumption that the population problem of Japan was a dependent phenomenon does not concern us here; the people who made decisions were influenced by their observations and their beliefs. Their observations over the two preceding decades had convinced them that population policies involving pessimistic evaluations of the future and recommendations for birth limitation were products of periods of economic depression and political difficulties, that policies developed in periods of economic prosperity and political confidence were nationalistic and pro-natalist. Support of policies of increase was politically feasible. Policies that involved the acceptance of economic retardation and population limitation violated the ethnocentrism of the people and the expansionism of the state. Moreover, these policies of defeat dealt with matters not properly subjects of open discussion and public action. There was still another political impediment. In the early years of the Occupation the population problem was espoused by left-wing parties. Mature consideration by conservative parties thus became difficult.

There is substantial evidence that the population policies whose recommendations emphasized contraception but condemned abortion were not in accord with the wishes of the Japanese people. If one contrasts the political processes in the prewar and postwar periods, it becomes apparent that the passage and the successive modifications of the Eugenic Protection Law as well as the activities it induced represent postwar democracy. The law as passed in 1948 and modified in 1949 and 1952 was not foisted on the people through the machinations of *zaibatsu*, military leaders, or Occupation forces. The "feudal" forces of Japan's past were opposed to it.

When considerations of population policy arose in Japan in the years from 1946 to 1948 or 1949, the problems requiring action were the simple ones faced by population commissions in many Asian countries. Birth rates were high; the problem was the stimulation of reduction in ways acceptable to the culture. It was assumed that reductions in marital fertility would come primarily as a result of contraceptive practices. By 1951 and 1952, however, the definition of the problem had altered in Japan. There had been a very rapid decline in fertility. In a sense, the goal of population adjustment policies was being accomplished so swiftly that it began to seem that the real problem was not the initiation and stimulation of fertility decline but how and when the process of decline could be halted. The difficulty was that the major means utilized to secure limitation was abortion, which the commissions and the scholars disapproved, rather than contraception, of which they approved. The major educational task became not so much the diffusion of the idea of family planning as the substitution of one means for another.

Since in fact contraception and abortion stood in sequential relation to each other, the decisions faced by those who wished to develop realistic policies with reference to induced abortions were difficult indeed. An approach to this problem was made in the activities of the Institute of Public Health. Here, in a public health setting, education as to the medical advantages of contraception was combined with instruction as to means of contraception. This approach, which combined education, medical assistance, and a voluntary choice of means, was utilized in the experimental village studies. These were medical personnel functioning as such, however. It was not within their province to deal with questions of social and ethical policy and political feasibility. These questions could not be avoided if the diffusion of contraception was considered as a segment of a broad population policy involving all aspects of the interrelations among people, economy, society, and state.

The rapid declines in fertility that presented such a dilemma to the formulation of population policy were not predictable on the basis of research on fertility immediately prior to the period when the declines began. Moreover, the paths and the rates of diffusion of abortion and contraception were predictable only in the broadest of outlines on the basis of current research in the various areas of the country and among the various segments of the population. In the formative years of the early postwar period, there had been considerable research on the demography and the social institutions of people who lived in agricultural, fishing, mining, and forest villages. The association between the ancient way of life and high fertility remained close. Universal education, electric lights, roads, radios, farmers' organizations, and contacts with sons and brothers in great cities and imperial areas had co-existed with a traditional role for married women that was relatively intact and a scarcely perceptible lessening of the age-specific rates of reproduction for these married women. Even in the postwar years few of the village women admitted knowledge of contraception and fewer still admitted the practice. It was widely believed that children were accepted as a natural part of an unquestioned way of life, though it was known on the basis of other studies that abortion persisted in critical situations and at ages where childbearing was inappropriate. There was no active search for information on how to avoid conception. Furthermore, the hesitancies were so deep that locally available contraception information remained largely unsought. In area after area where company health facilities or Health Centers had contraceptive supplies available at low cost, the women would pass them by. Purchases were made by husbands sent especially for that purpose.

The experimental village studies of the Institute of Public Health suggest that women may not have been as resigned to childbearing as they appeared to be. It is simple now to recall that in the late Tokugawa *bakufu* and the early Meiji period village women had taken the drastic step of infanticide to prevent family size from becoming too large. However, when early studies showed a resistance to abortions and contraception, it appeared reasonable to conclude that Japanese familism had survived the war, that frustrations, discontents, and positive action to limit family size had somehow failed to penetrate this world. In recent years, however, birth rates have moved sharply downward in the historic centers of the presumably highly resistant rural society. The initial explanation was resort to induced abortion, but current studies indicate an acceptance of contraception, at least to the extent of admitting the practice. Japan is achieving one of the major goals of population policy in all underdeveloped areas that have adopted population policies, a rapid decline in the marital fertility of the peasant. Yet that decline has occurred without population policy, unless the legalization of permissive induced abortions be defined as policy. The role of the educational activities concerning population and the national controversies over birth control and abortion is an important question. Here it would seem that research might contribute substantially to the formulation of policies in other areas, if not in Japan itself.

The structure of medical care in obstetrics and gynecology involved adjustments both to the reticences of women and to the low levels of income, and these were of a type that were conducive to the spread of abortion and sterilization rather than contraception. In the normal course of events, babies were delivered by midwives at home. Other things remaining equal and the number of midwives remaining constant, income increased in direct relation to the numbers of births. The pharmaceutical laws forbade midwives to sell chemical contraceptives, and they were not trained to give advice on contraceptive techniques. For the midwife to advise contraception would involve personal sacrifice. Abortion and sterilization, on the other hand, were performed by designated physicians who received a fee for their services. Hence the gynecologists and other designated physicians had a direct financial interest in the liberalization of abortion laws and the frequency of resort to abortion. This is not to suggest malpractice on any major scale, but only to indicate that there were groups interested in easing the regulations with reference to abortions. There were no comparable pressure groups with reference to contraception. Planned parenthood associations might have played such a role, but there were no major organizations of women working to secure acceptance for the principles of planned parenthood through contraception. There were many small groups, and there were birth control clinics, but it was not until September of 1953 that the desirability of inviting the International Planned Parenthood Conference to meet in Japan led to the consolidation of groups into a national Planned Parenthood Federation.

The retarded state of research on human conception and gestation must be mentioned as a final factor in the abortion-contraception balance in Japan. Suggestions of the need for an appropriate means of contraception are found occasionally in the reports and recommendations on population policy, but the depth of the problem is seldom admitted in demographic literature. In the early period after the war there was nation-wide advertising of miraculous products, and sales mounted rapidly. The products must have been inefficient or unsatisfactory, for production soon dropped sharply. Current contraceptive practice relies mainly on the widely known techniques subject to the control of men. Neither doctors nor birth control clinics have played major roles in dissemination. It is permissible to speculate that the national resort to abortions might have been far smaller in extent and might have lasted a briefer period of time if the contraceptives available in 1946-1947 and later years had been effective.

Given strong motivations to prevent increases in family size and the tradition of direct action to achieve limitation, the rapid diffusion of the resort to induced abortions is comprehensible. More unexpected is the rapid diffusion of contraceptive practices. The critical questions for research become the psychological interrelations between abortion and contraception and the influence of a general awareness of the population problem and the population controversy on the decision for limitation by either means or by some combination of the two.

New Moves Toward Policy on Fertility

The initiative for a renewal of efforts to achieve comprehensive national policies in the population field was taken by the Foundation Institute for Research on Population Problems (Jinko mondai kenkyu-kai).[47] A conference on the national population problem was held in Tokyo on May 25, 1952, on the twentieth anniversary of the founding of the Institute. A Committee on Population Policies was established under the chairmanship of Dr. Nagai, the chairman of the Foundation Institute. At its first general meeting on June 30, seven problems were recognized as within the cognizance of the Institute: (1) changes in population structure, especially the rapid increase of the population in the productive ages; (2) the industrial structure and population increase; (3) levels of living in relation to population increase; (4) the improvement of the quality of the population; (5) the diffusion of contraception; (6) overseas emigration in relation to the population problem; and (7) the geographic distribution of population. Two subcommittees were established, one on Population and the Standard of Living, the other on the Quantitative and Qualitative Adjustment of Population. The latter subcommittee considered the diffusion of family planning as a part of general population policy to be a matter of urgency and so reported to the General Committee on June 14. The "Resolutions concerning the diffusion of family planning as population policy" were accepted by the Committee on Population Policies, adopted by the Foundation Institute, and submitted

[47] Nihon. Kosei-sho, jinko mondai kenkyujo. *J.m.k.*, 9(1-2):68-70. November 1953.

to the Welfare Minister and other members of the Cabinet as recommendations of the Institute on June 30, 1954.[48]

The Committee on Population Policies of the Foundation Institute for Research on Population Problems proceeded on the assumption that the limitation of population increase was essential to the reduction of population pressure in Japan.[49] The birth control that it advocated was not merely a reduction in numbers of births, however achieved, but a planned parenthood by married couples that would regulate the numbers of children and the intervals between births in the interest of preserving and improving levels of living and health conditions. The means should be contraception, and every effort should be made to prevent the abuse of induced abortion and sterilization. We quote: "In view of the foregoing, it is necessary for the Government to adopt strong and adequate measures immediately for the thorough practice and diffusion of family planning as a part of the general population policy."[50] The Subcommittee recognized the historical reasons that had led to a justification of education and guidance in contraception solely in terms of maternal health. However, it stated its belief that policies for the diffusion of contraception needed a more positive motivation than the prevention of the morbidity and mortality associated with abortions, that in fact policies for the diffusion of contraception must form part of a general population policy.

The Subcommittee formulated general principles for a positive approach to family planning as an integral part of general population policy. A clear distinction was made between the diffusion of family planning and guidance in contraceptive techniques. In essence, it felt that the reasons for family planning lie in attitudes toward life based on modern rationalism; family planning should be considered as guidance for living. The Subcommittee recognized that special efforts would be necessary if planned parenthood as thus conceived was to spread in lower social-economic groups, farm villages, and the low income areas of cities. It believed that contraceptive facilities should be developed under the Daily Life Security Law (public relief), and that facilities should be available as benefits under health and social insurance systems.

In view of the existing demographic situation, the Subcommittee emphasized the need to spread knowledge of family planning among young married women. "Measures should be taken to guide their beginning at the time of their marriage."[51]

Specific operational recommendations were made: Guidance organizations such as Health Centers and marriage consultation offices should be strengthened and the training of instructors should be improved. The frictions and restrictions of the existing guidance system should be regulated and there should be positive co-operation of civilian guidance organizations with each other and with governmental groups. The conclusion was that continuing research was essential if means of contraception were to conform to the needs of the various strata of the population and to accord with the special characteristics of Japanese family life. Continuing studies of the status of contraceptive practice should serve as a guide in relation to further diffusion and guidance. Sex education should be increased, but there should be emphasis on morality in sex and family life.

Finally, the Subcommittee indicated the close associations between family planning and other aspects of individual aspirations and national policy. In their view, the advance of the national economy, the rise in standards of living, and the aspirations for a more cultured life were correlated with the general maturity required for family planning. It was pointed out that family planning becomes even more essential for individual families as their incomes reflect the pressures of an expanding population in the productive ages. Provisions for the aged may become essential as the structure of the population is altered, but the development of social provisions for old age will itself be conducive to a planned family among youth.[52]

Throughout the period after the lapse of the Cabinet Council on Population in 1950, research on population had been undertaken by Jinko mondai kenkyujo (Institute for Research on Population Problems). This research was done by a small staff within the Welfare Ministry and there was no procedure whereby its results could be related to policy or could be utilized in the formulation of policy. By decree of August 14, 1953, the Cabinet established a permanent Council for Population Problems.[53] The Council was to consist of not more than 40 members and not more than 22 expert consultants, all appointed by the Minister of Welfare from among persons with knowledge and experience in the relevant fields and from among the personnel of government agencies. Article 1 defined the functions of the Council as follows: "The Council for Population Problems . . . , responding to the request of the respective ministers concerned, shall investigate and deliberate matters, mentioned hereunder, relative to the Population Council and shall present to the same ministers such views as are deemed necessary on the [following] subjects: 1. Standard of living. 2. Structure of industry. 3. Natural resources. 4. The adjustment of conceptions. 5. The improvement of the quality of the people. 6. Any other important matters relating to the population problem."

Building on the work of the Committee on Population Policies of the Foundation Institute for Research on Population, the Council on Population Problems of the Welfare Ministry submitted its recommendations on fertility control on August 24, 1954.[54] In the preamble to this "Resolution on the quantitative adjustment of population," the Council recognized the persistent overpopulation of Japan and pointed out that "If the matter should be left to run its own course, it would intensify the instability of livelihood as well as the difficulty of establishing a self-supporting economy, thereby bringing about the confusion of social order and possibly further obstructing the promotion of international peace."

[48] Published in English translation by Jinko mondai kenkyu-kai as: Foundation Institute for Research on Population Problems. Committee on Population Policies. *Resolution for diffusion of family planning as population policy*. Tokyo, 1954. 15 pp.

[49] It was recognized that regulation could proceed through emigration or the control of births. Emigration was reserved for later consideration because it involved many other factors than population policy within Japan.

[50] Jinko mondai kenkyu-kai. *Op.cit.* P. 3.

[51] *Ibid.* P. 5.

[52] Eugenic factors were recognized as important but were reserved for later and more specific consideration.

[53] Government Decree No. 189 of August 14, 1953, pursuant to the provision of Article 29, Paragraph 2, of Law No. 151 of 1949, Law for the Establishment of the Welfare Ministry. See note, *J.m.k.*, 9(3-4):55-56. March 1954.

[54] The Council on Population Problems was divided into two subcommittees—one to consider population capacity, geographic distribution, and levels of living; the other to consider the quantitative control and qualitative improvement of population. In addition, a special committee was established to prepare a white paper on population and to issue yearly reports on population after study of the present situation and the future prospects. The yearly reports were to "present the essence of the population problems in our country." See: Nihon. Kosei-sho, jinko mondai kenkyujo. *J.m.k.*, 9(3-4):55-56. March 1954.

The importance of emigration and eugenics were noted, but priority was assigned to family limitation.

The basic resolution of this governmental council of 1954 follows:

> In order to solve the important problem of population now confronting our nation, it is necessary beyond dispute to adopt a policy for promoting the strength to support its population. However, in the light of the prevailing situation in which the pressure of population is only hampering the accumulation of capital and rationalization of industry, it is necessary for the Government to adopt a policy designed to check the growth of population.
>
> It is necessary that the government should take up the conception-control movement hitherto conducted from the standpoint of protection of maternity, but should now adopt it also from the standpoint of the planning of families as a link in the chain of the overall population policy, provide every person desiring birth control with adequate means and facilities, and further take steps to remove any obstacles and friction hindering the popularization of that practice.

The Council then proceeded to make specific recommendations for the implementation of this resolution. It felt that since the stimulation of family planning within the framework of a general population policy should be a direct responsibility of government, a department should be established to fulfill this function, and private groups should be urged to co-operate. All impediments to practical guidance in contraception should be removed; information on methods should be disseminated through health and other social insurance systems; supplies should be free for the destitute; welfare agencies in mines and other establishments should co-operate. Family planning and related matters should be included in the curricula of medical schools; doctors who perform induced abortions should be required to give contraceptive information to dissuade women from resort to further operations. Any wage or tax procedures that resulted in increased fertility should be eliminated. Finally, research on the quantitative and qualitative trends of population and studies of family planning should be conducted as guides to administration and policy.

The Problems of Policy

Population policies have been developed by the Japanese government in times of crisis. The motivations have been predominantly economic, although problems of morality and national destiny have been involved. If the policies as developed were in accord with the values of the culture and the power orientation of the state, they were adopted and implemented by specific actions. If the policies were not in accord with the familial mores of the people and the codes of propriety among the elite, they were not adopted. Twice a comprehensive policy has been eagerly implemented. The first case occurred in that rather remote period in the late Tokugawa and early Meiji eras when infanticide and abortion were to be eradicated as barbaric practices. The second was in the years only a decade and a half ago when abortion and contraception were to be eradicated as pernicious values of a materialistic and alien civilization. Both policies were positive. They were associated with the creation of a new and better order, rather than with adjustment to depressed economic and political conditions. In both instances, the people were enjoined to act in accord with the values of the culture, and material and psychological rewards were given for so acting.

Twice also population policies have been developed by government commissions but ignored by the agency of government to which recommendations were made. The first case was in the late 1920's and early 1930's, when a coincidence of large annual increase and economic depression made the population problem appear to be due to a surplus of people. The second was in the late 1940's, when the coincidence of the postwar boom of births and the economic limitations of the early postwar era focused national and international attention on the population problem. The population commissions of 1927-1930 and 1947-1950 cannot be dismissed cavalierly as unsuccessful because their general recommendations remained unacknowledged and their specific recommendations were ignored. In each instance, there was drastic action by government in the field of population-economic relations, though in neither instance was the action consistent with the social philosophy and the stated value premises of the men who had made the studies and framed the policies recommended to the government. In 1931 the decision for continental expansion and the creation of an economic domain in which Japan should be paramount was rendered almost irrevocable by the move into Manchuria. This was an economic solution that led within a decade to a situation in which the population problem was defined as one of numerical insufficiency, with an ensuing decision to increase the birth rate. In 1948-1949 the government that had ignored recommendations for the diffusion of contraception within the framework of broad population policy made sterilization, abortion, and contraception permissive on eugenic and health grounds.

In the years from 1951 to the present, the government has permitted increasingly effective work by private and governmental groups to reduce fertility, though their efforts have had to retain the guise of activities to reduce health hazards. In any realistic definition of the term, the liberalizations of the Eugenic Protection Law that made abortions and sterilizations available at low cost were government policy in the population field, whether the original Eugenic Protection Law of 1948 is defined as a genuine eugenic and health measure or as a ruse to make means of birth limitation available to the people. The executive agencies of government did not develop major policies to stimulate limitation *per se*, but public health programs to spread contraceptive practices were developed directly by government on order of Cabinet Ministers. Again, whether the real motivations were the protection of health or the reduction of population increase cannot be determined on objective evidence.

The considerations of policy have always had two aspects, one economic, the other demographic. The demographic aspect has concerned fertility and mortality. Recommendations to expand the internal economy, to increase international trade, and to seek areas where emigrants might go have been favorably received.[55] Recommendations to reduce mortality have been included in all policies, and the reception has always been favorable. The only questions with regard to economic and political expansion, emigration, reduced mortality, and improved health were those of feasibility. It is with reference to recommendations on fertility that the reports of population commissions have been accepted or rejected.

The present demographic, economic, and political situation of Japan differs so sharply from that of the century before the defeat of 1945 that answers as to the future of population or of policy cannot be derived directly from the record of

[55] Recommendations for economic and tax reforms that would result in an internal redistribution of income were not received with the favor accorded recommendations that concerned external economic and political expansion within the framework of the existing structure of economy and state.

the past. The economic imperatives for the future are not difficult to state, but they do not appear to be realizable in the present state of international tension. Political and economic factors have combined to maximize the population problem, and there is no escape from internal solutions through political and military adventures abroad.

The situation of Japan with reference to fertility today also differs markedly from that which existed in 1930 or in 1948. Then fertility was defined as high; the problem was to secure rapid reduction. The thinking and the recommendations were solely in terms of the diffusion of contraception. The barriers to action included deep resistance to government action in a field appropriate for family decision. Now the situation is quite different. Government, responsible civilian groups, and ordinary people alike recognize that the pressures of manpower on employment opportunities within the country are severe, and that there can be no evasion of the problem through external action. Fertility has declined greatly. In fact, it is not unlikely that sometime in the near future the problem of fertility will be redefined as that of the means whereby fertility can be maintained at levels adequate to renew the population. At present, the basic problem is the substitution of more acceptable for less acceptable techniques of family limitation. There is also the related problem of ensuring that practices of family limitation permeate all social and economic classes. The question of whether or not married couples should limit family size is now academic. Such limitation exists. The problem is control and guidance of the limitation in the interests of the preservation of basic institutions, the avoidance of sex behavior defined as immoral, and the prevention of differential reproduction believed to be harmful to the physical quality of the people.

CHAPTER XVIII

The Past and the Future

IN THE fifteenth and sixteenth centuries Japan sent great armies to the mainland. Her ships roamed the Pacific, and her trading settlements were scattered as far as Thailand. Possibilities for eastward expansion were great, for America north of the Rio Grande was sparsely settled, its agricultural and other resources waiting as a developmental area and a demographic safety valve for adventuresome and ambitious people. From the early seventeenth to the mid-nineteenth century, however, Japan remained in seclusion. There was peace and quiescence under a political and social order believed to be immutable. Only remote influences of the Renaissance, the Reformation, and the commercial, agricultural, and industrial revolutions reached Japan. Her people were largely illiterate, and poverty was severe. Death rates were high, while famines and epidemics occasionally decimated the populations of regions and cities.

While Japan developed so slowly, European peoples landed on the east coast of North America, established settlements, and expanded across the continent. By the middle of the nineteenth century, the territory of the United States of America extended from the Atlantic to the Pacific, from the Great Lakes to the Rio Grande. The population numbered 23.2 million. Japan had somewhere near 32 million people on the three islands of Honshu, Shikoku, and Kyushu. The only frontier was the island of Hokkaido, but it was far to the north and mountainous, and its resources were limited.

IMPERIAL JAPAN: 1868-1945

Evaluations of the somber prospects for Japan's resources, economy, society, and population did not deter the men who planned the Meiji Restoration and the new Japan. In the Pacific region all people except the Chinese had been reduced to colonial status, and China's future was hazardous. The statesmen of the Restoration realized that survival itself was the critical problem. Power in the world that Japan had entered required munitions and ships, fortifications and transportation systems, scientists and engineers. Military force rested on industry, and prudence dictated that this industry be located in Japan, manned by Japanese, and subject to Japanese control without interference by aliens who furnished capital. Thus the drive for industrialization at whatever cost was in considerable part derived from the decision to make Japan a military power. Initially, the causal sequence ran primarily from militarism to industrialism rather than vice versa. Neither welfare goals nor population pressure were the primary motivations in economic development.

The modern pattern of population growth evolved in the last half of the nineteenth century, though the rapidity of the transformations and their interrelations with the society and the economy altered within the nineteenth century itself and still more in the early twentieth century. There was colonization in Hokkaido and an increase in cultivated acreage in Japan, while productivity per unit of cultivated land was also growing. Industries were developing not only in cities, but in rural areas where the labor of the daughters of the peasants contributed to Japan's production for world markets. A dual economy developed. There were industries that employed workers in great modern factories, but there were also industries where family workers predominated. There were *mura* where people lived much as they always had, but there were also great cities where an industrial civilization developed rapidly. Rural living, dependence on agriculture, hard labor, and poverty were one cluster. Urban living, dependence on industry and commerce, labor for wages, and higher incomes formed another. The direction of the movement was from agriculture to industry, from rural area to city. Urban areas received youth, particularly males, and these areas grew so rapidly that their populations came to include large portions of people in the productive ages. In the cities marriage was postponed to later ages and ratios of young children to all women or to married women were lower than in the surrounding countryside.

When the increase in national population began is difficult to determine with any precision. By 1895, however, death rates had been reduced sufficiently to produce appreciable rates of natural increase at the levels of fertility then existing. Any assumptions that the population of the Tokugawa era had increased to the limits of subsistence had proved erroneous. Agricultural production had increased, natural resources were supplemented through widespread trade, and industry was adding both to production and to employment opportunities. By 1900, there were many more people living in Japan than there had been in the mid-nineteenth century. Levels of living were higher. Rising levels of education and lowered death rates suggested that the qualitative aspects of living had been changed in directions that the Japanese people found desirable.

The population increase that had occurred in the last half of the nineteenth century had as yet produced no tragic consequences, but neither was there freedom from worry about the upward course of population. Numbers had been about 36 million in 1875. By 1905 they were 47 million. The number of mouths was increasing steadily; soon rice produced at home would be inadequate to feed the nation. Each year there were more men in the productive ages than there had been the year before, and there was no longer much chance for the younger sons of the peasants to establish branch families on land in or near the village where the father lived. Jobs were difficult to secure in the cities, and people objected to the severe climate, the isolated living, and the low levels of income and culture in Hokkaido.

Japan achieved status as a world power with the defeat of Russia in the first decade of the twentieth century. She was the most advanced industrial nation in Asia, with levels of living far above those of many nations on the continent.

However, in Japan ancient arts and practices were intermingled with modern industrial production and wage remuneration. Disparities in the consumption and income levels of peasants and urban workers were great, and problems of markets were severe. Continuing population increase involved difficulties in employment and production.

Internal economic growth, expanding trade, and political expansion characterized the early decades of the twentieth century. With the annexation of Taiwan in the south and Korea, Kwantung, and the South Manchuria Railway Zone on the mainland of northeastern Asia, Japan controlled areas suitable for major investments of capital in economic development. In the Micronesian Islands to the far south she acquired strategic bases for defense or for further advance. However, the population situation remained serious, as the country was transformed into a rice-deficit area.

The pattern of population development in the 1920's illustrated both the industrialization and urbanization that had been achieved and the extent of the developments that were necessary if the population was to be balanced with employment opportunities. Fertility declined with consistency. Gross reproduction rates were lower in 1925 than in 1920, and lower in 1930 than in 1925. This downward drift occurred not only in Japan as a whole but in each of the 47 prefectures. There were persistent advances in the age at marriage for men and women in the rural areas, as in the cities. Increasing proportions of the population were living in cities and so subject to the higher ages at marriage that characterized urban dwellers. The fertility of married women was declining also, though the practice of planned parenthood was concentrated in the cities. Death rates were declining more rapidly than birth rates. Fertility was declining in response to altered ways of living and correlated changes in values and aspirations. This was a slow process of undirected cultural transformation. It was quite the opposite with mortality. Imported technologies and trained personnel operated with the resources of the government to prevent needless death and to reduce morbidity and ill-health. The death rate dropped so rapidly that the absolute number of deaths declined from year to year. And although fertility was declining, the numbers of women in the childbearing ages were increasing so rapidly that annual numbers of births increased from year to year. As the size of the annual increment to the population increased, the population problem became visible to the general public.

The military activities of the years from the end of the Russo-Japanese War to 1930 were limited. Armed forces were maintained, but numbers were not large enough to reduce the pressure of maturing youth on the employment market. There was some migration to imperial areas but it was more than compensated by an influx of Koreans into Japan. The change in the immigration laws of the United States to exclude Japanese and other Asians added further to the growing sense of desperation about the population problem.

Economic developments in the 1920's held to the village industry-textile factory mold. The exodus from agriculture continued; the number of households and the population gainfully occupied in agriculture changed little between 1920 and 1930. The data of the census of 1930 revealed a cumulation of unpaid family labor in retail trades, service trades, and other marginal economic positions. With the great depression in the United States, the virtual disappearance of the market for silk, and the proliferation of restrictive trade practices, the economic situation of Japan became very serious.

So precarious was the population-resources-economy relationship that a population problem would have existed in Japan in the absence of population increase. With population increasing by a million a year, rapid economic expansion was required to maintain levels of living. Three to four hundred thousand additional workers entered the non-agricultural labor market each year. Political stability and human welfare alike dictated that they have opportunities other than the unpaid family labor which was Japan's familial substitute for unemployment insurance or a public dole. In this period of the late 1920's, the government appointed a committee with a mandate to study the problem of food and population.[1] Its constitution, the problems with which it dealt, and the nature of its recommendations were summarized in the preceding discussion of the population policies planned by the government of Japan.[2] The recommendations were twofold. One part concerned the basic problem of the high fertility that resulted in the continuing production of ever larger total populations and ever more workers year by year and decade by decade. The other part concerned increases in production and trade as well as reforms of the production and distribution system to secure more equitable consumption among socioeconomic groups and to enlarge internal markets.

The report of the Commission on Population and Food dealt with the long-run interrelations of population growth and levels of living. Its recommendation that planned parenthood should be encouraged did not seem an immediately helpful one to an economy and a government in crisis. Even under the most optimistic assumptions as to the readiness of the people to accept contraceptive practice, diffusion would have been a slow process. Precipitant declines in fertility could not be expected to follow quickly after a decision of government to encourage contraceptive practice, and even immediate declines in fertility would produce substantial reductions in the labor force only in the distant future, not in the present period of crisis. Whatever the explanation may be, the recommendations of the Commission on Population and Food were not adopted as government policy.

In 1931 the intervention in Manchuria began, and in 1937 it was extended to North China. The consequences of this action have been considered as an aspect of the demography of war and need not be discussed here.[3]

In the late 1930's there was a major reorganization of the industrial structure, with rapid developments in those segments essential to war. Cities and industries grew rapidly in areas accessible to the Asian mainland; centers of light industries and the traditional crafts stagnated or declined. Youth poured out to Manchuria and, later, North China, either as civilians or as members of the armed forces. So rapid was the urbanization between 1930 and 1940 that 14 of the 47 prefectures lost in total population. In 1940, less than one-third of the gainfully occupied men in Japan were in agriculture. There were almost one and a half million Japanese civilians in Manchoukuo and Occupied China, and some 1.7 million men were in the armed forces. Manpower shortages were imminent in a nation in which population increase had led to predictions of demographic disaster only ten years earlier.

Natural increase remained appreciable during the 1930's, but it was slowing. Civilian mortality continued downward among youth of both sexes and among adult women, but tuberculosis was leading to increased mortality among young

[1] Chapter XVII, p. 366.
[2] *Ibid.*
[3] See Chapter XVI.

men. Fertility declined rather sharply, for age at marriage was advancing and the migrations of industrialization and war were separating increasing numbers of married couples. Projections of the trends in mortality and fertility indicated that eventually growth would cease.

The reaction of the Japanese government to the political, economic, and demographic situation of the late 1930's was the adoption of a strong pro-natalist policy. To describe this policy as purely militaristic is to oversimplify the situation. Military success and temporary economic prosperity associated with it provided an indispensable basis for population planning on the premise that the population problem was manpower deficiency rather than redundancy. Direct military elements were involved; the major goal of policy was to ensure manpower adequate to the civilian and military requirements of the nation. Beyond this, however, policy was positive, not negative. Government propaganda urged population increase in the interest of the nation's imperial destiny and as a contribution to the political stability, the economic development, and the cultural advance of all East Asia. The reports of the demographers to the Imperial Cabinet pointed out that political, economic, and health developments in the Co-Prosperity Sphere would result in rapid rates of population increase among the agricultural peoples of Asia. The increased reproduction which was advocated in the government policies was not for the sake of more soldiers, but for leaders competent to assume the responsibilities of peaceful development over vast areas with massive populations.[4]

Since we have noted the failure of the Japanese government to adopt policies designed to hasten the reduction of fertility, we should note here the limited effects of the policies designed to increase fertility. National fertility had been below its 1920-1937 trend line in 1938 and 1939. In the years from 1941 to 1943 it deviated little from its prewar trend line. A favorable evaluation of the effects of the policies would designate the absence of decline below this level as success. An unfavorable evaluation would deny any major efficacy to policy, pointing out that full employment and the *élan* of victory were associated with the maintenance of fertility in many countries where there were no pro-natalist policies.

In the years from 1938 onward, Japan's internal economy and her labor market were geared to military production and the maintenance of her armed forces, if not to war itself. Economic developments in Taiwan, Korea, and Manchoukuo were integrated segments of the over-all dedication of productive power to military preparation. The migration of rural youth from the land, the interchange of manpower between areas, the growth of cities, the increases in age at marriage, and even the declines in fertility were aspects of what was regarded until late in the Pacific War as a forward movement to a greatly enlarged area of economic development.

Government actions designed to alter rates of population growth were minor factors in the evolution of the Japanese population from the Meiji Restoration of 1868 to the surrender in 1945. Government problems were the urgent ones of survival in the short run. The emphasis was placed on economic measures to increase production and to utilize the manpower currently available. Actions on fertility were always postponed for mature consideration, for there were no simple solutions to problems of overabundant fertility. Restrictionist policies were not in accord with the values of the traditional culture. Moreover, it was difficult to see how the decisions of government could lead straight way to the practice of contraception by individual families. There were also disturbing questions that involved aspects of society other than the control of numbers. Many questioned whether customary morality could be preserved if techniques of contraception were widely known. Eugenic aspects were disturbing, for the limitation of family size among upper social-economic groups was believed to jeopardize the quality of the race. These were difficult questions on which to expect governments to act. Decisions were evaded in periods of crisis. When economic recovery came, there was official quiescence concerning the desirability of fertility control, the means of family limitation, and the political and economic implications of rates of population growth. Thus, throughout the history of Imperial Japan, fertility remained in the domain of cultural and traditional values. Its magnitude and its characteristics for the nation as a whole reflected the actions and the decisions of individual families without guidance on techniques of birth control as then known or appreciable research designed to advance scientific knowledge and practical applications in this field. On the other hand, mortality declined in direct relationship to guidance in techniques of death limitation as then known. Research designed to advance scientific knowledge and practical applications in regard to health and mortality received high priority, and the knowledge of other countries was assiduously sought and eagerly applied. Slow declines in fertility, more rapid declines in mortality, and long-continued population increase were necessary consequences of the differences in the nature of the forces influencing fertility and mortality and the differences in government action, scientific research, and technology as applied to the two sides of the population question. This was an expected development and it occurred in many countries other than Japan. Health was a positive value, and the continuity of the family was another such value. The prevention of conception or childbirth was not in itself a value, nor was it a practice tied to an approved value. Government was part of the culture; the people who determined policy and action in government were not only responsive to the values and the will of others but were themselves members of the culture.

The Years of Reconstruction: 1945-1950

The early assessments of the economic future of Japan by the Occupation Forces envisioned return to the per capita levels of production that had existed in 1935-1936. Emphasis was placed on agriculture—on the extension of the area of utilization, on improved crops and better practices, on a more equitable distribution of property rights in land, and on improved distribution through cooperative activity. Industry was to be of the traditional light type, without the heavy industries that had been associated with preparations for war in the past and that would permit similar preparations in the future. The requirements for the maintenance of an economy of this type were estimated on varying assumptions as to the economic conditions and trade possibilities in the Far East as a whole.

The facts of present and estimated future population growth soon complicated the plans for a desirable future for Japan. The population projections made in the Economic and Sci-

[4] There is no evidence of a long-run analysis of this situation, in which Japanese would be cooperating with agricultural countries whose increasing populations would force them also to adopt policies of industrialization if the lowered death rates were to be maintained.

entific Section of General Headquarters, SCAP, involved what were believed to be realistic assumptions as to rapid rates of decline in fertility. The "optimistic" assumption required a generation for fertility in Japan to decline to the level that existed in the United States in 1940. The population increase that lay ahead was so great that the population problem came to be regarded by many people as among the most serious of Japan's difficulties.

The official and quasi-official committees that reported on the population problem in the early years of defeat adopted positions similar to those of the years of economic depression in the late 1920's and the early 1930's. The population which the committees of the late 1930's and early 1940's had viewed as a source of strength was now viewed as a weakness. The policies that were recommended included economic development, emigration, and planned parenthood.

When the Korean War began in 1950, developments seemed to be comparable to that of the period of the great depression two decades earlier. Pessimism as to Japan's ability to maintain and employ her people in the future, general recommendations for economic development and trade, the cautious and neglected recommendations for government action to diffuse contraceptive practice—all these recurred. It was the reaction of the people that was different, perhaps because twenty years of arduous experience had been added to that of the years before the Manchurian incident, perhaps because of the sharp transition from great victory in the early years of war to defeat and frustration in the late war and early postwar years. Whatever the factor or combinations of factors involved, the people seized upon the permissive legislation of the Eugenic Protection Law to adopt abortion as a means of family limitation. Along with or after that resort to abortion there occurred a rapid resort to contraceptive practice. The presumably resistant fertility which the Occupation Forces and the Japanese alike had expected to decline slowly dropped quickly. By 1955 the crude birth rate was less than 20 and the gross reproduction rate was 1.2. The net reproduction rate was 1.1.

To observers of this period, the comparison that first suggested itself was the late Tokugawa era, when infanticide was widespread. This comparison was natural when abortions became common in 1949 and 1950 and it was assumed that the motivations were those of poverty and economic pressure. As research was extended and official statistics became somewhat more representative of all abortions, it became apparent that the parallel between abortions in modern Japan and infanticide in Tokugawa Japan was limited. Perhaps both indicate a constellation of attitudes and values that facilitate direct action to reduce childbearing if that childbearing threatens the present or future way of life of those now alive. The practice of abortion diffused with extraordinary rapidity during the postwar years when restored movements from agricultural to non-agricultural occupations and rapid urbanization were lessening the pressures of industrial and urban growth. Moreover, those who practiced abortion seemed to be the same groups who practiced contraception. They were the urban rather than the rural, the upper rather than the lower social-economic classes, the young and those with few children as well as the old and those with many children. Here the parallels end, whether considered in relation to Japan's own history or to that of Western nations. Today's Japan, with its high rates of abortion and contraception practice, has achieved substantial reductions in the fertility of married women in the predominantly agricultural populations of remote areas. Regional differentials persist, but whereas in 1925 a birth rate of 40 or over was necessary to qualify as high, today a birth rate of 26 is high.

The population problem of Japan appears to be approaching a solution insofar as the numerical aspects of growth are concerned. The decline in fertility has been rapid and nationwide, and the trends of the years since 1949 lead to the anticipation of further declines.

The Situation from 1950 to 1955

By 1950 Japan had progressed far toward the restoration of normality in economic and demographic processes. Most of the people who had fled the cities in the last year of the war and the early postwar period of hunger and disease had returned. Some of the youth of the rural villages and towns were migrating to employment in the cities. Industrialization and urbanization were again the basic processes, although the levels achieved in 1950 were still below those of the early war years. Mortality had been reduced below any levels that could have been anticipated on the basis of prewar trends. The postwar increase in births was past, and ratios of births to women in the reproductive years were already below the levels expected on the basis of prewar trends. Japanese who had been permanent residents in the colonies or other regions of Asia had been returned to Japan along with the armed forces and civilian migrants of the war years. There were many missing from this population of 1950, but already the scars were healing. The survivors of the youth who had been age 22 when war began in China in 1937 were now 35 years of age. The small birth cohorts of 1945 and 1946 had reached kindergarten age, while the large number of toddlers of two and three years of age indicated that there had been many births in 1947 and 1948.

The problem did not lie in any peculiar characteristics of the Japanese population or in any abnormalities in its behavior insofar as migration or vital rates were concerned. The problem was the attained size and rate of growth in relation to the amount of land and other natural resources, the state and the rate of development of the economy, and the level of international trade. Natural resources as utilized were inadequate to meet the needs of the population. The economy was unable to provide jobs for all who desired and needed them. Intra-regional trade was at only a fraction of its prewar level. People alone seemed abundant in the Japan of 1950.

In numerical terms, there were 83.4 million people in the present area of Japan on October 1, 1950. On October 1, 1955, the number had increased to 89.3 million. The increase in five years had amounted to almost six million people. The declines in rates had been rapid, but growth itself remained substantial.

The six million people added to the population of Japan between 1950 and 1955 are not abstract entities except for counting purposes. They are men, women, and children, youth and aged. The changes in this five-year period are shown in graphic form in FIGURE 28. The absolute and percentage changes in age groups were as follows:[5]

[5] Source: Chapter IV, Table 21.

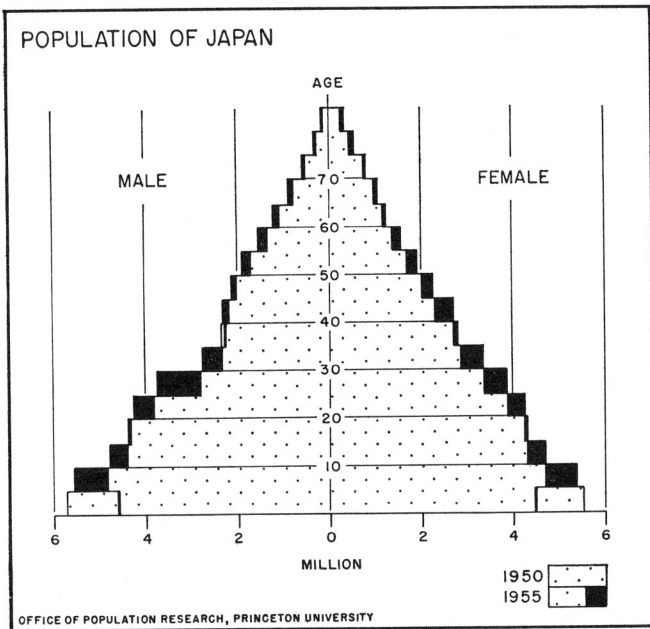

Figure 28. The population of Japan by sex and age, 1950 and 1955
Source: 1950: Nihon. Sori-fu, tokei-kyoku. *Showa 25-nen kokusei chosa hokoku.* VIII. Table 11. 1955: Footnote 7. Amami Oshima is excluded in 1955 as in 1950.

Age	*Number (in '000)* 1950	1955	*Change* Amount (in '000)	Per cent
Total	83,413	89,275	5,862	7.0
0-4	11,235	9,308	−1,927	−17.2
5-14	18,271	20,684	2,413	13.2
15-19	8,591	8,539	−52	−0.6
20-44				
Male	13,621	15,388	1,767	13.0
Female	15,088	16,766	1,678	11.1
45-64				
Male	6,241	6,876	635	10.2
Female	6,239	6,990	751	12.0
65 and over	4,128	4,724	596	14.4

The 7 per cent increase in total population in the years from 1950 to 1955 reveals little either of the inherent growth of the population or of the associated economic and political problems. Children below age 5 were 17 per cent fewer in 1955 than in 1950, whereas children aged from 5 to 14 were 13 per cent more numerous. Young men were receiving age groups untouched by war, while they were losing groups decimated by war. Older men, too, were increasing in numbers. There were 2.4 million more men aged from 20 to 64 in 1955 than there had been in 1950.

The forces of expansion inherent in the increase of the population may be shown by estimating the increase in the labor force that would be required by 1954 if participation rates for men and women remained at the level of October 1950.[6] In October 1950, there were 37.8 million people in the labor force. Population growth required a labor force of 40.7 million in October 1954 if participation rates for the sex and age groups remained unchanged. This is a total increase of 2.9 million, and an annual increase of 723 thousand. The required annual increase included 431 thousand men and 292 thousand women.

The actual labor force in October 1954 numbered 42.3 million rather than the 40.7 million required at 1950 participation rates. Average annual increases in this four-year period had amounted to 1.1 million, of whom 455 thousand were men and 672 thousand women. The percentages of men and women entering the labor force were changing rapidly. The following figures are percentages among the sex and age groups:[7]

Age	*Men* 1950	1954	*Women* 1950	1954
Total	84.3	85.1	53.0	58.0
14-19	56.3	55.0	51.8	51.6
20-24	92.3	88.5	69.0	74.2
25-29	96.6	95.5	51.6	61.1
30-34	98.2	97.3	51.7	58.2
35-39	97.9	97.9	54.5	60.8
40-44	97.4	97.9	59.9	64.3
45-54	95.9	96.4	57.7	62.5
55-64	84.9	88.5	47.7	52.0
65 and over	55.1	62.6	25.9	33.3

Participation rates were declining for men in the upper years of formal education, but they were increasing in late middle and old age. There were increases in participation rates for women at all ages over 20, and the increases were striking at the ages from 20 to 29. Advanced age at marriage and reduced childbearing in the early years of marriage would seem to be factors here.

The total labor force increased 12 per cent between October 1950 and October 1954, but the increase amounted to 8 per cent for men, 17 per cent for women. The patterns of changes by age as given in TABLE 138 reflect the combined influence of changing numbers in the sex and age groups and altered rates of participation in the labor force. Comparisons of the actual changes with those that would have been anticipated at 1950 participation rates indicate that 36 per cent of the total increase was associated with altered participation rates, 64 per cent with population increase. Only 5 per cent of the increase in the male labor force was due to altered participation rates, however. Ninety-five per cent was due to population increase. Fifty-six per cent of the increase in the number of women in the labor force was associated with increased participation rates for women of the various ages, while 44 per cent was associated with population increase.

The rapid increase in the labor force and the altered patterns of participation do not deny the existence of an economic problem in the provision of employment for the increasing population. They do demonstrate that changes in the numbers of people in the productive ages cannot be equated with changes in the labor force.

THE DIMENSIONS OF THE FUTURE: 1950-1980

Past estimates of future populations give little basis for assuming that the dimensions of the future can be seen with any degree of precision. At any given time, the makers of projections described the future inherent in a continuation of the

[6] Population, 1954: Nihon. Sori-fu, tokei-kyoku. *Rodoryoku chosa sogo hokokusho,* No. 2, March 1955. Broad groups, October 1954, Table 1. Detailed groups, September 1954, Table 2. Participation rates, 1950 and 1954, October, Table 5. Population adjusted to October 1954.

[7] *Ibid.* Table 5.

TABLE 138

Labor force, by sex and age, October 1950 and October 1954

	NUMBER (IN '000)						PER CENT CHANGE, 1950-1954		
	1950			*1954*					
Age	*Total*	*Male*	*Female*	*Total*	*Male*	*Female*	*Total*	*Male*	*Female*
14 and over	37,760	22,300	15,460	42,270	24,120	18,150	11.9	8.2	17.4
14-19	5,550	2,890	2,660	5,350	2,750	2,600	−3.6	−4.8	−2.2
20-24	5,840	3,230	2,610	6,030	3,160	2,870	3.2	−2.2	10.0
25-29	4,190	2,530	1,660	5,470	3,180	2,290	30.5	25.7	38.0
30-34	3,670	2,170	1,500	4,400	2,480	1,920	19.9	14.3	28.0
35-39	3,860	2,350	1,510	3,910	2,310	1,600	1.3	−1.7	6.0
40-44	3,630	2,210	1,420	4,080	2,330	1,750	12.4	5.4	23.2
45-54	5,900	3,700	2,200	6,660	4,010	2,650	12.9	8.4	20.4
55-64	3,490	2,250	1,240	4,230	2,690	1,550	21.2	19.6	25.0
65 and over	1,640	980	660	2,140	1,220	920	30.5	24.5	39.4

Source: 1950: Nihon. Sori-fu, tokei-kyoku. *Rodoryoku chose sogo hokokusho, 1947-1952.* Table 3. 1954: *Ibid. Rodoryoku chosa sogo hokokusho*, No. 2, March 1955. Population, Table 2. Labor force, Table 5. Amami Oshima is included in 1954 but not in 1950.

trends as of that time. In the late 1920's and early 1930's, for instance, the anticipated declines in fertility were slight. In the late 1930's and the early 1940's, rates of decline of a period of crisis were projected undiminished into the long-range future. There were analytical values in all these projections, for they showed what future populations would be under specific assumptions as to change.

Many new estimates of Japan's future population have been made in recent years. Some were made for use in government planning, while others were intended as models of the long-time results of hypothetical trends in fertility and mortality. None were presented as predictions. In the light of the kaleidoscopic changes of the war years and the recent precipitant declines in mortality and fertility, no one need tell the Japanese that their future population is not predictable.

THE ESTIMATES

TABLE 139 presents several estimates of future populations made in the years from 1949 to 1955. There are nine estimates in all, six made before the rapid decline in fertility began in 1949-1950, three made thereafter. Of the pre-1950 estimates, the first two were intended as assessments of probable developments, while the next four were illustrations of the influence of rapid declines in fertility on future populations. In 1948-1949 the Economic and Scientific Section of GHQ, SCAP, made estimates of the future based on the assumption that Japanese fertility and mortality would reach the low levels of the United States within a generation.[8] The staff of Jinko mondai kenkyujo made estimates using trends in England and Wales as a model. The resultant populations are strikingly similar for the years from 1950 to 1970. Continued slow declines in fertility and mortality such as those that had occurred in either the United States or England and Wales would have given Japan a population of 95 million in 1960 and 106 million in 1970. Growth would have continued throughout the twentieth century, with a population of more than 125 million by the year 2000. Estimates such as these underlay the pessimistic economic evaluations of the technical sections of SCAP as well as the Japanese Population Commission of 1948.

As fertility began to decline from its postwar peak, the demographers of Jinko mondai kenkyujo began to explore the consequences of rapid declines in fertility. In the first series of estimates they assumed that each Japanese woman had two children, while in the second series they assumed that each Japanese family had two children. In each case there were two estimates, one assuming that fertility dropped suddenly to its hypothetical level on April 1, 1950, the second assuming that it dropped on April 1, 1955. In all cases mortality was assumed to remain constant at the attained level of the period. These projections indicated that cessation of growth in a few decades would require extraordinary declines in fertility.

Appraisals of the future population made in the years after 1951 or 1952 differ sharply from those made from 1947 to 1949. Fertility had dropped more rapidly than expected. A radical estimate made in 1949 had assumed that the Japanese birth rate would decline to 20 by 1965. The actual birth rate was 20 in 1954. Mortality had also dropped rapidly, however, and projections assuming unchanging mortality were no longer realistic. In 1952 and later years, projections involved the dual assumptions of rapid declines in fertility from already low levels and continuing declines in mortality. A projection using a Swedish model for fertility and a New Zealand model for mortality yielded a total population of 100.7 million in 1970, a maximum population of 108.5 million in 1990, and a population of 107.0 million at the end of the twentieth century. Projections deriving declines in fertility and in mortality from Japan's own recent experience yielded similar results.

The analytical possibilities in estimates of future populations are apparent in the populations by age in TABLE 140. Mortality was reasonably low when the initial estimates were made, and it was lower still when the later estimates were made. In any event, death rates are now so low that future declines cannot be major factors in population growth except

[8] See Chapter XVII, pp. 370-371, for a further discussion of these estimates.

TABLE 139

Estimates of the future population of Japan, 1950-2000

(Numbers in '000)

Assumptions	*1950*	*1960*	*1970*	*1980*	*1990*	*2000*
Model: United States[a]	82,811	94,953	106,244	—	—	—
Model: England and Wales[b]	83,975	95,424	106,185	115,867	123,110	126,667
Two children per woman:[c]						
Adopted April 1, 1950	82,530	87,915	93,110	96,218	95,722	93,196
Adopted April 1, 1955	84,179	92,508	97,812	102,316	103,079	100,949
Two children per family:[d]						
Adopted April 1, 1950	81,995	81,981	81,185	78,042	71,427	62,373
Adopted April 1, 1955	84,118	87,885	87,110	84,870	78,805	69,753
Model: Sweden-New Zealand[e]	83,200	93,795	100,662	106,453	108,475	106,960
Recent Japanese trends						
First[f]	83,200	92,926	100,269	106,396	108,014	106,356
Second[g]	83,200	93,230	99,774	105,572	107,101	105,034

[a] SCAP. GHQ. Economic and Scientific Section. "Future population of Japan, 1950-1970." *Japanese Economic Statistics*, Bulletin No. 39. May 1949. See Chapter XVII, p. 370, for description.

[b] Nihon. Kosei-sho, jinko mondai kenkyujo. *Shuju no suikei shorai jinko.* Birth rate declines from 1947 to 1953 assumed parallel to England and Wales, 1920 to 1926; then decline to 20.0 in 1965, the rate of decline in 1953-1965 continuing to 2005. Mortality to reach that of England and Wales in 1938, by 1958; to decline to that of Sweden in 1931-1935, by 1968; and then to remain constant.

[c] *Ibid.* Estimates made in 1949 and based on 1947 census.

[d] Two children per married woman, assuming constant proportions married.

[e] Tachi, Minoru; Watanabe, Sadamu; Ueda, Masao; and Takagi, Naobumi. *Shorai jinko no suikei ni tsuite.* 1953 revisions presented here. Using maternal fertility rates, it was assumed that fertility would reach the Swedish level of 1937 by 1965 and remain constant thereafter. Mortality was assumed to reach that of New Zealand in 1934-1937, by 1965, and remain constant thereafter. Actual experience was used through August 1953.

[f] Tachi, Minoru. *An estimate of future population of Japan (revised).* Mortality and proportions of women married were projected to 1965 and held constant, projection being on the basis of trends from 1920 to the time of study. Trends in age-specific maternal fertility, 1948-1952, were projected to 1960 and held constant thereafter.

[g] Takagi, Naobumi. "Suikei shorai jinko. Showa 25-nen—Showa 40-nen." *J.m.k.*, No. 62, pp. 80-90. December 1955. Fertility was assumed to decline to an age-specific pattern that yielded a total fertility rate of 1,600 by 1960, 1962, or 1965 respectively and then remained constant. The medium estimate is given here. Mortality after 1956 was to decline linearly to a schedule derived from world experience that gave an expectation of life at birth of 66.47 for men and 70.89 for women.

at the older ages. Neither international migration nor deaths from natural disasters were considered in any of the estimates. The major differences among the estimates were products of differing assumptions concerning the initial levels and the rates of decline of fertility. These differences are relatively small in the later estimates, for all were based on an assumption of rapid decline.

Since fertility is the major unknown factor in the population change of the next few decades, it might seem that estimates of probable changes in the population involved great uncertainties. This is true if the total population is considered, but it is not true for all age groups. Estimates of the future numbers of the pre-school and early school-age children are highly conjectural, for within a decade any estimate of numbers depends in major part on assumptions concerning fertility. Numbers of men in the productive ages and women in the homemaking and childbearing ages can be estimated for 25 or 30 years in the future with reasonable certainty, for people who will be aged 25 or over in 1980 were born by 1955.

POPULATION GROWTH, 1950-1980

Discussion of the future growth of the population of Japan requires that one estimate be selected, and that a time period be specified. The estimate used will be the most recent one of the Jinko mondai kenkyujo. The period covered will terminate at 1980. The population below age 25 in 1980 represents primarily a reasoned guess as to the future of fertility. The population aged 25 and over may differ from the estimated one if mortality declines more or less rapidly than assumed, or if it fails to decline. Numbers of youth and adults alike may be influenced by international migration. The lack of agreement between past estimates and present populations cautions against assuming that projections of the present necessarily represent the realities of the future.

The total population of Japan was 55.4 million in 1920 and 83.4 million in 1950.[9] The estimated population for 1980 is 105.6 million.[10] Population will continue to increase to a maximum of 107.1 million in 1990. After this decline will occur, but the population that first exceeds 100 million between 1970 and 1975 will not fall below that figure until after the year 2010.

[9] This figure for 1950 includes the Ryukyu Islands returned to Japan by the end of 1953.

[10] Takagi, Naobumi. "Suikei shorai jinko. . . ."

TABLE 140

Estimates of the future population of Japan, by broad age groups, 1950-1980
(Numbers in '000)

Age	*England and Wales model*	TOTAL FERTILITY: 2 — *Adopted April 1, 1950*	TOTAL FERTILITY: 2 — *Adopted April 1, 1955*	2-CHILD SYSTEM — *Adopted April 1, 1950*	2-CHILD SYSTEM — *Adopted April 1, 1955*	*Swedish fertility—New Zealand mortality*	PROJECTION OF RECENT JAPANESE TRENDS — *I*	PROJECTION OF RECENT JAPANESE TRENDS — *II*[a]
1950	83,975	82,530	84,179	81,995	84,118	83,200	83,200	83,200[b]
Under 15	29,475	28,208	29,857	27,674	29,796	29,472	29,453	29,428
15-59	48,032	48,015	48,015	48,015	48,015	47,311	47,341	47,354
60 and over	6,468	6,306	6,306	6,306	6,306	6,417	6,406	6,413
1960	95,424	87,915	92,508	81,981	87,885	93,795	92,926	93,230
Under 15	29,351	22,472	27,065	16,538	22,442	28,062	27,320	27,308
15-59	57,777	56,883	56,883	56,883	56,883	57,574	57,428	57,688
60 and over	8,296	8,560	8,560	8,560	8,560	8,159	8,177	8,235
1970	106,185	93,110	97,812	81,185	87,110	100,662	100,269	99,774
Under 15	27,770	21,124	21,336	12,203	12,357	22,292	21,758	20,986
15-59	67,767	61,109	65,599	58,105	63,876	67,565	67,982	68,186
60 and over	10,647	10,877	10,877	10,877	10,877	10,806	10,528	10,602
1980	115,867	96,218	102,316	78,042	84,870	106,453	106,396	105,572
Under 15	28,447	21,307	23,153	11,524	12,897	22,249	22,343	21,756
15-59	74,380	61,927	66,178	53,534	58,989	71,073	71,179	70,929
60 and over	13,040	12,984	12,984	12,984	12,984	13,131	12,874	12,886

[a] Excluding Amami Oshima in 1950, but including it in the projected population.
[b] Five thousand of unknown ages not distributed.
Source: References, Table 139.

All age groups were increasing in number between 1920 and 1950, but the rates of increase were highest among younger workers (TABLE 141 and FIGURE 29). The changes between 1950 and 1980 will be strikingly different. The younger people of 1950 will move upward to constitute the prime workers, the aging and the aged. Birth cohorts will decrease in size from year to year, and there will be massive erosion at the base of the age pyramid. Between 1950 and

TABLE 141

The population of Japan, by sex and age, actual, 1920 and 1950, estimated 1980
(Numbers in '000)

Age	TOTAL *1920*	TOTAL *1950*	TOTAL *1980*	MALES *1920*	MALES *1950*	MALES *1980*	FEMALES *1920*	FEMALES *1950*	FEMALES *1980*
Total	55,391	83,413	105,572	27,769	40,911	52,028	27,622	42,502	53,544
Under 15	20,202	29,505	21,755	10,203	14,983	11,108	10,000	14,522	10,647
0-4	7,377	11,235	7,187	3,713	5,734	3,668	3,664	5,501	3,519
5-14	12,825	18,270	14,568	6,490	9,250	7,440	6,335	9,020	7,128
15-64	32,273	49,780	75,048	16,274	24,191	37,178	15,999	25,589	37,872
15-19	5,362	8,590	6,506	2,721	4,328	3,315	2,641	4,262	3,192
20-34	12,022	19,157	26,777	6,100	9,037	13,622	5,922	10,120	13,155
35-44	6,590	9,553	17,499	3,317	4,584	8,813	3,273	4,968	8,687
45-64	8,299	12,480	24,266	4,136	6,241	11,428	4,163	6,239	12,838
65 and over	2,917	4,123	8,768	1,294	1,734	3,743	1,623	2,389	5,025

Source: 1920 and 1950: Censuses of Japan and, for 1950, the Ryukyus. Citations in Bibliography. 1980: Takagi, Naobumi. "Suikei shorai jinko. Showa 25-nen—Showa 40-nen." *J.m.k.*, No. 62, pp. 80-90. December 1955.

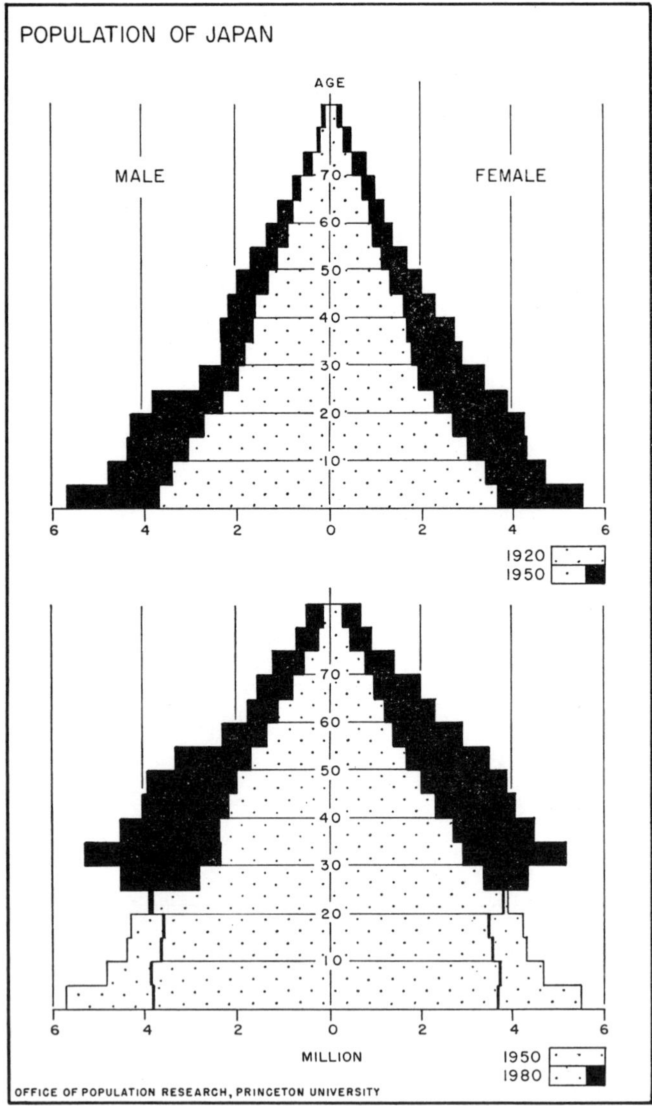

Figure 29. The population of Japan by sex and age, 1920, 1950, actual; and 1980, projected

Source: 1920 and 1950: Censuses, cited in Bibliography. 1980: Tachi, Minoru, *et al. Shorai jinko no suikei ni tsuite.* 1953 revision.

1980 there will be a total increase of 22.2 million, but this figure is a balance of increase in some age groups, decrease in others. During these three decades, more than one-fifth of the total increase will occur among people aged 65 and over. There will be a decrease among youth under age 15 that is one-third as large as the increase in the total population. The absolute increase of 25.3 in the population aged from 15 to 64 will be considerably larger than the increase in the total population. Major frictional difficulties will arise from changing age structures such as those summarized here in percentage terms:

Age	*1920-1950*	*1950-1980*
Total	50.6	26.6
0-4	52.3	−36.0
5-14	42.4	−20.3
15-19	60.2	−24.3
20-34	59.3	39.8
35-44	45.0	83.2
45-64	50.4	94.4
65 and over	41.3	112.7

Some of the imbalances in age groups will be conducive to economic advance and social developments, while others will act as depressants.

If the declines in fertility continue as estimated, there will be declines in the burdens that the society carries in the rearing of the new generation. In 1920 there were 802 children aged from 0 to 4 for each 1,000 women aged from 20 to 44; in 1950 there were 745. If the decline in the birth rate continues, there will be 329 children under 5 for each 1,000 women aged from 20 to 44 in the year 1980. Comparable declines will have occurred in the ratio of school-age children to women in the reproductive ages. Numerically viewed, the total burden of child care may be indicated by the ratio of children under 15 to each 1,000 women aged from 20 to 44. That ratio was 2,197 in 1920 and 1,956 in 1950, only a slight decline. By 1980 it will be 996, almost a 50 per cent reduction in a generation.

The replacement of the generations may also be considered from the economic point of view, for youth under 15 are a non-productive burden on men in the productive ages. In 1920 there were 1,241 youths under 15 for each 1,000 men aged from 15 to 64; in 1950 there were 1,220. If the decline in fertility continues, there will be 585 in 1980.

The dependent load on the productive members of a society consists not only of youth but also of the aged. A decrease in the number of children is likely to be followed eventually by an increase in the burden of the aged. In Japan this burden has been and remains low, for increasing numbers of births and rapidly declining infant and child mortality have sent increasing numbers of youth into the productive age groups decade after decade. In 1920 there were 179 persons aged 65 and over for each 1,000 men aged from 15 to 64; in 1950 there were 170. By 1980 there will be 236. The total dependency will decrease between 1950 and 1980, for the decrease in the number of children will be greater than the increase in the number of the aged.

Aging occurs within the productive ages as well as in the terminal groups of the life span. Thus aging of the labor force is inherent in the change from one type of growth to another. Given adequate trade, the changing structure of the labor force might be the major way in which population growth will become a social and economic problem. If economic development is not rapid enough, it may be growth itself which is defined as the problem.

The critical aspect of population growth in the years from 1950 to 1980 will be the growth of manpower in the productive ages, roughly from age 20 to 64. Practically all men in this age group must have employment if the society and government are to be stable. In other age groups, participation in the labor force may be marginal, or there may be alternatives to such participation. For the men who are married and heads of families, there are few alternatives to full-time employment.

The number of men aged from 20 to 64 increased from 13.6 million in 1920 to 19.9 million in 1950, an increase of 6.3 million or 47 per cent in thirty years. The 19.9 million men of 1950 will increase to 33.9 million in 1980, an increase of 14 million in thirty years. This increase of more than 70 per cent in the number of men in the productive ages is likely to occur. All persons who will be aged from 25 to 64 in 1980 were already born when the projections were made. Only increases in mortality or substantial out-migration could reduce the actual number below that projected for 1980.

If fertility continues downward to 1965 and remains low, there will be only slight increases in numbers of men in the productive ages after 1980. The rate of increase in the successive five-year periods from 1975 to 1990 will be 3.1, 1.7, and 1.3. After 1990, there will be declines in the numbers of men aged from 20 to 64.

The Japanese economy absorbed an increase of almost 50 per cent in men aged from 20 to 64 in the years from 1920 to 1950. Can it absorb a further increase of 70 per cent between 1950 and 1980? The absorption cannot come in agriculture, for here increased productivity requires a reduced rather than an expanded population. Migration is not a panacea, for even migration comparable to that which occurred at the height of prewar imperial expansion would not remove a substantial portion of an increase of 14 million men. The great increases in employment opportunities must come in the industrial segment of the economy and the services associated with it. The population problem of the near future is basically an economic problem.

THE POPULATION PROBLEM

There have been governmental, quasi-governmental, and private studies of the problems involved in the increasing numbers of people requiring employment. The quasi-official Foundation Institute for Research on Population Problems appointed an Inquiry Commission on Population Policies.[11] The Commission limited itself to the years from 1950 to 1956, so that elements of uncertainty in population increase would be minimal. The basis of their inquiry was an estimated increase of 17.3 million persons aged from 15 to 64 and a required labor force expansion of 11.4 million. This would mean an average annual increase of three-quarters of a million jobs. If trends in employment between 1950 and 1965 were similar to those between 1920 and 1935, the economy of 1965 would provide employment for 5.4 million of the 11.1 million additional persons requiring jobs.[12] Absorption in agriculture and small enterprises might disguise the situation, but ". . . the pressures of the surplus population will permeate the daily living of the masses and conceal the eruptive dangers from deep social uneasiness."[13]

The resolutions of the Foundation Institute on the problems of latent unemployment were issued in late 1956 after improvements in economic conditions, an increase in the labor force, the exodus from agriculture and the rural areas, and the growth of cities had occurred.[14] The Institute cited the entrance of women and the aged into the labor force, the increase in commerce and services, and the growth of the category of day-laborers as evidences of latent unemployment, low productivity, and low wages. The urgency of ameliorative economic and welfare measures was indicated by citing the parallel with the 1930's. To quote: "The rationalization of industry increased the stability of the national economy at the expense of the villages and the small and medium enterprises. The farmers and the small urban citizens lost their faith in democratic improvements and served as the social generators for militarism. The present situation reminds one of the past, except that the population pressure is greater than ever before."[15]

The activities and the conclusions of the late 1950's are indeed reminiscent of those of the late 1920's, when the Commission on Population and Food considered the interrelations of food deficits, inadequate markets, and increasing population in the productive ages.[16] Today, as in that period a generation ago, the difficulties inherent in the economic situation are viewed with deep pessimism. Analyses avoid the quicksands of the situation through considering public works and welfare activities that preserve large portions of the labor force at sub-marginal wages.

THE POSSIBILITIES

Barring catastrophe, the demographic facts for the next decade or so are known in outline. It is the economic developments that are problematical. If the next decade or so witnesses a slow economic development of the type that occurred between 1920 and 1935, millions of maturing youth will be marginal participants in the labor force of the industrial economy. A foretaste of what the years from 1955 to 1964 may hold is apparent in the experience of the years from 1950 to 1954. In those years there was movement from rural areas to cities and there was decline in the agricultural labor force. Increases in employment occurred in major part in the less productive segments of the economy where labor was already overabundant—retail trade, services, small manufacturing industries. There were steep upward movements in industrial production, but improved equipment and more efficient techniques eliminated the need for additional workers in mechanized production. Industries with thirty or more workers employed a relatively unchanging number of people and a declining portion of the total labor force.

The assumptions of continuity in a "normal" type of economic development as measured by changes from 1920 to 1935 are somber warnings of the economic deterioration and social instabilities that confront Japan if the projected future should become reality. However, the Japanese are an industrial people with many research institutions, scientists, and technicians, and will benefit from any developments in production that are made available by advances in world knowledge. If major new resources, a more rational organization of production and distribution, and larger purchasing power within Japan were combined with a lessening of political tensions and an expansion of trade, the dimensions of the population problem would be altered.

The Japanese have the great strength of their characteristics. They are more educated than any other Asian group, and they are disciplined to the requirements of life and labor in the industrial society. They are an Asian people with knowledge of the folkways of peasant agriculture but they are also a modern people with the productive techniques needed to

[11] Jinko mondai kenkyu-kai, zaidan hojin, "Zaidan hojin, jinko mondai kenkyu-kai no jinko taisaku iinkai dai-ikkai chukan hokoku no happyo." *J.m.k.*, 9(3-4):58-67. March 1954.

[12] *Ibid.* P. 67.

[13] The trends from 1920 to 1930 were regarded as inappropriate because 1930 was a year of depression and latent unemployment. The trends from 1930 to 1940 were avoided because of the influence of war on manpower utilization in 1940. The dilemma of a base period was not avoided, however; in the absence of census data for 1935, estimates for that year were secured by linear interpolation between the values for 1930 and those for 1940.

[14] Zaidan hojin jinko mondai kenkyu-kai. *Senzai shitsugyo taisaku ni kansuru ketsugi.* December 1956.

[15] *Ibid.* Part 2, Section 3. Quoting further: "The increase in latent unemployment deepens social instabilities and insecurities. It will lead to questions of the soundness of the present economic system. It is urgent to voice the great necessity for policies."

[16] The analysis that underlay the considerations of the Foundation Institute was also published: Nihon. Kosei-sho, jinko mondai kenkyujo. *Sengo Nihon no jinko mondai.* Similar conclusions were reached in the studies presented by Mainichi shimbun-sha, jinko mondai chosa-kai: *Japanese economy and problems of employment*, and *The future of Japan—her population and natural resources.*

continue industrialization at minimum cost. Japan's increasing population in the productive ages could be a major asset in the modernization of other countries in the Pacific region.

These optimistic possibilities exist, but so do the pessimistic ones. Economic development and political stability require increases in production that will yield rising levels of living. There must be adequate employment for the population in the productive ages, and it must be employment that uses available skills and yields wages that are reasonably high. These are difficult requirements for an economy such as that of Japan. The condition of the economy and the state would be difficult even if there were no increases in population. The continuing increase in the productive ages makes the situation both difficult and critical. And it is faced by a people who are not likely to remain quiescent in depression. The alternatives for Japan do not include a continuation of the low levels of living that existed a quarter of a century ago. They consist, on the one hand, of rapid economic development producing higher levels of living for an increasing population. On the other hand, there may be a failure to achieve such development, with a resultant loss of confidence in the future. In the latter case, there might be radical changes in social structure and political alignments with serious consequences for Japan, the Pacific region, and the West.

APPENDICES

CHRONOLOGY

Date	Period
To 645 A.D.	Age of clans (*uji*) and hereditary titles (*kabane*).
645-784.	Taika Reform and implementation. (710-784. Nara.)
794-1185.	Heian. (866-1160. Fujiwara.)
1185-1333.	Kamakura.
1336-1568.	Ashikaga, or Muromachi.
1568-1600.	Azuchi-Momoyama, or period of national unification.
1600-1868.	Tokugawa.
1868-1912.	Meiji. (Meiji 1, 1868, to Meiji 45, August 1912.)
1912-1926.	Taishō. (Taishō 1, August 1912, to Taishō 15, December 1926.)
1926—	Shōwa. (Shōwa 1, December 1926—)

This chronology is given by Edwin O. Reischauer in: Langer, William L., Compiler and Editor. *An encyclopedia of world history.* Revised Edition. Boston, Mass., Houghton Mifflin Co., 1948. xlvi, 1270 pp.

GLOSSARY

bakufu—The central government from the late twelfth to the mid-nineteenth century.
buraku—A settlement consisting of a group of houses and related buildings, together with the land used by the people within the area.
bushidō—The code of the *samurai*, or knightly class.

chō—See *machi*.
Chūgoku—A region in central Honshū, including the prefectures of Tottori, Shimane, Okayama, Hiroshima, and Yamaguchi.

daimyō—The possessors of the great domains of the *bakufu* period. The holders of estates were first called *myōden* and subdivided into *kokushu*, rulers of one or several *kuni*; *ryōshu*, rulers of a smaller area; and *jōshu*, rulers of castles. Under the Tokugawa, all whose revenues were more than 10 thousand *koku* of rice were *daimyō*.
dō—The regions of the country in the *bakufu* period, each including several *kuni*.
dōzoku—The extended kin group.

Emishi—The indigenous people in eastern Japan.
eta—The inferior class to whom specific occupations were assigned in the premodern period; a minority subject to discrimination.
Ezo—A former name for Hokkaidō, and also for the indigenous people. Sometimes spelled *Yezo*.

fu—An urbanized prefecture, specifically Kyōto and Ōsaka.
fudai-daimyō—*Daimyō* who supported the Tokugawa prior to the battle of Sekigahara in 1600.
Fujiwara—One of the great *han* of the early and medieval periods.

genjū jinkō—Resident population.
genjū kosū—Resident households.
gun—A subdivision of a prefecture, no longer politically functional. All land outside the *shi* is included in *gun*; *gun* in turn consists of *machi* and *mura*.

hakutei—Small cultivators.
han—The pseudo-consanguineous clan of the legendary and early historical periods; the great family; the fief or region ruled by a *daimyō*.
heimin—The common people—farmers, artisans, and merchants—below the *samurai* and above the *eta* and other disadvantaged classes.
hi'nin—An out-caste group below the *eta*.
Hokuriku—In the *bakufu* period, a region of northern Japan including the *kuni* of Wakasa, Echizen, Etchū, Echigo, Kaya, Noto, and Sado. In the modern period, a region of Honshū including the prefectures of Niigata, Toyama, Ishikawa, and Fukui.
honseki—Legal domicile, the place where the original *koseki* entry for the individual is maintained.
honseki jinkō—The legally domiciled population; the population with *honseki* in the area.
Honshū—The major island of Japan, including the regions of Tōhoku, Kantō, Hokuriku, Tōsan, Tōkai, Kinki, and Chūgoku.
hsien—The Chinese administrative area rather comparable to a county but larger, used in Manchoukuo.

ie—The traditional house, or extended family; the legal family of the civil code to 1945.

kakeochi—Escape.
kami—The deity or the principle of divinity in Shintō.
kan'i kokusei chōsa—Simplified national census.
Kantō—A region including Tōkyō and the surrounding areas. The following prefectures are in this region: Ibaraki, Tochigi, Gumma, Saitama, Chiba, Tōkyō, and Kanagawa.
ken—A prefecture.
Kinai—The inner *kuni* in the *bakufu* period, including Yamato, Kawachi, Naniwa, Yamashiro, and Izumi.
Kinki—A region in central Honshū including the following prefectures: Shiga, Kyōto, Ōsaka, Hyōgo, Nara, and Wakayama.
Kojiki—The Record of Ancient Matters, the compilation of Japanese "history" extending from the mythical beginning to the end of the reign of the Empress Suiko in 628 A.D.
koku—A measure of volume, 4.9629 bushels. It was in *koku* of rice that the revenues of the *daimyō* were estimated.
kokusei chōsa—National census.
koseki—The house, or *ie*, record book in which vital events and population movements were entered.
ku—The administrative areas or wards within the cities of Tōkyō, Ōsaka, Kyōto, Nagoya, Yokohama, and Kōbe.
Kumaso—The indigenous people of southern Kyūshū.
kuni—The provinces of the *bakufu* period.
Kyūshū—The large southern island of Japan, considered as a region of the country and including the following prefectures: Fukuoka, Saga, Nagasaki, Kumamoto, Ōita, Miyazaki, and Kagoshima.

mabiki—The thinning of the plants; infanticide.
machi—An administrative unit with fewer powers and a less complex organization than a *shi*, more powers and a more complex organization than a *mura*. The *machi* includes both the central settlement and the surrounding agricultural area; it is usually larger and more "urban" in character than the *mura*.
Meiji—The era that began with the Imperial Restoration of 1868.
Minamoto—The family name of the imperial families. One of the four great family names of Japan.
miyake—Area where rice was cultivated for the imperial household.
muko yōshi kon'in—Marriage by the adoption of the groom into the *ie* of the bride. The name of the adopted son is added to the *koseki* of the family of the girl, the name of her family is taken, and the adopted son then has rights of succession.
mura—The most agricultural and rural of the administrative units into which Japan is divided. A *mura* often includes several *buraku*, or village settlements.

Nanyō-guntō—South Sea Islands; Micronesia; the islands mandated to Japan by the League of Nations.
Nihon-shoki—Ancient chronicles of Japan, from the origin to the end of the reign of Jito in 696 A.D.
nyūfu kon'in—Marriage to an heiress and the assumption of the name of her *ie*, but without the adoption that would give the headship of the *ie* to the groom adopted as the son.

rōnin—The masterless and vagrant *samurai.*
ryō—Fief or possession.
ryōmin—Peaceful and law-abiding people.
Ryūkyū Islands—The Loochoo Islands; islands between Kyūshū and Taiwan.

samurai—A member of the military class in the service of the *daimyō.*
sankin-kōtai—The provision of the Tokugawa *bakufu* that all *daimyō* must reside in Edo in alternate years and leave their wives and children as hostages in that city.
shi—Incorporated municipalities, generally with populations larger than 30 thousand.
Shikoku—One of the four main islands of Japan, including the prefectures of Tokushima, Kagawa, Ehime, and Kōchi.
shintō—The indigenous beliefs of the Japanese, especially veneration of the ancestors and the worship of nature.
shiseiji—An illegitimate child not recognized by the father and therefore with a legal record in the *koseki* of the *ie* of the mother or in a new *koseki* established by her.
shōen—Domains with which the emperor rewarded princes and high officials; manors.
shōgun—The dictator of the government operating with investiture by the emperor; originally, the commander of the military forces operating against the barbarians on the frontiers.
shoshi—An illegitimate child who is recognized by the father and whose name is hence entered in the *koseki* of his *ie.*
Shōwa—The present era, 1926—.
shukuba-machi—Service stations located each eight to twelve kilometers along the great roads of Tokugawa Japan.
son—See *mura.*
suiheisha—The association for the abolition of prejudice against the *eta*; the water-leveling society.

Taihō code—The code of laws promulgated in the first year of the Taihō era, 701 A.D.
Taika Reform—The revision of administration from the beginning of the Taika era in 645 A.D. to the promulgation of the Taihō code by the Emperor Kotoku in 701 A.D.
Taira—One of the great *han*, or families, in Japanese history, struggling with the Minamoto for control of the country in the Middle Ages.
Taishō—The era from 1912 to 1926.
tennō—The emperor, and also the personification of the imperial institution.
to—A metropolitan administrative organization, used only for *Tōkyō-to.*
Tōhoku—The region of northeastern Honshū including the prefectures of Aomori, Iwate, Miyagi, Akita, Yamagata, and Fukushima.
Tōkai—The region of Honshū including the prefectures of Shizuoka, Aichi, and Mie.
Tōkaidō—The great outer road from Kyōto to Tōkyō; also one of the major administrative divisions of the Tokugawa shogunate.
Tokugawa—One of the great families of Japan; the family of the *shōgun* in the *bakufu* period from the early seventeenth to the mid-nineteenth century.
Tōsan—A region of Honshū, including the prefectures of Yamanashi, Nagano, and Gifu.
Tōsandō—The major administrative division of the Tokugawa that included northern Honshū.
tozama-daimyō—The *daimyō* who submitted to the Tokugawa *shōgun* only after the battle of Sekigahara in 1600.

uji—The consanguineous or pseudo-consanguineous group or clan that was the basic unit of the society of ancient Japan; family name; surname.
uji-no-kami—The head of the *uji*, or clan.

Yamato—The early people and culture in southwest Japan who gave their name to the presumed race of origin and culture of all Japan.
Yezo—See *Ezo.*
Yōrō code—The code promulgated in the first year of the Taihō era, 701 A.D.

zōshiki—Artisans; formerly people without court rank and hence allowed to dress as they chose.

AGENCIES AND INSTITUTIONS

NIHON—JAPAN

Gaimu-shō, chōsa-bu—Foreign Ministry. Investigation Section.
Gaimu-shō, Tōa-kyoku—Foreign Ministry. Bureau of East Asia.

Hikiage engo-chō—Repatriation Relief Board.
Hōmu-fu, minji-kyoku—Ministry of Law. Civil Affairs Bureau.

Jinkō mondai kenkyū-kai—Institute for Research on Population Problems.
Jinkō mondai kenkyū-kai, zaidan hōjin—Foundation Institute for Research on Population Problems.

Kan'i hoken-kyoku—Post Office Insurance Bureau.
Keizai antei hombu—Economic Stabilization Board.
Kōsei-shō, daijin kambō, tōkei chōsa-bu—Welfare Ministry. Secretariat. Statistical Bureau.
Kōsei-shō, eisei-kyoku—Welfare Ministry. Sanitation Bureau.
Kōsei-shō, eisei tōkei-bu—Welfare Ministry. Division of Health and Welfare Statistics.
Kōsei-shō, jinkō mondai kenkyūjo—Welfare Ministry. Institute of Population Problems.
Kōsei-shō, jinkō mondai shingi-kai—Welfare Ministry. Population Problem Council.
Kōsei-shō, kōshū hoken-kyoku—Welfare Ministry. Bureau of Public Health.
Kyōto-shi, eisei-kyoku—Kyōto Municipal Office. Public Health Bureau.

Mombu-shō—Ministry of Education.

Naikaku—Cabinet.
Naikaku insatsu-kyoku—Cabinet Printing Bureau.
Naikaku jōhō-kyoku—Cabinet Information Bureau.
Naikaku kampō-ka—Cabinet. Official Gazette Section.
Naikaku kikaku-in—Cabinet Planning Board.
Naikaku tōkei-kyoku—Cabinet Bureau of Statistics.
Naimu-shō, eisei-kyoku—Ministry of Interior. Sanitation Bureau.
Nihon taishi-kan—Japanese Embassy.
Nōrin daijin kambō, tōkei-ka—Ministry of Agriculture and Forestry. Statistics Section.
Nōrin-sho, nōgyō kairyō-kyoku, tōkei chōsa-bu—Ministry of Agriculture and Forestry. Bureau of Agricultural Improvement. Statistical Survey Division.
Nōrin-shō, tōkei chōsa-kyoku—Ministry of Agriculture and Forestry. Statistical Survey Department.
Nōshōmu-shō, shōkō-kyoku—Ministry of Agriculture and Commerce. Bureau of Commerce and Industry.

Ōsaka-fu—Ōsaka Prefecture.

Rōdō-shō, fujin shōnen-kyoku—Ministry of Labor. Women and Children's Bureau.
Rōdō-shō, rōdō tōkei chōsa-bu—Ministry of Labor. Labor Statistics Survey Bureau.

Shōkō daijin kambō, tōkei-ka—Secretariat for Commerce and Industry. Statistical Bureau.
Shokuryō-chō—Rationing Office.
Sōri-fu, tōkei-kyoku—Prime Minister's Office. Bureau of Statistics. Previously: Sōri-chō, tōkei-kyoku.
Sōri-fu, tōkei-kyoku, toshokan—Prime Minister's Office. Bureau of Statistics Library.

Takumu daijin—Minister for Colonial Affairs.
Takumu daijin kambō, bunsho-ka—Secretariat for Colonial Affairs. Documents Section.
Tōkyō-fu—Tōkyō Prefecture.
Tōkyō-shi—Tōkyō City.
Tōkyō shiyakusho—Tōkyō Municipal Office.
Tōkyō shiyakusho, rinji kokusei chōsa-bu—Tōkyō Municipal Office. Temporary Census Bureau.
Tōkyō-to—Tōkyō Metropolitan Government.

Un'yu-shō—Ministry of Transportation.

RYŪKYŪ ISLANDS

Ryūkyū seifu gyōsei shuseki, tōkei-kyoku—Government of the Ryūkyū Islands. Administrative Headquarters. Statistics Section.

Ryūkyū seifu, tōkei-bu—Government of the Ryūkyū Islands. Statistics Division.

HOKKAIDŌ AND KARAFUTO

Hokkaidō sōgō kaihatsu iinkai, jimu-kyoku—Hokkaidō United Development Committee. Business Office.
Hokkaidō sōmu-bu, tōkei-ka—Hokkaidō. General Affairs Division. Statistics Bureau.
Karafuto-chō—Government of Karafuto.

TAIWAN—FORMOSA

Sōtoku-fu—Government General.
Sōtoku kambō, bunsho-ka—Government General. Secretariat. Document Section.
Sōtoku kambō, chōsa-ka—Government General. Secretariat. Investigation Section.
Sōtoku kambō, rinji kokō chōsa-bu—Government General. Secretariat. Temporary Office of Household and Population Survey.
Sōtoku kambō, rinji kokusei chōsa-bu—Government General. Secretariat. Temporary Census Bureau.
Sōtoku kambō, tōkei-ka—Government General. Secretariat. Statistics Department.

NANYŌ-GUNTŌ—MICRONESIAN ISLANDS

Nanyō-chō—Government of Nanyō-gunto.
Rinji Nanyō-guntō bōbitai—Temporary Defense Troops of Nanyō-guntō.

CHŌSEN—KOREA

Sōtoku-fu—Government General.
Sōtoku-fu, bunsho-ka—Government General. Document Section.

KWANTUNG AND THE SOUTH MANCHURIA RAILWAY ZONE

Kantō-chō, rinji kokō chōsa-bu—Government of Kwantung. Temporary Census Office.
Kantō chōkan kambō, chōsa-ka—Governor of Kwantung, Secretariat. Survey Section.
Kantō-kyoku—Kwantung Bureau.
Minami Manshū tetsudō kabushiki kaisha, chihō-bu—South Manchuria Railway Company. Regional Bureau.

MANSHŪKOKU—MANCHURIA

Chian-bu, keimu-shi—Department of Public Peace. Police Section.
Harubin tokubetsu shi kōsho—Harbin Special City. Affairs Office.
Keimusō-kyoku—Police Bureau.
Kokumu-in, sōmu-chō—State Council. Department of Civil Affairs.
Kokumu-in, sōmu-chō, chōhō-sho—State Council. Department of Civil Affairs. Intelligence Section.
Kokumu-in, sōmu-chō, rinji kokusei chōsa jimusho—State Council. Department of Civil Affairs. Temporary Census Office.
Kokumu-in, sōmu-chō, tōkei-sho—State Council. Department of Civil Affairs. Statistics Division.
Kuo-wu yüan fa-chih ch'u—State Council. Bureau of Legislation.
Minami Manshū tetsudō kabushiki kaisha, chihō-bu—South Manchuria Railway Company. Regional Bureau.
Minami Manshū tetsudō kabushiki kaisha, sōmu-bu, chōsa-ka—South Manchurian Railway Company. General Affairs Section. Survey Unit.
Minami Manshū tetsudō kabushiki kaisha, Taiheiyō mondai chōsa jumbi-kai—South Manchuria Railway Company. Preparatory Committee for Investigating Pacific Problems.
Minsei-bu—Department of Welfare.

NON-OFFICIAL

Chōsen kōsei kyōkai—Korea. Police Bureau Welfare Association.
Chūo shakai jigyō kyōkai, shakai jigyō kenkyūjo—Central Social Work Association. Social Work Research Institute.

Hokkaidō takushoku ginkō, chōsa-ka—Hokkaidō Colonial Bank. Investigation Section.

Kokutetsu rōdō kumiai, funjin-bu—Japan National Railways Trade Union. Women's Division.
Kyōto koseki kenkyū-kai—Kyōto Koseki Research Association.

Mainichi shimbun-sha, jinkō mondai chōsa-kai—Mainichi Press. The Population Problems Research Council.
Manshū Nichi-nichi shimbun-sha—Manchurian Nichi-nichi Press.
Manshūkoku tsūshin-sha—Manchurian News Agency.
Minzokugaku kenkyūjo—Institute of Ethnology.

Nihon gakujutsu shinkō-kai—Japanese Learned Society.
Nihon jimbun kagaku-kai—Japanese Cultural Sciences Society.
Nihon minzokugaku kyōkai—Japanese Society of Ethnology.

Okinawa Asahi shimbun-sha—Okinawa Asahi Newspaper.
Okinawa kōshinji—Okinawa Information Agency.

Tōa keizai chōsa-kyoku—East Asiatic Economic Investigation Bureau.
Tōyō keizai shimpō-sha—Oriental Economist Publishing Company.

PERIODICALS

Annals of the Hitotsubashi Academy.
Archives of the Population Association of Japan. Nihon jinkō gakkai kiyō.

Bulletin of the Institute of Public Health. Kokuritsu kōshū eisei-in kenkyū hōkoku. Issued by: The Institute of Public Health, Nihon kokuritsu kōshū eisei-in.

Chigaku zasshi—Journal of Geography.
Chōsa geppō—Survey Monthly.
Chōsa kenkyū shuyō kekka—Major Results of Surveys and Research. Issued by: Nihon. Kōsei-shō, jinkō mondai kenkyūjo—Welfare Ministry. Institute of Population Problems.
Chōsen igakkai zasshi—Journal of the Chōsen Medical Association.
Chūō kōron—The Central Review.
Contemporary Japan. A Review of East Asian Affairs. Issued by: Foreign Affairs Association of Japan.

Eisei tōkei—Health Statistics. Issued by: Nihon eisei tōkei kyōkai—Japan Health Statistics Society.

Far Eastern Quarterly. Issued by: Far Eastern Association.
Fukuoka Journal of Medicine—Hukuoka igakkai zasshi. Issued by: The University of Kyūshū, Medical Faculty.

Harvard Journal of Asiatic Studies. Issued by: Harvard-Yenching Institute.
Hō shakaigaku—Sociology of Law. Issued by: Nihon hō shakai gakkai—Japanese Association of Sociology of Law.

Igaku kenkyū—Medical Research.

Japan Planned Parenthood Quarterly. Nihon sanji keikaku jōhō. Issued by: The Japan Birth Control Institute, Nihon ninshin chōsetsu kenkyūjo.
Jimbun chiri—Human Geography.
Jinkō mondai—Population Problems. Issued by: Jinkō mondai kenkyū-kai—Institute for Research on Population Problems.
Jinkō mondai kenkyū—Studies in Population Problems. Issued by: Nihon. Kōsei-shō, jinkō mondai kenkyūjo—Welfare Ministry. Institute of Population Problems.
Jinkō mondai shiryō—Materials for the Study of Population Problems. Issued by: Nihon. Kōsei-shō, jinkō mondai kenkyujo—Welfare Ministry. Institute of Population Problems.
Jinkō suikei geppō—Population Estimates Monthly. Issued by: Nihon. Sōri-fu, tōkei-kyoku—Prime Minister's Office, Bureau of Statistics.
Jōhō—Survey Reports. Issued by: Nanyō-guntō. Nanyō-chō—Government of Nanyō-guntō.
Journal of the American Oriental Society.
Journal of the Kōbe University of Commerce.

Kantō-kyoku kyokuhō—Official Gazette of the Kwantung Bureau.
Keizai ronsō—Economic Studies. Issued by: Kyōto University, Department of Economics.
Keizai shi kenkyū—Studies in Economic History. Issued by: Kyōto University.
Keizaigaku ronshū—Studies in Economics. Issued by: Tōkyō University, Department of Economics.
Keizaigaku zasshi—Journal of Economics. Issued by: Ōsaka University of Commerce.
Kokumin keizai zasshi—National Economic Review. Issued by: Kōbe University of Commerce.
Kokuritsu kōshū eisei-in kenkyū hōkoku. Bulletin of the Institute of Public Health. Issued by: Nihon. Kokuritsu kōshū eisei-in, The Institute of Public Health.
Kōsei kagaku—The Japanese Journal of Public Health.
Kōsei no shihyō—Welfare Index. Issued by: Nihon. Kōsei-shō, daijin kambō, tōkei chōsa-bu—Welfare Ministry. Secretariat. Statistical Bureau.
Kōshū eisei—Journal of Public Health. Issued by: Nihon kōshū eisei kyōkai—Japan Society of Public Health.
Kōshū eiseigaku zasshi—Journal of Public Health. Issued by: Gakujutsu shoin—Science Publishing Company.

Kyōto University Economic Review. Memoirs of the Department of Economics in the Imperial University of Kyōto. See also: *Keizai ronsō.*

Manshū igakkai zasshi—Journal of Oriental Medicine.
Minzoku eisei—Race Hygiene.
Minzokugaku kenkyū—The Japanese Journal of Ethnology. Issued by: Nihon minzokugaku kyōkai—The Japanese Society of Ethnology.
Minzokugaku nempō—Yearbook of Ethnology.
Mitsubishi Economic Research Bureau. Monthly Circular.
Mitteilungen aus der medizinischen Facultät der Kaiserlichen Universität zu Tōkyō. Issued by: Tōkyō University, Faculty of Medicine. 1887 to 1925.
Mittheilungen der deutschen Gesellschaft für Natur- und Völkerkunde Ostasiens. Issued by: Deutsche Gesellschaft für Natur- und Völkerkunde Ostasiens.
Monthly Circular. Survey of Economic Conditions in Japan. Issued by: Mitsubishi Economic Research Institute.

Nagasaki igakkai zasshi—Journal of the Nagasaki Medical Association.
Nagoya igakkai zasshi—Journal of the Nagoya Medical Association.
Nihon iji shimpō—Japanese Medical Journal.
Nihon jinkō gakkai kiyō. Archives of the Population Association of Japan.
Nihon sanfujinka gakkai shi—Journal of the Japanese Obstetrics and Gynecology Society.
Nihon sanji keikaku jōhō. Japan Planned Parenthood Quarterly. Issued by: Nihon ninshin chōsetsu kenkyūjo—The Japan Birth Control Institute.
Nihon tōkei geppō. Monthly Report on Agricultural Statistics. Issued by: Nihon. Nōrin-shō, nōgyo kairyō-kyoku, tōkei-bu—Ministry of Agriculture and Forestry. Bureau of Agricultural Improvement. Statistical Survey Division.
Nisshin igaku—New Japanese Medicine.

Oriental Economist. A Monthly Journal of Practical Finance and Economics for Japan and Eastern Asia.

Pacific Affairs. Issued by: International Council, Institute of Pacific Affairs.
Press Translations and Summaries. SCAP, GHQ, Military Intelligence Section, Allied Translator and Interpreter Section.

Rōdō jihō—Labor Gazette.
Rōdō kagaku kenkyū—Labor Science Research.
Rōdōryoku chōsa hōkoku. Monthly Report on the Labor Force Survey. Issued by: Nihon. Sōri-fu, tōkei-kyoku—Prime Minister's Office. Bureau of Statistics.
Ryokufū bunko—Green Breeze Magazine. Issued by: Ryokufūkai—Green Breeze Society, of the Upper House of the Diet.

Seifu kōhō—Government Gazette. Issued by: Manshūkoku. Kokumu-in, sōmu-chō—Manchuria. State Council. Department of Civil Affairs.
Shakai seisaku jihō—Social Policy Review.
Shūhō—Weekly Report. Issued by: Nihon. Naikaku jōhō-kyoku—Cabinet Information Bureau.

Taiwan igakkai zasshi—Journal of the Formosan Medical Association.
Tōkei-kyoku kenkyū ihō—Research Bulletin of the Bureau of Statistics.
Tōkyō Gazette. A Monthly Report on Current Policies, Official Statements, and Statistics. Issued by: Board of Information of the Government of Japan.
Tōkyō igakkai zasshi—Journal of the Tōkyō Medical Association.
Tōkyō iji shinshi—Tōkyō New Journal of Medicine.
Tōyō keizai shimpō—Oriental Economic Review. Issued by: Toyo keizai shimpō-sha—Oriental Economist Publishing Company.
Transactions and Proceedings, Japan Society of London.
Transactions of the Asiatic Society of Japan. First Series, 1872-1922, Vols. 1-50. Second Series, 1923—, Vol. 1—
Transactions of the Korea Branch of the Royal Asiatic Society.

BIBLIOGRAPHY

PREFACE

THE extent of the statistical publications and the demographic literature of Japan presents difficult problems in citation and annotation. Limitations of space precluded annotation, and citations are selective rather than comprehensive. All census volumes are cited specifically; elsewhere citation forms are indicative. The selection among studies, reports, descriptions, and policy statements involved value judgments that would be difficult to justify in each individual case. In general, an attempt was made to cite the basic studies and to indicate the scope of research, the direction of interest, and the changing policy orientations. Limitations of knowledge have perhaps forced errors that will be apparent to students in specialized aspects of the broad field that has been covered.

The classification scheme involves a separation of materials on Japan from those on the former imperial and related areas. Within each area the main distinction is that between the official demographic statistics and the other studies or literature. The subject classification is more detailed for Japan than for the related areas. In order to assist those interested in specific fields, a guide to the classification precedes the bibliography.

The Romanization of the Japanese is the work of Dr. Y. Scott Matsumoto. It is based on *Kenkyūsha's new Japanese-English dictionary*.[1] Word divisions are based primarily on meaning rather than on morphological criteria, a word being the minimal unit that can stand independently. Macrons are used to indicate the pronunciation of a, o, and u as long vowels. If publications are in Japanese only, an English translation of the title of the book or article is enclosed in brackets. The titles of bilingual publications are cited in Japanese first, then in English, and without the use of brackets. Translations of the names of institutions and the titles of periodicals are given in separate lists rather than being repeated in all citations.

The following abbreviations are used for commonly cited sources:

J.m.—*Jinkō mondai*
J.m.k.—*Jinkō mondai kenkyū*
K.U.E.R.—*Kyoto University Economic Review*
SCAP. GHQ.—Supreme Commander for the Allied Powers, General Headquarters
T.A.S.J.—*Transactions of the Asiatic Society of Japan*

[1] Takenobu, Yoshitarō. General Editor. *Kenkyūsha's new Japanese-English dictionary*. American Edition. Tokyo, 1939. Cambridge, Mass., Harvard University Press, 1942. iv, 2280 pp.

SUBJECT GUIDE

I. JAPAN

LAND AND RESOURCES 396

DEVELOPMENTS TO 1868 396
- Population 396
- Culture and economy 397

OFFICIAL STATISTICS 399
- Registration and vital statistics 399
- Population censuses 403
- Other censuses and surveys 407
- Compilations 408
- Exodus and repatriation 408
- Population estimates 408
- Yearbooks, compendia, serials 409
- Non-official sources 410

POPULATION STUDIES 411
- General 411
- Distribution 413
- Increase 414
- Structure 414
- Migration 416
- Natural movements 418
  - Natural increase 418
  - Marriage 419
  - Fertility 420
  - Mortality 423
  - Life tables 425
- Projections 426

POLICY 426
- Governmental and quasi-governmental 426
- Studies and literature on policies 427

CULTURE, ECONOMY, AND SOCIETY 430
- General 430
- Economy 430
- Society 433
  - General 433
  - Education 434
  - Family 434
  - Religion 435
- Government 436

WAR AND PEACE 437

SPECIAL AREAS 438

SOURCES, OTHER 439

II. IMPERIAL AND RELATED AREAS

GENERAL 440

RYŪKYŪ ISLANDS 440

HOKKAIDŌ AND KARAFUTO 441

TAIWAN 443

NANYŌ-GUNTŌ 445

KOREA 447

KWANTUNG AND THE S.M.R. ZONE 450

MANCHOUKUO 451

CITATIONS

I. JAPAN

LAND AND RESOURCES

Ackerman, Edward A.

Japan's natural resources and their relations to Japan's economic future. Chicago, Ill., University of Chicago Press, 1953. xxv, 655 pp.

Cressey, George B.

Asia's lands and peoples: A geography of one-third the earth and two-thirds its people. New York, McGraw-Hill Book Co., 1944. xi, 608 pp.

SCAP. GHQ.

Japanese natural resources: A comprehensive survey. Prepared in General Headquarters in 1948. Tokyo, Hosokawa Printing Co., 1949. xxii, 559 pp.; map supplement.

Trewartha, Glenn T.

Japan: A physical, cultural and regional geography. Madison, Wisc., University of Wisconsin Press, 1945. xv, 607 pp.

U.S. Office of Strategic Services.

Natural resources. Civil Affairs Handbook, Section 6. Washington, D.C., 1944.

DEVELOPMENTS TO 1868

POPULATION

Books

Honjō, Eijirō.

Nihon jinkō shi. [History of Japanese population.] Tōkyō, Nihon hyōron-sha, 1941. 429 pp.

Ishii, Ryōichi.

Population pressure and economic life in Japan. Chicago, Ill., University of Chicago Press, 1937. xvii, 259 pp.

Morita, Yūzō.

Jinkō zōka no bunseki. [Analysis of population increase.] Tōkyō, Nihon hyōron-sha, 1944. 464, 4 pp.

Nihon. Chūo shakai jigyō kyōkai, shakai jigyō kenkyūjo.

Datai mabiki no kenkyū. [Research on abortion and infanticide.] Tōkyō, 1936. 286 pp.

Sekiyama, Naotarō.

Kinsei Nihon jinkō no kenkyū. [Studies on the Japanese population in the modern era.] Tōkyō, Ryūjin-sha, 1948. With emphasis on the Tokugawa period.

Nihon jinkō shi. [History of Japanese population.] Tōkyō, 1942. 261 pp., 3 tables.

Smith, Neil Skene, Editor.

Materials on Japanese social and economic history: Tokugawa Japan. (1) Introduction. Resources and population. Communication and trade. London, P. S. King and Son, Ltd., 1937. xvi, 176 pp.

Takahashi, Bonsen.

Nihon jinkō shi no kenkyū. [Study in Japanese population history.] Tōkyō, Sanyū-sha, 1941. 853 pp.

Tsujimura, Tarō, Compiler.

Distribution maps on the regional geographical study of Japan. Text. Tokyo, 1952. 41 pp.

The following contributions concern developments prior to 1868: Oda, Takeo, and Tanioka, Takeo. "The *jō-ri* system. A rural land planning in ancient Japan," pp. 16-17. Fujioka, Kenjirō. "An explanation of Japanese castle towns," pp. 18-19. Asaka, Yukio, and Nagai, Masatarō. "Settlement originated in the medieval period, 15th-16th cen.," pp. 20-21.

Other

Bowles, Gordon.

"Population control." In: *The Walter Buchanan Cline memorial volume.* The Kroeber Anthropological Society, Papers, Nos. 8 and 9. Berkeley, Calif., 1953. xix, 159 pp.

Droppers, Garret.

"The population of Japan in the Tokugawa period." *T.A.S.J.*, 22:253-284. 1894.

Honjō, Eijirō.

"The population and its problems in the Tokugawa era." *Bulletin de l'Institut international de statistique*, 25(2):60-82. 1931.

Izukawa, Senkichi.

"Mino-no-kuni ni okeru jinkō no bumpu to zōgen." [Population distribution and change in *Mino-no-kuni.*] *J.m.*, 6(2): 19-48. November 1943.

Kanno, W.

["The increase of population in Japan in earlier times."] *Keizai shi kenkyū*, No. 7, p. 1. May 1930.

Katō, Umeshirō.

"Taihōrei ni okeru jinkō seido no gaiyō." [Outline of the population system in the *Taihōrei.*] Pp. 38-40 in: Nihon. Jinkō mondai kenkyū-kai. *Jinkō seisaku to kokudo keikaku.* Tōkyō, 1942.

Mayet, P.

"Japanische Bevölkerungsstatistik, historisch, mit Hinblick auf China, und kritisch betrachtet." *Mittheilungen der Deutschen Gesellschaft für Natur- und Völkerkunde Ostasiens in Tokio*, 4(36):245-264. July 1887.

Sekiyama, Naotarō.
"Baku matsu Chikugo-no-kuni ichi nōson no jinkō jōtai ni tsuite." [On the condition of population in a village of *Chikugo kuni* in the latter part of the *bakufu* period.] *J.m.k.*, 1(6):1-13, September 1940.
"Tokugawa jidai no kon'in nenrei ni kansuru ichi kōsatsu." [An observation concerning marriage age in the Tokugawa period.] *J.m.k.*, 2(3):17-25. March 1941.
"Tokugawa jidai no shussei ritsu oyobi shibō ritsu. Sono jakkan no jirei." [Birth and death rates in the Tokugawa period. Some examples.] *J.m.k.*, 1(3):32-43. June 1940.
Summary: Nihon. Kōsei-shō, jinkō mondai kenkyūjo. *Demographic Researches*, A-2(b). Tōkyō, 1948.
"Tokugawa jidai zenkoku jinkō no sai-gimmi." [A re-examination of the national population in the Tokugawa period.] *J.m.k.*, 2(8):1-15. August 1941.
Summary: Nihon. Kōsei-shō, jinkō mondai kenkyūjo. *Demographic Researches*, A-2. Tōkyō, 1948.
Sugino, Watarō.
"Waga kuni kodai no jinkō zōka." [Population increase in our country in ancient times.] *Keizai shi kenkyū*, No. 7, pp. 1-9. May 1930.
Takahashi, Bonsen.
"Mito han no jinkō seisaku." [The population policy of Mito clan.] *J.m.*, 5(1):121-131. September 1942.
"Nihon jinkō shi-jō no ninsanfu todokeide seido." [System of reporting pregnancy as reflected in Japanese population history.] Pp. 40-42 in: Jinkō mondai kenkyū-kai. *Jinkō seisaku to kokudo keikaku*. Tōkyō, 1942.
"Tokugawa jidai izen no jinkō no rekishiteki kenkyū no konnan." [Difficulties in historical studies of population before the Tokugawa period.] In: *Dai-ikkai jinkō mondai zenkoku kyōgi-kai hōkokusho*. [Report of the First National Conference on Population Problems.] Tōkyō, 1938. 828 pp.
Tamayama, Isamu.
"Edo jidai no jinkō mondai." [Population problems in the Edo period.] *Kokumin keizai zasshi*, 73(1):63-94. July 1942.
Uchida, Kan'ichi.
"Tokugawa jidai nōson ni okeru sanji." [The newborn baby in rural villages during the Tokugawa period.] Pp. 43-45 in: Jinkō mondai kenkyū-kai. *Jinkō seisaku to kokudo keikaku*. Tōkyō, 1942.
Yanagisawa, Yasutoshi.
"Histoire critique des travaux statistiques au Japon depuis l'antiquité jusqu'à la restauration impériale." *Bulletin de l'Institut international de statistique*, 19(3):249-307. 1911.
See also his "On the progress of statistics in Japan." *Ibid.*, 12(1):349-355. 1900.
Yuzuki, Jūgo, and Horie, Yasuzō.
"Hompō jinkō hyō." [Tables of the population of this country.] *Keizai shi kenkyū*, No. 7, pp. 188-210. May 1930.

CULTURE AND ECONOMY

Books

Asakawa, Kan'ichi.
The early institutional life of Japan: A study in the reform of 645 A.D. Tokyo, Tōkyō Shueisha, 1903. 6, 355 pp.
Aston, W. G.
Nihongi. Chronicles of Japan from the earliest times to A.D. 697. Transactions and Proceedings of the Japan Society, London, Supplement 1. London, Kegan, Paul, Trench, Trübner and Co., Ltd., 1886. Vol. I, xxii, 407 pp. Vol. II, 443 pp.
Borton, Hugh.
Peasant uprisings in Japan of the Tokugawa period. T.A.S.J., 2nd Series, Vol. XVI, 1938. 228 pp.
Boxer, Charles R.
The Christian century in Japan, 1549-1650. Berkeley and Los Angeles, Calif., University of California Press, 1951. xv, 535 pp.
Jan Compangie in Japan, 1600-1850. 2nd Rev. Ed. The Hague, Martinus Nijhoff, 1950. xii, 198 pp.
Brinkley, Frank, with Kikuchi, Baron.
History of the Japanese people. New York, The Encyclopaedia Britannica Co., 1915. xi, 784 pp.
Brown, Delmer M.
Money economy in medieval Japan: A study in the use of coins. Published for Far Eastern Association by Institute of Far Eastern Languages, Yale University. New Haven, Conn., 1951. 128 pp.
Chamberlain, Basil Hall.
Things Japanese, being notes on various subjects connected with Japan, for the use of travellers and others. 6th Ed., Rev. London, Kegan Paul, Trench, Trübner and Co., Ltd., 1939. xvi, 584 pp.
Translation of the Ko-ji-ki or record of ancient matters. T.A.S.J., Supplement, 1882. Kobe, J. L. Thompson and Co., Ltd., 1932. lxxxv, 495 pp.
Fuji, Naomoto; Hirayama, Toshirō; and Ishida, Kazuyoshi.
Hōken shakai no seijuku. [The development of the feudal society.] Kyō-dai Nihon shi [Kyōto University Japanese History Series], No. 4. Osaka, Sōgen-sha, 1951. 4, 172 pp.
Groot, Gerard J.
The prehistory of Japan. New York, Columbia University Press, 1951. 128 pp.
Honjō, Eijirō.
Nihon keizai shi gaisetsu. [An outline of the economic history of Japan.] Tōkyō, Nihon hyōron-sha, 1932. 433 pp.
The social and economic history of Japan. Kyoto, Institute for Research in Economic History of Japan, 1935. xii, 410 pp.
Kaempfer, Englebert.
The history of Japan, together with a description of the Kingdom of Siam, 1690-92. Translated by J. G. Scheuchzer. Glasgow, James MacLehose and Sons, 1906. 3 vols.
Vol. I. Book I. *A general description of the Empire of Japan.* Book II. *Of the political state of Japan.* lxxxix, 337 pp.
Vol. II. Book III. *Of the state of religion in Japan.* Book IV. *Of Nagasaki, the place of residence for foreigners; of their trade, accommodation, etc.* Book V. *The author's two journies to the emperor's court at Jedo, the city of his residence.* x, 397 pp.
Vol. III. Book V. *The author's two journies to the emperor's court at Jedo, the city of his residence. Continued. The appendix to the history of Japan.* ix, 386 pp.
Kuno, Yoshi S.
Japanese expansion on the Asiatic continent: A study in the history of Japan with special reference to her international relations with China, Korea, and Russia. Vol. II. *To the end of the seclusion period.* Berkeley, Calif., University of California Press, 1940. xi, 416 pp.

Kuroita, Katsumi.
Kokushi no kenkyū. [Study of Japanese history.] Tōkyō, Iwanami shoten, 1932. 3 vols.

Munro, N. Gordon.
Primitive culture in Japan. Tokyo, Asiatic Society of Japan, 1906. vii, 212 pp.

Murdoch, James.
A history of Japan. I. From the origins to the arrival of the Portuguese in 1542 A.D. II. During the century of early foreign intercourse, 1542-1651. (In collaboration with Isoh Yamagata.) *III. The Tokugawa epoch, 1652-1868.* Published by the Asiatic Society of Japan. Yokohama, Kelly and Walsh, Ltd., London, Kegan Paul, Trench, Trübner and Co., Ltd. Vol. I, 1910; Vol. II, 1903; Vol. III, 1926.

Nakamura, Kichiji.
Nihon shakai shi gaisetsu. [Outline of Japanese social history.] Tōkyō, Usui shobō, 1947. 336 pp.

Paske-Smith, C. B. E.
Western barbarians in Japan and Formosa in Tokugawa days, 1605-1868. Kobe, 1930. 227 pp.

Reischauer, Robert K.
Early Japanese history, c. 40 B.C.-A.D. 1167. Princeton, N.J., Princeton University Press, 1937. Part A, xiii, 405 pp. Part B, 249 pp.

Sansom, George B.
Japan: A short cultural history. Revised Edition. New York, D. Appleton Century Co., 1943. xviii, 554 pp.
The first edition was issued in 1931.

Takekoshi, Yosaburō.
The economic aspects of the history of the civilization of Japan. New York, The Macmillan Co., 1930. 3 vols.

Takizawa, Matsuyo.
The penetration of money economy into Japan and its effects upon social and political institutions. New York, Columbia University Press, 1927. 159 pp.

Toyama, Shigeki.
Meiji ishin. [Meiji Restoration.] Tōkyō, Iwanami shoten, 1951. 368 pp.

Tsuchiya, Takao.
An economic history of Japan. Translation by Michitarō Shidehara; revised by Neil Skene Smith; edited, with introduction and notes, by Kurt Singer. *T.A.S.J.*, 2nd Series, Vol. XV, 1937. xviii, 269 pp.

Wakamori, Tarō.
Nihon kodai shakai. [Japanese ancient society.] Tōkyō, Sōbun-sha, 1949. 154 pp.

Wedemeyer, André.
Japanische Frühgeschichte. Untersuchungen zur Chronologie und Territorialverfassung von Altjapan bis zum 5. Jahrh. n. Chr. Tokyo, Deutsche Gesellschaft für Natur- und Völkerkunde Ostasiens, 1930. xvi, 346 pp.

Other

Ariga, Kizaemon.
"Nihon kodai kazoku." [Japanese ancient family.] Pp. 103-150 in: Tanabe, Hisatoshi, Editor. *Kazoku* [Family.] Shakaigaku taikei [Sociology Series], No. 1. Tōkyō, Kokuritsu shoin, 1948. 239, 8 pp.

Asakawa, Kan'ichi.
"Agriculture in Japanese history." *Economic History Review*, 2:80-96. 1929.
"The early *shō* and the early manor: A comparative study." *Journal of Economic and Business History*, 1:177-207. 1928-1929.
"The life of a monastic *shō* in medieval Japan." *Annual Report of the American Historical Association for 1916*, 1:313-342. 1919.
"Notes on village government in Japan after 1600." *Journal of the American Oriental Society*, 30:259-300; 31:151-216. 1909-1910 and 1910-1911.
"Some aspects of Japanese feudal institutions." *T.A.S.J.*, 46(1):76-102. 1918.

Baelz, E.
"Prehistoric Japan." Pp. 523-547 in: U.S. Smithsonian Institution. *Annual report . . . for the year ending June 30, 1907.* Washington, D.C., Govt. Printing Office, 1908.

Bishop, Carl W.
"The historical geography of early Japan." *The Geographical Review*, 13:40-63. January 1923.
"Origin of Far Eastern civilizations: A brief handbook." Pp. 463-512 in: U.S. Smithsonian Institution. *Annual report . . . 1943.* Washington, D.C., Govt. Printing Office, 1944. xi, 609 pp.

Hall, J. C.
"The Tokugawa legislation." Parts I-III. *T.A.S.J.*, 38:269-331. 1911. Part IV, 41:683-804. 1913.

Hasebe, Kontondo.
"Jinrui no shinka to Nihonjin no kengen." [Evolution of man and the Japanese "manifestation."] *Minzokugaku kenkyū*, 13(3):197-206. 1948.

Honjō, Eijirō.
"The agrarian problem in the Tokugawa regime." *K.U.E.R.*, 12:75-93. December 1926.
The following articles were also published in the *Kyoto University Economic Review*:
"Changes of social classes during the Tokugawa period: A cause of the collapse of the feudal system of the Tokugawa regime." 3(1):56-74. July 1928.
"The commoner class of the Tokugawa period." 8(2):38-48. December 1933.
"The decay of the *samurai* class." 2(1):38-52. July 1927.
"Economic ideas in Tokugawa days." 13(1):1-22. July 1938.
"Economic thought in the early period of the Tokugawa era." 14(4):1-17. October 1939.
"The economic thought in the middle period of the Tokugawa era." 15(2):1-33. April 1940.
"Japan's overseas trade in the closing days of the Tokugawa shogunate." 14(2):1-23. April 1939.
"New economic policy in the closing days of the Tokugawa shogunate." 4(2):52-75. December 1929.
"A short history of social problems in Japan before the Restoration." 3(2):41-85. December 1928.
"A survey of economic thought in the closing days of the Tokugawa Period." 13(2):21-39. October 1938.
"The views of various *hans* on the opening of the country." 11(1):16-31. July 1936.

Horie, Yasuzō.
"The economic significance of the Meiji restoration." *K.U.E.R.*, 12(2):63-81. December 1937.
"The life structure of the Japanese people in its historical aspects." *K.U.E.R.*, 21(1):1-22. April 1951.

Hulse, Frederick S.
"Physical types among the Japanese." Pp. 122-133 in: Coon, Carleton S., and Andrews, James M., IV, Editors. *Studies in the anthropology of Oceania and Asia, presented in memory of Roland Burrage Dixon.* Papers of the Pea-

body Museum of American Archaeology and Ethnology, Harvard University, Vol. xx. Cambridge, Mass., 1943. xiv, 220 pp.

Kraus, Johannes B.
"Familiensystem und Wirtschaft im alten und neuen Japan." Pp. 346-394 in: Deutsche Gesellschaft für Natur- und Völkerkunde Ostasiens, Tōkyō. *Jubiläumsband . . . anlässlich ihres 60 jährigen Bestehens 1873-1933*, Teil I. Tokyo, 1933. xxii, 409 pp.

Kure, Shūzō.
"Einfluss der fremden, insbesondere den deutschen Medizin, auf die Japanische vom Anfang des 18 bis gegen das Ende des 19. Jahrhunderts." Pp. 76-91 in: Deutsche Gesellschaft für Natur- und Völkerkunde Ostasiens. *Jubiläumsband . . . 1873-1933*. Teil I. Tokyo, 1933.

McCune, George M.
"The exchange of envoys between Korea and Japan during the Tokugawa period." *The Far Eastern Quarterly*, 5:308-325. May 1946.

Matsumoto, H.
"Notes on the stone age people of Japan." *American Anthropologist*, 23(N.S.):50-76. January-March 1921.

Mitsukuri, K.
"The early study of Dutch in Japan." *T.A.S.J.*, 5(1):207-216. 1877.

Nishioka, Hideo, and Schenck, W. Egbert.
"An outline of theories concerning the prehistoric people of Japan." *American Anthropologist*, 39(N.S.):23-31. January-March 1937.

Oka, Masao; Yawata, Ichirō; and Egami, Namio.
"Nihon minzoku bunka no genryū to Nihon kokka no keisei—taidan to tōron." [Origin of the Japanese people and culture, and formation of the Japanese state. Round table discussion.] *Minzokugaku kenkyū*, 13(3):11-81. 1948.

Rabbit, James A.
"Rice in the cultural life of the Japanese people." *T.A.S.J.*, 2nd Series, 19:187-258. December 1940.

Reischauer, Edwin O.
"Japan and Korea." In: Langer, William L., Compiler and Editor. *An encyclopedia of world history, ancient, medieval, and modern, chronologically arranged*. Boston, Houghton, Mifflin Co., 1940 and 1948. xlvi, 1270 pp.

Sansom, George B.
"Early Japanese law and administration." *T.A.S.J.*, 2nd Series, 9:67-109; 11:117-149. 1932 and 1934.
"An outline of recent Japanese archaeological research in Korea, in its bearings upon early Japanese history." *T.A.S.J.*, 2nd Series, 6:5-19. 1929.

Satow, E. M.
"Notes on the intercourse between Japan and Siam in the seventeenth century." *T.A.S.J.*, 13:139-210. 1885.

Smith, Neil Skene.
"An introduction to some Japanese economic writings of the 18th century." *T.A.S.J.*, 2nd Series, 11:32-95. December 1934.
"Tokugawa Japan as a field for the student of social organization." *Monumenta Nipponica*, 1:165-172. 1938.

Smith, Thomas C.
"The Japanese village in the seventeenth century." *Journal of Economic History*, 12(1):1-20. Winter 1952.

Snellen, J. B., Translator.
"*Shoku-nihongi*, chronicles of Japan. Continued, from 697-791 A.D.," *T.A.S.J.*, 2nd Series, 11:151-240. 1934.

Whynant, A. Neville J.
"The oceanic theory of the origin of the Japanese language and people." *T.A.S.J.*, 2nd Series, 3:17-81. December 1926.

Zachert, Herbert.
"Social change during the Tokugawa period." *T.A.S.J.*, 2nd Series, 17:238-254. December 1938.

OFFICIAL STATISTICS

REGISTRATION AND VITAL STATISTICS

General

Official, national

Nihon. Hōmu-fu, minji-kyoku.
Jūmin tōroku kankei hōreishū. [Laws and regulations on national registration.] Tōkyō, 1952.
See also: *Jūmin tōroku chōsain hikkei.* [Handbook for the enumerators of national registration, July 1, 1952.] Tōkyō, 1952.

Nihon. Naikaku.
[Ordinance governing survey of population movement.] Imperial Ordinance No. 478, November 2, 1922, Amended, No. 245, 1926. *Genkō hōrei shūran*, Vol. II, Section 6, No. 3.
These regulations replaced the ordinance of November 1898, which first provided for individual transcripts centrally processed.

Nihon. Naikaku tōkei-kyoku.
Nihon teikoku tōkei nenkan, 1881-1939. [Statistical annual of the Japanese Empire.] Tōkyō, 1882-1940.
In 1881 a General Bureau of Statistics was established in the Supreme Council (Daijōkan), together with a Central Commission of Statistics composed of representatives from the different ministries and administrations. In a reorganization at the end of 1885 the General Bureau of Statistics (Tōkei-kyoku) was attached to the Imperial Cabinet (Naikaku), and commissioners of statistics were named in the various ministries and administrations. With the foundation of the Daijōkan in 1881, a yearbook was issued to summarize all statistical data collected by the government.
The annual estimates of the population from 1872 through 1897 were published in the statistical yearbook. In 1898 and later years, summary compilations from the registration "censuses" and annual "intercensal" estimates were included.

Other

Kimura, Masabumi.
"Waga kuni jinkō dōtai no hensen." [The development of vital statistics in our country.] *Tōkei-kyoku kenkyū ihō*, No. 5, pp. 23-49. September 1953.

Kyōto koseki kenkyū-ka.
Koseki no shikō kisoku. [Koseki act enforcement rules.] Kyōto, 1947. 104 pp.

McLaren, W. W., Editor.
Japanese government documents. T.A.S.J., Vol. XLII, Part 1. Tōkyō, 1914. ci, 681 pp.
Translation of the first four of the 33 articles of the "census of 1871," pp. 18-19.

Yanagisawa, Yasutoshi.
"On the progress of statistics in Japan." *Bulletin de l'Institut international de statistique*, 12(1):349-355. 1900.

Registration Compilations

Compilation, 1898

Nihon. Naikaku tōkei-kyoku. Bureau de la statistique imperiale.

Nihon teikoku jinkō seitai tōkei. Etat de la population de l'Empire du Japon au 31 décembre 1898. Tokyo, 1901.

The registration compilation was made in accordance with the provisions of Law Number 1 of the Instructions of the Imperial Cabinet as of 1898 to secure the legally domiciled population (*honseki jinkō*), the resident population (*genjū jinkō*), and the number of resident households (*genjū kosū*).

Compilation, 1903

Nihon. Naikaku tōkei-kyoku. Bureau de la statistique imperiale.

Nihon teikoku jinkō seitai tōkei. Etat de la population de l'Empire du Japon au 31 décembre 1903. Tokyo, 1906.

Partial contents: Legal and resident population and number of resident households for prefectures, *gun, shi, machi,* and *mura*; number of communes by size; legal population by age and year of birth; marital status by year of birth and age; legal population by caste.

Compilation, 1908

Nihon. Naikaku tōkei-kyoku. Bureau de la statistique imperiale.

Nihon teikoku jinkō seitai tōkei. Etat de la population de l'Empire du Japon au décembre 1908. Tokyo, 1911.

Procedures, report forms, etc., are described in the preface. Detailed tables are similar to those in the 1903 compilation. Appendix I, "Population résidente relevié par les autorités de police au 31 décembre 1908," reports a simultaneous census carried out by the police to determine *de facto* population. Appendix II is a summary compilation of data on the size, distribution, and age composition of the population of Japan from 1872 to 1908.

Compilation, 1913

Nihon. Naikaku tōkei-kyoku. Bureau de la statistique imperiale.

Nihon teikoku jinkō seitai tōkei. Etat de la population de l'Empire du Japon au décembre 1913. Tableaux. Tokyo, 1916.

Part I is similar to the 1903 survey. Part II presents tabulations of a police survey. An appendix reproduces the laws, modifications of rules, and instructions, beginning with 1898.

Taishō ni'nen matsu jinkō seitai chōsa no kekka ni yoru teikoku jinkō gaisetsu. [Outline of the Japanese population based on the results of the static survey of population as of the end of 1913.] Tōkyō, 1916.

The introduction is an analytical survey of the methods used in investigating the "legal domicile" and the "present residence" population from the Meiji Restoration to 1913. The data of the 1913 survey are presented in a series of chapters, each with descriptive text and tabulations, on the following subjects: Total population of the country; population of prefectures; density; number of cities, towns, and townships classified by present-resident population, and the population of urban and rural districts; sex composition, total country; sex composition, prefectures; urban and rural population; age composition in 1913, including a comparison of results with those of the four earlier surveys; and marital status, total and by age and sex.

There are two appendixes: 1. Age composition of the "present residence" population of prefectures. 2. The registered movements to and from prefectures.

Graphiques statistiques sur l'état de la population de l'Empire du Japon. Tokyo, 1916.

A cartographic and diagrammatic presentation of the major data of the survey of 1913.

Compilation, 1918

Nihon. Naikaku tōkei-kyoku. Bureau de la statistique imperiale.

Nihon teikoku jinkō seitai tōkei. Etat de la population de l'Empire du Japon au 31 décembre 1918. Tableaux. Tokyo, 1920.

The pattern of presentation is similar to that of previous compilations.

Vital Statistics

General, 1872-1945

Nihon. Naikaku tōkei-kyoku.

Jinkō dōtai tōkei. [Vital statistics.] *1899-1942.* Tōkyō, 1903-1943.

Jinkō dōtai tōkei kijutsu hen. [Vital statistics. Descriptive volume.] *1913-193—.* Tōkyō, 1917-193—.

Nihon. Naikaku tōkei-kyoku. Bureau de la statistique imperiale.

Nihon teikoku jinkō dōtai tōkei. Mouvement de la population de l'Empire du Japon pendant l'an . . . 1899-1918. Tokyo, 1902-1921.

The issues for 1899-1904 had the sub-title *genhyō no bu, tableaux*; those for 1905-1918 had the sub-title *Jissū oyobi hirei, nombre absolu et proportion.* The volume for 1918 was issued by Kokusei-in, Departement imperial de recensement, rather than by Naikaku tōkei-kyoku.

Résumé statistique du mouvement de la population de l'Empire du Japon. 1919-1940. Tokyo, 1922-1940.

A summary presentation of marriage, divorce, fertility, and mortality statistics from the three Japanese-language yearbooks: *Jinkō dōtai tōkei.* [Vital statistics], *Jinkō dōtai tōkei kijutsu hen* [Vital statistics, descriptive volume], and *Shiin tōkei* [Statistics of causes of death].

Nihon. Naikaku tōkei-kyoku.

Shi, chō, son betsu jinkō dōtai tōkei. [Vital statistics for minor civil divisions.] Tōkyō. Various years.

Taishō jūyo'nen. [1925.] 1927.

Shōwa go'nen. [1930.] 1932.

Shōwa jū'nen. [1935.] 1938.

A special volume presenting numbers and rates for *shi, gun, machi, mura,* and the *ku* of the largest *shi* was published for the census year when the population figures were available for the computation of rates.

General, 1945—

Nihon. Kōsei-shō, eisei tōkei-bu. Welfare Ministry. Division of Health and Welfare Statistics.

Jinkō dōtai tōkei. Vital statistics. 1946—. Tokyo, 1949—.

Jinkō dōtai tōkei nempō, kijutsu hen. Shōwa 24-nen. [Annual report on vital statistics, narrative part. 1949.] Tōkyō, 1953. 7, 146 pp.

Jinkō dōtai tōkei maigetsu gaisū. Shōwa 30-nen nenkei-bun. [Monthly schedule report of vital statistics. Yearly total for 1955.] No. 117, Tōkyō, 1956. 57 pp.

Vital and health statistics in Japan. Tokyo, 1953. 3 vols.
Part I. *General description.* 95 pp.
Part II. *Tables.* Pp. 95-329.
Appendix. [*Laws, regulations, report forms, etc.*] 45 pp.

Nihon. Kōsei tōkei kyōkai. Zaidan hōjin.
Kokumin eisei no dōkō. Shōwa 31-nen. [Trend of national health. 1956.] *Kōsei no shihyō,* Special Edition. Vol. III, No. 9. 1956.

Marriage and divorce, annual

Nihon. Naikaku tōkei-kyoku.
Jinkō dōtai tōkei. 1899-1942. Tōkyō, 1903-1943.

Marriage data, 1937: 2. Summary table. 3. Marriages for areas by kind by month. 4. Average age at first marriage. 5. Marriages by age of husband and wife. 6. Marriages by marital status of husband and wife before present marriage. 7. Divorces by method of recording in the *koseki,* and by month. 8. Divorce by length of marriage. 9. Divorce by age of partners at time of divorce. 10. Divorce by age of husband and wife. Appendix Table 3 gives marriages and divorces of 1937 by place of *honseki,* while Table 4 gives data for Karafuto.

Nihon. Kōsei-shō, eisei tōkei-bu. Welfare Ministry. Division of Health and Welfare Statistics.
Jinkō dōtai tōkei. Vital statistics. 1946—. Tokyo, 1949—.

Marriage data, 1950: 1. Marriage by place of residence and place of occurrence. 14. Marriage and divorces in each prefecture by urban and rural areas according to place of declaration. 15. Marriages by year and month of wedding ceremony and month of declaration in all Japan. 16. Marriages by combined ages (single years) of both first-married bridegrooms and first-married brides in all Japan. 17. *Ibid.,* first-married bridegrooms and remarried brides. 18. *Ibid.,* remarried bridegrooms and first-married brides. 19. *Ibid.,* remarried bridegrooms and remarried brides. 20. First-married and remarried persons by age (single years) in each prefecture and average age of first-married persons according to place of wedding ceremony. [Tables 16-20 are limited to marriages occurring in and reported during the year.] 21. Divorces by year and month of cessation of cohabitation and month of declaration in all Japan. 22. Divorces by combined ages (single year) of both husbands and wives in all Japan. 23. Divorces by duration of cohabitation and number of children between the husband and wife in all Japan. A. By number of children born between the husband and wife. B. By number of minor children between the husband and wife. 24. Divorces by number of children under parental authority of husband and wife in all Japan. 25. Divorces by type and divorces of court decision by reason in all Japan. 26. Divorces by sex in each prefecture by cities, towns, wards, and villages.

Marriage and divorce, other

Nihon. Kōsei-shō, eisei tōkei-bu. Welfare Ministry. Division of Health and Welfare Statistics.
Birthplaces of bridegrooms and brides who married in June, 1950. Tokyo, 1952. Special tabulation.

Fertility, annual

Nihon. Naikaku tōkei-kyoku.
Jinkō dōtai tōkei. [Vital statistics.] *1899-1942.* Tōkyō, 1903-1943.

Fertility data, 1937: 2. Summary table. 11. Deliveries, live births, and stillbirths by month. 12. Births by legitimacy status. 13. Births by occupation of father or mother. 14. Stillbirths by age of mother. 15. Stillbirths by length of pregnancy. 16. Multiple births, prefectures. The appendix includes tables on births of 1936 and earlier years reported in 1937, births and stillbirths in Karafuto, and historical summary data.

In 1937 and 1938, tabulations of births by legitimacy status by age of mother were published for the total country and for cities of 100,000 and over as a group. In 1939 and later years, the tabulation for cities of 100,000 and over was omitted, but a tabulation of births to Japanese women living outside Japan was added.

The vital statistics yearbooks also included a distribution of births by age of mother for Karafuto.

A tabulation for the total country and each prefecture of births by sex and legitimacy status according to the occupation of the father or mother was first published in 1937. Less detailed tabulations were given in later years.

Nihon. Kōsei-shō, eisei tōkei-bu. Welfare Ministry. Division of Health and Welfare Statistics.
Jinkō dōtai tōkei. Vital statistics. 1946—. Tokyo, 1949—.

Fertility data, 1950: 1. Live births by place of occurrence and place of residence. 2. Live births by sex and month of occurrence in each prefecture according to place of residence. 3. Live births by age (single years) of mother, sex, and legitimacy in all Japan. 4. Live births by age (5-year groups) of mothers, sex, and birth order in all Japan. 5. Live births by person in attendance. . . . 9. Stillbirths by sex and month of occurrence in each prefecture by urban and rural areas according to place of residence. 10. Stillbirths by sex, month of gestation, and nature (spontaneous or artificial) in each prefecture by urban and rural areas according to place of residence. 11. Stillbirths by age (5-year groups) of mother, sex, and birth order in all Japan. A. Total. B. Spontaneous. C. Induced. 12. Stillbirths by person in attendance. . . . 13. Stillbirths in attendance of physician from each cause. . . . 26. Births by sex in each prefecture by cities, towns, wards, and villages according to place of residence.

Fertility, other

Nihon. Naikaku tōkei-kyoku.
Fubo no nenrei to shussei to no kankei. [Births in relation to age of parents.] Chōsa shiryō [Research Materials], No. 1. Tōkyō, 1927. 55 pp.
Fubo no nenrei betsu shussei tōkei. Taishō 14-nen. [Statistics on births by age of parents. 1925.] Tōkyō, 1927. 99 pp.
Fubo no nenrei betsu shussei oyobi shisan tōkei. Shōwa go'nen. [Statistics of live births and stillbirths by age of parents in 1930.] Tōkyō, 1935.

Mortality, annual

Nihon. Naikaku tōkei kyoku.
Jinkō dōtai tōkei. [Vital statistics.] *1899-1942.* Tōkyō, 1903-1943.

Mortality data, 1937: 2. Summary data. 17. Deaths by month. 18. Deaths by month and age. 19. Deaths by year of birth and age. 20. Deaths by occupation. 21. Deaths by marital status and age. 22. Deaths of children less than 5 years old by day, month, and year. 23. Number of deaths by cause. 24. Numbers removed from the register by abandoning of infants, disappearance, or recognition of death.

Appendix Table 2 gives deaths of 1936 and earlier years reported in 1937, while Table 4 gives data on deaths in Karafuto.

Shiin tōkei. [Statistics of causes of death.] *1902-193—.* Tōkyō, 1909-194—.

Tables: 1. Number of deaths by cause (fine classification), total Japan, cities of 100,000 and over as a group, prefectures, and the six large cities individually. 2. Number of deaths by cause (fine classification) and by month, total Japan and cities of 100,000 and over. 3. Number of deaths by cause (fine classification) and by age, total Japan and cities of 100,000 and over. 4. Number of deaths by cause (fine classification) and by occupation (broad classification), all Japan and cities of 100,000 and over.

Similar tables for Karafuto were given in an appendix. There was also a general explanation of the classification procedures and a list of causes of deaths.

Based on the 1937 edition.

Statistiques des cause de décès de l'Empire du Japon . . . 1906-1918. Tokyo, 1909-1921.

Prior to 1905 all statistics on causes of death were included in the "Statistique du mouvement . . . de la population de l'Empire du Japon." This publication, bilingual with French, is divided into three parts: Causes of death by districts, causes of death in cities of 50,000 or more inhabitants, and rates.

Nihon. Kōsei-shō, eisei-kyoku.

Eisei nempō. [Annual health report.] *1938-1940.* Tōkyō, 1939-1941.

Issues for 1937 and earlier years were published by Naimu-shō, eisei-kyoku [Ministry of Interior. Sanitation Bureau].

Nihon. Kōsei-shō, kōshū hoken-kyoku.

Eisei nempō, Shōwa jūroku'nen, nijū'nen. [Annual health report, 1941-1945.] Tōkyō, 1947.

Nihon. Kōsei-shō, eisei tōkei-bu. Welfare Ministry. Division of Health and Welfare Statistics.

Jinkō dōtai tōkei. Vital Statistics, 1946—. Tokyo, 1949—.

Mortality data, 1950: 1. Deaths by place of residence and place of occurrence. 6. Deaths by sex, year of birth, and age (single years) in each prefecture according to place of residence. 7. Deaths of married persons by sex and combined ages (single years) of both decedents and surviving spouses in all Japan. A. Male decedents. B. Female decedents. 8. Deaths of all ages and of infants, inside and outside of institutions, in each prefecture by urban and rural areas and by individual cities according to place of occurrence. 26. Deaths in each prefecture by cities, towns, wards, and villages according to place of residence. 27. Deaths from each cause (detailed list) by sex and age (5-year groups) in all Japan. 20. Deaths from causes of death (abbreviated list) by sex in each prefecture by urban and rural areas and in six great cities according to place of residence. 29. Deaths from causes of deaths (abbreviated list) by sex and month of occurrence in all Japan. 30. Deaths of infants under 1 year of age from selected causes by sex in each prefecture by urban and rural areas and in six great cities according to place of residence. 32. Deaths of infants under 1 year of age from selected causes by sex and month of occurrence in all Japan. 33. Deaths classified by international abbreviated list by sex and age (5-year groups) in each prefecture according to place of residence.

Life tables

Nihon. Naikaku tōkei-kyoku.

[The first, second, and third life tables.] *Nihon teikoku tōkei nenkan.* [Statistical annual of the Japanese Empire.] Various issues. Also in summary form: *Résumé statistique de l'Empire du Japon.*

Shōwa go'nen shichi-gatsu. Dai-yonkai seimei hyō. [The fourth life table. July 1930.] Tōkyō, 1930.

Shōwa jūichi'nen ichi-gatsu. Dai-gokai seimei hyō [The fifth life table. January 1936.] Tōkyō, 1936.

Shōwa jūroku'nen ichi-gatsu. Dai-rokkai seimei hyō. [The sixth life table. January 1941.] Tōkyō, 1941.

The sixth life table for the Japanese population of Japan is based on the data of the 1935 census and the vital statistics for the period from April 1, 1935, to March 31, 1936. There are four appendixes: I. Actuarial functions. II. Summary statement and major functions by single years of age for the 1st through the 5th life tables. III. Life tables for Japanese and natives in Formosa (Taiwan), 1926-1930. IV. International comparisons.

The seventh life table was omitted. The eighth and ninth life tables were published by Kōsei-shō, daijin kambō, tōkei chōsa-bu.

Dai-hachikai, seimei hyō [The eighth life table.] Tōkyō, 1950. [1947.]

Dai-9-kai seimei hyō. [The 9th life table.] Tōkyō, 1955. [1950-1952.]

Nihon. Kōsei-shō, daijin kambō, tōkei chōsa-bu.

The abridged life tables, 1948. Tōkyō, 1951. 24 pp.

Including life tables for 1945 and 1946. Abridged life tables are published annually in: *Jinkō dōtai tōkei maigetsu gaisū* [Monthly schedule reports of vital statistics, yearly summary volume].

Nihon. Kōsei-shō, jinkō mondai kenkyūjo.

Dai-2-kai kanryaku seishi jinkō hyō, seimei hyō, yohō. [The 2nd abridged life table. Preliminary report.] Tōkyō, 1949.

Dai-3-kai kanryaku seishi jinkō hyō. [The 3rd abridged life table.] Data series, No. 63. Tōkyō, 1950.

Dai-4-kai kansoku seishi jinkō hyō, seimei hyō. [The 4th abridged life table with comparisons of the 6th and 8th complete tables and the 1st to 4th abridged tables.] By Takagi, Naobumi. Report No. 72. 1951.

Dai-5-kai kansoku seishi jinkō hyō, seimei hyō. [The 5th abridged life table, April 1, 1951-March 31, 1952.] Tōkyō, 1952.

Dai-6-kai kansoku seishi jinkō hyō, seimei hyō. [The 6th abridged life table, April 1, 1952-March 31, 1953.] Tōkyō, 1953.

Dai-7-kai kansoku seishi jinkō hyō, seimei hyō. [The 7th abridged life table. April 1, 1953-March 31, 1954.] Data series, No. 98. Tōkyō, 1954.

Dai-8-kai kansoku seishi jinkō hyō, seimei hyō. [The 8th abridged life table, April 1, 1954-March 31, 1955.] Tōkyō, 1955.

Nihon. Kōsei-shō, jinkō mondai kenkyūjo.

To, dō, fu, ken betsu kansoku seishi jinkō hyō, 1. Hokkaidō. [The abridged life table by prefecture, 1. Hokkaidō, April 1, 1950-March 31, 1951.] Data Series, No. 78. Tōkyō, 1952.

Migration, internal

Nihon. Shokuryō-chō.

Shokuryō kanri tōkei nempō. Shōwa 28-nen. [Statistical

yearbook on rationing administration. 1953.] Tōkyō, 1954. 17, 535 pp.

Population movements based on ration registrations, pp. 247-266.

Nihon. Sōri-fu, tōkei-kyoku.

Jūmin tōroku jinkō idō hōkoku sokuhō. [Preliminary report on population movement by registration.] Tōkyō, April 1954—.

Jūmin tōroku jinkō idō hōkoku nempō. Shōwa 29-nen—. [Annual report on the inter-prefectural population migration based on registration. 1954—.] Tōkyō, 1955—.

POPULATION CENSUSES

The system

Nihon. Naikaku.

Genkō hōrei shūran. Bunsho: Tōkei kokusei chōsa. [Regulations governing the collection and publication of census statistics.] Tōkyō, 1940.

Nihon. Naikaku tōkei-kyoku. Bureau de la statistique générale.

Bureau of Statistics of the Imperial Cabinet. Organization, functions, administration. Tokyo, 1930. 21 pp.

Nihon. Sōri-fu, tōkei-kyoku.

Sōri-fu, tōkei-kyoku annai. [Guide to the Statistics Bureau of the Prime Minister's Office.] Tōkyō, 1950.

Census, 1920

Nihon. Naikaku tōkei-kyoku.

I. *Kokusei chōsa sokuhō: shotai oyobi jinkō.* [Preliminary report of the census: households and population.] Tōkyō, 1920-1933.

II. *Dō, fu, ken, gun, to, shō, shi, ku, chō, son betsu jinkō.* [Population of minor civil divisions.] 1921.

III. *Chūshutsu hōhō ni yoru dai-ikkai kokusei chōsa no gaikan.* [A general view of the first national census, based upon abstracts.] 1924.

IV. A. 1. *Taishō ku'nen kokusei chōsa hōkoku.* [Reports of the 1920 census.] *Zenkoku no bu.* [Section on all Japan.] *Jinkō, taisei, shussei chi, nenrei, haigū kankei, kokuseki, minseki, shotai.* [Population, sex, place of birth, age, marital status, nationality, imperial status, and households.] 1928.

IV. A. 2. *Taishō ku'nen kokusei chōsa hōkoku.* [Reports of the 1920 census.] *Zenkoku no bu.* [Section on all Japan.] *Shokugyō.* [Occupations.] 1929.

IV. A. 3. *Taishō ku'nen kokusei chōsa hōkoku.* [Reports of the 1920 census.] *Zenkoku no bu.* [Section on all Japan.] *Futsū shotai no kōsei.* [Composition of ordinary households.] 1929.

For prefectures and cities of 100,000 and over: Composition of households; heads and members, by occupation, and domestic employment; households and members by occupation of head of household.

IV. B. *Taishō ku'nen kokusei chōsa hōkoku.* [Reports of the 1920 census.] *Fu, ken no bu.* [Prefectural volumes.] 47 vols. Various dates.

The major contents of each prefectural volume are as follows: 1. Population of *shi, machi,* and *mura,* including age, broad occupational class, place of birth, colonials and aliens. 2. Population and households. 3. Population of the prefecture, the large cities, and the remainder of the prefecture, by place of birth (in Japan, same commune, elsewhere in same prefecture, in another prefecture and, if so, which one). 4. Population by age and marital status, single years of age, prefectures and cities. 5. Population by occupation. 6. *Ibid.,* classification of medium fineness, prefecture and cities. 7. Population by occupation, broad classification, age and marital status. 8. People with subsidiary occupations attached to main occupation. 9. Main occupation and subsidiary occupation, classification of medium fineness. 10. Population by nationality, registration, age, and marital status. 11. Population by nationality, registration, and occupation, medium fineness.

V. *Taishō ku'nen kokusei chōsa shokugyō meikan.* [Occupational titles used in the 1920 census.] 1931.

VI. *Taishō ku'nen kokusei chōsa tōkei zu.* [Statistical charts based on the 1920 census.] 1931.

VII. *Taishō ku'nen kokusei chōsa kijutsu hen.* [Descriptive summary of the 1920 census.] 1933.

The text portion presents a general description and interpretation of the statistics on distribution, sex, place of birth, age, marital status, occupations, nationality, and households.

The appendix reproduces the census regulations for Japan and Korea. (The census of Korea was canceled because of the disturbed conditions following the Independence Movement of 1919.) It also includes summary tables.

Census, 1925

Nihon. Naikaku tōkei-kyoku.

I. *Taishō jūyo'nen kokusei chōsa sokuhō.* [Preliminary report of the 1925 census.] 1925.

II. 1. *Taishō jūyo'nen kokusei chōsa hōkoku.* [Reports of the 1925 census.] *Kijutsu hen.* [Descriptive summary.] 1934.

The text includes a description and interpretation of the statistics on population size and distribution, sex, age, marital status, and number of households. This section also includes the basic census law of 1902 as amended in 1905 and the regulations of the 1925 census for the Japanese Empire, Kwantung and the South Manchuria Railway Zone, and the South Sea Mandated Islands. There are also summary tables.

II. 2. *Taishō jūyo'nen kokusei chōsa hōkoku.* [Reports of the 1925 census.] *Zenkoku kekka hyō. Tableaux recapitulatifs pour le Japon propre.* 1926.

II. 3. *Taishō jūyo'nen kokusei chōsa hōkoku.* [Reports of the 1925 census.] *Shi, chō, son betsu shotai oyobi jinkō.* [Households and population of cities, towns, and villages.] 1926.

II. 4. *Taishō jūyo'nen kokusei chōsa hōkoku.* [Reports of the 1925 census.] *Fu ken hen.* [Prefectural volumes.] 47 vols. Various dates.

The major contents of each prefectural volume are as follows: 1. Population and households, for minor civil divisions, including the *ku* or wards of cities. 2. Population of minor civil divisions, selected ages, by sex. 3. Population by marital status, total, cities, and minor civil divisions. 4. Age and marital status, single years of age. 5. *Ibid.,* large cities. 6. Quinquennial age classes and marital status, prefecture, *ku* of large cities, *shi* and *gun.*

Census, 1930

Nihon. Naikaku tōkei-kyoku.

I. 1. *Shōwa go'nen kokusei chōsa sokuhō.* [Preliminary reports of the 1930 census.] 1. *Shotai oyobi jinkō.* [Households and population.] 1930.

I. 2. *Shōwa go'nen kokusei chōsa sokuhō.* [Preliminary reports of the 1930 census.] *Shitsugyō.* [Unemployment.] 1930.

This is a preliminary report of the statistics on unemployment. An appendix gives unemployment statistics, 1925 and 1930, for 27 cities and surrounding territory.

II. *Dō, fu, ken, gun, to, shō, shi, chō, son betsu jinkō.* [Population of the various administrative divisions.] 1931.

III. *Chūshutsu chōsa ni yoru Shōwa go'nen kokusei chōsa kekka no gaikan.* [A general survey of the 1930 census, based on abstracts of summary tables.] 1932.

This is a preliminary presentation and interpretation of the data.

IV. 1. *Shōwa go'nen kokusei chōsa hōkoku.* [Reports of the 1930 census.] *Jinkō, taisei, nenrei, haigū kankei, shusseichi, minseki, kokuseki, shotai, jūkyo.* [Population, sex, age, marital status, place of birth, imperial status, nationality, households, and residences.] 1935.

IV. 2. *Shōwa go'nen kokusei chōsa hōkoku.* [Reports of the 1930 census.] *Shokugyō oyobi sangyō.* [Occupations and industries.] 1935.

IV. 3. *Shōwa go'nen kokusei chōsa hōkoku.* [Reports of the 1930 census.] *Jugyō no basho.* [Place of work.] 2 vols. 1935.

IV. 4. *Shōwa go'nen kokusei chōsa hōkoku.* [Reports of the 1930 census.] *Fu ken hen.* [Prefectural volumes.] 47 vols. Various dates.

The major contents of each prefectural volume are indicated by the following list of tables: 1. Population of *shi, machi,* and *mura.* 2. *Ibid.*, by size classes. 3. *Ibid.*, by special ages. 4. *Ibid.*, by marital status. 5. The age composition of the total population of the prefecture, with marital status, by single years. 6. Age composition and marital status, quinquennial groups, urban and rural areas of the prefecture. 7. Population by place of birth, *shi, machi,* and *mura* (same commune, other commune, other prefecture). 8. Place of birth for total, urban, and rural population (born in prefecture or outside, by prefecture of birth). 9. Age composition of those born in and outside prefecture. 10. Distribution of colonials and aliens by *shi, machi,* and *mura.* 11. Colonials and aliens in eleven age groups. 12. Japanese, colonials, and aliens by place of birth. 13. Population by occupation, broad classification, *shi, machi,* and *mura.* 14. Population by fine classification, urban and rural. 15. Occupation (broad classification), age, and marital status by position in industry. 16. Occupation of colonials and aliens. 17. Population by industries, broad classification, *shi, machi,* and *mura.* 18. Population by industries, fine classification, urban and rural. 19. Employed population classified by industries and occupation. 20. Unemployment, *shi, machi,* and *mura.*

IV. 5. *Shōwa go'nen kokusei chōsa hōkoku.* [Reports of the 1930 census.] *Shi, chō, son betsu jinkō.* [Population of *shi, machi,* and *mura.*] 1931.

V. *Roku dai-toshi sangyō betsu chūkan jinkō.* [Daytime population of the six metropolises, classified by industries.] 1936.

The industrial composition of the population of the entire city and each *ku* or ward in Tōkyō, Yokohama, Nagoya, Ōsaka, Kōbe, and Kyōto is given for the daytime population and the enumerated population, together with the proportionate composition and the sex ratio in each type-of-residence group. The tabulation for each *ku* is presented for the broad (10 groups), medium (42 groups), and fine (280 groups) classification of industries.

VI. *Chōsa shiryō dai-go shū.* [Survey materials. Collection No. 5.] *Taishō ku'nen oyobi Shōwa go'nen kokusei chōsa sangyō betsu jinkō no hikaku.* [A comparison, by industries, of the census populations of 1920 and 1930.] 1936.

VII. *Kokusei chōsa no kekka hyōshō ni mochiubeki sangyō bunrui oyobi shokugyō bunrui.* [Industrial and occupational classifications to be used in tabulating the 1930 census.] 1931.

VIII. *Shōwa go'nen kokusei chōsa saishū hōkokusho.* [Final report of the 1930 census.] 1938.

This is the final description and interpretation of the data of the 1930 census of the Japanese Empire on population, sex, age, marital status, place of birth, occupations and industry, places of employment, nationality, households, and number of rooms in residences. The schedule and regulations for the census are reproduced.

Census, 1935

Nihon. Naikaku kampō-ka.

"Shōwa jū'nen kokusei chōsa shikō rei." [Census regulations, 1935.] *Kampō* [Official Gazette], No. 2481, pp. 414-417, 421-436, 447-450. April 13, 1935.

These regulations were also published in *Hōrei zensho* [Compilation of laws], April 1935.

Nihon. Naikaku tōkei-kyoku.

I. *Shōwa jū'nen kokusei chōsa sokuhō. Shotai oyobi jinkō.* [Preliminary report of the 1935 census. Households and population.] 1935.

II. 1. *Shōwa jū'nen kokusei chōsa hōkoku.* [Reports of the 1935 census.] *Zenkoku hen.* [Section on all Japan.] 1939.

II. 2. *Shōwa jū'nen kokusei chōsa hōkoku.* [Reports of the 1935 census.] *Fu ken hen.* [Prefectural volumes.] 47 vols. Various dates.

The major contents are as follows: 1. For minor civil divisions, the population, by sex in 1935, total for 1930, 1925, and 1920, with intercensal increase in comparable areas. 2. The number of places and the population by sex in places of specified sizes, 1935, 1930, 1925, and 1920. 3. The population of minor civil divisions, by sex, for special ages. 4. Marital status. 5. Population by quinquennial ages, total and by marital status, by sex, for the prefectures, the individual cities, and the remainder of the prefecture. 6. Total population by single years of age, by sex. 7. Ordinary families and population, with number of households, population, and members per household, for minor civil divisions. 8. Types of populations, for minor civil divisions: A. Population at midnight preceding October 1, 1935. B. Resident population. C. Population temporarily absent. D. *De jure* or constant population. Appendix: Non-Japanese temporarily present at the time of the census, total, from each part of the Empire, and from foreign countries. 9. Age distribution of the resident, the temporarily present, the temporarily absent, and the permanent, by sex. 10. *Ibid.*, by single years of age.

II. 3. *Shōwa jū'nen kokusei chōsa hōkoku.* [Reports of the 1935 census.] *Shi, chō, son betsu jinkō.* [Population of *shi, machi,* and *mura.*] 1936.

Census, 1940

Nihon. Naikaku.

Genkō hōrei shūran. [Complete collection of laws in force.] Section 6, Subsection 4: *Kokusei chōsa.* [The national census.] December 15, 1940, pp. 241/1-248.

The instructions on the census schedule itself are reproduced as a part of a larger section: *Shōwa jūgo'nen, kokusei chōsa shikō-rei.* [1940 census regulations.] Pp. 217-248. The complete section includes the laws and regulations relating to the 1940 census in Japan, Korea, Taiwan, Karafuto, and Nanyō-guntō, in addition to those for the 1939 provisional industrial census.

Nihon. Naikaku kampō-ka.
"Shōwa jūgo'nen kokusei chōsa no kekka ni yoru Shōwa jūgo'nen jūgatsu ichijitsu genzai no dō, fu, ken, to, shō, shi, ku, chō, son betsu jinkō." [Population of Japan as of October 1, 1940 for prefectures, *gun*, islands, *shi, ku, machi,* and *mura.*] *Hōrei zensho* [Complete laws and statutes.] Pp. 559-653. April 1941.

This same report was published in *Kampō* [Official Gazette], No. 4282, April 18, 1941, as "Kokuji" [Notification] No. 2, pp. 7-101. Only the population by sex is given. The basic data have been translated and published in English in the following sources:

U.S. Department of State. Division of Geography and Cartography. *Japan. Total population by sex, 1940 census, by ken, shi, gun, machi and mura.* Washington, D.C., 1944. And: *Japan. Area and population by ken, shi, and gun. 1930-1940.* Washington, D.C., 1945.

Nihon. Naikaku tōkei-kyoku.
Shōwa jūgo'nen kokusei chōsa naichi jinkō sū: Shi, chō, son betsu. [Population of Japan according to the 1940 census, for *shi, machi,* and *mura.*] Tōkyō, 1941.

Nihon. Naikaku tōkei-kyoku. Cabinet Bureau of Statistics.
Census of 1940. Selected tables. Microfilm copy, Library of Congress, Washington, D.C., 1946.

The following tables were compiled from data sheets:

1. Population by ethnic group and sex, and number of households, Japan, Korea, Karafuto, Kwantung, Taiwan, and Nanyō-guntō.

2. Population by ethnic group, sex and age, Japan, prefectures, and the six major cities. (Age is given by single years for each sex for the total population, Japanese, Koreans, and other colonials.)

3. Japanese population by sex, marital status, and age (0-10, single years 11 and over), Japan, prefectures, and the six major cities.

4. Employed population by sex and industry, detailed classification, for Japan, prefectures, and the six major cities, by sex. (Japanese nationals only, i.e., excluding aliens.)

5. Population by sex and industry, broad classification, for the total population, prefectures, *shi, ku,* and *gun.* [This table refers to employed Japanese (excluding colonials) resident in Japan or serving in the military forces or related thereto outside Japan. "Employed" includes the self-employed, unpaid family workers (except those attending school full-time), and those temporarily unemployed. Persons in the armed forces other than career officers were reported under their usual civilian occupations.]

6. Koreans in Japan by industry, detailed classification, by sex.

7. Employed population by sex, industry (detailed classification), and occupation (detailed classification), Japanese nationals.

8. Japanese population by sex, marital status, age and industry, broad classification.

Nihon. Sōri-chō, tōkei-kyoku.
Kekka hōkoku tekiyō, Shōwa 15-nen kokusei chōsa, Shōwa 19-nen jinkō chōsa, Shōwa 20-nen jinkō chōsa, Shōwa 21-nen jinkō chōsa. [Summary of results, census of 1940, and population surveys of 1944, 1945, and 1946.] Tōkyō, 1949.

For 1940: Population by households and nationality; *honseki* population by present residence, prefecture; population by age and marital status; five-year ages, by sex, prefectures; age and marital status, including reported marriages; industrial composition.

Survey, 1944

Nihon. Naikaku jōhō-kyoku.
Shōwa jūku'nen no jinkō chōsa. [1944 population survey.] Shūhō [Weekly Report] No. 381. February 9, 1944.

Nihon. Naikaku tōkei-kyoku. Cabinet Bureau of Statistics.
Special survey of 1944. Selected tables. Microfilm copy, Library of Congress, Washington, D.C.

The following tables were compiled from the data sheets.

1. Population of Japan, prefectures, *shi* and *gun*, by sex. [The area covered included Karafuto, but excluded certain local areas previously a part of Japan Proper. The survey included civilian Japanese nationals, plus a small number of military personnel in Japan who were living outside military installations. Koreans, Formosans, and other colonials were included, but foreigners were excluded. The data were secured by preliminary hand tabulations made in the local areas.]

2. Population by sex for prefectures, *shi, gun, machi,* and *mura,* censuses of 1940, 1944, and 1945.

3. Population by sex and age, total country, prefectures, and the six major cities. [In single years of age, Japanese system.]

4. Population by sex, age, and occupational status. [Koreans and other colonials are included. The classification is as follows: Manager, clerk, technician, laborer, official or professional, student, other, and unemployed.]

5. Population by sex and occupational status, prefectures and six major cities.

6. Employed population aged from 14 to 61, by sex and industry, civilian population only. [The basic data for prefectures and smaller areas for Tables 6 to 9 inclusive were destroyed.]

7. Employed population aged from 14 to 61, by sex, occupational status, and industry.

8. Employed male population aged from 14 to 61, by age, industry, and military service classification.

9. *Ibid.*, employed female population.

Nihon. Sōri-fu, tōkei-kyoku.
Kekka hōkoku tekiyō: Shōwa 15-nen kokusei chōsa, Shōwa 19-nen jinkō chōsa, Shōwa 20-nen jinkō chōsa, Shōwa 21-nen jinkō chōsa. [Summary of result reports: 1940 census, 1944 population survey, 1945 population survey, 1946 population survey.] Tōkyō, 1949. 153 pp.

For 1944: Occupied population by industry and age; age and occupational status; age by sex, five-year groups, prefectures.

Survey, 1945

Nihon. Naikaku tōkei-kyoku. Cabinet Bureau of Statistics.
Special census of 1945. Selected tables. Microfilm copy, Library of Congress. Washington, D.C., 1946.

The following tabulations are based on a preliminary count:

1. Population of prefectures, *shi* and *gun*, 1945 and 1944, by sex. (Civilian population, excluding "foreigners," living under the jurisdiction of the Imperial Japanese Government on November 1, 1945. Okinawa, Karafuto, parts of Hokkaidō, and Ōshima *gun* of Kagoshima prefecture are excluded. Presumably some Koreans and Taiwanese were included, some excluded, owing to their mobility and some confusion over their status as "foreigners" after Japan's surrender.

2. Populations for 1945, 1944, and 1940, total, prefectures, *shi, gun, machi*, and *mura*.

3. Population by sex and age, Japan, prefectures, and six major cities, 1945. (By single years, lunar.)

Nihon. Sōri-chō, tōkei-kyoku.
Kekka hōkoku tekiyō: Shōwa 15-nen kokusei chōsa, Shōwa 19-nen jinkō chōsa, Shōwa 20-nen jinkō chōsa, Shōwa 21-nen jinkō chōsa. [Summary of result reports: 1940 census, 1944 population survey, 1945 population survey, 1946 population survey.] Tōkyō, 1949.

1945: Population by single ages, lunar, total, *shi* and *gun*; population by quinquennial age groups, prefectures; Koreans and Taiwanese by single ages, lunar.

Survey, 1946

Nihon. Sōri-chō, tōkei-kyoku.
Kekka hōkoku tekiyō: Shōwa 15-nen kokusei chōsa, Shōwa 19-nen jinkō chōsa, Shōwa 20-nen jinkō chōsa, Shōwa 21-nen jinkō chōsa. [Summary of result reports: 1940 census, 1944 population survey, 1945 population survey, 1946 population survey.] Tōkyō, 1949.

1946: Population in agricultural and non-agricultural households; agricultural and non-agricultural population in *shi* and *gun*; population by industry; age, single years, lunar, all Japan, *shi* and *gun*; ages, quinquennial, prefectures; Koreans and Taiwanese by agricultural status; agricultural and non-agricultural, ordinary and other households, *shi* and *gun*, prefectures.

SCAP. GHQ. Economic and Scientific Section.
Age distribution of population of Japan, 26 April 1946. Tokyo, 1946.

Census, 1947

Nihon.
"Extraordinary census of 1947." *Official Gazette, Extra.* December 24, 1947, and later dates.

Population, by sex, for *shi, gun, machi*, and *mura*, specific prefectures.

Nihon. Sōri-fu, tōkei-kyoku.
Shōwa 22-nen rinji kokusei chōsa kekka hōkoku. [Reports on the special national census, 1947.] Tōkyō, 1948-1949.

Sono 1. *Jinkō no gaiyō.* [Population summary.] 1948.

Sono. 2. *Zenkoku to, dō, fu, ken, gun, shi, ku, chō, son betsu jinkō.* [Population by prefecture, *shi, machi*, and *mura.*] 1948.

Sono 3. *Rōdōryoku jinkō ni kansuru gaiyō.* [Summary of population in the labor force.] 1948.

Sono 4. *Shusshin chiiki oyobi kokuseki betsu jinkō no gaiyō.* [Summary of population by native origin and nationality.] 1948.

Sono 5. [Households.] 1948.

Sono 7. *Nenrei betsu jinkō.* [Population by age.] 1949.

Population by year of birth and month, by year of birth, and by full age, all Japan, each prefecture (total, urban, and rural areas), the big cities together and individually, and cities by size groups.

Nihon. Sōri-fu, tōkei-kyoku. Prime Minister's Office. Bureau of Statistics.
Population census of Japan, 1 October 1947. Summary report. Tokyo, 1949.

Also: "Towns and villages classified by industrial structure of the population (according to 1947 population census)." *Tōkei geppō, Monthly Bulletin of Statistics,* No. 15, pp. 72-87. June 1950.

Nihon. Nōrin-shō, nōgyō kairyō-kyoku, tōkei chōsa-bu.
Dai 24-ji Nōrin-shō tōkei-hyō, 1947. [The 24th statistical yearbook of the Ministry of Agriculture and Forestry.] Tōkyō, 1949.

Section 9, "Farm population," 1947 census data.

Nihon tōkei geppō [Monthly Report on Japanese Statistics.] No. 111, April 1948; No. 115, August 1948.

Agricultural population and labor force, census of 1947.

Census, 1948

Nihon. Naikaku. Cabinet.
"Resident population census, 1948." *Official Gazette, Extra* No. 42. December 7, 1948.

Population as of August 1, 1948, for *gun, shi, machi,* and *mura,* specific prefectures.

Nihon. Sōri-fu, tōkei-kyoku. Prime Minister's Office. Bureau of Statistics.
Report on the resident population census, 1948. Tokyo, 1948-1949. 2 vols.

I. *Resident population, ration population, self-supplying population, and number of households by prefecture.* 1948.

II. *Resident population and number of households by city, ward, town, and village; ration population or self-supplying population by city.* 1949.

Census, 1950

Morita, Yūzō.
"Nihon no jinkō tōkei no seikaku sa ni tsuite." Pp. 25-31. "On the accuracy of demographic statistics of Japan." Pp. 27-33. In: Nihon jinkō gakkai. The Population Association of Japan. *Nihon jinkō gakkai kiyō. Archives of the Population Association of Japan.* No. 3. Tokyo, 1954.
"Sampling tabulation of the 1950 population census in Japan." *Bulletin of the International Statistical Institute,* 33(4):47-54. 1954.

A description of the census plan, the sampling tabulation plan, and the problem of estimation and reliability.

Nihon. Sōri-fu, tōkei-kyoku. Prime Minister's Office. Bureau of Statistics.
Population census, 1950. Manual for enumerators and supervisors. Tokyo, 1950. Japanese, 98 pp.; preliminary English translation, 126 pp.

SCAP. GHQ. Economic and Scientific Section. And: Japanese Government. Statistics Committee.
Standard industrial classification for Japan. Tōkyō, 1950. 2 vols.

Nihon. Naikaku. Cabinet.
"Population of *to, dō, fu, ken, gun, shi, ku, machi* (*chō*) and *mura* (*son*)." Prime Minister's Notifications, Nos. 19 and 24. *Official Gazette, English edition. Extra* No. 10, February 10, 1951; *Extra* No. 12, February 15, 1951.

Nihon. Sōri-fu, tōkei-kyoku. Prime Minister's Office. Bureau of Statistics.
Shōwa 25-nen kokusei chōsa hōkoku. Population census of 1950. Tokyo, 1951-1955.

I. *Jinkō sōsū. Total population.* 1951.

II. *1% chūshutsu shūkei kekka. Results of one percent sample tabulation.* 1952.

III. *10% chūshutsu shūkei kekka, sono ichi. Danjo betsu, nenrei, haigū kankei, kokuseki mata wa shusshin-chi, kyōiku, shotai, jūtaku, shussanryoku. Results of ten percent sample tabulation.* Part 1. *Sex, age, marital status, citizenship, education, household, housing, fertility.* 1952.

III. *10% chūshutsu shūkei kekka, sono ni. Rōdōryoku jōtai, shokugyō, sangyō, jugyōjō no chii, shūgyō jikan. Results of ten percent sample tabulation.* Part 2. *Labor force status, occupation, industry, class of workers, hours worked.* 1952.

IV. *Zenkoku hen. 1. Danjo betsu, nenrei, haigū kankei, kokuseki mata wa shusshin-chi, shussei-chi, kyōiku, shotai, jūtaku. All Japan 1. Sex, age, marital status, citizenship, birthplace, education, household, housing.* 1954.

V. *Zenkoku hen. 2. Rōdōryoku jōtai, shokugyō, sangyō, jūgyōjō no chii. All Japan 2. Labor force status, occupation, industry, class of worker.* 1954.

VI. *Jōjū jinkō oyobi genzai jinkō. De jure population and de facto population.* 1954.

VII. *To, dō, fu, ken, hen, sono—. Report by prefecture. Part —.* 1952-1954. 46 vols.

VIII. *Saishū hōkokusho. Final report.* 1955.

Nihon. Sōri-fu, tōkei-kyoku.

Taishō 9-nen naishi Shōwa 25-nen kokusei chōsa, sangyō betsu shūgyōsha no hikaku. [Comparison of the gainfully occupied by industry in the censuses of 1920 through 1950.] Tōkyō, 1952. 35 pp.

Hikiage shinkokusha sū. Shōwa 25-nen kokusei chōsa 10% chūshutsu shukei kekka. [Number of reported repatriates. Result of 10% sample tabulation of 1950 census.] Tōkyō, 1953. 11 pp.

Nihon fujin no shussanryoku. Shōwa 25-nen kokusei chōsa tokubetsu shūkei. Fertility of Japanese women. Special report. Population census of 1950. Tokyo, 1957. ii, 251 pp.

Census, Amami-guntō

Nihon. Sōri-fu, tōkei-kyoku. Prime Minister's Office. Bureau of Statistics.

Amami-guntō jinkō chōsa kekka hōkoku. Report on the population census of the Amami Islands. Tokyo, 1954.

Also includes results of census of May 17, 1952, of Toshima-mura, Ōshima-gun, Kagoshima-ken.

Census, 1955

Nihon. Sōri-fu, tōkei-kyoku. Prime Minister's Office. Bureau of Statistics.

Zenkoku to dō fu ken gun shi ku chō son betsu shotai oyobi jinkō gaisū. Shōwa 30-nen 10-gatsu ichijitsu genzai. [Population and households by *son, chō, ku, shi, gun, ken, dō* and *to* for all Japan, as of October 1, 1955.] Tōkyō, 1955. 77 pp.

Shōwa 30-nen kokusei chōsa hōkoku. Dai-ikkan. Jinkō sōsū. 1955 population census of Japan, Vol. I. *Total population.* 1956. iv, 370 pp.

1% chūshutsu shukei ni yoru kekka sokuhō. Shōwa 30-nen kokusei chōsa. Zenkoku. [Results of the 1 per cent sample tabulation. Census of 1955. All Japan.] 1956. 8 parts.

OTHER CENSUSES AND SURVEYS

Agriculture

Nihon. Naikaku tōkei-kyoku.

Nōgyō chōsa kekka hōkoku, Shōwa yo'nen. [Report of the results of the agriculture survey of 1929.] Tōkyō, 1930.

The census of agriculture of 1929 covered only area of land, type of use, and whether owner or tenant cultivated. Land was classified as total and cultivated, the latter subdivided into wet rice fields and other fields. Other fields were further classified as ordinary and as fields for the cultivation of trees and shrubs (total, mulberry trees, tea, fruit trees, and other). The tabulations give areas of types of cultivated land, classified on the basis of self or tenant cultivation.

Nihon. Nōrin-shō tōkei chōsa-bu.

Denbata shoyū jōkyō chōsa. [Survey on the conditions of rice-paddy and vegetable-field holdings as of the end of April 1941.] Revised. Tōkyō, 1950.

Establishments

Nihon. Naikaku tōkei-kyoku.

Shōwa jūyo'nen rinji kokusei chōsa kekka hyō. [Tables of results of the special census of 1939.] 6 vols. Tōkyō, 1941.

The preface to Volume I notes that "This special census as of August 1, 1939, was conducted in order to make clear the state of the consumption of goods in the daily lives of the people of our nation. As a secondary aim, this census surveyed the firms and shops which were the organs for the supplying of the commodities." Tabulations were carried through rapidly. All volumes were published on March 31, 1941, and stamped "secret."

Vol. I. Number of firms, number of workers, and amount of business (in yen) by kind of enterprise and form of enterprise in the year prior to the census. [Firms employing one or more workers are included.]

Vol. II. Number of shops, position of worker (manager, working families, and employees), and amount of business by kind of enterprise and form of enterprise.

Vol. III. Number of shops and age and educational status of the workers by kind of enterprise.

Vol. IV. Number of shops, kinds of workers, and amount of business by kind of enterprise and number of workers.

Vol. V. Main firms and branch firms, and amount of business, by kind of enterprise, paid-up capital, amount of investment, and organization of enterprise.

Vol. VI. Amount of designated commodities sold in the year before the census (August 1, 1938-July 31, 1939) by form of enterprise.

Nihon. Sōri-fu, tōkei-kyoku.

Jigyōsho tōkei chōsa kekka hōkoku. Shōwa 26-nen. Establishment census of 1951. Tokyo, 1952. 6 vols.

Vol. I. 1952. [Number of establishments and workers by occupational status, by business organization, by size, and by minor groups of industries, in private and local government establishments, etc.: all Japan.]

Vol. II. 1952. [Number of establishments by number of workers and by medium groups of industries in private and local government establishments, by prefectures.]

Housing

Nihon. Sōri-fu, tōkei-kyoku.

Jūtaku chōsa kekka hōkoku, Shōwa 23-nen. Report on the housing census of 1948. Tokyo 1950.

These summary results of the first national housing census include data on dwelling units, *tatami*, households, and persons for provinces, *shi, ku,* and *gun*. There are classifications by type of building, ownership of house and land, and date of construction.

Shōwa 28-nen jūtaku tōkei chōsa kekka hōkoku. Report on the housing survey of 1953. Tokyo, 1954.

Labor Force

Nihon. Sōri-fu, tōkei-kyoku. Prime Minster's Office. Bureau of Statistics.

Rōdōryoku chōsa hōkoku. Monthly Report on the Labor Force Survey. Tokyo.

Rōdōryoku chōsa sōgō hōkokusho. Report on the Labor Force Survey, 1947-1952. Tōkyō, 1952. 172 pp.

Rōdōryoku chōsa sōgō hōkokusho. Dai-2-kai. Report on the Labor Force Survey. No. 2. Tokyo, March 1955. 5, 195 pp.

Shitsugyō jōkyō jittai chōsa hōkoku. [Survey report on actual status of unemployment.] Tōkyō, 1952. 36 pp.

Shi gun-kan oyobi sangyō-kan no jinkō idō ni kansuru chōsa hōkoku. [Report on the population movement between industries and between *shi* and *gun*.] Rōdōryoku chōsa shiryō [Labor force survey data], No. 4. Tōkyō, 1952. 25 pp.

COMPILATIONS

Nihon. Kōsei-shō, jinkō mondai kenkyūjo.

Saikin no jinkō ni kansuru shiryō. [Materials concerning the recent population.] Tōkyō, 1947—.

Issued periodically.

Saikin no jinkō ni kansuru tōkei shiryō. [Statistical materials concerning the recent population.] 7th Edition. Report No. 92. Tōkyō, 1954. 199 pp.

Nihon. Kōsei-shō, kenkyūjo, jinkō minzoku-bu.

Jinkō tōkei sōran. Shōwa 18-nen 9-gatsu. [General survey of population statistics, September 1943.] Tōkyō, 1943. 4, 371 pp.

A compilation of census and vital statistics materials, with emphasis on the data of the 1930 census and on the vital statistics of the late 1930's and early 1940's.

Nihon. Sōri-fu, tōkei-kyoku.

Kekka hōkoku tekiyō: Shōwa 15-nen kokusei chōsa, Shōwa 19-nen jinkō chōsa, Shōwa 20-nen jinkō chōsa, Shōwa 21-nen jinkō chōsa. [Summary of result reports: 1940 census, 1944 population survey, 1945 population survey, 1946 population survey.] Tōkyō, 1949. 153 pp.

U.S. Department of State. Division of Research for Far East.

Administrative subdivisions of Japan, with Appendix of 47 prefectural maps. A listing of Japanese prefectures, cities, counties, towns, and townships, giving for each the area, the population for 1940 (adjusted to 1943 boundaries), and the population for 1945, with characters, romanized names, and a code showing location on accompanying maps. All changes in civil status and names shown through November 1943. Washington, D.C. 1946. xiv, 652 pp., atlas.

Japan: Growth of official cities, 1935-1940. Map No. 10133. Washington, D.C., 1947.

EXODUS AND REPATRIATION

Nihon. Gaimu-sho, chōsa-bu.

Shōwa jū'nen zaigai hompōjin chōsa hōkoku. [Report of the 1935 investigation of the peoples of the Japanese Empire abroad.] Tōkyō, 1936.

Japanese abroad by sex, place of residence, age (eleven classes), and marital status, and colonials abroad by nationality.

Hokubei nikkei shimin gaikyō. [General condition of American citizens of Japanese origin in North America.] Tōkyō, 1936. 180 pp.

Detailed demographic data for Hawaii, the United States, and Canada.

Kaigai kakuchi zairyū hompōjin naichijin shokugyō betsu jinkō hyō. [Population tables for peoples of the Japanese Empire and Japanese abroad by occupation.] Tōkyō, 1937.

Japanese and colonials abroad by country of residence and occupation, October 1, 1936.

Kaigai zairyū hompōjin chōsa kekka hyō, Shōwa 15-nen. [Tables on results of research on Japanese residing overseas, 1940.] Tōkyō, 1943.

Nihon. Kōsei-shō, jinkō mondai kenkyūjo.

"Gaimu-shō no zai-Shi hōjin jinkō sucho." [The Ministry of Foreign Affairs' investigation of the peoples of the Japanese Empire in China.] *J.m.k.*, 1(5):77-78. August 1940.

A summary tabulation giving the numbers of Japanese, Koreans, and Formosans in North, Central, and South China, 1937-1940, and the number of Japanese, Koreans, and Formosans in Chinese cities, 1940.

"Gaimu-shō no zai-Nanyō chihō hompō naichijin shokugyō betsu jinkō shirabe." [The Ministry of Foreign Affairs' investigation of the Japanese population in the South Seas region by occupation.] *J.m.k.*, 1(5):78-81. August 1940.

Japanese in the Philippine Islands, the Netherlands East Indies, British Borneo and Sarawak, British Malaya, French Indo-China, and Thailand, by occupation, 1938.

Nihon. Hikiage engo-chō.

Hikiage engo no kiroku. [Record of repatriation relief.] Tōkyō, 1950. 185 pp.

SCAP. GHQ.

Selected data on the occupation of Japan. Tokyo, 1950. v, 214 pp.

Section xv, "Repatriation," gives the status as of March 31, 1950.

POPULATION ESTIMATES

Nihon. Kosei-shō, jinkō mondai kenkyūjo.

Estimated population by sex and ages in the inter-census years, 1916-1938. By Tachi, Minoru, and Kubota, Yoshiaki. Demographic Researches, A-5. Mimeo. Translation. Tokyo, 1948.

Annual estimates based on the official life tables for 1920-1935; extrapolation for other years.

Nihon. Naikaku tokei-kyoku. Bureau de la statistique générale.

Population du Japon depuis 1872. Tokyo, 1930.

The Cabinet Bureau of Statistics utilized the enumeration of 1872, the censuses of 1920 and 1925, and the data on births, deaths, and register changes from 1872 to 1920 to estimate the population present in Japan from 1872 to 1925. There is a detailed note on method and a brief résumé of estimates of the population from the seventh century to the end of the Tokugawa era.

Nihon. Sōri-fu, tōkei-kyoku.

Taishō 9-nen—Shōwa 25-nen, waga kuni nenji betsu jinkō no suikei. [Estimated annual population of Japan, 1920-1950.] Tōkyō, 1953. 34 pp.

"Shōwa 25-nen 10-gatsu igo maitsuki zenkoku suikei jinkō." [Monthly estimates of national population after October 1950.] *Jinkō suikei geppō*, Tokushū [Special edition]. October 1953—.

To, dō, fu, ken jinkō no suikei. Shōwa 27-nen oyobi 26-nen 10-gatsu ichijitsu genzai. [Estimated population by prefectures. As of October 1, 1951 and 1952.] Tōkyō, 1953. 42 pp.

Issued annually, 1953 and later years.

Zenkoku nenrei betsu jinkō no suikei. Shōwa 26-nen 10-gatsu ichijitsu genzai. [Estimated national population by age. October 1, 1951.] Tōkyō, 1953. 27 pp.

Issued annually for 1951 and later years.

Zenkoku nenrei betsu jinkō no suikei. Taishō 9-nen—Shōwa 15-nen oyobi Shōwa 22-nen—Shōwa 25-nen. [Estimate of national population by age. 1920-1940 and 1947-1950.] Tōkyō, 1956. 137 pp.

SCAP. GHQ. Economic and Scientific Section.

Annual changes in population of Japan Proper, 1 October, 1920-1 October 1947. By Allen Buchanan. Tokyo, 1948. 33 pp. [Revised edition, 1952. Unpublished.]

"Estimated population, 1 October 1947 to January 1951. . . ." *Japanese Economic Statistics*, Bulletin No. 54, Section III, p. 2. February 1951.

Revised estimates on the assumption that there was over—rather than under—enumeration in the 1947 census.

Takatsu, Hideo.

"Meiji go'nen ikō waga kuni jinkō no suikei." [Estimates of population in Japan since 1872.] *Tōkei-kyoku kenkyū ihō*, (1):9-47. March 1950.

YEARBOOKS, COMPENDIA, SERIALS

Demography

Nihon. Naikaku tōkei-kyoku.

Nihon teikoku tōkei nenkan. [Statistical annual of the Japanese Empire.] 1881-1939. Tōkyō, 1882-1940.

Nihon. Naikaku tōkei-kyoku. Bureau de la statistique générale.

Résumé statistique de l'Empire du Japon, 1886-1940. Tokyo, 1887-1941.

In the early years the titles of the tables in *Nihon teikoku tōkei nenkan* were translated into French. See: *Tables des matières de l'Annuaire statistique de l'Empire du Japon. Cinquième année, 1884—Neuvième année, 1888.* 1886-1890. 5 vols.

Nihon. Sōri-fu, tōkei-kyoku. Prime Minister's Office. Bureau of Statistics.

Nihon tōkei nenkan. Japan statistical yearbook. Tokyo, 1949—.

The volume for 1949 was issued in co-operation with Tōkei iinkai jimu-kyoku, Executive Office of the Statistics Commission. There was a combined issue for 1955-1956.

Tokei geppo. Monthly bulletin of statistics. Tokyo.

Nihon. Kōsei-shō. Welfare Ministry.

A brief report on public health administration in Japan. Tokyo, 1950—.

A brief report on tuberculosis control program in Japan. Tokyo, 1953. 59 pp.

Nihon. Kōsei-shō, daijin kambō, tōkei chōsa-bu.

Kōsei no shihyō. [Welfare Index.] Vol. I, 1954. Tōkyō, Kōsei tōkei kyōkai, 1954—.

A monthly publication, with three special issues per year.

Nihon. Kōsei-shō, jidō-kyoku, boshi eisei-ka. Ministry of Health and Welfare, Children's Bureau, Maternal and Child Health Section.

Boshi eisei no shu naru tōkei. Shōwa 27-nen. Statistics of maternal and child health. 1952. Tokyo, 1952. 47 pp.

Agriculture

Nihon. Noshō-shō. Department of Agriculture and Commerce.

Statistical report. 1884-1885 to 1917-1918. Tokyo, 1885-1919.

Continued in: *The statistics of agriculture, industries and commerce, 1919-1923.* Tokyo, 1921-1925.

Continued after 1923 in: *The statistics of the Department of Commerce and Industry*, and *The statistical abstract of the Department of Agriculture and Forestry.*

Nihon. Nōrin daijin kambō, tōkei-ka.

Nōrin-shō tōkei hyō [Statistics of the Ministry of Agriculture and Forestry.] Tōkyō, 1924—.

Résumé of the Japanese edition: *The statistical abstract of the Ministry of Agriculture and Forestry.* Tokyo, 1924—.

Nihon. Nōrin daijin kambō, tōkei-ka. Ministry of Agriculture and Forestry. Statistics Section.

Japanese agricultural land statistics. Translation. Tokyo, SCAP. GHQ. Natural Resources Section, 1948. 85 pp.

Nihon. Nōrin-shō, nōrin keizai-kyoku, tōkei chōsa-bu.

Nōka keizai chōsa hōkoku. [Survey report of agricultural economy, 1950.] Tōkyō, 1952. 3, 480 pp.

Nihon. Nōrin-shō, nōrin keizai-kyoku, tōkei chōsa-bu.

Nōrin suisan tōkei shiryō. [Statistical data on agriculture, forestry, and marine products.] Tōkyō, 1952-1954.

The following are illustrative of the types of data available:

No. 49. *Shōwa 27-nensan, jūyō nōsanbutsu, sakubutsu betsu gen tan'i chōsa seiseki oyobi sagyō betsu tsuki betsu rōdō, chikuryoku, dōryoku jikan chōsa seiseki. Dai 2-shū.* [Survey results by units of capacity by production and by primary farm produce, and survey results of hours of work, animal use, and labor by months. 1952 production. No. 2.] 1954. 114 pp.

No. 50. *Shōwa 28-nensan mugi rui seisan hi chōsa.* [Survey by types of grain on production cost, 1953.] 1954. 2, 391 pp.

No. 52. *Nōrin-shō, nōmin eiyō chōsa hōkoku. Shōwa 27-nendo.* [Ministry of Agriculture and Forestry's report on a survey of rural nutrition. 1952.] 1954. 1, 1, 135 pp.

No. 53. *Nōsanbutsu no shōhin-ka ni kansuru chōsa hōkoku. Nōka keizai chōsa. Shōwa 27-nendo.* [Survey report on the commercialization of farm produce. Rural economy survey. 1952.] 1954. 41 pp.

Economic, other

Nihon. Keizai antei hombu. Economic Stabilization Board.

"Index number of industrial production." *Japanese Economic Statistics*, Annex 1. May 1952. 48 pp.

Nihon. Keizai shingi hombu. Economic Council Board.

Japanese Economic Statistics. Tokyo, 1946—.

This serial was initiated and published by the Economic and Scientific Section of General Headquarters, Supreme Commander for the Allied Powers. With the termination of the Occupation, it was issued first by the Economic Stabilization Board, and then by the Economic Counsel Board. The following four sections are or have been included:

I. *Industrial production.*
II. *Foreign and domestic commerce.*
III. *Population, labor, food supply, and prices.*
IV. *Review.* [Initiated with Bulletin No. 37 of September 1949, and later suspended.]

Nihon. Kōsei-shō.

Shōwa ku'nenjū ni okeru shukka-sha ni kansuru chōsa gaiyō. [Summary of the report regarding labor migration during 1934.] Tōkyō, 1937. 140 pp.

Reports compiled by the Social Section of the Social Bureau.

Nihon. Naikaku tōkei-kyoku.

Rōdō tōkei yōran. [Conspectus of labor statistics.] Tōkyō, 1924—.

This yearbook presents historical series and detailed current data on the employed population. In addition, there are sections on labor organizations, hours of work, wages, health insurance, labor disputes, the education of laborers, conditions of labor in the cities, household expenses, and indices of production costs.

Nihon. Nihon ginkō. Bank of Japan.

Monthly Economic Review. July, 1954. Tokyo, 1954. 13 pp.

Nihon. Nihon ginkō, kawase kanri-kyoku. Bank of Japan. Foreign Exchange Control Department.

Gaikoku kawase tōkei geppō. Foreign Exchange Statistics Monthly. No. 47, August 1954. Tokyo, 1954. 63 pp.

Nihon. Nihon ginkō, tōkei-kyoku. Bank of Japan. Statistics Department.

Hompō keizai tōkei. Shōwa 27-nen. Economic statistics of Japan, 1952. Tokyo, 1953. 7, 339, 33 pp.

Nihon. Ōkura-shō. Department of Finance.

The financial and economic annual of Japan. Tokyo, 1901-194—.

In the 1937 issue a résumé of general conditions of finance and economy in 1936-1937 was followed by tabular sections on finance; agriculture, industry, and commerce; foreign trade; banking and the money market; communications; Chōsen; and Taiwan, Karafuto, and Kwantung Province. Tables are compiled from and cited to the various statistical publications of the government ministries.

Nihon. Ōkura-shō. Ministry of Finance.

Statistical abstract of Japanese finance and economy, 1950. No. 1. Tokyo, 1950. 191 pp.

Quarterly Bulletin of Financial Statistics, 4th quarter, 1951. Tokyo, 1952. 144 pp.

Nihon. Ōkura-shō, Nihon ginkō. Ministry of Finance and Bank of Japan.

Shōwa 23-nen zaisei keizai tōkei nempō. Statistical yearbook of finance and economy of Japan, 1948. Tokyo, 1948. 847 pp.

Nihon. Rōdō-shō, daijin kambō, rōdō tōkei chōsa-bu. Ministry of Labor, Division of Labor Statistics and Research.

Rōdō tōkei chōsa nempō, Shōwa 26-nen. Yearbook of labor statistics and research, 1951. Tokyo, 1952.

Monthly Labor Statistics Bulletin. No. 1, January 1948. Tokyo, 1948—.

Nihon. Rōdō-shō, shokugyō antei-kyoku, shitsugyō taisaku-ka.

Shitsugyō taisaku nempō. [Yearbook on unemployment.] Tōkyō, Rōdō hōrei kyōkai, 1953. 6, 480 pp.

Nihon. Shōkō daijin kambō, tōkei-ka.

Kōjō tōkei hyō. [Factory statistical tables.] Tōkyō, 1911—. 194—.

Shōkō-shō tōkei hyō: Kōgyō, shōgyō, shōkō shodantai bukka oyobi chinkin, tokkyo. [Statistical tables of the Ministry of Commerce and Industry: Industry, mining, commerce, commercial and industrial organizations, prices, wages, and patents.] Tōkyō, 1926—.

Nihon. Shōkō daijan kambō, tōkei-ka. Ministry of Commerce and Industry. Statistics Bureau.

The statistics of the Department of Commerce and Industry. 1924—. Tokyo, 1926—.

Continuation, with *The statistical abstract of the Department of Agriculture and Forestry,* of *The statistics of agriculture, industries and commerce,* issued 1919-1923 by the Department of Agriculture and Commerce.

Nihon. Shokuryō-chō.

Shokuryō kanri tōkei nempō. Shōwa 28-nen. [Statistical yearbook of rationing administration, 1953.] Tōkyō, 1954. 17, 535 pp.

Nihon. Sōri-fu, tōkei-kyoku. Prime Minister's Office. Bureau of Statistics.

Shōhi jittai chōsa nempō, Shōwa 27-nen. Annual report of family income and expenditure survey, 1952. Tokyo, 1953. 176 pp.

Nihon. Un'yu-shō. Ministry of Transportation.

Un'yu geppō. Monthly bulletin of transportation. Vol. IV, Tokyo, 1952-1953.

SCAP. GHQ. Economic and Scientific Section.

Japanese Economic Statistics. Tokyo, 1946—.

See: Nihon. Keizai antei hombu. *Japanese Economic Statistics.*

Number of establishments, employment and value of products in manufacturing industries in Japan, 1929-1942. Tokyo, 1947.

Social

Nihon. Kōsei-shō. Ministry of Health and Welfare.

Outline of child welfare works in Japan. Tokyo, 1951. 21 pp.

Prepared by the Children's Bureau.

Nihon. Kōsei-shō, eisei tōkei-bu. Ministry of Welfare. Division of Health and Welfare Statistics.

The social welfare statistics, 1951. No. 2, Tokyo, 1952.

Numbers and characteristics of recipients of aid, by type, all Japan and prefectures, with rates based on the 1950 census.

Nihon. Mombu-shō, chōsa fukyū-kyoku, tōkei-ka.

Mombu-shō dai-hichijūhachi nempō. Shōwa nijūgo-nendo. [78th yearbook of the Ministry of Education. 1950.] Tōkyō, 1952. 3, 532 pp.

Nihon. Mombu-shō, sōmu-kyoku, chōsa-ka.

Dai Nihon teikoku mombu-shō dai-rokujūgo nempō. Yori Shōwa 12-nen 4-gatsu, made Shōwa 13-nen 3-gatsu. Gekan. [Great Imperial Japan 65th yearbook of the Ministry of Education. From April 1937 to March 1938. Second volume.] Tōkyō, 1943. 6, 513 pp.

NON-OFFICIAL SOURCES

Asahi shimbun-sha.

Asahi nenkan. [Asahi yearbook.] Tōkyō, 1939. 1008 pp.

Dōmei tsūshin-sha.

Dōmei jiji nenkan. [Dōmei current events yearbook.] Tōkyō, Dōmei tsūshin-sha [Dōmei News Agency], 1943.

Keizai zasshi daiyamondo-sha.

Daiyamondo keizai tōkei nenkan. [Diamond economic statistics yearbook.] Tōkyō, 1938.

Kyōchō-kai.

Rōdō nenkan. [Labor yearbook.] Tōkyō, 1940.

This annual reproduced the employment statistics of the Welfare Ministry and the Bank of Japan. It also included a bibliography of important current publications on labor problems.

Mainichi shimbun-sha. Mainichi Press.

Mainichi nenkan. Mainichi yearbook. Tōkyō, 1943.

General population statistics for Japan and the Empire were summarized.

Mitsubishi Economic Research Institute.
Monthly Circular. Survey of Economic Conditions in Japan. No. 235. Tokyo, June 1949.
Nihon rōdō kagaku kenkyūjo.
Nihon shakai eisei nenkan. [Japan social hygiene yearbook.] Vol. XIX, 1940. Tōkyō, 1940.
Labor, hygiene, and demographic statistics were summarized. There was also a bibliography on hygiene and social science.
Ōhara shakai mondai kenkyūjo.
Nihon rōdō nenkan. [Labor yearbook of Japan.] 20th volume, 1939. Tōkyō, Kurida shoten, 1940. 485, 11, 7 pp.
Teikoku nōkai.
Nōgyō nenkan. [Agriculture yearbook.] Tōkyō, 1941.
Tōkyō shisei chōsa-kai.
Nihon toshi nenkan. [Japan municipal yearbook.] Tōkyō, 1931—.
An extensive compilation of data for the individual cities of Japan, with less comprehensive tabulations for the cities of the parts of the Empire.
Tōyō keizai shimpō-sha.
Tōyō keizai nenkan. [Yearbook of the Oriental Economist.] Tōkyō, 1943. 367 pp.

POPULATION STUDIES

GENERAL

Books

Crocker, Walter R.
The Japanese population problem: The coming crisis. London, G. Allen and Unwin, Ltd., 1931. 240 pp.
Inouye, Masaji.
Population of Japan. Report submitted to the International Population Conference. Tokyo, Bureau of Social Affairs, 1937. 27 pp.
Ishii, Ryōichi.
Population pressure and economic life in Japan. Chicago, Ill., University of Chicago Press, 1937. xvii, 259 pp.
Jinkō mondai kenkyū-kai.
Jinkō mondai kōen-shū. [Collection of lectures on population problems.] 13 vols. Tōkyō, 1933-1940.
A series of volumes including contributions on various aspects of the internal and international problems and opportunities confronting Japan at the time.
Waga kuni jinkō mondai ni kansuru sho-kenkyū. [Various studies on Japanese population problems.] Tōkyō, 1936. 101 pp.
Hompō jinkō zōka no keikō oyobi sūryōteki hendō ni tsuite. [On the trends of increase and quantitative changes in the Japanese population.] Tōkyō, 1935. 212 pp.
Sekai jinkō no dōkō narabini seisanryoku kakuchō to rōdō jinkō. [Tendencies of the world population, the expansion of production, and the working population.] Tōkyō, 1938. 118 pp.
Mainichi shimbun-sha, jinkō mondai chōsa-kai.
Nihon no jinkō. [Population of Japan.] Tōkyō, 1954. 320, 7 pp.
Terao, Takuma. "Jinkō chōsetsu no sho-mondai." [Various problems in population control.]
Inaba, Shūzō "Nihon no jinkō to keizairyoku." [The economy and the population of Japan.]
Tachi, Minoru. "Waga kuni jinkō no genjō." [The present condition of our country's population.]
Nihon no jinkō mondai. [Population problems of Japan.] Tōkyō, 1950. 6, 286pp.
Tachi, Minoru. "Sengo no Nihon jinkō." [Postwar Japanese population.] Pp. 3-109.
Inaba, Hidezō. "Jinkō to keizairyoku." [Population and economy.] Pp. 111-164.
Aki, Kōichi. "Jinkō to shigen." [Population and resources.] Pp. 165-217.
Kondō, Yasuo. "Shokuryō kara mita jinkō mondai." [Population problem from the viewpoint of food.] Pp. 219-242.
Minoguchi, Tokijirō. "Jinkō riron." [Population theory.] Pp. 243-286.
Minami, Ryōsaburō.
Jinkō ron hatten shi. [History of the development of population theory.] Tōkyō, Sanseidō, 1936. 226 pp.
Jinkō ron. [Population theory.] Kyōto, Sanwa shobō, 1954. 4, 6, 344, 8 pp.
Minoguchi, Tokijirō.
Jinkō riron no kenkyū. [Research on population theories.] Tōkyō, Chūo kōron-sha, 1949. 422 pp.
Morita, Yūzō.
Jinkō zōka no bunseki. [Analysis of population increase.] Tōkyō, Nihon hyōron-sha, 1944. 464, 4 pp.
Nihon. Kōsei-shō, jinkō mondai kenkyūjo.
Chōsa kenkyū shuyō kekka. [Principal results of surveys and research.] Tōkyō, 1950. 157 pp.
Collected studies, issued annually in one or two volumes.
Nihon. Kōsei-shō, jinkō mondai kenkyūjo.
Genka no jinkō mondai. [The pending population problem.] Tōkyō, Kokumin kyōiku-sha, 1949. 318 pp.
Okazaki, Ayanori. "Waga kuni no jinkō mondai to jinkō seisaku." [Population problem and population policy in our nation.] Pp. 1-29.
Tachi, Minoru. "Nihon jinkō no genjō to shōrai." [The present and future condition of Japanese population.] Pp. 31-84.
Ueda, Masao. "Nihon jinkō genshō no chiikiteki tokusei." [The areal characteristics of the Japanese population phenomenon.] Pp. 85-187.
Mikuni, Kazuyoshi. "Sangyō kōzō kara mita waga kuni jinkō shūyōryoku no bunseki." [An analysis of the absorption capacity of our nation as viewed from the industrial structure.] Pp. 189-222.
Hayashi, Shigeru. "Nihon nōgyō no tekido jinkō ni kansuru ichi kōsatsu." [An observation concerning the moderate population for Japanese agriculture.] Pp. 223-256.
Shinozaki, Nobuo. "Nihon ni okeru sanji seigen no jitsujō to sono shōrai." [The actual condition of birth control in Japan and its future.] Pp. 257-313.
Noma, Kaizō.
Nihon no jinkō to keizai. [Population and economics in Japan.] Tōkyō, Nihon hyōron-sha, 1941. 11, 25, 407 pp.
Okazaki, Ayanori.
Effects of the late war upon the population of Japan. Tokyo, Research Institute of Population Problems, 1949. 62 pp.
Jinkōgaku nyūmon. [Introduction to demography.] Tōkyō, Kōbun-sha, 1950. 2, 6, 247 pp.
Nihon jinkō no jisshōteki kenkyū. [Factual study of the Japanese population.] Tōkyō, Hokuryū-kan, 1950. 602, 50 pp.

Nihon jinkō zusetsu. (Explanatory diagrams on Japanese population.) Tōkyō, Tōyō keizai shimpō-sha, 1954. 2, 8, 177 pp.

Penrose, Ernest F.
Population theories and their application, with special reference to Japan. Stanford, Calif., Food Research Institute, 1934. 347 pp.

Schumpeter, Elizabeth B., Editor.
The industrialization of Japan and Manchukuo, 1930-1940: Population, raw materials and industry. New York, The Macmillan Co., 1940. xxviii, 944 pp.
Part I, *Population and raw materials*: Schumpeter, E. B., "The population of the Japanese Empire." Penrose, E. F., "Japan, 1920-1936."

Tachi, Minoru.
Jinkō mondai setsuwa. [Narrations on population problem.] Tōkyō, Hanyō-sha, 1943. 3, 264, 30, 7 pp.
Nihon jinkō no shōrai. [The future of Japan's population.] Tōkyō, Sekai keizai chōsa-kai, 1947. 162 pp.
Part I. The influence of war on the Japanese population.
Part II. Population estimates in the near future.

Tanabe, Hisatoshi, Editor.
Jinkō to minzoku. [Population and people.] Shakaigaku taikei [Sociology series], No. 4. Tōkyō, Kokuritsu shoin, 1948. 253, 8 pp.

Terao, Takuma.
Jinkō riron no tenkai. [Development of population theory.] Tōkyō, Tōyō keizai shimpō-sha, 1948. 5, 6, 296, 9 pp.

Thompson, Warren S.
Population and peace in the Pacific. Chicago, Ill., University of Chicago Press, 1946. 397 pp.

Ueda, Masao.
Jinkō mondai. [Population problem.] Tōkyō, Sanshōdō, 1949. 4, 8, 267, 4 pp.

Ueda, Teijirō, Editor.
Nihon jinkō mondai kenkyū. [Studies in Japanese population problems.] 3 vols. Tōkyō, Kyōchō-kai, 1933-1937.
The first volume included estimates of the future population of Japan and of Tōkyō, together with reviews of international situations and literature. The second volume emphasized future population and the course of vital rates, together with studies of population and occupation. The third volume was devoted to theory, occupation and industry, levels of living, and regional studies.

Yoshida, Hideo.
Nihon jinkō ron no shiteki kenkyū. [Historical study of discussions on the Japanese population.] Tōkyō, Kawade shobō, 1944. 536 pp.

Other

Allen, George C.
"The population problem in Japan." *Economica,* 6:170-186. 1926.

Frumkin, Grzegorz.
"Japan's demographic expansion in the light of statistical analysis." *The Sociological Review,* 30(1):1-28. January 1938.

Honda, Tatsuo.
"Nihon jinkō mondai no shiteki kaiseki: Nōson jinkō mondai kenkyū no tame no ichi josetsu." [Historical analysis of population problems in Japan: An introduction to the "study of agricultural population problems."] *J.m.k.,* 6(2):1-29. June 1950.
"Nihon jinkō no genjō bunseki—'Nihon jinkō hakusho' no happyō ni yosete." [Analysis of recent trends in the Japanese population, with the publication of the White Paper on Japanese population.] *J.m.k.,* 7(3):1-30. December 1951.

Inouye, Masaji.
"Les problèmes de la population au Japon." *Revue économique internationale,* 30(II,I):7-22. April 1938.

Minoguchi, Tokijirō.
"Jinkō to shakai keizai henka to no sōgō kankei." Pp. 16-18. "Interrelation of population, economic, and social changes." Pp. 17-19. In: Nihon jinkō gakkai. The Population Association of Japan. *Nihon jinkō gakkai kiyō. Archives of the Population Association of Japan.* No. 3. Tokyo, 1954. 50, 53 pp.
"The over-population problem in post-war Japan." *The Annals of the Hitotsubashi Academy,* 1(2):111-120. April 1951.

Morita, Yūzō.
Facts about the population of Japan—shown in figures and charts. Population Problems Series, No. 14. Tokyo, The Population Problems Research Council, The Mainichi Newspapers, 1956. 55 pp.

Nagai, K.
"Kajō jinkō to shitsugyō to no kankei ni tsuite." [On the relationship of surplus population and unemployment.] Pp. 7-19 in: Jinkō mondai kenkyū-kai. *Waga kuni jinkō mondai ni kansuru sho-kenkyū.* [Researches on population problem in our country.] Tōkyō, Tōe shoin, 1936. 101 pp.

Nasu, Shiroshi.
"Population and the food supply." Pp. 141-210 in: Gini, Corrado, *et al. Population. Lectures on the Harris Foundation, 1929.* Chicago, Ill., University of Chicago Press, 1930. 312 pp.

Nojiri, Shigeo.
"Kajō nōson jinkō to fukanzen kōyō rōdōryoku no seikaku." [Surplus farm population and the character of the incompletely utilized labor force.] Reprint, pp. 293-314 in: Hashimoto hakase kanreki ki'nen ronbun shū. [Collection of essays commemorating the 60th birthday of Professor Hashimoto.] *Nōgyō ni okeru keiei to seisaku.* [Policy and management in agriculture.] [Publisher and date not given.]
"Nōgyō ni okeru kajō jinkō no mondai." Pp. 37-40. "The agricultural overpopulation problem." Pp. 39-43. In: Nihon jinkō gakkai. The Population Association of Japan. *Nihon jinkō gakkai kiyō. Archives of the Population Association of Japan.* No. 3. Tokyo, 1954. 50, 53 pp.

Orchard, John E.
"The pressure of population in Japan." *Geographical Review,* 18:374-401. 1928.

Ozaki, Iwao.
"Jinkō kajō sokudo sokutei e no rironteki sekkin—seichō ritsu riron no keiryōteki kōsatsu." Pp. 28-34. "Theoretical approach to measurement of over-rate of population growth—econometric analysis of the rate of economic growth." Pp. 25-33. In: Nihon jinkō gakkai. The Population Association of Japan. *Nihon jinkō gakkai kiyō. Archives of the Population Association of Japan.* Tokyo, 1953. 92, 102 pp.

Steiner, Jesse F.
"Population trends in Japan." *American Sociological Review,* 9(1):36-40. February 1944.

"Japan's post-war population problems." *Social Forces*, 31(3):245-249. March 1953.

Tachi, Minoru.

"Jinkō to kindaiteki kōshū eisei to no kihonteki kankei." [Fundamental relations between population and modern public health.] *J.m.k.*, 7(4):1-23. March 1952.

Also: Pp. 106-142 in: *Tōkyō Shuppan kankō*, 1949.

"Jinkō to kōshū eisei." [Population and public health.] Pp. 107-142 in: Tōkyō ika daigaku [Tōkyō Medical University], Editor. *Igaku kōgi*. [Lectures on medicine.] Tōkyō, 1949. 158 pp.

"Nihon jinkō ron." [Discourse on Japanese population.] Pp. 53-116 in: Tanabe, Hisatoshi, Editor. *Jinkō to minzoku*. [Population and people.] Shakaigaku taikei [Sociology series], No. 4. Tōkyō, Kokuritsu shoin, 1948. 253, 8 pp.

Ueda, Teijirō.

"Jinkō mondai no rironjō no igi." [The meaning of the theory of population problem.] Pp. 21-36 in: Jinkō mondai kenkyū-kai. *Waga kuni jinkō mondai ni kansuru sho-kenkyū*. [Researches on population problem in our country.] Tōkyō, Tōe shoin, 1936. 101 pp.

"Bevölkerungsfrage und Wirtschaft im heutigen Japan." *Weltwirtschaftliches Archiv*, 46(1):93-115. July 1937.

Yasukawa, Masaaki.

"Tekido jinkō no gainen." Pp. 18-91. "General concept of optimum population." Pp. 113-119. In: Nihon jinkō gakkai. The Population Association of Japan. *Nihon jinkō gakkai kiyō. Archives of the Population Association of Japan*. 1952. 102, 130 pp.

DISTRIBUTION

General

Periodicals and pamphlets

Hall, Robert B.

"Cities of Japan: Notes on distribution and inherited forms." *Annals of the Association of American Geographers*, 24:175-200. December 1934.

"A map of settlement agglomeration and dissemination in Japan." *Michigan Papers in Geography*, 7:365-367. 1937. Reprinted from: *Papers of the Michigan Academy of Science, Arts and Letters*, Vol. XXII. 1936. Published, 1937.

Hama, Hidehiko.

"Jinkō bumpu keitai no henka ni kansuru chōsa kenkyū." [Analysis of changes in population distribution patterns.] Pp. 367-384 in: Nihon. Kōsei-shō, jinkō mondai kenkyūjo. *Chōsa kenkyū shuyō kekka*. [Major results of research.] Tōkyō, 1953. 384 pp.

Hoffman, Lawrence A.

"Japan: Main population concentrations." *Journal of Geography*, 46(2):62-69. February 1947.

Inouye, Shūji.

"Shōwa 5-nen Nihon zenkoku chō son betsu jinkō mitsudo bumpu ni tsuite." [On the density and distribution of population by *chō* and *son* for all Japan, 1930.] Pp. 79-97 in: Jinkō mondai kenkyū-kai. *Waga kuni jinkō mondai ni kansuru sho-kenkyū*. Tōkyō, Tōe shoin, 1936. 101 pp.

Itō, Kyōhei.

"Dai-toshi jinkō no chirigakuteki kenkyū." [A geographical study of the metropolitan population.] Pp. 218-221 in: Nihon. Jinkō mondai kenkyū-kai. *Jinkō seisaku to kokudo keikaku*. Tōkyō, 1942.

Kawaguchi, Takeo.

"Hokkaidō Nihon-kai shamen ni okeru ni san no jinkō genshō shu to shite jinkō genshō ni tsuite." [Two or three population phenomena in Hokkaidō on the side of the Japan Sea—primarily on the population decrease.] Pp. 51-62 in: Jinkō mondai kenkyū-kai. *Waga kuni jinkō mondai ni kansuru sho-kenkyū*. [Researches on population problem in our country.] Tōkyō, Tōe shoin, 1936. 101 pp.

Kojima, Reikichi.

"Waga kuni saikin no fu ken oyobi toshi jinkō, Shōwa jūgo'nen kokusei chōsa no kekka ni yoru." [Population of the prefectures and cities of Japan in most recent times, based on the results of the 1940 census.] *Toshi mondai panfuretto* [Municipal Problems Pamphlet], No. 41. July 1941. 35 pp.

A translation of this pamphlet was published by Edwin G. Beal, Jr., under the title: "The population of the prefectures and cities of Japan in most recent times." *Far Eastern Quarterly*, 3(4):313-362. August, 1944.

Matsuda, Teijirō, and Hayashi, Keikai.

Hompō naichi tohi betsu jinkō zōka ritsu no sokutei-hō Taishō ku'nen—Shōwa go'nen. [Calculation methods of population increase rate by urban and rural areas in Japan proper, 1920-1930.] Tōkyō, 1937. 6 pp.

Nihon, Kōsei-shō, jinkō mondai kenkyūjo. Institute for the Research of Population Problems.

Map of density of population in Japan. . . . Tokyo, 1934. 2, v, 50 pp.

Rathgen, K.

"Amtlich Bevölkerungsstatistik." *Mittheilungen der Deutschen Gesellschaft für Natur- und Völkerkunde Ostasiens*, Vol. IV, p. 324. 1876.

Satow, E.

"The geography of Japan." *T.A.S.J.*, 1:30-51. 1874.

Stedman, Frank H.

Urban population shifts in Japan, 1940-1946. Washington, D.C., 1947. 23 pp.

Unpublished manuscript.

Tachi, Minoru.

"Jinkō tōkeigaku josetsu, jinkō tōkei shudan." [An introduction to demographic statistics, demographic statistical group.] *J.m.k.*, 8(1):1-28. July 1952.

Tachi, Minoru, and Ishii, Kiichi.

"Sengo ni okeru Nihon jinkō no chiikiteki kenkyū—chūsū jinkō mitsudo. [Geographical study on population of post-war Japan—median density of population by prefectures, 1935, 1947, and 1950.] Pp. 97-102 in: Nihon. Kōsei-shō, jinkō mondai kenkūjo. *Chōsa kenkyū shuyō kekka*. [Major results of surveys and research, 1951.] Tōkyō, 1951. 134 pp.

Sengo ni okeru Nihonjin no chiikiteki kenkyū—jinkō mitsudo. [Geographical study on population of postwar Japan—population growth and density.] Nihon jinkō gakkai, dai-4-kai kenkyū happyō-kai. [The 4th study meeting of the Population Association of Japan.] Tōkyō, September 1950. 5 pp.

Tachi, Minoru, and Ueda, Masao.

"Jinkō." [Population.] Pp. 181-292 in: Kiuchi, Shinzō, Editor. *Jinkō shuraku chiri*. [Population and commune geography.] Shinchirigaku kōza [New geographical series], Vol. v. Tōkyō, Asakura shoten, 1955. 8, 338 pp.

"Shakai no ōkisa to kihonteki jinkō genshō no henka ni kansuru jinkō tōkeigakuteki ichi kenkyū." Pp. 71-85. "A statistical study on the variation of basic demographic phenomena by the size of communities." Pp. 94-112. In:

Nihon jinkō gakkai. The Population Association of Japan.
Nihon jinkō gakkai kiyo. Archives of the Population Association of Japan, No. 1. Tokyo, 1952. 102, 130 pp.
"Chiiki shakai no ōkisa to jinkō genshō." [Population phenomenon by size of commune.] *J.m.k.*, 8(2):10-72. October 1952.
"Shikoku chihō hachi shi jinkō hokyū chiiki no santei." [Computation of the hinterland of eight cities in Shikoku.] *J.m.*, 4(1):71-87. August 1941.

Tsujimura, Tarō, Compiler.
Distribution maps on the regional geographical study of Japan. Text. For the Japanese National Committee of International Geographical Union. Tokyo, 1952. 40 pp.
Fujioka, Kenjirō, "An explanation of Japanese castle-towns." Pp. 18-19.
Asaka, Yukio, and Nagai, Masatarō. "Settlement originated in the medieval period (15th-16th centuries)." Pp. 20-21.
Kiuchi, Shinzō. "Rehabilitation and reconstruction of war-damaged cities in Japan." Pp. 25-29.
Kiuchi, Shinzō, *et al.* "Distribution maps of manufacturing industries in Japan." Pp. 29-30.
Tachi, Minoru, *et al.* "Basic maps of Japanese population showing regional characteristics." Pp. 30-33. [Population density, rate of increase in resident population, crude birth rate, and crude death rate.]
Horiguchi, Tamoichi. "Distribution of diseases in Japan." Pp. 34-35.

Area Studies

Books

Cornell, John B., and Smith, Robert J.
Two Japanese villages: Matsunagi, a Japanese mountain community; Kurusu, a Japanese agricultural community. Center for Japanese Studies, Occasional Papers, No. 5. Ann Arbor, Mich., University of Michigan Press, 1956. xiv, 232 pp.

Embree, John F.
Suya mura: A Japanese village. Chicago, Ill., The University of Chicago Press, 1939.

Jinkō mondai kenkyū-kai.
Tōhoku chihō jinkō no jinkō ni kansuru chōsa. [Survey on population of the Tōhoku region.] Tōkyō, 1935. 87 pp.
Tōhoku jinkō. [Population of Tōhoku.] Tōkyō, 1941. 335 pp.

Norbeck, Edward.
Takashima: A Japanese fishing community. Salt Lake City, Utah, University of Utah Press, 1954. xi, 232 pp.

Sekiyama, Naotarō.
Kinsei Nihon jinkō no kenkyū. [Research on population of *kinsei* Japan.] Tōkyō, Ryūgin-sha, 1948. 4, 4, 282 pp.

INCREASE

Inoue, Kenji.
"Nōson jinkō zōkaryoku no gensui to sono gen'in ni tsuite." [The decline in the rate of increase of the rural population and its causes.] Pp. 381-386 in: *Dai-sankai jinkō mondai zenkoku kyōgi-kai hōkokusho.* [Report of the Third National Conference on Population Problems.] Tōkyō, Jinkō mondai kenkyū-kai, 1941.

Kitaoka, J.
"Jinkō zōka to shitsugyō to no kankei ni tsuite no shosetsu no kenkyū." [Research on various explanations on the relationship between population increase and unemployment.] *J.m.k.*, 2(3):1-16. March 1941.

Koyama, Y.
"Correlation between population growth and birth, death, and migration in Japan by geographical districts." *Journal of the Chōsen Medical Association* (Abstracts Section), 27:38-39. July 20, 1937.

Masuda, Shigeki.
"Hompō jinkō zōka no keikō oyobi sūryōteki hendō ni tsuite." [Concerning the trend of population increase in Japan and its numerical change.] *Jinko mondai shiryō* [Materials on population problems], No. 13, 1935.

Matsuda, Yasujirō, and Hayashi, K.
Hompō naichi tohi betsu jinkō zōka ritsu no sokutei-hō, Taishō ku'nen—Shōwa go'nen. [Calculation of the rate of population increase for the urban and rural areas of Japan, 1920-1930.] Tōkyō, 1937. 6 tables.

Okasaki, Ayanori.
"Toshi jinkō no hatten." [On the growth of the urban population.] *J.m.k.*, 5(10-12):1-9. October-December 1947.
Growth, 1920-1940.

Tachi, Minoru.
"Chiikiteki ni mitaru waga kuni seisanryoku no hatten to jinkō no sūsei." [The relation between the increase of production and the growth of population in the prefectures of Japan, 1925-1935.] *J.m.k.*, 5(2):15-44. February 1946.
Summary in English: Nihon. Kōsei-shō, jinkō mondai kenkyūjo. Social-Economical Researches, B-1. Tokyo, 1948.
Population increase and change in value of production, 1935, with the ratio of the proportionate increases used as a measure of changes in "pressure."

Tachi, Minoru; Ueda, Masao; and Takayasu, Hiroshi.
"Shakai genshō ni kansuru rojisuteikku kyokusen no ōyō ni kansuru kenkyū." [The application of the logistic curve to social data.] Pp. 1-12 in: Nihon. Kōsei-shō, jinkō mondai kenkyūjo. *Chōsa kenkyū shuyō kekka* [Major results of research], *1952.* Tōkyō, 1953. 384 pp.
Application of logistic curve to social phenomena. Data Paper, 20th Annual Meeting, Japan Statistical Society, 1952. Tokyo, 1952.
Including stillbirths, 1947-1951; growth of population of Tōkyō, 15 *ku*; and population of Hokkaidō, 1870-1950.

Ueda, Masao; Hama, Hidehiko; and Yamaguchi, Y.
"Chiiki shakai no ōkisa ni yotte mita jinkō zōka ni kansuru chōsa kenkyū." [Population increase by size of community.] Pp. 193-242 in: Nihon. Kōsei-shō, jinkō mondai kenkyūjo. *Chōsa kenkyū shuyō kekka* [Major results of research], 1952. Tōkyō, 1953. 384 pp.

Uyeda, Teijirō.
The growth of population and occupational changes in Japan, 1920-1935. Japanese Council Papers, No. 2. Institute of Pacific Relations, Conference, Yosemite, Calif., August 15-29, 1936. 19 pp.

STRUCTURE

Demographic

Periodicals and pamphlets

Ishiwara, Fusao, and Iidaka, Toshiko.
"Beikoku umare Nisei no taikaku seiseki to Nihonjin to no hikaku." [A comparative study of body structure of Nisei and of native Japanese.] Pp. 44-84 in: Nihon. Kōsei-shō, jinkō mondai kenkyūjo. *Konketsu oyobi imin ni yoru Nihon*

minzoku taii no eikyō ni tsuite. [Anthropometric influences of emigration and blood mixture on Japanese race.] Data Series, No. 97. Tōkyō, 1954. 84, 4 pp.

Ishiwara, Fusao, and Kubota, Yoshinobu.
"Nihonjin to hakujin oyobi kokujin to no konketsuji no chōsa." [Anthropometric study of mixed-blood children between Japanese and white or Negro races.] Pp. 1-43 in: Nihon. Kōsei-shō, jinkō mondai kenkyūjo. *Konketsu oyobi imin ni yoru Nihon minzoku taii no eikyō ni tsuite*. [Anthropometric influences of emigration and blood mixture on Japanese race.] Data Series, No. 97. Tōkyō, 1954. 84, 4 pp.

Katuki, S.
Sex-ratio in the population of Japan Proper. Kurashiki, Institute for Science of Labour, Report No. 29, I, 1934-35. Pp. 1-13.

Koya, Yoshio.
"Untersuchungen über das Geschlechtsverhältnis der Geburten bei Japanern und Aino." Text in Japanese. Pp. 59-93 in: *Rassenbiologische Untersuchungen aus dem hygienischen Institut der medizinische Fakultät zu Kanazawa*, No. 1. 1936.

Maruoka, Hiroo.
"Seihi ni kansuru kenkyū. Dai-3 hen. Kekkon tekirei jinkō no seihi." [Studies on sex ratio. 3. Sex ratio among population of marriageable age.] *Igaku kenkyū*, 22(3):101-104. March 1952.

Miyake, Masao.
"Nai-sen konketsuji no shintai hatsuiku ni tsuite." [On the physical development of mixed-blood children of Japanese-Koreans.] *J.m.*, 6(2):105-154. November 1943.

Mizushima, Haruo, and Miyake, Masao.
"Nai-sen konketsu mondai." [The problem of admixture of Japanese and Koreans.] Pp. 20-21 in: Nihon. Jinkō mondai kenkyū-kai. *Jinkō seisaku to kokudo keikaku*. Tōkyō, 1942.

Shinozaki, Nobuo.
The investigation of mixed blood families of Micronesian-European or other . . . as the materials of eugenics from a viewpoint of physical anthropology. Surveyed in 1941. Nihon. Kōsei-shō, jinkō mondai kenkyūjo. Social-Biological Researches, C-1. Tokyo, 1948. 19pp.

Tachi, Minoru.
"Jinkō no rōnen-ka." [On the aging of population.] *Nihon kōshū eisei zasshi*, 1(5):33-38. July 1954.
"Waga kuni jinkō rōnen-ka no jisshōteki kenkyū." [Studies on aging of the population of Japan.] *Jumeigaku kenkyū-kai nempō*. [Annual reports of the Gerontological Association of Japan.] 1956. Pp. 8-19.
Also: *"Gerontology" no ni-san no seikaku ni tsuite—"demographie" no tachiba kara*. [Some aspects of "gerontology"—from the viewpoint of demography.] Revised. Nihon. Kōsei-shō, jinkō mondai kenkyūjo. 1954. 20 pp.

Tachikawa, Kiyoshi.
"Seihi no tōkeiteki kenkyū." [Statistical study of the sex ratio.] *Kōsei kagaku*, 1(2):221-243. August 1940.

Economic and Social

Periodicals and pamphlets

Hayakawa, M.
"Jinkō no shotoku kaisō betsu kōsei." [The structure of population by income classes.] Pp. 178-183 in: Nihon. Jinkō mondai kenkyū-kai. *Jinkō seisaku to kokudo keikaku*. Tōkyō, 1942.

Hayashi, Shigeru.
"Nōgyō no kōzōteki shinka to nōgyō jinkō. Okayama-ken Kojima-gun Kōjō-son ni okeru jinkō atsuryoku to keizaiteki tekiō o chūshin to shite mitaru nōka kaisō hendō no bunseki." [Structural evolution in agriculture and agricultural population. An analysis of transformation of class structure of farms viewed from the point of population pressure and economic adaptation in Kōjo-sōn, Kojima-gun, Okayama-ken.] *J.m.k.*, 7(1):16-60. May 1951.
"Shōhin sakumotsu chitai ni okeru nōson jinkō no jittai bunseki." [Analysis of demographic status in rural areas where commercial crops are prevalent.] *J.m.k.*, 7(4):24-44. March 1952.

Honda, Tatsuo.
"Ichi suiden tansaku mura no jinkō shiteki kansatsu—Niigata-ken, Nishikanbara-gun, Kurosaki-mura nōson jinkō shūyōryoku chōsa hōkoku." [Some demographic observations on a paddy-field village with a single crop—Kurosaki-mura, Nishikanbara-gun, Niigata prefecture.] *J.m.k.*, 7(1): 1-15. May 1951.
"Iwayuru 'jiyū rōdōsha' no shokureki chōsa. Shōwa, nijūgo-'nendo shokugyō idō chōsa hōkoku no ichi." [Occupational survey of the so-called "casual laborers." Survey report No. 1 on occupational mobility, 1950.] *J.m.k.*, 8(1):29-50. July 1952.

Kōhashi, Masaichi.
"Sangyō kōzō to rōdō jonkō—ichi." [Industrial structure and labor population—1.] *J.m.*, 5(1):91-120. September 1942.

Kuroda, Toshio.
[Social security and population structure.] In Japanese. Nihon. Kōsei-shō, jinkō mondai kenkyūjo. Data Series, No. 71. Tōkyō, 1951.
"Nenrei genshō no jinkōgakuteki shakai keizaiteki kōsatsu—shu to shite Nihon no jijitsu ni tsuite." [Demographic and social economic observations on aging—with primary emphasis on the case of Japan.] *Jumeigaku kenkyū-kai nempō*. [Annual reports of the Gerontological Association of Japan.] 1956. Pp. 20-30.

Miyade, Hideo.
"Yūkyū mirōdōryoku no shozai to sono riyō hōhō." [The location of potential labor force and its utilization methods.] *J.m.*, 5(3):541-564, February 1943.

Nagazawa, R.
"Reisai shokugyōsha no shokugyō idō chōsa, Shōwa nijūgo'nendo shokugyō idō chōsa hōkoku no ni." [Survey report on occupational careers of street traders in Tōkyō city.] *J.m.k.*, 8(3-4):53-67. February, 1953.
"Shitauke chūshō kigyōtai jinkō no shokugyō idō." [The occupational mobility of the population in subsidiary companies.] Nihon. Kōsei-shō, jinkō mondai kenkyūjo, Report No. 82. Tōkyō, 1952. 27 pp.

Nakajima, R.
"Nōson jinkō atsuryoku to sono shokeitai—Iwate-ken, Shiba-gun, Iioka-mura oyobi Kagawa-ken, Kida-gun, Ido-mura." [Population pressure in agricultural villages and its effects—Iioka-mura, Shiba-gun, Iwate prefecture, and Ido-mura, Kida-gun, Kagawa prefecture.] *J.m.k.*, 7(1):61-104. May 1951.

Nihon. Kōsei-shō, jinkō mondai kenkyūjo.
"Nōgyō jinkō tekisei-ka no ichi shiryō—Saga-ken, Saga-gun Honjō-mura ni okeru chūkai nōka no dōkō bunseki—nōson jinkō shūyōryoku chōsa chūkan hōkoku." [Research

on the optimum population in agriculture—analysis of the movements of standard farmers in Honjō village in Saga province. Intermediate report on the research on the population capacity of agricultural villages.] By S. Hayashi. *J.m.k.*, 6(2):30-47. June 1950.

Saga-ken Chitose-mura no nōka jinkō ni kansuru jakkan no bunseki—nōson jinkō shūyōryoku chōsa chūkan hōkoku. [Some analyses of the farm population of Chitose-mura, Saga prefecture—an intermediate report on the population capacity of agricultural villages.] Jinkō mondai kenkyūjo, Research Series, No. 37. Tōkyō, 1950. 9 pp.

Nōson jinkō shūyōryoku chōsa kekka hyō—Okayama-ken. [Result tables of research on the population capacity of agricultural villages—Okayama province.] *Ibid.*, No. 40. Tōkyō, 1950. 23 pp.

Nihon nōgyō no saiteki jinkō shisan ni kansuru ichi shiryō. [On the estimation of the optimum population in Japanese agriculture.] *Ibid.*, No. 41. Tōkyō, 1950. 12 pp.

Kaitaku-son ni okeru junsui nyūshokusha no teichakusei ni kansuru ichi mura ni okeru nōson jinkō shūyōryoku chōsa kekka no chūkan hōkoku. [Data on the permanency of genuine migrants in colonized villages. An intermediate report on the population capacity of agricultural villages in Okayama prefecture, Kojima-gun, Fujita-mura.] *Ibid.*, No. 46. Tōkyō, 1950. 24 pp.

Nōson jinkō shūyōryoku chōsa kekka no kaiyō—tokuni saikin no chōsa-son o taishō to suru chūkan hōkoku. [Summary of an investigation of the population capacity of agricultural villages—an intermediate report on villages investigated recently.] *Ibid.*, No. 55. Tōkyō, 1950. 33 pp.

Similar reports were issued for individual *machi* or *mura* in various prefectures.

Nihon. Kōsei-shō, jinkō mondai kenkyūjo.

Roten sho ni kansuru shokugyō idō chōsa shukei kekka hyō. [Data from a survey of occupational mobility, street stalls.] Progress Report No. 11. Tōkyō, 1952. 57 pp.

Yawata seitetsujo shitauke kaisha no shokugyō idō chōsa shukei kekka hyō. [Data from a survey of occupational mobility, subsidiary companies of Yawata Iron Works.] Progress Report No. 12. 1952. 61 pp.

Waga kuni yūgyō jinkō no kōzōteki suii ni tsuite. [On the structural change of Japan's occupied population.] Series No. 45. Tōkyō, 1949.

Nihon. Naikaku tōkei-kyoku. Cabinet Imperial. Bureau de la statistique générale.

Nombre des ouvriers au Japon et leurs salaires. Tokyo, 1930. 49 pp.

Nojiri, Shigeo.

"Kajō nōson jinkō to fukanzen kōyō rōdōryoku no seikaku." [Surplus farm population and the character of the incompletely utilized labor force.] Reprint, pp. 293-314 in: *Hashimoto hakase kanreki ki'nen ronbun shū.* [Collection of essays commemorating the 60th birthday of Professor Hashimoto.] Nōgyō ni okeru keiei to seisaku [Policy and management in agriculture.] [Publisher and date not given.]

"Saikin no nōson jinkō idō ni yoru shokugyō bunsan no keikō." [The trend of occupational distribution as affected by recent rural population movements.] *J.m.*, 5(1):81-90. September 1942.

"Waga kuni nōgyō jinkō no ugoki to sangyō, jinkō koyō no jittai." Pp. 36-41. "Trend of farm population and industrial employment in Japan." Pp. 47-54. In: Nihon jinkō gakkai. The Population Association of Japan. *Nihon jinkō gekkai kiyō. Archives of the Population Association of Japan.* Tokyo, 1952. 102, 130 pp.

Nōson jinkō mondai kenkyū-kai, Editor.

Nōson jinkō mondai kenkyū. [Research on rural population problems.] Tōkyō, Nōrin tōkei kyōkai, 1951. 4, 8, 361 pp.

Yoshimiya, Yukihiko. "Saikin ni okeru nōson jinkō no dōkō." [Recent trends in the population of rural villages.] Pp. 3-33.

Hatai, Yoshitaka. "Sengo nōson jinkō mondai no shosō." [Situation of the population problem in postwar rural villages.] Pp. 37-104.

Nishimura, Kōichi. "Nihon nōgyō no jinkō shūyōryoku." [The population absorption capacity of Japanese agriculture.] Pp. 107-124.

Hayashi, Shigeru. "Nōgyō kindaika to nōgyō tekido jinkō ni kansuru ichi kōsatsu." [An observation on modernization and moderate population in agriculture.] Pp. 127-154.

Ōshima, Kiyoshi. "Toshi to nōson ni okeru rōdōryoku no idō keitai." [Movement forms of the labor force in cities and rural villages.] Pp. 157-231.

Hata, Genryū. "Toshi to nōson kan no jinkō idō." [Population movements between cities and rural villages.] Pp. 235-260.

Yamashita, Masanobu. "Waga kuni nōka ni okeru keiei kibo to jinkō oyobi rōdōryoku ni kansuru tōkeiteki kenkyū." [A statistical study of population and labor force, and the management scale of farms in our country.]

Tamai, Torao. "Nōson seikatsu suijun kenkyū nōto." [Research notes on the standard of living in rural villages.] Pp. 297-321.

Okazaki, Ayanori.

La grande industrie et la population des ouvriers d'usine du Japon. Tokyo, Institut d'étude des problèmes démographiques, 1954. 41 pp.

"Nihon no kōba kōgyō to kōgyō rōdō jinkō." [Manufacturing industries and their labor force in Japan.] *J.m.k.*, 9(3-4):1-25. March 1954.

"Rōmu jukyū no kenkyū, sono ichi." [Research on supply and demand of labor, No. 1.] *J.m.k.*, 6(1). January-March 1948.

MIGRATION

Within Japan

Book

Nojiri, Shigeo.

Nōson jinkō idō no jittai chōsa. [Field survey of population movement in rural villages.] Tōkyō, 1940.

Other

Fukutake, Tadashi.

"Waga kuni genzai ni okeru nōson ryūnyū jinkō no jittai." [The present condition of population influx into rural villages in our country.] *Shakaigaku kenkyū* [Sociological Research], 1(2):137-147. December 1947.

Hayashi, Shigeru.

"Kaitaku seisaku to jinkō mondai—Okayama-ken, Kojima-gun, Fujita-mura ni okeru nyūshoku nōka no teichaku to jinkō atsuryoku." [Inner colonization policy and and population problem—the settlers in Fujita-mura, Kojima-gun, Okayama prefecture.] *J.m.k.*, 7(2):29-51. September 1951.

Ishikawa, E.

"Kantō Hirano ni okeru seikatsu ken no jissō." [An actual study of the living radius of Hirano in Kantō.] Pp. 212-215 in: Nihon. Jinkō mondai kenkyū-kai. *Jinkō seisaku to kokudo keikaku.* Tōkyō, 1942.

Kōhashi, Masaichi.
"Rōdō jinkō no shūchū to bunsan—ichi." [Concentration and dispersion of labor population—1.] *J.m.*, 4(3):394-416. January 1942.
Ibid.—2. *J.m.*, 4(4):609-638. May 1942.

Mihara, Shin'ichi.
"Nihon ni okeru kokunai jinkō idō." Pp. 11-15. "Internal migration in Japan." Pp. 11-16. In: Nihon jinkō gakkai. The Population Association of Japan. *Nihon jinkō gakkai kiyō. Archives of the Population Association of Japan.* No. 3. Tokyo, 1954. 50, 53 pp.

Nihon. Kōsei-shō, jinkō mondai kenkyūjo.
Fu ken kan jinkō idō no gaikan. [An outline of population movements between prefectures.] Tōkyō, March 1954. 74 pp.
Sengo nōson jinkō idō no chiikiteki seikaku ni kansuru ichi kōsatsu. [An observation of the areal characteristics of postwar rural population movement.] Tōkyō, March 1954. 23 pp.

Nojiri, Shigeo.
"Nihon ni okeru kōgyōka no shinten to kokunai jinkō idō no seikaku." Pp. 33-36. "The true nature of development of industrialization and internal migration in Japan." Pp. 35-38. In: Nihon jinkō gakkai. The Population Association of Japan. *Nihon jinkō gakkai kiyō. Archives of the Population Association of Japan.* No. 3. Tokyo, 1954. 50, 53 pp.

Tachi, Minoru, and Ueda, Masao.
Birthplace composition of 109 cities in 1930. Nihon. Kōsei-shō, jinkō mondai kenkyūjo, Social-Economical Researches, B-12. Tokyo, 1948.

Yamaguchi, Y.
"Sanson ni okeru jinkō okikae genshō." [In- and out-movements in mountain villages.] *J.m.*, 4(2):228-248. November 1941.

Outside Japan Proper

Books

Fukutake, Tadashi, *et al.*
Influences of emigrants on their home village. Report of a survey of Amerika-mura. Mainichi shimbun-sha, jinkō mondai chōsa-kai. The Mainichi Newspapers, The Population Problems Research Council, Population Problems Series, No. 8. Tokyo, 1953. 36 pp.

Kuykendall, Ralph S.
The earliest Japanese labor immigration to Hawaii. Honolulu, University of Hawaii, 1935. 26 pp.

Normano, J. F., and Gerbi, Antonello.
The Japanese in South America: An introductory survey, with special reference to Peru. New York, International Secretariat, Institute of Pacific Relations, 1943. 135 pp.

Shapiro, Harry L.
Migration and environment: A study of the physical characteristics of the Japanese immigrants to Hawaii and the effects of environment on their descendants. New York, Oxford University Press, 1939. 594 pp.

Takekoshi, Yosaburō.
The story of the Wako: Japanese pioneers in the southern regions. Translated by Watanaba, Hideo. Tokyo, Kenkyūsha, Ltd., 1940. xvi, 183 pp.

U.S. Army. Western Defense Command and Fourth Army.
Final report, Japanese evacuation from the West coast. 1942. Washington, D.C., Govt. Printing Office, 1943. xxiii, 618 pp.
There were nine volumes in this comprehensive report.

Wagner, Edward W.
The Korean minority in Japan, 1904-1950. New York, International Secretariat, Institute of Pacific Relations, 1951. 108 pp.

Young, Charles H., and Reid, Helen R. Y.
The Japanese Canadians. Second part, *Oriental standards of living,* by W. A. Carrothers. Toronto, University of Toronto Press, 1938.

Other

Hisama, Kenichi.
"Chōsen nōmin no naichi ishutsu no hitsuzensei." [The necessity for the emigration of Korean farmers to Japan.] *Shakai seisaku jihō,* No. 244, pp. 113-128. January 1941.

Irie, Toraji.
"History of Japanese migration to Peru." *Hispanic American Historical Review,* 31(3):437-452; (4):648-664; 32(1):73-82. August and November 1951 and February 1952.
Translation by William Himel of: *Hōjin kaigai hatten shi.*

Noma, Kaizō.
"Waga kuni no saidai jinkō shūyōryoku to zaigai jinkō haibun ni tsuite." [On the distribution of population residing outside Japan and the maximum population absorption in our country.] Pp. 15-19 in: Jinkō mondai kenkyū-kai. *Jinkō seisaku to kokudo keikaku.* Tōkyō, 1942.

Ogishima, Tōru.
"Japanese emigration." *International Labour Review,* 34(5):618-651. November 1936.

Pelzer, Karl J.
"Japanese migration and colonization." In: Bowman, Isaiah, Editor. *Limits of land settlement: A report on present-day possibilities.* New York, Council on Foreign Relations, 1937. 380 pp.

Sebald, William J.
"Soviet Union refuses to cooperate in repatriation of Japanese." *U.S. Department of State Bulletin,* 22(548):24-28. January 2, 1950.

Shimojō, Yasumaro.
"Sekai jinkō no sai-haibun, toku ni Nihon ni kanren shite." Pp. 44-46. "Redistribution of population of the world, with special attention to Japan." Pp. 47-49. In: Nihon jinkō gakkai. The population Association of Japan. *Nihon jinkō gakkai kiyō. Archives of the Population Association of Japan.* No. 3. Tokyo, 1954. 50, 53 pp.

Takeda, Yukio.
"Naichi zaijū hantōjin mondai." [The problem of Korean residents in Japan.] *Shakai seisaku jihō,* (213):99-137. June 1938.

Thomas, Dorothy S.
"Differential fertility in California in 1930: The racial aspect." *Social Forces,* 20(2):146-154. December 1941. Also: Giannini Foundation of Agricultural Economics, Paper No. 97.

Tsubouchi, Shōji.
"Chōsenjin rōmusha naichi idō no gen'in ni tsuite." [On the reasons for migration of Korean workers to Japan.] *J.m.,* 6(2):155-176. November 1943.

United Nations, Population Division.
"International migrations in the Far East during recent times: The countries of emigration." *Population Bulletin,* No. 1, pp. 13-30. December 1951.

Characteristics and demographic significance of migration from the Far East, particularly China, India and Pakistan, Japan, and Korea.

NATURAL MOVEMENTS

Natural Increase

Periodicals

Eto, Masami.
"Tohi betsu jinkō shizen zōka ritsu no hikaku." [Comparison of rates of natural increase of urban and rural population.] *Hukuoka igakkai zasshi*, 34(5):492-508. May 1941.

Koyama, Yūkichi.
"Fu ken betsu shin no jinkō shizen zōka ritsu." [The true rates of natural increase of population for each prefecture in Japan, 1930.] *Chōsen igakkai zasshi*, 31(2):1-15. 1941.
"Fu ken betsu shin no jinkō shizen zōka ritsu dai-2-kai, Shōwa 6—10-nen." [The second true rates of natural increase of population for each prefecture in Japan, 1931-1935] *Chōsen igakkai zasshi*, 32(7):11-19. 1942.

Le Blanc, Thomas J.
"Specific vital indices for Japan, 1925." *Human Biology*, 1(2):198-213. May 1929. Also: "Vital index for the Ainu of Hokkaidō." *Tōhoku Imperial University, Science Reports*, Series 4, *Biology*, Vol. III, No. 4, Fasc. 2, pp. 689-698. November 1928. And, for Ōsaka, *ibid.*, pp. 713-725. November 1928.

Mizushima, Haruo.
"The true rate of natural increase of the population of Japan." *The Keijō Journal of Medicine*, 8(2):140-150. August 20, 1937. Also: "An amendment to 'The true rate of natural increase of the population of Japan.'" *Ibid.*, 9(3):210-214. October 1938.
"Hompō ni okeru makoto no jinkō shizen zōka ritsu." [The true rate of natural increase in Japan.] *Nisshin igaku*, Vol. XXVI, No. 12, 1937.
"Naichi roku dai-toshi no makoto no jinkō shizen zōka ritsu." [The true rate of natural increase in the six large cities of Japan.] *Tōkyō iji shinshi*, No. 3168, pp. 495-496. 1940. "Nihon ni okeru shinsei jinkō shizen zōka ritsu no chiriteki sai." Pp. 17-22. "Geographic variations in true increase rate of population in Japan." Pp. 22-29. In: Nihon jinkō gakkai. The Population Association of Japan. *Nihon jinkō gakkai kiyō. Archives of the Population Association of Japan.* Tokyo, 1952. 102, 130 pp.

Mizushima, Haruo; Kusukawa, Akira; and Fujimoto, Takashi.
"Shōwa 22-nen, fu ken betsu shinsei jinkō shizen zōka ritsu." [The true rate of natural increase of population for each prefecture in Japan, 1947.] *Eisei tōkei*, 4(8):1-5. 1951.

Nakagawa, Tomonaga.
"Antei jinkō no keisan." [The computation of a stable population.] *J.m.k.*, 1(1):14-20. April 1940.

Shinozaki, Kichirō, and Tachi, Minoru.
"Population curve no kenkyū." Pp. 35-42. "A study on population curve." Pp. 34-42. In: Nihon jinkō gakkai. The Population Association of Japan. *Nihon. jinkō gakkai kiyō. Archives of the Population Association of Japan.* Tokyo, 1953. 92, 102 pp.

Tachi, Minoru.
"Hitotsu no jinkō sai-seisan ritsu ni tsuite." Pp. 43-49. "On a replacement index population." Pp. 43-50. In: Nihon jinkō gakkai. The Population Association of Japan. *Nihon jinkō gakkai kiyō. Archives of the Population Association of Japan.* Tokyo, 1953. 92, 102 pp.
"Waga kuni saikin no shussei to shibō no hendō ga jinkō kōzō ni oyobosu eikyō ni kansuru kenkyū." [On a relation of the recent changes of fertility and mortality to the sex-age distribution of population in Japan—in view of "actual" and "potential."] *J.m.k.*, (60):1-74. March 1955.
Shibo ritsu no kaizen wa jinkō "aging" no gen'in de aruka? [Does the aging of the population arise from a lowering of mortality?] 23rd Annual Meeting, Japan Statistical Society, November 4-5, 1955. Tōkyō, 1955. 10 pp.
Tokushu no jinkō zōka keitai ni tsuite. [Some specific types of population growth.] 23rd Annual Meeting, Japan Statistical Society, November 4-5, 1955. Tōkyō, 1955. 9 pp.
Jikan no demogurafui—"Demodynamik" ni okeru seizon jikan to shite mita jinkō to jinkō dōtai. [The demography of time. Population and vital statistics seen as life span.] 23rd Annual Meeting, Japan Statistical Society, November 4-5, 1955. Tōkyō, 1955. 13 pp.
Demographic situation of population movement in Japan, 1920-1937. Nihon. Kōsei-shō, jinkō mondai kenkyūjo, Demographic Researches, A-6. Tokyo, 1948.
An observation on the correlation between standardized birth, death, and natural increase rate and some indices concerning social mode of life by prefectures, 1920, 1925, 1930 and 1935. Nihon. Kōsei-shō, jinkō mondai kenkyūjo, Social-Economical Researches, B-13. Tokyo, 1948.
Relations among reproduction rates, and reproduction rates and stable population by sex. The 17th General Meeting of the Statistical Association of Japan, November 4-5, 1949. Data Paper. Tokyo, 1949. 11 pp.
Japan, 1925, 1930, 1937, and 1947.

Tachi, Minoru, and Takayasu, Hiroshi.
Tokushu no keikō kyokusen ni yoru sengo Nihon no jinkō zōka keitai no hyōgen hōhō ni tsuite. [On the method of fitting curves to the population increase in postwar Japan.] Nihon. Kōsei-shō, jinkō mondai kenkyūjo, Report No. 86, 1952. Tōkyō, 1953. 25 pp.
With projections, 1950-1965.

Tachi, Minoru, and Ueda, Masao.
"Taishō ku'nen, Taishō jūyo'nen, Shōwa go'nen, Shōwa jū'nen. Dō fu ken betsu, shi gun betsu hyōjunka shussei ritsu, shibō ritsu oyobi shizen zōka ritsu." [Standardized birth rates, death rates and rates of natural increase, by prefectures, for 1920, 1925, 1930 and 1935.] *J.m.k.*, 1(1): 21-28. April 1940.
"Shōwa jū'nen naichi 127 shi hyōjun-ka shussei ritsu, shibō ritsu, oyobi shizen zōka ritsu, yohō." [Standardized birth rates, death rates, and rates of natural increase for the 127 cities in Japan in 1935. Preliminary report.] *J.m.k.*, 1(5): 20-27. August 1940.
Summary: Nihon. Kōsei-shō, jinkō mondai kenkyūjo. Demographic Researches, A-9. Tōkyō, 1948.
Standardized birth, death, and natural increase rate by rural and urban districts, 1920, 1925, 1930, and 1935. Nihon. Kōsei-shō jinkō mondai kenkyūjo. Demographic Researches, A-8. Tōkyō, 1948.
1947-nen no shi-bu gun-bu betsu oyobi to dō fu ken betsu hyōjunka shussei ritsu shibō ritsu oyobi shizen zōka ritsu. [Standardized birth rate, death rate, and rate of natural increase by rural and urban districts and by prefectures, 1947.] Tōkyō, 1949.

Takagi, Naobumi.
"Chihō betsu jinkō zōka no tōkeiteki kansatsu." [The statistical observation on population increase by regions.] *J.m.k.*, No. 63:1-15. March 1956.

Takagi, Naobumi, and Takayasu, Hiroshi.
"Senzen sengo ni okeru antei jinkō dōtai ritsu ni kansuru ichi shisan." [Birth, death, and natural increase rates of the stable population in pre- and post-war periods.] *J.m.k.*, No. 63:68-75. March 1956.

Ueda, Masao.
"Zenkoku to dō fu ken jinkō kaikyū betsu shi chō son jinkō dōtai." [Vital statistics of *shi-chō-son* by population size and prefectures.] Pp. 103-126 in: Nihon. Jinkō mondai kenkyūjo. *Chōsa kenkyū shuyō kekka.* [Major results of surveys and research, 1951.] Tōkyō, 1951. 134 pp.

Ueda, Masao; Yamaguchi, Y.; and Takayasu, Hiroshi.
"To dō fu ken kaku-shi kaku-gun betsu. Jinkō mitsudo—. Jinkō zōka wariai—." [Prefectures by *shi* and *gun*, population density—, percentage of population increase—, ordinary and standardized birth rates 1925, ordinary and standardized death rates 1925, ordinary and standardized rate of natural increase 1925.] Pp. 243-366 in: Nihon. Kōsei-shō, jinkō mondai kenkyūjo. *Chōsa kenkyū shuyō kekka* [Major results of research], 1952. Tōkyō, 1953. 384 pp.

MARRIAGE

Books

Ariga, Kizaemon.
Nihon kon'in shiron. [Treatise on Japanese marriage.] Tōkyō, Nikkō shoin, 1948. 296 pp.

Hozumi, Shigeto.
Kekkon tokuhon. [Reader on marriage.] Tōkyō, Chūo kōron-sha, 1950. 221 pp.

Yanagida, Kunio, Editor.
Sanson seikatsu no kenkyū. [Study of life in mountain villages.] Tōkyō, Iwanami shoten, 1937. 562 pp.

Other

Chiba, Masashi.
"Wakamono gumi no ichi ruikei—sonraku kōzō ni kanren shite." [A type of *wakamono gumi*, a kind of age-classes in Japan—concerning the social structure of villages.] *Hō shakaigaku*, 3:50-64. January 1953.

Fuetō, Toshio.
"Nō gyoson ni okeru kon'in mae no danjo kōsai no kanshū—Yamaguchi-kenka no kazoku seido no chōsa yori." [The custom of sex relations before marriage in the farm and fishing villages—from a field research on the family system in Yamaguchi prefecture.] *Hō shakaigaku*, No. 4, pp. 102-110. July 1953.

Hayashi, K.
"Shokugyō fujin no nenrei oyobi kon'in kankei chōsa." [A survey on the relationship of marriage and age of women with occupations.] Pp. 49-54 in: Jinkō mondai kenkyū-kai. *Jinkō seisaku to kokudo keikaku.* Tōkyō, 1942.

Homma, Yasumasa.
"Fukushima-ken ni okeru tohi no ketsuzoku kekkon no hindo ni tsuite." [On the frequency of consanguineous marriages in urban and rural areas, Fukushima Prefecture.] *Seibutsu tōkeigaku zasshi*, 2(3):32-34. October 1954.

Kawakami, Riichi, and Kō, T.
"Kekkon nenrei bumpū to shussei ritsu to no kankei." [Relationship of the birth rate and the age distribution of marriages.] Pp. 45-46 in: Jinkō mondai kenkyū-kai. *Jinkō seisaku to kokudo keikaku.* Tōkyō, 1942.

Neel, James V., *et al.*
"The incidence of consanguineous matings in Japan, with remarks on the estimation of comparative gene frequencies and the expected rate of appearance of induced recessive mutations." *American Journal of Human Genetics*, 1(2): 156-178. December 1949.

Okazaki, Ayanori.
Investigation on the regional scope in which marriages are made. Surveyed in 1941. Nihon. Kōsei-shō, jinkō mondai kenkyūjo, Social-Economic Researches, B-9. Tokyo, 1948.
"Kon'in ritsu no hendō." [Changes in the marriage rate.] *J.m.k.*, 2(9):1-12. September 1941.
An observation on the difference of actual formation of marriage and its official registration in Japan. Nihon. Kōsei-shō, jinkō mondai kenkyūjo. Demographic researches, A-13. Tokyo, 1948.
"Nihon ni okeru hōritsu kon, jijitsu kon oyobi kekkon tōkei." Pp. 41-43. "Mariages de fait, mariages légaux et statistique matrimoniale au Japon." Pp. 44-46. In: Nihon jinkō gakkai. The Population Association of Japan. *Nihon jinkō gakkai kiyō. Archives of the Population Association of Japan.* No. 3. Tokyo, 1954. 50, 53 pp.
"Shokonsha no shokugyō betsu kon'in nenrei." [The age of marriage by occupation of first marriages.] *J.m.k.*, 2(4): 1-9. April 1941.
"Yūhaigū jinkō no tōkeiteki kansatsu." Pp. 42-49. "A statistical observation concerning married population in Japan." Pp. 55-64. In: Nihon jinkō gakkai. The Population Association of Japan. *Nihon jinkō gakkai kiyō. Archives of the Population Association of Japan.* Tokyo, 1952. 102, 130 pp.

Ōtsuki, A.
"Joshi no mikon zanson ritsu ni tsuite." [On the rate of unmarried females.] *J.m.k.*, 2(12):43-57. December 1941.

Satō, Y.
"Fūfu no kekkon nenrei so ni tsuite." [On the age of marriage and its difference between husband and wife.] *J.m.k.*, 9(1-2):35-43. November 1953.

Schull, William J.
"The effect of Christianity on consanguinity in Nagasaki." *American Anthropologist*, 55(1):74-88. January-March, 1953.

Sekiyama, Naotarō.
"Shina jihen tōsho'nen no kon'in sū zōdai gen'in no bunseki." [An analysis of the cause for the great increase in number of marriages in the early years of the China Incident.] *J.m.k.*, 3(3):6-11. March 1942.

Shinozaki, Nobuo, and Aoki, H.
"Ketsuzoku kekkan buraku no yūseigakuteki chōsa gaihō—Niigata Nagano ken kyō 'Akiyamago' chōsa." [Report on a eugenic survey of consanguineous marriages—'Akiyamago' community at the boundary of Niigata and Nagano prefectures.] *J.m.k.*, 7(1):105-114. May 1951.
"Ketsuzoku kekkan buraku ni kansuru yūseigakuteki chōsa gaihō—Chiba-ken, Awa-gun, Nanaura-mura, Toyobusa-mura chōsa." [Eugenic survey of consanguineous marriages—Nanaura and Toyobusa-mura, Awa-gun, Chiba prefecture.] *J.m.k.*, 7(2):52-66. September 1951. [With Yoshida, K.]

Tachi, Minoru.
"Kekkon no seimei hyō." [Nuptiality tables, 1935 and 1949.] Pp. 51-78 in: Nihon. Kōsei-shō, jinkō mondai kenkyūjo. *Chōsa kenkyū shuyō kekka, 1952.* Tōkyō, 1953. 384 pp.
[Recent aspects of marriage in Japan.] In Japanese. *Jinkō mondai*, 1(1):123-174. February 1935.

Tachi, Minoru, and Arao, M.
[Marriage rate and the business cycle in Japan.] *J.m.*, 1(2): 205-220. October 1935.

Tachi, Minoru, and Ishii, Kiichi.
A specific divorce rate to marriage. Preliminary. Data Paper, 3rd General Meeting of the Population Association of Japan, November 13, 1949.

Tachi, Minoru; Kanno, Masao; and Yokoyama, Yasue.
An example of statistical studies at a health center. Some analyses of marriage statistics of Shinagawa ward, Tōkyō. Data Paper, 4th Meeting of the Population Association of Japan, September 15-16, 1950.

Tachi, Minoru, and Kawakami, Mitsuo.
Haigū kankei to kon'in ritsu. [Marriage rate by marital status.] Paper presented at the 6th Study Meeting of the Population Association of Japan. Tōkyō, 1952. 7 pp.
"Marriage table" of Japan and life table by marital status, 1935. Data Paper, 20th Annual Meeting, Japan Statistical Society, 1952.

Yokota, Nen, and Shinozaki, Nobuo.
Eugenical investigation on the inbreeding families. Surveyed in 1943. Nihon. Kōsei-shō, jinkō mondai kenkyūjo, Socio-Biological Researches, C-2. Tokyo, 1948. 8 pp.
A study of a village in Yamanashi province where cousin-marriage has been practiced for generations.

Fertility

Books

Honda, Tatsuo.
A survey of spread of birth control. Tokyo, Welfare Ministry, Institute of Population Problems, 1953. 37 pp.
Analysis of materials from a schedule given to the disappearing third of the national sample used for the Monthly Report on the Labor Force.
An analysis of post-war fertility in Japan—renewed tabulation of results of the fertility survey of 1952. Tokyo, The Institute of Population Problems, Welfare Ministry, September 1956. 17 pp.

Koya, Yoshio, *et al.*
Research on population health, especially test studies in three rural villages. Published on behalf of the Japan Association of Public Health. Tokyo, 1952. 27, 28 pp. Bilingual, Japanese and English.
"The new population phenomenon and its countermeasures: A study of three rural villages." Also published in: *Japan Medical Journal*, No. 1439, November 24, 1951.
"Test studies of family planning in three rural villages in Japan." Also published in: *Archives of the Population Association of Japan*, No. 1, pp. 1-15. 1952, and *Japan Medical Journal*, No. 1475. August 2, 1952.

Mainichi shimbun-sha. Jinkō mondai chōsa-kai. Mainichi Press. Population Problems Research Council.
A survey of public opinion in Japan on the readjustment of overpopulation. Population Problems Series, No. 3. Tokyo, 1951. 31 pp.
Public opinion survey on birth control in Japan. By Honda, Tatsuo. Population Problems Series, No. 7. Tokyo, 1952. 55 pp.
Third public opinion survey on birth control in Japan. By Honda, Tatsuo. Population Problems Series, No. 13, Tokyo, 1955. 38 pp.
Some facts about family planning in Japan. By Muramatsu, Minoru. Population Problems Series, No. 12. Tokyo, 1955. 120 pp.

Nihon. Kokuritsu yoron chōsa kenkyūjo. National Public Opinion Research Institute.
Public opinion research on population. Research No. A-10. Tokyo, 1950. 2, 47 pp.

Nihon. Kōsei-shō, jinkō mondai kenkyūjo.
Sanji chōsetsu no fukyū jokyō ni kansuru chōsa. [A survey of the extent of contraceptive practice.] Report No. 85, 1952. Tōkyō, 1953. 33 pp.
Dai-niji Shōwa 27-nen, shussanryoku chōsa no sokuhō. [Second preliminary report on the fertility survey.] Report No. 87, 1952. Tōkyō, 1953. 53 pp.

Nihon. Sōri-fu. Kokuritsu yoron chōsajo.
Jutai chōsetsu ni kansuru yoron chōsa. [Public opinion on birth control.] Survey No. 48. Tōkyō, March 1952. 35 pp.

Okazaki, Ayanori.
A fertility survey in Japan of 1952. Tokyo, Ministry of Welfare, Institute of Population Problems, 1953. 87 pp.

Shinozaki, Nobuo.
Nihonjin no sei seikatsu. [Sexual life of the Japanese.] Tōkyō, Bungei shuppan-sha, 1953. 265 pp.
Report on sexual life of Japanese. Nihon. Kōsei-shō, jinkō mondai kenkyūjo, Research-data C. No. 11. Tokyo, 1951. 38 pp.

Teruoka, Gito.
"An essay on the population problem of Japan in the light of social biology." *Reports of the Institute for Science of Labour*, Report No. 1. Kurashiki, 1931. 18 pp.

Other

Aoki, Hisao.
"Waga kuni ni okeru sanji seigen jikko kōka no sokutei—pāru no sokutei-hō ni yoru Tōkyō-to ka kiō chōsa kekka no sai-shūkei." [The effectiveness of contraceptive practice in Japan—a re-examination of past surveys in the Tōkyō metropolitan area by Pearl's method.] *J.m.k.*, 6(2):67-73. June 1950.
"Chihō ni okeru jutai chōsetsu no jikkō kōka ni tsuite—Yamagata-ken jūgo shi chō, son no moderu chōsa." [The effectiveness of contraceptive practice in local districts—Model survey in 15 cities, towns, and villages in Yamagata prefecture." *J.m.k.*, 7(2):19-28. September 1951.

Asahi shimbun.
"Solutions to population problems. Public opinion survey by The Asahi Shimbun, October 15-16, 1951." Translated from *The Asahi*, November 5, 1951. Nihon ninshin chōsetsu kenkyūjo. *Nihon sanji keikaku jōhō. The Japan Planned Parenthood Quarterly*, 2(3-4):30, 40. July-December 1951.

Dore, R. P.
"Japanese rural fertility: Some social and economic factors." *Population Studies*, 7(1):62-88. July 1953.

Hayashi, Shigeru.
"Shussei ritsu kōtei no shakaiteki yōin ni kansuru ichi kōsatsu—Okayama-kenka ni okeru nōson chōsa." [An observation on the social factors of high and low fertility—a survey report of agricultural villages in Okayama prefecture.] *J.m.k.*, 9(3-4):26-54. March 1954.
Shussei ritsu kōtei no shakaiteki yōin ni kansuru ichi kōsatsu. [An observation on the social causes of fluctuations in birth rates.] Nihon. Kōsei-shō, jinkō mondai kenkyūjo, Report No. 80. Tōkyō, 1952. 61 pp.

Henry, Louis.
"La fécondité des mariages au Japon." *Population*, 8(4): 711-730. October-December 1953.

Honda, Tatsuo.
Datai oyobi hi'nin ni yoru shussei yokusei sū no suikei. [Estimation of birth check through abortion and contraception.] Tōkyō, Nihon. Kōsei-shō, jinkō mondai kenkyūjo, 1952.
"Mainichi shimbun-sha no sansei mondai o chūshin to suru yoron chōsa ni tsuite." [On the public opinion survey on the readjustment of overpopulation in Japan conducted by the Population Problems Research Council of the Mainichi Press.] *J.m.k.*, 7(2):80-88. September 1951.
"Nihon ni okeru sanji chōsetsu no fukyū jōkyō ni tsuite." Pp. 1-5. "Extent of diffusion of fertility control in Japan." Pp. 1-5. In: Nihon jinkō gakkai. The Population Association of Japan. *Nihon jinkō gakkai kiyō. Archives of the Population Association of Japan.* No. 3. Tokyo, 1954. 50, 53 pp.
"Mainichi shimbun-sha no sanji chōsetsu ni kansuru dainikai yoron chōsa." [On the second public opinion survey on contraception practice conducted by the Mainichi Press.] *J.m.k.*, 8(2):73-91. October 1952.
"Sanji seigen mondai o shudai to suru jakkan no jinkō rironteki shōsatsu." [Some considerations concerning the contraception problem from the standpoint of the population problem.] *J.m.k.*, 5(7-8-9). July-August-September 1947.

Iwazaki, T.
"Nōka shufu no boseiteki katsudō ni kansuru kenkyū. Nōson fujin no ninshin, shussan hoiku ni kansuru kōsatsu." [Studies on motherhood activities of farm wives. Observations on pregnancy, births, and nursing of village women.] *Rōdō kagaku kenkyū*, 1935. Pp. 301-328.

Kawakami, Riichi.
"Shussei tōkei ni okeru kaisekiteki hōhō." [Analytical methods for dealing with birth statistics.] *Jinkō mondai shiryō*, No. 30, 1938.

Kimura, Masabumi.
[On the births during and after the war in Japan.] *Eisei tōkei*, Vol. IV, No. 11. November 1955.
"Haha no nenrei betsu shussei ritsu toku ni Kanagawa-ken shussei ritsu ni tsuite. Fertility rates by age of mothers in Japan, especially in Kanagawa Prefecture." *Kōshū eisei-in kenkyū hōkoku*, 3(2-3):25-32. December 1953.

Komai, Taku, and Fukuoka, G.
"Multiple births among the Japanese." *American Journal of Physical Anthropology*, 21(3). July-September 1936. Also: *Zeitschrift für Morphologie und Anthropologie*, 31: 167-172. 1933.

Koya, Yoshio.
"Keikaku shussan moderu mura no kenkyū." Pp. 1-11. "Test studies of family planning in three rural villages in Japan." Pp. 1-15. In: Nihon jinkō gakkai. The Population Association of Japan. *Nihon jinkō gakkai kiyō. Archives of the Population Association of Japan.* Tokyo, 1952. 102, 130 pp.
"Nihon no nōson oyobi tankō rōdōsha no kazoku keikaku." Pp. 6-10. "Present situation of family planning among farmers and coal mine workers in Japan." Pp. 6-10. In: Nihon jinkō gakkai. The Population Association of Japan. *Nihon jinkō gakkai kiyō. Archives of the Population Association of Japan.* No. 3. Tokyo, 1954. 50, 53 pp.
[A study of family planning of coal miners.] *Nihon iji shimpō*, No. 1573. June 19, 1954.

Koya, Yoshio, and Muramatsu, Minoru.
"Waga kuni ni okeru jinkō ninshin chūzetsu no kōshū eisei narabini jinkōgakuteki kenkyū shōhō. Sono ichi." "A survey of health and demographic aspects of induced abortion in Japan. Special Report No. 1." *Kōshū eisei-in kenkyū hōkoku*, 3(1):10-13. June 1953.
Special reports: No. 2. *Ibid.* 3(2-3). 1953. No. 3. *Ibid.* 4(1-2). 1954. No. 4. *Ibid.* 4(3). 1955. No. 5. *Ibid.* 5(3). 1956.

Koya, Yoshio; Muramatsu, Minoru; Agata, Sakito; and Koya, Tomohiko.
"Waga kuni ni okeru jinkō ninshin chūzetsu no kōshū eisei narabini jinkōgakuteki kenkyū." Pp. 1-9. "Preliminary report on a survey of health and demographic aspects of induced abortion in Japan." Pp. 1-9. In: Nihon jinkō gakkai. The Population Association of Japan. *Nihon jinkō gakkai kiyō. Archives of the Population Association of Japan*, No. 2. Tōkyō, 1953. 92, 102 pp.
In Japanese: *Nihon iji shimpō*, No. 1539. October 24, 1953. In English: *Milbank Memorial Fund Quarterly*, 32(3):282-293. July 1954.

Koya, Yoshio; Muramatsu, Minoru; Agata, Sakito; and Suzuki, Naruo.
"A survey of health and demographic aspects of reported female sterilizations in four health centers of Shizuoka Prefecture, Japan." *Milbank Memorial Fund Quarterly*, 33(4): 368-392. October 1955.
In Japanese: *Nihon kōshū-eisei*, 1(10):11-20. December 1954.

Koya, Yoshio, and Teramura, Rinko.
"Moderu mura no shussei sokudo ni tsuite. The speed of childbearing in three rural villages." *Kokuritsu kōshū eisei-in kenkyū hōkoku*, 1(2):75-77. October 1951.

Koyama, Chiaki.
"Otto no kon'in nenrei to shussei to no kankei ni tsuite." [On the relationship between births and the husband's age at marriage.] *J.m.k.*, 3(4):35-39. April 1942.

Koyama, Eizō.
Investigation on the fertility of Koreans in Japan. Surveyed in 1940 about 48,000 couples. Nihon. Kōsei-shō, jinkō mondai kenkyūjo, Social Economical Researches, B-5. Tokyo, 1948. 24 pp.

Kubo, Hideshi.
"Saikin no shussan chōsetsu no shussei ritsu ni taisuru eikyō." Pp. 12-16. "The influence of birth control against birth rate in Japan." Pp. 16-21. In: Nihon jinkō gakkai. The Population Association of Japan. *Nihon jinkō gakkai kiyō. Archives of the Population Association of Japan.* No. 1. Tokyo, 1952. 102, 130 pp.

Le Blanc, Thomas J.
"Some aspects of paternity in Sendai, Japan." *Human Biology*, 2(4):508-522. December 1930.

Maruoka, Hikoo.
"Seihi ni kansuru kenkyū. Dai-1 hen. Taiji no seihi." [Studies on sex ratio. 1. Sex ratio of foetus.] *Igaku kenkyū*, 22(3):75-86. March 1952.
"Seihi ni kansuru kenkyū. Dai-1 hen. Taiji no seihi." [Studies on sex ratio. 2. Sex ratio of live births.] *Ibid.* 22(3):87-100. March 1952.

Mizushima, Haruo.
"Nihon ni ogeru shussei ritsu no keikō." Pp. 19-24. "The trend of fertility in Japan." Pp. 20-26. In: Nihon jinkō

gakkai. The Population Association of Japan. *Nihon jinkō gakkai kiyō. Archives of the Population Association of Japan*. No. 3. Tokyo, 1954. 50, 53 pp.

"Shussan no jun'i to sono kankaku to no kankei." [Relationship between the order and time-intervals of births.] *J.m.*, 5(1):56-61. September 1942.

Muramatsu, Minoru.

"Waga kuni ni okeru jinkō ninshin chūzetsu no kōshū eisei narabini jinkōgakuteki kenkyū—yōyaku." P. 32. "Summary of the preliminary report of a survey of health and demographic aspects of induced abortion in Japan." P. 34. In: Nihon jinkō gakkai. The Population Association of Japan. *Nihon jinkō gakkai kiyō. Archives of the Population Association of Japan*. No. 3. Tokyo, 1954. 50, 53 pp.

Muramatsu, Minoru, and Ogino, Hiroshi.

[Estimation of the total numbers of induced abortions as well as of sterilization operations for females in Japan for the years of 1952 and 1953.] *Kōshū eisei-in kenkyū hōkoku*, 4(1-2):1-2. September 1954.

Nakagawa, T., and Koyama, Chiaki.

"Tsuma no kon'in nenrei to shussei to no kankei ni tsuite." [On the relationship of births and the marriage age of the wife.] *J.m.k.*, 2(10):1-30. October 1941.

Neel, James V., *et al.*

"The effect of exposure to the atomic bomb on pregnancy termination in Hiroshima and Nagasaki. Preliminary report." *Science*, 118:537-541. 1953.

Nihon. [Japan.]

[Eugenic Protection Law, Law No. 156 of 1948.] Tōkyō, 1948.

[Amended as of April, 1952.] 1952.

[Status as of August, 1954.] 1954.

Nihon. Kōsei-shō.

Summary of the program to promote conception control. Bureau of Public Sanitation. Western Pacific Regional Seminar in Vital Statistics/VS/13. Tokyo, 1952. 17 pp.

A statement prepared by Y. Koya, Institute of Public Health.

[Survey of prevalence of contraceptive practice in Japan—April, 1954.] *Kōsei no shihyō*, Vol. I, No. 12. October 1954.

English translation by M. Muramatsu.

Nihon. Kōsei-shō, jinkō mondai kenkyūjo.

Tōkyō-to chūshin to suru sanji seigen no jittai ni kansuru shiryō. [Materials on the actual situation of birth control centering in Tōkyō metropolitan area.] Tōkyō, 1949. 34 pp.

Revised. Tōkyō, 1949. 24 pp.

See also: Shinozaki, Nobuo. *The investigation of the actual state of the practice of contraception in Japan. Surveyed in 1947*. Social-Economical Researches, No. 11. Tokyo, 1948.

Ken betsu oyobi toshi chō, son betsu sanji chōsetsu jittai chōsa shukei kekka hyō. [Tables on results of survey on birth control by prefectures and by *toshi, chō,* and *son.*] Report No. 76. Tōkyō, 1952. 30 pp. [Results of survey of 17 prefectures in 1949 and 1950.]

Yūsei hogohō shikō go no jinkō ninshin chūzetsu no jōkyō ni kansuru kenkyū. Dai-ippō. [Study on induced abortion after enforcement of the Eugenic Protection Law.] Research data, No. 67. Tōkyō, 1950. 27 pp.

Nihon. Kōsei-shō, kōshū hoken-kyoku. Welfare Ministry. Public Health Bureau, General Affairs Section.

Activities under the Eugenic Protection Law for the year of 1949—. Tokyo, 1950—.

Nihon sanfujinka gakkai zasshi.

[*Induced abortions.*] Vol. XVII, 1950.

Kushima, K. "Harm to mothers caused by induced abortions and counter-measures." No. 1, pp. 9-14.

Yamamoto, S. "Reconsideration of Aburel's method." No. 5, pp. 30-33.

Hanaoka, K. "Infection by Aburel's method." No. 5, pp. 33-45.

Segi, M. "Various problems concerning eugenic protection law." No. 5, pp. 49-51.

Kashiwabara, N. "Reports on curetting." No. 6, pp. 4-13.

Ojima, N. "Surgical operation methods for induced abortions."

Segi, M. "Various problems on eugenic protection law."

Kojima, A. "Continuation of pregnancy after induced abortion." No. 11, pp. 6-10.

Okazaki, Ayanori.

"Shussanryoku chōsa kekka no gaisetsu." [Outline on fertility investigation results.] *J.m.k.*, 1(7):1-95. October 1940.

Birth-intervals according to birth-orders. A research from the result of investigation on fertility surveyed in 1940. Nihon. Kōsei-shō, jinkō mondai kenkyūjo, Demographic Researches, A-11. Tokyo, 1948.

"Fūfu kankai jizoku kikan to shussanryoku." [Duration of married life and fertility.] *J.m.k.*, 5(2):1-14. February 1946.

Investigation on the differential fertility by marriage ages, duration of married life, level of education, occupations, and economic ranks of husband and wife. Surveyed in 1940. Nihon. Kōsei-shō, jinkō mondai kenkyūjo, Social-Economical Researches, B-2. Tokyo, 1948.

"Nihon ni okeru saikin no shizan." [Stillbirths in Japan in recent years.] *J.m.k.*, 7(3):49-54. December 1951.

Les mort-nés au Japon dans ces dernières années. Tokyo, Institute for Population Problems, 1951. 11 pp.

"Nōgyōsha no shussanryoku ni kansuru tōkeiteki kansatsu." [Statistical observations on the fertility of farmers.] *J.m.k.*, 7(2):1-18. September 1951.

Fertility of the farming population in Japan. Tokyo, 1951. 17 pp.

"Toshi ni okeru kyūryō seikatsusha no shussanryoku." [Fertility of salaried men in an urban area.] *J.m.k.*, 8(2):1-9. October 1952. (With Sato, Y.)

Segi, Mitsuo, and Fukushima, Ichirō.

Some statistical observations on the cause of spontaneous stillbirth and induced interruption of pregnancy. Jan.-June, 1948. Japan. Tokyo, Ministry of Welfare, Division of Health and Welfare Statistics, 1949. 17 pp.

Shimamura, T.

Research on difference in fertility as occupations of wives vary. Surveyed 1943. Nihon. Kōsei-shō, jinkō mondai kenkyūjo, Social-Economical Researches, B-3. Tokyo, 1948.

Shinoda, Tadashi.

"Hompō fujin no nin'yō ritsu ni kansuru kenkyū." [A research relating to the conception rate of Japanese women.] Pp. 875-881 in: *Dai-nikai jinkō mondai zenkoku kyōgi-kai hōkokusho*. [Report of the Second National Conference on Population Problems.] Tōkyō, Jinkō mondai kenkyū-kai, 1939.

Shinozaki, Nobuo.

Gekkei shuki betsu seijuku kikan betsu ninshinryoku ni kansuru shukei kekka. [Data on conception by sterile and fertile periods of the cycle.] Nihon. Kōsei-shō, jinkō mondai kenkyūjo, Report No. 79. Tōkyō, 1952. 13 pp.

A preliminary analysis of survey data.
Hinin no jikkō fu jikkōsha betsu ni mita shi rejuzon ritsu ni kansuru ichi shiryō. [The abortion rate in relation to the avoidance of conception.] Nihon. Kōsei-shō, jinkō mondai kenkyūjo, Report No. 75. Tōkyō, 1951. 7 pp.
"Nihon ni okeru sanji chōsetsu fukyū no genjō." Pp. 50-57. "Present conditions of spread of birth control in Japan." Pp. 65-75. In: Nihon jinkō gakkai. The Population Association of Japan. *Nihon jinkō gakkai kiyō. Archives of the Population Association of Japan*, No. 1. Tokyo, 1952. 102, 130 pp.
"Shōwa nijūshi, nijūgo'nendo ni okeru sanji chōsetsu jittai chōsa kekka no gaiyō." [The major results of the surveys of contraceptive practice in 1949 and 1950.] *J.m.k.*, 7(4): 46-50. March 1952.
"Spontaneous and induced abortions. Their frequencies in order and number of pregnancies among the married." *The Planned Parenthood Quarterly*, 4(3-4):54-56. July-December 1953.
"Tōhoku, Kantō, Chūgoku chihō no nō-san-gyō son ni okeru sanji chōsetsu jittai chōsa kekka hōkoku." [A survey of contraceptive practice in farm-mountain-fishing villages, largely in northeastern Japan.] *J.m.k.*, 7(3):31-48. December 1951.
Tōhoku sanken ni okeru sanji chōsetsu jittai chōsa hyō miteishutsusha no miteishutsu riyū oyobi chōsa ni taisuru iken no jitsujō ni tsuite. [Reasons for refusals and the opinions of non-participants in the survey of birth control in three Tōhoku prefectures.] Nihon. Kōsei-shō, jinkō mondai kenkyūjo, Report No. 73, 1951. Tōkyō, 1951. 11 pp.
"Tōkyō kinkō shi, chō, son no sanji chōsetsu no jittai." Pp. 59-69. "The actual state of birth control practice in adjacent city, town, and village of Tōkyō." Pp. 62-75. In: Nihon jinkō gakkai. The Population Association of Japan. *Nihon jinkō gakkai kiyō. Archives of the Population Association of Japan.* Tokyo, 1953. 92, 102 pp.
Also: "Tōkyō kinkō shi, chō, son no sanji chōsetsu fukyū no jitsujō, chiikiteki seikaku no bunseki." [Diffusion of contraceptive practice in suburban areas of Tokyo. Analysis of areal characteristics.] *J.m.k.*, 8(3-4):30-52. February 1953.

Shinozaki, Nobuo; Kaneko, Akira; and Kobayashi, Kazumasa.
"Sanji seigen jittai chōsa no gaiyō." [Summary of the investigation of the actual state of the practice of contraception.] *J.m.k.*, 5(10-11-12):16-32. April 1948.
English summary: Nihon. Kōsei-shō, jinkō mondai kenkyūjo. Social-Economical Researches. No. 11. Tokyo, 1948.

Shirakawa, Isaburō, and Tokogawa, Tsuru.
"Nōson ni okeru shiryūzan ni tsuite." [On stillbirths and miscarriages in agricultural villages.] *Rōdō kagaku kenkyū*, 13(4):661-677. 1936.

Tachi, Minoru.
Hitotsu no jinkō saiseisan ritsu ni tsuite. [On a reproduction rate.] Tōkyō, November 1953. 8 pp.
Paper presented to the Annual Meeting of the Japan Statistical Society, November 6, 1953.
Jinkō saiseisan ritsu ni tsuite no hitotsu no kangae kata. [A consideration of a reproduction rate.] Paper presented at the 7th Meeting of the Population Association of Japan, October 17, 1953. Tōkyō, October 1953. 7 pp.
"Waga kuni jinkō no chihō betsu zōshokuryoku ni kansuru jinkō tōkeigakuteki ichi kōsatsu." [A statistical examination of the reproductive power of our population, by districts.] *J.m.*, 1(4):453-483; 2(1):217-238. December 1936 and June 1937.

Tachikawa, Kiyoshi.
"Ninshin to fujin no nenrei." [Pregnancy and age of women.] *Minzoku eisei*, 8(3):212-216. September 1940.

Takahashi, Eiji.
"Notes on Japanese birth statistics." *Human Biology*, 24(1):44-52. February 1952.

Takano, T., and Kojima, T.
"Jinkō ninshin chūzetsu o nikai ijō keizoku jisshi shita fujin no shoshu jittai chōsa." Pp. 66-70. "Studies on the women who had induced abortions more than once successively." Pp. 86-93. In: Nihon jinkō gakkai. The Population Association of Japan. *Nihon jinkō gakkai kiyō. Archives of the Population Association of Japan.* Tokyo, 1952. 102, 130 pp.

Takata, Yasuma.
"On the differential birth rate by classes." *Proceedings of the International Congress for Studies on Population*, Rome, 1931. Vol. VIII, pp. 69-83.

Terao, Takuma, and Ozaki, Iwao.
"Bankon to hinin no jinkō seigenteki kōka to sono sokutei." Pp. 58-65. "Restrictive effects of late marriage and contraception upon increase of population and measurement thereof." Pp. 76-85. In: Nihon jinkō gakkai. The Population Association of Japan. *Nihon jinkō gakkai kiyō. Archives of the Population Association of Japan.* Tokyo, 1952. 102, 130 pp.

Tsurumi, M., *et al.*
"Aichi-kenka ni, san no shō-toshi oyobi sono shūi nōson ni okeru kekkon oyobi shussan no suii ni kansuru kazoku chōsa." [A family survey on the changes in births and marriages in two or three small cities and surrounding rural villages in Aichi prefecture.] *J.m.*, 5(3):529-540. February 1943.

Yokota, T.
"Shussei ritsu no chiikiteki sai ni kansuru ichi kōsatsu." [An observation of the areal differences of birth rates.] *J.m.k.*, 2(12):1-23. December 1941.
"Tasan ni kansuri ni, san no tōkeiteki kansatsu." [Some statistical observations on fecundity.] *J.m.k.*, 2(8):16-22. August 1941.
"Tasansha kakei chōsa hōkoku—ni." [Report on fecundity by lineage—2.] *J.m.k.*, 3(3):12-20. March 1942.

MORTALITY

Periodicals and Pamphlets

Abe, Toshio.
"Shokugyō-byō yori mitaru shibō gen'in no tōkeiteki kenkyū." [Statistical study of causes of death from an occupational viewpoint.] *Rōdō kagaku kenkyū*, 13(3):351-413; 13(4):521-657. 1936.

Embree, John F.
"Sanitation and health in a Japanese village." *Journal of the Washington Academy of Sciences*, 34(4):97-108. April 1944.

Hirabayashi, Takeharu.
"Nōson oyobi shō-kōgyō toshi no shibō yūji shibō ni tsuite." [Deaths and infant mortality in agricultural villages and a small industrial city.] *Nagoya igakkai zasshi*, 51(6):1115-1142; 52(3):341-374. May and September 1940.

Matsumoto-*shi* and Higashi Tsukuma-*gun*, Nagano prefecture, 1925-1936.

Imamura, A.
The epidemiology and prevention of tuberculosis in Japan. Reported at the General Meeting of the 11th Japanese Medical Association, 1942. 12 pp.
Supplement, 1948. 23 pp., tables and charts.

Ishikawa, T., and Momiyama, M.
"Kisetsu-byō ni yoru shibō ritsu no nenkan bumpu no kenkyū." [Studies on the annual distribution of the death rate from seasonal diseases.] *Kōsei kagaku,* 7(1-2):42ff. May 1948.

Iwazaki, T.
Infant mortality in relation to the climate of Japan. Part 1. Reports of the Institute for Science of Labour, No. 23. Kurashiki, 1934.

Kasama, Naotake.
"Hompō bosei shibō no tōkeiteki kansatsu." [Statistical observations on the death of Japanese mothers.] *J.m.k.,* 2(11):49-87. November 1941.

Katsuki, S.
The influence of industrialism upon the mortality of young people and adults. Reports of the Institute for Science of Labour, No. 29, II. Kurashiki, 1934-1935. 30 pp.

Kawakami, Mitsuo.
Mortality by marital status. The 8th General Meeting of Kōsei kagaku [Health science]. Tokyo, 1951.

Kazama, N.
Maternal death in Japan. Analysis of the official statistical data from 1899 to 1938. Nihon. Kōsei-shō, jinkō mondai kenkyūjo, Social-Biological Researches, C-8. Tokyo, 1948. 29 pp.

Koyama, C., and Nakagawa, T.
"Shotoku kaikyū ni yoru shibō no hendō, fu shotoku kaikyū betsu kon'in oyobi shussei no jōkyō." [Mortality changes by income classes, with an appendix on conditions of marriage and birth by income classes.] *J.m.k.,* 2(5):1-32. May 1941.

League of Nations. Health Organization. Intergovernmental Conference of Far Eastern Countries on Rural Hygiene.
Report on Japan. Series, League of Nations Publications 1937, III, No. 12. Geneva, 1937.

Le Blanc, Thomas J.
"Density of population, mortality, and certain other phenomena in Japan." *American Journal of Hygiene,* 13(3): 781-802. May 1931.

Matsuda, Shin'ichi; Miyairi, Masato; and Hori, Kikuko.
"Tōkyō ni okeru kyūsei kaihaku zuien. Dai-ippō, Ryūkō no gaiyō. Poliomyelitis in Tōkyō. Part I. General Considerations." *Kōshū eisei-in kenkyū hōkoku,* 2(3):16-23. December 1952.

Mizawa, K.
"Kisetsu betsu shibō ritsu no kenkyū ni taisuru chiriteki chiiki no kōshō." [Relationship of geographical areas in research on death rate by seasons.] Pp. 71-78 in: Jinkō mondai kenkyū-kai. *Waga kuni jinkō mondai ni kansuru sho-kenkyū.* [Researches on the population problem in our country.] Tōkyō, Tōe shoin, 1936. 101 pp.

Nakagawa, Tomonaga.
Investigation on the differential death-rate by economic ranks. Surveyed in 1940. Nihon. Kōsei-shō, jinkō mondai kenkyūjo, Social-Economical Researches, B-6. Tokyo, 1948. 9 pp.
An investigation of 1,031,213 cases in 15 middle cities, utilizing house tax rates for differentiation of income classes and the *koseki* registers for population and death data.

Nihon. Naimu-shō, shakai-kyoku. Home Department. Social Bureau.
The great earthquake of 1923 in Japan. Tokyo, 1926.

Okazaki, Ayanori.
"A propos de la mortalité infantile au Japon." *Courrier du Centre international de l'enfance,* 3(3):125-135. March 1953.

Ōnishi, Seiji.
"Jinrui shibō ritsu ni kansuru shinkaronteki kōsatsu." [Observation on the theory of progress as concerned with the death rate of mankind.] Pp. 63-70 in: Jinkō mondai kenkyū-kai. *Waga kuni jinkō mondai ni kansuru sho-kenkyū.* [Researches on the population problem in our country.] Tōkyō, Tōe shoin, 1936. 101 pp.

Saitō, Kiyoshi.
"Hompō bosei shibō no tokusei ni tsuite. Certain characteristics of maternal mortality in Japan." *Kōshū eisei-in kenkyū hōkoku,* 2(3):4-8. December 1952.

Saitō, Kiyoshi, and Homma, H.
"Nyūyōji shibō o shiheisuru inshi ni kansuru kenkyū. Ibaraki-kenka nōson ni okeru chōsa kenkyū, Dai-ippō, jumbi chōsa to sono seiseki no kekka." [Causal factors in mortality of infants and pre-school children. An analysis of a village in Ibaraki-ken. Report 1. Results of preliminary survey and its statistical analysis.] *Kōshū eisei,* 4(1):76-88. January 1943.
Ibid. "Dai-nihō, nyūyōji shibō gen'in no shinsō." [Report No. 2. Causes of death of infants and pre-school children.] *Ibid.,* 6(1-2):6-10. September 1947.

Sams, Crawford F.
"American public health administration meets the problem of the Orient in Japan." *American Journal of Public Health,* 42(5, Part 1):557-565. May 1952.
"Medical care aspects of public health and welfare in Japan." *Journal of the American Medical Association,* 141(8):527-531. October 22, 1949.

Satō, T.
"Kiga hassei no shakai keizaiteki jōken ni tsuite." [Social and economic conditions of starvation.] *Kōsei kagaku,* 7(1-2):29-31. May 1948.

SCAP. GHQ. Public Health and Welfare Section.
Public health and welfare in Japan. Tokyo, 1949. 220 pp.; annex and charts, 54 pp.; tables, 86 pp.

Shimamura, T.
"Kekkaku shibō kaizen ga shōrai jinkō ni oyobosu eikyō ni tsuite." [Concerning the influence of the reduction of death by tuberculosis on the future population.] *J.m.,* 4(1):88-103. August 1941.

Tachi, Minoru.
[Death rates by marital status in Japan, 1930.] *J.m.,* 1(1): 203-210. February 1935.
[A method of measuring public health in Japan—standardized death rate in Japan.] *J.m.,* Vol. I, No. 3. April 1936.

Tachi, Minoru, *et al.*
"Saikin ni okeru waga kuni shibō ritsu no jakkan no keikō." [Some tendencies in recent death rates in our country.] *J.m.k.,* 2(1):39-42. January 1941.

Tachi, Minoru, and Ueda, Masao.
"Futsū shibō ritsu to seishi jinkō shibō ritsu to no kankei ni kansuru kenkyū yohō." [A study on the relation between death rates of actual population and stationary population.

Preliminary.] Pp. 67-84 in: Nihon. Kōsei-shō, jinkō mondai kenkyūjo. *Chōsa kenkyū shuyō kekka*, Tōkyō, 1951. 134 pp.

Takahashi, Eiji.
"The sex ratio of neonatal deaths in Japan." *Human Biology*, 26(2):133-142. May 1954.

Takarabe, Seiji.
"Suicide statistics in Japan classified according to sex." *K.U.E.R.*, 1(1):173-187. July 1926.

Tatai, Kichinosuke.
"Nihon ni okeru saikin no jisatsu keikō no bunseki. Recent trends of suicides in Japan." *Kōshū eisei-in kenkyū hōkoku*, 2(2):6-16. September 1952.
1910-1950.

U.S. Army. Far East Command.
The Fukui earthquake, Hokuriku region, Japan, 28 June 1948. Tokyo, General Headquarters, Far East Command, 1949. 2 vols.

U.S. War Department. Office of the Surgeon General.
Public health in the Japanese Empire. Civil Affairs Handbook, War Department Pamphlet No. 31-2. Washington, D.C., 1944. iv, 96 pp.

Yanagisawa, Comte de.
"Etude statistique sur la mortalité des enfants au dessous de cinq ans dans l'Empire du Japon." *Proceedings of the International Congress for Studies in Population, Rome, 1931*. Vol. v, pp. 181-186.

Yokota, T.
"Baidoku man'en jōkyō no chihō betsu kansatsu." [Observation on the extensiveness of syphilis by areas.] *J.m.k.*, 2(1): 43-58. January 1941.

Yoshioka, Hiroto, and Morooka, Taeko.
"Hompō tohi betsu rōnen shikkan shibō ritsu ni tsuite." Pp. 50-58. "Death rates of senile diseases in Japan by urban and rural." Pp. 51-61. In: Nihon jinkō gakkai. The Population Association of Japan. *Nihon jinkō gakkai kiyō. Archives of the Population Association of Japan*. Tokyo, 1953. 92, 102 pp.

LIFE TABLES

Periodicals and pamphlets

Higuchi, Haruo.
"Waga kuni ni okeru shuyō shiin no seimei hyō ni oyobosu eikyō, Shōwa 22-nen." [The influences of the principal causes of death in the life table in Japan in 1947.] *Igaku kenkyū*, 22(2):13-31. February 1952.

Majima, Yūjiro.
"1950-nen fu ken betsu seimei hyō." [Abridged life table for each prefecture, 1950.] *Igaku kenkyū*, 26(1):1-23. January 1956.

Mizushima, Haruo.
"Nihon ni okeru heikin yomei no chiriteki sai to kinnen no suii." Pp. 23-27. "Geographic variations of longevity in Japan and their recent change." Pp. 30-36. In: Nihon jinkō gakkai. The Population Association of Japan. *Nihon jinkō gakkai kiyō. Archives of the Population Association of Japan*. Tokyo, 1952. 102, 130 pp.
Complete expectation of life at birth, each prefecture, 1926-1930, 1931-1935, 1947, and 1948-1949.

Mizushima, Haruo, *et al.*
"Seitetsusho tankō oyobi nōson no seimei hyō." Pp. 10-27. "Life tables for an iron factory, a coal mine and agricultural villages." Pp. 10-24. In: Nihon jinkō gakkai. The Population Association of Japan. *Nihon jinkō gakkai kiyō. Archives of the Population Association of Japan*. Tokyo, 1953. 92, 102 pp.

Mizushima, Haruo; Harafuji, S.; Hosogami, T.; and Koyama, Y.
"Seison hi yori mitaru chiriteki bumpu." [Geographic distribution of the survival ratio in Japan.] *Chōsen igakkai zasshi*, 29:2137-2152. 1939.

Mizushima, Haruo; Hosogami, T.; and Harafuji, S.
"Fu ken betsu seimei hyō, dai-nikai." [The second abridged life tables of prefectures in Japan.] *Chōsen igakkai zasshi*, 29(9):1767-1803. September 1939.

Mizushima, Haruo; Koyama, Y.; Tsurusaki, T.; and Taniguchi, Y.
"Fu ken betsu seimei hyō, dai-ikkai." [An abridged life table for each prefecture of Japan, 1926-1930.] *Chōsen igakkai zasshi*, 28(8):1136-1175. August 1938.

Mizushima, Haruo; Kusukawa, Akira; and Fujimoto, Takashi.
"Dai-3-kai fu ken betsu seimei hyō, Shōwa 22-nen 4-gatsu—Shōwa 23-nen 3-gatsu." [The 3rd abridged prefectural life tables, April 1947-March 1948.] *Eisei tōkei*, 4(1):14-29. 1951.

Mizushima, Haruo; Kusukawa, Akira; and Majima, Yūjirō.
"Dai-4-kai fu ken betsu seimei hyō, 1948-1949." [The 4th prefectural life table, 1948-1949.] *Eisei tōkei*, 5(2):1-17. 1952.

Mizushima, Haruo; Kusukawa, Akira; Matsuura, Kōichi.
"1950-nen, 1951-nen, 1952-nen kanzen seimei hyō. 1953-nen, 1954-nen, 1955-nen kanryaku seimei hyō." [Complete life tables for 1950, 1951, 1952, and abridged life tables for 1953, 1954, 1955.] *Igaku kenkyū*, 26(11):2821-2847. November 1956.

Mizushima, Haruo, and Taniguchi, Yoshinori.
"Roku dai-toshi, Tōkyō, Ōsaka, Kyōto, Nagoya, Yokohama, Kōbe jūmin no seimei hyō." [Life tables for the six largest cities in Japan: Tōkyō, Ōsaka, Kyōto, Nagoya, Yokohama, Kōbe, 1926-1930.] *Nihon minzoku eisei kyōkai shi*, Vol. VIII, No. 1. March 1940.

Saitō, Hitoshi.
"Sur la table de mortalité des japonais No. 4." *Bulletin de l'Institut international de statistique*, 25(2):133-142. Tōkyō, 1931.

Tachi, Minoru, and Takagi, Naobumi.
Kan'i seimei hyō ni tsuite. [On the abridged life table.] Data Paper, 18th General Meeting of the Statistical Association of Japan. July 1950. 21 pp.
Rural and urban life tables of post-war Japan. Data Paper, 4th Meeting of the Population Association of Japan, September 15-16, 1950.
Text in Japanese, tables bilingual with English.

Takagi, Naobumi.
"Hokensho ni okeru tōkeiteki kenkyū no ichi jirei—Shinagawa-ku ni okeru kan'i seimei hyō." [An example of statistical studies at a Health Center—Abridged life table for Shinagawa Ward, Tōkyō.] Pp. 59-66 in: Nihon. Kōsei-shō, jinkō mondai kenkyūjo. *Chōsa kenkyū shuyō kekka*. Tōkyō, 1951. 134 pp. (With Kanno, Masao.)
"Fukui-ken oyobi Fukui hokensho ni okeru kansoku seimei hyō." [The abridged life tables of Fukui prefecture and Fukui Health Center.] Pp. 85-90 in: Nihon. Kōsei-shō, jinkō mondai kenkyūjo. *Chōsa kenkyū shuyō kekka*. Tōkyō, 1951. 134 pp.

Takagi, Naobumi, and Hama, Hidehiko.
Abridged life table for the period from April 1950 to March 1951. Data Paper, 5th Meeting, Population Association of Japan, 1951. Tokyo, 1951.

Taniguchi, Yoshinori.
"Hompō ni okeru kekkaku shibō ni yoru heikin yomei tanshuku no chiriteki bumpu." [Extension to the complete expectation of life for each prefecture in Japan by eliminating the deaths due to tuberculosis, 1925-1930, 1931-1935.] *Chōsen igakkai zasshi*, 29:2153-2170. 1939.
"How many years of expectation of life of Japanese would be increased if principal causes of death could completely be eliminated?" Reprint: *Keijō Journal of Medicine*, 9(3): 195-209. October 30, 1938.

Ueyama, Norie.
"A life table of deaths from tuberculosis, 1947." *Kyūshū Memoirs of Medical Sciences*, 2(1-2):23-31. June 1951.

PROJECTIONS

Nakagawa, Tomonaga.
"Shōrai jinkō no keisan ni tsuite." [Concerning estimates of the future population.] *J.m.k.*, 1(2):1-13. May 1940.
Summary: Nihon. Kōsei-shō, jinkō mondai kenkyūjo. Demographic Researches, A-3. Tōkyō, 1948.
"Jinkō no rojisutekku kyokusen ni tsuite." [On the logistic curve of population.] *J.m.k.*, 3(4):1-14. April 1942.

Nihon. Keizai antei hombu, tōkei kenkyū-kai, jinkō bunka-kai.
Shōrai jinkō no suikei ni kansuru hōkoku. Shōwa 21-nen 8-gatsu. [Report of the estimation of future population. August 1946.] Tōkyō, 1946. 3, 35 pp.

Nihon. Kōsei-shō, jinkō mondai kenkyūjo.
Chihō to-dō-fu-ken betsu suikei. [Estimates of future population for regions and prefectures.] Pp. 93-129 in: *Chōsa kenkyū shuyō kekka.* Tōkyō, 1950.
Shuju no suikei shōrai jinkō. [Various estimates of the future population.] Tōkyō, 1950. 17 pp.
Danjo nenrei kakusai betsu suikei shōrai jinkō, Shōwa 25-nen—35-nen. [Estimated future population by sex and age, 1950-1960.] Tōkyō, 1951. 20 pp.

SCAP. GHQ. Economic and Scientific Section.
"Future population of Japan, 1950-1970." *Japanese Economic Statistics, Bulletin*, No. 32, pp. 142-147. April 1949. *Ibid.*, No. 33, pp. 221-224. May 1949.

Sōda, Takeo.
"Jinkō zōka no suitei." [An estimate of population growth.] Pp. 76-110 in: Uyeda, Teijirō, Editor. *Nihon jinkō mondai kenkyū.* [Studies in Japanese population problems.] Vol. I. Tōkyō, Kyō chō-kai, 1933.

Tachi, Minoru.
[Population estimates in the near future.] Part II in: *Nihon jinkō no shōrai.* Tōkyō, Sekai keizai chōsa-kai, 1947. 162 pp.
"Nihon no shōrai jinkō no ichi suikei." Pp. 47-50. "An estimate of future population of Japan." Pp. 50-53. In: Nihon jinkō gakkai. The Population Association of Japan. *Nihon jinkō gakkai kiyō. Archives of the Population Association of Japan.* No. 3. Tokyo, 1954. 50, 53 pp.

Tachi, Minoru; Ueda, Masao; Kubota, Yoshiaki; and Takagi, Naobumi.
"Shōwa nijūgo'nen made no suikei jinkō no bunseki." [Analysis of the estimated population from 1946 to 1950.] *J.m.k.*, 5(3-4-5-6). March-April-May-June 1947.
"Shōwa nijūgo'nen made no suikei shōrai jinkō no kaisan." [Revision of the estimation of the population to 1950.] *J.m.k.*, 5(7-8-9). July-August-September 1947.

Tachi, Minoru; Ueda, Masao; and Takagi, Naobumi.
"Shōwa 24-nen yori Shōwa 90-nen ni itaru danjo nenrei gosai kaikyū betsu jinkō no suikei." [Projection of population, 1950 to 2015, by sex and age.] Pp. 79-94 in: Nihon. Kōsei-shō, jinkō mondai kenkyūjo. *Chōsa kenkyū shuyō kekka*, 1952. Tōkyō, 1953. 384 pp.

Tachi, Minoru; Watanabe, Sadamu; Ueda, Masao; and Takagi, Naobumi.
Shōrai jinkō no suikei ni tsuite. [On the estimation of the future population of Japan.] Tōkyō, 1952. 12 pp.
Paper read at the 6th Study Meeting of the Population Association of Japan, October 28, 1952.

Takagi, Naobumi.
"Suikei shōrai jinkō, Shōwa 25-nen—Shōwa 40-nen." [Estimated future population, 1950-1965.] *J.m.k.*, No. 62: 80-90. December 1955.

Uyeda, Teijirō.
"Chikaki shōrai ni okeru Nihon jinkō no yosoku." [Estimates of Japanese population for the near future.] Pp. 65-169 in: *Idem, Nihon jinkō seisaku.* [Japan's population policy.] Tōkyō Chikuno shobō, 1937. 356 pp.
Future of the Japanese population. Tokyo, Japanese Council, Institute of Pacific Relations, 1933, 25 pp.

POLICY

GOVERNMENTAL AND QUASI-GOVERNMENTAL

Jinkō mondai kenkyū-kai.
Dai-ikkai jinkō mondai zenkoku kyōgi-kai hōkokusho. [Report, First National Conference on Population Problems.] Tōkyō, 1938, 828 pp.
Dai-nikai jinkō mondai zenkoku kyōgi-kai kaihō. [Summary report. Second National Conference on Population Problems.] Tōkyō, 1938. 154 pp.
Dai-nikai jinkō mondai zenkoku kyōgi-kai hōkokusho. [Report, Second Conference on Population Problems.] Tōkyō, 1939. 1104 pp.
Dai-sankai jinkō mondai zenkoku kyōgi-kai kaihō. [Summary report. Third National Conference on Population Problems.] Tōkyō, 1940. 141 pp.
Dai-sankai jinkō mondai zenkoku kyōgi-kai hōkokusho. [Report, Third National Conference on Population Problems.] Tōkyō, 1941. 956 pp.
Dai-yonkai jinkō mondai zenkoku kyōgi-kai kaihō. [Summary report. Fourth National Conference on Population Problems.] Tōkyō, 1941. 142 pp.
Dai-gokai jinkō mondai zenkoku kyōgi-kai kaihō. [Summary report. Fifth National Conference on Population Problems.] Tōkyō, 1942. 124 pp.
Jinkō seisaku to kokudo keikaku. [Population policy and national planning.] Tōkyō, 1942. 9, 369, 5 pp.
Reports on the Fifth National Conference.

Jinkō mondai kenkyū-kai.
Waga kuni no shōrai jinkō. [Our nation's future population.] Tōkyō, Tōkō shoin, 1941. 66, 7 pp.
Reports from the twelfth of a series of meetings on population problems at the Ministry of Welfare, including the following contributions:
Minoguchi, Tokijirō. "Jinkō seisaku kakuritsu yōkō no mokuhyō to hōsaku." [The goals and plans of the Outline for Establishment of Population Policy.] Pp. 5-11.

Nakagawa, Tomonaga. "Waga kuni jinkō no sūsei to shōrai jinkō." [Our country's population trends and the future population.] Pp. 13-25.

Odahashi, Teiju. "Jinkō ichi-oku no kanōsei." [Possibility of a population of 100 million.] Pp. 27-36.

Kawakami, Riichi. "Ichi-oku jinkō no seibutsugakuteki kiso." [The biological base for a population of 100 million.] Pp. 37-51.

Jinkō mondai kenkyū-kai. Dai-gokai jinkō mondai zenkoku kyōgi-kai. [The Fifth National Conference on Population Problems.]

"Jinkō seisaku jisshi sokushin ni kansuru ken kengi." [Proposal to the Government concerning the hastening of putting the population policies into effect.] *J.m.*, 4(4):527-529. May 1942.

Resolution adopted by the Fifth National Conference on Population Problems, November 14-15, 1941.

Jinkō mondai kenkyū-kai. Dai-rokkai jinkō mondai zenkoku kyōgi-kai. [The Sixth National Conference on Population Problems.]

"Jinkō no toshi haichi ni kansuru keizoku iinkai setchi ketsugi." [Resolution for the establishment of a continuing committee on the urban distribution of population.] *J.m.*, 5(3):481-483. February 1943.

"Kekkon sokushin ni kansuru kengi." [Proposal for hastening marriages.] *J.m.*, 5(3):480-481. February 1943.

"Dai-tōa kensetsu ni shosuru minzoku jinkō seisaku ni kansuru kengi." [Proposal concerning the racial population policy for the establishment of Greater East Asia.] *J.m.*, 5(3):477-479. February 1943.

Jinkō mondai kenkyū-kai, zaidan hōjin, jinkō taisaku iinkai.

Proposal on the fundamental cause and aim of population policy. Tokyo, November 22, 1946.

Jinkō taisaku to shite no katei keikaku no fukyū ni kansuru ketsugi. [Resolution on promoting family planning as a population measure.] Tōkyō, July 22, 1954. 51 pp.

Appendix: "Jinkō taisaku to shite no katei keikaku no fukyū ni kansuru ketsugi setsumei shiryō." [Explanation material on the resolution on promoting family planning as a population measure.]

"Zaidan hōjin, jinkō mondai kenkyū-kai no jinkō taisaku iinkai dai-ikkai chūkan hōkoku no happyō." [Announcement of the first interim report, "Population and employment in the near future," by the Inquiry Commission for Population Policies in the Foundation Institute for the Research of Population Problems.] *J.m.k.*, 9(3-4):58-67. March 1954.

Jinkō shūyōryoku ni kansuru taisaku yōkō ketsugi. [Recommendations for measures on the supporting capacity of population.] Tōkyō, January 21, 1955. 64 pp.

Senzai shitsugyō taisaku ni kansuru ketsugi. [Resolution on measures on disguised unemployment.] Tōkyō, 1956. 55 pp.

Nihon. Jinkō shokuryō mondai chōsa-kai.

Jinkō-bu toshin setsumei. [Reports of the population section.] Tōkyō, 1930.

Nihon. Kōsei-shō, jinkō mondai kenkyūjo.

"Jihen-ka no jinkō mondai." [Population problems in relation to the current emergency.] Naikaku jōhō-kyoku. *Shūhō* [Weekly Bulletin], December 18, 1940. 11 pp.

Sengo Nihon no jinkō mondai. [Population problems in postwar Japan.] Revised edition. Research Data, No. 114. Tōkyō, March 1, 1956. 80 pp.

First edition. Research Data, No. 99. 1954. 44 pp.

"Zaidan hōjin jinkō mondai kenkyū-kai ni okeru jinkō mondai taisaku iinkai no settei." [Council for population policies newly organized in the Foundation Institute for the Research of Population Problems.] *J.m.k.*, 9(1-2):68-70. November 1953.

Nihon. Kōsei-shō, jinkō mondai shingi-kai.

"Jinkō mondai shingi-kai no jinkō no ryōteki chōsei ni kansuru ketsugi." [Resolution of the Council of Population Problems in Welfare Ministry on control of population increase.] *J.m.k.*, 10(1-4):110-112. March 1955.

Jinkō shūyōryoku ni kansuru ketsugi. [Resolution on the supporting capacity of population.] Tōkyō, August 1955. 23 pp.

Nihon. Naikaku.

Jinkō seisaku kakuritsu yōkō. [Outline for the establishment of population policy.] Tōkyō, 1941.

Reproduced in: Okazaki, Ayanori. *Shin-tōa kakuritsu to jinkō taisaku.* Pp. 259-264. Tachi, Minoru. *Jinkō mondai setsuwa.* Appendix, pp. 2-6. And: Jinkō mondai kenkyū-kai. *Jinkō seisaku to kokudo keikaku.* [Population policy and national planning.] Tōkyō, Tōkō shoin, 1942. Appendix, pp. 2-4.

Nihon. Naikaku kikakuin.

"Jinkō mondai o dō suru ka." [What should be done about our population problem?] Naikaku jōhō-kyoku, *Shūhō* [Weekly Bulletin], February 12 and February 19, 1941. Pp. 23-31 and 36-45.

Nihon. Naikaku. Jinkō mondai shingi-kai. Cabinet Population Problem Council.

Recommendations of the Population Problem Council in the Cabinet, Japanese Government, Nov. 29, 1949. Tokyo, 1949. 20 pp.

Specific recommendations with reference to economic development and population control. This is the report to the Cabinet. The Cabinet did not act on the report and, as of April 1950, the Population Problem Council itself passed out of existence.

STUDIES AND LITERATURE ON POLICIES

Books

Aomori, Kazuo.

Jinkōgaku kenkyū. [Study of demography.] Tōkyō, Shobunkan, 1944.

Iizawa, Shōji.

Nanshin seisaku no sai-ninshiki. [The new recognition of Southern policy.] Tōkyō, Takayama, 1939. 452 pp.

Iwakura, Tomohide.

Senji jinkō seisaku. [Wartime population policy.] Tōkyō, Keibundō, 1941. 6, 237 pp.

Jinkō mondai kenkyū-kai.

Sensō to jinkō o kataru. [Talk on war and population.] Tōkyō, 1941. 3, 70 pp.

A symposium on "war and population" sponsored by the Hōchi newspaper, November 15, 1940.

Kitaoka, Juitsu.

Jinkō seisaku. [Population policy.] Tōkyō, Nihon hyōronsha, 1943. 3, 7, 251 pp.

Jinkō mondai to jinkō seisaku. [Population problems and population policies.] Tōkyō, 1948. 238 pp.

Over-population and family planning in Japan. Economic Series, No. 14. Tokyo, Division of Economics & Commerce, The Science Council of Japan, 1957. 71 pp.

Kori, Kikunosuke.
Sensō to jinkō mondai. [War and population problems.] Tōkyō, Dōbun-kan shuppan-bu, 1942.
Koya, Yoshio.
Kokudo, jinkō, ketsueki. [Country, population, blood.] Tōkyō, Asahi shimbun-sha, 1941. 3, 266 pp.
Koya, Yoshio, and Tachi, Minoru.
Kindaisen to tairyoku jinkō. [Physical strength, population, and modern war.] Tōkyō, Sōgen-sha, 1944. 3, 199 pp.
Koyama, Eizō.
Minzoku to jinkō no riron. [Theory on race and population.] Tōkyō, Haneda shoten, 1941. 9, 4, 409, 10 pp.
Minoguchi, Tokijirō.
Jinkō seisaku. [Population policy.] Tōkyō, Chikura shobō, 1944. 3, 4, 447 pp.
Nihon. Kōsei-shō, jinkō mondai kenkyūjo.
Kokumin shishitsu, kokumin seikatsu. [National qualitative resources and national life.] Tōkyō, Jinkō mondai kenkyūkai, 1941. 325 pp.
Sengo Nihon no jinkō mondai. [The population problem in postwar Japan.] Research Data, No. 99. Tōkyō, 1954. 44 pp.
Nishino, Mutsuo.
Jinkō mondai to Nampō ken. [Population problem and the Southern sphere.] Tōkyō, Muroto shobō, 1943. 5, 8, 431 pp.
Ōba, Saneharu.
Jinkō mondai to shokuryō mondai. [Population problem and food problem.] Tōkyō, Kōdō-kan, 1920. 4, 3, 2, 18, 4, 628, 22 pp.
Okazaki, Ayanori.
Kekkon to jinkō. [Marriage and population.] Tōkyō, Chikura shobō, 1941. 3, 4, 242 pp.
Shin-tōa kakuritsu to jinkō taisaku. [Establishment of new East Asia and population countermeasure.] Tōkyō, Chikura shobō, 1941. 6, 4, 280 pp.
"Jinkō seisaku kakuritsu yōkō." [An outline of the establishment of population policy.] Pp. 259-264.
Ueda, Teijirō.
Nihon jinkō seisaku. [Japan's population policy.] Tōkyō, Chikura shobō, 1937. 356 pp.
See also: *Ibid.* "Bevölkerungsfrage und Wirtschaft im heutigen Japan." *Weltwirtschaftliches Archiv*, 46(1):93-117. July 1937.

Periodicals

Ando, Masakichi.
"Saitei seikatsu hi to ichioku jinkō." [Minimum living expense and a population of 100,000,000.] Pp. 278-280 in: Nihon. Jinkō mondai kenkyū-kai. *Jinkō seisaku to kokudo keikaku.* Tōkyō, 1942.
Ballon, Robert, S. J.
"Le problème de la population au Japon." *La vie économique et sociale*, 24:81-90. January-March 1953.
Hiraide, Yōichi.
"Jinkō hatten no kompon taru kōdō sekaikan ningensei kaifuku to shinchō ni tsuite." [On the diffusion and restoration of humanistic Imperial world view as the basis for population development.] Pp. 243-249 in: Nihon. Jinkō mondai kenkyū-kai. *Jinkō seisaku to kokudo keikaku.* Tōkyō, 1942.
Holland, W. L.
"Population problems and policies in the Far East." *The Annals of the American Academy of Political and Social Science*, 188:307-317. November 1936.
Honda, Tatsuo.
"Minzoku rippō to shite no jinkō seisaku." [Population policy as race legislation.] *J.m.k.*, 3(2):40-44. February 1942.
Ishikawa, H.
"Jinkō no shinteki shishitsu to toshi keikaku." [Psychological quality of population and city planning.] *J.m.*, 4(1): 57-64. August 1941.
Iwakura, Tomohide.
"Dai-tōa jinkō seisaku." [Greater East Asia population policy.] *J.m.*, 5(1):19-27. September 1942.
"Jinkō mondai no jikyokuteki kōshō jakkan." [Some considerations of population problems under the present situation.] *J.m.*, 4(3):362-366. January 1942.
"Jikyoku shita ni okeru jinkō mondai." [Population problems under the present situation.] *J.m.*, 4(4):555-559. May 1942.
"Minzoku mondai no kōshō jakkan." [Some inquiries in race problems.] *J.m.*, 5(3):484-489. February 1943.
Koya, Yoshio.
Whither the population problem in Japan? Report, 7th Annual Meeting of the Association of Public Health and Welfare. Tokyo, Institute of Public Health, 1950.
Koya, Yoshio, Chairman.
[Reports on the discussion of Eugenic Protection Problems which was held at the general meeting of the Public Health Section, Japan Medical Congress, Tokyo, April 3, 1951.] *Kōshū eisei*, 9:263-266. May 1951.
A report on several studies of contraception and induced abortion.
Koyama, Eizō.
"Nettai no fūdoteki jōken to imin tekikakusei no shomondai." [Various problems of the climatic conditions in the torrid zone and suitability for migration.] Part 1. *J.m.k.*, 2(1):1-38. January 1941. Part 2. *J.m.k.*, 2(2):1-32. February 1941.
Mitsubishi Economic Research Bureau.
"Basic principles for population policy." *Monthly Circular*, March 1941. Pp. 16-17.
Miyajima, Mikinosuke.
"Jinkō mondai to Nampō keirin." [Population problems and Southern administration.] *J.m.*, 5(1):1-4. September 1942.
Miyoshi, T.
"Minzoku rōdō seisaku no kichō." [Keynote in the racial labor policy.] *J.m.*, 5(3):490-496. February 1943.
Mizuno, T.
"Jinkō seisaku yori mitaru kekkon tekireiki no hoken kyōiku." [The health education of those in marriageable age as seen from population policy.] Pp. 273-275 in: Jinkō mondai kenkyū-kai. *Jinkō seisaku to kokudo keikaku.* Tōkyō, 1942.
Nagai, Tōru.
"Genka no jinkō mondai to shakai seisaku." [Present population problems and social policy.] Pp. 21-48 in: Jinkō mondai kenkyū-kai. *Jinkō mondai kōen shu.* [Collection of lectures on population problems.] Tōkyō, 1937. 81 pp.
Nakamura, Keinoshin.
"Jinkō seisaku no jisshi taisaku ni tsuite." [Concerning the measures for putting the population policies into effect.] *J.m.*, 4(4):529-533. May 1942.
Speech by the director of the Welfare Ministry's Population Bureau (Kōsei-shō, jinkō mondai kenkyūjo).

Nemura, T.
"Shokonsha no kekkon hi." [First marriages and wedding expenses.] *J.m.k.*, 3(1):1-14. January 1942.

Nihon. Kōsei-shō, jinkō mondai kenkyūjo.
"Kōsei-shō jinkō-kyoku ni okeru jinkō mondai keimō posutā no seisaku." [The production of information posters on population problems by the Population Bureau of the Ministry of Welfare.] *J.m.k.*, 3(6):31-36. June 1942.
Sanji seigen mondai no jinkō seisakuteki kōsatsu. [Considerations on the question of birth control from the viewpoint of population policy.] Data Series, No. 43. July 1949. 46 pp.
Investigation on the rearing cost of children. Report of the 1st survey in February, 1943. By Naotarō Sekiyama. *2nd survey in November, 1943.* By Tatsuo Honda. *On the results of 3rd survey.* By K. Mikuni. Social-Economical Researches, Nos. 10(a), (b), and (c). Tokyo, 1948.
Summary translation of studies published in *Jinkō mondai kenkyū*, Vol. v, No. 1, January 1946; Vol. v, No. 10-12, October-December 1947; and Vol. vi, No. 1, January 1948.
Also: *Investigation on the expenses to have new home.* By Ayanori Okazaki. Social-Economical Researches, B-8. Tokyo, 1948.

Nishinoiri, T.
"Jinkō seisaku kakuritsu yōkō no gutaika ni hitsuyō naru komponteki suishinryoku ni tsuite." [On the basic propulsions necessary for the materialization of the Outline for the Establishment of Population Policy.] Pp. 243-249 in: Jinkō mondai kenkyū-kai. *Jinkō seisaku to kokudo keikaku.* Tōkyō, 1942.

Noma, Kaizō.
"Jinkō mondai yori mitaru nanshin ron." [Advocacy of southward expansion viewed from a standpoint of population problems.] *J.m.*, 4(4):560-588. May 1942.

Okazaki, Ayanori.
"Shokonsha no kekkon hi." [The wedding expenses of first marriages.] (With Nemura, Tōzaburō.) *J.m.k.*, 2(7):1-8. July 1941.
"Nōka ni okeru shokonsha no kekkon hiyō." [The wedding expenses of rural first marriages.] *J.m.k.*, 3(3):1-5. March 1942.
Population problem of Japan. Nihon. Jinkō mondai kenkyūjo, Research Data, Extra No. 1. Tokyo, 1948. 8 pp.
Food crisis and birth control. Nihon. Kōsei-shō, jinkō mondai kenkyūjo, Research Data, Extra No. 2. Tokyo, 1948. 5 pp.
"Population problems of Japan." *Contemporary Japan*, 17(7-12):248-254. July-December 1948.
"Le problème et la politique démographiques au Japon." Institut national d'études démographiques, Revue trimestrielle, *Population*, 7(2):207-226. April-June 1952.
"Nihon jinkō no genjō to sono shōrai." [The condition and future of Japanese population.] Pp. 239-265 in: Arisawa, Hiromi, Editor. *Nihon no seikatsu suijun.* [Japan's standard of living.] Tōkyō, Tōkyō daigaku shuppan-kai, 1954. 10, 322 pp.
The present and future of Japan's population. Japanese Paper No. 4. 12th Conference, Institute of Pacific Relations, Kyōto, Japan, September-October 1954. Tokyo, Japan Institute of Pacific Relations, 1954. 13 pp.

Okazaki, Ayanori, *et al.*
"Zadankai: Jinkō mondai o megutte." [Symposium: On the population problem.] *Ryokufū bunko.* Special edition on "Jinkō mondai to sanji seigen." [Population problem and birth control.] 1(1):32-59. October 1949.
The magazine is published by the Ryokufū-kai [Green Breeze Society] of the Upper House of the Diet.

Ota, Tenrei.
"Sanji seigen ron." [Discourse on birth control.] Pp. 187-216 in: Shakai shugi kyōiku kyōkai. *Fūjin mondai.* [Women problem.] Tōkyō, Sangen-sha, 1949. 245 pp.

Ōzumi, Yukio.
"Ie to minzoku to kokka." [Family, race, and state.] *J.m.*, 4(2):189-196. November 1941.

Shimomura, H.
"Dai-tōa sen to jinkō mondai." [The war of Greater East Asia and population problems.] *J.m.*, 4(4):534-545. May 1942.

Steiner, Jesse F.
"Japanese population policies." *American Journal of Sociology*, 43(5):717-733. March 1938.

Sue, M.
"Jinkō kenkyū to kokkateki seikaku." [Population research and its nationalistic character.] *J.m.*, 6(2):14-18. November 1943.

Tachi, Minoru.
"Jinkō saihaibun keikaku no kiso to shite nitaru jinkō zōshokuryoku no chiikiteki tokusei." [Planning for population redistribution based on the areal characteristic of population increase.] *J.m.k.*, 3(2):1-39. February 1942.

Takahashi, Jirō.
"Sengo no jinkō mondai." [Postwar population problems.] *J.m.*, 4(2):210-222. November 1941.

Tanaka, Takako.
"Kekkon sōdan jigyō no shakaiteki igi." [The social meaning of marital consultation enterprise.] Pp. 261-267 in: Nihon. Jinkō mondai kenkyū-kai. *Jinko seisaku to kokudo keikaku.* Tōkyō, 1942.

Takano, Rokurō.
"Nampō hatten to jinkō mondai." [Expansion to the South and population problems.] *J.m.*, 4(4):546-554. May 1942.

Thompson, Warren S.
"Future adjustments of population to resources in Japan." *Milbank Memorial Fund Quarterly*, 27(2):191-202. April 1950.
"The need for a population policy in Japan." *American Sociological Review*, 15(1):25-33. February 1950.

Tsuda, S.
"Yūshūji no kakei chōsa." [Genealogical study of superior children.] *J.m.*, 6(2):83-104. November 1943.

Tsukahara, Jin.
"Dai-tōa kyōeiken no jinkō mondai gaikan." [Outline of the population problems of the Greater East Asia Co-prosperity Sphere.] *J.m.*, 5(1):8-18. September 1942.

Umezawa, Kikue.
"Shina jihen no nyūyōji shintai hatsuiku jōkyō ni oyoboshitaru eikyō ni tsuite." [On the influence of the China Incident on the physical development of infants and children.] *J.m.k.*, 2(12):24-42. December 1941.

Umino, Kōtoku.
"Jinteki shigen no zōka saku." [Policy for increase in human resources.] *J.m.*, 5(1):28-39. September 1942.

Whelpton, P. K.
"The outlook for the control of human fertility in Japan." *American Sociological Review*, 15(1):34-42. February 1950.

Yanaihara, Tadao.
"Jinkō mondai to ishokumin." [Population problems and migrants.] Pp. 23-40 in: Jinkō mondai kenkyū-kai. *Jinkō mondai kōen shū.* [Collection of lectures on population problems.] Vol. IV. Tōkyō, 1937. 93 pp.

CULTURE, ECONOMY, SOCIETY

GENERAL

Books

Allen, George C.
Japan: The hungry guest. New York, Dutton, 1938. 281 pp.
Asakawa, Kan'ichi, Editor.
Japan, from the Japanese government history, . . . with supplementary chapters. New York, P. F. Collier and Son Corporation, 1939. xxiii, 382 pp.
A revised edition of the *History of the Empire of Japan,* compiled in 1893 for the Imperial Japanese Commission of the World's Columbian Expedition and published in Tōkyō by order of the Department of Education.
Borton, Hugh.
Japan since 1931. New York, Institute of Pacific Relations, Inquiry Series, 1940. 141 pp.
Borton, Hugh, Editor.
Japan. Ithaca, N.Y., Cornell University Press, 1951. viii, 320 pp.
Ch. II, "Political divisions and population," by Robert B. Hall, and Ch. III, "The people," by John F. Embree.
Haring, Douglas G., Editor.
Japan's prospect. Cambridge, Mass., Harvard University Press, 1946. xiv, 474 pp.
With a chapter on "Population and social structure," by Talcott Parsons.
Holland, W. L., and Mitchell, Kate, Editors.
Problems of the Pacific, 1936: Aims and results of social and economic policies in Pacific countries. Chicago, Ill., University of Chicago Press, 1937. 470 pp.
Nitobe, Inazō, Editor.
Western influences in modern Japan. Chicago, Ill., University of Chicago Press, 1931. xii, 532 pp.
Reischauer, Edwin O.
The United States and Japan. The American Foreign Policy Library. Cambridge, Mass., Harvard University Press, 1950. xviii, 357 pp.
Wakefield, Harold.
New paths for Japan. New York, Oxford University Press, 1948. 223 pp.
Yanaga, Chitoshi.
Japan since Perry. New York, McGraw-Hill Book Co., 1949. x, 723 pp.
Yoshida, Tōgō.
Ishin shi hachikō. [Eight lectures on the history of the Meiji Restoration.] Tōkyō, Fuzambo, 1911.

ECONOMY

Books

Allen, George C.
Japanese industry: Its recent development and present condition. New York, International Secretariat, Institute of Pacific Relations, 1940. 124 pp.
A short economic history of modern Japan, 1867-1937. London, Allen and Unwin, Ltd., 1946. 200 pp.
Western enterprise in Far Eastern economic development: China and Japan. (With Audrey G. Donnithorne.) New York, The Macmillan Co., 1954. 291 pp.
Asahi, Isoshi.
The economic strength of Japan. Tokyo, The Hokuseidō Press, 1939. xix, 324 pp.
Ayusawa, Iwao F.
Industrial conditions and labor legislation in Japan. International Labour Office, Studies and Reports, Series B, No. 16. Geneva, 1926, 119 pp.
Barret, François.
L'évolution du capitalisme japonais. 1. L'évolution de la structure capitaliste: Trusts, cartels, concentration et sociétés d'économie mixte. Paris, Editions sociales, 1945.
Ch. I, Mitsui; Ch. VI, Mitsubishi.
Bisson, Thomas A.
America's Far Eastern policy. New York, The Macmillan Co., 1945. xiii, 235 pp.
Aspects of wartime economic control in Japan. New York, International Secretariat, Institute of Pacific Relations, 1945. 108 pp.
Japan's war economy. Ibid., 1945. xv, 267 pp.
Zaibatsu dissolution in Japan. Berkeley, Calif., University of California Press, 1954. xi, 314 pp.
Carus, Clayton D., and McNichols, Charles L.
Japan: Its resources and industries. New York, Harper, 1944. xvii, 252 pp.
Clark, Colin.
The economics of 1960. London, Macmillan and Co., Ltd., 1942. x, 118 pp.
Cohen, Jerome B.
The Japanese war economy, 1937-1945. Minneapolis, Minn., University of Minnesota Press, 1949. xix, 545 pp.
Economic problems of free Japan. Princeton University, Center of International Studies, Memorandum No. 2. Princeton, N.J., 1952. 92 pp.
Daniels, C., *et al.*
Sericulture in Japan. Tokyo, SCAP, GHQ, Natural Resources Section, 1947. 38 pp.
Dodson, Joseph C., with Milligan, Clark C.
Japanese crop and livestock statistics, 1878-1950. Tokyo, SCAP, GHQ, Natural Resources Section, 1951. 133 pp.
Espenshade, Ada V.
Japanese fisheries production, 1908-46. A statistical report. Tokyo, SCAP, GHQ, Natural Resources Section, 1947. 40 pp.
Farley, Miriam S.
Aspects of Japan's labor problems. New York, The John Day Company, 1950. x, 283 pp.
Fine, Sherwood M.
Japan's postwar industrial recovery. Tokyo, Foreign Affairs Association of Japan, 1953. 52 pp.
Grad, Andrew J.
Land and peasant in Japan: An introductory survey. New York, International Secretariat, Institute of Pacific Relations, 1952. xii, 262 pp.
Harada, Shuichi.
Labor conditions in Japan. New York, Columbia University Press, 1928. 289 pp.
Hubbard, Gilbert E., Comp.
Eastern industrialization and its effect on the West. London, Oxford University Press, 1938. 418 pp.

Inaba, Hidemi.
Nihon keizai no shōrai. [The future of Japanese economy.] Tōkyō, Chūo rōdō gakuen, 1948. 13, 5, 292 pp.

Institute of Pacific Relations.
The development of upland areas in the Far East. New York, International Secretariat, 1949 [*i.e.*, 1951]. 2 vols.
Vol. I includes a section on Japan by Glenn T. Trewartha.

Institute of Pacific Relations. Secretariat, Research Staff, Compilers and Translators.
Industrial Japan: Aspects of recent economic developments as viewed by Japanese writers. New York, 1941. ix, 230 pp.

Institute of Pacific Relations. 3rd Conference, Kyoto, Japan, 1929.
Documents . . . Vol. XVII. *Agriculture, mineral production, and labor of the Pacific; and Phases of the Japanese population problem.* Kyoto—.

Institute of Pacific Relations. 6th Conference, Yosemite National Park, 1936.
Papers presented . . . August 15 to 29, 1936, by the National Councils and the International Secretariat of the Institute.
Volumes VII, VIII, and IX concern the economy of Japan and Manchuria.

Institute of Pacific Relations. 9th Conference, Hot Springs, Va., 1945.
Security in the Pacific. A preliminary report of the 9th conference of the Institute of Pacific Relations, Hot Springs, Virginia, January 6-17, 1945. New York, International Secretariat, 1945. xiii, 169 pp.

Institute of Pacific Relations. 10th Conference, Stratford-upon-Avon, 1947.
Problems of economic reconstruction in the Far East. Report. New York, International Secretariat, 1949. xxix, 125 pp.

International Labor Office.
Industrial labour in Japan. Studies and Reports, Series A, No. 37. Geneva, 1933.

Isobe, Hidetoshi.
"Labour condition in Japanese agriculture." *Bulletin of the Utsunomiya Agricultural College*, Section B, Vol. II, No. 1, 1937. 88 pp.

King, F. H.
Farmers of forty centuries, or permanent agriculture in China, Korea and Japan. Edited by J. P. Bruce. Emmaus, Pa., [no date]. 379 pp.

Kobayashi, Ushisaburō.
The basic industries and social history of Japan, 1914-1918. New Haven, Conn., Yale University Press, 1930.

Kuznets, Simon; Moore, Wilbert E.; and Spengler, Joseph J., Editors.
Economic growth: Brazil, India, Japan. Durham, N.C., Duke University Press, 1955. xi, 613 pp.

Ladejinsky, Wolf I.
Farm tenancy in Japan: A preliminary report. Tokyo, SCAP, GHQ, Natural Resources Section, 1947. 54 pp.

Lederer, E., and Lederer-Seidler, E.
Japan in transition. New Haven, Conn., Yale University Press, 1938.

Lockwood, William W.
The economic development of Japan: Growth and structural changes. Princeton, N.J., Princeton University Press, 1954. xv, 603 pp.

Mainichi shimbun-sha. Jinkō mondai chōsa-kai. The Population Problems Research Council.
Various forms of invisible unemployment in agricultural districts. Tokyo, 1950. 22 pp.

Maurette, Fernand.
Social aspects of industrial development in Japan. International Labor Office, Studies and Reports, Series B, No. 21. Geneva, 1934. 69 pp.

Mitchell, Kate L.
Industrialization of the western Pacific, constituting Part III of an economic survey of the Pacific area. New York, International Secretariat, Institute of Pacific Relations, 1942. 322 pp.
Japan's industrial strength. American Council, Institute of Pacific Relations. New York, Knopf, 1942. 140 pp.

Moulton, Harold G.
Japan: An economic and financial appraisal. Washington, D.C., The Brookings Institution, 1931.

Nasu, Shiroshi.
Aspects of Japanese agriculture: A preliminary survey. New York, International Secretariat, Institute of Pacific Relations, 1941. ix, 168 pp.
Land utilization in Japan. Prepared for the 3rd Session, Conference, Institute of Pacific Relations, Kyoto, 1929. Tokyo, 1929. 4, 262, 6 pp.

Nihon. Keizai antei hombu, Editor.
Ari no mama no Nihon keizai. [The actual state of Japanese economy.] E. S. B. Series, No. 1. Tōkyō, Hokujō shoten, 1949. 98 pp.
Jinkō to shitsugyō. [Population and unemployment.] E. S. B. Series, No. 3. Tōkyō, Hokujō shoten, 1949. 92 pp.

Nihon. Keizai antei hombu. Economic Stabilization Board.
Analysis of post-war Japanese economy. Tokyo, 1950. 84 pp.
Ch. IX, "Overall report on damages caused to Japan by World War II," including deaths by type and location.

Nihon. Keizai shingi hombu. Economic Planning Board.
Economic survey of Japan, 1950-1951. Tokyo, 1951.
The *Survey* for 1955-1956 was issued in September 1956 (iv, 209, 78 pp.).

Nihon. Nihon ginkō. Bank of Japan.
Outline of the financial system of Japan. By the Economic Research Department. Tokyo, 1953. 23 pp.

Nihon. Rōdō-shō, daijin kambō, rōdō tōkei, chōsa-bu. Ministry of Labour. Division of Labour Statistics and Research.
Analysis of labour economy in 1949. Tokyo, 1950. 87 pp.

Nihon. Rōdō-shō, rōdō tōkei chōsa-bu.
Rōdō hakusho. [Labor white paper.] Tōkyō, Rōdō hōrei kyōkai, 1953. 246 pp.
Ibid. 1954. 361 pp.

Ohkawa, Kazushi.
International comparisons of productivity in agriculture. Ministry of Agriculture and Forestry, The National Research Institute of Agriculture, Bulletin No. 1. Tokyo, 1949. 35 pp.

Orchard, John E., with Orchard, Dorothy J.
Japan's economic position: The progress of industrialization. New York, Whittlesey House, 1930. 504 pp.

Oshima, Harry T.
Survey of various long-term estimates of Japanese national income. Conference on Economic Growth in Selected Countries, sponsored by the Social Science Research Council, April 25-27, 1952. New York, 1952.

Penrose, E. F.
"Agricultural and mineral production in Japan." In: Institute of Pacific Relations. *Agriculture, mineral produc-*

tions, and labor of the Pacific; and phases of the Japanese population problem. Vol. XVII. Documents of the 3rd Conference. Kyoto, 1929.

Food supply and raw materials in Japan: An index of the physical volume of production of foodstuffs, industrial crops, and minerals, 1894-1927. Chicago, Ill., University of Chicago Press, 1930. 75 pp.

Reubens, Edwin P.

Absorption of foreign capital in Japan's economic development: The middle stages (1896-1913). Conference on Economic Growth in Selected Countries, sponsored by the Social Science Research Council, April 25-27, 1952. New York, 1952.

Schultze, Ernst.

Japan als Weltindustriemacht. Stuttgart, W. Kohlhammer, 1935. 2 vols.

Schumpeter, Elizabeth B., Editor.

The industrialization of Japan and Manchukuo, 1930-1940: Population, raw materials and industry. New York, The Macmillan Co., 1940. xxviii, 944 pp.

Part I, *Population and raw materials*: Schumpeter, E. B., "The population of the Japanese Empire." Penrose, E. F., "Japan, 1920-1936." Schumpeter, E. B., "Japan, Korea and Manchukuo, 1936-1940." Part II. *Japanese industry: Its organization and development to 1937.* By George C. Allen. Conclusion: *Industrial development and government policy, 1936-1940.* By E. B. Schumpeter.

Takahashi, Kamekichi.

Factors in Japan's recent industrial development. Prepared for the Sixth Conference of the Institute of Pacific Relations, held at Yosemite, California, August 15 to 29, 1936. Tokyo, Japanese Council, Institute of Pacific Relations, 1936. 35 pp.

Nihon stangyō rōdō ron. [Industrial labor in Japan.] Tōkyō, 1937. 466 pp.

Nihon shihonshugi hattatsu shi. [History of the development of Japanese capitalism.] Tōkyō, Nihon hyōron-sha, 1930.

I. Collapse of the feudal system at the end of the Tokugawa era. II. Capitalist evolution of the Meiji Restoration. III. Early development of the capitalistic system. IV. Development of the Japanese industrial revolution.

Takano, Iwasaburo.

A recent aspect of the working population in Japan Proper. Translated by Naikaku tōkei-kyoku. Tokyo, 1938. 7 pp.

Tsuru, Shigeto.

Japan's economy—present and future. Institute of Pacific Relations, Lucknow Conference, Japanese Paper No. 1. New York, Institute of Pacific Relations, 1950. 18 pp.

U.S. Army Service Forces. Headquarters.

Japan. Civil affairs handbook. Prepared by various agencies for the Office of the Provost Marshal General, Military Government Division. Washington, D.C., 1944-1945.

1 A. *Population statistics.* By: U.S. Department of State, Division of Geography and Cartography. 1945. xiv, 113 pp.

2 B. *Government and administration. Local government.* 1944. viii, 38 pp.

3. *Legal affairs.* 1944. ix, 68 pp.

3 A. *The commercial code of Japan.* By William J. Sebald, 1945. viii, 140 pp.

4. *Government finance,* 1944. xii, 350 pp.

5. *Money and exchange.* By The Federal Reserve Bank of New York and the Board of Governors of the Federal Reserve System, 1944. xii, 132 pp.

6. *Natural resources.* 1944. xiii, 116 pp.

7. *Agriculture.* By U.S. Department of Agriculture. Office of Foreign Agricultural Relations. 1944. xii, 195 pp.

8 A. *Industry.* 1944. ix, 135 pp.

8 B. *Commerce.* 1944. x, 99 pp.

9. *Labor.*

10. *Public works and utilities.*

11. *Transportation systems.*

12. *Communications.* 1944. 108 pp., 18 tables.

13. *Public health and sanitation.*

14. *Public safety.*

15. *Education.* 1944.

16. *Public welfare.*

17 A. *Cultural institutions.* 1945.

18 A. *Japanese administration over occupied areas—Burma.* 1944. xii, 96 pp.

18 B. *Japanese administration of occupied areas—Malaya.* 1944. vii, 27 pp.

18 E. *Japanese administration over occupied areas—Thailand.* 1944. x, 43 pp.

Uyeda, Teijiro, and Inokuchi, Tosuke.

Cost of living and real wages in Japan, 1914-1936. Tokyo, Japanese Council, Institute of Pacific Relations, 1936. 30 pp.

Uyeda, Teijiro, *et al.*

The small industries of Japan: Their growth and development. Issued under the auspices of the Japanese Council, Institute of Pacific Relations. London and New York, Oxford University Press, 1938. xxii, 319 pp.

Uyehara, Shigeru.

The industry and trade of Japan. 2nd Edition. London, P. S. King and Son, Ltd., 1936.

Wickizer, Vernon D., and Bennett, Murray K.

The rice economy of monsoon Asia. Published in cooperation with the International Secretariat, Institute of Pacific Relations. Stanford University, Calif., Food Research Institute, 1941. 358 pp.

Yamasaki, Kakujiro, and Ogawa, Gotaro.

The effect of the World War upon the commerce and industry of Japan. New Haven, Conn., Yale University Press, 1929.

Other

Adachi, Ikutsune.

Analysis of over-population in farming community in Japan—a case of Ehime Prefecture. Memoirs of the Research Institute for the Integrated Study of Shikoku Province, Ehime University, Series A, No. 3. Matsuyama, 1955. v, 34 pp.

Aki, Koichi.

The future of Japan—her population and natural resources. Population Problems Series, No. 11. Tokyo, The Population Problems Research Council, The Mainichi Newspapers, 1955. 29 pp.

Allen, George C.

"The last decade in Japan." *Economic History,* Vol. II, No. 8. January 1933.

Hewes, Lawrence I., Jr.

"On the current readjustment of land tenure in Japan." *Land Economics,* 25(3):246-259. August 1949.

Horie, Yasuzo.

"Government industries in the early years of the Meiji era." *K.U.E.R.,* 12(1):67-87. January 1939.

Ike, Nobutaka.
"Taxation and land ownership in the Westernization of Japan." *Journal of Economic History*, 7(2):160-182. November 1947.
"The development of capitalism in Japan." *Pacific Affairs*, 22:185-190. June 1949.
Johnston, Bruce F.
"Agricultural productivity and economic development in Japan." *Journal of Political Economy*, 59(6):498-513. December 1951.
Kamii, Yoshio.
"Industrial transformation in Japan, 1929-1936." *International Labour Review*, 40(4):516-533. October 1939.
Kawada, Shiro.
"Agricultural problems and their solution in Japan." *K.U.E.R.*, 1:155-191. 1926.
"The Japanese agricultural community and the composition of its population." *Journal of the Osaka University of Commerce*, No. 3, pp. 1-30. December 1935.
Koo, Anthony U., and Liang, C. C.
"The role of Japan in the intraregional trade of the Far East." *The Review of Economics and Statistics*, 35(1):31-40. February 1953.
Ladejinsky, Wolf I.
"Agriculture in Japan: Prewar." *Foreign Agriculture*, 9(9):130-142. September 1945.
"Landlord vs. tenant in Japan." *Foreign Agriculture*, 11(6):83-88; 121-128. June and August-September 1947.
Nakayama, Ichiro.
"Accumulation of capital in the Japanese economy." *The Annals of the Hitotsubashi Academy*, 3(3):145-163. April 1953.
Japanese economy and problems of employment. Population Problems Series, No. 10. Tokyo, The Population Problems Research Council, The Mainichi Newspapers, 1954. 35 pp.
Nasu, Shiroshi.
"Ziele und Ausrichtung der japanischen Agrarpolitik in der Gegenwart." *Weltwirtschaftliches Archiv*, 46(1):157-184. July 1937.
Ohkawa, Kazushi.
"Measurements of standards of living of the working classes in Japan." *The Annals of the Hitotsubashi Academy*, 1(2):120-137. April 1951.
Orchard, Dorothy.
"Agrarian problems of modern Japan." *Journal of Political* Economy, 37(2):129-149. April 1929.
Orchard, John E.
"Can Japan develop industrially?" *The Geographical Review*, 19(2):177-200. April 1929.
Penrose, E. F.
"Agricultural and mineral production in Japan." *Bulletin de l'Institut international de statistique*, 25(2):221-282. Tokyo, 1931.
"Japan's basic economic situation." *Annals of the American Academy of Political and Social Science*, 215:1-6. May 1941.
Reischauer, Robert K.
"Alien land tenure in Japan." *T.A.S.J.*, 2nd Series, Vol. XIII, 1936.
Reubens, Edwin P.
"Small-scale industry in Japan." *Quarterly Journal of Economics*, 61:577-604. August 1947.
"Foreign capital in economic development: A case-study of Japan." *Milbank Memorial Fund Quarterly*, 27(2):173-190. April, 1950.
Suma, Yakichiro.
"Economic conditions in Japan." *Annals of the American Academy of Political and Social Science*, 199:243-253. September 1938.
Trewartha, Glenn T.
"Land reform and land reclamation in Japan." *Geographical Review*, 40(3):376-396. July 1950.
Yamada, Yuzo.
"The income growth and the rate of saving in Japan." *The Annals of the Hitotsubashi Academy*, 4(2):79-97. April 1954.
Subtitle: "A brief survey of recent estimates by Hitotsubashi group."
"The national income and industrial structure in Japan." *Ibid.*, 1(1):15-34. October 1950.
Yamanaka, Tokutaro.
"Japanese small industries during the industrial revolution." *The Annals of the Hitotsubashi Academy*, 2(1):15-36. October, 1951.
"The nature of small industries: A survey of the economic interpretation in Japan." *Ibid.*, 4(1):2-14. October 1953.
Yoshisaka, Shuzo.
"Labor recruiting in Japan and its control." *International Labour Review*, 12:484-499. October 1923.

SOCIETY

General

Books

Benedict, Ruth F.
The chrysanthemum and the sword: Patterns of Japanese culture. London, Secker and Warburg, 1947. 324 pp.
Embree, John F.
The Japanese nation: A social survey. New York, Farrar and Rinehart, Inc., 1945. xi, 308 pp.
Fuji, Naomoto; Hirayama, Toshirō; and Ishida, Kazuyoshi.
Hōken shakai no seijuku. [The development of the feudal society.] Kyō-dai Nihon shi [Kyōto University Japanese History Series], No. 4. Ōsaka, Sōgen-sha, 1951. 4, 172 pp.
Fukutake, Tadashi.
Nihon nōson no shakaiteki seikaku. [The social characteristics of the Japanese rural villages.] Tōkyō, Tōdai kyōkumi, 1949. 2, 298 pp.
Fukutake, Tadashi, and Hidaka, Rokurō.
Shakaigaku. [Sociology.] Tōkyō, Kōbun-sha, 1952. 410, 12 pp.
Hall, Robert K.
Shushin: The ethics of a defeated nation. New York, Bureau of Publications, Teachers College, Columbia University, 1949. xvi, 244 pp.
Hearn, Lafcadio.
Japan: An attempt at interpretation. New York, The Macmillan Co., 1905. v, 549 pp.
Isomura, Eiichi.
Toshi shakaigaku. [Urban sociology.] Tōkyō, Yūhikaku, 1953. 7, 397, 7 pp.
Minzokugaku kenkyūjo.
Minzokugaku no hanashi. [Talks on ethnology.] Tōkyō, Kyōdo shuppan-sha, 1949. 2, 2, 199 pp.

Nihon jimbun kagaku-kai.
Shakaiteki kinchō no kenkyū. [Research on social tension.] Tōkyō, Yūhikaku, 1953. 3, 478 pp.
See especially:
Ōhama, Hideko. "Kaji jiken kara mita kazoku no tenshon." [Family tension as viewed from domestic cases.] Pp. 62-75.
Kohama, Mototsugu. "Buraku jūmin no keishitsu ni tsuite." [On the physical character of the Eta.] Pp. 359-368.
Toyoda, Takeshi. "Burakumin no sabetsu sareru yō ni natta rekishiteki jijō." [Historical circumstances for the discrimination against the Eta.] Pp. 369-380.
Suzuki, Jirō. "Burakumin no chiikisei, shokugyō, kekkon." [Residence, job, and marriage of the Eta.] Pp. 381-394.
Koyama, Takashi. "Buraku ni okeru shakai kinchō no seikaku." [The character of social tensions concerning the Eta.] Pp. 395-410.

Raper, Arthur F., *et al.*
The Japanese village in transition. SCAP, GHQ. Natural Resources Section, Report No. 136. Tokyo, 1950. 272 pp.

Stoetzel, Jean.
Without the chrysanthemum and the sword: A study of the attitudes of youth in post-war Japan. A UNESCO Publication. New York, Columbia University Press, 1955. 334 pp.

Yanagida, Kunio.
Shintō to minzokugaku. [Shintō and ethnology.] Tōkyō, Meiseidō, 1943. 146 pp.

Yanagida, Kunio, Editor.
Sanson seikatsu no kenkyū. [Study of life in mountain villages.] Tōkyō, Iwanami shoten, 1937. 562 pp.
Kaison seikatsu no kenkyū. [Study of life in fishing villages.] Tōkyō, Nihon minzoku gakkai, 1949. 4, 472 pp.

Yanagida, Kunio, and Seki, Keigo.
Nihon minzokugaku nyūmon. [Introduction to Japanese ethnology.] Tōkyō, Kaizō-sha, 1942. 7, 477 pp.

Other

Hulse, Frederick S.
"Status and function as factors in the structure of organization among the Japanese." *American Anthropologist,* 149:154-157. January-March 1947.

Makida, Shigeru.
"Wakamono no seikatsu." [Life of young men.] Pp. 81-92 in: Minzokugaku kenkyūjo. *Minzokugaku no hanashi.* [Talks on ethnology.] Tōkyō, Kyōdo shuppan-sha, 1949. 2, 2, 199 pp.

Minami, Hiroshi.
"The post-war social psychology of the Japanese people." *The Annals of the Hitotsubashi Academy,* 1(2):104-110. April 1951.

Pelzel, John C.
"Japanese ethnological and sociological research." *American Anthropologist,* 50(1):54-72. January-March 1948.

Smythe, Hugh H., *et al.*
"The *eta* caste in Japan. Part II. Present status." *Phylon,* 13(2):157-162. 1953.
Also: "The *eta*: Japan's indigenous minority." *Sociology and Social Research,* 37(2):112-114. November-December 1952.

Takashima, Zenya.
"The social consciousness of the people in post-war Japan." *The Annals of the Hitotsubashi Academy,* 1(2):91-103. April 1951.

Education

Books

Japanese Education Reform Council.
Education reform in Japan: The present status and the problems involved, 1950. Tokyo, 1950. 196 pp.

Keenleyside, Hugh L.
History of Japanese education and present educational systems. Tokyo, 1937.

Nihon. Mombu-shō. Ministry of Education.
An outline history of Japanese education. Prepared for the Philadelphia International Exhibition, 1876, by the Japanese Department of Education. New York, D. Appleton and Company, 1876. 202 pp.
Other issues for various international exhibitions.
A general survey of education in Japan. Tokyo, Herald of Asia Press, 1926. 88 pp.
Issued in 1931, 1935, and 1937, perhaps in other years.
The latest national language readers of Japan, approved by the Japanese Education Department. With English translation of all reading selections, trans-literations with Roman characters, and annotations. By Oreste Vaccari and Enko Elisa Vaccari. Tokyo, O. Vaccari, 1940.
Kokutai no hongi. Cardinal principles of the national entity of Japan. Translation by John O. Gauntlett and edited with an introduction by Robert King Hall. Cambridge, Mass., Harvard University Press, 1949. viii, 200 pp.

U.S. Education Mission to Japan.
Report of the United States Education Mission to Japan, submitted to the Supreme Commander for the Allied Powers, Tokyo, 30 March 1946. Washington, D.C., 1946.

Yomi kaki nōryoku chōsa iinkai. [Literacy Survey Committee.]
Nihonjin no yomi kaki nōryoku. [Literacy of the Japanese people.] Tōkyō, Tōkyō daigaku shuppan-bu, 1951. 916 pp.

Family

Books

Ariga, Kizaemon.
Nihon kazoku seido to kosaku seido. [The Japanese family system and the tenant system.] Tōkyō, Kawate shobō, 1943. 732, 32 pp.

Bennett, John W., and Nagai, Michio.
Summary and analysis of T. Kawashima's The familistic structure of Japanese society. Report by the Ohio State University Research Foundation, Report No. 4, RF Project 483. ONR Contract Nonr 495(03) (NR 176 110). Columbus, Ohio, 1952. 18 pp.

Hani, Setsuko.
The Japanese family system, as seen from the standpoint of Japanese women. Tokyo, Nihon taiheiyō mondai chōsa kai, 1948. 41 pp.

Hayashi, Megumi.
Nōka jinkō no kenkyū. [A study of the population of farm households.] Tōkyō, Nikkō shoin, 1940. 6, 4, 133 pp.

Hozumi, Nobushige.
Ancestor worship and Japanese law. Tokyo, The Hokuseidō Press, 1940. xxxl, 205 pp.

Kawashima, Takeyoshi.
Nihon shakai no kazokuteki kōsei. [Familistic structure of Japanese society.] Tōkyō, Gakusei shobō, 1948. 207 pp.

Mainichi shimbun-sha. Jinkō mondai chōsa-kai.
Kazoku seido to nōsen jinkō. Chōsa kekka, hōkoku shiryō. [Family system and agricultural population. Report data.] Tōkyō, 1951. 19 pp.

Family system and population of farming communities in Japan. Prepared by Tadashi Fukutake. Population Problems Series, No. 6. Tokyo, [1952]. iii, 54 pp.

Nagai, Michio.

Dozoku: A preliminary study of the Japanese "extended family" group and its social and economic functions (based on the researches of K. Ariga). The Ohio State University Research Foundation, Report No. 7, RF Project 483. ONR, Contract Nonr 495(03) (NR 176,00). Columbus, Ohio, 1953. 76 pp.

Nihon. Kokutetsu rōdō kumiai, fujin-bu.

Kokutetsu fujin rōdō no seikatsu. Fujin-bu jittai chōsa no chūkan hōkoku. [Livelihood of women laborers of the Japan National Railways. Intermediate report on a survey by the Women's Bureau.] Tōkyō, 1952. 18 pp.

Nihon. Rōdo-shō, fujin shōnen-kyoku.

Nōson fujin no seikatsu. [Life of rural women. Report on survey of status.] Tōkyō, 1950. 157 pp.

Fujin rōdōsha narabini rōdōsha katei fujin no kōjōgai seikatsu jikan chōsa hōkoku. [A report on the life outside the factory for women laborers and the women of laborers' families.] Tōkyō, 1950. 84 pp.

Hōkensei ni tsuite no chōsa. [Survey on feudalistic way of living.] Tōkyō, 1951. 37 pp.

SCAP. GHQ. Civil Information and Education Section.

Interim report to Population and Labor Branch, ESS, on research on census concepts and field data. Prepared by Public Opinion and Sociological Research Division at the request of the Economic and Scientific Section. Typescript. Tokyo, 1949.

Data on the composition of households and families.

A survey of attitudes toward the law on adultery. Special Report AR-298-PO-E-13. Tokyo, 1947. 8 pp.

Tamaki, Hajime.

Nihon kazoku seido no hihan. [A critical analysis of the Japanese family system.] Tōkyō, 1948. 210 pp.

1st Edition: Tōkyō, Fukuda shobō, 1934. 340 pp.

Nihon kazoku seido ron. [Theory on the Japanese family system.] Kyōto, Hōritsu bunka-sha, 1953. 3, 2, 248 pp.

Tanabe, Hisatoshi, Editor.

Kazoku. [Family.] Shakaigaku taikei [Sociology Series], No. 1. Tōkyō, Kokuritsu shoin, 1948. 239, 8 pp.

A series of general articles.

Toda, Teizō.

Kazoku kōsei. [Family structure.] Tōkyō, Kōbundō shobō, 1937. 606 pp.

A detailed analysis of family composition for various cultural and economic areas of Japan, based primarily on an analysis of a 1 per cent sample of the 1920 census schedules for rural areas.

Ie to kazoku seido. [House and family system.] Tōkyō, Hata shoten, 1944. 202 pp.

Other

Ariga, Kizaemon, *et al.*

"The Japanese family." Pp. 83-89 in: *Transactions of the Second World Congress of Sociology, held in the University of Liége, Belgium, from 24-31 August 1951*. Vol. I. London, International Sociological Association, 1954. xxii, 258 pp.

Kada, Tetsuji.

"Ie no sonchō to sono jōken." [The respect of the house and its conditions.] *Nihon hyōron*, 16(1):44-50. January 1941.

Summary: "The family system in Japan." *Contemporary Japan*, 10(2):237-241. February 1941.

Kikuchi, Hiroshi.

"Nagasaki-ken Isahaya-shi Ono ni okeru basshi naishi hichōshi sōzokusei ni tsuite." (On the ultimogeniture and non-primogeniture system in Ono, Isahaya-shi, Nagasaki prefecture.) *Hō shakaigaku*, 4:111-126. July 1953.

Kitano, Seiichi.

"Dōzoku soshiki to oyakata-kokata kankō shiryō." [Material on the dōzoku system and the oyakata-kokata custom.] *Minzokugaku nempō*, 3:161-189. 1941.

Koyama, Takashi.

"Nihon kindai kazoku." [Japanese contemporary family.] Pp. 151-194 in: Tanabe, Hisatoshi, Editor. *Kazoku*. [Family.] Shakaigaku taikei [Sociology series], No. 1. Tōkyō, Kokuritsu shoin, 1948. 239, 8 pp.

Masuoka, Jitsuichi.

"The structure of the Japanese family in Hawaii." *American Journal of Sociology*, 46(2):168-178. September 1940.

Matsumiya, Kazuya.

"Family organization in present-day Japan." *American Journal of Sociology*, 53(2):105-110. September 1947.

Okada, Yuzuru.

"Kinship organization in Japan." In: Olsen, Arthur R., Editor. *Readings on marriage and family relations. . . .* Harrisburg, Pa., Stackpole Co., 1953. 465 pp.

Pelzel, John C.

"Some social factors bearing upon Japanese population." *American Sociological Review*, 15(1):20-25. February 1950.

Spencer, Robert F. and Imamura, Kanmo.

"Notes on the Japanese kinship system." *Journal of the American Oriental Society*, 7:165-172. 1950.

Steiner, Kurt.

"The revision of the civil code of Japan: Provisions affecting the family." *The Far Eastern Quarterly*, 9(2):169-184. February 1950.

Yonebayashi, Tomio.

"Kazoku to jinkō." [Family and population.] Pp. 37-50 in: Jinkō mondai kenkyū-kai. *Waga kuni jinkō mondai ni kansuru sho-kenkyū*. [Researches on population problems in our country.] Tōkyō, Tōe shoin, 1936. 101 pp.

RELIGION

Books

Anesaki, Masaharu.

History of Japanese religion, with special reference to the social and moral life of the nation. London, Kegan Paul, Trench, Trübner, and Co., 1930. xxii, 423 pp.

Aston, W. G.

Shinto: The way of the gods. London, Longmans, Green and Co., 1905.

Holtom, Daniel C.

National faith of Japan: A study in modern Shinto. London, Kegan Paul, Trench, Trübner and Co., 1938. 329 pp.

Modern Japan and Shinto nationalism. Chicago, Ill., University of Chicago Press, 1943. 178 pp.

Hozumi, Nobushige.

Ancestor-worship and Japanese law. 5th Edition, Revised by Shigeto Hozumi. Tokyo, The Hokuseido Press, 1940. xxxi, 205 pp.

1st Edition, 1901.

Latourette, Kenneth S.
A history of the expansion of Christianity. Vol. IV. *The great century in northern Africa and Asia, A.D. 1800-A.D. 1914.* New York, Harper and Brothers, 1944. ix, 502 pp.
Nihon. Mombu-shō. Department of Education. Bureau of Religions.
A general view of the present religious situation in Japan. Tokyo, 1920.
SCAP. GHQ. Civil Information and Education Section.
Religions in Japan. Tokyo, 1948. ix, 204 pp.

GOVERNMENT

General

Books

Beard, Charles A.
The administration and politics of Tokyo: A survey and opinions. New York, The Macmillan Co., 1923. vii, 187 pp.
Borton, Hugh.
Japan since 1931: Its political and social developments. New York, International Secretariat, Institute of Pacific Relations, 1940. xii, 149 pp.
The administration and structure of Japanese government. Department of State, Publication 2244. Far Eastern Series 8. Washington, D.C., Govt. Printing Office, 1945. 17 pp.
Brown, Delmer M.
Nationalism in Japan: An introductory historical analysis. Berkeley, Calif., University of California Press, 1955. viii, 336 pp.
Fahs, Charles B.
Government in Japan: Recent trends in its scope and operation. New York, International Secretariat, Institute of Pacific Relations, 1940. xv, 114 pp.
Hindmarsh, Albert E.
The basis of Japanese foreign policy. Cambridge, Mass., Harvard University Press, 1936. x, 265 pp.
Norman, E. Herbert.
Japan's emergence as a modern state: Political and economic problems of the Meiji period. New York, International Secretariat, Institute of Pacific Relations, 1940. 254 pp.
Feudal background of Japanese politics. New York, International Secretariat, Institute of Pacific Relations, 1945. v, 136 pp.
Quigley, Harold S.
Japanese government and politics: An introductory study. New York, Century, 1932.
Reischauer, Robert K.
Japan: Government-politics. New York, Thomas Nelson and Son, 1939. xiv, 194 pp.

Periodical

Maki, John M.
"The role of the bureaucracy in Japan." *Pacific Affairs,* 20(4):391-406. December 1947.

Law

Books

Becker, J. E. de, Translator.
Annotated civil code of Japan. 1st Edition. Yokohama, Kelly and Walsh, Ltd., 1910. Vol. III.
Kyōto koseki kenkyū-ka.
Koseki no shikō kisoku, furoku. [*Koseki* act enforcement rules.] Kyōto, 1947. 104 pp.
Nihon. Hōmu-fu. Attorney General.
Codes and statutes of Japan. No. 5. *The civil code.* Book IV. "Relatives." Book V. "Succession." Law No. 222 of 1947 as amended by Law No. 260 of 1948 and Law No. 141 of 1949. Tokyo, 1950.
Nihon. Hōrei. [Laws, Statutes, etc.]
The constitution of Japan. Tokyo, Cabinet Secretariat, 1946. 16 pp.
Certified official English translation.
The civil code of Japan. Tokyo, 1950. 189 pp.
Hōritsugaku jiten. [Dictionary of Law.] Tōkyō, Iwanami shoten, 1934-1939.
Official Gazette. English Edition. No. 1, April 4, 1946—. Tokyo, Government Printing Bureau, 1946—.
The criminal code of Japan. Translated and annotated by William J. Sebald. Kobe, Japan Chronicle Press, 1936. 2, iii-x, 287 pp.
The criminal code of Japan, as amended in 1947, and the minor offenses law of Japan. Translated by Thomas L. Blakemore. Tokyo, Nihon hyōron-sha, 1950. 186 pp.
Daily life security legislations. Tokyo, Social Affairs Bureau, Ministry of Welfare, Japan, 1950. 93 pp.
Nihon. Nōrin-shō. Ministry of Agriculture and Forestry.
Land reform law. Tokyo, Jiji Press, 1947. 156 pp.
Sebald, W. J., Translator.
The civil code of Japan. Kobe, J. L. Thompson and Co., 1934. xiii, 351 pp.

The Occupation

Books

Fearey, Robert A.
The occupation of Japan, second phase: 1948-50. New York, The Macmillan Co., 1950. xii, 239 pp.
Martin, Edwin M.
The allied occupation of Japan. Auspices American Institute of Pacific Relations. Stanford, Calif., Stanford University Press, 1948. xiv, 155 pp.
Pauley, Edwin W.
Report on Japanese assets in Soviet-occupied Korea to the President of the United States, June 1946. Washington, D.C., Govt. Printing Office, 1946. iv, 141 pp.
Rice, Stuart A., and Dedrick, Calvert L.
Japanese statistical organization. A report of the Second Statistical Mission to Japan to the Supreme Commander for the Allied Powers. Tokyo, SCAP, GHQ. Economic and Scientific Section, 1951. 29 pp.
SCAP. GHQ.
Organization and activities of General Headquarters, Supreme Commander for the Allied Powers and Far East Command. Tokyo, 1950. 214 pp.
Scapins. Supreme Commander for the Allied Powers' instructions to the Japanese Government, from 4 September 1945 to 8 March 1952. Tokyo, 1952. xi, 528 pp.
Orders from the Supreme Commander for the Allied Powers to the Japanese Government. Tokyo, 15 August 1945-1952.
Catalogue of SCAP directives to the Imperial Japanese Government. Tokyo, 1947-1952.
SCAP. GHQ.
Summation . . . non-military activities in Japan. No. 1, September-October 1945-October 1948. Tokyo, 1945-1948.
Issues from September-October 1945 through February 1946 had the title: *Summation . . . non-military activities*

in Japan and Korea. Beginning with No. 6, March 1946, the summation for Korea was issued separately by the U.S. Army Forces in the Pacific under the title: *Summation . . . United States Army Military Government activities in Korea.*

"Review of the Third Occupation Year, 1 September 1947-31 August 1948." *Summation of non-military activities in Japan*, No. 35, *Appendix*, pp. 295-337. August 1948.

"This volume constitutes the final issue of the monthly *Summation of non-military activities in Japan* prepared by General Headquarters, Supreme Commander for the Allied Powers."

SCAP. GHQ. Economic and Scientific Section.
Mission and accomplishments of the Occupation in the economic and scientific fields. Tokyo, 1949.

SCAP. GHQ. Government Section.
Political reorientation of Japan, September 1945 to September 1948. Washington, D.C., Govt. Printing Office, 1949. 2 vols. xxxvi, 1300 pp.

SCAP. GHQ. Natural Resources Section.
Mission and accomplishments of the Occupation in the natural resources field. Tokyo, 1950. 43 pp.

SCAP. GHQ. Public Health and Welfare Section.
Mission and accomplishments of the Occupation in the public health and welfare fields. Tokyo, 1949.
Public health and welfare in Japan. Tokyo, 1949. 220 pp.; annex and charts, 54 pp.; tables, 86 pp.

The final summary for 1951-1952 was issued in Tokyo in 1952.

U.S. Department of State.
Occupation of Japan. Policy and progress. Far Eastern Series, No. 17, Publication 2671. Washington, D.C., Govt. Printing Office, 1946. iv, 173 pp.

Periodical

Seki, Keigo.
P. 7 in: "CIE ni okeru shakai chōsa no tenkai." [Development of social research by the Civil Information and Education Section of SCAP.] In: Nihon minzokugaku kyōkai. *Shakai chōsa.* [Social research.] *Minzokugaku kenkyū*, 17(1):1-99. February 1953.

WAR AND PEACE

Books

Conference for Conclusion and Signature of Treaty of Peace with Japan, San Francisco, 1951.
Treaty of Peace with Japan. Signed at San Francisco, September 8, 1951. . . . Washington, D.C., Govt. Printing Office, 1952. iii, 173 pp.

U.S. Department of State, Publication 4613. Treaties and Other International Acts series, 2490.

Record of proceedings. San Francisco, September 4-8, 1951. Washington, D.C., Govt. Printing Office, 1951. v, 468 pp.

U.S. Department of State, Publication 4392. International Organization and Conference Series II, Far Eastern 3.

Hishida, Seiji.
Japan among the great powers. New York, Longmans, Green and Co., 1940. 480 pp.

Johnston, Bruce F., *et al.*
Japanese food management in World War II. Stanford, Calif., Stanford University Press, 1953. xii, 283 pp.

Maki, John M.
Japanese militarism: Its cause and cure. New York, Knopf, 1945. 258 pp.

Miki, Kiyoshi, and Hosokawa, Karoku.
Introductory studies on the Sino-Japanese conflict. Tokyo, Japanese Council, Institute of Pacific Relations, 1941. xiv, 104 pp.

Moulton, Harold G., and Marlio, Louis.
The control of Germany and Japan. Washington, D.C., The Brookings Institution, 1944. xi, 116 pp.

Norman, E. Herbert.
Soldier and peasant in Japan: The origins of conscription. New York, International Secretariat, Institute of Pacific Relations, 1943. xiv, 76 pp.

Ogawa, Gotaro.
Conscription system in Japan. Publications of the Carnegie Endowment for International Peace, Division of Economics and History. New York, Oxford University Press, American Branch, 1921. xiii, 245 pp.

Ōkōchi, Kazuo.
Sengo shakai no jittai bunseki. [Analysis of the real state of the postwar society.] Tōkyō, Nihon hyōron-sha, 1950. 20, 292 pp.

A collection of articles.

Ōsaka mainichi.
Construction of the Greater East Asia Co-Prosperity Sphere. Osaka, The Mainichi Publishing Co., 1943. 67 pp.

Peffer, Nathaniel.
Prerequisites to peace in the Far East. New York, International Secretariat, Institute of Pacific Relations, 1940. 121 pp.

Stedman, Frank H.
Urban population shifts in Japan, 1940-1946. Washington, D.C., 1947. Unpublished manuscript.

Tanaka, Giichi, Baron.
Japan's dream of world empire: The Tanaka memorial. London, G. Allen and Unwin, Ltd., 1943. 68 pp.

United Kingdom. Air Ministry and Home Office.
The effects of the atomic bombs at Hiroshima and Nagasaki. Report of the British Mission to Japan. London, H. M. Stationery Office, 1946.

U.S. Adjutant General's Office.
Army battle casualties and nonbattle deaths in World War II. Final report 7 December 1941-31 December 1946. Report Control Symbol CSCAP(OT)87. Washington, D.C., Department of the Army, 1953. 118 pp.

U.S. Office of Strategic Services.
Population and migration in Japan. Research and Analysis No. 2450. Declassified by authority of Order SEC ARMY by TAG 8L 103. Washington, D.C., September 5, 1945. 41 pp.

U.S. Strategic Bombing Survey. Pacific War.
Japanese wartime standard of living and utilization of manpower. Washington, D.C., Govt. Printing Office, 1947. xi, 146 pp.

U.S. Strategic Bombing Survey. Pacific War.
Reports . . . Washington, D.C., Govt. Printing Office, 1946.

1. *Summary report, Pacific war.*

3. *The effects of atomic bombs on Hiroshima and Nagasaki.*

12. *The effects of bombing on health and medical services in Japan.*

13. *The effects of atomic bombs on health and medical services in Hiroshima and Nagasaki.*

14. *The effects of strategic bombing on Japanese morale.*
53. *The effects of strategic bombing on Japan's war economy.*
55. *Effects of air attack on Japanese urban economy. Summary report.*
56-60. *Effects of air attacks on . . .* [Tokyo-Kawasaki-Yokohama, Nagoya, Osaka-Kobe-Kyoto, Nagasaki, Hiroshima].
90. *Effect of the incendiary bomb attacks on Japan. A report on eight cities.*
96. *A report on physical damage in Japan. Summary report.*

U.S. War Department. General Staff.
Biennial report of the Chief of Staff of the United States Army, July 1, 1943, to June 30, 1945, to the Secretary of War. By General of the Army George C. Marshall. . . . Washington, D.C., Infantry Journal Press, 1946. 243 pp.
"Manpower balance," pp. 189-202; "The price of victory," pp. 203-209.

Ward, Robert S.
Asia for the Asiatics? The techniques of Japanese occupation. Chicago, Ill., University of Chicago Press, 1945. xiv, 204 pp.

Wright, Fergus C.
Population and peace: A survey of international opinion on claims for relief from population pressure. International Studies Conference, Peaceful Change. League of Nations, International Institute of Intellectual Cooperation. Paris, 1939. 373 pp.

Periodicals

Bloch, Kurt.
"Japanese war economy." *Annals of the American Academy of Political and Social Science*, 215:17-23. May 1941.

Chen Han-seng.
"Conquest and population." *Pacific Affairs*, 10(2):201-207. June 1937.

Chih Meng.
"Some economic aspects of the Sino-Japanese conflict." *Annals of the American Academy of Political and Social Science*, 199:233-242. September 1938.

Cole, Allen B.
"Japan's population problems in peace and war." *Pacific Affairs*, 16(4):397-417. December 1943.

Fisher, Charles A.
"The expansion of Japan: A study in Oriental geopolitics." *Geographical Journal*, 115(1-3):1-19; (4-6):179-193. 1950.

Hankins, Frank H.
"Pressure of population as a cause of war." *The Annals of the American Academy of Political and Social Science*, 198:101-108. July 1938.

Haushofer, Karl.
"Gross-Asiens Menschenwucht und Lebenswille am japanischen Beispiel." *Archiv für Bevölkerungswissenschaft*, 5(4):225-231. August 1935.

Redman, H. Vere.
"The problem of Japan." *International Affairs*, 20(1):19-31. January 1944.

Rowe, David N.
"Collective security in the Pacific: An American view." *Pacific Affairs*, 18(1):5-21. March 1945.

Thompson, Warren S., and Whelpton, P. K.
"Levels of living and population pressure." *Annals of the American Academy of Political and Social Science*, 198:93-100. July 1938.

SPECIAL AREAS

TOKYO

Books

Tōkyō-fu.
Tōkyō-fu tōkeisho, dai-ippen: Tochi, jinkō, sonota. [Statistical reports of Tōkyō Prefecture. Vol. I. Land, population, etc.] Tōkyō, 1936. Published in 1938.
Detailed local area data are presented for Tokyo Prefecture. The 1936 volume includes the following data: Area and 1930 and 1935 census populations of cities, towns, and villages; estimated 1937 populations for minor civil divisions; 1935 census population by single years of age and marital status; many detailed tabulations of 1930 census data on population, households, occupations, place of birth, etc., aliens by nationality and sex, 1927-1936; Koreans and Formosans by sex, 1927-1936; vital statistics, 1927-1936.
Vol. II was devoted to education, Vol. III to industry.
An English summary was issued from 1908 to 1929 as: *Annual statistics of the City of Tokyo.* A new series was initiated with Vol. I, 1928, published in 1930, under the title: *Statistical abstract for Tokyo.*

Tōkyō-shi.
Tōkyō-shi shisei chōsa gaisū hyō Meiji 41-nen. [Tōkyō municipal census tables, 1908.] Tōkyō, 1909. 149, 16 pp.

Tōkyō shiyakusho. Rinji kokusei chōsa-bu.
Kokusei chōsa futai chōsa tōkeisho, Shōwa jū'nen. [Census special survey, Tōkyō City, 1935.] Tōkyō, 1938. Charts, 907 pp.
With questions on date and place of birth and date of last movement into Tokyo, the tabulations including migrant status by age and age at migration and movements between *ku.*
Kokusei chōsa futai chōsa ku hen, kyūshi bu, Shōwa jū'nen. [Census special survey, *ku* volume, old city section, 1935.] 15 vols.
Ibid. Shin shi-bu. [New city section.] 20 vols.

Tōkyō shiyakusho.
Tōkyō-shi chūkan idō jinkō. [Tokyo city daytime population movement.] Tōkyō, 1933. 173 pp.
Tōkyō-shi kazoku tōkei, Shōwa ku'nen chōsa. [Family statistics of Tokyo, 1934 survey.] 1935. 8, 370 pp.
Tōkyō-shi naishoku chōsa, Shōwa jū'nen. [Family-industry survey in Tokyo, 1935.] 1936. 105 pp.
Tōkyō-shi nōzei jinkō chōsa, shotokuzei hen, Shōwa jū'nen. [Tokyo city tax-paying population survey. Income tax volume, 1935.] Tōkyō, 1939. 67 pp.

Tōkyō-to.
Dai-6-kai Tōkyō-to tōkei nenkan, Shōwa 29-nen. [The 6th Tokyo statistical yearbook, 1954.] Tōkyō, 1956. 107 pp.

Periodicals

Tachi, Minoru, *et al.*
"Demographic aspects of Tokyo. Summary." [In Japanese.] In: *Associations of Geography, Anthropology, Ethnology, Sociology, Philology, Archeology, Folklore, Science of Religion and Psychology of Japan, Associated Meeting.* Tokyo, 1950.

Takagi, Naobumi.
"Tōkyō-to shōrai jinkō no suitei." [Estimate of the future population of Tōkyō-to.] Pp. 91-96 in: Nihon. Jinkō mondai kenkyūjo. *Chōsa kenkyū shuyō kekka.* Tōkyō, 1951. 134 pp.

Toyoura, Senkichi.
"Tōkyō-shi ni okeru jinkō kōshin no ryō to shitsu." [Quantity and quality of Tokyo population renewal.] *Shakai seisaku jihō,* (223):48-65; (224):69-82; (225):41-64. April, May, and June 1939.

Other

Books

Kyōto-shi. Eisei-kyoku.
Kyōto-shi eisei tōkei nempō. [Public health statistical yearbook of Kyoto.] Kyōto, 1951. 150 pp.

Ōsaka-fu.
Statistical abstract for Osaka, 1917-1935. Osaka, 1919-1937.

Yokohama-fu.
Summary of the Yokohama city annual statistics, 1905-1920. Yokohama.

SOURCES, OTHER

Books

Hasencliver, Christa.
"Bibliographie zur Industrialisierung Japans. Aus dem Institut für Weltwirtschaft." *Weltwirtschaftliches Archiv,* 46(1):332-366. July 1937.

Japanese National Commission for Unesco, and Unesco Committee of Science Council of Japan.
Literature on population problems in Japan, 1945-1951. Tokyo, October 1952. 67, 20 pp.

Kerner, Robert J.
Northeastern Asia: A selected bibliography. Contributions to the bibliography of the relations of China, Russia, and Japan, with special reference to Korea, Manchuria, Mongolia, and Eastern Siberia, in Oriental and European languages. Berkeley, Calif., University of California Press, 1939. Vol. I, 675 pp.; Vol. II, 621 pp.

Nachod, Oskar.
Bibliographie von Japan, 1906-1926—1938-1943, enthaltend ein ausführliches Verzeichnis der Bücher und Aufsätze über Japan, die seit der Ausgabe des zweiten Bandes des Wenckstern "Bibliography of the Japanese Empire" . . . in europäischen Sprachen erschienen sind. Leipzig, K. W. Hiersemann, 1928-1944. 7 vols.

Bd. 1 and 2, to 1927. Bd. 3, 1927-1929. Bd. 4, 1930-1932. Bd. 5, 1933-1935, by H. Praesent and W. Haenisch. Bd. 6, 1936-1937, by W. Haenisch and H. Praesent. Bd. 7, 1938-1943. Part I, *Deutschsprachige Literatur,* by H. Praesent.

Nihon. Kōsei-shō, jinkō mondai kenkyūjo. Welfare Ministry. Institute of Population Problems.
Manual of the Institute of Population Problems. Tokyo, 1950. 22, 28 pp. [In Japanese and English.]

History and organization of the Institute; subjects of research and study during 1950; works undertaken since 1946; main publications.

Nihon. Naikaku insatsu-kyoku.
Kanchō kankō tosho mokuroku. [Bibliography of government publications.] Tōkyō, 1927-1937.

Continued as *Kanchō kankō tosho geppō.* [Government Publications Monthly.]

Nihon. Naikaku tōkei-kyoku.
Tōkei shiryō kaidai. [Bibliography of statistical materials.] Tōkyō, Zenkoku keizai chōsa kikan rengō kai, 193—.

An annotated bibliography of statistical publications, primarily those of the national government, but including local statistics of extraordinary value and the important statistical publications of such private institutions as banks, industrial societies, and schools.

There is a cross-referenced index of subjects and an alphabetical index of titles. [Based on issue for 1936.]

Periodical statistical publications in Japan. Tokyo, 1930. 32 pp.

Nihon. Sōri-fu, tōkei-kyoku, toshokan.
Hōbun jinkō kankei bunken narabi shiryō kaidai. [Bibliography on materials and literature on population in the Japanese language.] Tōkyō, 1951. 244, 163 pp.

Appendix: "Jinkō kankei ronbun mokuroku." [Listing of articles on population.]

Zōsho mokuroku, Washo no bu. Shōwa 29-nen. [Library catalogue. Section on Japanese. 1954.] Tōkyō, 1955. vii, 568 pp.

Nihon jinkō gakkai. The Population Association of Japan.
Nihon jinkō gakkai kiyō. Archives of the Population Association of Japan. Tokyo, 1952.

Nihon u'nesuko kokunai iinkai. [National committee of Japan UNESCO.]
Nihon ni okeru jinkō mondai kenkyū no tembō. [Prospects of population problem research in Japan.] Vol. I. *Jinkō riron.* [Population theory.] Tōkyō, 1955. 49 pp.

Pritchard, Earl H.
Far Eastern bibliography: 1936-1940. Washington, D.C., American Council of Learned Societies. 5 vols.

Supplements in issues of *Far Eastern Quarterly.*

Tachi, Minoru.
"Population statistics." *Japan Science Review—Economic Sciences,* No. 3:5-10. 1956.

Taeuber, Irene B., and Beal, Edwin G., Jr.
Guide to the official demographic statistics of Japan. Part I. Japan Proper, 1868-1945. Supplement, Population Index, Vol. XII, No. 4, October 1946. 36 pp.

Wenckstern, Friedrich von.
A bibliography of the Japanese Empire: Being a classified list of all books, essays and maps in European languages relating to Dai-Nihon (Great Japan) published in Europe, America and in the East from 1859-93 A.D. Leiden, E. J. Brill, 1895 (1894). xiv, 338 pp.

Idem. Bibliography of the Japanese empire . . . Vol. II. Comprising the literature from 1894 to the middle of 1906 . . . with additions and corrections to the first volume and a Supplement to Leon Pages Bibliographie japonaise. Tokyo, Maruzen kabushiki kaisha, 1907. xvi, 486 pp.

II. IMPERIAL AND RELATED AREAS

GENERAL

Books

Nihon. Naikaku tōkei-kyoku.
Nihon teikoku tōkei nenkan. [Statistical yearbook of the Japanese Empire.] Tōkyō, 1920-1943.

Nihon. Takumu daijin.
Takumu tōkei. [Colonial statistics.] Tōkyō, Takumu daijin kambō, bunsho-ka, 1937. 242 pp.

RYŪKYŪ ISLANDS

As Okinawa Prefecture and Ōshima *gun* in Kagoshima Prefecture, the Ryūkyū Islands were included in the censuses and registration statistics of Japan prior to 1945.

CENSUSES

1940 and 1944

U.S. Army. Far East Command. Commander-in-Chief. General Headquarters.
The Ryukyu Islands. Pre-war population and employment. Census data for 1940 and 1944. (Okinawa-ken and O-shima-gun.) Tokyo, 1950. 42 pp.

1950

U.S. Military Government of the Ryukyu Islands. Headquarters. Programs and Statistics Section.
Population Census. All Ryukyus. 1 December 1950. [No place or date of publication.]
Book 100. All Ryukyus. Books 200, 200:01-200:56. Okinawa gunto. Books 300, 300:60-300:79. Amami gunto. Books 400, 400:80-400:85. Miyako gunto. Books 500, 500:90-500:93. Yaeyama gunto. Book 600. Northern Okinawa. Book 700. Southern Okinawa.

U.S. Civil Administration of the Ryukyu Islands. Headquarters. Programs and Statistics Section.
Ryukyu Island Economic Statistics. Bulletin No. 18. June-October 1952. 153 pp.
Agricultural census, pp. 97-113; population census of 1 December, 1950, pp. 119-149.

Ryūkyū seifu gyōsei shuseki tōkei-kyoku.
Ryūkyū tōkei hōkoku. 1950-nen kokusei chōsa tokushu gō. [Monthly statistics of the Ryūkyū Islands. Special edition on the 1950 national census.] Vol. II, No. 5. Naha, 1952. 132 pp.

1954

Nihon. Sōri-fu, tōkei-kyoku.
Amami-guntō jinkō chōsa kekka hōkoku. Report on the population census of the Amami Islands. Tokyo, June 1954. iii, 19, 41 pp.

REGISTRATION SYSTEM

Ryūkyū seifu, tōkei-bu.
Ryūkyū tōkei hōkoku. Monthly statistics of the Ryūkyū Islands. Tokushū: 1952-nen shi, chō, son-sei yōran. [Special edition: Essential outline of *shi, chō,* and *son* for 1952.] Naha, 1953. 186 pp.

OTHER STATISTICS

Okinawa Asahi shimbun-sha.
Okinawa taikan. [Okinawa today.] Tōkyō, Nippon tsushin-sha, 1953. 799 pp.

Okinawa kōshinjo.
Rkūkyū nenkan, 1955-nen. [Ryūkyū yearbook, 1955.] Published, Kyōto; distributed, Naha, 1955. Sections separately paged.

Ryūkyū seifu, tōkei-bu.
Ryūkyū tōkei hōkoku. [Monthly statistics of the Ryukyu Islands.] Naha, 1952—.

U.S. Army Forces. Pacific. Commander-in-Chief.
Summation of United States Military Government Activities in the Ryukyu Islands. No. 1, July-November 1946. No. 12, July-August 1948.
Nos. 3-12 issued by: U.S. Army. Far East Command.

U.S. Military Government of the Ryukyu Islands. Headquarters. Programs and Statistics Section.
Ryukyu Statistical Bulletin. Vol. I, No. 1, January 1950—.

U.S. Civil Administration of the Ryukyu Islands. Programs and Statistics Section.
Economic Statistics. Bulletin No. 18, June-October 1952. 153 pp.

U.S. Civil Administration of the Ryukyu Islands.
Civil Affairs Activities in the Ryukyu Islands for the period ending June 1953. Vol. I, No. 2. 236 pp.
Issued semi-annually; last issue available, Vol. II, No. 1, for the period ending 30 June 1954. 169 pp.

U.S. Civil Administration of the Ryukyu Islands. Programs and Statistics Section.
Statistical Appendix for period ending 31 December 1952. Vol. I, No. 1. 122 pp.
Civil Affairs Statistics of the Ryukyu Islands for period ending 31 March 1953. Vol. I, No. 2. 99 pp.

OTHER

Books

Appleton, Roy E., *et al.*
Okinawa, the last battle. U.S. Army in World War II. Historical Division, Department of the Army. Washington, D.C., 1948.

Binkenstein, Rolf.
Beitraege zu einen kulturhistorischen Bibliographie der Ryuku (Okinawa)-Inseln. Berkeley, Calif., 1954. 66 pp.

Burd, William W.
Karimata, a village in the southern Ryukyus. SIRI, Report No. 3. Washington, D.C., Pacific Science Board, National Research Council, 1952. xii, 141 pp.

Glacken, Clarence J.
Studies of Okinawan village life. SIRI, Report No. 4. Washington, D.C., Pacific Science Board, National Research Council, 1953. ii, 382 pp.

Haring, Douglas G.
The island of Amama Oshima in the Northern Ryukyus. SIRI, Report No. 2. Washington, D.C., Pacific Science Board, National Research Council, 1952. xiii, 85 pp.

Iba sensei ki'nen ronbun shu hensan iin. [Committee on the compilation of essays dedicated to Dr. Iba.] Editor.

Nantō ronsō. [Collected essays on the southern islands.] Naha, Okinawa Nippō-sha, 1945. 2, 3, 457 pp.

Studies of the customs and dialects, including the following: Yanagida, Kunio. "Gyokuigen no mondai." [The problem of *Gyokuigen.*] Pp. 1-22. Nobori, Shomu. "Amami Ōshima no sairei to noro no seiryoku." [The festivals of Amami Islands and the role of the priestesses.] Pp. 80-94.

Inamine, Ichiro. President, Ryukyus Overseas Association. *The economy and population of the Ryukyu Islands.* Naha, 1953. 59 pp.

Kerr, George H.
Ryukyu: Kingdom and Province before 1945. SIRI Report. Washington, D.C., Pacific Science Board, National Research Council, 1953. iii, 240 pp.

Smith, Allan H.
Final field report on anthropological research in Yaeyama. SIRI Report. Washington, D.C., Pacific Science Board, National Research Council. 1952. 40 pp.

Tigner, James L.
The Okinawans in Latin America. (Investigation of Okinawan communities in Latin America with exploration of settlement possibilities.) SIRI Report No. 7. Washington, D.C., Pacific Science Board, National Research Council, 1954. xx, 656 pp.

Torigoe, Kenzaburō.
Ryūkyū kodai shakai no kenkyū. [Study of the ancient society of Ryūkyū.] Tōkyō, Mikasa shobō, 1944. 216 pp.

Torigoe, Kenzaburō, Editor.
Ryūkyū sono go. [Ryūkyū thereafter.] Asahi shashin bukku [Asahi pictorial book], No. 15. Tōkyō, Asahi shimbun-sha, 1955. 64 pp.

U.S. Army. Civil Affairs and Military Government.
Ryukyu Islands. Signed, Colonel King and Mr. Hauge. Washington, D.C., 1954.

U.S. Navy Department. Office of the Chief of Naval Operations.
Civil Affairs Handbook. Ryukyu (Loochoo) Islands. OPNAV 13-31. Washington, D.C., 1944. xiv, 334 pp.

Periodicals

Bennett, Henry S.
"The impact of invasion and occupation on the civilians of Okinawa." *U.S. Naval Institute Proceedings,* 72:263-275. February 1946.

Bickenstein, Rolf.
"Okinawa Studien." *Monumenta nipponica,* 3:554-566. 1940.

Chamberlain, Basil Hall.
"The Luchu islands and their inhabitants." *Geographical Journal,* 5:289-319, 446-462, 534-545. 1895.

Newman, Marshall T., and Eng, Ransom L.
"The Ryukyu people: A biological appraisal." *American Journal of Physical Anthropology,* 5(2):113-158. 1947.
"The Ryukyu people: A cultural appraisal." Pp. 379-405 in: Smithsonian Institution. *Annual report, 1947.* Washington, D.C., 1948.

Nihon minzokugaku kyōkai, Editor.
Okinawa kenkyū, tokushū. [A survey of Ryūkyūan research. Special number.] *Minzokugaku kenkyū,* 15(2):67-239. 1950.

The following articles were included, all in Japanese:
Ishida, Eiichirō. Ryūkyūan studies: Achievements and problems.
Kinjō, Chōei. A history of Ryūkyūan studies.
Suda, Akiyoshi. The physical anthropology of the Ryūkyūans.
Yawata, Ichirō. Some notes on the prehistory of the Ryūkyū Islands.
Higa, Shunchō. Structure of the Ryūkyūan rural community.
Bibliography of Ryūkyū, pp. 121-135.

Segawa, Kiyoko.
"Okinawa no kon'in." [Marriage in Okinawa.] *Minzokugaku kenkyū,* 13(3):285-296. 1948.

Spencer, Robert S.
"The Noro priestesses of Loochoo." *Transactions of the Asiatic Society of Japan,* 2nd Series, Vol. VIII, pp. 94-112. December 1931.

Steiner, Paul E.
"Okinawa and its people." *Scientific Monthly,* 64(3):233-241; (4):306-312. March and April 1947.

HOKKAIDŌ AND KARAFUTO

CENSUSES

Hokkaidō was a prefecture of Japan and so included in the censuses and other official statistics of the home country. Karafuto was a part of the Empire and so subject to special enumeration in the period from 1920 through 1940. It was included in the census of Japan for 1944 as a prefecture. After the war it was occupied by the U.S.S.R.

1920

Karafuto-chō.
Taishō ku'nen jūgatsu ichijitsu genzai, dai-ikkai kokusei chōsa yōran hyō. [The first census, October 1, 1920. Summary tables.] Toyohara, 1922. 41 pp., tables; 20 pp., description.
Taishō ku'nen jūgatsu ichijitsu genzai, dai-ikkai kokusei chōsa kekka hyō. [The first census, October 1, 1920. Result tables.] Toyohara, 1922. 889 pp.

1925

Karafuto-chō.
Taishō jūyo'nen jūgatsu ichijitsu genzai, Taishō jūyo'nen kokusei chōsa kekka hōkoku. [The report of the results of the census of 1925, as of October 1, 1925.] Toyohara, 1927. 215 pp.

1930

Karafuto-chō.
Kokusei chōsa yōran, Shōwa go'nen. [Census of 1930. Summary of results.] Toyohara, 1932. 88 pp.
Kokusei chōsa kekka hyō, Shōwa go'nen. [Census of 1930. Result tables.] Tōkyō, 1934. 925, 8 pp.

The tables for Karafuto are similar to those of the general volume of the 1930 census for Japan. For the Japanese there are detailed data on immigration by date of first and last arrival, occupation and industry, and on present residence and place of birth by *honseki.* Tabulations for natives include detailed distributions by ethnic groups.

Kokusei chōsa hōkoku. Fu, zuhyō, Shōwa go'nen. [Census of 1930. Reports. Appendix: Charts.] Toyohara, 1934. 34 charts, 59 pp.

1935

Karafuto-chō.
Kokusei chōsa kekka hōkoku, Shōwa jū'nen. [Census of 1935. Reports.] Toyohara, 1937. 497 pp.

1939

Karafuto-chō.
Rinji kokusei chōsa kekka hyō, Shōwa jūyo'nen. [Results of the special census, 1939.] Toyohara, 1941. 437 pp.
Census of distribution.

OTHER STATISTICS

Hokkaidō. Sōmu-bu, tōkei-ka.
Shōwa 26-nen Hokkaidō jōjū jinkō chōsa hōkoku, sono 1. Shotai oyobi jinkō. [Report on the constant population of Hokkaidō, 1951. I. Households and population.] Sapporo, 1952. 13 pp.

Hokkaidō takushoku ginkō, chōsa-ka.
Hokkaidō oyobi Karafuto keizai tōkei yōran. [Economic statistical summary of Hokkaidō and Karafuto.] Available: 1931, 1936, and 1938.
Detailed tabulations of immigration and immigrant population were included for Karafuto.

Karafuto-chō.
Karafuto-chō, tōkeisho. [Statistical yearbook of Karafuto.] Available: 1925, 1926, and 1928.

Otaru shimbun keiei kabushiki kaisha. [Otaru News Management Company.]
Hokkaidō Karafuto nenkan. [Hokkaidō and Karafuto yearbook.] Otaru, 1940. 606 pp.
Annual estimates of population in Hokkaidō and Karafuto, with data on immigrant households and population and number of workers in Hokkaidō.

OTHER

Books

Berg, Lev Semenovich.
Natural regions of the U.S.S.R. New York, The Macmillan Co., 1950. xxxi, 436 pp.
Ch. XVIII, "Sakhalin."

Chamberlain, Basil Hall.
The language, mythology, and geographical nomenclature of Japan viewed in the light of Aino studies. . . . Including "An Ainu Grammar," by John Batchelor . . . and a catalogue of books relating to Yezo and the Ainos. Tokyo, Imperial University, 1887. 174 pp.

Harrison, John A.
Japan's northern frontier: A preliminary study in colonization and expansion, with special reference to the relations of Japan and Russia. Gainesville, Fla., University of Florida Press, 1953. xii, 202 pp.

Hokkaidō sōgō kaihatsu iinkai, jimu-kyoku.
Hokkaidō no jinkō mondai—jinkō shūyōryoku ni kansuru chōsa. [Population problem of Hokkaidō—survey on population absorption.] Hokkaidō, 1952. 122 pp.

Nihon. Gaimu-shō. Ministry of Foreign Affairs.
Ueber die landwirtschaftlichen Verhaeltnisse Japan's und die Kolonisation Hokkaidos. . . . Tokyo, 1887. 89 pp.
Pp. 67-89: Fesca, Max. "Die Kolonisation Hokkaido's. Amtlicher Bericht."

Nihon. Office of Commissioner and Adviser of the Kaitakushi.
Reports and official letters to the Kaitakushi by Horace Capron, Commissioner and Adviser, and his foreign assistants. Tokyo, 1875. iii, 748 pp.

Schwind, Martin.
Die Gestaltung Karafutos zum japanischen Raum. Petermanns geographische Mitteilungen, Erganzungsheft Nr. 239. Gotha, J. Perthes, 1942. 230 pp.

U.S. Navy. Pacific Fleet and Pacific Ocean Areas.
Kurile Islands. CINCPAC-CINCPOA, Information Bulletin No. 60-45. April 1, 1945. 76 pp.

Periodicals

Cutshall, Alden.
"Urban settlement in Hokkaido." *Economic Geography,* 25(1):17-22. January 1949.

Erckert, F. C. von.
"Die wirtschaftlichen Verhältnisse des Hokkaido." *Mittheilungen der Deutschen Gesselschaft für Natur- und Völkerkunde Ostasiens,* 10(1):17-74. 1904.

Friis, H. R.
"Pioneer economy of Sakhalin Island." *Economic Geography,* 15(1):55-79. January 1939.

Harrison, John A.
"The Capron mission and the colonization of Hokkaido, 1868-1875." *Agricultural History,* 25(3):135-142. July 1951.

Scheinpflug, Alfons.
"Die japanische kolonisation in Hokkaido." *Mitteilungen der Gesellschaft für Erdkunde zu Leipzig,* 53:5-132. 1935.

Taeuber, Irene B.
"Hokkaido and Karafuto: Japan's internal frontier." *Population Index,* 12(1):6-13. January 1946.

Takagi, Naobumi.
"Hokkaidō shōrai jinkō no suikei." [Projection of the population of Hokkaidō.] Pp. 95-192 in: Nihon. Kōsei-shō, jinkō mondai kenkyūjo. *Chōsa kenkyū shuyō kekka* [Major results of research], 1952. Tōkyō, 1953. 384 pp.

Uyehara, T.
"Hokkaidō no jinkō to ijūsha." [Population and settlers of Hokkaidō.] *J.m.,* 4(1):22-30. August 1941.

Vries, Maertens G.
"Korte beschrijvinghe van het eylandt by de Iapanders Eso genaent . . . 500 als het eerst inden jare 1643, van't schip castricom bezeylt ende ondervonden is." Pp. 95-104 in: Brouwer, Hendrik. *Journael . . . van de reyse gedaen by oosten de straet le Maire.* Amsterdam, 1646.

Yoshida, Hideo.
"Jakkan no shoki Hokkaidō takushoku ron." [Some theories on developing Hokkaidō in her early stage.] *J.m.,* 4(1):104-112. August 1941.
"Kampō to Hokkaidō takushoku." [The *Kampō* and colonization of Hokkaidō.] *J.m.,* 5(1):132-147. September 1942.

Yoshida, Tōgo.
"Genroku-chū Matsumae han no Karafuto ni okeru hanto." [Karafuto under Prince Matsumae, 1688-1703.] *Chigaku zasshi,* 17(200):538-550; 17(201):638-646. August and September 1905.

TAIWAN

CENSUSES

1905

Taiwan. Rinji Taiwan kokō chōsa-bu.

I. *Rinji Taiwan kokō chōsa yōkei hyō, Meiji 38-nen, gaishōsha betsu jinkō oyobi kokō tō.* [Taiwan. Important statistical tables of the special household and population survey, 1905. Residence, household and population, towns and aboriginal areas.] Taihoku, 1907. 331 pp.

II. *Rinji Taiwan kokō chōsa shūkei gempyō, zentō no bu, Meiji 38-nen.* [Taiwan. Special household and population survey, 1905. Schedules. Island volume.] 1907. 1361 pp.

III. *Rinji Taiwan kokō chōsa shūkei gempyō, chihō no bu, Meiji 38-nen.* [Taiwan. Special household and population survey, 1905. Schedules. Provincial volume.] 1907. 1481 pp.

IV. *Rinji Taiwan kokō chōsa kekka hyō, Meiji 38-nen.* [Taiwan. Results of special household and population survey, 1905.] 1908. 467 pp.

V, VI, and VII. *Rinji Taiwan kokō chōsa kijutsu hōbun, Meiji 38-nen.* [Taiwan. Special household and population survey, 1905. Descriptive volume, Japanese language.] 1908. 558, 4 pp.

Issued in Japanese, English, and Chinese.

VIII. *Rinji Taiwan kokō chōsa shokugyōmei jii, Meiji 38-nen.* [Taiwan. Dictionary of titles of occupations used for special household and population survey, 1905.] 1907. 150 pp.

IX. *Rinji Taiwan kokō chōsa temmatsu.* [Not seen.]

Japan. Provisional Bureau of Census Investigation in Formosa. *The special population census of Formosa, 1905. Report of the Committee of the Formosan Special Census Investigation.* Tokyo, Imperial Printing Bureau, 1909. v, figures, 210 pp.

1915

Taiwan. Sōtoku kambō rinji kokō chōsa-bu.

I. *Dai-niji rinji Taiwan kokō chōsa kekka hyō, Taishō yo'nen.* [The second temporary household and population survey in Taiwan, 1915. Tabular results.] Taihoku, 1918. 537 pp.

II. *Dai-niji rinji Taiwan kokō chōsa kijutsu hōbun, Taishō yo'nen.* [The second temporary household and population survey in Taiwan, 1915. Descriptive volume.] 1917. 439 pp.; tables; 565 pp.

III. *Dai-niji rinji Taiwan kokō chōsa shukei gempyō, zentō no bu, Taishō yo'nen.* [The second temporary household and population survey in Taiwan, 1915. Original worksheets. Volume on whole island.] 1917. 1503 pp.

IV. *Dai-niji rinji Taiwan kokō chōsa shukei gempyō, chihō no bu, Taishō yo'nen.* [The second temporary household and population survey in Taiwan, 1915. Original worksheets. Provincial volume.] 1917. 1479 pp.

V. *Dai-niji rinji Taiwan kokō chōsa shokugyōmei jii, Taishō yo'nen.* [Taiwan. Dictionary of titles of occupations used for special household and population survey, 1915.] 1917. 153 pp.

VI. *Dai-niji rinji Taiwan kokō chōsa temmatsu, Taishō yo'nen.* [The second temporary population and household survey in Taiwan, 1915. Report on procedures.] 1918. 368 pp.

1920

Taiwan. Sōtoku kambō, rinji kokusei chōsa-bu.

I. *Dai-ikkai Taiwan kokusei chōsa, dai-sanji rinji Taiwan kokō chōsa, jūkyo shotai oyobi jinkō, Taishō ku'nen, 10-gatsu ichijitsu.* [The first census of Taiwan, the third special household and population survey, October 1, 1920. Present household and population.] Taihoku, 1921. 131 pp.

II. *Dai-ikkai Taiwan kokusei chōsa kekka gaisū.* [First census of Taiwan. Summary of results.] 1921. 66 pp.

III. *Dai-ikkai Taiwan kokusei chōsa, dai-sanji rinji Taiwan kokō chōsa, yōran hyō.* [The first census of Taiwan, the third special household and population survey. Summary of results.] 1922. 4, 19, 831, 67 pp.

IV. *Dai-ikkai Taiwan kokusei chōsa, dai-sanji rinji Taiwan kokō chōsa. Kijutsu hōbun, fu kekka hyō.* [The first census of Taiwan, the third special household and population survey, 1920. Descriptive volume, with tabular section.] 1924. 487, 475 pp.

V. *Dai-ikkai Taiwan kokusei chōsa, dai-sanji rinji Taiwan kokō chōsa, shukei gempyō, zentō no bu, Taishō ku'nen.* [The first census of Taiwan, the third special household and population survey, original work-sheet. Volume on entire island. 1920.] 1923.

VI. *Dai-ikkai Taiwan kokusei chōsa, dai-sanji rinji Taiwan kokō chōsa, shukei gempyō, shū chō no bu, Taishō ku'nen jūgatsu tōka.* [The first census of Taiwan, the third temporary household and population survey. Original tabulation tables. Provincial volume, October 10, 1920.] 1924. 971 pp.

VII. *Dai-ikkai Taiwan kokusei chōsa, Taishō ku'nen jūgatsu ichijitsu. Dai-sanji rinji Taiwan kokō chōsa, shokugyōmei jii.* [The first census of Taiwan, October 1, 1920, the third temporary household and population survey. Dictionary of titles of occupations. . . .] 1922. 204 pp.

1925

Taiwan. Sōtoku kambō, rinji kokusei chōsa-bu.

Kokusei chōsa kekka gaisū, Taishō jūyo'nen. [Census of 1925. Summary of results.] Taihoku, 1926. 68 pp.

Kokusei chōsa kekka hyō, Taishō jūyo'nen. [Census of 1925. Results.] 1927. 4 charts, 1175 pp.

1930

Taiwan. Sōtoku kambō, rinji kokusei chōsa-bu.

I. *Kokusei chōsa kekka gaisū, Shōwa go'nen.* [Census of 1930. Summary of results.] Taihoku, 1931. 80 pp.

II. *Kokusei chōsa kekka chūkan-hō, Taihoku-shū, Kaizan-gun, Shōwa go'nen.* [Census of 1930. Intermediate reports. Taihoku province, Kaizan *gun*.] 1932. 36, 10 pp.

Separate reports were issued for each *shū* and *gun*.

III. *Kokusei chōsa kekka hyō, zentō hen, Shōwa go'nen.* [Results of the 1930 census. All-island volume.] 1934. 528, 15 pp.

IV. *Shōwa go'nen kokusei chōsa kekka hyō, shū chō hen. Taichū-shū.* [Tabular results of the 1930 census. Provincial volumes. Taichu province.] Taihoku, 1933. 235, 10 pp.

A special volume with tabulations comparable to those for the Island as given in Vol. I was issued for each province.

1935

Taiwan, Sōtoku kambō, rinji kokusei chōsa-bu.

I. *Kokusei chōsa kekka gaihō, Taiwan, Shōwa jū'nen.*

[Census of 1935. Summary report.] Taihoku, 1935. 156 pp. II. *Kokusei chōsa kekka hyō, Shōwa jū'nen.* [Census of 1935. Tables.] 1937. 767 pp.

1939

Taiwan. Sōtoku-fu.

Rinji kokusei chōsa kekka hyō, Shōwa jūyo'nen. [Special census of 1939. Results.] Vol. I, 7 parts. Vol. II, 2 parts. Vol. III. Taihoku, 1942[?].

Vol. I of this special census of distribution includes six detailed tables, first for Taiwan, then for each province. There are tabulations of number of employees by sex and age, employment status, and education. Vol. II gives data on volume of sales, while Vol. III is an inquiry into inventories.

1940

Taiwan. Sōtoku kambō, bunsho-ka.

"Shōwa jūgo'nen kokusei chōsa shotai oyobi jinkō." [Census of households and population, 1940.] *Fuhō*, No. 4170, pp. 130-131. April 22, 1941.

Numbers by sex and nationality, provinces and cities.

"Shōwa jūgo'nen kokusei chōsa shikō rei." [Census enforcement ordinance, 1940.] *Fuhō*, No. 3915, pp. 56-57. June 17, 1940.

Succeeding pages, 57 to 90, include the rules for enforcement, the specifications of skills in accordance with census enforcement ordinances, and the rules for writing reports.

China. Taiwan. Provincial Government. Bureau of Accounting and Statistics.

Results of the seventh population census of Taiwan, 1940, including appendix with partial results of special households surveys of 1944 and 1945. Bilingual with Chinese. Taipei, 1953. xi, 190 pp.

REGISTRATION AND VITAL STATISTICS

Taiwan. Sōtoku kambō, tōkei-ka.

Taiwan genjō jinkō tōkei. . . . [Present population statistics of Taiwan, 1905-1933.] Taihoku, 1918-1936.

Taiwan jōjū kokō tōkei. . . . [Present population and household statistics of Taiwan, 1934-1940.] Taihoku, 1935-1941.

Earlier volumes included population and its changes by provinces, villages, and cities; population of the present year based on the population of the previous year, changes being divided into births and in-movements, deaths and out-movements, and given separately by sex. The volume for 1919 and those for 1934 and later years gave populations and households for provinces, cities, districts, towns, and villages; population by place of registration and nationality; and the population of aboriginal areas.

Taiwan. Sōtoku kambō, tōkei-ka.

Taiwan jinkō dōtai tōkei. . . . [Vital statistics of Taiwan, 1906-1942.] Taihoku, 1906-1943.

Taiwan jinkō dōtai tōkei kijutsu hen. . . . [Vital statistics of Taiwan. Descriptive volume.] 1909-1942. Taihoku, 1910-1943.

LIFE TABLES

Taiwan. Sōtoku kambō, chōsa-ka.

Taiwan jumin no seimei hyō, dai-ikkai. [Life tables for the residents of Taiwan, No. 1.] Taihoku, 1936.

A life table was computed but not published in 1930, using the data for the eight years from the end of 1920 to the end of 1928. These first official life tables cover the period 1926-1930; separate tables are presented for Taiwanese and Japanese in Taiwan.

China. Taiwan. Provincial Government. Department of Statistics.

Life tables of Taiwan (second issue), 1936-1940. [Bilingual.] Taipeh, 1947. x, 176 pp.

Taiwanese population only.

OTHER STATISTICS

Taiwan. Sōtoku-fu.

Taiwan jijō. [Taiwan annual.] Taihoku, Vol. I—, 1916—.

Taiwan. Sōtoku kambō, bunsho-ka.

Fuhō. [Official Gazette.] Taihoku.

Current population statistics are included. See: "Kokō tōkei" [Population statistics], no. 3992, pp. 44-45. September 15, 1940.

Taiwan. Sōtoku kambō, chōsa-ka.

Taiwan sōtoku-fu tōkeisho. [Statistical yearbook of Taiwan, 1898—.] Taihoku, 1898—.

Books

Barclay, George W.

Colonial development and population in Taiwan. Princeton, N.J., Princeton University Press, 1954. xviii, 274 pp.

Campbell, Rev. William.

Formosa under the Dutch. Described from contemporary records. . . . London, Kegan Paul, Trench, Trübner and Co., Ltd., 1903. xiv, 629 pp.

Davidson, James W.

The island of Formosa. Yokohama, Kenny and Walsh, 1903.

Grajdanzev, Andrew J.

Formosa today: An analysis of the economic development and strategic importance of Japan's tropical colony. New York, International Secretariat, Institute of Pacific Relations, 1942. v, 193 pp.

Malthus, T. R.

An essay on the principle of population. . . . A new edition, very much enlarged. London, Printed for J. Johnson, in St. Paul's Church-Yard, 1903. viii, 610 pp.

Formosa, pp. 60-61.

Pickering, W. A.

Pioneering in Formosa: Recollections of adventures among mandarins, wreckers and head-hunting savages. London, Hurst and Blackett, Ltd., 1898. xvi, 283 pp.

Taiwan. Sōtoku-fu.

The progress of Taiwan (Formosa) for ten years, 1895-1904. Taihoku, 1905. v, 79 pp.

A record of Taiwan's progress, 1936-1937. Tōkyō, Kokusai Nihon kyōkai, 1938 [?].

Taiwan, a unique colonial record, 1937-38. Tōkyō, Kokusai Nihon kyōkai, 1939. vii, 350, 6 pp.

Report on the control of the aborigines in Formosa. Bureau of Aboriginal Affairs, Taihoku. Tokyo, Tōyō Printing Co., 1911. 45 pp.

Taiwan jihō. [Current review of Taiwan.] Taihoku, Taiwan jihō hakkōsho, 1919—.

A general review of Taiwan.

Takekoshi, Yosaburo.
Japanese rule in Formosa. With preface by Baron Shimpei Goto, Chief, Civil Administration of Formosa. New York, Longman's, Green and Co., 1907. xv, 342 pp.

Tang, Chi-yu.
Studies of land settlement in successive dynasties. [In Chinese.] Shanghai, Tseng Chung Book Co., 1945. 2 vols.

U.S. Navy. Bureau of Medicine and Surgery.
Epidemiology of diseases of naval importance in Formosa. NAVMED 266. Washington, D.C., Bureau of Medicine and Surgery, Navy Department, 1944.
Health facilities, morbidity, and mortality from infectious diseases.

U.S. Navy. Office of the Chief of Naval Operations. Military Government Section.
Civil Affairs handbook: OPNAV. . . . Washington, D.C., 1944.
The handbooks are "factual studies of general information pertaining to civil affairs in specific areas." The handbook for Taichu province is a publication of 235 pp. Part I, "Provincial data," includes chapters on geography and land use; population; agriculture and industry; forestry; finance, industry and trade; communications; transportation; government; etc. Part II, "Local data," gives summary descriptions and tabulations for each *gun.* There is an appendix of statistical tables.
The following handbooks were issued:
Taiwan (Formosa). 50 E-12.
Taiwan (Formosa). Economic supplement. 50 E-13.
Japanese administrative organization in Taiwan (Formosa). 50 E-14.
Taiwan (Formosa). The Pescadores Islands. 13-21.
Taiwan (Formosa). Takao Province. 13-22.
Taiwan (Formosa). Karenko and Taito Provinces. 13-24.
Taiwan (Formosa). Shinchiku Province. 13-25.
Taiwan (Formosa). Taichu Province. 13-26.
Taiwan (Formosa). Taihoku Province. 13-27.
Taiwan (Formosa). Tainan Province. 13-28.

Periodicals

Dooman, Eugene H.; Borton, Hugh; and Coville, Cabot.
"Formosa." *U.S. Department of State Bulletin,* 12(310): 1018-1030. June 3, 1945.

Kerr, George H.
"Formosa: Island frontier." *Far Eastern Survey,* 14(7): 80-85. April 11, 1945.

Kirk, William.
"Social change in Formosa." *Sociology and Social Research,* 26(1):10-26. September-October 1941.

Ri, Togaku.
"Taiwan zaijū naichijin no shibō ritsu oyobi shibō gen'in no tōkeiteki kansatsu." [Statistical observations on the mortality rates and the causes of death among the Japanese population in Taiwan.] Parts 1 and 2. *Taiwan igakkai zasshi,* 37:1042-1075. 1938.

Sōda, C.
"Taiwan hontōjin no shōrai jinkō ni tsuite." [On the future population of the main islands of Taiwan.] Pp. 25-30 in: Nihon. Jinkō mondai kenkyū-kai. *Jinkō seisaku to kokudo keikaku.* Tōkyō, 1942.

Sung-ken, Quo.
"The population growth of Formosa." *Human Biology,* 22(4):293-301. December 1950.

Taeuber, Irene B.
"Colonial demography: Formosa." *Population Index,* 10(3):147-157. July 1944.

NANYŌ-GUNTŌ

CENSUSES

1920

Rinji Nanyō-guntō bōbitai.
Nanyō-guntō, tōsei chōsa hōkoku. [Report on Nanyō-guntō, 1920.] 1922. Tables, 13, 19, 83 pp. Text, 20 pp.

1925

Nanyō-guntō. Nanyō-chō.
Nanyō-guntō tōsei chōsa hōkoku, Taishō jūyo'nen. [Report on Nanyō-guntō, 1925.] 1927. 174 pp.

1930

Nanyō-guntō. Nanyō-chō.
Shōwa go'nen Nanyō-guntō tōsei chōsa sho. [Census reports of the Japanese Mandated Islands, 1930.] Palau, 1932.
I. *Sōkatsu hen.* [General volume.] 1932. 255, 4 pp.
II. *Tōmin hen.* [Islanders.] 614, 4 pp.
III. *Hōjin gaikokujin hen.* [Japanese and foreigners.] 465, 4 pp.
IV. *Temmatsu.* [The details.] 103 pp.; maps.

1935

Nanyō-guntō.
Shōwa jū'nen Nanyō-guntō tōsei chōsa sho, dai-ikkan, tōkei hyō. [Census reports of the Japanese Mandated Islands, 1935. Vol. I. Statistical tables.] Tōkyō, 1937. 731 pp.
Vol. II, presumably the administrative report, was not located.

1939

Nanyō-guntō. Nanyō-chō.
Nanyō-guntō rinji tōsei chōsa sho, Shōwa jūyo'nen. [Reports of the special census of Nanyō-guntō, 1939.] 1940.
I. *Dai-ikkan, tōkei hyō.* [Tabular section.] 683 pp.
II. *Dai-nikan, temmatsu.* [Report on procedure.] 19 maps, 115 pp.
Census of distribution.

OTHER STATISTICS AND ADMINISTRATION

Nanyō-guntō

Nanyō-guntō. Nanyō-chō.
Nanyō-chō shisei jū'nen shi. [History of ten years of South Seas administration.] Tōkyō, 1932. 476 pp.
Nanyō-chō tōkei nenkan. [Statistical yearbook of the South Sea Islands.] Tōkyō, 1933-1939.
Available: Vols. I, IV, V, VII, and IX for 1933, 1936, 1937, 1939 public and 1939 secret.
Nanyō-guntō yōran. [Survey of the South Sea Islands.] Tōkyō, 1940. 179 pp.

League of Nations

League of Nations.
The mandates system: Origin principles, application. Mandates, 1945 VI.A.I. Geneva, 1945. 120 pp.

League of Nations. Permanent Mandates Commission.
Minutes. . . . Geneva, 1921—.
Report on the work of the . . . session of the Commission to the Council of the League of Nations. Geneva, 1924-1938.

JAPAN

Japan. South Seas Bureau.
Laws and regulations appended to the annual report on the administration of the South Sea Islands under Japanese Mandate for the year 1926. Tokyo, 1926. v, 243 pp.
Published irregularly in this form. Instructions on statistics, the "census registers," and the "rules for the demographic survey of the South Sea Islands" were included.
Annual report on public health in the South Sea Islands for the year 1930. Attached to: Japanese Government. Annual report to the League of Nations on the administration of the South Sea Islands under Japanese mandate for the year 1930. Tokyo, 1930.
Published in varying detail from year to year.
Japanese Government.
Annual report to the League of Nations on the administration of the South Sea Islands under Japanese Mandate for the year. . . . Tokyo, 1923-1938.

GERMANY

Germany. Kolonialamt.
Die deutschen Schutzgebiete in Afrika und der Sudsee 1909-10, 1910-11, 1911-12, 1912-13. *Amtliche Jahresberichte. . . .* Berlin, 1911-1914. 4 vols.
Deutsches Kolonialblatt. Amtsblatt des Reichskolonialamt. I—. Berlin, 1890-19—.
Mitteilungen aus den deutschen Schutzgebieten. Mit Benutzung amtlicher Quellen. Berlin, 1888—.
Medizinal-berichte über die deutschen Schutzgebiete . . . Karolinen-, Marshall- und Palau-Inseln und Samoa. 1903-04-1911-12. Berlin, 1905-1915.
Germany. Reichstag.
Denkschrift über die Entwickelung des Schutzgebiets von Deutsch-Neu-Guinea, einshliesslich des Inselgebiets der Karolinen, Palau und Marianen im Jahre 1899/1900—, Stenographische Berichte über die Verhandlungen des Reichstages, . . . Berlin, 1901—.
Annual reports to the Reichstag on colonial administration, development, and problems.

UNITED STATES

U.S. Navy Department.
Trust Territory of the Pacific Islands. Information on the Trust Territory of the Pacific Islands transmitted by the United States to the Secretary-General of the United Nations. . . . Washington, D.C., 1948—.
U.S. Navy Department. Office of the Chief of Naval Operations.
Civil affairs guides [Micronesian Islands]. Washington, D.C., 1944.
Agriculture in the Japanese Mandated Islands. Prepared by the Office of Foreign Agricultural Relations, U.S.D.A. OPNAV 13-17.
The fishing industry of the Japanese Mandated Islands. Prepared by the Foreign Economic Administration. OPNAV 50 E-20.
Population and economic planning during the U.S. Naval Occupation of the Marshall Islands. OPNAV 50 E-6.
The sugar industry of the Japanese Mandated Islands. OPNAV 50 E-11.
Civil affairs hand book [Micronesian Islands]. Washington, D.C., 1943-1944.
East Caroline Islands. OPNAV 50 E-5. 213 pp.
Mandated Marianas Islands. OPNAV 50 E-8. 205 pp.
Marshall Islands. OPNAV 50 E-1. 1943. 113 pp. [Designated as "Military Affairs Handbook."]
West Caroline Islands. OPNAV 50 E-7. 222 pp.
Handbook on the Trust Territory of the Pacific Islands. Prepared by the School of Naval Administration, Hoover Institute, Stanford University. Washington, D.C., 1948. viii, 311 pp.
U.S. Tariff Commission.
Japanese Mandated Islands: A survey of pertinent information. Washington, D.C., 1943.

OTHER

Books

Bascom, William R.
Economic and human resources, Ponape, Eastern Carolines. U.S. Commercial Co., 1947. (Microfilm, Library of Congress.)
Bryan, E. H., Jr.
Geographic summary of Micronesia. U.S. Commercial Co., 1946. (Microfilm, Library of Congress.)
Clyde, Paul H.
Japan's Pacific Mandate. New York, The Macmillan Co., 1935. vi, 242 pp.
Decker, John A.
Labor problems in the Pacific mandates. Shanghai, Kelly and Walsh, Ltd., 1940. xiii, 246 pp.
Finsch, Otto.
Ethnologische Erfahrungen und Belegstücke aus der Sudsee. Vienna, 1893. 437 pp.
Gallahue, E. E.
Economic and human resources: Mariana Islands. U.S. Commercial Co., 1947. (Microfilm, Library of Congress.)
Hamburgische wissenschaftliche Stiftung.
Ergebnisse der Südsee-Expedition 1908-1910. Edited by G. Thilenius. Hamburg, L. Friederichsen and Co., 1913-1938. 29 vols.
I. *Allgemeines, Plan der expedition. . . .*
II. *Ethnographie*: A. *Melanesien.* 3 vols.
II. *Ethnographie*: B. *Micronesien.*
Bd. 1. Hambruch P. *Nauru.* 1914-1915. 2 vols.
Bd. 2. Muller, W. *Yap.* 1917-1918. 2 vols.
Bd. 3. Kramer, A. F. *Palau.* 1917-1929. 6 vols.
Bd. 4. Sarfert, E. G. *Kusae.* 1919-1920. 2 vols.
Bd. 5. Kramer, A. F. *Truk.* 1932.
Bd. 6. Kramer, A. F. *Inseln um Truk.* 1935. 2 vols.
Bd. 7. Hambruch, P., and Eiler, A. *Ponape.* 1932-1936. 3 vols.
Bd. 8. Eilers, A. *Inseln um Ponape.* 1934.
Bd. 9. Eilers, A. *Westkarolinen.* 1935. 2 vols.
Bd. 10. Krämer, A., and Damm, H. *Zentralkarolinen.* 1937-1938. 2 vols.
Bd. 11. Krämer, A., and Nevermann, H. *Ralik-Ratak*, Marshall Inseln. 1938.
Bd. 12. Sarfert, E. G., and Damm, H. *Luangiua und Nukumanu.* 1929-1931. 2 vols. in 1.
Hunt, Edward E.; Kidder, Nathaniel R.; *et al.*
The Micronesians of Yap and their depopulation. Report

of the Peabody Museum (at Harvard) Expedition to Yap Island, Micronesia, 1947-1948. Washington, D.C., Pacific Science Board, National Research Council, 1949. iii, 198 pp.

Keesing, Felix M.
Education in Pacific countries. Shanghai, Kelly and Walsh, Ltd., 1937. viii, 226 pp.
The South Seas in the modern world. Revised edition. New York, The John Day Co., 1945. xxiv, 391 pp.

Krieger, Herbert W.
Island peoples of the Western Pacific: Micronesia and Melanesia. Washington, D.C., Smithsonian Institution, 1943. 104 pp.

Mason, L. E.
Economic and human resources: Marshall Islands. U.S. Commercial Co., 1947. (Microfilm, Library of Congress.)

Matsue, Haruji.
Nanyō kaitaku jū'nen shi. [History of ten years' development in the South Sea Islands.] Tōkyō, 1932. 239 pp.

Matsumura, Akira.
Contributions to the ethnography of Micronesia. Journal of the College of Science, Imperial University of Tokyo, Vol. XL, Art. 7, 1918. Tokyo, 1918. 174 pp.
A summary for the East and West Caroline groups.

Matsuoka, Shizuo.
Mikuroneshia minzoku shi. [Ethnography of Micronesia.] Tōkyō, 1927. 716 pp.

Murdock, George P.
Social organization and government in Micronesia: Final report. Coordinated Investigation of Micronesian Anthropology, 1947-1949. Washington, D.C., Pacific Science Board, National Research Council, 1949.

Oliver, Douglas, Editor.
Economic survey of Micronesia. Vol. I. *Summary of findings and recommendations*. U.S. Commercial Co., 1946. ii, 148 pp.

Pelzer, Karl J., and Hall, E. T.
Economic and human resources: Truk Islands. U.S. Commercial Co., 1947. (Microfilm, Library of Congress.)

Price, Willard.
The South Sea adventure: Through Japan's equatorial empire. Tokyo, The Hokuseido Press, 1936. xiv, 313 pp.

Shinozaki, Nobuo.
The investigation of mixed blood families of Micronesian-European or other . . . as the materials of eugenics from a viewpoint of physical anthropology. Nihon. Kōsei-shō, jinkō mondai kenkyūjo, Research Data C, No. 1. Tokyo, 1948. 19 pp.

Thompson, Laura.
Archaeology of the Marianas Islands. Bernice P. Bishop Museum, Bulletin 100. Honolulu, Hawaii, 1932. 82 pp.
The native culture of the Marianas Islands. Bernice P. Bishop Museum, Bulletin 185. Honolulu, Hawaii, 1945. 48 pp.
Guam and its people: A study of cultural change and colonial education. New York, American Council, Institute of Pacific Relations, 1941.

Useem, John.
Economic and human resources, Yap and Palau, Western Carolines. 3 vols. U.S. Commercial Co., 1947. (Microfilm, Library of Congress.)

Yanaihara, Tadao.
Pacific islands under Japanese mandate. London, Oxford University Press, 1940. x, 312 pp.
An English translation and abridgement of: *Ibid. Nanyō-guntō no kenkyū*. [A study of the South Sea Islands.] Tokyo, 1935. 543 pp.

Periodicals

Coulter, J. W.
"Impact of the war on South Sea Islands." *Geographical Review*, 36(3):409-419. 1946.

Embree, John F.
"Military government in Saipan and Tinian." *Applied Anthropology*, 5(1):1-39. 1946.

Hermann, R.
"Zur Statistik der Eingeborenen der deutschen Südseegebiete." *Zeitschrift für Kolonialpolitik, Kolonialrecht und Kolonialwissenschaft*, No. 7-8. 1910.

Taeuber, Irene B., and Han, Chungnim C.
"Micronesian Islands under United States trusteeship: Demographic paradox." *Population Index*, 16(2):93-115. April 1950.

KOREA

CENSUSES

1920

No census was taken in Korea in 1920, but the temporary household and population survey usually taken as of the last of December was taken as of October 1. Japanese in Korea were included in the Empire census, however, the head of the house being responsible for the report which was collected by the police and sent to Japan. Information requested from the Japanese included name, sex, date of birth, marital status, *honseki*, and nationality.

Source: Chōsen. Sōtoku-fu. *Kan'i kokusei chōsa kekka hyō, Taishō jūyo'nen*. P. 1.

1925

Chōsen. Sōtoku-fu.
Kan'i kokusei chōsa kekka hyō, Taishō jūyo'nen. [Census result tables, 1925] Keijō, 1926. 576 pp.

Households and population by city and *men*; population by age and marital status, total, province, city, *gun*, and island; population by *honseki*, total, province, city, *gun*, island; population and household in ports.

1930

Chōsen. Sōtoku-fu.
I. *Chōsen kokusei chōsa hōkoku, Shōwa go'nen. Zensen hen, kekka hyō*. [Census reports for Korea, 1930. Section on all Korea. Table of results.] Keijō, 1934. 403, 14 pp.
II. *Chōsen kokusei chōsa hōkoku, Shōwa go'nen. Zensen hen, dai-nikan, kijutsu hōbun*. [Census reports for Korea, 1930. Section on all Korea. Vol. II, Descriptive report.] 1935. 332, 65 pp.
III. *Chōsen kokusei chōsa hōkoku, Shōwa go'nen. Dō hen*. [Census reports for Korea, 1930. Provincial volumes.] 1932-1935.

Keiki-dō [Kyonggi Do]
Chūsei-hokudō [Ch'ungch'ŏng Pukto]
Chūsei-nandō [Ch'ungch'ŏng Namdo]
Zenra-hokudō [Chŏlla Pukto]
Zenra-nandō [Chŏlla Namdo]
Keishō hokudō [Kyŏngsang Pukto]

Keishō-nandō [Kyŏngsang Namdo]
Kōkai-dō [Hwanghae Do]
Heian-nandō [P'yŏngan Namdo]
Heian-hokudō [P'yŏngan Pukto]
Kōgen-dō [Kangwŏn Do]
Kankyō-nandō [Hamgyŏng Namdo]
Kankyō-hokudō [Hamgyŏng Pukto]

1935

Chōsen. Sōtoku-fu.
Chōsen kokusei chōsa, Shōwa jū'nen. Fu yū men betsu chōjū jinkō. [Census reports for Korea, 1935. Permanent resident population by cities, towns, and villages.] Keijō, 1937. 32 pp.
I. *Chōsen kokusei chōsa hōkoku, Shōwa jū'nen. Zensen hen, kekka hyō oyobi kijutsu hōbun.* [Census reports for Korea, 1935. Section on all Korea. Result tables and descriptions.] 1939. 163, 41 pp.
II. *Chōsen kokusei chōsa hōkoku, Shōwa jū'nen, dō hen.* [Census reports for Korea, 1935. Provincial sections.] 1937-1938.
A volume for each province.

1940

Chōsen. Sōtoku-fu.
Chōsen kokusei chōsa kekka yoyaku, Shōwa jūgo'nen. [Census report for Korea, 1940. Summary.] Keijō, 1944. 255 pp.
The detailed volume for all Korea and the provincial volumes were not published.

1944

Chōsen. Sōtoku-fu.
Jinkō chōsa kekka hōkoku, Shōwa jūku'nen go-gatsu ichijitsu. [Report of population survey results, May 1, 1944. Vol. II.] Keijō, 1945. 169 pp.
Japanese and Korean populations separately by sex and single years of age for all Korea and each province for the following characteristics: occupational status; not gainfully occupied by status; educational status.

OTHER STATISTICS

Chōsen. Sōtoku-fu.
Annual report on administration of Chōsen, 1907—. Keijō, 1908—.
Compiled by His Imperial Japanese Majesty's Residency General, 1907-1908/1909; by the Government General of Chōsen, 1909/10 and later years. The title varied: 1907, *Annual report for 1907 on reforms and progress in Korea . . .* ; 1908/09-1909-10, *The second-third annual report. . .* ; 1910/11-1918/21, *Annual report on reforms and progress in Chōsen. . .* ; 1921/22 on, *Annual report on administration of Chōsen. . . .*
Chōsen sōtoku-fu hōkoku rei, Taishō go'nen, Chōsen sōtoku-fu kunrei dai-nijūgo. Taishō shichi'nen ichi-gatsu ichijitsu kaisei. [Korean Government reporting forms. Government regulations, No. 25, 1912, as revised January 1, 1918.] Keijō, 1918. Korea. 506 pp.
Similar publications issued for 1921, 1926, and 1934.
Chōsen sōtoku-fu tōkei nempō. [Statistical yearbook of the Government General of Korea.] Keijō, 1911-1942.
Chōsen no jinkō tōkei. [Population statistics of Korea.] Keijō, 1939. 49 pp.
This issue included a résumé of data, 1928-1937. The annual issues included registered population by nationality, sex, and occupations for provinces and smaller divisions; households and population in towns; vital statistics; and deaths by cause and age.
Chōsen. Sōtoku-fu, bunsho-ka.
[Vital statistics and registered population.] *Chōsa geppō*, Vol. I, July 1930—.
Vital statistics and data on registration populations compiled by the Bunsho-ka [Documents Section] were published here prior to inclusion in *Chōsen sōtoku-fu tōkei nempō.*
Manshūkoku. Kokumu-in, sōmu-chō.
[Population by age, province of. . . , census of 1940.] *Manshūkoku seifu kōhō* [Gazette of the Government of Manchoukuo]. Various issues, 1941-1942.
Koreans in Manchoukuo.
Nihon. Sōri-chō, tōkei-kyoku.
Kekka hōkoku tekiyō, Shōwa 15-nen kokusei chōsa, Shōwa 19-nen jinkō chōsa, Shōwa 20-nen jinkō chōsa, Shōwa 21-nen jinkō chōsa. [Summary of results, 1940 census and surveys of 1944, 1945, and 1946.] Tōkyō, 1949. 153 pp.
Data on Koreans in Japan.
U.S. Army Forces, Pacific. Commander-in-Chief.
Summation of United States Army Military Government activities in Korea. Nos. 15-22. December 1946-July 1947.
U.S. Military Governor, Korea (Territory under United States Occupation).
Repatriation from 25 September 1945 to 31 December 1945. Prepared by William J. Gane. Seoul, 1946. 97 pp.

OTHER

Books

Brunner, Edmund de S.
Rural Korea: A preliminary survey of economic, social and religious conditions. In: *The Christian mission in relation to rural problems.* Report of the Jerusalem meeting of the International Missionary Council, March 24-April 8, 1928. Vol. VI. London, 1928.
Chōsen kōsei kyōkai.
Chōsen ni okeru jinkō ni kansuru shotōkei. [Statistics relating to the population of Korea.] Keijō, 1943. 127 pp.
A general summary of developments during the Japanese period.
Chōsen. Sōtoku-fu.
Chōsen no jinkō genshō. [Demography of Korea.] Keijō, 1927. 482 pp.
A historical survey of population reports, with an analysis of size, composition, density, urban population, and vital statistics.
Chōsen. Sōtoku-fu. Government General.
Thriving Chosen: A survey of twenty-five years' administration. Keijo, Taishō shashin kōgeisho, 1935. 94 pp.
Illustrative of the types of materials issued in Western languages.
Ferrand, Gabriel.
Arab accounts of the geography of Korea. Arranged and translated by Shannon McCune. Korean Research Associates, Research Monographs on Korea, Series G, No. 1. Hamilton, N.Y., 1948. 7 pp.
With this is bound: Pawlowski, Auguste. *History of the geography of Korea.*
Grajdanzev, Andrew J.
Modern Korea. International Secretariat, Institute of Pacific

Relations. New York, The John Day Co., 1945. x, 330 pp.
Han, Chŏngnim Ch'oe.
Social organization of Upper Han hamlet in Korea. Ann Arbor, Mich., University Microfilms, 1949. 271 pp.
Korean American Cultural Association.
The culture of Korea: Racial background, sketch of geography, history of Korea, religion, literature, art, science, music, economic background, and history of revolutionary movement. Edited by Changsoon Kim. Honolulu, 1945. 334 pp.
See especially: Hrdlička, Aleš. "The Koreans." And: Grajdanzev, Andrew. "Korea in the postwar world."
Lautensach, Hermann.
Korea: Eine Landeskunde auf Grund eineger Reisin und der Literatur. Leipzig, Koehler, 1945. 542 pp.
Korea: Land, Volk, Schicksal. Stuttgart, Koehler, 1950. 135 pp.
Lee, Hoon K.
Land utilization and rural economy in Korea. London, Oxford University Press, 1936. xii, 302 pp.
Population, pp. 39-49. Ancient figures cited from: *Chingbo moonhuen biko* [Supplementary book of records], Vol. 161, Part 1.
McCune, George M., with Grey, Arthur L.
Korea today. Cambridge, Mass., Harvard University Press, 1950. xxi, 372 pp.
Osgood, Cornelius.
The Koreans and their culture. New York, Ronald Press Co., 1951. xvi, 387 pp.
Pauley, Edwin W.
Report on Japanese assets in Soviet-occupied Korea to the President of the United States, June 1946. Washington, D.C., Govt. Printing Office, 1946. iv, 141 pp.
U.S. Army. Office of the Provost Marshal General. Military Government Division.
Civil affairs handbook. Korea. Section 7. Agriculture. Prepared by the Office of Foreign Agricultural Relations. Washington, D.C., 1944. x, 113 pp.
U.S. Navy. Bureau of Medicine and Surgery.
Epidemiology of the diseases of naval importance in Korea. By Tsai-Yu Hsiao. NAVMED P-1289. Washington, D.C., Govt. Printing Office, 1948. ix, 89 pp.
Wagner, Edward W.
The Korean minority in Japan, 1904-1950. New York, International Secretariat, Institute of Pacific Relations, 1951. v, 108 pp.

Periodicals

Bowman, N. H.
"The history of Korean medicine." *Transactions of the Korea Branch of the Royal Asiatic Society*, 6(1):1-34. 1915.
Bunce, Arthur.
"Economic and cultural bases of family size in Korea." Pp. 18-28 in: *Milbank Memorial Fund. Approaches to problems of high fertility in agrarian societies.* New York, Milbank Memorial Fund, 1952. 171 pp.
Coulter, John W., and Kim, Bernice Bong Hee.
"Land utilization maps of Korea." *The Geographical Review*, 24:418-422. July 1934.
Harafuji, S.
"Dō betsu Chōsenjin seimei hyō." [Life table for Koreans by provinces.] *Chōsen igakkai zasshi*, 30(7-8):1-32. August 1940.
For the years 1934-1936.
Hisama, Ken'ichi.
"Chōsen nōmin no naichi ishutsu no hitsuzensei." [The necessity for the emigration of Korean farmers to Japan.] *Shakai seisaku jihō*, No. 244, pp. 113-128. January 1941.
Komatsu, Midori.
"The old people and the new government." *Transactions of the Korea Branch, Royal Asian Society*, 4(1):1-12. 1912.
Ladejinsky, Wolf.
"Chosen's agriculture and its problems." *Foreign Agriculture*, 4(2):95-122. February 1940.
McCune, Shannon.
"Physical basis for Korean boundaries." *The Far Eastern Quarterly*, 5(3):272-288. 1946.
"Regional diversity in Korea." *Korean Review*, 2(1):3-13. September 1949.
Mizushima, Haruo.
[Life table, 1939.] *Chōsa geppō*, Vol. XI, No. 6. June 1940.
Ochiai, Tokinori.
"Zai-sen naichijin no shibō tōkei ni kansuru kenkyū." [Studies on mortality statistics of Japanese in Korea.] *Chōsen igakkai zasshi*, 30(7-8):1390-1410. August 1940.
Death rates by cause and ratio of rates of Japanese in Korea to Japanese in Japan, 1933-1937.
Sai, Kiei. [Choe, Huiyong.]
"Chōsen jūmin no seimei hyō." [Korean life tables.] *Chōsen igakkai zasshi*, 29(11):2180-2220. November 1939.
Koreans and Japanese, 1925-1930 and 1930-1935.
"Chōsen ni okeru shussei ritsu oyobi shibō ritsu ni kansuru shakaigakuteki kōsatsu." [A sociological observation on the birth and death rate in Korea.] *Chōsen igakkai zasshi*, 27:101-125. February 1937.
The relations between population density, fertility, mortality, size of household, doctors per 10,000 population, etc., for 1921-1926.
Sansom, George B.
"An outline of recent archaeological research in Korea. . . ." *T.A.S.J.*, 2nd Series, 6:5-19. December 1929.
Sawamura, Tokei.
"Chōsen nōgyō no rōryoku kōsei." [The structure of agricultural labor in Korea.] *Shaikai seisaku jihō*, No. 208, pp. 114-141. January 1938.
South Manchuria Railway Co.
"Koreans in Manchuria." *Contemporary Manchuria*, 4(2): 49-69. April 1940.
Taeuber, Irene B.
"The population potential of postwar Korea." *The Far Eastern Quarterly*, 5:289-307. May 1946.
"Korea in transition: Demographic aspects." *Populatîon Index*, 10(4):229-242. October 1944.
"Korea and the Koreans in the Northeast Asian Region." With George W. Barclay. *Ibid.*, 16(4):278-297. October 1950.
Takeda, Yukio.
"Naichi zaigū hantōjin mondai." [Koreans resident in Japan.] *Shakai seisaku jihō*. No. 213, pp. 99-137. June 1938.

SOURCES

Courant, Maurice.
Bibliographie Coréenne. Tableau littéraire de la Coreé contenant le nomenclature des ouvrages publiés dans ce pays jusqu'en 1890, ainsi que la description et l'analyse détailliés des principaux d'entre ces ouvrages. Publications

de l'Ecole des langues orientales vivantes. Paris, E. Leroux, Editeur, 1895. 2 vols.

U.S. Library of Congress.

Korea: An annotated bibliography of publications in Far Eastern languages. By Edwin G. Beal, Jr., with Robin L. Winkler. Washington, D.C., 1950. 167 pp.

Also: *Korea: An annotated bibliography of publications in the Russian language.* By Albert Parry, *et al.* 1950. 84 pp.

And: *Korea: An annotated bibliography of publications in Western languages.* By Helen D. Jones and Robin L. Winkler. 1950. ix, 155 pp.

KWANTUNG AND THE S.M.R. ZONE

CENSUSES

1920

Kwantung. Kantō-chō, rinji kokō chōsa-bu.

I. 1. *Taishō ku'nen jūgatsu ichijitsu, rinji kokō chōsa, hirei hen.* [Temporary household survey as of October 1, 1920. Tabular section.] Dairen, 1924. 283 pp.

I. 2. *Taishō ku'nen jūgatsu ichijitsu, rinji kokō chōsa, kijutsu hen, fu byōgazu.* [Temporary household survey as of October 1, 1920. Descriptive section, appendix, charts.] 1924. 335, 24 pp.

I. *Taishō ku'nen, rinji kokō chōsa. Gempyō, dai-ikkan.* [Original schedules of the temporary household survey, 1920. Vol. I.] 1924. 800 pp.

II. 1. *Taishō ku'nen, rinji kokō chōsa. Gempyō, dai-nikan, jinkō no bu, sono ichi.* [Original schedules of the temporary household survey, 1920. Vol. II, Population section, Part 1.] 1924. 807 pp.

III. 2. *Taishō ku'nen, rinji kokō chōsa. Gempyō, dai-sankan, jinkō no bu, sono ni.* [Original schedules of the temporary household survey. Vol. III. Population section, Part 2.] 1924. 979 pp.

1925

Kwantung. Kanto-chō.

Taishō jūyo'nen kokusei chōsa shotai oyobi jinkō. [Census of households and population, 1925.] Dairen, 1926. 29 pp.

Kwantung. Kantō-chō, rinji kokō chōsa-bu.

Taishō jūyo'nen jūgatsu ichijitsu, Kantō-chō kokusei chōsa kijutsu hen: fu; byōgazu oyobi hirei hyō. [Census of Kwantung Province, October 1, 1925. Descriptive section, appendix; charts and tables.] Dairen, 1927. 5 charts; description, 72 pp.; regulations, 15 pp.; tables, 117 pp.

1930

Kwantung. Kantō chōkan kambō, chōsa-ka.

Shōwa go'nen, kokusei chōsa shotai oyobi jinkō. [Census of households and population, 1930.] Dairen, 1931. 17 pp.

I. *Kantō-chō kokusei chōsa kekka hyō, dai-ikkan, shotai oyobi jinkō, Shōwa go'nen.* [Kwantung. Census of 1930. Result tables. I. Households and population.] Dairen, 1933. 865 pp.

II. *Kantō-chō kokusei chōsa kekka hyō, dai-nikan, Shōwa go'nen. Jinkō, taisei, nenrei, haigū kankei, honseki, minseki, kokuseki, futsū kyōiku no yūmu, shusseichi, raiō no toshi.* [Kwantung. Census of 1930. Result tables. II. Population, sex, age, marital status, *honseki* and *minseki*, nationality, elementary education, place of birth, and year of arrival.] 1933. 371 pp.

III. 1. *Kantō-chō kokusei chōsa kekka hyō, dai-sankan, sono ichi, shokugyō, sangyō oyobi shitsugyō, Shōwa go'nen.* [Kwantung. Census of 1930. Result tables. III. 1. Occupation, industry and unemployment.] 1934. 896 pp.

III. 2. *Kantō-chō kokusei chōsa kekka hyō, dai-sankan, sono ni, shokugyō, sangyō oyobi shitsugyō, Shōwa go'nen.* [Kwantung. Census of 1930. Result table. III. 2. Occupation, industry and unemployment.] 1934. 773, 11 pp.

Kantō-chō kokusei chōsa kijutsu hen, Shōwa go'nen. [Kwantung. Census of 1930. Descriptive volume.] Dairen, 1934. 196, 19 pp., maps, graphs.

1935

Kwantung. Kantō-kyoku.

Shōwa jū'nen kokusei chōsa shotai oyobi jinkō. [Census of households and population, 1935.] Dairen, 1936. 29 pp.

Shōwa jū'nen, Kantō-kyoku kokusei chōsa kekka hyō. [Results of the census of Kwantung province, 1935.] 1939. 483 pp.

Shōwa jū'nen, Kantō-kyoku chōsa kijutsu hen. [Census of Kwantung province, 1935. Descriptive volume.] 1939. 131, 16 pp.

1939

Kwantung. Kantō-kyoku.

Shōwa jūyo'nen, rinji Kantō-shū kokusei chōsa kekka hyō. [Results of the special census of Kwantung Province, 1939.] Dairen, 1941. 465 pp.

A census of distribution, with information on numbers of employees and their characteristics, separately for Japanese and Manchurians.

1940

Kwantung. Kantō-kyoku.

"Kantō-shū kokusei chōsa kisoku, Shōwa jūgo'nen." [Regulations for the Kwantung census, 1940.] *Kanto-kyoku kyokuhō*, No. 754, pp. 37.40. July 9, 1940.

"Kantō-shū kokusei chōsa shiko saisoku, Shōwa jūgo'nen." [Detailed regulations for the Kwantung census, 1940.] *Ibid.*, No. 754, pp. 40-45. July 9, 1940.

"Kantō-shū kokusei chōsa shikō kisoku dai-sanjō daishichigō no kitei ni yoru ginōsha shitei, Shōwa jūgo'nen." [Listing of industrial skills in accordance with the provisions of Section 7, Article 3, Regulations for the Kwantung census.] *Ibid.*, No. 754, pp. 45-48. July 9, 1940.

"Kantō-shū kokusei chōsa iin kokoroe, Shōwa jūgo'nen." [Kwantung census of 1940. Rules for enumerations.] *Ibid.*, No. 785, pp. 1-12. July 20, 1940.

"Kantō-shū kokusei chōsa no kekka ni yoru jinkō oyobi shotai, Shōwa jūgo'nen." [Population and households census of 1940. Kwantung.] *Ibid.*, No. 858, Supplement, pp. 1-4. April 19, 1941.

Number of households and population by ethnic status and sex, total and major administrative divisions.

OTHER STATISTICS

Kwantung. Kantō-shū, minsei-sho.

Kantō-shū genjū kokō, dai 1-2. [Population of present residents, Kwantung Province, No. 1 and 2.] Dairen, 1906. 2 vols.

Kwantung. Kantō-kyoku.

Kantō-kyoku dai-sanjū tōkeisho, Shōwa jū'nen. [Thirtieth

statistical book of the Kwantung Bureau, 1935.] Dairen, 1936. 417 pp.
"Genjū jinkō gaiyō. Shōwa jūgo'nen gogatsu matsu." [Summary report on the resident population as of the end of May 1940.] *Kantō-kyoku kyokuhō*, No. 752, Supplement, pp. 1-2. July 6, 1940.
Kantō-kyoku kannai genzai jinkō tōkei, Shōwa ku'nen. [Statistics on the population present within the jurisdiction of the Kwantung Government, 1934.] Dairen, 1935. 85 pp.
Issued annually.
"Jinkō dōtai gaiyō." [Summary of vital statistics.] *Kantō-kyoku kyokuhō*, No. 860, *Supplement*, pp. 1-4. April 23, 1941.
Vital statistics by nationality and sex were published quarterly, with annual summations.
Jinkō dōtai tōkei. [Vital statistics.] Dairen.
Issued annually.
Minami Manshū tetsudō kabushiki kaisha, chihō-bu.
Chihō keiei tōkei nempō, Shōwa san'nendo. [Statistical yearbook of local administration, 1928.] Dairen, 1930. 336 pp.
Including population data.

OTHER

Kawahito, Sadao.
"Saikin ni okeru zai-Man Nihon naichijin shibō tōkei." [Recent mortality statistics of the Japanese in Manchuria.] *Manshū igakkai zasshi*, 19:289-333; 335-356. 1933. Also: 24:109-130. 1936.
Data refer to Kwantung and the South Manchuria Railway Zone.
Mizushima, Haruo, and Hosogami, Tsuneo.
"Manshū Kantō-kyoku kannai jūmin no seimei hyō." [Life tables for Kwantung and the South Manchuria Railway Zone.] *Chōsen igakkai zasshi*, 30(4):579-597. April 1940.
Single years, Japanese and "Manchurians," 1931-1935.

MANCHOUKUO

CENSUSES AND SURVEYS

First Provisional Survey

Manshūkoku. Kuo-wu yuan fa-chih ch'u.
Manchoukuo fa-ling chi-lan. Manshūkoku hōrei shūran. [Complete collection of laws in force in Manchoukuo.] Supplements 117, 119, 121 and 125. Hsinking, Manchou hsing-cheng hsueh-hui, 1934.
The provisional census law and the regulations for enforcement were translated by Edwin G. Beal and published as: "The 1940 census of Manchuria." *The Far Eastern Quarterly*, 4(3):243-262. May 1945.
Manshūkoku. Kokumu-in, sōmu-chō.
"Dai-ichiji rinji jinkō chōsa yōkō." [First provisional population survey ordinance.] *Seifu kōhō*, No. 477, pp. 167-168. October 14, 1935.
This same issue included the survey regulations, pp. 168-169.
"Dai-ichiji rinji jinkō chōsa ni yoru Shinkyō tokubetsu shi gai nijūshi toyū jōjū jinkō gaisu." [Permanent population of Hsinking and 24 other cities, first provisional population survey.] *Seifu kōhō*, No. 633, pp. 563-564. April 30, 1936.
Data on populations as of December 31, 1935, were given in the following issues of *Seifu kōhō* for 1936: No. 607, Harbin; No. 612, Fengtien city; No. 614, Yenkih and Tsitsihar; No. 618, Hwaiteh, Kaiyuan, Chengteh, Tiehling, and Changtu; No. 621, Kirin, Heiho, Antung, Chamussu, and Fushun; No. 624, Liuoyang, Szepingkai, Kaiping, Haicheng, Yingkow, Fengcheng, and Penhsi; No. 625, Chinhsien and Lishu.
Manshūkoku. Kokumu-in, sōmu-chō, tōkei-sho.
Dai-ichiji rinji jinkō chōsa hōkokusho, toyū hen, dai-ikkan, Shinkyō tokubetsu shi. [The first provisional population survey report. City Volume I. Hsinking Special City.] Hsinking, 1937. 275, 9 pp.
Dai-ichiji rinji jinkō chōsa hōkokusho, toyū hen, dai-sankan, Hōten-shi. [The first provisional population survey report. City Volume III. Mukden.] Hsinking, 1937. 305, 9 pp.
Dai-ichiji rinji jinkō chōsa hōkokusho, toyū hen, dai-yonkan, Kirin-shi. [The first provisional population survey report. City Volume IV. Kirin City.] Hsinking, 1937. 310 pp.
Manshūkoku. Harubin tokubetsu shi kōsho.
I. Part 1. *Harubin tokubetsu shi kokō chōsa kekka hyō, dai-ikkan, kokō.* [Harbin Special City. Results of household survey. Vol. I. Households.] Harbin, 1935. 127, 8 pp.
II. *Harubin tokubetsu shi kokō chōsa kekka hyō, dai-nikan, shokugyō.* [Harbin Special City. Results of household survey. Vol. II. Occupations.] Dairen, 1935. 305 pp.
IV. *Harubin tokubetsu shi kokō chōsa kekka hyō, dai-yonkan. Dai-yonshū, kyōiku. Dai-goshū, haigū. Dai-rokushū, nenrei. Dai-shichishū, shusseichi. Dai-hasshū, nenrei to haigū. Dai-kyūshū, nenrei to kyōiku.*
[Harbin Special City. Results of household survey. Vol. IV. Section 4, Education. Section 5, Marital status. Section 6, Age. Section 7, Place of birth. Section 8, Age and marital status. Section 9, Age and education.]

Second Provisional Survey

Manshūkoku. Kokumu-in, sōmu-chō.
"Dai-niji rinji jinkō chōsa shikkō kitei." [Regulations for conducting the second provisional population survey.] *Seifu kōhō*, No. 710, pp. 414-415. July 31, 1936.
Manshūkoku. Kokumu-in, sōmu-chō, tōkei-sho.
Dai-niji rinji jinkō chōsa hōkokusho, sōkatsu hen. [Second provisional population survey report. General volume.] Hsinking. 1073 pp.
This survey covered 53 areas. Data include population by age and ethnic group, single years, and occupation (large, medium, and small classifications) by ethnic group.

Police Surveys, 1932-1936

Manshūkoku. Kokumu-in, sōmu-chō, tōkei-shō.
Manshū teikoku genjū jinkō tōkei, Daidō 1-nen—Kōtoku 3-nen. [Manchoukuo Empire. Population statistics.] Hsinking, 1932-1936.

Police Survey, 1939

Manshūkoku. Chian-bu, keimu-shi.
Manshū teikoku genjū jinkō tōkei, Kōtoku roku'nen jūgatsu ichijitsu genzai, shokugyō betsu jinkō tōkei hen. [Manchoukuo Empire. Population statistics as of October 1, 1939. Population by occupation.] Hsinking, 1941. 470 pp.
Manshū teikoku genjū jinkō tōkei, Kōtoku roku'nen jūgatsu ichijitsu genzai, sō hen oyobi nenrei betsu jinkō hen.

[Manchoukuo Empire. Population statistics as of October 1, 1939. General section on population by age.]

Police Survey, 1940

Manshūkoku. Kokumu-in, sōmu-chō, tōkei-sho. Chian-bu, keimu-shi.

Manshū teikoku genjū jinkō tōkei, Kōtoku shichi'nen jūgatsu ichijitsu genzai, shokugyō betsu jinkō tōkei hen. [Manchoukuo Empire. Population statistics as of October 1, 1940. Population by occupation.] Hsinking, 1940. 469 pp.

Manshū teikoku genjū jinkō tōkei, Kōtoku shichi'nen sue. [Manchoukuo Empire. Population statistics at end of 1940.] Hsinking, 1942. 333 pp.

Police Survey, 1941

Manshūkoku. Kokumu-in, sōmu-chō, tōkei-sho. Keimusōkyoku.

Manshū teikoku genjū jinkō tōkei, Kōtoku hachi'nen jūgatsu ichijitsu genzai sō hen oyobi nenrei betsu hen. [Manchoukuo Empire. Population statistics as of October 1, 1941. General section and section by age.] Hsinking, 1943. 467 pp.

Police Survey, 1942

Manshūkoku. Kokumu-in, sōmu-chō, tōkei-sho. Keimusōkyoku.

Manshū teikoku genjū jinkō tōkei, Kōtoku ku'nen jūgatsu ichijitsu genzai, sō hen oyobi nenrei betsu hen. [Manchoukuo Empire. Population statistics as of October 1, 1942. General section and section by age.] Hsinking, 1944. 473 pp.

Census of 1940

Manshūkoku. Kokumu-in, sōmu-chō.

"Kokumu-in sōmu-chō rinji kokusei chōsa jimukyoku bunka kitei." [Regulations for divisions of Provisional Census Branch, General Affairs Bureau, State Affairs Council.] *Seifu kōhō* [Government Gazette], No. 1831, p. 30. June 3, 1940.

"Rinji kokusei chōsa hō." [Provisional census act.] *Seifu kōhō*, No. 1845, pp. 1-25. June 20, 1940.

The act, pp. 1-2; regulations for enforcement, pp. 2-4; investigation in special areas such as army and navy, police, jails, etc., pp. 4-5; detailed rules for enumeration in provinces, *hsien*, and minor civil division, pp. 5-16; procedures for schedule examination, pp. 16-19; rules for enumerators and supervisors of enumerators, pp. 19-25.

An analysis of the legal basis, procedure, and contents, together with preliminary data, was prepared by Edwin G. Beal, Jr.

"The 1940 census of Manchuria." *The Far Eastern Quarterly*, 4(3):243-262. May 1945.

"Manchoukuo. Lin-shih kuo-shi tiao-cha su-pao jen-k'ou." [Preliminary report of the 1940 census.] *Seifu kōhō*, No. 2003. December 26, 1940.

Rinji kokusei chōsa sokuhō Kōtoku shichi'nen. [Preliminary report on the provisional census, 1940.] Hsinking, 1940. 58 pp.

In Japanese and Chinese. Population of provinces and Hsinking; by city, *hsien*, and banners; by streets and villages. There are appendixes giving the provisional census act and the regulations.

Manshūkoku. Kokumu-in, sōmu-chō.

[Population by ethnic groups and age, census of 1940.] *Seifu kōhō*, 1941 and 1942.

Specific citations for total Manchoukuo, Hsinking, and the provinces are as follows:

Manchoukuo, total. No. 2503, September 22, 1941, pp. 256-258.

Hsinking Special Municipality. No. 2108, May 15, 1941, pp. 222-223.

Kirin. No. 2278, December 10, 1941, pp. 189-191.
Lunkiang. No. 2407, May 26, 1942, pp. 399-402.
Peian. No. 2343, March 6, 1941, pp. 68-71.
Heiho. No. 2408, May 27, 1942, pp. 416-418.
Sankiang. No. 2343, March 6, 1941, pp. 71-73.
Tungan. No. 2409, May 28, 1942, pp. 435-436.
Mutankiang. No. 2212, September 18, 1941.
Pinkiang. No. 2343, March 6, 1941, pp. 73-75.
Chientao. No. 2136, June 19, 1941, pp. 314-316.
Tunghua. No. 2410, May 29, 1942, pp. 458-460.
Antung. No. 2439, July 3, 1942, pp. 55-57.
Ssuping. No. 2278, December 10, 1941, pp. 191-193.
Fengtien. No. 2236, October 21, 1940, pp. 365-367.
Fengtien City. No. 2122, June 3, 1941, pp. 28-29.
Chinchou. No. 2483, August 25, 1941, pp. 399-401.
Jehol. No. 2492, September 4, 1942, pp. 51-53.
West Hsingan. No. 2411, May 30, 1942, pp. 475-477.
South Hsingan. No. 2343, March 6, 1941, pp. 751-777.
East Hsingan. No. 2189, August 21, 1941, pp. 380-381.
North Hsingan. No. 2413, June 2, 1941, pp. 24-26.

The following tables are included: 1. Quinquennial ages, lunar, 1-5 to 61 and over, by sex, for total, Japanese (total, Japanese, Korean, other), Manchurians (total, Chinese, Manchu, Mongol, Moslem, other), and other (total, nationals of third powers, and without nationality). 2. Numbers by politico-ethnic groups by sex for total population, provinces, *hsien*, and municipality.

Manshūkoku. Kokumu-in, sōmu-chō, rinji kokusei chōsa jimu-kyoku.

Zai-Manshūkoku Nihonjin chōsa kekka hyō. Kōtoku shichi'nen rinji kokusei chōsa, zenkoku hen. [Reports of the survey of the Japanese in Manchoukuo. Special census of 1940. Section of the whole country.] Hsinking, 1944, 460 pp.

Zai-Manshūkoku Nihonjin chōsa kekka hyō. Kōtoku shichi'nen rinji kokusei chōsa, chihō hen. [Reports of the survey of the Japanese in Manchoukuo. Special census of 1940. Section of provinces.] Hsinking, 1944. 460 pp.

Manshūkoku. Kokumu-in, sōmu-chō, rinji kokusei chōsa jimu kyoku.

Vol. I. *Kōtoku shichi'nen, rinji kokusei chōsa hōkoku. Zenkoku hen.* [Reports of the special census, 1940. Section of the whole country.] Hsinking, 1943. 199 pp.

This is a census of the "civilian" population. Military personnel were surveyed by the authorities of the Kwantung army and the Japanese navy. The armed forces of allied powers and their dependents were not included insofar as they were only temporary residents in Manchoukuo.

The plans for the census included four volumes: Vol. I. The total country. Vol. II. Provinces. Vol. III. Descriptive section. Vol. IV. The history of the census. Vol. I includes three tables. The first gives the population of the provinces by sex, the sex ratio, and density. The second gives the population by sex and age (single years, lunar, counting) for Hsinking City and the provinces. The third gives the population of the *hsien* by ethnic group by sex.

Vol. II. *Kōtoku shichi'nen, rinji kokusei chōsa hōkoku. Chihō hen.* [Reports of the special census, 1940. Section of provinces.] Hsinking, 1941-1943. 19 parts.

These provincial volumes are comparable to that for the country as a whole, age being given for ethnic groups by sex for the *hsien* within the provinces, and ethnic groups by sex, but not by age, for towns and villages.

Shinkyō-shi, Kichirin-sho. [Hsinking City and Kirin Province.] 1942. 197 pp.
Ryuko-sho. 1943. 188 pp.
Hokuan-sho. 1943. 161 pp.
Kokuka-sho. 1943. 87 pp.
Sanko-sho. 1943. 135 pp.
Toan-sho. 1943. 61 pp.
Botanko-sho. 1941. 59 pp.
Hinko-sho. 1943. 195 pp.
Kanto-sho. 1941. 59 pp.
Tsuka sho. 1943. 95 pp.
Anto-sho. 1943. 83 pp.
Shihei-sho. 1942. 129 pp.
Hoten-sho. 1942. 245 pp.
Kinshu-sho. 1943. 169 pp.
Nekka-sho. 1943. 161 pp.
Koan-sei-sho. 1943. 85 pp.
Koan-nan-sho. 1943. 95 pp.
Koan-to-sho. 1942. 55 pp.
Koan-hoku-sho. 1943. 79 pp.

OTHER STATISTICS

Official

Manshūkoku. Kokumu-in, sōmu-chō.
"Zenkoku tochi menseki tōkei ni kansuru ken." [Quantitative data on national areas.] *Seifu kōhō*, No. 291, pp. 208-214. February 28, 1935.
A regular source for information on areas of provinces, *hsien*, and banners.
"Genjū kōkō sū tōkei." [Statistics on resident population.] *Seifu kōhō*, No. 243, pp. 5-19. October 21, 1933.
Current materials, usually total population without classification by ethnic group, sex, or age.

Manshūkoku. Kokumu-in, sōmu-chō, tōkei-sho.
Manshū teikoku kokō tōkei, Kōtoku 2-nen matsu. [Resident population statistics of Manchoukuo, end of 1935.] 1936. 25 pp.
An annual publication giving population by province, city, *hsien*, banner, and village, total and by nationality. An appendix gave comparable data for Kwantung and the South Manchuria Railway Zone.
Dai-ikkai Manshū teikoku tōkei nenkan. [The first Imperial Manchoukuo statistical yearbook.] Hsinking, 1941. 349 pp.
Niji Manshū teikoku nempō. [The second Imperial Manchoukuo yearbook.] Dairen, Manshū bunka kyōkai [Manchoukuo Cultural Association], 1933.

Manshūkoku. Minsei-bu.
Dai-niji tōkei nempō, Kōtoku san'nen. [The second statistical yearbook, 1936.] Mukden, 1936. 319 pp.
There are detailed data on the population in the cities by whether the street of residence was within or outside the jurisdiction of the police of the South Manchuria Railway Company. Data on Japanese immigrants include whether under the auspices of the Ministry of Colonization or independently, movements within the settlements in Manchoukuo, *honseki* in Japan, etc.

Nihon. Gaimu-shō, Tōa-kyoku.
Dai-nijūkyūkai Manshūkoku oyobi Chūka Minkoku zairyū hōjin oyobi gaikokujin jinkō tōkei hyō, Shōwa jūichi'nen jūni-gatsu matsujitsu genzai. [The 29th population statistics of the Japanese and foreigners in Manchoukuo and China as of the end of December 1936.] [No date of publication.] 159 pp.
Manchoukuo included Kwantung Province; China included Hongkong and Mãçāo.

Non-official

China Yearbook Publishing Company.
The China yearbook, 1935-1936. Premier issue. Edited by Kwei Chungshu. Shanghai, The Commercial Press, 1935.

Far East Year Book Company.
The Far East Yearbook. Tokyo. Various issues.

Japan-Manchoukuo Year Book Company.
Japan-Manchoukuo yearbook. Tokyo, 1938. xxiv, 1227 pp.

Manshū Nichi-nichi shimbun-sha.
Manshū nenkan. [Manchurian yearbook.] Dairen, 1931.

Manshūkoku tsūshin-sha.
Kōtoku go'nen han, Manshūkoku gensei. [Present conditions in Manchuria, 1938 edition.] Hsinking, 1938. 533 pp.

Tōa keizai chōsa-kyoku.
The Manchoukuo yearbook. Tokyo, 1931.
Title varies. The issue for 1941 was published in Hsinking.

Tōyō keizai shimpō-sha.
Tōyō keizai nenkan. [Yearbook of the Oriental Economist.] Tōkyō. Various issues.

SOUTH MANCHURIA RAILWAY COMPANY

South Manchuria Railway Company.
Report on progress in Manchuria, 1907-1928. Dairen, 1929. vii, 238 pp.
The following reports were issued: 2nd, to 1930; 3rd, 1907-1932; 4th, to 1934; 5th, to 1936; 6th, to 1939.

Minami Manshū tetsudō kabushiki kaisha, shomu-bu, chōsa-ka.
Waga kuni jinkō mondai to Mammō. [Our national population problem and Manchuria and Mongolia.] Mantetsu chōsa shiryō [Survey data of Manchurian Railway], No. 75. Dairen, 1928. 4, 247 pp.

Minami Manshū tetsudō kabushiki kaisha, chōsa-bu.
Manshū keizai nempō. Shōwa jūsan'nen han. [Manchoukuo economic annual, 1938 edition.] Tōkyō, Kaizō-sha, 1939. 624, 40 pp.

Minami Manshū tetsudō kabushiki kaisha.
Minkoku jūroku'nendo, Manshū dekasegi mono. [Immigrants into Manchuria, 1927.] Mantetsu chōsa shiryō [Survey data of Manchurian Railway], No. 70. Dairen, 1927. 166 pp.
Issued annually or semi-annually.
Minkoku jūhachi'nen, Manshū dekasegi imin idō jōkyō. [General condition of the movement of immigrants into Manchuria. 1929.] Mantetsu chōsa shiryō [Survey data of Manchurian Railway], No. 130. Dairen, 1930. 91 pp.
A study of the migrants from Shantung, Hopei, and Honan by regions in Manchuria.
Shōwa san'nendo, Manshū Shina imin tōkei. [Statistics on

Chinese immigrants in Manchuria, 1928.] Dairen, 1929. 53 pp.

By place of arrival and settlement.

Manshū ni taisuru Shina no shokumin. [Chinese immigrants in Manchuria.] Dairen, 1929.

Manshū ni okeru hōjin no genkyō, shita no maki. [Condition of Japanese in Manchuria. Vol. II.] Dairen, 1931. 249, 22 pp.

Minami Manshū tetsudō kabushiki kaisha, Taiheiyō mondai chōsa jumbi-kai.

Manshū ni okeru Shina ijūmin ni kansuru sūteki kenkyū. [Numerical study on Chinese immigrants in Manchuria.] Taiheiyō mondai panfuretto [Pacific problem pamphlet], No. 8, 1931. 165, 96 pp.

Manchurian immigrants, 1923-1930.

OTHER

Books

Bowman, Isaiah, Director.

Limits of land settlement: A report on present-day possibilities. New York, Council on Foreign Relations, 1937. vii, 380 pp.

Chang Chun-jo.

A study on military colonization during the successive dynasties. [In Chinese.] Shanghai, Commercial Press, 1939.

Chinese Eastern Railway Co.

North Manchuria and the Chinese Eastern Railway. Harbin, China, C.E.R. Printing Office, 1924. xvii, 454 pp.

Russian studies of the history, economy, and population of northern Manchuria are summarized.

Fochler-Hauke, Gustav.

Die Mandschurei: Eine geographisch-geopolitische Landeskunde, auf Grund eigener Reisen und des Schrifttums. Heidelberg, K. Vowinckel, 1941. xv, 448 pp.

Ho, Franklin L.

Population movements to the north eastern frontier in China. Preliminary paper presented to the Fourth Biennial Conference of the Institute of Pacific Relations to be held in Hangchow, . . . 1931. Shanghai, Institute of Pacific Relations, 1931. 51 pp.

Hsu, Hsing-chong, Editor.

Administrative documents relating to the Three Eastern Provinces. [In Chinese.] 40 vols. 1911.

Kasamori, Denhan.

Manshū kaitaku nōson. [Colonization of farm villages in Manchuria.] Tōkyō, Iwamatsu shobō, 1940, 304 pp.

Lattimore, Owen.

Manchuria, cradle of conflict. New York, The Macmillan Co., 1932. xiii, 311 pp.

The Mongols of Manchuria: Their tribal divisions, geographical distribution, historical relations with Manchus and Chinese and present political problems. New York, John Day Co., 1934. 311 pp.

Inner Asian frontiers of China. American Geographical Society, Research Series, No. 21. New York, 1940. xxiii, 585 pp.

League of Nations.

Appeal by the Chinese Government. Report of the Commission of Enquiry. Series of League of Nations Publications, VII. Political. 1932. Official No.: C. 663. M.320.1932. Geneva, 1932.

Nagao, Sakurō, Editor.

Manshū nōgyō imin jū kō. [Ten lectures on Manchurian agricultural immigrants.] Tōkyō, Chijin shokan, 1938. 384 pp.

Nihon gakujutsu shinkō-kai.

Nichi-Man keizai tōsei to nōgyō imin. [Control of Japanese and Manchurian economy and agricultural immigrants.] Tōkyō, 1935. 135 pp.

Manshū nōgyō imin bunken mokuroku. [Bibliography of literature on agricultural emigration to Manchuria.] Tōkyō, 1936. 166 pp.

Mammō nōgyō imin kikan no soshiki oyobi kantoku. [Organization and direction of the organs promoting agricultural emigration to Manchuria and Mongolia.] Tōkyō, 1937. 40 pp.

Nihon. Nihon taishi-kan.

Zai-Man Chōsenjin gaikyō. [General condition of Koreans in Manchoukuo.] Hsinking, 1936. 417 pp.

Pauley, Edwin W.

Report on Japanese assets in Manchuria to the President of the United States, July, 1946. Washington, D.C., 1946. xi, 255 pp.; 14 appendixes.

Tang, Chi-Yu.

Studies of land settlement during various dynasties. [In Chinese.] Shanghai, Tseng Chung Book Co., 1945. 2 vols.

U.S. Army. Office of the Provost Marshal General. Military Government Division.

Civil affairs handbook. Manchuria. Section 7: Agriculture. Prepared by the Office of Foreign Agricultural Relations. Army Service Forces Manual M367-7. Washington, D.C., 1944. 67 pp.

U.S. Navy. Bureau of Medicine and Surgery.

Epidemiology of diseases of naval importance in Manchuria. Prepared by Tsai-yu Hsiao. NAVMED 958. Washington, D.C., 1946. 54 pp.

Wang, Chin-fu.

China's northeast: An introductory physical, economic and human geography of the northeast. [In Chinese.] Shanghai, Commercial Press, 1935.

Wittfogel, Karl A., and Feng, Chia-sheng.

History of Chinese society: Liao, 907-1125. New York, The Macmillan Co., 1949. xv, 752 pp.

Young, C. Walter.

Chinese colonization and the development of Manchuria. Honolulu, Institute of Pacific Relations, 1931.

Japanese jurisdiction in the South Manchuria Railway areas. Baltimore, Md., The Johns Hopkins Press, 1931. xxii, 332 pp.

Other

Ahnert, E. E.

"Manchuria as a region of pioneer settlement: Its natural conditions and agricultural possibilities." Pp. 313-329 in: *Pioneer settlement.* American Geographical Society, Special Publication No. 14. New York, 1932. 473 pp.

Germany. Statistisches Reichstamt.

"Arbeiterwanderung und Arbeiterpolitik in Mandschukuo." *Wirtschaft und Statistik*, 23(1):265-270. December 1943.

Grajdanzev, Andrew J.

"Manchuria: An industrial survey." *Pacific Affairs*, 18(4): 321-339. December 1945.

"Manchuria as a region of colonization." *Pacific Affairs*, 19(1):5-19. January 1946.

Horiuchi, Hidenori.

"Japan's development policy in Manchoukuo." *Contemporary Manchuria*, 5(1):30-42. January 1941.

With special reference to the agricultural settlement of Japanese.

Iwakura, T.
"Manshū jinkō shokuryō mondai no ichi kōsatsu." [A consideration of the problem of population and food of Manchoukuo.] *J.m.*, 4(1):8-12. August 1941.

Kasama, Naotake.
"Shakai seibutsugakuteki kenchi yori mitaru Manshū kaitaku nōson." [The colonization villages in Manchuria from the viewpoint of social biology.] *J.m.k.*, 2(5):33-43; 2(7): 9-24. May and July 1941.

Kishimoto, Eitarō.
"Gendai Manshū no rōdō seisaku to sono kadai." [Labor policy of present Manchuria and its task.] *Shakai seisaku jihō*, pp. 99-157. August 1941.

Koyama, Eizō.
"Shina Manshū ni okeru shōrai jinkō no suitei." [An estimate of the future population of China and Manchoukuo.] *J.m.k.*, 1:60-70. 1940.
"Manshū ni okeru idō jinkō: Rōdōryoku to shite no kūri." [Migratory population in Manchuria: Coolies as labor potential.] *J.m.k.*, 1(3):1-31; (4):1-38. June and July 1940.

Ladejinsky, Wolf I.
"Agriculture in Manchuria: Possibilities for expansion." *Foreign Agriculture*, 1(4):157-182. April 1937.
"Manchurian agriculture under Japanese control." *Foreign Agriculture*, 5(8):309-349. August 1941.

Lattimore, Owen.
"Chinese colonization in Manchuria." *Geographical Review*, 22:177-195. 1932.

Lee, Hoon K.
"Korean immigrants in Manchuria." *Geographical Review*, 22:196-204. 1932.

Liu, Hsuan-min.
"The colonization of the Three Eastern Provinces during the Ch'ing Dynasty." [In Chinese.] *Historical Annual, Historical Society, Yenching University, Peiping*, 2(4): 67-120. December 1938.

Miura, Un'ichi, and Shinozuka, Fusaji.
"Zai-Man Mōkojin no jinkō seitai." Pp. 28-35. "Population ecology of the Mongolians in Manchuria." Pp. 37-46. In: Nihon jinkō gakkai. The Population Association of Japan. *Nihon jinkō gakkai kiyō. Archives of the Population Association of Japan.* Tokyo, 1952. 102, 130 pp.

Moyer, Raymond T.
"The agricultural potentialities of Manchuria." *Foreign Agriculture*, 8(8):171-191. August 1944.

Murakoshi, Nobuo, and Trewartha, Glenn T.
"Land utilization maps of Manchuria." *Geographical Review*, 20:480-493. 1930.

Nihon. Kōsei-shō, jinkō mondai kenkyūjo.
"Takumu-shō Manshū shūdan kaitaku nōmin oyobi seishōnen giyū-gun chō." [Ministry of Overseas Affairs investigation on Manchurian group-colonizing farm population and youth volunteer army.] *J.m.k.*, 1(2):75-76. 1940.

Numata, S.
"Shinkyō oyobi Hōten no jinkō kōsei ni tsuite." [Concerning the population structure of Hsinking and Mukden.] *J.m.*, 4(2):223-227. November 1941.

Pan, Chia-lin, and Taeuber, Irene B.
"The expansion of the Chinese: North and West." *Population Index*, 18(2):85-108. April 1952.

Sato, Hiroshi.
"Study on the palisade in Manchuria." Pp. 32-44 in: *The Annals of the Hitotsubashi Academy*, Supplement No. 1. February 1951. 44 pp.

Schwind, Martin.
"Schwierigkeiten und Erfolge japanischer Kolonisation in Mandschukuo." *Geographische Zeitschrift*, 46(2):41-56. 1940.

Taeuber, Irene B.
"Manchuria as a demographic frontier." *Population Index*, 11(4):260-274. October 1945.

Tanaka, Kaoru.
"Emigration to Manchuria in the light of climatological geography." *Journal of the Kobe University of Commerce*, 1:85-108. December 1939.

Young, C. Walter.
"Chinese colonization in Manchuria: Part I. Motives and characteristics; Part II. Settlement zones and economic effects." *Far East Review*, 24:241-250; 296-303. 1928.

Zenshō, E.
"Manshūkoku no jinkō genshō." [Population phenomenon of Manchukuo.] *J.m.*, 4(3):388-393. January 1942.

INDEX

This index is a supplement to the table of contents and the lists of tables, figures, and maps. Official entries are limited, since detailed citations to the censuses and the vital statistics of Japan and the former imperial areas are included in the bibliography.

abortion, 29, 269-70, 275-83, 367-68, 372-73
adoption, 101-02
Agata, Sakito, 275, 373
age, change by, 45-46, 73-76, 335-42, 348-50, 383-89
age at marriage, 209-13, 227-28
age at migration to Tokyo, 162-64
age composition of labor force, 96-97
age groups, in eighth century, 9-10; errors, 42-43; Japan and areas, 74, 76-78; prefectures by industrial type, 78-79, 129-30; in Okinawa, 179-80; relation to vital rates, 320-23; armed forces, 333-34; war period, 335-42, 348-50; 1950 to 1955, 383-84; future population, 385-89
age groups, industrial structure of, 93-94
age patterns of mortality, 303-05
aged, numbers and increase in nation and in prefectures by type, 73-76; numbers, structures, and sex ratios, communes by size, *shi* and *gun*, and prefectures by type, 76-79
agriculture, 5-8, 12-15, 19, 20, 92-93, 96-99. *See also* prefectures by industrial type
agriculture and fertility in *gun*, 254
agriculture and food, 63-64
agricultural holdings, 98
agricultural labor force, 88-90, 92-93, 95-97
agricultural population and industrialization, 39
Aichi prefecture, *see* Nagoya
air attacks, 340
aliens in Tokugawa period, 17-18
Allen, George C., 38, 62
Allied Powers, *see* SCAP. GHQ
Aoki, Hisao, 272
Aomori, migrants, 127; children ever born, 250, 266; mortality, 295-96
area, prewar, 3; postwar, 347
armed forces, 9-10, 329, 331-35; in labor force ages, 82-84; unrecorded marriages, 219; in war, 340-41; repatriation, 345-48
army, deaths, 334-35
arrangements for marriage, 208
Asaka, Yukio, 25
Asakawa, Kan'ichi, 7, 14, 17
Ashikaga *shoguns*, 17
Asia, population with *honseki* in Japan, 198-201
Aston, W. G., 5, 6, 12, 13

balance of war and repatriation, 361
Balfour, Marshall C., 284
Barclay, George W., 182-83
Beal, Edwin G., Jr., 80, 192
Becker, J. E. de, 100, 207
Berg, Lev S., 175
birth limitation, in Tokugawa period, 16, 29-33; legal status, 269-70; means, 282-83; policies, 366. *See also* abortion, contraception, infanticide, sterilization
birth rates, in Tokugawa, 28-29; Meiji, precensal, 40-43, 50, 52-53; in Nanyo-gunto, 181; in nation, 231-38; prefectures, 238-43; prefectures by industrial type, 245; correlation with natural increase, 315. *See also* child-women ratios, children ever born, and gross reproduction rates
birth rates by age of mothers, nation, 233-38; prefectures, 239-45; prefectures by industrial type, 245-46; in large cities, 251-52
birth rates by order of birth, 236-38
birth registration, completeness before 1920, 42-43, 52; residence allocation, 231
births expected, 235; deficits to women, 259-61; deficits to men, 259-60; war deficit, 254-56
births in war period, 348, 350, 352, 354-56
boom cities, *see* migrant cities
branch houses, 101
Brazil, Okinawans in, 180; Japanese in, 199
Buddhism, 6, 14, 39, 64
Buddhists, transfers in Tokugawa, 32
bus transportation, 65

Canada, Japanese in, 199-200
capital formation in early industrialization, 38-39
catastrophes, 15-16, 24-25
causes of death, 288-90
census, reputed early counts, 9; plans prior to 1920, 40n
Chamberlain, Basil H., 5
Chiba, Masashi, 207
child-women ratios, in precensal period, 52-55; in census period, 74, 76, 78; Japanese abroad, 199
children ever born, by age of women, prefectures by industrial type, 245; in *shi* and *gun*, 250; to ever-married women, 265-68
China, early contacts, 3-5; cultural influences, 6, 8; technologies, 12
China, occupied, Japanese in, 343-46; repatriation, 344-46
Chinese in Manchoukuo, 192-93
cholera, 51
Christianity, 18
Christians, 64
cities, planned in Taika Reform, 8; in period of seclusion, 25-28. *See also shi*
cities by size, populations, 71-72, 76-78; economic activities, 84-86
cities of 100,000 and over, growth, 148-49; migrant status, 149-57; net migration, 157-59; mortality, 297, 299-300; infant mortality, 302. *See also shi*, six cities
civil code, prewar, 100-02; postwar, 102-03; on marriage, 208
civil wars, 13, 17
civilian population, *see* population behind the front class of worker, *shi, gun*, and prefectures by industrial type, 91-93
climate, 3-4
Coale, Ansley J., 323, 358
colonization, Tokugawa period, 19; Hokkaido, 173-75; Karafuto, 175-79; southern areas, 180-81; Taiwan, 182-83; Manchoukuo, 191-97
Commission on Population and Food, 366, 381
communes by size, precensal, 49-50; censal, 71-72; age groups, 76-77; economic activity, 84; industrial structure, 90-91; fertility, 247-48; influence of war, 350, 353
communication media, 66
Confucian teachings, 10
conscription, 19, 38, 331
constitution, postwar, 102, 207-08
contacts in period of seclusion, 18-19
contraception, premodern, 29; in Eugenic Protection Law, 269-70; extent, 272-75; government activity, 275; relation to abortions, 282-83; in war years, 367-68; Eugenic Protection Law, 372-73; policy resolution, 377-78
Co-Prosperity Sphere, 344
Council for Population Problems, 377-78
cultivated land, to the twelfth century, 3, 6-8, 12-15; in Tokugawa period, 19, 27; density in *gun*, 97-98
cultural homogeneity, 64

daimyo, residence in Edo, 18
Dajokan, reclamation policies, 14
day population, large cities, 152-54; *ku* of Tokyo, 166-67
death rates, in Tokugawa period, 28-29; in precensal period, 40-43, 50-51; Japanese in Nanyo-gunto, 181; crude and standardized rates, 286-88; prefectures, 289-94; prefectures by industrial type, 295-96; *shi, machi*, and *mura*, 297-98; correlation with natural increase, 315
death registration, 285-86
deaths in war period, 350, 352, 354-56, 358, 360
deaths of armed forces, 334-35
demographic diversities, 79
demographic structure of active population, 93-96
demographic transition, 37, 380-82
density, eighth century, 13; Tokugawa period, 22; census period, 67-68; in *gun*, 97-98; in Manchoukuo and Kwantung, 192
dependency burdens, 76; in households, 111-14; future, 388-89
dependent and productive age groups, 74-79
depopulation of rural areas, 68
differential fertility, 356-57
distance in migration, 127-28; to Tokyo, 161-62
distribution, Tokugawa period, 22; early Meiji period, 45-48; census period, 68, 70-71; prefectures by industrial type, 90; Japanese in the world, 201-03
divorce, in the Taika code, 10; definition, 209; statistics, 208-09; rates, 223-24, 228-30
doctors, prior to 1920, 51
Droppers, Garrett, 29
duration of marriage and fertility, 267-68
dysentery, 50-51

economic activity, by marital status, 215-18; persons in unrecorded marriages, 220-22
economic development, to twelfth century, 12; in Tokugawa period, 19; in 1850, 37-38; Hokkaido, 173-74; Karafuto, 175-77; Nanyo-gunto, 181; Taiwan, 182-83; Korea, 188-89; Manchoukuo, 191-93; postwar, 382-84
economic growth and population increase, 61-62
Economic Stabilization Board, population estimates, 371
economically active population, proportions by age and sex, 80-81; increase, 82-84; by size of commune and age in *shi* and *gun*, 84-86; by industry, 86-88. *See also* labor force
Edo, *see* Tokyo

education, in early Meiji, 39; subjects, 66; attendance and achievement, 66-68; status in Korea, 188-89; status of Japanese outside Japan, 200; levels and fertility, 268. *See also* school attendance
educational reforms of SCAP. GHQ, 67
emigration, armed forces, 333-34; questions of policy, 377
Emperor, status in postwar years, 347-48
Empire, as place of birth, 155-56; migrants in Hokkaido, 176. *See also* Japanese Empire
enumeration of children, 231
epidemics, in early period, 13; thirteenth century, 16-17; Tokugawa period, 24-25; nineteenth and early twentieth centuries, 50-51; postwar, 348
eta, see suiheisha
ethnic composition, Nanyo-gunto, 181-82; Taiwan, 183-84; Korea, 187-88; Manchoukuo, 193
ethnic homogeneity, 64
ethnic Japanese, increase of, 82-84
Eugenic Marriage Consultation Offices, 372
Eugenic Protection Law, 269-70, 372-73
ever-married women by age, prefectures by industrial type, 258-59. *See also* marital status, married exodus of native-born, *see* out-migrants
expansion of Japanese, 60-61
expectation of life, in nation, 287-88; prefectures, 290-94; in large cities, 297-300; at end of war, 355
extended family, *see* family structure
Ezo, 9, 11, 13

factory employment, 39, 115-16
family, in the Taika codes, 10-11; in eighth century records, 11; in centuries of insecurity, 17; in civil code, 101-02; relations to house, 103-04; stabilization, 229-30. *See also* house, household
family allowances, in the Tokugawa period, 32
family limitation, *see* birth limitation
family system, sanction of limitation in Tokugawa period, 30-22; relation to migration, 169-70
family wages and population policy, 374-75
famines, in the early period, 13; in the thirteenth century, 16-17; Great Famine of 1783-1787, 24-25; Great Famine of 1836-1837, 25; birth and death rates during, 28-29
farm households, employment outside agriculture, 98
farm labor in 1945, 340
fertility by age of women, and marital status, 259; prefectures by industrial type, 264-65; children ever born, 265-68
fertility, by duration of marriage, 267-68; by occupation and education, 268-69; by social-economic status, 268-69; induced abortions, 275-77; relation to infant mortality, 301; relation to age structures, 320-23
fertility by legitimacy, live births, 261-64; stillbirths, 270-72
fertility levels, in early centuries, 10, 15; in period of seclusion, 32-33; changes, 1880 to 1920, 52, 53, 55; late precensal period, 232-33; census period, 233-38
fertility variations, in frontier and colonial areas, 190; in prefectures, 238-45; convergence, 246; in *shi* and *gun*, 248; communes by size in prefectures by industrial type, 248; convergence, 248-50; in *machi* and *mura*, 255-57; declines, 259-61
feudalism, institutions, 13; lines of vassalage, 17
Fine, Sherwood M., 348
flight from cities, 341-43
food production, 63-64
Foundation Institute for Research on Population Problems, *see* Jinko mondai kenkyu-kai, Zaidan hojin
Fueto, Toshio, 207
Fujioka, Kenjiro, 25
Fujiwara family, 13
Fukuoka prefecture, 47
Fukuoka-Yamaguchi conurbation, growth, 155; migration, 155-57, 157-60
Fukutake, Tadashi, 103
future population estimates, 323, 325, 365-67, 370-71, 384-89

gainfully occupied population, concepts and definitions, 80; civilian population in 1944, 337; women in war years, 340. *See also* economic activity, economically active population, labor force
grade of school completed, *see* education
Grajdanzev, Andrew J., 182
great cities, Tokugawa period, 25-26; Meiji precensal, 47; censal, 154-57; migration, 167. *See also* cities of 100,000 and over, six cities, and the specific cities
Great Reform, *see* Taika Reform
Groot, Gerard J., 3
gross reproduction rates, nation, 231-38; prefectures, 243-44; prefectures by industrial type, 246; *shi* and *gun* of prefectures, 248-49; places by size, 250; *shi* and *gun*, prefectures by industrial type, 253
growth potential, 324-25
gun, definition, 43n; population changes, 72-73; age composition, 76-78; economic activity, 84-86; class of worker, prefectures by industrial type, 91-92; industrial composition of labor force, 96; households by size, 108; migrant status, 126-27; population in absence of migration, 145; per cent single, by age, 210-12; economic activity by marital status, 217-18; natural increase, 317-18; industrial composition of repatriates, 347; age, 1940-50, 353-54
gun, fertility, levels and changes, 248; gross reproduction rates in prefectures, 248-49; variations, 253-55; children ever born, 265-67; contraceptive practice, 272-75; ratios of children to women, 356

Hasegawa, T., 81
Hawaii, Okinawans in, 180; people with *honseki* in Japan, 198-99
head of house, responsibilities, 101, 207-09. *See also* house
Health Centers, 284-85
hinin, see suiheisha
Hiroshima, fatalities, 360
Hoffman, Lawrence A., 68
Hokkaido, increase, 47, 71; migrants, 162, 173-75, 177-78
Homma, H., 272
Honda, Tatsuo, 268-69, 272, 282
honseki of Japanese outside Japan, 177-78, 181, 186, 198-201. *See also koseki*
Honjo, Eijiro, 3, 5, 6, 18-23, 27, 29-32
Horie, Yasuzo, 20, 22, 23, 26
house, definition, 100-01; in postwar civil code, 102-03; relations to family, 103-04; powers in marriage, 207-09
household, definition, 104; structure of relations, 105-06; size, 107-09; sex ratios, 109; characteristics by industry of head, 111-14
household heads, characteristics, 109-11
household industries in late nineteenth century, 39
household labor in *ku* of Tokyo, 166-67
household law, of Taika Reform, 9-11
household members, relations to head by industry, 111; dependency burdens, 111-14; gainful employment, 112-14
household registers, *see koseki*
Hozumi, Nobushige, 100
Hulse, Frederick S., 3
Hyogo prefecture, *see* Kobe

ie, see house
illegitimacy, *see* legitimacy status
immigration, limitations, 64
imperial migration and marriage, 210
Imperial Restoration, 19, 38, 100
income distribution, 65
incorporation of cities, 71n
increase, prior to Meiji Restoration, 13-14, 16, 20, 33-34; precensal, 40-42, 44-47; census period, 60-61, 73-75
industrial composition, 62-63, 86-88; by size of commune, 90-91; age groups, 93-95; age groups in *shi* and *gun*, 96; in war years, 337
industrial composition in imperial areas, in-migrants in Karafuto, 177; ethnic groups in Taiwan, 183-86; ethnic groups in Korea, 188-89; Japanese in Manchoukuo, 195
industrial prefectures as areas of concentration, 70-71
industrialization, late nineteenth century, 38; internal migration, 168-70; marital status, 212-15; stability of marriage, 229-30; fertility, 245-47; mortality, 293-97; natural increase, 317; population growth, 380-82
infant mortality, incomplete reporting, 50n; trends and variations, 286-88, 301-02
infanticide, 9, 16, 29-33, 52, 271-72, 278-79
influenza, 51
influx, *see* in-migrants
informal marriage, *see* unrecorded marriage
in-migrants, definition, 124n; prefectures, 124-26; by age and sex, prefectures by industrial type, 134-35; in Tokyo by age at arrival, 162-63; by year of arrival in Karafuto, 176-77; and fertility in *gun*, 256. *See also* internal migration
inoculations, 285
Inquiry Commission on Population Policies, 389
Institute of Population Problems, *see* Nihon. Kosei-sho, Jinko mondai kenkyujo
Institute of Public Health, *see* Nihon. Kosei-sho, kokuritsu koshu eisei-in
internal migration, measurement before 1920, 143-44; relation to economic activity, 85; in Manchoukuo, 196; relation to natural increase, 320. *See also* in-migrants, net migration, out-migrants
irrigation, introduction and development, 12ff
Ishii, Ryoichi, 14, 20, 29, 365-66
Ishikawa, mortality by age, 295-96
Isobe, Hidetoshi, 98

Japan. Cabinet Bureau of Statistics, *see* Nihon. Naikaku tokei kyoku
Japan. Department of Education, *see* Nihon. Mombu-sho
Japan. Economic Planning Board, 63
Japan. Economic Stabilization Board, *see* Nihon. Keizai antei hombu
Japan. Embassy, United States, 344
Japan. First Demobilization Board, 334, 360
Japan. Office of Commissioner and Adviser of Kaitakusi, 173
Japan. Welfare Ministry, *see* Nihon. Kosei-sho
Japan. Welfare Ministry. Institute of Population Problems, *see* Nihon. Kosei-sho, Jinko mondai kenkyujo
Japan. Welfare Ministry. Institute of Public Health, *see* Nihon. Kosei-sho, kokuritsu koshu eisei-in
Japanese Empire, population, 60-61
Japanese outside Japan, 1850 to 1920, 45n; 1920 to 1940, 60-61; in imperial areas, 183-86, 188-89, 194-95; in world, 202-03; in Co-Prosperity Sphere, 343-44
Jinko mondai kenkyu-kai, Zaidan hojin, 371-72, 374, 376-77, 389
Jinko mondai shingi-kai, 372

Kaempfer, Engelbert, 26
Kamakura *bakufu*, 16; reports of abortion, 29
Kamii, Yoshio, 62
Kanagawa prefecture, migrants to Tokyo, 162. *See also* Yokohama
Karafuto, 60-61, 175-79; fertility of Japanese, 247; Japanese armed forces, 332;

Japanese population and repatriation, 343-46
Kasama, Naotake, 301
Kawakami, Mitsuo, 224
Kawashima, Takeyoshi, 103, 207
kinship organization, 102
Kirk, Dudley, 358
Kiser, Louise, 358
Knibbs, George H., 365
Kobe, growth, 154; migration, 155-60, 167; gross reproduction rates, 250; fertility in *ku*, 253
Kojiki (Record of Ancient Matters), 5
Kojima, Reikichi, 60, 71, 148, 154-55
Korea, 60-61, 64, 186-89; fertility of Japanese, 247; Japanese armed forces, 332; Japanese population and repatriation, 343-46
Koreans, migrants in early period, 12; movements to Japan, 188; movements to Manchoukuo, 193-94; mortality, 296-97; in Japan, 345
koseki, in Taika Code, 7; to twelfth century, 9-11, 14; in Tokugawa period, 21, 23, 27; changes at Restoration, 64; relations to *ie*, 101; transfers of *honseki*, 168; marriage entries, 207-09, 218-22; vital records, 231, 285-86; during war, 354
Koya, Yoshio, 269, 275, 277, 373
Koyama, Eizo, 189
ku of Tokyo, migration, 162-66
Kubota, Yoshiaki, 371
Kuno, Yoshi S., 17, 29
Kurile Islands, repatriation, 344-45
Kusakawa, Akira, 303
Kwantung Leased Territory, 60-61; fertility of Japanese, 247; Japanese armed forces, 332; Japanese population, 343-46
Kyoto, origin, 9; in fifteenth and sixteenth centuries, 17; in Tokugawa period, 25-27; growth, 154-55; migration, 155-61, 167; gross reproduction rates, 250; fertility in *ku*, 253
Kyoto prefecture, *see* Kyoto
Kyoto-shi. Eisei kyoku, 281

labor force, participation, prefectures by industrial type, 89-90; status of repatriates, 347; postwar growth, 384; as a population problem, 389. *See also* economic activity, economically active population, labor force
land holdings, 98
land redistribution, in Taika Code, 6-7; to twelfth century, 12-14; by Tokugawa *shogun*, 18; in postwar period, 348
land settlement, limitations to, 189-90
Latin America, population with *honseki* in Japan, 198-99
legitimacy status, definitions and types, 101; in postwar civil code, 102; live births, 261-64; stillbirths, 270-72
life cycles and mortality, 306-08
life tables, *see* expectation of life at birth, mortality
linguistic homogeneity, 64
location, 3
Lockwood, William W., 38, 61
Lorimer, Frank, 323
Lotka, A. J., 313

mabiki, see infanticide
machi, definition, 47n; characteristics, 71n, 73n; migrant status, 126; birth rates, 225-27; death rates, 297-98; natural increase, 318-19
Mainichi Newspapers. Population Problems Research Council, *see* Mainichi shimbun-sha. Jinko mondai chosa-kai
Mainichi shimbun-sha. Jinko mondai chosa-kai, 272-73, 277, 282, 374
Majima, Yujiro, 316-17
malaria, 51
Manchoukuo, population, 60; migration of Koreans, 189; Japanese in, 343-46
Manchuria, 191-97; repatriation, 344-46
manufacturing industry, class of worker, prefectures by industrial type, 92-93
marital status, of heads of households, 110-11; and economic activities of women, 116-19; Japanese in Manchoukuo, 194-95; and economic activity, 215-18; and deficits of births, 260; and children ever born, 267
market, development in Tokugawa period, 19
marriage, in seventh and eighth centuries, 10-11; in Tokugawa period, 32; in civil codes, 101-02, 207-09; patterns and statistics, 207-09; postponement, 209-13; rates by type, 223-27; stabilization, 227-28. *See also* unrecorded marriages
married, definition, 209; per cent in younger ages, 210-13; proportion by sex and age, 213-14; relation to fertility, 259. *See also* ever-married women
Maruoka, Hikoo, 279
maternal health, effect of induced abortions, 277; as reason for birth limitation, 372-73
Matsuura, Koichi, 303
medical care, 285
Meiji Restoration, *see* Imperial Restoration
metropolitan centers, 148-51. *See also* cities of 100,000 and over
metropolitan prefectures, 47, 68-70. *See also* prefectures by industrial type
Micronesian Islands, addition to Japan, 60. *See also* Nanyo-gunto
midwives, 51
migrant cities, migrant status, 150-51; per cent single, 212-13
migrant interchanges, Japan and Korea, 189
migrant status, 123-26; *shi, machi*, and *mura*, 126; prefectures by industrial type, 127; by age, 129; cities by size and type, 149-51; large cities, 152-54; great cities, other large cities, and outside, 155-57; in Hokkaido, 175-76; in Karafuto, 176, 177-78; in Taiwan, 185-86. *See also* in-migrants, migrants, internal migration, migration, net migration, out-migrants
migrants at successive ages, 130-32, 134n
migrants within prefectures, 138, 139-41
migration, in late Tokugawa, 26-27; registration, 40-41; in late precensal period, 49n; to and from Japan, 59; age impact, 83-84; younger sons, 103; stage movement, 127; relation to growth, 144-46; selectivities, 169; Hokkaido, 174-75; relation to population pressure, 189-90; relation to fertility and mortality, 256-57, 304-05; armed forces, 333-34; postwar, 348; influence of war, 354. *See also* migrant status
migrations to Manchoukuo, Chinese, 193; Koreans, 194; Japanese, 195
military mortality, 334-35
military status of civilian Japanese in Manchoukuo, 194-95
Minamoto, 13; as *shogun* at Kamakura, 16
Miyazaki, mortality by age, 295-96
Mizushima, Haruo, 165, 290, 301, 303, 312, 315-18, 365
mobility, in periods of instability, 17; in late Tokugawa period, 25-27; in modern period, 65; in large cities, 152-54; in colonial areas, 203-04
money, use in Tokugawa period, 19
Mongol invasions, 17
Morita, Yuzo, 51
mortality, in early period, 11, 13-15; in Tokugawa period, 16, 24-25; in precensal period, 51, 53, 55; trends, 286-88; probability of death, 289; by age and sex in prefectures, 295-97; in and outside large cities, 297-300; women, 300-01; patterns by age and sex, 303-06; relation to population growth, 319; influence on age structure, 320-23
Mortara, Giorgio, 224
mothers, children ever born, prefectures by industrial type, 266-67
Moyer, Raymond T., 197
muko yoshi kon'in, 227
Munro, N. Gordon, 5
mura, definition, 47n; characteristics, 71n, 73n; migrant status, 126; birth rates, 255-57; death rates, 297-98; natural increase, 317-18
Muramatsu, Minoru, 269, 275, 276, 281, 373
Murdoch, James, 8, 24

Nagasaki, fatalities, 360
Nagoya, growth, 154; migration, 155-61, 167; gross reproduction rates, 250; fertility in *ku*, 253
Nakagawa, Tomonaga, 367
Nanyo-gunto, 60-61, 180-82; fertility of Japanese, 247; Japanese population, 343-46
Nara, early capital, 9
Nasu, Shiroshi, 97
nationals of colonies in Japan, 83
native born, regional and prefectural interchanges, 123-26
natural increase, in Tokugawa period, 28-29; precensal, 40-42; in Manchoukuo, 196; crude and refined rates in nation, 310-13; in prefectures, 313-17; convergence, 317; war period, 350, 352, 354-56
navy, deaths, 334-35
neighborhood groups, in the Taika Code, 7; in the Tokugawa *bakufu*, 18
Neolithic culture, 3-4
neonatal mortality, by legitimacy of births, 271-72; trends, 286-87
net civilian migrations, 344-47
net migration, prefectures, 124-26; by age and sex, 134, 137; by age and sex, prefectures by industrial type, 135-39; intercensal periods, prefectures, and by industrial type, 142-44; relation to natural increase, 145-46; prewar and postwar, by age, prefectures by industrial type, 145-47; by age, 1925-35, great cities and prefectures, 157-61; Tokyo, 162, 165; 1920-35 and 1935-50, prefectures by industrial type, 354
net migration to and from Japan and colonies, Karafuto, 178-79; Okinawa, 179; Japanese in Japan and Empire, 201-03; Japanese to and from Japan, 343-44, 350, 352
net reproduction rates, *see* natural increase
night population, large cities, 152-54; *ku* of Tokyo, 166-67. *See also* individual great cities
Nihon. Homo-fu, 102
Nihon. Keizai antei hombu, 348, 371
Nihon. Kokuritsu yoron chosa kenkyujo, 272
Nihon. Kosei-sho, 272, 371
Nihon. Kosei-sho, Jinko mondai kenkyujo, 72, 77, 84, 97, 312-13, 366, 371, 373-74, 386
Nihon. Kosei-sho, kokuritsu koshu eisei-in, education for family planning, 275, 375-76; village studies, 373
Nihon. Mombu-sho, 39, 66
Nihon. Naikaku, kikaku-in, 366-68
Nihon. Naikaku tokei-kyo, 41-42, 45, 118, 354
Nihon. Sori-fu, tokei kyoku, 87, 94
Nihon. Tokyo shiyakusho, 106
Nihon-shoki (Chronicles of Japan), 5ff
Niigata, migrant status, 150-51; per cent single by age, 212-13
Nishioka, Hideo, 3
Noh, Toshio, 13
non-family living, 106-07
non-Japanese in Japan, 60n
Norman, E. Herbert, 39
North America, people with *honseki* in Japan, 198-201
Notestein, Frank W., 325, 358
nuclear family, 103-04
nyufu kon'in, 227

occupational composition, late Tokugawa and early Meiji, 28; in-migrants in Hok-

kaido, 177-78; ethnic groups in Manchoukuo, 194-95. *See also* industrial composition
occupational mobility in agriculture, 95-96
occupations of fathers and fertility, 268-69
Occupied China, 60, 197-98
Oda, Takao, 7
Ogawa, Gotaro, 329
Ogino, Hiroshi, 276, 281
Okazaki, Ayanori, 268
Okayama, mortality by age, 295-96
Okinawa, 24n, 60-61, 179-80; out-migrants to Nanyo-gunto, 181; fertility of Japanese, 247; separation from Japan, 343n
Osaka, growth in Tokugawa period, 25-27; growth, 154; migration, 155-61, 167; gross reproduction rates, 250; fertility in *ku*, 253; mortality by age, 295-96
Osaka prefecture, *see* Osaka
Oshima, Harry T., 61
out-migrants, definition, 124n; prefectures, 124-26; by age, prefectures and by industrial type, 130-34; from Tokyo, 162-65; to Hokkaido, 174-75; from Okinawa, 180; from agriculture in relation to marriage, 212

patriarchal family, in eighth century records, 11
patrilineal residence, 105-06
patrilineal succession, in eighth century records, 11
Pearl, Raymond, 365
peasants, role in Tokugawa period, 19-20
Penrose, E. F., 63
Perry, Commodore, 19
Peru, people with *honseki* in Japan, 199
Pharmaceutical Law, 373
Philippines, Okinawans in, 180; people with *honseki* in Japan, 199-200
place of birth, questions in censuses, 123n, 124n; interchanges among prefectures, 125, 128; large cities, 148, 151-54, 155-57. *See also* migrant status, migration, etc.
place of work, 152-54
plague, 51
police counts, 43n, 53-54
population behind the front, 330, 335-43
population change and war, 348, 350, 352
population changes in period of seclusion, 21-23; in the *do* and the *kuni*, 24-25
population expected without war, 357-60
population growth, Hokkaido, 173-75; Karafuto, 175-78; Okinawa, 179-80; Nanyo-gunto, 181-82; Taiwan, 183; Korea, 187-88; Japan, 380-84
population in productive ages without migration, 1920-40, 82
population policies, Tokugawa period, 31-32; Co-Prosperity Sphere, 366-69; postwar, 371-72, 375-76. *See also* population problems
Population Problem Council, 1949, 372-73
population problems, in early centuries, 15; in period of seclusion, 19-20; definitions, 364-65; in early 'forties, 366; postwar, 383-84; future, 384, 389
population projections, *see* future population estimates
population research, fields, 375-76
population with *honseki* in Japan, annually, 1875-1919, 40-43; in rural and urban areas, 43-44; child-women ratios for prefectures, 53-55
Portugal, contacts in sixteenth century, 17
prefectures, population, 1903-1918, 47-48; ratios of children to women, 52-54; population, 1920-1940, 68-70; migration, 124-32, 142-44; fertility, 238-45; mortality, 289-94, 298-99; infant mortality, 301-02; natural increase, 313-18; differential fertility in war period, 356-57
prefectures by industrial type, education, 66-67; population change, 70-71; population by age and sex, 74-75, 78-79; classification, 88-89; labor force participation, 89-90; class of worker, 91-93; households and economic activities, 108-09, 113-14; migration, 127, 132-36, 137-42, 144-47; marital status, 214-16, 220, 258-59; fertility, 245-46, 248, 253, 264-67; stillbirths, 281; mortality, 295; natural increase, 317-19; women in reproductive ages, 320; age structures of female population, 337-39, 341-43, 350-52; net migration by age, 354; ratios of children to women in war years, 356-57
pregnancy wastage, 276
production indices, 61-62
productive ages, number and increase in nation and in prefectures by type, 73-76; numbers, structures, and sex ratios, communes by size, *shi* and *gun*, and prefectures by type, 76-79
public health, 51, 284-85
puerperal deaths, 301

racial policy, 367
railroads and rail travel, 65
Rathgen, K., 46
ratios of children to women, 245n, 356-57. *See also* fertility
recognized illegitimate births, 261-63. *See also* legitimacy status
recognized illegitimate stillbirths, 270-72. *See also* legitimacy status
redistribution, 1750-1918, 45-48; intercensal periods, 68-71; war years, 337-39, 341-43. *See also* distribution
registers of population, in Taika codes, 6-7; to the twelfth century, 9-11, 14; in the Tokugawa period, 21, 23, 27; annual additions, 1875-1919, 40-42; inaccuracies, 42-43. *See also koseki*
registration system, *kosei-ho* of 1871, 40; enumeration of 1871, 40; compilation of registers, 40
Reischauer, Robert K., 5, 6, 8, 18
religious adherents, 64
remarriage, 214, 226-27
repatriation, 59-60, 214-15, 344-48
repatriation area, enumerated and expected populations, 358-60
residence allocations, 43-44
resources, in Japan, 62-63; in East Asia, 63
restoration of population in postwar period, 347-50
Reubens, Edwin P., 38, 61
rice movements in Tokugawa period, 25-26
roads, to the ninth century, 12; in the Tokugawa period, 25; modern, 65
rural areas, population changes by type of area, 73. *See also gun*
rural population, problems of measurement, 43-44; measures, 47-50. *See also gun*
Ryukyu Islands, addition to Japan, 60; Japanese population, 343-46. *See also* Okinawa

Sabagh, George, 200
Sai, Kiei, 52
Saitama, migrants to Tokyo, 162
Saito, K., 272
Sakhalin Island, *see* Karafuto
Sanger, Margaret, 370, 374
Sansom, George B., 3-5, 7, 8, 10, 11, 16, 17, 20
Sasebo, migrant status, 150-51; per cent single, 212-13
savings, 65
SCAP. GHQ., 348, 369-71
SCAP. GHQ. Civil Information and Education Section, 67, 370
SCAP. GHQ., Economic and Scientific Section, 61, 62, 343, 370, 386
SCAP. GHQ. Government Section, 102, 207
SCAP. GHQ. Natural Resources Section, 3-5, 63, 370
SCAP. GHQ. Public Health and Welfare Section, 369
Scheinpflug, Alfons, 173
Schenck, W. Egbert, 3
school attendance, late nineteenth century, 39; prefectures by industrial type, 66-67; in large cities, 153-54. *See also* education
school-age children in nation and in prefectures, 73-76, 78
Schumpeter, E. B., 63
Sebald, W. J., 207
seclusion, 18-34
Sekiyama, Naotaro, 9, 10, 21, 24, 27, 28, 32
Sendai, migrant status, 150-51; per cent single by age, 212-13
settlement, in Hokkaido, 173-76; in Manchoukuo, 191-92
sex differences in mortality, 305-06
sex ratios, by age, 76; by age, prefectures by industrial type, 79; migrants by distance, 162; in Manchoukuo, 196; Japanese outside Japan, 199; in population increase, 322-23; in stable populations, 323-24; by age in war period, 335-36, 340-41, 348-50
sex ratios, in births by legitimacy status, 262; in births by age of mother and order of birth, 278-79
shi, definition and measurement, 43-44; increase and concentration, 47-50, 68-72, 76-78; economic characteristics, 84-86, 91-92, 96; households, 108; migration, 126-27; marital status, 210-12, 217-18; fertility, 248-53, 256, 265-67; stillbirths, 270-72; contraceptive practice, 272-75; death rates, 297-98; natural increase, 318-19; changes in war period, 339, 353-54, 356; industrial composition of repatriates, 347. *See also* urbanization
Shinozaki, Nobuo, 272-73, 282
Shintoists, 6, 64
shiseiji, see legitimacy
Shizuoka, migrant status, 150-51; per cent single by age, 212-13
shoen, 12-13, 16
shoshi, see legitimacy
Siberia, repatriation, 344-46
single, 209, 210-13, 223-25, 259
single person households, 109
six cities, age composition, 77-78; mortality of women, 300-01; changes in war period, 353-54, 356. *See also* cities of 100,000 and over, *shi*, urbanization, and individual cities
Smith, Neil Skene, 16, 25
social mobility, in the Tokugawa *bakufu*, 18
social structure, in the Taika codes, 6; seventh to twelfth centuries, 9; in the Tokugawa period, 18, 27-28; continuity in imperial restoration, 38-39
Soda, Takeo, 365
Southeast Asia, early relations with, 17
South Manchuria Railway Zone, fertility of Japanese, 247; Japanese armed forces, 332. *See also* Kwantung Leased Territory
stable (non-migrant) in resident populations, 141-42
stable cities, migrant status, 150-51; per cent single by age, 212-13
stable populations, 323-25
stability in large cities, 152-54
stability in the period of seclusion, 16, 20-25
statistics during war, 330-31
Steiner, Kurt, 100
sterilization, 269-70, 281-83, 372-73
stillbirths, 270-72; frequency, 278; sex ratios and type, 278-80; order of gestation and age of mother, 279-81; prefectures by industrial type, 281; trends, 287
Stolnitz, George, 297, 323
strictly illegitimate births, 261-63, 270-72. *See also* legitimacy status
Sugi, Kyoji, 40
Sugino, Wataro, 9, 15
suiheisha (water-level people), addition to registers, 39; low status, 64
Supreme Commander for the Allied Powers, *see* SCAP
Suzuki, Naruo, 275, 373

Tachi, Minoru, 66, 74, 84, 90, 224, 290, 291, 297, 316-17, 354, 371, 386
Taika Reform, 6-12
Taira family, 13
Taiwan, 60-61, 63-64, 181-86; unrecorded

marriages, 219-20; fertility of Japanese, 247; mortality by age, 296-97; Japanese armed forces, 332; Japanese population, 343-46
Takagi, Naofumi, 313, 323, 371, 386
Takahashi, Bonsen, 29-31
Takayasu, Hiroshi, 313, 323
Takekoshi, Y., 18
Takizawa, Matsuyo, 16
Taniguchi, Yoshinori, 307
Tanioka, Takeo, 7
tenancy, 98
territories, additions to Empire, 173
territorial organization, in the Taika Code, 7; in the Kamakura Shogunate, 16; in the Tokugawa Shogunate, 18
Teruoka, Gito, 52
Thomas, Dorothy S., 200
Toda, Teizo, 11, 105-06
Tokugawa *bakufu*, 17-34
Tokugawa period, population problem and policy, 364
Tokugawa report on commoners, 16; changes, late seventeenth and early eighteenth centuries, 20-21; reports, 1726-1852, 21-24; excluded groups, 21; validity, 22-23
Tokyo, in Tokugawa period, 25-27; migrant status, 124; growth, 154; migrant status in 1930, 155-57; net migration, 157-61; migrant selection, 161-62; age at migration, 162-66; migration, 1940-1955, 167; migrant status in *ku*, 162-66; out-migrants to Nanyo-gunto, 181; fertility, 250, 266; mortality by age and sex, 295-96
Tokyo prefecture, *see* Tokyo
Toyoura, Senkichi, 162
Trewartha, Glenn T., 3, 154, 173
Tsuchiya, Takao, 12, 25
tuberculosis, 51, 289-90, 308
typhoid and paratyphoid, 51

Uchida, Kan'ichi, 32
Ueda, Musao, 84, 90, 248, 290, 291, 297, 316-17, 365-66, 371, 386
uji, 5-6, 8
U.S.S.R., repatriation from, 344-46
United States, people with *honseki* in Japan, 199-200
U.S. Army, 50
U.S. Office of Foreign Agricultural Relations, 63-64
U.S. Military Government, Ryukyu Islands, 95
U.S. Office of Strategic Services, 39, 63, 369
U.S. Strategic Bombing Survey, 81, 335, 337, 340, 355
U.S. War Department. General Staff, 334
unpaid family workers, 91-93
unrecorded marriages, 208-09, 218-23
urbanization, precensal, 47, 49-50; growth of *shi* and communes by size, 71, 72; within the *gun*, 73; of age groups, 77-78; and internal migration, 168-70; in settlement and imperial areas, 175, 183, 188, 192; and marriage, 212-13, 229-30; and fertility, 247-57; and mortality, 293-95, 297-300; and natural increase, 317-18; in war period, 350-52; and population growth, 380-82. *See also* cities of 100,000 and over, *shi*, six cities, and individual cities

vital statistics, tests of accuracy in late nineteenth century, 50n; for large cities, 251
war, in early period, 9; and marriage, 210-13; 214-15; and fertility, 246-47, 261
war damage in cities, 348
war losses, 358-60, 362-63
Watanabe, Sadamu, 386
widow (widower), definition, 209
widowed and separated, 213-14; economic activities, 220-22
widowhood, relation to fertility, 244n
Wigmore, H., 26
Wilkinson, H. L., 365
women, family status and gainful employment, 114-16; numbers in reproductive ages, 319-20

Yamada, Yuzo, 61
Yamanaka, Tokutaro, 62
Yamato, 5-6, 11-12, 13, 15
Yanagida, Kunio, 207
Yanagisawa, Yasutoshi, 9
Yawata, marital status, 150-51; per cent single by age, 212-13
Yokohama, growth, 154; migration, 155-60, 167; gross reproduction rates, 250; fertility in *ku*, 253
Yokosuka, migrant status, 150-51; per cent single by age, 212-13
Yokoyama, Y., 9
Yoshida, Togo, 20, 173
youth, numbers and increase in nation and in prefectures by type, 73-76; numbers, structures, and sex ratios, communes by size, *shi* and *gun*, and prefectures by type, 76-79
youth-women ratios, 76
Yuzuki, Jugo, 20, 22, 23, 26